Gavin Rees

MILLINGTON AND SUTHERLAND WILLIAMS ON THE PROCEEDS OF CRIME

MILLINGTON AND SUTHERLAND WILLIAMS ON

THE PROCEEDS OF CRIME

THIRD EDITION

TREVOR MILLINGTON *OBE LLB (Hons) Wales*
Barrister of the Middle Temple

MARK SUTHERLAND WILLIAMS *LLB (Hons) Exon*
Barrister of the Inner Temple

OXFORD
UNIVERSITY PRESS

OXFORD

UNIVERSITY PRESS

Great Clarendon Street, Oxford OX2 6DP

Oxford University Press is a department of the University of Oxford.
It furthers the University's objective of excellence in research, scholarship,
and education by publishing worldwide in

Oxford New York

Auckland Cape Town Dar es Salaam Hong Kong Karachi
Kuala Lumpur Madrid Melbourne Mexico City Nairobi
New Delhi Shanghai Taipei Toronto

With offices in

Argentina Austria Brazil Chile Czech Republic France Greece
Guatemala Hungary Italy Japan Poland Portugal Singapore
South Korea Switzerland Thailand Turkey Ukraine Vietnam

Oxford is a registered trade mark of Oxford University Press
in the UK and in certain other countries

Published in the United States
by Oxford University Press Inc., New York

British Library Cataloging in Publication Data

Data available

Library of Congress Cataloging-in-Publication Data

Millington, Trevor.
   Millington and Sutherland Williams on the proceeds of crime / Trevor Millington,
Mark Sutherland Williams. -- 3rd ed.
      p. cm.
   Rev. ed. of : The proceeds of crime. 2nd ed. 2007.
   Includes bibliographical references and index.
   ISBN 978-0-19-956612-9 (hardback: alk. paper) 1. Forfeiture--England. 2. Forfeiture--Wales.
3. Great Britain. Proceeds of Crime Act 2002. I. Williams, Mark Sutherland. II. Millington, Trevor.
The proceeds of crime. III. Title.
   KD8460.M55 2010
   345.42'0773--dc22   2009050907

Typeset by Glyph International, Bangalore, India
Printed in Great Britain
on acid-free paper by
CPI Antony Rowe, Chippenham, Wiltshire

ISBN 978-0-19-956612-9

1 3 5 7 9 10 8 6 4 2

For Angela

For Jayne

In memory of Frank Trevor Leslie Millington 1922–2009

FOREWORD TO THE THIRD EDITION

With the laudable aim of stripping criminals, especially professional criminals, of the proceeds of their crimes, successive governments have introduced a large volume of legislation. Since 1986 there have been seven major Acts of Parliament. The principal Act is now the Proceeds of Crime Act 2002, as amended.

Good legislation needs to be well thought out and clear, and it should be no longer than is necessary to serve its purpose. This is easier said than done. It takes more time to prepare a shorter and clearer Act than one which is longer and less well constructed. It is an irony of the present legislative system that, whatever party is in power, its legislative programme tends not to allow such time to be taken in the first place, although it does allow time for successive criminal law amendments and re-enactments.

Our current proceeds of crime legislation is complex and over-engineered. It is unsurprising that it is a *bete noir* of those who sit as judges in the Crown Court. The object of depriving criminals of the proceeds of their crimes could have been approached in a simpler way by establishing the basic structure of the confiscation regime and setting out the principles in general terms but leaving it to the courts to work out their practical application. There would then have been less need for repeated amendments and re-enactments. But we are where we are, and it is hard to see a realistic prospect of any government seeking to replace our present legislation by a simpler model.

In 2008 the House of Lords clarified some important aspects of the legislation in a trio of cases (*May*, *Green*, and *Jennings*), but problems remain in other areas which the courts are attempting to work out. The challenge is to interpret and apply the legislation in a way which is loyal to the language and at the same time is just and coherent.

To grapple with these matters the busy and perplexed practitioner or judge needs help. Here is the considerable value of this book. For those seeking to find their way through the legislative and case law jungle, the authors have provided a well organised and comprehensive guide.

Lord Justice Roger Toulson
Royal Courts of Justice
September 2009

vii

FOREWORD TO THE SECOND EDITION

In *R v Sekhon* [2003] 1 WLR 1655, Lord Woolf CJ began his judgment by noting that one of the most successful weapons that can be used to discourage offences that are committed in order to enrich the offender is to ensure that any profit which is made from the offending is confiscated. He went on to say that Parliament had repeatedly introduced legislation designed to enable the courts to confiscate the proceeds of crime. These comments were made in the context of a number of appeals against sentence in which errors had occurred in confiscation proceedings before the Crown Court. These appeals were themselves only some of the many which made their way to the Court of Appeal. The legislation had become a trap for the unwary. The difficulties were compounded by the fact that different statutory regimes existed for drug trafficking, other crime, and terrorism. Moreover, which regime applied did not only depend upon the nature of the offence but also on the date of its commission. Now, the principal legislation is the Proceeds of Crime Act 2002, which runs to about 320 pages and which has been amended by, amongst other statutes, the Serious and Organised Crime and Police Act 2005. This combination of legislation amounts to a dense thicket of law and there are many problems still to be resolved.

Mark Sutherland Williams and Trevor Millington, who are both extremely able and experienced lawyers in this field, have performed an invaluable service to the law by producing a book which explains the legislation and the formidable body of case law it has accumulated. They are to be congratulated for producing a work that satisfies all the requirements of an enquiring and demanding reader. It is well written and even the most obscure statutory provisions are illuminated by the authors' knowledge and understanding. It is analytical and comprehensive, dealing with everything from absconding defendants to warrants of commitment. It contains helpful practical observations on the operation of the legislation and helpfully explains the rationale for many of the provisions. The précis of the case law is a model of its kind.

In short, it is a practical and accessible guide whose value will be as great as the care and effort the authors have taken over its preparation. All those who have the responsibility for advising on or resolving the intricate problems which arise in this field will be grateful for such an excellent work.

David Perry QC
6 King's Bench Walk Temple
January 2007

FOREWORD TO THE FIRST EDITION

Crime can be extremely profitable. Examples abound of fraudsters, drug dealers, racketeers, and other professional criminals living lives of luxury on the proceeds of crime. In recent years the need to convict and sentence the guilty has been supplemented by the need to separate the criminal from his ill-gotten gains. The Proceeds of Crime Act 2002 is a statute of great size and importance. It is difficult. It is complex. It is a legal minefield. Moreover, it will impose burdens on judges in Crown Courts who will be required to fit countless urgent and complicated applications of a novel kind into their crowded lists. In addition, High Court judges will have to grapple with the new civil recovery provisions in cases where the Assets Recovery Agency seek to recover property which it alleges to be the proceeds of crime where no one has been convicted—and even where the defendant has been acquitted. All this calls for the most detailed examination by practitioners and judges. It requires the striking of a balance between the need to ensure that criminals do not prosper and the guarantee of fair treatment for defendants and third parties.

All those involved with this rapidly developing area of legal practice will benefit from this authoritative book. Trevor Millington and Mark Sutherland Williams are two acknowledged experts with great experience in the field. I welcome and pay tribute to the fruits of their labours.

The Honourable Sir Maurice Kay (now Lord Justice Maurice Kay)
The Royal Courts of Justice
July 2003

PREFACE TO THE THIRD EDITION

Some eight years have passed since we originally sat down and started planning a book on the law relating to restraint, confiscation, and forfeiture. The principal Acts we then focused upon were the Criminal Justice Act 1988 and the Drug Trafficking Act 1994, two Acts which, though not quite, are now fading into the legal sunset in terms of the recovery of the proceeds of crime. Another Act was just around the corner, the Proceeds of Crime Act 2002, which was due to eclipse the earlier legislation and take pride of place in the then Government's determination to tackle crime and the causes of crime. The rationale, like its predecessors, was in part to act as a deterrent to criminals, who would know that their assets would be in jeopardy if they were caught and found guilty of acquisitive offences. That new Act also took matters one step further. It introduced the concept of civil recovery: recovery of property and assets, even on acquittal, or where no criminal charges had been laid. The creation of the Assets Recovery Agency heralded a new era in what has always been described as draconian legislation.

Only a few years on and the Assets Recovery Agency has now been abolished. A nationwide Serious Organised Crime Agency now takes on the primary mantle for civil recovery, with the Directors of other agencies, most notably the Director of Public Prosecutions and the Director of Revenue and Customs Prosecutions, also vested with civil recovery powers. The Assets Recovery Agency, however, remains something more than a footnote in history. It dealt successfully with many of the legal challenges that inevitably arose, particularly with reference to the human rights legislation, and to a large degree has paved the way for enforcement agencies to carry forward its legacy.

The abolition of the Assets Recovery Agency is not the only change in recent years. The original Act has become punctured by amendments, substitutions, and additions as a result of further legislation, most particularly the Serious Organised Crime and Police Act 2005, the revised Money Laundering Regulations, and the Serious Crime Act 2007. While some of these changes may be welcomed by those who police the legislation, many of the new powers given to the various agencies are yet to be fully embraced by them, and as a result, are yet to be fully tested in the courts. Other major changes include the merger of the Revenue and Customs Prosecutions Office into the CPS, and the introduction of the UK Border Agency, which will take over many of the responsibilities traditionally held by Customs at the ports. Indeed, it is at least possible to anticipate that by the time this book is ready for a fourth edition, the term 'Customs Officer' may well be consigned to the past.

We remain optimistic. The post-*May* decisions of the Court of Appeal, led by the judgments of Toulson LJ, have given to this area of the law a new vitality. There remains much to be achieved and clarified. The next few years are likely to be as busy as the last few.

In this third edition, we have strived to keep to the original formula, namely that of a straightforward, easily digestible work on this, at times, complex area of the law. Whether we have succeeded we will leave for others to decide. We have refrained from including in this text the same amount of detail about the Criminal Justice Act 1988 and the Drug Trafficking Act 1994 as we included in earlier editions. During the lifetime of this book the Proceeds of Crime Act 2002 will have been in existence for some 10 years, and the impact of the earlier legislation is therefore likely to be considerably diluted.

We are grateful, as always, for the positive and encouraging feedback we have received about the second edition. Its circulation exceeded our expectations, and it continues to give us considerable pride to know that members of our profession find it a useful source of reference.

The mistakes in this third edition are our own, as are any views expressed, which are neither intended to be nor are representative of any government department or other organisation.

Trevor Millington writes: The period since the publication of the second edition of this work has been something of a roller coaster ride for me. The high point was learning that I had been awarded the OBE in the 2008 Birthday Honours List and attending Buckingham Palace to be presented with my insignia by Her Majesty The Queen. Only a few months later, my colleagues and I at the Revenue and Customs Prosecutions Office learned that we were to be merged with the Crown Prosecution Service, thereby bringing to an end an association with Customs which, in my case, spans over 22 years. As with the abolition of the Assets Recovery Agency, whether this will result in any appreciable benefits remains to be seen. Whatever the outcome, I would like to say a particular word of thanks to David Green, QC, Director of the Revenue and Customs Prosecutions Office, not only for his unfailing support, but for restoring our reputation for excellence in the prosecution of Revenue and Customs cases. As our most recent annual report shows, we now have a 92 per cent conviction rate and are one of the most successful law enforcement agencies for restraining and confiscating the proceeds of crime. We all owe David an enormous debt of gratitude. A special thank you too to 'MSW', my extremely able and learned co-author: as always working with Mark on the book project has been a real pleasure for me. I must also thank Alun Milford, Head of the Asset Forfeiture Division at RCPO and all my colleagues in the AFD, too many to mention here, for their support, friendship and helpful sugges-tions—I am grateful to you all. My sincere thanks go once more to those dearest to me, to Margaret for her unfailing support and understanding even through the most difficult times, and to my dear friends John and Marion O'Loughlin and their now very grown up children, Susan and Thomas. Finally, these acknowledgements would not be complete without expressing a sincere thank you to Angela whose extraordinary kindness never ceases to be a source of inspiration and to whom, once again, I dedicate this book with my affection, admiration, and grateful thanks.

As this third edition of *The Proceeds of Crime* went to press, my father and sole surviving parent died aged 87. I also dedicate this book to his memory. I should also like to express my heartfelt thanks and gratitude to my cousins, Tony and Grenville, and their wives Hazel and Linda, for all the help and support they have given me at this sad time.

Mark Sutherland Williams would like to thank: firstly, my distinguished co-author and friend, Trevor Millington OBE, for his continued commitment to this project. At the launch of the Proceeds of Crime Review, Trevor was dubbed by Lord Carlile of Berriew QC 'the Proceeds of Crime Tsar' and a few months later he was awarded the honour of an OBE. It has once again been a pleasure to collaborate with him on this book. Secondly, I thank all those who make working in this field the adventure that it is. Usually at this point I produce a list of those who I have recently worked with and single them out for thanks. My concern in this third edition is that I may leave someone out and then risk causing offence, so I shall take the easier route: Thank you, you know who you are. In terms of the book itself, may I thank Mathew Gullick, my junior in *Sivaraman*, for his outstanding assistance with the revised confiscation chapter, and equally Charlotte Hadfield of my chambers and my former pupil James Chegwidden, for their respective contributions. My particular thanks also go to Master Evan Bell for keeping me updated with developments in civil recovery, my pupil Tom Jaggar, for his proof reading and enormous assistance, and to Peter Brunning, of the London Regional Confiscation Unit and the City of Westminster Magistrates' Court, for his indispensable assistance with the reconsideration and enforcement chapters. Above all, I thank my wife Jayne; for ten exceptional years.

Both my and Trevor's thanks go to Faye Judges, Jodi Towler, and Roxanne Selby at OUP for their kind assistance and patience.

Lastly, we thank Lord Justice Toulson, who has in part been responsible for re-writing the confiscation scheme post-*May*, for kindly agreeing to pen the Foreword to this third edition.

Trevor Millington OBE
New Kings Beam House
London

Mark Sutherland Williams
3 Paper Buildings
Temple
January 2010

BIOGRAPHIES

Trevor Millington

Trevor Millington is a Barrister and Senior Lawyer in the Asset Forfeiture Division of the Revenue and Customs Prosecutions Office (formerly the Solicitor's Office of HM Customs and Excise). He was responsible for setting up the Customs and Excise Asset Forfeiture Unit in 1989 and since that time has specialised exclusively in the law relating to the restraint and confiscation of the proceeds of crime. He has been involved in many of the reported cases concerning this increasingly complex area of law, including *Re T (Disclosure Orders)*, *Hare v Commissioners of Customs and Excise* (piercing the corporate veil of companies), *Commissioners of Customs and Excise v Hughes*, *Capewell v HMRC*, and *Sinclair v Glatt* (liability to pay costs of management receivers), and *Re S* (release of funds subject to a Proceeds of Crime Act restraint order to meet the defendant's legal fees). In 1994 he was seconded to Gibraltar, where he was responsible for drafting legislation to implement the EC Money Laundering Directive and to provide for the restraint and confiscation of the proceeds of crime. His first book, *Restraint and Confiscation Orders*, was published by FT Law and Tax in 1996. He is on the editorial board of The Proceeds of Crime Review and is a member of the Society of Authors. He is a founder member and committee member of the Proceeds of Crime Lawyers Association and is a member of the Fraud Advisory Panel, the Commercial Fraud Lawyers Association, and the Association of Certified Asset Forfeiture Specialists. He is regularly asked to speak at continuing professional development courses organised by Central Law Training, Lexis Nexis, barristers' chambers, solicitors, chartered accountants, and professional associations. He was awarded the OBE by Her Majesty the Queen in the 2008 Birthday Honours List and is a Liveryman of the Worshipful Company of Scriveners. Away from work, his interests include a passionate love of opera and classical music.

Mark Sutherland Williams

Mark Sutherland Williams has appeared as counsel in a number of the most significant cases that have been decided in the proceeds of crime field in recent years. He co-drafted the receivers guidelines in *Capewell*. He was the first counsel to be instructed by the Director of the Assets Recovery Agency to draft an interim receiving order under POCA and a property freezing order under SOCPA, and was the first counsel to be instructed by the RCPO to obtain a restraint order under the 2002 Act. In 2006 he drafted and obtained the first external restraint order under the new legislation. He was junior counsel in the House of Lords cases of *Capewell*, *Briggs-Price*, and *Islam*. His career has also been notable for his involvement in a number of the country's most high-profile drug importation cases, including Operations *Stealer* and *Extend*. In 1999 he was instructed to draft the witness statement of Baroness Thatcher and John Major for the BSE public inquiry. He is currently the Treasurer of the Proceeds of Crime Lawyers Association and a member of the Fraud Advisory Panel. He has spoken at both national and international conferences on asset forfeiture and is head of the 3 Paper Buildings Asset Forfeiture Group. He sits as deputy Tribunal Judge and has recently run both the New York and Paris marathons.

CONTENTS—SUMMARY

CONTENTS

Contents

9. The Confiscation Hearing

10. Reconsideration of Confiscation Orders

Contents

TABLE OF CASES

TABLES OF LEGISLATION

A. PRIMARY LEGISLATION

B. SECONDARY LEGISLATION

TABLES OF EUROPEAN LEGISLATION

TABLE OF INTERNATIONAL TREATIES
AND CONVENTIONS

LIST OF ABBREVIATIONS

The following abbreviations are used throughout this work:

AJA	Access to Justice Act 1999
ARA	Assets Recovery Agency
ASBO	Anti-social behaviour order
ASP	Accountancy Service Provider
CCR	County Court Rules
CCRC	Criminal Cases Review Commission
CDD	Customer due diligence
CEMA	Customs & Excise Management Act 1979
CJA 1988	Criminal Justice Act 1988
CJA 1993	Criminal Justice Act 1993
CLS	Community Legal Service
CPR	Civil Procedure Rules
CPS	Crown Prosecution Service
CrimPR	Criminal Procedure Rules 2005
DTA	Drug Trafficking Act 1994
DTOA	Drug Trafficking Offences Act 1986
DWP	Department of Work and Pensions
ECHR	European Convention on Human Rights
ECtHR	European Court of Human Rights
FSA	Financial Services Authority
HMRC	HM Revenue and Customs
HVD	High Value Dealer
IRO	Interim Receiving Order
JARD	Joint Asset Recovery Database
LA	Limitation Act 1980
LIVR	Limited Intelligence Value Report
LSC	Legal Service Commission
MCA	Matrimonial Causes Act 1973
MRO	Management Receiving Order
MSB	Money Service Business
NCIS	National Criminal Intelligence Service
OFT	Office of Fair Trading
PACE	Police and Criminal Evidence Act 1984
PCC(S)A	Powers of Criminal Courts (Sentencing) Act 2000
PFO	Property Freezing Order
PII	Public Interest Immunity
POCA	Proceeds of Crime Act 2002
POCA 1995	Proceeds of Crime Act 1995
RCPO	Revenue and Customs Prosecutions Office
RSC	Rules of the Supreme Court
SAR	Suspicious Activity Report

SCA	Serious Crime Act (2007)
SCA	Supreme Court Act 1981
SFO	Serious Fraud Office
SOCA	Serious Organised Crime Agency
SOCPA	Serious Organised Crime and Police Act 2005
TCSP	Trust or Company Service Provider
UKBA	UK Border Agency

1

SETTING THE SCENE

A. Introduction

The purpose of this introductory chapter is to consider why Parliament decided to enact **1.01** confiscation legislation and to give a brief overview of the mechanics of the Acts. We also outline the functions of the key law enforcement agencies having the conduct of restraint and confiscation cases under the legislation and provide a summary of some of the most significant recent developments that have taken place in this fast moving area of law since the publication of the second edition of this work. As this is essentially a practical work, we do not intend to consider in any great detail the philosophy behind confiscation legislation, or to give a full academic critique of the provisions. The aim of this work is to consider the legislation against the background of the practical problems it is likely to cause, both to the prosecuting and to the defending lawyer.

B. Why was Confiscation Law Enacted?

The genesis of the confiscation regime

1.02 The first confiscation enactment to reach the statute book was the Drug Trafficking Offences Act 1986 (DTOA) which came into force on 10 January 1987. It was introduced following a recognition by Parliament that the profits made from drug trafficking were so great that the deterrent effect of even lengthy terms of imprisonment were negligible: the convicted criminal could spend his sentence secure in the knowledge that his ill-gotten gains (often well invested in the meantime) would be available to him on his release. The legislation also reflected the recognition by Parliament that existing forfeiture provisions were inadequate for the purpose of depriving the offender of the fruits of his crime.

1.03 The inadequacy of the old law is well illustrated by the decision of the House of Lords in *R v Cuthbertson* [1980] 2 All ER 401. The defendants had been convicted of offences of conspiring to produce and supply LSD following a police exercise known as 'Operation Julie'. The investigating officers traced assets to the value of approximately £750,000, which represented the defendants' proceeds of drug trafficking. The judge made a forfeiture order under s 27 of the Misuse of Drugs Act 1971 in this amount. This section empowers the court to order anything shown to relate to the offence to be forfeited. The House of Lords, however, quashed the order because the defendants had not been convicted of 'an offence under the Act' but of statutory conspiracies contrary to the Criminal Law Act 1977. Further, their Lordships ruled that the power of forfeiture was restricted to the physical items used to commit the offence and not to choses in action or other intangibles. In the words of Lord Diplock, at page 406:

> . . . section 27 can never have been intended by Parliament to serve as a means of stripping the drug traffickers of the total profits of their unlawful enterprises.

Accordingly, the monies remained the property of the defendants to do with as they pleased on their release from prison.

1.04 In 1984, a committee chaired by Mr Justice Hodgson recommended that the courts should be empowered to confiscate the proceeds of criminal offences of which defendants had been convicted. This led to the enactment of the DTOA, which imposed a mandatory obligation on the court to confiscate the proceeds of drug trafficking of those convicted of such offences. Some two years later, Parliament passed the Criminal Justice Act 1988 (CJA 1988), which, in broad terms, extended the confiscation regime imposed by the 1986 Act to cover all indictable offences together with a small number of offences triable only summarily where the benefits accruing to the defendant were likely to be unusually high.

1.05 The DTOA confiscation regime was augmented by a number of provisions in the Criminal Justice (International Co-operation) Act 1990 which came into force on 1 July 1991. Section 15 of the Act provided for the payment of interest on unpaid confiscation orders and s 16 empowered the prosecutor to apply to the court for confiscation orders to be increased where further realisable property was identified. Part III of the Act introduced entirely new provisions empowering customs officers to apply to a magistrates' court for the detention and forfeiture of drug trafficking money being imported or exported in cash.

On 3 February 1995, the Drug Trafficking Act 1994 (DTA) came into force. It consoli- **1.06** dated the provisions of the DTOA and the Criminal Justice (International Cooperation) Act 1990. It also strengthened the provisions of the DTOA by implementing many of the recommendations of the Home Office Working Group on Confiscation.

In October 1998 the Performance and Innovation Unit of the Cabinet Office examined **1.07** once again the UK's asset recovery arrangements with a view to improving the efficiency of the recovery process and increasing the amount of illegally obtained assets recovered. It proposed the creation of a new agency with lead responsibility for asset recovery and the consolidation of existing laws on confiscation and money laundering into a single piece of legislation. It also proposed the introduction of new powers to recover criminal assets through civil proceedings without, controversially, the need for a criminal conviction. As a result the Proceeds of Crime Act 2002 (POCA) consolidated the law and created the Assets Recovery Agency (ARA). In 2008, following some criticism in the press directed at the financial sustainability of the Agency, ARA was abolished and its civil recovery powers transferred to the Serious Organised Crime Agency (SOCA) and the Directors of the lead prosecuting agencies.

C. The Object of the Confiscation Regime

It is important to appreciate at the outset of any study of the law relating to restraint and **1.08** confiscation orders that POCA, the DTA, and the CJA 1988 are concerned with confiscat-ing the *value* of the defendant's proceeds of the offences of which he has been convicted, and not the actual proceeds themselves. It follows from this that once the court has deter-mined the amount by which the defendant has benefited from his criminal conduct, all assets in which he has an interest, whether legitimately acquired or not, are vulnerable to confiscation up to the amount of that benefit. The Crown Court (under POCA) and the High Court (under the DTA and CJA 1988) are thus entitled, pre-conviction, to restrain the defendant from dissipating assets which have been acquired perfectly legitimately for the purpose of ensuring that they remain available to satisfy a confiscation order in the amount of his benefit.

It is also important to appreciate that, contrary to the position in some countries (eg the **1.09** USA), a confiscation order is not an *in rem* order against the defendant's realisable property, but an *in personam* order against the defendant himself. This has a number of important consequences. In particular, the mere making of a confiscation order does not divest the defendant of his legal title to whatever realisable property was taken into account by the court in making the order. Thus the making of a confiscation order does not, itself, entitle any person in possession of the defendant's property to pass the same over to the enforcing magistrates' court in satisfaction of the confiscation order. Unless the property is being handed over pursuant to a receivership order or the defendant has expressly consented to the property being forwarded to the court, any person who does so will be vulnerable to a civil action for conversion.

D. The Drug Trafficking Act 1994: A Summary

> It is plain that the object of the Act is to ensure, so far as is possible, that the convicted drug trafficker is parted from the proceeds of any drug trafficking which he has carried out. The provisions are intentionally draconian.
>
> *R v Dickens* [1990] 2 QB 102, Lord Lane CJ

1.10 Where a defendant is convicted of a drug trafficking offence, as defined by s 1(3) of the Act, the Crown Court must enquire as to whether he has at any time benefited from drug trafficking. If the court answers in the affirmative, it must go on to assess the value of the defendant's proceeds from drug trafficking. The court must then make a confiscation order against the defendant in the amount by which he has benefited, unless he proves on a balance of probabilities that the value of his realisable property is less than this amount. In assessing the defendant's proceeds of drug trafficking, the court is not only required to take into account his proceeds from the offences of which he has been convicted, but of any drug trafficking activities carried on by him at any time.

1.11 The High Court is also given jurisdiction to make certain orders under the Act. Firstly, the court is empowered, normally at the pre-conviction stage, to make restraint and charging orders to prevent a defendant dissipating assets that may be made the subject of a confiscation order. Restraint orders have been described by Lord Donaldson MR in *Re Peters* [1988] QB 871 as being 'closely analogous' to *Mareval* freezing injunctions. The court may also appoint a receiver for the purposes of preserving and maintaining the value of the defendant's realisable property pending the conclusion of the criminal proceedings. Once a confiscation order has been made which is no longer subject to appeal, a receiver may be appointed to realise the defendant's assets in satisfaction of the order. The monies are paid to the enforcing magistrates' court and the magistrates are given concurrent powers of enforcement, which entitle them to enforce confiscation orders, by similar means to fines and other financial penalties.

E. The Criminal Justice Act 1988: A Summary

> One of the most successful weapons which can be used to discourage offences that are committed in order to enrich the offenders is to ensure that if the offenders are brought to justice, any profit which they have made from their offending is confiscated.
>
> *R v Sekhon*, 16 December 2002, The Lord Chief Justice

1.12 The 1988 Act, in broad terms, extended the confiscation regime in respect of drug trafficking offences to cover all acquisitive indictable offences together with a limited number of summary offences from which peculiarly high profits could be gained. There are, however, a number of differences between the two regimes and these will be considered in more detail in subsequent chapters. In general, the provisions of the CJA 1988 are less draconian than those of the DTA, although the Criminal Justice Act 1993 (CJA 1993), which came into force on 3 February 1995, and the Proceeds of Crime Act 1995, which came into force on 1 November 1995, removed many of the differences between the two regimes.

F. The Proceeds of Crime Act 2002: A Summary

The Proceeds of Crime Act 2002 received Royal Assent on 24 July 2002. It was intended to **1.13** replace and improve the existing legislation, namely the DTA and the CJA 1988. The main implementation date for Part 2 of the Act, the confiscation provisions, was 24 March 2003. The transitional provisions stipulate that the CJA 1988 and the DTA shall continue to apply to all offences committed before 24 March 2003 or which overlap that date. The three Acts are therefore likely to co-exist side by side for some time to come. In practice, most new confiscation orders are now being made under POCA, although many orders under the old legislation are still being enforced in the High Court and elsewhere. In effect, therefore, for some time to come one can expect the three Acts to co-exist side by side. The other implementation dates on which POCA came into force are considered in the relevant chapters herein.

POCA provides for confiscation orders in relation to persons who benefit from criminal **1.14** conduct and for restraint orders to prohibit persons from dealing with property. It also allows for the recovery of property that is or represents property obtained through unlawful conduct or is intended to be used in unlawful conduct; and it made new provisions about money laundering and investigations relating to benefit from criminal conduct or to property that is or represents property obtained through unlawful conduct.

POCA will eventually provide a complete code governing confiscation law. Under it there **1.15** is no distinction between drug trafficking offences and other offences (except in relation to the 'criminal lifestyle' provisions). Powers that were formerly exercised by the High Court in relation to restraint orders and the supervision and enforcement of confiscation orders are exercised by the Crown Court. The Act also made provision for 'civil recovery' where the defendant has been convicted or not even charged with an offence.

G. Agencies Responsible for the Enforcement of the Legislation

The Assets Recovery Agency

Section 74 of the Serious Crime Act 2007 (SCA) abolished the Assets Recovery Agency **1.16** (ARA) with effect from 1 April 2008. Schedule 8 to the SCA transferred the civil recovery powers of ARA to the Serious Organised Crime Agency (SOCA) and extended those powers to the Director of Public Prosecutions, the Director of the Revenue and Customs Prosecutions Office (now merged with the CPS), and the Director of the Serious Fraud Office. The Revenue functions formerly exercised by the Director of ARA are also transferred to SOCA. Responsibility for the training and accreditation of financial investigators is transferred to the National Policing Improvement Agency. Part 1 of POCA established ARA and Sch 1 sets out the terms of appointment for the Director.

The Serious Organised Crime Agency

As noted above, the effect of Sch 8 to the Serious Crime Act 2007 is to transfer the civil **1.17** recovery and revenue functions of the ARA to SOCA. SOCA is itself a creature of statute established by s 1 of the Serious Organised Crime and Police Act 2005 (SOCPA). By s 2(1) of the Act:

SOCA has the functions of—

(a) preventing and detecting serious organised crime, and

(b) contributing to the reduction of such crime in other ways and to the mitigation of its consequences.

1.18 By s 3(1) of SOCPA, SOCA has the following function as to information in relation to crime:

... gathering, storing, analysing and disseminating information relevant to—

(a) the prevention, detection, investigation or prosecution of offences, or

(b) the reduction of crime in other ways or the mitigation of its consequences.

1.19 By s 3(2) of SOCPA, SOCA is empowered to disseminate such information to police forces, special police forces, law enforcement agencies or such other persons as it considers appropriate in connection with its functions under s 3(1). Section 3(4) defines 'law enforcement agencies' in very broad terms to include the Commissioners of HM Revenue and Customs or any other government department, the Scottish Administration, any other person charged with the duty of investigating offences or charging offenders, and any other person outside the UK carrying on activities similar to those carried on by SOCA or a police force.

1.20 The general powers of SOCA are set out in s 5(2) of the Act which provides as follows:

SOCA may—

(a) institute criminal proceedings in England and Wales or Northern Ireland;

(b) at the request of the chief officer of a police force or of a special police force, act in support of any activities of that force;

(c) at the request of any law enforcement agency, act in support of any activities of that agency;

(d) enter into other arrangements for co-operating with bodies or persons (in the United Kingdom or elsewhere) which it considers appropriate in connection with the exercise of SOCA's powers under section 2 or 3 or any activities within subsection (3).

1.21 By s 5(3) of SOCPA, SOCA may carry on activities in relation to other crime if they are carried on for the purposes of any of the functions conferred on SOCA.

1.22 On any view, these provisions give SOCA a very wide remit indeed. It is noteworthy that SOCA was established in response to the Government's White Paper 'One Step Ahead: A 21st Century Strategy to Defeat Organised Crime' (Cm 6167) and, when it was launched in April 2006, was heralded in the media as 'the British FBI'. The extent to which it succeeds in meeting these aims remains to be seen.

1.23 It should also be noted that SOCA has no prosecutorial function and is not responsible for the conduct of criminal proceedings in relation to the offences it investigates. By s 38 of the Act, prosecutions for 'designated offences' are conducted by the Director of Revenue and Customs Prosecutions, and prosecutions for 'non designated offences' are conducted by the Director of Public Prosecutions. The expression 'designated offences' is not defined in the Act, but s 39 provides that the Directors may give directions to enable SOCA to determine whether cases should be referred to the Director of Revenue and Customs Prosecutions or to the Director of Public Prosecutions.

In so far as the transfer of ARA's civil recovery powers to SOCA is concerned, its purpose **1.24** was described in the Home Office Asset Recovery Action Plan published in May 2007 as being:

> . . . to build on the successes ARA has secured and give additional momentum to the use of the civil recovery powers in POCA.

The criteria that SOCA require to be satisfied before it will embark on a civil recovery **1.25** or revenue investigation are set out on the Agency's website at <http://www.soca.gov.uk> and are:

- Criminal investigation and prosecution must have been considered and either failed or been impossible e.g. because of lack of resources within the law enforcement agency.
- For Civil Recovery, there must be evidence of criminal conduct that is supported to the civil standard of proof (i.e. on the balance of probabilities) and that has generated the funding or acquisition of the referred recoverable property. The Civil Evidence Rules will apply and evidence may include hearsay, statements by co-accused or other material that could not be used in a criminal case. The professional opinion of an experienced police officer who knows the subject may also be used as evidence from an expert witness.
- For Tax Cases, there must be material to give rise to reasonable suspicion that there is criminality that has produced an untaxed income. There suspicion may rest in whole or in part on reliable intelligence.
- Recoverable property must have been identified to a value of at least £10,000 and acquired within the previous 12 years (or 20 years for Part 6 Tax).
- All relevant case papers both criminal and financial (where applicable) are to be made available for inspection and use by the Agency in assessing this referral for adoption. (If documents are not made available to the Serious Organised Crime Agency then this may affect whether the case is adopted.)

This criteria is very similar to those previously used by the ARA. In particular, it follows the guidance given to the former Director of ARA by the Secretary of State under s 2(5) of POCA to the effect that the institution of criminal proceedings should always be considered first and either have failed or proved impossible to complete.

The Crown Prosecution Service

The Crown Prosecution Service (CPS) is responsible for the restraint and confiscation aspects **1.26** of all prosecutions instituted by the police. The Central Confiscation Branch, located at CPS Headquarters, has the conduct of all restraint and confiscation proceedings brought under the DTA and CJA 1988 in police cases. POCA cases are generally dealt with locally in CPS area offices. The Central Confiscation Branch also has the conduct of the restraint and confiscation aspects of cases brought by SOCA in those cases where the CPS is the lead prosecuting authority. Following the merger of the CPS with the RCPO, the Central Confiscation Branch and the Asset Forfeiture Division have combined, within the auspices of the Organised Crime Division, and is now referred to as 'The Proceeds of Crime Unit'.

The Revenue and Customs Prosecutions Office

The Revenue and Customs Prosecutions Office (RCPO) was established under s 34 of **1.27** the Commissioners for Revenue and Customs Act 2005 and came into existence on

18 April, 2005. The Office was initially headed by a Director appointed under s 34(1) of the Act by the Attorney-General.

1.28 The RCPO was established following much criticism of its predecessor, the Customs and Excise Prosecutions Office within the Solicitor's Office of HM Customs and Excise. A number of inquiries into failed prosecutions had criticised the lack of independence of the Office which reported through its Solicitor to the Commissioners of Customs and Excise.

1.29 The restraint and enforcement aspects of all RCPO prosecutions, whether under the DTA, CJA 1988, or POCA, were dealt with by its Asset Forfeiture Division (AFD) working independently of, but in close liaison with, the prosecuting lawyer. The AFD also had the conduct of the restraint and confiscation aspects of SOCA-led investigations and prosecutions in those cases where the RCPO was the lead prosecution agency.

1.30 In April 2009, the Attorney General announced her intention of merging the RCPO and the Crown Prosecution Service into a single prosecutions agency. That merger has resulted in the overhaul of the Organised Crime Division, of which the Proceeds of Crime Unit (incorporating the former AFD), will be one component part.

HM Revenue and Customs

1.31 On 18 April 2005 the Inland Revenue and HM Customs and Excise merged to form one new Department known as HM Revenue and Customs (HMRC). HMRC is responsible for mounting criminal investigations into precisely the same offences for which its predecessors had responsibility, including money laundering and tax frauds. The one significant difference is that HMRC has no prosecutorial function: as noted above, this is the responsibility of the Revenue and Customs Division of the merged CPS. HMRC does, however, retain responsibility for applications before the magistrates' court for the inland detention and forfeiture of cash under Pt V of POCA. The effect of ss 5, 6, and 50 of the Commissioners for Revenue and Customs Act 2005 is such that references in any enactment, statutory instrument, or other document to the 'Commissioners of Customs and Excise' is deemed to be a reference to the Commissioners of HMRC, and similarly references to 'Customs Officers' are deemed to be references to officers of HMRC.

The UK Border Agency

1.32 The UK Border Agency (UKBA) takes over the role of Customs at airports and ports throughout the UK from 5 August 2009. While the force of the cash forfeiture and condemnation provisions will remain unchanged, the switch will involve the handing over of responsibility from HMRC to the UKBA of seizures and investigations in relation to travellers found in possession of cash in excess of the minimum amount and excise goods.

1.33 Section 26 of the Borders, Citizenship and Immigration Act 2009 makes various transfer provisions. The Scheme gives effect to the transfer of specified property, rights, and liabilities from the Commissioners for Revenue and Customs to the Secretary of State for the Home Department and the Director of Border Revenue in connection with the exercise of the Commissioners' functions. The Secretary of State's functions will be exercised by delegation to the Chief Executive of UKBA.

The changes include: **1.34**

> The liabilities and legal proceedings transferred in Parts II and III of this Scheme shall include statutory reviews and appeals pursuant to sections 14 and 16 of and Schedule 5 to the Finance Act 1994, condemnation proceedings pursuant to Schedule 3 to CEMA, requests, notices and appeals pursuant to the Freedom of Information Act 2000 and requests pursuant to the Data Protection Act 1998.

The Serious Fraud Office

The Serious Fraud Office (SFO) was established under the Criminal Justice Act 1987 to inves-   **1.35**
tigate and prosecute cases of serious fraud. The Act gives the SFO a number of investigatory powers not vested in other law enforcement agencies, including the power under s 2 to require any person whom the Director has reason to believe has relevant information, or a person under investigation, to attend for interview and provide information and documentation.

The Act provides no definition of what constitutes a 'serious fraud' and the SFO does not   **1.36**
take on every case referred to it. According to the SFO website (<http://www.sfo.gov.uk>), the following matters are taken into account in deciding whether to adopt a case:

(a) Does the value of the alleged fraud exceed £1,000,000?
(b) Is there a significant international dimension?
(c) Is the case likely to be of widespread public concern?
(d) Does the case require highly specialised knowledge, eg of financial markets?
(e) Is there a need to use the SFO's special powers such as those under s 2?
(f) Does the fraud appear to be complex and one where the use of the s 2 powers might be appropriate?

Offences prosecuted by the SFO are caught by the restraint and confiscation elements of the CJA 1988 and POCA and the SFO has its own specialist confiscation unit, the Asset Recovery Unit, handling this aspect of their cases.

Regional Asset Recovery Teams

Regional Asset Recovery Teams (RART) have been set up in London, Wales, North West   **1.37**
and North East England, and the West Midlands. The teams are formed of police and customs officers, as well as National Criminal Intelligence Service (NCIS) staff and provide advice, support, and assistance to law enforcement authorities within their areas. They will take over the financial investigations in particular cases and prepare witness statements in support of restraint applications and, where the defendants are convicted, will prepare the prosecutor's statement of information. Many of the officers attached to the RARTs are accredited financial investigators under POCA.

HMCS Regional Confiscation Units

There were originally 63 independent offices in 42 areas that dealt with confiscation   **1.38**
enforcement through magistrates' courts. There are now nine dedicated Regional Confiscation Units (RCUs) which are located in the South West, South East, London, North West (Bolton), North West (Merseyside and Cheshire), North East, Wales, Midlands East, and Midlands West. The benefits of those RCUs include:

• delivery of 'total confiscation' by ensuring the end-to-end multi-agency confiscation process has been designed into the delivery mechanism;

- a central point of contact for internal colleagues and stakeholders from other agencies, eg police prosecutors;
- improved communication links with other asset recovery agencies/stakeholders;
- opportunities for joint training/awareness with other agencies raising the profile and ensuring all are working to the same goal;
- consolidating casework management processes;
- driving forward best practice;
- ensuring a singular and dedicated focus;
- performance improvement; and
- engagement with Local Criminal Justice Boards.

H. The International Element

1.39 Drug trafficking, in nearly every case, at some stage involves the smuggling of controlled drugs from one country to another. There is also an international element in many other organised criminal activities, including tax frauds, people smuggling, and money laundering. It is not surprising therefore that the various Acts make provision for assets held in the UK by defendants being prosecuted in other jurisdictions to be restrained and ultimately realised in satisfaction of a foreign confiscation order. Similarly all UK confiscation legislation applies to assets a defendant owns overseas, and prosecuting authorities frequently seek the assistance of overseas jurisdictions, by means of letters of request, to restrain such assets and, after conviction, realise the same in satisfaction of a confiscation order. The High Court and Crown Court also has the power to make a 'repatriation order' directing a defendant to bring within the jurisdiction of the court assets he holds overseas.

I. Money Laundering

1.40 Closely related to restraint and confiscation law is the law relating to money laundering. Those who participate in drug trafficking and other criminal offences that yield huge profits need to conceal their proceeds from law enforcement authorities to prevent confiscation and also to disguise the true source of their ill-gotten gains. Consequently, confiscation legislation has criminalised money laundering activities and, as the threat of money laundering has increased, so the provisions have become increasingly more draconian. The legislation now extends to financial institutions and others who hold money on behalf of clients. The Money Laundering Regulations 2003 and 2007 make it a criminal offence not to report suspicious transactions to law enforcement authorities, and impose a positive obligation to introduce systems and staff training with a view to detecting such transactions.

J. Recent Developments in Confiscation Law

1.41 Since the second edition of this work was published in 2007 we have seen many significant developments in confiscation law, both in terms of statute and case law. We summarise below the most important developments which are considered in greater detail in the following chapters.

Assessment of benefit: *R v May, Jennings,* and *Green*

In 2008 the House of Lords handed down its long-awaited ruling in *R v May and Others* **1.42**
[2008] UKHL 28. The case is of the greatest importance to practitioners in proceeds of
crime cases. In summary, the House had to determine how the court should assess the
benefit derived from criminal conduct by one defendant when he has obtained property
jointly with co-conspirators. The House of Lords held that in such circumstances the court
should not apportion the property between the defendants, and each is taken to have
received and to be accountable for the total value of the property obtained. The fact that
this may lead to double recovery is immaterial. At the end of the judgment, their Lordships
took the opportunity of giving important advice to courts dealing with applications for
confiscation orders.

The Court of Appeal has subsequently begun the task of determining the large number of **1.43**
appeals that have been held up awaiting the House of Lords ruling in *May*. The indications
are that the Court is adopting a less robust approach following the *May* decision and a
number of appeals against confiscation orders under all three statutory regimes have been
allowed. The effect of the *May* ruling is fully considered in Chapter 9.

Release of restrained funds to meet legal expenses in POCA cases

The release of restrained funds to pay legal fees, under all three Acts, has continued to **1.44**
generate much controversy as the courts attempt to achieve the right balance between
ensuring that defendants are properly represented on the one hand and preventing the
dissipation of restrained assets on the other. Four cases should be highlighted.

In the much publicised case of *Re P, Harrow Crown Court*, 18 March 2008, His Honour **1.45**
Judge Mole QC stayed a confiscation hearing under POCA because no counsel could be
found who was prepared to act for the defendant, a convicted drug trafficker, at legal aid
rates. On hearing that 18 sets of chambers had been approached and no one was prepared
to act for the defendant at the prescribed rate of £178.25 per day, the judge found that the
defendant would not receive a fair hearing and stayed the confiscation proceedings.

In *U Limited v Revenue and Customs Prosecutions Office* [2007] EWCA Crim 3128 the **1.46**
Court of Appeal held that the prohibition on the release of restrained funds to pay legal
expenses in POCA extended to judicial review proceedings that related to the offence with
which the defendant was charged or in respect of which he was under investigation.

In *Irwin Mitchell v Revenue and Customs Prosecutions Office and another* [2008] EWCA **1.47**
Crim 1741 the Court of Appeal held that a POCA restraint order did not apply to an
amount of £5,000 paid by the defendant into a solicitor's client account before the order
was made, where the firm had already incurred fees up to that amount.

In CJA and DTA cases, where restrained funds may still be released to pay legal fees, in a **1.48**
series of rulings, the courts have held that the right to draw on the restrained assets for such
purposes does not continue indefinitely. In *Revenue and Customs Prosecutions Office v
Briggs-Price* [2007] EWCA Civ 568 the Court of Appeal held that the release of funds to
meet legal expenses was ultimately a matter for the court's discretion which must be exercised judicially and proportionately. In general the right to draw on the restrained fund

would come to an end when a defendant had exhausted all domestic avenues of appeal against his conviction and confiscation order.

1.49 In two subsequent cases, *Re S* [2008] EWHC 1295 (Admin) and *Re L* [2008] EWHC 3321 (Admin) the High Court has ruled that payments of restrained funds for legal and living expenses should come to an end where confiscation orders remain unsatisfied long after all domestic avenues of appeal have been exhausted.

Management receivers—the *Capewell* decisions

1.50 One of the most significant developments in confiscation law in recent times concerns the appointment of management receivers at the pre-conviction stage. The courts have expressed considerable concern as to the costs incurred by management receivers which have, on occasion, been disproportionate to any benefit derived to the defendant's estate, particularly in the light of the decision in *Hughes v Customs and Excise Commissioners* [2002] 4 All ER 633, where the Court of Appeal held that the defendant is liable to meet the receiver's costs even when the order has been discharged following his acquittal.

1.51 In January 2007 the House of Lords gave its opinion in the appeal of *Capewell v HM Revenue and Customs* [2007] UKHL 2, (2007) 1 WLR 386, following the Court of Appeal's decision in a CJA (High Court) receivership case that r 69.7(2) of the Civil Procedure Rules (CPR) was designed to give the Court some discretion in relation to who would pay the court-appointed receiver's remuneration. The Court of Appeal had accordingly made an order requiring Customs to be responsible for payment of the receiver's remuneration for part of the period of the receivership.

1.52 The central issue in *Capewell* therefore concerned whether the case of *Hughes* remained good law as a result of the introduction of CPR 69.7. The House of Lords reversed the Court of Appeal's ruling and as a result, the common law position in *Hughes* has now been re-affirmed, and all receiverships under the DTA, CJA 1988, and POCA legislation will proceed on the basis that the overall costs of the receivership will be drawn from assets within the receivership estate, even if the defendant is subsequently acquitted, not proceeded against, or the receivership is successfully discharged.

Restraint orders: failure to comply with the duty to give full and frank disclosure

1.53 In *Jennings v CPS* [2005] 4 All ER 391 the Court of Appeal ruled that the public interest in restraining assets to make them available for confiscation was such that restraint orders should not always be discharged where there has been a failure by the prosecutor to give full and frank disclosure. The Court observed that in many such cases it is sufficient for the court to express its displeasure by penalising the prosecutor's actions in costs and that the remedy of discharging the order entirely should be reserved for cases whether the prosecutor's failure to disclose has been 'appalling'.

Release of restrained funds to pay unsecured third party creditors

1.54 In CJA and DTA cases, there appear to be two conflicting authorities as to whether the legislative steer permits the release of restrained funds to pay unsecured third party creditors of the defendant. The decision of Buckley J in *Re W* The Times, 15 November 1990 suggests that restraint orders may not be varied for this purpose to meet debts owed by the defendant to unsecured third party creditors. But in *Re X* [2004] 3 WLR 906 Davis J ruled that *Re W* was wrongly decided and that the court did have a discretion to release restrained funds for such purposes in appropriate circumstances.

In *Serious Fraud Office v Lexi Holdings PLC (In Administration)* [2008] EWCA Crim 1443 **1.55** the Court of Appeal considered whether the differently worded legislative steer in s 69 of POCA permitted funds to be released to pay third party creditors when the restraint order had been made under that Act. The Court concluded that there was no such discretion. The Court also gave important guidance as to how cases involving complex points of law far removed from the usual work of the Crown Court should be dealt with in future. The Court suggested that henceforth such applications should be adjourned for hearing by a specialist Chancery Circuit Judge or a High Court Judge assigned to the Chancery Division. The Court also reminded practitioners of their obligation under s 58(5) and (6) of POCA in relation to restrained assets over which they are litigating on behalf of third parties. These provisions require that the prosecutor and any receiver appointed under the Act are to be given the opportunity of making representations before the Court decides whether to stay third party litigation in respect of restrained assets or allow it to continue. The implications of the *Lexi Holdings* ruling are considered in Chapters 5 and 16.

Delay in enforcing confiscation orders

The ruling of the Divisional Court in *Lloyd v Bow Street Magistrates' Court* [2003] EWHC **1.56** Admin 2294 to the effect that an unreasonable delay in taking action to enforce confiscation orders by way of implementation of the default sentence constitutes a breach of the offender's Art 6 rights, has resulted in a number of challenges to orders made by enforcing magistrates' courts.

These challenges, however, have had little success. In *Joyce v Dover Magistrates' Court* [2008] **1.57** EWHC 1448, the enforcing magistrates' court accepted that the delay had been such as to preclude implementation of the default sentence and sought to rely on civil remedies instead. The defendant submitted that the delay had been such that it would amount to an abuse of process to continue with the enforcement proceedings. The District Judge rejected this argument and this was upheld on appeal to the Divisional Court. The Court held that although civil enforcement proceedings could be stayed as an abuse of process, the reasons given by the District Judge for refusing a stay were, on the facts, unassailable. In *Minshall v Marylebone Magistrates' Court* [2008] EWHC 2800 (Admin) the defendant accepted that the prosecutor had in no way been responsible for the delay in the enforcement process, but nonetheless contended that a delay caused by his appeal against the confiscation order was such that proceedings to consider implementation of the default sentence should be stayed. The Court rejected the defendant's contention, finding that there was nothing unreasonable or unjustified in the delay given that, with his agreement, his appeal had been held up awaiting a ruling from the House of Lords in a case that turned on the same point. The Court did, however, accept that a delay in the appeals process, for which the State was responsible, could, in appropriate circumstances, amount to a breach of Art 6. These cases are considered in more detail in Chapter 11.

The international element

1.58   In *King v Serious Fraud Office* [2009] UKHL 19, the House of Lords held that the Proceeds of Crime Act 2002 (External Requests and Orders) Order 2005 (SI 2005/3181) only empowered the Crown Court to restrain a defendant from dealing with assets held in England and Wales. It did not give the Court jurisdiction, in making a restraint order pursuant to an external request, to restrain assets held by the defendant outside the jurisdiction. In another case involving the SFO, *Director of Serious Fraud Office v A* [2007] EWCA Crim 1927, the Court of Appeal held that a failure by the applicant for a restraint order to disclose that the Iranian judge making the external request was a military judge rather than a civilian judge did not amount to a breach of the duty of full and frank disclosure sufficiently to justify the restraint order being set aside. These cases are considered in more detail in Chapter 19.

1.59   After much delay, the Proceeds of Crime Act 2002 (External Requests and Orders) Order 2005, SI 2005/3181, made under s 444 of POCA, came into force on 1 January 2006. It revoked the Drug Trafficking Act and Criminal Justice Act Designated Countries and Territories Orders, and provides a comprehensive code for the enforcement of external orders in the UK and for the making of restraint orders in support of external investigations and proceedings. The most significant difference is that applications in relation to such orders and proceedings are now made to the Crown Court rather than the High Court. The effect of the Order is considered in more detail in Chapter 19.

2

RESTRAINT ORDERS

A. Introduction

An application for a restraint order to prevent the dissipation of assets is frequently the first **2.01** step a prosecutor will take in the confiscation process. Restraint orders are most commonly sought shortly before or just after criminal proceedings have been commenced, but they can be sought at any stage prior to the conclusion of those proceedings. Indeed, it is by no means unusual for a restraint order to be made after a confiscation order has been made for the purpose of protecting assets against dissipation during the enforcement process. Further, under POCA, a restraint order may be made as soon as a criminal investigation is started in England and Wales with regard to an offence.

Purpose of restraint orders

Many months, or even years, may elapse between a criminal investigation getting under- **2.02** way and a defendant ultimately standing trial. The aims of the legislation would clearly be defeated if a defendant against whom a confiscation order may be made could deal freely with his assets while awaiting trial: he would be able to dispose of his property to ensure he was effectively 'judgment proof' by the time the trial takes place. POCA, in common with the legislation that preceded it, gives the court jurisdiction to make restraint orders to prevent a defendant dealing with his property pending the conclusion of the criminal proceedings brought against him. Restraint orders may also be made to prevent a defendant dealing in his property pending the determination of an application to increase a confiscation order that has already been made.

Freezing orders distinguished

2.03 Although the Court of Appeal held in *Re Peters* [1988] QB 571 that the jurisdiction to make restraint orders is 'clearly analogous' to the jurisdiction to make freezing orders (formerly *Mareva* injunctions), there are a number of important distinctions between the two forms of relief. The jurisdiction to make freezing orders stemmed initially from the inherent jurisdiction of the High Court before being enshrined in s 37(3) of the Supreme Court Act 1981, whereas the restraint order has always been a creature of statute. Further, the purpose of the freezing order is to preserve assets to meet any award of damages that might be made in favour of the claimant in a civil action. The restraint order, in contrast, is intended to preserve a defendant's assets with a view to making them available to satisfy any confiscation order that might be made against him following his conviction for a criminal offence.

2.04 Of most practical importance, POCA makes specific provision as to the way in which the court must exercise its discretion when considering applications for restraint and receivership orders and applications by defendants and affected third parties to vary or discharge such orders. By s 69(2) of POCA:

(2) The powers—
  (a) must be exercised with a view to the value for the time being of realisable property being made available (by the property's realisation) for satisfying any confiscation order that has been or may be made against the defendant;
  (b) must be exercised, in a case where a confiscation order has not been made, with a view to securing that there is no diminution in the value of realisable property;
  (c) must be exercised without taking account of any obligation of the defendant or a recipient of a tainted gift if the obligation conflicts with the object of satisfying any confiscation order that has been or may be made against the defendant;
  (d) may be exercised in respect of a debt owed by the Crown.

This provision, often referred to as 'the legislative steer', led the Court of Appeal in *Serious Fraud Office v Lexi Holdings PLC (In Administration)* [2008] EWCA Crim 1443 to hold that the Court has no jurisdiction to vary a restraint order to allow an unsecured bona fide creditor of the defendant to be paid from restrained funds. This is in marked contrast to the position in relation to freezing orders where the court will not allow a claimant who has not obtained judgment to gain priority over other creditors of the defendant.

2.05 A further distinction between restraint orders and freezing orders is that the court has no power, when making a restraint order, to require the prosecutor to give an undertaking to indemnify third parties in respect of any liability which may flow from compliance with the order: see *Re R (Restraint Order)* [1990] 2 All ER 569. A freezing order, in contrast, will not normally be granted unless such an undertaking is given by the claimant. Similarly, as an essential prerequisite to obtaining a freezing order, the claimant will be required to give an undertaking to pay damages to the defendant if it later transpires that the order should not have been granted. In relation to restraint orders, however, r 59.2(4) of the Criminal Procedure Rules 2005 provides that a prosecutor applying for a restraint order shall not be required to give any such undertaking. Further, s 72 of POCA imposes strict limitations on the circumstances in which an acquitted defendant can seek compensation from the prosecutor for any loss he has suffered as a result of being subject to the restraint order.

Finally, and perhaps most controversially of all, s 41(4) of POCA precludes the release of   **2.06**
restrained funds to meet legal fees incurred by the defendant if they relate to the offence
with which he is charged or in respect of which he is under investigation. This provision not
only includes the criminal proceedings but extends to the restraint proceedings themselves:
see *Customs and Excise Commissioners v S* [2005] 1 WLR 1338.

B. Restraint Orders

When does POCA apply?

Under the Proceeds of Crime Act 2002 (Commencement No 5, Transitional Provisions,   **2.07**
Savings and Amendment) Order 2003, SI 2003/333, from 24 March 2003 all applications
for restraint orders are made to the Crown Court under POCA where it is alleged that the
offences to which the application relates were committed on or after that date. Proceedings
that have been instituted in the High Court prior to that date under the Criminal Justice
Act 1988 (CJA 1988) and the Drug Trafficking Act 1994 (DTA) will continue to be heard
in that court even after the commencement date. Applications for the variation or discharge of such orders, for the appointment of management and enforcement receivers, or
for certificates of inadequacy therefore remain within the jurisdiction of the High Court.
Similarly, new applications for restraint orders in cases where the offences are alleged to
have been committed before POCA came into force will continue to be made in the High
Court under the CJA 1988 and DTA.

Difficult questions may arise as to whether it is appropriate to proceed under POCA where   **2.08**
the offences charged or under investigation straddle the 24 March 2003 commencement
date. Article 5 of the 2003 Order provides that:

Section 41 (restraint orders) and section 74 (enforcement abroad) of the Act shall not have effect
where—
(a) the powers in those sections would otherwise be exercisable by virtue of a condition in section 40(2)
     or (3) of the Act being satisfied; and
(b) the offence mentioned in section 40(2)(a) or 40(3)(a), as the case may be, was committed before
     24th March 2003.

Further, Art 3(1) provides that s 6 of POCA, which gives the court power to make confiscation orders, shall not have effect where any of the offences were committed before 24
March 2003.

It appeared that the combined effect of these provisions in the 2003 Order was that the CJA   **2.09**
1988 and DTA applied whenever one or more of the offences were committed before 24
March 2003. This interpretation was, however, held to be incorrect in *Revenue and Customs
Prosecutions Office v Hill* [2005] EWCA Crim 3271. In March 2003 HMRC began an
investigation into the affairs of two companies allegedly involved in a dishonest scheme to
perpetrate a fraud on the Revenue. In July 2005 search warrants were obtained and three
potential defendants were arrested and interviewed. Initial analysis of the documentation
suggested that between £6 and £10 million had been transferred overseas between 2003
and 2005. The prosecutor took the view that these transfers amounted to money laundering offences. It is clear, however, that if any offences of tax evasion had been committed,

they had either been committed before 24 March 2003 or were continuing offences which had begun before and continued after 24 March 2003. Indeed, enquiries revealed evidence of tax evasion going back to 1999.

2.10   The prosecutor, wishing to take advantage of the provision in POCA enabling the Crown Court to make a restraint order as soon as a criminal investigation has started, decided to focus on the money laundering offences which, with one exception, had taken place after 24 March 2003. The prosecutor applied, without notice, for restraint and management receivership orders under POCA and these were granted by the Crown Court. The defendants subsequently applied for the orders to be set aside and, on an *inter partes* application, the Crown Court judge agreed the orders should be discharged, ruling that they should have been made by the High Court under the CJA 1988.

2.11   The Crown exercised its right of appeal under s 43 of POCA, contending that the judge had erred in law in holding that the CJA 1988 regime applied. The Court of Appeal upheld the prosecutor's appeal, ruling, in the words of Smith LJ:

> In our view, the judge erred in his approach to the requirement of section 40(2)(a) when read in conjunction with Article 5 of the Commencement Order. The test to be applied is whether an investigation has begun into an offence which took place after 24 March 2003. In order to satisfy section 69, the offence must be one in respect of which a confiscation order may be made following conviction. For the purpose of establishing jurisdiction to make an order, it matters not whether the investigating authority is also investigating one or more offences which occurred before 24th March 2003. Nor does it matter, for the purpose of jurisdiction, that there is criminal conduct occurring before 24th March 2003, which underlies the post March 2003 offences—as may occur with money laundering. In our view, the time at which the test is to be applied is the time when the application is made not when the investigation began. That is clear from the words of section 40(2)(a). All that is required therefore, to establish jurisdiction, is that an offence that may, following conviction, give rise to a confiscation order is under investigation at the time of the application.

The Court remitted the matter back to the Crown Court so the judge could determine whether it would be appropriate to make another restraint order having regard to the fact that the defendants' assets had subsequently been frozen in civil proceedings.

2.12   It is submitted that prosecutors should proceed with caution when relying on the restraint provisions of POCA in cases where the alleged offences straddle the commencement date. If the prosecutor has a settled intention to prefer charges to which the CJA 1988 or DTA apply, applications for restraint orders should be made to the High Court under that legislation. Where, however, at the commencement of an investigation, the prosecutor intends to focus only on offences committed after 24 March 2003, he may properly proceed under POCA. If, at a later date, it becomes apparent to him that charges will be preferred to which the CJA 1988 or DTA apply, he should forthwith apply to the High Court for an order under the appropriate Act and seek the discharge of the POCA order.

2.13   Those acting for individuals subject to POCA restraint orders should be vigilant to ensure that the prosecutor has used the jurisdiction appropriately. Any attempt by a prosecutor to rely on POCA simply to obtain a restraint order when a defendant is still subject to investigation, or to preclude the release of funds to meet legal expenses would, it is submitted, amount to an abuse of process to which the court should be alerted immediately.

Conditions for obtaining restraint orders under POCA

Section 40(1) of POCA provides that the Crown Court may make a restraint order if any   **2.14**
of the following conditions are satisfied.

The first condition: criminal investigations

By s 40(2) the first condition is that: **2.15**

(a) a criminal investigation has been started in England and Wales with regard to an offence; and
(b) there is reasonable cause to believe that the alleged offender has benefited from his criminal conduct.

This condition represents a significant departure from the position under the old legislation. Restraint orders can only be made under the CJA 1988 and DTA when the defendant has been charged with an offence to which the legislation applies or the prosecutor is in a position to say that he will be so charged at a future date.

A 'criminal investigation' is defined in s 88(2) of POCA in the following terms: **2.16**

> A criminal investigation is an investigation which police officers or other persons have a duty to conduct with a view to it being ascertained whether a person should be charged with an offence.

The term therefore extends to investigations conducted by all law enforcement authorities and not just the police. By s 40(9)(a) of POCA, references to 'the defendant' are to be construed as references to the alleged offender and, by s 40(9)(b), references to 'the prosecutor' are to the person the court believes will have the conduct of any proceedings for an offence.

The second condition: criminal proceedings already started

By s 40(3), the second condition is that: **2.17**

(a) proceedings for an offence have been started in England and Wales and not concluded, and
(b) there is reasonable cause to believe that the defendant has benefited from his criminal conduct.

This condition is in similar terms to the previous legislation and is the provision under which most applications for restraint orders are made. By s 85(1), proceedings for an offence are started:

(a) when a justice of the peace issues a summons or warrant under section 1 of the Magistrates' Courts Act 1980 in respect of an offence;
(b) when a person is charged with the offence after being taken into custody without a warrant;
(c) when a bill of indictment is preferred under section 2 of the Administration of Justice (Miscellaneous Provisions) Act 1933 in a case falling within subsection (2)(b) of that section (preferment by Court of Appeal or High Court judge).

Again, this definition will be familiar to practitioners as being in identical terms to the CJA 1988 and DTA. Section 85(3) to (6) provides a much more comprehensive definition of the phrase 'proceedings are concluded' than under the old legislation, and is in the following terms:

(3) If the defendant is acquitted on all counts in proceedings for an offence, the proceedings are concluded when he is acquitted.

(4) If the defendant is convicted in proceedings for an offence and the conviction is quashed or the defendant is pardoned before a confiscation order is made, the proceedings are concluded when the conviction is quashed or the defendant is pardoned.

(5) If a confiscation order is made against the defendant in proceedings for an offence (whether the order is made by the Crown Court or the Court of Appeal) the proceedings are concluded—
  (a) when the order is satisfied or discharged, or
  (b) when the order is quashed and there is no further possibility of an appeal against the decision to quash the order.

2.18 It is a common misconception that proceedings conclude on the making of a confiscation order and that any restraint order is discharged at that point. Section 85(5)(a) makes it plain that proceedings only conclude when the confiscation order is satisfied and the restraint order may thus remain in force until full payment is made. Indeed, it is by no means uncommon for restraint orders to be sought for the first time after the making of a confiscation order for the purpose of preventing any dissipation of assets pending the enforcement of the order or the determination of any appeal.

2.19 Section 85(6) to (8) sets out the rules for determining when proceedings conclude in circumstances where the prosecutor exercises his right of appeal under s 31(2) of the Act. The section provides:

(6) If the defendant is convicted in proceedings for an offence but the Crown Court decides not to make a confiscation order against him, the following rules apply—
  (a) if an application for leave to appeal under section 31(2) is refused, the proceedings are concluded when the decision to refuse is made;
  (b) if the time for applying for leave to appeal under section 31(2) expires without an application being made, the proceedings are concluded when the time expires;
  (c) if on appeal under section 31(2) the Court of Appeal confirms the Crown Court's decision, and an application for leave to appeal under section 33 is refused, the proceedings are concluded when the decision to refuse is made;
  (d) if on appeal under section 31(2) the Court of Appeal confirms the Crown Court's decision, and the time for applying for leave to appeal under section 33 expires without an application being made, the proceedings are concluded when the time expires;
  (e) if on appeal under section 31(2) the Court of Appeal confirms the Crown Court's decision, and on appeal under section 33 the House of Lords confirms the Court of Appeal's decision, the proceedings are concluded when the House of Lords confirms the decision;
  (f) if on appeal under section 31(2) the Court of Appeal directs the Crown Court to reconsider the case, and on reconsideration the Crown Court decides not to make a confiscation order against the defendant, the proceedings are concluded when the Crown Court makes that decision;
  (g) if on appeal under section 33 the House of Lords directs the Crown Court to reconsider the case, and on reconsideration the Crown Court decides not to make a confiscation order against the defendant, the proceedings are concluded when the Crown Court makes that decision.

(7) In applying subsection (6) any power to extend the time for making application for leave to appeal must be ignored.

(8) In applying subsection (6) the fact that a court may decide on a later occasion to make a confiscation order against the defendant must be ignored.

The effect of these provisions is to permit the restraint order to remain in force until appeal proceedings have been determined by the Court of Appeal or House of Lords in accordance with ss 31 and 33 of the Act.

The third condition: application for reconsideration to be made

By s 40(4) (as amended by para 22 (2) of Pt 1 to Sch 8 of the Serious Crime Act 2007), the **2.20** third condition is that:

(a) an application by the prosecutor has been made under sections 19, 20, 27 or 28 and not concluded, or the court believes that such an application is to be made, and
(b) there is reasonable cause to believe the defendant has benefited from his criminal conduct.

Sections 19 and 20 allow the prosecutor to apply to the Crown Court to reconsider a case in **2.21** the light of fresh evidence where no confiscation order was made. Sections 27 and 28 permit the prosecutor to apply to the Crown Court for confiscation orders to be made against defendants who abscond. The effect of s 40(4) is to give the court jurisdiction to make restraint orders to prevent assets being dissipated while such applications are pending.

By s 86(1), such applications are concluded: **2.22**

(a) in a case where the court decides not to make a confiscation order against the defendant, when it makes the decision;
(b) in a case where a confiscation order is made against him as a result of the application, when the order is satisfied or discharged, or where the order is quashed and there is no further possibility of an appeal against the decision to quash the order;
(c) in a case where the application is withdrawn, when the person who made the application notifies the withdrawal to the court to which the application was made.

The effect of this section is very similar to s 85 in that it defines the word 'concluded' in such a way as to allow the restraint order to remain in force pending any appeal or until such time as any confiscation order has been satisfied.

The fourth condition: reconsideration of benefit

By s 40(5) (as amended by para 22(3) of Pt 1 to Sch 8 of the Serious Crime Act 2007), the **2.23** fourth condition is that:

(a) an application by the prosecutor has been made under section 21 and not concluded, or the court believes that such an application is to be made, and
(b) there is reasonable cause to believe that the court will decide under that section that the amount found under the new calculation of the defendant's benefit exceeds the relevant amount (as defined in that section).

Section 21 permits the court, on an application by the prosecutor, to make a new calcula- **2.24** tion of benefit and increase the confiscation order accordingly in the light of evidence that was not available at the time the original order was made.

The fifth condition: reconsideration of available amount

By s 40(6) (as amended by para 22(4) of Pt 1 to Sch 8 of the Serious Crime Act 2007), the **2.25** fifth condition is that:

(a) an application by the prosecutor has been made under section 22 and not concluded, or the court believes that such an application is to be made, and
(b) there is reasonable cause to believe that the court will decide under that section that the amount found under the new calculation of the available amount exceeds the relevant amount (as defined in that section).

Under s 22 the Crown Court may, on the application of the prosecutor or an enforcement **2.26** receiver, increase a confiscation order when it appears that the value of the defendant's realisable property exceeds that found to be available at the time the confiscation order was made. In such circumstances, the court may increase the order to such amount as it believes just, provided it does not exceed the amount found to be the defendant's benefit from the criminal conduct concerned.

2.27 By s 86(2) applications under ss 21 and 22 are concluded:

(a) in a case where the court decides not to vary the confiscation order concerned, when it makes that decision;

(b) in a case where the court varies the confiscation order as a result of the application, when the order is satisfied or discharged, or when the order is quashed and there is no further possibility of an appeal against the decision to quash the order;

(c) in a case where the application is withdrawn, when the person who made the application notifies the withdrawal to the court to which the application was made.

2.28 Section 40(8) provides that the third, fourth, and fifth conditions are not satisfied if the court believes there has been undue delay in continuing the application or that the prosecutor does not intend to proceed.

Conduct and benefit

2.29 Each of the five conditions in s 40 requires the prosecutor to prove that there is reasonable cause to believe the defendant has benefited from his criminal conduct. Section 76(1) of POCA defines 'criminal conduct' in these terms:

(1) Criminal conduct is conduct which—

(a) constitutes an offence in England and Wales, or

(b) would constitute such an offence if it occurred in England and Wales.

2.30 In many cases it will be obvious from the circumstances of the alleged offence that there is reasonable cause to believe that the defendant has benefited from such conduct: the bank robber who steals vast sums of money from a bank or the fraudster who evades paying substantial sums in tax have both clearly benefited. There are, however, many situations in which the position is less clear—what, for example, of the professional man who launders the proceeds of a client's crime through his client account and only retains control over it for a very short time? Or the tobacco smuggler who is arrested and has his bounty seized before he has the chance to sell it on?

2.31 The Act itself provides some assistance in defining benefit in s 76(4) to (7) which provides:

(4) A person benefits from conduct if he obtains property as a result of or in connection with the conduct.

(5) If a person obtains a pecuniary advantage as a result of or in connection with conduct, he is to be taken to obtain as a result of or in connection with the conduct a sum of money equal to the value of the pecuniary advantage.

(6) References to property or a pecuniary advantage obtained in connection with conduct include references to property or a pecuniary advantage obtained both in that connection and some other.

(7) If a person benefits from conduct his benefit is the value of the property obtained.

2.32 The leading authority on benefit is the decision of the House of Lords in *R v May* [2008] 2 WLR 1131. This decision will be considered in greater detail in Chapter 9, para 9.12 *et seq* but, in summary, their Lordships ruled that:

(1) Benefit is the total value of the property or advantage obtained, not the defendant's net profit after deductions of expenses and payments to co-conspirators.

(2) In determining whether the defendant has obtained property or a pecuniary advantage, the Court should apply ordinary common law principles governing entitlement and ownership.

(3) A defendant obtains property if in law he owns it, whether alone or jointly, which will ordinarily connote a power of disposition or control.

(4) A defendant ordinarily obtains a pecuniary advantage if (amongst other things) he evades a liability to which he is personally subject.

(5) Mere couriers or other minor contributors to an offence, rewarded by a specific fee and having no interest in the property or the proceeds of sale, are unlikely to be found to have obtained that property. It may, however, be otherwise in the case of money launderers.

The question of pecuniary advantage was considered by the House of Lords in the earlier **2.33** case of *R v Cadman-Smith* [2002] 1 WLR 54. The defendant had pleaded guilty to an offence of being knowingly concerned in the fraudulent evasion of excise duty. He had attempted to smuggle 1.25 million cigarettes into the country in a boat which he sailed up the Humber estuary past Customs' posts at Immingham and Hull before he reached Goole, where the boat was stopped and searched and the contraband seized by customs' officers. At the confiscation hearing the court determined that he had benefited from the offence to the extent of £130,000, the amount of the duty evaded, and a confiscation order for £46,250 was made. The Court of Appeal quashed the order on the basis that the defendant had not benefited because the cigarettes had been seized by customs officers before he had the opportunity of selling them. The prosecution appealed to the House of Lords and, in allowing the appeal, their Lordships ruled that the defendant had obtained a pecuniary advantage by evading duty on the cigarettes at the point of importation and it was immaterial that he had not been able to sell them on at the time of his arrest.

There is a plethora of authority on the issue of benefit, and further rulings can be expected **2.34** from the Court of Appeal as it applies the decision in *May and Others* to the facts of individual cases. It should be borne in mind, however, that these cases are of limited relevance in the context of an application for a restraint order made at the early stages of an investigation or prosecution. As Laws LJ observed in *Jennings v CPS* [2005] EWCA Civ 746 where a restraint order had been made under the CJA 1988:

> The sense to be attributed to 'benefit' in section 71(4) of the Act of 1988 has been the subject of a good deal of authority. We have of course to consider this learning, not least given the divide in the positions taken by counsel, but it comes, so to speak, with a health warning. The cases are generally concerned with the court's function under section 71 to make a confiscation order. But this appeal is about the prior stage arising under section 77 relating to restraint orders, which is the subject of the legislative steer given by section 82(2). I think it very important to have in mind that in deciding whether to make a restraint order under section 77 (and, if so, in what terms) the court's task is not to reach firm conclusions as to the precise extent of a respondent's benefit, or realisable property, for the purposes of section 71; though of course if those matters are plain they will be put before the judge. Rather, under section 77 the court's duty is to decide whether to make a protective order so that in the particular case the satisfaction or fulfilment of any confiscation order made or to be made will be efficacious.

Proving a risk of dissipation of assets

An applicant for a freezing order must satisfy the court that there is a real risk of assets being **2.35** dissipated in order to be entitled to relief. There is no express provision in POCA, or in the previous legislation, requiring the prosecutor to establish such a risk exists as a condition precedent to obtaining a restraint order. As no such requirement appeared in the legislation, prosecutors initially contended that, on an application for a restraint order, it was unnecessary for them to establish a risk of dissipation.

2.36 This argument was rejected by the Court of Appeal in *Re AJ and DJ* (Unreported, 9 December 1992). The defendants had been charged in July 1990 with alleged mortgage fraud offences. They were granted bail and committal proceedings were continually adjourned until, in December 1990, a voluntary bill of indictment was preferred. During the time they were on bail, the defendants made no attempt to dissipate assets but, shortly before their trial was due to commence, the CPS obtained restraint orders against them at an *ex parte* hearing. At a subsequent hearing *inter partes*, Laws J. (as he then was) discharged the orders on the basis, amongst others, that the prosecutor had failed to establish there was a risk of assets being dissipated.

2.37 On an appeal by the CPS, the Court of Appeal upheld the decision of Laws J to discharge the orders. Glidewell LJ observed at page 23C of the transcript:

> It follows in my judgment that Laws J was entirely correct to conclude that he had a discretion whether or not to make or discharge a restraint or charging order and to consider that such an order should only be made if there is a reasonable apprehension that, without it, realisable property may be dissipated. I agree with the judge that, to quote him, 'if there is not such risk, or the risk is merely fanciful, the order ought not to be made, since ex hypothesi, it would not be necessary for the achievement of its only proper purpose.

2.38 In many cases, the risk of dissipation will speak for itself. As Glidewell LJ acknowledged in *Re AJ* and *DJ*:

> I accept that in many and perhaps the substantial majority of cases where offences involving a gain exceeding £10,000 are concerned, the circumstances of the alleged offences themselves will lead to a reasonable apprehension that, without a restraint or charging order, realisable assets are likely to be dissipated. In drug trafficking offences, this is likely to be so in almost every case. Thus the onus on the prosecution will often not be difficult to satisfy.

2.39 Similarly, in relation to cases where there is an allegation of dishonesty, Longmore LJ observed in *Jennings v CPS* [2005] 4 All ER 391:

> In a case where dishonesty is charged, there will usually be reason to fear that assets will be dissipated. I do not therefore consider it necessary for the prosecutor to state in terms that he fears assets will be dissipated merely because he thinks there is a good arguable case of dishonesty. As my Lord has said, the risk of dissipation will generally speak for itself. Nevertheless prosecutors must be alive to the possibility that there may be no risk in fact. If no asset dissipation has occurred over a long period, particularly after a defendant has been charged, the prosecutor should explain why asset dissipation is now feared at the time of application for the order when it was not feared before.

2.40 In *Jennings v CPS* the defendant had been arrested on suspicion of conspiracy to defraud and fraudulent trading on 22 May 2003, was charged with conspiracy to defraud on 4 February 2004, and a CJA 1988 restraint order was made on 2 November 2004. The defendant applied to have the order discharged, amongst other things, on the grounds of delay. Leveson J refused to discharge the order on the basis that, the delay notwithstanding, the case was still in its early stages, the trial was not due to commence for some months, and there was sufficient justification for a restraint order being in place in the meantime. The Court of Appeal held that this was the correct approach and dismissed the defendant's appeal. Laws J. held:

> The principal question for the court must always be whether the protection of a restraint order is on the facts necessary to ensure so far as possible that any confiscation order will be efficacious. There remains the theoretical possibility of the eccentric case where the Crown delay on purpose for some collateral or mischievous reason. That, I am sure, can generally be discounted in the real world, as it can certainly be dismissed in this case.

Longmore LJ added:

> Delay will not usually be a significant fact on its own. It may be relevant if there has been delay between the defendant being charged and the date of the application, if there has been no dissipation of the assets meanwhile. It is then incumbent on the Crown to explain why dissipation was not seen as a major risk but now is.

2.41 These cases, relating to orders made under the old legislation after defendants had been charged, were decided by the Civil Division of the Court of Appeal. In *R v B* [2008] EWCA Crim 1374 the Court of Appeal (Criminal Division) had to consider the issue of delay and the risk of dissipation in relation to a restraint order made under POCA at a time when the defendant was still under investigation. On 17 May 2007 the defendant was arrested by officers from the Serious Organised Crime Agency (SOCA) investigating an alleged offence of concealing or disguising criminal property contrary to s 327 of POCA. Thereafter, he was admitted to bail and re-interviewed by SOCA officers on four occasions, during which time he made no attempt to dissipate assets. On 20 November 2007, on the application of the Revenue and Customs Prosecutions Office (RCPO), a restraint order was made under POCA. The order included a provision requiring the defendant to disclose the full extent of his assets and, in compliance with this provision, he made a witness statement which disclosed the existence of a donor account with a credit balance in excess of US$1 million of which the prosecutor was wholly unaware. He made no attempt to dissipate the funds in that account. Further, on 26 November the restraint order was varied to release a company bank account that had been restrained without justification and thereafter the defendant did not take the opportunity to remove any of the funds held in that account.

2.42 The defendant applied to discharge the restraint order on the grounds that there was no evidence to show that he would dissipate assets, but this was refused by the Crown Court judge. The defendant's appeal to the Court of Appeal was allowed and the restraint order discharged. Moses LJ said:

> Furthermore, in the light of the facts that we have identified of this appellant not taking the opportunity with which he was presented to dissipate his assets, it was incumbent both on the prosecution and the judge by way of reasoning to explain how it could be said that there was a real risk that he would dissipate his assets in the future when he had had every opportunity to do so in the past. In our view no such explanation has ever been forthcoming, no reasoning has been advanced upon which such a conclusion could be based.

He added:

> Of course in many cases a Crown Court Judge will have a better opportunity than this court to evaluate evidence, but it should be noted that in a case such as this the only proper safeguard of the rights of one whose property is to be interfered with by a restraint order is careful scrutiny

by the judge both on the ex parte hearing and on any application to vary or discharge not only of the issue as to whether there is reasonable course to believe that the alleged offender has benefited from his criminal conduct, but whether there is a real risk that assets will be dissipated. It should be noted that in the case on which the prosecution founded its argument, *Jennings*, the application was made after the subject of the restraint order had been prosecuted and indeed during the trial. Here, where a citizen has not even been charged, and still has not been charged, it is particularly important to see that there is a proper basis for such a serious order.

2.43 The longer the prosecutor delays in making his application for a restraint order, the more difficult it will be to establish there is a risk of assets being dissipated and the greater will be the duty on him to justify the necessity for a restraint order. Those acting for defendants and affected third parties should be vigilant in ensuring the prosecuting authority has established a risk of dissipation in relation to restraint orders obtained without notice, particularly where there has been a considerable delay between the start of the investigation and the application for a restraint order being made.

The scope and duration of restraint orders

Parties restrained by the order

2.44 Section 41(1) of POCA provides that:

If any condition set out in section 40 is satisfied the Crown Court may make an order (a restraint order) prohibiting any specified person from dealing with any realisable property held by him.

Section 41(1) gives the court very wide powers to restrain dealing in realisable property not only by the defendant, but by any other person or body holding assets in which he has an interest. Members of a defendant's family and business associates often find themselves affected by restraint orders. Wives frequently find themselves restrained from dealing with the matrimonial home and with funds held in joint bank accounts. Banks and other financial institutions holding accounts belonging to the defendant will also be bound by the terms of the restraint order. Business assets held by the defendant in conjunction with an innocent business partner are equally vulnerable to restraint.

Property restrained by the order

2.45 By s 41(2) of POCA:

A restraint order may provide that it applies—
(a) to all realisable property held by the specified person whether or not the property is described in the order;
(b) to realisable property transferred to the specified person after the order is made.

By s 83 of POCA, 'realisable property' includes any free property held by the defendant and any free property held by the recipient of a tainted gift. Section 82 provides that property is free unless an order is in force in relation to it under a number of provisions including s 27 of the Misuse of Drugs Act 1971, s 143 of the Powers of Criminal Courts (Sentencing) Act 2000, s 23 or 111 of the Terrorism Act 2000, or s 246, 266, 295(2), or 298(2) of POCA.

2.46 Section 84 contains a number of important provisions in relation to property. It provides:

(1) Property is all property wherever situated and includes—
(a) money;
(b) all forms of real or personal property;
(c) things in action and other intangible or incorporeal property.

(2) The following rules apply in relation to property—
    (a) property is held by a person if he holds an interest in it;
    (b) property is obtained by a person if he obtains an interest in it;
    (c) property is transferred by one person to another if the first one transfers or grants an interest in it to the second;
    (d) references to property held by a person include references to property vested in his trustee in bankruptcy, permanent or interim trustee (within the meaning of the Bankruptcy (Scotland) Act 1985) or liquidator;
    (e) references to an interest held by a person beneficially in property include references to an interest which would be held by him beneficially if the property were not so vested;
    (f) references to an interest, in relation to land in England and Wales or Northern Ireland, are to any legal estate or equitable interest or power;
    (g) reference to an interest, in relation to land in Scotland, are to any estate, interest, servitude or other heritable right in or over land, including a heritable security;
    (h) references to an interest, in relation to property other than land, include references to a right (including a right to possession).

In determining whether a defendant has an interest in property for the purposes of making a restraint order the court will have regard to the practical realities of the situation. In *D (UK) Ltd v Revenue and Customs Prosecutions Office* [2005] EWCA Crim 2919, a restraint order was varied, on the prosecutor's application, to include some £366,000 held in the account of a company known as 'R' on the basis that it should be available for confiscation at the end of a trial involving an alleged fraudster, Mrs S. On appeal, it was argued that the order should not have been so varied as Mrs S had no interest in the money in the company bank account. This argument was rejected by the Court of Appeal and, in dismissing the appeal, Longmore LJ said: **2.47**

> If, therefore, Revenue and Customs can show that there is a good arguable case that the money in R's account in R's bank was part of the benefit obtained by the alleged fraudster, Mrs S, that money will be liable to restraint until a confiscation order is made. In our judgment, Revenue and Customs do not have to show that there is any enforceable right to the money as between the fraudsters. If they can show an arguable case of fraud in which R (or any other party which may claim entitlement to the money) were participating, money retained in the execution of the fraud is, for the purposes of this legislation, the fraudster's money. No doubt the legal title to the chose in action constituted by R's account at the bank while it is in credit is in R, but the beneficial interest lies with any of the fraudster participants in the fraudulent scheme. It is thus an existing beneficial interest which can be subject to a restraint order, not, as Counsel sought to persuade the full court in his supplemental skeleton argument in order to obtain leave to appeal, 'an inchoate future benefit'.

In *R v Walbrook and Glasgow* [1994] Crim LR 613, the Court of Appeal held that a contingent interest under a will was capable of constituting 'property'. **2.48**

Restraint orders are often obtained at an early stage of an investigation or prosecution before the full extent of the defendant's realisable property is known, but when restraint action is considered appropriate to prevent dissipation. Prosecutors frequently rely on the wide terms of s 41(2) to restrain all assets in which the defendant has an interest whether in his possession at the time the order was made, or coming into his possession at some time thereafter. The prosecutor must not, however, seek a restraint order over assets having a value substantially in excess of the amount by which the defendant is alleged to have benefited. By way of example, if it is suggested that a defendant has benefited from a crime **2.49** to the extent of £1 million, it would clearly be oppressive for the order to restrain assets worth over £5 million. In *Re K* The Times, 30 September 1990 the court accepted that the prosecutor must be entitled to some latitude during the early stages of a case because it may not be possible to quantify the full extent of the defendant's benefit. Further, the prosecutor will be entitled to pray in aid the statutory assumptions that may be applied at a confiscation hearing. In *Re K* [2005] EWCA Crim 619 it was contended that the maximum amount of benefit of which there was *prima facie* evidence was £477,000 and there was no justification for making a restraint order to cover a greater amount. The judge rejected this argument ruling that he was entitled to have regard to the statutory assumptions which, if applied, may result in a confiscation order being made in a much larger amount. The Court of Appeal upheld the judge's ruling and rejected the contention that the restraint order should be restricted to assets to the value of £477,000. In delivering the judgment of the Court, Laws LJ said:

> In our view, the judge's reasoning demonstrates a common sense approach to the facts and we see no reason why this Court should interfere with it. It seems to us the judge was perfectly justified in looking to these assumptions as a feature of the case that might very well be in play at a later stage. The reality here is, in our judgment, that at the stage at which the judge was dealing with the matter in January 2005, and in the light of such information as he then had, he was entitled to make an order unlimited in amount. There was strong evidence of control of the companies by S and M. The companies were significantly engaged, on the Commissioners' evidence, in the defendants' criminality. We have already referred to the judge's finding, unchallenged here, that there is a substantial case that the defendants have used the companies as a façade behind which they were hiding the proceeds of smuggling. In our judgment, it would have been artificial for the judge to conclude that the realisable assets were to be treated as strictly limited to the ill gotten gains that were expressly demonstrated.

2.50 In cases to which the statutory assumptions do not apply because it cannot be shown that the defendant has a 'criminal lifestyle' and where the amount of the defendant's benefit can be readily ascertained, the prosecutor should not restrain assets significantly in excess of that benefit. Those acting for defendants subject to restraint orders should be vigilant in ensuring that the order does not restrain more assets than necessary and, if it does, invite the prosecutor to consent to an appropriate variation, failing which an application to the court should be made.

Limited companies

2.51 It is by no means uncommon for a defendant subject to a restraint order to have an interest in a limited company incorporated under the Companies Acts. As limited companies enjoy a legal personality of their own, company assets will not normally constitute 'realisable property' of the defendant within the meaning of POCA. There are, however, a number of exceptions to this general rule. Firstly, property that a defendant gifts to a company will be caught by the Act in the same way as property gifted to any other third party. The second and most important exception relates to companies under the control of the defendant that have been used to facilitate the commission of the criminal offences with which he has been charged or is subject to investigation. This occurs most frequently in money laundering cases and in so called 'MTIC' (missing trader intra community) or VAT 'carousel' frauds where a series of buffer companies are created to facilitate the fraudulent activity. In these circumstances, the court may lift the corporate veil of the company and treat the assets of the company as being the assets of the defendant and therefore liable to restraint and confiscation under the Act.

The leading authority is *Re H (Restraint Order: Realisable Property)* [1996] 2 All ER 391. **2.52**
The three defendants had been charged with excise duty evasion offences in relation to which it was alleged there was a loss to the Exchequer in excess of £100 million. They owned, together with a third party, 100 per cent of the issued share capital of two family companies through which it was alleged the frauds had been committed. On this basis, the High Court made restraint and management receivership orders that included the assets of the companies. The defendants sought variations to the orders removing all references to the companies, contending that the court had no jurisdiction to restrain them. The Court of Appeal rejected the defendants' contention ruling that, where a corporate structure had been used as a device or façade to conceal criminal activity, the court could lift the corporate veil and treat the assets of the company as the realisable property of the defendant for the purposes of the Act. Rose LJ (with whom Aldous LJ and Sir Iain Glidewell agreed) said:

> As to the law, the general principle remains that which was enunciated in *Salmon v Saloman* [1897] AC 22, [1895–9] namely that a company duly formed and registered is a separate legal entity and must be treated like any other independent person with its own rights and liabilities distinct from those of its shareholders.

> But a succession of cases throughout the twentieth century show, as Danckwerts LJ said in *Merchandise Transport Ltd v British Transport Commission, Arnold Transport (Rochester) Ltd v British Transport Commission* [1961] 3 All ER 495 at 518, [1962] 2 QB 173 at 206-207:

> . . . where the character of a company, or the nature of the persons who control it is a relevant feature, the court will go behind the mere status of the company as a legal entity and will consider who are the persons as shareholders or even as agents who direct and control the activities of a company which is incapable of doing anything without human assistance.

> In *Adams v Cape Industries plc* [1990] CH 433; 2 WLR 657 Slade LJ, giving the judgment of **2.53**
> the Court of Appeal (of which Mustill and Ralph Gibson LJ were the other members), cited this passage and added:

> The correctness of this statement has not been disputed. The court also assumed to be correct the proposition that the court will lift the corporate veil where the defendant by the device of a corporate structure attempts to evade (i) limitations imposed on his conduct by law . . .

> Clearly, as a matter of law, the corporate veil can be lifted in appropriate circumstances.

The Court then went on to review the facts in *Re H* and concluded:

> As to the evidence, it provides a prima facie case that the defendants control these companies, that the companies have been used for fraud, in particular the evasion of excise duty on a large scale; that the defendants regard the companies as carrying on a family business and that company cash has benefited the defendants in substantial amounts.

In these circumstances, the Court held it was appropriate to lift the corporate veil of the companies and treat them as the realisable property of the defendants.

The court is entitled to lift the corporate veil even if it is shown that the company in ques- **2.54**
tion is engaged in significant legitimate trading activity. In *Re K* [2005] EWCA Crim 619

the judge found there was a substantial arguable case that the defendants had used various companies as a façade behind which they were hiding the proceeds of their smuggling activities. He lifted the corporate veil on the companies notwithstanding that he accepted they were also engaged in legitimate trading activity. The companies appealed, contending that the judge had failed to ask himself the correct question, namely whether the companies were façades or shams set up by the defendants to conceal the true position. The Court refused the defendants permission to appeal on this point. Laws LJ in delivering the judgment of the Court observed:

> In our judgment the judge's ruling here did no more than reflect the reality of the situation. There was a pressing case on the evidence that albeit none of the defendants had formal control of the companies as office holders they used the companies without the least let or hindrance to facilitate and execute their fraudulent designs. The judge's decision was, in our judgment, plainly in line not only with the dictum from *Re H* but also other authority, not least *Merchandise Transport Limited v British Transport Commission* [1962] 2 QB 173, *Adams v Cape Industries plc* [1990] 1 Ch 433, *Yukong Line* [1998] 1 WLR 794 and *Compton* to which we have already referred and which in truth replicated the test in *H*.

The Court held that the phrase 'lifting the corporate veil' may be somewhat misleading and in reality the true question is whether assets of the company may be treated as realisable property of the defendant.

2.55 This approach was followed by Ouseley J in *Re D* [2006] EWHC Admin 254. The facts of this case were unusual to the extent that the application to lift the corporate veil was made for the first time long after the defendant had been convicted. The defendant had been convicted of drug trafficking offences and a confiscation order was made against him for £800,000. The order remained largely unsatisfied and in 2005 he was returned to prison to serve the default sentence for non-payment. In 2004 or 2005, he set up a business with a Mr J known as X Limited which was engaged in property development. Each of them owned one of the two issued shares and both of them put some capital into the company —in the case of D in breach of the restraint order. On discovering this, the Revenue and Customs Prosecutions Office applied, without notice, for the restraint order to be varied to include the assets of the company and for a management receiver to be appointed in relation to D's assets, including the company. After these orders were made, X Limited applied for them to be varied to remove therefrom references to the company assets, contending that the corporate veil should not have been lifted. Ouseley J rejected this contention, observing that:

> In my judgment the real question which the judge faced with an application for a restraint or receivership order is whether the order of the extent sought and now obtained is appropriate or necessary in view of the two legislative objectives set out in section 31(2) and (4) of the 1994 Act. The question whether the effect of such an order is to pierce the corporate veil or whether some particular test related to that concept requires to be satisfied is not, in my judgment, the ultimate object of the inquiry the court has to carry out. The object of the Act is to enable proceeds of crime to be ascertained, protected and realised. The first question therefore is whether there are corporate assets which should be treated as the defendant's assets and the second question is whether, if that is the case, a restraint and receivership order of the extent sought is necessary. The position, in my judgment, is the same where there is an intermingling of the assets of a criminal, who is seeking to evade the effect of a confiscation order,

with the assets of innocent business partners of a company. If it is established that some or all of the assets of the company are to be treated as assets of the defendant, the question of how their intermingling with the assets of someone who is innocent of wrongdoing is to be dealt with, is a matter for resolution by deciding whether an order should be made and if so on what terms, rather than a matter which has to be resolved by simply asking whether the corporate veil should be pierced. As I have said, the question is whether it is necessary to impose an order of the terms sought bearing in mind that there would be, necessarily, someone who is innocent whose interests would be adversely affected by such an order. This involves a balancing of interests as is inherent in the statutory provisions of section 31.

The cases to which I have been referred do not deal with the problem of the intermingling of a criminal's realisable assets with those of an innocent person in a company which has legitimate business activities but in part carries them out using the criminal's realisable assets. There would obviously be a very considerable lacuna in the ability of the Act to achieve its objective if in principle, because such a company was not a one man band or wholly criminal in its origin, funding or activities, assets held in it could not be subject to receivership or restraint order provisions.

The judge then considered whether the restraint and receivership orders in relation to the assets of X Limited were necessary having regard to the facts of the case. He concluded that the orders were necessary, saying: **2.56**

The starting point is the background of Mr. D in crime with a substantial unsatisfied confiscation order. There is also evidence of a serious set of breaches by him of the restraint order and of the use by him of a personal account, the scale of transactions in which suggest that he was carrying on a business as he himself appeared to assert. There is evidence that Mr. D had a practice of putting property in the names of others but nonetheless controlling the destiny of the property and the assets with which it is purchased—in other words, there is a personal façade as opposed to a corporate façade in a number of transactions he has engaged in. There was evidence of investment in X Limited through the provision of cash, the shareholding, his role as an officer, his role as a signatory to accounts as director and as company secretary. He took part in the activities of the company and it represented some of the funds which he had sought to place beyond the R&CPO. The relationship of his loans to the company to those of Mr. J is unclear because there is no written documentary material, and nothing which could be described as a paper trail in relation to the loans made to the company. Although it is not said that Mr. J was involved in laundering or drug activities, the precise power or control relationship, the beneficial ownership of the assets is not wholly resolved and the documentary material or accounts in relation to that are rudimentary. There is no dispute but that Mr. D put money into the company and has a shareholding both of which are the proceeds of crime being dealt with through the company. In my judgment, it would be absurd not to treat the company's assets as being his in part. Any other approach would enable, as I have said, somebody with criminal proceeds to incorporate himself with one other, who might be an innocent dupe, and thereby put his assets beyond the reach of the R&CPO.

In *R v Seager and Blatch* [2009] EWCA Crim 1303, the Court of Appeal considered the issue of lifting the corporate veil in the context of cases where a defendant has been convicted of managing a company in breach of a director's disqualification order. On the facts of these cases, the Court of Appeal found that the corporate veil on the companies in question should not have been lifted. Aikens LJ, in delivering the judgment of the court said: **2.57**

A court can 'pierce' the carapace of the corporate entity and look at what lies behind it only in certain circumstances. It cannot do so simply because it considers it might be just to do so. Each of these circumstances involves impropriety and dishonesty. The court will then be entitled to look for the legal substance, not just the form. In the context of criminal cases the courts have identified at least three situations where the corporate veil can be pierced. First if an offender attempts to shelter behind a corporate façade, or veil to hide his crime and his benefits from it: see *Re H and others,* per Rose LJ at 402A; *Crown Prosecution Service v Compton and others* [2002] All ER (D) 395, paragraph 44–48, per Simon Brown LJ; *R v Grainger,* paragraph 15 per Toulson LJ. Secondly, where an offender does acts in the name of the company which (with the necessary *mens rea*) constitute a criminal offence which leads to the offender's conviction, then 'the veil of incorporation is not so much pierced as rudely torn away': per Lord Bingham in *Jennings v CPS,* paragraph 16. Thirdly, where the transaction or business structures constitute a 'device', 'cloak' or 'sham', i.e. an attempt to disguise the true nature of the transaction or structure so as to deceive third parties or the courts: *R v Dimsey* [2000] QB 744 and 772 (per Laws LJ), applying *Snook v London and West Riding Investment Ltd* [1967] 786 at 802 per Diplock LJ

2.58 Applying these principles to the case of Blatch, Aikens LJ said:

> Mr Blatch was not hiding behind the companies to conceal his offence of contravening the disqualification to act as a company director. He was doing the opposite. He was brazenly continuing to operate and control the companies despite his ban. That was the essence of his offence. There was no question of Mr Blatch using the companies for any illegal purpose, such as avoiding the payment of VAT or money laundering, or defrauding his creditors from which he benefited. There was no evidence before the judge that Mr Blatch used the companies as a shield to hide benefits that he had obtained from his offence of contravening the disqualification.

> We accept that Mr Blatch performed acts in the names of the companies whilst illegally acting as a 'director' of them. But the position is very different from that in *Jennings v CPS*. There the company was the vehicle used to perpetrate the 'advanced fee fraud' of the appellant (an employee) and his co-accused, who was the controlling shareholder and director of the company. The corporate structure was, effectively, a sham. Once the corporate veil was pierced, or torn aside, then the property in question was to be regarded as the joint property of those who controlled the company. That was why the restraining order against dissipation of the appellant's property was held to be effective, because the property restrained was to be regarded as the appellant's (jointly with his co-accused), rather than that of the company. In the present case the acts of Mr Blatch, when purporting to be a director, were done on behalf of the companies and they meant that he contravened the disqualification. But the existence of the companies themselves and the legitimacy of their business cannot be in doubt. No one has said that they are to be disregarded as legitimate legal entities.

2.59 The Court found that the facts were very different from those in *Re H*. Aikens J said:

> The case of *Re H* was different on the facts. There, Rose LJ, who gave the leading judgment, held that the evidence showed that the defendants controlled the family companies, which had been used for fraud to evade excise duty on a large scale and that company cash had benefited the defendants in substantial amounts: see page 402A. In those circumstances it was obviously appropriate to lift or pierce the corporate veil.

The Court took a similar view of the facts in *Seager*. Aikens LJ said:

> Mr Seager did not use (the company) as a façade to hide benefits from his crime of contravening the undertaking. He did not use the company for other illegal activities. The business of the company was legitimate. Although Mr Seager purported to do acts in the name of the company (eg enter the lease and operate a bank account in its name), there was no evidence that this was a 'sham', with the consequence that he was, in practice, the lessee or the person beneficially entitled to any credit in the bank account. Even if Mr Seager did, as a 'shadow'

director, dispose of property and money on behalf of the company, that would not, by itself, prove that he owned it.

The Court of Appeal's decision in *Blatch and Seager* serves as a reminder of the limits on the   **2.60** powers of the court to lift the corporate veil on companies in which those subject to restraint and confiscation orders have an interest. It appears that the decision of Ouseley J in *Re D* [2006] EWHC Admin 254 was not cited in the Court of Appeal in *Blatch and Seager*. Whether it remains good law in the light of the Court of Appeal's decision must now be open to some doubt, since there was never any dispute that the company involved in *Re D* was trading legitimately and openly. The defendant in *Re D* was nonetheless operating a bank account in breach of a High Court restraint order, in relation to which he was ulti- mately sent to prison for contempt of court. Against this background it is submitted that Ouseley J reached the correct decision on the facts. Nonetheless, some statutory interven- tion may become necessary to clarify the precise limits on the court's jurisdiction to lift the corporate veil on companies if their use to evade the effect of restraint and confiscation orders is to be prevented.

Another avenue open to a prosecutor wishing to secure company assets would be to insti-   **2.61** tute criminal proceedings against the company itself if the evidence justified such a course. In this event the company would become a defendant in its own right and be liable to restraint and confiscation action. This did not, however, find favour with the Court of Appeal in *Re H*. Rose LJ said in this regard:

> In my judgment the Customs and Excise are not to be criticised for not charging the compa- nies. The more complex commercial activities become, the more vital it is for prosecuting authorities to be selective in whom and what they charge, so that issues can be presented in as clear and short a form as possible. In the present case, it seems to me that no useful purpose would have been served by introducing into criminal proceedings the additional complexi- ties as to the corporate mind and will, which charging the companies would have involved. Conversely, there could have been justified criticism had the companies been charged merely as a device for obtaining orders under the Act in relation to their assets.

Legitimately acquired assets

It is a common misconception that restraint orders may only be made in relation to assets   **2.62** that represent, directly or indirectly, the proceeds of the defendant's criminal conduct. This view is erroneous because, as we have seen, s 83 defines realisable property as any free prop- erty held by the defendant or the recipient of a tainted gift, and s 84 defines property as being 'all property' wherever situated.

These definitions make no distinction between assets that have been acquired legitimately   **2.63** and those which have not. All realisable property of the defendant is liable to restraint and ultimately confiscation up to the full amount of his benefit, even if it is acquired legiti- mately many years before the commission of the offences. This was confirmed in *R v Chrastny (No 2)* [1991] 1 WLR 1385 where, in delivering the judgment of the court in a case to which the Drug Trafficking Offences Act 1986 applied, Glidewell LJ said:

> In our view it is quite clear that that definition embraces legitimately acquired property. We cannot read into the Act of 1986 any inference that that definition is limited to illegitimately acquired property; that is to say the proceeds of drug trafficking. The statute is undoubtedly draconian and the decision on that point may seem harsh; the statute is harsh. The statute is

in essence one that seeks to ensure that anybody who has benefited from drug trafficking shall, to the extent to which he or she can do so, be deprived of the whole of that benefit.

Assets held overseas

2.64 Realisable property of a defendant is subject to restraint and confiscation regardless of whether it is located in England and Wales or overseas. Section 84(1) of POCA provides that 'property is all property wherever situated'. Any dissipation of restrained assets held overseas will therefore amount to a breach of the order punishable as a contempt of court by the courts in England and Wales.

2.65 The contempt remedy will only be effective to the extent that the contemnor is amenable to the jurisdiction of the court: it will be of little concern to a person resident overseas who has no intention of returning to the UK. However, as will be seen in Chapter 19, mutual legal assistance arrangements exist in most countries whereby a restraint order made in England and Wales can be protected by obtaining a further order in the overseas jurisdiction in which assets are located. The prosecutor may also apply to the Crown Court under s 41(7) of POCA for a repatriation order requiring the defendant to bring within the jurisdiction of the court realisable property he holds overseas. The court's power to make repatriation orders is considered in more detail in Chapter 3.

Duration of restraint orders

2.66 By r 59.2(7) of the Criminal Procedure Rules 2005 (CrimPR):

> (7) Unless the Crown Court directs otherwise, a restraint order made without notice has effect until the court makes an order varying or discharging the restraint order.

In practice, the Crown Court rarely 'directs otherwise' and the majority of restraint orders remain in force until a further order of the court is made. The court will invariably give all parties affected by the order permission to apply to vary or discharge it upon giving the court and prosecutor two clear days' notice in writing. In any event r 59.3 of the CrimPR allows any person affected by a restraint order to apply for it to be varied or discharged on giving two clear days' notice.

2.67 This procedure met with the approval of the Court of Appeal (Civil Division) in *Ahmad v Ahmad* [1998] EWCA Civ 1246 when complaint was made by the appellant third party that a CJA 1988 restraint order did not have a return date on which she could attend and argue why the order should not continue in that form. In rejecting this criticism, Thorpe LJ said:

> In my opinion that would not be a sensible practice since in the majority of cases I suspect that the return date, inter partes, would achieve little useful purpose. I can see no objection to the practice whereby the order obtained ex parte contains an obligation to serve with liberty to apply on short notice. This is certainly the practice that obtains in ancillary relief litigation in the Family Division and it has proved to work effectively.

This is not to say that the prosecutor should automatically seek a restraint order of indefinite duration. Indeed, in the later case of *Customs and Excise Commissioners v S* [2005] 1 WLR 1338 the Criminal Division of the Court of Appeal expressed a somewhat different view. Scott Baker LJ said:

> It also seems to us, in the light of the statutory prohibition on the use of restrained funds for legal expenses, that these orders should ordinarily be made with a short return date rather

than left open ended for the defendant to apply to vary or discharge. In that way the court can exercise close supervision over orders that are by their nature draconian.

It is submitted that prosecutors should consider each case on its own particular facts. If **2.68** the circumstances of a particular case are such that there should be an early hearing at which the court can determine whether the order should remain in force and, if so, on what terms, the prosecutor should always consider asking the court to fix a return date rather than inviting the court to leave the order open ended.

Exceptions

By s 41(3) of POCA: **2.69**

> (3) A restraint order may be made subject to exceptions, and an exception may in particular—
> (a) make provision for reasonable living expenses and reasonable legal expenses;
> (b) make provision for the purpose of enabling any person to carry on any trade, business, profession or occupation;
> (c) be made subject to conditions.

Section 41(3) gives statutory effect to many of the practices of the High Court in CJA 1988 and DTA cases as to the type of exceptions that can be permitted. The section gives the court a discretion, which must be exercised in accordance with the legislative steer in s 69 of the Act, as to what exceptions and conditions should be made on making a restraint order. The exceptions made and conditions imposed will inevitably depend on the particular facts of individual cases, but the more usual requirements are detailed below.

Reasonable living expenses

The court will normally require the order to make provision for the release of reasonable **2.70** sums (typically £300 per week) for the payment of general living expenses. As restraint orders are normally made before the defendant has been convicted of any offence and he is therefore entitled to the benefit of the presumption of innocence, it is right and proper that he should be allowed to meet his general living expenses pending the determination of the criminal proceedings. As Lawton LJ observed in *CBS United Kingdom Limited v Lambert* [1982] 3 All ER 537:

> Even if a plaintiff has good reason for thinking that a defendant intends to dispose of assets so as to deprive him of his anticipated judgment, the court must always remember that rogues have to live and that all orders, particularly interlocutory ones, should as far as possible do justice to all parties.

Further, where a restraint order prevents a spouse or partner of the defendant from dealing with realisable property (eg money in a bank account) the order should also make provision for the release of funds to meet his or her reasonable living expenses unless there is evidence to show that he or she has access to adequate unrestrained funds. The order should also make provision for the defendant to deal freely in any payments he receives from the Department for Work and Pensions by way of state benefits.

If the defendant or an affected third party considers the amounts payable under the restraint **2.71** order by way of general living expenses is insufficient for his legitimate needs, he should invite the prosecutor to agree to the order being varied by consent to allow a greater amount to be released for such purposes. If the prosecutor does not agree to the variation sought, it will be necessary for a formal variation application to be made to the court. This subject is considered in more detail in Chapter 5 where it will be seen that, in determining such applications, the court has to strike a difficult balance between ensuring the defendant has sufficient funds available to meet reasonable living expenses on the one hand and complying with the 'legislative steer' imposed by s 69 of POCA to ensure that the value of the defendant's realisable property is made available to satisfy a confiscation order on the other.

Businesses

2.72 The court will not, at the pre-confiscation stage, allow a restraint order to operate in such a way as to prevent a business in which the defendant has an interest from trading profitably and legitimately. As Stanley Burnton J said in *Re G* [2001] EWHC (Admin) 606:

> Particular caution is required if it appears that, in addition to engaging in fraudulent transactions, the company is carrying on a legitimate business that may be closed down by the order. It may not be appropriate to treat the assets of the company as those of the defendant in such circumstances. Freezing injunctions in civil proceedings normally contain an exception to the prohibition against dealing with property to enable the person restrained to deal with his assets in the ordinary course of business.

Accordingly, most restraint orders will make provision for the release of business bank accounts for the purpose of facilitating legitimate trading activity subject to profit and loss accounts, bank statements, and related documentation being produced to the prosecutor on a regular basis. The standard form of words used appears in paragraph 20 of the precedent restraint order in Appendix 1. In more complex cases, or where there is evidence to suggest the business may be being used to facilitate the commission of offences, the appointment of a management receiver to run the business may prove necessary. This is considered in Chapter 4.

Legal expenses

2.73 Although s 41(3)(a) of POCA gives the court jurisdiction to make provision in a restraint order for the release of funds to pay reasonable legal expenses, s 41(4) imposes strict limitations on the court's powers in this regard. It provides:

> (4) But an exception to a restraint order must not make provision for any legal expenses which:
> (a) relate to an offence which falls within subsection (5), and
> (b) are incurred by the defendant or by the recipient of a tainted gift.

2.74 Section 41(5) provides that the offences caught by s 41(4)(a) are:

> (a) the offence mentioned in section 40(2) or (3) if the first or second condition (as the case may be) is satisfied;
> (b) the offence (or any of the offences) concerned, if the third, fourth or fifth condition is satisfied.

2.75 In *Customs and Excise Commissioners v S* [2005] 1 WLR 1338 the Court of Appeal held that s 41(4) prohibited the release of restrained funds to meet legal expenses incurred in relation to the restraint proceedings as well as such expenditure incurred in defending the criminal proceedings. The Court upheld the prosecutor's contention that the words 'relate to an offence' in s 41(4) are sufficiently wide to cover the restraint proceedings as no restraint order could be made unless an investigation was underway in relation to an offence or a person had been charged with an offence. In reaching this conclusion, the court found it significant that the prohibition in s 41(4) extended to legal expenses incurred by recipients of tainted gifts. As Scott Baker LJ observed:

> This makes clear that the legislation is not directed simply at excluding legal expenses in connection with the defendant's criminal proceedings—the underlying offence—but in the restraint proceedings themselves, otherwise the provision in relation to recipients of tainted gifts would be unnecessary.

The Court was influenced by the fact that Sch 11 para 36(4) to POCA expressly amended the Access to Justice Act 1999 to make public funding available in relation to restraint proceedings, and that s 252 of the Act imposed a similar prohibition on the release of funds to meet legal expenses incurred in relation to proceedings for an interim receiving order brought under the civil recovery provisions.

The Court considered, but rejected, a submission by the defendant that s 41(4) amounted **2.76** to a breach of his right to a fair trial under Art 6 of the European Convention on Human Rights. The Court observed that the defendant faced 'an overwhelming factual difficulty' because he was represented throughout and it was not suggested that he did not have a fair hearing. The Court noted that Art 6(3) applied only to criminal hearings where the defendant had been charged with an offence and found, following *R (McCann) v Crown Court at Manchester* [2003] 1 AC 787, that it was 'impossible to conceptualise the restraint proceedings as criminal'. Further, the Court noted that in *X v UK* (1984) 6 EHRR 366 the European Commission distinguished civil proceedings from criminal proceedings holding that:

> Only in exceptional circumstances, namely where the withholding of legal aid would make the assertion of a civil claim practically impossible, or where it would lead to an obvious unfairness of the proceedings, can such a right be invoked by virtue of Article 6(1).

Finally, the Court considered whether s 41(4) amounted to a breach of the defendant's **2.77** right to peaceful enjoyment of his possessions under Art 1 of the First Protocol to the Convention. Again, the Court answered in the negative, noting that *Raimondo v Italy* [1994] 18 EHRR 237 made it plain that there is a distinction to be drawn between depriving a person of his possessions and temporary measures to prevent him using them. As Scott Baker LJ said:

> A restraint order constitutes a control in the use of property which will be lawful if, as in the present case, it serves a legitimate aim, namely the preservation of property believed to be the proceeds of crime for confiscation so as to deprive offenders of their benefit from crime.

The Court was nonetheless troubled by the possible consequences of its ruling on those affected by restraint orders. In the concluding paragraph of the judgment, Scott Baker LJ stressed that 'This is not a conclusion we have reached with any enthusiasm'.

The Court of Appeal followed the decision of *Customs and Excise Commissioners v S* in *AP* **2.78** *& U Limited v Crown Prosecution Service and Revenue & Customs Prosecutions Office* [2007] EWCA Crim 3128. The defendant applied to the Crown Court for the release of restrained funds to secure legal representation at the confiscation hearing. The Crown Court judge refused the application, ruling that he was bound by the decision in *S*. The defendant appealed, arguing that his rights under the European Convention on Human Rights had been violated. The Court followed the decision in *S*, refused to make a declaration of incompatibility, and dismissed the appeal. In delivering the judgment of the Court Latham LJ said:

> An important point, not dealt with, at least expressly, in any of the cases to which we have been referred, is that a restraint order relates to funds which the prosecution believe could well be the proceeds of crime. To permit, therefore, monies which could well be the proceeds of crime being used to pay lawyers for the benefit of the defendant who is either suspected of being, or has been found to be, a criminal raises a clear social issue. Parliament, it seems to us, is entitled to take the view that funds which may have criminal origins should not be so used. Parliament had to take into account the consequences, namely that other means would have to be provided to enable defendants to have legal representation during restraint and confiscation proceedings. The course adopted was to provide state aid.

2.79 The case of *AP* had an interesting sequel in that the trial judge, His Honour Judge Mole QC, ultimately stayed the confiscation proceedings as an abuse of process because no Counsel of sufficient experience could be found who was prepared to act for the defendant at the legal rate of £178.25 per day. The solicitors acting for the defendant had approached 18 sets of chambers in London and in the provinces, but no one was prepared to act for those rates of payment. In staying the proceedings the trial judge said:

> I am driven to the conclusion, I have to say reluctantly, that in the exceptional, possibly unique position of P, he cannot have a fair trial of this confiscation issue without representation by the counsel he wishes to have and, in my view, needs. To use the language of *McLean and Buchanan*, I do think it is inevitable he will suffer real prejudice without the assistance of counsel.

> The principle underlying confiscation is a just one so long as the confiscation is carried out justly. The overriding principle is, in my judgment, that for these serious matters, the defendant must be able to have a fair trail and in this case I am confident that he cannot, unrepresented by counsel. I therefore stay these proceedings as an abuse of the process of the Court.

2.80 The Crown Prosecution Service did not appeal the judge's ruling. It is submitted that the outcome of this litigation is most unsatisfactory. In consequence, a convicted drugs dealer was allowed to retain his ill gotten gains in a case where the Crown alleged his benefit from criminal conduct exceeded £4 million. Section 41(4) of POCA was introduced to overcome some of the abuses that occurred in cases to which the CJA 1988 and DTA applied where vast amounts of restrained funds were being dissipated in legal fees. Particular care had been taken by the draftsman to amend the Access to Justice Act 1999 to make it clear that public funding should be available for proceedings under POCA (see Sch 11 para 36(4) to POCA). There is an urgent need, it is submitted, for the Legal Services Commission to ensure that defence solicitors and counsel are adequately remunerated to ensure that those facing restraint and confiscation proceedings are properly represented to enable justice to be done between the parties.

2.81 In the meantime, in August 2008, the Bar Council issued a Guidance Note on 'Confiscation and Graduated Fee Cases' to assist barristers faced with such issues when representing a defendant. The Guidance is available on the Bar Council's website: see <http://www.barcouncil.org.uk/guidance>.

Section 41(4) does not preclude the release of restrained funds to meet legal expenses **2.82** incurred in connection with proceedings that are wholly unrelated to the offence. If, for example, the defendant wishes to pursue or defend civil proceedings or even criminal proceedings totally unrelated to the offences in relation to which the restraint order has been made (eg proceedings for a road traffic offence) the prohibition will not apply. The authorities suggest, however, that the court will take a broad view as to the nature of proceedings that relate to the offence. In *AP & U Limited v Crown Prosecution Service and Revenue and Customs Prosecutions Office* [2007] EWCA Crim 3128, one of the issues the Court of Appeal had to consider was whether the prohibition extended to judicial review proceedings. U Limited, a company describing itself as a money transmitting business, transferred some €7 million on behalf of clients to the account of a company called Currency Solutions Ltd at the Laiki Bank in the UK. On 6 February 2007, Currency Solutions made a formal disclosure report under POCA to SOCA requesting consent to continue providing facilities to U Limited. After initially giving consent, SOCA refused permission to the bank to provide further facilities to U Limited who thereupon commenced judicial review proceedings.

U Limited was under investigation for alleged money laundering offences and was subject **2.83** to a restraint order made under POCA. The company sought a variation to the restraint order for the purpose of meeting legal fees incurred in connection with the judicial review proceedings. The Crown Court judge agreed that funds should be released for this purpose and varied the restraint order accordingly, but the Crown exercised its right of appeal against that decision. The key issue for the Court of Appeal was whether the judicial review proceedings related to the offence within the meaning of s 41(4). The Court held that they did and allowed the Crown's appeal. Latham LJ said:

> The Crown's case is simply that the events in February 2007, that is the circumstances surrounding the disclosure reports, were all matters connected with the money laundering which, in general terms, was the offence into which the criminal investigation had been started, as disclosed in the witness statement relied upon by the Crown before the Judge applying for the restraint order. [Counsel for U Ltd] has valiantly attempted to persuade us that there is no proper connection between the events of February 2007 and the offence or offences into which the criminal investigation began. In particular he pointed to the fact that no money laundering offences were committed if consent was given for the transaction disclosed. But that fails to grapple with the Crown's argument. Consent may relieve the bank of any criminal responsibility for a transaction in question; but that does not mean that in relation to others involved in the transaction, it may not amount to or form part of a dishonest money laundering scheme. The Crown's case is that the disclosure reports were triggered by transactions which were suspected of being part of such a scheme. That being so, it seems to us that there is a sufficiently clear connection between the offence or offences into which there was the investigation to mean that the judicial review proceedings 'related to' that offence or offences.

Further, it is not possible to avoid the prohibition in s 41(4) by arguing that the payment **2.84** of legal fees constitutes a living expense allowable under s 41(3)(a). In *McInerney v Financial Services Authority* [2009] EWCA Crim 997, the defendant was being prosecuted by the Financial Services Authority for alleged money laundering offences. A restraint order had been made which released £250 per week to him for ordinary living expenses. The defendant applied to the Legal Services Commission for public funding to seek a judicial review of the Financial Services Authority's power to prosecute offences contrary to POCA. The Legal Services Commission agreed to provide public funding, but subject to the defendant making a contribution of £117.66 per month. This contribution was assessed on the basis of the defendant's entitlement to £250 per week living expenses from restrained funds. The defendant thereupon sought confirmation from the Financial Services Authority that the monthly contributions could be paid from the allowance made for his ordinary living expenses. The authority refused to give the confirmation sought, contending that payment of the contribution would constitute a breach of s 41(4) of POCA as it was not possible to make an exception to the order for the payment of legal expenses. The defendant then sought a variation to the restraint order to make it clear that he was not prohibited from paying the contribution. The judge refused the application saying that to accede to it would be 'an attempt to do serious injury to the wording of the statute'.

2.85 The defendant thereupon appealed to the Court of Appeal, contending that, on a proper reading of s 41 of the Act, it places no limitations on what the defendant may do with any money allowed to him by way of general living expenses. He contended that he could spend the £250 per week allowed in any way he pleases without being in breach of the Act or in contempt of court. He could therefore choose to use the money to instruct a lawyer to defend him in the restraint proceedings or on the criminal charges. The Court of Appeal rejected this argument and dismissed the appeal. Hooper LJ said:

> We agree with the judge. Payments to the LSC are not ordinary living expenses and thus McInerney would be in contempt of court to pay money to the LSC and the LSC would be in breach of the restraint order to receive it. Furthermore section 41(3)(a) makes a distinction between living expenses and legal expenses and if a contribution to the LSC is a legal expense, a payment to the LSC would not be a payment towards ordinary living expenses.

He added:

> It follows that a judge who discovers that a contribution is being made to the LSC is likely to impose a condition that no such contribution should be made, indeed if not bound to do so in the light of sections 41(4) and 69.

2.86 The terms and conditions on which the court will release restrained funds to pay legal expenses in cases where the s 41(4) prohibition does not apply, are considered in more detail in Chapter 5.

Costs and expenses incurred in complying with the restraint order

2.87 Third parties affected by restraint orders will from time to time incur costs in ensuring they are properly complied with. Banks and other financial institutions, for example, will incur costs in identifying accounts affected by the order and freezing them in compliance with it. By r 59.2(5) of the CrimPR:

(5) The Crown Court may require the applicant for a restraint order to give an undertaking to pay the reasonable expenses of any person other than a person who is prohibited from dealing with realisable property by the restraint order, which are incurred in complying with the restraint order.

As this requirement does not extend to persons who are prohibited from dealing with realisable property, the defendant, his spouse or partner, any company in relation to which the corporate veil has been lifted and any recipient of a tainted gift will generally be excluded from the terms of any such undertaking given by the prosecutor.

Undertakings in damages

Rule 59.2(4) of the CrimPR provides that the Crown Court must not require the applicant **2.88** for a restraint order to give any undertaking to pay damages sustained as a result of the order to any person who is prohibited from dealing with assets by it. This is in marked contrast to the position in relation to freezing orders where the applicant will normally be required to give an undertaking in damages as a condition precedent to the making of the order.

Restrictions

Section 58 of POCA imposes a number of restrictions on third parties exercising various **2.89** rights they may otherwise have in relation to realisable property caught by a restraint order. By s 58(2), no distress may be levied against property subject to a restraint order except with the leave of the Crown Court and subject to any conditions it may impose.

Similarly, by s 58(3) and (4), where a restraint order applies to a tenancy of any premises, **2.90** no landlord or any person to whom rent is payable may exercise a right of forfeiture by way of peaceable re-entry without the leave of the Crown Court. This is in contrast to the position under the old legislation where it has been held that the exercise of a right to forfeiture does not constitute a breach of any restraint order affecting the property: see *Re R (Restraint Order)* [1990] 2 All ER 569.

By s 58(5), where a court in which proceedings are pending in relation to any property is **2.91** satisfied that a restraint order has been applied for or made in respect of that property, it may either stay the proceedings or allow them to continue on such terms as it thinks fit. Although s 58 appears to give the Crown Court a very wide discretion as to how it may exercise its powers, it is submitted that the discretion must be exercised in accordance with the legislative steer in s 69. This is considered in more detail in Chapter 5.

Further, s 58(6) provides that before the court exercises its power under s 58(5), it must give **2.92** the applicant for the restraint order and any receiver appointed under the Act an opportunity to be heard. In *Serious Fraud Office v Lexi Holdings PLC (In Administration)* [2008] EWCA Crim 1443, the Court of Appeal reminded practitioners of the importance of complying with s 58 where property in respect of which they are litigating is subject to a restraint order. In noting that the section had not been complied with, Keene LJ said:

> We entirely accept that the reason why section 58 was not drawn to the attention of those judges was because counsel then appearing for Lexi was himself unaware of it. It was an innocent oversight. Nonetheless, steps do need to be taken to ensure that the terms of section 58 are observed. Some thought might usefully be given to the possibility of creating a register of restraint orders and applications for such orders, though that would not have cured the problem in the present case, since all involved were aware of the existence of the restraint order. The SFO and other prosecuting authorities could usefully publicise more widely the general tenor of section 58 and no doubt the relevant Bar Associations could play a role. This is not just a matter for the criminal courts and criminal lawyers: the duty under section 58 applies to all courts in which proceedings about such property take place and very often those will be the civil courts.

Variation and discharge of restraint orders

2.93 Section 42(3) to (7) deals with the variation and discharge of restraint orders. This is dealt with in more detail in Chapter 5 below.

C. Charging Orders

2.94 It should be noted that, in contrast to the CJA 1988 and DTA, POCA does not give the Crown Court power to make charging orders. In practice, very little use was made of charging orders under the old legislation, with most prosecutors preferring to obtain restraint orders and, where they affected real property, to protect them by registering a restriction at the Land Registry. Section 47 of POCA allows this practice to continue as it provides that 'the registration acts' (defined as the Land Registration Act 1925, the Land Charges Act 1972, and the Land Registration Act 2002) shall apply to restraint orders as they apply in relation to orders which affect land and are made by the court for the purpose of enforcing judgments and recognisances.

D. Protecting Restraint Orders in Relation to Real Property

2.95 By r 93(1) of the Land Registration Rules 2003 (SI 2003/1417) a POCA restraint order may be registered as a restriction against the title to the property at the Land Registry. By r 92(1), the application must be made by the prosecutor on Form RX1. The restriction will be entered in the charges register in Form EE set out in Sch 4 to the Land Registration Rules 2003 and will preclude any dealing in the property without the consent or the prosecutor or further order of the court.

3

ANCILLARY ORDERS: SEIZURE, DISCLOSURE, AND REPATRIATION OF ASSETS

A. Introduction

Practitioners may be surprised, on seeing a restraint order for the first time, to note the **3.01** extent and breadth of its terms. In many instances, the order will go way beyond restraining the defendant from dealing in his assets but, in addition, will require him to make a witness statement disclosing the full extent and location of all his realisable property and even to repatriate assets held overseas. In DTA and CJA cases, the jurisdiction to make disclosure and repatriation orders flows from the inherent jurisdiction of the court to make such ancillary provision as is necessary to ensure that its orders are properly policed. In POCA cases, the power is to be found in the statute itself. Section 41(7) empowers the Crown Court to make any such order as it believes appropriate for the purpose of ensuring the restraint order is effective. In this chapter, we examine the powers of the court to make such orders and the conditions and limitations to which they are subject.

B. Seizure of Assets

By s 45 of POCA: **3.02**

(1) If a restraint order is in force, a constable or a customs officer may seize any realisable property to which it applies to prevent its removal from England and Wales.

(2) Property seized under subsection (1) must be dealt with in accordance with the directions of the court which made the order.

The Act is silent as to the degree of proof the officer must have that the asset may be removed from England and Wales before he can seize it. It is submitted that the standard must be the same as that required to obtain a restraint order, namely that there is a good arguable case that the asset may be removed: see *Compton v CPS* [2002] EWCA Civ 1720. Substantial proof is not required and, it is submitted, there is no requirement that the evidence should be in a form admissible in a criminal trial.

3.03 Once an asset has been seized, it must be dealt with in accordance with the court's directions under s 45(2). Although no procedures are laid down in POCA or in rules of court, it is submitted that the proper course is for the prosecutor to issue an application seeking the court's directions as to how the asset should be dealt with. The application notice should be served on all parties who, to the prosecutor's knowledge, claim to have an interest in the property. If the asset is of particularly high value, it may be appropriate for the prosecutor to apply for the appointment of a management receiver to take possession of it pending the conclusion of the proceedings.

3.04 POCA appears to confer an unlimited discretion on the court to give such directions as it sees fit as to how the seized property should be dealt with. It is submitted that the court must exercise its discretion in accordance with the legislative steer in s 69 of the Act. The court should be particularly mindful of its power under s 69 (4) to order that property must not be sold if it cannot be replaced.

C. Disclosure Orders

3.05 The prosecutor should have full information as to the nature, extent, and location of all the defendant's realisable property to police the restraint order effectively. When the prosecutor applies for a restraint order, he will have much information about the defendant's realisable property from a variety of sources. In the last analysis, however, the extent of a defendant's realisable property is a matter within his own knowledge. Thus, from the very early days of the legislation, prosecutors have asked courts making restraint orders to include a provision requiring the defendant to swear an affidavit disclosing the full extent of his realisable property. Although the early cases required disclosure on affidavit, since the advent of the Civil Procedure Rules the usual requirement is for the defendant to make the required disclosure in a witness statement verified by a statement of truth.

Jurisdiction to make the order: a brief history

3.06 In CJA and DTA cases, the power of the High Court to make disclosure orders emanated not from the legislation but from the court's inherent jurisdiction to make such orders as it considers just and convenient. The first reported case in which the court held it had jurisdiction to make a disclosure order is *Re A Defendant*, The Independent, 2 April 1987, a decision of Webster J at first instance. A restraint order including a disclosure provision had been made under the Drug Trafficking Offences Act 1986 at an *ex parte* hearing. At a later hearing, held *inter partes*, the defendant challenged the court's power to include the disclosure requirement in the order. He contended that if the power to make disclosure existed at all, it could only be granted in favour of a receiver because it was his function, and not that of the prosecutor, to get the property. Webster J rejected that argument, ruling that the principal purpose to be achieved by the appointment of a receiver was the management of assets which, for whatever reason, the defendant could not manage himself.

The High Court's power to make disclosure orders in CJA and DTA cases was first consid- **3.07** ered by the Court of Appeal in *Re O* [1991] 1 All ER 330. Restraint orders had been made under the CJA 1988 containing an exception allowing the release of £100 per week for general living expenses. The defendants applied to vary the order by increasing the amount payable to £500 per week. The prosecutor contended that the variation should not be entertained unless the defendants swore affidavits disclosing the extent of their assets. Macpherson J acceded to that submission and made an order requiring the defendants:

> to swear an affidavit disclosing the full value of any salary, money, goods or other assets what-soever within and without the jurisdiction identifying with full particularity the nature of all such assets, their whereabouts and whether the same be held in their own names or jointly with some other person or persons, or by nominees or otherwise howsoever on their behalf.

He then adjourned the application pending compliance with the disclosure order. The defendants appealed contending that the judge had no jurisdiction to make the disclosure order.

The Court of Appeal dismissed the appeal, finding that the court had an inherent juris- **3.08** diction to order disclosure of assets in support of restraint orders. Lord Donaldson of Lymington MR said:

> Equally, in my judgment, the High Court must have been intended to have power to render effective a restraint order made under section 77 of the 1988 Act.
>
> Under that section notice of the order has to be given to persons affected by it (s 77(5)(c)). In addition there is power to appoint a receiver and manager of any realisable property (s 77(8)). Finally, there is an obvious necessity to be able to police compliance with the order. All these features dictate that there should be some means of identifying and ascertaining the where-abouts and value of assets affected by the restraint order and this need is reinforced when it is realised that, whatever may be the position in an individual case, the legislative contempla-tion is that restraint orders will be made in circumstances in which it is thought that some of those having interests in the property may well be of a dishonest disposition. I therefore have no doubt that there is jurisdiction to make an order for disclosure in the nature of that made in this case.

Although *Re O* related to restraint orders made under the CJA 1988, it was assumed that **3.09** the principle applied equally to orders made under the DTA and its predecessor, the Drug Trafficking Offences Act 1986, particularly as Lord Donaldson MR noted in his judgment that:

> The jurisdiction to make restraint orders under the Drug Trafficking Offences Act 1986 is mirrored by that under the Criminal Justice Act 1988 and a decision in relation to one Act will apply equally to the other.

An attempt was nonetheless made in *Re T (Restraint Order: Disclosure of Assets)* [1992] 1 WLR 949 to argue that *Re O* had no application in drug trafficking cases. In that case a restraint order under the 1986 Act had been made that contained a disclosure provision in precisely the same terms as that considered by the Court of Appeal in *Re O*. The defendant made an application to Schiemann J for the disclosure provision to be removed from the order. The learned judge refused the application, ruling that he could find no good reason for distinguishing between disclosure provisions included in restraint orders made under the 1986 Act from those in orders made under the CJA 1988.

3.10 The defendant appealed to the Court of Appeal contending that notwithstanding the remarks of Lord Donaldson in *Re O*, given the material differences between the confiscation regimes in the two Acts, the decision did not apply in drug trafficking cases. The Court of Appeal dismissed the appeal, ruling that any differences there may be between the two Acts were of little substance. Parker LJ said of Lord Donaldson's observations in *Re O*:

> It is in my view clear from the passage from Lord Donaldson's judgment immediately following the passage which I have quoted, that his reference to a 'mirror image' related only to the sections in the two Acts dealing with the jurisdiction of the High Court to make restraint and charging orders. Those sections are not identical but I can detect no difference in substance.

Concluding his judgment, Parker LJ said:

> The context of the restraint order provisions of the two Acts is certainly different, but the difference is such that it is in my judgment clearer under the Act of 1986 than under the Act of 1988 that the jurisdiction to make a disclosure order in support of a restraint order exists.

Jurisdiction to make disclosure orders under POCA

3.11 As we have seen, the power of the High Court to make disclosure orders under POCA flows from the inherent jurisdiction of the court. As the Crown Court is a creature of statute and has no such inherent jurisdiction, POCA makes express statutory provision empowering the court to make ancillary orders. Section 41(6) and (7) of POCA provides as follows:

(6) Subsection (7) applies if—
    (a) a court makes a restraint order, and
    (b) the applicant for the order applies to the court to proceed under subsection (7) (whether as part of the application for the restraint order or at any time afterwards).
(7) The court may make such order as it believes is appropriate for the purpose of ensuring the restraint order is effective.

This provision enables the Crown Court to continue making disclosure and repatriation orders in precisely the same way as the High Court together with any other form of order it considers necessary to ensure the restraint order is effective. An example of a POCA restraint order, including disclosure and repatriation provisions, is found at Appendix 7.

The problem of self-incrimination

3.12 There is a real risk that by requiring a defendant to disclose his assets he might incriminate himself both in relation to the offence with which he has been charged and other offences as well. Full compliance with a disclosure order might, for example, result in the defendant admitting money laundering offences. The courts have from the outset been vigilant to protect the defendant's right against self-incrimination by insisting that the prosecutor must not make any use of the disclosure statement during any criminal trial. In *Re a Defendant*

The Independent, 2 April 1987, Webster J ruled that the disclosure order was only to take effect upon the prosecutor giving an undertaking:

> not to use any of the information obtained as a result of compliance with the order for any purpose or in connection with any criminal proceedings taken or contemplated against the defendant or for any purpose other than a purpose arising under the Drug Trafficking Offences Act 1986.

The Court of Appeal made it clear in *Re O* [1991] 1 All ER 330 that the CJA 1988 could **3.13** not be construed in such a way as to abrogate the privilege against self incrimination. The Court ruled, however, that the privilege was capable of protection by the imposition of conditions upon the use to which information provided in disclosure statements may be put. The Court considered the practice that had developed following *Re a Defendant* and Lord Donaldson MR said:

> We were told that in another case the CPS was required to give an undertaking limiting the class of person to whom the disclosed information could be given and the purposes for which it could be used. I would not wish to be taken to criticise such an approach, but consider it preferable to impose a condition in the order rather than seek an undertaking.

The Court suggested that the condition should be in the following terms:

> No disclosure made in compliance with this order shall be used as evidence in the prosecution of an offence alleged to have been committed by the person required to make that disclosure or by any spouse of that person.

In *Re T (Restraint Order: Disclosure of Assets)* [1992] 1 WLR 949 the defendant contended **3.14** that this condition was insufficient to protect his privilege against self-incrimination in a drug trafficking case. It was contended that, by complying with the disclosure order, the defendant would suffer an enhanced penalty by increasing the size of the confiscation order that would be made against him and, in consequence, render him liable to serve a longer term of imprisonment in default of payment than would otherwise be the case. The Court of Appeal rejected this argument ruling that the purpose of the legislation is to compel the defendant to make reparation in respect of the unjust enrichment he has obtained from his criminal activities and, that by making such reparation, he did not incur punishment. There is thus no question of self-incrimination. As Leggatt LJ said:

> Compliance with the order to swear an affidavit does not expose the defendant to any such risk: the condition to which the order is subject precludes the risk of further prosecution on that account; a confiscation order is different in nature from forfeiture: and even if it were right to regard a confiscation order as penal in character, disclosure on affidavit does not render the defendant liable to the imposition of a form of order to which he would not otherwise be subject.
>
> Disclosure of assets in conjunction with the statutory assumptions merely facilitates assessment of the amount to be recovered in the defendant's case, once it has been determined that he has benefited from drug trafficking, and does not in my view amount to self incrimination. Confiscation applies to the value of the defendant's proceeds of drug trafficking, whereas forfeiture extends to things used for the commission of crime and is therefore punitive. It is true that disclosure of assets exposes the defendant to the risk of a confiscation order greater in amount than could be made in the absence of disclosure. But it is not self incriminating because a person does not by making reparation incur punishment.

3.15 In *R v Martin and White* (1998) 2 Cr App R 385 the Court of Appeal had to consider a complaint by a defendant that the condition approved in *Re O* had been breached by the prosecutor during the course of his trial. Prosecuting counsel, who had been supplied with a copy of the disclosure affidavit by those instructing him, had cross-examined the defendant on inconsistencies between the evidence he gave on oath to the jury and the contents of the affidavit. The defendant contended that this represented a breach of the condition and, furthermore, that there should be a species of 'Chinese Wall' preventing the affidavit coming into the possession of those having conduct of the prosecution until such time as the defendant is convicted.

3.16 The Court of Appeal ruled that there had been no such breach by the prosecutor because the affidavit had not been adduced as evidence in the prosecution of an offence but merely in cross examination as to credit. Rose LJ added that it would be 'an affront to common sense' if the defendant could make two wholly contradictory statements on oath and avoid being challenged in any way as to the inconsistency. Further, the Court rejected the suggestion that the disclosure affidavit should have been withheld from those having the conduct of the prosecution until after conviction. Rose LJ said:

> We cannot accede to the submission that such an affidavit should remain detached from those engaged in prosecution. To attempt to debar the prosecution from sight of such an affidavit would be both impracticable and wrong, not least because the conduct of the prosecutor is or should be under the immediate supervision of the court. We are not prepared to contemplate the prosecution being kept in ignorance of any such affidavit until a confiscation order is sought.

3.17 The Court was nonetheless troubled by the use to which the affidavit had been put and the circumstances in which it had been used without prior reference to the trial judge. Rose LJ emphasised that:

> We cannot envisage circumstances in which any such affidavit could become admissible in evidence during a criminal trial at the behest of the Crown, either in the course of the prosecution or, as was thought to have happened here, by being purportedly proved by way of cross examination of the accused. We would hope and expect that, in future cases, the Crown and the court will be alert to the limitations subject to which an order for disclosure by affidavit is made.

3.18 The Court also held that prosecuting counsel should not rely on the disclosure statement without first seeking the leave of the judge. Rose LJ said:

> Such use of the affidavit should be subject to safeguards aimed at reconciling the proviso with the immediate needs of the Crown. In our judgment, prosecuting counsel should seek prior directions from the judge as to the precise use which can be made of the affidavit. This will alert the judge and defence counsel as to the situation and enable the judge to maintain an oversight that reconciles use of the affidavit with the proviso.

3.19 The wording of the condition as approved in *Re O* has subsequently been reviewed by the High Court in the light of the incorporation of the European Convention on Human Rights into English law. In *Re C (Restraint Order: Disclosure)* (4 September 2000) the prosecutor sought an order of committal against the defendant for failing to comply with the disclosure provisions in a DTA restraint order. In response, counsel for the defendant expressed concern that compliance with the disclosure order might put those investigating the criminal case on the track of some evidence they would otherwise have been unaware of which could prove gravely prejudicial to the defendant. Collins J held that this submission had considerable force and that any such use of the disclosure statement would constitute a breach of the defendant's right to a fair trial under Art 6 of the Convention given the ruling of the European Court of Human Rights in *Saunders v UK* [1996] 23 EHRR 313. The judge also expressed doubt as to whether the decision in *Martin and White*, which was made prior to the Convention being incorporated in English law, was consistent with Art 6. Collins J said:

> It does not matter in what form the information is used, whether as evidence, whether because it enables other evidence to be obtained which could not otherwise have been discovered or whether it is used merely as a weapon in cross examination of the defendant. Whatever use in the criminal trial is prima facie a breach, it seems to me, of Article 6.

Collins J ruled that the wording of the condition should be tightened to make it plain that **3.20** the information disclosed should not be used against the defendant in the course of the criminal trial. The revised wording of the condition is set out in paragraph 8 of the draft restraint order in Appendix 7. Collins J recognised that there may be circumstances in which the interests of justice dictate that the contents of a disclosure statement should be disclosed to a co-accused. It may be, for example, that the contents of a disclosure statement made by defendant A may exonerate or at the very least assist the defence of defendant B. The judge emphasised that, whatever the circumstances, the court must retain ultimate control over the use to which the disclosed information is put and that in circumstances such as these an application for directions should be made to determine how, if at all, the disclosed information might be revealed to the co-accused.

It should be noted that the condition as revised by the ruling of Collins J in *Re C* does not **3.21** preclude the use of the disclosure statement in a confiscation hearing after the defendant has been convicted. In *Re E and Re H* (Unreported, 24 May 2001) an application by the defendants for an order preventing the prosecutor relying on the disclosure statement at the confiscation hearing was robustly rejected by the High Court. In delivering his judgment, Henriques J said:

> The absurd consequence of counsel's submission is that where a prosecuting authority are aware of assets disclosed and verified they would not be able to rely on that information in the confiscation proceedings. Nothing could be more absurd. If the defendant gave different information or no information when it was sought under section 73(A) known assets would have to be returned. Counsel suggests that is a necessary consequence of Parliament not clearly revoking the privilege against self incrimination. He suggests, in any event, that individuals might themselves obtain Mareva injunctions. Such a course is fanciful and it would dismember a now sophisticated and highly developed procedure for recovering assets from criminals and returning them to their rightful source. The absurdity of the consequence exposes the fallacy of the argument which unhappily falls at the first hurdle of binding precedent.

Dyson LJ took a similar line in refusing permission to appeal against the ruling of Henriques **3.22** J. In *Customs and Excise Commissioners v El Heri* [2001] EWCA Civ 1782 he said:

> Counsel submits that unless the prohibition on the use of disclosed material is extended to the confiscation proceedings, then there will be a significant erosion of the privilege against self incrimination, an erosion for which there is no sufficiently clear statutory authority. I am not persuaded that the confiscation proceedings attract the privilege against self incrimination.

I accept that the outcome of confiscation proceedings may properly be described as a penalty and may also be described as part of the sentencing process, since they arise in criminal proceedings. But no authority has been cited to me which shows that the privilege against self incrimination extended to proceedings which take place following a conviction. Be that as it may, the authorities to which I have referred clearly point to the conclusion that the judge was right in this case. I do not accept that the law has been materially changed in this regard by Article 6 of the European Convention on Human Rights.

3.23   Disclosure orders are also subject to the usual rule of civil procedure that they may not be used for any ancillary or collateral purpose. In *Re R* (Unreported, 21 October 1992) a third party creditor of a defendant subject to a CJA restraint order had obtained an *ex parte* order from a Practice Master giving leave to inspect the court file and copy the defendant's disclosure affidavit for the purpose of determining what assets might be available for satisfying any judgment that may be obtained against him. The prosecutor, fearing that the use of disclosure affidavits for such purposes may cause defendants to be less than frank about the extent of their assets, appealed against the order to a High Court judge. In allowing the appeal, Macpherson J said:

> As a matter of general principle, it seems to me in the highest degree undesirable that these affidavits should go to anybody other than the court and the parties involved. The reasons for that are obvious. They may not be used in other criminal proceedings. There will be reticence, if not downright secretion of facts by individuals, if they feel that these affidavits may go elsewhere. In ordinary circumstances—this appears to be such a case—these affidavits should be kept locked in the Central Office and not disclosed to anyone.

3.24   Macpherson J. was also concerned that the application for inspection had been made *ex parte*. He ruled that henceforth any third party who wished, for some exceptional reason, to inspect the court file for such purposes should make application on notice both to the defendant and the prosecutor.

Disclosure and third parties

3.25   It has been seen that restraint orders can, and frequently do, bind third parties not charged with any offence who may have control or possession of realisable property or claim an interest in it. In *Re D (Restraint Order: Non party)* The Times, 26 January 1995 the High Court held that the power to order disclosure extended to such third parties. The father of the defendant had been restrained from dealing with a number of bank accounts and was required to swear an affidavit disclosing details of transactions through accounts held in his name. Turner J dismissed the father's application to remove the disclosure requirement from the order in so far as it affected him. The judge held that the court did have jurisdiction to compel a third party to make such disclosure. He held that as the purpose of requiring disclosure was to police compliance with the restraint order and that third parties could be restrained from dealing with realisable property, it followed that the inherent jurisdiction of the court to order disclosure applied equally to third parties as it did to the defendant.

Disclosure orders against solicitors

3.26   Solicitors from time to time may hold information that may assist the prosecutor in policing a restraint order and the question arises as to the extent to which they may be compelled to disclose such information. The information may take many forms and may include, for example, the name and address of persons known to be affected by the order and details of assets caught by the order such as a bank account used by the defendant or an affected third party to pay the solicitor's fees. The leading authority is *Re W* [2008] EWHC 2780 (Admin). The background to the case was the defendant's conviction for fraud which resulted in a finding that he had benefited from criminal conduct to the extent of £33 million and the making of a confiscation order for £9.4 million. The defendant escaped from prison and was eventually arrested in Switzerland. An enforcement receiver was appointed, but he was only able to recover a small proportion of the amount outstanding under the order.

One of the defendant's assets was a development plot in Spain which the trial judge found **3.27** had been purchased in the name of a Spanish company by the defendant's wife using money supplied by the defendant. The defendant contended that the property was not realisable because it had been stolen by a Spanish lawyer, but the judge rejected this contention. Two days before the hearing of the application to appoint a management receiver, London solicitors applied to intervene in the proceedings on behalf an entity referred to as Estevez Consulting Group who claimed that the property was not owned by the defendant but by a Mr Estevez. Two days later, the solicitors advised the prosecutor that in fact a company called Achedina Veinte SL owned the property. It appeared to the prosecutor that this company was owned beneficially by the defendant.

Thereafter the intervenor failed to comply with a court order to file evidence as a result of **3.28** which the prosecutor applied to strike the intervention out. In response, it was contended that Mr Estevez, who was alleged to be the agent for Achedina, was dealing with the solicitors through an interpreter, and was eager to put in evidence, but had not yet had the opportunity to do so. On the evening prior to the strike out hearing, the solicitors served a witness statement to the effect that they had discovered the interpreter was in fact the sole director of the company and the person who had been giving them instructions. The interpreter herself produced a witness statement referring to Mr Estevez as a friend and accountant. She said that the company was owned by a British Virgin Islands trust company known as Candis. The court thereupon ordered the production of the trust deed. Eleven days before the deadline for compliance, the solicitors sent a letter to the prosecutor advising that their client was unable to comply with the disclosure order, in consequence of which the prosecutor instituted another strike out application. Shortly before the hearing, the solicitors advised that their clients would no longer be pursuing the intervention and the court struck it out, ordering the intervenor to pay the prosecutor's costs of £17,849.63. The costs were never paid.

The prosecutor believed that the defendant and his wife were the beneficiaries of Candis **3.29** and the owners of the land in Spain and that it was they who initiated and controlled the third party intervention. The prosecutor thereupon sought disclosure from the solicitors for the dual purposes of enabling the receiver to take possession of the property and enforcing the costs order made in his favour. The information sought included details as to when the solicitors first received instructions to act, whether the instructions were oral or in writing, the identity of the person who instructed them, and their address and telephone number. The prosecutor also sought disclosure of the date on which funds were remitted to the solicitors to cover the costs of the proceedings, the identity of the person remitting the funds, and the sort code and account number of any cheque transfer. The solicitors provided the names and addresses sought, but not the date on which they were instructed or the financial information requested by the prosecutor.

3.30   Ouseley J ordered the solicitors to disclose the information sought by the prosecutor. He found as a fact that where one saw the involvement of the defendant's wife as beneficiary of the trust owning the property, one also saw the hand of the defendant. The judge expressed himself as being satisfied that the disclosure sought would be of value to the enforcement receiver in preventing the defendant evading the confiscation order and of assistance in making sure that the defendant's assets were realised. As to the legal basis for making the disclosure order Ouseley J said:

> Counsel (for the prosecutor) puts the legal principles which he says should govern the exercise of the admitted jurisdiction as follows. He says that I should follow the principles in *Norwich Pharmacal v Customs & Excise Commissioners* [1973] AC 133. He adopts the succinct summary of those principles from Mr Justice Lightman in *Mitsui & Co Ltd v Nexen Petroleum (UK) Ltd* [2005] EWHC 625 Ch in which, at paragraph 21, he said the principles required for *Norwich Pharmacal* relief were:
> 'i)   a wrong must have been carried out, or arguably carried out, by an ultimate wrongdoer;
> ii)   there must be the need for an order to enable an action to be brought against the ultimate wrongdoer;
> iii)   the person against whom the order is sought must: (a) be mixed up in so as to have facilitated the wrongdoing; and (b) be able or likely to be able to provide the information necessary to enable the ultimate wrongdoer to be sued.'

> He points out that in *Re D (Restraint Order: Non-Party)* TLR, 25 January 1995, Mr Justice Turner had held that disclosure could be ordered within the context of a restraint order under section 8 of the Drug Trafficking Offences Act 1986 against a person who was not a party in the criminal proceedings, and he applied the broad principles of *Norwich Pharmacal* although the precise test is not discussed.

> Counsel for the solicitors, whilst accepting that an order for disclosure can be made, submits that because it is confidential information, whether applying *Norwich Pharmacal* or not, a stricter test or an additional point needs to be added. For these purposes he relies on *Finers and Others v Miro* [1991] 1 WLR 35, 40D to 41C, where Lord Justice Dillon, with whose judgment the others concurred, made a number of comments about the circumstances in which disclosure could be ordered in respect of privileged information. The court said that privilege could not apply if the solicitors were consulted—even though he did not realise it or was himself acting innocently—to cover up or stifle a fraud:

>> 'On the material before us I conclude that it does seem probable that the defendant may have consulted Mr Stein for the purpose of being guided and helped, albeit unwittingly on the part of Mr Stein, in covering up or stifling a fraud on the insurance company of which there is a prima facie case resting on solid grounds.'

> Counsel submits that it is necessary for there to be a higher test to reflect the fact the information sought here is confidential, whereas in *Norwich Pharmacal* cases the information may well not be confidential but merely information which the third party simply does not wish to supply.

> In support of his submission, Counsel referred to Article 8 of the European Convention on Human Rights and the tests there to be satisfied in Article 8(2) for an interference with

Article 8 rights to be justified. It is not necessary separately to consider that issue. Counsel was minded to agree—and he would have been certainly wrong not to have done—that if the *Finers v Miro* test was satisfied then Article 8(2) would also have been satisfied. There is in my judgment nothing in Article 8 which imposes a higher test than that which emerges from *Finers v Miro*.

Counsel for the prosecutor was not disposed to take issue, as I understand his submissions, with the sort of language put forward in *Finers v Miro* in relation to confidential information.

For my part, I consider that Counsel for the solicitors makes a sound point in relation to the approach which a court ought to adopt in relation to confidential information. However I accept Counsel for the prosecutor's submission that on the application of that test it is manifestly satisfied here for the reasons I have given. There is a substantial amount outstanding on a confiscation order made as a result of a conviction for a very serious fraud on the public purse.

The judge emphasised that he was making the order for the purpose of advancing the **3.31** enforcement of the confiscation order and hindering the 'manifest attempts' of the defendant at evading it. The order was not made, nor was it refused, for the other purpose sought by the prosecutor, namely the enforcement of the costs order made against the intervener. He said:

> Quite what the test should be for that may be debatable, certainly very debatable in the absence of the background to which I have described. If an abuse of process is required I am minded to consider that that is exactly what the intervention was. But in the light of the way in which the arguments have developed on what I see as the main basis for the making of this order, it is unnecessary for me to reach any firm conclusion. If there are any difficulties in relation to the use of the information I am ordering to be disclosed for the purpose of enforcement of costs it will be open to the prosecutor to revert to this court for the purpose of seeing whether it can indeed use the information to that end.

It should be noted that information sought by the prosecutor in *Re W* is not protected by **3.32** legal professional privilege since it has nothing to do with the provision of legal advice by the solicitor to the client. The authority for this is *R (On the application of Miller Gardner Solicitors) v Minshull Street Crown Court* [2002] EWHC 3077 (Admin). In that case the police needed to establish a link between a particular telephone number and two brothers, referred to as AH and NH, who were indicted for firearms offences. The Crown Court judge made an order requiring the solicitors, who at various times had acted for the defendants, to disclose any personal records they held related to AH and NH together with desk diaries of the solicitors representing them. It was contended on an application for judicial review of the Crown Court's order that it should never have been made because the information sought was subject to legal professional privilege. The Divisional Court rejected this argument. Fulford J, with whom Rose LJ agreed, said:

> In *R v Manchester Crown Court ex parte Rogers* [1999] 1 WLR 832 this court held that a record of an attendance at a solicitor's office by a client for an appointment, which I observe must involve giving the name of the client, was a communication between client and solicitor, but not one that attracted legal professional privilege. In his judgment at page 839, Lord Bingham CJ considered the function and nature of the document with which the court was concerned, and he concluded that:
>
> > 'It records nothing which passes between the solicitor and the client and it has nothing to do with obtaining legal advice. It is the same sort of record as might arise if a call were

> made to a dentist or a bank manager. A record of an appointment does involve a communication between the client and the solicitor's office but it is not in my judgment, without more, to be regarded as made in connect with legal advice. So to hold would extend the scope of legal privilege beyond its proper sphere …'

That decision provides strong support for the proposition that the provision of an individual's name, address and contact number cannot, without more, be regarded as being made in connection with legal advice. It records nothing which passes between the solicitor and client in relation to the obtaining of or giving of legal advice. Taking down the name and telephone number is a formality that occurs before the legal advice is sought or given. As My Lord observed during argument, provided these details does no more than create the channel through which advice may later flow: see in this regard the case of *Studdy v Sanders and others* [1823] 2 D and R 347.

It follows, in my judgment, that the identity of the person contacting the solicitor is not information subject to legal professional privilege and the telephone numbers of the brothers, equally, are not covered by this protection; neither are the dates when one or other of those men phoned the office. Moreover, the record of appointments in the office diary and attendance notes, insofar as they merely record who was speaking to the solicitor and the number they were calling from, fall within the same category.

3.33 Further, information or documentation is not protected by legal professional privilege if it is held with the intention of furthering a criminal purpose: see *R v Central Criminal Court ex parte Francis and Francis* [1988] 3 All ER 775 considered in more detail in Chapter 17 below.

3.34 The fact that the information has been provided to the solicitors is not necessarily a bar to disclosure. In *A v A; B v B* [2000] 1 FLR 701 Charles J reviewed the extent to which confidential information is protected from disclosure to persons having a legitimate interest in gaining access to it: the issue that fell to be determined was the extent of the court's power to disclose financial information revealed during the course of ancillary relief proceedings to the Inland Revenue. At p 713F Charles J summarised the position in these terms:

> Generally, in the absence of a statutory provision or rule that prohibits, or restricts, the proposed use, or disclosure of material there is no absolute duty of confidence and a court has a discretion to authorise, or order, disclosure of confidential information.

3.35 The court will normally exercise its discretion in favour of disclosure where the proper administration of justice would otherwise be defeated. In *Price Waterhouse v BCCI Holdings (Luxembourg) SA* [1992] BCLC 583 at 601f Millet J (as he then was) said:

> The duty of confidentiality … is subject to a limiting principle. It is subject to the right, not merely the duty, to disclose information where there is a higher public interest in disclosure than in maintaining confidentiality.

3.36 In *A v A; B v B* Charles J went on to consider the types of case where the public interest in disclosure should outweigh the duty of confidentiality. At p 722C he said:

> There is a well accepted and strong public interest in the proper and efficient investigation and prosecution of crime.

At p 722E–F he added:

> There is also a well accepted and strong public interest in the proper, fair and efficient administration of justice. A part of the public interest in the administration of justice, and also a free standing public interest, is that solicitors, as officers of the court, and the persons

employed by them should perform their duties honestly and efficiently and thus, for example, not mislead the court.

It is submitted that there is compelling public interest in divesting criminals of the proceeds **3.37** of their nefarious activities and, to that end, in ensuring the proper and effective enforcement of restraint, confiscation, and receivership orders. In most circumstances this should outweigh any duty of disclosure owed by solicitors to their clients.

Form of disclosure orders

A typical disclosure order appears in paragraphs 12 and 13 of the draft restraint order at **3.38** Appendix 7. Many orders impose two distinct obligations on the defendant: firstly, to give initial disclosure in writing within 72 hours of the order being served and, secondly, within 14 days thereafter to serve a witness statement on the prosecutor, supported by a statement of truth, verifying the information provided in the initial disclosure. In *Re E and Re H* (Unreported, 24 May 2001) the defendant disputed the necessity for his disclosure statement to be verified by a statement of truth. In rejecting this submission, Henriques J said:

> It is particularly appropriate in a case involving very large sums of money such as this that a disclosure of assets should be accompanied by a statement of truth. With prosecution for contempt as the only sanction and a two year maximum sentence discounted by way of good character, pleas and possible parole, many a fraudster would not be deterred from a partial or inaccurate disclosure of assets.

Disclosure may not be ordered against the prosecutor

The defendant does not have the right to seek disclosure of information or documentation **3.39** held by the prosecutor for the purpose of assisting him to comply with his disclosure obligations under a restraint order. In *Re S and W* (Unreported, 7 February 2000) the defendants, who were both in custody, sought orders requiring the prosecutor to disclose documents they claimed were in his possession and which they required to assist in complying with the disclosure provisions in DTA restraint orders made against them. Tucker J dismissed the application saying:

> The point taken on behalf of Her Majesty's Customs and Excise is that if these defendants were aware of the information which Customs and Excise had obtained, they might have been tempted to tailor their own information to that which they were aware that Customs and Excise already had. I see the force in that submission. I rather doubt whether the court has the power, in any event, to order disclosure on the part of Her Majesty's Customs and Excise. Even if I had that power, I would not be minded in my discretion to exercise it.

> These orders are, and are intended to be, Draconian in their provisions. They are aimed at restricting the use by the defendants of ill-gotten gains obtained by them by allegedly criminal activities. The terms of the order are clear. The accounts may be numerous and it may be expensive for the defendants to obtain the information from their banks but the obligation is, nevertheless, laid on the defendants to do so. I am not going to relieve that obligation by making any order against Her Majesty's Customs and Excise; therefore, I decline to do so. It is for the defendants to obtain the information.

The judge nonetheless indicated that he had some sympathy with the position in which the defendants found themselves and, without making any order, invited the prosecutor to assist in so far as he felt able to do so.

Advising the defendant or third party required to disclose

3.40   The practitioner's task in advising a client, whether he be a defendant or an affected third party, who is required to make disclosure under the terms of a restraint order, is an important and complex one. Serious consequences for the client may flow from a failure to give full and complete disclosure of assets, whereas too much disclosure may cause unnecessary prejudice to the client at a later stage in the proceedings. Although each case must be considered on its own particular facts, we endeavour in this section to offer practical guidance to the practitioner faced with this important task.

3.41   The disclosure order usually requires compliance within a relatively short timescale: most orders require initial disclosure within 72 hours and full disclosure in a witness statement verified by a statement of truth within 14 or 21 days thereafter. The practitioner needs to consider at the outset whether it will be possible for the client to comply within these time frames. There may be many legitimate reasons why compliance will not be possible: for example, the client may be remanded in custody at a prison some distance from his solicitor's office and a legal visit may take some time to arrange. If it is not going to be possible to comply with the time limits imposed by the order, the prosecutor should be approached as a matter of urgency and asked to agree to the order being varied by consent to extend the time for compliance. It is unlikely that the prosecutor will refuse to agree a short extension provided a proper explanation is advanced as to why it is necessary. However, given that the prosecutor requires the disclosure information to police the restraint order effectively, a lengthy or open ended extension is unlikely to be acceptable and any extension agreed will be expressed in terms of days rather than weeks or months. If the prosecution will not consent to the order being varied, an application should be made to the court for an extension of time. The matter should not be left in abeyance, because the prosecutor may well institute contempt proceedings in the absence of proper compliance with the order or an application to court for further time to comply.

3.42   As far as initial disclosure is concerned, the client should be asked to list all the assets in which he has an interest in as much detail as possible. As initial disclosure has to be given within 72 hours, the prosecutor will not expect it to be full and comprehensive provided the defendant has listed all the assets in which he has an interest to the best of his ability. If time permits, the list should be typed and the client invited to check it carefully and sign it before it is sent to the prosecutor. A handwritten list will suffice if there is insufficient time to provide the prosecutor with a typed copy before the deadline expires.

3.43   Once the initial disclosure has been provided, work should begin on the preparation of the witness statement which will need to be served usually no later than 14 days thereafter. Great care should be taken in the preparation of the statement because the order requires it to be verified by a statement of truth, and potentially serious consequences will flow from any material inaccuracy or non-disclosure. The client should be advised very carefully of these possible consequences, which include proceedings for contempt of court and criminal prosecution together with the risk of serious damage to the client's credibility at any confiscation hearing if he has been shown to be untruthful in his disclosure statement. Further, the client should not assume that the full extent of the prosecutor's knowledge of the defendant's assets is set out in the officer's witness statement in support of the restraint application. The prosecutor's investigation will inevitably continue until the confiscation hearing takes place and, indeed, may even continue after a confiscation order has been made given the court's powers under POCA to increase orders in the light of fresh evidence. The client would therefore be well advised to disclose all his assets at the outset, whether the prosecutor appears to be aware of them or not, in order to avoid any risk of contempt proceedings or being embarrassed at the confiscation hearing.

The client should be taken through every subparagraph of the disclosure order and asked **3.44** to provide full details of the assets he holds that are caught by each provision. If he cannot remember the precise details, the relevant financial institutions should be approached for confirmation of the position: banks may be contacted, for example, to advise as to account numbers and the balances standing to the credit of all the client's accounts. The prosecutor may also be approached for assistance if he has taken up documentation relating to the client's assets during house searches at the time of the arrest. The prosecutor may, however, rely on *Re S and W* (Unreported, 7 February 2000) as authority for the proposition that he is not required to provide such documentation.

Once the client has provided all the required information, work should commence on **3.45** drafting the witness statement. It is submitted that the proper approach is to address each subparagraph of the disclosure order in turn, in the order in which they appear in the restraint order, and identify with full particularity each and every asset required to be disclosed. Once the draft has been completed and typed, the client should check it and the effect of his signing the statement of truth fully explained. If he is satisfied it sets out fully all the assets in which he has an interest, he should sign the statement of truth and it should be served on the prosecutor.

After the disclosure statement has been served, the defendant's legal representatives should **3.46** be vigilant to ensure it is not abused by the prosecutor or put to any improper use. The legal representative's suspicions should be aroused if, within a short time of a disclosure statement being served, the prosecutor serves further evidence in the criminal proceedings that appears to mirror facts disclosed by the defendant. In such circumstances, an enquiry of the prosecutor as to how the new evidence was obtained would be perfectly justified. If the evidence has been obtained legitimately and quite independently of the disclosure statement, the prosecutor should be able to demonstrate this through a proper audit trail. As Collins J said in *Re C (Restraint Order: Disclosure)* (Unreported, 4 September 2000):

> I am not prepared to assume that any prosecuting authority is going deliberately to fail to comply with the requirements and surreptitiously obtain evidence based on the material disclosed as a result of the order. I cannot approach my task, nor could any court, on that assumption. If there is a misuse, if there is an attempt to produce and rely on material obtained as a result of disclosure it would, I would have thought, normally be difficult to conceal that exercise because of the requirements of prior disclosure and because of the need for there to be a prima facie case before the High Court could be persuaded to make a restraint order.

> A restraint order is based upon an affidavit by the applicant which is itself based upon information given by the officer in the case. If further information suddenly came to light after disclosure it would indeed be suspicious. I do not doubt that the trial judge who could see among other things the affidavit of the officer which had obtained the restraint order would be able to ascertain whether there had been any bad faith, which is what it would amount to

on the part of the prosecution. That, as I say, is not something I should take into account in my judgment in deciding whether the order in a particular form should or should not be made.

3.47   If the trial judge finds there has been 'bad faith' on the part of the prosecutor he has ample powers, it is submitted, to exclude any evidence obtained in consequence under s 78 of the Police and Criminal Evidence Act 1984.

D. Repatriation of Assets

Introduction

3.48   The legislation applies to all realisable property of the defendant wherever it is situated in the world: see s 84(1) of POCA, s 102(3) of the CJA 1988, and s 62(2) of the DTA. As most serious organised crime involves an international element, it is by no means an infrequent occurrence that those involved in such offences have the ability to invest their ill-gotten gains in overseas jurisdictions. Indeed, as money laundering operations have become more sophisticated and funds can be transferred from country to country more or less instantaneously by means of electronic transfer, those involved in criminal activity can move the proceeds of their nefarious activities overseas with ease in an attempt to conceal them from the UK law enforcement agencies.

3.49   As we shall see in Chapter 19, international cooperation between countries can often facilitate the restraint and confiscation of assets in foreign jurisdictions in support of criminal proceedings brought in the UK. The process can, however, be a long and drawn out one and not all countries are willing to cooperate, particularly in cases involving tax fraud. In such circumstances the prosecutor may seek a repatriation order requiring the defendant to bring the asset in question within the jurisdiction of the court pending the determination of the proceedings.

Jurisdiction to make repatriation orders

3.50   As with disclosure orders, the Crown Court's jurisdiction to make repatriation orders is to be found in s 41(7) of POCA. In CJA and DTA cases, the High Court's power to make such orders stems from its inherent jurisdiction. The Court of Appeal first recognised the power of the court to order the repatriation of assets when exercising the jurisdiction to make freezing orders in civil proceedings. In *Derby v Weldon (No 6)* [1990] 3 All ER 263 the Court of Appeal held that as the court's power to grant freezing orders depended not on its territorial jurisdiction but on its unlimited jurisdiction *in personam* against any person properly made a party to proceedings before it, the court had power to order the repatriation of assets held overseas. Dillon LJ, with whom the other members of the court agreed, said:

> I see no reason why that should not extend, in principle and in an appropriate case, to ordering the transfer of assets to a jurisdiction in which the order of the English court after the trial of the action will be recognised from a jurisdiction in which that order will not be recognised and the issue would have to be relitigated if, which may not be entirely the present case, the only connection of the latter jurisdiction with the matters in issue in the proceedings is that monies have been placed in that jurisdiction in order to make them proof against the

enforcement, without a full retrial in the foreign court, of any judgment which may be granted to the plaintiffs by the English court in this action or indeed, if the only connection with the latter jurisdiction is financial, as a matter of controlling investments.

In *Re WJT* (Unreported, 5 October 1992) the High Court considered the jurisdiction to **3.51** make a repatriation order in support of a restraint order made under the CJA 1988. The defendant had been charged with VAT fraud offences from which it was alleged he had benefited to the extent of some £250,000. A restraint order was obtained after which it was discovered that £187,000 had been taken from an account in the defendant's name by his sister acting on his authority. May J made an order requiring the repatriation of the money to a bank account within the jurisdiction of the court. The defendant challenged the court's power to make this order, submitting that the court should not take upon itself a jurisdiction which Parliament had not expressly given it.

Brooke J rejected this argument ruling that the court had an inherent jurisdiction to require **3.52** the repatriation of assets held overseas. He said:

> In my judgment, in principle, the jurisdiction exists if the court considers it just and convenient to grant an injunction of the type to which the Court of Appeal referred in *Derby v Weldon (No 6)* in aid of a restraint order made under section 77 of the Act. We are living in a world where money can be transferred very rapidly from one jurisdiction to another. On the face of it, it would be surprising if this court was powerless to make orders *in personam* against a defendant which had the effect of making safe assets and preventing them from being dissipated prior to the outcome of the criminal proceedings merely because the assets were outside the jurisdiction at the time the original restraint order was made. All I am concerned about is an application to make an order *in personam* against the defendant and, in my judgment, on an analogy with the judgment of the Court of Appeal in *Re O*, in order to achieve the purposes of Parliament in Part VI of the Criminal Justice Act 1988 and to render effective a restraint order made under section 77 of the Act, the court has the power to grant an injunction of the type which the Customs and Excise sought in this case. Accordingly, as a matter of principle, I am satisfied, as I am told other judges sitting in chambers exercising jurisdiction under part VI of the Criminal Justice Act 1988 have also been satisfied, that I have jurisdiction to make the type of order which May J made in the case.

Although WJT was given leave to appeal, the appeal was not pursued and it was not until **3.53** the case of *DPP v Scarlett* [2000] 1 WLR 515 that the jurisdiction to make repatriation orders was considered by the Court of Appeal. The Court had no hesitation in confirming that the jurisdiction to make repatriation orders in support of restraint proceedings did indeed exist. Beldam LJ (with whom Roch and Judge LJJ agreed) said:

> If a power to order full disclosure of assets on affidavit is inherent in a restraint order, the order should also include power to order the return of those assets within the jurisdiction. Both powers are essential to the purpose of the restraint order and to the realisation of those assets which is the purpose of the express statutory power given by Parliament.

The power to order repatriation is a discretionary one and it does not follow that the court **3.54** will order it in every case where assets are located overseas. In *Re WJT*, by way of example, having satisfied himself that he had jurisdiction to make the repatriation order, Brooke J went on to discharge it on the basis that the defendant had sufficient assets within the jurisdiction to satisfy a confiscation order in the amount by which he was alleged to have benefited from criminal conduct. Further, the court will not make an order with which it is impossible for the defendant to comply given the possible sanctions available if he breaches the order. The court will therefore need to satisfy itself that the defendant is in fact capable of repatriating the asset before making the order. Finally, the court may well require an explanation as to why the prosecutor has chosen to rely on the repatriation remedy rather than seeking mutual legal assistance to restrain the asset in the jurisdiction in which it is located. There may be many reasons why such action would prove impractical: the country in question may not be prepared to assist, a letter of request may have been sent and not been met with a timely response, or the necessity to prevent threatened dissipation of assets may require urgent action to be taken. Whatever the reason, the prosecutor must be prepared to justify the use of the repatriation remedy to the court's satisfaction.

Form of repatriation orders

3.55 The draft restraint order at Appendix 7 incorporates repatriation provisions at paragraph 16. The usual form of order requires the asset to be brought within the jurisdiction within 21 days and for the prosecutor to be informed of its location within 7 days thereafter. If the asset is in the form of money, the order will require it to be deposited in an interest bearing account and for the prosecutor to be notified of its location within the same period. As with disclosure orders, if compliance within the periods specified in the order proves impossible for any reason, the prosecutor must be approached with a view to an extension of time being agreed by consent and, in default of agreement, an application to the court should be made.

4

MANAGEMENT RECEIVERS

A. Introduction

A restraint order, coupled with disclosure and repatriation provisions, will in most cases **4.01** prove sufficient to preserve the value of realisable property pending the making and enforcement of a confiscation order. Banks will immediately freeze a defendant's accounts on being served with a copy of the order and the registration of a restriction at the Land Registry will effectively prevent any dealing in real property. As to the running of businesses caught by the order, conditions requiring the defendant to deliver accounts, bank statements, and associated documentation at regular intervals will normally be sufficient for the prosecutor to satisfy himself that the business is being properly run for legitimate trading activities. The defendant himself will also be aware that any dealing in realisable property in breach of the order will constitute a contempt of court for which he may be committed to prison.

In some cases, however, a restraint order alone will not be an effective means of preserving **4.02** the value of a defendant's assets pending the determination of the proceedings. The defendant may, for example, be in custody or have absconded leaving valuable assets unmanaged. In consequence, a house, often the most valuable asset in a defendant's estate available for confiscation, may be left unoccupied or fall into a state of disrepair and attract the attention of squatters, burglars, or vandals. It may be left uninsured and mortgage payments may fall into arrears. Similar considerations may apply to other valuable assets including cars, boats, and light aircraft. A business or company under the control of the defendant may need closer supervision than that afforded by requiring the defendant to submit business records on a regular basis. Further, the prosecutor has neither the qualifications nor experience necessary to make important decisions relating to the management of a restrained business. It would not, for example, be in a position to judge whether the release of a large sum of money from a restrained bank account to fund a particular business venture represents a good business risk or not.

4.03   In circumstances such as these, further measures need to be taken to manage and preserve the realisable property of the defendant while the restraint order remains in force. POCA gives the court power, on the application of the prosecutor, to appoint a receiver to take possession of and manage the defendant's realisable property pending the conclusion of the proceedings. Receivers appointed for such purpose are referred to as 'management receivers' to distinguish them from 'enforcement receivers' who are appointed after a confiscation order has been made to realise the defendant's assets in satisfaction of the order. Similar powers are conferred on the court under the CJA 1988 and DTA.

4.04   There have, in recent years, been many significant developments affecting the law relating to the appointment of management receivers and, in particular, as to the basis on which they are entitled to be remunerated for their services. In *Hughes v Customs and Excise Commissioners* [2002] 4 All ER 633 the Court of Appeal held that the costs and disbursements of management receivers are to be paid from the estate under management, even when the defendant is acquitted. Although the House of Lords refused leave to appeal against that decision, it is clear that the courts have become increasingly concerned about the level of costs incurred by management receivers and the potential injustice that may be caused as a result of such costs having to be met by an acquitted person.

4.05   In *Capewell v Customs and Excise Commissioners* [2005] 1 All ER 900 the Court of Appeal emphasised how management receivership orders can seriously interfere with the business and personal life of the defendant, and that the costs of appointing a receiver should always be proportionate to the benefits to be derived from the appointment. Once the overall objective of the receivership has been achieved and there is no further benefit to be derived without disproportionate cost, the receiver should be discharged. The Court also approved a number of guidelines drawn up by counsel which should be followed by the court and the prosecutor on the hearing of applications for the appointment of management receivers and adhered to by all parties once the appointment has been made.

4.06   It is of considerable importance to any study of the law and procedure relating to receivers under POCA and the previous legislation to note that the court has had power to appoint receivers for various purposes for many hundreds of years and that a considerable body of case law has developed in relation thereto. In *Capewell v HM Revenue and Customs* [2007] UKHL 2 Lord Walker of Gestingthorpe summarised the position in these terms:

> The Court's power to appoint a receiver, as part of its auxiliary equitable jurisdiction is of very ancient origin. It was described in *Hopkins v Worcester and Birmingham Canal Proprietors* (1868) LR 6 Eq 437, 447 as one of the oldest remedies in the Court of Chancery. It was used in a wide variety of situations where there was a need for the interim protection of property (and the income of property), including disputes about partnerships, sales or mortgages of land, and administration of estates. Receivers could also be appointed by way of equitable execution. The receiver, being appointed by the Court, was an officer of the Court. His duty

was to act impartially, and in accordance with the directions of the Court in administering the property to which the receivership extended.

In short, the appointment of a receiver was in many cases the most effective way of 'holding the ring' between warring litigants until the disputed issues could be finally determined. Because it is a useful procedure, Parliament has from time to time extended the range of situations in which a receiver or manager could be appointed—for instance, in order to enforce the repairing obligations of the absentee landlord of a block of flats (see Landlord and Tenant Act 1987 section 21). The provisions of section 77(8) of CJA 1988, section 26(7) of DTA 1994 and section 48 of POCA 2002 are a further important extension of the situations in which the court has a statutory power to appoint a receiver. Sections 48, 50 and 52 of POCA 2002 provide for three types of receivers (management receivers, enforcement receivers and Director's receivers, the latter appointed by the Director of the Assets Recovery Agency) but it is unnecessary to go into those details on this appeal.

B. Jurisdiction to Appoint Management Receivers

The power to appoint management receivers

Sections 48 and 49 of POCA give the Crown Court jurisdiction to appoint management **4.07** receivers for the purpose of managing and preserving the value of realisable property pending the conclusion of the criminal proceedings. By s 48 of POCA:

(1) Subsection (2) applies if—
    (a) the Crown Court makes a restraint order, and
    (b) the applicant for the restraint order applies to the court to proceed under subsection (2) (whether as part of the application for the restraint order or at any time afterwards).
(2) The Crown Court may by order appoint a receiver in respect of any realisable property to which the restraint order applies.

Section 48(1)(b) gives statutory effect to what had become the practice by prosecutors of **4.08** applying for restraint and management receivers under the old legislation at the same time. In *Re P (Restraint Order: Sale of Assets)* [2000] 1 WLR 473 the Court of Appeal suggested that restraint and management receivership orders should only be sought simultaneously in cases of urgency. Simon Brown LJ (as he then was) said:

> But to justify the making of composite orders on an ex parte basis there must, in my judgment, be an urgency about the matter (or a need not to alert the defendant) such as to preclude putting the defendant on notice, and the order initially made should be in the narrowest terms necessary to meet the strict requirements of the situation.

It is important to note that under s 48(1)(b) only the applicant for the restraint order may **4.09** make an application for the appointment of a management receiver: neither the defendant nor an affected third party (such as a judgment creditor) may apply for the appointment of a receiver to manage restraint assets. In *Re M* [1992] 1 All ER 537 a defendant did apply, under the old legislation, for the appointment of a management receiver. Otton J held that he had no *locus standi* to make the application saying:

> . . . in my judgment, it is unthinkable that an application for the appointment of a receiver by or on behalf of an accused to preserve assets intended for the satisfaction of a confiscation order could be entertained by the court. A restraint order may only be made upon the application of a prosecutor and, bearing in mind that the making of an order appointing a receiver can only be exercised upon the making of a restraint order, it would follow, in my judgment,

that an application for the appointment of a receiver can similarly only be made by a prosecutor.

Powers of management receivers

4.10 The powers the court may confer on management receivers are set out in POCA as supplemented by the general law of receivership as it has developed over the years. By s 49 of POCA:

(1) If the court appoints a receiver under section 48 it may act under this section on the application of the person who applied for the restraint order.

(2) The court may by order confer on the receiver the following powers in relation to any realisable property to which the restraint order applies—
    (a) power to take possession of the property;
    (b) power to manage or otherwise deal with the property;
    (c) power to start, carry on or defend any legal proceedings in respect of the property;
    (d) power to realise so much of the property as is necessary to meeting the receivers remuneration and expenses.

(3) The court may by order confer on the receiver power to enter any premises in England and Wales and to do any of the following—
    (a) search for or inspect anything authorised by the court;
    (b) make or obtain a copy, photograph or other record of anything so authorised;
    (c) remove anything which the receiver is required or authorised to take possession of in pursuance of an order of the court.

(4) The court may by order authorise the receiver to do any of the following for the purpose of the exercise of his functions—
    (a) hold property;
    (b) enter into contracts;
    (c) sue and be sued;
    (d) employ agents;
    (e) execute powers of attorney, deeds or other instruments;
    (f) take any other steps the court thinks appropriate.

(5) The court may order any person who has possession of realisable property to which the restraint order applies to give possession of it to the receiver.

(6) The court—
    (a) may order a person with an interest in realisable property to which the restraint order applies to make to the receiver such payment as the court specifies in respect of a beneficial interest held by the defendant or the recipient of a tainted gift.
    (b) may (on payment being made) by order, transfer, grant or extinguish any interest in the property.

(7) Subsections (2), (5) and (6) do not apply to property for the time being subject to a charge under any of these provisions—
    (a) section 9 of the Drug Trafficking Offences Act 1986 (c32);
    (b) section 78 of the Criminal Justice Act, 1988 (c33);
    (c) Article 14 of the Criminal Justice (Confiscation) (Northern Ireland) Order 1990 (SI1990/2588 (NI17);
    (d) section 27 of the Drug Trafficking Act 1994 (c37);
    (e) Article 32 of the Proceeds of Crime (Northern Ireland) Order 1996 (SI1996/1299 (NI9)).

(8) The court must not—
    (a) confer the power mentioned in subsection (2)(b) or (d) in respect of property, or
    (b) exercise the power conferred on it by subsection (6) in respect of property,
unless it gives persons holding interests in the property a reasonable opportunity to make representations to it.

(9) The court may order that a power conferred by an order under this section is subject to such conditions and exceptions as it specifies.

(10) Managing or otherwise dealing with property includes—

    (a) selling the property or any part of it or interest in it;

    (b) carrying on or arranging for another person to carry on any trade or business the assets of which are or are part of the property;

    (c) incurring capital expenditure in relation to the property.

Most of the powers the court may vest in the receiver under s 49 reflect powers the High Court **4.11** has for many years conferred on receivers appointed under the CJA 1988 and DTA pursuant to its inherent jurisdiction. Section 49(8) imposes an important restriction on the court's power to confer powers on management receivers. The power to manage or otherwise deal with property (s 49(2)(b)), to realise assets to meet the costs and expenses of the receiver (s 49(2)(d)), and to require a person holding realisable property to make payments to the receiver after which property rights may be granted, transferred, or extinguished (s 49(6)), may not be exercised until persons having an interest in the property have been given a reasonable opportunity to make representations to the court. Thus, in cases where the receiver is appointed without notice to the defendant or interested third parties, a further application on notice will have to be made before any of the powers referred to in s 49(8) can be conferred on the receiver.

There is, however, an important exception to this rule in relation to property that is **4.12** perishable or needs to be sold before its value diminishes. Section 82(1) of the Serious Crime Act 2007 adds a new s 49(8A) to POCA which provides:

(8A) Subsection 8 so far as relating to the power mentioned in subsection (2) (b) does not apply to property which—

    (a) is perishable, or

    (b) ought to be disposed of before its value diminishes.

The effect of this new subsection is that defendants and affected third parties need not be given an opportunity to make representations before the court empowers a receiver to manage or otherwise deal with property where that property is perishable or ought to be disposed of before its value diminishes. This is a useful power for receivers because the delay caused by giving an opportunity to make representations can often result in the property diminishing in value to the detriment of all concerned. It is submitted that the power should be exercised sparingly where there is a genuine risk of the property in question depreciating in value and the prosecutor or receiver should be in a position to justify the urgent necessity to deal with property without giving the defendant or affected third parties the opportunity to make representations. Particular care should be exercised in relation to property which is irreplaceable or may have considerable sentimental value to those claiming an interest in it.

The powers conferred on management receivers are not, however, necessarily confined to **4.13** those set out in s 49 of POCA. A receiver is a recognisable creature of the common law, an officer of the court whose powers and duties have been established over many hundreds of years. By using the expression 'receiver' in the Act, Parliament clearly intended that the powers of a management receiver should include those vested in common law receivers, save to the extent that the statute provides otherwise. As Simon Brown LJ observed in *Hughes v Customs and Excise Commissioners* [2002] 4 All ER 633:

> Statutory receivers are to be treated precisely as their common law counterparts save to the extent that the legislation provides otherwise. The statute is not to be regarded as an entirely

self contained code incorporating nothing from the common law. The fact that, unusually (but not uniquely—consider such cases as *Hoffman-la-Roche v Secretary of State for Trade and Industry* [1975] AC 295 and *Attorney General v Wright* [1988] 1 WLR 164) the prosecutor cannot be required to give a cross-undertaking in damages does not constitute so fundamental a difference between statutory and common law receivers as to give rise to wholly discrete schemes for their remuneration.

4.14 When a management receiver is appointed, he assumes the power, and indeed the duty, to police compliance with the restraint order and to bring any breaches to the attention of the court. In *Re G, Manning v G (No 4)* EWHC Admin 1732 Munby J said:

> Prior to the appointment of a receiver it is, no doubt, a matter for the prosecution to 'police' the restraint order. But it is perfectly proper for the receiver, once he has been appointed, to police the order. So if it is said that there has been a breach of the restraint order by the defendant it is perfectly proper for the receiver to take steps to investigate the matter, whether for the purpose of locating and retrieving assets which he is entitled to have under his control and/or for the purpose of punishing the defendant for any contempt of court that can be proved. The receiver is simply acting in pursuance of his statutory duties, exercising powers which are conferred on him: those duties and powers are vested in the receiver, not the prosecutor, though the prosecutor will no doubt support the receiver as necessary. It is implicit in the entire statutory scheme that it is the receiver's duty to ensure that all the realisable property is under his control, not the control of the prosecutor.

4.15 The powers of management receivers extend to intangible property. In *Manning and Sinclair v Glatt* [2003] EWCA Civ 1977 the Court of Appeal, in refusing an application for permission to appeal, rejected the contention that a management receiver's powers were confined to tangible property. Jacob LJ said:

> We explored with Counsel the various possibilities of different kinds of action that might involve receivers who have been appointed. Could they, if appointed as receivers over a lease, take proceedings for unpaid rent or for possession? Or could they defend proceedings if, for example, there was an application for a third party debt order? All those examples to my mind indicated very clearly that unless this Act was restricted to physical objects Counsel's arguments disintegrated. I can think of no reason whatever why the Act should have been limited, as Counsel submitted. The power is to take possession of any realisable property. One focuses on anything, therefore, which can be converted into money. Almost all forms of property can be so converted. The word 'possession' takes its flavour from the kind of property. The Act would serve no useful or meaningful purpose if confined to chattels . . . once one has arrived at the position that the receiver can take possession of all realisable property, it must follow that he has the power to look after that property by taking proceedings or defending them, as well as any other necessary action. Of course if the receiver acts in some improper way there may well be proceedings which can be taken, and if the receiver is ever in doubt as to what he should be doing he has, of course, express power to apply to the court. But that is much the same as the position of any other receiver appointed by the court, or indeed others concerned with insolvency, for example trustees in bankruptcy or liquidators of companies. The remedy lies not in challenging the receiver's powers, but in any misuse of them.

Sedley LJ added:

> . . . Receivers must have an implied power to resort to the courts in order to preserve the defendant's property. Once this is accepted there can be no bright line which restricts either the kinds of proceedings which the receiver may bring or defend, or the kinds of realisable property to which the receivership may relate. The proper control of the receiver, precisely

because he is an officer of the court, lies where necessary in the hands of the court. There is no reason why the defendant himself should not be able to alert the court to any possible irregularities of the kind with which Counsel is understandably concerned in the present case.

Management receivers' power of sale

The power of selling realisable property causes particular problems in relation to manage-   **4.16**
ment receiverships. The primary role of a management receiver is, of course, to manage and preserve the defendant's realisable property pending the making or enforcement of a confiscation order. This is in contrast to the position of an enforcement receiver who is appointed to sell off realisable property and pay the proceedings into court in satisfaction of a confiscation order that has already been made and that is no longer subject to an appeal. Nonetheless, a situation may arise in which a management receiver wishes to sell a particular asset because, for example, it is depreciating in value. The course of action may be opposed by a defendant who claims that the asset in question is of sentimental value or irreplaceable and that sale would preclude the return of the asset to him in the event of an acquittal.

This problem was first considered by the Court of Appeal, in the context of the old legisla-   **4.17**
tion, in *Re P (Restraint Order: Sale of Assets)* [2000] 1 WLR 473. The defendant had been arrested and charged with drug trafficking offences in relation to which he had been remanded in custody, and the High Court had made restraint and management receivership orders under the DTA without notice to him. The assets caught by the orders included three race horses, one of which, named 'Nipper Read', apparently had race-winning potential and was also alleged to be a 'much loved pet' by the defendant's family. The receiver wished to sell the horses believing them to be depreciating assets. This course of action was strongly opposed by the defendant who made an application to the High Court for an order directing the receiver not to sell the horses unless it proved necessary to satisfy any confiscation order made in the event of his conviction. The application was dismissed by Scott Baker J at first instance, but the defendant succeeded on appeal to the Court of Appeal.

Simon Brown LJ (with whom Chadwick LJ and Rattee J agreed) considered why the legis-   **4.18**
lation gave the court power to appoint management receivers and said:

> In part, no doubt this is because appointment is to guard against attempts by determined defendants, less concerned than most at the thought of the sanctions attending breach of restraint orders, to salt away their assets beyond the reach of any eventual confiscation order. In short, I see as the primary task of an interim receiver the safeguarding of the defendant's assets from dissipation and secretion rather than their realisation so as to maximise the amount of any confiscation order.

He concluded:

> On the material then before the judge I for my part would not have thought it right to allow these three horses to be sold. There was no suggestion that the defendant was dissipating his assets (in the sense of incurring excessive or unusual expenditure beyond what for him was the norm), still less that he was attempting to salt them away. While the defendant remains unconvicted, his assets should not be sold against his wishes except for compelling reason. The possibility, even the probability, that these horses could be more profitably sold now than at some future date is not such a compelling reason.

4.19 It would appear, however, that *Re P* is no longer good law in relation to management receiverships made under POCA and that its effect is confined to receivership orders made under the CJA 1988 and DTA. This is because the legislative steer under POCA is worded in very different terms to the old legislation. In particular, s 69(2)(b) provides that the powers of a receiver appointed under s 48:

> must be exercised, in a case where a confiscation order has not been made, with a view to securing that there is no diminution in the value of realisable property.

4.20 As the Guidance Notes to the Act say, this provision 'requires the powers to be exercised with a view to maintaining the value available for confiscation.' In *Re P* the Court of Appeal found that the purpose of the legislation was to 'impoverish defendants and not enrich the Crown' by selling assets to ensure assets do not depreciate in value. It would appear that, to this extent, *Re P* is no longer good law in relation to restraint and receivership orders made under POCA.

4.21 POCA does not, however, leave the defendant without a remedy in such circumstances. By s 69(3)(c) of POCA:

> in a case where a confiscation order has not been made against a defendant, property must not be sold if the court so orders under subsection (4).

Section 69(4) provides:

> If on an application by the defendant, or by the recipient of a tainted gift, the court decides that property cannot be replaced it may order that it must not be sold.

4.22 By s 69(5) an order made under subs (4) may be revoked or varied. It should be noted that the court is not compelled to order that irreplaceable assets should not be sold: the Act provides that the court 'may' order that the asset is not to be sold, not that it must do so. Unless, however, there are very compelling reasons to the contrary, it is submitted that the proper course would be to order that irreplaceable assets should not be sold prior to the defendant's conviction. This is not to say that it will never be appropriate for a court to empower a management receiver to sell assets. If a defendant is deliberately exposing his assets to the risk of dissipation or depreciation, for example, by not paying the mortgage and insurance premiums on a property, or not effecting essential repairs, by abandoning an asset or causing wanton damage, an order for sale may well be entirely appropriate. The sale of an asset may also be appropriate to make funds available to meet receivership costs and expenses or the general living expenses of the defendant where no other funds are available within the receivership estate.

4.23 The Court of Appeal in *Re P* also gave helpful guidance as to the circumstances in which the court should interfere with decisions made by a receiver in the exercise of his powers. At first instance Scott Baker J ruled that it was only appropriate for the court to interfere where it is satisfied the receiver has 'clearly fallen into error' The Court of Appeal ruled that this was not the correct approach and the court was entitled to interfere wherever the judge's view differs from that of the receiver. The Court was nonetheless at pains to emphasise that this should not be seen as a charter for aggrieved defendants to complain to the court as to every decision made by the receiver. As Simon Brown LJ observed:

> All that said, a court faced with a dispute between the receiver and the defendant as to the proposed course of the receivership is likely to give great weight to the essentially disinterested

views of the former, particularly where they are supported by professional advice and expertise. This judgment should certainly not be seen as a charter for niggling complaints by disgruntled defendants.

C. Exercising the Discretion to Appoint Management Receivers: The *Capewell* Guidelines

The power to appoint a management receiver is a discretionary one, although the court **4.24** must have regard to the 'legislative steer' in s 69 of POCA in determining how that discretion should be exercised. While the need to preserve property to meet any confiscation order must carry great weight, it is not the only issue the court must take into account in the exercise of its discretion. As the Court of Appeal observed in *Re P (Restraint Order: Sale of Assets* [2000] 1 WLR 473, a balance has to be struck between the preservation of property and allowing the defendant to continue with the ordinary course of his life at a time when he is presumed innocent. The court will need to be satisfied that a restraint order alone will be insufficient to prevent dissipation of the defendant's realisable property and the appointment of a receiver is an appropriate and proportionate measure in all the circumstances. The appointment of a receiver is inevitably an expensive exercise and the court will need to be satisfied that the costs involved do not outweigh the potential benefits to the defendant's estate. Further, in *Hughes v Customs and Excise Commissioners* [2000] 4 All ER 633 the Court of Appeal held that the court must always take account of the fact that, if acquitted, significantly depleted assets may be returned to the defendant given that the receiver is entitled to look to the receivership estate for the payment of his remuneration and expenses. Simon Brown LJ said:

> Given that restraint orders can, as perhaps these very cases show, bear heavily upon the individuals involved and may leave acquitted defendants with substantially depleted assets, the court should, in deciding whether initially to make and whether thereafter to vary or discharge such orders, weigh up the balance of the competing interests with the greatest care. The Court's concern to safeguard an accused's property against dissipation or removal abroad must always be weighed against the possibility that the price to be paid will fall upon an innocent man.

Since the Court of Appeal judgment in *Hughes*, courts have become increasingly concerned **4.25** about the costs of management receiverships and the risk that they could have to be borne by a defendant who is ultimately acquitted. In *Capewell v Customs and Excise Commissioners* [2005] 1 All ER 900 at the Court's invitation, counsel on both sides prepared a set of Guidelines for the appointment of management receivers. Although the Court did not hear detailed argument on the Guidelines, it commended them as a 'useful checklist' for those involved in future cases. The Guidelines are in the following terms:

Application by the Prosecutor
1. Within the witness statement in support of the application to appoint a management receiver, the prosecutor should set out the reasons the prosecutor seeks the appointment of a receiver, and what purpose the prosecutor believes the receivership will serve.
2. The witness statement in support of the application should also give an indication of the type of work that it is envisaged the receiver may need to undertake, based on the facts known to the prosecutor at the time of the appointment.

3. The witness statement in support of the application should specifically draw to the Court's attention the proposition that the assets over which the receiver is appointed will be used to pay the costs, disbursements and other expenses of the receivership (even if the defendant is acquitted or the receivership is subsequently discharged).

4. The letter of acceptance of appointment from the receiver, which must be exhibited to the applicant's witness statement, should contain the time charging rates of the staff the receiver anticipates he may need to deploy.

5. In appropriate cases, where it is possible, and this will not be in every case, the receiver should give in his letter of acceptance an estimate as to how much the receivership is likely to cost.

6. The prosecutor's witness statement in support of the application should inform the Court of the nature of the assets and their approximate value (if known) and the income the assets might produce (if known).

7. If the prosecutor or receiver is unable to comply with any of the above requirements the prosecutor should explain the reasons for the failure in the prosecutor's application to the court and the matter will be left at the discretion of the court.

Upon appointment

8. Upon the appointment of a receiver, the Judge should consider whether it is appropriate, in all the circumstances, to reserve any future applications to himself, with a view to minimising costs.

9. Upon the appointment of a receiver, the Judge should consider whether it is appropriate, in all the circumstances, to set a return date, balancing the need for such a hearing with the interests of the defendant, who ultimately will bear the costs of such a hearing.

10. The receiver should inform the parties by written report as soon as reasonably practicable, if it appears to him that any initial costs estimate will be exceeded, or receivership costs are increasing, or are likely to increase to a disproportionate level. Such a report should also be filed with the Court. In such circumstances the parties and the receiver shall be at liberty to seek directions from the Court.

Reporting requirements

11. Unless the Court directs otherwise, the receiver should report 28 days after his appointment and quarterly thereafter.

12. Unless the Court directs otherwise, the report should be served on the prosecutor and the defendant and filed with the Court.

13. Every report should set out the costs incurred to date; the work done; the projected costs until the next report; a summary of how those costs attach to the matters that led to the appointment or to the matters that may have arisen; and, where appropriate, an estimated final outcome statement.

14. Every report should contain a statement that the receiver believes that his costs are reasonable and proportionate in all the circumstances.

15. If the receiver is unable to fulfil any of the above reporting requirements, he should give, as soon as reasonably practicable, an explanation, by way of written report to be filed at Court and served on the parties, of why this is the case, and those parties shall be at liberty to seek directions from the Court.

Lawyers and other agents

16. The parties should always be told that lawyers or other agents have been instructed unless it is not practicable or in the interests of justice to do so (for example, to make an urgent without notice application to secure assets).

17. If lawyers or other agents are instructed the receiver should ask for monthly bills or fee notes. The receiver should endeavour to keep a close control on such fees and satisfy himself that the costs being incurred are reasonable and proportionate in all the circumstances.

18. The receiver should notify the parties as soon as reasonably practicable if it appears to him that any lawyers' or other agents' costs are rising to a disproportionate level, and those parties shall be at liberty to apply to the Court for directions.

General

19. Nothing in these guidelines should be read as surplanting the appropriate rules of court, particularly CPR 69, and the relevant statutory provisions.

20. Judges appointing receivers should always bear in mind that the costs of the receivership may fall on an innocent man. They should also bear in mind that the interests of justice dictate that receiverships are a necessary and essential tool of the criminal justice system for preserving and managing assets to satisfy confiscation orders if the defendant is convicted.

21. Management receivership orders should be endorsed with the appropriate penal notice. It will be a term of most orders that defendants should cooperate with and comply with, as soon as possible and forthwith, directions and requests of the receiver, so as to enable the receiver to efficiently and cost-effectively carry out the duties, functions and obligations of his office. It is therefore in the defendant's interest to avoid, as far as possible, the need for the receiver to return to Court for further orders or directions, the cost of which will ultimately fall on the defendant's estate.

The *Capewell* Guidelines seek to achieve a balance between the rights of all concerned: the **4.26** prosecutor, concerned to protect and preserve the value of realisable property pending the determination of the proceedings; the defendant, anxious to prevent his business and personal life being unduly interfered with and the costs of any receivership escalating out of control; and the receiver's desire to have sufficient powers to act effectively and be properly remunerated for his work. The guidelines achieve this by making it clear that, although the power to appoint a management receiver is an essential tool in the criminal justice system to ensure assets are properly preserved, prosecutors must give proper thought to the objectives the receivership is intended to achieve and consider whether the cost will be proportionate having regard to the benefits likely to accrue to the defendant's estate. The receiver too is enjoined to have proper regard to the principle of proportionality, to report regularly to the parties and the court on the state of progress and the likely costs involved. He must also advise the parties promptly if costs are likely to increase to an amount beyond that estimated in his reports or to the extent that they cease to be proportionate. If a defendant fails to cooperate with the receiver in the proper discharge of his duties after being given due warning, the receiver should bring the matter promptly to the court's attention on an application for directions rather than allow the matter to drift with further unnecessary costs being incurred.

It should also be noted that the defendant has an important role to play in ensuring that **4.27** receivership costs do not escalate out of control. As Guideline 21 makes plain, it is incumbent on the defendant to cooperate with the receiver by complying promptly and fully with his requirements to enable him to discharge his duties, functions, and obligations as an officer of the court efficiently and cost-effectively. Indeed, it is in the defendant's interests to cooperate because the consequence of any failure to do so is likely to be an application by the receiver for further directions. In particularly serious cases, any such failure could result in the receiver or prosecutor instituting contempt proceedings.

D. Status of the Receiver on Appointment

4.28 On appointment, a management receiver becomes an officer of the court, accountable to the court for his actions. Although appointed on the application of the prosecutor, the receiver must act entirely independently and the prosecutor does not have the right to direct him to exercise his powers in a particular way. When the court appoints a management receiver, it effectively assumes the management of the defendant's estate and the receiver is entitled to refer to the court all issues that arise about that management and about the nature and extent of the estate for it to determine: see *Re G, Manning v G (No 4)* [2003] EWHC Admin 1732. It is inevitable that the receiver will work very closely with the prosecuting authority because they will have access to a great deal of information as to the location and status of assets subject to the receivership order. Further, where there is no conflict of interest between the receiver and the prosecuting authority, they may arrange, with a view to saving costs, to be represented by the same counsel on the hearing of any subsequent application in relation to the receivership. This practice was approved by Munby J in *Re G, Manning v G (No 4)*. The judge said:

> I can see no overriding objection to HM Customs and Excise using the same counsel as the receiver where there is no reason to think there is any conflict of interest. Indeed, other things being equal, there are obvious financial advantages both to the receivership estate and to the public purse that duplication of work and effort should be avoided wherever possible.

4.29 The court may from time to time ask the prosecutor to litigate a particular issue on behalf of the receiver, such as the ownership of a particular asset identified in the receivership order. The advantage of this course is that the prosecutor can often litigate such issues more economically than the receiver, to the mutual advantage of all concerned. Where the prosecutor litigates such issues pursuant to an order of the court, he is entitled to the same indemnity from the receivership estate as the receiver: see *Heath Sinclair (The former court appointed receiver) v Louis Glatt & Others* [2008] EWHC 798 (Admin).

4.30 As the receiver is entirely independent of the prosecutor, it follows that the prosecutor cannot be held liable for any default by the receiver.

4.31 It follows from the receiver's status as an officer of the court that any obstruction of the receiver in the performance of his duties under the court's order will constitute a contempt of court. It is for this reason that the standard practice is to endorse all receivership orders with a penal notice (see *Capewell* Guideline 21). A wide range of acts and omissions can constitute obstruction of the receiver including: putting assets beyond the receiver's reach; refusing to deliver up assets or documents of title relating to them; refusing to sign powers of attorney or other documents allowing the receiver to take control of assets; submitting false or forged documents to the receiver intending him to act on them as genuine; and threatening or assaulting the receiver, members of his staff, or agents.

E. Duties and Liabilities of the Receiver

Liability in negligence

Like all professionals, a receiver owes a duty of care to those affected by his actions during **4.32** the course of a receivership. This does not, however, mean that the receiver will be held liable in relation to every act or omission that results in loss to the state. If, for example, the receiver is managing a business, he is entitled to take decisions in relation to the running of the business that involve an element of risk, provided that the risk is not such that no reasonable and prudent person in the receiver's position would have taken it. In order to succeed in an action against a receiver, the defendant or aggrieved third party would have to establish negligence on the part of the receiver.

Further, POCA itself gives the receiver some protection against liability to the defendant **4.33** and third parties. By s 61:

If a receiver appointed under section 48, 50 or 52—
(a) takes action in relation to property which is not realisable property,
(b) would be entitled to take the action if it were realisable property, and
(c) believes on reasonable grounds that he is entitled to take the action,
he is not liable to any person in respect of any loss or damage resulting from the action, except so far as the loss or damage is caused by his negligence.

Thus, even where the receiver acts in relation to property that turns out not to be realisable property under the legislation, he will enjoy protection from liability for his actions provided that he was not negligent and had reasonable grounds for believing he was entitled to act in relation to the property in question.

The receiver will be personally liable in relation to any contracts he enters into in his capacity **4.34** as receiver. He will not, however, be liable in relation to any contracts already in force at the time of his appointment, save to the extent that he adopts them and allows them to continue.

Employment of agents

In all but the most straightforward cases, the receiver will need to instruct agents to assist **4.35** and advise him in the proper discharge of his duties and the receivership order will normally empower him to do so. The receiver will frequently need to instruct a solicitor to provide legal advice and litigation support, expert valuers to value assets subject to the receivership, and property management agents to manage real property. The receiver must ensure that the costs of any such agents are reasonable and proportionate having regard to the benefits that are likely to accrue to the receivership estate. It is the practice of some receivers to instruct City solicitors to advise them and, although it is normally possible to negotiate a discount on the firms' charge out rates, the costs of these firms can rapidly escalate. Although it may be justifiable for the receiver to instruct a City firm in highly complex receivership cases, the use of such a firm to act on a straightforward conveyancing transaction in relation to a property located in the provinces would not. In such a case the receiver would be expected to instruct a high street solicitor in the area where the property is located. In Re D [2006] EWHC Admin 254, solicitors acting for a company affected by restraint and management receivership orders sought the release of some £110,000 by way of legal fees for advising and representing the company. This amount represented a third of the company's entire asset base. Ouseley J ruled that this was disproportionate and released only £50,000 to the solicitors. It is submitted that the same principle applies to receivers and their agents: the services of agents must be obtained at a cost that is proportionate in all the circumstances and not necessarily from the receiver's first choice of professional advisers.

4.36 When the receiver intends to instruct an agent, he should notify the parties as soon as possible except where this is not practicable or in the interests of justice to do so (see *Capewell* Guideline 16). The receiver should also ask for monthly bills or fee notes and satisfy himself that the amounts claimed are reasonable and proportionate (see *Capewell* Guideline 17). The duties of the receiver in this regard are considered in more detail at paragraph 4.52 below. Finally, the receiver must notify the parties immediately if it appears to him that the costs of his agents are rising to a disproportionate level (see *Capewell* Guideline 18).

4.37 Receivers must, therefore, take great care to ensure the reasonableness and proportionality of their actions in relation to the appointment of agents. If they are unable to satisfy the court that their agents fees and disbursements are reasonable and proportionate having regard to all the circumstances of the case, they run the risk of the same being disallowed in whole or in part. The court will not expect receivers to get it right every time and, it is submitted, should be willing to give receivers appointed under POCA rather more latitude than those appointed in civil cases because, as Lord Donaldson MR observed in *Re O* [1991] 1 All ER 330, the legislative contemplation is that some of those claiming an interest in realisable property may be of a 'dishonest disposition' who do their expert best to deal with it in such a way that it is outside the grasp of the court and the receivers whom it appoints.

Receivers' accounts and reports

4.38 By r 60.7(1) of the Criminal Procedure Rules 2005 (CrimPR) the Crown Court may order a management or enforcement receiver to prepare and serve accounts. The letter of agreement between the receiver and the prosecuting authority on whose application he is appointed will invariably require the preparation and service of accounts on the court, prosecutor, and defendant at regular intervals, and the receivership order itself will provide that the receiver must act in accordance with that letter of agreement.

4.39 CrimPR Pt 60.7 gives all parties served with the receiver's accounts certain important rights. Firstly, under CrimPR 60.7(2) any party served with the accounts may apply for an order permitting him to inspect any document in the possession of the receiver relevant to those accounts. This does not entitle a defendant or affected third party to have full access to the receiver's file, but merely to documents that are of relevance to the accounts he has submitted. Secondly, by CrimPR 60.7(3), any party may, within 14 days of being served with the accounts, serve notice on the receiver:

(a) specifying any items in the accounts to which he objects;
(b) giving the reason for such objection; and
(c) requiring the receiver within 14 days of receipt of the notice, either—
　　(i) to notify all the parties who were served with the accounts that he accepts the objection, or
　　(ii) if he does not accept the objection to apply for an examination of the accounts in relation to the contested item.

By CrimPR Pt 60.7(4), when the receiver applies for the examination of the accounts he **4.40** must file the accounts and a copy of the notice served him under paragraph (3). If the receiver fails either to accept the objection or apply for an examination of his accounts under CrimPR Pt 60.7(3)(c), any party to the receivership proceedings may apply to the Crown Court for an examination of the accounts in relation to the contested item: CrimPR 60.1(5). At the conclusion of the examination of the accounts the court shall certify the result: CrimPR 60.7(6).

The duty of the receiver to serve accounts on the defendant also extends to any reports he **4.41** may prepare as to the progress of the receivership. If the receiver considers that particularly sensitive issues alluded to in his report should be withheld from the defendant he should refer the matter to the court and be in a position to justify departing from the usual rule: see *Re G, Manning v G (No 4)* [2003] EWHC Admin 1732 and *Capewell* Guideline 12. In *Re G, Manning v G (No 4)* Munby J said:

> . . . it seems to me that orders of this sort should, as a matter of standard practice, require the prompt submission to the defendant of copies not merely of the accounts prepared by the receiver but also of the reports prepared by him. Indeed, as appears from *Hughes* at para [19] that has in fact now become a 'standard provision' in orders of this kind. If it is to be said that for some special reason a different form of order is appropriate in a particular instance then the case for departing from the usual form of order must be made out. Likewise if it is to be said that, notwithstanding an order in the usual form, the receiver should be relieved from what would otherwise be his obligation to give the defendant a copy of some particularly sensitive report.

F. Remuneration of Receivers

Those appointed as management receivers under POCA are normally chartered accoun- **4.42** tants or licensed insolvency practitioners working for large accountancy firms. They accept appointments under the legislation because they are a commercially viable enterprise from which they are entitled to charge fees and make a profit for themselves or their employers. The remuneration of receivers has been one of the most controversial aspects of management receiverships in recent years as there is a real danger that the costs can escalate out of control unless there is careful monitoring by the court, the prosecutor, and the defendant. This gives rise to two distinct but interrelated issues which have been the subject of much litigation, namely who is liable to pay the receiver's fees and how is control exercised over the amounts claimed?

The historical background

The position at common law has always been that the receiver looks to the estate under **4.43** management for payment of his remuneration, costs, and expenses. This rule flows from the status of the receiver as an independent officer of the court rather than an agent of the prosecutor or parties or other parties to the proceedings. In *Boehm v Goodall* [1911] 1 Ch 151 Warrington J summarised the position thus:

> I think it is of the utmost importance that receivers and managers in this position should know that they must look for their indemnity to the assets which are under the control of the court. The court cannot indemnify receivers but can, and will, do so out of the assets, so far as they extend, for expenses properly incurred, but it cannot go further.

4.44 This principle was upheld by the Court of Appeal in the more recent case of *Evans v Clayhope Ltd* [1988] 1 WLR 358. In that case, the court had appointed a receiver and manager to manage property which was the subject of an action pending the trial. The court held that it had no power, before the issues in the action had been determined, to make an interim order requiring one of the parties to pay the remuneration or expenses of the receiver and that, accordingly, the receiver was entitled to recover his remuneration and expenses only from such funds as were under the control of the court pursuant to the receivership. Nourse LJ said:

> *Boehm v Goodall* was a decision based on statements of principles of high authority. In my judgment it was correctly decided and it applies in this case. Moreover the decision is one of jurisdiction, and unless any part of the receiver and manager's remuneration and expenditure can be treated as 'costs', no question of discretion arises.

4.45 The position at common law is thus clear: the receiver is entitled to look only to the estate under management for the payment of his remuneration and expenses. In a number of cases, the Court of Appeal and House of Lords have had to consider the extent to which this rule applies to receivers appointed under confiscation legislation and, in particular, whether the position is different where the defendant is acquitted or the management receiver is discharged for any reason. In *Re Andrews* [1999] 1 WLR 1236 a management receiver appointed under the CJA 1988 was discharged following the defendant's acquittal. The defendant thereafter discovered that some £10,000 had been taken from his estate by way of receiver's fees and he sought an order that this sum be reimbursed by the prosecuting authority. The Court of Appeal upheld the judge's ruling that he had no power to do so and that, the acquittal notwithstanding, he the receiver was entitled to draw his remuneration and expenses from the estate under management. Aldous LJ said:

> Despite the persuasive submissions of Counsel who appeared for the appellant, in my judgment the remuneration of the receiver was not costs incidental to proceedings in the civil division of the High Court. By order of the Court the receiver assumed control of the company and of the £42,000. Most of the time of the receiver was spent supervising the running of the company. For example, she spent time supervising disposal and acquisition of lorries for the benefit of the company. As yet the receiver has not produced accounts but they will show expenditure and income. Part of the expenditure will consist of her charges which were paid for at least in part out of the money available from the £42,000 that came from the appellant. Such charges cannot in my view be recoverable in these proceedings. These charges are expenses of the receivership and are therefore not recoverable by a successful party in proceedings in which a receiver has been appointed. That conclusion can be demonstrated to be right if it be assumed that the only property that was taken into receivership was the company. If so, receiver's remuneration would be incurred as a charge for running the company which hopefully would have made a profit even after the remuneration of the receiver had been deducted. It would by no means have been certain that the same position would have been achieved without the accountancy advice of the receiver. In such a case would the receiver's remuneration be recoverable by the owners of the company, if they were successful in the proceedings in which the receiver was appointed? If so would the amount recoverable be the amount charged by the receiver or that sum less the income derived from work done by the receiver? I believe the first question should be answered in the negative. The remuneration of a receiver is an expense of the receivership not costs incidental to the proceedings in which he is appointed. To answer in the affirmative would lead to the difficulty posed by the second question.

The Court also agreed with the prosecutor's submission that the defendant's claim was in **4.46** reality a claim for compensation under s 89 of the CJA 1988 dressed up as a claim for costs because he could not bring himself within the strict requirements of the section. Aldous LJ said:

> I would add that in my judgment counsel was right in his submission that this really was a claim for compensation dressed up as an application for an award of costs; and it is therefore most significant that by section 80 Parliament laid down a carefully regulated code for such a claim. Consequently, in my judgment section 89 is the proper avenue for a compensation claim of this kind, provided of course the claimant can bring himself within the rather strict requirements of the section.

The Court of Appeal in *Andrews* made it clear that it had not considered the provisions **4.47** of the European Convention on Human Rights in reaching its decision. The issue came before the Court of Appeal again in *Hughes v Customs and Excise Commissioners* [2002] 4 All ER 633, and on this occasion the court considered it afresh in the light of the Convention. In this case, the acquitted defendant claimed that it would represent a breach of his rights under Art 1 of the First Protocol to the Convention for the costs of the management receivership to be met from the estate under management. It would, he contended, be disproportionate and arbitrary to deprive an unconvicted or acquitted defendant of his assets in the absence of provision for the payment of compensation. He was successful at first instance but, on the prosecutor's appeal, the Court of Appeal upheld its earlier decision in *Andrews*. The Court ruled that statutory receivers appointed under the DTA and CJA 1988 should be treated in precisely the same way as their common law counterparts except where the legislation provided to the contrary. Accordingly, the costs of the receiver were to be met from the fund under management rather than by the prosecutor, even when the defendant is acquitted or the receiver discharged.

The Court found nothing in its decision that conflicted with the European Convention on **4.48** Human Rights. Simon Brown LJ said:

> It is common ground that acquitted defendants are not, save in the most exceptional circumstances, entitled to compensation for being deprived of their liberty while on remand or indeed for any other heads of loss suffered through being prosecuted. In my view, it is no more unfair, disproportionate or arbitrary that they should be uncompensated too for any effects that restraint and receivership orders may have had upon their assets.

The decisions in *Hughes* and *Andrews* may not be as harsh as they first appear. The defen- **4.49** dant will have benefited from a professional manager administering his assets and business. In many cases, following his acquittal, the defendant will get back assets that are far better managed and maintained than at the time the receiver took office. Inevitably, managing those assets incurs much expenditure. Houses and other real property will need to be insured, kept in good repair, and mortgage repayments and council tax liabilities met. If there is a business to run, staff and trading expenses will need to be paid and proper accounts prepared and maintained. All these items of expenditure are essential to the proper management of the defendant's estate and would have to be met regardless of whether a receiver is in office.

4.50 Section 49(2)(d) of POCA allows the Crown Court to give management receivers power to:

> realise so much of the property as is necessary to meet the receiver's remuneration and expenses.

Similarly, CrimPR Pt 60.6 makes specific provision for the payment of the receiver's remuneration from the estate under his management. It is submitted that the combined effect of these provisions is to apply the common law rules in relation to the remuneration of receivers to management receivers appointed under POCA. Part 60.6 is considered at paragraph 4.55 below.

4.51 In many cases the prosecutor will undertake, in the letter of agreement, to indemnify the receiver as to his remuneration and expenses in the event that there are insufficient assets available within the estate under his management. Such indemnities are often made subject to conditions, such as a requirement that the receiver notify the prosecutor immediately if he considers there is a risk he may need to call on the indemnity, and/or a provision capping the amount the prosecutor is prepared to pay. Many receivers are now prepared to act without an indemnity or subject to a conditional fee agreement.

Controlling the receiver's remuneration and expenses

4.52 In the *Hughes* case, the Court of Appeal ruled that receivers' remuneration and expenses must be approved by the court and the previous practice of such fees being vetted and approved by the prosecutor alone was wrong. Arden LJ drew attention to paragraph 22.6 of the Chancery Guide which provides that:

> The receiver's remuneration must be authorised by the Court. Unless the court directs it to be fixed by reference to some fixed scale, or percentage of sums collected, it is assessed by the court, but in the first instance the receiver should submit his remuneration claim to the parties for approval. If the claim is accepted by the parties, the court should not normally be concerned to intervene, but it must at least formally authorise the remuneration.

This, it is submitted, is a more equitable regime because it gives the defendant the right to make representations if he considers the receiver's claim is excessive. The previous system whereby fees were simply agreed between the prosecutor and the receiver left no avenue of redress open to a defendant who wished to challenge the receiver's claim.

4.53 Indeed, it must be thought that a receivership order gives the receiver a 'blank cheque' to charge whatever fees he thinks appropriate, pursue whatever enquiries he chooses, or pay the fees of agents he engages without holding up their invoices to critical scrutiny. In *Mirror Group Newspapers v Maxwell* [1998] BCC 324 Ferris J described as 'profoundly shocking' a receivership in which nothing at all had been realised for the benefit of creditors in an estate valued in excess of £1.5 million, and the majority of the funds had been applied in satisfaction of the costs of the receivers and their lawyers. He issued a timely reminder to receivers as to their duties as office holders and fiduciaries. He said that the test for determining whether a receiver had acted properly in undertaking particular tasks at a particular cost must be:

> whether a reasonable prudent man, faced with the same circumstances in relation to his own affairs, would lay out or hazard his own money in doing what the office holders have done.

It is not sufficient, in my view, for office holders to say that what they have done is within the scope of the duties or powers conferred on them. They are expected to deploy commercial judgment, not to act regardless of expense. This is not to say that a transaction carried out at a high cost in relation to the benefit received, or even an expensive failure, will automatically result in the disallowance of expenses or remuneration. But it is to be expected that transactions having these characteristics will be subject to close scrutiny.

The learned judge took a similarly robust line in relation to the fees of lawyers and other **4.54** professionals engaged to advise receivers. He said:

At the very least they must subject the bills to critical scrutiny. If they simply pay them without scrutiny they will obviously be vulnerable. They may be able to negotiate certain reductions, thus facilitating an argument that the negotiated reductions are preferable to the possibility of obtaining greater reductions at greater costs. In an appropriate case (but not I would expect one where the issues are as complex and the amounts as large as in this case) they may be able to obtain a certificate from the Law Society as to the proper amount of their solicitors bill. Finally they can require the bills to be taxed pursuant to Section 70 of the Solicitors Act 1975.

The concerns expressed by Ferris J led to new rules being introduced in the High Court in **4.55** relation to remuneration of receivers with effect from 2 December 2002. In so far as CJA and DTA cases are concerned the new rules are to be found in Pt 69.7 of the Civil Procedure Rules (CPR). In relation to POCA cases, the rules, which are in almost identical terms, are to be found in Pt 60.6 of the Criminal Procedure Rules 2005. Part 60.6 provides:

(1) This rule applies where the Crown Court appoints a receiver under section 48 or 50 of the Proceeds of Crime Act 2002 and the receiver is not a member of staff of the Crown Prosecution Service or the Revenue and Customs Prosecutions Office (and it is immaterial whether the receiver is a permanent or temporary member or he is on secondment from elsewhere).
(2) The receiver may only charge for his services if the Crown Court—
    (a) so directs; and
    (b) specifies the basis on which the receiver is to be remunerated.
(3) Unless the Crown Court orders otherwise, in determining the remuneration of the receiver, the Crown Court shall award such sum as is reasonable and proportionate in all the circumstances and which takes into account—
    (a) the time properly given by him and his staff to the receivership;
    (b) the complexity of the receivership;
    (c) any responsibility of an exceptional kind or degree which falls on the receiver in consequence of the receivership;
    (d) the effectiveness with which the receiver appears to be carrying out, or to have carried out, his duties; and
    (e) the value and nature of the subject matter of the receivership.
(4) The Crown Court may refer the determination of a receiver's remuneration to be ascertained by the taxing authority of the Crown Court and rules 78.4 and 78.7 shall have effect as if the taxing authority was ascertaining costs.
(5) A receiver appointed under section 48 of the 2002 Act is to receive his remuneration by realising property in respect of which he is appointed in accordance with section 49 (2) (d) of the 2002 Act.
(6) A receiver appointed under section 50 of the 2002 Act is to receive his remuneration by applying to the magistrates' court office for payment under section 55 (4) (b) of the 2002 Act.

All parties to the proceedings should examine receivers' claims for remuneration with **4.56** care and challenge any discrepancies or concerns. In particular, the hourly rates claimed should be checked to ensure they are in accordance with the letter of agreement between the prosecutor and the receiver which will always be annexed to the witness statement in support of the receivership application. The number of hours spent on each task should also be examined to ensure reasonableness and proportionality, having regard to the particular circumstances of the case. The grade of fee earner performing particular tasks is also open to challenge: it does not, for example, require the receiver himself to write letters about routine issues; this can properly be delegated to more junior staff on lower charge out rates. Care should also be taken to check that receivers are not claiming for overheads such as handover meetings when a fee earner is leaving the firm, drawing cheques, bank reconciliations, and the like. All these overheads are included in the hourly rate and should not attract separate entries on the invoices. Similar checks should be undertaken in relation to invoices rendered by agents engaged by the receiver such as solicitors, surveyors, estate agents etc. In many cases it will be possible to resolve any disputes by negotiation with the receiver but, if this proves impossible, the Crown Court should be asked to refer the matter to the taxing authority in accordance with CrimPR 60.6(4).

4.57   In *Capewell v Customs and Excise Commissoiners (No 2)* [2005] EWCA Civ 964 the Court of Appeal held that the similarly worded provisions of Pt 69.7 of the Civil Procedure Rules gave the court a discretion to require the prosecutor, in special circumstances, to pay the remuneration of the receiver, the decision in *Hughes* notwithstanding. Carnwath LJ said:

> On its face, it gives an unlimited discretion in respect of the receiver's remuneration. Without more detailed information as to the background, I am prepared to assume that this rule was not intended to make a radical change to the previous practice. However, it seems clearly designed to give the court some discretion in the matter, at least in special circumstances where application of the ordinary rule would cause unfairness or hardship. *Andrews* may have been one example in the draftsman's mind.

4.58   In a concurring judgment, Longmore LJ added:

> I would add only a reference to paragraph 60 of the judgment of Simon Brown LJ in *Hughes v Customs and Excise Commissioners* [2003] 1 WLR 177 where he said this:
>
>> 'It is important that this legislation continues to be operated to strip criminals of their ill gotten gains. But it is important too that the court keeps a close control over those it appoints to act as receivers on its behalf and that costs are not too readily incurred, particularly before any confiscation order is made.'
>
> It is only by making, in appropriate cases, orders of the kind we have decided to make in the present case that the courts can exercise the sort of control envisaged by Simon Brown LJ to be necessary.

4.59   The Court of Appeal's decision in *Capewell (No 2)* was reversed by the House of Lords on a successful appeal by the prosecutor. In *Capewell v HM Revenue and Customs* [2007] UKHL 2 the House of Lords held that the Court of Appeal had been wrong to assume that CPR Pt 69.7 could have the effect of overruling the Court's previous ruling in *Hughes*. Lord Walker of Gestingthorpe said:

> In my opinion, CPR 69.7 has not had that far-reaching and surprising result. The function of CPR 69 is to set out a procedural code applicable to the generality of receiverships of all types. Its text gives no indication that its draftsman had particularly in mind the new species of receiverships in support of restraint orders and confiscation orders. No doubt its provisions do in general apply to such receiverships but they cannot override the scheme inherent

in the detailed provisions of the CJA 1988. That scheme is for the receiver's remuneration and expenses to be paid out of the receivership assets, but in a way which counts towards satisfaction of any confiscation order, and subject to the statutory long-stop already mentioned. If an individual subject to a restraint order is not ultimately convicted and made subject to a confiscation order, section 89 of the CJA gives a statutory right to compensation in some circumstances. But Parliament has deliberately framed the right to compensation in narrow terms. That is an aggrieved individual's only right to compensation as such. He would not normally have the benefit of an undertaking in damages since (as Simon Brown LJ observed in *Hughes* at para 50) a prosecutor cannot be required to give an undertaking in damages as a condition of obtaining the appointment of a receiver. An aggrieved individual's only other recourse would be to challenge the amount of the receiver's remuneration as the respondent has done in this case. There is a similar scheme under POCA 2002 and the Crown Court (Confiscation, Restraint and Receivership) Rules 2003 (SI 2003/421) made under that Act, but in these new provisions it is made perfectly clear that receivership expenses and remuneration are to come out of the assets subject to the receivership.

The Court of Appeal was in my opinion wrong to suppose that CPR 69.7 has made (or could have made) a fundamental change either in the general law of receivership, or in the position of receiverships under CJA 1988 and other comparable statutory powers. I would allow this appeal on that ground. There is also a further, narrower ground for concluding that the order of the Court of Appeal cannot be upheld. In the original order appointing Mr Sinclair as receiver, Jackson J directed that 'the costs of the receivership' (which in the context must mean expenses and remuneration) were to be paid in accordance with the agreement letter of 21 November 2002. That order was not appealed at the time (although it was contemplated that an early application would be made for discharge of the receiver) nor has there been any subsequent application for permission to appeal from it out of time. A receiver takes on heavy responsibilities when he accepts appointment, and he is entitled to the security of knowing that the terms of his appointment will not be changed retrospectively—even if an appellate court later decides that the receivership should have been terminated at an earlier date.

The decision in *Hughes* therefore remains good law, Pt 69.7 of the Civil Procedure Rules **4.60** and Pt 60.6 of the Criminal Procedure Rules notwithstanding.

The receiver's lien

The receiver has a lien over the assets forming part of the receivership estate for payment of **4.61** his remuneration and expenses. In *Mellor v Mellor & others* [1992] 1 WLR 517 it was held by the High Court that the receiver's lien over the assets gave him a continuing right to possession even after the discharge of the receivership order. In *Sinclair v Glatt and others* [2009] EWCA Civ 176 the Court of Appeal held that the receiver's lien extended to assets over which the defendant only had a bare legal interest. The defendant had been subject to restraint and management receivership orders which were ultimately discharged when his confiscation order was quashed by the Court of Appeal. During the course of the management receivership, Munby J made a ruling to the effect that the executors of the defendant's late mother's estate were beneficially entitled to various assets subject to the order and that the defendant merely held a bare legal title to them. The receiver thereafter asserted a lien for his remuneration and expenses against those assets and, in a further ruling, Munby J upheld the receiver's claim notwithstanding that the estate of the defendant's late mother was beneficially entitled to them. The Court of Appeal upheld the judge's ruling that the receiver was entitled to exercise his lien over the assets. Longmore LJ, with whom Stanley Burnton and Elias LJJ agreed, held that there was an element of 'artificiality' in the submission that the lien could not attach to property over which the defendant only had a bare legal interest. He said:

> A further reason why Counsel cannot be right to say that 'realisable property' cannot include a defendant's bare legal interest is its artificiality. Counsel has to accept that if a defendant has a 10% (or even 1%) beneficial interest in the property, it would then be realisable property and that the receiver's lien would then attach. Such a construction would create anomaly and defy practical sense.

4.62 The Court also rejected a submission from the defendant's wife that the receivership assets should not be made available to meet the receiver's lien until her own ancillary relief application in divorce proceedings had been determined. Longmore LJ said:

> Mrs Glatt has not yet obtained any property adjustment or other order in her matrimonial proceedings; she is, therefore, in no position to make any claim to the receivership assets in her own name. There is no suggestion by her or by Mr Glatt that any assets are not properly the subject-matter of the receivership order. The fact that if the confiscation order had not been quashed, Mrs Glatt would have been afforded an opportunity before any asset was realised to show that she had an interest of her own in such assets (see *Re Norris*) is nothing to the point since she does not currently assert that she has any such interest. The most she has is the hope that, in due course, a court might make a property transfer order in her favour. If she does obtain such an order, and the receivership order had been outstanding, she might have been able to extract what by then would have become her assets but there is no reason why the receiver could not exercise his lien for his charge up to the time of any such transfer. It follows that there is no point in preventing the receiver from now exercising his lien and Counsel's first argument that the entire proceedings should be deferred until after the resolution of Mrs Glatt's proceedings for ancillary relief must fail.

4.63 The Court was similarly unimpressed with an argument advanced on behalf of the wife to the effect that the court had a discretion to balance the competing claims of the wife and receiver and conclude that the receiver should look to his indemnity from the prosecutor for payment of his remuneration and expenses. Longmore LJ said:

> That would be contrary to the decisions of this court in *Mellor* and *Hughes* in which it was determined that a receiver appointed under the Act had the same powers as his common law counterpart and that he must be entitled to assess the value of the receivership assets included in the receivership order when determining whether or not to take on the receivership.

4.64 Finally, the court considered whether the decision represented a breach of property rights under Art 1 to the First Protocol of the European Convention on Human Rights and concluded that it did not. The Court held that the statutory measures in relation to the receiver's costs were in the public interest, appropriate for and achieving their aim, proportionate in striking a fair balance between the demands of the general interests of the community and the requirements of the protection of individual rights. Longmore LJ noted that Counsel for the receiver and prosecutor had conceded that in an extreme case, where a party wholly unconnected with the defendant stood to lose an entire asset because it was eaten up by receiver's costs, Art 1 might have a part to play in determining how much the receiver was entitled to claim and from which asset it would be payable. He emphasised that, in the instant case, none of the parties could claim to have no connection with the defendant. The court observed that the wife's claim under Art 1 to the First Protocol was 'even more hopeless' since she had no property interest of which she would be deprived if the receiver exercised his lien.

G. Discharge of the Receiver

Receivers and the prosecuting authorities that apply for their appointment should be **4.65** vigilant in reviewing both the economic viability of the receivership and the continued necessity for having a receiver in office. If the point comes when it is apparent that the receivership would no longer serve any useful purpose or that it is no longer economically viable, an application should be made to the Crown Court for the receiver's discharge.

A defendant who considers that a management receivership order should be discharged for **4.66** these reasons should initially invite the receiver and the prosecutor to justify why it is necessary for the receiver to stay in office. If he considers the response unsatisfactory, the defendant should himself apply to discharge the receivership. He should serve a witness statement in support of his application setting out his grounds for seeking the discharge of the receiver together with his own proposals for the effective management of his assets pending the conclusion of the proceedings.

Section 63 of POCA (as amended by para 30 of Sch 8 to the Serious Crime Act 2007) **4.67** makes provision for the discharge and variation of receivership orders. It provides:

(1) The following persons may apply to the Crown Court to vary or discharge an order made under any of sections 48 to 51—
  (a) the receiver;
  (b) the person who applied for the order;
  (c) any person affected by the order.
(2) On an application under this section the court—
  (a) may discharge the order;
  (b) may vary the order.
(3) But in the case of an order under section 48 or 49—
  (a) if the condition in section 40 which was satisfied was that proceedings were started or an application was made, the court must discharge the order on the conclusion of the proceedings or of the application (as the case may be);
  (b) if the condition which was satisfied was that an investigation was started or an application was to be made, the court must discharge the order if within a reasonable time proceedings for the offences are not started or the application is not made (as the case may be).

It is thus a matter for the court's discretion as to whether the receivership order should be **4.68** discharged or not, save where s 63(3) applies when the court must discharge the order. When exercising its discretion under s 63(2), the court must have regard to the legislative steer in s 69. In *Capewell v Customs and Excise Commissioners (No 2)* [2005] EWCA Civ 964 the Court of Appeal gave guidance as to the issues the court should take into account in determining whether a management receivership order should be discharged. Carnwath LJ said:

> On the question of discharge, cost is of course a factor, but it is not the primary issue. The overriding consideration is whether the receivership is still serving a valid purpose, within the overall objective set by section 82. The relevant questions for the court are likely to be—
> (i) For what purposes, within the overall objective, was the receivership authorised?
> (ii) To what extent have those purposes been achieved or overtaken?
> (iii) To the extent that they have not yet been achieved or overtaken, is the continuation of the receivership (as opposed to a restraint order or some other order) necessary to achieve them?

(iv) In any event, having regard both to the overall objective and to fairness to the defendant, is the additional cost of continuing the receivership proportionate to the likely financial gain?

We would add that fairness to the defendant cannot be measured purely in financial terms. Even without accepting all of Mr Capewell's evidence, it requires little imagination to understand how a receivership of this kind can seriously interfere with the ordinary business and personal life of those affected and their families. The premise of the 1988 Act is that such a burden may have to be accepted in the public interest. But it is for the court to decide in individual cases where the balance lies, weighing all the benefits and burdens, both public and private.

4.69 Even if there are insufficient grounds to justify the discharge of the receiver, the defendant or an affected third party is always entitled to seek the court's directions if he considers the receiver is abusing his power or is otherwise acting improperly: see *Manning & Sinclair v Glatt* [2003] EWCA Civ 1977.

4.70 Section 64 of POCA (as amended by para 31 of Sch 8 to the Serious Crime Act 2007) makes provision for the discharge of management receivers on the appointment of an enforcement receiver. It provides:

(1) This section applies if—
    (a) a receiver stands appointed under section 48 in respect of realisable property (the management receiver), and
    (b) the court appoints a receiver under section 50.
(2) The court must order the management receiver to transfer to the other receiver all property held by the management receiver by virtue of the powers conferred on him by section 49.
(3) *repealed by para 31(3) of Schedule 8 to the Serious Crime Act 2007.*
(4) Subsection (2) does not apply to property which the management receiver holds by virtue of the exercise by him of his power under section 49(2)(d).
(5) If the management receiver complies with an order under subsection (2) he is discharged—
    (a) from his appointment under section 48;
    (b) from any obligation under this Act arising from his appointment.
(6) If this section applies the court may make such a consequential or incidental order as it believes is appropriate.

4.71 The management receiver cannot be compelled to deliver up to the enforcement receiver assets he holds for the purpose of meeting his remuneration and expenses: see s 64(4). Once he complies with an order under s 64(2), the management receiver is discharged from office and from any obligation consequent upon it: see s 65(5).

H. Taxation and Receivers

4.72 Management and enforcement receivers appointed under POCA are not liable to pay tax pursuant to the Taxes Management Act 1970 in respect of their dealings in and realisations of realisable property pursuant to their orders of appointment: see s 448 and Pt 1 of Sch 10 to POCA. The same principle applies to receivers appointed under the CJA 1988 and DTA: see *IRC v Dayman and Piacentini* The Times, 10 February 2003.

5

APPLICATIONS TO VARY AND
DISCHARGE RESTRAINT ORDERS

A. Introduction

By s 42(3) of POCA: **5.01**

An application to discharge or vary a restraint order or an order under section 41(7) may be made to the Crown Court by—
(a) the person who applied for the order;
(b) any person affected by the order.

Further, the restraint order itself will invariably give all parties affected by it permission to apply for its discharge or variation on giving two clear days notice in writing to the court and the prosecutor. A party aggrieved by a restraint order should always apply for the order to be varied or discharged before embarking on an appeal. Indeed, an appeal to the Court of Appeal by a person affected by a restraint order only lies against a decision of the Crown Court on an application made under s 42(3) of the Act. There is no immediate right of appeal against the making of a restraint order without first seeking its variation or discharge: see s 43 of the Act. In this chapter we consider the grounds on which applications for the variation and discharge of POCA restraint orders might be made by prosecutors, defendants and third parties.

B. Applications to Discharge Restraint Orders

On the conclusion of proceedings

5.02   By s 42(6) of POCA:

> If the condition in section 40 which was satisfied was that proceedings were started or an application was made, the court must discharge the order on the conclusion of the proceedings or of the application (as the case may be).

Once proceedings conclude the restraint order must be discharged: s 42(6) gives the court no discretion in the matter. It should, however, be noted that the definition of the expression 'conclusion of proceedings' in s 85 of POCA is such that proceedings do not conclude when the defendant is convicted and sentenced, but only upon the satisfaction of any confiscation order. In practice, the prosecutor will apply promptly for the restraint order to be discharged in the event of the defendant being acquitted or on the satisfaction of a confiscation order. If he does not, in the absence of a satisfactory explanation, the defendant should make his own application for the order to be discharged.

Delay by the prosecutor

5.03   A restraint order can, and often does, have a significant impact on a defendant and others affected by it. The order imposes draconian restrictions on the extent to which he is entitled to deal with his assets at a time when he has not been convicted of any offence and is entitled to be presumed innocent. Accordingly, the prosecutor is expected to proceed expeditiously once a restraint order has been obtained and to prosecute the associated criminal proceedings without undue delay. This principle has been applied for many years by the civil courts in cases where freezing orders (formerly 'Mareva injunctions') have been granted: see, for example, *Lloyds Bowmaker Ltd v Britannia Arrow Holdings Ltd* [1988] 1 WLR 1337.

5.04   Section 42(7) of POCA puts this principle on a statutory footing in cases where the restraint order has been made pre-charge when a person is subject to a criminal investigation. It provides:

> If the condition in section 40 which was satisfied was that an investigation was started or an application was to be made, the court must discharge the order if within a reasonable time proceedings for the offence are not started or the application is not made (as the case may be).

5.05   What constitutes a 'reasonable time' is an issue of fact to be determined on the facts of individual cases. If the investigation being conducted relates to a complex fraud with a vast quantity of documentation to examine and overseas enquiries to pursue, it is clearly reasonable for the investigation to take longer to complete than a more straightforward investigation where all the evidence is to be found in the UK. In determining what constitutes a 'reasonable time' the court is entitled to take into account the progress of the investigation from the time it started and not just from the date on which the restraint order was made. Where an investigation is taking longer to complete than was expected at the time a restraint order was made, in compliance with his ongoing duty to give full and frank disclosure of all material facts, the prosecutor should inform the court of the position so it may determine whether it is appropriate for the restraint order to remain in force and, if so, on what terms.

Procedural irregularities by the prosecutor

A procedural irregularity by the prosecutor in obtaining the restraint order may be a suffi-   **5.06**
cient basis to seek its discharge although, as indicated above, this could prove a short-lived
victory for the defendant because it is always open to the prosecutor to remedy the defect
and apply for a new order. If the irregularity is of a minor or technical nature that can easily
be remedied, the defendant and any affected third party would be well advised not to pursue an application for the discharge of the order as litigating the matter could prove costly
and may even serve no useful purpose.

If the irregularity is a serious one, an application to discharge the order may well be appro-   **5.07**
priate, particularly if it is not easily capable of remedy. A classic example of this is a failure
by the prosecutor to demonstrate a risk that assets will be dissipated in the absence of a
restraint order. In *Re AJ and DJ* (Unreported, 9 December 1992) there had been a delay in
excess of two years between the defendants being charged and an application for a restraint
order being made. During this time, no attempt had been made by the defendants to dissipate their assets other than expending reasonable sums on normal living expenses. The
Court of Appeal found there was no evidence to establish a real risk of assets being dissipated and the decision of the judge to discharge the order was upheld. If there has been a
lengthy delay by the prosecutor in applying for a restraint order, the witness statement in
support should provide a detailed explanation as to why it is now believed that assets
will be dissipated in the absence of a restraint order. It does not follow from the fact that
there has been a delay that the prosecutor is not entitled to seek a restraint order and he may
be able to justify his actions. For example, at the time a defendant is charged there may be
no evidence to suggest a real risk of dissipation but, some time later as his trial approaches,
he may start removing large sums of money from bank accounts or put properties on the
market. In such circumstances his actions would establish a real risk of further assets being
dissipated and a restraint order may well be appropriate. But, without an explanation for a
lengthy delay in the prosecutor's witness statement, an application to discharge the order
may well be justified on the basis of insufficient evidence to establish a risk of dissipation.

A discharge application may also be appropriate where the statutory criteria that have to   **5.08**
exist before a restraint order can be made have not been established. Applications for the
discharge of the order on this basis should be confined to cases where there is no evidence
to show that one or more of the statutory criteria exist. The Crown Court judge will not
attempt to usurp the function of the jury by assessing the strengths and weaknesses of the
criminal case—if the statutory criteria have been made out, it is unlikely the court will
consider discharging an order in the absence of some serious procedural irregularity by the
prosecutor.

Failure to give full and frank disclosure

Applications for restraint orders made without notice to the defendant are subject to the   **5.09**
same procedural rule that the applicant for such relief must give full and frank disclosure of
all material facts. The defendant has neither the right nor the opportunity to be present or
represented when the application is made. The procedure therefore constitutes an exception to the principle of natural justice that both sides should be heard before the court

makes an order. In consequence, the prosecutor is required to give full and frank disclosure of all material facts in his witness statement in support of the application. This obligation requires him to disclose any weaknesses in his cases of which he is aware, any information that might be favourable to the defendant and any innocent explanation that he may have advanced when being interviewed. The prosecutor's duty of full and frank disclosure is considered in more detail in Chapter 7 below, and it will be seen that a serious failure to comply with this duty may result in the order being discharged. Some caution does need to be exercised in considering whether an application to discharge the order should be made on this basis, because it is always open to the prosecutor to apply for a further order on the basis of an amended witness statement that remedies any previous deficiencies in his case.

5.10   Further, in *Jennings v Crown Prosecution Service* [2005] 4 All ER 391 the Court of Appeal held that the public interest in the restraint and confiscation of the proceeds of crime dictated that the court should not be too ready to discharge a restraint order where there has been a failure to give full and frank disclosure. Lloyd LJ said:

> The fact that the Crown acts in the public interest does, in my view, militate against the sanction of discharging an order if, after consideration of all the evidence, the court thinks that an order is appropriate. That is not to say that there could never be a case where the Crown's failure might be so appalling that the ultimate sanction of discharge might be justified.

C. Applications to Vary the Restraint Order

5.11   In the majority of cases, the most appropriate means of seeking to mitigate the harsher effects of a restraint order is to apply for it to be varied in some respect. Applications to vary restraint orders are most commonly made to release funds to pay legal fees and to increase the amount payable to the defendant and his dependants by way of general living expenses.

Legal fees

5.12   We have seen in Chapter 2 that s 41(4) of POCA imposes strict limitations on the release of restrained funds to pay legal fees. Funds may not be released to the defendant or the recipient of a tainted gift in connection with the offence or offences with which the defendant has been charged or is under investigation. This prohibition includes the restraint proceedings (see *Commissioners and Customs and Excise v S* [2005] 1 WLR 1338) and any related judicial review proceedings (see *AP & U Limited v Crown Prosecution Service and Revenue and Customs Prosecutions Office* [2007] EWCA Crim 3128).

5.13   The effect of the prohibition imposed by s 41(4) is that restrained funds may now only be released to meet legal fees incurred in proceedings wholly unrelated to the criminal prosecution. In such circumstances the court may be prepared to accede to the release of restrained funds to permit the defendant's legal expenses to be paid. The court will not, however, sign a 'blank cheque' allowing the defendant to expend whatever sums he wishes on legal expenses. The order will limit such expenditure to expenses actually, reasonably, and properly incurred in the proceedings. As a condition precedent to the release of funds for such purposes the variation order will provide that the following details must be provided to the prosecutor:

(a) the source of the fund to be used to meet the costs;
(b) the general nature of the costs incurred;
(c) the time spent and the grade of fee earners involved; and
(d) the hourly rate charged by each grade of fee earner.

The variation order will also make provision for the resolution of any dispute between the **5.14** parties as to the amount payable by providing that, in the event of prosecutor considering the amount claimed has not been actually, reasonably, and properly incurred, the claim shall be subject to detailed assessment by a costs judge with 65 per cent of the amount claimed being paid in the interim. The assessment will be on the indemnity basis in accordance with Part 48.8 of the Civil Procedure Rules (CPR) but without the provisions of CPR Part 48.8(2) applying.

The authority for the inclusion of this provision is the decision of the High Court in *Re L* **5.15** *The Times*, 10 July 1996. In that case, to which the provisions of the the the Drug Trafficking Act 1994 (DTA) applied, the prosecutor sought the imposition of conditions to prevent any extravagant expenditure. Latham J ruled that given the legislation identifies a clear public interest in ensuring that the defendant's assets should be secured in so far as is reasonable, the imposition of such safeguards was justified. The judge decided that the balance between allowing reasonable sums to be released by way of legal fees against the necessity to preserve assets to make them available to meet any confiscation order could best be achieved by directing that, in default of agreement with the prosecutor, the costs be assessed on an indemnity basis, but without the presumptions in CPR Part 48.8(2) applying. Latham J rejected the prosecutor's contention that the assessment should be on the standard basis saying:

> It seems to me it gives inadequate expression to the defendant's right to use the funds which are prima facie his for the purpose of defending himself. In instructing his solicitor he should be entitled, subject to proper safeguards against extravagance, to expect that his solicitor would be remunerated on a solicitor and own client basis, and not as constrained by a process of taxation based upon the protection of a losing litigant.

The judge went on to hold that, where the claim is disputed by the prosecutor, the full **5.16** amount claimed should not be released from the restrained fund prior to the determination of the assessment proceedings. He upheld the prosecutor's submission that only 65 per cent of the amount claimed should be paid at that stage saying:

> It seems to me to be unsatisfactory for there to be payment out of a protected fund of sums which might thereafter have to be recovered. It follows that the most satisfactory solution is to provide for the retention of such amount as will obviate so far as is fair to both interests, the risk of that happening. In the circumstances of the present case, bearing in mind the amounts which have been mentioned as counsel's fees, which may well need close scrutiny on taxation, I consider that the suggested retention of 35% is entirely appropriate.

Further, and in contrast to the position in relation to freezing orders, where a defendant **5.17** or affected third party seeks the release of funds to meet legal expenses, the expenditure incurred must be proportionate in all the circumstances. Thus, as long as the party concerned has access to proper legal advice, he may not necessarily be entitled to call on the services of his preferred solicitors if the expense incurred would be disproportionate. In *Re D* [2006] EWHC Admin 254 a company, referred to as X Limited, obtained an order authorising the release of up to £35,000 to instruct a firm of solicitors based in the City of London to apply to vary DTA restraint and management receivership orders by which it was affected. The solicitors exceeded the £35,000 ceiling without referring the matter back to the court and, by the hearing of the substantive application to vary the order, their costs had increased to £90,000 plus VAT. This sum represented approximately one-third of the company's entire asset base. Ouseley J refused to increase the ceiling to £90,000 plus VAT and, adopting what he described as 'a fairly generous approach', permitted the release of only £50,000 plus VAT. He said:

> Counsel urged on me in relation to the consideration of costs the approach adopted by Ferris J in *Cala Crystal SA v Emran Al-Borno,* The Times, 6th May 1994 in which, when dealing with freezing injunctions and the dissipation of assets and costs, he said that the expenditure by a company on legal costs was not prima facie the dissipation of the assets and it was not for the parties or indeed the court to criticise either the rate of charge or the hours spent or the nature of the solicitors, city firm or otherwise, who had been chosen to represent the defendant. Hence, said Counsel, it did not lie in the mouth of the receiver to object to his application to the court for an increase in the sum of money which could be spent on legal fees in relation to the receiver and his application, by reference to the hourly rate, time spent or purposes upon which it was spent by the solicitor provided that it reasonably and properly related to the permitted objectives.

> Counsel's submissions seem to me to get very close to say that the ceiling had no purpose other than exclude quite absurd expenditure. I do not accept that. The object of it is not merely to prevent money being spent unnecessarily, it is to avoid disproportionate expenditure in relation to the assets. The avoidance of disproportionate expenditure might very well involve a court saying there is to be a ceiling on the amount of money spent because of the relationship which that bears to the assets of the company; if that means that the preferred choice of solicitors is not available then, provided advice can properly be obtained, it has to be obtained within that ceiling.

5.18 The court is also entitled to enquire as to the purpose for which the release of funds to meet legal fees is sought. If the court concludes that the defendant's case is frivolous or without merit, it is entitled to refuse the application. In *Revenue and Customs Prosecutions Office and another v Briggs-Price* [2007] EWCA 568 Wall LJ said:

> Counsel was, I think, also minded to accept that (and this would certainly be my view) there would be pre-POCA applications to release funds which, on their facts would result in a refusal to vary the restraint order. Thus if, for example, the application for which the release of funds was sought was manifestly unmeritorious or if the sums sought to be expended were clearly disproportionate to the proposed objective, the court would be entitled to refuse the application.

5.19 The court will look at claims for the release of funds to meet legal costs with some scepticism where they are made by a defendant who already has the benefit of legal aid or who has not yet made an application for public funding. In *Re W* (QBD (Admin), unreported 1992) the defendant had been granted legal aid subject to a contribution of £5,000. Shortly thereafter a restraint order was served on him and he decided that he no longer wished to have legal aid and would pay the full costs of his defence privately. He applied for a variation to the restraint order to enable funds to be released for this purpose. Potts J upheld the prosecutor's view that, having sought and been granted legal aid prior to the restraint order being made, the defendant was only entitled to have £5,000 released to meet his legal aid contribution rather than the full costs of his defence. Similarly, in *Re T* (QBD (Admin), unreported, 17 December 2002) the defendant had an application for legal aid outstanding at the time he applied to the High Court for the release of funds to meet his legal expenses.

Davis J adopted a similar approach in *T v Customs and Excise Commissioners* [2004] EWHC   **5.20** Admin 3256 where the defendant sought the release of restrained funds to seek legal advice and representation in relation to a prosecutor's application to appoint an enforcement receiver in relation to an outstanding DTA confiscation order. After T admitted that he had not made any application for civil legal aid, Davis J refused the application for the release of funds saying:

> I can see where Mr. T is coming from but, unfortunately, as I see it, the difficulty for him is that he has produced no evidence before me to show that he has actually applied for civil legal aid and been turned down. Indeed, he frankly told me that he had not, although he did tell me that he had approached a number of firms of solicitors who, in view of the lack of funds, were not able to assist him. I must of course bear in mind the legislative steer behind the Act and I also note, although I do not perhaps need to attach much weight to it, Counsel's stated concerns that this is an attempt to open the door a little bit and thereafter the door will then be opened wide, giving rise to numerous applications with the eventual effect that such funds as there are available will be dissipated, thereby failing to achieve the statutory purpose behind restraint orders and confiscation orders.

> I do not think it right to accede to this application for the reasons I have given and not least because there is no evidence before me as to any application for civil legal aid having actually been pursued by Mr. T and also, I have to say, my unease at the lack of precise evidence as to whether or not funds might not be available to him for this purpose.

There are now many ways in which civil litigation can be funded including through insur-   **5.21** ance policies, membership of trade unions and professional associations, conditional fee agreements, and 'no win, no fee' arrangements. It is submitted that a defendant subject to a POCA restraint order who wishes to have funds released to pursue or defend unrelated civil litigation must also establish that funding through these means is not available to him. Ultimately, however, it is a matter for the discretion of the court to decide whether funds caught by a POCA restraint order should be released to meet legal fees incurred in connection with proceedings unrelated to the criminal offence with which the defendant is charged or for which he is under investigation. In *Revenue and Customs Office v Briggs-Price* [2007] EWCA Civ 568 the Court of Appeal refused to interfere with the decision of Wilkie J to allow the release of restrained funds to finance an appeal against a confiscation order even though the defendant previously had the benefit of a legal aid order. The court emphasised, however, that any exercise of discretion by the judge must be 'judicial and proportionate'. It is submitted that the discretion must also be exercised in a manner that is consistent with the legislative steer in s 69 of POCA.

General living expenses

Most restraint orders will make provision for the release of funds (usually £350 per week) to a   **5.22** defendant not in custody for the purpose of meeting his general living expenses. At the time the prosecutor applies for a restraint order, the information he has as to the personal circumstances of the defendant may well be very limited. He may not, for example, know the defendant's marital status, or whether he has any dependant children to care for. It is also unlikely that the prosecutor will know the extent of the defendant's legitimate financial commitments such as mortgage repayments, public utility bills, and the like. If the defendant considers the amount allowed by way of general living expenses is insufficient, he may ask the prosecutor to consent to the order being varied to permit an upward variation and, in default of agreement, can apply to the court for the restraint order to be so varied. The leading authority on the variation of restraint orders to meet general living expenses is *Re Peters* [1988] 3 WLR 182 where the Court of Appeal considered an application by the defendant for the release of restrained funds to meet school fees for his children. In delivering his judgment, Lord Donaldson MR observed:

> Mr. Peters as an unconvicted accused person who might be acquitted, was entitled to ask that his son's education should not be interrupted, that he himself should be adequately clothed and that he should be able to pay the costs of his defence.

Similarly, Mann LJ said:

> In my experience a restraint order does not, and properly does not, prevent the meeting of ordinary and reasonable expenditure. That which is or is not ordinary expenditure may vary from time to time.

5.23   What constitutes 'ordinary and reasonable expenditure' is an issue to be determined having regard to the circumstances of each individual case and the principles on which the court acts are considered at para 5.30 below.

5.24   It is unlikely that the court will sanction any increase until the defendant has fully complied with his disclosure obligations under the order because, until such time as the required information has been supplied, it is unlikely that sufficient information will be available on which to reach a decision. Indeed, it will be recalled that in *Re O* [1991] 1 All ER 330 the court specifically adjourned an application for an increase in the amounts payable by way of general living expenses until such time as the defendants had sworn affidavits. A detailed breakdown of the expenditure the proposed variation is intended to fund will also be required so the court might be satisfied that it is genuinely necessary for the purpose of meeting ordinary and reasonable expenditure. A defendant who wishes to have funds released to meet such expenses as mortgage repayments, pension and life insurance policies etc is unlikely to encounter any resistance from the court or prosecutor: indeed, in most cases, it will be in the prosecutor's interests to ensure that mortgages do not fall into arrears as the properties to which they relate will then become liable to repossession by the lender and therefore no longer available to meet a confiscation order. A defendant who seeks to have funds released to fund an extravagant lifestyle is likely to incur more resistance from the prosecutor and find the court reluctant to accede to his requests. The court will only sanction the release of such funds as are necessary to enable the defendant to meet ordinary and reasonable expenditure and not to enable him to continue to pursue the lifestyle he enjoyed prior to the making of the order.

Companies and other business entities

5.25   It is by no means unusual, especially in tax fraud cases, that the defendant has an interest in a company or other business entity engaged in legitimate trading. In the absence of special provision, the business bank accounts would be frozen and it would not be able to deal with its assets. This would have the effect of preventing the business trading and cause it to close down. The court will not, however, allow a restraint order to prevent a defendant or his business trading legitimately prior to him being convicted: see *Re G* [2001] EWHC Admin 606. If a restraint order does not provide for such a business to trade legitimately, the defendant would be entitled to apply to the court for the order to be varied appropriately. The court will require safeguards to be incorporated to prevent any such variation being abused. In particular, the court is likely to insist on accounts and other business records being produced to the prosecutor at regular intervals. The usual provisions of the release of business accounts and assets appear in para 19(6) of the draft restraint order at Appendix 7. Where the affairs of a restrained business are unusually complex, or it has a very high turnover, or there is a suggestion that it has been used to facilitate the commission of criminal offences, the appointment of a management receiver may well be appropriate.

Unsecured third party creditors

5.26 The Crown Court has no jurisdiction to vary a POCA restraint order to release funds to enable an unsecured third party creditor of the defendant to be paid. This is in marked contrast to the position under a freezing order made in support of a civil claim, where a third party credit may intervene and apply for the order to be varied so as to enable, but not compel, the defendant to make payment of the amount owed. The reason for this is that a claimant who obtains a freezing order does not acquire an interest in the frozen assets, nor does he acquire precedence over other creditors of the defendant: see *Iraqi Ministry of Defence v Arcepey Shipping Co SA (The Angel Bell)* [1981] QB 65.

5.27 The position is very different where a defendant's assets are frozen pursuant to a restraint order. Since its inception, confiscation legislation has made specific provision as to the way in which the court must exercise its discretion to make, vary, and discharge restraint orders. In *Re Peters* [1988] 3 WLR the court described these provisions as a 'legislative steer' as to the manner in which the discretion should be exercised. There are conflicting authorities as to the extent to which CJA 1988 and DTA restraint orders may be varied to enable third party creditors to be paid. In *Re W* The Times, 15 November 1990 Buckley J held that the legislative steer in the old legislation (to be found in s 82 of the CJA 1988 and s 31 of the DTA) precluded the variation of a restraint order for such purposes. He ruled that the legislative steer gave priority to the satisfaction of a confiscation order over general creditors of the defendant. In *Re X* [2004] 3 WLR 906, however, Davis J refused to follow *Re W* holding that it had been wrongly decided. The judge held that the words 'with a view to making available' in s 82(2) of CJA 1988 should not be construed as meaning 'to make available'. He also noted that s 77(1) of CJA 1988 was drafted in wide terms providing that restraint orders may be made 'subject to such exceptions as may be specified in the order'. He found that these words conferred a wide discretion on the court, empowering it to sanction the payment of creditors over and above living expenses and legal fees.

5.28 The position of unsecured third party creditors therefore remains somewhat uncertain under the old legislation. The legislative steer in s 69 of POCA is worded very differently and, in *Serious Fraud Office v Lexi Holdings PLC (In Administration)* [2008] EWCA Crim 1443, the Court of Appeal held it precluded the release of funds restrained by POCA restraint orders for the purpose of paying third party creditors of the defendant. The effect of the decision is that unless the creditor can assert a proprietary claim over restrained assets, he will be unable to secure their release for the purpose of satisfying his claim. The *Lexi Holdings* decision is considered in more detail at para 5.31 below.

Burden of proof

5.29 It is for the application for a variation to a restraint order to satisfy the court that he should be entitled to the variation he seeks. In *Serious Fraud Office v X* [2005] EWCA Civ 1564, a case concerning the release of restrained funds to meet legal fees under the old legislation, Sir Anthony Clarke MR (with whom Brooke and Buxton LJJ agreed) said:

> If a defendant against whom a restraint order has been made wishes to vary the order in order to enable him to use the funds or assets which are the subject of the order, which I will call 'the restrained assets', in order to pay for his defence, it is for him to persuade the court that it would be just for the court to make the variation sought. I would call that the burden of persuasion.

As X had failed to show that he did not have assets overseas which could be used to meet his legal expenses, the Court held that the order should not be varied for this purpose.

D. The Principles on which the Court Acts: the 'Legislative Steer'

5.30 In determining applications for the release of restrained funds for whatever purpose the court has to achieve a difficult balance between ensuring assets are available to satisfy a confiscation order on the one hand and ensuring that the defendant has sufficient funds available to meet legitimate expenditure on the other. Section 69 of POCA contains mandatory provisions with which the court is required to comply when exercising its powers under the Act, and these are particularly relevant in the context of variation applications. It is therefore convenient to consider them here. Section 69 (as amended by para 34 of Sch 8 to the Serious Crime Act 2007) provides:

(1) This section applies to—
    (a) the powers conferred on a court by sections 41 to 59 and sections 62 to 67;
    (b) the powers of a receiver appointed under section 48 or 50.
(2) The powers—
    (a) must be exercised with a view to the value for the time being of realisable property being made available (by the property's realisation) for satisfying any confiscation order that has been or may be made against the defendant.
    (b) must be exercised, in a case where a confiscation order has not been made, with a view to securing that there is no diminution in the value of realisable property;
    (c) must be exercised without taking account of any obligation of the defendant or a recipient of a tainted gift if the obligation conflicts with the object of satisfying any confiscation order that has been or may be made against the defendant;
    (d) may be exercised in respect of a debt owed by the Crown.
(3) Subsection (2) has effect subject to the following rules—
    (a) the powers must be exercised with a view to allowing a person other than the defendant or a recipient of a tainted gift to retain or recover the value of any interest held by him;
    (b) in the case of realisable property held by a recipient of a tainted gift, the powers must be exercised with a view to realising no more than the value for the time being of the gift;

    (c) in a case where a confiscation order has not been made against the defendant, property must not be sold if the court so orders under subsection (4).

(4) If on an application by the defendant, or by the recipient of a tainted gift, the court decides that property cannot be replaced it may order that it must not be sold.

(5) An order under subsection (4) may be revoked or varied.

Similar, but by no means identical, provisions appear in s 82 of the CJA 1988 and s 31 of **5.31** the DTA. These provisions under the old legislation were described in *Re Peters* [1988] 3 WLR 182 as amounting to a 'legislative steer' as to the manner in which the court's discretion should be exercised. The legislative steer in s 69 is drafted much more tightly than under the previous legislation and its construction fell to be determined by the Court of Appeal in *Serious Fraud Office v Lexi Holdings PLC (In Administration)* [2008] EWCA Crim 1443.

A restraint order had been obtained by the Serious Fraud Office (SFO) against an indi- **5.32** vidual known as 'M' on the basis that he was subject to a criminal investigation into an alleged offence of conspiring to defraud the Cheshire Building Society and associated money laundering offences. The administrators of Lexi alleged it had been the victim of substantial frauds committed by M and others and judgment in default was eventually entered in its favour for some £625,250 plus interest. Lexi thereafter applied to the Central Criminal Court for the restraint order to be varied to permit M to satisfy the judgment. Lexi sought the variation both on the basis that it had a proprietary claim and as a bona fide judgment creditor. The application was opposed by the SFO, but the judge made the variation sought so as to allow payment to be made to Lexi from M's restrained assets. The Judge held that the court had a 'reasonably wide discretion' under POCA so as to do justice. He held that there was no significant change in statutory policy or underlying principle from the pre-2002 Act regime and agreed with the reasoning of Davis J in *Re X* [2004] 3 WLR 906. The SFO appealed, with permission, to the Criminal Division of the Court of Appeal.

The Court (which included Davis J in its composition) allowed the SFO's appeal. The **5.33** Court noted that there were significant differences between the wording of the legislative steer in s 69 of POCA and under the previous legislation. Keene LJ said:

> It is true that some of the provisions in that section contain the phrase 'with a view to' which as has been said in several of the authorities indicates a degree of flexibility in the court's approach and simply gives a 'legislative steer'. Section 69(2)(c), however, is different. It does not contain that phrase and does appear to be in mandatory terms: the powers 'must be exercised without taking account of any obligation . . .' Moreover, the feature of its equivalent provision in the earlier legislation which so influenced Davis J. in *Re X* has changed: it is now clear that this provision does apply in the situation where there is a restraint order but no confiscation order in existence, because the words 'or may be made' have been added. This must be taken to represent a deliberate tightening up of the legislation by Parliament.

He went on:

> On the face of it, section 69(2)(c) does require the courts to ignore any debt owed by the restrained person to an unsecured third party creditor, so that the existence of such a debt would not empower the court to vary a restraint order unless there was no conflict 'with the object of satisfying any confiscation order'. On that last aspect we are wholly unpersuaded

by Counsel for Lexi's argument about the meaning to be attached to those words. His contention that the 'object' is that of depriving the offender of the proceeds of crime is unsustainable. That is the object of the confiscation order itself, whereas this provision is referring to the object of 'satisfying' any confiscation order, i.e. providing a sufficient quantum of assets to meet the sum identified, already or in due course, in a confiscation order. Counsel's interpretation would render the presence of that word 'satisfying' unnecessary and would, in our judgment, distort the natural meaning of section 69(2)(c). If he were right, the provision would enable any third party creditor to obtain a variation of the restraint order and so to be paid and indeed Counsel submits that this is what should happen. The provision would in fact have virtually no effect in practice. In our view, the latter part of paragraph (c) is, as Counsel for the SFO argues, indicating merely that if the court can see that a confiscation order, existing or prospective relates to an amount which the defendant has ample assets to meet, then it may be that a debt to a third party creditor can properly be allowed to be paid from the restrained assets.

5.34 The Court also noted that Lexi's argument appeared inconsistent with the procedures to be followed at the confiscation stage. Keene LJ said:

> . . . of the greatest significance, the payment of third party creditors at the restraint order stage seems to us to be inconsistent with the position which obtains at the confiscation order stage. Section 9 of the 2002 Act provides that the available amount of the defendant's assets when one comes to quantify the amount to be specified in the confiscation order is to be ascertained in the following way:
>
> '(1) For the purpose of deciding the recoverable amount, the available amount is the aggregate of—
>> (a) the total of the values (at the time the confiscation order is made) of all the free property then held by the defendant minus the total amount payable in pursuance of obligations which have priority, and
>> (b) the total of the values (at that time) of all tainted gifts.
> (2) An obligation has priority if it is an obligation of the defendant—
>> (a) to pay an amount due in respect of a fine or other order of a court which was imposed or made on conviction of an offence and at any time before the time the confiscation order is made, or
>> (b) to pay a sum which would be included among the preferential debts if the defendant's bankruptcy had commenced on the date of the confiscation order or his winding up had been ordered on that date.
> (3) "Preferential debts" has the meaning given by section 386 of the Insolvency Act 1986 (c45).'
>
> It will be seen that, when the court decided on the amount to be specified in the confiscation order, it has to use the total of the values of the property the defendant holds, less only 'priority' obligations such as fines and preferential debts. The existence of obligations owed to ordinary third party creditors is to be disregarded when a confiscation order is made. It seems to this court that it would have been wholly illogical for the legislature to have decided to allow third party debts to be paid during the period when assets are supposedly being preserved by a restraint order when such debts are to be left out of account at the stage when the confiscation order is made. We can see no reason why Parliament should have decided to allow unsecured creditors to reduce the assets during the restraint phase when such creditors could not reduce the assets at the confiscation stage. If that were the position, it would put a premium on well advised creditors getting in quickly during the restraint phase before their opportunity is lost, and we do not accept that that situation is one which was ever intended.

Although the effect of s 69 may appear to be harsh so far as innocent third parties are **5.35** concerned, the Court emphasised that they were not necessarily left without a remedy. The Court noted that a restraint order is essentially a temporary measure preserving assets pending the making and enforcement of a confiscation order. As Keene LJ said.

> A restraint order is therefore performing a holding operation. Of course, it has to be acknowledged that that operation may, and has been known to, last a considerable time. Nonetheless, the limited duration of restraint orders is a relevant factor when considering its adverse effects on third party creditors and when seeking to ascertain the intention of Parliament. The restraint order will eventually be discharged and either replaced by some other order such as a confiscation order or not replaced at all.

The Court also noted that the potential harshness of s 69(2)(c) was mitigated to some **5.36** extent by other powers available to the Crown Court once an offender is convicted. As Keene LJ observed:

> ... the court has the power under section 130 of the Sentencing Act to make a compensation order in favour of a person who has suffered loss resulting from the offence or any other offence which is taken into consideration. As Counsel for the SFO points out, such a compensation order takes priority over a confiscation order: see section 13(5) and (6) of the 2002 Act. Not every creditor will be helped by this provision, since he may not qualify under section 130, but some will be assisted. Indeed, if a victim of the defendant's criminal conduct has started or intends to start civil proceedings against him 'in respect of loss, injury or damage sustained in connection with the conduct', then the court, by virtue of section 6(6) need not make a confiscation order at all. The duty to make one where it is determined that the defendant has benefited from his criminal conduct becomes simply a power in those circumstances described in section 6(6). When one bears in mind that the criminal conduct leading to 'loss, injury or damage' may be *general* criminal conduct if the defendant has a criminal lifestyle and not merely the *particular* criminal conduct covered by the offences in question (plus those taken into consideration), it can be appreciated that a considerable number of persons may qualify as 'victims' for this purpose. This too must tend to reduce the number of third parties ultimately affected adversely by the 2002 Act.

Finally, the court noted that the victims themselves may benefit from the defendant's assets **5.37** being held under restraint pending the determination of the criminal proceedings. They too could lose out if the total value of the defendant's assets was reduced by claims brought by other third party creditors being entertained by the court at the restraint stage.

This important decision makes it clear that the effect of s 69(2)(c) is such that POCA **5.38** restraint orders may not be varied to allow third party creditors of the defendant to be paid from restrained funds. In relation to POCA restraint orders at least, it is clear that the decision of Buckley J in *Re W* remains good law. The Court avoided making any observations as to whether the *Re W* or *Re X* approach was to be preferred in relation to restraint orders made under the old legislation, merely noting that the treatment of third party creditors had:

> produced a number of judicial decisions, not all of which were reconcilable with each other.

It is submitted that the Court's approach in the *Lexi Holdings* case should be welcomed, **5.39** bringing back, as it does, some much needed certainty into the law relating to the release of assets to pay unsecured third party creditors of a defendant. Prosecutors can now take a consistent approach to all applications to vary POCA restraint orders for such purposes, and defendants, victims, and creditors alike know where they stand in relation to such matters. This consistency of approach will ensure that no unsecured creditor can 'jump the gun' and gain an advantage over others, including a victim, by reducing the amount of assets available to meet compensation and confiscation orders.

5.40 This approach will also overcome the risk of abuse by associates of a defendant making bogus third party claims at his behest with a view to reducing the fund available for confiscation. Although defendants are of course entitled to a presumption of innocence at the pre-conviction stage, one must remain mindful of the fact that, as Lord Donaldson MR observed in *Re O* [1991] 1 All ER 330:

> Whatever may be the position in an individual case, the legislative contemplation is that restraint orders will be made in circumstances in which it is thought that some of those having interests in the property may well be of a dishonest disposition.

5.41 Of course, not all payments to third parties will fall foul of s 69(2)(c). There is, for example, no difficulty with a management receiver paying off trade debts with a view to retaining and preserving the value of the business of a company, since the payment of such a debt would preserve an asset greater in value. Similarly, there can be no objection to allowing rent or mortgage payments to be made either on the basis that it constitutes a living expense or because it preserves and maintains the defendant's interest in property. In both cases the value of the realisable property is not diminished or reduced in value overall because the payment allows a company to continue trading, making profits, and prevents the mortgagee foreclosing.

5.42 Section 69 also represents a tightening up of the legislation in other respects, in particular in relation to the sale of assets that are likely to depreciate in value. Section 69(2)(b) would appear to overrule the decision of the Court of Appeal in *Re P (Restraint Order: Sale of Assets* [2000] 1 WLR 473. In that case, the restraint and management receivership orders were made against the defendant under the DTA. The assets caught by the order included three racehorses, one of which had race-winning potential. The receiver wished to sell the horses considering them to be depreciating assets. This course of action was strongly opposed by the defendant who made application to the High Court for an order directing the receiver not to sell the horses unless it proved necessary to satisfy any confiscation order made in the event of conviction. The application was dismissed by Scott Baker J at first instance, but the defendant succeeded on appeal to the Court of Appeal. The Court found that purpose of the Acts was to 'impoverish defendants, not to enrich the Crown' and ruled that the horses should not be sold. The provision in s 69(2)(b) to the effect that the powers must be exercised, in circumstances where no confiscation order has yet been made, with a view to securing that there is no diminution in the value of realisable property must, it is submitted, mean that *Re P* is no longer good law in relation to restraint and management receivership orders made under POCA.

5.43 POCA protects the position of unconvicted defendants in possession of property that 'cannot be replaced' in that it gives the court a power to order that it must not be sold in cases where a confiscation order has not yet been made. The reason for this new provision is set out in the Guidance Notes to the Act in these terms:

> The provision has regard to the fact that the defendant has not been convicted at this stage and should not, therefore, be obliged to lose irreplaceable assets.

It should be noted that the court is not compelled to order that irreplaceable assets should **5.44** not be sold: s 69(4) provides that the court 'may' order that the asset is not to be sold, not that it must do so. Unless there are very compelling reasons to the contrary, such as a deliberate intention on the part of the defendant to dispose of property or it is depreciating significantly in value, it is submitted that the proper course would be to order that irreplaceable assets should not be sold prior to the defendant's conviction. It is likely therefore that the racehorses in *Re P* described by the defendant as 'well loved family pets', would not have been sold even if POCA had been in force at the time the decision was made.

Another consequence of the legislative steer is that the court will not give effect to a pro- **5.45** posed variation which allows a defendant to pursue a luxurious lifestyle or live beyond his legitimate means: see *Re D and D* (Unreported, 28 October 1992). In that case Hutchison J. commented:

> As I suggested, perhaps a court which is making a variation will think that he may have to content himself in the exigencies in which he finds himself with something less than a Rolls Royce lifestyle until his guilt or innocence is established.

The defendant may well find that he has to tighten his belt and economise on his normal expenditure while the restraint order remains in force.

Further, and quite independently of the legislative steer, the Court of Appeal held in *Serious* **5.46** *Fraud Office v X* [2005] EWCA 1564 that the authorities in relation to the variation of freezing orders (formerly Mareva injunctions) are also relevant to applications to vary restraint orders. The Court drew particular attention to the judgment of Robert Goff J in *A v C (No 2)* [1981] QB 962 at p 963:

> In the present case, I have had to consider the position where the defendant has, or may have, other assets from which the relevant payment may be made. I have still to apply the basic principle, i.e. that I can only permit a qualification to the injunction if the defendant satisfies the court that the money is required for a purpose which does not conflict with the policy underlining the Mareva jurisdiction. I do not consider that in normal circumstances a defendant can discharge that burden of proof simply by saying 'I owe someone some money'. I put to the defendants' counsel, in the course of argument, the example of an English based defendant with two bank accounts, one containing a very substantial sum which was not subject to the Mareva injunction, and the other containing a smaller sum which was. I asked counsel whether it would be sufficient for the defendant simply to say, 'I owe somebody some money, please qualify the injunction to permit payment from the smaller account without giving any consideration to the possibility of payment from the larger account.' Counsel was constrained to accept that that would not be sufficient because it would not satisfy the court that the payment out of the smaller account would not conflict with the principle underlying the Mareva jurisdiction. The whole purpose of selecting the smaller account might be to prevent the money in that account from being available to satisfy a judgment in the pending proceedings. In my judgment, a defendant has to go further than that; precisely what he has to prove will depend, no doubt, upon the circumstances of the particular case. At all events, in the present case, if the defendants making the application have other assets freely available—and I do not know, on the evidence, whether they have or not—it would be open to counsel for the plaintiffs to submit, on the evidence, that it would be wrong for the court to vary the Mareva injunction. All I can say at present is that, on the evidence before the court, the defendants have not discharged the burden of proof which rests upon them.

5.47   The Court in *Serious Fraud Office v X* also held that two judgments of Sir John Donaldson MR in relation to Mareva injunctions were relevant to applications to vary restraint orders. In *Campbell Mussells v Thompson* The Times, 30 May 1984 Sir John said:

> ... if there is reason to believe that people are asking for money for solicitors costs ... simply as a means of avoiding bring free money into this country, or as a means of not having to use other monies which have not been discovered and which they wish to keep out of the clutches of the court, of course they will be refused.

5.48   In a similar vein, in *Southern Cross Commodities Proprietary Ltd v Martin* (Unreported, Court of Appeal, 11 February 1986) Sir John said:

> It is quite clear that the court will not allow expenditure to be channelled into funds which are subject to a Mareva injunction where there are other free funds proved to be available to meet the expenditure. It is also clear that the courts should exercise a healthy scepticism over claims that the only monies available are in the funds which are subject to a Mareva injunction.

5.49   A defendant seeking to have restrained funds released, for whatever purpose, must therefore produce credible evidence that he has no unrestrained assets, either within the jurisdiction or overseas, which might be used for this purpose.

E. The Source for Payment of Legal Fees and General Living Expenses

5.50   The order will require the defendant to nominate a source for the payment of any sums released by way of legal fees and general living expenses. As a general rule, he has an unfettered right to nominate any restrained source he chooses for this purpose. He must, however, bear in mind that if he fails to disclose the nominated asset in his disclosure statement or claims it does not belong to him, the court and prosecutor may have some difficulty in acceding to its release for such purposes.

Assets not legitimately acquired

5.51   It would seem that a defendant is entitled to use assets the Crown alleges have not been legitimately acquired as the source for payment of any sums released to him. In *Re D and D* (Unreported, 28 June 1992) large sums of money were found in the homes of the defendants when they were arrested. They were later charged with alleged drug trafficking offences and restraint orders were obtained that specifically identified the seized money as one of the restrained assets. The order further provided that the money was to be paid into an interest bearing account if it was not required as an exhibit in the criminal proceedings. The prosecutor decided the money was not so required and duly paid it into an interest bearing account in accordance with the terms of the order. The defendants then applied for the money to be released to paid their legal fees and general living expenses. The prosecutor objected, contending that the money had not been legitimately acquired and should not therefore be released for these purposes.

5.52   Hutchison J overruled the prosecutor's objections and acceded to the defendant's application for the release of the seized funds. The learned judge ruled that it would breach the presumption of innocence for a finding to be made prior to the defendants' trial that the funds had not been legitimately acquired. In any event, given that both legitimately and illegitimately acquired assets could be used to satisfy any confiscation order, it was inappropriate, the learned judge ruled, to restrict a defendant to using only assets the prosecutor was satisfied were legitimately acquired to pay his legal fees and general living expenses prior to conviction.

Assets that are prosecution exhibits

It happens from time to time that restrained assets (particularly cash taken up at the time **5.53** of a defendant's arrest) become an exhibit in the criminal proceedings. In *Re C* (Unreported, 1993) the court considered the extent to which exhibited assets could be released to fund general living expenses. The defendant was found in possession of substantial sums of money when he was arrested and which were duly included in a DTA restraint order. In due course the money became an exhibit in the criminal case and, at committal proceedings, the prosecutor gave an undertaking to the examining magistrates to produce the money along with all the other exhibits at trial. Laws J ruled that the court did have a discretion to order the release of the money notwithstanding that it was an exhibit in the criminal case and notwithstanding the prosecutor's undertaking. The judge said:

> In my judgment, the court is not deprived of the jurisdiction to release money for living expenses simply on the Crown's assertion that it intends to put the relevant cash before the jury. Nor do I accept that where money in cash form, or for that matter any other property, has been accorded the formal status of an exhibit, this court lacks all power to release it in whole or in part to permit living expenses within the general context of a restraint order. Any undertaking by the Crown given to the magistrates' court to produce exhibits at trial will surely be released pro tanto by the High Court's superior order. The question, therefore, is one of discretion.

The judge then went on to consider the manner in which the court should exercise its **5.54** discretion. The crucial test seems to me whether it is essential that the original exhibit must be produced to the criminal court if the prosecutor is to do justice to his case. Laws J said:

> The court will certainly give great weight to what after proper consideration are said to be the evidential needs of the prosecution. There will be situations in which that weight is obviously conclusive. Not only that: in my judgment there can be no question of making allowances for living or other expenses within a restraint order if to do so would curtail or circumscribe the Crown's function of properly presenting, by evidence, the case to the jury.

The judge found in the instant case that there was no reason why the prosecution could not **5.55** produce photographs of the money and describe in the fullest detail the circumstances in which it was found and still do justice to its case. He therefore ordered the release of some of the money to meet the general living expenses of the defendant's family.

F. Release of Funds after a Confiscation Order has been Made

The right of defendants and affected third parties to draw on restrained funds for whatever **5.56** purpose does not continue indefinitely. It is submitted that this right comes to an end on the making of a confiscation order or, if there is an appeal against conviction and/or the confiscation order, when all domestic avenues of appeal have been exhausted. Many of the authorities make reference to the defendant being entitled to have funds released to fund general living expenses because, at the time the restraint order is made, he has not been convicted of any offence and is therefore entitled to a presumption of innocence. In *Re Peters* [1988] 3 WLR 182, by way of example, Lord Donaldson MR justified the release of funds to meet general living expenses on the basis that Mr Peters was an unconvicted accused person who might be acquitted and therefore entitled to ask that his son's education should not be interrupted and that he himself should be adequately clothed. Clearly, this consideration does not apply after the defendant has been convicted and all domestic avenues of appeal have been exhausted.

5.57 In *Re P* [1998] EWHC Admin 1049 the defendant had been convicted of drug trafficking offences and a confiscation order made. An appeal to the Court of Appeal (Criminal Division) had been dismissed but the defendant sought the release of funds for various purposes in connection with pursuing the matter with the European Court of Human Rights and the Criminal Cases Review Commission, including studying for a law degree to assist him in conducting his legal affairs. Laws J rejected the application saying:

> I am afraid that it is clear beyond any doubt that none of these matters could justify a variation of the restraint order. The fact is that, so far as the domestic criminal litigation is concerned in this case, Mr. P is well past the end of the road.

5.58 In *Re C* [2008] EWHC 3377 (Admin) Sullivan J, sitting in the High Court, took the view that the fact of the defendant's conviction entitled the court to draw in the purse strings somewhat so far as the release of funds to meet general living expenses is concerned. The defendant had been convicted of conspiracy to defraud, the amount involved being in the region of £1.8 million. She was subject to a CJA restraint order which had been varied to allow the release of £420 per week by way of general living expenses and £750 per month to pay rent. Further one-off payments had been authorised in relation to a Spanish property she owned. The defendant made a further application for the restraint order to be varied to allow the release of a lump sum payment of £1,000 to buy Christmas presents for her children before the likely imposition of a custodial sentence on 12 December. Sullivan J refused the application saying:

> Whilst I of course have sympathy with the position in which the applicant finds herself, it has to be said it is one of her own making, and if she does not have funds, one is not in the position to buy presents for other people. That sadly will be the position of many people this Christmas. The applicant has funds only as a result of the fraud, so in effect she would be buying Christmas presents for her children out of money which is not by rights hers to give away as presents.

> The other factor is this: I have indicated the amount of her weekly allowance and her monthly rental allowance. By my calculation that amounts to a net payment equivalent to more than £30,000 a year. It does seem to me that since that comfortably exceeds the gross national average wage and those on average wages are able by careful saving to give presents to their children, there is no good reason why this particular applicant should not be in a similar position. The presents might not be as generous as she might wish, but there certainly is no reason why someone who is on 'net earnings' in excess of £30,000 a year should not be able to buy presents out of those monies.

In *Stodgell v Stodgell* [2009] EWCA Civ 243 the Court of Appeal refused permission to **5.59** appeal to a wife against a decision from of Holman J to the effect that all payments by way of general living expenses from the restrained fund should come to an end. The defendant husband had been convicted of tax fraud offences and a CJA confiscation order was made against him for £903,453. The order remained unpaid in its entirety whilst substantial payments were being made from the restrained fund to pay general living expenses for the wife together with legal fees incurred in ancillary relief payments. Holman J noted that everyone except the Crown, who were the victims of the offence, appeared to be drawing on the restrained fund and ruled the payments had to stop. He said:

> I have already expressed my great sympathy for the wife and indeed for (the child), but I echo also a comment from Lord Justice Mann in *Re Peters* [1988] 1 QB 871 at 881 that
>
>> 'There is, in light of section 13(2) [viz the identical legislative steer in an earlier Act] no room for the intrusion of sympathy.'
>
> Unless and until the confiscation order has been satisfied in full, both the wife and (the child) will have to live at the standard and by the means provided by the state out of welfare and other benefits and entitlements.

He added:

> The result has been that the funds needed to satisfy the confiscation order have been even further reduced by a combination of maintenance payments for the wife and, separately, (the children), and by the provision of her and her husband's legal costs. In my view this has simply got to stop. All members of this family have got to face and bear the reality of what has happened and of the criminal confiscation order and that the available funds cannot continue simply to be drawn as if from a piggy-bank.

The Court of Appeal refused the wife permission to appeal against the judge's decision. **5.60** Hughes LJ (with whom Lloyd and Thorpe LJJ agreed) said:

> . . . I am for my part entirely sure that the judge was right. Indeed, as it seems to me he would have been wrong to make any other order. He was right for the reasons which he gave and which I have only imperfectly summarised. They also included the very rapid haemorrhaging of the pot by the incurring of very substantial costs.

The judge also noted that s 69 of POCA represented a 'significant tightening of the rules' in cases to which it applies.

Cranston J followed the ruling of Holman J at first instance in *Stodgell* in *In the Matter of* **5.61** *L* [2008] EWHC 3327 (Admin). In that case the defendant had been convicted of fraudulent trading offences. Calvert-Smith J made an order allowing the release of restrained funds to meet legal fees incurred in connection with the confiscation proceedings and to commission a report from BDO Stoy Hayward, a firm of chartered accountants. In the confiscation proceedings, the defendant was found to have benefited from those offences to the extent of £99 million and a confiscation order was made under the CJA 1988 for £16.25 million. The defendant continued to expend restrained funds on legal expenses: it being estimated that the total legal fees incurred amounted to some £1.5 million of which some £380,000 was said to have been incurred since the defendant's conviction. The prosecutor and management receiver jointly applied to the High Court for an order that these payments should stop.

5.62 Cranston J agreed and allowed the receiver's application. He said:

> In my judgment it is time to draw a line. The circumstances are different from those which faced Calvert-Smith J. in December 2006. At that point there was no confiscation order. It followed about nine months later. There was no receiver. The extent to which the defendant had benefited had not been determined. That required the detailed work of BDO Stoy Hayward. So the circumstances were quite different.

5.63 It is submitted that it is clear from these authorities that the right to draw on the restrained fund, for whatever purpose, comes to an end once domestic avenues of appeal against a confiscation order and the underlying conviction have been exhausted. This is particularly so where, as in *Stodgell v Stodgell*, the lifestyle enjoyed by the defendant and his family has been funded by offences of dishonesty and no recompense has been made to the victim of those offences.

5.64 In consequence, restraint orders made for the first time after all domestic appeals against a confiscation order have been exhausted need not contain a provision for the payment of general living expenses. Further, all parties who are dependent on restrained funds to meet general living expenses would be well advised to make contingency plans as to how such expenses will be met in the event of the defendant being convicted. If they do not, they may well find that in this eventuality restrained funds are no longer available to meet these expenses or, at the very least, the court significantly reduces the amount payable.

5.65 The legislative steer also precludes the release of funds to an affected third party to resist an application for the appointment of an enforcement receiver to realise assets in satisfaction of the confiscation order. In *Re D* [2006] EWHC Admin 1519 a confiscation order had been made against the defendant which took into account his interest in a number of properties. On the Crown's application to appoint a receiver to realise the properties in satisfaction of the confiscation order, a number of third parties intervened claiming ownership of them. They applied for an order for the properties to be sold and for some of the proceeds to be used to meet their legal and other expenses in making their claim. The application was rejected by Collins J who said:

> The court is enjoined to ensure so far as possible (a) that the property is retained and its full value is available in order to meet the confiscation and (b) that anyone who has an interest in that property is able to have the opportunity to establish the existence of that interest. Counsel, as I understand the argument, submits that that extends in an appropriate case to ensuring that the third party has legal representation and the only way in which that can be achieved in certain circumstances is to provide him with monies available from the proceeds of the property the subject of the restraint order and in which he is asserting an interest. That seems to me, as I indicated, to be a quite hopeless submission.
>
> The powers must be exercised to ensure that the third parties have a proper opportunity of pursuing their claim. That they will do in the way that any litigation is to be pursued. If they have the means, then they will have to pay for it: if they do not have sufficient means, then they may apply for public funding. But what they cannot do is to obtain funding from the property which they are asserting they have an interest in when that interest is being disputed.

5.66 Once the position is reached where the prosecutor is applying for the appointment of an enforcement receiver, the defendant not only stands convicted but all appeals against the order and the underlying conviction will have been dismissed. At this stage, it would seem entirely consistent with the legislative steer and the policy underlying the legislation for affected third parties to rely on public funding or, if they are available, unrestrained assets for the purpose of securing advice and representation in relation to the receivership application or any associated litigation. Similarly, where this point has been reached, neither the defendant nor any affected third party is entitled to continue drawing on the restrained fund for the payment of general living expenses.

6

ENFORCEMENT OF RESTRAINT AND RECEIVERSHIP ORDERS: CONTEMPT OF COURT

A. Introduction

Restraint and receivership orders can only serve their intended purpose to the extent that **6.01** there are effective sanctions available to the court to deal with any breach of the order committed by a defendant or third party affected by it. In this chapter we examine the powers of the court to deal with breaches of restraint and receivership orders, the procedures that must be followed to bring a person before the court in relation to any such breach, and to offer guidance to practitioners who are instructed to act on behalf of those against whom such proceedings are brought.

Ways in which breaches may be committed

Breaches of restraint and receivership orders may be committed in a variety of ways. The **6.02** most common types of breach brought before the court are:

(a) a defendant or affected third party dealing or attempting to deal with restrained assets;
(b) a defendant failing to comply with the terms of a disclosure order either by not disclosing at all or by failing to disclose his interest in a particular asset;

(c) a defendant failing to comply with the terms of a repatriation order;

(d) a defendant or affected third party failing to comply with the terms of a receivership order, for example by refusing to deliver up assets to the receiver or refusing to sign a power of attorney in favour of the receiver; and

(e) obstructing the receiver in the performance of his duties, for example by assaulting, threatening, or abusing him, producing forged documentation intending the receiver to act on it as being genuine, or making untruthful statements to the receiver as to the extent of his realisable property.

Sanctions available for breaches of restraint and receivership orders

6.03 POCA and indeed the old legislation do not give the prosecutor or receiver any specific remedy in relation to breaches of restraint and receivership orders. Any breach of the order is to be dealt with as a contempt of court in the same way as a breach of another form of court order. As with other instances of disobedience to an order of the court, the ultimate sanction available to the court is an order committing the contemnor to prison or, if the contemnor is a body corporate, an order sequestrating the company's assets.

In which court are contempt proceedings to be brought?

6.04 When POCA transferred the power to make restraint and receivership orders from the High Court to the Crown Court no provisions were made, either in the Act itself or in rules of court, as to how breaches of such orders should be dealt with. This led to some uncertainty as to the correct venue for contempt proceedings and, in particular, to doubts as to whether the Crown Court had any jurisdiction at all to entertain applications by a prosecutor or receiver for the committal of a defendant alleged to be in breach of such orders. These doubts were laid to rest by the Court of Appeal in *R v M* [2008] EWCA Crim 1901. A restraint order had been made against M under POCA and the prosecutor alleged that thereafter he had made a number of transactions in breach of the order. The prosecutor contended that these breaches amounted to a contempt of court and applied to the Crown Court for an order for committal. The Crown Court held that it had jurisdiction to entertain the prosecutor's application and M appeal against that that ruling to the Court of Appeal.

6.05 The Court of Appeal held that s 45(4) of the Supreme Court Act 1981 clearly gave the Crown Court jurisdiction to determine contempt proceedings brought in relation to breaches of POCA restraint and receivership order. The section provides:

> The Crown Court shall in relation to . . . Any contempt of court, the enforcement of its order and all other matters incidental to its jurisdiction have the like powers, rights, privileges and authority as the High Court.

6.06 The defendant contended that the word 'contempt' in s 45(4) could only be construed as meaning criminal contempt because, when the Supreme Court Act was enacted, there were no restraint orders nor any other order which could be made by the Crown Court which carried the contempt sanction in the event of a breach. The Court rejected this argument, Bean J saying:

> We do not accept that the meaning of the statute is that only such types of contempt as might have arisen in the Crown Court in 1981 are covered, nor that only such orders as the Crown Court would have been enforcing as the law stood in 1981 are covered.

The defendant also sought to rely on *DPP v Channel 4 Television Company Limited* [1993] **6.07**
2 All ER 517. In that case a Crown Court judge had made production orders against
Channel 4 under terrorism legislation. Channel 4 refused to comply, relying on the journal-
ist's duty of protecting the confidentiality of his source. The DPP brought proceedings for
contempt in the Divisional Court. In the course of his judgment Woolf LJ said that in 'this
type of case' the contempt proceedings should invariably be heard by a Divisional Court.
The Court of Appeal held that the reference to 'this type of case' by Woolf LJ meant an application against the media which raised substantial issues of principle. He was not, the Court
held, referring to all contempt applications, nor even all civil contempt applications emanating from the work of the Crown Court. In a clear statement of principle, Bean J said:

> We can see no reason why the contempt proceedings should not be tried by a single judge in
> the court whose restraint order the defendant has said to have breached, just as would occur
> in the case of a freezing injunction.

It is submitted that this statement of principle must be correct as the clear intention of **6.08**
Parliament in enacting POCA was to make the Crown Court a 'one stop shop' dealing with
all matters relating to restraint, receivership, and confiscation orders and their enforcement. This dispensed with the rather cumbersome procedure under the old legislation
whereby cases passed to and fro between the High Court and the Crown Court, with the
former responsible for making restraint, management, and enforcement receivership orders
and determining applications for certificates of inadequacy, and the latter being responsible
for making the confiscation order and reducing the same when a certificate of inadequacy
has been granted. The Criminal Procedure Rules have now been amended to incorporate
Crown Court contempt hearings. The new rules are set out at para 6.49.

B. Procedure on High Court Applications

Contempt of the High Court

The parties follow the provisions of the Civil Procedure Rules in relation to contempt pro- **6.09**
ceedings in the High Court. The rules in relation to High Court proceedings are to be
found in sc52 and in the Practice Direction accompanying the rules which is cited in the
White Book as scpd52.

The High Court's power to punish breaches of its orders by committal and sequestration of **6.10**
assets is set out in sc45 r 4 which provides as follows:

(1) Where–
  (a) a person required by a judgment or order to do an act within a time specified in the judgment
      or order refuses or neglects to do it within that time or, as the case may be, within that time as
      extended or abridged under a court order or CPR 2.11; or
  (b) a person disobeys a judgment or order requiring him to abstain from doing an act,
  then, subject to the provisions of these rules, the judgment or order may be enforced by one or more
  of the following means, that is to say—
   (i) with the permission of the court, a writ of sequestration against the property of that person;
   (ii) where that person is body corporate, with the permission of the court, a writ of sequestration
        against the property of any director or other officer of the body;
   (iii) subject to the provisions of the Debtors Act 1869 and 1878, an order of committal against that
         person, or where the person is a body corporate, against any such officer.

This provision applies with equal force in the Crown Court by virtue of s 45(4) of the Supreme Court Act 1981 considered above. The Crown Court procedure and related rules are considered at para 6.49 below

Strict compliance required

6.11 At the outset, it must be emphasised that the court has held on many occasions that, as the liberty of the subject is at stake, strict compliance with all the required procedures is essential: see, for example, *Gagnon v McDonald* The Times, 14 November 1984. Any failure by the prosecutor to comply with these procedures may result in the application being dismissed, although a court may waive any procedural defect in the commencement or conduct of a committal application if it is satisfied the defendant has suffered no injustice as a result: see scpd52.10.

The burden and standard of proof

6.12 The burden is on the person bringing the contempt proceedings (in this context, the prosecutor or receiver) to prove his case. The respondent to the application cannot be compelled to adduce evidence in his defence, although in most cases he would be well advised to file an affidavit responding to the allegations of contempt made against him. The standard of proof required is proof beyond reasonable doubt. This is an exception to the usual rule that the standard of proof in civil proceedings is proof on a balance of probabilities and is justified on the basis that in contempt proceedings the liberty of the subject is at stake.

6.13 In *R (on the application of Minshall) v City of Westminster Magistrates' Court & HM Revenue and Customs* [2007] EWHC 214 (Admin) the High Court had to consider whether a defendant would be guilty of contempt of court if he genuinely believed the restraint order had been discharged. In the event, the court did not need to make a definitive ruling because it rejected the evidence of the defendant in this regard but, in a helpful review of the cases, Langstaff J said:

> As to this, I was invited to give consideration to the case of *Intelli v Squatriti and Others* [1993] 1 QB 83, a decision of the Court of Appeal. In that case Farquharson LJ said:
>
> > 'The question for us is whether the evidence now available establishes beyond a reasonable doubt that they did intend to act in contempt of the court's authority.'
>
> He referred to finding it impossible on the evidence to say that he was convinced that the appellants had the necessary intention. Taylor LJ applied the same test, that the judge could not have been sure that the appellant had knowingly breached the court order. The Vice-Chancellor, Sir Donald Nicols, said in the last sentence of the report, 'that the conclusion had to be that a knowing breach of the order by the appellants had not been proved'. All three members of the court, therefore, approached the question whether contempt was made out by asking whether or not the respondent, the appellants in that case, had known that what they did was in breach of the order.
>
> However, shortly after that decision, the House of Lords had cause to consider the question of knowledge in the case of *Director General of Fair Trading v Pioneer Concrete (UK) Ltd and Another* [1995] 1 AC 456. There, following extensive citation of authority, their Lordships adopted the earlier view, which had been expressed by Warrington J in the case of *Stancomb*

v Trowbridge Urban District Council [1910] 2 Ch 190 at 194. Lord Nolan said that in his judgment the decision in the *Stancomb* case was good law.

It is plain that their Lordships considered that it was not necessary for an alleged contemnor to know that what he did was in breach of the relevant order. The decision in *Irtelli* was one in which it appears from the note of argument that no argument was addressed to the requisite mental intention of the respondent. No case was cited which related to it. Although *Irtelli* was itself not cited to their Lordships in *Pioneer Concrete*, other relevant authority was. It is plain that what was in issue in *Pioneer* was the mental element. I have no hesitation in concluding that I am bound by the view expressed in the House of Lords, which I consider to be ratio.

I am fortified in this conclusion by considering the cases of *Bird and Hadkinson* 4 March 1999 a decision of Neuberger J, as he then was, and *Adam Phones Limited v Goldsmidt and Others* [1999] 4 All ER 486, a decision of Jacob J, as he then was, in each of which the court followed the *Pioneer Concrete* approach and not that indicated by *Irtelli*.

Langstaff J then addressed directly the issue of whether a defendant who believed the **6.14** restraint order had been discharged would be in breach. He said:

It seems to me that this is an interesting question of law which, as will be plain from my conclusions of fact, I do not need to decide in the present case. I do not, therefore, do so. However, should it be relevant I consider that in any case in which a defendant knows of the existence of an order, but subsequently forms a view that it may very well have been discharged, without making any adequate inquiry (as it were, a wilful shutting of eyes) he will be bound by the order. This seems to me to represent the policy and principle underlying the cases of *Pioneer Concrete* and those others, to which I have referred.

I leave for further consideration the question whether if he knew of the existence of the order, but then believed genuinely that the order had been discharged, he should be treated as guilty of contempt rather than the matter simply going to a question of penalty. There is much force in the observations which Jacob J made in saying that had it been a matter open to him in that particular case, that of *Adam v Goldsmidt*, he might have inclined to finding that there had been no contempt.

It is submitted that this approach is correct. If the defendant genuinely believes on reason- **6.15** able grounds (for example, because his solicitor told him so) that the restraint order had been discharged, it would be wrong to find him guilty of contempt. If, however, he fails to make due enquiry, or wilfully shuts his eyes to the question of whether the order has been discharged or not, he can properly be found guilty of contempt and his belief as to the position of the restraint order would only amount to mitigation.

Commencing proceedings

In the High Court, proceedings for contempt of court are normally commenced by the **6.16** issue of a claim form but, as will inevitably be the case in restraint and receivership cases, where the application is brought in existing proceedings, they may be commenced by the issue of an application notice: see scpd52.2. A practice has developed in some Crown Courts of commencing proceedings by way of a letter to the proper officer of the court requesting that the defendant be required to attend court to answer the allegations of contempt made against him. The revised Crown Court procedure is set out at para 6.49 below.

Contents of the application notice

6.17   The High Court application notice must state that the application is made in the proceedings in question and set out its title and reference number which must correspond with the title and reference number of those proceedings. In accordance with scpd52.2.6(4) the application notice must:

> set out in full the grounds on which the committal application is made and must identify, separately and numerically, each alleged act of contempt, including, if known, the date of each of the alleged acts.

6.18   Once the application notice has been issued, it may only be amended with the court's permission: see scpd52.2.6(3). The test as to whether an application notice provides sufficient detail as to the alleged acts of contempt complained of is set out in the judgment of Nicholls LJ in *Harmsworth v Harmsworth* [1988] 1 FLR 349:

> The test is, does the notice give the person alleged to be in contempt enough information to enable him to meet the charge? In satisfying this test it is clear that in a suitable case if lengthy particulars are needed, they may be included in a schedule or other addendum either at the foot of the notice so as to form part of the notice rather than being set out in the body of the notice itself. The rules require that the notice itself must contain certain information. The information is required to be available to the respondent to the application from within the four corners of the notice itself. From the notice itself the person alleged to be in contempt should know with sufficient particularity what are the breaches alleged.

6.19   The application notice or letter must also contain a prominent notice setting out the possible consequences of the court making a committal order and the respondent not attending the hearing: see scpd52.2.6(5). The annex to the Practice Direction incorporates a form of notice that might be used to comply with scpd52.2.6(5) that reads as follows:

IMPORTANT NOTICE

The court has power to send you to prison and fine you if it finds that any of the allegations against you are true and amount to a contempt of court.

You must attend court on the date shown on the front of this form. It is in your own interests to do so. You should bring with you any witnesses and documents you think will you put your side of the case.

If you consider the allegations are not true you must tell the court why. If it is established that they are true, you must tell the court of any good reason why they do not amount to a contempt of court, or if they do, why you should not be punished.

If you need advice you should show this document at once to your solicitor or go to a Citizens Advice Bureau.

It is submitted that this form of words should be used in every case so the defendant is left under no illusions as to the gravity of the proceedings and what he should do in response to them.

The evidence in support of the application

6.20   The High Court application notice must be accompanied by an affidavit setting out the evidence relied on in support of each and every allegation of contempt made against the defendant: see sc52.4 (1). The affidavit should exhibit all documentation on which the applicant wishes to rely. This is the only instance in restraint and confiscation proceedings where a witness statement verified by a statement of truth will not suffice: the evidence must be in affidavit form.

Proving service of the order

The first issue the affidavit must address is the service of the restraint or receivership order **6.21** on the person who is alleged to be in breach of it. In all but the most exceptional circumstances, the prosecutor must be in a position to prove that the order was personally served on the person who is said to have disobeyed it. It is obviously only right and proper that a person should not face the loss of his liberty for disobeying an order unless it can be proved that he had knowledge of the terms of that order at the time he disobeyed it.

Further, the prosecutor must prove that the order was endorsed with a penal notice in **6.22** accordance with sc45 r 7(4) which provides that:

There must be prominently displayed on the front of the copy of an order served under this rule a warning to the person on whom the copy is served that disobedience to the order would be a contempt of court punishable by imprisonment or (in the case of an order requiring a body corporate to do or abstain from doing an act) punishable by sequestration of the assets of the body corporate and by imprisonment of an individual responsible.

The penal notice appears at the top of the draft restraint and receivership orders at **6.23** Appendices 1 and 2 respectively. In rare circumstances, the court may dispense with proof of personal service of the order. The court is given this discretion under sc45 r 7 (6) which provides that in respect of an order requiring the defendant to abstain from doing any act, the order may be enforced by committal notwithstanding that service has not been effected in the prescribed manner where the party sought to be committed has notice of the order either by:

(a) being present when the order was made; or
(b) being notified of its terms, whether by telephone, telegram, or otherwise.

It should be noted that this provision can only be used where the contemnor is alleged to **6.24** be in breach of the prohibitory terms of a restraint order: ie the provisions restraining him from dealing with assets. Where it is sought to commit the defendant for breach of a requirement in the order to perform a positive act (eg to make a disclosure statement or repatriate assets) only personal service will suffice. The affidavit should provide full details of the circumstances in which the order was served on the alleged contemnor and, it is submitted, should exhibit a copy of the order to enable the court to be satisfied it contains all the required information. Crown Court procedure is considered at para 6.49 below.

Proving the breach

The prosecutor's affidavit should set out clearly and fully the facts relied on to prove each **6.25** breach alleged against the defendant. The affidavit should also exhibit all documentation relied on by the prosecutor to establish the breach. As the liberty of the subject is in issue, the court will require the best evidence possible to establish the breach and, it is submitted, hearsay evidence should be avoided, particularly when direct evidence is readily available.

Serving the application

Once the proper officer of the Court has issued the application and given it a return date it **6.26** must, together with the supporting evidence, be served personally on the alleged contemnor unless the court otherwise directs. If it proves impossible to effect personal service because, for example, the defendant is deliberately evading service, then an application should be made to the court for an order allowing service by an alternative method (for Crown Court see r 57.12 of the Criminal Procedure Rules (CrimPR)). Once service has been effected, the prosecutor should cause an affidavit of service to be sworn to enable the court to proceed in the alleged contemnor's absence should he fail to attend.

The defendant's response

6.27 Any written evidence by the defendant in response to the contempt application must also be given on affidavit: see scpd52.3.1. Even if the defendant has not filed any such evidence, he may still give oral evidence at the hearing if he chooses, but if he does so he will be liable to cross-examination: see scpd52.3.3. Further, he may with the permission of the court, call witnesses to give oral evidence regardless of whether they have sworn an affidavit: see scpd52.3.4. The court does, however, have power to direct the alleged contemnor to swear an affidavit or produce statements from witnesses of fact upon whom he wishes to rely and serve them in sufficient time to enable the prosecutor to consider them and file any necessary evidence in reply. The alleged contemnor retains the right not to have such evidence adduced at the hearing, although the wise course is normally to file evidence setting out his case in detail and, if appropriate to make a full and frank admission of the contempt: see *Re B (A Minor) (Contempt Evidence)* The Times, 11 November 1995. Further, the rule in criminal proceedings precluding the prosecutor from commenting on the defendant's failure to give evidence does not apply in contempt cases and the judge is entitled to make appropriate inferences from the alleged contemnor's failure to offer any explanation to the court as to his conduct.

6.28 For all these reasons, it is submitted that the best course is for a person facing contempt proceedings for an alleged breach of a restraint or receivership order to file affidavit evidence addressing each and every allegation made by the prosecutor in his notice of application and accompanying affidavit. If the breach is admitted, an affidavit should be filed making full and frank admissions and setting out any facts relied on in mitigation. The affidavit should also offer an unequivocal apology and an undertaking not to commit any further breaches. If the breach is capable of remedy, the affidavit should set out the defendant's proposals in this regard. For Crown Court procedure see para 6.49 below.

C. The Hearing

Preliminary matters

6.29 In Crown Court cases, the hearing will take place before a Crown Court judge sitting in open court. Advocates should therefore be robed. In High Court cases, the court is given jurisdiction under sc52.6(1)(d) to hear the application in private if the interests of justice of national security so dictate. It is submitted that the Crown Court has similar jurisdiction to direct the hearing should be in private in such circumstances. A defendant in a high profile case that has attracted a lot of publicity may wish to ask the court to hear the application in private if there is a risk that hearing it in public could prejudice his defence in the criminal proceedings. If the court does decide to hear the application in private and decides to make a committal order it must, under sc52.6, state in public:

(a) the name of the person committed;
(b) in general terms the nature of the contempt of court in respect of which the order of committal is being made; and
(c) the length of the period for which he is being committed.

Crown Court procedure is considered at para 6.49 below.

The court may at any time give case management directions, including directions as to the **6.30** service of written evidence by the alleged contemnor and written evidence in response by the prosecutor and may hold a directions hearing: see scpd52.4.3. By scpd52.4.4., the court may, on the hearing date:

(1) give case management directions with a view to a hearing of the committal application on a future date; or
(2) if the committal application is ready to be heard, proceed forthwith to hear it.

Crown Court procedure is considered at para 6.49 below.

The court must always have regard to the need for the alleged contemnor to have details of **6.31** the alleged acts of contempt and the opportunity to respond to the application: see scpd52.4.5. Further, by scpd52.4.6, the court must also have regard to the need for the respondent to be:

(1) allowed a reasonable time for responding to the committal application including, if necessary, preparing a defence;
(2) made aware of the availability of assistance from the Community Legal Service and how to contact the service;
(3) given the opportunity, if unrepresented, to obtain legal advice; and
(4) if unable to understand English, allowed to make arrangements, seeking the assistance of the court if necessary, for an interpreter to attend the hearing.

In *Togher v Customs and Excise Commissioners* [2001] EWCA Civ 474 the Court of Appeal **6.32** emphasised the importance of those facing contempt proceedings being legally represented whenever imprisonment was contemplated as the appropriate sanction for the breach. Robert Walker LJ said:

> I consider next the criticisms which Mr. Togher makes of the procedure followed at the committal hearing, including the absence of any legal representation for Mr. Togher in a matter in which is personal liberty was at stake. Counsel for the Commissioners has pointed out, correctly, that the restraint order gave Mr. Togher the opportunity of applying for a variation of the restraints on his bank account so as to enable him to pay for legal representation but that he did not make such an application, nor did he ask for an order for cross-examination of the Customs and Excise witnesses on their affidavits.
>
> These observations are no doubt correct but they seem to me rather to miss the point. Legal representation is important for defendants because lawyers understand the need for applications of that sort and defendants who are not lawyers may not do so, even assuming them to be hardened criminals. It is easy for for anyone who is not a lawyer, especially if he is under stress, to overlook the need to interrupt Counsel (which is what Mr. Togher would have had to do) in order to raise this sort of preliminary point. This court has said that in matters of civil contempt, as soon as it appears that there is an appreciable risk of imprisonment, an unrepresented defendant should be asked by the judge whether he or she wishes to be represented: see *Newman v Modern Bookbinders* [2000] 2 All ER 814, 822. It does not appear that Mr. Togher was asked that question at the hearing on 15th November 1995.

6.33   The court may, either of its own motion or on the application of the alleged contemnor, strike out a committal application if it appears to the court:

(1) that the committal application and the evidence served in support of it disclose no reasonable ground for alleging that the respondent is guilty of contempt of court;

(2) that the committal application is an abuse of the court's process or, if made in existing proceedings, is otherwise likely to obstruct the just disposal of those proceedings, or

(3) that there has been a failure to comply with a rule, practice direction or court order.

6.34   If the prosecutor brings a contempt application during the course of the criminal trial or shortly before it is due to commence, the defendant may be able to argue with some force that it would be oppressive to require him to respond to it at that time when all his resources need to be directed towards defending the criminal proceedings. This is particularly so if it can be shown that the prosecutor has been aware of the facts giving rise to the committal application, but has been guilty of an unreasonable delay in bringing the proceedings. In such circumstances, the court would be entitled to strike out the committal application as an abuse of process or adjourn it pending the determination of the criminal proceedings. The court is, however, unlikely to strike out or adjourn a committal application where the alleged breach occurs shortly before or during the criminal trial.

6.35   Once a committal application has been issued, it may only be discontinued with the permission of the court. Thus the prosecutor is not entitled to withdraw a committal application, even if the defendant has remedied the breach complained of by, for example, filing a disclosure statement or repatriating assets. The proper course is for the prosecutor to write to the court, enclosing a letter of agreement from the defendant, seeking permission to discontinue the application. If the court agrees, the application can be discontinued without the necessity for the parties to attend court and the hearing date can be vacated.

Procedure at the hearing

6.36   The court clerk or associate will open proceedings by identifying the defendant, reaching each of the allegations of contempt contained in the application to him and asking whether he admits or denies them. The prosecutor, upon whom the burden of proving the contempt rests, will then open his case, read his affidavits, and call any witnesses required to attend for cross examination. The defendant will then have the opportunity of addressing the court, reading his affidavits and calling evidence. By sc52.6(4), if the person sought to be committed expresses a wish to give oral evidence on his own behalf, he shall be entitled to do so. The parties will then have the right to make closing addresses before the judge considers his decision. If the court concludes that the prosecutor has not proved his case beyond reasonable doubt, the committal application will be dismissed. If, however, the court finds the case has been proved to the criminal standard, it will proceed to consider the appropriate sentence. The 2009 Order in relation to Crown Court procedure is considered at para 6.49 below.

6.37   It is important to appreciate that proceedings for contempt of court are separate and distinct from the criminal proceedings and serve entirely different purposes. In *Re S* [1999] EWHC Admin 466 a restraint order had been obtained against the defendant which included a term requiring him to repatriate funds held in a named bank account in Jamaica.

The defendant failed to comply with this requirement and, in the meantime, a confiscation order was made against him at Nottingham Crown Court in the sum of £47,851.45, 18 months' imprisonment to be served in default of payment. The CPS took proceedings against him alleging that he was guilty of contempt of court by failing to comply with the repatriation requirement. In his defence, the defendant contended that the contempt proceedings exposed him to double jeopardy because he was already liable to serve the default sentence if he did not pay the sums held in the Jamaican bank account in satisfaction of the confiscation order. Ognall J rejected this argument saying:

> It seems to me that that argument, however ingeniously clothed, is doomed to failure. First, on a narrow construction of fact, it fails because there is no material before me which serves to satisfy me that in making the confiscation order in the quantum that he did, the judge paid any account whatever to the assets there might be in the Jamaican bank account. Even if I be wrong in that conclusion, the argument is fatally flawed because of this consideration. The jeopardy in which the Respondent before me stands (in relation to the order made at Nottingham) is a jeopardy which would be triggered by his failure to pay the monies the subject of the confiscation order. The jeopardy in which he stands before the High Court is by reason not of his failure to pay any money. It stems from his wilful failure to bring assets within that Jamaican bank account into this jurisdiction as required by the court. The fact that in the event were he to have done so were he to do so now, any proceeds to be derived from it might go in satisfaction of the confiscation order is neither here nor there. The fact is, the contingency which put him in contempt of this Court is his failure to comply with an order to bring the proceeds of that account within this jurisdiction. It is a quite different contingency from that which triggers the sanction imposed by way of a default term at Nottingham.

The judge ruled that the contempt had to be marked with a separate and consecutive terms of imprisonment and imposed a sentence of six months.

Sentence

If the defendant admits the contempt, or the court finds the case proved, the court must **6.38** then proceed to sentence. The contemnor will of course have the right to address the court in mitigation before sentence is imposed. Any such mitigation should include an unequivocal apology, an undertaking not to commit any further breaches of the order and, if possible, proposals for remedying the contempt. The maximum sentence that may be imposed for contempt of court is two years' imprisonment: see s 14(1) of the Contempt of Court Act 1981. Consecutive sentences may be imposed for separate breaches, so long as the total sentence imposed on any one occasion does not exceed the maximum. Sentences of imprisonment for contempt of court are subject to the early release provisions set out in the Criminal Justice Act 1991. By s 33(1), as substituted by s 47 of the Act, as soon as the contemnor has served one-half of his sentence if he has been committed for less than 12 months, or one-third of the sentence if he has been committed for more than 12 months, he must be released unconditionally.

The court will invariably treat breaches of restraint and receivership orders very seriously, **6.39** especially where the dissipation of assets is involved. Unless the contemnor has taken prompt steps to recover assets so dissipated, the almost inevitable consequence will be an immediate sentence of imprisonment. Indeed, in relation to freezing orders, there is clear authority to the effect that any dissipation of assets should be visited by immediate imprisonment. In *Popishal v Phillips* The Times, 20 January 1988, the Court of Appeal said that it was:

> of the highest importance to the public as well as to the parties that Mareva injunctions issued to prevent the dissipation of assets should be obeyed and not disregarded and certainly not flouted.

The Court held that where property had been sold in breach of such an order, an immediate custodial sentence was appropriate, irrespective of whether it was necessary to ensure compliance with the injunction.

6.40   A similar approach was adopted by Stanley Burnton J in *R v Selby* (Unreported, QBD (Admin) 16 June 2006) where a six month sentence of imprisonment was imposed for dissipating assets in breach of a CJA restraint order. In passing sentence the learned judge said:

> Any order of this court is regarded by the court as a matter of the greatest importance. It is necessary that they be complied with and, if not complied with, that punishment follows, otherwise the orders become pointless; compliance with the law would fall into disrepute. The courts necessarily regard a breach of any court order, particularly an order of the kind involved in this case, as a serious matter.

6.41   Keith J adopted the same approach in *CPS v Ellis* [2009] EWHC 876 (Admin) where the defendant had failed to disclose the existence of bank accounts and used funds in those accounts in breach of the restraint order. He imposed a sentence of nine months' imprisonment, saying to the defendant:

> These were serious contempts of court. You deliberately set out to do what you could to conceal your assets in order to avoid having to comply with the confiscation order and you disposed of at least some of your assets.

He added:

> I have to say that your breaches are too serious for a sentence of imprisonment of immediate effect to be avoided.

6.42   If the contemnor is already serving a sentence of imprisonment at the time of being sentenced for contempt of court, the contempt sentence will be consecutive to the earlier sentence unless the court otherwise directs.

6.43   The contemnor has the right under s 258 of the Criminal Justice Act 2003 to be released from custody after serving one half of the term for which he was committed. The 2009 Crown Court procedure is considered at para 6.49 below.

Suspended committals

6.44   The court has power under sc52.7(1) to direct that the execution of an order for committal be suspended for such period or on such terms or conditions as it may specify. In the context of restraint orders, this provision gives the court jurisdiction to suspend the committal provided the defendant remedies his breach by, for example, serving his disclosure statement or repatriating assets within a specified period of time. The court may also suspend the committal on terms that the defendant henceforth comply with the terms of the order, notwithstanding that the effect of this is to suspend the committal indefinitely: see *Griffin v Griffin* The Times, 28 April 2000. If the committal is suspended and the contemnor thereafter commits another breach of the restraint order, the court can activate the suspended committal and impose another sentence for the new contempt to be served consecutively, provided the overall limit of two years imposed by s 14 of the Contempt of Court Act 1981 is not exceeded: see *Villiers v Villiers* [1994] 2 All ER 149.

Effect of being in contempt

The potential consequences of being in contempt extend well beyond being sentenced to a term of imprisonment. The court has a discretion to refuse to hear a person who is in contempt until such time as the contempt has been purged: see *Hadkinson v Hadkinson* [1952] 2 All ER 567 and *X Ltd v Morgan Grampian* [1990] 2 All ER 1. The discretion may only be exercised on an application made by the contemnor and may not be used to prevent him defending an application brought by the prosecutor in the proceedings. This can be a powerful weapon against a defendant who flagrantly disobeys a restraint or receivership order as it can preclude him seeking a variation while he remains in contempt.

6.45

Purging contempt

A defendant imprisoned for contempt of court has the right under sc52.8(1) to go back to court at any time and seek his discharge on the ground that he has purged his contempt. In order to convince a judge that it is appropriate to release him, the defendant will have to show that he is now suitably contrite and henceforth will comply with the terms of the order. The chances of a defendant being discharged will be enhanced if he is able to advance proposals as to how the harm caused by his breach of the order might be remedied.

6.46

The application for the contemnor's discharge should be made on application notice, supported by an affidavit setting out the grounds relied on. If he is available, the application should be made to the judge who heard the original application. The judge has a wide discretion as to what cause of action to take: he may refuse the application which will mean the original sentence remains unchanged; he may accede to it, in which case the contemnor will be released immediately; or alternatively he may direct the contemnor's release at a future date prior to the end of the original sentence.

6.47

Appeals

The contemnor has the right of appeal to the Court of Appeal (Criminal Division) against the Crown Court's finding of contempt or the sentence it imposes. Permission to appeal against a contempt sentence is not normally required and the court has jurisdiction to grant bail pending the determination of the appeal.

6.48

D. Procedure in Crown Court Applications

Contempt of the Crown Court

The Criminal Procedure (Amendment) Rules 2009 (SI 2009/2087) came into force on 5 October 2009, and for the first time codify the procedure that should be followed in Crown Court contempt cases. The general principles are as those stated under the High Court procedures set out above.

6.49

New Criminal Procedure Rules

6.50 Rule 23 and Sch 6 of the 2009 rules introduce a new Part 62 of the CrimPR to deal with applications for the punishment for contempt of court of those who disobey court orders, or who disclose prosecution material without authority.

6.51 It appears these rules were introduced to provide clarity about the procedure to be followed when dealing with disobedience of a respondent to a restraint order made under POCA. In *R v M* [2008] EWCA Crim 1901, the appellant questioned the jurisdiction of the Crown Court to punish him for alleged disobedience to a restraint order made under POCA. The court commented on the fact that there were at that stage no relevant Criminal Procedure Rules. It found that the Crown Court had the necessary powers, but that in the absence of relevant rules the procedure was unclear. In response to that case, the Criminal Procedure Rules Committee introduced new rules about this type of application to punish for contempt of court, so that applicants, and those accused of failing to obey this type of order or requirement, could find the relevant procedure rules in a single place.

6.52 Rule 62.1 confirms that the rules in Part 62 of the CrimPR apply in the Crown Court and in magistrates' courts. Rule 62.2 states that the court must not exercise its power to punish for contempt of court in the respondent's absence, unless he has had at least 14 days in which to make representations and introduce evidence.

6.53 In terms of procedure, r 62.3 deals with applications to punish for contempt of court. The rules set out what a person who wants the court to exercise its power to punish the respondent must do. The application must be made in writing, identifying the respondent and giving details about the conduct that they consider amounts to contempt of court. The application must include a warning notice to the respondent that the court can impose imprisonment or a fine, or both, for contempt of court; and that the court may deal with the application even if the respondent does not turn up at the hearing. Applications of this type must be handed to the person accused of the contempt. Rule 62.12 sets out the court's power to vary requirements under Part 62. The court can extend or shorten a time limit. If a person wants an extension of time, they must apply when serving the statement, notice or application for which the extension of time is needed and they must explain the delay.

6.54 The accompanying guidance summarises the other main rule changes thus:

- Rule 62.4 deals with Notice of suspension of punishment. Where the person accused of the contempt (the respondent) is absent and the court decides to impose a punishment but suspends it for a period, or conditionally, the applicant must serve a notice of the terms of the court's order on the respondent.

- Rule 62.5 sets out the procedure to be followed when the respondent wants to apply to discharge the order for imprisonment for contempt of court. A written application must be made, explaining why it would be appropriate for the order to be discharged. The respondent must serve the application on the court and on the applicant who applied to the respondent's punishment. If the respondent wants one, they can ask for a hearing.

- Rule 62.6 deals with the introduction of a written witness statement or other hearsay. It sets out the procedure to be followed when a party wants to introduce the written statement, or notice of other hearsay, in evidence. A note to the rule explains hearsay evidence.

- Rule 62.7 requires any written statement served in accordance with r 62.6 to contain a declaration that it is true to the best of that person's knowledge and belief.

- Rule 62.8 provides a power for the Crown Court to punish anyone who makes a statement in such a witness statement without an honest belief in its truth. The court can do that either of its own accord or when a party makes an application.

- Rule 62.9 confirms that a notice of hearsay served under r 62.6 must set out the evidence or attach the document that contains it; and identify the person who made the hearsay statement.

Rule 62.10 deals with the cross-examination of someone who has made a written witness **6.55** statement or other hearsay. The party wanting the court's permission to cross-examine that person must make a written application, giving reasons. They must serve a copy of the application on the court and on the person who served the hearsay. A person accused of disobeying an order, 'the respondent', must apply within seven days of service of the hearsay to cross-examine the person. When an applicant wants to cross-examine a person, they must apply to do so not more than three days after service of the hearsay by the respondent. The court may decide an application of this type without a hearing, but must not dismiss an application unless the person making it has had an opportunity to make representations at a hearing.

Finally, r 62.11 describes the procedure to be followed when someone wants to challenge **6.56** the credibility or consistency of the maker of a written witness statement, or other hearsay statement, which has been served under r 62.6. Rule 62.11 introduces the following procedure to be followed:

- Rule 62.11(2) states that they must serve a written notice of their intention to challenge the credibility or consistency of that person, on the court officer and on the person who served the hearsay. In that notice, they must identify any statement or other material on which the party that they want to challenge relies.

- Rule 62.11(3) provides that a person accused of disobeying an order, 'the respondent', must serve their notice of intention to challenge the credibility or consistency of the person within seven days of service of the hearsay.

- Rule 62.11(4) provides that when an applicant wants to challenge the credibility or consistency of a person, they must serve their written notice of intention to do so not more than three days after service of the hearsay by the respondent.

- Rule 62.11(5) provides that a party who served the hearsay may call the person to give oral evidence instead. They must serve a notice of intention to do so on the court officer and the other party, as soon as possible after service of the notice of challenge served under r 62.11(2).

7

PRACTICE AND PROCEDURE IN CROWN COURT RESTRAINT AND MANAGEMENT RECEIVERSHIP CASES UNDER POCA

A. Introduction

One of the most striking features of confiscation legislation is the extent to which it makes **7.01** use of remedies normally employed in the civil courts for the purpose of protecting assets against dissipation and realising assets in satisfaction of a confiscation order after conviction. The use of restraint and receivership orders in proceeds of crime cases can create a dilemma for experienced criminal practitioners who rarely have cause to venture into the civil courts where these remedies are more commonly employed. Court procedures and terminology are different and the practitioner who gets it wrong runs the risk of doing irreparable damage to his client's case and suffering adverse consequences in costs. In this chapter, we examine the rules and procedures in so far as they affect restraint and management receivership applications in the Crown Court to assist the practitioner in pursuing the right course from the outset so as to protect the client's interests and avoid incurring judicial displeasure and adverse costs orders.

B. The Overriding Objective

7.02   It is important to note at the outset that the overriding objective in r 1 of the Criminal Procedure Rules 2005 (SI 2005/384) (CrimPR) applies equal force to restraint and receivership applications as it does to criminal proceedings in general. Rule 1 provides as follows:

1.1   The overriding objective

   (1)   The overriding objective of this new code is that criminal cases be dealt with justly.

   (2)   Dealing with a criminal case justly includes—

      (a)   acquitting the innocent and convicting the guilty;

      (b)   dealing with the prosecution and the defence fairly;

      (c)   recognising the rights of the defendant, particularly those under Article 6 of the European Convention on Human Rights;

      (d)   respecting the interests of witnesses, victims and jurors and keeping them informed of the progress of the case;

      (e)   dealing with the case efficiently and expeditiously;

      (f)   ensuring that appropriate information is available to the court when bail and sentence are considered; and

      (g)   dealing with the case in ways that take into account—

         (i)   the gravity of the offence alleged,

         (ii)   the complexity of what is in issue,

         (iii)   the severity of the consequences for the defendant and others affected, and

         (iv)   the needs of other cases.

1.2.   The duty of the participants in a criminal case

   (1)   Each participant, in the conduct of each case, must—

      (a)   prepare and conduct the case in accordance with the overriding objective;

      (b)   comply with these Rules, practice directions and directions by the court; and

      (c)   at once inform the court and all parties of any significant failure (whether or not that participant is responsible for that failure) to take any procedural step required by these Rules, any practice direction or any direction of the court. A failure is significant if it might hinder the court in furthering the overriding objective.

   (2)   Anyone involved in any way with a criminal case is a participant in its conduct for the purposes of this rule.

1.3.   The application by the court of the overriding objective

The court must further the overriding objective in particular when—

(a)   exercising any power given to it by legislation (including these Rules);

(b)   applying any practice direction; or

(c)   interpreting any rule or practice direction.

7.03   By r 3.1 of the CrimPR, the court must further the overriding objective by actively managing the case. By r 3.2, 'active case management includes:

(a)   the early identification of the issues;

(b)   the early identification of the needs of witnesses;

(c) achieving certainty as to what must be done, by whom, and when, in particular by the early setting of a timetable for the progress of the case;

(d) monitoring the progress of the case and compliance with directions;

(e) ensuring that evidence, whether disputed or not, is presented in the shortest and clearest way;

(f) discouraging delay, dealing with as many aspects of the case as possible on the same occasion and avoiding unnecessary hearings;

(g) encouraging the participants to co-operate in the progression of the case; and

(h) making use of technology.

By r 3.3 the parties are under a duty to assist the court in fulfilling its duties under r 3.2 and **7.04** to apply to the court for directions if they are needed to further the overriding objective. The expression 'overriding objective' was first used in the Civil Procedure Rules which brought into effect the recommendations of Lord Woolf's report on the civil justice system. The aim of the overriding objective, in the context of civil proceedings, is to encourage the parties to resolve their differences without recourse to litigation and, in those cases where litigation is unavoidable, to narrow down the issues in dispute as much as possible. In the context of restraint and receivership proceedings, the parties will be expected to serve their evidence on each other and on the court well in advance of any hearing, together with skeleton arguments summarising the case they propose to advance. They will also be expected to agree bundles of documents and serve them on the court so the judge may have the opportunity of considering them in advance of the hearing. In the more complex cases, the judge will give directions as to the various steps the parties must take and the timescale within which they must be completed. Any party to the proceedings who does not comply with such directions risks sanctions being imposed in costs. The duty of active case management imposed on the court by the rules means that the court takes a much more 'hands on' approach to case management than has hitherto been the case. In the past, particularly in civil cases, case management was largely in the hands of the parties who were able to agree amongst themselves how the case would progress, often granting one another significant extensions of time in which to carry out various steps in the litigation prescribed by the rules or by order of the court. This is no longer the case under the overriding objective, and the parties will be expected to comply with their obligations within the period specified by the rules or in the court's directions and, if they are unable to do so, will be expected to advance very compelling reasons to the court.

C. Procedure on Applications for Restraint Orders

Applications for restraint orders

By r 59.1: **7.05**

(1) This rule applies where the prosecutor or an accredited financial investigator makes an application for a restraint order under section 42 of the Proceeds of Crime Act 2002.

(2) The application may be made without notice.

(3) The application must be in writing and supported by a witness statement which must—

    (a) give the grounds for the application;

    (b) to the best of the witness's ability, give full details of the realisable property in respect of which the applicant is seeking the order and specify the person holding that realisable property;

    (c) give the grounds for, and full details of, any application for an ancillary order under section 41(7) of the 2002 Act for the purposes of ensuring that the restraint order is effective; and

    (d) where the application is made by an accredited financial investigator, include a statement that he has been authorised to make the application under section 68 of the 2002 Act.

7.06   Rule 59.1 closely follows the provisions of sc115 in relation to applications for restraint orders in the High Court. Rule 59(1) expressly provides that the application may be made without notice to the defendant and persons holding realisable property. As the Court of Appeal emphasised in *Re AJ and DJ* (Unreported, 9 December 1992) the mere fact that applications 'may' be made without notice does not mean that the prosecutor should automatically make his application without notice in every case. Where there is little likelihood of assets being dissipated in the short period between notice of an application being given and the hearing taking place, the prosecutor should always consider whether it would be more appropriate for the application to be heard on notice. The position was summarised by Leggatt LJ in *Re AJ and DJ* (Unreported, 9 December 1992) in these terms:

> In the ordinary case the prosecution would no doubt be unwise not to proceed *ex parte*, and will need, in support of the application, no more than an affidavit which concisely and truthfully summarises the facts, but in an unusual case such as the present in which it is not established that there was any need for a restraint order to be made the order will be discharged. Rare though such cases will be, this represents a cautionary reminder for all prosecutors that they are not entitled to assume that an order will made automatically once the conditions of section 76 (of the CJA) have been satisfied.

The duty of full and frank disclosure

7.07   Rule 59.1(3) sets out the issues the prosecutor's witness statement in support of the restraint application must address. It should not, however, be thought that the prosecutor need do no more than provide in his witness statement the information required by r 59.1(3). Applications for restraint orders are subject to the usual rule of civil procedure that a litigant who asks the court to make an order without giving notice to the other parties to the action must give full and frank disclosure of all material facts whether they support his case or not. The requirement to give full and frank disclosure is imposed because the defendant has no opportunity to attend and address the court as to why the order should not be made. If granted, a restraint order can have a drastic effect on the defendant, his family and business, and, in contrast to the position in relation to freezing orders, he will only have very limited rights to compensation in the event of his acquittal. In *Director of the Serious Fraud Office v A* [2007] EWCA Crim 1927 Hughes LJ explained the duty of full and frank disclosure in the context of applications for restraint orders as follows:

> A restraint order is a far-reaching order. Although it takes away no property or assets from the person under investigation, and is by definition temporary in application, it prevents him from using the frozen property in any way until the criminal investigation and any ensuing prosecution is over. That may restrict him considerably in what he can do by way of business or private activity. If it turns out that the person is not shown to be guilty of crime, he may in the meantime have lost a good deal because of the restrictions put upon him by the order. His ability to recover any losses from those who asked for the order is in a domestic case strictly limited by section 72 to cases in which there has been serious default by an investigator of a kind which caused the investigation to continue when otherwise it would not have done.

The restriction of a restraint order may sometimes last for a long time, though it can be reviewed if it is persisting unfairly. The order has been called draconian, and so it may (deliberately) be.

Because the initial application is commonly made without notice, the court will not at that stage hear evidence on both sides. For this reason, as with other without notice applications, the court insists on full and complete disclosure by the applicant of everything which might affect the decision whether or not to grant the order. There is a high obligation on the applicant to put everything relevant before the Judge, whether it may help or hinder his cause.

In short, full and frank disclosure is essential to enable the court to determine the application for a restraint order fairly.

What additional matters should be disclosed?

There can be no exhaustive list of the matters which should be disclosed as each case is dif- **7.08** ferent and must be judged on its own particular facts. It is submitted that the following matters should be disclosed by the prosecutor if he is to comply with his duty of full and frank disclosure:

(a) particulars of any defence put forward by the defendant in interview or which would appear to be available to him from the facts known to the prosecutor;

(b) details of any innocent explanation advanced by the defendant as to his possession of substantial assets that appear to be inconsistent with his known legitimate sources of income;

(c) details of any legitimate business operated by the defendant, so the court can be satisfied any restraint order makes proper provision to enable the company to continue in bona fide trading pending the conclusion of the proceedings;

(d) details, in so far as they are known, of the defendant's domestic circumstances and financial commitments, including his martial status, details of any children or other dependent relatives he may have, and the extent of any mortgage obligations. If the defendant has at any time been made bankrupt, this too should be disclosed;

(e) particulars of any interest held by a third party in realisable property in respect of which the order is being sought;

(f) where it is alleged that a company controlled by the defendant has facilitated the criminal conduct complained of, all the facts relied on in support of this contention should be disclosed together with full details of the corporate structure, including the date on which the company was incorporated, the share capital, the names of the company's officers and shareholders, and, when known, the approximate annual turnover of the company;

(g) details of any civil proceedings brought against the defendant by any victim of the offence and any efforts the defendant may have made to compensate the victim voluntarily; and

(h) full details of all facts relied on in support of the contention that the defendant will dissipate assets if a restraint order is not made.

The duty to give full and frank disclosure is a continuing one that does not come to an end **7.09** once a restraint order has been made. The duty extends to disclosing subsequently discovered facts, so if further information comes to light after the order has been made that could be relevant to the exercise of the court's discretion whether or not to make a restraint order and, if so, on what terms, the prosecutor must make full and prompt disclosure. The proper course in such circumstances is for the prosecutor to make a further witness statement deposing as to the new matters and then refer the matter back to the court, on notice to the defendant and affected third parties, to enable the court to determine what action should be taken having regard to those matters.

The consequences of non-disclosure

7.10 The usual consequence of material non-disclosure is that the court will discharge the order. The court will also be at pains to ensure that a prosecutor who obtains a restraint order without full disclosure will be deprived of any advantage he may have derived from the failure to disclose. As the Court of Appeal made clear in *Brinks Mat Ltd v Elcombe* [1988] 1 WLR 1350, the court does nonetheless have some discretion in the matter and, if it considers any non-disclosure to be of a minor nature, it may either direct the order to continue or discharge it and make a new order on the same or different terms.

7.11 In *Re AJ and DJ* (Unreported, 9 December 1992) the Court of Appeal upheld a decision of Laws J (as he then was) to discharge a restraint order *inter alia* on the basis of material non disclosure where the prosecutor's affidavit wrongly deposed that:

(a) the benefit from the alleged offences was £450,000 when in reality it was nearer £40,000;

(b) no civil proceedings had been instituted by victims of the offences when one of the building societies affected had in fact instituted such proceedings;

(c) the defendants had been uncooperative with the police when this was not the case and there was evidence that the defendants were attempting to dissipate assets when in reality there was no such evidence.

7.12 The Court emphasised that not every instance of non-disclosure would result in the order being discharged. Leggatt LJ said:

> Even if there is material non-disclosure in applying for a restraint order, the court will hesitate to discharge the order on that ground alone. Instead, it will normally be content to vary the order so as to apply only to that realisable property which it has been satisfactorily proved should be subject to the order, and will mark the breach of duty to the court in swearing an exceptionable affidavit by an appropriate order for costs.

7.13 The Court of Appeal took a similar approach in *Jennings v CPS* [2005] 4 All ER 391 and was at pains to stress the public interest in ensuring that assets were available to meet any confiscation order that might be made in the defendant's cases. Longmore LJ said:

> The fact that the Crown acts in the public interest does, in my view, militate against the sanction of discharging an order if, after consideration of all the evidence, the court thinks that an order is appropriate. That is not to say that there could never be a case where the Crown's failure might be so appalling that the ultimate sanction of discharge would be justified.

7.14 As Laws LJ observed in *Jennings v CPS* this has to be balanced against the importance of requiring the Crown to comply strictly with the rules. He said:

> It seems to me that there are two factors which might point towards a different approach being taken to without notice applications for restraint orders in comparison to applications in ordinary litigation for freezing orders; but they pull in different directions. First, the application is necessarily brought (assuming of course that it is brought in good faith) in the

public interest. The public interest in question is the efficacy of s71 of the Act of 1988. Here is the first factor: the court should be more concerned to fulfil this public interest if that is what on the facts the restraint order would do, than to discipline the applicant—the Crown—for delay or failure of disclosure. But secondly, precisely because the applicant is the Crown, the court must be alert to see that its jurisdiction is not being conscripted to the service of any arbitrary or unfair action by the State, and so should particularly insist on strict compliance with its rules and standards, not least the duty of disclosure.

Further, a failure to give full and frank disclosure will only attract the sanction of the restraint **7.15** order being discharged if the facts that have not been disclosed are material to the exercise of the court's discretion whether or not to grant the order and, if so, on what terms. Minor failings to disclose peripheral issues will not normally result in the order being discharged. In the *Jennings* case the defendant's solicitors had written to the Greater Manchester CPS advising of his intention to re-mortgage his home in order to pay off some outstanding liabilities. As a result of an oversight this letter was not passed on to the Central Confiscation Branch of the CPS in London and complaint was made that it was not disclosed in the witness statement made in support of the restraint application. In rejecting the contention that the restraint order should have been discharged on this basis, the Court of Appeal pointed out that the letter did necessarily assist the defendant because it showed that he was living beyond his means. As Laws LJ said:

> Plainly the letter displayed a willingness on the applicant's part to disclose to the CPS transactions which he intended to carry out relating to his property. But it cuts both ways. The letter tends also to show that the appellant was living beyond his means. He was having to borrow to pay tax: and he was proposing to turn unsecured debt into a secured loan, thus giving the lender a statutory priority over the Crown. At the very least Leveson J was not plainly wrong to hold that the impact of disclosure of the letter would only have been 'to increase the concern of dissipation of assets, rather than reduce it'. And the failure to disclose it was inadvertent. In the circumstances I am quite unable to hold that the failure was such as to require the court to discharge the restraint order, and then consider as a separate exercise whether to impose a fresh order.

The Court of Appeal took a similar approach in *Director of the Serious Fraud Office v A* **7.16** [2007] EWCA Crim 1927. In that case the Director appealed against the decision of a Crown Court judge to discharge a restraint order it had obtained following a request from the Government of Iran pursuant to the Proceeds of Crime Act 2002 (External Requests and Orders) Order 2005. The non-disclosure complained of, and which led the judge to discharge the order, was a failure by the Iranian judge who made the original request for the order to disclose that it came from the military branch of the Iranian judicial organisation. The Court of Appeal held that this was not sufficiently material to justify the discharge of the order and allowed the Director's appeal. Hughes LJ said:

> . . . the difficulty lies in ascertaining why he found that the fact that the investigation judge was in this instance operating within the framework of the military courts made a crucial difference to whether a restraint order should be made. If the investigating judge's explanation of his own position and of the nature of the investigation is correct, it is not easy to see why it should. If he is right, it is not easy to see why it makes a significant difference that, as a career lawyer, he is in this instance investigating a case proceeding within the military court structure when he operates in a similar way in what he says is a parallel system of civil courts governed essentially by the same rules. If he is right, it is not easy to see why even if the investigator were a military officer that makes a significant difference where the trial will be before a properly constituted civil court. It might or might not be different if (the defendant) were being investigated by a biased or politically motivated officer with a view to a show trial with

a pre-ordained end. But there is no finding that that is the case, or even that the contrary has not been sufficiently shown.

He added:

> To say, as the Judge did, that the fact that the external request emanated from the military branch of the judicial organisation of Iran would have been a factor relevant to his decision is to beg the question of what its effect would have been upon that decision and why. To answer that unanswered question involves answering the antecedent questions likewise unresolved, (i) how much if any of the investigating judge's explanation of the non-disclosure can be accepted, and (ii) what is the import of the undisclosed origin of the request. Without the answer to any of those questions, it is impossible to know whether the non-disclosure was sufficiently significant to justify the immediate discharge of the order. In any event, the Judge has not considered whether the order should, on its merits, stand or fall. If the conclusion drawn by the Crown Court had been one of deliberate deception, then providing there was sufficient reason for reaching it that might well provide a basis for discharging the restraint order, but in the absence of such a conclusion and, if it be reached, consideration whether or not the order should stand on its merits, we are unable to say that the Judge directed himself correctly.

7.17   Prosecutors must nonetheless remain vigilant to ensure that witness statements in support of applications for restraint orders made without notice to the defendant give full and frank disclosure of all material facts. If a prosecutor has any doubt as to whether a particular fact should be disclosed, he should err on the side of disclosure. This is not to say that it is incumbent on him to disclose every minute detail of the case and the court must, it is submitted, give the prosecutor some latitude to reflect the fact that in many cases restraint orders have to be obtained as a matter of great urgency to prevent assets of substantial value being dissipated. Indeed, in *Brinks Mat Ltd v Elcombe* [1988] 1 WLR 1350 Slade LJ deprecated the practice of applying for orders to be discharged alleging non-disclosure on very slender grounds.

7.18   When material non-disclosure does occur in restraint cases, it is rarely attributable to bad faith on the part of the prosecutor. In most instances, it arises from a breakdown in communication between those responsible for the financial investigation and those dealing with the prosecution side of a case at a time when there is an understandable concern to have a restraint order in place at the earliest opportunity to prevent any dissipation of assets. In such circumstances, it is perhaps not surprising that, from time to time, misunderstandings arise in the passing of information between those having the conduct of different aspects of the case. The failure to pass on the letter in the case of *Jennings v CPS* [2005] 4 All ER 391 is a classic example of this and was, rightly it is submitted, described by Laws LJ as 'unimpressive but, plainly, not malicious'. Minor failings of this nature are, in the absence of bad faith on the part of the prosecutor, unlikely to result in the restraint order being discharged.

The order

7.19   By r 59.2 of the CrimPR:

(1)   The Crown Court may make a restraint order subject to exceptions, including but not limited to, exceptions for reasonable living expenses and reasonable legal expenses and for the purpose of enabling any person to carry on any trade, business or occupation.

(2)   But the Crown Court must not make an exception for legal expenses where this is prohibited by section 41(4) of the Proceeds of Crime Act 2002.

(3)   An exception to a restraint order may be made subject to conditions.

(4) The Crown Court must not require the applicant for a restraint order to give any undertaking relating to damages sustained by a person who holds realisable property as a result of the restraint order.

(5) The Crown Court may require the applicant for a restraint order to pay the reasonable expenses of any person, other than a person who holds realisable property, which are incurred in complying with the restraint order.

(6) A restraint order must include a statement that disobedience of the order, either by a person to whom the order is addressed, or by another person, may be contempt of court and the order must include details of the possible consequences of being held in contempt of court.

(7) Unless the Crown Court directs otherwise, a restraint order made without notice has effect until the court makes an order varying or discharging the order.

(8) The applicant for a restraint order must—
    (a) serve copies of the restraint order and of the witness statement made in support of the application on the defendant and any person who holds realisable property to which the restraint order applies; and
    (b) notify any person affected by the restraint order of the terms of the restraint order.

Rule 59.2 mirrors very closely sc115 r 4 in relation to restraint orders made in the High **7.20** Court under the old legislation although some of the provisions are new. Rule 59.2(1) makes it clear for the first time that the restraint order may be made subject to an exception permitting a person to carry on any trade, business, or occupation. Rule 59.2(2) limits the court's power to make an exception for the payment of legal expenses where this is prohibited by s 41(4) of POCA. Rule 59.2(7) is drafted in entirely different terms to sc115 r 4(2). By sc115 r 4(2), a High Court restraint order is to have effect only until a return date for an *inter partes* hearing, unless the court otherwise directs. Rule 59.2(7), in contrast, provides that a POCA restraint order has effect until the court makes an order varying or discharging it unless the court directs otherwise. In fact, this provision merely gives effect to what had been the practice of the High Court for many years and which was expressly approved by the Court of Appeal in *Ahmad v Ahmad* [1998] EWCA Civ 1246. We saw in Chapter 2 that there was some conflict between this ruling and the later judgment of the Court of Appeal in *Customs and Excise Commissioners v S* [2005] 1 WLR 1338 where it was suggested that restraint orders should normally be given a short return date given the potential consequences of the prohibition on releasing funds for legal expenses.

The court also suggested in *Customs and Excise Commissioners v S* that POCA restraint **7.21** orders should contain a provision advising as to the availability of public funding. Scott Baker LJ said:

> We think these orders should state clearly on their face that public funding is available. It is plainly desirable that defendants to restraint orders should in the ordinary course of events have legal representation. It would also be helpful if such orders direct defendants to the central unit at which their public funding application will be processed. Time will often be of the essence; it is crucial that public funding applications in these matters should be dealt with, with the greatest expedition.

By CrimPR r 61.10(1) the order must state the name and judicial title of the person mak- **7.22** ing it, bear the date on which it was made, and be sealed by the Crown Court. The seal may be placed on the order by hand or by printing a facsimile of the seal on the order whether electronically or otherwise: see r 61.10(2). The standard practice is for the prosecutor to submit a draft of the order he seeks with the application and to be responsible for drawing up the final version of the order as approved by the court. This is in accordance with r 61.15(1) which provides that orders shall be drawn up by the court unless it directs a party to draw it up or a party, with the permission of the court, agrees to draw it up. A draft POCA restraint order appears at Appendix 7.

Hearings

7.23 Where the prosecutor applies for the restraint order without notice, there is rarely a formal hearing of the application, the judge considering the matter in his private room without any attendance by the parties. This is in accordance with r 61.3 of the CrimPR which provides that applications in restraint and receivership proceedings are to be dealt with without a hearing unless the Crown Court orders otherwise. This rule gives effect to the procedure that applies in the High Court in relation to applications under the old legislation where the judge considers the application without a hearing and only requires the prosecutor to attend if there are aspects of the application that concern him. Of course it is always open to the prosecutor to request a hearing and, it is submitted, he should always do so where there are unusual features to the application that call for an explanation.

7.24 In *R v B* [2008] EWCA Crim 1374 the Court of Appeal held that the Crown Court judge should normally give reasons for making a restraint order. Moses LJ said:

> ... those facts do serve to demonstrate how serious it is to make an order such as this and therefore the obligation upon any judge either considering it *ex parte* or on an application to vary or discharge to see that those bases are not only established but that there are good reasons for making and reaching the conclusion that they have been established. After all, the giving of reasons for making such a decision not only tells the subject of such an order why they have been made, but afford a powerful discipline to the judge who is obliged to consider whether the grounds have been established. We note that pursuant to the Criminal Procedure Rules 61.3 such applications are to be dealt with without a hearing unless the Crown Court orders otherwise. But we wish to stress that the fact that they are to be dealt with without a hearing does not in any way obviate the need for careful scrutiny by the court on an *ex parte* application, lest rights enshrined in the European Convention on Human Rights should be infringed. In the instant case it is by no means clear why it was that the judge on the *ex parte* application made this order notwithstanding the fact that there had been an opportunity to dissipate the assets which had not been taken.

7.25 Where a hearing does take place, in accordance with the procedure established in relation to freezing injunctions in *Interroute Telecommunications (UK) Ltd v Fashion Group Ltd* [1999] TLR 762, the prosecutor should take a full note of the hearing and serve the same on the defendant along with a copy of the restraint order and supporting evidence. In *Director of the Assets Recovery Agency v Singh* [2004] EWHC Admin 2335 McCombe J held that the *Interroute* principle in relation to freezing orders applied equally to applications for interim receiving orders under Pt V of POCA. He said:

> I can see no reason why the common practice in relation to without notice applications in the High Court should not be followed in cases of this type, unless the judge hearing the application expressly decides that, for good reason, a note should not be served on the affected parties and provided that that decision is recorded on the face of the order, so that all affected parties may know that that decision also is susceptible to the customary provision to apply to vary or discharge the order.

It is submitted that this principle should also apply to applications for restraint orders made **7.26** without notice and that the best practice is for the prosecutor to prepare and serve a note of the hearing on the defendant.

Service of the order

Once the restraint order has been made the prosecutor must serve it together with the **7.27** witness statement in support and, if applicable, his note of the hearing, on the defendant and any person holding realisable property and must notify any person affected by the order of its terms: see CrimPR r 59.2(8). The rules as to service, service by an alternative method, and service outside the jurisdiction are found in r 57 and are considered at para 7.62 below.

The court will normally expect the prosecutor to give an undertaking to serve the order as **7.28** soon as reasonably practicable. In *PS Refson & Co Ltd v Saggars* [1982] 3 All ER 111. The High Court held that 'as soon as reasonably practicable' meant 'forthwith'. Nourse J, with the concurrence of the Vice-Chancellor, gave a warning to the profession that any failure to comply with undertakings as to service constitute a contempt of court and that solicitors acting on behalf of a party can also be held in contempt for failing to implement any such undertakings given on behalf of a client.

D. Procedure on Applications to Vary or Discharge the Order

In Chapter 5 we considered the grounds on which a defendant or affected third party might **7.29** apply to the court for a restraint order to be varied or discharged. In this section we examine the procedures that should be followed on the making of such an application. Applications to discharge the order should normally be confined to those instances where the prosecutor's evidence appears to be insufficient to justify the making of the order or where there has been a serious breach of the duty to give full and frank disclosure of all material facts. In most cases, it will be more appropriate to make an application to vary the order to mitigate its harsher effects. In practice, the most commonly made applications for variations include:

(a) requests for more time to comply with disclosure and repatriation requirements;
(b) requests for an increase in the amount payable by way of general living expenses; and
(c) applications to release a particular asset either to effect a sale or on the ground that it is not realisable property of the defendant.

Variation by consent: consulting the prosecutor

Any person seeking a variation to a restraint order should always approach the prosecutor **7.30** before making an application to the court to discover whether the proposed variation, or a mutually acceptable compromise, can be agreed on a 'by consent' basis. A person who applies directly to the court for the order to be varied without first consulting the prosecutor risks being penalised in costs and, if the application is made on the advice of his legal representatives, the court might be minded to make a wasted costs order against those responsible.

In approaching the prosecutor, the applicant should provide precisely the same information **7.31** that he would incorporate in his evidence in support were the matter to be determined by the court. Further, if the variation requested is an increase in the amount payable by way of general living expenses, the applicant should ensure that he has first complied with his disclosure obligations under the order. It is unlikely that the prosecutor would be in a position to accede to a request for an increase prior thereto because he will not have sufficient information on which to base a decision in the absence of full details of the defendant's assets. In *Re O* [1991] 1 All ER 330 the Court of Appeal upheld the decision of Macpherson J not to entertain a variation application until the defendants had given full disclosure of their assets.

7.32 Any consent order agreed must be drawn up by the parties in terms that comply with CrimPR r 61.11. It must be expressed as being 'by consent' and must be signed by the legal representative acting for each of the parties to whom the order relates or by the party if he is a litigant in person: see r 61.11(4). The application may be dealt with without a hearing in accordance with r 61.11(3).

7.33 Defendants, affected third parties, and their legal advisors should take care in agreeing the terms of 'by consent' variations and only agree to the same if they are content to be legally bound by them. A consent order is treated as a binding contract between the parties and, as the Court of Appeal held in *Weston v Dayman* [2006] EWCA Civ 1165, the Court will only entertain an application to vary an order made by consent in exceptional circumstances. Arden LJ said:

> I would accept that the court should accede to an application for variation where it is just to do so but in my judgment one of the aspects of justice is that a bargain freely made should be upheld. Mr. Weston clearly obtained benefits under the order. It may well be that those benefits are not as great as he thought, but that is not a matter for the court. In those circumstances I do not consider it would be right for this court to exercise its discretion to vary the order as sought

Applying to the court

7.34 Where an approach to the prosecutor does not result in agreement as to the terms of any variation, the only way forward is for an application to be made to the court for the order to be varied. The procedure is set out in r 59.3 of the CrimPR which provides:

(1) This rule applies where a person affected by a restraint order makes an application to the Crown Court under section 42(3) of the Proceeds of Crime Act 2002 to discharge or vary the restraint order or any ancillary order made under section 41(7) of the Act.
(2) The application must be in writing and may be supported by a witness statement.
(3) The application and any witness statement must be lodged with the Crown Court.
(4) The application and any witness statement must be served on the person who applied for the restraint order and any person who holds realisable property to which the restraint order applies (if he is not the person making the application) at least 2 days before the date fixed by the court for hearing the application, unless the Crown Court specifies a shorter period.

7.35 This Rule is in very similar terms to sc115 r 5 in relation to applications in the High Court to vary restraint orders made under the old legislation. The interpretation provisions in rr 57.1, 57.2, and 57.3 provide assistance in computing time. By r 57.2(2):

A period of time expressed as a number of days shall be computed as clear days.

7.36 'Clear days' is defined in r 57.2(3) in these terms:

(3) In this rule 'clear days' means that in computing the number of days—
   (a) the day on which the period begins; and
   (b) if the end of the period is defined by reference to an event, the day on which that event occurs
are not included.

Further, under r 57.2(4), when the period is five days or less and includes a day that is not a business day, that day does not count for the purpose of computing time. 'Business day' is defined in r 57.1 as being any day other than:

(i) a Saturday, Sunday, Christmas Day or Good Friday; or
(ii) a bank holiday under the Banking and Financial Dealings Act 1971 in England and Wales.

The effect of these provisions is to provide very similar rules as to service as applied under **7.37** sc115 in relation to applications under the old legislation. The position remains that two clear days notice must be given by the defendant or affected third party of any application to vary or discharge a restraint order. Thus, if an application to vary or discharge a restraint order is served on the prosecutor on a Monday, the first day on which the same may be heard at the Crown Court would be the following Thursday.

Variation applications by the person who applied for the order

Thus far, we have considered only the procedures to be followed when an application to **7.38** vary a restraint order is made by the defendant or an affected third party. There may, however, be circumstances in which the prosecutor wishes to apply for the order to be varied, for example by including new assets discovered since the restraint order was made or, indeed, by deleting assets from the order if further enquiries reveal that he has restrained more assets than are necessary to satisfy a confiscation order in the amount of the defendant's benefit.

The procedure to be adopted on such applications is set out in r 59.4 of the CrimPR which **7.39** provides:

(1) This rule applies where the applicant for a restraint order makes an application under section 42(3) of the Proceeds of Crime Act to the Crown Court to vary the restraint order or any ancillary order made under section 41(7) of the 2002 Act (including where the court has already made a restraint order and the applicant is seeking to vary the order in order to restrain further realisable property).
(2) The application may be made without notice if the application is urgent or there are reasonable grounds for believing that giving notice would cause the dissipation of realisable property which is the subject of the application.
(3) The application must be in writing and must be supported by a witness statement which must—
    (a) give the grounds for the application; and
    (b) where the application is for the inclusion of further realisable property in the order, to the best of the witness's ability give full details of the realisable property in respect of which the applicant is seeking the order and specify the person holding that realisable property;
    (c) when the application is made by an accredited financial investigator, include a statement that he has been authorised to make the application under section 68 of the 2002 Act.
(4) The application and witness statement must be lodged with the Crown Court.
(5) Except where, under paragraph (2), notice of the application is not required to be served, the application and witness statement must be served on any person who holds realisable property to which the restraint order applies at least 2 days before the date fixed by the court for hearing the application, unless the Crown Court specifies a shorter period.
(6) If the court makes an order for the variation of a restraint order, the applicant must serve copies of the order and of the witness statement made in support of the application on—
    (a) the defendant;
    (b) any person who holds realisable property to which the restraint order applies (whether before or after the variation); and
    (c) any other person whom the applicant knows to be affected by the order.

7.40   Rule 59.4 is in very similar terms to sc115 r 6 in relation to such applications made to the High Court under the old legislation, and introduced no procedural changes to the way in which applications for variations by the prosecutor should be made.

Hearing the variation application: the *Lexi Holdings* decision

7.41   Where an application for the variation of a restraint order is contested a hearing will almost certainly be necessary. Any such hearing may be held in chambers: see CrimPR r 61.4. In many cases the issues the court is required to determine will be relatively straightforward: for example, whether the defendant should be entitled to an increase in the amount payable by way of general living expenses and will not occupy a great deal of court time. Some applications, however, will be more complicated and may even occupy a number of days of court time. In such circumstances the court should consider listing the matter for directions initially so that it can make orders as to the timescale for the service of evidence and skeleton arguments and the agreement of bundles by the parties.

7.42   A small number of variation applications can prove highly complex and may well involve issues of law far removed from those normally determined by the Crown Court. Just such a situation arose in *Serious Fraud Office v Lexi Holdings PLC (In Administration)* [2008] EWCA Crim 1443 where the Court had to determine whether a third party creditor had a proprietary claim to restrained assets and, if not, whether a restraint order could properly be varied to allow a third party judgment creditor of the defendant to be paid. The Court, having determined the point of law at issue, gave some important guidance as to how complex cases of this nature should be dealt with in the future. Keene LJ said:

> We cannot leave this appeal without commenting on some procedural matters which have come to light during the hearing. First, there can be little doubt that the issues which arose in this case concerning beneficial interests, equitable charges and tracing were far from straightforward. They are not part of the daily work of most Crown Court judges, and indeed this constitution of the Court of Appeal was deliberately arranged to ensure that appropriate expertise in matters normally falling within the jurisdiction of the Chancery Division was available. Sometimes issues may arise in restraint order proceedings about equitable interests which are not unduly complicated and can readily be dealt with in the Crown Court. In other cases the sums involved may not warrant any unusual steps. But there may be other times when the complexities are such that it may not be wise for the Crown Court judge to embark on seeking to decide those issues. In such a case where a relaxation of the restraint order is sought, consideration should be given to adjourning those variation proceedings to enable the issues to be determined in proceedings before a specialist Chancery Circuit Judge or High Court Judge of the Chancery Division. Alternatively, those arranging the listing of such cases in the Crown Court should seek to ensure that they are heard before a judge with the relevant experience and expertise.

7.43   Where such issues are involved, the parties should inform the court as soon as possible so arrangements can be made for the case to be listed before a judge with the appropriate expertise.

E. Receivership Proceedings

7.44   The CrimPR makes extensive provision in relation to applications for the appointment of management and enforcement receivers. These are necessary because the Crown Court, being a creature of statute, does not have the same inherent jurisdiction as the High Court.

In consequence most of the provisions are not replicated in sc115 dealing with the High Court's jurisdiction under the old legislation.

The application for appointment

Rule 60.1 provides: **7.45**

(1) This rule applies to an application for the appointment of a management receiver under section 48(1) of the Proceeds of Crime Act 2002 and an application for the appointment of an enforcement receiver under section 50(1) of the 2002 Act.
(2) The application may be made without notice if the application is—
  (a) joined with an application for a restraint order under rule 59.1;
  (b) the application is urgent; or
  (c) there are reasonable grounds for believing that giving notice would cause the dissipation of realisable property which is the subject of the application.
(3) The application must be in writing and must be supported by a witness statement which must—
  (a) give the grounds for the application;
  (b) give full details of the proposed receiver;
  (c) to the best of the witness's ability, give full details of the realisable property in respect of which the applicant is seeking the order and specify the person holding that realisable property;
  (d) where the application is made by an accredited financial investigator, include a statement that he has been authorised to make the application under section 68 of the 2002 Act;
  (e) if the proposed receiver is not a member of staff of the Crown Prosecution Service or the Revenue and Customs Prosecutions Office and the applicant is asking the court to allow the receiver to act—
    (i) without giving security, or
    (ii) before he has given security or satisfied the court that he has security in place,
  explain the reasons why that is necessary.
(4) Where the application is for the appointment of an enforcement receiver, the applicant must provide the Crown Court with a copy of the confiscation order made against the defendant.
(5) The application and witness statement must be lodged with the Crown Court.
(6) Except where, under paragraph (2), notice of the application is not required to be served, the application and witness statement must be lodged with the Crown Court and served on—
  (a) the defendant,
  (b) any person who holds realisable property to which the application relates, and
  (c) any person whom the applicant knows is affected by the application,
  at least 7 days before the date fixed by the court for hearing the application, unless the Crown Court specifies a shorter period.
(7) If the court makes an order for the appointment of a receiver, the applicant must serve copies of the order and of the witness statement made in support of the application on—
  (a) the defendant;
  (b) any person who holds realisable property to which the order applies; and
  (c) any other person whom the applicant knows to be affected by the order.

Most law enforcement authorities who apply for the appointment of receivers select the **7.46** person they apply to the court to appoint from an approved panel that have agreed to adhere to prescribed standards in the conduct of the receivership. The members of the panel are typically insolvency practitioners who are partners in firms of chartered accountants or solicitors. The prosecutor will select a member of the panel either on a rota basis or because of his known expertise in a particular type of case and invite him to accept the appointment by sending him a 'letter of agreement' setting out the terms of the proposed appointment and inviting him to confirm his acceptance of them. The letter of agreement forms the basis of a contractual relationship between the prosecutor and the proposed receiver and an example of such a letter may be found in Appendix 10. The letter of agreement should always be exhibited to the prosecutor's witness statement in support of the application and the receivership order will usually provide that the receiver must act in accordance with the letter of agreement.

7.47 Rule 60.1(2) permits applications for the appointment of management receivers to made without notice in urgent cases or where there are reasonable grounds to believe assets would be dissipated were notice to be given. In appropriate circumstances, the application may be made at the same time as an application for a restraint order. Prosecutors must, however, have due regard to the decision of the Court of Appeal in *Re P (Restraint Order: Sale of Assets)* [2000] 1 WLR 473 where the Court emphasised that such applications should only be made in cases of genuine urgency and that the receiver's powers should be confined to those strictly necessary to meet the justice of the situation. A draft management receivership order appears at Appendix 8 and an enforcement receivership order at Appendix 9.

Applications for the conferment of powers on receivers

7.48 Rule 60.2 of the CrimPR deals with applications for the conferment of powers on receivers made pursuant to s 49 of POCA. As r 60.2 is in almost identical terms, to r 60.1, it is not reproduced here.

Applications to vary or discharge receivership orders

7.49 Rule 60.3 makes provision for applications to vary or discharge receivership orders. These, too, must be made in writing and served on all affected parties at least seven days before the hearing unless the court specifies a shorter period. If the court decides to make an order varying or discharging the order, the applicant must serve copies of the order on any persons whom he knows to be affected by it.

Security

7.50 Rule 60.5 deals with the provision of security by receivers who are not members of staff of the Crown Prosecution Service or the Revenue and Customs Prosecutions Office. By r 60.5(2):

> (2) The Crown Court may direct that before the receiver begins to act, or within a specified time, he must either—
> (a) give such security as the Crown Court may determine; or
> (b) file with the Crown Court and serve on all parties to any receivership proceedings evidence that he is already has in force such security,
> to cover his liability for his acts and omissions as a receiver.

The Crown Court may terminate the receiver's appointment if he fails to give security or satisfy the court as to the security he has in place by the date specified: see r 60.5(3).

7.51 The Crown Court has a discretion whether or not to require the receiver to give security and does not have to require it in every case. It is submitted that the Crown Court could properly dispense with the provision of security where the person the prosecutor seeks to appoint comes from an experienced receiver in the employ of a reputable firm of chartered accountants which has a proven track record for conducting receiverships in a proper manner. The purpose of the security is to ensure the defendant's estate is properly protected in the event that the receiver acts improperly. If, in reality, there is no real risk that the receiver will abuse his position, it is submitted that security could properly be dispensed with. It is worthy of note that the High Court, where it appoints a receiver under the DTA and CJA 1988, is not bound to require security in cases where the proposed receiver has already acted in previous cases under the legislation. The Crown Court, it is submitted, could properly apply the same rule in deciding whether or not to exercise its discretion in favour of requiring security.

Receivers' remuneration and accounts

Rule 60.6 and Rule 60.7 respectively deal with receivers' remuneration and accounts. As these provisions are dealt with in detail in Chapter 3, they are not reproduced again here. **7.52**

Non-compliance by a receiver

Rule 60.8 makes provision for dealing with a receiver who fails to comply with any rule, practice direction, or direction of the Crown Court. By r 60.8(1) the Crown Court may order him to attend a hearing to explain his non-compliance. At the hearing the court may make any order it considers appropriate, including an order terminating the receiver's appointment, reducing or disallowing his remuneration, or requiring him to pay the costs of any party. **7.53**

F. Provisions as to Evidence and the Service of Documents

Evidence

Rule 61.5 of the CrimPR gives the Crown Court power to control the evidence in restraint and receivership proceedings by giving directions as to: **7.54**

(a) the issues on which it requires evidence;
(b) the nature of the evidence which it requires to decide those issues; and
(c) the way in which the evidence is to be placed before the court.

The court may use its powers under r 61.5(1) to exclude evidence that would otherwise be admissible (see r 61.5(2)), and may limit the scope of cross examination (see r 61.5(3)).

Evidence should be in writing

Rule 61.6 of the CrimPR imposes a general rule that unless the court otherwise orders, evidence in restraint and receivership proceedings should be in writing. The parties may apply under r 61.6(2) for permission to cross-examine a person who has tendered written evidence. If a person is required to attend for cross-examination and fails so to attend, his evidence may not be used unless the court gives permission: see r 61.5(3). This accords with the procedures of the High Court in restraint and receivership applications under the old legislation where evidence is normally given in affidavit or witness statement form. It is submitted that cross-examination should be ordered only in cases where there is a complete conflict of evidence between the parties. Rule 61.7 empowers the court, on the application of any party to the proceedings, to issue a witness summons requiring a witness to attend court to give evidence or produce documents to the court. **7.55**

7.56 Witness statements required to be served under the rules must be verified by a statement of truth contained in the statement itself: see r 57.7(1)). By r 57.7(2) a statement of truth is defined as:

> . . . a declaration by the person making the witness statement to the effect that the witness statement is true to the best of his knowledge and belief and that he made the statement knowing that, if it were tendered in evidence, he would be liable to prosecution if he wilfully stated in it anything which he knew to be false or did not believe to be true.

The effect of this provision appears to be that statement of truth should be in the same form as that in witness statements tendered under s 9 of the Criminal Justice Act 1967 rather the form required under the Civil Procedure Rules (CPR). If a person making a witness statement fails to verify the witness statement by a statement of truth, the court may direct that it shall not be admissible in evidence: see r 57.7(4).

Hearsay evidence

7.57 Rule 61.8 of the CrimPR makes provision as the admission of hearsay evidence in restraint and receivership proceedings. It provides that the duty imposed by s 2(1) of the Civil Evidence Act 1995 to give notice of an intention to rely on hearsay evidence does not apply to evidence in restraint and receivership proceedings.

Expert evidence

7.58 By r 57.9(1) of the CrimPR, a party to restraint or receivership proceedings who wishes to adduce expert evidence (whether of fact or opinion) must, as soon as practicable:

(a) serve on the other parties a statement in writing of any findings or opinion which he proposes to adduce by was of such evidence; and

(b) serve on any party who request it in writing, a copy of (or if it appears to the party proposing to adduce the evidence to be more practicable, a reasonable opportunity to examine)—

    (i) the record of any observation, test, calculation or other procedure on which the finding or opinion is based; and

    (ii) any document or other thing or substance in respect of which the observation, test, calculation or other procedure mentioned in sub-paragraph (i) has been carried out.

7.59 A party may waive his right to be served with r 57.9(1) but, if he does not waive that right, expert evidence that has not been served in accordance with this rule may not be admitted without the leave of the court (see r 57.9(1)(c) and (d)). Rule 57.10 makes special rules to deal with cases where a party fears that compliance with r 57.9 might lead to intimidation or attempted intimidation of the witness or that the course of justice may otherwise be interfered with. In such circumstances, he shall not be obliged to comply with r 57.9 but must serve a notice on the other party stating that the evidence is being withheld and the reasons for withholding it.

Disclosure and inspection of documents

7.60 Where any issue arises in restraint or receivership proceedings as to whether property is realisable property the Crown Court may make an order under r 61.9 of the CrimPR for disclosure and inspection of documents. In such circumstances Pt 31 of the CPR has effect as if the proceedings were proceedings in the High Court: see r 61.9(3). Part 31 of the CPR makes provisions for the disclosure and inspection of documents and for the service of lists of documents by the parties.

Court documents

Rule 61.10 of the CrimPR makes various miscellaneous requirements as to court docu- **7.61**
ments. These are primarily administrative provisions that give effect to the practices and
procedures that apply in High Court proceedings under the old legislation. Rule 61.10(1)
provides that Crown Court orders must state the name and judicial title of the judge that
made them and the date on which they are made, and must be sealed by the court. By
r 61.10(2), the Crown Court may place the seal on the order by hand or by printing a
facsimile of it on the order, whether electronically or otherwise. A document purporting to
bear the court's seal is admissible in evidence without further proof (see r 61.10(3)).

Service of documents

Rule 57.11(2) of the CrimPR provides that, unless the court directs otherwise, documents **7.62**
in restraint and receivership proceedings may be served by any of the following methods:

(a) in all cases, by delivering the document personally to the person to be served;
(b) if no solicitor is acting for the party to be served by delivering the document at, or by sending it by
first class post to his residence or his last known residence;
(c) if a solicitor is acting for the person to be served—
  (i) by delivering the document at, or sending it by first class post to, the solicitor's business
  address, or
  (ii) where the solicitor's business address includes a numbered box at a document exchange, by
  leaving the document at that document exchange or at a document exchange which transmits
  documents on every business day to that document exchange, or
  (iii) by sending a legible copy of the document by facsimile transmission to the solicitor's office.

By r 57.11(3), documents served by post or left at a document exchange are deemed to have **7.63**
been served on the second day after posting or being deposited at the document exchange.
Where documents are served by fax, they are deemed to have been served on the same day
or, if they were transmitted after 4pm, on the next business day.

Rule 57.11(4) allows an order made in restraint and receivership proceedings to be enforced **7.64**
against a defendant or party affected by it notwithstanding that it has not been served in
accordance with the rules, provided the court is satisfied that he had notice of it by being
present when it was made.

Service by an alternative method

Rule 57.12 of the CrimPR makes provision for service by an alternative method where **7.65**
there is good reason to do so. This would include, for example, cases where a defendant or
affected third party is deliberately evading service. The application must be supported by
evidence and may be made without notice (see r 57.12(2)). The court's order authorising
service by an alternative method must specify the method of service allowed and the date
when the document will be deemed to have been served (see r 57.12(3)).

Service outside the jurisdiction

Rule 57.13 of the CrimPR allows documents to be served outside England and Wales with **7.66**
the permission of the court. The document may be served by any method permitted by the
law of the country in which it is to be served (see r 57.13(2)). However, nothing in the rule

or in any court order authorises or requires any person to do anything in the country where the document is to be served which is against the law of that country (see r 57.13(3)). Where a document is required to be served a certain time before the date of a hearing and the recipient does not appear at the hearing, that hearing must not take place unless the Crown Court is satisfied the document has been duly served (see r 57.13(4)).

Proof of service

7.67 By r 57.14 of the CrimPR, where the rules require an applicant for an order to serve a document on another person, he must lodge a certificate of service with the Crown Court within seven days of the service of the document stating the method and date of service and, where the document is served in accordance with an order for service by an alternative method, such other information as the court may require (see r 57.14(2)). Where a document in restraint and receivership proceedings is to be served by the court, and the court is unable to serve it for any reason, it must send a notice of non-service stating the method attempted to the party who requested service (see r 57.14(3)).

Consent orders

7.68 Rule 61.11 of the CrimPR makes provision in relation to consent orders. By r 61.11(2) any party to the proceedings may apply for a judgment or order in agreed terms and such an application may be dealt with without a hearing. By r 61.11(4) such a judgment or order must be drawn up in the terms agreed, must be expressed as being 'by consent', and must be signed by the legal representative acting for each of the parties or by the party himself if he is a litigant in person.

Slips and omissions

7.69 Rule 61.12 of the CrimPR introduces a 'slip rule' whereby the Crown Court may at any time correct an accidental slip or omission made in an order in restraint and receivership proceedings. A party may apply for a correction without notice (see r 61.12(2)).

Supply of documents from court records

7.70 By r 61.13(1) of the CrimPR, no document relating to restraint or receivership proceedings may be supplied to any person to inspect or copy unless the Crown Court gives permission. Given the sensitivity of restraint proceedings, the court should normally be very reluctant to give such permission, especially at the pre-conviction stage. This is particularly so in relation to the defendant's disclosure statement or any document he produces to the court under compulsion. The court should, it is submitted, follow the ruling given by Macpherson J in *Re R* (Unreported, 21 October 1992) to the effect that such statements should be held in the court office 'under lock and key' and disclosed to no one (see Chapter 3 para 3.23). An application for permission under r 61.13(1) must be made on notice to the parties to the proceedings (see r 61.13(2)).

7.71 Rule 61.14(2) provides that the judge presiding at proceedings for the offence may be supplied with documents relating to restraint and receivership proceedings but otherwise such documents must not be disclosed in proceedings for an offence (see r 61.14(2) and (3)).

Preparation of documents

Rule 61.15 of the CrimPR makes provision for the preparation of documents by the court **7.72** and the parties. By r 61.15(1), orders in restraint and receivership proceedings should be drawn up by the Crown Court unless:

(a) the Crown Court orders a party to draw it up;
(b) a party, with the permission of the Crown Court agrees to draw it up; or
(c) the order is made by consent under r 61.10.

By r 61.15(2) the Crown Court may direct that orders drawn up by a party must be checked **7.73** by the court prior to sealing, or that before an order is drawn up by the court the parties must lodge an agreed statement of its terms. It is submitted that the better course in most cases would be for the parties to draw up the order for the court's approval given the length and complexity of most restraint and receivership orders. Where an order is to be drawn up by a party to the proceedings, he must do so within seven days after the date on which he was ordered or permitted to draw it up and, if he fails to lodge it within that period, any other party may draw it up and lodge it at the court for sealing (see r 61.15(3)).

Change of solicitor

Rule 16.16 of the CrimPR requires a party who changes his solicitor to notify the court **7.74** and all the other parties to the proceedings. By r 61.17, a solicitor may apply to the court for an order that he has ceased to act for a party to restraint and receivership proceedings. If the solicitor has died, been made bankrupt, ceased to practise, or cannot be found, any other party to the proceedings may apply to the court for an order that he has ceased to act (see r 61.18).

Costs

Rules 61.19 to 61.21 make provision for the payment of costs in restraint and receivership **7.75** proceedings. The rules as to costs are considered in detail in Chapter 22 below and are therefore not reproduced here.

8

PREPARING FOR CONFISCATION HEARINGS

A. Introduction

The evolution of confiscation

8.01 In *Sekhon v R* [2002] EWCA Crim 2954, [2003] 3 All ER 508, the then Lord Chief Justice considered the evolving history of confiscation law, concluding that one of the most successful weapons that could be used to discourage offences that are committed in order to enrich offenders is to ensure that if the offenders are brought to justice any profit which they have made from their offending is confiscated.

8.02 The Hodgson committee report, 'The Profits of Crime and their Recovery, Howard League for Penal Reform, 1984', made a number of recommendations which form the background of the modern confiscation provisions. The report recommended the repeal of the Criminal Bankruptcy Order and its replacement with confiscation and sentences in default, designed to catch the profits of major crime. Following these recommendations, a confiscation regime was introduced in relation to drug trafficking under the guise of the Drug Trafficking Offences Act 1986 (DTOA). As well as including the powers of restraint and confiscation, that Act also contained a statutory assumption to the effect that a drug trafficker's assets were the proceeds of crime and therefore liable to confiscation. The Criminal Justice Act 1988 (CJA 1988) introduced a new power to make a confiscation order in the case of certain crimes other than drug trafficking offences.

8.03 Section 1 of the DTOA imposed a mandatory obligation on the court to hold a financial enquiry whenever a defendant was convicted of a drug trafficking offence. This resulted in a considerable waste of court time, both in cases where it was patently obvious that there had been no benefit (or any benefit was of a purely nominal amount) and also in cases where the defendant was accepted to have no realisable property.

8.04 In cases that commenced after the Drug Trafficking Act 1994 (DTA) came into force (on 1 February 1995), the mandatory obligation on the court to hold a financial enquiry in every case was relaxed. Under s 2(1) of the DTA, the court was only obliged to hold a mandatory enquiry when either the prosecutor asked it to proceed under s 2 or if the court considered it appropriate to proceed under s 2, even though the prosecutor had not asked it to do so.

Under s 71(1) of the CJA 1988, a confiscation hearing could be held by the Crown Court **8.05** whenever a defendant had been convicted of an indictable offence (other than a drug trafficking offence), but it was contingent upon the prosecutor giving written notice and/or the court considering it appropriate to proceed.

Under POCA the Crown Court must hold a confiscation hearing if a defendant has either **8.06** been convicted of an offence in the Crown Court, or has been committed to the Crown Court for sentencing (or committed with a view to a confiscation order being considered) and the court has been asked to proceed by the prosecutor or the court believes it is appropriate to do so. The amended Act is set out in Appendix 1.

The transitional arrangements

The transitional arrangements introduced following the commencement of POCA antici- **8.07** pate that offences committed before the effective date of the legislation, namely 24 March 2003, should remain under the DTA or the CJA 1988 (SI 2003/333).

For the purposes of this third edition, we have focused almost exclusively on POCA as **8.08** opposed to the two preceding Acts. During the lifetime of this edition some 10 years will have elapsed since the passing of POCA. The effects of the transitional provisions, therefore, are now considerably diluted, with the vast majority of cases now falling squarely within the scope of POCA. For cases where the DTA or CJA 1988 do still apply, the second edition of this work gives a detailed commentary on the practice and procedure to be followed. In terms of general practice, however, this chapter should still be of assistance, not least because we refer to the case law that had developed under the DTA and the CJA 1988, which still remains persuasive under POCA.

Introduction: the wake-up call

The purpose of this first of two chapters on confiscation hearings is to focus on the steps **8.09** usually required prior to the hearing. The concerns of the Court of Appeal in relation to preparation for confiscation hearings were summarised concisely in the Court of Appeal case of *R (on the prosecution of BERR) v Baden Lowe* [2009] EWCA Crim 194, where the Court made the following two important observations (para 21):

> (i) It is essential that the court hearing the proceedings finds and sets out all the relevant facts in its ruling (or judgment), including the facts that are agreed before it. It is evident that many confiscation hearings are not prepared in advance as they should be. There are many complaints that Defence Statements are inadequate. Timetables set out in the Criminal Procedure Rules or the court's directions frequently slip. Sometimes it is only at the last minute, either immediately before the court sits or even in the course of a hearing, that some matters are agreed and the real issues emerge, considerably burdening the task of the judge hearing the proceedings. If identifying the issues is left to the last minute, then insufficient attention is paid to ensuring that any procedural steps needed for the evidence to be admissible are taken. In an occasional case, where difficult issues arise, it may be the case that counsel with more experience of such issues is needed. Difficulties are from time to time compounded by the lack of a properly paginated bundle. It is, in the experience of many in this court, that, for reasons such as those we have outlined, it is not always clear from the ruling (or judgment) below what the facts were on which the issues which arose were determined. As the task of the court hearing the confiscation proceedings is to apply

the statutory provisions to the facts (as agreed or found), it is essential that the ruling (or judgment) sets out all the relevant facts, as agreed and as found.

(ii) Too many authorities are cited to courts. Advocates should bear the observations in *May* at paragraph 48(4) clearly in mind before any authority is cited to the judge hearing the proceedings or in this court. We were provided with a large bundle of authorities which were unnecessary.

When do POCA confiscation hearings have to be held?

8.10 Under s 6(1) of POCA the Crown Court must proceed with a confiscation hearing if the following two conditions are satisfied:

(2) The first condition is that a defendant falls within any of the following paragraphs:
  (a) he is convicted of an offence or offences in proceedings before the Crown Court;
  (b) he is committed to the Crown Court for sentence in respect of an offence or offences under Section 3, 4 or 6 of the Sentencing Act;
  (c) he is committed to the Crown Court in respect of an offence or offences under Section 70 of the Proceeds of Crime Act 2002 (committal with a view to a confiscation order being considered).

(3) The second condition is that:
  (a) the Prosecutor has asked the Court to proceed under [Section 6 of POCA]; or
  (b) the Court believes it is appropriate to do so.

Section 6(1) therefore imposes a mandatory obligation on the court to hold a financial enquiry whenever subss (2) and (3) are satisfied. The Sentencing Act referred to is the Powers of Criminal Courts (Sentencing) Act 2000 (see s 88(5) of POCA).

8.11 In *R v Moulden* (2009) 2 All ER 912; (2009) 1 Cr App R 27 the Court of Appeal held that the words 'proceedings before the Crown Court' in s 6(2)(a) meant proceedings under a single indictment. The Court found that where there were two sets of proceedings, one under POCA and one under the CJA 1988, the two statutory frameworks should be independently applied.

The steps to confiscation—in a nutshell

8.12 In summary, the route to the confiscation hearing is likely to include:

(a) *Conviction of the defendant for an acquisitive crime.* While the confiscation process may commence prior to conviction, ordinarily the court and prosecutor are only likely to focus on the timetable for confiscation once a conviction has been secured, not least because of resource issues and the potential that the defendant may be acquitted.

(b) *The prosecutor will ask the court to proceed under s 6 of POCA.* In the alternative, although rarely applied in practice, the court may proceed to hold a confiscation hearing of its own motion. The application is often made orally after the jury has returned its verdict. The court may at this stage order the defendant to provide information pursuant to s 18 of POCA to assist in the enquiry.

(c) *The prosecutor will provide or the court will order a statement of information from the prosecutor, pursuant to s 16 of POCA.* This is essentially the Crown's opportunity to state its case. It will often be the product of an ongoing financial investigation and will make reference to restraint proceedings where assets have been frozen. The Crown will put figures on what it believes to be the defendant's benefit, the burden of which rests with the Crown on the balance of probabilities. The Crown may also make reference to available assets and whether it contends there are hidden assets, although the burden of proving the same rests with the defendant.

(d) *Within the statement of information the Crown will identify whether the case is a particular or general criminal conduct matter.* If it is a general criminal conduct matter or a lifestyle offence, the statutory assumptions under s 10 of POCA will apply. If it is a particular criminal conduct matter they will not.

(e) *The defendant will be required to respond to the statement of information within a set time frame, pursuant to s 17 of POCA.* A failure to address the issues may lead to the court treating the defendant as accepting the allegations in the prosecutor's statement.

(f) *The prosecutor may serve a further statement of information (at any time), pursuant to s 16(6).*

(g) *The court may order the defendant to provide further specified information, pursuant to s 18 of POCA.*

(h) *The court may postpone confiscation proceedings and sentence the defendant, pursuant to s 14 of POCA.* However, if it decides to do this it cannot exercise its powers to order s 16 and s 17 statements when it is not proceeding under s 6. It may postpone for beyond two years if exceptional circumstances apply.

(i) *The court may sentence the defendant, if it is proceeding under s 6, prior to making the confiscation order.* (*CPS Swansea v Gilleeney* [2009] EWCA Crim 193). There is no requirement to complete the proceedings under s 6 within a particular period, or before sentence.

The confiscation hearing itself is considered in more detail in the next chapter of this book. A draft directions order may be found at the end of this chapter, and the relevant sections are reproduced at Appendix 1. Whilst deceptively simple, the path to confiscation can be full of pitfalls, and the practice and procedure is considered in more detail below. **8.13**

The discretion to ask the court to proceed and abuse of process

In *R v Paulet* [2009] EWCA Crim 288 the Court of Appeal found that there may be limited and exceptional cases where it might be considered oppressive for the Crown to seek a confiscation order. It invited the Director of Public Prosecutions (DPP) to give guidance to prosecutors about the policy to be followed and to identify proceedings in which the commencement of confiscation proceedings would be appropriate, in order to establish a consistency of approach. **8.14**

In May 2009 that policy was issued by the CPS in a document entitled: 'Guidance for Prosecutor's on the Discretion to Instigate Confiscation Proceedings'. The guidance is only that, and it undoubtedly will need to be updated from time to time. **8.15**

The guidance confirms that while prosecutors have a duty to carry out their functions in accordance with the intention of Parliament, it is important that they also remember that they retain a discretion whether or not to instigate confiscation proceedings. In considering how to exercise their discretion, prosecutors need to consider their role as ministers of justice and should remember the three legitimate aims of confiscation set out in *R v Rezvi, R v Benjafield* [2003] 1 AC 1099, namely to 'punish convicted offenders, to deter the commission of further offences and to reduce the profits available to fund further criminal enterprises' (per Lord Steyn, para 14). **8.16**

8.17 The guidance adds that the prosecutor should consider in each case whether the statutory regime would operate in a way that would be oppressive. The concern being that, although following a request by a prosecutor, the courts no longer hold a discretion whether or not to make a confiscation order against a defendant who falls within the statutory regime, the courts still retain a jurisdiction to stay confiscation proceedings as an abuse of process. This jurisdiction may be invoked in order to halt proceedings which ought not to have been instigated by the prosecutor. However, the jurisdiction should only be exercised with 'considerable caution' and is ordinarily confined to cases of 'true oppression' (*R v Shabir* [2008] EWCA Crim 1809).

8.18 While the categories of the abuse jurisdiction are not closed, the guidance identifies four situations where proceedings may be stayed if confiscation proceedings are unreasonably instigated:

i. Where the Crown has reneged on an earlier agreement not to proceed.

ii. In a simple benefit case, where the defendant has voluntarily paid full compensation to the victim or victims, or is ready, willing and able immediately to repay all of the victims to the full amount of their losses, and has not otherwise profited from his crime (*R v Morgan* [2009] 1 Cr App R (S) 60).

iii. Where proper application of the relevant statute to a defendant's case would, if the court were asked to proceed to confiscation, compel the court to find that property obtained in the most part legitimately by the defendant, and to which the defendant would have been entitled but for his criminal conduct, must be treated as benefit. An example of this situation arose in the case of *R v Shabir* [2009] 1 Cr App (S) 84. In that case the defendant was a pharmacist who had submitted false, inflated claims to the NHS. The total amount obtained by deception was approximately £179,000, but the defendant had been entitled to most of the money claimed, except £464. It was held to be inappropriate to proceed to confiscation, but such examples will be rare and confined to cases of 'true oppression' (per Hughes LJ, at para 23).

iv. Where a defendant has obtained paid employment by a false representation to his employer. The defendant's wages may be his benefit (*R v Carter* [2006] EWCA Crim 416), but some cases will arise where the link between the criminality and the receipt of payment from dishonestly obtained employment is too remote, for example, where had the representation been corrected, the employment would have continued, or where after many years of otherwise lawful employment, a relatively minor previous conviction is discovered.

8.19 It should be emphasised that cases in which an abuse argument will succeed will be rare (see *R (on the prosecution of BERR) v Baden Lowe* [2009] EWCA Crim 194, para 16, where the Court observed that it was not an abuse of process to seek to recover more than a defendant has profited from his crime nor an abuse where he has made restitution outside the very narrow circumstances identified in *Morgan and Bygrave* [2008] EWCA Crim 1323). In *Morgan and Bygrave* the Court of Appeal held that it may amount to an abuse of process for the Crown to seek a confiscation order which would result in an oppressive order to pay double the full restitution which the defendant had made or was willing to make (para 30). In *CPS v N, P and Paulet* [2009] EWCA Crim 1573, the Court of Appeal indicated that Crown Courts were 'too readily' staying confiscation proceedings and that the court lacks discretion to interfere with the Crown's decision to invoke confiscation proceedings (paras 34 and 35).

8.20 The discretion to commit a confiscation matter from the magistrates' court is considered in more detail below.

For the necessity of keeping compensation payments separate from the issues of confisca- **8.21**
tion in a social security fraud case, and the lack of discretion to take into account such
payments under the confiscation scheme, see *R v Bartaby* [2007] EWCA Crim 2313.

In *R v Chatha* [2008] EWCA Crim 2597 the defendant was convicted of participation in **8.22**
a substantial conspiracy to facilitate unlawful immigration. The conspirators used a 'banker'
named Aujla. Prior to Aujla's arrest, the defendant had been seen to give him three items;
one of these was a plastic bag containing £17,000 in cash. The defendant was later heard
during an intercepted phone call with one of the other conspirators referring to having
handed over this money to Aujla. The judge found at a Newton hearing that the defendant
was involved throughout the conspiracy, that he knew it involved a considerable number
of illegal immigrants, and that he was an important member of the conspiracy, knew that
its purpose was to make money, and that he had benefited from it financially. At the confiscation hearing, the defendant asserted that half the £17,000 was his (albeit going to be
passed on to another conspirator) and that half belonged to his friends, and that it was all
legitimate.

This was a 'criminal lifestyle' case, as the offence was a Sch 2 offence under POCA. The **8.23**
judge found that there was no evidence to show that any of the monies handed to Aujla
were legitimate and rejected the defendant's explanation. He included the sum of £17,000
in the calculation of the defendant's benefit.

Counsel for the defendant then raised the fact that the £17,000 had already been seized **8.24**
from Mr Aujla, and submitted that it should be either deducted from the amount of the
order, or used to discharge part of the order. Money laundering and tax evasion charges had
been brought against Aujla, which included the possibility that there would be a forfeiture
or confiscation order in relation to the cash, and any 'double counting' would (it was submitted) be unfair to the defendant. The judge refused to alter the amount of the order.
Subsequently, although criminal proceedings against Aujla were discontinued, the £17,000
cash was made the subject of a forfeiture order.

The defendant argued on appeal that since the £17,000 was available at the time of sen- **8.25**
tence, and had since been forfeited, that should be reflected by an adjustment to the order,
or by the discharge of part of the order. The Crown argued that the sum had been found to
be a benefit from the defendant's criminal lifestyle, and that as he had assets in excess of
the total benefit figure (£122,000) then an order in respect of the total sum had to be
made. The Crown Court submitted that neither the seizure of the cash from Aujla nor its
subsequent forfeiture made any difference, and this was far from an 'oppressive' case in
which a stay for abuse of process might be granted. The Court considered the line of cases
beginning with *May* and agreed with the Crown, finding that there was 'no unfairness in
the appellant having to pay for his benefit from his criminal lifestyle from his surviving
assets, whilst, at the same time, the £17,000 in cash has been the subject of a forfeiture order
in different proceedings in relation to a different individual'.

The standard and burden of proof

The court must decide any question arising under s 6(4) and (5) of POCA on the 'balance **8.26**
of probabilities' (pursuant to s 6(7), see Appendix 1).

8.27 In *R v Barwick* (2001) 1 Cr App R(S) 129 the Court of Appeal held that in confiscation proceedings under the CJA 1988 it was for the prosecution to establish that the defendant had benefited from an offence and the value of that benefit. Once that had been established, it was for the offender to prove, on a balance of probabilities, that the amount that might be realised was less than the value of his calculated benefit (see also *R v Layode* (CA, 12 March 1993), *R v Carroll* [1991] Crim LR 720, and *R v Ilsemann* 12 Cr App R(S) 398).

8.28 In *R v Barnham* [2005] Crim LR 657, [2006] 1 Cr App R (S) 83 the Court confirmed:

> 40... Once the prosecution has established the benefit there is no requirement on it to provide a *prima facie* case. At the second stage the burden of proof shifts to a defendant to establish, if he can, his realisable assets to the satisfaction of the court. By the second stage a defendant will know exactly how the court has determined the benefit attributable to him and must prove by evidence what his realisable assets are. It is for him to show why the confiscation order should not be 'the value of (*his*) proceeds of drug trafficking'. If he proves that he has no, or appreciably less, realisable assets than the amount of the benefit determined by the court the order will be made in the lesser sum. Provided the judge keeps well in mind the principle that the risk of serious injustice to the defendant must be avoided and does not just pay lip service to that principle, the order will be in the amount assessed as either the amount of benefit or such other sum as the defendant shows represents his realisable assets.

> 41. To hold that the prosecution must, in some way, show a *prima facie* case that the defendant has hidden assets in our judgment would defeat the object of the legislation. It is designed to enable the court to confiscate a criminal's ill-gotten gains. The expression 'hidden assets' is indicative of the fact that the prosecution can have no means of knowing how and where a defendant may have dealt with or disposed of the proceeds of his criminal activities.

8.29 Similarly, the Court of Appeal in *R v Granger* [2007] EWCA Crim 139 held that:

> 13. Moreover, it is not enough for a defendant to accept that he has had money and say in general terms that it has disappeared. A defendant seeking to avert or minimise a proposed confiscation order needs to be specific about where his money has come from and gone to, if the judge is to be invited to hold a defendant has no realisable assets.

Victims and restitution

8.30 As with most acquisitive crime, frequently an innocent third party will have suffered a loss, eg householders and insurance companies in burglary cases, building societies in mortgage fraud cases, HM Revenue and Customs in VAT and income tax frauds etc. Section 6(6) of POCA permits the court to treat its duty to decide the recoverable amount and make a confiscation order as a discretionary power if it believes that a victim of the criminal conduct has at any time started or intends to start proceedings against the defendant in respect of loss, injury, or damage sustained in connection with the conduct.

8.31 If, for example, it transpires that a building society which has suffered loss as a result of a mortgage fraud has instituted civil proceedings against the defendant in which it is seeking the recovery of a sum equating to the benefit the defendant has derived from the offence, the court may form the view that it would not be proper to make a confiscation order against the defendant because of the element of double recovery involved. Section 7(3) specifies how the court should approach the recoverable amount in such circumstances; see Appendix 1.

However, the potential for such a claim is not something upon which the court should **8.32** speculate. In *R v Hockey* [2008] Crim LR 59; [2008] 1 Cr App R (S) 50, the Court of Appeal found that the judge at first instance had erred by expressing the view that a confiscation order would be inappropriate in circumstances where financial institutions may have a legitimate interest. The lenders concerned had not at any time indicated that they had started or intended to start proceedings. In such circumstances a confiscation order ought to have been made.

The case of *Hockey* is a salutary reminder to financial institutions (and those who represent **8.33** them) that if they wish to make a claim against a defendant then they must notify the prosecutor or court expeditiously, or risk losing the opportunity to mount a purposive action.

The Court of Appeal considered *Hockey*, amongst other cases, in *Morgan and Bygrave v R* **8.34** [2008] EWCA Crim 1323. In that case the court, striking a cautionary note, found:

> 30... it may amount to an abuse of process for the Crown to seek a confiscation order which would result in an oppressive order to pay up to double the full restitution which the defendant has made or is willing immediately to make, and which would thus deter him from making it ... Whilst confiscation may well be draconian or penal in effect, it does not, as the House of Lords observed in *R v May* [2008] UKHL 28, at paragraph 48(1), operate as a fine.

However, this will not always be the case. In *R (on the prosecution of BERR) v Baden Lowe* [2009] EWCA Crim 194) the Court of Appeal stated:

> 16. We have emphasised these passages to underline, contrary to the fears of some (as for example set out in [2008] Crim LR 991 at 995) that it will now be difficult to know when the jurisdiction to stay is applicable. The cases in which it is likely to be applicable are very rare. Indeed, if the principles set out in *Morgan and Bygrave* are observed by prosecutors, it may never arise. It is not, for example, an abuse of process to seek to recover more than a defendant has profited from his crime nor where he has made restitution outside the very narrow circumstances identified in *Morgan and Bygrave*. If it were otherwise the case and the jurisdiction exercised more widely, the court would be defeating the clear decision of Parliament, by enacting the legislation in the terms in which it did, not only to impose a draconian policy but also to remove the discretion of the court to avoid those consequences, save in a case where abuse was established.

B. Confiscation in the Magistrates' Court

Introduction

Section 97 of the Serious Organised Crime and Police Act 2005 (SOCPA) permits magis- **8.35** trates' courts to make confiscation orders under Pt 2 of POCA in a sum less than £10,000. Whilst the Act came into force on 1 July 2005 (for the enabling provision, see SI 2005/1521, Art 3, and s 97(2)), the actual provisions have, at the time of writing, yet to be implemented (although we understand that steps are now being taken to rectify this).

When they do, magistrates will have the power to fix confiscation hearings pursuant to the **8.36** POCA scheme following a trial or a guilty plea, where the sum to be confiscated is less than £10,000.

8.37 To some extent these provisions, once introduced, will ease the burden on prosecutors in determining whether or not to ask the magistrates to refer a case to the Crown Court. However, the issue of whether to commit will still arise in a number of cases.

Section 70: committal by a magistrates' court

8.38 Section 70 of POCA states:

(1) This section applies if—
  (a) a defendant is convicted of an offence by a magistrates' court, and
  (b) the prosecutor asks the Court to commit the defendant to the Crown Court with a view to a confiscation order being considered under Section 6.
(2) In such a case the magistrates' court must—
  (a) commit the defendant to the Crown Court in respect of the offence and
  (b) may commit him to the Crown Court in respect of any other offence within sub-section (3).
(3) An offence falls within this sub-section if—
  (a) the defendant has been convicted of it by the magistrates' court or any other Court, and
  (b) the magistrates' court has power to deal with him in respect of it.

The effect of s 70 is that a defendant may be committed to the Crown Court for confiscation proceedings following a conviction of any offence (triable either way or summary) in the magistrates' court. The requirement to commit a defendant to the Crown Court is mandatory once the prosecutor has asked the magistrates' court to do so (see s 70(2)).

8.39 Where the defendant is convicted of an either way offence, s 70(5) requires the magistrates' court to state whether it would have committed the defendant to the Crown Court for sentencing in any event. It appears this subsection is required because, under s 71(3)(b), the Crown Court's sentencing powers following a committal for confiscation are otherwise limited to the sentencing powers of the magistrates' court.

The circumstances where a magistrates' court may commit

8.40 When considering s 6(2)(b) of POCA, the Powers of Criminal Courts (Sentencing) Act 2000 (PCC(S)A) specifies the powers under which a magistrates' court may commit to the Crown Court. Section 3 of the PCC(S)A provides a general power to commit adult offenders summarily convicted of an offence triable either way; s 4 confers a power to commit adult offenders convicted of a triable either way offence as a result of a guilty plea indicated before the mode of trial procedures have been embarked upon; and s 6 gives a general power to commit for sentence, which may be used to supplement a committal under the various provisions of the PCC(S)A.

8.41 It follows that defendants appearing before the Crown Court on appeal from decisions of the magistrates' court do not fall under s 6(2)(b) of POCA, nor do those defendants who are committed outside of s 3, 4, and 6 of the PCC(S)A, eg committal for breach of a community order or return to custody under s 116 of PCC(S)A.

The discretion to commit

8.42 We have already referred to the 2009 guidance for prosecutors to instigate confiscation proceedings. That guidance is also likely to have a direct bearing on whether prosecutors should seek the committal of defendants in confiscation matters before magistrates' courts.

As well as abuse of process arguments, public policy considerations may also arise because **8.43** s 70(1)(a) confers on the prosecutor a discretion as to whether he should ask the magistrates' court to commit following a defendant's conviction. How and when that discretion is exercised will ultimately depend on the circumstances of the individual case. The Code for Crown Prosecutors emphasises that deciding on what is in the public interest is not simply a matter of adding up factors on each side. It will be for the lawyer who has control of the case to determine how important each factor is in the circumstances of the individual case and go on to make an overall assessment. This approach was confirmed by the Court of Appeal in *R v Benjafield* [2001] 3 WLR 75, a DTA case, where the Court held that the discretion 'will have to be exercised taking into account all relevant considerations, so as to avoid the risk of injustice'.

It has long been the view that it is not in the public interest to automatically make referrals; **8.44** not least because such a course would entail no exercise of any discretion and would leave prosecutors exposed to potential judicial review actions (see para 5.6 et seq of the Code for Crown Prosecutors).

However, there are a number of factors that are common to all confiscation matters, which **8.45** may assist the prosecutor on the decision he is being asked to make in relation to s 70(1)(b):

  i. It is an established principle that prosecutors should seek to carry out a financial enquiry in every case where such an enquiry would be both relevant and appropriate. There is therefore a presumption that a case lawyer should consider whether the confiscation scheme is likely to be applicable.

  ii. The fact that Parliament has legislated for the prosecutor to seek confiscation orders in summary matters is a clear indication that this power is to be considered and *used* by prosecutors.

  iii. It would not be in the public interest to allow a repeat offender to see the benefit from his criminality go unchecked.

Arguments concerning the First Protocol of the European Convention of Human Rights, **8.46** proportionality, and the protection of an individual's property are somewhat diminished if one accepts that confiscating the proceeds of crime is in the overriding public interest. This view was confirmed by the House of Lords in *R v Benjafield* [2002] 1 All ER 815, applying *McIntosh v Lord Advocate* [2001] 2 All ER 638 and *Phillips v UK* [2001] 11 EHRC 280.

Whether it is a proportionate response to ask the magistrates' court to refer a case to the **8.47** Crown Court will depend very much on the facts of the individual case, including the seriousness of the matter, whether the individual is a repeat offender, and the sums/loss involved. The fact that the chances of recovering realisable assets ('the available amount') are very low is a consideration, but may not be determinative.

The burden of proof in confiscation proceedings rests on the prosecutor to demonstrate on **8.48** the balance of possibilities that the defendant has benefited from his criminal conduct. Where the alleged benefit is not likely to be significant there will be instances when the benefit is so low that asking the bench to commit the case up to the Crown Court would be disproportionate. However, to set a financial cut off point below which referrals should not be made would amount to a fettering of the prosecutor's discretion. Inevitably, internal resources may also be a factor in influencing matters.

Committal: practice and procedure

8.49 In relation to confiscation proceedings themselves, the timetable in the magistrates' court is likely to be as follows:

  i. The defendant is convicted;.
  ii. The prosecutor asks the magistrates' court to commit.
  iii. The matter is listed at the Crown Court for directions.
  iv. The directions hearing deals with the serving of the prosecutor's statement, the defence reply, the time estimate for the confiscation hearing etc.
  v. The defendant is sentenced. (A timetable should ideally be set and the matter postponed in relation to the confiscation hearing before sentence is passed.)
  vi. A confiscation hearing may be postponed for up to two years from the date of conviction to allow for the financial reports etc to be prepared (s 14(5)).

8.50 Once committed, the Crown Court will follow the confiscation procedure set out in s 6 et seq of POCA (see s 70(4)(a)).

No confiscation in absolute or conditional discharge cases

8.51 In *Clarke v R* [2009] EWCA Crim 1074 the Court considered committals under s 70 and whether the Crown Court could make a confiscation order in a case where there had been either an absolute or conditional discharge. It concluded that there was no reference to confiscation proceedings under s 12 or s 14 of the PCC(S)A, which deals with conditional and absolute discharges and suggests that absolute or conditional discharges 'shall be deemed not to be a conviction for any other purpose . . .'. It concluded, having considered s 12(7) in some detail, that the Crown Court had no power to make a confiscation order against a defendant if he receives an absolute or conditional discharge (para 77).

C. The Basics of Confiscation under POCA

If section 6(1)–(3) is satisfied, how must the court proceed?

8.52 Section 6(4) states:

The court must proceed as follows:
(a) it must decide whether the defendant has a criminal lifestyle;
(b) if it decides that he has a criminal lifestyle it must decide whether he has benefited from his general criminal conduct;
(c) if it decides that he does not have a criminal lifestyle it must decide whether he has benefited from his particular criminal conduct.

8.53 Under s 6(4) the court must, when considering a confiscation hearing, decide whether the defendant has a 'criminal lifestyle'. If it decides he has (or presumably had) a criminal lifestyle the court must then decide whether he has benefited from his 'general criminal conduct'. If the court decides that the offender does not have a criminal lifestyle, it must decide whether he has benefited from his 'particular criminal conduct'.

How is 'criminal lifestyle' defined?

Section 75 of POCA provides: **8.54**

(1) A defendant has a criminal lifestyle if (and only if) the following condition is satisfied.
(2) The condition is that the offence (or any of the offences) concerned satisfies any of these tests—
    (a) it is specified in Schedule 2;
    (b) it constitutes conduct forming part of a course of criminal activity;
    (c) it is an offence committed over a period of at least six months and the defendant has benefited from the conduct which constitutes the offence.

In respect of s 75(2)(a), the offences specified in Sch 2 are termed 'lifestyle' offences.

What are 'lifestyle offences'?

Lifestyle offences are defined under Sch 2 to POCA, and include drug trafficking offences, **8.55** namely:

(1) An offence under any of the following provisions of the Misuse of Drugs Act 1971—
    (a) Section 4(2) or (3) (unlawful production or supply of controlled drugs);
    (b) Section 5(3) (possession of controlled drugs with intent to supply);
    (c) Section 8 (permitting certain activities relating to controlled drugs);
    (d) Section 20 (assisting in or inducing the commission outside the UK of an offence punishable under a corresponding law).
(2) An offence under any of the following provisions of the Customs & Excise Management Act 1979 if it is committed in connection with a prohibition or restriction on importation or exportation which has effect by virtue of Section 3 of the Misuse of Drugs Act 1971—
    (a) Section 50(2) or (3) (improper importation of goods);
    (b) Section 68(2) (exploration of prohibited or restricted goods);
    (c) Section 170 (fraudulent evasion).
(3) An offence under either of the following provisions of the Criminal Justice (International Co-operation) Act 1990—
    (a) Section 12 (manufacture or supply of a substance for the time being specified in Schedule 2 to that Act); or
    (b) Section 19 (using a ship for illicit trafficking of controlled drugs).

Other offences specified in Sch 2 include money laundering, namely s 327 of POCA **8.56** (concealing, etc criminal property) and s 328 of POCA (assisting another to retain criminal property). Lifestyle offences also include: directing terrorism under s 56 of the Terrorism Act 2000; people trafficking under ss 25, 25A, or 25B of the Immigration Act 1971; arms trafficking under s 68(2) of the Customs & Excise Management Act 1979 (exportation of prohibited goods), and s 170 of the same Act (fraudulent evasion); or an offence under s 31 of the Firearms Act 1968 (dealing in firearms or ammunition by way of trade or business).

Also included under Sch 2 are: trafficking for sexual exploitation; asylum and immigration **8.57** exploitation; counterfeiting; intellectual property under the Copyright, Designs and Patents Act 1988 and the Trade Marks Act 1994 (unauthorised use of trade marks); certain prostitution and child sex offences under the Sexual Offences Acts of 1956 and 2003; blackmail under s 21 of the Theft Act 1968; and acting as a gangmaster.

Paragraph 10 of Sch 2 incorporates inchoate offences, namely: attempting; conspiring; **8.58** inciting; aiding or abetting; or counselling or procuring, the commission of any offence specified in Sch 2.

'Criminal lifestyle' and relevant benefit of not less than £5,000

8.59 Under s 75(4) an offence does not satisfy the test in s 75(2)(b) or (c) unless the defendant obtains a relevant benefit of not less than £5,000. The term 'relevant benefit' is given two definitions under s 75, dependant upon whether or not the court is proceeding under s 75(2)(b) or s 75(2)(c).

How is 'relevant benefit' defined?

8.60 Under s 75(5), 'relevant benefit' for the purposes of s 75(2)(b) (where the offence constitutes conduct forming part of a course of criminal activity), is defined as:

(a) benefit from conduct which constitutes the offence;

(b) benefit from any other conduct which forms part of the course of criminal activity and which constitutes an offence of which the defendant has been convicted;

(c) benefit from conduct which constitutes an offence which has been or will be taken into consideration by the Court in sentencing the defendant for an offence mentioned in paragraph (a) or (b).

8.61 Under s 75(6), 'relevant benefit' for the purposes of subs (2)(c) (where the offence has been committed over a period of at least six months and the defendant has benefited from the conduct which constitutes the offence), is defined as:

(a) benefit from conduct which constitutes the offence;

(b) benefit from conduct which constitutes an offence which has been or will be taken into consideration by the court in sentencing the defendant for the offence mentioned in paragraph (a).

Criminal conduct and benefit

8.62 Section 6(4)(b) and (c) refers to 'criminal conduct'. Criminal conduct is defined at s 76(1) as being:

(1) conduct which (a) constitutes an offence in England and Wales; or (b) would constitute such an offence if it occurred in England and Wales.

Section 76 adds:

(4) A person benefits from conduct if he obtains property as a result of or in connection with the conduct.

(5) If a person obtains a pecuniary advantage as a result of or in connection with conduct, he is to be taken to obtain as a result of or in connection with the conduct a sum of money equal to the value of the pecuniary advantage.

(6) References to property or a pecuniary advantage obtained in connection with conduct include references to property or a pecuniary advantage obtained in both that connection and some other.

(7) If the person benefits from conduct his benefit is the value of the property obtained.

General criminal conduct

8.63 Section 76(2) states:

General criminal conduct of the defendant is all his criminal conduct, and it is immaterial—

(a) whether conduct occurred before or after the passing of this Act;

(b) whether property constituting a benefit from conduct was obtained before or after the passing of this Act.

The phrase 'general criminal conduct' therefore encompasses all of the defendant's criminal conduct, both conduct for the offence(s) in question and criminal conduct other than the offence in question on the basis that the defendant has a criminal lifestyle.

Particular criminal conduct

Section 76(3) defines the 'particular criminal conduct' of the defendant as being: **8.64**

(3) . . . all his criminal conduct which falls within the following paragraphs—
- (a) conduct which constitutes the offence or offences concerned;
- (b) conduct which constitutes offences of which he was convicted in the same proceedings as those in which he was convicted of the offence or offences concerned;
- (c) conduct which constitutes offences which the court will be taking into consideration in deciding his sentence for the offence or offences concerned.

The relationship between general and particular conduct

By virtue of its definition, 'general criminal conduct' is inclusive of 'particular criminal   **8.65**
conduct'. Under the POCA regime courts must therefore consider the defendant's benefit from his general criminal conduct, where the court has found, upon conviction, that the defendant has a criminal lifestyle. If the court concludes that the defendant does not or has not had a criminal lifestyle, confiscation is by reference to his benefit from the particular criminal conduct on which he has been convicted (this is similar, although not identical, to the former provisions of the CJA 1988 that dictated simple and extended benefit).

When does a defendant's conduct form part of his criminal activity?

Under s 75(3):   **8.66**

Conduct forms part of a course of criminal activity if the defendant has benefited from the conduct and—
- (a) in the proceedings in which he was convicted he was convicted of three or more other offences, each of three or more of them constituting conduct from which he has benefited, or
- (b) in the period of six years ending with the day when those proceedings were started (or if there is more than one such day, the earliest day) he was convicted on at least two separate occasions of an offence constituting conduct from which he has benefited.

When does a person benefit from criminal conduct?

Under s 76(4) a person benefits from criminal conduct if he obtains property as a result of   **8.67**
or in connection with that conduct. If a person benefits from criminal conduct, his benefit is the value of the property obtained (s 76(7)).

Under s 6(5) of POCA, if the court decides under s 6(4)(b) or (c) that the defendant has   **8.68**
benefited from criminal conduct, it must next decide the recoverable amount (see s 7 of POCA) and then make a confiscation order requiring him to pay that amount in full.

Transitional provisions

Conduct shall not form part of a course of criminal activity under s 75(3)(a) of the Act   **8.69**
where any of the three or more offences mentioned in s 75(3)(a) (see para 8.66 above) was committed before 24 March 2003 (SI 2003/531). (See *R v Moulden* (2009) 2 All ER 912; (2009) 1 Cr App R 27.)

The transitional provisions set out in SI 2003/531 state that where the court is applying the   **8.70**
rule in s 75(5) of the Act in relation to the calculation of relevant benefit for the purposes of determining whether or not the test in s 75(2)(b) is satisfied by virtue of conduct forming

part of a course of criminal activity under s 75(3)(a), the court must not take into account benefit from conduct constituting an offence mentioned in s 75(5)(c) of the Act which was committed before 24 March 2003.

8.71 However, conduct shall form part of a course of criminal activity under s 75(3)(b) of the Act if the offences that the defendant was convicted of on at least two separate occasions in the period mentioned in s 75(3)(b) were committed before 24 March 2003.

8.72 Similarly, where the court is applying the rule in s 75(5) in relation to the calculation of relevant benefit for the purposes of determining whether or not the test in s 75(2)(b) of the Act is satisfied by virtue of conduct forming part of a course of criminal activity under s 75(3)(b), the court may take into account benefit from conduct constituting an offence committed before 24 March 2003.

8.73 Under SI 2003/531, where the court is applying the rule in s 75(6) in relation to the calculation of relevant benefit for the purpose of determining whether or not the test in s 75(2)(c) of the Act is satisfied, the court must not take into account benefit from conduct constituting an offence mentioned in s 75(6)(b) of the Act which was committed before 24 March 2003.

D. Postponement of POCA Confiscation Hearings

The statutory scheme

8.74 Under s 14(1) of POCA the court may:

(a) . . . proceed under Section 6 before it sentences the defendant for the offence (or any of the offences) concerned, or
(b) postpone proceedings under Section 6 for a specified period.

The court may order more than one postponement and the period of postponement may be extended (as per s 14(2)). However, a period of postponement must not end after the 'permitted period' has finished (s 14(3)).

8.75 It will be noted, pursuant to r 58.2 of the Criminal Procedure Rules, the Crown Court may grant a postponement without holding a hearing.

What is the 'permitted period'?

8.76 'Permitted period' is defined at s 14(5) as being a period of two years starting with the date of conviction. This section therefore extends the period of postponement previously permitted under the DTA and CJA 1988 from six months to two years. This means that the court no longer has to find 'exceptional circumstances' to postpone beyond six months. Further, it appears the court may now postpone a confiscation hearing under POCA for any reason, eg because no court is available. Previously it had to be on the grounds that 'further information' was required. Where the court is satisfied exceptional circumstances exist, the period may be extended beyond two years, adopting similar considerations to those that have developed under the DTA and CJA 1988 (see s 14(4) and para 8.80 below).

Date of conviction

The defendant's date of conviction is defined in s 14(9) as being the date on which the **8.77** defendant was convicted of the offence concerned, or where there are two or more offences and the convictions were on different dates, the date of the latest.

Further postponements

Section 14(8) provides that where proceedings have been postponed already for a period **8.78** and an application to extend the period further is made before the previous period of postponement ends, the application may be granted, even though the previous period (by the time the application is heard) may have ended. In effect this means that provided the application is submitted to the court before the postponed period comes to an end, the application may be granted.

Postponement beyond two years

There is no limit to the period of postponement where the court finds that there are **8.79** 'exceptional circumstances' (s 14(4)). The Act does not define when circumstances are exceptional, although some guidance may be found from previous case law in relation to the DTA or CJA 1988. In practice, only in exceptional circumstances should the need for postponement take the final date of making any confiscation order beyond the two-year period and the timetabling should reflect this.

What amounts to exceptional circumstances?

In *R v Jagdev* [2002] 1 WLR 3017 the court held that the purpose of the power to postpone **8.80** confiscation proceedings was to enable the judge to reach a fair conclusion on the confiscation issue; and that where there was a real prospect that the hearing might have been wasted and an unjust order made if the judge had proceeded to hear the case (in *Jagdev* because of an awaited decision of the Court of Appeal), then the judge was entitled to hold that there were exceptional circumstances.

In *R v Cole* The Independent, 30 April 1998 (CA), the trial judge had become ill after a **8.81** difficult and complex trial. The issue was whether this constituted exceptional circumstances. Judge LJ stated:

> The judgment whether circumstances are exceptional or not must be made by the Court considering whether to make a confiscation order. Here the Judge was in hospital on the date when he had indicated that he would determine the confiscation issue . . . Having studied the statutory code we do not consider that it was intended or drafted so as to preclude the Listing Officer making sensible arrangements for the conduct of the Crown Court business, normally after discussion with the Trial Judge or the Resident Judge . . .

The Court of Appeal has shown a marked reluctance to interfere with the exercise of the **8.82** discretion of the sentencing judge to find exceptional circumstances. It is not a question of whether or not the Court of Appeal would find the circumstances in question to be exceptional, but whether the judge was entitled to conclude that they were (see *R v Gadsby* (2002) 1 Cr App R(S) 97). Nor is it necessary for the sentencing judge to use the expression 'exceptional circumstances' (although it is submitted it is better that he does) (see *R v Chuni* (2002) Cr App R(S) 420).

8.83 In *Steele and Shevki* [2001] 2 Cr App R(S) 40; [2001] Crim LR 153 Judge LJ returned to this subject and stated:

> These decisions involved the Courts discretion, judicially exercised when the statutory conditions are present, taking full account of the preferred statutory sequence . . . For example, to take account of illness on one side or the other, or the unavailability of the Judge, without depriving a subsequent order for confiscation of its validity.

8.84 In *Sekhon* [2003] 1 WLR 1655 the Court of Appeal held that the decision as to whether to postpone and as to whether exceptional circumstances existed involved the consideration of the same types of issues that courts were regularly required to determine when engaged in case management and that the strict compliance with procedural requirements relating to issues of that nature would not normally be expected to go to jurisdiction.

8.85 This rationale is reflected in s 14(11) of POCA which provides:

> (11) A confiscation order must not be quashed only on the ground that there was a defect or omission in the procedure connected with the application for or the granting of a postponement.
> (12) But subsection (11) does not apply if before it made the confiscation order the court—
> (a) imposed a fine on the defendant;
> (b) made an order falling within section 13(3);
> (c) made an order under section 130 of the Sentencing Act (compensation orders)

Case law under the DTA and CJA 1988

8.86 Earlier case law needs to be approached with some caution when considering the issue of postponement and the related issue of exceptional circumstances. Under the DTA and the CJA 1988 the period of postponement was limited to six months, as opposed to the permitted period of two years given under POCA. As a result, the arguments that regularly arose over postponements (due often to court listing pressures) will be less prevalent under the more recent legislation. It is also important to note that there must be some finality to confiscation proceedings, and that the period of two years should not be viewed as an invitation to treat by either prosecutors or defendants. Two years should be sufficient to commence most hearings. The elasticity the appeal courts may have previously demonstrated towards courts and prosecutors who were required to squeeze a sometimes burdensome process to within a six-month period may be less generous in a scheme that permits postponement to run for two years from the date of the conviction. That having been said, the legislation clearly contemplates that exceptional circumstances may arise, which could take the confiscation process beyond two years, and in such circumstances an extension is still permissible.

8.87 In *R v Soneji and Bullen* (2005) UKHL 49, [2006] 1 AC 340, the House of Lords held that non-compliance with the terms of s 72A(3) of the Criminal Justice Act 1988 (the mirror provisions under the CJA 1988) did not deprive the court of its duty to consider the making of a confiscation order (applied in *CPS Swansea v Gilleeney* [2009] EWCA Crim 193, para 14).

8.88 In *Soneji,* the defendant had pleaded guilty to an offence of conspiracy to convert property and to remove it from the jurisdiction knowing or suspecting that it represented the proceeds of criminal conduct. The Court of Appeal had quashed the confiscation orders on the basis that they had been made beyond (the then) six-month time limit. The House of Lords were invited to consider two points:

(1) whether or not the court's common law jurisdiction to adjourn confiscation proceedings was subject to a mandatory time limit from the date of conviction save where exceptional circumstances were present and

(2) whether or not, once the court had assumed jurisdiction, its jurisdiction was extinguished by a failure to comply with the provisions of s 72A of the CJA 1988 or any common law requirement relating to the postponement or adjournment of the proceedings.

8.89 The House of Lords held that when interpreting statutory provisions, the approach of distinguishing between mandatory requirements and directory requirements should not be applied, as it served to deflect attention from the real issue of whether an act done in breach of the legislative provision was invalid (see *Project Blue Sky Inc v Australian Broadcasting Authority* (1998) 194 CLR 355).

8.90 The House found that a purposive interpretation of the legislation was required, including considering the scope and object of the whole statute. It found generally that the argument of prejudice was over-stated and that Parliament's intention of a specific time limit would not be necessarily rendered ineffective because courts would still be able to police the scheme adopted by Parliament through the abuse of process jurisdiction.

8.91 In *Soneji and Bullen* there had been no suggestion of the Crown or Court having acted in bad faith and the House of Lords found that the potential prejudice was decisively outweighed by the overriding public interest in not allowing a convicted defender to escape confiscation for what were no more than *bona fide* errors in the judicial process. Importantly, their Lordships also found that there was no common law jurisdiction to adjourn confiscation proceedings. As a result, the court must comply with the time-limit requirement wherever possible but, where difficulties arose, for example through listing, these could amount to exceptional circumstances and afford the court the power to postpone the proceedings beyond the set requirement.

Postponement for a specified period

8.92 Under s 14(1)(b) of POCA, the period of the postponement must be for a specified period. However, that does not mean that a judge must specify the very date the substantive hearing is to begin. In *R v Knights* [2005] 3 WLR 330, a CJA 1988 case, the judge purported to postpone the confiscation proceedings under s 72(A)(1) of the CJA 1988 by arranging for the case to be mentioned with a view to fixing a hearing. The appeal was heard immediately following the case of *Soneji and Bullen*. Both cases raised broadly similar questions as to whether non-compliance with the strict requirements of the 1988 Act (which correspond with the DTA and, save for the extension to two years, POCA) disabled the court from making confiscation orders.

8.93 The argument advanced suggested that the court was only allowed to postpone for a precise period of time and had to stipulate a date when the actual determination was to take place. It was argued that a date for mention was insufficient because it did not deal with the substantive hearing. Because it was anticipated that there would have to be a further postponement, it was argued that the initial postponement should not have been made without the court expressing itself satisfied that there were exceptional circumstances to justify such a course.

8.94 Lord Brown stated that when postponing the determination in confiscation proceedings, the judge was required to specify the particular period of the postponement: he could not simply adjourn the proceedings generally. However, the judge was not bound to specify the very date when the substantive hearing was to begin; it was sufficient when postponing the proceedings to give directions for the service of statements and to specify a date when the proceedings were next to be listed, whether for disposal or for such further directions as might be needed (or to fix a final hearing date).

8.95 In *Knights* the House of Lords held that it was only if the timetable initially set made it likely that the limit would ultimately be exceeded that the court had on the occasion of the first postponement to address the question of whether exceptional circumstances existed to justify the directions proposed. Although the House of Lords held that the judge *should* have addressed the question of exceptional circumstances, it found that that did not deprive the court of jurisdiction to make the confiscation order. Even if a judge were to postpone confiscation proceedings in a particular case without specifying any return date at all, the court would not, applying the approach now laid down in *Soneji*, be precluded from restoring the proceedings to the list for hearing and thereafter making an appropriate order (in *R v Soneji and Bullen* (2005) UKHL 49, [2006] 1 AC 340, the House of Lords held that a failure to comply with the procedural requirements of s 72(A) of the CJA 1988 did not result in the invalidity of the proceedings, where a judge had made the order more than six months after conviction, owing to listing difficulties, without having made a finding of exceptional circumstances).

No requirement to find further exceptional circumstances

8.96 In *R v Steel and Shevki* [2001] 2 Cr App R(S) 40; [2001] Crim LR 153 it was held that once the court had postponed a determination on the grounds that there are exceptional circumstances it is not then necessary for the court to find further exceptional circumstances for subsequent postponements (see also *R v Zelzele* (2002) 1 Cr App R(S) 62).

Who may apply for a postponement?

8.97 A postponement or extension may be made upon application by either the defendant, or by the prosecutor, or alternatively by the court of its own motion (see s 14(7)).

The effect of the court failing to follow the postponement provisions

8.98 Section 14(11) states that a confiscation order *must not* be quashed on the sole ground that there was a defect or omission in the procedure connected with the application for the granting of a postponement.

8.99 In effect this prevents confiscation orders being quashed because of some procedural irregularity in the postponement procedures. There is an exception to this rule if, before the court made the confiscation order, it imposed a fine on the defendant, or made an order falling within s 13(3) of POCA (ie a compensation order, a forfeiture order, or a deprivation order), or made an order under s 130 of the PCC(S)A (compensation orders), then, under s 14(12), a procedural irregularity of that type is likely to lead to the confiscation order being quashed.

However, in *R v Donohoe* The Times, 20 October 2006, the Court of Appeal held that the **8.100** making of a technically erroneous order for the forfeiture of illegal drugs did not have the effect of depriving the court of the jurisdiction to make a confiscation order. The Court held that it would frustrate the object of the 2002 Act to hold that the erroneous imposition of a trivial fine rendered the court powerless to proceed with the substantive confiscation proceedings.

Postponement pending appeal

Under s 14(6) of POCA, if: **8.101**

(a) the defendant appeals against his conviction for the offence (or any of the offences) concerned, and
(b) the period of three months (starting with the day when the appeal is determined or otherwise disposed of) ends after the period found under sub-section (5), the permitted period is that period of three months.

Section 14(6) provides in circumstances where a defendant has appealed that the postponement shall not, save where the court is satisfied that there are exceptional circumstances, exceed three months after the date on which the appeal is determined or otherwise disposed of.

Sentencing

In *CPS Swansea v Gilleeney* [2009] EWCA Crim 193 (commentary CLW/19/14/09) the **8.102** Court of Appeal considered the disjunctive nature of s 14(1) and emphasised the importance of judges stating plainly whether they were acting under s 14(1)(a) and going ahead with confiscation proceedings under s 6 or whether they were postponing the whole issue of confiscation, pursuant to s 14(1)(b).

In *Gilleeney*, the court concluded that the judge at first instance had been proceeding under **8.103** s 14(1)(a) (and thereby s 6) when he had ordered the Crown to supply a s 16 statement of information within six months. Importantly, the Court found that the fact that the judge was proceeding under part 6, and had not postponed the proceedings, did not prevent the court from then sentencing the defendant (para 14):

> A power to sentence in advance of the completion of the s 6 proceedings can be read into s 14(1), a view reinforced by *Soneji*.

The Court added, at para 15:

> Section 14(1)(a) plainly contemplates that proceedings under section 6 may commence before sentences are imposed. The present tense is used in the paragraph and proceedings under section 6 commenced with the requirement that the prosecution give the court statements of information within 6 months, under section 16(1). There is no requirement to complete the proceedings under section 6 within a particular period, or before sentence, or that a direction under section 14(1)(a) requires directions beyond that to provide statements of information.

This is an important development, as courts and commentators had previously proceeded **8.104** on the basis that the court could only move to sentence in cases where the court had postponed the confiscation proceedings. Nevertheless, the Court of Appeal's ruling does appear to be consistent with the more recent relaxing of the statutory scheme to ensure that technical arguments on the legislation do not overcome the overriding object, an example of which is reflected in *R v Soneji and Bullen* (2005) UKHL 49, [2006] 1 AC 340 which held that a confiscation order *must not* be quashed on the sole ground that there was a defect or omission in the procedure.

8.105   Similarly, if the court postpones proceedings under s 6 it may proceed to sentence the defendant for the offence (or any of the offences) concerned, by virtue of s 15(1). Section 15(2) provides:

> In sentencing the defendant for the offence (or any of the offences concerned) in the postponement period the Court must not (a) impose a fine on him, (b) make an order falling within section 13(3) [ie a compensation order, a forfeiture order, or a deprivation order], or (c) make an order for the payment of compensation under Section 130 of the Sentencing Act.

The purpose of this section is to prevent sentencing being delayed while confiscation is being considered.

8.106   It is suggested that in certain cases the defendant may benefit if the judge decides not to sentence until the confiscation hearing is over. For example, where new information surfaces concerning the defendant's criminal lifestyle, or lack of it, during the confiscation hearing, or where an assumption may have been made in respect of the defendant, which is also relevant to sentencing, and the defence are able to show at the confiscation hearing that it has no application. In those circumstances it may be to the defendant's benefit if the judge does not sentence until the confiscation hearing is over, and all of the facts have been considered.

Power to vary sentence

8.107   Under s 15(3), if the court decides to sentence the defendant for the offence concerned in a postponement period, once that period has ended the court may vary the sentence by imposing a fine on him, or making an order falling within s 13(3) (compensation, for-feiture, or deprivation orders), or making an order for the payment of compensation under s 130 of the PCC(S)A. However, the court may only proceed under s 13(3) within a period of 28 days starting from the last day of the postponement period (s 15(4)). In practice this means that a court may vary the sentence within 28 days of the end of the postponement period by making one or more of the orders referred to in s 13(3), ie a fine or ancillary order. This is intended to enable the court to order, for example, the forfeiture and destruction of drugs, if the court had not done so already.

8.108   The postponement provisions set out in s 15 only apply to circumstances where the court has passed sentence following a postponement under s 14(1)(b) of the Act. The court should take care therefore to specify whether it is proceeding under s 14(1)(a), namely going ahead with confiscation proceedings, or whether it is postponing the same under s 14(1)(b).

E.   Preparatory Steps for a POCA Hearing

Section 16 statements of information

8.109   Under s 16(1) of POCA if the court is proceeding under s 6(3)(a) (where the prosecutor has asked the court to proceed under the confiscation provisions), the prosecutor must provide the court with a statement of information, within 'any period' that the court orders. Section 16 is set out in Appendix 1.

Alternatively, if the court is proceeding under s 6(3)(b) (where the court believed it **8.110** was appropriate to proceed to a confiscation hearing without an invitation from the prosecutor), it may order the prosecutor to give it a statement of information, and the prosecutor must present such a statement within the time frame the court orders (see s 16(2)).

It is important to note that s 16 statements may only be ordered if the court is proceedings **8.111** under s 6, and not if the court has decided to postpone the confiscation proceedings under s 14(1)(b).

The purpose of section 16 statements

Section 16(3) provides that if the prosecutor believes the defendant has a criminal lifestyle, **8.112** the statement of information should include matters the prosecutor believes are relevant in connection with deciding the following issues:

(a) whether the defendant has a criminal lifestyle;
(b) whether he has benefited from his general criminal conduct;
(c) his benefit from the conduct.

The prosecutor's statement serves a number of purposes. Firstly, it enables the defence and **8.113** the court to be put on notice of the Crown's case and prevent the defence from being taken by surprise. Secondly, it identifies the real issues in terms of the Crown's case, thereby saving court time in relation to matters that are not really disputed. In *R v Comiskey* (1991) 93 Cr App R 227, Turner J, in delivering the judgment of the Court, said (at p 231): 'it is very desirable that those responsible for the prosecution of offences should make full use of this (section)' (when dealing with the use of the corresponding s 11 statements under the DTA).

The Court of Appeal considered the purpose of the prosecutor's statement in *R v Benjafield* **8.114** (2001) 2 Cr App R(S) 221, at para 107. In finding that such statements did not contravene Art 6 of the European Convention of Human Rights the Court held that:

> A statement serves the useful purpose of forewarning the defendant of the case of the prosecution which he will have to meet as to his assets. It should assist the defendant by making clear the matters with which he has to be prepared to deal. It is right that, as the rules require, the prosecution should identify any information which would assist the defendant.

The content of section 16 statements

Under s 16 of POCA, the prosecutor should give to the court a statement with as much **8.115** relevant detail as possible relating to the defendant's benefit from criminal conduct. It should achieve what it says on the can, namely it should be a 'statement of information'.

The actual content of the statement will partly depend on whether the prosecutor alleges **8.116** the defendant has had a criminal lifestyle. Under s 16(4), the statement should include information relevant to the making of the assumptions if the prosecutor believes that the defendant has had a criminal lifestyle.

If the prosecutor does not believe the defendant has had a criminal lifestyle, the statement **8.117** of information becomes a statement of matters the prosecutor believes are relevant in deciding whether or not the defendant has benefited from his *particular* criminal conduct and, if so, his benefit from that conduct (see s 16(5)).

8.118 Under r 58.1 of the Criminal Procedure Rules (CrimPR), when the prosecutor is required under s 16 of the Act to give a statement to the Crown Court, the prosecutor must also, as soon as practicable, serve a copy of the statement on the defendant. Any statement given to the Crown Court by the prosecutor under s 16 of the Act must, in addition to the information required by the Act, include the following information, pursuant to r 58.1(2) of the CrimPR:

(1) the name of the defendant;
(2) the name of the person by whom the statement is made and the date on which it is made; and
(3) where the statement is not given to the Crown Court immediately after the defendant has been convicted, the date on which, and the place where the relevant conviction occurred.

8.119 It will be noted, pursuant to r 57.7 of the CrimPR, that witness statements should be verified with a statement of truth in confiscation proceedings.

8.120 In practice, the statement of information will ordinarily include:

i. an outline of the nature of the offence(s) that the defendant has been convicted of, together with references to the indictment, the factual background, the date of conviction, any sentence that has been passed, and the timetable for confiscation;

ii. a portrait of the defendant himself, including age, address, marital status, and dependants. This will also include reference to previous occupations, income derived from the same, and any previous relevant convictions;

iii. the history of any restraint order proceedings, including whether a receiver has been appointed;

iv. the extent of the benefit alleged, and whether the case is one of general or particular criminal conduct. This will often include reference to admissions made at trial or the evidence given. It may also extend to relevant sentencing remarks and the basis of plea;

v. if a general criminal conduct matter, or a lifestyle offence, reference to the assumptions that the court is being invited to draw;

vi. the nature of the assets the Crown maintains are realisable. Whilst there is no duty upon the Crown to prove the available amount (formerly the 'realisable assets') it is clearly helpful if it refers to what is known in terms of the defendant's property and wealth;

v. the extent of any allegation of hidden assets and the basis for such a belief;

vi. the amount of the confiscation order the Crown is seeking;

vi. occasionally statements of information will make reference to decided case law or the statute itself.

A duty of full and frank disclosure?

8.121 If the prosecutor believes that the defendant has a criminal lifestyle, the statement must include information relevant to the making of the assumptions (s 16(4)). To avoid criticism of the Crown, it is suggested that the statement should also include information about matters known to the prosecutor that might contribute to the court concluding that making an assumption would amount to a serious risk of injustice.

The financial investigation

The financial investigator has a number of tools upon which he can call when conducting **8.122**
his enquiry. These include:

- Production Orders—s 345 of POCA, requiring disclosure of information;
- Account Monitoring Orders—s 370 of POCA, placing an ongoing duty on financial institutions to provide information for a period of up to 90 days from the day on which it is made;
- Customer Information Orders—s 364 of POCA, requiring a financial institution to provide any customer information in relation to a specified individual;
- Search and Seizure Warrants—s 352 of POCA, giving power to the court to make warrants authorising officers to enter premises and seize material likely to be of substantial value to the investigation, where a production order has been made and not complied with.

When should the section 16 statement be served?

Under s 16(1) and (2) the prosecutor must give the statement of information to the court **8.123**
'within the period the Court orders'. It is submitted, however, that in matters flowing from criminal trials the best practice is to serve the s 16 statement prior to said trial whenever possible and, except in the most complex cases, not later than the return of the jury. This will enable the trial judge to be in the best possible position to give directions as to how the POCA enquiry should proceed after conviction or a timely guilty plea.

Upon whom should the prosecutor's statement be served?

Section 16(1) of POCA states that the statement of information must be given to the court. **8.124**
At the same time as the court orders a statement to be prepared, it may also direct that a copy be served on the defendant and/or the defendant's solicitors.

There is no requirement in the CrimPR that a statement should be served on solicitors **8.125**
acting on behalf of the co-accused. This is possibly because statements frequently disclose personal matters relating to the defendant's financial affairs and exhibit his disclosure statements sworn in compliance with a restraint order. Because it is in the public interest that the defendant should be encouraged to make full and frank disclosure of all his realisable property in such statements, it is suggested that he is not likely to do so if the statement was to come into the hands of third parties.

The defendant's statement

Section 17 of POCA reads as follows: **8.126**

(1) If the Prosecutor gives the Court a Statement of Information and a copy is served on the defendant, the Court may order the defendant—
   (a) to indicate (within the period it orders) the extent to which he accepts each allegation in the statement, and
   (b) so far as he does not accept such an allegation to give particulars of any matters he proposes to rely on.

The purpose of s 17 is to identify areas of dispute for the confiscation hearing, so that evidence may be adduced only in relation to the disputed points, thus narrowing the issues and saving court time. Under r 58.1 of the CrimPR where, under s 17 of the Act, the Crown Court orders the defendant to indicate the extent to which he accepts each allegation in a statement given by the prosecutor, the defendant must state in writing his position and provide a copy to the Crown Court. One of the other purposes of s 17 is to avoid the defendant ambushing the Crown by not disclosing in advance what his case is. In addition, s 17(1) anticipates giving the prosecution the opportunity of making enquiries into the correctness of the defendant's assertions.

8.127   Once again it is important to note that a defence statement under s 17 may only be triggered if the court gives a statement of information and the court is therefore proceeding under s 6, and not if the court has decided to postpone the confiscation proceedings under s 14(1)(b).

8.128   When considering s 17(1)(a), the defence should consider the prosecutor's statement paragraph by paragraph and state whether each allegation is admitted or denied. (This is analogous to a defence in civil proceedings and a similar approach should be adopted when drafting the defendant's statement.) Where an allegation is denied, any facts relied upon to support that denial should be fully set out, with exhibits/evidence if necessary. The statement should also be verified by a statement of truth (r 57.7 of the CrimPR).

8.129   The importance of obtaining independent corroboration of the defendant's assertions cannot be overemphasised. In *R v Walbrook and Glasgow* [1994] Crim LR 613, the Court of Appeal held that where a defendant wanted to show that the amount of his realisable assets available for confiscation was less than the amount of his benefit as certified by the court, he had to produce clear and cogent evidence; 'vague and generalised assertions unsupported by evidence would rarely if ever be sufficient'.

8.130   It must also be remembered that at this stage the defendant is likely to stand convicted of an offence, whether by guilty plea or by the verdict of a jury, and may therefore have something of a credibility problem.

Defendant's acceptance conclusive

8.131   Under s 17(2) of POCA, if the defendant accepts to any extent an allegation in the statement of information, the court may treat his acceptance as conclusive of the matters to which it relates for the purpose of deciding the issues referred to in s 16(3) (general criminal conduct) or s 16(5) (particular criminal conduct), as the case may be. Great care therefore should be taken only to admit assertions made in the prosecutor's statement that are genuinely accepted.

8.132   It should be noted, however, that the defendant's acceptance will not necessarily be binding on appeal. In the case of *R v Emmett* [1997] 3 WLR 1119, a DTOA case, the defendant pleaded guilty at the Crown Court stage. It was agreed between counsel that the benefit figure amounted to £100,000 and various sums were agreed in respect of his realisable assets. The judge made an agreed confiscation order. In the Court of Appeal the Crown submitted that the general right to appeal against a confiscation order was excluded by virtue of the DTOA's corresponding provision to s 17(2) of POCA, following the defendant's acceptance of any allegation in a statement tendered by the prosecutor which had been acted upon by the court. However, the Court of Appeal ruled that there was a strong presumption that, except by specific provision, the legislature will not exclude a right of appeal as of right, or with leave, where such a right is ordinarily available (as per *R v Cain* [1985] AC 46, 55g–56d). In *Emmett* Lord Steyn held that unless the Act expressly or by necessary implication excluded a right of appeal, there is, as a matter of jurisdiction, a right of appeal against a confiscation order in all cases. However, he went on to state, at p 1123, that:

> it is of course true that if there is an appeal, the Court of Appeal may have to take account of the fact that a Judge has decided to treat an acceptance of an allegation in a prosecution statement as conclusive, and the Court of Appeal may have to give proper and due weight to that consideration.

Failure to respond by the defendant

If the defendant fails in any respect to comply with an order under s 17(1) he may be **8.133** treated, under s 17(3), as having accepted every allegation in the statement of information, apart from:

(a) any allegation in respect of which he has complied with the requirement;
(b) any allegation that he has benefited from his general or particular criminal conduct.

Thus, if the defendant fails to respond to a statement of fact in relation to his assets or the available amount, that fact may be deemed by the court to be true.

However, there should not be any automatic assumption that the defendant has accepted **8.134** an allegation that he has benefited from general or particular criminal conduct. This is because, at the time this legislation was introduced, and as part of the explanatory notes that accompanied POCA, it was considered inappropriate that the defendant's silence should be conclusive of the two principal issues before the court.

Consequences of the defendant failing to respond to the prosecutor's statement

The defendant who fails to respond to orders of the court made under s 17 of POCA runs **8.135** the risk of having a confiscation order made in the full amount of the benefit figure as alleged by the prosecution.

In *R v Comiskey* (1991) 93 Cr App R 227, the Court of Appeal held that once the prosecu- **8.136** tion have proved benefit, the burden then passes to the defendant to show, on a balance of probabilities, the value of his realisable property was less than this sum. If he fails to discharge that burden, the court must make a confiscation order in the full amount by which it has certified he has benefited from his crime.

As a result, the Court of Appeal has shown a reluctance to interfere with confiscation orders **8.137** made in circumstances where the defendant has failed to respond to the prosecutor's statement and has failed to give evidence at the confiscation hearing.

In *R v Layode* (Unreported, CA, 12 March 1993) the defendant failed to respond to the **8.138** prosecutor's financial statement or give evidence at the confiscation hearing. The Court of Appeal dismissed the defendant's appeal against the confiscation order. McPhearson J, in delivering the judgment of the court, observed that:

> if the Judge was wrong about the realisable assets and the bank accounts, the Appellant had nobody but himself to blame in this regard.

He added that the case underlined the importance of a defendant submitting evidence.

Disclosure evidence inadmissible: section 17(6)

8.139   A potential danger arises if information is passed to the criminal case team before or during the trial that reveals matters contained within the defendant's disclosure statement, following disclosure ordered pursuant to a restraint order. The prosecutor must be alert to the fact that such disclosure is protected from cross examination by the Crown, pursuant to the restraint order itself and *Re O (Restraint Order)* [1991] 2 QB 520, 530 (CA); *Re C (Restraint Order: Identification)* The Times, 24 April 1995; *Re C (Restraint Order: Disclosure)* (4 September 2000) (DTA 7/2000) at paras 42, 43; and *Re D* [2001] EWHC Admin 668.

8.140   A similar danger may arise if the prosecutor was allowed to utilise disclosures made in a defendant's reply to a s 16 statement, particularly if the trial were on-going or further trials were anticipated. As a result some protection is included within POCA. Under s 17(6):

> No acceptance under section 17 (the defendant's response to the prosecutor's statement) that the defendant has benefited from criminal conduct is admissible in evidence in proceedings for an offence.

8.141   This protection is also given to witness statements generally in POCA matters by r 57.8 of the CrimPR, although r 57.8 does not apply where:

   (a)   the witness gives consent in writing to some other use of it;
   (b)   the Crown Court gives permission for some other use; or
   (c)   the witness statement has been put in evidence at a hearing held in public.

The problem of self-incrimination

8.142   One of the purposes of s 17(6) is to prevent the defendant invoking his privilege against self-incrimination as a justification for failing to respond to a prosecutor's statement. This provision is analogous to the condition which disclosure orders are made in restraint order cases and which are designed to protect the defendant's privilege against self-incrimination.

8.143   The purpose of a s 17 defendant's statement in response is not to assist the prosecution to advance their case. However, the reality, it is suggested, is that there will often be an overlap between the criminal investigation and preparation for the confiscation hearing, particularly in criminal cases involving financial investigations, and often to the detriment of the defendant (see *Re J* [2001] EWHC Admin 713 at para 20 challenging *R v Martin and White* (1998) 2 Cr App R 385, and *Re C (Restraint Order: Disclosure)*, (4 September 2000) (DTA/7/2000); and on self incrimination: *Re E and Re H* [2001] EWHC Admin 472; *Istel v Tully* [1993] AC 45 at pp 55–57; and *Re: T (Restraint Order: Disclosure of Assets)* (1993) 96 Cr App R 194).

8.144   Section 17(6) is intended to encourage the defendant to be more forthcoming in his disclosure, whereas if the protection afforded by s 17(6) did not exist, the defendant may be reluctant to admit benefit from criminal conduct that had not been the subject of a prosecution.

Further provision of information by the defendant

8.145   Section 18 of POCA makes the obligations on the defendant yet more onerous. Section 18 applies either where the court is proceeding under s 6 of POCA in a matter where s 6(3)(a) applies (namely where the prosecutor has asked the court to proceed) or where s 6(3)(b) applies (where the court believes it is appropriate to do so).

Section 18(2) enables the court to order the defendant to provide information 'at any time' **8.146** for the purpose of assisting the court to carry out its confiscatory function.

Under r 58.1(4) of the CrimPR, where the Crown Court orders the defendant to give to **8.147** it any information under s 18 of the Act, the defendant must provide the information in writing and must, as soon as practicable, serve a copy of it on the prosecutor.

The primary purpose of s 18 is to allow the court to make an order where the defendant is **8.148** relying, or has relied, on certain matters, and the court considers it requires more information to assist it in determining the point in question.

It would appear that because s 18 is triggered when the court is proceeding under s 6 it may **8.149** not exercise its s 18 powers in circumstances where it has postponed the confiscation proceedings, unless it can be argued that it requires the information to determine whether it should now entertain proceedings itself under s 6.

If the defendant fails to comply with the court's order, without reasonable excuse, **8.150** s 18(4) allows the court to draw any inference it believes appropriate. Section 18(5) states that:

> Subsection 4 does not affect any power of the Court to deal with the defendant in respect of a failure to comply with an order under this section.

For example, the court's power to punish the defendant for contempt of court in refusing to comply with the order would exist in addition to the court's power to draw an inference or rely on an assumption as a result of the defendant's failure to comply.

It will be noted that pursuant to r 57.7 of the CrimPR, statements provided should bear a **8.151** statement of truth.

In terms of the type of information the court may require to assist it with its functions, there **8.152** can be no exhaustive list, but examples would include:

(a) particulars of any sources of income, including bequests;
(b) identification of all bank and building society accounts, whether jointly or solely held;
(c) particulars of any real property in which the defendant holds an interest;
(d) details of any unit trusts, bonds, shares, or debentures the defendant holds an interest in;
(e) details of any cash held and from where it was sourced;
(f) particulars of any motor vehicles, boats, works of art, livestock, or jewellery owned;
(g) details of any safe deposit boxes held;
(h) details of all charge and credit cards held;
(i) details of any other transfers made to or from the defendant in the previous six years.

Further protection against self-incrimination

Section 18(9) contains a similar provision to that in s 17(6), in that it protects the defendant **8.153** from incriminating himself and others in the making of any admission or reply to s 18. However, if the information disclosed leads the prosecuting authority to other new information or evidence, s 18 does not appear to prevent the authorities from using that other evidence.

Prosecutor's acceptance conclusive

8.154   Under s 18(6) of POCA, any acceptance by the prosecutor of any assertion contained in a defendant's statement may be treated by the court as being conclusive for the purposes of the POCA enquiry.

Failure to provide the information ordered

8.155   The position of a defendant who fails to provide information under s 18(2) of POCA is dealt with in s 18(4) which provides as follows:

> If the Defendant fails without reasonable excuse to comply with an order under this section the Court may draw such inference as it believes is appropriate.

Further statements by the prosecutor

8.156   Section 16(6) provides:

> (6) If the Prosecutor gives the Court a statement of information—
> (a) he may at any time give the Court a further statement of information;
> (b) he must give the Court a further statement of information if it orders him to do so and he must give it within the period the Court orders.

A practice developed under the DTA and the CJA 1988 of the prosecutor submitting a further statement if there were matters in the defendant's statement with which he disagreed or which called for further comment. Section 16(6) of POCA endorses this practice and provides for a further statement to be tendered by the prosecutor either acting on his own volition or in compliance with an order of the court.

Securing the attendance of witnesses

8.157   Once s 16 and s 17 statements have been served, the parties should advise each other of which witnesses they require at the hearing. It should be borne in mind that certain civilian witnesses, especially those employed by financial institutions, may not be prepared to attend the court voluntarily. In such cases witness summonses should be sought from the appropriate officer of the Crown Court.

Expert evidence

8.158   The procedure to be followed for adducing expert evidence in confiscation hearings and the exceptions to same are set out in rr 57.9 and 57.10 of the CrimPR.

Service of documents

8.159   The procedure relating to the service of documents in relation to Pt 2 of POCA is set out in r 57.11 of the CrimPR. The procedure for alternative service and service outside of the jurisdiction is contained in rr 57.12 and 57.13 of the CrimPR respectively.

An example timetable for confiscation

8.160   While each case will always have its own peculiar attributes and many cases may begin with a s 18 order against the defendant, a typical timetable and directions towards confiscation, may look something like this:

A FAILURE TO ADDRESS AN ALLEGATION IN A STATEMENT OF INFORMATION MAY LEAD TO THE COURT TREATING SUCH A FAILURE AS AN ACCEPTANCE OF THE MATTERS SET OUT THEREIN. A FAILURE TO COMPLY WITH THIS ORDER WITHOUT REASONABLE EXCUSE MAY LEAD THE COURT TO DRAW SUCH INFERENCES AS IT CONSIDERS APPROPRIATE.

IN THE CROWN COURT

SITTING IN TORBAY

R V ALFREDO GERMONT

_____

DIRECTIONS IN RELATION TO CONFISCATION

_____

UPON HEARING [COUNSEL] on behalf of the Crown

AND UPON HEARING [COUNSEL] on behalf of the Defendant

AND UPON the request of the Crown that confiscation proceedings be instituted and the Court proceeding pursuant to section 6 of the Proceeds of Crime Act 2002 –

IT IS ORDERED THAT:

1. The confiscation hearing shall be heard on Monday 5th July 2010, time estimate 5 days.
2. By 4pm on Friday 12th February 2010, the Crown shall serve upon the Defendant and the Court a statement of information in this matter, including any evidence and exhibits upon which it seeks to rely in a paginated bundle. Said statement shall include:
   i. Whether the Crown believes the Defendant has a criminal lifestyle and the basis for that belief;
   ii. The amount alleged to be the Defendant's benefit from his criminal conduct;
   iii. (If applicable) any information relevant to the making or otherwise of the required assumptions;
   iv. Any other information the Crown considers relevant to the issue of benefit;
   v. Any information the Crown considers relevant to the issue of the available amount; whether hidden assets are being alleged, the basis for that belief; and the amount the Crown has identified as realisable (if any).
3. By 4pm on Friday 12th March 2010 the Defendant shall serve on the Crown and the Court a response to the Crown's statement of information, in a witness statement bearing a statement of truth. Said statement shall include any evidence and exhibits upon which he seeks to rely in a paginated bundle and:
   i. Indicate the extent to which he accepts each allegation in the Crown's statement of information;
   ii. Where he does not accept an allegation, give particulars of any matters he proposes to rely upon;
   iii. Give details of any available assets to meet any confiscation order that may be made, and if assets identified by the Crown are not available, give an explanation for the same.
4. By 4pm on Friday 2nd April 2010 the Crown shall serve on the Defendant and the Court a reply (if any) to the Defendant's statement. Said reply shall include a supplementary statement of information and any further evidence and exhibits upon which it seeks to rely in a paginated bundle.

5. By 4pm on Friday 16th April 2010 the Defendant shall serve on the Crown and the Court any further statement or evidence upon which he seeks to rely (if any), including any further evidence and exhibits in a paginated bundle.

6. By 4pm on Friday 30th April 2010 the Defendant and the Crown shall exchange witness requirements, and notify the Court accordingly.

7. By 4pm on Friday 21st May 2010 the Defendant and the Crown shall serve any skeleton arguments upon which they seek to rely, upon each other and the Court, together with authorities. Said skeleton arguments shall also indicate the main areas of dispute and/or agreement between the parties, and shall include any admissions that may be made.

8. By 4pm on Friday 4th June 2010 the Defendant and the Crown shall serve any reply to the skeleton arguments served, upon each other and the Court, together with any authorities upon which they seek to rely.

9. By no later than 4pm on Friday 11th June 2010 the Defendant and the Crown shall notify the court list office if there has been any change to the time estimate in this matter.

10. Permission to apply.

11. Costs reserved.

By the Court

This 5th day of February 2010

9

THE CONFISCATION HEARING

A. Introduction

9.01 Whether the hearing is under the Proceeds of Crime Act 2002 (POCA), the Drug Trafficking Act 1994 (DTA), or the Criminal Justice Act 1988 (CJA 1988), the purpose of the confiscation hearing remains very similar. It is to determine:

(a) whether or not the defendant has financially benefited from the offence(s) that he has been convicted of;

(b) the amount of that benefit; and

(c) the value of the defendant's assets that are available to meet any confiscation order that may be made.

9.02 In the Chapter 8 we considered the steps that are generally taken when preparing for a confiscation hearing. In this chapter we look at what is likely to take place during the confiscation hearing itself. We also consider some of the problems that regularly arise, with reference to the ever-growing body of case law.

9.03 The transitional arrangements introduced following the commencement of POCA anticipate that offences committed before the effective date of the legislation, namely 24 March 2003, should remain under the DTA or the CJA 1988 (SI 2003/333). For the purposes of this third edition, we have focused almost exclusively on POCA as opposed to the two preceding Acts. This is because during the lifetime of this edition some 10 years will have elapsed since the passing of POCA. The effects of the transitional provisions are therefore now considerably diluted, with the vast majority of cases now falling squarely within the scope of POCA. For cases where the DTA or CJA 1988 do still apply, the second edition of this work gives a detailed commentary on the practice and procedure to be followed. However, in terms of general practice, this chapter should still be of assistance, not least because we refer to the case law that had developed under the DTA and the CJA 1988 that still remains persuasive under POCA. A best practice guide is set out at para 9.224 and a recent case digest is at para 9.223.

Steps to confiscation: a summary

The legislation sets out a step-by-step process that will lead to the making of the confisca- **9.04**
tion order. In the last chapter we set out that process up to the time of the hearing. In terms
of the steps that happen next the following may provide a helpful summary:

1. *Mandatory effect.* The Crown Court must proceed to determine a confiscation application if the defendant is convicted of an offence before the court and the prosecution ask
   the court to proceed or it decides to do so of its own motion (ss 6(1),6(2)(a) and 6(3)(a)
   of POCA).

2. *Standard of proof on all issues.* In order to determine whether the defendant has benefited
   from his criminal conduct, the court must decide the issue on the balance of probabilities (s 6(7)).

3. *Value.* The determination of the 'value' of each piece of property must be carried out in
   accordance with ss 79 and 80. Section 79(1) and (2) provides that the value of the property is its 'market value'.

Particular criminal conduct cases

4. *Not a general criminal conduct case: so has the defendant benefited?* If the court has determined that the defendant has not had a criminal lifestyle, it must decide whether the
   defendant has benefited from his particular criminal conduct, (s 6(4)(c));

5. *Was it an acquisitive offence?* In order to determine whether the defendant has benefited
   from his particular criminal conduct/the offence concerned, the court must resolve
   whether the defendant received property as a result of or in connection with the conduct
   or obtained a pecuniary advantage as a result of or in connection with the conduct
   (which is equated to a sum of money equal to that advantage) (s 76(5)).

6. *What was the defendant's benefit?* The benefit is the value of the property (including
   money) obtained (ss 76(3)(a), 76(4) and (5) and s 76(7));

7. *What is the recoverable amount?* The amount of the confiscation order is a sum equal to
   the defendant's benefit from the conduct, unless the defendant shows that the available
   amount, which is all his free property together with any tainted gifts, is less than that
   sum (ss 7(1), 7(2), 9(1));

General criminal conduct cases

8. *What constitutes a criminal lifestyle?* The court must find that the defendant had a
   criminal lifestyle if the offence concerned is specified in Sch 2 of POCA or if it constitutes conduct forming part of a course of criminal activity or it is an acquisitive
   offence committed over a period of at least 6 months (s 75(2), s 6(4)(a)) (considered in
   Chapter 8);

9. *Has the defendant benefited from his offending?* The court must then decide whether
   the defendant has benefited (essentially financially) from his general criminal conduct
   (s 6(4)(b), s 76(1) and (2)).

10. *What is the amount of the benefit?* A person benefits from conduct if he obtains property
    (money or other real property) as a result or in connection with the conduct (s 76(4));

11. *Apply the assumptions.* If the court decides the defendant has benefited from general
    criminal conduct, it must make the assumptions set out in s 10. The assumptions are
    not to be made if they or part are shown to be incorrect or a serious risk of injustice may
    arise (ss 10(1), (2), (6));

12. *What is the recoverable amount?* The amount of the confiscation order is a sum equal to
    the defendant's benefit from the conduct, unless the defendant shows that the available

amount, which is all his free property together with any tainted gifts, is less than that sum (ss 6(5)(a), 7(1), 7(2), 9(1));

Sentencing

13. Having determined the recoverable amount, the court must:
    a. *Give its reasons.* Once the court has decided the available amount, it must include in the confiscation order a statement of its findings as to the matters relevant for deciding that amount.(s 7(5)).
    b. *Set a time for payment,* which must be immediate unless the defendant can show further time is required, in which case the period must not exceed 6 months (a period which can be extended, on application, to a maximum of 12 months in exceptional circumstances) (s 11(3),(4));
    c. *Set a period of imprisonment in default of payment* (s 38(2) POCA and s 139(4) PCC(S)A).

A further 'shopping list' of best practice is set out at para 9.224.

Understanding confiscation

9.05 Recent authorities have established a number of principles, which relate to the purpose of the confiscation of assets generally:

(a) Confiscation orders are designed to deter those who consider embarking upon criminal conduct (see *R v Rezvi* (2002) 2 Cr App R(S) 70).

(b) Confiscation orders are designed to deprive a person of profits received from criminal conduct and to remove the value of the proceeds received from criminal conduct from possible future use in criminal conduct (see *Re T (Restraint Order: Disclosure of Assets)* [1992] 1 WLR 949; *R v Tivnan* (1999) 1 Cr App R(S) 92).

(c) Confiscation orders are designed essentially to impoverish defendants, not to enrich the Crown (*Re P (Restraint Order: Sale of Asset)*, [2000] 1 WLR 473).

(d) Confiscation orders are a penalty and are a measure to which Art 1 of Protocol 1 of the European Convention on Human Rights (ECHR) is applicable (see *Welch v UK* (1995) 20 EHRR 247).

9.06 In *R v Levin* The Times, 20 February 2004 the Court of Appeal confirmed:

(1) the court could make far-reaching assumptions;

(2) the court could require the defendant to provide information and could draw inferences from the failure to do so; and

(3) the court might rely on evidence given at trial and any relevant information properly obtained either before the trial or thereafter in order to determine a defendant's benefit and the amount to be recovered;

(4) these factors did and were intended to separate the confiscation proceedings from the criminal proceedings.

Purpose

9.07 In *R v Forte* [2004] EWCA Crim 3188, the Court stated (at para 9):

It has been argued, in this court and in the House of Lords, that the legislation operates unfairly. The House of Lords has emphasised, in particular in the recent case of *Cadman-Smith*

(2002) 2 Cr App R (S) 37, that the legislation has to be considered as having a dual purpose. It is aimed at depriving offenders of the proceeds of their criminal conduct, and it is also an act which has the purpose of punishing convicted offenders in order to deter the commission of further offences so as to reduce the profits available to fund further criminal enterprises. In that respect it is therefore described as penal, or indeed draconian in its operation.

Interpretation: confiscation and POCA

We have already set out in Chapter 8 what may be considered the 'basics' of confiscation **9.08** under POCA (para 8.52). By way of easy reference, the relevant statutory provisions are as follows:

Criminal lifestyle—s 75
Conduct and benefit—s 76
Tainted gifts—s 77
Gifts and their recipients—s 78
Value: the basic rule—s 79
Value of property obtained from conduct—s 80
Value of tainted gifts—s 81
Free property—s 82
Realisable property—s 83
Property: general provisions—s 84
Proceedings—s 85
Confiscation orders—s 87
Other interpretative provisions—s 88

The importance of following the provisions of POCA

The House of Lords decisions in *R v May* [2008] UKHL 28, *CPS v Jennings* [2008] UKHL **9.09** 29, and *R v Green* [2008] UKHL 30 contain authoritative statements of principle on the definition of 'benefit' for the purposes of the confiscation legislation, and on apportionment between co-conspirators. The leading case is *May* (cited in the other two decisions), but both *Jennings* and *Green* also contain important statements on the way forward in terms of confiscation. All three cases were decided by a single joint opinion of the Law Lords, delivered by Lord Bingham.

The House emphasised repeatedly the need to focus on the statutory language and not **9.10** on judicial pronouncements. Emphasis was placed on the centrality of the evidence (ie evidence before the judge conducting the confiscation hearing), with particular emphasis on the role that the defendant played and the way in which he obtained the money or property that he held or holds. Key considerations include whether the defendant had or has some power of control or disposition over the property in question, or whether he held or holds the property on his own behalf or jointly on behalf of himself and others or whether a pecuniary advantage was obtained (ie the defendant evades a liability to which he is personally subject).

The findings of the House of Lords in *May* and the subsequently decided Court of **9.11** Appeal decisions are considered in some detail in this chapter. They are essential reading for practitioners who aspire to a better understanding of this area of the law. A case digest of recent decisions following *May* can be found at para 9.223.

Summary: *May, Jennings,* and *Green*

9.12 The House of Lords in *May* included at para 48 what is described as an 'endnote'. This contains a concise, yet important, restatement of the relevant principles:

1. The legislation is intended to deprive defendants of the benefit they have gained from relevant criminal conduct, whether or not they have retained such benefit, within the limits of their available means. It does not provide for confiscation in the sense understood by schoolchildren and others, but nor does it operate by way of fine. The benefit gained is the total value of the property or advantage obtained, not the defendant's net profit after deduction of expenses or any amounts payable to co-conspirators.

2. The court should proceed by asking three questions posed above:
   (i) Has the defendant (D) benefited from relevant criminal conduct?
   (ii) If so, what is the value of the benefit D has so obtained?
   (iii) What sum is recoverable from D?

   Where issues of criminal lifestyle arise the questions must be modified. These are separate questions calling for separate answers, and the questions and answers must not be elided.

3. In addressing these questions the court must first establish the facts as best it can on the material available, relying as appropriate on the statutory assumptions. In very many cases the factual findings made will be decisive.

4. In addressing the questions the court should focus very closely on the language of the statutory provision in question in the context of the statute and in the light of any statutory definition. The language used is not arcane or obscure and any judicial gloss or exegesis should be viewed with caution. Guidance should ordinarily be sought in the statutory language rather than in the proliferating case law.

5. In determining, under the 2002 Act, whether D has obtained property or a pecuniary advantage and, if so, the value of any property or advantage so obtained, the court should (subject to any relevant statutory definition) apply ordinary common law principles to the facts as found. The exercise of this jurisdiction involves no departure from familiar rules governing entitlement and ownership. While the answering of the third question calls for inquiry into the financial resources of D at the date of the determination, the answering of the first two questions plainly calls for a historical inquiry into past transactions.

6. D ordinarily obtains property if in law he owns it, whether alone or jointly, which will ordinarily connote a power of disposition or control, as where a person directs a payment or conveyance of property to someone else. He ordinarily obtains a pecuniary advantage if (among other things) he evades a liability to which he is personally subject. Mere couriers or custodians or other very minor contributors to an offence, rewarded by a specific fee and having no interest in the property or the proceeds of sale, are unlikely to be found to have obtained that property. It may be otherwise with money launderers.

9.13 The Court of Appeal in *R v Sivaraman* [2008] EWCA Crim 1736 also set out a number of statements of principle, derived from the *May, Jennings,* and *Green* cases:

i. The legislation is intended to deprive the defendants of the benefit they have gained from the relevant conduct within the limits of their available means. It does not operate by way of fine: *May*, paragraph 48(1); *Jennings*, paragraph 13.

ii. The benefit gained is the total value of the property or pecuniary advantage obtained, not the particular defendant's net profit: *May*, paragraph 48(1).

iii. In considering what is the value of the benefit which the defendant has obtained, the court should focus on the language of the statute and apply its ordinary meaning (subject to any statutory definition) to the facts of the case: *May*, paragraph 48(3) and (4); *Jennings* paragraph 13.

iv. 'Obtained' means obtained by the relevant defendant: *Jennings*, paragraph 14.

v. A defendant's acts may contribute significantly to property, or to a pecuniary advantage, being obtained without that defendant obtaining it: *Jennings*, paragraph 14.

vi. Where two or more defendants obtain property jointly, each is to be regarded as obtaining the whole of it. Where property is received by one conspirator, what matters is the capacity in which he receives it, that is whether for his own personal benefit, or on behalf of others, or jointly on behalf of himself and others. This has to be decided on the evidence: *Green*, paragraph 15. By parity of reasoning, two or more defendants may or may not obtain a joint pecuniary advantage; it depends on the facts.

B. A Mandatory Regime

Section 6 sets out the circumstances in which confiscation orders may be made under **9.14** Pt 2 of POCA. It is a mandatory regime. A confiscation order under s 6 is an order for a convicted defendant to pay a sum of money representing the defendant's benefit from crime. Section 6 is considered more fully in Chapter 8.

The principal points, however, are as follows: **9.15**

(1) The Crown Court must proceed under s 6 if the following two conditions are satisfied:
   (a) the defendant falls within s 6(2) (ie he is convicted of an offence or offences in proceedings before the Crown Court; or he is committed to the Crown Court for sentence by a magistrates' court under ss 3, 4, or 6 of the Powers of Criminal Courts (Sentencing) Act 2000 (PCC(S)A); or he is committed to the Crown Court in respect of an offence or offences under s 70 of POCA (committal with a view to a confiscation order being made));
   (b) the prosecutor has asked the court to proceed under s 6 or the court believes it is appropriate to do so.

(2) Once the above is satisfied, the court must proceed in the following way:
   (a) it must decide whether the defendant has a criminal lifestyle;
   (b) if it decides that he has a criminal lifestyle it must decide whether he has benefited from his general criminal conduct;
   (c) if it decides that he does not have a criminal lifestyle it must decide whether he has benefited from his particular criminal conduct (s 6(4)).

(3) If the court decides under s 6(4)(b) or (c) that the defendant has benefited from either general or particular criminal conduct it must:
   (a) decide the recoverable amount; and
   (b) make an order (the confiscation order) requiring him to pay that amount (as per s 6(5)).

(4) Under s 6(6), the court must treat the duty to make a confiscation order in s 6(5) as a power (an option) if it believes that any victim of the conduct has at any time started or intends to start proceedings against the defendant in respect of loss, injury, or damage

sustained in connection with the conduct. By s 6(6), discretion is invested in the court to dispense with deciding the recoverable amount and making an order, but only in circumstances where it appears the victim of the offence is seeking through the courts some form of restitution for the offence committed (see Chapter 8). Section 7(3) specifies how the court should approach the recoverable amount in such circumstances.

9.16 The mandatory nature of confiscation orders is further considered in *R v Brack* [2007] EWCA Crim 1205 and *R v Hockey* [2007] EWCA Crim 1577.

Confiscation orders made by magistrates' courts

9.17 Section 97 of SOCPA allows for provision to be made for magistrates' courts to make confiscation orders under Pt 2 or 4 of POCA. Section 97(2) provides that the power of the magistrates' courts to make a confiscation order is subject to a restriction that the amount does not exceed £10,000. Whilst introduced five years ago, the actual provisions have, at the time of writing, yet to be implemented, although we understand that steps are now being taken to rectify this. Orders above this amount can only therefore be made by the Crown Court (see Chapter 8, para 8.35).

Basis of pleas

9.18 Care should be taken when drafting and agreeing to basis of pleas, particularly on behalf of the prosecution. See *R v Lunnon* (2005) 1 Cr App R(S) 24 and *R v Lazarus* [2005] Crim LR 64, where the Court of Appeal (Hughes J) stated:

> In some cases the Crown may be in a position to make the kind of express acknowledgment that was made in Lunnon, that the indicated offence is the defendant's first involvement in relevant crime, and to do so knowing that that acknowledgment will be carried forward into confiscation proceedings. In other cases . . . the Crown may be able to say no more than that for the purposes of sentence it does not and cannot dispute a particular assertion made by the defendant, but that it cannot say what information may arise in any subsequent confiscation proceedings . . . We have no doubt that the Crown ought, as a matter of good practice, when responding to a basis of plea which is advanced in a case where confiscation proceedings might follow, to bear in mind the question of whether it will be asking for a confiscation enquiry to be made and, if so, what if any admission is now being made which will apply to that enquiry.

9.19 In *R v Byatt* [2006] EWCA Crim 904, the defendant pleaded guilty to conspiracy to rob. In his basis of plea, not challenged by the prosecution, he stated he withdrew from the conspiracy prior to the robbery taking place. It was found that he had not obtained the cash stolen in any realistic way. In those circumstances the Court held there was no benefit under POCA.

9.20 The issue of basis of pleas was considered more recently in *R v Chambers* [2008] EWCA Crim 2467, a case in which the defendant pleaded guilty on a written basis, which was that he had never been to the warehouse in question prior to his arrest, but had been invited to work on that day at the warehouse by his co-defendant, for which he was to be paid £50. He became aware that the work at the warehouse would involve handling the dutiable tobacco, but agreed to carry it out.

9.21 The Crown did not request a *Newton* hearing for the purpose of sentencing, but had made clear that it would not be bound by the basis of plea so far as confiscation was concerned.

The Court of Appeal rejected Chambers' submission that because there was no *Newton* hearing then the judge was bound in the confiscation hearing to accept that Chambers' role was limited to that set out in his basis of plea. The Court of Appeal approved the trial judge's comments that where the Crown agrees a basis of plea, that basis is binding on both the Crown and the court considering confiscation. If the basis is not agreed, then the judge will be required to hear evidence and reach his own conclusion on the defendant's role. The fact that the sentencing judge does not conduct a *Newton* hearing before sentencing a defendant is 'neither here nor there when it [comes] to the confiscation proceedings'. The Court held that it was for the defendant to call evidence to explain his role; the law in this respect was clear and the Crown had set its position out at the time of the guilty plea.

The burden and standard of proof

The standard of proof in determining whether the defendant has a criminal lifestyle and the recoverable amount is on the balance of probabilities (s 6(7)).   **9.22**

The issue of whether the defendant has benefited from the offences of which he has been convicted and the amount of that benefit is a matter for the prosecution to prove. In terms of the value of the defendant's assets available to meet a confiscation order it is for the defendant to establish that the value of the realisable property is less than the amount of the benefit. In all circumstances, the standard of proof is on a balance of probabilities. (See *R v Barwick* (2001) 1 Cr App R(S) 129 where the Court of Appeal confirmed that in confiscation proceedings (under the CJA 1988) it was for the prosecution to establish that the defendant had benefited from an offence and the value of that benefit. Once that had been established, it was for the offender to prove, on a balance of probabilities, that the amount that might be realised is less than the value of his calculated benefit (see also *R v Granger* [2007] EWCA Crim 139 and Chapter 8).   **9.23**

Unlike the DTA and the CJA 1988, where the standard of proof is expressed as being 'to the civil standard', under POCA the standard is expressed as being on the 'balance of probabilities'. This imports that the courts will be entitled to apply a test that is more akin to a 51/49 percentage basis.   **9.24**

Public interest immunity

In *R v May* [2005] EWCA Crim 97, the Court of Appeal held that where a judge was confident that he could put undisclosed material (namely, material subject to public interest immunity applications) out of his mind for the purposes of a decision in relation to confiscation proceedings, then he was neither obliged to recuse himself nor to appoint special counsel.   **9.25**

Is the court limited to the prosecutor's statement?

In short, no. In *R v Atkinson* [1992] Crim LR 749, a DTOA case, the court held that the statute was imperative in its terms, which were mandatory. The court was obliged to determine the amount to be recovered under the Act, and the amount of the order was to be the amount which the court assessed to be the value of the defendant's proceeds of his crime, and not the prosecutor's. The sentencer was therefore bound to reject any suggestion that the scope of the enquiry should be limited.   **9.26**

Is the court limited to the jury's finding?

9.27 Again, it appears not. In *R v Sangha* [2008] EWCA Crim 2562 the defendants were convicted of cheating the public revenue in a VAT carousel fraud and were subject to CJA 1988 confiscation proceedings. On appeal, the defendants contended that, given the way the matter had been left to the jury at trial, the factual basis of their conviction was narrow and they could not be said to have benefited from the criminal conduct of which they were convicted.

9.28 The Court held that where there has been a contested trial, the jury's verdict and the factual basis upon which it was reached (to the extent that this can be determined from what happened at the trial) will of course have an important part to play in setting the parameters of the confiscation proceedings, and it will not be open to the judge to act inconsistently with the verdict or its factual basis when dealing with matters of confiscation. However, the defendants in this case sought to place:

> unwarranted limitations upon the confiscation proceedings by reference to the verdict and its factual basis. The questions that have to be determined in the confiscation proceedings (whether the defendant has benefited from the relevant criminal conduct, the amount of any such benefit, and the amount recoverable from him) are distinct from those falling for determination during the trial process itself eg the standard of proof is different, namely that applicable in civil proceedings. There will normally be evidence additional to that led at the trial. The court responsible for making the relevant determinations is the judge, not the jury. Whilst the judge must act consistently with the jury's verdict and its factual basis, it is open to him, in the light of the evidence as a whole, to make additional and more extensive findings of fact than those upon which the verdict was based.

For example, said the Court, the 'criminal lifestyle' provisions of POCA require the court to decide whether a defendant has benefited from general criminal conduct, not limited to the offences which he had been convicted of, and to make assumptions that property had been obtained from general criminal conduct. The Court held that provided that the judge acted consistently with the verdict and its factual basis, the judge was entitled to take into account all the evidence he had heard and to make his own relevant findings of fact when determining the question of the defendants' benefit.

Is the court limited to the offences charged?

9.29 No, providing the judge is satisfied that other criminal conduct has beyond reasonable doubt been committed. In *R v Briggs-Price* [2009] UKHL 19, the defendant had been convicted of a conspiracy to import heroin, albeit none had been imported, and there was other evidence adduced during the course of the trial that the defendant had been dealing in cannabis, albeit such an offence had not been pursued. The judge made a specific finding, during the course of the confiscation proceedings, that he was satisfied to the criminal standard that the cannabis offending was made out on the evidence he had seen and heard. Whilst the House of Lords was divided on the issue as to whether in such circumstances the court needs to be satisfied to the criminal or the civil standard, their Lordships were unanimous in dismissing the appeal. *Per* Lord Rodger:

> The judge plainly thought that the appellant's involvement had been proved to the criminal standard, beyond a reasonable doubt. On any view, therefore, the presumption of innocence in article 6(1) was fully respected in the confiscation proceedings. (at [75]).

The majority of the House (Lords Rodger, Brown, and Neuberger) reached the conclusion **9.30** that in respect of such uncharged offences, the standard must be the criminal standard. While they accepted that the civil standard is intended by the Act to apply presumptively in confiscation proceedings, and that for most of the purposes of the Act the civil standard can properly apply, that standard would not be acceptable under the ECHR when taking into account other drug trafficking offences for which no conviction had been reached. This would breach the presumption of innocence implied into Art 6(1). More recently, the Court of Appeal have stated that *Briggs-Price* was not authority for the proposition that the only means of establishing that a defendant had obtained property in the past was by proof of criminal offences (see *R v Whittington* (2009) EWCA Crim 1641). *Briggs-Price* is considered further at para 9.198, below.

C. The Defendant's Benefit

Section 8(1) of POCA provides: **9.31**

(1) If the court is proceeding under Section 6 this section applies for the purpose of—
    (a) deciding whether the defendant has benefited from conduct; and
    (b) deciding his benefit from the conduct.
(2) The court must—
    (a) take account of conduct occurring up to the time it makes its decision;
    (b) take account of property obtained up to that time.

Section 6 envisages that there will be confiscation of the defendant's benefit from either his **9.32** 'general criminal conduct' or his 'particular criminal conduct'.

The three central questions

The facts in *R v May* [2008] UKHL 28 were relatively straightforward. May had pleaded **9.33** guilty to a charge of conspiracy to cheat in connection with a £4.4 million VAT carousel fraud. There were a number of co-conspirators. He appealed against the confiscation order made against him on the ground that there should have been apportionment of the benefit between him and his co-conspirators. The House, rejecting the apportionment argument, considered the law generally, and identified three central questions that should be asked by courts when conducting confiscation proceedings:

- Has the defendant benefited from the relevant criminal conduct?
- What is the value of the benefit obtained by the defendant?
- What sum is recoverable from the defendant?

In the case of POCA, the court must first decide whether the offender has a 'criminal life- **9.34** style': s 6(4)(a). If the answer is 'yes', then the court must decide whether the offender has 'benefited from his general criminal conduct'. If the answer to the first question is 'no', then the court must decide whether the offender has 'benefited from his particular criminal conduct': s 6(4)(b) and (c). In each case, 'benefit' is defined by s 76(4) of POCA, as follows: 'a person benefits from conduct if he obtains property as a result of or in connection with the conduct'. Section 76(7) stipulates that '. . . if a person benefits from conduct his benefit is the value of the property obtained'. Thus, as the House of Lords has made clear, the questions to be asked are essentially the same whether the confiscation proceedings arise under the CJA 1988 or the DTA or POCA.

The first question: has the defendant benefited from the relevant criminal conduct?

9.35 The first question the court has to determine is whether the defendant has benefited from his criminal conduct. In many cases, this will be obvious from the evidence adduced during the trial. As Lord Lane CJ said in *Dickens* [1990] 2 All ER 626, a DTOA case (at p 629D):

> The evidence on which the judgment is based will come in part from the trial, if there has been one, in part from the statements rendered by the parties to the court and in part from evidence adduced before the court.

9.36 Under POCA, in determining benefit, the court must take account of both conduct and property obtained (s 8(2)). By s 76(4), a person benefits from conduct if he obtains property as a result of or in connection with the conduct, or (pursuant to s 76(5)) if he obtains a pecuniary advantage.

9.37 In terms of guidance when considering this question the House of Lords in *May* indicated that the word 'obtain' does *not* exclude either joint receipts or cases where payment is made to a third party at the defendant's behest. The House considered and approved both *R v Moran* [2002] 1 WLR 253, CA, which holds that pecuniary advantage in tax fraud is the amount of tax underpaid plus interest, and *Cadnam Smith* [2002] 1 WLR 52, where the House of Lords had previously decided that a defendant derived a pecuniary advantage in the sum of the duty evaded at the moment when he imported cigarettes, irrespective of what happened to them later.

9.38 It also approved *R v Olubitan* [2004] 2 Cr App R (S), a case where the Court of Appeal had found that a defendant obtained nothing in circumstances where he had only joined a conspiracy to defraud on the day that police action had brought it to an end, stating:

> On these facts the Court of Appeal rightly held that the defendant had obtained nothing from his participation in this conspiracy, observing . . . that section 71(1A) and (5) [of the CJA 1988 as amended] are 'not to be construed so that a person may be held to have obtained property or derived a pecuniary advantage when a proper view of the evidence demonstrates that he has not in fact done so'.

It should be noted that there is no obligation on the Crown to recall evidence adduced in the trial for these purposes, the Court being entitled to rely on that evidence in so far as it may be relevant to the issues it has to determine: see *R v Paul Jenkins* [1991] Crim LR 481–2.

9.39 Evidence adduced in the trial, for example, that the defendant was observed selling drugs in the street or has been involved in fraud, will provide almost irrefutable evidence of benefit from criminal conduct. The court will take notice of the fact that defendants participate in activities such as drug trafficking for the purpose of making a profit, rather than a desire to keep drug addicts supplied with narcotics.

Obtains

9.40 Ordinarily, the word 'obtains' means ownership (whether alone or jointly), which will ordinarily connote a power of disposition or control. *R v Jennings* [2008] UKHL 29 concerned an appeal against a restraint order made under the CJA 1988 (as amended). Jennings was charged with conspiracy to defraud. He had participated in an 'advance fee fraud' orchestrated through a company. Jennings was neither a director nor a shareholder of the company, but an employee. Jennings received a salary and other payments. The total amount defrauded was £584,637.64. Jennings argued that over the period of the conspiracy, he and his wife could have received no more than £50,000. The Crown alleged that Jennings had obtained the full amount of over £584,000.

In the Court of Appeal, Laws LJ had stated that the word 'obtain' meant that a defendant **9.41** should have been:

> instrumental in getting the property out of the crime. His acts must have been a cause of that being done. Not necessarily the only cause: there may, plainly, be other actors playing their parts. All that is required is that the defendant's acts should have contributed, to a non-trivial (that is, not *de minimis*) extent, to the getting of the property. This is no more than an instance of the common law's conventional approach to questions of causation.

Laws LJ did not believe that there was a separate requirement that the defendant should be **9.42** shown to have control over the property. The House of Lords disagreed with Laws LJ. It stated that:

> The focus must be and remain on the language of the legislation. It is, however, relevant to remember that the object of the legislation is *to deprive the defendant of the product of his crime or its equivalent, not to operate by way of fine.* The rationale of the confiscation regime is that the defendant is deprived of what *he* has gained or its equivalent.

> He cannot, and should not, be deprived of what he has never obtained or its equivalent, because that is a fine. This must ordinarily mean that he has obtained property so as to own it, whether alone or jointly, which will ordinarily connote a power of disposition or control, as where a person directs a payment or conveyance of property to someone else.

> A person's acts may contribute significantly to property (as defined in the Act) being obtained without his obtaining it. But under section 71(4) [of the CJA 1988] a person benefits from an offence if he obtains property as a result of or in connection with its commission, and his benefit is the value of the property so obtained, which must be read as meaning 'obtained by him'.

It is not necessarily therefore enough that a defendant's actions have contributed significantly to property being obtained, as he may nonetheless not have obtained it himself.

The second question: what is the value of the benefit obtained by the defendant?

If a person benefits from conduct his benefit is the value of the property obtained (s 76(7)). **9.43** Under s 84(2)(b) of POCA, property is obtained by a person if he obtains an interest in it and its value is defined by ss 79 and 80.

The relevant statutory definitions are set out both in this chapter and in Chapter 8. We set **9.44** out below a number of the common issues that regularly arise in confiscation matters, together with a practical guide to confiscation hearings.

The House of Lords in *May* considered s 71(4) of the CJA 1988, which also deals with **9.45** when a person benefits from an offence, and found that it:

> called for an essentially factual enquiry: what is the value of the property the defendant obtained?

Proceeds, not profits

9.46 It is important to note that the court is concerned at this stage to assess the defendant's proceeds of crime and not merely his profits. Consequently, in assessing the value of his proceeds, the court is not required to deduct the cost of any expenses of the enterprise such as the travelling expenses incurred in their importation. In *R v Versluis* [2004] EWCA Crim 3168, the Court of Appeal stated that in a case where a defendant had adduced no evidence as to his realisable assets and as a result a confiscation order had been made in the sum of his benefit from the proceeds of drug trafficking, there was no need to make a deduction to reflect the expenses that must have been incurred by the defendant in the drug trafficking, pursuant to the concept of commercial reality observed in *R v Comiskey* (1990) 12 Cr App R(S) 562.

Value of property obtained from criminal conduct

9.47 When deciding the value of property obtained by a person as a result of, or in connection with, his criminal conduct, s 80 of POCA applies. Section 80(1) states that the material time for valuing property is the time when the court makes its decision.

9.48 Section 80(2) provides:

(2) The value of the property at the material time is the greater of the following—
    (a) the value of the property (at the time the person obtained it) adjusted to take account of later changes in the value of money;
    (b) the value (at the material time) of the property found under subsection (3).
(3) The property found under this subsection is as follows:
    (a) if the person holds the property obtained, the property found under this subsection is that property;
    (b) if he holds no part of the property obtained, the property found under this subsection is any property which directly or indirectly represents it in his hands;
    (c) if he holds part of the property obtained, the property found under this subsection is that part and any property which directly or indirectly represents the other part in his hands.

9.49 In *Crown Prosecution Service (Nottinghamshire) v Rose* (2008) EWCA Crim 239, (2008) 1 WLR 2113, The Times, 6 March 2008 the Court of Appeal confirmed that when calculating the benefit to a thief or handler of his acquisition or possession of criminal property, the market value of it was the amount it would have cost him to obtain the property legitimately, or the economic value to the loser, rather than what the thief or handler could get for the property if he sold it. It held:

> On that basis there is no need to consider the nature of the defendant's interest in the property obtained or the market value of that interest: the focus is on the incoming value of the property, not the value of the property in his hands. (para 87)

Value of illicit goods and illegal drugs

9.50 In *R v Islam* [2009] UKHL 30, the House of Lords confirmed (by a majority of 3 to 2) that when calculating a defendant's benefit in confiscation proceedings under POCA, goods of an illegal nature, found in the possession of or seized from a defendant, could be attributed a market value, and said value could include their black market value. Their Lordships concluded that it was correct to take into account the market value for goods seized, such as illegal drugs, when assessing the benefit a defendant had obtained, but their market value should be ignored in terms of the available amount, as the illicit goods in question would have been seized and could not be sold lawfully.

Their Lordships' finding appears to overcome an apparent anomaly that had arisen as a **9.51** result of earlier case law, namely that, in terms of confiscation, a defendant who smuggled drugs would potentially find himself in a better position than a defendant who had smuggled tobacco, because tobacco could be valued in a lawful market and drugs could not.

The facts in *Islam* were straightforward. The defendant had pleaded guilty to two **9.52** counts of being knowingly concerned in the importation of 3.53kg of heroin through Southampton in February 2005 and a further 0.438kg of heroin through Felixstowe in March 2005. Both consignments were seized by HMRC following their importation, the latter after a controlled delivery to a location selected by the defendant. The Crown Court judge had included in the benefit calculation the wholesale value of the drugs seized.

The defendant initially appealed against the order on the basis that he could not be said to **9.53** have obtained the drugs within the meaning of POCA; that ground of appeal was rejected and was not resurrected before the House of Lords. A further issue arose, however, in relation to the trial judge's decision to take into account the value of the drugs in the defendant's hands. POCA and its statutory predecessors, the CJA 1988 and the DTA, provide that in assessing a defendant's benefit from his criminal conduct, the court must take into account the market value of the defendant's property (POCA, s 79(2), DTA, s 7(1), CJA 1988, s 74), although there has never been a statutory definition of 'market value'. There was, however, a line of Court of Appeal authorities, including *R v Dore* [1997] 2 Cr App R(S) 152 and ending with *R v Hussain* [2006] EWCA Crim 621 to the effect that the term 'market value' was to be read as meaning 'value in a lawful market', meaning that illicit goods such as drugs would have to be taken as having nil value.

In *Dore*, Lord Bingham CJ had commented, *obiter*, that for the purposes of calculating the **9.54** defendant's *realisable* property drugs could not be sold lawfully and therefore could have no market value. In *R v Berry* [2000] 1 Cr App R (S) 352, Tuckey LJ referred to *Dore*, and commented, also *obiter*, that the same would not necessarily apply to the benefit calculation. It was not until *R v Ajibade* (2006) EWCA Crim 368 that the definition of 'market value' as 'value in a lawful market' was applied to the benefit calculation as well as the calculation of the available amount. In that case, the appeal proceeded upon a concession by the prosecutor, adopted by the Court, that Lord Bingham's *obiter* comment applied equally to the benefit calculation. The Court of Appeal in *Hussain* considered that it was bound by *Ajibade*.

Peculiarly, therefore, the definition of 'market value' as 'lawful market value' bound the Court **9.55** of Appeal without having been fully argued. Toulson LJ, who delivered the Court of Appeal's judgment in *Islam*, felt that too much significance had been placed upon Lord Bingham's *obiter* comments in *Dore*, but nonetheless considered that the Court was bound by *Hussain*.

The House of Lords approached the question as a matter of statutory construction. The ques- **9.56** tion was simply whether Parliament had intended, in enacting s 79(2) of POCA, to accept that the term 'market value' was to be limited to lawful markets, *as per* the *Dore* line of authority. Lord Hope, Baroness Hale, and Lord Mance took the view that it did not. Earlier cases in other legislative contexts supported the view that 'the essence of market value is simply . . . the price that would be paid for the goods as between a willing buyer and a willing seller' (per Lord Hope at para 16). Their Lordships held that there was no anomaly in defining 'market value' widely at the stage of the benefit calculation, and more narrowly at the stage of the available amount calculation, because the context of the expression was different at each stage.

9.57 The dissenting view, Lord Walker and Lord Neuberger, considered that as the *Dore* line of authority was well established when the POCA Bill came before Parliament, the term 'market value' could have been replaced with language that made it clear that the defendant's property did not have to be valued by reference to a lawful market, but Parliament had chosen not to do this; and that the term 'market value' should bear the same definition in the same Act and in the same way when calculating the benefit and available amount.

9.58 Whilst essentially permitting a fast track route to valuing illicit goods without recourse to the assumptions, this judgment nevertheless does not absolve Crown Courts of the obligation to carefully consider whether, on the facts of any particular case, a defendant found in possession of drugs or illegal goods can be said to have benefited from them for the purposes of the benefit calculation; that remains a matter to be decided on the evidence available at the time of the hearing. It does, however, provide a simpler approach to the question of the valuation of drugs, and was followed in *R v Mejia and Sneath* (2009) EWCA Crim 1940, where the Court of Appeal stated it was 'absurd' to suggest that cocaine had no market value and that *Islam* had 'demolished' the point.

Particular criminal conduct

9.59 Particular criminal conduct means the offences of which the defendant has been convicted in the current proceedings, together with any taken into consideration by the court in passing sentence (s 76(3)). For a definition of criminal conduct see s 76 (see Chapter 8 for more detail about these provisions).

General criminal conduct

9.60 Section 8(3) to (8) deals with situations where the court is holding confiscation proceedings in respect of the defendant's general criminal conduct. General criminal conduct means any criminal conduct of the defendants, whenever the conduct occurred (s 76(2)).

Rule against double counting

9.61 Theoretically, because of the broad nature of the way in which general criminal conduct is defined, where a defendant has been the subject of a confiscation order in the past, a court making a general criminal conduct confiscation order could potentially confiscate the same benefit twice, unless the legislation prevented it.

9.62 Section 8(4) prevents double counting by ensuring that a calculation of benefit once made in relation to an offence would apply for the purposes of any subsequent calculation of benefit in respect of general criminal conduct:

8(3) Subsection (4) applies if—
    (a) the conduct concerned is general criminal conduct,
    (b) a confiscation order mentioned in subsection (5) has at an earlier time been made against the defendant, and
    (c) his benefit for the purpose of that order was benefit from his general criminal conduct.

(4) His benefit found at the time of the last confiscation order mentioned in subsection (3)(c) was made against him must be taken for the purposes of this section to be his benefit from his general criminal conduct at that time.

(5) If the conduct concerned is general criminal conduct the court must deduct the aggregate of the following amounts—
   (a) the amount ordered to be paid under each confiscation order previously made against the defendant;
   (b) the amount ordered to be paid under each confiscation order previously made against him under any of the provisions listed in subsection (7).

Section 8(5) does not apply to an amount that has been taken into account for the purposes of a deduction of that subsection on any earlier occasion (s 8(6)).

The provisions in s 8(7) include the Drug Trafficking Offences Act 1986 (DTOA), Pt VI **9.63** of the CJA 1988, Pt I of the DTA, and Pts 3 and 4 of POCA. The reference to general criminal conduct in the case of a confiscation order made under any of the provisions listed in s 8(7) is a reference to conduct in respect of which the court is required or entitled to make one or more assumptions for the purpose of assessing the person's benefit from the conduct (see s 8(8)).

The assumptions: section 10

As we have seen, the burden is on the prosecution to prove on the balance of probabilities **9.64** the benefit and the value of the defendant's proceeds from criminal conduct. The Crown's responsibility in this regard is considerably lightened in general criminal conduct cases, by the application of the statutory assumptions.

Section 10 of POCA creates a single scheme under which certain assumptions are manda- **9.65** tory. Under the DTA they were mandatory, but discretionary in all other confiscation cases. Now they are mandatory in all cases where a person has a criminal lifestyle (for a definition of criminal lifestyle, see s 75 and Chapter 8).

Section 10 requires the court to make a number of assumptions in determining the **9.66** question of benefit and the amount received from general criminal conduct. Section 10(1) provides:

(1) If the court decides under Section 6 that the defendant has a criminal lifestyle it must make the following four assumptions for the purpose of—
   (a) deciding whether he has benefited from his general criminal conduct, and
   (b) deciding his benefit from the conduct.

Section 10 only applies where the court has decided that the defendant has a criminal lifestyle and it is, accordingly, considering the defendant's benefit from general criminal conduct.

The four assumptions

The four assumptions are as follows: **9.67**

(1) That any property transferred to the defendant at any time after the relevant day was obtained by him:
   (a) as a result of his general criminal conduct, and
   (b) at the earliest time he appears to have held it (s 10(2)).

(2) That any property held by the defendant at any time after the date of conviction was obtained by him:

    (a) as a result of his general criminal conduct, and

    (b) at the earliest time he appears to have held it (s 10(3)).

(3) That any expenditure incurred by the defendant at any time after the relevant day was met from property obtained by him as a result of his general criminal conduct (s 10(4)).

(4) For the purpose of valuing any property obtained (or assumed to have been obtained) by the defendant, he obtained it free of any other interest in it (s 10(5)).

The 'relevant day'

9.68 Under s 10(8), the 'relevant day' is the first day in the period of six years ending with:

    (1) the day when proceedings for the offence concerned were started against the defendant, or

    (2) if there are two or more offences and proceedings for them were started on different days, the earliest of those days.

However, where a previous confiscation order has been made against the defendant, the relevant day will only stretch back to the date of the making of that order, as a means of avoiding double counting. Pursuant to s 10(9), if a confiscation order mentioned in s 8(3) (c) has been made against the defendant at any time during the six-year period, then the 'relevant day' becomes the day when the defendant's benefit was calculated for the purposes of the last confiscation order and the second assumption (that any property held by the defendant at any time after the date of conviction obtained by him as a result of his general criminal conduct) does not apply to any property which was held by him on or before the relevant day.

The 'date of conviction'

9.69 Under s 10(10) the date of conviction is:

    (1) the date on which the defendant was convicted of the offence concerned, or

    (2) if there are two or more offences and the convictions were on different dates, the date of the latest.

When the assumptions do not apply

9.70 Pursuant to s 10(6), the court must not make a required assumption in relation to particular property or expenditure if:

    (1) the assumption is shown to be incorrect, or

    (2) there would be a serious risk of injustice if the assumption were made.

9.71 By s 10(7), if the court does not make one or more of the required assumptions, it must state its reasons. Where the court does not make any of the assumptions specified in the legislation, it must nevertheless continue to decide whether the defendant has benefited from general criminal conduct and decide the recoverable amount, albeit without the assistance of the assumptions.

9.72 In *R v Jones (Confiscation Orders)* The Times, 8 August 2006, the Court of Appeal held that 'serious risk of injustice' does not refer to hardship that would be sustained by the offender by virtue of the making of the confiscation order, and it does not operate so as to confer discretion on the court to determine whether it is fair to make a confiscation order at all. Parliament's plain intention was that a confiscation order should be made in every case where the court concludes that the offender has benefited from his general criminal conduct.

No other assumptions may be made

In *R v Williams*, The Times, 11 January 2001 the Court of Appeal held that while the **9.73** Crown Court is bound to make the assumptions set out in the Act for the purposes of determining whether a defendant has benefited, and, if he has, of assessing the value of the proceeds, no other assumption other than those specifically provided for may be made.

At what stage are the assumptions applied?

The court may decide to apply the assumptions at any stage of the enquiry, including **9.74** before the defendant's case has commenced (*R v Redbourne* [1992] 1 WLR 1182). In delivering the judgment in *Redbourne*, a DTOA case, Staughton LJ said (at p 1187):

> The Act does not specify the stage of the proceedings at which the assumptions may be made. . . . A judge's decision whether or not to make the assumptions is an interim one which falls to be made on his way to reaching his final decision, such final decision involving a full consideration of the defendant's case and whether (once fully deployed) it is sufficient to negate any assumptions made. In an appropriate case, the judge is entitled to make the assumptions at the start of his enquiry, for example, if he has reason to do so from the circumstances of the offence for which the defendant has been convicted. Or the judge may do so at any later stage, up to the time when he makes his final decision.

Effect of applying the assumptions

In *Redbourne* Staughton LJ observed (at p 1188) that: **9.75**

> An assumption, in this context is the acceptance of something as true which is not already known or proved, and therefore may or may not be true. If the Court is directed or empowered to make an assumption, that means that the Court must or may take the assumed fact as true.

While *Redbourne* is now to a degree historic, as it was determined under the DTOA, it is submitted that it must be indicative of the law on the effect of the assumptions once applied, namely that the assumed fact is deemed to be true except to the extent that the defendant succeeds in rebutting it. In *R v Whittington* (2010) Crim LR 65, the Court of Appeal confirmed that the assumptions set out in s 10 of POCA operated in such a way that it was for the prosecution to prove to the civil standard that property was transferred to the defendant and the assumptions were engaged once that has been proved.

Rebutting the assumptions

When the judge decides to apply one or more of the assumptions, this is not necessarily **9.76** conclusive against the defendant. Section 10(6) of POCA provides that the court must apply the assumptions except to the extent that they are shown to be incorrect in the defendant's case or there would be a serious risk of injustice if the assumption were made. The burden of disproving an assumption rests on the defendant and the standard of proof is on a balance of probabilities. If a defendant wishes to succeed in showing the assumptions are incorrect he must produce clear and cogent evidence: see *R v Walbrook and Glasgow* [1994] Crim LR 613, where the Court held:

> vague and generalised assertions unsupported by evidence would rarely, if ever, be sufficient to discharge the burden on the defendant.

9.77   In *R v Jones (Confiscation Orders)* The Times, 8 August 2006, the Court of Appeal held that 'serious risk of injustice' does not refer to hardship that would be sustained by the offender by virtue of the making of the confiscation order, and it does not operate so as to confer discretion on the court to determine whether it is fair to make a confiscation order at all. In *R v Hesketh* (2006) 150 SJ 1468, the Court of Appeal determined that where a defendant was able to show transfers in and out of a bank account were as a result of gambling activities, that would be sufficient to rebut the assumptions.

Pecuniary advantage

9.78   Section 76(5) and (6) of the Act makes reference to, but does not define, the concept of 'pecuniary advantage'. It often happens in POCA cases that, rather than obtaining property as a result of the offence, the defendant obtains a pecuniary advantage, for example the evasion of VAT which he would otherwise be liable to pay. Pursuant to the Act, the defendant is liable to have a confiscation order made against him in the amount of the pecuniary advantage he derived from the offence in the same way as if he had obtained property to that value.

9.79   In *R v David Cadman-Smith* [2002] 1 WLR 54, a CJA case, the House of Lords held that 'pecuniary advantage' should be given its ordinary natural meaning, and that included cases where a debt was evaded or deferred. It stated that the court was concerned simply with the value of the property as obtained by the defendant, and it made no difference if, after he had obtained it, it was destroyed or damaged or forfeited. In so finding they held that the defendant had derived a pecuniary advantage when he had evaded payment of an excise duty, even though the goods in question (cigarettes) had been forfeited before he had been able to dispose of them.

9.80   In *R v Dimsey and Allen* (2000) 1 Cr App R(S) 497 the main point argued was that failure to pay tax did not amount to a pecuniary advantage for the purpose of s 71(4) of the CJA 1988 because the tax remained payable. The court held that the deferment of payment of tax was a pecuniary advantage in the amount of the tax deferred. Allen was convicted of 13 counts of cheating the public revenue in an amount of £4 million. Laws LJ stated at p 501:

> Had these grave frauds succeeded then, in crude terms, Mr Allen would have been better off to the tune of £4 million. That represents in our judgement, the measure of his pecuniary advantage.

9.81   The Court of Appeal considered the question again in *A-G v Moran* [2001] EWCA Crim 1770. In *Moran* the defendant was a market trader. He traded in his own right and there was no company. For 20 years he had understated his income on his tax returns. There was no misappropriation of money *per se*. He was charged with cheating and making false statements. In confiscation proceedings it was alleged that the benefit he had received was the whole of his undeclared profits—£386,584. The judge rejected that submission and made a confiscation order in the sum of £190,000 representing the under payment of tax and interest. Mantell LJ stated (at para 8):

> What is plain and has been accepted before this court, as it was before the judge, is that we are dealing with the pecuniary advantage. On the face of things the pecuniary advantage would seem to be represented by the underpayment of tax which resulted from the failure to

fully disclose profits. On the wording of the Act the pecuniary advantage must be taken to include any interest accrued or investment returned upon that sum. Giving the words of the Act their ordinary and natural meaning it is hard to see how the balance of the profits which are the product of lawful trading can be said to represent a pecuniary advantage which has resulted from or come about in connection with the commission of an offence. We reject the argument that where there has been systematic and persistent non-disclosure of profits the whole enterprise is to be regarded as fraudulent and the proceeds liable to forfeiture. It seems to us, therefore, that, authority apart, the judge was plainly right.

In *R v Foggon* [2003] EWCA Crim 270 the Court of Appeal, including Mantell LJ, consid- **9.82**
ering the above authorities held:

> ... where a person misappropriates money from a company as an essential part of a fraud on
> the Inland Revenue, and is convicted of that fraud, he is liable to a confiscation order in the
> amount of the monies which he has misappropriated on the ground that the monies are
> property obtained as a result of or in connection with the fraud.

Pecuniary advantage and the liability to pay excise duty

The courts' approach to the expression 'pecuniary advantage' was recently considered **9.83**
by the Court of Appeal in *R v Chambers* [2008] EWCA Crim 2467. Chambers had been
convicted of being knowingly concerned in the fraudulent evasion of excise duty in relation
to 600kg of tobacco. The duty evaded was £66,120. The tobacco had been bought in
Belgium in September 2006 and seized at a warehouse in England the next day; Chambers
and his co-defendant were present at the site. He pleaded guilty on a written basis, which
was that he had never been to the warehouse prior to his arrest but had been invited to
work on that day at the warehouse by his co-defendant, for which he was to be paid £50.
He became aware that the work at the warehouse would involve handling the dutiable
tobacco but agreed to carry it out. He also said that he had not travelled to Belgium to
purchase the goods.

The judge at first instance neither expressly accepted nor rejected the basis of plea. He **9.84**
concluded that on the Crown's evidence and Chambers' admissions that Chambers had
obtained a pecuniary advantage equal to the value of the unpaid duty. The Court of Appeal,
however, concluded that:

- The defendant would only have obtained a benefit by way of a pecuniary advantage in
  the form of the evasion of excise duty if he was himself under a liability for the payment
  of that duty which he dishonestly evaded;

- To help someone else to evade the payment of duty payable by that other person, with
  intent to defraud, is no less criminal, but in confiscation proceedings the focus is on the
  benefit obtained by the relevant offender.

- An offender may derive other benefits from helping a person who is under a liability
  for the payment of duty to avoid that liability, eg by way of payment for the accessory's
  services, but that is another matter.

- In order to decide whether the offender has obtained a benefit in the form of the evasion
  of a liability, it is necessary to determine whether the offender had a liability which he
  avoided.

The result in the case thus turned on whether Chambers was liable for the payment of excise duty on the relevant goods under the relevant Regulations. The Crown had relied on the Excise Goods Regulations 1992, which the Court had concluded in a draft judgment gave rise to a liability on Chambers' part to pay duty. However, before the judgment was handed down, the Revenue and Customs Prosecutions Office (RCPO) alerted the Court to the fact that the 1992 Regulations no longer applied to tobacco products and had been superseded by the Tobacco Product Regulations 2001 with materially different (and narrower) provisions relating to the liability to pay duty. As the trial judge had been invited to make findings of fact and to decide the case on the basis of inapplicable law, and the Court of Appeal was not in a position to make further findings of fact, the Court rejected the Crown's submission that it should decide the appeal on the basis of the 2001 Regulations, and the appeal was allowed.

9.85 In *R v Mitchell* [2009] EWCA Crim 214, the facts were as follows: Mitchell was convicted of being knowingly concerned in the fraudulent evasion of duty payable on the importation of tobacco contrary to s 170(2) of the Customs and Excise Management Act 1979. This was not a 'criminal lifestyle' case. The Crown argued that his 'benefit' was £304,123.71 being the aggregate of the value of the tobacco (£86,020) as having been property obtained under s 76(4), and the value of the duty evaded (£280,103.71) as being a pecuniary advantage obtained under s 76(5). Mitchell said that he had been paid £100 in cash for helping to load the tobacco, and this was his only benefit. In the Crown Court, the Recorder made a confiscation order in the sum of £100. The Crown appealed against that order under s 31 of POCA

9.86 The Court of Appeal rejected the Crown's contention that the Recorder had been wrong to reach his conclusions as to the facts, given the evidence. It was not prepared to hold that the Recorder was wrong in not finding that the defendant was an importer or co-importer of the goods. The Court then considered whether Mitchell nonetheless obtained a benefit for the purposes of POCA greater than the £100 he had admitted. The Crown accepted that, in the light of *May*, Mitchell if not an importer or co-importer could not be said to have 'obtained' the tobacco. It did, however, argue that he had obtained a pecuniary advantage through the evasion of the payment of duty. The Court described as 'rightly made' the Crown's concession that it had to show that Mitchell was personally liable for the payment of that duty. As a loader, was the defendant liable for the payment of duty?

9.87 The Court considered the various pieces of applicable legislation, including in particular the Tobacco Products Regulations 2001. Regulation 13(1) provides that the person liable to pay the duty is the person holding the products at the excise duty point. In addition, Regulation 13(3) makes any person who (amongst other things) 'caused the tobacco products to reach' the excise duty point jointly and severally liable for the duty.

9.88 The Court stated that it was:

> ... important to keep separate in one's mind the distinction between civil liability under the regulations and criminal liability under section 170 of the 1979 Act, which may trigger confiscation proceedings under POCA. A person who dishonestly evades the civil liability will commit an offence and be liable to a confiscation order, but it is wrong to approach the construction of the civil liability imposed by regulation 13 on the footing that this regulation

is aimed at crooks; it is aimed at importations in general, which will include some dishonest importations but of which the vast majority will be lawful.

The Court rejected the Crown's submission that anybody who contributed to the importa- **9.89** tion (eg by loading the goods) would be a person who 'caused' the goods to reach the excise duty point. The Court considered the impact of the European Council Directive 92/12/ EEC on the construction of the Regulations (which implemented the Directive) and in particular Art 7(3) which states:

> Depending on all the circumstances, the duty shall be due from *the person making the delivery or holding the products intended for delivery or from the person receiving the products* for use in a Member State other than the one where the products have already been released for consumption, or from the relevant trader or body governed by public law. (Emphasis added)

The Court held, particularly in the light of the wording of the Directive, that the civil liability created by the Regulations was 'not intended to have the wide sweep contended for by the prosecution'. They did not put a precise definition on the phrase in Regulation 13(3), but said that it appeared to be 'directed at that person or body who had real and immediate responsibility for causing the product to reach that point, which will typically and ordinarily be the consignor'. The Court held that the defendant in this case did not have a personal liability to pay the duty, and the prosecution's appeal was dismissed.

Apportionment and multiple recovery

The House of Lords in *May* found that the sum fraudulently obtained by May, jointly with **9.90** others, was as much his as if he had acted alone; and that the confiscation order made was neither unjust nor disproportionate. The confiscation legislation was held to be:

> a precise, fair and proportionate response to the important need to protect the public—*per* Lord Steyn in *Rezvi* [2003] 1 AC 1099, para 17.

The House held that apportionment of benefit between parties jointly liable was:

> a procedure which would be contrary to principle and unauthorised by statute.

The House disapproved of making an apportionment on ECHR grounds (rejecting the view of the Northern Ireland Court of Appeal in *R v Leslie* [2008] NICA 28).

The House of Lords in *May* disapproved *R v Porter* [1990] 1 WLR 1260, a case where the **9.91** Court of Appeal had quashed orders that two defendants should each pay the total amount of their joint benefit (£9,600) and substituted orders that they should only pay £4,800 each. The House of Lords stated that:

> this might as later authorities show, have been a proper disposal had there in fact been no evidence of the parties' shares in the proceeds. But the judge's finding, not challenged on appeal, was that the proceeds had been received jointly. That being so each had received a payment or other reward in the full sum of £9,600 and orders in that sum should have been made against each of them severally.

It is not relevant what a defendant who receives money does with that money afterwards. **9.92** The House of Lords in *May* approved *R v Patel* [2000] 2 Cr App R (S) 10, CA, a case where a defendant had been convicted of obtaining pecuniary advantage by deception and the court had rightly held that he had benefited to the full extent of the money received by him, even though he had paid a share of the proceeds of the fraud to an accomplice. If the accomplice had been before the court then (if he had not been found to have obtained the full sum jointly with the defendant), he would have benefited to the extent of the payment that he received.

9.93 Their Lordships in *May* similarly approved *R v Sharma* [2006] 2 Cr App R (S) 416, CA, where defendants had *not* jointly obtained benefit, but there had been a disposal by one member of a criminal enterprise to another. In such circumstances each is treated as the recipient of a benefit to the extent of the value of the money which has come into the possession of each of them. The amount of the benefit is *not* affected by the amount obtained by others when the defendant transfers it. A person who receives money into his bank account obtains it from the source from which it is derived, and where he is sole signatory he obtains that money and has possession of it for his own benefit.

9.94 The extent to which the evidence is likely to play a crucial part in determining the facts is illustrated by their Lordships approval of *R v Gibbons* [2003] 2 Cr App R (S) 169, CA, a case which goes against the judicial grain indicated above. In *Gibbons* four conspirators had obtained £220,000 by fraud. There was no evidence before the judge to enable a finding that the sum had been jointly obtained or how the proceeds had been divided. In such circumstances an order for equal division between the four defendants was appropriate. The House of Lords held that the equal division was 'rightly upheld' by the Court of Appeal which was the 'fairest solution available in the circumstances' given the lack of evidence.

9.95 In *R v Green* [2008] UKHL 30, Green pleaded guilty to offences of conspiracy to supply controlled drugs, launder the proceeds of drug trafficking and import controlled drugs. A number of fellow conspirators were also convicted. He argued that the judge had been wrong to hold that money retained by two of his co-defendants from the sale of drugs were held by them jointly with him, as proceeds in which they were all fully interested.

9.96 The House approved (and indeed called 'admirable') the judgment of the Court of Appeal, in which David Clarke J had stated:

> ... where money or property is received by one defendant on behalf of several defendants jointly, each defendant is to be regarded as having received the whole of it ... It does not matter that proceeds of sale may have been received by one conspirator who retains his share before passing on the remainder; what matters is the capacity in which he received them ... *Whether the proceeds of sale received by [the appellant's associates] ... were initially received on their own personal behalf or on behalf of the conspirators as a whole was a matter of fact for the judge to decide on the evidence before him.* In fact, there was evidence on which he could find that the appellant was the ringleader and controller of the conspiracy and in those circumstances he was entitled to infer that the others were acting in accordance with his instructions, receiving proceeds of sale on behalf of the conspirators as a whole before retaining for themselves such amounts as had been agreed with the appellant. In our view this part of the judge's decision is not open to criticism. (Emphasis added)

9.97 In *Green* the House approved *Simons* (1993) 98 Cr App R 100, which held that there may be multiple recovery through the confiscation process, where there is a chain of contracts with payments to different individuals.

The House in *Green* stated that it was 'not disproportionate to make an order depriving a **9.98** defendant of a benefit which he has in fact and in law obtained, within the limits of his realisable assets . . .' It noted that challenges to the proportionality of the confiscation regime had not succeeded; see *Phillips v UK* (2001) 11 BHRC 280 and *Rezvi* [2003] 1 AC 1099.

In *R v Sivaraman* [2008] EWCA Crim 1736 the defendant pleaded guilty to conspiracy to **9.99** evade excise duty in respect of agricultural 'red diesel' which had been converted into road vehicle diesel (DERV) for sale to the general public. Sivaraman was the manager of the service station where the diesel, purchased by his employer, was sold. He pleaded guilty on a written basis, in which he stated that he had accepted a number of deliveries of the converted diesel (the duty on which was in excess of £128,000) but that he had been paid only £15,000 for his role. The trial judge stated that, 'with reservation', he was 'constrained' to find that S's benefit was £128,000.

The Court of Appeal held that participants in a joint criminal offence (including conspir- **9.100** acy) may benefit jointly to the same extent by each obtaining the same property or pecuniary advantage; or the value of the benefit received by them may differ as between one and another. This is a matter of applying straightforward concepts (obtaining property or obtaining a pecuniary advantage) to the facts as established and trying to avoid becoming enmeshed in case law in the process. The court needs to find the facts and to apply the words of the statute to them in as commonsensical a way as possible. The greater the involvement in a conspiracy, the greater the appropriate level of punishment; but it does not follow that the greater the involvement, the greater the benefit to that defendant. What benefit a defendant gained is a question of fact, within the statutory framework. The court must examine the facts before determining the benefit gained by a particular defendant on those facts.

In Sivaraman's case, it had not been the Crown's case that he was a joint purchaser and seller **9.101** of the fuel. It would be one thing if he had acted as a joint purchaser with his employer, but another if he had received the fuel in his capacity as an employee. There was no liability to pay duty which Sivaraman himself had evaded; in this context the case was different to tobacco importation cases such as *Rowbotham*. The appeal was accordingly allowed, and the amount of the benefit reduced to £15,000.

Apportionment and companies

In *R v Grainger* [2008] EWCA Crim 2506, Grainger was the director of companies which **9.102** had received large advances from its bankers as a result of representing that fraudulent invoices were genuine records of debts. Over £40 million was advanced to the companies in this way. This money enabled the companies to continue trading when they would otherwise have become insolvent; as a result Grainger's employment with the companies continued. Grainger was convicted of fraudulent trading. The trial judge was invited by the Crown to apportion (as a matter of discretion) the benefit (defined as the total sum obtained from the banks) between the various defendants. The Crown contended that the defendants had obtained the benefit jointly. The judge adopted the Crown's approach, and the figure set as Grainger's benefit was £4.1 million. His recoverable assets were far less than this.

9.103 The appeal was successful on the basis that payments made by the banks to the companies were not as a matter of fact payments to Grainger (although the Court did stress that the corporate veil might be pierced in appropriate cases):

> The moral is that in such cases it is essential, first, for the prosecution and then for the judge to look to see what real benefit the offender has obtained and to examine the evidence relating to it in order to arrive at a fair valuation … If an offender chooses to use a company as a shield to hide his benefits from crime, it is open to the court to look behind the corporate veil in order to ascertain the true position. Again, it is necessary in each case for the prosecution in the first instance and then the judge to examine the facts in order to see what benefit the offender has in truth obtained and how it should be valued.

9.104 The Court of Appeal held that it was necessary to draw a distinction between legal culpability, which goes to punishment, and benefit, which goes to the issue of confiscation. It was wrong for the trial judge to state that anybody whose conduct contributed in a more than *de minimis* way to the obtaining of benefit was to be treated as having obtained such benefit. What benefit an offender has obtained was a question of fact to be determined in each case, applying the language of the statute in a common sense way. The payments had been made to the various companies. Grainger was instrumental, with others, in causing those payments to be made, but he did not himself obtain a direct benefit. They were not monies that he received or in which he had any direct beneficial interest. It was plain that Grainger derived benefit from his fraudulent conduct, as he obtained employment in a company which would otherwise have gone into liquidation. Whilst he may have benefited to the tune of the salary and benefits he received from his continued employment, the Crown had not invited the trial judge to assess these, and the Court of Appeal was in no position to do so itself.

9.105 In *R v Xu* [2008] EWCA Crim 2372 the facts were as follows: the defendants were convicted of facilitating breaches of immigration law. They owned a restaurant in which for a period of time several illegal immigrants were employed, constituting one-quarter of the workforce. The trial judge found that the entirety of the receipts of the restaurant from the time at which the defendants started to employ illegal immigrants until they ceased to employ the illegal immigrants was the 'benefit' for the purposes of the confiscation orders.

9.106 The Crown conceded on appeal that, had the illegal immigrants not been employed at the material time, then the business would still have operated, albeit at a reduced capacity. The Court of Appeal held that the case was distinguishable from *Neuberg* [2007] EWCA Crim 1994, which the judge had followed, on the basis that in *Neuberg* the business would not have survived but for the defendant's criminal conduct. The Court of Appeal held that:

> We have no doubt that the appellants did obtain a benefit from the employment of illegal immigrants, which might be looked at either in terms of receipts generated by their employment or expenses avoided, but in our judgment it is not realistic or just to conclude that the entirety of the receipts from each and every customer flowed from the employment of these illegal immigrants. That would be tantamount to a finding that the business would otherwise not have been sustainable, contrary to the agreed position that it would indeed have continued.

9.107 The Court of Appeal found itself in a difficult position of deciding what order should be made. The defendants had not been forthcoming before the judge about the real part played in the business by the illegal immigrants, which the Court noted may have been relatively modest given that they were employed in lowly positions. The Court in the absence of this evidence took a 'robust approach' and inferred, absent any better basis for assessing the benefit, that a quarter of the receipts for the relevant period came from their employment, basing this on the fact that the illegal immigrants represented one quarter of the workforce.

In *R v Seager and Blatch* [2009] EWCA Crim 1703 at para 68, the Court of Appeal **9.108** confirmed that company director disqualified under the Company Directors Disqualification Act 1986, were to be treated no differently from any other defendant's for the purposes of the confiscation scheme. In addition to the fundamental questions posed by *May* the Court added:

> 73. Two further general principles must apply to an offender who has been found guilty of contravening a director's disqualification order or who has contravened an equivalent undertaking. First, in *R v May*, the House of Lords stated that the benefit gained is the total value of the property (or pecuniary advantage) gained, not the particular defendant's net profit: see paragraph 48(1). In *Jennings v CPS* the House of Lords held that 'obtained' meant obtained by the relevant defendant: see paragraph 14. Secondly, however, it is important to recognise that a defendant's acts may contribute significantly to property (or to a pecuniary advantage) being obtained, without the relevant defendant obtaining it himself: ibid.

Partnerships

The issues that arise out of partnerships and their effect on confiscation were considered **9.109** in *R v W Stephenson and Sons and Bick* [2008] EWCA Crim 273. The court held (at para 30):

> In as much as business activities are conducted in the name of a partnership and the partnership has identifiable assets that are distinct from the personal assets of each partner there is no reason why a partnership should not be treated for the purposes of the criminal law as a separate entity from the partners who are members of it.

The court held that proceedings could only be brought against an individual partner if that **9.110** partner is complicit in the offence committed by the partnership. Where a partnership alone is indicted, any fine imposed can only be levied against the assets of the partnership. The court stated (para 37) that confiscation proceedings apply to the 'offender'. In cases where the charge is brought against the partnership, as opposed to the individual partner, the individual partners are not 'offenders'. As a result, confiscation proceedings cannot properly be brought against their personal assets, when the 'individual' convicted is the Partnership.

The corporate veil

The circumstances in which a court may pierce or lift the corporate veil are discussed in **9.111** some detail in the restraint chapter of this book (see para 2.51). However, the principles that apply were recently concisely distilled in *R v Seager and Blatch* [2009] EWCA Crim 1703 at para 76, as follows:

> . . . It is 'hornbook' law that a duly formed and registered company is a separate legal entity from those who are its shareholders and it has rights and liabilities that are separate from its

shareholders: *Salomon v A Salomon & Co Ltd* [1897] AC 22; referred to by Rose LJ in *Re H and others (restraint order: realisable property):* [1996] 2 All ER 391 at 401F. A court can 'pierce' the carapace of the corporate entity and look at what lies behind it only in certain circumstances. It cannot do so simply because it considers it might be just to do so. Each of these circumstances involves impropriety and dishonesty. The court will then be entitled to look for the legal substance, not the just the form. In the context of criminal cases the courts have identified at least three situations when the corporate veil can be pierced. First if an offender attempts to shelter behind a corporate façade, or veil to hide his crime and his benefits from it: see *Re H and others,* per Rose LJ at 402A; *Crown Prosecution Service v Compton and others* [2002] All ER (D) 395, paragraph 44–48, per Simon Brown LJ; *R v Grainger,* paragraph 15, per Toulson LJ. Secondly, where an offender does acts in the name of a company which (with the necessary *mens rea)* constitute a criminal offence which leads to the offender's conviction, then '*the veil of incorporation is not so much pierced as rudely torn away':* per Lord Bingham in *Jennings v CPS,* paragraph 16. Thirdly, where the transaction or business structures constitute a 'device', 'cloak' or 'sham', ie an attempt to disguise the true nature of the transaction or structure so as to deceive third parties or the courts: *R v Dimsey* [2000] QB 744 at 772 (per Laws LJ), applying *Snook v London and West Riding Investment Ltd* [1967] 2 QB 786 at 802, per Diplock LJ.

Benefit and money launderers

9.112 *R v Allpress & Others* [2009] EWCA Crim 8 involved a specially convened five judge Court of Appeal (Latham, Hughes, and Toulson LJJ, Rafferty and Maddison JJ) to address the issue of money laundering in the light of the judgments in the *May* trilogy of cases. None of those cases had involved money laundering, and the House of Lords had stated that the position of a money launderer might be different from that of a 'mere courier' or custodian of tangible property who was rewarded by a fee and had no interest in the property.

9.113 The Court considered the general principles in the *May* trilogy, as explained in *Sivaraman.* It affirmed the correctness (in stating the effect of *May*) of para 12(6) of Sivaraman, ie that 'Where property is received by one conspirator, what matters is the capacity in which he receives it, that is, whether for his own personal benefit, or on behalf of others, or jointly on behalf of himself and others'.

9.114 The Court also repeated its criticism of:

> two misconceptions which subsequent cases suggest may still be common. One was that in assessing benefit in a conspiracy case each conspirator is to be taken as having jointly obtained the whole benefit obtained by 'the conspiracy'. A conspiracy is not a legal entity but an agreement or arrangement which people may join or leave at different times. In confiscation proceedings the court is concerned not with the aggregate benefit obtained by all parties to the conspiracy but with the benefit obtained, whether singly or jointly, by the individual conspirator before the court.

The Court continued:

> The second misconception is a variant of the first. It is that anybody who has taken part in a conspiracy in more than a minor way is to be taken as having a joint share in all benefits obtained from the conspiracy. This is to confuse criminal liability and resulting benefit. The more heavily involved a defendant is in a conspiracy, the more severe the penalty which may be merited, but in confiscation proceedings the focus of the inquiry is on the benefit gained by the relevant defendant. In the nature of things there may well be a lack of reliable evidence

about the exact benefit obtained by any particular conspirator, and in drawing common sense inferences the role of a particular conspirator may be relevant as a matter of fact, but that is a purely evidential matter.

The Court considered the arguments for a different approach to that set out in *May* in the **9.115** case of money laundering. The Crown argued that, firstly, money laundering offences constituted a 'special category of offences' to which a separate approach should apply. This was rejected by the Court. The various offences of which the defendants had been convicted might involve dealing with money or other forms of property, and there was no justification for treating them as a special category of offence for the purpose of confiscation if the offending took the form of dealing with money.

The second argument for the Crown was that different considerations apply to cash from **9.116** any other form of property, and that the holder of cash has a power of disposition or control over it which is different from that of a bailee of tangible property. The Court took an everyday example of a checkout supervisor who is handed cash to put into a till. Nobody would think that the supervisor had benefited from the cash in terms of it being within his power of disposition or control. The Court did not see why (even with tainted money) a person who collects money which he delivers to a receiver should be regarded as having an interest in the money, even if he knew that the property was stolen.

The third was that the statutory language required a different approach to be taken to **9.117** money. The Crown argued that where a courier or custodian receives cash to safeguard or pass on in return for a fee, both the fee and the cash constitute a payment received by that person, or property obtained by him. The Court held that this was wrong: the phrase 'payment or other reward' under the DTA implied that the payment must be in the nature of a reward in order to be caught. Neither the DTA nor the CJA 1988 compelled a different approach to sums of cash than to other forms of property. In respect of POCA, and in particular the definition in s 84(2), 'the answer to the question whether a person is intended to be regarded as holding an interest in property by mere manual possession, or whether something more is required, is put beyond doubt by the words "a right to possession"'. The Court of Appeal noted that a person holding cash in these circumstances did not have a right to possession for his own benefit. Even if the mere custodian were held to have a limited interest in property, the relevant value would be 'the value of that interest, which if the property was being held purely for another would be nil'. It held that the observations in the *May* cases were equally applicable to POCA.

Accordingly, if a defendant's only role in relation to property connected with his criminal **9.118** conduct, whether in the form of cash or otherwise, was to act as a courier on behalf of another, or mere custodian of cash for another, such property does not amount to property obtained by him within the meaning of POCA or the CJA 1988, or to 'payment or other reward' under the DTA. The appeals of Allpress, Symeou, Casal, and Martin were therefore allowed.

A different approach was applied to Morris, who was a money launderer through the **9.119** banking system. The money had gone into an account operated by Morris and his partners, and the Court of Appeal found that the judge had been entitled to reject the argument that he was simply a bare trustee. Payment of the money into his account meant that the starting point was that it was his property. Morris had sole operational control of the account. The Court did not exclude the possibility of a case where money was paid into a bank account in the defendant's name, but in reality operated entirely by another person for his benefit, where it would be wrong to conclude that the defendant obtained the monies paid in, although this would be more likely to arise in a domestic setting (eg spouse or parent operating an account in the name of the other spouse or child).

9.120   Morris had received funds of which he had legal ownership and practical control. The case was no different in principle to where a money changer had been paid £1 million and agreed to transfer it to an offshore account in a different currency. The £1 million received would have been money obtained by him. Morris had received funds into his account in England, which he then sent on to the USA and to Spain.

Property, mortgages, and benefit

9.121   The House of Lords in *May* approved *R v Walls* [2003] 1 WLR 731, confirming that if a defendant applies £10,000 of tainted money to the purchase of a £250,000 house, legitimately borrowing the remainder:

> it cannot plausibly be said that he has obtained the house as a result of or in connection with the commission of his offence.

9.122   In *R v Nadarajah* [2007] EWCA Crim 2688 the Court of Appeal rejected the submission that mortgage money was not 'obtained' by the appellant because, at his request and following usual practice, it was probably paid by the mortgage company direct to the vendor.

9.123   In *R v Roach* [2008] EWCA Crim 2562, there were two main points on appeal: firstly, where a property is acquired on a mortgage, what is the interest to be valued when assessing the offender's benefit—the freehold interest or the equity? The Court of Appeal held that, applying s 79 of POCA, 'the relevant value was the value of the appellant in the property at the material time, subject to the charge in favour of the building society'. Accordingly, the benefit figure was half the equity in the property, which represented the defendant's half share after the building society's interest had been taken into account. The Court also stated that there was no scope for disapplying s 79 where the mortgage had been obtained by fraud; it was a fact that at the material time, the building society had an interest in the property.

9.124   Secondly, what is the position where funds for the property come partly from tainted and partly from untainted money? One of Roach's properties had been acquired half by means of a loan and half with money which was treated as tainted money. She argued that half of the value of that property should not be regarded as the proceeds of crime. The Court of Appeal applied by analogy s 306 of POCA which would have, in civil proceedings, led to the result that half the property would indeed not have been treated as the proceeds of her offending, applying *R v Olupitan* [2008] EWCA Civ 104. It could not discern 'any rational ground' upon which a different approach should be taken in criminal confiscation proceedings and stated that there was 'fairness and simplicity' in the outcome, stating that it would be unjust to deprive someone of a property largely acquired with untainted funds. The Court reserved for future decision a case in which the property was acquired by a mortgage and the mortgage instalments were paid either out of tainted or innocent funds, in which 'other questions may arise'.

Such other questions did arguably arise in the case of *R v Barry Ward* [2008] EWCA Civ **9.125** 2955, where the Court found (at para 10):

> 10. . . . the contention [is] that the remortgage moneys should not have been included in the benefit from the Appellant's general criminal conduct because they came from a legitimate source. However, the legitimacy of the source of moneys is not sufficient to displace the assumption. What must be shown in addition is that the property in question, here the remortgage money, was obtained lawfully, and that the Appellant's criminal lifestyle was irrelevant to its obtaining. Because of his general lack of credibility, the Appellant failed to show that the moneys had been obtained lawfully. We see no fault in the judge's reasoning.
>
> 11. Moreover, the false accounts made it virtually impossible for the Appellant to displace the statutory assumption. The judge was entitled to infer in the circumstances that the accounts had been submitted by the Appellant or on his behalf. The suggestion that they were made up and submitted to the Building Society without his participation, at a time when, because of his detention in prison, he had no earnings, is simply incredible. In these circumstances, it is clear that these moneys were obtained by his criminal conduct.

Similar issues arose in the case of *R v Agombar* [2009] EWCA Crim 903, where the Court **9.126** of Appeal confirmed that where it had been concluded that an offender's matrimonial home represented the proceeds of crime, any money raised by way of a mortgage against the property itself would also be considered the proceeds of crime. Legitimate documentation backing the mortgage did not mean that the sums borrowed did not represent the proceeds of crime.

D. The Recoverable Amount

The third question: what sum is recoverable from the defendant?

Section 7 of POCA provides that: **9.127**

(1) The recoverable amount for the purposes of section 6 is an amount equal to the defendant's benefit from the conduct concerned.
(2) But if the defendant shows that the available amount is less than that benefit the recoverable amount is—
(a) the available amount, or
(b) a nominal amount, if the available amount is nil.

It will be noted that under s 7 the method of calculation in terms of assessing the recoverable amount is the same as in the DTA and the CJA 1988. The recoverable amount is the amount of the defendant's benefit from either his general criminal conduct or his particular criminal conduct (as the case may be). However, if the amount available for confiscation is, after consideration by the court, found to be less than the benefit in question, the confiscation order must be made in the lesser amount. The word 'nominal' is defined in the Oxford English Dictionary as meaning 'virtually nothing'.

9.128 The House of Lords in *R v May* [2008] UKHL 28 noted that:

> The answering of this third question is a very important stage in the procedure for making confiscation orders since, however great the payments a defendant may have received or the property he may have obtained, he cannot be ordered to pay a sum which it is beyond his means to pay.

The House continued (para 41):

> In many cases the assessment of the realisable amount poses complex and difficult problems for the trial judge, often exacerbated by lack of information . . . But the statutory provisions governing the assessment are detailed, and the problems which arise are not, in the main, questions of principle. It is not in doubt that assets legitimately acquired may be included within the realisable amount, provided of course that the defendant's total benefit from the relevant criminal conduct is not exceeded.

The 'available amount'

9.129 Section 9(1) and (2) of POCA provides:

(1) For the purposes of deciding the recoverable amount, the available amount is the aggregate of—
  (a) the total of the values (at the time the confiscation order is made) of all the free property then held by the defendant minus the total amount payable in pursuance of obligations which then have priority, and
  (b) the total of the values (at that time) of all tainted gifts.
(2) An obligation has priority if it is an obligation of the defendant—
  (a) to pay an amount due in respect of a fine or other order of a Court which was imposed or made on conviction of an offence and at any time before the time the confiscation order is made, or
  (b) to pay a sum which would be included amongst preferential debts if the defendant's bankruptcy had commenced on the date of the confiscation order or his winding up had been ordered on that date.

9.130 Under s 9(1), the 'available amount' is the value of all the defendant's property, minus certain prior obligations of the defendant, such as earlier fines, plus the value of all tainted gifts made by the defendant. It is, in effect, equivalent to the term 'the amount that might be realised' in the earlier confiscation legislation, and is calculated in the same way.

9.131 Section 82(3) defines free property as follows:

Property is free unless an order is enforced in respect of it under any of these provisions:
(a) forfeiture orders under Section 27 of the Misuse of Drugs Act 1971;
(b) . . .
(c) . . .
(d) deprivation orders under Section 143 of the Sentencing Act;
(e) Section 23 or 111 of the Terrorism Act 2000 (forfeiture orders);
(f) Section 246, 266, 295(2) or 298(2) of this Act (certain civil recovery orders under Pt 5).

In *R v Chen* (2009) EWCA Crim 2669, the Court confirmed that whilst a pension policy did constitute free property, the judge at first instance had been wrong in his assessment of its value, as the policy could not be realised.

Burden of proof

9.132 Thus far, the burden of proof, at each stage, has been on the Crown. Once the Crown has discharged the burden of satisfying the court of the fact of benefit and the amount of the defendant's proceeds, the burden shifts onto the defendant to show that the value of his realisable assets is less than the amount of his benefit (see *R v Comiskey* [1991] 93 Cr App R 227). The reason for this is that the defendant is the person who is in the best position to know the extent and value of his own assets. As Tucker J said in delivering the judgment of the Court of Appeal in *Comiskey* (at p 231):

> The Act was intended to avoid a situation where a drug dealer serves his sentence with equanimity, knowing that on his release substantial funds will be available to enable him to live in comfort. With this in mind, a successful drugs dealer will take care to ensure, so far as he can, that the proceeds of his trade will be hidden away so as to be untraceable. The Act is designed to oblige him to disclose his assets, or to face the risk that if he does not do so, the court will make certain assumptions against him, and that he may have to serve an additional sentence of imprisonment if he does not comply with an order.

The standard of proof is on a balance of probabilities (s 6(7)). If the defendant fails to participate in the hearing or fails to discharge this burden, a confiscation order will be made in the full amount of his benefit. **9.133**

In *R v Benjafield* (2002) 2 Cr App R(S) 70, Lord Steyn confirmed (at para 12): **9.134**

> The fact that the appellant did not testify is a powerful point against him.

In *R v Afraz Siddique* [2005] EWCA Crim 1812, the Court held that in circumstances where a defendant had failed to provide evidence about his realisable assets for the purposes of the confiscation order, the judge was entitled to conclude that the appellant had not satisfied him that his realisable assets were less than the benefit of the drug trafficking. The Court held (at para 27) that: **9.135**

> The appellant had the opportunity of seeking to persuade the court about his realisable assets. He declined to take it, for no doubt the very good reason that either there was no, or no credible, evidence he could give and/or he would be exposed to penetrating cross-examination which could only make his position worse. The fact that his credibility may already have been badly damaged is not a shield behind which he can hide. If it were, defendants in the position of the appellant would refuse to give evidence and yet successfully maintain that their realisable assets were less than the benefit. Such a position would be nonsensical, given the structure of the DTA and its compliance with Article 6, and would place judges hearing confiscation proceedings in an impossible position.

Hidden assets

In *R v Ilsemann* [1991] Crim LR 141 the Court of Appeal considered the issue of 'hidden assets' and held: **9.136**

> it was a misconception to say that the amount of the confiscation order should be limited to the amount which the prosecution could prove to be the value of the defendant's assets known to them. If the defendant wished to say that that was all that was realisable, it was for him to satisfy the court to this effect.

(See also *R v Cokovic* (1996) 1 Cr App R(S) 131.)

In *R v Wright* [2006] EWCA Crim 1257, the Court of Appeal returned to the subject of hidden assets. In *Wright* the judge at first instance had made a confiscation order in the sum of £100,000 but had not given specific reasons as to how he had come to that conclusion. A benefit figure of £4,630,823 had been identified and the appellant's realisable assets were put at a sum of just over £50,000. It was apparent and assumed therefore that the judge had **9.137** concluded that the appellant must have hidden assets in the sum of the balance. The appellant appealed on the basis that there was no evidence that he had such hidden assets. The principles in *R v Barwick* (2001) 1 Cr App R(S) 129 were accepted by the Court of Appeal. They make clear that the burden of establishing that the realisable assets are in a lesser sum than the benefit is with the defendant. The question for the Court in *Wright* was whether the judge was entitled to add £50,000 by way of realisable assets upon the evidence before him. The Court of Appeal (Pill LJ) stated:

> Of course there are many ways in which assets can be hidden, including assets being held temporarily by some other person on the defendant's behalf. The burden was on the appellant, an appellant who hitherto had had a lavish lifestyle. It was for the judge to form a judgement on realisable assets in those circumstances. As he correctly pointed out, he had had no assistance from the appellant himself by way of oral evidence, or even by way of signed statements. (See para 20).

9.138 The Court of Appeal concluded in *Wright* that the judge was entitled to reach the conclusion he did. There was, the Court said, no rule of law that a judge was not entitled to find on appropriate facts that there are hidden assets. The Court concluded that the judge had been modest in his assessment of the situation.

9.139 In *R v Barnham* [2005] EWCA Crim 1049, the Court of Appeal had to consider the issue of whether the Crown was required to make out a *prima facie* case that a defendant had hidden assets before a defendant could be expected to deal with such an allegation. The defendant submitted that Art 6(1) of the European Convention on Human Rights would be engaged in relation to the second stage of the confiscation proceedings, namely after a benefit figure had been found, contending that the assumptions flowed through to the second stage and accordingly the Crown should be required to establish a *prima facie* case of hidden assets before the burden of proof shifted to the defendant. The Court ruled that the correct approach was that once the prosecution had established the existence of benefit, there was no requirement on it to provide a *prima facie* case in relation to realisable or hidden assets. At the second stage, the burden of proof shifted to the defendant to establish, if he could, his realisable assets to the satisfaction of the court. By that stage the defendant would know exactly how the court had determined benefit attributable to him and he had to prove by evidence what his realisable assets were. It was for him to show why the confiscation order should not be the value of the proceeds of drug trafficking. The Court of Appeal stated that to hold that the prosecution should, in some way, show a *prima facie* case that the defendant had hidden assets would defeat the object of the legislation (which was designed to enable the court to confiscate the criminal's ill-gotten gains). It confirmed that the expression 'hidden assets' was indicative of the fact that the prosecution could have no means of knowing how and where a defendant might have disposed of or dealt with the proceeds in question; see further *R v Valentine* [2006] EWCA Crim 2717.

9.140 The above rationale was echoed in the DTA case of *R v Peacock and Gillett* [2009] EWCA Crim 654 where the Court held (at para 24):

> Realisable property . . . is not confined to that which is specifically identified. Money received is a realisable asset even though its source is described generically and its exact provenance is not established. Further, a court is entitled to draw reasonable inferences as to the existence of realisable assets from evidence satisfying it to the requisite standard of proof.

Assets not restricted to those derived from criminal activity

As with DTA and CJA cases, any asset of the defendant, whether legitimately acquired or **9.141** not, is vulnerable to confiscation in order to satisfy a confiscation order made under POCA (see *R v Currey* (1995) 16 Cr App R(S) 421).

In *R v Chrastny (No 2)* [1991] 1 WLR 1385, a DTOA case but of application in terms of **9.142** POCA, Glidewell LJ stated at p 1395:

> . . . one of the questions that arises is if a defendant has legitimately acquired property which is not part of his or her proceeds of drug trafficking, and if the amount realisable from the proceeds of drug trafficking are less than the total proceeds attributable to her, whether an order can be made in the total sum of the proceeds of drug trafficking, which will mean that she has to turn to some of her legitimate assets in order to satisfy the order. I have read the definition of realisable property within section 5(1). In our view it is quite clear that that definition embraces legitimately acquired property. We cannot read into the Act of 1986 any inference that the definition is to be limited to illegitimately acquired property; that is to say, the proceeds of drug trafficking. This statute is undoubtedly draconian and the decision on that point may seem to be harsh; the statute is harsh. The statute is in essence one that seeks to ensure that everyone who has benefited from drug trafficking shall to the extent to which he or she can do so be deprived of the whole of that benefit.

Market value

Section 79 states that in deciding the value at any time of property held by a person, its value **9.143** is the market value of the property at that time (s 79(2)). But if at that time another person has an interest in the property, its value, in relation to the person who holds the property, is the market value at the time of the person who holds the property's interest, ignoring any charging order (see s 79(3) and s 79(4) for the provisions relating to charging orders).

Costs of sale

In *R v Davies* [2004] EWCA Crim 3380, the Court of Appeal held that it was 'quite right' **9.144** to deduct the costs of any sale (eg estate agent's costs) from the value of the house that was to be sold in order to satisfy the confiscation order, (see para 15, reflecting *R v Kramer* (1992) 13 Cr App R(S) 390 and the terms of the order in *Lemmon* (1991) 13 Crim App R (S) 66).

Contract services

In *Re Adams* (2005) LS Gaz January 13, 28, QBD (Lightman J), the Court held that a con- **9.145** sultancy contract entered into by the defendant under which he would be entitled to £52,000 pa for his services, was not 'realisable property' within s 74(1) and s 102(1) of the CJA 1988, because the contract was for the provision of services where the identity of the provider was the essence and any entitlement to payment under the contract for services would only arise if the services were provided by the defendant. The Court found that such conditional and future entitlement 'was not property' but a chose in action personal to the party. In *R v Najafpour* (2009) EWCA Crim 2723, the Court of Appeal stated that commission, owed as a debt, could not be treated as a realisable asset under the confiscation scheme.

Assets jointly held with third parties

If the defendant owns an asset jointly with an innocent third party (eg a matrimonial **9.146** home held jointly with his wife) it constitutes a realisable asset of the defendant to the extent of his interest in it. Thus, if the defendant has a 50 per cent interest in an asset with another party, 50 per cent of its value can be taken into account in assessing the amount to be realised. The means by which such assets are realised, the procedure, and the rights of third parties in relation thereto are considered fully in Chapter 16. It should be emphasised at this stage that any third party claiming to have an interest in realisable property does not have the right to be heard or be legally represented at the confiscation hearing except in his capacity as a witness on behalf of the defendant, if he chooses to call him. The third party's right to be heard arises at the enforcement stage. For the proposition that private pension funds can form part of confiscation orders, see *R v Ford* (2008) EWCA 966. Once assets have been identified as realisable property they may be recovered from any trust or company; see *In the matter of May* (2009) EWHC 1826 (QB).

Matrimonial homes

9.147   The issue of matrimonial homes and their fate in confiscation proceedings, together with case law relating thereto, is considered fully in Chapter 16.

Recoverable amount: victims

9.148   By ss 6(6) and 7(3), where the victim of the criminal conduct has started or intends to start proceedings against the defendant in respect of loss, injury, or damage sustained in connection with the conduct, the recoverable amount will be an amount which:

(1) the court believes is just, but
(2) does not exceed the amount found under s 7(1) or (2) as the case may be.

Court must give reasons

9.149   Under s 7(5) if the court decides the available amount, it must include in the confiscation order a statement of its findings as to the matters relevant for deciding that amount. In *Birmingham City Council v Ram* [2007] EWCA Crim 3084 Toulson J commented (at para 28):

> the judge was not required as a matter of law to deal with each point on which there was a conflict of evidence. He had to deal with the essential issues in dispute and state his reasons for his conclusions.

E. Tainted Gifts

9.150   The legislature is alive to the possibility that defendants and those involved in nefarious activities may seek to divest themselves of valuable assets in order to circumvent the confiscation regime. In order to ensure such 'gifts' are caught as realisable assets, the Act makes specific provision for them to be taken into account.

9.151   Under s 77(1) of POCA, the issue of whether a gift of assets or property is tainted will be considered if:

(a) no court has made a decision as to whether the defendant has a criminal lifestyle, or
(b) the court has decided that the defendant has a criminal lifestyle.

When is a gift tainted?

Under s 77 of POCA, a gift becomes tainted if: **9.152**

(2) ... it was made by the defendant at any time after the relevant day.
(3) A gift is also tainted if it was made by the defendant at any time and was of property—
  (a) which was obtained by the defendant as a result of or in connection with his general criminal conduct, or
  (b) which (in whole or in part and whether directly or indirectly) represented in the defendant's hands property obtained by him as a result of or in connection with his general criminal conduct.

Under s 77(9), the 'relevant day' referred to in s 77(2) is the first day of the period of six   **9.153**
years ending with:

(a) the day when proceedings for the offence concerned were started against the defendant, or
(b) if there are two or more offences and proceedings for them were started on different days, the earliest of those days.

Under POCA, therefore, a gift is tainted: **9.154**

(1) if it is made by the defendant to any person in the period beginning six years before the commencement of proceedings, (under s 77(2))
(2) if it was made by the defendant at any time and the gift was from the proceeds of crime (under s 77(3)).

Section 77(5) adds a further situation where a gift will be tainted, but, by virtue of s 77(4),   **9.155**
it only applies if the court has decided that the defendant does not have a criminal lifestyle:

(5) A gift is tainted if it was made by the defendant at any time after—
  (a) the date on which the offence concerned was committed, or
  (b) if his particular criminal conduct consists of two or more offences and they were committed on different dates, the date of the earliest.

For the purposes of s 77(5), an offence which is a continuing offence is committed on the   **9.156**
first occasion when it is committed (as per s 77(6)), and the defendant's particular criminal conduct for the purposes of s 77(5), includes any conduct which constitutes offences which the court has taken into consideration in deciding his sentence for the offence or offences concerned (s 77(7)).

It should be noted that the gift might be a tainted gift whether it was made before or after   **9.157**
the passing of POCA (as per s 77(8)). Further, like the earlier legislation, gifts made by the defendant to other persons may be placed under restraint prior to the criminal trial or confiscation hearing.

Gifts and their recipients

Section 78(1) provides: **9.158**

If the defendant transfers property to another person for a consideration whose value is significantly less than the value of the property at the time of the transfer, he is to be treated as making a gift.

This section is designed to prevent defendants from benefiting under the legislation if they sell property for an under value. Under POCA a 'gift' includes a transaction for a consideration which is significantly less than the value of the gift at the time of the transfer, eg if a defendant sells a painting worth £100,000 for £5,000.

9.159 This is a departure from the earlier legislation, where an undervalued transaction was defined as the difference between the value of the property when the defendant received it and its value at the time of the transfer.

9.160 References to a recipient of a tainted gift are to a person to whom the defendant has made the gift (s 78(3)).

Value of tainted gifts

9.161 Under s 81 of POCA:

(1) The value at any time (the material time) of a tainted gift is the greater of the following—
  (a) the value at the time of the gift of the property given, adjusted to take account of later changes in the value of money;
  (b) the value (at the material time) of the property found under subsection (2).
(2) The property found under this subsection is as follows—
  (a) if the recipient holds the property given, the property found under this subsection is that property;
  (b) if the recipient holds no part of the property given, the property found under this subsection is any property which directly or indirectly represents it in his hands;
  (c) if the recipient holds part of the property given, the property found under this subsection is that part and any property which directly or indirectly represents the other part in his hands.

9.162 Section 81 sets out how the court is to work out the value of property held by a person. These principles broadly reproduce the previous legislation. The references under s 81 to value are to the value found in accordance with s 79 (as per s 81(3)).

Defendant does not have to be able to realise gift

9.163 In *R v Tighe* [1996] Crim LR 69 the Court of Appeal held that Parliament had contemplated that money might continue to be realisable even though it had been the subject of a gift or gifts by the defendant. The fact that a gift had been made would not save the offender from a confiscation order. The recovery of the money was only one factor of which the court must take account in exercising its discretion. In *Tighe* the appellant had deliberately put out of his control monies already outside of the jurisdiction. On that basis the judge had been correct in refusing to take account of the fact that the appellant might not be able to recover the money. See also *R v Wallace Duncan Smith* (1996) 2 Cr App R 1. For the proposition that private pension funds can form part of confiscation orders, see *R v Ford* (2008) EWCA Crim 966.

9.164 In the post-*May* Court of Appeal decision of *R v Richards* [2008] EWCA Crim 1841 (Toulson LJ) the Court came to consider once again the application of the gift provisions. The facts were as follows: Richards had had transferred into his name five properties from an associate named Rogers, who was convicted of drug trafficking offences. There was no consideration for these transfers. Richards was then convicted of money laundering contrary to ss 328 and 329 of POCA. The total value of the five properties (or their sale proceeds, as appropriate) at the time of the confiscation hearing was £241,000. This sum was included by the judge in the benefit and recoverable amount figures for both Richards and Rogers. Richards submitted that it was inconsistent to treat the property as available to both Richards and Rogers to meet the confiscation order. If it was available to Rogers then it was held by Rogers and not by Richards. If it was held by Richards and of benefit to him, he must be allowed to use it to discharge the order.

Richards' evidence at the confiscation hearing was that, although he was the legal owner **9.165** of the properties, they were in truth the assets of Rogers. The trial judge found that Richards benefited by obtaining the properties and his benefit was the value of the properties obtained. He did not address the question of whether Richards was the full beneficial owner or merely a nominee. The Court of Appeal held that Richards obtained a benefit when he obtained legal title to the properties, even if he was a bare nominee. However, the judge had clearly treated the properties as belonging to Rogers. The most that Richards had was a bare legal title to the properties, with Rogers retaining the full beneficial interest.

The Crown submitted that the properties had to be returned to Rogers because of the **9.166** operation of the tainted gift provisions of s 77 of POCA, and that the beneficial interest in the properties which had initially passed to Richards re-vested in Rogers by operation of law upon the making of the confiscation order by the judge.

The Court held that the tainted gift provisions could not determine what Richards' interest **9.167** was; this was to be determined by the law of property. The judge should not have found that Richards received the full beneficial interest in the properties, as he was holding them for Rogers. The appeal was allowed and the confiscation order quashed. The Court noted that some form of order might have been merited on the basis that Richards had received rent from the properties, but the Court had not been invited to make any alternative order. There would be no injustice in the result, as the value of the properties would pass to the State by reason of the confiscation order against Rogers.

F. Time for Payment

Section 11 indicates the period the court should allow the defendant to pay the amount **9.168** due under the confiscation order. Section 11(1) states that the amount ordered to be paid must be paid on the making of the order (ie immediately), but this is subject to certain provisions:

(2) If the defendant shows that he needs time to pay the amount ordered to be paid, the court making the confiscation order may make an order allowing payment to be made in a specified period.

(3) The specified period—
  (a) must start with the day on which the confiscation order is made, and
  (b) must not exceed six months.

It is for the defendant to show that he needs more time to pay (eg because he envisages the **9.169** sale of his home). If within the specified period the defendant applies to the Crown Court for the period to be extended and the court believes there are exceptional circumstances, it may make an order extending the period (see s 11(4)). However, the court must not make an order under either s 11(2) or (4) unless it gives the prosecutor a right to be heard and make representations at any such application.

9.170 Section 11(5) states the extended period:

(a) must start with the day on which the confiscation order is made, and
(b) must not exceed 12 months.

Similarly, an order under s 11(4) may be made after the end of the specified period, but must not be made after the end of the period of 12 months starting on the day on which the confiscation order is made (see s 11(6)). Therefore, no more than 12 months may be granted from the day on which the confiscation order is made.

9.171 The court may direct payment of any amount ordered to be paid under a confiscation order by instalment (see s 139(1)(b) PCC(S)A). Payment should be made to the magistrates' court, pursuant to CrimPR 52.2. Occasionally, the court will split the time-to-pay period, eg £10,000 within one month of the making of the order, the balance within six months.

Appeal does not stop clock

9.172 In circumstances where an appeal had been lodged, the Court of Appeal took a robust approach to the period set for payment in the case of *R v May, Lawrence* [2005] EWCA Crim 97, where Keene LJ held at para 5 that the:

> proposition that the time to pay a confiscation order runs from the date of the determination of an appeal was 'unsound in law'. In principle the fact that an appeal is pending does not operate so as to suspend the operation of any sentence or order.

He added at para 7 that:

> There is no reason why steps preparatory to the raising of the money specified in the confiscation order should not have been taken while an (the defendant May's) appeal was pending. The appellant was not entitled to assume that his appeal would be successful and, as indicated above, as a matter of law time was running during that period. Moreover, it would be wrong as a matter of principle for appellants to be encouraged to believe that bringing an appeal would be likely to lengthen the time given for payment, even if the appeal was unsuccessful.

Imprisonment in default

9.173 Under s 38(2) and (5) of POCA, the provisions of the PCC(S)A apply to the enforcement of a confiscation order in the same way as they apply to the imposition of a fine by the Crown Court. The effect of this provision is that the court must impose a prison sentence to be served in default of payment. It will be noted that, as with the previous legislation, the serving of the sentence in default does not extinguish the debt.

9.174 The penalties available for default in payment are set out in s 139(4) of the PCC(S)A and are as follows:

An amount not exceeding £200	7 days
An amount exceeding £200 but not exceeding £500	14 days
An amount exceeding £500 but not exceeding £1,000	28 days
An amount exceeding £1,000 but not exceeding £2,500	45 days
An amount exceeding £2,500 but not exceeding £5,000	3 months
An amount exceeding £5,000 but not exceeding £10,000	6 months
An amount exceeding £10,000 but not exceeding £20,000	12 months

An amount exceeding £20,000 but not exceeding £50,000	18 months
An amount exceeding £50,000 but not exceeding £100,000	2 years
An amount exceeding £100,000 but not exceeding £250,000	3 years
An amount exceeding £250,000 but not exceeding £1,000,000	5 years
An amount exceeding £1,000,000	10 years

The imposition of a default sentence was held to be mandatory in *R v Popple* [1992] **9.175**
Crim LR 675 and s 38(2) of POCA provides that the default sentence must be served
consecutively to any sentence of imprisonment imposed for the substantive offence.
It should be noted, however, that the above sentences are the maximum that may be
imposed and it does not follow that the maximum sentence available for a particular
amount should automatically be imposed in every case.

In *R v Szrajber* (1994) 15 Cr App R (S) 821, Crim LR 543 a CJA confiscation order **9.176**
was made against the defendant in the sum of £407,188 and a five-year sentence of
imprisonment imposed for default in making payment, being the maximum period that
could be ordered in respect of a sum between £250,000 and £1 million. The trial judge
imposed the maximum sentence assuming it was a fixed period that she was required to
impose. The Court of Appeal ruled, however, that the periods set out in the table were
maximum periods and the court had discretion to impose a period below the maximum.
The normal procedure would be for the court to impose a default sentence that fell
between the maximum and minimum of the band being considered. So, for a confiscation
order in the sum imposed against the defendant, a default sentence between three and five
years should normally be imposed. In determining the proper sentence the court had to
have regard to the circumstances of the case, to the overall seriousness of the matter, and in
particular to the purpose for which the default sentence was imposed, namely to secure
payment of the sum ordered to be confiscated. It was not necessary to approach the matter
on a strict arithmetical basis. In the circumstances, the court varied the default sentence to
four years. *Szrajber* was followed in the case of *R v Cox* [2008] EWCA Crim 3007, where
the five-year maximum was reduced to four years, and where the Court commented that
the judge should have been given more assistance on the issue than she was.

In *R v French* (1995) 16 Cr App R(S) 841, the court held that the period of imprison- **9.177**
ment in default should be such, within the maximum permitted, as to make it completely
clear to the defendant that he had nothing to gain by failing to comply with the order. In
R v Simon Price, Court of Appeal, 14 December 2009, the Court adopted the reasoning
in *R v Pigott* (2009) EWCA Crim 2292, in determining that the purpose of the default
sentence was to ensure that the defendant complied with the order, and that it was wrong
in principle to take into account the sentence for the substantive offence, ie the principle of
totality in sentence did not have application.

Serving the default sentence does not extinguish the debt

Under s 38(5) where the defendant serves the term of imprisonment or detention in default **9.178**
of paying any amount due under a confiscation order, his serving that term does not prevent the confiscation order from continuing to have effect, so far as any other method of
enforcement is concerned.

Early release

9.179   The liability to serve the full default sentence is reduced by half following the introduction of s 258 of the Criminal Justice Act 2003. It applies to those defendants committed to prison after 4 April 2005 as a result of a default in the payment of a sum adjudged to be paid on conviction:

> (2)   As soon as a person to whom this section applies has served one-half of the term for which he was committed, it is the duty of the Secretary of State to release him unconditionally.
>
> (3)   Where a person to whom this section applies is also serving one or more sentences of imprisonment, nothing in this section requires the Secretary of State to release him until he is also required to release him in respect of that sentence or each of those sentences.

Interest on unpaid sums

9.180   If the amount to be paid by a person under a confiscation order is not paid by the time it was required to be paid, the defendant must pay interest on that amount for any period after which it remains unpaid (see s 12(1)). Under s 12(2), the rate of interest is the same as that for interest on civil judgment debts (see s 17 of the Judgments Act 1838, currently 8 per cent). The payment of interest is mandatory in all cases, the interest being treated as part of the amount to be paid under the confiscation order (s 12(4)).

Term in default: a penalty

9.181   In *Togher (Appellant) v Revenue & Customs Prosecutions Office (Respondent) & Doran (Intervenor)* (2007) EWCA Civ 686 Collins J had held at first instance that the term of imprisonment in default was not a penalty, but a means of enforcement. The Court of Appeal however rejected this, Thomas LJ, delivering the judgment of the court, finding (at para 470):

> The confiscation order and the default sentence were imposed following a conviction for a criminal offence. The nature and purpose of the confiscation and the term in default is to punish the offender. In *R v Clark & Bentham* [1997] 2 Cr App (S) 99, Lord Bingham CJ giving the judgment of the Court of Appeal Criminal Division made it clear that a judge should approach the period of imprisonment to be served in default by asking the question— what period of imprisonment not exceeding the statutory maximum is necessary to coerce the defendant into realising and paying the sum due under the confiscation order? The procedures for the making of the confiscation order and the imposition of the term in default were those of a criminal court. Both the confiscation order and the term in default were severe in their consequences. In my view it is artificial to seek to categorise separately the confiscation order and the term in default; to categorise the term in default as the means by which the penalty is to be enforced is to disregard the overall scheme and to put form before substance. In my view each is a penalty within the meaning of Article 7(1), but both should be considered together. If they are, they plainly are a penalty within the meaning of Article 7(1).

Unreasonable delay

9.182   In *Bullen and Soneji v UK* [2009] ECtHR 28, The Times, 2 February 2009, the ECtHR held that there had been a violation of Art 6.1 following a delay of approximately five years and six months (including appeals to the Court of Appeal (Criminal Division) and the House of Lords) in the final determination of the confiscation proceedings. The ECtHR reiterated that the reasonableness of the length of the proceedings must be assessed in the light of the circumstances of the case with reference to: the complexity of the case; the conduct of the applicants and the relevant authorities; and what was at stake for the applicants (para 58, applying *Pelissier and Sassi v France* no 25444/94 and *Caplik v Turkey* no 57019/00).

In *Lloyd v Bow Street Magistrates' Court* [2003] EWHC Admin 2294 the court ruled **9.183** that an unreasonable delay on the part of the prosecutor in taking enforcement action would amount to a breach of the defendant's rights under Art 6 of the European Convention on Human Rights if an attempt was made to implement the default sentence. The Court made it plain, however, that its decision applied only where enforcement action took the form of implementing the default sentence and had no application in respect of the use of civil remedies, such as the appointment of an enforcement receiver. This position has, however, been slightly modified by *R (on the application of Deamer) v Southampton Crown Court* (DC, 13 July 2006) where the court held that where there had been no unexplained or unjustifiable delay on the part of the prosecutor a committal in default was not unreasonable even though six years had elapsed. The issue of delay is returned to in the enforcement chapter of this book (at para 11.140). Recent cases include *Minshall v Marylebone Magistrates' Court* [2008] EWHC 2800, where the court found that an unusually long delay would not prevent enforcement in circumstances where it had been caused by the defendant pursuing every avenue of appeal open to him and *R (on the application of Stone) v Plymouth Magistrates' Court* [2007] EWHC 2519 (Admin), where a confiscation order was quashed following a 13-year delay in enforcement.

G. The Effect of a Confiscation Order on Sentence and the Court's Other Powers

Once the court has made a confiscation order it must then proceed in respect of the offence **9.184** or offences concerned in the terms set out in s 13(2) and (4) of POCA:

(2) The court must take account of the confiscation order before—
    (a) it imposes a fine on the defendant, or
    (b) it makes an order falling within subsection (3).
(3) ...
(4) Subject to subsection (2) the court must leave the confiscation order out of account in deciding the appropriate sentence for the defendant.

Orders falling within subs (3) include compensation orders under s 130 of the Sentencing **9.185** Act; forfeiture orders under s 27 of the Misuse of Drugs Act 1971; deprivation orders under s 143 of the Sentencing Act 2000; and forfeiture orders under s 23 of the Terrorism Act 2000.

Section 13 therefore requires the court to have regard to the confiscation order before **9.186** imposing a fine or other order involving payment by the defendant, except for a compensation order, but otherwise it directs the court to ignore the confiscation order when sentencing the defendant.

The relationship between the confiscation order and compensation

9.187 Under s 13(5):

> (5) Subsection (6) applies if—
>
> (a) the Crown Court makes both a confiscation order and an order for the payment of compensation under section 130 of the Sentencing Act against the same person in the same proceedings, and
>
> (b) the court believes he will not have sufficient means to satisfy both the orders in full.
>
> (6) In such a case the court must direct that so much of the compensation as it specifies is to be paid out of any sums recovered under the confiscation order; and the amount it specifies must be the amount it believes will not be recoverable because of the insufficiency of the person's means.

Orders for the payment of prosecution costs

9.188 Orders for the payment of costs should only be made where the defendant has the ability to pay them. If a confiscation order is made in what the court finds to be the full value of a defendant's realisable property, no order for costs should be made. In *R v Szrajber* (1994) Crim LR 543 the defendant's benefit from the offences was found to be £524,000, but his realisable property was valued at £407,188 and a confiscation order accordingly made in this lesser sum. In addition, an order for the payment of costs was made in the sum of £65,428. The Court of Appeal quashed the order for costs on the basis that a confiscation order had been made in the full amount of the defendant's benefit from the offence and accordingly he had no further assets at his disposal from which the order for costs could be paid.

9.189 In *R v Ghadami* [1997] Crim LR 606 the Court of Appeal held that when it came to considering the question of an order to pay the costs of the prosecution, other debts should be taken into account (eg a confiscation order). It could then be seen that the appellant was a man without assets. In *Ghadami* the order to pay the costs of the prosecution was quashed (see also *R v Ruddick* The Times, 6 May 2003 (CA)).

H. Confiscation and the ECHR

9.190 It is now fairly well established that confiscation proceedings, following on and attaching to a criminal conviction, represent a penalty (see *R v Benjafield* [2002] UKHL 2 (para 82); *Rezvi* [2002] UKHL 1; and *Phillips v UK* [2001] EHRR No 41087/98.)

9.191 Case law also dictates that the confiscation procedures do not involve the determination of a criminal charge, but are properly to be regarded as part of the sentencing procedures of the court, following conviction of a criminal offence. Accordingly Art 6(2) of the European Convention on Human Rights (ECHR) has no application as to the right to a fair trial under Art 6(1) or in respect of the determination of the defendant's civil obligations.

9.192 In *R v Benjafield* [2002] UKHL 2 the House of Lords considered the relationship between confiscation orders under the DTA and the Human Rights Act 1998. The defendant had pleaded guilty to two counts of conspiracy to supply drugs, and was sentenced to a total of 14 years' imprisonment. Subsequently, the court made a confiscation order against him. The order was imposed before the implementation of the Human Rights Act 1998. On the defendant's appeal against the confiscation order, which was heard after the implementation of the 1998 Act, the Court of Appeal considered whether the reverse assumptions in s 4(3) of the 1994 Act were compatible with the provisions of the ECHR (as set out in the Schedule to the 1998 Act), particularly Art 6(1) (the general right to a fair hearing) and Art 6(2) (the presumption of innocence in respect of those charged with a criminal offence). The House of Lords held that a defendant who was the subject of criminal proceedings before the implementation of the 1998 Act was not entitled to rely on Convention rights in an appeal after the implementation of that Act. It followed that in the case of *Benjafield* the defendant's Convention rights were not engaged, and his appeal was dismissed (applying *R v Kansal (No 2)* [2002] 1 All ER 257). However the House of Lords also held that Art 6(2) of the Convention did not apply to confiscation proceedings under the 1994 Act. Such proceedings, it held, were part of the sentencing process following a conviction, and are not a criminal charge within the meaning of Art 6(2). The Court held that although a person who is subject to confiscation proceedings had the full protection of Art 6(1), the reverse burden provisions in s 4(3) of the 1994 Act were compatible with that article. Further, the Court held any interference with the right of peaceful enjoyment of possessions under Art 1 of the First Protocol of the Convention was also justified (applying *McIntosh v Lord Advocate* [2001] 2 All ER 638 and *Phillips v UK* (2001) 11 EHRR 280 No 41087/98).

In Lord Steyn's judgment he held (at para 8):   **9.193**

> Making due allowance for the differences between the confiscation procedures under the 1988 Act and under the 1994 Act, the reasoning in *R v Rezvi* (2002) 1 All ER 801 applies with equal force in this case. The 1994 Act pursues an important objective in the public interest and the legislative measures are rationally connected with the furtherance of this objective. The procedure devised by Parliament is a fair and proportionate response to the need to protect the public interest. The critical point is that under the 1994 Act, as under the 1988 Act, the judge must be astute to avoid injustice. If there is or might be a serious risk of injustice, he must not make a confiscation order. In these circumstances a challenge to the compatibility of the legislation must fail.

In *McIntosh v Lord Advocate* [2001] 3 WLR 107 the Privy Council had considered whether   **9.194** the assumptions set out in the Proceeds of Crime (Scotland) Act 1995 were incompatible with the presumption of innocence afforded by Art 6(2) of the ECHR. The court held that the presumption of innocence guaranteed by Art 6(2) applied only to persons 'charged with a criminal offence'; and that although a person against whom an application for a confiscation order was made faced a financial penalty with a custodial penalty in default of payment, it was a penalty imposed for the offence with which he had already been convicted and involved no accusation of, or enquiry into, any other offence. Therefore in relation to the application for a confiscation order made against him the respondent was not a person entitled to rely on the presumption of innocence guaranteed by Art 6(2).

Further, on the assumption that Art 6(2) did apply to an application for a confiscation   **9.195** order following conviction, it was not unreasonable or oppressive to call on a proven drug trafficker to proffer an explanation for any significant discrepancy which could be established between his property and expenditure on the one hand and his known sources of income on the other. Accordingly, the assumptions that the court was entitled to make were not incompatible with the presumption of innocence under Art 6(2).

9.196 In *Welch v UK* [1995] 1/1994/448/527, the European Court of Human Rights held that the DTOA constituted a violation of Art 7 of the ECHR on the basis that Art 7(1) provides, *inter alia*, that a defendant may not be subject to a heavier penalty than that which was applicable at the time the offence was committed, and that the retrospective parts of the DTOA amounted to just that. See also *R v Togher*.

9.197 In *Welch* the Court specifically upheld the legality of the use of confiscation orders in combating drug trafficking; stating in its conclusion that it:

> does not call into question in any respect the powers of confiscation conferred on the courts as a weapon in the fight against the scourge of drug trafficking.

9.198 The ECHR was returned to in *R v Briggs-Price* [2009] UKHL 19, where their Lordships held that the confiscation proceedings in issue were both compatible with and followed from the legislation. In *R v Briggs-Price*, the defendant had been convicted of a conspiracy to import heroin, albeit none had been imported, and there was other evidence adduced during the course of the trial that the defendant had been dealing in cannabis, albeit such an offence had not been pursued. The judge made a specific finding, during the course of the confiscation proceedings, that he was satisfied to the criminal standard that the cannabis offending was made out on the evidence he had seen and heard. The appellant contended that the confiscation order should be quashed, since its imposition was incompatible with the fair trial guarantee in Art 6(2) of the Convention. Article 6(2) provides that 'everyone charged with a criminal offence shall be presumed innocent until proved guilty according to law'.

9.199 The appellant's case was that to impose a confiscation sum for any cannabis dealing effectively amounted to finding him guilty of that criminal offence. Having been neither tried for that offence, nor found guilty of it, the appellant asserted that the confiscation hearing breached his right to the presumption of innocence until proven guilty in Art 6(2).

9.200 As outlined above, in *Phillips v United Kingdom* (41087/98) and *HM Advocate v McIntosh* [2003] 1 AC 1078, the Strasbourg Court and Privy Council respectively had already confirmed that in confiscation proceedings no one is 'charged with a criminal offence' and therefore Art 6(2) did not apply. Their reasoning was that, other than the trigger offence for which a defendant has been convicted and which has resulted in confiscation proceedings, there is no new criminal offence being tried or added to the defendant's record at the confiscation stage. Rather, confiscation is really no more than a sentencing procedure for an offence that has already been proven. The sole purpose of such hearings is to assess the level of penalty.

9.201 The House of Lords found that the confiscation order that has been made, although involving a calculation on the basis of 'drug trafficking . . . at any time' and not only for the trigger offence, was no different in substance from the confiscation hearings upheld in *Phillips*. No matter how high the sum imposed, it still did not amount to any new 'charge'. The appellant was found guilty of conspiracy to import heroin. There was no question of his being charged in the confiscation proceedings of some new offence involving cannabis. Since he was not being 'charged with a criminal offence', the Art 6(2) protection did not extend beyond the appellant's substantive trial before a jury, where, it was conceded, those rights had been observed.

Lord Phillips found the recent Strasbourg cases of *Grayson & Barnham v United Kingdom* **9.202** (19955/05 and 15085/06), also concerning confiscation, to be instructive. In these cases, the European Court of Human Rights approved a confiscation order which was inferred partly from amounts that one defendant must have paid to purchase two consignments of cannabis which he had disclosed to an undercover police officer but which had not formed part of the charges against him. Art 6(2) was of no application in those circumstances. Lord Phillips noted (at [40]):

> Those cases required a finding that the property confiscated was derived from criminal offending, albeit that the precise offences did not have to be specified but could be inferred. The Strasbourg Court accepted that the safeguards of Article 6(2) did not apply in such circumstances. It would seem illogical to impose them where the details of the offending are alleged with more particularity [as they were here].

In *Geerings v the Netherlands* (2007) 46 EHRR 1222, the ECtHR declared as incompatible **9.203** with the Convention a procedure in the Netherlands whereby a defendant had been tried for a number of offences, convicted only of some and acquitted of others, but was nevertheless then made subject to a confiscation order for the total benefit of all of the offences charged.

The Judicial Committee observed that this case was not on par with the facts of *Briggs-* **9.204** *Price*. In *Geerings*, the defendant had in fact been tried and found not guilty of some of the offences for which he was later made subject to a confiscation order. Here, the confiscation order was made on the basis of activities that were simply not charged (but which were in any event found proven by the trial judge). There was no acquittal, as in *Geerings*. Where those facts prevail, '*Geerings does not decide that question one way or another*' (Lord Phillips at para [39]) and Art 6(2) did not apply.

Lord Brown dissented on this point, holding that in circumstances such as these, Art 6(2) **9.205** did apply, but held that on the facts it was satisfied in any case because the cannabis activities had been proved beyond reasonable doubt according to the judge, and therefore no violation had occurred.

I. Appeals

The defendant's right of appeal in relation to POCA confiscation matters is considered **9.206** fully in Chapter 18.

Under s 31(1) and (2) and s 89 of POCA, the prosecutor's right of appeal is without restric- **9.207** tion, subject to leave. Section 32(1) confirms that on an appeal the Court of Appeal may confirm, quash, or vary the confiscation order.

J. Defendants who Die or Abscond

Introduction

Sections 27 and 28 of POCA give the court jurisdiction, in certain circumstances, to make **9.208** confiscation orders in relation to s 6 of POCA for defendants who abscond. It will be noted that previously these powers were vested in the High Court and that in effect the power to deal with absconded defendants now rests with the Crown Court.

The defendant who dies

9.209 There is no provision in POCA for the court to proceed in terms of confiscation in circumstances where the defendant dies following his conviction, but before a confiscation order is made. The previous provision under s 19 of the DTA for the High Court to make a confiscation order against a drug trafficker who died after conviction, but before the Crown Court could make a confiscation order was not re-enacted under POCA (it was considered, according to the explanatory notes that accompany POCA, that the recovery of benefit where the perpetrator is dead was better dealt with under the Civil Recovery Procedures in Pt 5 of POCA).

The defendant who absconds post-conviction

9.210 Section 27(2) and (3) of POCA gives the Crown Court the power to make confiscation orders post-conviction and provides as follows:

(1) The section applies if the following two conditions are satisfied.

(2) The first condition is that a defendant absconds after—

    (a) he is convicted of an offence or offences in proceedings before the Crown Court,

    (b) he is committed to the Crown Court for sentencing in respect of an offence or offences under section 3, 4 or 6 of the Sentencing Act, or

    (c) he is committed to the Crown Court in respect of an offence or offences under section 70 (committal with a view to a confiscation order being considered).

(3) The second condition is that—

    (a) the prosecutor or the director applies to the Crown Court to proceed under this section, and

    (b) the court believes it is appropriate to do so.

Procedure

9.211 If this section applies the court must then proceed under s 6 in the same way as it would proceed if the two conditions mentioned in s 6 were otherwise satisfied; but in the case of the absconded defendant this is subject to s 27(5):

(5) If the court proceeds under section 6 as applied by this section, this Part has effect with these modifications—

    (a) any person the court believes is likely to be affected by an order under section 6 is entitled to appear before the court and make representations;

    (b) the court must not make an order under section 6 unless the prosecutor has taken reasonable steps to contact the defendant;

    (c) Section 6(9) applies if the reference to subsection (2) were to subsection (2) of this section;

    (d) sections 10, 16(4), 17 and 18 must be ignored;

    (e) sections 19, 20 and 21 must be ignored while the defendant is still an absconder.

Subsection (5)(c) imports that the defendant must fall within the paragraphs set out in 6(2).

9.212 For the purposes of s 27 the following sections of POCA must be ignored: s 10 (assumptions to be made cases of a criminal lifestyle); s 16(4) (the requirement that a statement of information by the prosecutor under s 16(3) must include information the prosecutor believes is relevant in connection to the making of the required assumptions or for the purpose of enabling the court to decide if the circumstances are such that it must not make an assumption); s 17 (the defendant's response to the statement of information); and s 18 (provision of information by the defendant). It is suggested that the requirement that the defendant need not respond to the prosecutor's statement is perhaps not surprising in the circumstances.

Furthermore, ss 19 (no order made: reconsideration of case), 20 (no order made: reconsid- **9.213** eration of benefit), and 21 (order made: reconsideration of benefit) must be ignored while the defendant is still an absconder (see s 27(5)(e)).

However, once the defendant ceases to be an absconder s 19 has effect as if subs (1)(a) **9.214** read:

(a) at a time when the first condition in Section 27 was satisfied the court did not proceed under Section 6.

Similarly if the court does not believe it is appropriate for it to proceed under s 27, once the **9.215** defendant ceases to be an absconder, s 19 has effect as if subs (1)(b) read:

(b) there is evidence which was not available to the prosecutor on the relevant date.

The defendant who absconds pre-conviction

Section 28 deals with the position where proceedings have been instituted against the **9.216** defendant, but at the relevant time there has been no conviction recorded against him. Section 28 provides as follows:

(1) This section applies if the following two conditions are satisfied.
(2) The first condition is that—
    (a) proceedings for an offence or offences are started against a defendant but are not concluded,
    (b) he absconds, and
    (c) the period of two years (starting with the date the court believes he absconded) has ended.
(3) The second condition is that—
    (a) the prosecutor applies to the Crown Court to proceed under this section, and
    (b) the Court believes it is appropriate for it to do so.

Two-year rule

In the circumstances set out in s 28, it will be noted that a confiscation order may only **9.217** be made against an absconder if two years have elapsed from the time he absconds (s 28(2)(b)).

Procedure

If s 28 applies, the court must proceed under s 6 in the same way as it would proceed if the **9.218** two conditions mentioned in s 6 are satisfied (s 28(4)). Any person the court believes is likely to be affected by an order under s 6 is entitled to appear before the court and make representations (s 28(5)(a)).

The court is not entitled to make an order under s 6 unless the prosecutor has taken reason- **9.219** able steps to contact the defendant (s 28(5)(b)).

Under s 28(5)(b)–(e), the following sections of the confiscation provisions of POCA must **9.220** be ignored when proceeding under s 28: s 10 of POCA (assumptions to be made in case of a criminal lifestyle); s 16(4) (the requirement that a statement of information by the prosecutor under s 16(3) must include information the prosecutor believes is relevant in connection to the making of the required assumptions or for the purpose of enabling the court to decide if the circumstances are such that it must not make an assumption); ss 17 to 20 (the defendant's response to a statement of information; provision of information by the defendant; and where no confiscation order is made: reconsideration of case and benefit); as must be s 21, while the defendant is still an absconder (confiscation order made: reconsideration of benefit). However, once the defendant had ceased to be an absconder s 21 does have effect.

What happens if the defendant later returns?

9.221 If the court makes an order under s 6 as applied by s 28, and the defendant is later convicted in proceedings before the Crown Court of the offence or any of the offences concerned, s 6 does not apply so far as that conviction is concerned (s 28(7)). In other words, when a court has made a confiscation order under s 28 it cannot go on to make another confiscation order if the defendant returns and is convicted.

Variation and discharge of absconder's confiscation order

9.222 Section 29 deals with varying orders made under s 28 and s 30 deals with the discharging of orders made under s 28. Both are considered in more detail in Chapter 10.

K. Case Digest: Key Post-*May* Cases in the Court of Appeal

The definition of 'benefit' and the process for determining 'benefit'

9.223 • *Sivaraman* [2008] EWCA Crim 1736, (Toulson LJ) (24 July 2008): Interpretation/ clarification of the House of Lords' opinions in the *May* cases; central question is benefit to the individual defendant considering civil law principles.

• *Richards* [2008] EWCA Crim 1841 (Toulson LJ) (23 July 2008): Benefit of a legal owner of property who held it on trust for another defendant was nil, as this was the value of the legal owner's true interest in the property.

• *Grainger* [2008] EWCA Crim 2506 (Toulson LJ) (14 October 2008): Defendant did not 'benefit' in the amount of the payments made to companies, as he had not received them himself and the corporate veil was not pierced.

• *Xu* [2008] EWCA Crim 2372 (Toulson LJ) (15 October 2008): 'Benefit' where business employed illegal workers was not the whole of the business' takings, as the business would have continued without the illegal workers.

• *Moss* [2008] EWCA Crim 2454 (Toulson LJ) (15 October 2008): Sufficiency of evidence for finding extent of co-conspirators' 'benefit'.

• *Roach* [2008] EWCA Crim 2562 (Toulson LJ) (15 October 2008): Relevance of basis of plea in confiscation proceedings; procedure where property is acquired with tainted and untainted money.

• *Chambers* [2008] EWCA Crim 2467 (Toulson LJ) (17 October 2008): Procedure for assessing when defendant has obtained 'benefit' in cases involving evasion of liability for payment of duty; applicability of civil regulations on payment of duty. Need to apply correct civil regulations.

- *Chatha* [2008] EWCA Crim 2597 (Sweeney J) (27 October 2008): Not unfair to include cash obtained by defendant, passed on to third party, and subsequently forfeited in calculation of 'benefit' or in amount to be paid.

- *Sangha* [2008] EWCA Crim 2562 (Richards LJ) (18 November 2008): Evidence and findings of fact in confiscation proceedings can go beyond that at trial.

- *Allpress & Others* [2009] EWCA Crim 8 (Toulson LJ) (20 January 2009): 'Benefit' received by certain types of money launderers, including cash couriers—definition of 'obtaining' in relation to cash.

- *Mitchell* [2009] EWCA Crim 214 (Toulson LJ) (21 January 2009): Defendant who, on judge's findings, merely loaded, for a fee, cigarettes onto lorry for import into the UK did not 'benefit' by the value of the goods or the amount of duty evaded. Narrow interpretation of civil regulations governing liability to pay duty in tobacco cases.

L. A Final Summary

Pre-hearing

See Chapter 8.   **9.224**

1. The starting point:

- The force of the judgments emanating from the Court of Appeal at present require that parties should be in as strong a position as possible to be able to deal with confiscation from the point at which the defendant is convicted (*Baden Lowe*).

- Too often in the past has the financial investigation only begun at the point of conviction, no doubt on the basis that there may be little merit in conducting a thorough financial analysis when the defendant may yet be acquitted.

- It is clear from the implications of *May*, *Green* and *Jennings* that the role of the prosecutor will include identifying the defendant's actual benefit (as opposed to some fanciful figure) and that this will require a proper analysis of the defendant's financial affairs from the outset.

- The prosecution will ordinarily keep financial unused material schedules. Make sure that you are provided with a copy.

- Consider abuse of process, although it is only likely to apply in rare cases. The Crown has a duty to recognise when a defendant has effectively repaid the proceeds of his offending, and should in certain circumstances consider whether or not to press for confiscation—*Morgan* and the subsequent cases. There is a discretion as to whether or not to ask the judge to proceed to confiscation.

2. Carefully consider the basis of plea:

- A basis of plea is not binding if it is not accepted by the Crown. The parties should make it clear when the basis of plea is offered whether it is accepted or not for the purposes of confiscation—see *Chambers* and *Roach*. If not, invite judge to make findings as appropriate.

3. Be prepared for the hearing:

- Be prepared for the financial investigator to give evidence/be cross examined.

- Be prepared at the confiscation hearing to call or cross-examine the defendant and other potential witnesses.

- Be prepared to help your judge and lead him to the findings of fact that you want him to make—they may be unfamiliar with how to apply property law concepts in a confiscation context, such as one person holding property on behalf of another (*Richards*).

- Emphasise the Regulations and know them. It is essential that the Regulations upon which the parties rely in terms of establishing or arguing the benefit from a defendant's offending are cited and clearly set out—see *Chambers*. In practical terms this will mean in an alcohol duty evasion conspiracy, for example, one would need to refer to the Regulations which make the defendant liable for the duty to be paid (or not as the case may be).

At the hearing

4. The figure for a defendant's benefit will come from the facts as found at the confiscation hearing:

- *May* at para 48—when determining whether an offender has benefited, and the amount of that benefit, the court must first establish the facts as best it can on the material available, relying as appropriate on the statutory assumptions. In very many cases the factual findings made will be decisive.

- It is necessary in each case for the prosecution in the first instance and then the judge to examine the facts in order to see what benefit the offender has in truth obtained and how it should be valued (*Grainger* at paras 14–15).

5. Focus on the statutory language, not on old case law:

- *May* para 48—'In addressing the questions the court should focus very closely on the language of the statutory provision in question in the context of the statute and in the light of any statutory definition. The language used is not arcane or obscure and any judicial gloss or exegesis should be viewed with caution. Guidance should ordinarily be sought in the statutory language rather than in the proliferating case law.'

6. Focus on the facts:

- Take the judge through the evidence and the findings you want him to make and inferences you want him to draw.

- Cross-examine on income/expenditure and payment.

- Have a *Newton* style hearing if necessary—*Chambers*.

7. Focus on the conclusions you wish the judge to draw:

- Assess in each case whether the statutory assumptions ought to apply. If they should not, it is essential that the court hears argument on the application of s 4(4) and that the judge give formal reasons, should he choose to disapply the assumptions regime. Section 4(4) makes it clear that it is the court, not the parties, that must make the decision as to the applicability of the assumptions, so such a decision should not be presented as an agreement between the parties, as it was here.

- If the judge finds that other offences which have not been charged or tried have occurred as well as the trigger offence, those findings must be to the criminal standard and the judge must expressly state this fact. While the civil standard applies in most cases and for most purposes in the Act, in view of the majority reasoning in *Briggs-Price*, findings to the civil standard alone cannot validly ground any element of a confiscation order in these circumstances.

8. No apportionment of benefit amongst those who jointly obtain property or a pecuniary advantage:

- Where conspirators put the proceeds of fraud into their joint bank account, each is entitled to the full amount in the account. Each individual 'obtains' the property jointly held. Someone who has joint control of property has 'obtained' that property within the meaning of the legislation (para 45 of *May*). See also the discussion about how property is 'obtained' in *Allpress & Others*.

- Paragraph 46 of *May*—apportionment is 'a procedure which would be contrary to principle and unauthorised by statute'.

- Multiple recovery is permissible—see para 15 of *Green*, approving *Simons*.

- Paragraph 16 of *Green*—it is not disproportionate to make an order depriving a defendant of a benefit which he has in fact and in law obtained, within the limits of his realisable assets. Challenges to the proportionality of the confiscation regime (as in *Phillips v United Kingdom* (2001) 11 BHRC 280 and *R v Rezvi* [2002] UKHL 1, [2003] 1 AC 1099) have not succeeded.

9. Where possible, an assessment needs to be made in terms of roles:

- The mere fact that a defendant is involved in a conspiracy does not necessarily make him liable for the whole of the benefit obtained as a result of that conspiracy—*Sivaraman* at para 13.

- Some participants may contribute to obtaining a benefit *for others* without gaining it themselves—see *Sivaraman* at para 12.

- What did the conspirators agree among themselves?

- Who ultimately was to receive the proceeds of the crime? How were the proceeds to be divided?

- Were the proceeds truly held for the group jointly, or for some only?

- Were some conspirators rewarded by fixed fees only?

10

RECONSIDERATION OF CONFISCATION ORDERS

A. Introduction

10.01 When it makes a confiscation order the Crown Court will usually attempt to determine accurately the value of the defendant's realisable property. Nonetheless the valuation process is something of an inexact science and it frequently happens that the sum realised on sale of a particular asset is either less or more than that anticipated at the time a confiscation order is made. For example, fluctuations in the property market may mean that when a house is sold it may be worth significantly more or less than was originally anticipated. Further, as the objective of many criminals is to conceal the extent of their benefit from criminal conduct and the extent and location of their assets, it may well be that at the time of a confiscation hearing the prosecutor is unable to put before the court evidence which gives a full picture of a defendant's wealth.

10.02 Accordingly, the three main Acts concerned with confiscation, the Proceeds of Crime Act 2002 (POCA), the Drug Trafficking Act 1994 (DTA), and the Criminal Justice Act 1988 (CJA 1988), give the prosecutor the right to apply to the court for the various determinations made during the course of a confiscation hearing to be revised in the light of new evidence. Similarly, the Acts give the defendant the right to seek a reduction in the amount of a confiscation order where the value of his realisable assets proves inadequate to satisfy the order in full.

It will be noted that the relevant provisions of the CJA 1988 and DTA were repealed on **10.03** 24 March 2003, but they continue to have effect in respect of proceedings for offences committed before that date and there remain a significant number of DTA and CJA cases within the system.

In this chapter, we primarily consider the variation and discharge of orders made under **10.04** POCA, not least because during the lifetime of this edition some 10 years will have elapsed since the passing of that Act. The numbers of DTA and CJA cases are inevitably decreasing and the effects therefore of the transitional provisions are now considerably diluted. At the end of this chapter we also consider variation and discharge under the DTA and CJA 1988, and the reader should find the entire chapter helpful in terms of general practice, as we also refer herein to the case law that had developed under the DTA and the CJA 1988 and which still remains persuasive under POCA.

B. Variation and Discharge under the Proceeds of Crime Act 2002

In the rest of this chapter we consider the various provisions concerning the reconsidera- **10.05** tion, variation, and discharge of confiscation orders under POCA.

The slip rule

Section 155(1) of the Powers of Criminal Courts (Sentencing) Act 2000 (PCC(S)A) **10.06** provides as follows:

. . . a sentence imposed, or other order made, by the Crown Court when dealing with an offender may be varied or rescinded by the Crown Court within the period of 28 days beginning with the day on which the sentence or other order was imposed . . .

The application of this section to confiscation cases was confirmed in the case of *R v Bukhari* [2008] EWCA Crim 2915, but only within the strict 28-day limit, thereafter the correct route was by way of appeal. Appeals against confiscation orders are considered separately in Chapter 18.

C. Reconsideration of Case where no Confiscation Order was Originally Made

Section 19 of POCA applies where no confiscation hearing was held after the original **10.07** conviction.

Section 19(1) states: **10.08**

This section applies if—
(a) the first condition in section 6 is satisfied, and no court has proceeded under that section;
(b) there is evidence which was not available to the prosecutor on the relevant date;
(c) before the end of the period of six years starting with the date of conviction the prosecutor applies to the Crown Court to consider the evidence; and
(d) after considering the evidence the Court believes it is appropriate for it to proceed under section 6.

10.09 The first condition of s 6 of POCA (s 6(2)) is that a defendant must fall within one of the following categories:

(a) he is convicted of an offence or offences in proceedings before the Crown Court;

(b) he is committed to the Crown Court for sentencing in respect of an offence or offences under ss 3, 4, or 6 of the Powers of Criminal Courts (Sentencing) Act 2000 (PCCSA); or

(c) he is committed to the Crown Court in respect of an offence or offences under s 70 of POCA (committal with a view to a confiscation order being considered).

Once the court has established that s 19(1) is satisfied the court must proceed under s 6 (s 19(2)) and in doing so must apply s 19(3) to (8).

Time limit

10.10 Importantly, it will be noted that in all cases, an application must be made to the Crown Court within six years of the original conviction (see s 19(1)(c)),

How are the 'relevant date' and the 'date of conviction' defined?

10.11 The 'relevant date' referred to in s 19(1)(b) is defined in s 19(9) as either:

(a) if the court made a decision not to proceed under section 6, the date of that decision; or

(b) if the court did not make such a decision, the date of conviction.

Under s 19(10) the date of conviction is either:

(a) the date on which the defendant was convicted of the offence concerned, or

(b) if there were two or more offences and the convictions were on different dates, the date of the latest.

10.12 It should be noted that the purpose of s 19 is to allow the prosecutor to return to court when new evidence in relation to confiscation arises. It is therefore inappropriate for a prosecutor who had possession of evidence relating to the defendant's assets and conduct etc at the time of his trial and conviction, but chose not to apply for a confiscation order then, to apply for reconsideration under s 19 at a later date in circumstances where no new evidence has arisen.

The status of previous orders of the court and compensation

10.13 Section 19(8) states that where a compensation order under s 130 of the PCC(S)A was made following the trial, the court cannot order payment of that compensation out of a confiscation order made at a reconsideration hearing under s 19. It follows that the payment of any compensation should only be ordered out of confiscated monies under s 13(6) of POCA where a confiscation order was also made in the original proceedings.

10.14 Under s 19(7)(c), POCA requires the court to take into account certain orders already made against the defendant in the original proceedings, namely fines, forfeiture, and compensation orders.

Procedure: applications under section 19 of POCA

10.15 See para 10.40 below.

Statements of information

Under s 26 of POCA, if the court proceeds under s 6 (the making of a confiscation order) **10.16** in pursuance of s 19, the prosecutor must give the court a statement of information within the period the court orders (see para 10.41 below).

D. Reconsideration of Benefit: No Confiscation Order Originally Made

Section 20 of POCA applies when a confiscation hearing was originally held and the court **10.17** decided on that occasion that the defendant had a criminal lifestyle, but had not benefited from his general criminal conduct; or did not have a criminal lifestyle and did not benefit from his particular criminal conduct. Section 20 of POCA only applies if two specified conditions are satisfied.

The first condition

Section 20(2) states: **10.18**

The first condition is that in proceeding under section 6 the court has decided that—
(a) the defendant has a criminal lifestyle but has not benefited from his general criminal conduct, or
(b) the defendant does not have a criminal lifestyle and has not benefited from his particular criminal conduct.

The second condition

The second condition under s 20(4) is that: **10.19**

(a) there is evidence that was not available to the prosecutor when the court decided that the defendant had not benefited from his general or particular criminal conduct,
(b) before the end of the period of six years starting with the date on which the prosecutor applies to the Crown Court to consider the evidence, and
(c) after considering the evidence the court concludes that it would have decided that the defendant would have benefited from his general or particular criminal conduct (as the case may be) if the evidence had been available to it.

The 'date of conviction' is defined at s 19(10) as the date on which the defendant was convicted of the offence concerned or, if there are two or more offences and the convictions were on different dates, the date of the latest (see s 20(13)).

The status of previous orders of the court

Under s 20(11)(c) and (d), POCA requires the court to take into account certain orders **10.20** already made against the defendant in the original proceedings, namely fines, forfeiture, and compensation orders.

Compensation

Section 20(12) states that where a compensation order under s 130 of the PCC(S)A was **10.21** made following the trial, the court cannot order payment of that compensation out of a confiscation order made at a reconsideration hearing under s 20. It follows that the payment of any compensation should only be ordered out of confiscated monies under s 13(6) of POCA where a confiscation order was also made in the original proceedings.

Procedure: applications under section 20 of POCA

10.22 See para 10.40 below.

Statements of information

10.23 Under s 26 of POCA, if the court proceeds under s 6 (the making of a confiscation order) in pursuance of s 20, the prosecutor must give the court a statement of information within the period the court orders (see para 10.41 below).

E. Where a Confiscation Order has been Made: Reconsideration of Benefit

10.24 Section 21 of POCA applies if:

(1) ...

(a) the court has made a confiscation order,

(b) there is evidence which was not available to the prosecutor at the relevant time,

(c) the prosecutor . . . believes that if the court were to find the amount of the defendant's benefit in pursuance of this section, it would exceed the relevant amount,

(d) before the end of the period of six years starting from the date of conviction the prosecutor . . . applies to the Crown Court to consider the evidence, and

(e) after considering the evidence the court believes it is appropriate for it to proceed under this section.

10.25 When reconsidering the defendant's benefit, the court must make a new calculation of the defendant's benefit from the conduct concerned (s 21(2)). In effect this enables a confiscation order already made to be increased.

10.26 Under s 21 there is no restriction as to the number of times that the prosecutor may return to the Crown Court to seek an increase in the defendant's benefit figure, although it will have been noted that s 21(1)(d) imports a limitation date of six years starting from the date of conviction.

10.27 If a court has already sentenced the defendant for the offence (or any of the offences) concerned, s 6 of POCA has effect as if the defendant's particular criminal conduct included conduct which constitutes offences which the court has taken into consideration in deciding his sentence for the offence or offences concerned (as per s 21(3)).

10.28 When the court is reconsidering the defendant's benefit under s 21, s 8(2) of POCA does not apply. Instead the court must:

(4) ...

(a) take account of conduct occurring up to the time it decided the defendant's benefit for the purposes of the confiscation order;

(b) take account of the property obtained up to that time;

(c) take account of property obtained after that time if it was obtained as a result of or in connection with conduct occurring before that time.

10.29 In terms of general criminal conduct and the deducting of aggregate amounts, when applying s 8(5) of POCA in relation to reconsidering a defendant's benefit, the confiscation order previously made against the defendant must be ignored (s 21(5)).

When is the relevant time?

By s 21(12), the relevant time is: **10.30**

(a) when the court calculated the defendant's benefit for the purposes of the confiscation order, if this section [21] has not applied previously;
(b) when the court last calculated the defendant's benefit in pursuance of this section, if this section has applied previously.

What is the relevant amount?

Under s 21(13) the relevant amount is: **10.31**

(a) the amount found as the defendant's benefit for the purposes of the confiscation order, if this section [21] has not applied previously;
(b) the amount last found as the defendant's benefit in pursuance of this section, if this section has applied previously.

When is the date of conviction?

The date of conviction is: **10.32**

(a) the date on which the defendant was convicted of the offence concerned; or
(b) if there are two or more offences and the convictions are on different dates, the date of the latest (see s 21(14) applying s 19(10)).

The assumptions

When considering s 10 of POCA (assumptions to be made in cases of criminal lifestyle) in **10.33** s 21 cases:

(a) the first and second assumptions do not apply with regard to property first held by the defendant after the time the court decided his benefit for the purposes of the confiscation order;
(b) the third assumption does not apply with regard to expenditure incurred by him after that time;
(c) the fourth assumption does not apply with regard to property obtained (or assumed to have been obtained) by him after that time (see s 21(6)).

Revised benefit and relationship with the recoverable amount

If the amount found under the new calculation of the defendant's benefit under s 21 exceeds **10.34** the relevant amount, the court must make a new calculation of the recoverable amount for the purposes of s 6, and, if it exceeds the amount required to be paid under the confiscation order previously ordered, the court may vary the order by substituting for the amount required to be paid such amount as it believes is just (s 21(7)).

When making the new calculation for the recoverable amount for the purposes of s 6, **10.35** the court must take the new calculation of the defendant's benefit and apply s 9 of POCA (the available amount) as if references to the time the confiscation order was made were to the time of the new calculation of the recoverable amount, and as if references to the date of the confiscation order were to the date of that new calculation (s 21(8)).

10.36 Under s 21(9), in applying s 21(7)(b) (where the court is considering varying an order to substitute it for an amount it believes 'just') the court must have regard to:

(a) any fine imposed on the defendant for the offence (or any of the offences) concerned;

(b) any order which falls within section 13(3) of POCA [compensation orders, forfeiture orders or deprivation orders] which have been made against the defendant in respect of the offence (or any of the offences) concerned and have not already been taken into account by the court in deciding what is the free property held by him for the purposes of section 9;

(c) any order which has been made against the defendant in respect of the offence (or any of the offences) concerned under section 130 of the Sentencing Act (compensation orders).

The purpose of s 21(9)(b) and (c) is to avoid double recovery and equally to prevent a defendant from being allowed a reduction twice in respect of the same property.

The status of previous orders of the court

10.37 Under s 21(9)(b) and (c), POCA requires the court to take into account certain orders already made against the defendant in the original proceedings, namely fines, forfeiture, and compensation orders.

Exception to rule

10.38 By s 21(10), the court cannot take a compensation order into account in one specified circumstance when reconsidering the defendant's benefit. If the court has made a direction under s 13(6) (compensation to be paid out of any sums recovered under the confiscation order), in applying s 21(7)(b) (where the defendant's benefit exceeds the amount required to be paid under the confiscation order) the court must not have regard to an order falling within s 21(9)(c) (compensation orders).

Changes in the value of money

10.39 When deciding under s 21 whether one amount exceeds another, the court must take account of any change in the value of money (s 21(11)).

F. Procedure: Applications under Sections 19, 20, or 21 of the Act

10.40 Where the prosecutor makes an application under s 19, 20, or 21 of the Act (application for reconsideration of a decision to make a confiscation order or benefit assessed for purposes of a confiscation order) the application must be in writing and give details of:

(a) the name of the defendant;

(b) the date on which and the place where any relevant conviction occurred;

(c) the date on which and the place where any relevant confiscation order was made or varied;

(d) the grounds for the application;

(e) an indication of the evidence available to support the application (see r 58.3 of the Criminal Procedure Rules (CrimPR)). Under r 58.3(3) any application for reconsideration of a decision to make a confiscation order or reconsideration of benefit assessed for the purposes of a confiscation order, must be lodged with the Crown Court, and the application must be served on the defendant at least seven days before the date fixed by the court for hearing the application, unless the Crown Court specifies a shorter period (see r 58.3(4)).

Statements of information

Under s 26 of POCA if the court proceeds under s 6 (the making of a confiscation order) **10.41** in pursuance of either s 19 (no order made: reconsideration of case) or s 20 (no confiscation order made: reconsideration of benefit) or the prosecutor applies under s 21 of POCA (where a confiscation order has been made and the court has to reconsider the benefit figure), the prosecutor must give the court a statement of information within the period the court orders (see s 26(1) and (2)(a)).

Section 16 of POCA (the provision of a statement of information) applies accordingly **10.42** (with appropriate modification where the prosecutor applies under s 21); as does s 17 (the defendant's response to the statement of information), and s 18 (the provision of informa-tion by the defendant) where s 6(3)(a) or s 6(3)(b) applies (ie the prosecutor has asked the court to proceed under s 6 or the court believes it is appropriate for it to do so), or the court is considering whether or not to proceed under s 6 (s 26(2)(b)).

G. Increase in Available Amount

Where a confiscation order has been made: reconsideration of the available amount

The purpose of s 22 of POCA is to allow the court to recalculate the available amount in **10.43** circumstances where a confiscation order has been previously made in an amount lower than the defendant's assessed benefit, because at that time there was insufficient realisable property to satisfy an order in the full amount. Under the previous legislation this was sometimes referred to as a 'Certificate of Increase'.

Section 22 of POCA applies if: **10.44**

(1) ...
   (a) a court has made a confiscation order,
   (b) the amount required to be paid was the amount found under section 7(2) [where the defendant was able to show that the available amount was less than the benefit figure], and
   (c) an applicant falling within section 22(2) [ie the prosecutor or a receiver appointed under section 50 of POCA (an enforcement receiver)] applies to the Crown Court to make a new calculation of the available amount.

Where the above circumstances apply the court must make the new calculation, and in **10.45** doing so it must apply s 9 of POCA (calculation of the available amount) as if references to the time the confiscation order is made were to the time of the new calculation, and as if reference to the date of the confiscation order were to the date of the new calculation (s 22(3)). This section operates in a similar way as the 'Certificate of Increase' provisions operated under the DTA. The purpose of these provisions was identified by Rose LJ in *R v Tivnan* (1999) 1 Cr App R(S) 92 who held:

> ... we see no ambiguity. The plain words of the statute, in our judgment, provide for the making of an application for a further certificate and for an increase in the amount recovered under the confiscation order at any time after the original confiscation order was made.

By this means drug dealers can be deprived of their assets until they have disgorged an amount equivalent to all the benefit which had accrued to them from drug dealing.

It will be noted that, unlike ss 19, 20, and 21, there is no limitation to the time when an application may be made and the prosecutor or a receiver may apply on more than one occasion.

10.46 Under s 22(4), if the amount found under the new calculation exceeds the relevant amount the court may vary the order by substituting for the amount required to be paid such amount as:

(a) it believes is just, but

(b) does not exceed the amount found as the defendant's benefit from the conduct concerned.

10.47 In deciding what is 'just' the court must have regard in particular to:

(5) ...

(a) any fine imposed on the defendant for the offence (or any of the offences) concerned;

(b) any order which falls within section 13(3) (compensation orders, forfeiture orders or deprivation orders) and has been made against him in respect of the offence (or any of the offences) concerned and has not already been taken into account by the court in deciding what is the free property held by him for the purposes of section 9 of POCA [the available amount];

(c) any order which has been made against the defendant in respect of the offence (or any of the offences) concerned under Section 130 of the Sentencing Act (compensation orders).

10.48 In deciding what is 'just' the court must have regard to an order falling within subs (5)(c) (orders made under s 130 of the Sentencing Act (compensation orders)), if a court has made a direction under s 13(6) of POCA, to avoid the defendant being able to off-set the impact of the compensation order on both occasions (subs (6)).

What is the 'relevant amount' under section 22?

10.49 Under s 22(8) the relevant amount is:

(a) the amount found as the available amount for the purposes of the confiscation order, if section 22 had not applied previously;

(b) the amount last found as the available amount in pursuance of section 22, if section 22 has applied previously.

10.50 The amount found as the defendant's benefit from the conduct concerned is:

(9) ...

(a) the amount so found when the confiscation order was made, or

(b) if one or more new calculations of the defendant's benefit have been made under section 21 of POCA, the amount found on the occasion of the last such calculation.

Changes in the value of money

10.51 When deciding under s 22 whether one amount exceeds another, the court must take account of any change in the value of money (see s 22(7)).

Procedure: applications under section 22 of the Act

10.52 Under r 58.4 of the CrimPR, where the prosecutor or a receiver makes an application under s 22 of the Act for a new calculation of the available amount, in circumstances where a confiscation order has already been made, the application must be in writing and must be supported by a witness statement. That application and any witness statement must be lodged with the Crown Court and served upon:

(a) the defendant;
(b) the receiver, if the prosecutor is making the application and a receiver has been appointed under s 50 of the Act (an enforcement receiver); and
(c) the prosecutor if the receiver is making the application,

at least seven days before the date fixed by the court hearing the application, unless the Crown Court specifies a shorter period (see r 58.4(1) to (4)).

Increase in the available amount: ECHR

In *Saggar* [2005] EWCA Civ 174, the Court of Appeal held that where the State had **10.53** granted to itself the right to re-open the issue of confiscation under s 16 of the DTA (for a certificate of increase), the reasonable time requirement under Art 6(1) of the European Convention of Human Rights (ECHR), was triggered and extended throughout the period starting from the original proceedings, and not just from the institution of the s 16 application.

H. Inadequacy of Available Amount

Introduction

The intention of s 23 of POCA is to replace the previous procedure where defendants or **10.54** the receiver had to apply to the High Court for a certificate of inadequacy.

Applications by defendants attaching to the inadequacy of their realisable assets, and **10.55** thereby their inability to meet their confiscation orders, are commonplace. Pending applications are regularly raised as a reason for the default sentence not to be implemented at enforcement hearings.

Prior to s 23, the legislative provisions for subsequent applications by defendants in respect **10.56** of confiscation orders were contained in s 17 of the DTA and s 83 of the CJA 1988, each as amended by POCA and by the PCC(S)A. They were in the same terms, save for provisions in the latter referring to magistrates' courts. The sections provided for an application to the High Court for a certificate of the inadequacy of the defendant's realisable property to pay the amount previously ordered. Where a certificate was issued by the High Court the defendant could apply to the Crown Court to have substituted for the amount originally ordered such lesser amount as the Crown Court thought just in all the circumstances.

The earlier sections thus provided a wholly different procedure to enable a defendant to **10.57** come back to the Crown Court to ask for a reduction in the amount originally ordered. It was formerly the High Court which had to consider the adequacy of realisable property: it is now the Crown Court which has to consider whether the available amount is inadequate for the payment of the outstanding balance. In terms of procedure, if a defence solicitor wishes to seek public funding for a s 23 application, he should apply to the Crown Court, not to the enforcement magistrates' court (which has no power to grant a representation order for s 23 proceedings).

Section 23

10.58   Section 23 applies to POCA cases if:

(1) ...

    (a) a court has made a confiscation order, and

    (b) the defendant, or a receiver appointed under Section 50 of POCA [an enforcement receiver], applies to the Crown Court to vary the order under section 23.

When an application is being considered under s 23, the Crown Court must calculate the available amount, and in doing so it must apply s 9 of POCA (calculation of the available amount) as if references to the time the confiscation order was made were to the time of the current calculation and as if references to the date of the confiscation order were to the date of the current calculation (see s 23(2)). As a result, under s 23 the available amount is to be assessed as under section 9, but at the time of the calculation under s 23.

10.59   The court may disregard any inadequacy which it believes is attributable (wholly or partly) to anything done by the defendant for the purpose of preserving property in circumstances where it is held by the recipient of a tainted gift (s 23(5)).

10.60   Under s 23(3), if the court finds that the available amount (as so calculated) is inadequate for the payment of any amount remaining to be paid under the confiscation order, it may vary the order by substituting it for a smaller amount as the court believes is just.

10.61   If the defendant or others are going to rely upon this provision they must demonstrate to the court firm and clear evidence of their reduced circumstances—per *Gokal v SFO* [2001] EWCA Civ 368 where Keene LJ stated:

> As has been said many times in the authorities, it is not enough for the defendant to come to court and say that his assets are inadequate to meet the confiscation order, unless at the same time he condescends to demonstrate what has happened since the making of the order to the realisable property found by the trial judge to have existed at the time when the order was made.

10.62   *Gokal* was applied in *R v Younis* [2008] EWCA Crim 2950 where the Court held, applying the 'hard edged rule' in *Re McKinsley* [2006] 1 WLR 3420, that s 23 should not be seen as an opportunity to re-litigate matters already determined against the defendant in the Crown Court (para 11).

Procedure: variation of confiscation order due to inadequacy of available amount

10.63   Rule 58.5 of the CrimPR applies where the defendant or a receiver makes an application under s 23 of POCA for the variation of a confiscation order to a lower amount. Under r 58.5 the application must be in writing and may be supported by a witness statement, and any application and accompanying witness statement must be lodged with the Crown Court. That application and any witness statement must be served on:

(a) the prosecutor;

(b) the defendant, if the receiver is making the application; and

(c) the receiver, if the defendant is making the application and a receiver has been appointed under s 50 (an enforcement receiver)

at least seven days before the date fixed by the court for hearing the application, unless the Crown Court specifies a shorter period. Where appropriate, the application should also include any accrued interest.

It will also be noted that in *Re T* [2005] EWHC 3359 (Admin) Collins J held (in a DTA **10.64** case) that the court did have jurisdiction to grant bail in an appropriate case where the outcome of a certificate of inadequacy application was awaited.

Practice

In *Re B* [2008] EWHC 3217 (Admin), DHCJ Holgate QC gave a helpful distillation of **10.65** the principles that have been established with regard to the consideration of inadequacy applications in a CJA matter (para 74):

(1) The burden lies on the applicant to prove, on the balance of probabilities, that his realisable property is inadequate for the payment of the confiscation order (see *Re O'Donoghue* (2004) EWCA Civ 1800, per Laws LJ at para 3).

(2) The reference to realisable property must be to 'whatever are his realisable assets as a whole at the time he applies for the certificate of inadequacy. If they include assets he did not have when the confiscation order was made, that is by no means a reason for leaving such fresh assets out of consideration.' (ibid and see also *Re Phillips* [2006] EWHC 623 (Admin)).

(3) A section 83 application cannot be used to go behind a finding made at the confiscation hearing or embodied in the confiscation order as to the amount of the defendant's realisable assets. Such a finding can only be challenged by way of an appeal against the confiscation order. (See *Gokal v Serious Fraud Office* (2001) EWCA Civ 368, Per Keene LJ at paras 17 and 24).

(4) It is insufficient for a defendant to say under section 83 'that his assets are inadequate to meet the confiscation order, unless at the same time he condescends to demonstrate what has happened since the making of the order to the realisable property found by the trial Judge to have existed when the order was made' (see *Gokal* at para 24 and *Re O'Donoghue* at para 3).

(5) The confiscation hearing provided an opportunity for the Defendant to show that his realisable property was worth less than the Prosecution alleged. It also enabled the Defendant to identify any specific assets which he contended should be treated as the only realisable property. The section 83 procedure, however, is intended to be used only where there has been a genuine change in the Defendant's financial circumstances. It is a safety net intended to provide for post-confiscation order events. (See *McKinsley v Crown Prosecution Service* (2006) EWCA Civ 1092 per Scott Baker LJ at paras 9, 21–24, 31 and 35).

(6) A section 83 application is not to be used as a 'second bite of the cherry'. It is not an opportunity to adduce evidence or to present arguments which could have been put before the Crown Court Judge at the confiscation hearing (para 38 of *Gokal* and paras 23, 24 and 37 of *McKinsley*).

(7) The clarification of a third party's interest in property may be a post confiscation order event. The extent of any such interest may have to be decided by a civil court. (*Re Norris* (2001) UKHL 34 and *McKinsley* at para 39).

(8) In a section 83 application the definition of realisable property includes a chose in action or a right to a sum of money which the applicant is entitled to recover, irrespective of any difficulty in its actual recovery, unless the applicant proves on the balance of probabilities that

it is impossible to recover that sum (*R v Liverpool Magistrates' Court ex parte Ansen* [1998] 1 All ER 692 at page 701d-e and *Re Houssan Ali* [2002] EWCA Civ 1450 at para 1.11).

Not a route to appeal

10.66 An inadequacy application should only be sought in cases where, since the making of the confiscation order, the value of the defendant's realisable property has decreased for some reason. It is not an appropriate remedy for a defendant who is aggrieved by the Crown Court's findings when it made the confiscation order: in such circumstances the defendant's remedy is an appeal to the Court of Appeal (Criminal Division).

10.67 Recent case law has confirmed this to be the position. In *Re N* [2005] EWHC QBD (Admin) 3211, Toulson J endorsed a 'hard-edged rule' in respect of certificate of inadequacy applications. He expressed concern that the provisions set out in s 17 of the DTA and the corresponding provisions of POCA, were being used by defendants as an appeal route, whereas the proper course would have been to pursue the matter in the Court of Appeal.

10.68 This was further confirmed in *P v Customs and Excise Commissioners* [2005] EWHC (Admin) 877, where Beatson J stated (at para 18) that it was:

> ... well established that the procedure under [s 17] ... is not to be used as a device to appeal against the original finding that an item of property is realisable property within the legislation.

He added at para 20:

> In applying for a certificate of inadequacy, an applicant must show what has happened to the realisable property or to part of it since the making of the confiscation order.

Evidence

10.69 In *Gokal v Serious Fraud Office* [2001] EWCA Civ 368, at paras 16 and 17 Keene J considered a similar problem:

> The evidence in support of the recent application for a certificate took the form of a witness statement ... In the witness statement it is said that the appellant 'seeks to prove that he has no realisable property to be applied in satisfaction of the confiscation order'. Apparently an attempt was going to be made to produce evidence at this stage to show that the money which went into the appellant's personal bank account has been dissipated. This would take the form of schedules produced by accountants which were available at the time of the appeal to the Court of Appeal but not produced to that court. This is not a proper basis on which to seek a certificate. It amounts to an attempt to go behind the original confiscation order finding as to the amount of the defendant's realisable assets. Such a finding can only be challenged by way of an appeal against the confiscation order ... An application for a certificate does not provide an opportunity to try to make good deficiencies in the case presented at the time of the confiscation order or at the appeal against it.

10.70 In *R v T* (QBD (Admin), 1 February 1996) McCullough J said:

> It is not sufficient for a defendant simply to assert at the time of his application for a certificate of inadequacy that he has no realisable property. He must explain what has become of the realisable property whose existence formed the basis of the confiscation order. If a defendant is at liberty simply to rely upon the assertion of the present lack of realisable property to justify the issue of a certificate of inadequacy, then it is open to him ... to subvert

the decision which formed the basis of the confiscation order. That is plainly wrong in principle. The scheme of the Act is quite clear. If a confiscation order is to be challenged, that must be by way of appeal and only by way of appeal.

Hidden assets

A particular difficulty arise for a defendant where there has been a finding of hidden assets **10.71** by the Crown Court. The finding implies that he has been less than frank about the extent of his assets. In such cases it would appear to be near impossible to obtain a certificate of inadequacy, particularly in cases where the defendant is still maintaining that he has. In *Telli v RCPO* [2007] EWHC 2233 the court held that:

> . . . absent identification of all the realisable property held by him, a defendant normally will be unable to satisfy the court that the amount that might be realised at the time the confiscation order is made is less than the amount assessed to be the proceeds of his drug trafficking. Assets which he hides from the gaze of Customs and Excise may, for all anyone knows, be equal to or in excess of the value of his proceeds of drug trafficking. For that reason, no court should be satisfied that they are to be quantified at a lesser amount.

> 37 Secondly, it is incumbent upon a court to assess the *current* value of the realisable property in order to determine whether it is inadequate to meet the outstanding sum. Once it is appreciated that the property held by the defendant includes unidentified assets forming part of the total value of the realisable property at the time of the order, it is impossible for Telli to establish that the realisable property is inadequate now to meet payment of the outstanding amount. The order was made in 1996. If a defendant fails to identify all the assets he holds, no-one will know their true value and by the time of the application, the value of the assets he failed to identify may have increased, particularly after 10 years. Absent consideration of current value, no court could be satisfied that the realisable property was inadequate. If the assets remain unidentified no conclusion can be reached as to their current value.

Burden and standard of proof

In *Re O'Donoghue* [2004] EWHC (Admin) 176, Lightman J reaffirmed that the burden of **10.72** proof was on the defendant to establish that the value of his assets were inadequate to satisfy the whole value of the confiscation order. He added that it was not sufficient for him to merely state that his assets were inadequate, without demonstrating what had happened since the making of the confiscation order that had made them so.

Assets difficult to realise

The fact that particular assets prove difficult for a defendant to realise does not necessarily **10.73** mean they cease to be realisable property (see *Re R*, The Independent, 4 November 2002). In *R v Liverpool Justices ex p Ansen* [1998] 1 All ER 692 the assets taken into account in making a confiscation order included a deposit he had put down on a summer house in Turkey and held by German agents; a deposit he had put down and was entitled to reclaim in relation to some Waterford Wedgwood articles; and a loan he had apparently made to his junior counsel at trial. He had been unable to realise any of these amounts in satisfaction of a confiscation order and accordingly applied for a certificate of inadequacy. In refusing the defendant's application, May J said:

> [Counsel for the Prosecutor] submits that the fact that an asset may be difficult to realise is simply not relevant. The provisions of the Act, he submits, define 'realisable property'

in terms of section 5 and do not address any question of whether in practical terms it is difficult to recover the money. I agree with that submission for two reasons. Firstly, the definition of 'realisable property' includes property held by the defendant and by definition 'property' is held by any person if he holds an interest in it and the 'interest' in property includes a right. Accordingly, if as Mr. Ansen's affidavit indicates, the sum of approximately £8,500 held by agents in Germany is an amount which he is entitled to recover, then it is realisable property by definition irrespective of any difficulty in its actual recovery.

Secondly, s 5(1)(b) of the DTA, referring, as it does, to 'realisable property' including 'gifts caught by the Act', necessarily means that circumstances may arise where gifts which an applicant has made may be practically, even legally, irrecoverable, but they are nevertheless still regarded as realisable property under this draconian Act. The purpose of these draconian procedures is obvious: they are intended, as has often been said, to make it as difficult as possible for those who traffic in drugs to get away with the proceeds of that traffic.

Inadequacy of available amount in bankruptcy cases

10.74 Section 23(4) states that if a person has been adjudged bankrupt or his estate has been sequestrated (or if an order for the winding up of a company has been made), the court must take into account the extent to which realisable property held by that person or that company may be distributed among creditors ('company' for these purposes means any company that may be wound up under the Insolvency Act 1986 (see s 23(6)).

Court must give its reasons

10.75 In *Re Forwell* [2003] EWCA Civ 1608, the Court of Appeal held that where a court, when dealing with an inadequacy application, decided to disregard any inadequacy, it was expressly required to set out its reasons for so doing.

Inadequacy of available amount: discharge of confiscation order

10.76 Section 24 is a provision that previously did not exist under either the DTA or the CJA 1988. Section 24 of POCA applies if:

(a) a court has made a confiscation order,
(b) the designated officer for a magistrates' court applies to the Crown Court for the discharge of the order; and
(c) the amount remaining to be paid under the order is less than £1,000. (s 24(1))

In such a case the court must calculate the available amount and in so doing it must apply s 9 (calculation of available amount) as if references to the time the confiscation order is made were to the time of the original calculation and as if references to the date of the confiscation order were to the date of the original calculation (see s 24(2)).

10.77 Under s 24(3) if the court:

(a) finds that the available amount (as so calculated) is inadequate to meet the amount remaining to be paid, and
(b) is satisfied that the inadequacy is due wholly to a specified reason or a combination of specified reasons,
it may discharge the confiscation order.

Under section 24 what are 'specified reasons'?

The specified reasons are: **10.78**

(4) ...
    (a) in a case where any of the realisable property consists of money in a currency other than sterling, the fluctuations in currency exchange rates occurred;
    (b) any reason specified by the Secretary of State by Order.

For the procedure to be followed by magistrates' courts for applications under s 24, see para 10.81.

Small amount outstanding: discharge of confiscation order

Under s 25 of POCA, if: **10.79**

(a) a court has made a confiscation order,
(b) a justices' chief executive applies to the Crown Court for the discharge of the order, and
(c) the amount remaining to be paid under the order is £50 or less,

the court may discharge the order (see s 25(1) and (2)).

This section only applies where the magistrates' court is enforcing a confiscation order. The **10.80** intention is that certain confiscation orders should be discharged where their final recovery becomes uneconomic.

Procedure: application by magistrates' court to discharge a confiscation order

Under r 58.6 of the Criminal Procedure Rules, where a magistrates' court makes an appli- **10.81** cation under s 24 or s 25 of POCA for the discharge of a confiscation order, the application must be in writing and supported by a witness statement which must give details of:

(a) the confiscation order;
(b) the amount outstanding under the order; and
(c) the grounds for the application (see r 58.6(2)).

That application and witness statement must be served on: **10.82**

(a) the defendant;
(b) the prosecutor; and
(c) any receiver appointed under s 50 (enforcement receiver) of the Act, under r 58.6(3).

Once such an application has been made the Crown Court may determine the application **10.83** without a hearing, unless any of the persons listed in r 58.6(3) indicates, within the period of seven days beginning on the day after the day on which the application was served on him, that he would like to make representations (see r 58.6(4)).

Procedure where the Crown Court discharges a confiscation order

Under r 58.6(5) of the CrimPR, if the Crown Court makes an order discharging the con- **10.84** fiscation order, the appropriate court officer must at once send a copy of the order to:

(a) the designated officer of the magistrates' court who applied for the order;
(b) the defendant;
(c) the prosecutor; and
(d) any receiver appointed under s 50 of the Act (an enforcement receiver).

I. Variations and Discharge for Defendants who Abscond

Introduction

10.85 Sections 27 and 28 of POCA give the court jurisdiction, in certain circumstances, to make confiscation orders in relation to s 6 of POCA for defendants who abscond. These powers were considered in some depth in Chapter 9. Here we consider applications to vary and discharge such orders.

Variation and discharge of orders under section 28

10.86 Section 29 deals with varying orders made under s 28, and s 30 deals with the discharging of orders made under s 28. If the court discharges a confiscation order under s 30 it may make such consequential or incidental orders as it believes are appropriate (see s 30(5)).

Variation of order

10.87 POCA identifies certain circumstances where, if the court makes a confiscation order in circumstances where the defendant has absconded, such an order may later be varied. The variation provisions have effect only where the defendant applies to the court on the grounds the original order, made in his absence, is too large.

10.88 The circumstances are set out in s 29(1) which apply if:
   (a) the court makes a confiscation order under s 6 as applied by s 28 (where the defendant is neither convicted nor acquitted);
   (b) the defendant ceases to be an absconder;
   (c) he is convicted of an offence (or any of the offences) mentioned in s 28(2)(a) (ie he is now convicted of an offence where previously proceedings had been started against him, but had not been concluded);
   (d) the defendant believes that the amount required to be paid was too large (taking the circumstances prevailing when the amount was found for the purposes of the order), and
   (e) before the end of the relevant period the defendant applies to the Crown Court to consider the evidence on which his belief is based.

What is the relevant period?

10.89 Under s 29(3) the relevant period referred to in subs (1)(e) is the period of 28 days starting with:
   (a) the date on which the defendant was convicted of an offence mentioned in section 28(2)(a), or
   (b) if there are two or more offences and the convictions were on different dates, the date of the latest.

It should be noted that the defendant only has 28 days from his conviction to apply for a variation of an order made in his absence under s 29.

Procedure on applications for a variation made by a former absconder

10.90 Under r 58.7 of the CrimPR, where the defendant makes an application under s 29 of the Act for a variation of a confiscation order, that application must be made in writing and supported by a witness statement which must give details of:
   (a) the confiscation order made against an absconder under section 6 of the Act as applied by section 28 of the Act;
   (b) the circumstances in which the defendant ceased to be an absconder;
   (c) the defendant's conviction of the offences concerned; and

(d) the reason why he believes the amount required to be paid under the confiscation order was too large. (Rule 58.7(2))

That application and witness statement must be lodged with the Crown Court and must **10.91** be served on the prosecutor at least seven days before the date fixed by the court for hearing the application, unless the Crown Court specifies a shorter period (r 58.7(3) and (4)).

Powers of the court

If (after considering the evidence) the court concludes that the defendant's representations **10.92** are well founded:

29(2) (a) it must find the amount which should have been the amount required to be paid (taking the circumstances prevailing when the amount was found for the purposes of the order), and
     (b) it may vary the order by substituting for the amount required to be paid such amount it believes is just.

However, in a case where s 28(2)(a) applies to more than one offence the court must not make an order under s 29 unless it is satisfied that there is no possibility of any further proceedings being taken or continued in relation to any such offence in respect of which the defendant has not been convicted (s 29(4)).

Discharge of confiscation order where the defendant has absconded

Under s 30 of POCA, if the court makes a confiscation order under s 6, as applied by s 28 **10.93** (defendant neither convicted nor acquitted) and the defendant is later tried for the offence (or offences) concerned and acquitted on all counts, and the defendant then applies to the Crown Court to discharge the confiscation order made in his absence, the court must discharge that confiscation order (see s 30(1) and (2)).

Discharge of order: undue delay or proceedings not continuing

Under s 30(3) if the court makes a confiscation order under subs 6, as applied by s 28 **10.94** (a confiscation order in circumstances where the defendant is neither convicted nor acquitted, ie pre-conviction), and the defendant ceases to be an absconder, and the defendant was never tried for the offence(s) concerned, the defendant may apply to the Crown Court to discharge the order.

The court may discharge the order if it finds that there has been undue delay in continuing **10.95** the proceedings mentioned in s 28(2) (ie the proceedings for the offence(s) have been started against the defendant, but have not been concluded), or the prosecutor does not intend to proceed with the prosecution.

Unlike s 30(2), s 30(4) is discretionary. If the court discharges a confiscation order under s 30 it **10.96** may make such other consequential or incidental orders as it believes are appropriate (s 30(5)).

Procedure: application for discharge made by a former absconder

Under r 58.8 of the CrimPR, if a defendant makes an application under s 30 of the Act for **10.97** discharge of a confiscation order, that application must be in writing and supported by a witness statement which must give details of:

(a) the confiscation order made under section 28 of the Act;
(b) the date on which the defendant ceased to be an absconder;

(c) the acquittal of the defendant if he had been acquitted of the offences concerned; and

(d) if the defendant has not been acquitted of the offence concerned—

    (i) the date on which the defendant ceased to be an absconder;

    (ii) the date on which the proceedings taken against the defendant were instituted; and a summary of steps taken in the proceedings since then; and

    (iii) any application given by the prosecutor that he does not intend to proceed against the defendant.

10.98 Under r 58.8(3) once that application and witness statement have been made they must be lodged with the Crown Court. Further, under r 58.7(4) they must be served on the prosecutor at least seven days before the date fixed by the court for hearing the application, unless the Crown Court specifies a shorter period.

10.99 If the Crown Court orders the discharge of the confiscation order, the court must serve notice on the magistrates' court responsible for enforcing the order (see r 58.8(5) CrimPR).

Compensation: confiscation order made against absconder

10.100 Rule 58.11(1) of the CrimPR applies to an application for compensation under s 73 of the Act (where a confiscation order has been varied or discharged under either s 29 or s 30 of POCA and an application has been made to the Crown Court by a person who held realisable property and who has suffered a loss as a result of the making of that order). Under r 58.11(2) the application must be in writing and supported by a witness statement which must give details of:

(a) the confiscation order made under s 28 of the Act;

(b) the variation or discharge of the confiscation order under s 29 or 30 of the Act;

(c) the realisable property to which the application relates; and

(d) the loss suffered by the applicant as a result of the confiscation order.

10.101 Once the application and witness statement are made they must be lodged with the Crown Court (r 58.11(3)) and served on the prosecutor at least seven days before the date fixed by the court for hearing the application, unless the Crown Court specifies a shorter period.

10.102 The rules applying to general compensation under s 72 of POCA are set out in r 58.10 of the CrimPR.

Increase in term of imprisonment in default

10.103 Under s 39(5) of POCA there is provision for the prosecutor to make an application to increase the term of imprisonment in default of payment of a confiscation order. The CrimPR in relation to same are found at r 58.9, which provides:

(2) The application must be made in writing and give details of—

    (a) the name and address of the defendant;

    (b) the confiscation order;

    (c) the grounds for the application; and

    (d) the enforcement measures taken, if any.

(3) On receipt of the application, the court must—

    (a) at once send to the defendant and the magistrates' court responsible for enforcing the order, a copy of the application; and

    (b) fix a time, date and place for the hearing and notify the applicant and the defendant of that time, date and place.

(4) If the Crown Court makes an order increasing the term of imprisonment in default, the court must, at once, send a copy of the order to—
   (a) the applicant;
   (b) the defendant;
   (c) where the defendant is in custody at the time of the making of the order, the person having custody of the defendant; and
   (d) the magistrates' court responsible for enforcing the order.

J. Variations to Confiscation Orders under the Drug Trafficking Act 1994

Applications by the prosecutor

The DTA permits the prosecutor to seek a redetermination of the findings made during the **10.104** course of a confiscation hearing with a view to the confiscation order being increased. The DTA allows the prosecutor to make such applications in the light of new evidence in the following circumstances:

(1) where, on conviction, the court did not proceed under the DTA at all;
(2) where the court has determined that the defendant did not benefit from drug trafficking;
(3) where it appears that the defendant's proceeds of drug trafficking are greater than that determined by the court; and
(4) where it appears that the value of the defendant's realisable assets is greater than that determined by the court.

The case law relating to certificates of increase and inadequacy is set out in the preceding **10.105** part of this chapter, where now relevant to POCA.

Section 13: where the court has not proceeded under the Act

If, at the time of conviction, the prosecutor has no evidence to show that the defendant has **10.106** benefited from drug trafficking, the court will not proceed under the DTA at all. Where this has occurred, s 13 of the DTA allows the prosecutor to return to the court and ask the court to make a confiscation order in the light of evidence obtained subsequently that shows the defendant has benefited from drug trafficking.

It is an essential prerequisite to proceeding under s 13 that the evidence the prosecutor **10.107** wishes the court to consider was not available to him at the time the defendant was sentenced. Once the court is satisfied the provisions of s 13 have been met, it shall proceed under s 2 if, having considered the evidence, it is satisfied it is appropriate to do so (see s 13(3)). By s 13(4), in deciding whether it is appropriate to proceed under s 2, the court shall have regard to all the circumstances of the case. This gives the court an element of discretion in deciding whether to act under s 2 that it does not have if asked by the prosecutor to proceed under the DTA immediately following conviction. If the court does decide to proceed under s 2, it has jurisdiction to order the parties to file prosecutor's and defendant's statements under s 11 and require the defendant to provide information in accordance with s 12.

10.108 In other respects, however, the provisions of s 13 are significantly less draconian than those that apply when the court proceeds under s 2 immediately after conviction. When the court decides to proceed under s 13, the confiscation order shall be for such amount as it thinks just in all the circumstances of the case: see s 13(5). The court may therefore make a confiscation order in a sum less than the defendant's benefit from drug trafficking. Further, in considering the circumstances of the case, s 13(6) requires the court to have regard, in particular, to the amount of any fine or fines imposed on the defendant in respect of the offence or offences in question. The court may take account of any payment or other reward received by the defendant on or after the date of his conviction, but only if the prosecutor shows that it is received by him in connection with drug trafficking carried on before that date: see s 13(8). Section 13(9) precludes the court from applying the assumptions under s 4 in relation to any such payment or reward.

Time limits

10.109 Section 13(10) provides that no application under the section shall be entertained if it is made more than six years after the date of conviction. Section 13(12) defines 'date of conviction' as meaning the date on which the defendant was convicted or, where there appear to be sentences in respect of more than one conviction and those convictions were not all on the same date, the date of the latest conviction.

Section 14: where the court determines the defendant has not benefited from drug trafficking

10.110 Section 14 of the DTA deals with the position where the court does proceed under s 2, but determines that the defendant has not benefited from drug trafficking and accordingly makes no confiscation order against him.

10.111 The court has jurisdiction to order the parties to serve statements under s 11 and to require the defendant to provide information under s 12 (see s 14(8)). Section 14(5) and (6) make the same provision as to the acceptance of payments and rewards by the defendant and the application of the assumptions as s 13. Again, a six-year time limit from the date of conviction is imposed (see s 13(7)).

Section 15: revised assessment of the proceeds of drug trafficking

10.112 Section 15 applies where the court proceeds under s 2, and it later appears to the prosecutor that the defendant's proceeds from drug trafficking are greater than the amount determined by the court.

10.113 If the court is satisfied, having considered the evidence, that the real value of the defendant's proceeds of drug trafficking is greater than their assessed value, the court must make a fresh determination under s 2(4) (see s 15(4)). Again, the court is given power to require the parties to serve statements and order the defendant to provide information (see s 15(3)). Section 15(10) and (11) make the same provision in relation to payments and rewards and the application of the assumptions as ss 13 and 14. If the amount of the fresh determination of the defendant's proceeds of drug trafficking exceeds the amount of the confiscation order, the court may increase the order to such greater sum as it thinks just in all the circumstances (see s 15(12)).

The court may also make an appropriate increase in the default sentence to be served in the event of non-payment (see s 15(13)). Section 15(14), however, provides that this power may only be exercised in circumstances where the effect of the increase in the order would be to make the defendant liable to serve an increased default sentence. By way of example, an increase in a confiscation order from £150,000 to £200,000 would not necessarily make the defendant liable to an increased default sentence, but an increase from £150,000 to £275,000 would. Again, there is a six-year time limit on applications from the date of conviction (see s 15(15)).

Procedure on applications

By r 56.3 of the CrimPR, any application by the prosecutor under ss 13, 14, or 15 or under   **10.114**
the equivalent sections in the CJA 1988 must be in writing and a copy served on the defendant. Rule 56.3(2) requires that the application must include the following particulars:

(a) the name of the defendant;
(b) the date on which and the place where any relevant conviction occurred;
(c) the date on which and the place where any relevant confiscation order was made or, as the case may be, varied;
(d) the grounds on which the application is made;
(e) an indication of the evidence available to support the application.

It is suggested that the most appropriate course is for the proper officer of the Crown   **10.115**
Court, on receipt of such an application, to issue a summons requiring the defendant to attend on a particular date for the court to give directions as to how the application should proceed, eg by directing the service of s 11 statements by the parties and the provision of information by the defendant under s 12, within a specified timescale.

Section 16: increase in realisable property

Drug traffickers and others who commit financially motivated crime can be adept at con-   **10.116**
cealing their true wealth from law enforcement authorities. It is therefore by no means uncommon for further assets to come to light after a confiscation order has been made in a sum considerably less than the sum by which the court certifies he has benefited from drug trafficking. Further, after a confiscation order is made against a defendant in a sum less than his certified benefit, he may acquire other assets that could be made available to meet the shortfall between the amount of the benefit and the amount of the order. This situation is dealt with in s 16 of the DTA which provides as follows:

(1) This section applies where, by virtue of section 5(3) of this Act, the amount which a person is ordered to pay by a confiscation order is less than the amount assessed to be the value of his proceeds of drug trafficking.
(2) If, on an application made in accordance with subsection 3 below, the High Court is satisfied that the amount that might be realised in the case of the person in question is greater than the amount taken into account in making the confiscation order (whether it was greater than was thought when the order was made or has subsequently increased) the court shall issue a certificate to that effect, giving the court's reasons.
(3) An application under subsection (2) above may be made either by the prosecutor or by a receiver appointed in relation to the realisable property of the person in question under section 26 or 29 of this Act or in pursuance of a charging order.

(4) Where a certificate has been issued under subsection (2) above the prosecutor may apply to the Crown Court for an increase in the amount to be recovered under the confiscation order; and on that application the court may—

    (a) substitute for that amount such amount (not exceeding the amount assessed as the value referred to in subsection (1) above) as appears to the court to be appropriate having regard to the amount now shown to be realisable; and

    (b) increase the term of imprisonment or detention fixed in respect of the confiscation order under subsection (2) of section 139 of the Powers of Criminal Courts (Sentencing) Act 2000 (as it has effect by virtue of section 9 of this Act) if the effect of the substitution is to increase the maximum period applicable in relation to the order under subsection (4) of that section.

Practice

10.117 It should be noted that the practice and procedure under s 16 is significantly different from that under ss 13, 14, and 15. Under s 16, the Crown Court has no immediate jurisdiction to increase the confiscation order. An application must first be made to the High Court for a certificate under s 16(2) to reflect that the amount that might be realised is greater than the amount of the order. Only when the High Court has issued such a certificate does the Crown Court have jurisdiction to increase the order. The application may be made by the prosecutor or by a receiver appointed under the Act.

10.118 The section applies to all property owned by the defendant, whether he acquired ownership of it before or after the making of the order. Further, the prosecutor is not required to show that it represents the proceeds of drug trafficking or any other criminal activity. If the confiscation order is made for an amount less than the defendant's benefit from drug trafficking, any other assets he may acquire, whether legitimately or otherwise, may form the subject matter of a s 16 application until such time as the defendant has paid the full amount of his certified benefit (see *R v Tivnan* (1999) 1 Cr App R(S) 92).

Unfettered discretion

10.119 In *R v Bates* [2007] 1 Cr App R (S)(2) the Court of Appeal held that the Crown Court's discretion under s 16 of the DTA to increase the amount to be recovered under a confiscation order was unfettered. A judge could take into account certain matters, or reject them as being of little significance, depending on the circumstances of the case before him.

Procedure on applications

10.120 By scl15.9A, the High Court application for a certificate of increase must be served with any supporting evidence at least seven days before the hearing. The application must be served on the defendant and any receiver appointed under the Acts. Where the application is made by a receiver, he must serve it on the prosecutor. The application is issued out to the Administrative Court Office at the Royal Courts of Justice and is heard by a High Court Judge of the Queen's Bench Division assigned to Administrative Court business.

10.121 Rule 56.3 of the CrimPR does not apply to applications under s 16 and there appears to be no further guidance in the legislation as to the procedure to be followed in the Crown Court once a certificate has been granted. It is suggested that the proper course is for the prosecutor to write to the Crown Court providing all relevant information in relation to the defendant and the order and enclosing a copy of the High Court's certificate.

The defendant should then be required to attend before the court for directions to be given as to the hearing of the prosecutor's application for the order to be increased.

Certificates of inadequacy under the DTA

The relevant provisions are to be found in s 17 of the DTA which provides: **10.122**

(1) If, on an application made in respect of a confiscation order by—
   (a) the defendant, or
   (b) a receiver appointed under section 26 or 29 of this Act or in pursuance of a charging order,
   the High Court is satisfied that the realisable property is inadequate for the payment of any amount remaining to be recovered under the confiscation order, the court shall issue a certificate to that effect, giving the court's reasons.
(2) For the purposes of subsection (1) above—
   (a) in the case of realisable property held by a person who has been adjudged bankrupt or whose estate has been sequestrated the court shall take into account the extent to which any property held by him may be distributed among creditors; and
   (b) the court may disregard any inadequacy in the realisable property which appears to the court to be attributable wholly or partly to anything done by the defendant for the purpose of preserving any property held by a person to whom the defendant had directly or indirectly made a gift caught by this Act from any risk of realisation under this Act.
(3) Where a certificate has been issued under subsection (1) above, the person who applied for it may apply to the Crown Court for the amount to be recovered under the confiscation order to be reduced.
(4) The Crown Court shall, on an application under subsection (3) above—
   (a) substitute for the amount to be recovered under the order such lesser amount as the court thinks just in all the circumstances of the case; and
   (b) substitute for the term of imprisonment or of detention fixed under subsection (2) of section 139 of the Powers of Criminal Courts (Sentencing) Act 2000 in respect of the amount to be recovered under the order a shorter term determined in accordance with that section (as it has effect by virtue of section 9 of this Act) in respect of the lesser amount.

Commentary on the burden and standard of proof, the fact that assets maybe merely difficult to realise, and that certificate of inadequacy applications should not be seen as an alternative route to appeal are set out in the preceding paragraphs of this chapter. **10.123**

It should be noted that not every application for a certificate of inadequacy meets with unadulterated success. In *R v Briggs* (Crown Court, 31 October 2003), although the defence were successful in obtaining a certificate of inadequacy in the High Court, when the matter was referred to the Crown Court, the Crown Court judge took the view, on the particular facts, that the confiscation order in the sum of £40,586.97 should only be reduced by £1. **10.124**

Certificates of inadequacy: procedure

The procedure for making the application for the certificate of inadequacy to the High Court is set out in sc115.9. The application must be made by way of application notice which must be served together with any supporting evidence not less than seven days before the hearing on the prosecutor and, as the case may be, on either the defendant or the receiver, where one has been appointed. The application must be issued out of the Administrative Court Office at the Royal Courts of Justice. District Registries of the High Court have no jurisdiction to entertain such applications. The application should be **10.125** accompanied by a witness statement from the defendant verified by a statement of truth setting out in detail why his assets have proved insufficient to meet the confiscation order in full. Any relevant documentation, including receiver's reports, should be exhibited to the statement. In some circumstances, particularly where any receiver that may have been appointed accepts that the assets are inadequate to meet the order, the prosecutor may be prepared to consent to the issue of a certificate without the necessity for a court hearing. Where a defence solicitor wishes to apply for public funding, he should make application to the High Court, not to the enforcement magistrates' court, which has no power to grant a representation order for such proceedings.

10.126 Where the court grants a certificate of inadequacy whether by consent or otherwise, the defendant's solicitor must draw it up and arrange for it to be sealed by the Administrative Court Office. Care should be taken to ensure the order incorporates the court's reasons for granting the certificate. Once this has been done, the certificate should be lodged at the Crown Court where the order was originally made and arrangements made for the matter to be listed for the hearing of the defendant's application for the confiscation order to be reduced. At the hearing the court shall, by s 17(4) of the DTA substitute such lesser sum as it thinks just in all the circumstances and make any necessary reduction in the default sentence. It is submitted that at this stage the Crown Court can enquire into the reasons for the inadequacy and if, eg, it transpires that it has been caused by the defendant dissipating assets to make them unavailable for confiscation, it would be entitled to reduce the order only by a nominal sum and leave the default sentence undisturbed.

K. Variations to Confiscation Orders under the Criminal Justice Act 1988

10.127 The CJA 1988, as originally enacted, did not make provision for the prosecutor to return to court to apply for the original determinations made in a confiscation hearing to be revised. This changed in 1995 when the Proceeds of Crime Act 1995 added new ss 74A, 74B, and 74C to the CJA 1988 to give the prosecutor similar powers to those already in force under the DTA.

Section 74A: review of cases where the proceeds of crime have not been assessed

10.128 Section 74A is in very similar terms to s 13 of the DTA and s 74A(1) applies where:

(1) a person has been convicted before the Crown Court or a Magistrates' Court of an offence of a specified description;

(2) the prosecutor did not give written notice under s 71(1)(a); and

(3) a determination was made under s 71(1)(b) not to proceed under that section or no determination was made for those purposes.

10.129 By s 74A(2), where these conditions are satisfied and the prosecutor has evidence:

(a) which, at the date of conviction or, if later, when any determination not to proceed under section 71 was made, was not available to the prosecutor (and, accordingly, was not considered by the court); but

(b) which the prosecutor believes would have led the court to determine, if—

(i) the prosecutor had given written notice for the purposes of subsection (1)(a) of that section, and

(ii) the evidence had been considered by the court,

that the defendant had benefited from relevant criminal conduct, the prosecutor may apply to the relevant court for it to consider that evidence.

The relevant court is defined as meaning the Crown Court before which the defendant was **10.130** convicted or, where he was convicted in a magistrates' court, any magistrates' court for the same area (see s 74A(12)).

By s 74A(3), where the court is satisfied on the evidence, the court shall proceed under s 71 **10.131** as if it were doing so before sentencing the defendant. In considering whether it is appropriate so to proceed, the court must have regard to all the circumstances of the case (see s 74A(4)). If, having proceeded under s 71, the court determines the defendant did benefit from relevant criminal conduct, it then has a power rather than a duty to make a confiscation order and may make the order for such sum as it thinks fit, not exceeding the amount of that benefit: see s 74A(5).

Section 74A contains many similar provisions to those in s 13 of the DTA. Section 74A(9) **10.132** imposes similar restrictions in relation to the use of the assumptions and s 74(10) imposes the same six-year time limit for the bringing of applications. Section 74A(11) gives the court jurisdiction to order the parties to file s 73 statements and require the defendant to provide information in the same way as if the hearing was taking place immediately after conviction.

Section 74B: revision of assessment of the proceeds of crime

Section 74B is in similar terms to s 14 of the DTA and applies in circumstances where there **10.133** has been a determination under s 71(1A) that the defendant has not benefited from any relevant criminal conduct.

If the court is satisfied the conditions are met, the procedure to be followed is very similar **10.134** to that under s 74A. The court shall, by s 74B(3), proceed to make a fresh determination as to whether the defendant has benefited from relevant criminal conduct, make a determination under s 71(1B)(a), and then make an order requiring the defendant to pay such sum as it thinks fit. Similar restrictions on the use of the assumptions are imposed by s 74B(9) (see Chapter 12), and s 74B(10) again imposes a six-year time limit for bringing applications. The court is given jurisdiction to order the parties to file statements under s 73 and to require the defendant to provide information under s 73A (see s 74B(11)).

Section 74C: revision of assessment of amount to be recovered

Section 74C is in similar terms to s 15 of the DTA and applies where the prosecutor is of **10.135** the opinion that the value of the defendant's benefit from relevant criminal conduct is greater than that assessed by the court. In these circumstances, the prosecutor can apply under s 74C for the court to consider the evidence on which he has formed this opinion. If the court is satisfied that the amount of the defendant's benefit is greater than that assessed by the court it may make a fresh determination under s 71 and has the power to increase, to such extent as it thinks just in all the circumstances, the amount to be recovered and vary the confiscation order accordingly (see s 74C(3)). The default sentence may also be increased (see s 74C(7) and (8)). There is again a six-year time limit on bringing applications (see s 74C(9)) and the court is again given jurisdiction to order the parties to file s 73 statements and require the defendant to provide information under s 73A (see s 74C (11)).

Increase in realisable property

10.136   Of import, the CJA 1988 contains no equivalent of s 16 of the DTA giving the court jurisdiction to increase confiscation orders in circumstances where further realisable property is discovered. There does not seem to be any logical reason for this omission which has been remedied under POCA.

Certificates of inadequacy under the CJA 1988

10.137   The relevant provisions are to be found in s 83 of the CJA 1988. Section 83 is in virtually identical terms to s 17 of the DTA which is reproduced above.

10.138   Commentary on the burden and standard of proof, the fact that assets maybe merely difficult to realise, and that certificate of inadequacy applications should not be seen as an alternative route to appeal are set out in the preceding paragraphs of this chapter.

Certificates of inadequacy: procedure

10.139   The procedure for making the application for the certificate of inadequacy to the High Court is set out in sc115.9. The application must be made by way of application notice which must be served together with any supporting evidence not less than seven days before the hearing on the prosecutor and, as the case may be, on either the defendant or the receiver, where one has been appointed. The application should be accompanied by a witness statement from the defendant verified by a statement of truth setting out in detail why his assets have proved insufficient to meet the confiscation order in full. Any relevant documentation, including receiver's reports, should be exhibited to the statement.

10.140   Where the court grants a certificate of inadequacy whether by consent or otherwise, the defendant's solicitor must draw it up and arrange for it to be sealed by the Administrative Court Office. Care should be taken to ensure the order incorporates the court's reasons for granting the certificate. Once this has been done, the certificate should be lodged at the Crown Court where the order was originally made and arrangements made for the matter to be listed for the hearing of the defendant's application for the confiscation order to be reduced. At the hearing the court shall, by s 83(4) of the CJA 1988 substitute such lesser sum as it thinks just in all the circumstances and make any necessary reduction in the default sentence.

10.141   In *Escobar v DPP* [2009] 1 WLR 64 the court held that when making an order under s 83(4) the Crown Court had jurisdiction to fix a time for payment. Although there was no express power to extend time in s 83, s 75(1) had application by incorporating the provision of s 139(1) to (4) of the PCC(S)A.

11

ENFORCEMENT OF
CONFISCATION ORDERS

A. Introduction

11.01   A confiscation order is an *in personam* order against the defendant requiring him to pay a sum of money and is not an *in rem* order against the property taken into account by the court in making the order. A confiscation order does not therefore divest the defendant or any interested third party of title to the property and any person who attempts to realise the same in satisfaction of the order will be vulnerable to civil proceedings for conversion if he does so without consent or an appropriate order of the court. This principle must be borne in mind by all those in possession of a defendant's realisable property, particularly officers of prosecuting authorities who may, for example, be in possession of money taken from the defendant on his arrest.

11.02   A further order of the court is necessary to enforce a confiscation order unless the defendant cooperates with the prosecuting authority and enforcing magistrates' court in satisfying the order voluntarily. In some cases, particularly those involving third party claims to the assets (especially ancillary relief applications in relation to the matrimonial home) and assets located overseas, enforcement proceedings can become lengthy and protracted. In other cases, especially those involving so-called 'hidden assets' the respective law enforcements agencies will rarely have much success in locating and realising the property in the absence of cooperation from the defendant and, in practice, there will be little the court can do other than consider activation of the default sentence for non-payment. In this chapter, we examine the powers available to the court under the Proceeds of Crime Act 2002 (POCA) and the old legislation to enforce confiscation orders.

11.03   In 2003 the Home Office published its 'National Best Practice Guide to Confiscation Order Enforcement'. It was revised in 2005 and its purpose is to improve performance and promote consistency of approach in the enforcement of confiscation orders. The Guide is in the public domain and may be assessed on the internet at <http://www.homeoffice.gov.uk/about-us/publications/home-office-circulars/circulars-2005/027-2005>.

11.04   It should be emphasised the Guide is precisely that and does purport to prescribe the legal procedures that must be followed in individual cases. In the words of the Introduction:

> The guide aims to set the minimum acceptable standards for the confiscation order process. It is not intended to be prescriptive, so where local processes already deliver the same standard or better there may be no need for change.

11.05   The Guide does not have the force of law and the mere fact that a particular law enforcement agency has failed to follow the procedures it recommends does not, without more, give the defendant a right of redress.

B. Roles of Law Enforcement Agencies in the Satisfaction of Confiscation Orders

11.06   The legislation gives different agencies a variety of roles in the enforcement process which can appear at first sight to be confusing. The position is set out below.

The enforcing magistrates' court

Primary responsibility for the enforcement of confiscation orders rests with the magistrates' **11.07** court. All moneys realised in satisfaction of the order are paid to the designated officer at the court (CrimPR 52.2). As confiscation orders may be enforced as if they were fines, the magistrates' court has power to issue distress warrants. The magistrates' court may also make orders under s 67 of POCA directing banks, other financial institutions and law enforcement agencies to pay over funds they are holding and which belong to the defendant, in satisfaction of the confiscation order. It is the enforcing magistrates' court that has power to activate the default sentence imposed by the Crown Court if the defendant fails to satisfy the order. The enforcing magistrates' court normally takes the lead in enforcing confiscation orders where the amounts involved are relatively small and there are no third party claims to the assets involved. The court should liaise closely with the prosecutor who has the right to attend and make representations at any hearing when the activation of the default sentence is being considered. Section 109 of the Coroners and Justice Act permits a live video link to be used in magistrates' court enforcement proceedings. The bench will wish to know why the order has not been paid and will wish to have detailed proposals for prompt payment if it is not to consider committing the defaulter to prison. For further on the role of the magistrates' court and the Regional Confiscation Units, see para 1.38.

The prosecutor

The prosecutor too has an important role to play in the enforcement of confiscation **11.08** orders. It is the prosecutor, and only the prosecutor, who may apply to the Crown Court for the appointment of an enforcement receiver under s 50 of POCA or to the High Court under s 82 of the CJA 1988 or s 29 of the Drug Trafficking Act 1994 (DTA). The enforcing magistrates' court and, indeed, the defendant himself, have no standing under these sections to apply for an enforcement receiver to be appointed. As the National Best Practice Guide makes clear, the prosecutor is under a continuing duty to assist the enforcing magistrates' court in the efficient and expeditious enforcement of confiscation orders. It says:

> The financial investigator and prosecuting authority have a continuing responsibility to support the enforcement authority wherever their assistance could improve enforcement outcomes.

In practical terms, this involves close liaison with the enforcing magistrates' court, keeping **11.09** the court abreast of what action the prosecutor himself is taking to realise assets (for example, by the appointment of a receiver) advising the court of the location of assets and, in appropriate circumstances, appearing at enforcement hearings before the justices to assist them in discharging their responsibilities under the legislation.

The Crown Court

Once a confiscation order has been made, the Crown Court has little part to play in its **11.10** enforcement other than to determine applications by the prosecutor for the appointment of enforcement receivers in POCA cases.

The Serious Organised Crime Agency

11.11 Since the demise of the Assets Recovery Agency, the Serious Organised Crime Agency (SOCA) has been responsible for maintaining the Joint Assets Recovery Database (JARD) which plays a key role in the enforcement of confiscation orders and is described in more detail below.

C. The Joint Asset Recovery Database

11.12 JARD records all restraint, confiscation, cash seizure and civil recovery orders made throughout the United Kingdom and brief details of the assets taken into account in the making of such orders. It also shows the balance outstanding on confiscation orders at any time, and the daily rate of interest being charged where applicable.

11.13 The following agencies have access to and maintain data on JARD: all Police Services; Regional Asset Recovery Teams; HM Revenue and Customs; SOCA; the Department for Work and Pensions; the Department for Business, Enterprise and Regulatory Reform; the Crown Prosecution Service; the Revenue and Customs Prosecutions Office (as was); the Northern Ireland Director of Public Prosecutions; magistrates' courts in England and Wales; the Financial Crime Unit (in Scotland); and the Civil Recovery Unit (also in Scotland). It is estimated that the system is used by over 2,500 officers and staff across the asset recovery community.

11.14 JARD is described in these terms in the National Best Practice Guide:

> JARD was a brainchild of the Concerted Inter Agency Criminal Finance Action group (CICFA) in 2003. Its purpose is to improve the overall performance of the criminal justice system (CJS) in removing the proceeds of crime through better day to day management of asset recovery at case and order level.
>
> It is the master repository for data concerning asset recovery activity in the UK and is used to produce national statistics for the agencies involved, CICFA and other government departments including the Home Office. In addition, statistics from JARD enable CICFA and others concerned with CJS performance regarding asset recovery to identify where systemic problems exist and can identify projects or legislative changes needed to address them.

D. Voluntary Satisfaction by the Defendant

11.15 In most circumstances, the prosecutor should give the defendant the opportunity to satisfy the confiscation order voluntarily before taking enforcement action in the courts. It is very much to the defendant's advantage to cooperate with the court and prosecutor in the voluntary satisfaction of the confiscation order for the following reasons:

(1) He will be liable to pay interest, at the same rate applicable to civil judgments, currently 8 per cent, on any amount outstanding when the time allowed for payment expires: see s 10 of the DTA, s 75A of the CJA 1988, and s 12 of POCA. These provisions also give the court power, on the application of the prosecutor, to increase the default sentence if the effect of adding interest to the capital sum due is to increase the maximum period of imprisonment for which he would be liable. Interest is added to

the amount outstanding by operation of law and the court does not have a discretion not to add interest to the amount due, see *Hansford v Southampton Magistrates Court* [2008] EWHC 67 (Admin).

(2) It will reduce the risk of the prosecutor applying for the appointment of an enforcement receiver to realise the defendant's assets in satisfaction of the order.

(3) If the order is satisfied prior to time to pay expiring, the defendant will avoid any risk of having to serve the default sentence for non-payment.

(4) Any restraint order made in the defendant's case does not come to an end once a confiscation order is made, but remains in force until the confiscation order is satisfied. The sooner the defendant satisfies the confiscation order, the sooner he will be free of the restrictions imposed by the order and be able to resume a normal lifestyle.

(5) Voluntary satisfaction of an order may avoid assets being sold by bailiffs at a public auction where they may not realise the values attributed to them in the Crown Court proceedings.

Once a confiscation order has been made, the prosecutor will invariably write to the defen- **11.16** dant or his solicitors inviting proposals for payment and, for the reasons outlined above, it is very much in the defendant's interests to reply positively and constructively. If the defendant fails to respond in positive terms, he may well find that the court is unsympathetic if the prosecutor invites the court to appoint an enforcement receiver or consideration is being given to the implementation of the default sentence. Conversely, if the defendant demonstrates his willingness from the outset to satisfy a confiscation order voluntarily, the court may be reluctant to accede to a prosecutor's application for a receiver to be appointed until the defendant has been afforded that opportunity.

There will, of course, be some circumstances where voluntary satisfaction is inappropriate: **11.17** for example, where a defendant has shown, by his previous conduct, that he cannot be trusted to realise assets himself or where the assets in question are subject to third party claims that need to be determined. In many cases, the defendant will be in some difficulty in satisfying the confiscation order voluntarily because he will be serving a lengthy sentence of imprisonment. This need not, however, prevent him signing letters of authority permitting the prosecutor to pay over to the court money taken up at the time of his arrest or permitting banks to pay over money held in his bank accounts. Similarly, in so far as real property is concerned, there is no reason why the defendant cannot give his solicitor instructions to effect a sale notwithstanding the fact that he is in prison.

If a restraint order is in force, it may be necessary to seek a variation to authorise the **11.18** payment of money to the enforcing magistrates' court or to put a restrained property on the market with a view of its realisation in satisfaction of the confiscation order. It is important that those holding assets on behalf of a defendant or who are instructed to act for him on the sale of property should check the terms of the restraint order very carefully before taking any action. It will not normally be necessary for the restraint order to be varied to enable money held by the defendant or a third party to be paid into court in satisfaction of the confiscation order. This is because most restraint orders contain a provision to the effect that nothing in the order shall prevent the payment of money into court in satisfaction of a confiscation order: see para 19(7) of the draft restraint order at appendix 7.

11.19   In so far as other assets are concerned, a variation to the restraint order will normally be necessary and solicitors should be vigilant to ensure that such a variation is obtained prior to taking steps to realise restrained property on behalf of a client. In the absence of such a variation, a solicitor or any other professional person instructed to effect a sale of realisable property on behalf of a client could be vulnerable to proceedings for contempt of court if he assists in any way in the sale of an asset subject to a restraint order. In most instances, the prosecutor will be prepared to agree that the restraint order should be varied by consent to allow a sale to take place, but he will want to be assured that the property is not sold at an undervalue, possibly to an associate of the defendant, and that, once the sale is completed, the net proceeds are paid directly into court and not given to the defendant or placed under his control. These concerns can normally be met by the inclusion of a number of conditions in the variation order. These usually include the following:

(1)   A term that the property shall be valued by at least two independent valuers who are members of a recognised trade association and be sold in an arm's length transaction to a bona fide purchaser for value, for not less than the average of the two valuations.

(2)   An undertaking by the defendant to instruct a named solicitor to act for him in relation to the transaction and that he will not terminate that solicitor's retainer without the agreement of the prosecutor or, in default of agreement, the permission of the court.

(3)   An undertaking by the solicitor to pay the net proceeds of sale into court in satisfaction of the order forthwith on completion of the transaction.

(4)   A term that all fees payable to solicitors, valuers, estate agents, and other professionals in relation to the transaction shall be agreed with the prosecutor in advance of being incurred.

11.20   Where real property is involved, it is usual for the prosecutor to give an undertaking to apply for the discharge of any restriction registered at the Land Registry on being notified that the proceeds of sale have been paid into court. The above conditions and undertakings are by no means exhaustive and others may be required having regard to the particular circumstances of individual cases.

11.21   Defendants and affected third parties should take great care when agreeing consent orders with the prosecutor to check the terms proposed and ensure they are content to be bound by them. Once a consent order has been agreed, it has the status of a contract between the parties and will be interpreted as such. In *Weston v Dayman* [2006] EWCA Civ 1165 the claimant, who had been subject to CJA restraint and management receivership orders, agreed a consent order dealing with the discharge of the receiver on his acquittal. One of the terms of the consent order was that the receiver would not be liable for any failure by her to properly manage the claimant's estate. Notwithstanding this provision, the claimant instituted proceedings against the receiver claiming damages, alleging she had acted in breach of duty by failing to take proper care of a motor yacht. The Court of Appeal upheld the judge's ruling that summary judgment should be entered in favour of the defendant receiver, holding that the claimant was bound by the terms of the consent order he had freely entered into whereby the receiver was released from any such liability. Although it would be open to a defendant to apply for a consent order to which he is party to be varied or set aside, it is submitted this would only be appropriate in exceptional circumstances. As Arden LJ observed in *Weston v Dayman*:

> I would accept that the court should accede to an application for variation where it is just to do so but in my judgment one of the aspects of justice is that a bargain freely made should be upheld. Mr. Weston clearly obtained benefits under the order. It may well be that those benefits are not as great as he thought, but that is not a matter for this court. In those circumstances I do not consider it would be right for this court to exercise its discretion to vary the order as sought.

A variation to a restraint order will not be sanctioned by the court if it does not result in the **11.22** full value of the defendant's interest in the property to which it relates being realised in satisfaction of the confiscation order. In *Re Barnes and Barnes* [2004] EWHC Admin 2620 CJA confiscation orders were made against the defendants (who were husband and wife) in the sums of £42,845.73 and £63,320.73 respectively. The realisable assets of the defendants included their half shares in the matrimonial home which amounted to some £21,316.50. They sought a variation to the restraint order to permit them to take out a second mortgage on the property which would enable them to pay £38,715 into court in part satisfaction of the confiscation orders. They proposed to pay off the balance in monthly instalments of £60. The prosecutor refused to agree a variation to the restraint order in these terms and the defendants made an application to court for the order to be so varied. Lightman J refused the defendants' application, ruling that the variation sought was incompatible with the legislative steer in s 82(2) of the CJA 1988. He said:

> In my judgment, the language of section 82(2) of the Criminal Justice Act 1988 is mandatory and requires the power to be exercised with a view to securing the full realisation of the realisable property, so far as necessary to secure the full satisfaction of the confiscation order. An exercise of power for the purpose of anything less than full realisation of value can only be sanctioned if it is clear that that exercise, or that exercise jointly with something else (for example, a further payment to the Crown) will fully discharge the debt due to the Crown.
>
> In this case, assuming—and this is a considerable assumption—that the building society, after being correctly informed as to the full and true facts, is prepared to agree to the proposed remortgage, there will be a shortfall due to the Crown of some £8,000 to £10,000, and this shortfall will arise because the defendants propose a remortgage and not a sale. I do not think that the court has jurisdiction to vary the restraint order with a view to authorising a transaction which does not realise the full value of the property, or at least sufficient to enable the confiscation order to be satisfied. The adverse consequences for the defendant (which are the plight of their own criminal conduct) and the adverse consequences to the community in the costs of providing housing are nothing to the point.

If a defendant refuses to cooperate in the voluntary satisfaction of a confiscation order, or, **11.23** for whatever reason, it is inappropriate to allow him to do so, it will be necessary to invoke the powers of the court to ensure the order is paid, and we examine below the various sanctions available to the court.

E. General Living Expenses and Legal Fees

We saw in Chapter 5 that the right to draw on restrained funds for the payment of general **11.24** living expenses and, in cases to which the CJA 1988 and DTA apply, for the payment of legal fees, does not continue indefinitely but comes to an end on the making of a confiscation order or, if an appeal is lodged, when all domestic avenues of appeal have been exhausted. Many restraint orders now make provision for such payments to come to an end on the making of a confiscation order but, if they do not, it is likely that the prosecutor will invite the defendant to consent to a variation precluding the release of further funds for such purposes and, if consent is not forthcoming, make an appropriate application to the court.

11.25 This is particularly so in cases where a defendant has been found guilty of an offence of dishonesty and the funds which he is seeking to use for these purposes are tainted. The principle is not, however, confined to cases where the assets can be traced directly to the proceeds of crime, but applies equally where the assets have only been accumulated as a result of the defendant's dishonest failure to pay tax. The authority that supports this proposition is *Stodgell v Stodgell* [2009] EWCA Civ 243, a CJA case in which considerable sums had been released to pay general living expenses of the defendant's family and to meet her legal expenses incurred in ancillary relief proceedings. Holman J directed the payments to cease and this decision was upheld by the Court of Appeal. Hughes LJ said:

> The spouses both lived well on a domestic economy which included the non-payment of tax and penalties. For the same reason, counsel's careful submissions about 'taint' do not, as it seems to me, provide the wife with any arguable ground of appeal. 'Taint' is not a statutory expression. Of course it is relevant where assets can be traced to acquisition from the proceeds of crime, but that is not the only case in which justice requires that the confiscation order should be met before there can be any question of allocating the assets between husband and wife. Another such case, of which this is one, is where the domestic economy and the assets accumulated are only of the size they are because the husband failed to pay the tax due. If this husband had paid his tax and penalties, his assets would be nil rather than either £880,000 or £750,000. For that reason, it is not critical that the Devon house and the London flat were not acquired from crime. What is critical, as it seems to me, is that they could not have been and cannot be preserved without non payment of the tax and the penalties.

11.26 The court indicated that in its view the judge would have been wrong to make any other order. Although this case was decided under the CJA 1988, the Court noted that the legislative steer in POCA represented a 'significant tightening of the statutory rules'. It is likely therefore that, at the enforcement stage, the court will not allow the dissipation of further funds by way of general living expenses and legal fees, and defendants and affected third parties should prepare for this contingency by arranging other sources of funding or, if appropriate, apply for state benefits.

F. Enforcement Receivers under POCA

The power to appoint enforcement receivers

11.27 Section 50 of POCA empowers the Crown Court to appoint receivers for the purpose of enforcing confiscation orders. In contrast to the position in relation to management receivers, the primary purpose of an enforcement receiver is to realise assets in satisfaction of the confiscation order, although enforcement receivers will inevitably have to manage the assets prior to realisation.

Section 50 provides: **11.28**

(1) This section applies if—
    (a) a confiscation is made,
    (b) it is not satisfied, and
    (c) it is not subject to appeal.
(2) On the application of the prosecutor the Crown Court may by order appoint a receiver in respect of realisable property.

The remedy is a discretionary one and the court is not bound to appoint a receiver even   **11.29**
when the conditions in s 50(1) have been met. The court may, for example, consider
whether the defendant could reasonably satisfy the order voluntarily and, if so, whether
he has been given sufficient opportunity to do so. The court may also consider whether
other less expensive methods of enforcement might be equally effective. The court must,
however, exercise its discretion judicially and in accordance with the legislative steer in s 69.
It is submitted that the correct approach is that outlined by Munby J in *Re HN* [2005]
EWHC Admin 2982, a case heard in the High Court under the CJA 1988. He said:

> On the face of it, once a confiscation order has been made, the Crown is entitled to demand
> the appointment of an enforcement receiver in order to realise the funds with which to
> discharge the confiscation order. That, after all is no more than the 'legislative steer' in section
> 82(2) would normally demand. On the other hand, since the effect of my ruling is poten-
> tially to throw onto the defendant's assets the burden of meeting the receiver's costs, disburse-
> ments and fees, it may be proper, in an appropriate case to defer the appointment of a receiver
> for a short period to give the defendant the opportunity himself (subject of course to suitable
> safeguards) to realise the assets—something he may perhaps be able to do more advanta-
> geously and at lesser expense than a receiver.

The court will not, on an application for the appointment of an enforcement receiver,   **11.30**
entertain any challenge by the defendant to the validity of the confiscation order to which
it relates. In *Customs and Excise Commissioners v Togher* [2005] EWCA 274 the defendant
contended that a confiscation order made against him under the DTA was invalid because
it should have been made under the Drug Trafficking Offences Act 1986. Sedley LJ, in
refusing the defendant leave to appeal, said:

> This submission is, in my judgment, entirely misconceived. The confiscation order exists. It
> has the authority of the Criminal Division of the Court of Appeal and of the Crown Court.
> Customs and Excise are not only entitled but are required, as a matter of public duty, to
> enforce it if they can. The time for challenging its validity is past. The place of challenging its
> validity in any event is not the receivership proceedings consequent upon it.

> I am tempted to go into the reasons why it seems to me that the underlying argument is a bad
> one. But to do so would be to accept the very thing that I do not accept, which is that it
> is open to the Administrative Court, or therefore to this court, in receivership proceedings,
> to embark upon the question whether the order upon which Customs and Excise rely is a
> properly made order. The time and place for such a challenge are not here and are not now.

Section 50 does not require that any time allowed for payment by the Crown Court should   **11.31**
have elapsed before an enforcement receiver can be appointed. An application to appoint
an enforcement receiver may therefore be made before the time allowed for payment has
expired. Although the fact that time to pay has not expired will be a matter the court will
wish to take into account in exercising its discretion whether or not to make the order, it is

submitted there is nothing wrong in principle in making an enforcement receivership order before the expiration of the period. The prompt appointment of an enforcement receiver after the making of a confiscation order will assist in ensuring that the order is satisfied within the time allowed for payment and so is entirely consistent with the legislative steer. This is particularly so in cases where assets are going to take a considerable time to realise, where there are third party claims to resolve, or where the defendant fails to advance his own proposals for the voluntary satisfaction of the order.

Orders subject to appeal

11.32 Section 50(1)(c) precludes the appointment of an enforcement receiver when the confiscation order is subject to appeal. By s 87(2) of POCA:

> A confiscation order is subject to appeal until there is no further possibility of an appeal on which the order could be varied or quashed; and for this purpose any power to grant leave to appeal out of time must be ignored.

A confiscation order is therefore only subject to appeal if an appeal has been lodged within the time limits prescribed by rules of court or if permission to appeal has been granted out of time. If an application for permission to appeal out of time has been lodged but not determined, or if the defendant merely indicates an intention to appeal out of time, the order will not be 'subject to appeal' within the meaning of s 87(2). Although a confiscation order will not technically be 'subject to appeal' if an application for permission to appeal out of time has been made, the fact that such an application has been lodged may be a matter the court will wish to consider in exercising its discretion whether or not to appoint an enforcement receiver.

11.33 If a confiscation order is 'properly subject to appeal' the prosecutor may, of course, still apply for the appointment of a management receiver to manage and preserve realisable property pending the determination of the appeal, but, unlike an enforcement receiver, he would not have power to realise assets in satisfaction of the confiscation order.

11.34 In *Re P* [1998] EWHC Admin 1049 it was held that a confiscation order is not 'subject to appeal' if there is a pending application to the Criminal Cases Review Commission or to the European Court of Human Rights in relation to it. Laws J said:

> The fact is that, so far as the domestic criminal litigation is concerned in this case Mr. P is well past the end of the road. The Commission may, of course, investigate a matter after all other criminal legal processes have been exhausted. Indeed, that is their very role. However, it is quite clear to me that while they are doing so, and the fact that they are doing so, are no basis for altering, suspending or varying the effect of a restraint order and therefore, the execution of a confiscation order once that has been made. The same applies in relation to his application to the European Court of Human Rights.

11.35 *Re P* was followed in *R v Bullen and Soneji* [2006] EWCA Crim 1125 where the Court of Appeal expressed itself as being:

> ... wholly unimpressed by the suggestion that the period allowed for payment should be extended uncertainly into the future so that the defendants can pursue their petition before the European Court of Human Rights.

Further, it is important to appreciate that, in the absence of a specific order of the court, a pending appeal does not suspend the obligation to pay the confiscation order and time continues to run. In *R v May* [2005] EWCA Crim 367 the Crown Court made a confiscation order for £3,264,277 and ordered the defendant to pay within three years. He appealed against the order to the Court of Appeal, but his appeal was dismissed. He then contended that the three-year period for payment should run from the date on which his appeal was dismissed and not from the date on which the confiscation order was made. Keene LJ described this proposition as 'unsound in law' and said:

> We do not find this argument persuasive. There is no reason why steps preparatory to the raising of the money specified in the confiscation order should not have been taken while May's appeal was pending. The appellant was not entitled to assume that his appeal would be successful and, as indicated above, as a matter of law time was running during that period. Moreover, it would be wrong as a matter of principle for appellants to be encouraged to believe that the bringing of an appeal would be likely to lengthen the time given for payment, even if the appeal was unsuccessful.

The decision in *May* was followed by the Court of Appeal in *R v Bullen and Soneji* [2006] **11.36**
EWCA Crim 1125. In that case, confiscation orders were made against the defendants for £375,000 and £30,284 respectively. The trial judge, being aware of the defendants' intention of appealing against the orders, allowed 18 months to pay from the date on which the Court of Appeal determined the appeals. In due course, the Court of Appeal allowed the appeals and quashed the confiscation orders.

The Crown thereafter successfully appealed to the House of Lords and the confiscation **11.37**
orders were reinstated. The defendants contended that the 18-month period should run from the date on which the House of Lords allowed the Crown's appeal. The Court of Appeal rejected this argument and ordered the defendants to pay in full within 28 days. In delivering the judgment of the Court, Fulford J said:

> . . . in our view they have had ample time to raise, speedily, adequate funds. Given the time that has elapsed, it is our view a sufficient—indeed generous—opportunity has been afforded to the defendants to put their affairs in order so they can pay these sums. As the decision of this Court in *R v May* [2005] EWCA Crim 367 makes clear, the obligation to pay a confiscation order within a specified period remains in force from the date it was imposed. The clock does not stop running whilst an appeal is pending, save by judicial authorisation, in other words, time continues to run unless there is a court order to the contrary.

Defendants subject to confiscation orders who appeal against the order, or against the **11.38**
conviction that resulted in the order being made, would be well advised to make contingency plans for the prompt satisfaction of the order in the event that the appeal is unsuccessful. If they do not do so, they may find enforcement action being taken shortly after the appeal is dismissed.

Powers of enforcement receivers

The powers the Crown Court may give an enforcement receiver are set out in some detail **11.39**
in s 51 of POCA which provides:

(1) If the court appoints a receiver under section 50 it may act under this section on the application of the prosecutor.
(2) The court may by order confer on the receiver the following powers in relation to the realisable property—
  (a) power to take possession of the property;

    (b) power to manage or otherwise deal with the property;

    (c) power to realise the property, in such manner as the court may specify;

    (d) power to start, carry on or defend any legal proceedings in respect of the property.

(3) The court may by order confer on the receiver power to enter any premises in England and Wales and to do any of the following—

    (a) search for or inspect anything authorised by the court;

    (b) make or obtain a copy, photograph or other record of anything so authorised;

    (c) remove anything which the receiver is required or authorised to take possession of in pursuance of an order of the court.

(4) The court may by order authorise the receiver to do any of the following for the purpose of the exercise of his functions—

    (a) hold property;

    (b) enter into contracts;

    (c) sue and be sued;

    (d) execute powers of attorney, deeds or other instruments;

    (e) take any other steps the court thinks appropriate.

(5) The court may order any person who has possession of realisable property to give possession of it to the receiver.

(6) The court—

    (a) may order a person holding an interest in realisable property to make to the receiver such payment as the court specifies in respect of a beneficial interest held by the defendant or the recipient of a tainted gift;

    (b) may (on the payment being made) by order transfer, grant or extinguish any interest in the property.

(7) Subsections (2), (5) and (6) do not apply to property for the time being subject to a charge under any of these provisions—

    (a) section 9 of the Drug Trafficking Offences Act 1986 (c32);

    (b) section 78 of the Criminal Justice Act 1988 (c33);

    (c) Article 14 of the Criminal Justice (Confiscation) (Northern Ireland) Order 1990 (SI 1990/2588 (NI 17));

    (d) section 27 of the Drug Trafficking Act 1994 (c37);

    (e) Article 32 of the Proceeds of Crime (Northern Ireland) Order 1996 (SI 1996/1299 (NI 9)).

(8) The court must not—

    (a) confer the power mentioned in subsection (2)(b) or (c) in respect of property, or

    (b) exercise the power conferred on it by subsection (6) in respect of property,

    unless it gives persons holding interests in the property a reasonable opportunity to make representations to it.

(9) The court may order that a power conferred by an order under this section is subject to such conditions and exceptions as it specifies.

(10) Managing or otherwise dealing with property includes—

    (a) selling the property or any part of it or interest in it;

    (b) carrying on or arranging for another person to carry on any trade or business the assets of which are or are part of the property;

    (c) incurring capital expenditure in respect of the property.

11.40 These powers are in very similar terms to those given to management receivers under s 49 of POCA and which are considered in Chapter 4 above. There is, however, one significant difference in that s 51(2)(c) allows the court to empower the receiver to realise the property in such manner as it may direct. The equivalent power in relation to management receivers in s 49(2)(d) is confined to the realisation of assets to pay the receiver's remuneration and expenses. This difference reflects the different purposes for which management and enforcement receivers are appointed: the primary role of the management receiver being to manage and preserve property, and the primary role of the enforcement receiver being to realise assets in satisfaction of the confiscation order. Section 51(8) of the Act protects the interests of third parties to the extent that the powers set out in s 51(2)(b) and (c) and (6) cannot be conferred on the receiver unless and until they have been given a reasonable opportunity to make representations.

Application of the proceeds of realisation

Sections 54 and 55 of POCA deal with the way in which the proceeds of realisation must be dealt with both by the management receiver and the enforcing magistrates' court. Section 54(1) and (2) provide as follows: **11.41**

(1) This section applies to sums which are in the hands of a receiver appointed under section 50 if they are—
    (a) the proceeds of the realisation of property under section 51;
    (b) sums (other than those mentioned in paragraph (a) in which the defendant holds an interest.
(2) The sums must be applied as follows—
    (a) first, they must be applied in payment of such expenses incurred by a person acting as an insolvency practitioner as are payable under this subsection by virtue of section 432;
    (b) second, they must be applied in making any payments directed by the Crown Court;
    (c) third, they must be applied on the defendant's behalf towards satisfaction of the confiscation order.

By s 54(6), the receiver applies the sums in satisfaction of the confiscation order under s 54(2)(c) by paying them to the designated officer of the magistrates' court responsible for enforcing the order. It is important to note that an enforcement receiver appointed under POCA is not entitled to deduct his own remuneration and expenses before paying the proceeds of realisation into court. The only payments he is permitted to make under s 54 prior to remitting funds to the enforcing magistrates' court are the expenses of an insolvency practitioner pursuant to s 432 of POCA and any payments the Crown Court directs should be made, such as compensation to a victim of the offence. Once the receiver has paid the sums he holds to the enforcing magistrates' court, he must apply to the Magistrates' Court Executive to be reimbursed in respect of his fees. The purpose of this provision is to ensure that the gross amount realised by the receiver is credited against the amount outstanding under the confiscation order.   **11.42**

Section 51(3) to (5) deals with the position where the receiver remains in possession of funds after the confiscation order has been paid in full. By s 51(3) he must distribute such funds among such persons who held (or hold) interests in the property concerned as the Crown Court directs and in such proportions as it directs. The Crown Court must give persons who held (or hold) interests in the property concerned a reasonable opportunity to make representations before making a direction under s 54(3): see s 54(4).   **11.43**

Section 55 sets out how funds must be dealt with when received by the Magistrates' Court Executive. By s 55(1) the section applies to all funds received on account of the amount payable under a confiscation order, whether received from an enforcement receiver or otherwise. Section 55(2) provides that the receipt of those sums by the court reduces   **11.44** the amount payable under the order, but he is required to apply the sums received as follows:

(3) First, he must apply them in payment of such expenses incurred by a person acting as an insolvency practitioner as—

    (a) are payable under this subsection by virtue of section 432, but

    (b) are not already paid under section 54(2)(a).

(4) If the justices' chief executive received the sums under section 54 he must next apply them—

    (a) first, in payment of the remuneration and expenses of a receiver appointed under section 48 to the extent that they have not been met by the exercise by that receiver of a power conferred under section 49(2)(d);

    (b) second, in payment of the remuneration and expenses of the receiver appointed under section 50.

(5) If a direction was made under section 13(6) for an amount of compensation to be paid out of sums recovered under the confiscation order, the justices chief executive must next apply the sums in payment of that amount.

11.45 The effect of these provisions is that the court must first pay the costs of an insolvency practitioner in accordance with s 432 if the receiver himself has not already paid those costs. Next he must pay any remuneration and expenses still owed to a management receiver and then, but only then, may he pay the remuneration and expenses of the enforcement receiver. Finally, the court may pay any compensation ordered by the Crown Court to be paid under s 13(6) which applies in cases where the court believes there will be insufficient funds available to meet both the compensation order and the confiscation order.

11.46 The question arises as to whether the receiver is entitled to realise sufficient assets to pay both the confiscation order and his own remuneration and expenses. It is submitted that he can. Firstly, it is well settled law that the remuneration and expenses of a receiver appointed under the legislation fall to be paid from the receivership estate: see in particular the decision of the House of Lords in *Capewell v HM Revenue and Customs* [2007] UKHL 2.

11.47 Secondly, the appointment of the enforcement receiver in the first place is necessitated by the defendant's failure to discharge the confiscation order voluntarily. As Munby J said in *Re HN & Others* [2005] EWHC 2982 (Admin):

> If it becomes necessary to have a receiver, why should the Crown be left paying his costs, disbursements and fees? On the contrary, in most such cases, at least where there is a sufficiency of assets, the only proper order is that the burden of meeting those costs, disbursements and fees should be thrown on the defendant rather than on the Crown. Why, after all, should the public purse be expected to pay for something necessitated by a solvent criminal's failure to discharge a confiscation order? I can think of no good reason.

G. Procedure on Applications for the Appointment of Enforcement Receivers

Initiating the application

11.48 The procedures to be followed on applications for the appointment of enforcement receivers are set out in r 60 of the Criminal Procedure Rules 2005 (CrimPR). By r 60.1(3) the application must be in writing and supported by a witness statement which must:

(a) give the grounds for the application;

(b) give full details of the proposed receiver;

(c) to the best of the witness's ability, give full details of the realisable property in respect of which the applicant is seeking the order and specify the person holding it;

(d) if the proposed receiver is not a member of staff of the Crown Prosecution Service or the Revenue and Customs Prosecutions Office and the applicant is asking the court to allow the receiver to act—

(i) without giving security, or

(ii) before he has given security or satisfied the court that he has security in place,

explain the reasons why that is necessary.

The applicant must provide the Crown Court with a copy of the confiscation order it is **11.49** sought to enforce against the defendant (see r 60.1(4)). It is submitted that the best practice is to exhibit a copy of the order to the witness statement in support of the application. Although not specifically required by the rules, it is submitted that the letter of agreement between the prosecutor and the receiver should also be exhibited to the witness statement. The letter of agreement is, in essence, a contractual document between the receiver and the applicant prosecutor dealing with such matters as reporting arrangements, the maintenance and inspection of records, the instruction of agents, drawing remuneration, and maintaining confidentiality. A draft letter of agreement appears at Appendix 10. The receiver's response, which will normally include an estimate of the likely costs involved and a table setting out the rates to be claimed by each grade of fee earner likely to be involved, should also be exhibited.

Letters of agreement have for many years included an indemnity under which the prosecu- **11.50** tor agrees to indemnify the receiver in relation to his remuneration and expenses in the event that the value of any assets realised proves insufficient to meet the same. Increasingly, however, receivers are agreeing to agree without any indemnity being provided or subject to a conditional fee agreement in enforcement cases.

Finally, the prosecutor should also exhibit or lodge with the Crown Court a draft of the **11.51** receivership order he seeks.

Service of the application

Although r 60.1(2) of the CrimPR allows applications for the appointment of enforcement **11.52** receivers to be made without notice, it is submitted that it would rarely, if ever, be appropriate for such applications to be made other than on notice to the defendant and affected third parties. Where the application is to be made on notice, the application and witness statement in support must be lodged with the Crown Court and served on the defendant, any person who holds realisable property to which the application relates, and any other person whom the applicant knows to be affected by it, at least seven days before the date of the hearing (see r 60.1(6)).

The defendant's response to the application

It is important that the defendant should determine well in advance of the hearing date **11.53** what his response should be. Where a defendant has been sentenced to a long term of imprisonment and has a substantial confiscation order to meet he will, in most instances, have no grounds for resisting the application. In such circumstances, he should write promptly to the court and prosecutor consenting to the appointment of the receiver so that the matter may proceed on a 'by consent' basis, thereby saving the time and expense of a contested hearing in the Crown Court. If the defendant is in a position to satisfy the order voluntarily, he should make a witness statement setting out realistic proposals as to how this might be achieved. The court will need to be satisfied that any such proposal is genuine and the court will almost certainly insist on the consent order setting out a clear timescale within which assets must be realised together with conditions and undertakings to ensure assets are sold to bona fide purchasers at the proper market value and the proceeds of sale paid promptly into court.

11.54 One argument that will find little favour with the court is that the defendant would prefer to serve the default sentence for non-payment rather than satisfy the confiscation order. As the Divisional Court emphasised in *R v Harrow Justices ex p DPP* [1991] 1 WLR 395 this is not an option open to the defendant. As Stuart-Smith LJ said in delivering the judgment of the court:

> The object of a confiscation order is to divest the defaulter of money or other realisable assets. Consequently, it is not a matter of choice for the defaulter to 'buy' his way out of such an order by serving the term of imprisonment imposed in default of responding to the order for confiscation: see *R v Clacton Justices ex pare Customs and Excise* (1987) 152 JP 129.

In any event, serving the default sentence imposed for non-payment of the order no longer expunges the debt: see s 38(5) of POCA.

11.55 If the defendant contends that an asset the prosecutor wishes to have incorporated in the enforcement receivership order does not constitute realisable property, this should be dealt with in his witness statement and documentary evidence exhibited to confirm the position. Ideally, evidence should also be obtained from the person the defendant alleges to be the true owner of the property. Indeed, wherever possible, independent evidence should be obtained to corroborate the defendant's testimony. It must be remembered that at the enforcement stage the defendant stands convicted and, particularly if he pleaded not guilty at trial, may face something of a credibility problem having been disbelieved by the jury. For the application of *Wednesbury* unreasonableness in magistrates' decisions and enforcement cases, see *Barnett v DPP* (2009) EWHC 2004.

Third parties

11.56 Section 51(8) of POCA precludes the court from empowering receivers to realise property in which a third party has an interest until such time as the person in question has been given a reasonable opportunity to make representations to the court. This is an important protection for third parties because they have no right to appear or be represented at the confiscation hearing when the court is determining the extent and value of the defendant's realisable property. Indeed, the only opportunity the law allows a third party to prevent property in which he claims an interest being realised in satisfaction of a confiscation order is in the receivership proceedings. This was confirmed by the House of Lords in *Re Norris* [2001] 1 WLR 1388, a case under the Drug Trafficking Offences Act 1986. Mr Norris had been convicted of drug trafficking offences and a confiscation hearing was held under the 1986 Act. There was a dispute as to whether the matrimonial home (registered in the name of Mrs Norris) belonged beneficially to her or to her husband. Mrs Norris was called as a witness at the confiscation hearing by her husband and gave evidence on his behalf to the effect that she was the beneficial owner of the property. Her evidence was rejected by the trial judge and the value of the property was included in the confiscation order. Thereafter, the prosecutor applied to the High Court for the appointment of an enforcement receiver to sell the property in satisfaction of the confiscation order. After the receiver was appointed, Mrs Norris made application to the High Court for the order to be varied to recognise her interest in the property. The prosecutor objected, contending that Mrs Norris had already litigated the issue before the Crown Court at the confiscation hearing and it was an abuse of process for her to attempt to re-litigate it before the High Court. The High Court upheld the prosecutor's objection and the application was dismissed, as was an appeal to the Court of Appeal. The House of Lords unanimously allowed a further appeal by Mrs Norris. In considering the different purposes of the confiscation and receivership proceedings, Lord Hope of Craighead said:

> The scheme of the Act, so far as third party interests are concerned, is for their claims to be resolved in the High Court. The question for the High Court, when proceedings reach this stage, relates not to the amount of money which the defendant must pay—that has already been fixed by the order made in the Crown Court—but to the powers which the receiver is to be authorised to exercise. It is at this stage that third parties are entitled to have their claims heard and determined. This is when, as a matter of both substance and procedure, representations may be made as to their interests, if any, in the property which the receiver wishes to realise.

> Provisions designed to protect the interests of third parties are conspicuously absent from the rules of procedure that apply at the stage of the hearing in the Crown Court. Third parties are not entitled to participate in the criminal proceedings in that court. But the issue for the Crown Court is not whether any property in which a third party might have an interest is to be confiscated. The order which it makes is an order which is directed against the defendant only, and it is simply an order for the payment of a sum of money. The question of realisation, if the exercise of powers by a receiver is needed in order to make good the order which the defendant is required to satisfy, is reserved for the High Court.

> I do not therefore, with respect, agree with the observation by Tuckey LJ, that the situation which has arisen in this case is exactly that which the doctrine of abuse of process is designed to prevent. The scheme of the Act itself shows that this proposition must be unsound. It cannot be an abuse of process for a third party holding an interest in property, to which a right is given by section 11(8) of the Act to make representations to the High Court, to seek to exercise that right just because he or she gave evidence in the Crown Court in support of the defendant's case that the property was not to be valued and taken into account as realisable property.

Although POCA has transferred the power to make enforcement receivership orders from **11.57** the High Court to the Crown Court, the principle clearly remains the same. As Lord Hobhouse of Woodborough observed in *Re Norris*, the interests of the defendant of a third party are not necessarily identical. He said:

> It was wrong to say that her interests were identical with those of her husband. Indeed their proprietary interests were in principle opposed to each other. There were competing rights of property giving rights to one spouse against the other. It was in the interests of the defendant to put forward to the Crown Court the interest of his wife because he could use it to get a reduction in the confiscation order which was going to be made against him. But the wife's interests were not and are not the same as those of her husband. She wishes to preserve for

herself and her children the right to live at [the matrimonial home] against her husband if necessary and against anyone claiming through him. The defendant also has an interest in mitigating the sentence of imprisonment he was going to receive. The proceedings in the Crown Court were for the benefit of the defendant and the Customs and Excise and not Mrs Norris.

11.58 The legislative steer in s 69 of POCA provides further protection for third parties and the recipients of tainted gifts. Section 69(3) lays down a number of rules with which the court and enforcement receiver must comply in exercising powers under the Act. Section 69(3) provides:

Subsection (2) has effect subject to the following rules—
(a) the powers must be exercised with a view to allowing a person other than the defendant or recipient of a tainted gift to retain or recover the value of any interest held by him;
(b) in the case of realisable property held by a recipient of a tainted gift, the powers must be exercised with a view to realising no more than the value for the time being of the gift;
(c) in a case where a confiscation order has not been made against the defendant, property must not be sold if the court so orders under subsection (4).

11.59 Section 69(3)(c) clearly does not apply to enforcement receivers as, at the stage they are appointed, a confiscation order will have been made. The protection third parties are given by s 69 is not absolute. It does not prevent the court from empowering receivers to sell assets in which the defendant and a third party have a joint interest: they are concerned with protecting the value of the third party's interest in such property. If, for example, a defendant and a third party each have a half share in a property, although the court will be vigilant to protect the third party's interest, s 69(3) does not preclude the court from ordering a sale to ensure the defendant's share is realised in satisfaction of the confiscation order. The court will merely direct that an amount of money proportionate to the third party's interest should be paid to him from the proceeds of sale with the balance being paid into court in satisfaction of the confiscation order. An alternative way of proceeding is to give the third party the option of buying out the defendant's interest in the property. In this event, the court will order the third party to pay to the receiver a sum of money equivalent to the value of the defendant's interest in the property and, on payment being made, direct that the defendant's interest in the property be transferred to the third party.

Advising third parties served with an application to appoint an enforcement receiver

11.60 As soon as a solicitor is instructed by a third party affected by an application to appoint an enforcement receiver, he should notify the court, the prosecuting authority, and any solicitor acting on behalf of the defendant of his interest in the matter. If the client is unable to fund the case privately and meets the eligibility criteria, an emergency application for public funding should be made. As third parties, like defendants, are only entitled to seven days' notice of the hearing of an application to appoint an enforcement receiver, the solicitor may find it necessary to seek an adjournment. Although the court will view such a request sympathetically, given that the public interest dictates that the confiscation order should be satisfied promptly, it may well not be prepared to adjourn the entire receivership application. The court will frequently order that the enforcement receiver be appointed with powers to realise assets that are free from third party claims, but impose a stay on the receiver's powers of realisation over those assets which are subject to third party claims pending their determination. At the same time, the court may exercise its case management functions to impose directions as to how the third party claim should proceed, imposing requirements, for example, as to the timescale within which the third party's evidence must be served, along with any response by the prosecutor and the defendant.

11.61 Once any necessary adjournment has been obtained and funding secured, the third party's witness statement in support of his claim should be prepared. Where documentary evidence exists to support the claim, it should be exhibited to the witness statement. If there are other persons who are in a position to confirm the veracity of the third party's claim, witness statements should also be taken from them. Such independent evidence is particularly important in cases where no documentary evidence exists to support the third party claim.

11.62 Once the third party's evidence has been served, it may be prudent to enter into without prejudice negotiations with the prosecutor and the defendant. In many cases, the fact of the third party having an interest in the asset in question will be beyond dispute. The real issue is more commonly the extent of that interest. As all the parties will be anxious to resolve the matter expeditiously with the minimum of costs, and the court will encourage the parties to reach agreement wherever possible, it may well be that all concerned would be willing to take a commercial view and not press for the highest amount for which they could contend.

11.63 Although the prosecutor acts in the public interest in taking proceedings to enforce a confiscation order, this does not mean that he should not negotiate with the defendant and interested third parties to reach a mutually acceptable compromise where this is justified by the evidence. In *Grimes v CPS* [2003] EWCA Civ 1814 the Court of Appeal accepted that the prosecutor had public duties to perform in relation to the confiscation order but, in the words of Brooke LJ:

> That does not in my judgment mean that the CPS were entitled to behave, as litigants far too often behaved before the CPR came in, by simply standing back and saying 'We will make no offer at all for the court to consider when it decides what order as to costs is a reasonable one to make. We will simply see you in court.'
>
> The CPS has a duty under CPR 1.3 to help the court to further the overriding objective, and it would be the reverse of justice if the court were to be perceived to be upholding a policy which led the CPS to think that it did not have to make any offer at all and could come to court for an expensive contested hearing, simply leaving the successful party to lose much of its success by an order for costs which it could not recover.

He added:

> To some extent both parties were at fault for not doing all they could to resolve this dispute without the uneconomic costs of a hearing before a High Court judge, and it may well be that mediation is a more appropriate way of resolving many of these disputes now that experience of mediation, and of successful mediation, has grown so much.

11.64 All parties to receivership proceedings should, it is submitted, bear these remarks very much in mind and should be willing to make what Brooke LJ described as a 'well pitched offer' to compromise the proceedings. A party to the proceedings who refuses to accept such an offer is at risk of having costs awarded against him.

The matrimonial home: rights of spouses

11.65 It should be noted that different rules apply in relation to the matrimonial home and, in certain circumstances, the spouse of a defendant may be allowed to remain in the property notwithstanding that he or she has less than a 100 per cent interest in it, or indeed no proprietary interest at all. This subject is given detailed consideration in Chapter 16.

The court's order

11.66 If the parties cannot reach agreement, the application for the appointment of an enforcement receiver will proceed to a full contested hearing before a Crown Court judge. In most cases, where there is a substantial confiscation order that remains unsatisfied where the defendant has made little effort to satisfy the order voluntarily, or it is impracticable to allow him to do so, the court will exercise its discretion in favour of appointing a receiver. The terms of the appointment will depend on the findings the court makes in determining any third party claims. If a third party is successful in resisting the prosecutor's claim that the defendant has an interest in the asset, it will of course form no part of the receivership order. If, however, the court finds that the asset is owned by the defendant it will be included in the order. If the court determines the asset is owned by the defendant and a third party, it may proceed in one of two ways:

(1) the court may order the defendant and third party to give possession of the asset to the receiver to realise and that the receiver should pay to the third party a sum of money from the proceeds of sale proportionate to his interest in it; or

(2) the court may order the third party to pay to the receiver a sum of money equivalent to the defendant's interest in the property. On payment of this sum, the court will direct that the defendant's interest in the property should be extinguished and transferred to the third party. The court will need to be satisfied that the third party has sufficient funds before making an order in these terms, but will usually be prepared to give the third party a reasonable time in which to raise any necessary finance (see s 51(6) of POCA).

Status of the enforcement receiver on appointment

11.67 As with a management receiver, on appointment an enforcement receiver becomes an officer of the court accountable to the court for his actions. Although appointed on the application of the prosecutor, an enforcement receiver is entirely independent of the prosecutor who has no power to require him to exercise his powers in a particular way. This is not to say that the prosecutor and receiver should not work closely together during the course of the receivership. Indeed, in practice, the prosecuting authority's financial investigation officers will work very closely with the receiver and his staff as they are in the best possible position to advise as to the realisable property owned by the defendant and its current location. Similarly where, during the course of a receivership, the defendant or a third party makes an application to the court, the prosecutor frequently liaises closely with the receiver because he may well have access to information and documentation relevant to the court's consideration of the claim. Where no conflict of interest arises, the prosecutor and receiver frequently instruct the same counsel with a view to saving costs. It is submitted that these practices are perfectly proper provided the receiver does nothing to compromise his independence as an officer of the court.

The prosecutor is also responsible for monitoring the receiver's fees and, prior to applying to the **11.68** enforcing magistrates' court to draw his remuneration and expenses, must seek the prosecutor's approval. The defendant should also be given the opportunity to make representations if he has any interest in the amount being claimed. In many cases he will have no such interest since the full amount realised by the receiver will be paid in gross and credited towards the confiscation order. Most letters of agreement will also require the receiver to seek approval from the prosecutor to the appointment of agents such as solicitors, property managers, and valuers.

H. Enforcement Receivers under the CJA 1988 and DTA

Introduction

Although POCA has now been in force for over six years, there remain many confiscation **11.69** orders falling to be made or enforced under the old legislation. There are many reasons for this. Firstly, POCA does not apply to offences committed before 24 March 2003 and many complex cases, in particular fraud prosecutions, relate to offences committed before that date. Secondly, a considerable backlog of appeals in relation to DTA and CJA confiscation orders developed pending the decision of the House of Lords in *R v May and Others* [2008] AC 1028. These orders cannot be enforced until such time as the appeals have been determined. In consequence, prosecutors are likely to be applying to the High Court for the appointment of enforcement receivers throughout the lifetime of this work, and the provisions of the DTA and CJA 1988 cannot therefore be completely ignored. A summary of the relevant provisions is set out below. For a more detailed account of the old legislation, the reader is referred to the second edition of this work.

The jurisdiction of the High Court to appoint enforcement receivers under the DTA and CJA 1988

Section 29 of the DTA and s 80 of the CJA 1988 empower the High Court and, in the case **11.70** of the DTA, a county court, to appoint receivers for the purpose of enforcing confiscation orders made under the old legislation. As the two sections are worded somewhat differently, it is necessary to consider each section individually. By s 29 of the DTA:

(1) Where a confiscation order—
    (a) has been made under this Act,
    (b) it is not satisfied, and
    (c) is not subject to appeal,
    the High Court or a county court may, on an application by the prosecutor, exercise the powers conferred by subsections (2) to (6) below.
(2) The court may appoint a receiver in respect of realisable property.
(3) The court may empower a receiver appointed under subsection (2) above, under section 26 of this Act or in pursuance of a charging order—
    (a) to enforce any charge imposed under section 27 of this Act on realisable property or on interest or dividends payable in respect of such property; and

    (b) in relation to any realisable property other than property for the time being subject to a charge under section 27 of this Act to take possession of the property subject to such conditions or exceptions as may be specified by the court.

(4) The court may order any person having possession of realisable property to give possession of it to any such receiver.

(5) The court may empower any such receiver to realise any realisable property in such manner as the court may direct.

(6) The court may—

    (a) order any person holding an interest in realisable property to make to the receiver such payment as it may direct in respect of any beneficial interest held by the defendant or, as the case may be, the recipient of a gift caught by this Act; and

    (b) on the payment being made, by order transfer, grant or extinguish any interest in the property.

(7) Subsections (4) to (6) above do not apply to property for the time being subject to a charge under section 27 of this Act or section 9 of the Drug Trafficking Offences Act 1986.

(8) The court shall not in respect of any property exercise the powers conferred by subsection (3)(a), (5) or (6) above unless a reasonable opportunity has been given for persons holding any interest in the property to make representations to the court.

11.71   By s 80 of the CJA 1988 (as amended by s 8(6) of the Proceeds of Crime Act 1995):

(1) Where—

    (a) a confiscation order is made in proceedings instituted for an offence to which this Part of this Act applies or an order is made or varied on an application under section 74A, 74B or 74C above;

    (b) the proceedings in question have not, or the application in question has not been concluded; and

    (c) the order of variation is not subject to appeal;

    the High Court may, on an application by the prosecutor, exercise the powers conferred by subsections (2) to (6) below.

(2) The court may appoint a receiver in respect of realisable property;

(3) The court may empower a receiver appointed under subsection (2) above, under section 77 above or in pursuance of a charging order—

    (a) to enforce any charge imposed under section 78 above on realisable property or on interest or dividends payable in respect of such property;

    (b) in relation to any realisable property other than property for the time being subject to a charge under section 78 above, to take possession of the property subject to such conditions or exceptions as may be specified by the court.

(4) The court may order any person having possession of realisable property to give possession of it to any such receiver.

(5) The court may empower any such receiver to realise any realisable property in such manner as the court may direct.

(6) The court may order any person holding an interest in realisable property to make such payment to the receiver in respect of any beneficial interest held by the defendant or, as the case may be, the recipient of a gift caught by this Part of this Act as the court may direct and the court may, on such payment being made, by order transfer, grant or extinguish any interest in the property.

(7) Subsections (4) to (6) above do not apply to property for the time being subject to a charge under section 78 above.

(8) The court shall not in respect of any property exercise the powers conferred by subsection (3)(a), (5) or (6) above unless a reasonable opportunity has been given for persons holding any interest in the property to make representations to the court.

11.72   Under both statutes and in common with POCA, the remedy is a discretionary one and the court is not bound to appoint a receiver even when the provisions of the Acts have been satisfied. Similarly, the Acts do not require that any time allowed for payment of the confiscation order must have expired before an application for the appointment of an enforcement receiver can be made. The discretion whether or not to make the order must be exercised in accordance with the legislative steer set out in s 31 of the DTA and s 82 of the CJA 1988.

Definitions of the principal terms used

The principal terms used in the CJA 1988 and DTA are defined in very similar terms to **11.73** POCA. These terms are defined in the following sections.

'A confiscation order is not satisfied' (DTA cases only)
The expression is defined in s 41(6) of the DTA.   **11.74**

'Proceedings have not been concluded' (CJA cases only)
The expression is defined in s 102(12) and (12A) of the CJA 1988.   **11.75**

'Subject to appeal'
The expression is defined in s 29(1) of the DTA and s 80(1) of the CJA 1988.   **11.76**

Powers of enforcement receivers under the DTA and CJA 1988

The powers that may be given to enforcement receivers are set out in s 29(3) and (5) of the **11.77** DTA and s 80(3) and (5) of the CJA 1988. They are:

(a) power to enforce any charge imposed on realisable property or on interest or dividends payable on such property;
(b) power to take possession of any realisable property except property subject to a charging order under s 27 of the DTA or s 78 of the CJA 1988, subject to such conditions and exceptions as the court may specify; and
(c) power to realise any realisable property in such manner as the court may direct.

It should be noted that where the receiver is given power to enforce a charging order on realis- **11.78** able property, he cannot be given power to take possession of the property. The reason for this is that his interest in the property is sufficiently protected by the charge and there is no need for him to take physical possession of the property pending the enforcement of the charge.

Ancillary orders

The court is empowered to make the following ancillary orders to enable the receiver to **11.79** discharge his duties effectively:

(a) that any person having possession of realisable property deliver it up to the receiver (see s 29(4) of the DTA and s 80(4) of the CJA 1988);
(b) that any person holding an interest in realisable property make such payment to the receiver in respect of any beneficial interest held by the defendant as the court may direct and, on payment being made, the court may transfer, grant, or extinguish any interest in the property (see s 29(6) of the DTA and s 80(6) of the CJA 1988).

Again these powers may not be exercised in respect of property subject to a charging order (see s 29(7) of the DTA and s 80(7) of the CJA 1988).

Third parties

11.80 Section 29(8) of the DTA and s 80(8) of the CJA 1988 preclude the court for empowering receivers to realise assets in which a third party has an interest until such time as the person has been afforded a reasonable opportunity to make representations to the court.

Procedure on applications

11.81 Applications for the appointment of enforcement receivers in DTA and CJA cases are made to the High Court and the procedures are set out in sc115 r 7. The application is made by issuing an application notice at the Administrative Court Office at the Royal Courts of Justice. Where there have been no previous High Court proceedings in the matter, the application is made by the issue of a claim form (see sc115 r 7(1)).

11.82 The application notice or claim form must be served, together with the evidence in support, at least seven days prior to the date of the hearing on:

(a) the defendant;

(b) any person holding an interest in any of the property to which the application relates; and

(c) if a management receiver has already been appointed, on that receiver (see sc115 r 7(2)).

11.83 The evidence in support may either be in an affidavit or a witness statement and matters which must be included are set out in sc115 r 7(3) which provides:

> The application shall be supported by a witness statement or affidavit which shall, to the best of the witness's ability, give full particulars of the realisable property to which it relates and specify the person or persons holding such property, and a copy of the confiscation order, of any certificate issued by the Crown Court under section 5(2) (of the DTA) and of any charging order made in the matter shall be exhibited to such witness statement or affidavit.

11.84 The prosecutor should also, it is submitted, exhibit any statements under s 11 of the DTA or s 73 of the CJA 1988 tendered at the Crown Court confiscation hearing, together with any disclosure statements made by the defendant or affected third parties in accordance with the requirements of the restraint order.

11.85 The witness statement should also exhibit all relevant correspondence passing between the prosecutor and the proposed receiver. This will include the letter of agreement in which the prosecutor sets out the terms of the proposed receivership and the receiver's reply agreeing to accept the proposed appointment and to abide by those terms. A precedent letter of agreement appears at Appendix 10. Save in cases where the proposed receiver has previously acted in this capacity under the legislation, he must provide a fidelity bond and affidavit of fitness. The affidavit, sworn by a reputable person known to the proposed receiver, confirms his fitness to act, and the fidelity bond is a form of insurance policy should the defendant's assets go astray whilst in the receiver's possession as a result of his default. Where these documents are required, they should also be exhibited to the prosecutor's witness statement.

Dealing with the proceeds of realisation

11.86 The sole purpose for which an enforcement receiver is appointed is to realise assets in satisfaction of the confiscation order. It follows that the receiver must pay to the enforcing magistrates' court all funds he realises whilst he is in office. Section 81 of the CJA 1988 and s 30 of the DTA make provision as to how the receiver should deal with the proceeds of realisation. Section 81(1) provides:

(1) Subject to subsection (2) below, the following sums in the hands of a receiver appointed under this Part of this Act or in pursuance of a charging order, that is—
   (a) the proceeds of the enforcement of any charge imposed under section 78 above;
   (b) the proceeds of the realisation, other by the enforcement or such a charge, of any property under section 77 or 80 above; and
   (c) any other sums, being property held by the defendant;
   shall first be applied in payment of such expenses incurred by a person acting as an insolvency practitioner as are payable under section 87(2) below and then shall, after such payments (if any) as the High Court may direct have been made out of those sums, be applied on the defendant's behalf towards the payment of the confiscation order.

Section 81(3) to (6) provides: **11.87**

(3) The receipt of any sum by a justices' chief executive on account of an amount payable under a confiscation order shall reduce the amount so payable, but the justices' chief executive shall apply the money received for the purposes specified in this section and in the order so specified.
(4) The justices' chief executive shall first pay any expenses incurred by a person acting as an insolvency practitioner and payable under section 87(2) below but not already paid under subsection (1) above.
(5) If the money was paid to the justices' chief executive by a receiver appointed under this Part of this Act or in pursuance of a charging order, the justices' chief executive shall next pay the receiver's remuneration and expenses.
(6) After making—
   (a) any payment required by subsection (4) above, and
   (b) in a case in which subsection (5) above applies, any payment required by that subsection,
   the justices chief executive shall reimburse any amount paid under subsection 88(2) below.

Section 30 of the DTA is drafted in similar terms and is therefore not reproduced here. In   **11.88**
Hansford v Southampton Magistrates' Court [2008] EWHC 67 (Admin) the Divisional Court had to determine whether a receiver appointed under the CJA 1988 was entitled to retain funds sufficient to pay his remuneration and expenses prior to making payment to the court under s 81. The court held that, in the absence of a specific direction to the contrary in the receivership order, the receiver had no such power and that the gross realisations must be paid into court. The defendant had been convicted of an offence of conspiracy to cheat the public revenue and a confiscation order for £276,153 was made. The receiver, initially appointed as a management receiver, realised £120,036.50 from the sale of the former matrimonial home, but retained £77,163.50 in respect of his remuneration and disbursements incurred during the course of the receivership. When accrued interest was taken into account, this left £266,263 outstanding under the order. The District Judge at Southampton Magistrates' Court thereafter activated the default sentence for non-payment of the balance. The defendant appealed to the Divisional Court by way of case stated contending, amongst other things, that the receiver was not entitled under s 81(1).

The Divisional Court held that s 81(1) gave the High Court power to direct that receiver   **11.89**
should be entitled to withhold his fees before making payment to the enforcing magistrates' court but, in the absence of such a direction from the court, the receiver must pay the gross amount realised to the designated officer of the court. The court found that, on a true

construction of the receivership order made in relation to the defendant, the High Court had made no such direction and the receiver was not entitled to retain funds to meet his fees before making payment to the court. After noting the general rule of common law that receivers are entitled to draw their costs, expenses, and remuneration from the estate under their control, Dyson LJ said:

> But where a confiscation order has been made, section 81(1) makes provision for the applications of proceeds of the realisation. The core provision is that the receiver must apply the proceeds towards the satisfaction of the confiscation order, ie to pay them to the justices' chief executive. Section 81(4) provides that the justices' chief executive shall first pay any sums payable to an insolvency practitioner under section 87(2) 'But not already paid under subsection (1) above'. Section 81(5) provides that the justices' chief executive shall next pay the receiver's remuneration and expenses. It is worth noting that the words 'not already paid under subsection (1) above' do not appear in subsection (5). Although not determinative of the retention of fees issue, this omission suggests that it may not have been contemplated by Parliament that subsection (1) would be used by the High Court to direct payments of the receiver's remuneration and expenses.

11.90   Further, the court held that the receiver is not entitled to retain the proceeds of realisation pending approval of his remuneration and expenses. Dyson LJ said:

> Once the proceeds are in his hands, he must forthwith apply them towards the satisfaction of the confiscation order after making such payments (if any) as the High Court has directed may be made. I do not consider that, upon its true construction, section 81(1) permits the receiver to defer applying the proceeds towards the confiscation for a reasonable time. The subsection does not expressly provide that the proceeds shall be applied towards the confiscation order within a reasonable time; nor can it be construed as having this effect by necessary implication.
>
> Such an interpretation would introduce uncertainty into the statutory scheme. There would be scope for argument as to what constitutes a reasonable time. That would obviously be undesirable.

11.91   The Court found that any delay by the receiver in paying over the proceeds of realisation could lead to injustice. Dyson LJ observed:

> More fundamentally, to allow a receiver to delay applying the proceeds towards the satisfaction of a confiscation order can work real hardship to a defendant where enforcement proceedings are instituted after property has been realised. That is because until the proceeds are so applied, they are not taken into account in calculating the custodial term that will have to be served in default of payment. I would not interpret the statutory scheme as permitting such a result unless compelled to do so by clear language.

11.92   The court held that s 75A of the CJA 1988, providing for interest to be paid if the confiscation order remains unsatisfied after the period allowed for payment has expired, was a further reason why the full proceeds of realisation should be applied towards the order as soon as they are received. Dyson LJ concluded:

> It seems to me that the meaning of section 81(1) is clear. The receiver is obliged to pay the proceeds of realisation to the justices' chief executive as soon as they are in his hands less any authorised payments. Unless he has authority to make those payments at the time the proceeds come into his hands, he may not deduct them from the proceeds. There is nothing surprising or unfair about that interpretation. The receiver is obliged to pay the proceeds to

the justices' chief executive, but he will receive his remuneration and disbursements pursuant to section 81(5).

Receivers must therefore be vigilant in paying the proceeds of realisation into court forth- **11.93** with upon receipt unless the court has made a specific order to the contrary. Further, it should be noted that the decision applies not only to enforcement receivers, but also to management receivers once a confiscation order has been made. If a defendant has suffi- cient assets to meet both the receivers' fees and the confiscation order, prosecutors should consider seeking a direction under s 81(1) that the receiver is entitled to withhold his fees before making payment to the justices' chief executive. As the Court of Appeal held in *Re Brian Roger Allen* [2003] EWCA Civ 1168, in appropriate circumstances the High Court is entitled to order that the receiver should have power to withdraw his remuneration and expenses from the proceeds of sale. Similarly, in *Re HN and others* [2005] EWHC 2982 (Admin) Munby J held at first instance that it was wrong in principle for the Crown to have to bear the costs of an enforcement receiver where sufficient assets are available.

If a receiver brings in more funds than are necessary to satisfy the confiscation order and his **11.94** remuneration and expenses, he must apply to the High Court for directions as to how the surplus should be distributed between interested parties: see s 30(3) of the DTA and s 81(2) of the CJA 1988.

The magistrates' court has no role to play in the assessment of the receiver's remuneration **11.95** and expenses. The receiver will be required to submit his accounts to the parties for approval at regular intervals and, if there are any challenges to the amounts claimed that cannot be resolved by negotiation, they will fall to be assessed by a costs judge in accordance with Pt 69 of the Civil Procedure Rules. As Pt 69 is in very similar terms to rr 60.6 and 60.7 of the Criminal Procedure Rules, it is not reproduced here.

I. The Powers of the Magistrates' Court

The appointment of an enforcement receiver, although a highly effective remedy to secure **11.96** payment of the amount due under a confiscation order, is also an expensive one. Its use should normally be confined to larger and more complex confiscation orders and those where there are houses or other substantial assets to be sold, overseas properties to be dealt with, third party claims to be determined, or other compelling reasons why the magistrates' court's powers are inadequate. In cases where there are no third party claims and the assets are easy to realise, such as money held in bank accounts or by the prosecutor, jewellery, or motor vehicles of relatively low value, recourse should always be had to the sanctions available to the magistrates' court responsible for enforcing the order.

Magistrates' courts are involved in the enforcement process because s 35 of POCA provides **11.97** that ss 139(1) to (4) and 140(1) to (3) of the Powers of Criminal Courts (Sentencing) Act 2000 (PCC(S)A) shall apply in relation to the enforcement of confiscation orders in the same way as they apply to the enforcement of fines. Section 9(1) of the DTA and s 75(1) of the CJA 1988 make similar provision in relation to confiscation orders made under the old legislation. In consequence, all the powers of the magistrates' court that are available for the enforcement of fines are also available for the purpose of enforcing confiscation orders.

Distress warrants

11.98 Section 76 of the Magistrates' Courts Act 1980 empowers the court to issue a distress warrant. Such a warrant empowers bailiffs to take possession of and sell property belonging to the defendant to satisfy the confiscation order. It is particularly useful in relation to motor vehicles, jewellery, and other goods belonging to the defendant providing, as it does, a quick and inexpensive means of realisation. Distress warrants may also assist in cases where the prosecutor is in possession of property taken from the defendant at the time of his arrest and which the defendant will not authorise the prosecutor to hand over to the court. In such circumstances, the issue of a distress warrant protects the prosecutor from any civil action for conversion if he hands the property over to the bailiff. A distress warrant may not be issued until time to pay has expired. It is arguable that once a distress warrant (or warrant of commitment) has been made, the magistrates are *functus officio*. See *R v Sheffield City Justices ex p Foster* (1999) The Times, 2 November, DC and *Hereford and Worcester Magistrates' Court ex p MacRae* ((1998) 163 JP 433).

Third party debt orders

11.99 By s 87 of the Magistrates' Courts Act 1980, the magistrates' court may enforce the order in the High Court or in a county court otherwise than by the issue of a writ of *fieri facias*, imprisonment, or attachment of earnings. This, in effect, restricts him to applying for a third party debt order (formerly known as a 'garnishee order') under Pt 72 of the Civil Procedure Rules. The application is in two stages: the county court will first make an interim order freezing the funds in question pending a hearing at which the third party must attend and provide information regarding any funds he holds belonging to the defendant. At the second stage, a hearing will take place at which the county court will decide whether to make a final third party debt order instructing the third party to pay the sum in question to the enforcing magistrates' court. Further enforcement measures include an application for deduction of benefit.

11.100 Such orders are likely to be sought less frequently now the enforcing magistrates' court has its own powers in relation to seized funds under s 67 of POCA which are considered below.

Seized money

11.101 Section 67 of POCA gives the enforcing magistrates' court power to direct banks and building societies holding money belonging to a defendant to pay it to the court in satisfaction of the confiscation order. The section also applies to money held by police and customs officers. Section 67(1) to (3) specifies the money to which the section applies and provides:

(1) This section applies to money which—
    (a) is held by a person, and
    (b) is held in an account maintained by him with a bank or building society.
(2) This section also applies to money which is held by a person and which—
    (a) has been seized by a constable under section 19 of the Police and Criminal Evidence Act 1984 (c60) (general power of seizure, etc.), and
    (b) is held in an account maintained by a police force with a bank or building society.
(3) This section also applies to money which is held by a person and which—
    (a) has been seized by a customs officer under section 19 of the 1984 Act as applied by an order made under section 114(2) of that Act, and

(b) it is held in an account maintained by the Commissioners of Customs and Excise with a bank or building society.

If the seized cash falls into any one of these categories, the justices may make an order **11.102** requiring the bank or building society to pay the money to the court, provided the conditions set out in s 67(4) of POCA (as amended by para 33 of Pt 1 of Sch 8 to the Serious Crime Act 2007) have been satisfied. These are:

(a) a restraint order has effect in relation to the money;
(b) a confiscation order is made against the person by whom the money is held;
(c) any period allowed under s 11 for payment of the amounts ordered to be paid under the confiscation order has ended.

It is important to note that the section only applies when a restraint order is in force and **11.103** any time allowed for payment by the Crown Court has ended. If no restraint order is in force, a third party debt order will have to be sought. If the bank or building society fails to comply with an order under s 67 it may be fined up to £5,000 (see s 67(6)). For the purposes of the section, a bank is a deposit-taking institution within the meaning of the Banking Act 1987 and 'building society' has the same meaning as in the Building Societies Act 1986 (see s 67(8)).

Rule 58.12(1) of the Criminal Procedure Rules sets out the information that an order **11.104** under s 67 must contain. It provides:

An order under section 67 of the Proceeds of Crime Act 2002 requiring a bank or building society to pay money to a magistrates' court officer ('a payment order') shall—
(a) be directed to the bank or building society in respect of which the payment order is made;
(b) name the person against whom the confiscation order has been made;
(c) state the amount which remains to be paid under the confiscation order;
(d) state the name and address of the branch at which the account in which the money ordered to be paid is held and the sort code of that branch, if the sort code is known;
(e) state the name in which the account in which the money ordered to be paid is held and the account number of that account, if the account number is known;
(f) state the amount which the bank or building society is required to pay to the court officer under the payment order;
(g) give the name and address of the court officer to whom payment is to be made; and
(h) require the bank or building society to make payment within a period of seven days beginning on the day on which the payment order is made, unless it appears to the court that a longer or shorter period would be appropriate in the particular circumstances.

By r 58.12(2) the order shall be served by leaving it at, or sending it by first class post to, **11.105** the principal office of the bank or building society in question. If the order is served by first class post, unless the contrary is proved, it is deemed to have been served on the second business day after posting: see r 58.12(3).

Activation of the default sentence

Introduction: the enforcement hearing

Section 76 of the Magistrates' Courts Act 1980 gives the court power to issue a warrant of **11.106** commitment to activate the default sentence imposed by the Crown Court in the event of non-payment. In order to give consideration to the activation of the default sentence, it will be necessary to convene an enforcement hearing at which the defendant will be required to attend. If the defendant fails to attend, a warrant may be issued for his arrest under s 83 of the Magistrates Courts Act 1980: the default sentence may not be activated in his absence. The power to issue a warrant for the defendant's arrest only applies in cases where the justices are considering activation of the default sentence and does not extend to cases where only civil remedies are being considered. In *R (on the application of Rustim Necip) v City of London Magistrates' Court* [2009] EWHC 755 (Admin) the defendant had already served his default sentence, but the magistrates' court convened a further enforcement hearing to consider whether any other means of enforcement might be appropriate. The defendant did not appear and a warrant was issued for his arrest. The Divisional Court quashed the warrant holding that the power to issue a warrant under s 83 was ancillary to the power under s 82 to activate the default sentence. As it was no longer open to the court to impose the default sentence, there was no power to issue a warrant under s 83. Richards LJ said:

> An arrest warrant can be issued under section 83 only for the purpose of enabling inquiry to be made under section 82 or for securing attendance at a hearing required under section 82(5). But the provisions of section 82 are all concerned with the issue of a warrant of commitment. They impose a raft of restrictions on the exercise of the power to issue such a warrant, so as to ensure in effect that a warrant of commitment is a remedy of last resort. They are not dealing with the situation where a period of imprisonment in default of payment has already been served and where there can therefore be no possible question of the issue of a warrant of commitment.

He added:

> Thus there is nothing in section 82, as it seems to me, to cover a case where there is no question of a warrant of commitment being issued and the court is concerned only with whether some other method of enforcement of the confiscation order should be adopted.
>
> As I read section 83, it is purely ancillary to section 82. It can be used to secure attendance for section 82 purposes but it cannot be used so as to secure attendance for some other purpose.

11.107   The decision in *Necip* has unfortunate consequences for enforcing magistrates' courts wishing to consider civil methods of enforcement when, for whatever reason, activation of the default sentence is no longer an available remedy. If defendants realise that the court has no means of compelling their attendance for such purposes they will simply refuse to attend court, with the consequence that the justices are effectively powerless to enforce the order.

11.108   The hearing does not take the form of a means enquiry as would take place in the case of a fine defaulter. In the words of the National Best Practice Guide:

> An enforcement hearing before the magistrates' court is held when the payment period has expired, all enforcement actions have been exhausted and there is still an amount outstanding on the confiscation order. It is not a means enquiry hearing, the means (realisable assets) having been established by the Crown Court in the confiscation hearing.

11.109   In *R v Hastings and Rother Justices ex p Anscombe* (1998) (Unreported, 5 February 1998) the Divisional Court refused to quash a warrant of commitment where no means enquiry had been conducted. Schiemann LJ said:

> The basic submission on behalf of the application is that the magistrates had no power to commit the applicant to prison without first holding a means enquiry. That submission was

based on section 82 of the 1980 Act. I would reject it for the simple reason that the inhibition in section 84(3) only bites if the magistrates' court is bound by section 82(3) to inquire into the offender's means. They are only so bound if they have not on a previous occasion fixed a term of imprisonment to be served in default of payment. In the present case a term of imprisonment in default of payment has been fixed on conviction by the Crown Court. The effect of the legislation is to treat this term as having been fixed by the magistrates.

The only duty of the justices is to enquire into the defendant's proposals for payment and **11.110** to determine whether any other method of enforcement might be effective. If the defendant advances no such proposals, or no other methods of enforcement appear to the court to be appropriate, it is entitled to issue the warrant of commitment.

It is important that the justices should resist the temptation to act as a court of appeal **11.111** against the making of the confiscation order. The court is only concerned with the enforcement of the order and, if the defendant is aggrieved by it, he has the right to appeal to the Court of Appeal. Similarly, if he claims that his assets are insufficient to meet the confiscation order, he may apply for a certificate of inadequacy. As Stuart-Smith LJ observed in the *Harrow Justices* case:

> The mere fact that a confiscation order has been made is evidence that, at the date of its imposition, there were realisable assets available to meet the requirements of the order. Even if at the date when the Justices have to consider the question of enforcement, the value of realisable assets are less than they were at the date of the confiscation order, it is open to the defendant to apply for a certificate of inadequacy . . . which will lead to a reduction in the amount of the original order.

The prosecutor has the right to attend and make representations

When the justices are determining whether or not to issue the warrant of commitment, **11.112** they are entitled to hear representations from the prosecuting authority as to the position in relation to the confiscation order. In *R v Hastings and Rother Justices ex p Anscombe* (1998) (above) Schiemann LJ observed:

> The applicant also seeks to quash the decision of the justices to hear the representative of the Customs and Excise who informed them as to the current situation as best it was known to him and who informed them amongst other things of the undisputed fact that, in breach of bail, the applicant had previously left the jurisdiction. I see nothing wrong either in the fact that the representative was heard or that he saw it appropriate to put this fact before the magistrates who were being asked to adjourn the proceedings. Had they adjourned Mr Anscombe would have been released from prison and might have chosen this opportunity to go abroad again.

Similar sentiments were expressed by the Divisional Court in *R v Harrow Justices ex p DPP* **11.113** [1991] 1 WLR 395. In that case Stuart-Smith LJ said:

> Given the *inter partes* nature of the procedure leading to the making of a confiscation order, it will be in the nature of things that the prosecution will in all probability have information available which would be relevant to the justices' consideration. More compellingly, the prosecution has a legitimate interest in being heard before the justices come to any decision.

It is submitted that the court and the prosecutor should as a matter of course liaise before **11.114** an enforcement hearing is listed. In the *Harrow Justices* case, the court reminded the justices that two Home Office circulars numbered 98/1986 and 10/1988 advised that such liaison should take place. The latter circular advises that in every case where either a confiscation order for a sum in excess of £10,000 is made, or it appears that a restraint order is in force, the justices should always liaise with the prosecutor before listing an enforcement hearing. Indeed, it is submitted that the court would always be well advised to contact the prosecutor who may be in a position to provide a wealth of information, including copies of statements of information relied on in the Crown Court, disclosure statements made in response to restraint orders, and receivers' reports.

11.115 In *Garrote v City of London Magistrates' Court* [2002] EWHC 2909 the Divisional Court quashed a committal warrant where the enforcing magistrates' court failed to adjourn the case to give the prosecutor the opportunity to attend and make representations. A confiscation order had been made against the defendant in the sum of £1,373,405.47 under the CJA 1988 in its unamended form and a receiver had been appointed to realise assets in satisfaction of the order. After realising assets located within the jurisdiction to the extent of £114,725.72, the receiver was discharged. The prosecutor and the receiver were satisfied that all the assets within the jurisdiction had, so far as possible, been realised, and there was no suggestion that the defendant had failed to cooperate or had misled the authorities. The prosecutor sought the realisation of overseas assets by means of letters of request to the countries in which they were located.

11.116 The enforcing magistrates' court nonetheless had the defendant produced from prison for an enforcement hearing. The prosecutor did not attend and was not represented. The defendant's counsel sought an adjournment to allow enquiries to be made as to whether the prosecutor was aware of the hearing and wished to attend to make representations and to establish the position in relation to letters of request forwarded to overseas countries in which assets were located. The court refused the application and issued the committal warrant to activate the default sentence. The defendant sought judicial review of the justices' decision. The High Court found that the justices had acted unreasonably in not adjourning to seek the prosecutor's representations and quashed the committal warrant. Gibbs J said:

> My conclusions about this regrettable chain of events already summarised, and about this application, are as follows. The justices apparently failed to consider all methods of enforcement short of issuing the committal warrant. Despite receiving the letter dated 18th January 2002 from the Crown Prosecution Service saying that assets were still being pursued, the magistrates failed to offer the prosecution the opportunity to be heard in relation to the legitimate public interest that their position should be known. There is no sign that the magistrates conducted, or even considered conducting, the balancing exercise which Silber J rightly referred to as being necessary in a situation such as this. Alternatively, if the justices did attempt to conduct such a balancing exercise, they did so without the benefit of any, or any adequate, information.
>
> In the result, it follows that the magistrates' decision was neither a rational one, nor was it conducted with regard to the appropriate legal considerations. The only way in which the magistrates could have dealt with the matter properly was to adjourn for the purposes of obtaining information about the progress of the prosecution regarding assets pursued both in this country and abroad, but in particular abroad.

11.117 It is therefore essential that the enforcing magistrates' court should consult the prosecutor before listing an enforcement hearing and give him the opportunity to attend and make representations. If the court neglects to do this and issues the committal warrant, the decision will be vulnerable to challenge by way of judicial review at the instance both of the prosecutor and the defendant.

The decision in *Garrote* was followed by the Divisional Court in *Barnett v Director of Public*   **11.118**
Prosecutions [2009] EWHC 2004 (Admin). In that case a POCA confiscation order had been made against the defendant for £86,605.74 to be paid within six months and with a default sentence of two years' imprisonment. The main assets available to satisfy the order were funds in a bank account and the defendant's equity in a property valued at £59,000. The property proved difficult to market and in November 2007 the court extended time to pay until April 2008. Enforcement proceedings were taken in the magistrates' court but adjourned on a number of occasions as it appeared that a sale of the property was imminent. One week before the adjourned hearing was to take place in January 2009 the sale fell through because the proposed purchaser failed to put his solicitor in funds. In the light of this, the defendant's solicitors wrote to the court and the prosecutor asking for a further adjournment. The prosecutor consented, but, in view of the imminence of the hearing, the court took the view that the case should remain in the list. The application for an adjournment was ultimately refused and the district judge concluded that the only way of enforcing the order was to commit the defendant for the default sentence which he duly did. The defendant appealed by way of case stated to the Divisional Court.

The court held that the district judge had been wrong to refuse the adjournment and   **11.119**
activate the default sentence as alternative methods of enforcement were available. Maddison J said:

> There is no statutory requirement that a court should be satisfied that no alternative means of enforcement are available for it to commit a defendant to prison in circumstances such as these. But there is clear case law authority to that effect in cases such as *R v Harrow Justices ex parte DPP* [1991] 1 WLR 935 and *R v City of London Justices ex parte Garrote* [2003] EWHC 2909.

> In my judgment the district judge was wrong in both his conclusions. He should have granted the application for a further adjournment. The fact that the application was made with the agreement of the Crown Prosecution Service, as the enforcement authority, was not determinative of the issue but it was certainly an important matter to be taken into account. Despite the disappointing and very recent collapse of the intended sale of the property for £130,000, there was no reason to believe at the time that the property could not be sold for some such amount. There was never a suggestion that the property was inherently unsaleable. It could have been sold at auction if all else failed or by the mortgagees following repossession or indeed still on the open market. There was no suggestion that the appellant would block or refuse to co-operate with any such sale. The district judge had previously adjourned the enforcement hearings because efforts were being made to sell the property. The memorandum of 19 January 2009 which was before the district judge spoke of the appellant's wish that the sale proceed without delay. Depending on the price achieved, it might well then be necessary to apply to the court for a variation of the confiscation order under Section 23 of the 2002 Act by reducing the amount specified in the order to be paid. But there remained the prospect that the sum still due under the confiscation order would, at least in part, be satisfied.

> It follows, in my view, that the district judge was demonstrably wrong to refuse the application to adjourn the proceedings and to conclude that no other method of enforcement

remained other than to commit the appellant to prison. In my view, his decisions can properly be described as *Wednesbury* unreasonable.

11.120 This case is clear authority for the proposition that, although it is not necessary to prove wilful refusal or culpable neglect to pay as a condition precedent to activating the default sentence, the court must be satisfied that no other alternative methods of enforcement are appropriate.

Legal representation of the defendant

11.121 The defendant is, of course, entitled to be legally represented at the enforcement hearing and, in appropriate circumstances, public funding is available for representation by a solicitor. The right to funding does not, however, extend to representation by counsel or an advocate at public expense. In *Taylor v City of Westminster Magistrates' Court* [2009] EWHC 1498 (Admin) the defendant was facing an enforcement hearing in relation to a confiscation order for £633,530.45 made in 1996 of which £258,530.47 remained outstanding. He sought public funding for representation by counsel. The basis of the application was that it would be necessary to argue complex delay points relating to the European Convention on Human Rights (ECHR) as to whether the default sentence should be served concurrently or consecutively with a sentence imposed for an unrelated offence and that it would be necessary to consider copious amounts of correspondence reflecting the conduct of the parties. The defendant's application was refused by the District Judge on the basis that the conditions set out in Regulation 12(1) of the Criminal Defence Service (General) (No 2) Regulations 2001 (SI 1473/2001) had not been met. Regulation 12 provides:

> (1) A representation order for the purpose of proceedings before a magistrates' court may only include representation by an advocate in the case of:
>   (a) any indictable offence, including an offence which is triable either way; or
>   (b) extradition hearings under the Extradition Act 2003
>   where the court is of the opinion that because of circumstances which make the proceedings unusually grave or difficult, representation by both a litigator and an advocate would be desirable.

11.122 The District Judge found that the enforcement hearing did not amount to 'proceedings before a magistrates' court in the case of an indictable offence' but was merely incidental to such proceedings. As to the second limb regarding the proceedings being unusually grave or difficult, the District Judge found that the defendant's case was 'far too vague and rather woolly', the delay point under the ECHR not being particularly complex. The defendant applied for judicial review of the District Judge's decision, but his application was dismissed by the High Court. The court found that the District Judge had been correct to hold that the enforcement hearing did not amount to proceedings before a magistrates' court in the case of an indictable offence within the meaning of Regulation 12(1). Cranston J (with whom Pill LJ agreed) said:

> In my view, regulation 12 does not extend to confiscation enforcement proceedings in the magistrates' court, however serious the underlying events. The District Judge was correct to conclude that he had no jurisdiction to make a representation order in this case. The basic principle of interpretation is that a regulation such as this must be construed in context. That means that consideration must be given to this regulation in the context of the 2001 regulations themselves but also against the background legislative scheme, its scope and purpose.

Confiscation enforcement proceedings are criminal proceedings for the purposes of the 1999 Act and the 2001 Regulations and fall within the scope of section 12(2)(b) of the 1999 Act. However, the confiscation legislation makes clear that enforcement of a confiscation order is deemed to be equivalent to the enforcement of a fine through the magistrates' court. That is far from being proceedings in the case of an indictable offence.

He added:

Regulation 12 has no application as a matter of statutory interpretation because such proceedings are not 'in the case of . . . an indictable offence'. Rather they are, in their statutory context, quite separate proceedings: the enforcement of a confiscation order is to be treated as the enforcement of a fine. In my view, the meaning of regulation 12 within its statutory context is that a representation order in the magistrates' court may only be extended to cover the instruction of a court advocate where the case before the court involves proceedings in the case of an indictable offence in the strict sense or extradition proceedings.

Applications to adjourn the enforcement hearing

The court has a discretion to adjourn the enforcement hearing if it considers it appropriate **11.123** to do so. It not infrequently happens that the listing of an enforcement hearing focuses the defendant's attention on applying for a certificate of inadequacy. The mere fact that the defendant asserts he is taking such steps does not necessarily mean that the justices must adjourn the enforcement hearing pending the outcome of the application for a certificate of inadequacy. The justices must, of course, exercise their discretion judicially but, if there has been a long delay by the defendant in lodging his application for a certificate of inadequacy, the court would be entitled to refuse an application for an adjournment. If, on the other hand, the defendant has acted with all due expedition and a hearing is pending, the better course may be to adjourn the enforcement proceedings to await the outcome of the application. In *R v Liverpool Magistrates' Court ex p Ansen* [1998] 1 All ER 692 there had been a delay of two years between the confiscation order being made and the justices issuing the warrant of commitment during which time no application had been made by the defendant for a certificate of inadequacy. He brought judicial review proceedings against the justices for, *inter alia*, refusing his application for the hearing to be adjourned to allow an application for a certificate of inadequacy to be made. In rejecting this argument, May J said:

The next matter relied upon is that the magistrate did not adjourn the matter before him so that the applicant could be given time to make an application to the High Court for a certificate of inadequacy. The evidence of the magistrate here is that he did not do so because he reckoned that the applicant had had quite adequate time to do this and that an adjournment for that purpose should be refused. In my judgment, that was a perfectly proper decision for the magistrate to make.

The court took a similar view in *R v Hastings and Rother Justices* (1998) (above) where it **11.124** found that an application for a certificate of inadequacy would have had no prospect of success. Schiemann LJ said:

The justices could have adjourned the proceedings in front of them in order to see whether or not the High Court would issue a certificate of inadequacy and, if so, whether an application would be made by the defendant to the Crown Court to reduce the amount of the order and of the period to be served in default. An application for an adjournment was made to them. The only grounds put forward appear to have been the promised application to the

High Court for the certificate of inadequacy which in turns seems to have been based on the contention that the sums which the Crown Court had held had been salted away had never been salted away. That assertion was not open to the appellant as I have indicated earlier in this judgment. I see no error of law in the failure by the justices to exercise in Mr Anscombe's favour their discretion to adjourn.

11.125 The refusal of an enforcing magistrates' court to adjourn an enforcement hearing was again challenged in *McLeod v City of Westminster Magistrates' Court* [2009] EWHC 897 (Admin). A CJA confiscation order for £170,962 was made against the defendant on 18 October 2007 to be paid in full by 18 July 2008. On 30 January 2008 the Revenue and Customs Prosecutions Office wrote to the defendant advising that they were the enforcing authority and inviting his proposals for payment. The letter contained a warning that, in the absence of satisfactory proposals, the appointment of an enforcement receiver would be considered. No response was received to this letter, but on 8 July 2008 the defendant's solicitors asked the prosecutor to agree a three-month extension of time in which to pay. The prosecutor responded advising that there was no power under the CJA to extend time to pay. An enforcement hearing was then listed before the magistrates' court on 23 September 2008 on which occasion the defendant appeared unrepresented. The hearing was adjourned until 4 November 2008 to allow the defendant the opportunity to secure legal representation and on this date he appeared represented by Counsel. Counsel sought a further adjournment to enable both parties to consider the possibility of a receiver being appointed and to allow the defendant to realise his share of the matrimonial home which was held in his wife's name. Counsel explained that the defendant was going through divorce proceedings and the property had been on the market since the confiscation order was made. The prosecutor pointed out that the defendant had provided no evidence he was going through a divorce or that the property was on the market. The defendant had only raised the possibility of a receiver being appointed on the day of the hearing. In the light of these submissions, the District Judge refused the application for an adjournment and activated the default sentence. The District Judge found that the defendant had been given every opportunity to produce evidence and said he was not prepared to act on his unsupported assertions. He found that the adjournment application amounted to a 'delaying tactic' by the defendant.

11.126 The defendant sought judicial review of the District Judge's decision. Whilst the application was pending the Revenue and Customs Prosecution Office (RCPO) wrote to the defendant's solicitors asking for confirmation of the position in relation to the divorce proceedings as it was necessary to consider whether to intervene in any related ancillary relief application. Again, no response was forthcoming. The Divisional Court dismissed the application and was critical of the defendant's contention that the District Judge had failed to exercise his discretion judicially. May LJ said:

> To my mind this is an unfortunate submission, taken alone, when the District Judge plainly addressed all the submissions that were made to him and made a reasoned judicial decision on them.

He added:

> In my judgment the case that the District Judge failed to properly exercise his judicial discretion, and/or that he came to a wrong decision on 4 November, is simply not made out.

The date for payment of the amount ordered by agreement in the confiscation proceedings was well past, and the applicant had had more than a year to arrange to sell the house to raise the amount required. In practice, he had had an additional period after the expiry of the nine month period that he had been given at the confiscation proceedings as time to pay.

The Divisional Court was also critical of the defendant's failure to produce evidence and **11.127** respond to correspondence from the prosecutor. May LJ said:

> There was no evidence before the court and in my judgment it was well within the District Judge's judicial discretionary competence to decline to accept assertions by counsel, unsupported by evidence from one who had been convicted of conspiracy to cheat. The applicant had been warned on 23 September 2008 when the matter was first adjourned that he risked a committal order, and he had had six weeks or so in which to produce evidence. He had had legal aid since the beginning of October 2008.

Referring to the prosecutor's correspondence, he added:

> The submission in that respect is simply not helped by the fact that we are told that no response was received to that letter nor to the one that had been written to the applicant's wife. In those circumstances, this court is in no better position from the point of view of evidence than was the District Judge.

In *Barnett v Director of Public Prosecutions* [2009] EWHC 2004 (Admin) the Divisional **11.128** Court reached a different conclusion and held that the court should have adjourned an enforcement hearing in circumstances where an anticipated sale of a property had fallen through a week before the hearing was due to take place. This case is clearly distinguishable from *McLeod* because the defendant was in no way responsible for the sale falling through and he and his solicitors cooperated throughout with the court and prosecutor in attempting to realise the property in satisfaction of the confiscation order. It is submitted that a number of principles can be established from these cases. Firstly, the magistrates' court has a discretion whether or not to accede to applications for the adjournment of enforcement hearings. The discretion must be exercised judicially and, if it is found to have been exercised in a manner which is *Wednesbury* unreasonable, it will be vulnerable to challenge. A defendant who asks the court to exercise the discretion to adjourn in his favour must be able to show the court that he has cooperated with the enforcement authorities in responding to correspondence, realising assets voluntarily where possible, and by carrying out any stated intention of seeking a certificate of inadequacy promptly. Further, he must provide evidence to support his assertions: in the absence of evidence to corroborate a defendant's assertions, the court is entitled to reject his claims, particularly in cases where he has been convicted of offences of dishonesty.

Applications to extend the time allowed for payment

Neither the enforcing magistrates' court nor the Crown Court has the power to extend **11.129** the time allowed for payment in CJA and DTA cases. In POCA cases, the Crown Court alone has a power to extend the time to pay provided the total period allowed for payment does not exceed 12 months and that any application for an extension is made prior to the expiration of the initial period allowed for payment: see s 11 of POCA. In cases to which the old legislation applies, there is no statutory provision similar to s 11 of POCA allowing time to pay to be extended and it has been held that the court has no inherent jurisdiction to so order. In *Revenue and Customs Prosecutions Office v Kearney* [2007] EWHC 640 (Admin) a CJA confiscation order was made against the defendant for £143,000 and he was given 12 months in which to pay. After the expiration of the 12-month period, the defendant applied to the Crown Court for the time to pay to be extended. The prosecutor opposed the application, contending the court had no jurisdiction to extend time to pay, but the judge held that the Crown Court had an inherent jurisdiction to grant an extension and noted that s 11 of POCA gave the court such a power in cases to which that Act applied. He extended time to pay by a further four months. The prosecutor appealed to the Divisional Court by way of case stated.

11.130 The Divisional Court allowed the prosecutor's appeal, holding there was no inherent jurisdiction to extend time to pay CJA and DTA confiscation orders. Gross J (with whom Smith LJ agreed) said:

> The reality of the confiscation order is that it is to pay a given amount within a given period or face a sentence of imprisonment in default. The given period of time to pay is an integral part of the order. For my part, I am satisfied that the introduction of any power such as that purportedly exercised by the judge here into the pre-POCA regime would, as submitted by the prosecutor, give rise to some difficulty. But that is in a sense by the by. There is no such power which is capable of being inferred from the provisions of POCA, a different regime which in any event would not have assisted the respondent as he was out of time. The right answer was for the respondent to seek to persuade the Magistrates in the exercise of their discretion, not then to activate the default sentence so that any injustice, if such there was, could have been addressed. Here that course was not followed. The learned judge had, with respect, no jurisdiction to make the order which he did.

11.131 A similar approach was adopted by the Divisional Court in the later case of *Crown Prosecution Service v Greenacre* [2007] EWHC 1193 (Admin) in which it was held that the enforcing magistrates' court similarly had no power to extend time to pay. A confiscation order for £818,953.45 was made against the defendant under the CJA 1988 and he was given six months to pay. When the six-month period expired, the defendant applied to the Crown Court for an extension of the time to pay. The Crown Court judge correctly found that he had no power to grant the extension, but concluded that the magistrates' court did have such power. He therefore proceeded to sit as a District Judge in accordance with s 66 of the Courts Act 2003 and granted an extension of time. A number of further extensions were granted by the magistrates' court until, nearly a year later, the prosecutor wrote to the court contending that it had no power to grant an extension of time. The District Judge concluded that he did have such power under s 75(2) of the Magistrates' Courts Act 1980 and granted a further extension of time. The prosecutor appealed to the Divisional Court by way of case stated.

11.132 The Divisional Court allowed the prosecutor's appeal, holding that the enforcing magistrates' court too had no jurisdiction to extend the time to pay. Laws LJ (with whom Tomlinson J agreed, said:

> First, it is to be noted that the effect of section 75(5)(a) of the Criminal Justice Act 1988 is that the magistrates' court has no power to remit the whole or any part of a confiscation order. One then notes that section 75A(1)(b) of the same Act provides that the amount of interest required to be paid when a confiscation order is not paid on time 'shall, for the purposes of

enforcement, be treated as part of the amount to be recovered under the confiscation order'. If the magistrates' court can, under section 75(2) of the 1980 Act, allow further time to pay in the case of a Crown Court confiscation order, that would vary the date from which interest began to accrue and thereby, as it seems to me, would be tantamount to a partial remittal of the confiscation order; but that the magistrates' court cannot do. This is in my judgment a powerful consideration militating against any legislative intent that section 75(2) of the Magistrates' Courts Act might be deployed to allow the magistrates' court to extend time for payment of a Crown Court confiscation order.

In the light of these judgments, a defendant who needs further time to realise assets in sat- **11.133**
isfaction of a confiscation order would be better advised to seek an adjournment of the enforcement hearing rather than to seek an extension of time to pay. The court will want to be satisfied that an adjournment will serve a useful purpose and is not merely delaying the inevitable, and it will no doubt require clear and cogent evidence from the defendant that there is a very real likelihood of further assets being realised if the proceedings are so adjourned.

The court has no discretion to waive interest payments

The enforcing magistrates' court has no power to waive interest payments due on an **11.134**
unpaid confiscation order. In *Hansford v Southampton Magistrates' Court* [2008] EWHC 67 (Admin) the defendant sought to argue that the enforcing magistrates' court had a discretion, in appropriate circumstances, not to make a defaulter liable to pay the full amount of interest due from the date on which he becomes liable to pay until the date of the enforcement hearing. The defendant contended that the words 'shall be liable to pay interest' in s 75A(1)(a) of the CJA 1988 were ambiguous and could be given an 'absolute construction' meaning bound to pay or a 'discretion construction' meaning at risk of paying and, as the Act is a punitive statute, the ambiguity should be resolved in his favour. The court held that there was no such ambiguity and that the court had no discretion to waive any interest that had accrued on an unpaid confiscation order. Dyson LJ said:

> Section 75A(1) and (2) are provisions which prescribe the consequences of court orders. There is no role for the court here. They follow automatically if the necessary conditions are satisfied. One of the conditions is that a court has made a confiscation order. If a confiscation order has been made and the sum required to be paid under it has not been paid when it is required to be paid, the consequence follows that the defendant pays interest at the rate defined in subsection (3). The provision accords no role to the court here. The lack of role for the court is not only to be contrasted with those other provisions where a court function is specified; it is to be contrasted with subsection (2) where the court is given the power (but not the duty) to increase the default term of imprisonment or detention if the effect of sub-section (1) is to increase the maximum period applicable.

> The contrast between subsection (2) on the one hand and subsections (1) and (3) on the other is striking and fatal to counsel's argument. Where Parliament intends to give the court a discretion, it does so expressly and uses the word 'may' which is well understood to connote a discretion.

Issuing the warrant of commitment

The enforcing magistrates' court should only issue the warrant of commitment after **11.135**
considering all the other available enforcement options and concluding that they are

unlikely to be effective: see *R v Harrow Justices ex p DPP* [1991] 1 WLR 395 and *Garotte v City of London Magistrates' Court* [2002] EWHC 2909.

11.136 Where the committal warrant is issued by the justices, the sentence is to be served consecutively to the sentence imposed for the substantive offence: see s 38 of POCA, s 9(2) of the DTA, and s 75(3) of the CJA 1988. Section 38 of POCA provides as follows:

(1) Subsection (2) applies if—
  (a) a warrant committing the defendant to prison or detention is issued for a default in payment of an amount ordered to be paid under a confiscation order in respect of an offence or offences, and
  (b) at the time the warrant is issued the defendant is liable to serve a term of custody in respect of the offence (or any of the offences).
(2) In such a case the term of imprisonment or detention under section 108 of the Sentencing Act (detention of persons aged between 18 to 20 for default) to be served in default of payment of the amount does not begin to run until after the term mentioned in subsection (1)(b) above.
(3) The reference in subsection (1)(b) above to the term of custody the defendant is liable to serve in respect of the offence (or any of the offences) is a reference to the term of imprisonment or detention in a young offender institution, which he is liable to serve in respect of the offence (or any of the offences).
(4) For the purposes of subsection (3) consecutive terms and terms which are wholly or partly concurrent must be treated as a single terms and the following must be ignored—
  (a) any sentence suspended under section 118(1) of the Sentencing Act which has not taken effect at the time the warrant is issued;
  (b) in the case of a sentence of imprisonment passed with an order under section 47(1) of the Criminal Law Act 1977 (c45) (sentences of imprisonment partly served and partly suspended) any part of the sentence which the defendant has not at that time been required to serve in prison;
  (c) any term of imprisonment or detention fixed under section 139(2) of the Sentencing Act (term to be served in default of payment of fine etc) for which a warrant committing the defendant to prison or detention has not been issued at that time.
(5) If the defendant serves a term of imprisonment or detention in default of paying any amount due under a confiscation order, his serving that term does not prevent the confiscation order from continuing to have effect so far as any other method of enforcement is concerned.

11.137 In *R v City of London Justice ex p Chapman* (1998) 162 JP 359, a case under the Drug Trafficking Offences Act 1986, the defendant sought to argue that where he had been released on licence from the sentence of imprisonment imposed for the substantive offence, the default sentence could not start until the end of the licence period since he was still 'liable to serve' the remainder of his sentence. The Divisional Court rejected this argument, Gage J (with whom Pill LJ agreed) observing:

> It seems to me that the scheme of the Drug Trafficking Offences Act was to require that sentences in default be served consecutively immediately following the period in custody in respect of the offence or offences . . . In my judgment, 'liable to serve a term of custody in respect of the offence' is to be construed as currently liable to serve a term of imprisonment. It is not apt to include a prisoner who is released on licence.

11.138 The decision in *Chapman* was followed by the High Court in *R v City of London Justices ex p Peracha* (Unreported, 31 March 1998). In that case Rose LJ said:

> For my part, I see no reason to regard *Chapman* as having been wrongly decided. On the contrary, I agree with those passages in the judgments of Mr. Justice Gage and Lord Justice

Pill which I have cited in relation to the construction of section 6: that is to say, 'liable' in section 6 means 'presently liable'. The history of the legislation, in so far as it provides any assistance, to my mind suggests that the words 'liable to serve' which appear in section 6(3) should, if anything, be given a restricted meaning, because they are no longer immediate preceded by the word 'serving'.

In any event, for my part, I am satisfied that 'liable' means 'bound to serve' and not 'exposed to the risk of serving.' There is a separate regime for sentences for substantive offences and default terms imposed if confiscation orders are not complied with. This is demonstrated, to my mind, both by the definition of sentence of imprisonment in the 1967 Act, which is repeated in the 1991 Criminal Justice Act section 51, and by the separate regime which is provided in the 1991 Act for default terms as compared with sentences of imprisonment.

To my mind, it would be absurd to suppose that in the draconian provisions in relation to drug trafficking, Parliament intended that a person, subject to a default term should be able to avoid serving that term by taking advantage of a period of liberty stretching to months or, as in the present case, to years, in order to abscond either in this country or abroad. If this were the case, there would, as it seems to me, never be any practical purpose in a court making an order for committal in default, for it would not have the effect of encouraging regurgitation of drug profits.

Offenders committed to prison to serve the default sentence for non-payment of a confis- **11.139** cation order have the right to be released from custody unconditionally under s 258 of the Criminal Justice Act 2003 after serving half of the default term.

J. Delay in Taking Enforcement Action

Introduction

Delays in the enforcement of confiscation orders can occur for a variety of reasons: the **11.140** defendant may abscond or be obstructive or there may be administrative failings or a break-down in communication by the law enforcement agencies responsible for enforcing confis-cation orders. Lengthy appeal processes can also cause delay since prosecutors may not normally enforce confiscation orders whilst they remain subject to appeal. In *R v Chichester Magistrates' Court ex p Crowther* [1998] EWHC Admin 960 the High Court held that even a culpable delay by the prosecutor does not constitute a bar to the order being enforced. This changed, however, with the decision of the Divisional Court in *Lloyd v Bow Street Magistrates' Court* [2003] EWHC Admin 2294 where the decision of a magistrates' court to activate the default sentence was quashed by reason of a lengthy delay by the prosecutor in taking action to enforce a confiscation order. As a result of the decision in *Lloyd*, a substantial body of case law has built up dealing with the circumstances in which a delay will result in enforcement proceedings being stayed.

Activation of the default sentence

It is now well settled law that an unreasonable delay in taking enforcement proceedings will **11.141** act as a bar to the activation of the default sentence. Whether the delay is unreasonable is a matter of fact to be determined having regard to the circumstances of individual cases. In *Lloyd* a CJA confiscation order had been made against the defendant on 21 June 1996 for £33,236 with an 18-month sentence of imprisonment to be served in default of payment.

On 10 July 1997, when £26,897.37 was still outstanding, the Crown Prosecution Service (CPS) wrote to the defendant advising him of their intention to apply for the appointment of an enforcement receiver unless the amount owing was paid within 14 days. No further payments were made, but it was not until 30 November 1998 that the CPS issued an application for the appointment of a receiver. The receiver was duly appointed by an order of the court dated 15 January 1999. Thereafter, it appears there was a breakdown of communication between the CPS and the receiver, the latter claiming never to have received a copy of the order appointing him. The CPS did not write to the receiver to establish what progress had been made in realising the defendant's assets but, on 6 December 1999, wrote to the enforcing magistrates' court saying that no assets had been realised and inviting the court to issue the warrant of commitment. In January 2001 the court issued a summons requiring the defendant to attend for consideration to be given to the warrant being issued, but the hearing did not take place until 9 October 2002 when the defendant was committed to prison.

11.142 The High Court quashed the warrant of commitment, holding that the delay constituted a breach of the defendant's right under Art 6.1 of the ECHR to a fair trial within a reasonable time. At first sight this might seem surprising, because the primary obligation to satisfy a confiscation order is on the defendant and not on the prosecuting authority or enforcing magistrates' court. If there is a delay it is normally the result of the defendant failing to comply with the terms of the order. This contention was firmly rejected by Dyson LJ in Lloyd. He said:

> We do not see how the fact that the defendant is in breach of his continuing duty to satisfy the confiscation order can be relevant. In our view, the conduct of the defendant can have no bearing on the question whether he has a right to have proceedings against him in respect of that conduct instituted and determined within a reasonable time. It is common ground that a defendant is entitled to have a substantive criminal charge against him determined within a reasonable time. That right is predicated on the basis that the defendant is alleged to have broken the law by committing a crime. The fact that a defendant is alleged to have committed a crime is plainly not a reason for denying him the right to have the criminal charged determined within a reasonable time. Indeed, the existence of the criminal charge is the very reason why he has that right. Similarly, in our view, the fact that a defendant is alleged to be in breach of a confiscation order is no reason to deny him the right to have proceedings brought to enforce the order by commitment to prison determined within a reasonable time.

He added:

> Convicted criminals who are the subject of confiscation orders do not attract sympathy and are not entitled to favoured treatment. But there is nothing surprising about a requirement that, if the prosecuting authorities/magistrates' court seek to enforce a confiscation order, they should do so within a reasonable time. It is potentially very unfair on a defendant that he should be liable to be committed to prison for non-payment of sums due under a confiscation order many years after the time for payment has expired, and long after he has been released from custody and resumed work and family life.

11.143 In a clear warning to the enforcement authorities, Dyson LJ concluded:

> If the authorities whose task it is to enforce confiscation order are so slow in communicating with one another, or in activating enforcement mechanisms that they become in breach of Article 6.1, then the appropriate remedy my well be (as in this case) that the weapon of

imprisonment in default is lost. The sooner this is appreciated by all agencies of the criminal justice system, the better.

If, of course, the defendant himself is responsible for the delay or, due to the complexity of **11.144** his financial affairs, his assets take an unusually long time to realise, Art 6.1 will not assist him. As Dyson LJ said:

> It follows that, in deciding what is a reasonable time, regard should be had to the efforts made to extract the money by other methods, for example (as in the present case) by the appointment of a receiver. If a receiver has been appointed within a reasonable time and has proceeded with reasonable expedition, then the fact that all of this may have taken some time will not prevent the court from concluding that there has been no violation of the defendant's Article 6.1 rights if the unsuccessful attempts to recover the money have led to delay in the institution of proceedings to commit. Likewise, if the defendant has been evasive and has avoided diligent attempts to extract the money from him, he will be unable to rely on the resultant delay in support of an argument that his right to a determination within a reasonable time has been violated.

In *R (on the application of Deamer) v Southampton Magistrates' Court* [2006] EWHC Admin **11.145** 2221, the High Court reiterated that a stay on enforcement would only be granted where the delay by the enforcing authority was unreasonable and unjustified. In that case a confiscation order for £5,448,200 had been made against the defendant on 1 March 1999. The order was to be paid in fully by 29 January 2000 and a default sentence of six years' imprisonment was imposed. On 18 February 2000 an enforcement receiver was appointed, but he only succeeded in bringing in £5,456.06 before his discharge on 24 May 2001. On 23 January 2002, a further £350,182.85, representing funds taken up by HM Customs and Excise at the time of the defendant's arrest, was also paid into court in part satisfaction of the order.

Thereafter, between 2002 and 2006 extensive correspondence passed between the RCPO **11.146** and the defendant's solicitors concerning the payment of the balance due under the order. At various points the solicitors suggested they were intending to make an application for a certificate of inadequacy and were pursuing enquiries as to the availability of assets in the USA to satisfy the order. In the event, no application for a certificate of inadequacy was made and the order remained unsatisfied. On a number of occasions, RCPO warned the defendant's solicitors that in the absence of acceptable proposals for payment, the matter would be referred to the enforcing magistrates' court.

On 3 April 2006, one day before the claimant was eligible for release on parole, he appeared **11.147** before Southampton Magistrates' Court for an enforcement hearing. He contended that having regard to the delay in enforcing the order, the court should direct that the proceedings be stayed, relying on the ruling in *Lloyd*. The District Judge concluded that the mere passage of time was not enough to order a stay and there had to be some delay that is 'unjustifiable and unreasonable'. The District Judge concluded that the period while the receiver was in office should be disregarded because it was proper for the receiver to have been appointed and the time allowed for him to bring in the assets was reasonable. As to the period between May 2001 and February 2006, the District Judge reviewed the correspondence between RCPO and the defendant's solicitors and concluded that the prosecutor had not been indolent. She found that the prosecutor had regularly sought information from the defendant's solicitors and the correspondence made it plain that it was RCPO's continuing intention to enforce the order. Although RCPO may have been naïve in accepting some of the assurances given by the defendant's solicitors, the District Judge found that they had not allowed the case to become dormant and their decision to await further information from the defendant as to the availability of further assets was neither unreasonable nor unjustified. The District Judge refused a stay of proceedings and activated the six-year default sentence.

11.148 The defendant applied for judicial review of the District Judge's decision. The Court dismissed the application, Aikens J observing:

> In my view, the District Judge cannot be criticised for her conclusion that the period up to the end of the appointment of the receiver is unexceptional. As to the period when Mr Deamer's solicitors were apparently seeking evidence for the application of a certificate of inadequacy, it seems to me that they were trying to get information to back such an application. At the same time the RCPO were hoping that the information would provide material to show that Mr Deamer indeed had assets to pay the confiscation order. I agree with the District Judge's view that the RCPO might have been naïve in this regard. But I have reached the firm conclusion that it cannot be said that the District Judge's finding on the facts was in any way unreasonable. The solicitors for Mr Deamer did indicate that investigations were going on in the USA, even if they had produced no results.

> In my view it cannot be said that the District Judge's conclusion on the reasonableness of RCPO's activity and their stance in relation to these investigations is either irrational or perverse or unreasonable.

11.149 The decision in *Deamer* makes it clear that mere delay by itself will not be sufficient to justify a stay of the enforcement proceedings. The delay must be one for which the enforcement agency is responsible and which is unreasonable and unjustifiable on the facts. If the defendant causes or contributes to any such delay, it will not normally be appropriate to order a stay of proceedings. This is particularly so where, as in *Deamer*, the enforcement agency had throughout made its intention of enforcing the order abundantly clear.

11.150 In *Stone v Plymouth Magistrates' Court* [2007] EWHC 2519 (Admin) the Divisional Court quashed a committal warrant that had been issued some 13 years after a confiscation order had been made in relation to drug trafficking offences. The court said it 'had no doubt' that the delay had been such as to breach the defendant's Art 6.1 rights.

11.151 In all the cases examined thus far, the allegation was that the prosecutor was responsible for the delays that occurred. In *Minshall v Marylebone Magistrates' Court* [2008] EWHC 2800 (Admin) the High Court had to consider the position when all parties accepted that the prosecutor was not at fault, but that the delay had occurred during the appeal process as the defendant exercised his right of appeal against conviction and confiscation. The essential timetable was that the defendant had been arrested on 1 October 1997 on suspicion of excise duty offences. On 3 February 2000 he was convicted having changed his plea to guilty and on 13 October 2000 a confiscation order was made for £80,000 and the defendant was ordered to pay in full by 13 April 2001. A sentence of 18 months' imprisonment was imposed in default of payment. The defendant decided to appeal against the confiscation order and on 20 March 2001 the enforcing magistrates' court agreed to suspend enforcement action pending the determination of the appeal. Leave to appeal was duly granted on 19 July 2001. Thereafter, there was a lengthy delay in the appeal process because the point of law on which the defendant was given leave to appeal was awaiting determination by the House of Lords in the case of *R v Soneji and another* [2005] UKHL 49. The defendant's appeal clearly could not be heard until the House of Lords delivered its ruling in the case of *Soneji*. The House delivered its ruling on 21 July 2005 in terms which were unfavourable to the defendant's case in consequence of which his counsel withdrew. The defendant changed his solicitors and counsel who, on 7 February 2006 settled amended grounds of appeal against the confiscation order and an application for leave to amend the grounds of appeal out of time. This was dismissed by the Court of Appeal on 14 February 2006. Two days later the defendant lodged an application to the European Court of Human Rights claiming a breach of Art 6.1. On 20 February 2006 the prosecutor wrote to the defendant asking for his proposals for the satisfaction of the confiscation order. No satisfactory proposals were advanced and by 2 May 2006 the amount outstanding under the order had increased to £112,052.60 after the addition of accrued interest. On that day, the enforcing magistrates' court fixed an enforcement hearing for 2 June 2006 which was later adjourned to 23 August 2006. The defendant claimed that the delay breached his Art 6.1 rights and applied to the District Judge for the hearing to be stayed, but this was refused and she ordered the hearing to continue. The defendant sought judicial review of the District Judge's decision. The High Court ruled that as the State is responsible for the appeal mechanism, a delay in the appeal process could amount to an unreasonable delay within the meaning of Art 6.1, but held that on the facts of the defendant's case the delay was reasonable. Pitchford J said:

> While the prosecutor may not be permitted to take enforcement proceedings when the underlying conviction or sentence is the subject of appeal it remains the duty of the State to ensure that the proceedings as a whole are completed within a reasonable time. Nevertheless, the institution of appeal proceedings is, in my view, a significant and weighty factor to be considered in a judgment of reasonableness of the length of the enforcement proceedings as a whole.

> Here, the period between imposition of the confiscation order (October 2000) and the conclusion of the claimant's appeal against conviction (June 2004) was 3 years 8 months. The responsibility for that lapse of time was neither the prosecutor's nor the State's. It was a consequence of the claimant's wish to pursue every avenue available to him on appeal notwithstanding his plea of guilty at trial. That is something he was perfectly entitled to do but in view of the complexity of the appeal it was bound to take a significant period of time to resolve. The period following the judgments in *Knights* and *Soneji* (July 2005) to the dismissal of the claimant's appeal against the confiscation order (February 2006) was 7 months. That period was reasonable given the claimant's decision to make substantial amendments to his grounds of appeal having instructed his present solicitors.

Pitchford J also had regard to the conduct of the parties and noted that the prosecutor had **11.152** never given the defendant the impression he was not going to enforce the order and had never been guilty of inaction. The defendant had dissipated assets in breach of a restraint order and had been found guilty of contempt of court. The judge dealing with the contempt application had described the defendant's actions as 'serious breaches in respect of which false evidence had been given to me, as I find it, simply compounds the contempt'. Pitchford J concluded:

> While the period between imposition of the confiscation order and the enforcement proceedings was unusually long, I have concluded, as did the District Judge that it was not

unreasonable within the meaning of Article 6. I accept that there may be some cases in which delay caused by the appeals process, for which the State is responsible, may without more be unreasonable in itself; if so, a breach of article 6 is at risk. Having regard to the particular exigencies of the appeal process which were presented here, I agree with the central plank of her judgment that there is 'nothing to suggest that that [the time taken in the appeals process] was unreasonable or unjustifiable'. That alone would, in my view, have been sufficient to dispose of the current claim. It now appears that while, as he was quite entitled, the claimant utilised the appeal process to its full extent, he was at the same time frustrating the purpose of the restraint order by dissipating his money assets. Once all the circumstances are examined I do not consider that the District Judge erred in reaching the conclusion she did.

11.153 The European Court of Human Rights took a somewhat different view in *Bullen and Soneji v The United Kingdom* [2009] ECHR 28. As a result of appeals against confiscation orders being pursued, by the applicants in the Court of Appeal and by the Crown in the House of Lords, there had been a lengthy delay and applicants complained that their Art 6 rights had been violated. The Court found that the relevant period of delay had been five years and six months between the applicants being convicted and therefore liable to have confiscation orders made against them and the decision of the House of Lords to allow the Crown's appeal and reinstate the confiscation orders. The Government contended that the prosecutor had acted with reasonable expedition at all times and that any delays were not attributable to the State. If the applicants had not raised objections to the Crown Court's jurisdiction to make the confiscation orders, the proceedings would have been concluded much earlier.

11.154 The European Court of Human Rights held unanimously that the applicants' Art 6.1 rights had been violated. The Court reiterated that Art 6.1 rights applied throughout proceedings for the determination of a criminal charge and extended to the confiscation proceedings. The Court held that the reasonableness of the length of the proceedings must be assessed:

> In the light of the circumstances of the case and with reference to the following criteria: the complexity of the case, the conduct of the applicants and the relevant authorities and what was at stake for the applicants.

11.155 The Court found that the applicants could not be criticised for exercising their legal entitlement to have the question of the Crown Court's jurisdiction to make the confiscation orders challenged on appeal and the delay that arose in consequence could not be attributed to their conduct. The Court went on to consider what was at stake for the applicants and noted that they faced confiscation orders in which they were required to pay substantial sums of money—£30,284 and £75,350 with default sentences of 12 and 21 months respectively. The Court concluded that:

> In the light of the importance of what was at stake for the applicants in this case and without discounting the complexity of the legal issue in question, the Court finds the period of delay attributable to the State, when taken cumulatively, to be unreasonably long and in breach of the reasonable time requirement as provided in Article 6 of the Convention.

11.156 The Court went on to reject as manifestly ill-founded a complaint by the applicants that the imposition of the confiscation orders outside the statutory time limit, without consideration as to whether there were exceptional circumstances, made the proceedings against them unfair. The Court noted that the House of Lords had given 'full and reasoned judgments' on the issue and said:

> The applicants acknowledged that the Crown Court's jurisdiction to impose confiscation orders outside the statutory time limit was a contested issue which had resulted in a spate of related cases being heard before the Court of Appeal. There are no grounds to suggest that the ultimate re-imposition of the confiscation orders against the applicants, albeit significantly delayed, was inconsistent with the essence of the offences to which they had pleaded guilty or that they were not reasonably foreseeable, given the contentious legal debate over the domestic courts' jurisdiction outside the time-limit provided by section 72A(3) of the CJA 1988. In sum, the Court finds no evidence to substantiate the applicants' complaint that the imposition of the confiscation orders against them outside the statutory time limit rendered the proceedings unfair within the meaning of Article 6.1 of the Convention.

As the applicants did not make a claim for just satisfaction, the Court made no order other **11.157** than declaring that there had been a violation of the applicants' Art 6.1 rights in relation to the delay.

Delays in the appeal process may therefore give rise to a breach of Art 6.1 in certain circum- **11.158** stances. The conduct of the parties will clearly be a highly relevant feature: this will particularly be so where, as in the case of *Minshull*, the defendant sought to frustrate enforcement of the order by disposing of assets in breach of a restraint order. The Court will, however, also need to consider what is at stake for the defendant and, where a substantial confiscation order and lengthy default sentence is involved, the Court is likely to look at any delay with particular care. The case should act as a reminder to prosecutors to pursue confiscation investigations with all due expedition.

Other methods of enforcement

In *Lloyd v Bow Street Magistrates' Court* [2003] EWHC Admin 2294 the Divisional Court **11.159** emphasised that its decision applied only to the enforcement of confiscation orders by means of committal to prison and did not extend to civil methods of enforcement. In *Joyce v Dover Magistrates' Court* [2008] EWHC Admin 1448 the High Court had to consider the effect of a delay when an attempt was being made to enforce a confiscation order by the employment of civil remedies. A confiscation order had been made against the defendant as long ago as 1993. It was accepted that the delay was such that it was no longer appropriate to enforce the confiscation order by activation of the default sentence, but the court proceeded to hold an enforcement hearing to determine whether any of the civil means of enforcing the order would be appropriate. The defendant asked the District Judge to stay the enforcement hearing as an abuse of process, but he declined to do so giving the following reasons:

> (1) Mr Joyce has made no payments whatsoever in the 14 years since this order was made; (2) that there has never been any offer of any sort of satisfaction in any form from Mr Joyce relating to this order; (3) not only has there never been any attempt by Mr Joyce to reach a resolution of the order, he himself delayed enforcement proceedings for some significant period by indicating periodically that he would be seeking a certificate of inadequacy, which in the event he never pursued; (4) Mr Joyce has throughout been aware of his continuing liability to satisfy this order; (5) for the 3 year period from March 2004 to April 2007 Mr Joyce was unlawfully at large, fully aware of his duty to surrender to the court, but failed to do so.

> I cannot see how, taking these factors into account, that it can be maintained that it would be an abuse of the process of this court to enforce any of the methods of enforcement available, other than committal to prison. Given Mr Joyce's own responsibility for some significant periods of delay, his complaint that the enforcement authorities should be prevented by this court from seeking satisfaction of this long outstanding debt is in my view wholly unsustainable.

11.160 The defendant sought judicial review of the District Judge's decision. There was an issue between the parties as to whether Art 6.1 rights extended to the enforcement of confiscation orders by the employment of civil remedies, but the Court declined to rule on this point because it was accepted that the law of abuse of process applied to such proceedings and that these gave the defendant as much protection as the ECHR. Maurice Kay LJ said:

> There is a debate in the skeleton arguments about the position under Article 6 of the ECHR, and the right to a fair hearing within a reasonable time. The submission on behalf of the respondent is that Article 6 does not apply to this stage of the enforcement of a confiscation order by means other than a warrant of commitment, because it does not involve a determination of civil rights and obligations, nor is it now the determination of a criminal charge. However, this is something of a sterile debate, because it is common ground that the common law of abuse of process is applicable to these proceedings and that this is no less protective than Article 6 would be. In the circumstances, I propose to deal with the case on a common law basis.

11.161 The Court concluded that there was no abuse of process in the defendant's case and dismissed his claim for judicial review. Maurice Kay LJ said:

> For my part I do not doubt that enforcement proceedings such as these do not fall outside the ambit of abuse of process. For example, if the enforcement authority were to manipulate the procedure, a finding of abuse could follow. But in the present case, no manipulation or bad faith is suggested. It is put as a case of culpable delay, pure and simple. Moreover, it is not suggested that the passage of time would prevent a fair assessment of the claimant's means and ability to discharge the order. Such matters are within the knowledge of the claimant.

11.162 The Court also stressed that an application for judicial review could only succeed if it could be shown that the decision of the enforcing magistrates' court was *Wednesbury* unreasonable. Maurice Kay LJ concluded:

> In this application for judicial review the question becomes whether that conclusion and the reasoning which led to it are vitiated on *Wednesbury* grounds. This is common ground. In my judgment, they are not so vitiated. I accept that there may be cases in which delay is so extensive and so culpable, or unexplained, that a stay will be appropriate. However, the District Judge's reasons for refusing a stay in the present cased are, in my judgment, unassailable.

11.163 It is clear therefore that the employment of civil methods of enforcement is vulnerable to challenge where the delay is such as to amount to an abuse of process. In the case of *Joyce* a significant factor in the failure of the application was the defendant's own conduct which had played a major part in the delay. If he had cooperated with the enforcement authorities, not absconded, and pursued his stated intention of applying for a certificate of inadequacy the outcome may well have been different.

12

THE INSOLVENT DEFENDANT

A. Introduction

It is not unusual for a defendant to become insolvent either before or during the course of **12.01** restraint and confiscation proceedings. There are a number of possible reasons for this. A defendant who has a business experiencing cash flow difficulties may be tempted to commit criminal offences as a means of alleviating his problems. He may, for example, commit income, corporation, or value added tax offences, or even become involved in other criminal offences such as drug trafficking in the hope of raising funds to overcome his financial difficulties. Once a defendant has been arrested and charged he may be unable to continue to work and meet his debts, especially if he has been remanded in custody, and third party creditors may launch institute civil proceedings to recover debts owing to them. It is also not uncommon for a defendant to try and make himself bankrupt with a view to rendering any restraint or confiscation proceedings ineffective. Finally, in cases where the Crown has suffered a significant loss, for example in a VAT carousel of 'MTIC' fraud as it has become known, law enforcement agencies may institute civil proceedings to recover their loss and seek the appointment of a provisional liquidator over the companies involved. In this chapter we examine the provisions of POCA and the previous legislation in relation to the insolvent defendant.

B. The Position under POCA

Part 9 of the Proceeds of Crime Act 2002 (POCA) deals with insolvency and maintains the **12.02** 'first come, first served' rule in the old legislation: that is to say that, in most circumstances, a restraint order will take priority provided it was first in time and, similarly, insolvency proceedings will take precedence if they were brought before a restraint order is made.

Bankruptcy

12.03 Bankruptcy is dealt with by ss 417 to 419 of POCA. Section 417 deals with the position where the bankruptcy post-dates the restraint order and provides that in such circumstances the restrained assets shall be excluded from the defendant's estate for the purposes of the bankruptcy. By s 417(1) and (2) of POCA (as amended by para 69 of Pt 1 to Sch 8 of the Serious Crime Act 2007):

(1) This section applies if a person is adjudged bankrupt in England and Wales.
(2) The following property is excluded from his estate for the purposes of Part 9 of the 1986 Act—
  (a) property for the time being subject to a restraint order which was made under section 41, 120 or 190 before the order adjudging him bankrupt;
  (b) any property in respect of which an order under section 50 is in force;
  (c) any property in respect of which an order section 128 (3) is in force;
  (d) any property in respect of which an order under section 198 is in force.

12.04 References to 'the 1986 Act' are to the Insolvency Act 1986: see s 434(1)(d) of POCA. It is important to note that the key date for determining priority is the date on which a restraint or enforcement receivership order is made. The date on which a confiscation order is made is immaterial for this purpose. Thus, if a confiscation order is made in a case where there is no restraint or an enforcement receivership order is in force, the bankruptcy order will take precedence even if it post-dates the restraint order. If a prosecutor wishes to protect assets to satisfy a confiscation order, he should always seek a restraint order in any cases where there is a real risk of a bankruptcy order being made. The date on which the bankruptcy order is made determines which order has priority and not the date on which the petition is lodged: see s 417(1).

12.05 Section 418 of POCA (as amended by para 70 of Pt 1 of Sch 8 to the Serious Crime Act 2007) deals with the position where the bankruptcy order is first in time and provides:

(1) If a person is adjudged bankrupt in England and Wales the powers referred to in subsection (2) must not be exercised in relation to the property referred to in subsection (3).
(2) These are the powers—
  (a) the powers conferred on a court by sections 41 to 67 and the powers of a referred appointed under section 48 or 50;
  (b) the powers conferred on a court by sections 120 to 136 and Schedule 3 and the powers of an administrator appointed under section 125 or 128(3).
  (c) the powers conferred on a court by sections 190 to 215 and the powers of a receiver appointed under section 196 or 198.
(3) This is the property—
  (a) property which is for the time being comprised in the bankrupt's estate for the purposes of Part 9 of the 1986 Act;
  (b) property in respect of which his trustee in bankruptcy may (without leave of the court) serve a notice under section 307, 308 or 308A of the 1986 Act (after acquired property, tools, tenancies etc);
  (c) property which is to be applied for the benefit of creditors of the bankrupt by virtue of a condition imposed under section 280 (2) (c) of the 1986 Act;
  (d) in a case where a confiscation order has been made under section 6 or 156 of this Act, any sums in the hands of a receiver appointed under section 50 or 198 of this Act after the amount required to be paid under the confiscation order has been fully paid;

(e) in a case where a confiscation order has been made under section 92 of this Act, any sums remaining in the hands of an administrator appointed under section 128 of this Act after the amount required to be paid under the confiscation order has been fully paid.

12.06 This section again gives effect to the 'first come, first served' rule by providing that if the order adjudging the defendant bankrupt comes first in time, the court may not make restraint or receivership orders over any property referred to in s 418(3).

12.07 Section 419 makes provision in relation to tainted gifts and provides that no order under the Insolvency Act 1986 may be made in relation to property that amounts to a tainted gift provided it is subject to a restraint or enforcement receivership order.

Winding up of companies

12.08 Section 426 of POCA makes similar provision in relation to the winding up of companies. By s 426(2)(a), where a court has made a winding-up order or the company passes a resolution for its voluntary winding up, the functions of the liquidator (or any provisional liquidator) may not be exercised in relation to property subject to a restraint order made before the relevant time. Section 426(9) defines the relevant time as:

(a) if no order for the winding up of the company has been made, the time of the passing of the resolution for voluntary winding up;
(b) if such an order has been made, but before the presentation of the petition for the winding up of the company by the court such a resolution has been passed by the company, the time of the passing of the resolution;
(c) if such an order has been made, but paragraph (b) does not apply, the time of the making of the order.

12.09 Section 426(4) and (5) deals with the situation where the order or resolution for winding up pre-dates a restraint order and provides that the powers of the court to make restraint orders and management and enforcement receivership orders must not be exercised in a way mentioned in s 426(6) in relation to property held by the company and in relation to which the functions of the liquidator are exercisable. Section 426(6) provides:

(6) the powers must not be exercised—
(a) so as to inhibit the liquidator from exercising his functions for the purpose of distributing property to the company's creditors;
(b) so as to prevent the payment out of any property of expenses (including the remuneration of the liquidator or any provisional liquidator) properly incurred in respect of the property.

Floating charges

12.10 Creditors, particularly financial institutions, frequently hold a floating charge over a company's assets as security for a loan. The terms of the charge will normally empower the creditor to appoint an administrative receiver, without the necessity to make an application to court, for the purpose of taking control of the assets subject to the charge. The relationship between such charges and restraint orders and court appointed receivers is provided for in s 430 of POCA. Again, the rule is generally one of 'first come, first served'. By s 430(2) the functions of a receiver appointed pursuant to a floating charge are not exercisable in relation to property subject to a restraint order made prior to the appointment of the receiver. Similarly, if the receiver is appointed prior to the application for the restraint order, s 430(4) provides that the administrative receivership shall take precedence, and the powers of the court to make restraint orders and to appoint management and enforcement receivers shall not be used in a way mentioned in s 430(6). By s 430(6):

The powers shall not be exercised—

(a) so as to inhibit the receiver from exercising his functions for the purpose of distributing property to the company's creditors;

(b) so as to prevent the payment out of any property of expenses (including the remuneration of the receiver) properly incurred in the exercise of his functions in respect of the property.

Limited liability partnerships

12.11 By s 431 of POCA, the provisions as to the winding up of companies and floating charges apply equally to limited liability partnerships that are capable of being wound up the under the Insolvency Act 1986.

Protection of insolvency practitioners

12.12 Section 432(1) and (2) give protection to insolvency practitioners who mistakenly deal in realisable property providing that they will only be liable to pay damages for their actions if they are negligent. The section also empowers them to recover their remuneration and expenses, and gives them a lien over the property and the proceeds of sale for payment.

C. The Position under the Old Legislation

12.13 The old legislation makes very similar provision in relation to insolvency. The relevant provisions are to be found in s 32 of the Drug Trafficking Act 1994 (DTA) and s 84 of the CJA 1988 in relation to bankruptcy, and in s 34 of the DTA and s 86 of the CJA 1988 in relation to the winding up of companies. For a detailed account of these provisions, the reader is referred to the second edition of this work.

12.14 In the recent case of *R v Shahid* [2009] EWCA Crim 831 the Court of Appeal held that the mere fact that a bankruptcy order has been made does not necessarily preclude the making of a confiscation order under the CJA 1988 even though difficulties might arise at the enforcement stage. On 30 September 2005 a confiscation order was made against the defendant for £135,524.60 notwithstanding that on 1 September 2005 a bankruptcy order had been made in respect of the defendant on his own petition for bankruptcy. He argued that the bankruptcy order deprived the judge of jurisdiction to make the confiscation order some four weeks later. The Court of Appeal disagreed and dismissed the appeal. Keith J said:

> As a matter of principle, we do not think that a bankrupt's assets being in the hands of the trustee in bankruptcy affects the position at all. The bankruptcy may be highly relevant to the enforcement of a confiscation order, but not to the making of such an order in the first place. That, we think, is the explicit effect of section 102(8) of the 1988 Act, which defines what is meant by the phrase 'property held by a person' which relates back, inter alia, to the definition of 'realisable property' in section 74(1) of the 1988 Act, which refers to 'any property held by the defendant'. Section 102(8) reads:
>
> > 'References to property held by a person include a reference to property vested in the trustee in bankruptcy, permanent or interim trustee within the meaning of the Bankruptcy (Scotland) Act 1985 or liquidator.'

So if the property held by the defendant for the purposes of making a confiscation order includes property vested in his trustee in bankruptcy, it is impossible to say that a confiscation order cannot be made against a bankrupt.

Keith J added: 12.15

> In our view, the difficulties which are said to arise as a result of the tension between these two legal processes are significantly reduced when one focuses, once again, on the making of the confiscation order as opposed to its enforcement. The prosecution accepts that its powers may well be severely restricted when it comes to the enforcement of a confiscation order, which is where the tension really lies. We have not been persuaded that the making of a confiscation order, which will focus on what the offender's realisable assets are rather than how their realisation can be enforced, brings the tension between confiscation and bankruptcy into play. Indeed, as Hallett LJ pointed out in the course of argument, if the public interest is a relevant factor at all, the public interest would not be served if a defendant was able to avoid a confiscation order by the simple expedient of applying for his own bankruptcy before the hearing of the application for a confiscation order takes place. It is no argument to say that the prosecution could protect itself by making an application for a restraint order, because the circumstances entitling the prosecution to apply for a restraint order may either not be known to the prosecution or may not even exist.

As Keith J acknowledged, the problem is likely to come at the enforcement stage where,   12.16
absent a restraint order coming first in time, the bankruptcy order will take precedence over the confiscation order and, unless the value of the defendant's estate is greater than that necessary to pay off his creditors, the confiscation order will stand little chance of being satisfied. If the prosecutor had obtained a restraint order prior to the bankruptcy order being made, this problem would not have arisen as the confiscation order would have taken priority. Although Keith J was right to observe that circumstances justifying an application for a restraint order by the prosecutor might not exist, in the case of *Shahid* the defendant had been convicted in April 2005, some six months earlier, of the offences for which he had been indicted, namely two specimen counts of cheating the public revenue. In most circumstances, convictions for offences of dishonesty of this nature would give rise to a reasonable apprehension that the defendant would dissipate his assets which would justify an application for a restraint order. Prosecutors and financial investigators should always be alive to the risk of a defendant petitioning for his own bankruptcy as a means of evading a confiscation order, and also of the risk that third party creditors may seek to protect their position by means of bankruptcy proceedings and, wherever the circumstances justify it, seek a restraint order to protect assets for the purpose of satisfying the confiscation order.

D. Interaction between Restraint and Insolvency Proceedings

It is by no means uncommon for restraint and insolvency actions to proceed concurrently   12.17
in respect of companies holding realisable property. This is particularly common in VAT 'carousel' or 'MTIC' fraud cases where there has been a significant loss—often many millions of pounds to the Exchequer. It is understandable that, in such circumstances, the Government Department suffering the loss, usually HM Revenue and Customs, wishes to pursue every remedy at its disposal to recoup the loss that has been sustained. In circumstances where the

restraint and insolvency proceedings are serving separate and distinct purposes it is submitted this course of action is entirely unobjectionable.

12.18 Problems can arise, however, when restraint and insolvency proceedings are pursued in relation to the same assets. This is particularly so where a management receiver has been appointed and both he and a liquidator or provisional liquidator are pursuing the same assets. They will both be seeking to claim their remuneration and expenses from the assets under their control and may well each have solicitors and other agents acting for them at considerable expense. In such circumstances, there is a real risk of a duplication of effort and the receiver and liquidator fighting over the same assets which, one way or another will all go to the benefit the Crown if the proceedings are successful, whether in the liquidation proceedings or by way of the satisfaction of a confiscation order.

12.19 It is submitted that it cannot be right for this to be allowed to occur and that all law enforcement agencies should have regard to the following principles:

(1) A restraint order is not a remedy in itself but is an interim order intended to preserve assets to make them available to satisfy a confiscation order. It follows from this that once a restraint order is in place, law enforcement agencies should not, without good and sufficient reason, change tactics and institute proceedings in the civil courts in relation to the same assets.

(2) If civil proceedings are instituted, the duty under s 6 of POCA to make a confiscation order becomes a mere power: see s 6(6). The institution of civil proceedings in these circumstances would represent a significant change in circumstances and, in compliance with his ongoing duty to give full and frank disclosure, the prosecutor should notify the court forthwith.

(3) Guidance issued by the Home Secretary and Attorney General indicates that benefit derived from criminal activities should normally be recovered through prosecution and the making of confiscation orders.

12.20 This does not necessarily mean that civil proceedings should never be brought in cases where restraint and confiscation orders are actively being pursued. Indeed, there may be compelling reasons, why, on the facts of individual cases, civil proceedings should be brought. If, for example, civil proceedings will allow assets to be recovered that would otherwise be unavailable then such a course would be entirely justified. Law enforcement agencies should, however, proceed with caution and only bring resort to civil proceedings where there is some appreciable benefit to be gained from doing so. There should also be close liaison with prosecutors to ensure that there is no duplication of effort and that ongoing duties to provide full and frank disclosure are complied with.

13

CIVIL RECOVERY: PROPERTY
FREEZING ORDERS; RECEIVERS;
AND LEGAL EXPENSES

A. Introduction

13.01   Civil recovery of the proceeds of crime includes both recovery in the High Court (under Chapter 2 of Pt 5 of the Proceeds of Crime Act 2002 (POCA)) and the recovery of cash in summary proceedings (under Chapter 3 of Pt 5 of POCA). As a result, Pt 5 of the Act has two purposes: firstly, to enable the relevant agency to recover in civil proceedings before the High Court property that is, or represents, property obtained through unlawful conduct; and secondly, to enable cash which is, or represents, property obtained through unlawful conduct, or which is intended to be used in unlawful conduct, to be forfeited in civil proceedings before a magistrates' court.

The second of these objectives is considered fully in Chapter 15.   **13.02**

The first objective, to enable the relevant agency ('the enforcement authority') to recover prop-   **13.03**
erty in civil proceedings before the High Court, is considered in this and the next chapter.

For ease of reference we have divided civil recovery into two parts. First, in this chapter, we give   **13.04**
an overview of the legislation in relation to civil recovery and then look at the interim measures
anticipated by the Act, namely Property Freezing Orders (PFOs), Management Receiving
Orders, and Interim Receiving Orders (IROs), before considering insolvency, compensation,
and how to obtain the release of funds to cover legal expenses in civil recovery cases.

In the next chapter we consider recovery orders themselves; decisions concerning the   **13.05**
European Convention on Human Rights (ECHR); the pension provisions; and the Pt 6
taxation powers.

B. Overview in Relation to Civil Recovery

The rise and fall of the Assets Recovery Agency

The civil recovery provisions came into force on 24 February 2003, SI 2003/120. The Act,   **13.06**
in its original form, created a new government agency, known as the 'Assets Recovery
Agency' (ARA). ARA's task was to implement the new legislation and spearhead the new
powers in relation to civil recovery. By June 2005 ARA had collected £4.6 million, and had
targeted some 200 individuals. In addition, the Agency had been given recovery orders to
liquidate assets amounting to a further £5.5 million against a target of £13 million. It had
also frozen a further £16.8 million worth of assets.

Whilst ARA enjoyed a measurable success before the courts (particularly with challenges   **13.07**
to the legislation), it nevertheless failed to come close to collecting its target figures. One of
the problems cited was delays with legal aid, which created a considerable backlog in claims.
The cost of the ARA, which employed 162 staff, to June 2005 was £29 million. This led the
press and other commentators to question its value for money's worth, and this, perhaps
inevitably, applied pressure on ministers to consider yet more reform.

As a result, s 74 of the Serious Crime Act 2007 (SCA) abolished the ARA with effect from   **13.08**
1 April 2008. Schedule 8 of the SCA transferred the civil recovery powers of the ARA to the
Serious Organised Crime Agency (SOCA) and extended those powers to the Director of
Public Prosecutions (DPP), the Director of the Revenue and Customs Prosecutions Office
(RCPO) (now merged with the CPS), and the Director of the Serious Fraud Office (SFO).

In SOCA's first year it collected £16.7 million in relation to civil and tax recovery, exceeding   **13.09**
the Government's target of £16 million, with the other agencies contributing a further £2
million plus. This compared with £7.7 million in ARA's last year of operation (SOCA
annual report 2009).

The main changes

The SCA introduced a number of amendments to the existing legislation: **13.10**

• The ARA was abolished and its functions redistributed (s 74).

- Schedule 8 amended POCA and other relevant legislation to repeal or transfer functions previously conferred on the ARA and its Director.

- Under Pt 1 of the Schedule, the role of the Director of ARA under Pts 2 and 4 of POCA in respect of confiscation and restraint orders in England and Wales and Northern Ireland, respectively, were repealed.

- References to receivers of the Director under Pts 2 (for example ss 52 and 53) and 4 of POCA were also repealed.

- Under Pt 2 of Sch 8, powers under Pt 5 of POCA (civil recovery of the proceeds of 'unlawful conduct') were transferred to SOCA. Powers under Pt 5 were also transferred, in respect of England and Wales, to the DPP, the Director of the RCPO, and the Director of the SFO, and, in relation to Northern Ireland, to the Director of Public Prosecutions for Northern Ireland.

- Under Pt 4 of Sch 8, powers under Pt 8 of POCA (the power to apply for investigation orders to investigate confiscation cases and civil recovery cases) were transferred from ARA to SOCA.

- Under Pt 5 of Sch 8, the role of the ARA to train, accredit, and monitor performance of financial investigators under s 3 of POCA was transferred to the National Policing Improvement Agency. (This Agency was established under Pt 1 of the Police and Justice Act 2006 with the function of training and developing police officers.)

The purpose of the changes

13.11 The broadening of the powers to other agencies and the various directors may be seen as consistent with one of the main purposes of the Act, namely the reduction of crime.

13.12 Under s 2A of the amended POCA, SOCA and the directors are required to exercise their functions under POCA 'in the way best calculated to contribute to the reduction of crime'.

13.13 In doing so the directors must have regard to guidance issued by the Secretary of State and the Attorney-General. Importantly, pursuant to s 2A(4), that guidance must indicate that 'the reduction of crime is in general best secured by means of criminal investigations and criminal proceedings'.

13.14 Section 2A(4) appears to give a steer in that it signals that criminal investigations and criminal proceedings should be seen as the preferential route for the reduction of crime. As a secondary route, POCA anticipates that where criminal investigations or proceedings cannot be taken forward, other methods, such as civil recovery, may be deployed.

The enforcement authority

13.15 The power to recover in civil proceedings before the High Court is reserved to the 'enforcement authority'. The definition of enforcement authority is set out at s 316(1) of the Act and includes SOCA, the Director of Public Prosecutions (the CPS), the Director of the RCPO, and the Director of the SFO.

Proceedings even on acquittal

13.16 Under s 240(2) it is possible to invoke civil recovery and cash forfeiture proceedings even though proceedings have not been brought for a criminal offence in connection with the property, eg where there may be insufficient grounds for a prosecution, or the suspect is outside of the jurisdiction, or has died:

The powers conferred by this Part are exercisable in relation to any property (including cash) whether or not any proceedings have been brought for an offence in connection with that property.

It should be noted that cases where criminal proceedings have been brought include cases **13.17** where a defendant has been acquitted, as they too fall within the scheme of Pt 5. In *Director of the Assets Recovery Agency v Taher and Ors* [2006] EWHC 3402 (Admin), Collins J confirmed the effect of the legislation:

The legislation provides that if the Director is able to establish on the balance of probabilities that assets are the proceeds of crime, they are recoverable even if there has been a prosecution, which has not succeeded and even if there has been no prosecution, because, for example, the view has been taken that evidence would not be sufficient to establish criminality beyond reasonable doubt.

This reasoning has been extended to circumstances where the respondent's conviction had been quashed because his arrest had been unlawful (*Serious Organised Crime Agency v Olden* [2009] EWHC 610).

Standard and burden of proof

Section 241(3) states: **13.18**

The court . . . must decide on *a balance of probabilities* whether it is proved:
(a) that any matters alleged to constitute unlawful conduct have occurred, or
(b) that any person intended to use any cash in unlawful conduct.

The standard of proof applicable is that which normally applies to civil matters, ie the balance of probabilities, and not the criminal standard of beyond reasonable doubt. It will be noted that the Act is specific in that it states that the burden is on 'the balance of probabilities' and not to the 'civil standard'. In many civil cases the degree of probability required to establish proof may vary according to the allegation to be proved (see *Hornal v Neuberger Products Ltd* [1957] 1 QB 247) and the court is often reluctant, when considering claims by the Crown, to apply merely a 51/49 per cent test where an individual's property or other assets are in jeopardy (see *Bater v Bater* [1950] 2 All ER 458 and *B v Chief Constable of Avon and Somerset* [2001] 1 All ER 562). POCA, however, is proactively encouraging the courts to apply a strict 51/49 per cent 'balance of probabilities' test.

Griffith Williams J considered the issue of standard and burden of proof in *SOCA v Gale* **13.19** *and others* [2009] EWHC 1015. He observed as follows (at 9):

The burden of proof is on the claimant and the standard of proof they must satisfy is the balance of probabilities. While the claimant alleged serious criminal conduct, the criminal standard of proof does not apply, although 'cogent evidence is generally required to satisfy a civil tribunal that a person has been fraudulent or behaved in some other reprehensible manner. But the question is always whether the tribunal thinks it more probable than not'—see *Secretary of State for the Home Department v Rehman* [2003] 1 AC 153 at paragraph 55 *per* Lord Hoffmann. In *In Re D* [2008] 1 WLR 1499 at paragraph 27 Lord Carswell, with whose speech the other Law Lords agreed, said the proper state of the law on the topic had, subject to one qualification [at para 28], been summarised by

Richards LJ in *R(N) v Mental Health Review Tribunal (Northern Region)* [2006] QB 468 at paragraph 62:

'Although there is a single civil standard of proof on the balance of probabilities, it is flexible in its application. In particular, the more serious the allegation or the more serious the consequences if the allegation is proved, the stronger must be the evidence before a court will find the allegation proved on the balance of probabilities. Thus the flexibility of the standard lies not in any adjustment to the degree of probability required for an allegation to be proved (such that a more serious allegation has to be proved to a higher degree of probability), but in the strength or quality of the evidence that will in practise be required for an allegation to be proved on the balance of probabilities'.

13.20 The standard of proof appropriate in deciding whether matters alleged to constitute unlawful conduct have occurred was considered by Collins J in *R (on the application of the Director of the Assets Recovery Agency) v (1) Jia Jin He and (2) Dan Dan Chen* (2004) EWHC Admin 3021, in which he found that 'cogent' evidence, although no gloss, was required. He stated:

As a general rule, no doubt, criminal conduct may be regarded as less probable than non-criminal conduct. But where there is evidence from which a court can be satisfied that it is more probable than not that criminal conduct has been involved, it does not seem to me that that is something that is so improbable as to require a gloss on the standard of proof. However, I recognise, and it is no doubt right, that since it is necessary to establish that there has been criminal conduct in the obtaining of the property, the court should look for cogent evidence before deciding that the balance of probabilities has been met. But I have no doubt that Parliament deliberately referred to the balance of probabilities, and that the court should not place a gloss upon it, so as to require that the standard approach is that appropriate in a criminal case. Apart from anything else, if that were necessary, then the effectiveness of, in particular, Part 5 of the Act would be to a considerable extent removed . . . It is plain that Parliament deliberately imposed a lower standard of proof as the standard appropriate for these proceedings.

13.21 In the *Director of the Assets Recovery Agency v Jeffrey David Green* [2005] EWHC (Admin) 3168, The Times, 27 February 2006, Sullivan J stated (at para 19) that when read in the context of s 240 and the remainder of s 241, it was plain that Parliament envisaged that in civil recovery proceedings the Director would identify the matters alleged to constitute unlawful conduct in sufficient detail to enable the court 'not to decide whether a particular crime had been committed by a particular individual, but to decide whether the conduct so described was unlawful under the criminal law of the UK' (or the criminal law of the United Kingdom and the foreign country in question). He stated that any litigant in civil proceedings seeking to recover property upon the basis that it had been obtained by unlawful conduct would be expected to identify (a) the property, and (b) the conduct that was said to be unlawful (para 23).

Civil proceedings

13.22 In *Jia Jin He* Collins J stated that there was 'no doubt' that in domestic law proceedings under Pt 5 are classified as civil proceedings (para 47). In so finding, he adopted the decision of Coghlin J in the *Director of the Assets Recovery Agency v Walsh* [2004] NIQB 21 where his Lordship considered the three principal criteria identified in

Engel v The Netherlands (No 1) (1976) 1 EHRR 647 (para 13) for civil proceedings namely:

(i) the manner in which the domestic state classifies the proceedings, [although this normally carries comparatively little weight and is regarded as a starting point rather than determinative—see *Ozturk v Germany* (1984) 6 EHRR 409 at 421 and 422];

(ii) the nature of the conduct in question classified objectively bearing in mind the object and purpose of the Convention;

(iii) the severity of any possible penalty—severe penalties, including those with imprisonment in default and penalties intended to deter are pointers towards a criminal classification of proceedings—see *Schmautzer v Austria* (1995) 21 EHRR 511.

Having applied the approach in *Engel* (confirmed as appropriate by the House of Lords in **13.23** *R v H* [2003] 1 All ER 497) Coghlin J found the civil recovery scheme to be civil in nature, a view Collins J in *Jia Jin He* concurred with.

The distinction between recovery proceedings and confiscation proceedings

There are a number of fundamental differences between the two schemes, including the **13.24** distinct procedural requirements that govern the appropriate proceedings.

In the *Director of the Assets Recovery Agency v Ashton* [2006] EWHC 1064 Newman J endorsed **13.25** (at para 50) the following distinctions between civil recovery and confiscation proceedings:

• No conviction is necessary in recovery order proceedings (indeed civil recovery proceedings may be brought where no offence has been charged or where a defendant has been tried and acquitted), whereas a confiscation order can only be made if there has been a conviction.

• No one stands in jeopardy.

• Enforcement is through a Trustee, as opposed to an enforcement magistrates' court.

• Confiscation proceedings are dealt with by criminal courts (albeit operating on the civil standard—see the Criminal Procedure Rules, SI 2005/384 r 56 *et seq*) and often by the Judge who oversaw the criminal trial.

• Confiscation proceedings are initiated by the prosecutor, or the judge of his own motion.

• A confiscation order is not directed towards particular assets *per se*. A defendant may use any resource to satisfy the order made against him. Whereas in civil recovery the property itself is the target of the claim.

Civil recovery in the High Court: proceedings for recovery orders

Proceedings for a recovery order may be taken by the appropriate Director in the High **13.26** Court against any person who the enforcement authority thinks holds recoverable property (see s 243(1)).

Definitions within POCA

Chapter 4 of Pt 5 of POCA sets out various definitions which apply to both the civil **13.27** recovery scheme and the cash forfeiture provisions. It deals particularly with recoverable property, namely:

Property obtained through unlawful conduct	s 304
Tracing property	s 305

Mixing property	s 306
Recoverable property accruing profits	s 307
General and other exceptions and exemptions	ss 308 and 309
Granting interests	s 310
Obtaining and disposing of property	s 314
Property	s 316(4)

These sections are considered more closely below.

Definition of 'property'

13.28   Under s 316(4) property is all property wherever situated and includes:

(a) money,
(b) all forms of property, real or personal, heritable or moveable,
(c) things in action and other intangible or incorporeal property.

It should be noted that under s 308(9), property is not recoverable if it has already been taken into account when calculating the amount to be paid under a confiscation order.

13.29   Under s 316 'recoverable property' (defined in s 304 as 'property obtained through unlawful conduct') is to be read in accordance with ss 304 to 310, which deal with property obtained through 'unlawful conduct'; tracing property; mixing property; recoverable property and accruing profits; and general exceptions and exemptions including the granting of interests. In short, recoverable property is property that has been obtained through unlawful conduct or property that represents such property (see *Singh v Director of the Assets Recovery Agency* [2005] EWCA Civ 580, (2005) 1 WLR 3747).

13.30   Under s 316(5) any reference to a person's property (whether expressed as a reference to the property he holds or otherwise) is to be read as follows:

(1) In relation to land, it is a reference to any interest which he holds in the land.
(2) In relation to property other than land it is a reference to the property (if it belongs to him), or to any other interest which he holds in the property (s 316(5) to (7)).

Property obtained through unlawful conduct

13.31   Under s 242(1) a person obtains property through unlawful conduct (whether his own conduct or another's) if he obtains property by or in return for that conduct.

13.32   In deciding whether any property was obtained through unlawful conduct, it is immaterial 'whether or not any money, goods or services were provided in order to put the person in question in the position to carry out the conduct in question' (s 242(2)(a)). Nor is it necessary to show that the conduct was of a particular kind, if it can be shown that the property was obtained through conduct of one of a number of kinds, each of which would have fallen within the definition of 'unlawful conduct' (see s 242(2)).

13.33   It follows that a person will obtain property through unlawful conduct if he obtains it by his conduct, eg by stealing, or if he obtains it in return for unlawful conduct, eg by taking a bribe to award a contract.

Unlawful conduct

Conduct occurring in any part of the UK is unlawful conduct if it is unlawful under the criminal law of that part of the UK (s 241(1)).   **13.34**

Furthermore, under s 241(2) conduct which: **13.35**

(a) occurs in a country outside the United Kingdom and is unlawful under the criminal law of that country, and

(b) if it occurred in a part of the United Kingdom, would be unlawful under the criminal law of that part, is also unlawful conduct.

The effect of s 241(2) is to enable property obtained through unlawful conduct abroad to be recovered.

How is 'recoverable property' defined?

'Recoverable property' is defined as property obtained though unlawful conduct (s 304). The definitions of 'property' and 'unlawful conduct' are set out at paras 13.28 and 13.34 above.   **13.36**

How is 'associated property' defined?

Associated property is defined by s 245(1):   **13.37**

(1) 'Associated property' means property of any of the following descriptions (including property held by the Respondent which is not itself the recoverable property)—
(a) any interest in the recoverable property,
(b) any other interest in the property in which the recoverable property subsists,
(c) if the recoverable property is a tenancy in common, the tenancy of the other tenant,
(d) if (in Scotland) the recoverable property is owned in common, the interest of the other owner,
(e) if the recoverable property is part of a larger property, but not a separate part, the remainder of that property.

This broad definition is intended to deal with circumstances in which only part of the property is recoverable, or where there is more than one interest in the property and some of it is not recoverable. In those circumstances the non-recoverable part is described as 'associated property'.   **13.38**

The guidance notes that accompanied POCA give the following examples in terms of (a) to (e) above: **13.39**

In paragraph (a) the associated property might be a tenancy in a recoverable freehold. In paragraph (b), where a lease in a freehold block of flats has been purchased with recoverable property, another lease in the same block bought with legitimate money would be associated property. In paragraphs (c) and (d) where two people buy a car together, one with recoverable cash and one with legitimate cash, the share of the person who bought with legitimate cash is the associated property. In paragraph (e), where a painting is recoverable property but it had been framed using legitimate money, the frame would be associated property.

Section 245(2) adds that references to property 'being associated with recoverable property' are to be read accordingly, and that no property is to be treated as associated with the recoverable property where the recoverable property consists of rights under a pension scheme (within the meaning of ss 273 to 275 of POCA) (see s 245(3)).   **13.40**

The tracing of property

13.41 The Act envisages the tracing of property (s 305), which may include an audit trail exercise. Where property was originally obtained through unlawful conduct (or would have been recoverable property), property that represents the original property is also recoverable. For example, a person steals a valuable painting (the original property), it is sold and the cash received from the sale is later used to purchase a Mercedes motor car. The Mercedes becomes recoverable property, being representative of the proceeds of a crime.

Mixed property

13.42 The Act also stipulates that where a person's 'recoverable property' is mixed with other property, the portion of the mixed property that is said to relate to unlawful conduct becomes 'recoverable property' (see s 306—mixing property). For example, where there are two joint company directors, one uses the company account for legitimate monies, the other to launder the proceeds of crime. The 'honest' director withdraws a large sum of cash and as part of an investigation that cash is seized. The portion of the cash that he has on him that relates to legitimate money from the business does not fall within the recovery scheme. However, the portion that he holds that represents the proceeds of a crime does stand to be forfeited, whether that particular director knew about it or not.

Accruing profits

13.43 As one might expect, where a person who has 'recoverable property' obtains further property because of profits that have accrued on that recoverable property, those profits also become recoverable and are to be treated as 'property obtained through unlawful conduct' (eg increase in the value of an investment or in the value of a house) (see s 307—accruing profits).

Granting interests

13.44 Section 310 provides:

(1) If a person grants an interest in his recoverable property, the question of whether the interest is also recoverable is determined in the same manner as it is in any other disposal of recoverable property.
(2) Accordingly, on his granting an interest in the property in question,
  (a) where the property in question is property obtained through unlawful conduct, the interest is also to be treated as obtained through that conduct;
  (b) where the property in question represents property, in his hands, obtained through unlawful conduct, the interest is also to be treated as representing, in his hands, the property so obtained.

In other words, gifting a property or granting an interest in any other way is unlikely to save the property from civil recovery.

C. Property Freezing Orders

Introduction

13.45 The Serious Organised Crime and Police Act 2005 (SOCPA) introduced various amendments to the Civil Recovery Scheme. The former ARA had, at an early stage, taken a conscious decision not to appoint an interim receiver in every case, eg where the location and the value of the assets said to be the proceeds of unlawful conduct were known and where the functions therefore of an interim receiver were limited. By avoiding the appointment of an interim receiver, ARA also avoided the costs incurred by such an appointment, the costs of which fell upon the Agency.

To get around this problem, the ARA started using freezing orders pursuant to CPR 25.1 (formerly known as Mareva orders), as an interim remedy to restrain respondents from dealing with their assets and prohibit them from removing assets from the jurisdiction. However, the use of freezing orders in this way was not something originally envisaged by the legislation and as a result SOCPA introduced a purpose-built freezing order, known as a Property Freezing Order (PFO), as a device to be utilised in civil recovery.   **13.46**

Section 98 of SOCPA inserted s 245A into POCA. Section 245A(1) states: **13.47**

Where the enforcement authority may take proceedings for a recovery order in the High Court, the authority may apply to the court for a property freezing order (whether before or after starting the proceedings).

Section 245A reflects s 246(1) of POCA, in that it anticipates that the Director will be at liberty to apply for a PFO before he has started his Civil Procedure Rules (CPR) Pt 8 claim for civil recovery (s 316(1), as amended, defines 'enforcement authority').   **13.48**

Draft PFO

A draft PFO is found at Appendix 16.   **13.49**

Definition

Section 245A(2) defines a PFO as an order that: **13.50**

(a) specifies or describes the property to which it applies, and
(b) subject to any exclusions (see section 245C(1)(b) and (2)), prohibits any person to whose property the order applies from in any way dealing with the property.

PFO without notice

By s 245A(3), the relevant Director may apply for a PFO without giving notice, if the circumstances are such that notice of the application would prejudice any right of the enforcement authority to obtain a recovery order in respect of any property. This provision, like IROs and restraint orders under POCA, is to safeguard against the possibility that a respondent may attempt to either secrete his assets or transfer them out of the jurisdiction once put on notice that the relevant Director intends to seek a PFO. Clearly, whilst that risk is always a possibility, when making an *ex parte* application it is still incumbent upon the enforcement authority to at least state what its belief is in relation to the risk of dissipation and the facts upon which it bases that belief.   **13.51**

Factors giving rise to the risk of dissipation

One of the purposes of seeking a PFO is the risk that assets may be lost which might otherwise be the subject of a civil recovery order. In *Assets Recovery Agency v Keenan* [2005] NIQB 67, Coughlin J stated that assets obtained through the proceeds of crime were '. . . by their very nature assets likely to be at particular risk of dissipation'.   **13.52**

13.53 In many cases, the risk of dissipation will speak for itself. But of relevance will be the nature of the allegations against the respondent; whether or not those allegations have been proven (and therefore impact upon his credibility and integrity as a result); the ease with which the assets can be transferred, including whether or not the respondent has any bank accounts or connections overseas; and whether or not he has attempted to deal with his assets in the past. His cooperation with the authorities may also be relevant, particularly if he has a history of either evading court orders or failing to cooperate. The respondent's geographical location may also be a factor: a defendant who is either out of the country or being detained in prison is still able to deal with his assets fairly easily through the cooperation of others, particularly (it might be said) bearing in mind the technological age in which we live.

Duty of full and frank disclosure

13.54 It is important to remember that a person applying for an injunction without notice is under a duty of full and frank disclosure of all the material facts. The grant of either a PFO (or an IRO) is a discretionary remedy, and the enforcement authority is not therefore entitled to either order as of right. Accordingly, it is very important that the evidence put before the court should be as complete as possible and should demonstrate compelling reasons why such relief is necessary.

13.55 In *R v Kensington Income Tax Commissioners ex p de Polignac* [1917] 1 KB 486, the court held that there was a duty on all applicants to make full and fair disclosure of all material facts. In *Siporex Trade SA v Condel Commodities Ltd* [1986] 2 Lloyd's Rep 428, Bingham J (as he then was) said:

> The scope of the duty of disclosure of a party applying *ex parte* for injunctive relief is, in broad terms, agreed between the parties. Such an applicant must show the utmost good faith and disclose his case fully and fairly. He must, for the protection and information of the defendant, summarise his case and the evidence in support of it . . . must identify the crucial points for and against the application, and not rely on general statements and the mere exhibiting of numerous documents.

13.56 In *Brinks Mat Ltd v Elcombe* [1988] 1 WLR 1350, Ralph Gibson LJ said that the duty to make full and frank disclosure encapsulated the following duties and principles:

(1) the duty of the applicant to make a full and fair disclosure of all material facts;

(2) the material facts are those which it is material for the judge to know in dealing with the application as made, materiality is to be decided by the court and not by the assessment of the applicant or his legal advisers;

(3) the applicant must make proper inquiries before making the application;

(4) the extent of the inquiries which will be proper and therefore necessary, must depend on all the circumstances of the case;

(5) if material non-disclosure is established the court will be astute to ensure that a plaintiff who obtains an *ex parte* injunction without full disclosure is deprived of any advantage he may have derived by that breach of duty;

(6) whether the fact not disclosed is of sufficient materiality to justify or require immediate discharge of the order without examination of the merits, depends on the importance of the fact to the issues which were to be decided by the judge on the application;

(7) It is not for every omission that the injunction will be automatically discharged. The court has a discretion, notwithstanding proof of material non-disclosure which justifies or requires the immediate discharge of the *ex parte* order, nevertheless to continue the order or to make new terms.

Lord Justice Slade added to the above remarks: **13.57**

> . . . the principle is, I think a healthy one. It serves the important purposes of encouraging persons who are making *ex parte* applications to the court diligently to observe their duty to make full disclosure of all material facts and to deter them from any failure to observe this duty, whether through deliberate lack of candour or innocent lack of due care. Nevertheless, the nature of the principle, as I see it, is essentially penal and in its application the practical realities of any case before the court cannot be overlooked. By their very nature *ex parte* applications usually necessitate the giving and taking of instructions and the preparation of the requisite drafts in some haste. Particularly, in heavy commercial cases, the borderline between material facts and non-material facts may be somewhat uncertain. While in no way discounting the heavy duty of candour and care which falls on persons making *ex parte* applications, I do not think the application of the principle should be carried to extreme lengths. In one or two other recent cases coming before this court, I have suspected signs of a growing tendency on the part of some litigants against whom *ex parte* injunctions have been granted or of their legal advisers to rush to the *R v Kensington Income Tax Commissioners* (1917) 1 KB 486 principle . . . alleging material non-disclosure on sometimes rather slender grounds, as representing substantially the only hope of obtaining the discharge of injunctions in cases where there is little hope of doing so on the substantive merits of the case or on the balance of convenience.

In *Director of the Assets Recovery Agency v Satnam Singh* [2004] EWHC Admin 2335 **13.58** McCombe J considered the above authorities (at para 42 of the judgment) and the duty upon the Director to make full and frank disclosure at the time of a without notice hearing (in *Singh* the court was considering an application for an IRO). Having considered the authorities, His Lordship found that there had been a failure to disclose certain things to the court, but that this did not afford grounds to discharge the order. He stated he considered it a situation to which the remarks of Slade LJ in *Brinks Mat* were particularly applicable. The non-disclosure was attributable to an innocent lack of knowledge on the part of the Director and her advisers and the order should therefore be maintained. He did, however, adopt the procedure established in *Interoute Telecommunications (UK) Ltd v Fashion Gossip Ltd* The Times, 10 November 1999, which establishes that the applicant should provide to the respondent a note of what has taken place during the *ex parte* hearing. McCombe J stated (para 47):

> For the future, I can see no reason why the common practice in relation to without notice applications in the High Court should not be followed in cases of this type, unless the judge hearing the application expressly decides that, for good reason, a note should not be served on affected parties and provided that that decision is recorded on the face of the order, so that all affected parties may know that the decision also is susceptible to the customary permission to apply to vary or discharge the order.

It follows that if the enforcement authority is going without notice for an application, it **13.59** is important that notes are made during the hearing and that those notes are provided to any party affected by the injunction. In *Interoute* Lightman J said that this was essential so that each party might know exactly what had occurred, and the basis for granting the injunction, in order to be able to make an informed application for discharge. It should also be noted that the duty to provide full notes applies regardless of whether the respondent asks for them (see *Thane Investments Ltd v Tomlinson* The Times, 10 December 2002 (ChD)). (While these cases relate to freezing orders one can see that there must be an overlap between the jurisdictions and it is submitted that they represent good practice in relation to applications for both PFOs and IROs.)

13.60 The reasoning of McCombe J in *Singh* was adopted by Coghlin J in *Director of the Assets Recovery Agency v Gerard Malachy Keenan* (NIHC, 23 September 2005) (para 23). See also *Jennings v CPS* [2005] 4 All ER 391 for full and frank disclosure in relation to restraint orders.

Criteria for granting a PFO

13.61 The court may make a PFO if it is satisfied that the conditions in s 245A(5), and where applicable s 245A(6) are met. Section 245A(5) states:

The first condition is that there is a good arguable case
(a) that the property to which the application for the order relates is or includes recoverable property, and
(b) that if any of it is not recoverable property, it is associated property.

Section 245A(6) reads:

The second condition is that, if
(a) the property to which the application for the order relates includes property alleged to be associated property, and
(b) the enforcement authority has not established the identity of the person who holds it, the authority has taken all reasonable steps to do so.

Once again, these conditions mirror those that relate to an application for an IRO under s 246 of the Act.

13.62 Whilst the expression 'good arguable case' is not defined in the Act, it is a familiar expression to practitioners seeking injunctions under the freezing order scheme. In *The Niedersachsen* [1983] 2 Lloyd's Rep 600, 605A it was held a good arguable case related to the merits of the substantive claim and the evidence as a whole.

13.63 In *Derby & Co Ltd v Weldon (No 1)* [1990] 1 Ch 48 (CA) Parker LJ stated that a freezing injunction would only be made if the applicant could demonstrate that: (1) there is a good arguable case; (2) the respondent has assets (either in or outside the jurisdiction) over which such an order can bite; (3) there is a real risk that, if the freezing injunction is not granted, the respondent will remove assets from the jurisdiction or otherwise deal with or dispose of assets so as to render worthless any judgment subsequently obtained by the applicant.

Variation and setting aside of the PFO

13.64 Pursuant to s 245B of the amended Act, the court may at any time vary or set aside a PFO (s 245B(1)).

13.65 Section 245B(2) requires the court to set aside a PFO if it subsequently makes an IRO that applies to all of the same property which a PFO covers. Where the court makes an IRO that applies to some *but not all* of the property to which the PFO applies, it must vary the PFO so as to exclude any property to which the IRO applies (s 245B(3)). It is therefore also apparent that as a result of s 245B(3), the legislation anticipates that IROs and PFOs will not be mutually exclusive and may operate in tandem with each other.

If the court decides that any property to which the PFO applies is neither recoverable **13.66** property nor associated property it must vary the order so as to exclude the property (s 245B(4)). This subsection is directory and clearly affords the court little discretion once property has been identified as no longer being recoverable. However, before exercising any power to vary or set aside a PFO, the court must (as well as giving the parties to the proceedings an opportunity to be heard) give such an opportunity to any person who may be affected by the court's decision (see s 245B(5)) (although this subsection does not apply where the court is acting as required by s 245B(2) or (3) (see subs (6)). For practice and procedure in applying for variations, see para 13.94 below.

Exclusions and variations

The power to vary a PFO includes (in particular) power to make certain exclusions. These **13.67** include:

(a) power to exclude property from the order; and
(b) power, otherwise than by excluding property from the order, to make exclusions from the prohibition on dealing with the property to which the order applies (see s 245C(1)).

Exclusions from the prohibition on dealing with the property to which the order applies **13.68** may also be made when the order is made. Such exclusions may make provision for the purpose of enabling any person to:

(a) meet his reasonable living expenses; or
(b) carry on any trade, business, profession, or occupation.

However, such an exclusion may be made subject to conditions (see s 245C (2) to (4)). Section 245C(5) states that where the court exercises the power to make an exclusion for the purpose of enabling a person to meet legal expenses that he has incurred, or may incur, in proceedings under this part of the Act (note, not legal expenses in relation to other proceedings), it must ensure that the exclusion:

(a) is limited to the reasonable legal expenses that the person has reasonably incurred or that he reasonably incurs,
(b) specifies the total amount that may be released for legal expenses in pursuance of the exclusion, and
(c) is made subject to the required conditions (see section 286A (below)) in addition to any conditions imposed under sub-section (4).

The court has a discretion in deciding whether to make an exclusion for the purpose of **13.69** enabling a person to meet legal expenses and in exercising that discretion it:

(a) must have regard (in particular) to the desirability of the person being represented in any proceedings under Pt 5 of the Act in which he is a participant, and
(b) must, where the person is the respondent, disregard the possibility that legal representation of the person in any such proceedings might, were an exclusion not made, be funded by the Legal Services Commission.

13.70 The test the court is likely to apply was set out by Stanley Burnton J in *Director of the Assets Recovery Agency v Creaven* [2005] EWHC Admin 2726. For practice and procedure in applying for such an exclusion, see para 13.223 below.

13.71 The issue of obtaining funding from frozen assets to meet legal expenses is considered in detail at para 13.210 *et seq.* below.

The legislative steer

13.72 What can be described as a 'legislative steer' is found at s 245C(8), where the amended Act states that the power to make an exclusion must, subject to s 245C(6), be exercised with a view to ensuring, so far as practicable, that the satisfaction of any right of the enforcement authority to recover the property obtained through unlawful conduct is not unduly prejudiced. (Section 245C(8) does not apply where the court is acting as required by s 245B(3) or (4), (see s 245C(9).)

13.73 It is perhaps worthy of note that whilst judicial precedent is sometimes useful when looking at freezing orders/Mareva injunctions and considering them in the light of the PFO powers, it must be borne in mind that, unlike the freezing order jurisdiction, POCA contains this legislative steer that courts are required to consider. Courts are also likely to have regard to the overall purpose of the Act: namely to recover the proceeds of crime. So, for example, whilst in *PCW (Underwriting Agencies) Ltd v Dixon* [1983] 2 All ER 158 (QBD) Lloyd J stated 'justice and convenience require that [the frozen respondent] should be able to pay his ordinary bills and continue to live as he has been accustomed to live before' the same considerations may not necessarily apply in a POCA matter.

13.74 See para 13.191 below for further on the legislative steer.

Restriction and staying of other proceedings

13.75 Under s 245D, while a PFO has effect, the court must stay any action, execution, or other legal process in respect of the property to which the order applies and no distress may be levied against the property to which the order applies except with the leave of the court and subject to any terms the court may impose.

13.76 Similarly, under s 245D(2), if a court (whether the High Court or any other court) in which proceedings are pending in respect of any property is satisfied that a PFO has been applied for or made in respect of the property, it may either stay the proceedings or allow them to continue on any terms it thinks fit.

13.77 If a PFO applies to the tenancy of any premises, no landlord or other persons to whom rent is payable may exercise the right of forfeiture by peaceable re-entry in relation to the premises in respect of any failure by the tenant to comply with any terms or conditions of the tenancy, except with the leave of the court and subject to any terms the court may impose (see s 245D(3)).

13.78 Before exercising any power conferred by s 245D of POCA, the court must (as well as giving the parties to any of the proceedings concerned an opportunity to be heard) give such an opportunity to any person who may be affected by the court's decision.

Further SOCPA amendments

Schedule 6 to SOCPA makes various amendments to legislation affected by the changes it **13.79** introduces. Section 27A(3) of the Limitation Act 1980 (time limits for bringing proceedings for recovery orders) inserts para (aa) to include an application made for a PFO. POCA is further amended by paras 4 *et seq* of Sch 6 to SOCPA to incorporate, where appropriate, property freezing orders into the legislation. See, eg, s 248 which is amended at subs (1)(a) to read 'Property freezing orders, and in relation to interim receiving orders' to allow for PFOs to be registered at Land Registries.

Similarly, paras 16 and 17 of Sch 6 amend ss 271(4) and 272(5) to allow certain payments **13.80** to trustees for civil recovery to be reduced to take into account any loss caused by PFO's and/or to compensate for any loss caused by PFOs (see also para 19 in relation to s 283).

Paragraph 20 of Sch 6 to SOCPA also inserts after s 286 of POCA new conditions in relation **13.81** to legal expenses excluded from freezing. Section 286A allows for the Lord Chancellor to make regulations specifying the conditions which exclude legal expenses from being frozen pursuant to ss 245C(5) or 252(4) and those conditions may restrict who can receive sums released in pursuance of the exclusion (by, eg, requiring released sums to be paid to professional legal advisers) or be made for the purpose of controlling the amount of any sum released in pursuance of the exclusion in respect of an item of expenditure (discussed fully at para 13.223 below).

Ancillary orders

In *AJ Bekhor & Co Ltd v Bilton* [1981] QB 923 (CA) the Court held that it had an inherent **13.82** power to make such ancillary orders (including disclosure) as appears to be just and convenient in order to ensure that a freezing order was effective. See also *SOCA v Perry* (2009) EWHC 1960 (Admin). A draft property freezing order is found at Appendix 16.

Undertakings for damages

Under the legislation (it should be borne in mind that PFOs are creatures of statute, unlike **13.83** freezing injunctions) there appears to be no requirement on the Director to give an undertaking to pay the reasonable costs incurred by anyone other than the respondent as a result of the injunction (known as a 'Seatrain proviso' after the case of *Searose Ltd v Seatrain UK Ltd* [1981] 1 All ER 806 (QBD) in the freezing injunction jurisdiction).

PFOs: practice and procedure

The Civil Recovery Proceedings Practice Direction sets out the procedure to be followed in **13.84** relation to proceedings in the High Court under POCA.

Paragraph 2.1 stipulates that the venue for issuing applications should be the Administrative **13.85** Court. Paragraph 5.1 states that an application for a PFO must be made to a High Court judge in accordance with Pt 23 of the Civil Procedure Rules. Under CPR r 23.3 the general rule is that an applicant must file an Application Notice which must then be served on each respondent (see r 23.4).

Paragraph 5.3 of the Practice Direction allows for applications to be made without notice **13.86** pursuant to s 245A(3) of the Act, and Art 147(3) of the Order in Council (meaning the Proceeds of Crime Act 2002 (External Requests and Orders) Order 2005).

13.87   Paragraph 5.4 provides that an application for a PFO must be supported by written evidence which must:

(1) set out the grounds on which the order is sought; and

(2) give details of each item or description of property in respect of which the order is sought, including:

    (a) an estimate of the value of the property; and

    (b) the additional information referred to in para 5.5

13.88   The additional information referred to in para 5.5 requires that the written evidence must state in relation to each item or description of property in respect of which the PFO is sought:

(a) whether the property is alleged to be (i) recoverable property or (ii) associated property, and the facts relied upon in support of that allegation; and

(b) in the case of any associated property (i) who was believed to hold the property; or (ii) if the enforcement authority is unable to establish who holds the property, the steps that have been taken to establish their identity; and

(c) identify a nominee . . .

13.89   Paragraph 5.6 of the Practice Direction stipulates that a draft of the order which is sought must be filed with the Application Notice. This should, if possible, also be supplied to the court in an electronic form compatible with the word processing software used by the court.

13.90   Rule 23.8 CPR deals with situations where applications may be dealt with without a hearing, and it was not unheard of in relation to restraint orders under the Drug Trafficking Act 1994 (DTA) and the CJA 1988 for High Court judges to make orders without requiring the attendance of counsel on behalf of the prosecuting authority (see r 23.8(c) CPR). However, while some judges will be prepared to deal with PFO applications on the papers alone, many still require the attendance of counsel on behalf of the Director to explain the history and necessity of the order being applied for.

13.91   Rule 23.9 CPR deals with the service of the application and r 23.11 sets out the powers of the court to proceed in the absence of a party. Rule 23.10 does not apply to PFOs (see para 5.2).

13.92   Paragraph 5A of the Practice Direction states that where a PFO is made before a claim for a recovery order has been commenced it must:

(1) specify a period within which the enforcement authority must either start the claim or apply for the continuation of the order while it carries out its investigation; and

(2) provide that the order shall be set aside if the enforcement authority does not start the claim or apply for its continuation before the end of that period.

Exclusions when making a PFO: legal costs

13.93   Paragraph 5B.1 of the Civil Recovery Practice Direction sets out the court's power to make exclusions for the purpose of enabling a respondent to meet his reasonable legal costs so that he may:

(1) take advice in relation to the order;

(2) prepare a statement of assets in accordance with para 7A.3; and

(3) if so advised, apply for the order to be varied or set aside.

The total amount specified in the initial exclusion will not, according to the Practice Direction, normally exceed £3,000. This exclusion is dealt with in detail at para 13.227 below.

Applications to vary or set aside a PFO

Pursuant to para 7.1 of the Practice Direction an application to vary or set aside a PFO can be made at any time by (1) the enforcement authority, or (2) any person affected by the order. **13.94**

Unless the court otherwise directs or exceptional circumstances apply, a copy of the application notice must be served on every party to the proceedings and any other person who may be affected by the court's decision. **13.95**

This is an important proviso as it appears that the Practice Direction accompanying the legislation does not make any provision for return dates where applications for discharge and variation might otherwise be argued. **13.96**

Compensation

The compensation provisions within Pt 5 are considered at para 13.202 below. **13.97**

D. Management Receiving Orders

Introduction

Section 83 of the Serious Crime Act 2007 (SCA) was introduced on 6 April 2008 (SI 2008/755) and amends POCA to provide for a new type of receiver in civil recovery proceedings whose only function is to manage property subject to a property freezing order. **13.98**

The role of the management receiver is distinct from the role of the interim receiver as the latter has the additional responsibility of investigating the property that he manages and then reporting his findings to the enforcement authority and the court. The new management receiver will have no investigation function and so theoretically will have less of an influence on the progress and final outcome of the case. Accordingly, the role does not have the same level of independence and therefore can be performed by a member of staff of the enforcement authority that is pursuing the civil recovery case. **13.99**

The legislative scheme

Section 83(1) of the SCA inserts after s 245D of POCA the following provision: **13.100**

245E *Receivers in connection with property freezing orders*
(1) Subsection (2) applies if—
    (a) the High Court makes a property freezing order on an application by an enforcement authority, and
    (b) the authority applies to the court to proceed under subsection (2) (whether as part of the application for the property freezing order or at any time afterwards).
(2) The High Court may by order appoint a receiver in respect of any property to which the property freezing order applies.

13.101 Section 245E(4) and (5) provide that the enforcement authority must nominate a suitably qualified person for appointment as a receiver and that such a person may be a member of staff of the enforcement authority.

13.102 The term 'suitably qualified person' is not defined in the amended legislation, although in the past management receivers have been insolvency practitioners who hold accountancy qualifications.

Independence

13.103 There appears to be little requirement for the receiver to be seen as independent in this role, as it is apparent that the legislation anticipates that the appointment can be made 'in house'. This is likely to give rise to challenge, not least because a respondent may have justifiable reservations about cooperating with a receiver who is employed by the claimant pursuing his property.

13.104 Theoretically, a receiver appointed by the High Court is an officer of the court, and has historically been seen as an individual who could 'hold the ring' between the parties, (albeit defendants and respondents might greet such an assertion with some scepticism, as receivers in a management or enforcement role have generally been viewed as an extension of the State, in that they were often perceived as doing the bidding for those who sought their appointment and upon whom, to a degree, they depend for future work).

13.105 It is perhaps a reflection of this concern that s 245G(1) specifies that in terms of the supervision of the receiver, any of the following persons may at any time apply to the High Court for directions as to the exercise of the functions of a receiver appointed under s 245E:

(a) the receiver,
(b) any party to the proceedings for the appointment of the receiver or the property freezing order concerned,
(c) any person affected by any action taken by the receiver,
(d) any person who may be affected by any action proposed to be taken by the receiver.

13.106 The court may make such directions it considers appropriate, provided that the court has given the opportunity for the receiver, the parties to the proceedings for the appointment of the receiver and for the property freezing order concerned, and any other person who may be interested to be heard (s 245G(2)).

13.107 The amended Act does not limit the role of management receiver exclusively to those employed by the agency seeking the appointment, and it is apparent that an outside receiver may be appointed, or even an individual who is seconded to the agency concerned (s 245E(6) and (7)).

13.108 The purported independence of court appointed receivers is considered further at para 13.125 below.

Power to apply without notice

13.109 Pursuant to s 245E(3) an application for a management receiving order may be made without notice if the circumstances are such that notice of the application would prejudice any right of the enforcement authority to obtain a recovery order in respect of any property.

(6) The enforcement authority may apply a sum received by it under section 280(2) in making payment of the remuneration and expenses of a receiver appointed under this section.

(7) Subsection (6) does not apply in relation to the remuneration of the receiver if he is a member of the staff of the enforcement authority (but it does apply in relation to such remuneration if the receiver is a person providing services under arrangements made by the enforcement authority).

Remuneration of the management receiver

Section 245E(6) allows for the remuneration and expenses of the receiver to be met **13.110** from the realised proceeds of a recovery order, *unless* he is an employed member of staff (s 245E (7)).

The receiver's powers

The management powers of the receiver are set out in para 5 of Sch 6 (set out in Appendix 6 **13.111** of this book), and pursuant to s 245F (2), the High Court may authorise or require the receiver to exercise any of the powers mentioned therein (which includes the power of sale over property which is diminishing in value or is perishable; and the power to carry on any trade or business within the receivership estate).

In addition, the High Court has a broad discretion to order any other steps be taken in **13.112** connection with the management of the property (including securing the detention, custody, or preservation of the property concerned, s 245F(2)(b)).

Furthermore, the court may order any person in respect of whose property the receiver **13.113** is appointed to transfer or repatriate his assets pursuant to the receiver's direction or to do anything else he is 'reasonably required to do by the receiver' (s 245F(3)). What amounts to 'reasonable' in this context is not defined, although it is apparent that for the receivership to function the receiver must have some form of control over those holding the assets or property over which he is appointed, and the receiver and court will want to ensure that those assets are preserved and maintained without the repeated need to return to the court for further directions, directions that may be costly both in terms of the legal fees, but also in terms of the risk that assets will be dissipated in the intervening period.

In a similar vein, the court may order that any person in respect of whose property the **13.114** receiver is appointed should bring any documents relating to the property which are in his possession or control to a place specified by the receiver or to place them in the custody of the receiver (s 245F(4)). Subs (5) provides that 'document' means anything in which information of any description is recorded, and could therefore encompass computer records.

Whilst an individual could suggest that he was prohibited from following the receiver's **13.115** request by virtue of the extant PFO, which prevents any dealing with the property, the legislation anticipates this by incorporating within s 245F(6) a clause which permits a person to comply with the requirements imposed.

Protection for the receiver

13.116   By s 245F(7), if the receiver deals with property which is not property in respect of which he is appointed (ie property outside of the receivership estate), but at the time of dealing with it he believes on reasonable grounds that he is entitled to do so, the management receiver will not be liable to any person in respect of any loss or damage resulting from his dealing with the property concerned, except so far as any loss or damage is caused by his negligence.

13.117   This proviso gives the receiver a large degree of protection and reassurance in terms of the powers he has to operate, save for any steps he takes in relation to property outside of the receivership which could be categorised as negligent (eg failing to make proper enquiries in terms of ownership, or overlooking information that he had previously been provided with, which has led to a loss to the true owner).

Variations to management receiving orders

13.118   The court may at any time vary or set aside the powers of the management receiver or any of the directions it has set, or equally set aside the appointment of the receiver as a whole (s 245G(3)).

13.119   Before exercising this power the court must ensure that the relevant parties have been given an opportunity to be heard, including the receiver, the parties to the proceedings, and any other person affected by the court's decision (s 245G(4)).

Practice and procedure

13.120   The Civil Recovery Proceedings Practice Direction sets out the procedural steps that relate to applications for management receiving orders. Pursuant to para 5.1, the applications must be made to a High Court judge in accordance with CPR Pt 23.

13.121   The right to go without notice set out by s 245E(3) is confirmed by para 5.3, and para 5.6 requires the applicant to file a draft of the order sought at the time the application is made.

13.122   Applications for directions are provided for by paras 6.1 and 6.2 of the Practice Direction, and equally the procedure to be followed for applications to vary or set aside the order are set out in paras 7.1 and 7.2. Unless exceptional circumstances apply, in both cases the application must be served on all parties to the proceedings, including the receiver, the enforcement authority, and any other person who may be affected by the court's decision.

E. Interim Receiving Orders

The role of the interim receiver

13.123   The role of the interim receiver is two-fold. Firstly, there is a management role which is to secure the detention, custody, or preservation of property to which the order applies (s 247(1)) (similar to that of a management receiver appointed while a restraint order is extant). Secondly, there is an investigative role whereby the interim receiver should investigate on behalf of the court: (a) whether the property to which the order applies is recoverable property; and (b) whether there is any other recoverable property (related to the same unlawful conduct) and, if there is, who holds it (see s 247(2)).

In *Director of the Assets Recovery Agency v Wilson and Wilson* [2007] NIHC (HIGF5852)   **13.124**
Higgins J observed (at 10):

> The role of the interim receiver is that of a court-appointed expert to investigate the origin
> and ownership of assets and to report to the court on those assets. In the absence of evidence
> to the contrary, such a report will be compelling evidence in any application based upon it.
> Its detailed contents relating to accountancy matters are accepted as fact unless shown
> otherwise.

The status and independence of the interim receiver

Interim receivers should be considered independent officers of the court. It is the court that   **13.125**
appoints them. Their independence is underlined in that the Act stipulates they must not
be a member of the enforcement authority's staff. The interim receiver is under a duty to
report to *the court* any material change in circumstances (s 255(1)). It is the court that
determines the receiver's powers on a case-by-case basis within the framework prescribed
by s 247 and Sch 6 to POCA. At any time, the interim receiver can apply to the court for
directions as to the exercise of his powers (s 251(1)). Only the court is able to direct an
interim receiver, and it follows that he or she should be beyond the direction of the parties.
In addition, the court may vary or set aside an IRO at any time (s 251(2)). It will also be
noted that there is no requirement for an independent person to supervise when the interim
receiver is exercising the powers conferred by Sch 6.

Once an IRO is made, the relevant director is deemed no longer to be carrying on a civil   **13.126**
recovery investigation (s 341(3)(b)). While the director may still receive information by
virtue of the gateway provisions in Pt 10 of POCA, in practice it is generally the position
that the investigation will cease on the granting of an IRO. The imposition of the investigative function upon the interim receiver confers a unique role amongst receivers in UK
jurisprudence. A vital aspect of the scheme is that the interim receiver is not a witness for
the enforcement authority and is not supervised by the enforcement authority. He is the
court's investigator and it can be expected that the report will be used to determine which
issues can be agreed and which remain in dispute.

In *The Director of the Assets Recovery Agency v Jackson* [2007] EWCA (QB) 2553 King J said: **13.127**

> 29. It is obviously clear from this legislative framework and these statutory provisions gov-
> erning the appointment of the Receiver and her investigative and reporting functions under
> the supervision of the court rather than the Director, that the Receiver is not the agent of any
> of the parties. In my judgment, she is kin to an officer of the court and is reporting and giving
> evidence to the court in that capacity independent of the parties. It is further obviously right
> that the Receiver's report should be used in advance of the final hearing as a means by which
> to establish such facts as can be agreed between the parties and to identify the matters in
> dispute in need of resolution by the court. Further, in principle, I am prepared to accept that
> the Receiver's findings as to recoverable property should be given considerable persuasive
> weight by the court and to that extent her report enjoys special status.
>
> 30. However, this said, I also agree with the respondent's submissions that the Receiver's
> findings of recoverable property are not binding on the court, that it is the primary evidential

material underlying her finding and said by her to justify them, which is of crucial importance together with any additional evidence called before the court and that it is the duty of the court, in determining any area of dispute between the parties carefully to scrutinise and weigh that evidence in order to determine whether the claim to recoverable property is made out . . . The statutory provisions referred to do not alter either the burden or standard of proof which is upon the claimant to establish the existence of recoverable property on the balance of probabilities by cogent evidence. The findings of the receiver do not in themselves reverse the burden of proof so as to put any onus on the respondent to disprove her findings . . .

Challenging the findings of the interim receiver

13.128 If a party wishes to dispute the correctness of the findings of an interim receiver, they should in the first instance notify the receiver in writing of the matter that they take issue with for the receiver to consider. Similar considerations apply where a party believes that a receiver has taken account of evidence which is either not relevant or is incorrect. Thereafter the interim receiver should either reply in writing or prepare a further report for the court. Whether it is desirable for interim receivers to meet with the parties in the absence of the other parties is a moot point. Clearly there will be occasions where it is appropriate to give the other party notice that a meeting is going to take place and to invite their observations and/or attendance. On the other hand, to require a third party to attend on every occasion will not only lead to additional costs for that party, as well as potential inconvenience, but may well inhibit the subject matters that need to be discussed. The interim receiver is not acting as mediator, but is trying to establish the facts in order to report them to the court. The minutes of any such meeting, if a party has not attended, can thereafter be circulated, subject to the agreement of the party attending.

13.129 Occasionally, respondents may wish to appoint their own forensic accountant or expert witness to deal with issues that arise. For funding in relation to the same, see para 13.247 below.

Applications for an IRO

13.130 Where the enforcement authority is considering taking proceedings for a recovery order in the High Court, the relevant director may apply to the court for an IRO (whether before or after starting proceedings) (see s 246(1)). An example of such an order is found at Appendix 15.

13.131 An application for an IRO may be made without notice if the circumstances are such that notice of the application would prejudice any right of the enforcement authority to obtain a recovery order in respect of any property (see s 246(3)), for example, because of the risk of dissipation (see para 13.52 above).

13.132 It is a requirement of s 247(2) that an IRO must require the interim receiver to take any steps which the court thinks necessary to establish:

(a) whether or not the property to which an order applies is recoverable property or associated property;

(b) whether or not any other property is recoverable property (in relation to the same unlawful conduct) and if it is, who holds it (s 247(1)).

Loss of power to investigate

It should be noted that up to the issuing of the claim form or until an IRO is made the **13.133** enforcement authority has access to the civil investigation powers set out in Pt 8 of POCA. Once an IRO is made or a claim form for civil recovery is issued the enforcement authority ceases to have the powers set out in Pt 8 (s 341(3)) and the duty of taking further steps to establish facts about the property is placed with the interim receiver acting under the court's direction.

The relevant authority also loses the power to obtain a disclosure order under s 357. This is **13.134** because s 391(3) provides that an application for a disclosure order must state that certain property specified in the application is subject to a civil recovery investigation. Section 341(3) provides that an investigation is not a civil recovery investigation if an IRO applies in relation to the property. Therefore the only person who can use compulsory questioning powers is the interim receiver. The enforcement authority would thus be prohibited from doing so.

Previous interim receiver investigations

In *Director of The Assets Recovery Agency v Szepietowski and others* [2006] EWHC 2406 **13.135** (Admin) The Times, 25 October 2006, the Court considered whether, on an application for the appointment of an interim receiver over certain property, an enforcement agency would be entitled to rely on information about property which had only come to light as a result of investigations conducted pursuant to a previous IRO which related to *different* wrong-doing by the proposed defendant. Silber J found it would be permissible, on the basis that:

(1) if the applicant could not use information obtained by the interim receiver relating to *different* unlawful conduct, it would undermine the 'general purposes' of the civil recovery provisions;
(2) there would be a serious loophole in the Act that would confer a form of immunity from the provisions of the Act on a wrongdoer who had property, which had been obtained through 'unlawful conduct';
(3) there was no basis at common law for restricting the use of that information in the absence of a provision in the first IRO preventing the use of the information obtained.

Purpose and conditions

Under s 246(2) an IRO is an order for: **13.136**

(a) the detention, custody, or preservation of property; and
(b) the appointment of an interim receiver.

A court may make an IRO on the application of the relevant director if it is satisfied that **13.137** either of the following two conditions is met:

(1) that there is a good arguable case that the property to which the application for the order relates is or includes 'recoverable property', and that, if any of it is not recoverable property, it is 'associated property' (see s 246(5));
(2) that if the property to which the application for the order relates includes property alleged to be associated property, and the enforcement authority has not established the identity of the person who holds it, the authority has taken all reasonable steps to do so (see s 246(6)).

If either of these conditions is met, an application can be made to the High Court to make an IRO and this may be done before the director issues a claim form for a recovery order. The application may also be without notice if the enforcement authority believes that giving notice would prejudice its right to recover the property (s 246(3)).

13.138 Often it may be necessary to apply *ex parte* in circumstances where alerting the potential parties may cause the property to be either hidden or dissipated (see para 13.51 above).

'Good arguable case'

13.139 The expression 'good arguable case' is not defined in the Act although it is already used in applications for injunctions to freeze disputed property in civil courts under the freezing injunction regime formerly known as Mareva injunctions. In *The Niedersachsen* [1983] 2 Lloyd's Rep 600, 605A it was held a 'good arguable case' related to the merits of the substantive claim and was described as 'one which is more than barely capable of serious argument, but not necessarily one which the judge considers would have a better than 50 per cent chance of success'. The courts have also observed that 'it is not enough to show an arguable case, namely one which a competent advocate can get on its feet. Something markedly better than that is required, even if it cannot be said with confidence that the Plaintiff is more likely to be right than wrong' (*Orri v Moundreas* [1981] Com LR 168, Mustill J QBD).

13.140 In *The Director of The Assets Recovery Agency and Szepietowski and others* [2007] EWCA 766, The Times, 21 August 2007 Waller LJ stated:

> the ARA must first establish a good arguable case that a certain kind of unlawful conduct occurred and then a good arguable case that property was obtained though that kind of unlawful conduct. What the ARA is not required to do is to establish a good arguable case that any property was obtained through a specific criminal offence, even of the general kind alleged. [para 26].

He added at para 28:

> . . . in considering whether a good arguable case has been established, it will be necessary to examine first whether it is arguable on the evidence that unlawful conduct of the kind asserted by the ARA has taken place i.e. mortgage fraud. Next needs to be considered whether it is arguable that the property sought to be frozen represents property originally obtained through such unlawful conduct, but not necessarily through specific examples of that conduct; and finally, if there is some evidence that property was obtained though unlawful conduct, consideration needs to be given to any untruthful explanation or a lack of explanation where opportunity has been given to provide it. An untruthful explanation or a failure to offer an explanation may add strength to the arguability of the case.

Application for an IRO: practice and procedure

13.141 Under para 5.1 of the Civil Recovery Proceedings Practice Direction, an application for an IRO must be made:

(1) to a High Court judge; and
(2) in accordance with CPR Pt 23.

Rule 23 CPR requires both written evidence in support and a draft order.

13.142 The application may be made without notice in the circumstances set out in s 246(3) of the Act (para 5.3(2)).

Under para 5.5, CPR Pt 69 (the court's power to appoint a receiver) and its Practice **13.143**
Direction apply to an application for an IRO with the following modifications:

(1) paragraph 2.1 of the PD supplementing Part 69 does not apply;
(2) the enforcement authority's written evidence must, in addition to the matters required by para-
    graph 4.1 of that PD, also state in relation to each item or description of property in respect of
    which the order is sought—
    (a) whether the property is alleged to be—
        (i) recoverable property;
        (ii) associated property,
    and the facts relied upon in support of that allegation; and
    (b) in the case of any associated property—
        (i) who is believed to hold the property;
        (ii) if the enforcement authority is unable to establish who holds the property, the steps that
            have been taken to establish their identity; and
(3) the enforcement authority's written evidence must always identify a nominee and include the
    information in paragraph 4.2 of the PD [claim form for a recovery order].

There must, under para 5.6, be filed with the application notice a draft of the order sought. **13.144**
This should if possible also be supplied to the court in electronic form. An example draft
order is found at Appendix 15.

In *R (on the application of the Director of the Assets Recovery Agency) v H* The Independent, **13.145**
8 November 2004, McCombe J held that it is important that the jurisdiction within s 246
of POCA should be exercised carefully, so that people are not wrongfully injuncted, or
injuncted for a period longer than is required. Equally, a court should not permit an individual to attack the basis upon which the order is made simply by choosing a snapshot in
time where the evidence remains incomplete and thereby 'crawl away' from the consequences of various suspicions until the investigation is complete and matters are capable of
clear resolution.

IRO made before commencement of claim for civil recovery

Pursuant to para 5A of the Civil Recovery Proceedings Practice Direction, an IRO which **13.146**
is made before a claim for a recovery order has been commenced must:

(1) specify a period in which the enforcement authority must either start the claim or
    apply for the continuation of the order while it carries out its investigations; and
(2) provide that the order shall be set aside if the enforcement authority does not start the
    claim or apply for its continuation before the end of that period.

Duty of full and frank disclosure

This is considered at para 13.54 above. **13.147**

The need for expedition

In *Director of the Assets Recovery Agency v (1) Jia Jin He (2) Dan Dan Chen* [2004] EWHC **13.148**
(Admin) 3021 Collins J commented at para 81:

> . . . It is plain that there is a need for expedition. The receiver has an obligation to report
> as soon as practicable and there is a serious interference with Mr. He's property and his
> ability to carry on business if the reality is that he is not in any way involved in criminal

conduct and it is not to be regarded as recoverable property. The matters which the receiver has to investigate are of some complexity, and it is not surprising that she has taken some time to resolve them. But the time is nigh when enquiries must be brought to a conclusion.

Other powers of the High Court

13.149 The High Court has an inherent discretion in civil proceedings to make such and any orders in law that it considers appropriate when making interlocutory injunctions (see *AJ Bekhor & Co Ltd v Bilton* [1981] QB 923 (CA)). This discretion is reflected in s 246(8) which states that the power to make an IRO is not limited by ss 247 to 255 of POCA.

Functions of an interim receiver

13.150 The enforcement authority must nominate a suitably qualified person for appointment as an interim receiver. This will usually be an independent licensed insolvency practitioner. It may not be a member of the staff of the agency in question (s 246(7)).

13.151 The IRO made by the High Court may authorise or require the interim receiver to:

(a) exercise any of the powers mentioned in Sch 6 to POCA;

(b) take any other steps the court thinks appropriate,

for securing the detention, custody or preservation of the property to which the order applies or of taking any steps under subs (2) (s 247(1)).

Contents of the order

13.152 Schedule 6 of POCA is reproduced at Appendix 6. The powers it invests in an interim receiver include the following:

(1) The power to seize property to which the order applies.

(2) The power to obtain information or require a person to answer any questions.

(3) The power to enter any premises in the UK to which the interim order applies and take the following steps:

(a) carry out a search or inspection of anything described in the order;

(b) make or obtain a copy, photograph, or other record of anything so described, and

(c) remove anything which the receiver is required to take possession of in pursuance of the order.

(4) The power to manage any property to which the order applies, including selling or otherwise disposing of assets comprised in the property which are perishable or which ought to be disposed of before their value diminishes, or where the property comprises assets of a trade or business, or incurring capital expenditure in respect of the property.

13.153 The power to sell depreciating assets remains the most controversial of these, and can include cars and other high value items. In such circumstances it is submitted that the receiver should give the respondent/owner sufficient notice of the sale to allow them the opportunity to make representations, either by correspondence or by way of an application to the High Court, if the costs of such a course are not prohibitive.

13.154 Schedule 6 also anticipates that the IRO may give the interim receiver access to any premises that he may need to enter in pursuance of Sch 6 para 3. The order may also require any person to give the interim receiver any assistance he may need for taking the steps mentioned above.

An IRO may also require any person to whose property the order applies to bring or repatri- **13.155** ate the property to a place in England and Wales specified by the interim receiver, or place it into the custody of the interim receiver (if, in either case the person to whose property the order applies is able to do so), and/or to do anything he is reasonably required to do by the interim receiver for the preservation of the property (see s 250(1)).

The IRO may also require any person to whose property the order applies to bring any **13.156** documents relating to the property which are in his possession or control to a place (in England and Wales) specified by the interim receiver or to place them in the custody of the interim receiver. For these purposes 'document' means anything in which information of any description is recorded (s 250(2)). This presumably would extend to computer files.

These 'duties of the respondent' graphically illustrate just how far-reaching the powers of **13.157** the interim receiver actually are, and that they extend to dictating the control of assets held outside of the UK.

A person who ignores or contravenes such an order would be potentially liable to **13.158** committal proceedings in the High Court for contempt (see *SOCA v McKinney* [2008] NIQB 111).

Restrictions on dealing with property

Under s 252(1) of POCA: **13.159**

An interim receiving order must, subject to any exclusion made in accordance with this section, prohibit any person to whose property the order applies from dealing with the property.

Exclusions may be made when the IRO is made or on an application to vary the order (see s 252(2)).Under s 252(3) an exclusion may, in particular, make provision for the purpose of enabling any person:

(a) to meet his reasonable living expenses or
(b) to carry on any trade, business, profession or occupation, and may be made subject to conditions.

The purpose of this section is to ensure that IROs prevent any dealing with the property **13.160** that they cover. It also anticipates that from time to time there will be exclusions to that rule. 'Dealing' with property includes disposing of it, taking possession of it, or removing it from the UK (see s 316(1)).

Any excluded property must either be specified or described in general terms in the order **13.161** (s 252(5)).

Contents of the order in terms of reporting by the receiver

Section 255(2) states that an IRO must require the interim receiver to report his findings **13.162** to the court and serve copies of his reports on the enforcement authority, and on any person who holds any property to which the order applies or who may otherwise be affected by the report. This requirement is considered in more detail at para 13.188 below.

Protection against self-incrimination

Under Sch 6 para 2(3) to POCA, any answer given by a person in pursuance of the **13.163** requirements set out in para 2 may not be used in evidence against him in criminal proceedings (see also para 2(4)(b)). However, it should be noted that contempt proceedings for any failure to cooperate or fully disclose may arise.

Protection for the receiver

13.164 Section 246(3) provides legal protection for the receiver if he mistakenly, but honestly, deals with property that is not the property specified in the order, providing that those dealings are not caused by his or her own negligence.

Applications to clarify the receiver's powers

13.165 The interim receiver, any party to the proceedings, and any person affected by any action taken by the interim receiver, or who may be affected by any action proposed to be taken by him, may at any time apply to the court for directions in relation to the interim receiver's functions. Once such an application has been made and the matter is before the court, before giving any directions the court must (as well as giving the parties to the proceedings an opportunity to be heard) give such an opportunity to the interim receiver and to any person who may be interested in the application (see s 251(1) and (2)). Such directions may be used to clarify the powers of the receiver in relation to certain property.

Applications for directions

13.166 Under para 6.1 of the Practice Direction, an application for directions in relation to the interim receiver's functions may, under s 251 of the Act, be made at any time by:

(1) the interim receiver;
(2) any party to the proceedings; and
(3) any person affected by any action taken by the interim receiver, or who may be affected by any action proposed to be taken by him.

13.167 The application must always be made by application notice, which must be served on:

(1) the interim receiver (unless he is the applicant);
(2) every party to the proceedings; and
(3) any other person who may be interested in the application.

Power to vary or set aside

13.168 The court may at any time vary or set aside an IRO (see s 251(3)). However, before exercising that power the court must give such opportunity to the interim receiver, and to any person who may be affected by the court's decision, an opportunity to be heard, including the parties to the proceedings themselves (s 251(4)).

13.169 Section 252(6) of POCA provides that the power to make exclusions to an IRO has to be exercised with a view to ensuring that the satisfaction of any right of the Agency to recover property obtained through unlawful conduct is not unduly prejudiced. The power to make exclusions to a freezing order made in support of a claim under Pt 5 should be exercised on that basis. In general a court is unlikely to permit a respondent who has property available that is not recoverable property to use property that is claimed to be recoverable property to meet his expenditure pending the hearing.

Application to vary or discharge an IRO: practice and procedure

Under the Civil Recovery Practice Direction (para 7.1), an application to vary or discharge **13.170** an IRO may be made at any time by:

(1) the enforcement authority; or
(2) any person affected by the order.

Paragraph 7.2 of the Practice Direction states that a copy of the application notice must be **13.171** served on:

(1) every party to the proceedings;
(2) the interim receiver; and
(3) any other person who may be affected by the court's decision.

In *R (on the application of the Director of the Assets Recovery Agency) v H* [2004] EWHC **13.172** (Admin) 2166, McCombe J held that since the making of an IRO was a draconian power, it was very important for the jurisdiction to be exercised carefully so that people were not wrongly injuncted, or injuncted for a longer period than was required. He added, however, it should not be permitted for any respondent, when faced with what was an inherently suspicious business activity, to 'crawl away' from the consequences of the various suspicions simply by choosing a snapshot in time when the evidence remained incomplete.

The difficulty in making an application for discharge prematurely was illustrated in *Director* **13.173** *of the Assets Recovery Agency v Molloy* [2006] NIQB 49, where Coghlin J dealt with an application to discharge in circumstances where it was suggested the ARA had not identified any relevant unlawful conduct on the part of the respondent, nor identified any property alleged to have been obtained as a result of such unlawful conduct. Coghlin J held that while no property had been specifically identified as representing the product of unlawful conduct, such identification may have been unlikely at the stage of the application he was dealing with because of extensive and complex property arrangements. He added:

> it is the specific task of the interim receiver to investigate that property for the purposes of establishing whether or not it is recoverable property ... a good deal of progress has already been made and it has become necessary to amend Sch 2 of the original receiving order so as to exclude a substantial amount of property which is no longer regarded as recoverable. However, at this stage, I remain of the view that there is a good arguable case that the property to which this interim receiving order relates is or includes recoverable property ... and, accordingly, I dismiss this application.

Non-specified recoverable property

As soon as an interim receiver believes that property not specifically referred to in the **13.174** order is recoverable then he should take steps to seize and take possession of that property. It is only by doing this that the risk of dissipation is minimised pending an application to the court to seek directions in respect of the non-specified property. Such an application therefore should be made forthwith in order to protect the interests of all the parties affected, as well as to inform the court as to what has happened. It may also be that the interim receiver will be required to give evidence and be cross-examined in relation to the property itself.

13.175   The court may then order either that the property be returned or extend the order itself to specifically include it and in so doing clarify that the newly discovered asset is potentially recoverable property. Such a conclusion is essential to the effective working of Pt 5 of POCA and its purpose of recovering the proceeds of crime.

Exclusion of property which is not recoverable

13.176   If the court decides that any property to which an IRO applies is neither recoverable property nor associated property, it must vary the order so as to exclude it (s 254(1)).

13.177   Under s 254(2) the court may (importing discretion) also exclude property providing the enforcement authority's rights to recover the remaining property is not prejudiced:

> The court may vary an interim receiving order so as to exclude from the property to which the order applies any property which is alleged to be associated property if the court thinks the satisfaction of any right of the enforcement authority to recover the property obtained through unlawful conduct will not be prejudiced.

13.178   Under s 245(3) the court may exclude any property within this section on any terms or conditions that the court thinks 'necessary or expedient'.

Exclusion of property to cover legal expenses

13.179   The issue of release of restrained funds to cover a respondent's legal costs is set out in detail at para 13.210 below.

Interim receiver's expenses

13.180   Section 99 of the Serious Organised Crime and Police Act 2005 (SOCPA) amended s 280 of POCA (Applying realised proceeds) to insert after subs (2):

> (3)   the enforcement authority may apply a sum received by it under sub-section (2) in making payment of the remuneration and expenses of
>
> (a)   the trustee or
>
> (b)   any interim receiver appointed in, or in anticipation of, the proceedings for the recovery order.
>
> (4)   Sub-section (3)(a) does not apply in relation to the remuneration of the trustee if the trustee is a member of the staff of the enforcement authority concerned.

This effectively allows for the enforcement authority to recompense the interim receiver (and the trustee for civil recovery) from sums which represent the realised proceeds of property following a successful civil recovery order claim, after payments referred to in s 280(2) of POCA have been made. This directly mirrors the manner in which receivers are paid pursuant to Pts 2 and 4 of the Act.

Interim receiverships over land

13.181   The purpose of s 248 of POCA is to ensure that where an IRO is made over land, its effect may be reinforced by taking action at the Land Registry to prevent the disposal or dissipation of the land in question. The 'Registration Acts' (namely the Land Registration Act 1925, the Land Charges Act 1972, and the Land Registration Act 2002) apply in relation to IROs as they would apply in relation to orders which affect any other land where an order is made by the court for the purpose of enforcing judgments or other pending land actions (see s 248(1) and (2)).

Section 248(3) prohibits the registering of title under the Land Registration Act 2002 in **13.182** respect of property covered by an IRO.

It should be noted that a person applying for an IRO should be treated for the purposes of **13.183** s 57 of the Land Registration Act 1925 (inhibitions) as an interested person in relation to any registered land to which the application relates (see s 248(4)).

Restriction on existing proceedings and rights

Whilst an IRO has effect, the court may stay any action, execution, or other legal process **13.184** in respect of the property to which the order applies. Nor may any distress be levied against the property to which the order applies except with the leave of the court and subject to any terms the court may impose (see s 253(1)).

Section 253(2) allows the court in which proceedings are pending in respect of the property **13.185** to stay them or impose terms on their continuation.

Section 253(3) deals with the situation where IROs apply to tenancies on premises. A landlord **13.186** may not exercise a right of forfeiture by peaceful re-entry on a property affected by an order.

When exercising the powers conferred by s 253 the court must give the opportunity to the **13.187** interim receiver (if appointed) and any other person who may be affected by the court's decision, including the parties, to be heard (s 253(4)).

Reporting to the enforcement authority and the court

Section 255(1) reads: **13.188**

(1) An interim receiving order must require the interim receiver to inform the enforcement authority and the court as soon as reasonably practicable if he thinks that—
    (a) any property to which the order applies by virtue of a claim that it is recoverable property is not recoverable property,
    (b) any property to which the order applies by virtue of a claim that it is associated property is not associated property,
    (c) any property to which the order does not apply is recoverable property (in relation to the same unlawful conduct) or associated property, or
    (d) any property to which the order applies is held by a person who is different from the person it is claimed holds it, or if he thinks that there has been any other material change of circumstances.

The Act therefore lays a pro-active duty upon the receiver to inform both the enforcement authority and the court of circumstances where, eg, he believes that property covered by an IRO claimed to be recoverable property, is in fact not recoverable. By virtue of this section, it is submitted, there must also be on an on-going duty within the receivership to keep matters under review to ensure that s 255 is complied with.

This duty is a corollary to s 247(2) which requires the interim receiver to take any steps **13.189** which the court thinks are necessary to establish whether or not the property in which the order applies is recoverable property or associated property.

Under s 255(2), an IRO must require the interim receiver: **13.190**

(a) to report his findings to the court,
(b) to serve copies of his reports to the enforcement authority and on any person who holds any property to which the order applies or who may otherwise be affected by the report.

This formalises the receiver's duty to produce a formal report of his findings and ensure that he serves copies of that report on all those who may be affected by it. These reports may then be used as a basis to establish agreed facts in relation to disputed matters.

F. The Legislative Steer and Third Party Creditors

13.191 Section 252(6) of POCA states:

> The power [of the Court] to make exclusions [regarding the general prohibition against dealing with receivership property] must be exercised with a view to ensuing, so far as is practicable, that the satisfaction of any right of the enforcement authority to recover the property … is not unduly prejudiced.

There is a distinct contrast between s 69(2)(c) of POCA (which deals with the legislative steer under Pt 2 of the Act (restraint and confiscation)) and s 252(6) under Pt 5. This may well be deliberate and designed to reflect that one section is concerned with confiscation of a criminal's benefit, whereas the other concerns the civil recovery of property. As a result it may be inappropriate to draw too much upon the case law that has arisen in relation to, for example, the payment of third party debts/creditors, under the earlier legislation. Nevertheless, in *Serious Fraud Office v Lexi Holdings PLC (In Administration)* [2008] EWCA Crim 1443 the Court of Appeal held that restraint orders made under POCA may not be varied to permit defendants to pay off unsecured third party creditors, and it is submitted that their Lordships' reasoning therein may have persuasive application to any variations sought (outwith legal expenses) under the civil recovery scheme.

13.192 Should s 252(6) of POCA be interpreted by reference to case law in the civil law jurisdiction of freezing/Mareva injunctions? It is submitted that the answer is no, and that s 252(6) is *sui generis*. Under freezing order/Mareva injunctions a *bona fide* creditor can recover their debts. This was confirmed by Lord Donaldson in *Re Peters* at p 879, who stated:

> The interest of the potential judgement creditor has to be balanced against those of actual creditors, whether secured or unsecured, and of the defendant himself who may succeed in the action and should be fettered in his dealing with his own property to the least possible extent necessary to ensure the interests of justice are not frustrated.

13.193 In IRO and PFO matters it is appropriate for the court or the receiver to consider all approaches for the settlement of secured or unsecured debts (which are bona fide) on their merits. It would not, however, be appropriate, it is suggested, to release property from civil restraint when that property was the probable proceeds of unlawful conduct, because to do so would be to frustrate the purpose of the Act.

13.194 An interim receiver will often be able to assist the court with this question, and where a court is faced with a dispute between the receiver and a respondent (or third party) as to the proposed course of a receivership, the court is likely to give greater weight to the disinterested views of the receiver, particularly if supported by professional advice and expertise (see *Re Piper* [2000] 1 WLR 473).

13.195 Although s 252(6) may not be particularly robust, it must still be considered by the court, and the approach of the court therefore cannot be as liberal as that which a court might adopt when considering freezing order injunctions. A distinction may also be drawn in cases where the nexus to unlawful conduct has not yet been established in relation to any given asset and where the possibility at least must exist that that property will not be subject to civil recovery.

G. The Insolvent Respondent

Introduction

Receiverships where an individual has been adjudged bankrupt have always been subject **13.196** to different rules in proceeds of crime legislation—see eg s 15(2) of the DTOA and its corresponding provisions, together with s 32 of the DTA and s 84 of the CJA 1988. In such cases the powers of a receiver have never been exercisable in relation to property within the bankrupt's estate or to property that is to be applied for the benefit of creditors.

Voluntary arrangements were not similarly protected (see *Re M* [1992] QB 377 at p 381). **13.197** So a receiver could have utilised his full powers before a defendant was adjudged bankrupt under the CJA 1988 or DTA. In *Re M*, Otton J concluded that the restraint order prohibits 'any person' from dealing with any realisable property, 'This prevents the debtor from petitioning for his own bankruptcy' (p 382).

Section 311 of POCA deals with insolvency in civil recovery proceedings under Pt 5. **13.198** Proceedings for a recovery order may not be taken or continued in respect of property:

(1) that is an asset of a company which is being wound up;
(2) where the company or an individual has entered into a voluntary arrangement;
(3) where an interim trustee has already been appointed over it, pursuant to the Insolvency Acts; or
(4) where it is an asset comprised in the estate of an individual who has been adjudged bankrupt (see s 311(3) of POCA).

A potential flaw exists in that, knowing this, an individual may prefer to rack up debts/force **13.199** his petition for bankruptcy rather than be subjected to civil recovery proceedings.

Unlike the situation in *Re M*, s 311 does not merely provide for a respondent who has **13.200** actually been adjudged bankrupt, but also for individuals and companies who have entered into a voluntary arrangement under Pt 1 or Pt 8 of the Insolvency Act 1986. As a result, the diluted legislative steer in s 252 and the broadening of the categories to include voluntary arrangements has potentially made it easier for respondents to avoid civil recovery. Whether in practice individuals would pursue such a line is a moot point. Any suggestion of contrivance would be likely to be viewed dimly by the court, and might lead to the court interpreting s 252(6) in a more robust fashion.

Insolvency and IROs

In *Q3 Media Ltd* [2006] EWHC 1553 (Ch D) Rimer J considered the issue of insolvency **13.201** where an interim receiver had been appointed. The effect of a company being subject to an IRO and the supremacy of such an order was underlined. In relation to an application by a company's prospective creditor for an administration order over the company, although the court was satisfied that the company was unable to pay its debts, it was not satisfied that an order was likely to achieve the purpose of administration, as the company was subject to an IRO under s 246 of POCA. It was likely that all the company's assets were recoverable property and not available to creditors. Rimer J held that the basis of W's claim was that X were creditors and their claim was a claim in restitution, not a claim for a debt. Therefore it might be that W's claim was on behalf of prospective creditors, not creditors, and Q was waiting to see how X would make good their claim. However, in the circumstances, the court was satisfied that Q was unable to pay its debts as even if the applicants were regarded as prospective creditors, the unexplained failure to pay justified the inference that it was unable to pay. There was a good arguable case that all of Q's assets were recoverable property, given the IRO, and that Q was unable to pay its debts, so that the Insolvency Act 1986, Sch B1, para 11(A) had been satisfied. However, the court could not be satisfied under para 11(B), Sch 1 to the 1986 Act that the making of the administration order would be reasonably likely to achieve the purpose of administration, because if Q's assets were recoverable property they would be available to meet the creditors' demands. An administration order therefore was not granted at that stage.

H. Compensation in IRO and PFO Cases

Ability to claim

13.202   Where an IRO or a PFO is made by the court, and the court later decides that the property is neither recoverable property nor associated property, the person whose property it is may make an application to the High Court for compensation (see s 283(1) and s 316(1)).

13.203   The ability to claim compensation does not extend to property in respect of which a declaration has been made under s 281 (victims of theft), or in circumstances where an order under s 276 has been made (a consent order) (see s 283(2)).

13.204   Under s 272(5):

> (5) If—
>   (a) a property freezing order, an interim receiving order . . . applied at any time to the associated property or joint tenancy, and
>   (b) the court is satisfied that the person who holds the associated property or who is an excepted joint owner has suffered loss as a result of the [order] . . ., a recovery order making any provision by virtue of subsection (2) or (3) [of section 272] may require the enforcement authority to pay compensation to that person.

The criterion which the court is to apply is set out in s 272(6) and it is an amount the court thinks reasonable, having regard to the person's loss and any other relevant circumstance.

Time limit for compensation application

13.205   Where the court has decided that no recovery order should be made in respect of property the application for compensation must be made within a period of three months beginning:

> . . . in relation to a decision of the High Court, with the date of the decision, or if any application is made for leave to appeal, with the date on which the application is withdrawn or refused or (if the application is granted) on which any proceedings on appeal are finally concluded (s 283(3)(a).

If the proceedings in respect of the property have been discontinued, the application **13.206** for compensation must be made within the period of three months beginning with the discontinuance (see s 283(4)).

If, but for s 269(2) (circumstances where a right of pre-emption, right of irritancy, right of **13.207** return, or other similar right does not operate as a result of the vesting of any property under a recovery order), any right would have operated in favour of, or become exercisable by any person, that person may make an application to the court for compensation. Such an application must be made within three months beginning with the vesting referred to in s 269(2) as per (s 269(6)).

The test the court should apply

If the court is satisfied that the applicant has suffered loss as a result of the PFO or IRO, **13.208** it may require the relevant enforcement authority to pay compensation to him under s 283(5). Similarly, if the court is satisfied that in consequence of the operation of s 269, the right of the applicant can no longer be operated or exercised by him, it may require the relevant agency to pay compensation to him. (It will be noted that these are discretionary awards and will clearly depend on the facts and evidence in the case.)

The amount of compensation to be paid under s 283 is the amount that the court 'thinks **13.209** reasonable' having regard to the loss suffered and any other relevant circumstances (see s 283(9)).

I. Legal Expenses in Civil Recovery Proceedings

Introduction

Section 98 and Sch 6 of SOCPA amends POCA to allow respondents, who are subject to **13.210** civil proceedings, to have access to their frozen assets in order to fund the costs of their legal representation. Such access was originally prohibited by s 252(4) of POCA.

The amended legislation is aimed at resolving funding difficulties and allowing matters to **13.211** proceed at a faster pace. It has the advantage of avoiding frustrating delays whilst Legal Services Commission (LSC) funding is explored. Equally, it has the disadvantage that defence firms must now go to the enforcement authority and in effect make their case for funding arrangements in which the relevant authority is not only a party, but the claimant of the property concerned. The concept of what are 'reasonable' legal expenses is left somewhat open by the amended legislation. It is intended that the courts will resolve any disagreement between the parties, although one can see that this has the potential to give rise to delay, with potential arguments being made in relation to both the Human Rights Act and judicial review, particularly bearing in mind that the new legislation appears to afford employees of the relevant authority a discretion.

It is important to note that the regulations are designed to ensure that the assets can only **13.212** be used to fund what is described as 'a reasonable defence', and presumably therefore not to fund proceedings that extend or frustrate the legal process by unjustifiably diminishing the assets on legal fees. At the time of their introduction the Legal Aid Minister, Bridget Prentice, said:

> These measures will achieve a balance that will ensure that the tax payer does not foot the bill for defendants who can afford to pay their own legal costs, while also ensuring that frozen assets are not misused to fund a 'champagne defence'. They will ensure that funds are only released for legal costs where reasonable and proportionate.

In a press release issued at the time it was anticipated that the new measures would save around £3 million a year from the Legal Aid budget.

13.213 Whilst the intention of the legislation may be sound, it is suggested that Sch 6 to SOCPA which seeks to amend s 286A of POCA and the amended Practice Direction in civil recovery proceedings together with the Proceeds of Crime Act 2002 (Legal Expenses in Civil Recovery Proceedings) have made this process unnecessarily complicated. As will be seen, defence firms are expected to carry out the work and only then submit their invoices to the enforcement authority for consideration of payment. Although the regulations anticipate a controlled and staged cost plan, clearly some work undertaken will lead to other enquiries which may not be anticipated at the beginning of an application. Furthermore, a respondent's solicitors may not wish to disclose every aspect of the work that they anticipate they will carry out to the person bringing the claim against them.

Background to the new provisions

13.214 Paragraph 15 of Sch 6 to SOCPA inserts into s 266 (Recovery Orders) subs 8(A) and 8(B), which state:

> 8(A) A recovery order made by a court in England and Wales or Northern Ireland may provide for payment under section 280 of reasonable legal expenses that a person has reasonably incurred, or may reasonably incur, in respect of—
> (a) the proceedings under this Part in which the order is made, or
> (b) any related proceedings under this Part.
> 8(B) If regulations under section 286B apply to an item of expenditure, a sum in respect of the item is not payable under section 280 in pursuance of provision under section 8(A) unless—
> (a) the enforcement authority agrees to its payment, or
> (b) the court has assessed the amount allowed by the regulations in respect of the item and the sum is paid in respect of the assessed amount.

13.215 Section 280(2) (application of the realised proceeds of a recovery order) is amended by para 18 of Sch 6 to SOCPA to insert after para (a)

> (aa) Next, any payment of the legal expenses which, after giving effect to section 266(8B), are payable under this sub-section in pursuance of a provision under section 266(8A) contained in the recovery order.

13.216 Paragraph 20 of Sch 6 inserts a new para 286B into POCA which sets out the Lord Chancellor's powers in terms of making provision for the purposes of remuneration allowable to representatives for work undertaken in civil recovery cases (which he has done, see below).

The legal expenses regulations

13.217 Provision for legal expenses were introduced by the Proceeds of Crime Act 2002 (Legal Expenses in Civil Recovery Proceedings) Regulations 2005, SI 2005/3382 (as amended by SI 2008/523), which came into force on 1 January 2006 (see regulation 1).

Legal expenses at the conclusion of proceedings

Part 4 of the Regulations deals with the agreement or assessment of expenses at the conclusion of civil recovery proceedings. It sets out the procedure for determining the amount payable in respect of legal expenses once the High Court has made a recovery order which vests property in the trustee for civil recovery and provides for the payment of those expenses out of that property. If the expenses are not agreed with the enforcement authority, proceedings must be commenced for them to be assessed by the court. Part 4 applies regardless of whether interim payments have been made under Pt 3, and the amount which must be paid is reduced by the amount of any interim payments. **13.218**

Regulation 12 applies where a person seeks the enforcement authority's agreement to the payment of a sum in respect of his legal expenses pursuant to s 266(8B)(a) of the 2002 Act or Art 177(11)(a) of the Proceeds of Crime Act 2002 (External Requests and Orders) Order 2005. **13.219**

In determining the amount which may be paid in respect of legal expenses with its agreement, the enforcement authority must have regard to the provisions of Pt 5 of the Regulations which apply on the assessment of those expenses by the court (regulation 12(2)). Regulation 12(3) states: **13.220**

Where the enforcement authority agrees to the payment of the sum which a person seeks in respect of his legal expenses—
(a) it shall give that person and the trustee for civil recovery notice of the agreed sum; and
(b) the sum payable in respect of those expenses shall be the agreed sum.

Expenses to be assessed if not agreed

Unless the enforcement authority agrees to the payment of the sum which a person seeks in respect of his legal expenses pursuant to a provision made in a recovery order, that person must commence proceedings for the assessment of those expenses in accordance with regulation 13(2). **13.221**

Two-month time limit

Regulation 13(2) states: **13.222**

(a) In relation to civil recovery proceedings in England and Wales, [a person] must commence proceedings for the detailed assessment of those expenses in accordance with CPR Part 47, subject to the modifications that—
  (i) r 47.7 shall have effect as if it provided that he must commence those proceedings not later than two months after the date of the recovery order; and
  (ii) r 47.14(2) shall have effect as if it is provided that he must file a request for a detailed assessment hearing not later than two months after the expiry of the period for commencing the detailed assessment proceedings.

Practice and procedure

The Proceeds of Crime Act 2002 (Legal Expenses in Civil Recovery Proceedings) Regulation 2005 came into force on 1 January 2006 (SI 2005/3382, as amended by SI 2008/523). Part 2 of those Regulations set out the general conditions required before money can be released to pay legal fees. Pursuant to regulation 4 an exclusion must specify: **13.223**

(a) the stage or stages in civil recovery proceedings to which it relates; and

(b) the maximum amount which may be released in respect of legal expenses for each stage to which it relates.

13.224 If the solicitor acting for the person to whose legal expenses the exclusion relates, becomes aware that:

(a) that person's legal expenses in respect of any stage in civil recovery proceedings have exceeded or will exceed the maximum amount specified in the exclusion for that stage; or

(b) that person's total legal expenses in respect of all the stages to which the exclusion relates have exceeded or will exceed the total amount that may be released pursuant to the exclusion,

the solicitor must give notice to the enforcement authority and the court as soon as reasonably practicable. This obviously places a pro-active duty upon the solicitor and the respondent's legal advisers (see reg 5 and PD7A.8).

13.225 Where a person has incurred legal expenses in relation to a stage in civil recovery proceedings specified in an exclusion:

(a) during any period when a property freezing order or IRO has effect, a sum may only be released in respect of those expenses in accordance with Pt 3 of the Regulations;

(b) where the court makes a recovery order which provides for the payment of that person's reasonable legal expenses in respect of civil recovery proceedings, the sum payable in respect of his legal expenses shall be determined in accordance with Pt 4 of the Regulations, regardless of whether a sum has been released in respect of any of these expenses under Pt 3.

Legal expenses at the commencement of proceedings

13.226 Paragraph 5B.1 of the Civil Recovery Proceedings Practice Direction (not to be confused with the Legal Expenses in Civil Recovery Proceedings Regulations) sets out the court's power to make exclusions for the purpose of enabling a respondent to meet his reasonable legal costs so that he may:

(1) take advice in relation to the order

(2) prepare a statement of assets in accordance with para 7A.3; and

(3) if so advised, apply for the order to be varied or set aside.

As a result, when a court makes a PFO or an IRO it may also make an exclusion to enable the respondent to meet his reasonable legal costs so that (for example) when the claim is commenced: (1) he may file an Acknowledgment of Service and any written evidence on which he intends to rely; or (2) he may apply for a further exclusion for the purpose of enabling him to meet his reasonable costs of the proceedings (see PD 5B.2).

13.227 The total amount specified in the initial exclusion will not, according to the Practice Direction, normally exceed £3,000. This clearly affords both the enforcement authority and the court some latitude in relation to the amount and there may be instances where initial exclusions will exceed that figure (particularly, for example, if the respondent has to make inquiries overseas or if a preliminary hearing or conference is envisaged which require further work, or if the respondent is separated from the individual who now holds the appropriate records).

The Practice Direction also provides that when an exclusion is made for the purpose of **13.228** enabling a person to meet his reasonable legal costs, it should specify:

(1) the stage or stages in civil recovery proceedings to which it relates;
(2) the maximum amount which may be released in respect of legal costs for each specified stage; and
(3) the total amount which may be released in respect of legal costs pursuant to the exclusion (para 7A.7).

Considerations for the court

The court, in deciding whether to make an exclusion for the purpose of enabling a person **13.229** to meet legal expenses in respect of proceedings must:

(a) have regard (in particular) to the desirability of the person being represented in any proceedings under this Part in which he is a participant; and
(b) where the person is the respondent, disregard the possibility that legal representation of the person in any such proceedings might, were an exclusion not made, be funded by the LSC.

The steer set out at s 252(6) of POCA, namely that the court's power 'be exercised with a **13.230** view to ensuring that the satisfaction of any right of the enforcement authority to recover the property obtained through unlawful conduct is not unduly prejudiced', is now subject to s 252(4A).

Section 252(6) requires the court to have regard to equality arms arguments and the desir- **13.231** ability of persons being legally represented. It tells the court to disregard the possibility that legal representation might be funded by the LSC.

The amended subs (4) states: **13.232**

Where the court exercises the power to make an exclusion for the purpose of enabling a person to meet legal expenses that he incurred, or may incur, in respect of proceedings under this Part, it must ensure that the exclusion (a) is limited to reasonable legal expenses that the person has reasonably incurred or that he reasonably incurs, (b) specifies the total amount that may be released for legal expenses in pursuance of the exclusion, and (c) is made subject to the required conditions (see section 286A) in addition to any conditions imposed under sub-section (3).

The issue of legal funding was considered by Morgan J in *The Director of the Asset Recovery* **13.233** *Agency v Patrick Fleming and others* [2007] NIQB 16. His Lordship indicated that for an exclusion to be made in respect of legal expenses:

1. The defendants must file an affidavit containing a statement of assets.
2. The court must be satisfied that the defendants had no other assets, beyond those subject to the IRO, available to them to discharge their legal expenses.
3. The court must have regard in particular to the desirability of the person being represented in proceedings under part 5 of the Act.
4. Subject to section 252(4A) the power to make exclusions must be exercised with a view to ensuring, so far as practicable, that the satisfaction of any right of the enforcement authority to recover the properly obtained through unlawful conduct is not unduly prejudiced.
5. The exclusion must be limited to the legal expenses that are reasonable.
6. The exclusion must be limited to reasonable legal expenses that must have been or will be reasonably incurred.

7. The exclusion must specify the stage or stages in civil recovery proceedings to which it relates.

8. The exclusion must specify the maximum amount which may be released in respect of legal expenses for each stage to which the exclusion relates and the total for the entire exclusion if it covers more than one stage.

9. Any question over the amount of an exclusion for a reasonable legal expenses should normally be referred to the Taxing Master.

10. The defendant shall then comply with the procedure set out in the 2005 regulations for payment and notification.

Practice and procedure: Part 3 of the regulations

13.234 Part 3 sets out the procedure for the release of frozen property to make interim payments of legal expenses during civil recovery proceedings. Once expenses have been incurred, the person may seek the enforcement authority's agreement to the release of an interim payment in respect of those expenses. The amount which may be released is the amount which the relevant agency agrees or 65 per cent of the amount claimed, whichever is the greater.

13.235 A request for the enforcement authority's agreement to the release of a sum in respect of legal expenses must be made in writing to the relevant agency by the person to whose expenses the exclusion relates (see regulation 8).

13.236 The request must describe the stage or stages in the civil recovery proceedings in relation to which the legal expenses were incurred; summarise the work done in connection with each stage; be accompanied by any invoices, receipts, or other documents which are necessary to show that the expenses have been incurred; and identify any item or description of property from which the person making the request wishes the sum to be released.

13.237 A person may not make a request under this regulation in respect of legal expenses which he has not yet incurred; or more than once in any two-month period.

The enforcement authority's response

13.238 Pursuant to regulation 9, the enforcement authority is required to respond to a request to release legal fees not later than 21 days after it receives the request and such a response must set out:

(a) whether it agrees to the release of the requested sum; and
(b) if it does not agree to the release of the requested sum:
    (i) the amount (if any) which it agrees may be released; and
    (ii) the reasons for its decision.

13.239 Where an IRO applies to the property from which it is proposed that the requested sum should be released, the enforcement authority must at the same time send copies of the request and the notice referred to in regulation 9(1) to the interim receiver.

13.240 In determining the amount which may be released in respect of legal expenses with its agreement, the enforcement authority must have regard to the provisions of Pt 5 of the Regulations, which set out the basis for assessment of legal expenses and which apply on the assessment of those expenses by the court (regulation 9(3)).

Release of an interim payment

Pursuant to the Legal Expenses Regulations (regulation 10), the sum which may be released **13.241** is the greater of:

(a) the amount which the enforcement authority agrees may be released; and
(b) 65 per cent of the requested sum.

The sum may only be released to (i) the solicitor who is instructed to act in the civil recovery proceedings for the person to whose legal expenses the exclusion relates; or (ii) where appropriate, to the solicitor who was so instructed when the legal expenses to which the sum relates were incurred.

There is no provision for the sum that is to be released to go to the respondents themselves. **13.242** If the enforcement authority does not agree the amount to be released, only 65 per cent of the requested sum may be released at this stage.

Evidence for the purpose of meeting legal costs

Pursuant to para 7.3 of the Practice Direction, the evidence in support of an application for **13.243** the purpose of enabling a person to meet his reasonable legal costs must:

(1) contain full details of the stage or stages in civil recovery proceedings in respect of which the costs in question have been or will be incurred;
(2) include an estimate of the costs which the person has incurred and will incur in relation to each stage to which the application relates (see precedent H of the Costs Precedent annexed to the Practice Direction);
(3) include a statement of assets containing the information set out in paragraph 7A.3 (unless the person has previously filed such a statement in the same civil recovery proceedings and there has been no material change in the facts set out in the statement);
(4) where the court has previously made an exclusion in respect of any stage to which the application relates, explain why the persons costs will exceed the amount specified in the exclusion for that stage; and
(5) state whether the terms of the exclusion have been agreed with the enforcement authority.

Ongoing opportunity

The Practice Direction goes on to say that when the court makes an order or gives directions **13.244** in civil recovery proceedings, it will at the same time consider whether it is appropriate to make or vary an exclusion for the purpose of enabling any person affected by the order or directions to meet his reasonable legal costs (see para 7A.1).

Statement of assets

The court will not make an exclusion for the purpose of enabling a person to meet his **13.245** reasonable legal costs (other than as provided for by para 5B.1) unless that person has made and filed a statement of assets. Paragraph 7A.3 defines a statement of assets as being a witness statement which sets out all the property which the maker of the statement owns, holds, or controls, or in which he has an interest, giving the value, location, and details of all such property. To that extent it is similar to a disclosure statement provided in restraint proceedings, albeit without the requirement to give details dating back six years. Such a statement must bear a statement of truth.

13.246 Paragraph 7A.3 also provides that the information given in a statement of assets under the Practice Direction will be used only for the purpose of the civil recovery proceedings. What it does not do is provide that the maker of the statement will be afforded some form of guarantee that the information that he or she supplies will not then be utilised by the enforcement authority in terms of pursuing further assets.

Legal costs and forensic accountants

13.247 In *The Director of the Asset Recovery Agency v Patrick Fleming and others* [2007] NIQB 16 Morgan J was asked by the respondent to consider making an exclusion for legal expenses in order for a forensic accountant to be employed. He indicated that the following matters should be taken into account in such applications (para 20):

(a) If a party considers that the interim receiver has not considered relevant evidence, he should first request of the receiver in writing that the matter be investigated. If this request is not met sufficiently or is not accepted then the defendant can apply to the court for a direction that the receiver so investigate.

(b) If a party considers that the interim receiver has considered evidence which is not relevant, or is incorrect, it should notify the interim receiver in writing of this view. If this request is not met sufficiently or is not accepted then the defendant can apply to the court for a direction in respect of same.

(c) If a party has taken action as above, the interim receiver should make a further report to the court stating her conclusions as to the matters raised.

(d) If a party wishes to explore the methodology or findings of a report, that party may request a meeting with the interim receiver. If such a meeting occurs, all parties should be invited and the meeting should be properly minuted for the court.

(e) If a party then wishes to challenge the methodology or findings in an interim receiver's report, that party should apply to the court for a legal expenses exclusion for the retention of a forensic accountant with an affidavit setting out in a focused way which aspects of the report it takes issue with.

(f) If a sufficiently detailed affidavit is sworn and served, the court should allow time for both the interim receiver and the other parties to make any replying affidavits they wish.

(g) Upon receipt and consideration of any replying affidavits, the court should reach a determination as to whether there are any issues on which it may be reasonable to incur expenditure for expert witnesses through a legal expenses exclusion.

(h) In reaching a decision the court may wish to hear from its interim receiver in a preliminary hearing in order to be satisfied as to whether there is any substance to the defendant's claims and also to ensure that the court's interim receiver is carrying out her functions properly.

(i) The court should set out the specific areas on which the defendant will be entitled to have his own expert witness and the exclusion orders shall specify those areas.

13.248 He added that where the court decides to make a legal expenses exclusion in respect of a forensic accountant the respondent should normally file an affidavit setting out the hourly rate of the forensic accountant who is going to do the work, the basis for that rate, the work involved in dealing with the issues, the time required to be spent on a specific issue including the time for any meetings, and the length of time envisaged in respect of evidence. Where there is a dispute in relation to these matters the court will normally rely upon the Taxing Master (para 21).

Legal expenses following the making of a recovery order

Pursuant to para 7B.1 of the Civil Recovery Proceedings Practice Direction, where the **13.249**
court:

(1) makes a recovery order in respect of property which was the subject of a property freezing order or interim receiving order; and

(2) had made an exclusion from the property freezing order or interim receiving order for the purpose of enabling a person to meet his reasonable legal costs, the recovery order will make provision under section 266(8A) of POCA or Art 177(10) of the External Requests Order.

Effectively where the court makes a recovery order which provides for the payment of a person's reasonable legal costs in respect of civil recovery proceedings, it will at the same time make an order for the detailed assessments of those costs, if they are not agreed. Parts 4 and 5 of the Regulations, Pt 47 of the Civil Procedure Rules, and r 49A of the Practice Direction on Costs apply to a detailed assessment pursuant to such an order (see para 7B.2).

Part 4 of the regulations

Part 4 sets out the procedure for determining the amount payable in respect of legal expenses **13.250**
once the High Court has made a recovery order which vests property in the trustee for civil recovery and provides for the payment of those expenses out of that property. If the expenses are not agreed with the enforcement authority, proceedings must be commenced for them to be assessed by the court. Part 4 applies regardless of whether any interim payments have been made under Pt 3, and the amount which must be paid is reduced by the amount of any interim payments.

Other assets

The court may set aside any exclusion which it has made for legal expenses or reduce any **13.251**
amount specified in such an exclusion, if it is satisfied that the person has property which the PFO or IRO does not apply to and from which he may meet his legal costs (Practice Direction 7A.4).

Costs judge assessment

Where there is dispute, the court will normally refer to a costs judge any question relating **13.252**
to the amount which an exclusion should allow for reasonable legal costs in respect of proceedings or a stage of the proceedings (Practice Direction 7A.5).

Basis for assessment of legal expenses

Part 5 of the Legal Expenses Regulations provides that the court is to assess legal expenses **13.253**
on the standard basis. It also specifies the hourly rates of remuneration which may be allowed in respect of work done by legal representatives. Higher rates may be allowed for cases involving substantial novel or complex issues of law or fact, and the rates are increased for legal representatives whose offices are situated in certain London postal code areas and districts.

Pursuant to regulation 16, the court must give effect to (a) any provision made in the **13.254**
recovery order for the purpose of enabling a person to meet his reasonable legal expenses in

civil recovery proceedings; and (b) subject to subpara (a), the terms of any exclusion made for the purpose of enabling that person to meet those legal expenses (including the required conditions).

13.255   The standard basis of assessing a person's legal expenses is set out in CPR r 44.4.

13.256   Remuneration for work done by a legal representative may only be allowed by the appropriate hourly rate shown in the table below:

Rates of remuneration for legal representatives

Solicitors and their employees		
Senior solicitor (of at least 8 years' standing)	£187.50	£225.00
Solicitor (of at least 4 years' and less than 8 years' standing)	£150.00	£187.50
Junior solicitor (of less than 4 years' standing)	£107.50	£131.25
Trainee solicitor, paralegal, or other fee earner	£75.00	£93.75
Counsel		
Queen's Counsel	–	£275.00
Senior junior counsel (of at least 10 years' standing)	£150.00	£225.00
Junior counsel (of less than 10 years' standing)	£100.00	£150.00

13.257   Several points arise from this table. Firstly, in relation to England and Wales, a reference to a number of years' standing as a solicitor or counsel is to be interpreted as referring to the number of years of general qualification within the meaning of the Courts and Legal Services Act 1990.

13.258   Secondly, the higher hourly rates as specified in the third column may only be allowed where the case involves substantial novel or complex issues of law or fact. These are not defined further in the Regulations; however, most courts will be adept at recognising same.

13.259   Thirdly, the rates specified in the table can be increased by 20 per cent for legal representatives whose offices are situated in central London, namely EC1–4, SW1, W1, and WC1–2, and increased by 10 per cent for legal representatives whose offices are situated in outer London (meaning all other post code districts and post code areas including BR, CR, DA, E, N, NW, SE, SW, UB, and W).

13.260   Fourthly, it is perhaps indicative of the current climate that there has been no movement in the fees since the rates were introduced over four years ago.

Civil legal aid

13.261   It is important to note that civil legal aid remains available for cases where access to assets is not possible.

14

CIVIL RECOVERY: RECOVERY ORDERS; THE ECHR; AND TAXATION

A. Introduction

14.01 For ease of reference we have divided civil recovery into two parts. In this chapter we consider recovery orders themselves; the European Convention on Human Rights (ECHR); the pension provisions; and the Pt 6 taxation powers.

14.02 In the previous chapter we gave an overview of the legislation in relation to civil recovery and considered the interim measures anticipated by the amended Act, namely Property Freezing Orders (PFOs), Management Receiving Orders (MROs), and Interim Receiving Orders (IROs), together with the provisions for the release of funds to cover legal expenses in civil recovery cases.

The purpose of civil recovery

14.03 The purpose of the legislation was considered in *R (on the application of the Director of the Assets Recovery Agency) v Ashton (Paul)* [2006] EWHC (Admin) 1064, where Newman J stated (at para 41):

> What, in my judgment, Parliament is here doing is seeking to enforce some measure of recovery for the benefit of the State. It is seeking to make a recovery for the State which is in the public interest of the State, so that the proceeds of crime should not be at large in society for the benefit of those who happen to be in possession of it at the time.
>
> Crime, when it is committed, is not simply a crime against the individual victim of the crime. Crime, when it occurs, is an offence against the good order of the State and, apart from the victim, it puts the State to enormous expense to resolve questions in connection with [it].

14.04 In *Director of the Assets Recovery Agency v Creaven* [2005] EWHC Admin 2726, [2006] 1 WLR 622, Stanley Burnton J held that it was the clear policy of the Act to deprive respondents of property obtained through unlawful conduct (unless they could establish a statutory defence), and for that property to be transferred for the benefit of the community.

The reduction of crime

14.05 Section 2A of the Proceeds of Crime Act 2002 (POCA) (as amended by the Serious Crime Act 2007, ss 74(2) and Sch 8 (para 124) and brought into force by SI 2008/755 on 1 April 2008) provides that:

(1) A relevant authority must exercise its functions under this Act in the way which it considers is best calculated to contribute to the reduction of crime.

(2) In this section 'a relevant authority' means—
- (a) SOCA,
- (b) the Director of Public Prosecutions,
- (c) the Director of Public Prosecutions for Northern Ireland,
- (d) the Director of Revenue and Customs Prosecutions, or
- (e) the Director of the Serious Fraud Office.

The various directors must have regard to guidance issued by the Secretary of State and the **14.06** Attorney-General. Importantly, pursuant to s 2A(4), that guidance must indicate that 'the reduction of crime is in general best secured by means of criminal investigations and criminal proceedings'. Section 2A(4) appears to give a steer in that it signals that criminal investigations and criminal proceedings should be seen as the preferential route for the reduction of crime. As a secondary route, POCA anticipates that where criminal investigations or proceedings cannot be taken forward, other methods, such as civil recovery, may be deployed.

B. Recovery Orders

Introduction

Proceedings for a recovery order may be taken by the relevant enforcement authority in the **14.07** High Court against any person who the enforcement authority thinks holds recoverable property (see s 243(1) of POCA).

Section 266(1) of POCA enables the court, if satisfied that any property is recoverable, to **14.08** make a 'recovery order'. Once made, the recovery order must vest the recoverable property in the 'trustee for civil recovery' (see s 266(2)). In practice this will either be the interim receiver (an insolvency practitioner) or an employee of SOCA or the agency concerned. For the recent operation of the civil recovery scheme, see the recent case of *SOCA v (1) Mathews (2) Scurlock (3) Wilson* [2009] LTL 8/6/2009.

Financial threshold

Section 287 of the Act anticipates the setting of a figure below which the relevant enforce- **14.09** ment authority will not be able to seek a recovery order. That figure has been set at £10,000 (see SI 2003/175).

Claims for a recovery order: practice and procedure

Under the Practice Direction for Civil Recovery Proceedings a claim by the enforcement **14.10** authority for a recovery order must be made using the Civil Procedure Rules (CPR) Pt 8 procedure (see para 4.1). The claim form must:

(1) identify the property in relation to which a recovery order is sought;
(2) state, in relation to each item or description of property—
- (a) whether the property is alleged to be recoverable property or associated property; and
- (b) either—
  - (i) who is alleged to hold the property; or
  - (ii) where the enforcement authority is unable to identify who holds the property, the steps that have been taken to try to establish their identity;
(3) set out the matters relied upon in support of the claim;

(4) give details of the person nominated by the enforcement authority to act as trustee for civil recovery in accordance with section 267 of the Act [or article 178 of the Order in Council in external request matters].

14.11 The evidence in support of the claim must include the signed, written consent of the person nominated by the relevant enforcement authority to act as trustee for civil recovery if appointed by the court (Practice Direction 4.4)

14.12 References to the claim form also include the Particulars of Claim when they are served subsequently (s 243(4)).

A stand-alone claim

14.13 In *Director of the Assets Recovery Agency v Creaven* [2005] EWHC Admin 2726, [2006] 1 WLR 622, Stanley Burnton J held that a claim under Pt 5 of the Act differed from both the conventional personal and conventional proprietary claim. It differed from a conventional personal claim in that it was confined to identified property, although not all of the property needed to be identified when the initial claim was brought. It differed from a conventional proprietary claim in that a respondent held no personal liability.

14.14 After an order was made the property was transferred to a trustee for civil recovery. Accordingly, a claim under Pt 5 was to be regarded as *sui generis*, a statutory creation of a special kind.

Procedure the enforcement authority must follow

14.15 Under s 243(2) the enforcement authority must serve a claim form:
(a) on the respondent, and
(b) unless the court dispenses with service, on any other person who the authority thinks holds any associated property which the authority wishes to be subject to a recovery order, wherever domiciled, resident or present.

Settlement agreements

14.16 The enforcement authority will usually be prepared to settle matters, providing that they are suitable for settlement, and the settlement does not abuse the agency's strategic aims. As a result SOCA has been amenable to see civil recovery claims settled by mediation and agreement. A draft Civil Recovery agreement may be found at Appendix 17.

Consent orders

14.17 The court may make an order staying any proceedings for a recovery order on terms agreed by the parties for the disposal of proceedings if each person to whose property the proceedings, or the agreement, relates, is a party both to the proceedings and the agreement (s 276(1)). A consent order, as well as staying the proceedings, may make provision under 276(2) for:
(a) . . . any property which may be recoverable property to cease to be recoverable, [and]
(b) make any further provision which the court thinks appropriate.

14.18 Section 280 applies to property vested in the trustee for civil recovery, or money paid to him, in pursuance of an agreement. Under s 280(2) the trustee must pay out of the sums that he receives:
(a) first, any payment required to be made by him by virtue of section 272,

(b) second, any payment or expenses incurred by a person acting as an insolvency practitioner which
   are payable . . . by virtue of section 432(10),
and any sum which remains to be paid to the enforcement authority.

(Section 432(10) states that whether or not an insolvency practitioner has ceased or
disposed of any property, he or she is entitled to payment of their expenses under s 280.)

This section should also be read in the light of amendments made to s 280(2) by the Serious **14.19**
Organised Crime and Police Act 2005 (SOCPA), which inserted subpara (aa) and allows
for payment of a respondent's agreed legal expenses (see Chapter 13).

For consent orders involving pensions, see para 14.147 below. **14.20**

A draft civil recovery order may be found at Appendix 17. **14.21**

Summary judgment

The enforcement authority is entitled to apply for summary judgment, pursuant to Pt 24 **14.22**
of the Civil Procedure Rules (CPR), in cases where the evidence lodged reveals that a respondent has no real prospect of succeeding on the claim or issue, and where there is no other
compelling reason for the case not to be disposed of before a hearing (see CPR r 24.2).

In *Director of the Assets Recovery Agency v Brian Colin Charrington* [2005] EWCA Civ 334, **14.23**
the Court of Appeal considered the position of summary judgments following a decision
of Collins J where an order for summary judgment under Pt 24 of the CPR had been
made. The genesis of the Director's claim was a seizure by Customs in June 1992 of some
£2.25 million in cash at the respondent's home, after the respondent had been arrested in
connection with the importation of very substantial quantities of cocaine into the UK.
Factually, the respondent had been an informant and had told officers at the time he was
interviewed that he had been acting as an informant and that he had been asked to launder
money from the sale of drugs. A note had been found at his premises which appeared to
corroborate this. Partly as a result of this a decision was taken that the respondent should
not be prosecuted (see para 4 of their Lordships' judgment). The burden therefore fell on
the Director to prove that the cash in question was the proceeds of crime.

The defence put forward by the respondent was that the cash represented a commission **14.24**
paid to him for his part in a legitimate transaction concerning diamonds and had nothing
whatsoever to do with the importation of drugs or laundering the proceeds of criminal
drug sales. Two statements were deployed in support of this case. Collins J held at first
instance that:

> It is a strong thing to give summary judgment without the matter being tested by the giving
> of evidence and cross-examination of relevant witnesses. But it is necessary for me to form a
> view if this application is brought before me. It seems to me that the story that is now given
> is truly incredible. Everything that was said at the material time and the note that was discov-
> ered (and I of course recognise that he now says it was a fabrication) all point in the direction
> that Charrington was indeed involved and heavily involved in these importations of cocaine
> and was laundering the money on behalf of those who were behind the importation. That is
> what he admitted, that is what he told a number of officers, that was the information that he
> himself gave in order to enable himself not to be prosecuted. At no time was the diamond
> suggestion raised until the question arose of seeking this confiscation, for want of a better
> word, on behalf of the Director of the Assets Recovery Agency.

14.25 Collins J stated that in the circumstances he had no hesitation in rejecting the evidence that was now sought to be relied upon. He said:

> I cannot imagine that any judge would believe it, were it to be put forward.

14.26 In the Court of Appeal, Laws LJ held that in his judgment, on the material before him, Collins J was not only right but 'obviously right' to dismiss the respondent's explanation out of hand for the reasons which he had given.

14.27 In *Woodstock v Director of the Assets Recovery Agency* [2006] EWCA Civ 741, however, the Court of Appeal held that where at a summary judgment stage it was not possible to say that a respondent was bound to be disbelieved, on his contention that the source of his money was loaned from friends as opposed to being from unlawful conduct, there was a triable issue that needed to be determined and in such circumstances summary judgment was not an appropriate remedy.

14.28 In *Woodstock* the respondent had been in custody for a substantial part of the period during which he had been directed to supply evidence as to his assets, and Legal Service Commission (LSC) funding had not been in place for most of that time. In their Lordships' opinion the Assets Recovery Agency (ARA) had a prima facie case that the source of the money must have been from unlawful conduct given the absence of any known legitimate source; but this needed to be balanced with the fact that the respondent also had a prima facie case that the money had been borrowed from friends.

14.29 There is nothing to prevent respondents also seeking summary judgment in a civil recovery claim (or its striking out) if the particulars of claim are not sufficiently clear or pertinent, or contain insufficient material to support the claim. However, where inferences may be drawn from the particulars, or where the pleadings were sufficiently clear, such an application would be unlikely to succeed (see *Director of the Assets Recovery Agency v Olupitan and Makinde* [2006] EWHC (Admin) 1906).

What the enforcement authority needs to prove

14.30 The purpose and object of the Act is to ensure that individuals who are enjoying the benefit of crime are deprived of its proceeds. It should be remembered that the burden of proof that the property is recoverable is with the enforcement authority, albeit on a civil standard.

14.31 In *Director of the Assets Recovery Agency v He and Chen* [2004] EWHC 3021 (Admin), Collins J held (at para 66) that the standard of proof required under s 241(3) is the balance of probabilities, a standard to which the court 'should not place a gloss upon, so as to require that the standard approaches that are appropriate in a criminal case' (confirmed in *Director of the Assets Recovery Agency v Taher* [2006] EWHC 3406 (Admin)).

14.32 Section 242(2)(b) provides that it is not necessary to show that the conduct was a particular kind, if it is shown that the property was obtained through conduct of one of a number of kinds, each of which would have been unlawful conduct. In *Serious Organised Crime Agency v Perry and Others* (2009) ACD 254(68), QBD, the Court confirmed that civil recovery proceedings may relate to property obtained as a result of unlawful conduct abroad (provided that conduct would have been criminal in the UK).

Does the enforcement authority need to establish a specific criminal offence?

The short answer is no. In the *Director of the Assets Recovery Agency v Green* [2005] EWHC **14.33**
(Admin) 3168 The Times, 27 February 2006, Sullivan J held that the director need neither
allege nor prove the commission of any specific criminal offence. However, nor should he
merely set out the matters that are alleged to constitute the particular kind or kinds of
unlawful conduct (para 47). He must prove that, on the balance of probabilities, the
property was obtained by or in return for a particular kind or one of a number of kinds of
unlawful conduct (para 50).

He also held that a claim for civil recovery could not be sustained solely upon the basis that **14.34**
a defendant had no identifiable lawful income to warrant his lifestyle:

> The purpose of the Act was to strike a fair balance between the interests of the State and
> society in general and the civil rights of the individual. If Parliament had wished the Agency
> to be able to recover property simply by alleging and thereafter persuading the court on
> the balance of probabilities that it had been obtained by or in return for some unspecified
> unlawful conduct, it could have said so, but it had not.

Sullivan J's view was approved by the Court of Appeal in *The Director of Assets Recovery* **14.35**
Agency v Szepietowski & Ors [2006] EWHC (Admin) 3228, with the possible qualification
in the judgment of Moore-Bick LJ, who said at para 107:

> . . . It is sufficient in my view for the director to prove that a criminal offence was committed,
> even if it is impossible to identify precisely when or by whom or in what circumstances and
> that the property was obtained by or in return for it. In my view Sullivan J was right therefore
> to hold that in order to succeed the Director need not prove the commission of any specific
> criminal offence in the sense of proving that a particular person committed a particular
> offence on a particular occasion. Nonetheless, I think it is necessary for her to prove that
> specific property was obtained by or in return for a criminal offence of an identifiable kind
> (robbery, theft, fraud or whatever) or, if she relies on Section 242 (2), by or in return for one
> or other of a number of offences of an identifiable kind. If, as I think, that is what the judge
> meant in paragraph 50 of his judgment, I respectfully agree with him.

Griffith Williams J considered the same issue in *SOCA v Gale and others* [2009] EWHC **14.36**
1015 and held:

> With respect to Sullivan J, I consider his second answer is too restrictive. While a claim for
> civil recovery may not be sustained solely upon the basis that a respondent has no identifiable
> lawful income to warrant his lifestyle, the absence of any evidence to explain that lifestyle
> may provide the answer because the inference may be drawn from the failure to provide an
> explanation or from an explanation which was untruthful (and deliberately so) that the
> source was unlawful.

Griffith Williams J concluded this aspect of his ruling by citing *The Director of the Assets
Recovery Agency v Olupitan* [2007] EWHC (QB) 162 (at 22); *The Director of the Assets
Recovery Agency v Jackson* [2007] EWHC (QB) 255 (at 115); and *R v Anwoir & Others*
[2008] 2 Cr App R 36 at para 21 at p 539, and finding:

> . . . that there are two ways in which the Crown can prove in money laundering offences that
> property was derived from crime—either by proving it derived from unlawful conduct of a
> specific kind or kinds or by evidence of the circumstances in which the property was handled,
> such as to give rise to the irresistible inference that it could only have been derived from crime.

What is a 'trustee for civil recovery'?

14.37   A trustee for civil recovery is a person appointed by the court to give effect to a recovery order (s 267(1)). Whenever a court makes a recovery order or a consent order under s 276, the court must also appoint a trustee for civil recovery. It is the duty of the enforcement agency to nominate a suitably qualified person for the appointment (see s 267(2)).

14.38   The person nominated is likely to be the interim receiver in situ, or an insolvency practitioner (the agencies concerned retain an 'approved' list of suitably qualified individuals and firms), or an employee of the enforcement authority. Much will depend upon the complexity and issues involved in realising the assets in question. If, for example, assets are held outside of the jurisdiction, a Trustee in the form of an insolvency practitioner is likely to be appointed, because of the jurisdictional issues involved. If, on the other hand, the realisation is a straightforward matter over a modest number of assets, the relevant authority is likely to nominate a member of its own staff, not least because it is more cost effective to do so.

What are the functions of the trustee?

14.39   Pursuant to s 267(3) the functions of the trustee are:
  (a) to secure the detention, custody or preservation of any property vested in him by the recovery order,
  (b) in the case of property other than money, to realise the value of the property to the benefit of the enforcement authority, and
  (c) to perform any other functions conferred on him by virtue of [Chapter 5].

Under s 267(4) of the Act, in performing his functions the trustee acts on behalf of the enforcement authority and must comply with any directions given by that authority.

14.40   The trustee's duty is to realise the value of the property vested in him by the recovery order, so far as practicable, in the manner best calculated to maximise the amount payable to the enforcement authority (section 267(5)).

Powers of the trustee for civil recovery

14.41   Schedule 7 of POCA sets out the powers of the trustee for civil recovery, as follows:
  (1) The power to sell the property or any part of it or interest in it.
  (2) The power to incur expenditure for the purpose of—
    (a) acquiring any part of the property, or any interest in it, which is not vested in him,
    (b) discharging any liabilities, or extinguishing any rights, to which the property is subject.
  (3)
    (a) The power to manage property;
    (b) Managing property involves doing anything mentioned in paragraph 5(2) of Schedule 6. [See Appendix 6]
  (4) The power to start, carry on or defend any legal proceedings in respect of the property.
  (5) The power to make any compromise or other arrangements in connection with any claim relating to the property.
  (6)
    (a) For the purposes of or in connection with, the exercise of any of his powers—
      (i) power by his official name to do any of the things mentioned in subparagraph (2),

    (ii) power to do any other act which is necessary or expedient.
  (b) Those things are—
      (i) holding property,
     (ii) entering into contracts,
    (iii) suing and being sued,
    (iv) employing agents,
     (v) executing a power or attorney, deed or other instrument.

14.42 It has already been observed that references to a recovery order include an order under s 276 (consent orders) and references to 'property vested in a trustee by a recovery order' include property vested in him in pursuance of an order under s 276 (see s 267(7)).

The 12-year limitation

14.43 Section 288 of POCA adds s 27A to the Limitation Act 1980 (LA). It deals with actions for recovery of property obtained through unlawful conduct and states that none of the time limits given in the LA apply to any proceedings under Chapter 2 of Pt 5 of POCA (civil recovery of the proceeds of unlawful conduct). Under s 27A(2):

Proceedings under that chapter [Chapter 2 of Pt 5 of POCA] for a recovery order in respect of any recoverable property shall not be brought after the expiration of the period of 12 years from the date on which the Director's cause of action accrued.

Proceedings are brought when (a) a claim form is issued, or (b) an application is made for an interim receiving order, whichever is the earlier.

14.44 The application of the 12-year rule was considered in *The Director of The Assets Recovery Agency v Szepietowski and others* [2007] EWCA 766 (para 18) The Times, 21 August 2007. Importantly, the Court held that the burden was on the respondent to persuade the Court that a limitation defence had such good prospects of success that it fatally undermined the Director's case. In *Szepietowski*, by failing to provide an explanation for the source of the funds used, the respondent had provided no relevant dates by reference to which the limitation point could at an interim stage be decided (para 42). The Court of Appeal held that s 32(1)(b) of the LA applied and that concealment from the ARA during the course of an investigation would lead to the limitation period recommencing on discovery of the concealment (or when the matter concealed could have been discovered with reasonable diligence) (para 58). (The application of s 32 LA was further endorsed in *SOCA v Gale and others* [2009] EWHC 1015 at para 145.)

Can civil recovery powers be used retrospectively?

14.45 The answer appears to be yes. Retrospectivity is made express by s 316(3) of POCA. This subsection was considered in the judgment of Waller LJ in the case of *The Director of The Assets Recovery Agency v Szepietowski and others* [2007] EWCA 766 (para 18) The Times, 21 August 2007.

14.46 Further, the powers can be used prior to the creation of the enforcement authority, subject to the limitation issue outlined above. Provided the property is recoverable the identity of the enforcement authority is irrelevant. The allocation of the claimant does not qualify the cause of action.

Rights of pre-emption

14.47   Under s 269 of POCA, recovery orders take precedence and have effect in relation to any property, even in circumstances where provision (of whatever nature) would otherwise prevent, penalise, or restrict the vesting of the property.

14.48   The right of pre-emption, the right of irritancy, the right of return, or other similar rights do not operate or become exercisable once property has been vested under a recovery order. (Section 269(2) defines a right of return as any right under a provision for the return or aversion of property in specified circumstances.)

14.49   It follows that a person who has the first right to buy a property when it changes hands will not be able to exercise his right to prevent the vesting of recoverable property in the trustee. He should, however, have first right to buy the property when the trustee comes to sell it (s 269(3)).

14.50   Under s 283(6), if a person holding any such right suffers a loss as a result of the property vesting in the trustee, he is entitled to apply to the court for compensation and the court may order compensation to be paid (s 283(8)).

The vesting of recoverable property

14.51   By s 266(8) a recovery order may impose conditions about the manner in which the trustee for civil recovery deals with the property vested for the purpose of realising it, and under s 266(7) a recovery order may sever any property. It should be noted that s 266 is subject to both s 270, which deals with associated and joint property (below) and sections 271 to 278, which deal with associated and joint property, payments in respect of pension schemes, consent orders, and limits on recovery.

Associated and joint property

14.52   Section 271 of POCA (agreements about associated and joint property) and s 272 (associated and joint property: default of agreement) apply if the court makes a recovery order in respect of any recoverable property which falls into the following four categories (see s 270(1) to (3)):

(a) the property to which the proceedings relate includes property which is associated with the recoverable property and is specified or described in the claim form, and
(b) if the associated property is not the respondent's property the claim form or application form has been served on the person whose property it is or the court has dispensed with service,
(c) the recoverable property belongs to joint tenants, and
(d) one of the tenants is an excepted joint owner.

14.53   Sections 270 to 272 have been created because joint tenants are, as a matter of law, treated as though they are the single owner of the property in issue. That would also include joint bank accounts or real property held jointly.

'Excepted joint owner'

14.54   Under s 270(4) which came into force on 30 December 2002 (SI 2002/3015):

> An excepted joint owner is a person who obtained the property in circumstances in which it would not be recoverable as against him; and references to the excepted joint owner's share of the recoverable property are to so much of the recoverable property as would have been his if the joint tenancy had been severed.

For a definition of associated property, see s 245 and para 13.37 of Chapter 13.

Associated and joint property: agreements

Section 271 is intended to deal with situations where an agreement can be reached with the **14.55** enforcement authority to permit a person to make a payment to the trustee rather than vesting property in the trustee.

Where s 271 of POCA applies, and the enforcement authority and the person who holds **14.56** the associated property who is the excepted joint owner agree, the recovery order may, instead of vesting the recoverable property in the trustee for civil recovery, require the person who holds the associated property or who is the excepted joint owner to make a payment to the trustee (s 271(1)).

A recovery order which includes such a requirement may, so far as is required for giving **14.57** effect to the agreement, include provision for vesting, creating, or extinguishing any interest in property. In effect, the joint owner is buying out the interest the enforcement authority has in the property.

Associated and joint property: calculating the amount

The amount to be paid is the amount which the enforcement authority and the person who **14.58** holds the associated property (or who is the excepted joint owner) agree represents:

(a) in a case within s 270(2), the value of the recoverable property;
(b) in a case within s 270(3), the value of the recoverable property less the value of the excepted joint owner's share.

Section 270(2) deals with situations (a) and (b) mentioned at para 14.52 above. **14.59** Section 270(3) deals with (c) and (d) also mentioned at para 14.52 above (s 271(1) to (3)).

However, if an IRO applied at any time to the associated property or joint tenancy, and the **14.60** enforcement authority agrees that the person has suffered a loss as a result of the IRO, the amount of the payment may be reduced by any amount the enforcement authority and that person agree is reasonable, having regard to that loss and to any other relevant circumstances (see s 271(4)).

If there is more than one such item of associated property or excepted joint owner, the total **14.61** amount to be paid to the trustee and the part of that amount which is to be provided by each person who holds any such associated property or who is an excepted joint owner, is to be agreed between both (or all of them) and the enforcement authority.

Upon agreement, the recovery order must provide that the property concerned ceases to be **14.62** recoverable (see s 271(6)).

Associated and joint property: default of agreement

Section 272 applies where no agreement can be reached in relation to either associated **14.63** or joint property, but the court thinks it would be just and equitable to make provision concerning that property (see s 272(1)). Under s 272(2) the recovery order may provide:

(a) for the associated property to vest in the trustee for civil recovery or (as the case may be) for the excepted joint owners interest to be extinguished or,
(b) in the case of an excepted joint owner, for the severance of his interest.

14.64 In relation to s 272(2)(a) above, a recovery order may also provide:

(a) for the trustee to pay an amount to the person who holds the associated property or who is an excepted joint owner, or

(b) for the creation of interests in favour of that person, or the imposition of liabilities or conditions, in relation to the property vested in the trustee, or for both. (s 272(3))

14.65 Pursuant to s 272(4), when making provision in a recovery order under subss (2) or (3) the court must have regard to the following:

(a) the rights of any person who holds the associated property or who is an excepted joint owner and the value to him of that property or, as the case may be, of his share (including any value which cannot be assessed in terms of money),

(b) the enforcement authority's interest in receiving the realised proceeds of the recoverable property.

Section 272(4)(a) particularly acknowledges the rights of third parties and directs the court to take into account those rights.

Interests

14.66 An interest in relation to land held in England and Wales means any legal estate and any equitable interest or power. In relation to property other than land, 'interest' includes any right 'including a right of possession of the property' (see s 316(1)).

Public interest immunity

14.67 The issue of public interest immunity in civil recovery proceedings arose in the case of *Director of the Assets Recovery Agency v Personal Representative of Paul Patrick Daly (Dec'd)* [2006] NIQB 36, where Coghlin J was shown some 87 intelligence documents referred to in an affidavit. It was thereafter submitted that having carried out an *ex parte* exercise he should recuse himself from sitting as a judge for the purpose of determining the substantive recovery order proceedings. Coghlin J accepted that the concept of fairness enshrined in Article 6 of the ECHR should be considered in this context. He balanced the interests of the parties with the efficient operation of the justice system, including additional delays, expense, and frustration on the part of other litigants which were likely to result from a decision to split the function of determining disclosure from that of determining the substantive issues (paras 8 and 9). Taking those matters into account, he stated that the basic test remained that set out by Lord Steyn in *Lawal v Northern Spirit Ltd* [2004] 1 All ER 197 at para 22, namely the 'indispensable requirements of public confidence in the administration of justice'.

14.68 He observed that in *R v May* [2005] 3 All ER 523, the judge had dealt with several public interest immunity (PII) applications and then went on to deal with confiscation proceedings brought under the Criminal Justice Act 1988. In that case the appellant had relied upon the decision of the Strasbourg Court in *Edwards v UK* [2004] ECHR 39647/98. In the Court of Appeal, Keene LJ attributed considerable importance to the judge's statement in *May* that he had ignored anything revealed to him which attracted public interest immunity, and felt able to distinguish the case of *May* from *Edwards v UK*.

14.69 In *Edwards* the court was not pronouncing upon a situation in which the judge had expressly stated that he had ignored the undisclosed material for the purpose of a subsequent ruling, but had been concerned with a situation in which the judge made a determinative ruling on an issue of fact which he had decided by reference to undisclosed material. And there it seems the distinction lies. As a result, in *Daly* Coghlin J was quite satisfied that he could exclude from his consideration the reports/observations that he had been shown in *ex parte* hearings, and thus was able to go on and consider the recovery order claim.

C. Safeguards and Exemptions in Civil Recovery

Overview

Civil recovery is subject to a number of safeguards and restrictions to ensure fairness and **14.70** compatibility with relevant civil law principles. These include the following:

- Parties will have the same rights of appeal as in other High Court actions.

- There is protection for third parties who have an interest in the property in the provisions about associated and joint property (ss 270 to 272).

- Where the true owner of the property concerned comes forward during civil recovery proceedings, the property will be returned to the true owner and will not be recovered by the enforcement authority (s 281).

- Property will not be recoverable from people who obtain recoverable property where they have purchased it for full value, in good faith and without notice of its unlawful origins (s 308).

- The court may refuse or limit a recovery order if a person satisfies it that he obtained the property in good faith; that as a result of receiving the property (or in anticipation of receiving it) he took steps which he would not otherwise have taken; that when he took the steps he had no notice that the property was recoverable; and that recovery would cause him to suffer detriment as a result of those steps (s 266(3) and (4)).

- There are limits on recovery in order to prevent double recovery (ss 278 and 279).

- The court cannot include in a recovery order measures that are incompatible with rights under the ECHR (s 266(3)(b)).

- If the enforcement authority loses the case, the court will be able to award compensation for any financial loss suffered by the respondent as a result of an interim receiving order applying to his property (s 283).

- As mentioned in paragraph 11 above, there is to be a financial threshold below which civil recovery proceedings may not be pursued (s 287). This has been set at £10,000.

- There is a 12-year limitation period on when civil recovery proceedings can be brought, starting at the time the original property was generated by unlawful conduct (s 288).

- There are certain exemptions which provide that proceedings for civil recovery may not be taken in respect of certain people in prescribed circumstances (s 282, which provides an order-making power to add further exemptions). Further exemptions in relation to property are set out in s 308 and may be made by order under s 309. An order has been made under s 309 (SI 2003/336).

Exclusions, exemptions, and exceptions

14.71   Exclusions to recovery orders are provided for under s 266(3) and the court may not make in a recovery order:

(a)   any provision in respect of any recoverable property if each of the conditions in subsection (4) is met and it would not be just and equitable to do so, or

(b)   any provision which is incompatible with any of the convention rights (within the meaning of the Human Rights Act 1998).

14.72   Under s 266(4) the conditions referred to in subs (3)(a) are that:

(a)   the respondent obtained the recoverable property in good faith,

(b)   he took steps after obtaining the property which he would not have taken if he had not obtained it or he took steps before obtaining the property which he would not have taken if he had not believed he was going to obtain it,

(c)   when he took the steps, he had no notice that the property was recoverable,

(d)   if a recovery order were made in respect of the property, it would, by reason of the steps, be detrimental to him.

14.73   In deciding whether it would be 'just and equitable' to make a provision in the recovery order where the conditions set out in s 266(4) are met, the court must have regard to:

(6) ...

(a)   the degree of detriment that would be suffered by the respondent if the provision were made,

(b)   the enforcement authority's interest in receiving the realised proceeds of the recoverable property.

(See also s 308(1).) It should be further noted that the exemptions set out at s 281 (victims of theft) and s 282 (other exemptions) apply to this section of the Act.

Where the court must not make a recovery order

14.74   Under s 278(3), the court is not to make a recovery order if it thinks that the enforcement authority's right to recover the original property has been satisfied by a previous recovery order or a consent order under s 276.

14.75   If an order is made under s 298 for the forfeiture of cash, and the enforcement authority subsequently seeks a recovery order in respect of related property, the order under s 298 is to be treated, for the purposes of s 278, as if it were a recovery order obtained by the relevant authority in respect of the forfeited property. This avoids double counting and/or the proceeds of the same criminal conduct being recovered twice (see also s 282(1)).

14.76   However, by s 278(6) where the court has made the recovery order in respect of any property, s 278 does not prevent the recovery of any profits which have accrued in respect of that property.

14.77   In *Satnam Singh v Director of the Assets Recovery Agency* [2005] EWCA Civ 580, (2005) 1 WLR 3747, it was held that if an order were quashed on appeal (in *Singh* a confiscation order), eg on a technicality, the fact the order was made over the property in question once before did not prohibit the agency from making a further claim (see para 14.92 below).

The Proceeds of Crime Act 2002 (Exemptions from Civil Recovery) Order 2003, SI **14.78**
2003/336 provides that certain property is not recoverable property for the purposes of Pt
5 of POCA, eg s 27 of the Misuse of Drugs Act 1971, s 6 of the Knives Act 1997, s 43 of
the Drug Trafficking Act 1994 (DTA), s 3 of the Obscene Publications Act 1959, and s 23
of the Terrorism Act 2000, and less used statutes such as the Salmon and Freshwater
Fisheries (Protection) (Scotland) Act 1951 and other enactments. This is because these
sections make particular provision for forfeiture themselves.

Victims of criminal conduct

Section 278(8) is designed to ensure that where a victim of unlawful conduct has recovered, **14.79**
through civil litigation, property which was obtained through unlawful conduct, the
enforcement authority cannot secure an order under the civil recovery scheme for that
property (see also s 281).

Recovery orders and confiscation orders

Sections 278(9) and (10) envisage circumstances where property has been taken into **14.80**
account in deciding the amount of the person's benefit from criminal conduct for the making of a confiscation order and the enforcement authority subsequently seeks a recovery
order in respect of the same property. For the purposes of s 278(9), the confiscation order
is to be treated as if it were a recovery order. This again avoids double counting and/or the
proceeds of the same criminal conduct being recovered twice.

As stated above in *Satnam Singh v Director of the Assets Recovery Agency* [2005] EWCA Civ **14.81**
580, (2005) 1 WLR 3747, it was held that if a confiscation order was quashed on appeal
the ARA would not be prevented from making a civil recovery claim (see para 14.92 below
and s 308(9)).

Supplementary provisions to recovery

Section 279 gives examples of the enforcement authority's right to recover original prop- **14.82**
erty (meaning property obtained through unlawful conduct, s 278(2)). Section 279(2)
states:

(2) If—
    (a) there is a disposal, other than a part of disposal, of the original property, and
    (b) other property (the representative property) is obtained in its place,
the enforcement authority's right to recover the original property is satisfied by the making of a recovery
order in respect of either the original property or the representative property.
(3) If—
    (a) there is a part disposal of the original property and
    (b) other part property (the representative property) is obtained in place of the property disposed
        of, the enforcement authority's right to recover the original property is satisfied by the making
        of a recovery order in respect of the remainder of the original property together with either the
        representative property or the property disposed of.

Exemptions to the recovery scheme

Sections 281 and 283 set out exemptions to the recovery order scheme. Under s 281(1), **14.83**
where a person affected by a recovery order claims that any property alleged to be recoverable

property, or any part of the property, belongs to him, he may apply for a declaration under s 281. The court may make a declaration to the effect sought by the person claiming the property providing the following conditions are met:

(3) . . .

    (a) the person was deprived of the property he claims, or of property which it represents, by unlawful conduct,

    (b) the property he was deprived of was not recoverable property immediately before he was deprived of it, and

    (c) the property he claims belongs to him.

The person who makes the claim must have true title to the property concerned (s 281(3)(c) and s 278(8)).

14.84 If the innocent individual is successful in his application and the court makes a declaration, the property is no longer recoverable (subs (4)). Section 281 therefore gives a true owner precedence over the enforcement authority for property which, for example, has been stolen in the past. 'The court' means the High Court (see s 316(1)).

Other exemptions

14.85 Section 282 lists the circumstances in which proceedings for a recovery order may not be taken. They include:

(1) Proceedings in respect of cash alone (unless the proceedings are also taken in respect of other property). This means that the enforcement authority may not take civil recovery proceedings in respect of cash; unless they are simultaneously taking proceedings against other property held by the same person. (Cash seizures fall within the domain of either the police or HM Revenue and Customs.)

(2) Proceedings against the Financial Services Authority in respect of any recoverable property held by the Authority.

(3) Proceedings which relate to a collateral security charge; a market charge; a money market charge; or a system charge (s 282(4)).

(4) Proceedings against any person in respect of any recoverable property which he holds by reason of his acting, or having acted, as an insolvency practitioner ('acting as an insolvency practitioner' is defined by s 433).

14.86 Further the Secretary of State may add to this list of exemptions in a prescribed order (see s 282(1)). Any such order must be approved by both Houses of Parliament (see s 459(6)(a)).

Exemptions or exceptions to property being 'recoverable'

14.87 Under ss 308 to 310 there are certain general exceptions and exemptions to the civil recovery rules, some of which appear to be repetitive of the above.

14.88 General exceptions include a situation where a person disposes of recoverable property and the person who obtains it on the disposal does so in good faith, for value and without notice that it was recoverable property. In such circumstances the property may not be followed into the persons hands and, accordingly it ceases to be recoverable (s 308(1) and s 266(4)).

14.89 Similarly, if in pursuance of a judgment in civil proceedings the defendant makes a payment to the claimant or the claimant otherwise obtains property from the defendant (which may otherwise have been recoverable property), that payment (property) ceases to be recoverable (see s 308(3)). Alternatively, if a payment is made to a person in pursuance of a compensation order under s 130 of the PCC(S)A 2000, the payment (property) ceases to be recoverable (s 308(4)).

If a payment is made to a person in pursuance of a restitution order under s 148(2) of the **14.90** PCC(S)A 2000 or a person otherwise obtains any property or money in pursuance of such an order, the property ceases to be recoverable. A similar provision applies in respect of restitution orders under s 308(6) and (7).

Under s 308(8), the property is not recoverable while a restraint order applies under ss 41, **14.91** 120, or 190 of POCA. Nor is it recoverable if it has already been taken into account in deciding the amount a person has benefited from for the purpose of making a confiscation order (see s 308(9) and s 278(9) and (10)).

In *Satnam Singh v Director of the Assets Recovery Agency* [2005] EWCA Civ 580, (2005) 1 **14.92** WLR 3747, the Court of Appeal held (at para 18) that where a previous court had quashed a confiscation order it must inevitably follow that no order was made 'under the corresponding provision' of a relevant enactment for the purposes of s 308(9) of POCA. This, in the view of Latham LJ, was 'precisely what Parliament intended'. The purpose of s 308(9) was to prevent double recovery. He stated at para 19:

> Its effect is to ensure that the only mechanism for recovery in relation to property taken into account if a confiscation order has been made is that provided for under the confiscation order. But if criminal proceedings are brought, but no confiscation order is made or the property in question has not been taken into account in determining benefit for the purpose of any confiscation order that has been made, I can see no justification under the 2002 Act for precluding the respondent from seeking to obtain a recovery order in relation to the proceeds of crime.

He went on to hold that the clear intention of Parliament was to ensure that, so far as pos- **14.93** sible, criminals should be deprived of the possibility of benefiting from their own crimes:

> To permit the technicality which resulted in the confiscation order being quashed to preclude recovery by the civil recovery route would be to perpetrate a mischief which the 2002 Act was clearly designed to prevent.

Other exemptions within the Act include where an order provides that property is not **14.94** recoverable if it is prescribed property or if it is disposed of in pursuance of a prescribed enactment (see s 309(1) and (2)). 'Prescribed property' means prescribed by an order made by the Secretary of State (see s 309(4)). (Any order made by the Secretary of State is subject to the affirmative resolution procedure provided under s 459(6)(a) of POCA.)

Insolvency and recovery orders

Proceedings for a recovery order may not be taken or continued in respect of property **14.95** which falls under the following categories, unless the appropriate court gives leave and the proceedings are taken or (as the case may be) continued in accordance with the terms imposed by that court (see s 311(1) and (3)):

(a) an asset of a company being wound up;
(b) an asset of a company and a voluntary arrangement under Pt 1 of the Insolvency Act 1986;

(c) an order under s 286 of the Insolvency Act 1986;

(d) an asset comprised of an estate of an individual who has been adjudged bankrupt;

(e) an asset of an individual and a voluntary arrangement under Pt 8 of the Insolvency Act 1986.

14.96 An application under s 311, or under any provision of the Insolvency Act 1986, for leave to take proceedings for a recovery order may be made without notice to the person. That, however, does not affect any requirement for notice of an application to be given to any person acting as an insolvency practitioner or to the official receiver (see s 311(4) and (5)).

14.97 Insolvency and civil recovery are also considered at para 13.196 of Chapter 13.

Publicity and civil recovery

14.98 It was previously commonplace for ARA to post on its website recent successes and issue corresponding press releases, and SOCA have tended to adopt a similar policy. The High Court in Northern Ireland considered the use of website publicity in *In the matter of Colin Armstrong* [2007] NIQB 20. Gillen J concluded that the use of the website in this manner was both proportionate and furthered the legitimate aim of ensuring that crime was reduced (para 15). In so finding, he dismissed arguments based upon Art 2 and Art 8 of the ECHR.

D. The Impact of the European Convention on Human Rights on Civil Recovery

14.99 The ECHR has featured in a number of civil recovery cases, as perhaps it inevitably would bearing in mind the controversial nature of the legislation.

Article 1—interference with property

14.100 In *Director of the Assets Recovery Agency v (1) Jia Jin He (2) Dan Dan Chen* [2004] EWHC (Admin) 3021 Collins J considered Art 1 of the First Protocol which prohibits interference with property. He referred to the Italian cases of *Arcuri v Italy (Application No 52024–99)* and *M v Italy (Application No 12386–86)*, where the European Court had held that recovery provisions did not fall foul of Art 1, provided that the measure in question was regarded as proportionate. At para 74 Collins J stated, in upholding the principle:

> Whilst the situation in this country is not, I hope, as dire as that represented by the activities of the Mafia in Italy, nonetheless Parliament has quite clearly decided that these measures are necessary in order to fight crime, and in particular to ensure, as far as possible, that those involved in crime should be unable to enjoy the fruits of their criminal activities.

Article 6(1)

14.101 In the *Director of the Assets Recovery Agency v Satnam Singh* [2004] EWHC Admin 2335, (2005) ACD 36, McCombe J rejected an argument advanced in relation to Art 6(1) of the ECHR that sought to join the overall length of the criminal proceedings with those of the recovery proceedings (a total of nine years from arrest for the substantive matter). While Art 6(1) provides that in the determination of the civil rights and obligations of an individual (or in criminal proceedings), everyone is entitled to a fair and public hearing 'within a reasonable time', McCombe J was inclined to the view that the recovery proceedings represented separate civil proceedings in which no question of relevant delay arose (para 40).

Article 6(2)

In *Director of the Assets Recovery Agency v Walsh* [2004] NIQB 21, Coghlin J held that pro-   **14.102**
ceedings under the 2002 Act were civil proceedings to which Art 6(2) did not apply. Coghlin J held:

> It seems to me that, in substance, proceedings by way of a civil recovery action under the provisions of Part 5 of POCA differ significantly from the situation of a person charged with a criminal offence within the meaning of Article 6.

In *R (on the application of the Director of the Assets Recovery Agency) (Paul) v Ashton* [2006]   **14.103**
EWHC (Admin) 1064, Newman J held that the imposition of a civil recovery order under s 243 of POCA was not punitive and could not therefore violate Art 6 of the ECHR (no punishment without law). He held that civil recovery orders had a compensatory aspect in that they are a manifestation of Parliament's intention to recover expenses incurred in investigating crime, and the fact that deprivation of property is involved does not consti- tute a penalty because the holder of the property to which the order relates had no right to hold it in the first place. (See also *Director of the Assets Recovery Agency v Charrington* [2005] EWCA Civ 334.)

Article 7—civil proceedings

Article 7 was specifically referred to in the case of *Director of the Assets Recovery Agency v (1)*   **14.104**
Jia Jin He (2) Dan Dan Chen [2004] EWHC (Admin) 3021. In that matter Collins J held that there was 'no doubt' recovery proceedings were civil, and that Art 7 did not apply as no penalty was involved (para 69).

In a considered judgment, His Lordship reviewed the structure and basis of the Act (para 1   **14.105**
et seq), together with the tests in *Engel v Netherlands (No 1)*(1976) 1 EHRR 647 (at 678– 679) which dictate whether proceedings should be classified as civil or criminal (para 49). Furthermore he considered two European authorities, namely *Arcuri v Italy* and *M v Italy (17 DR 59)*, where the European Court settled that preventative confiscation measures that did not involve a finding of guilt do not constitute a penalty (and therefore were not in contravention of Art 7) (see para 56 of the judgment).

His Lordship went on to consider the standard of proof required in such claims, and   **14.106**
concluded that Parliament had intentionally imposed a lower standard in civil recovery proceedings, namely that of the balance of probabilities (para 66).

In *R (on the Application of the Director of the Assets Recovery Agency) v Paul Ashton* [2006]   **14.107**
EWHC (Admin) 1064, Newman J adopted the decision of Collins J in *Jia Jin He* and noted that his Lordship had rejected the suggestion that a heightened civil standard of proof applied where criminal conduct was said to be involved. At para 39 Newman J stated that he regarded the judgments which had preceded this matter to be 'an impeccable catalogue of features which are relevant when considering the issue of Article 7'.

Article 7—a criminal penalty?

14.108   It is now established that confiscation proceedings, following on and attaching to a criminal conviction, represent a 'penalty', not least because a prison sentence in default flows from non-payment, and the confiscation order is treated as a fine, pursuant to (eg) s 9 of the Drug Trafficking Act 1994. (See *R v Benjafield* [2002] UKHL 2 (para 82), *Rezvi* [2002] UKHL 1, and *Phillips v UK* [2001] EHRR No 41087/98). Part of the reasoning in *Rezvi* was that the purpose of confiscation proceedings was to '. . . punish convicted offenders'.

14.109   The impact of Art 7 and the issue of 'penalty' in civil recovery proceedings was considered by the Court of Appeal in *Director of Assets Recovery Agency v Charrington* [2005] EWCA Civ 334, where Laws LJ embraced the argument that it was untenable to suggest that recovery orders should be treated as criminal (para 17). He described as 'entirely right' both Collins J's ruling (which was not appealed), and that of Coghlin J in the case of *Director of Assets Recovery Agency v Walsh* (QBD NI, 1 April 2004) where Coghlin J said:

> . . . what seems to me of greater importance is the fact that there is no arrest nor is there any formal charge, conviction, penalty or criminal record . . . (para 18).

14.110   Laws LJ roundly dismissed the argument that the case of *Charrington* should be classified as criminal proceedings for the purposes of Art 6 and Art 7 of the ECHR (para 14). His Lordship adopted the submissions the Director, who maintained that the argument that proceedings for recovery orders should be treated as criminal for Convention purposes was untenable. He cited the fact that the European Court of Human Rights (ECtHR) has twice considered and rejected that argument in cash forfeiture proceedings under the DTA (see *Butler v UK* (2002) App No 41661-98 and *Webb v UK* (2004) App No 56054-00). It was submitted that it was inconceivable that the reasoning of the ECtHR would not apply equally to the cash forfeiture provisions in Pt 5 of POCA (s 298) which replaced the DTA provisions. It followed that the argument being advanced on behalf of *Charrington* involved inviting the Court of Appeal to decide that the High Court civil recovery procedures under Pt 5 were 'criminal' in nature, whereas the magistrates' court procedures under Pt 5 were to be regarded as 'civil'. The Director submitted that there was no prospect of the court so holding and Laws LJ concurred with that view and adopted it in his judgment.

14.111   The case of *Walsh* went to appeal in Northern Ireland (Kerr LCJ, Nicholson LJ, and Campbell LJ, *Walsh v Director of the Assets Recovery Agency* [2005] NICA 6), and the Court found, applying the three tests set out in *Engel v Netherlands* that:

(1) all the available indicators point strongly to recovery cases being classified as a form of civil proceedings.
    'the Appellant is not charged with a crime . . . He is not liable to imprisonment or fine if the recovery action succeeds. There is no indictment and no verdict. The primary purpose of the legislation is restitutionary rather than penal.' [para 27]
(2) In terms of the nature of the proceedings the allegation made does not impute guilt and there is no prosecutorial function [para 29].
(3) The primary purpose of the legislation is to recover the proceeds of crime; it is not to punish the appellant in the sense normally entailed in a criminal sanction [para 39].

The Court in *Walsh* (which was primarily considering Art 6(1)) refrained from expressing **14.112** any final view as to whether recovery of assets was penal within the autonomous meaning of the term (see para 39)).

Subsequently, the matter was further considered in *Scottish Ministers v McGuffie* [2006] **14.113** SC(D) 26/2, in which the Court was invited to find that the petitioners were seeking to impose a criminal penalty retrospectively by asking for the appointment of an interim administrator pursuant to s 256 of the Act. It was accepted by the respondent that if there was no criminal penalty then his challenge to the petition would fail. Lord Kinclaven, having considered *Walsh* above, stated (see para 127):

> The proceedings are directed against property (*in rem*) rather than against Mr. McGuffie's person. The recovery procedures are under the control of the civil court. Mr. McGuffie's guilt is not in issue. He is not facing a criminal charge. He is not an accused person. He cannot be arrested or remanded or compelled to attend. There has been no formal accusation by the prosecuting authorities. He will not be subject to a criminal conviction or finding of guilt. He will not be imprisoned. He will not receive a sentence. A civil recovery order will not form any part of his criminal record.

Lord Kinclaven went on to list further features which distinguished civil recovery **14.114** proceedings:

- The orders sought by the petitioners did not amount to a retrospective criminal penalty within the meaning of art 7 of the Convention.
- The orders sought by the petitioners were part of a regime for the civil recovery of property that was, or represented, property obtained through unlawful conduct rather than a regime of punishment.
- They were not at the instance of the Lord Advocate or a prosecuting authority.
- They had been initiated by civil petition.
- They were being heard in a civil court.
- The procedures involved for making and implementing the order were clearly civil rather than criminal.
- The proceedings were directed against property rather than against the respondent's person.
- The respondent would not be subject to a criminal conviction or a finding of guilt.
- A civil recovery order would not form any part of his criminal record.

For features that distinguish confiscation and civil recovery proceedings, see para 13.25 of Chapter 13.

Article 7—retrospectivity

In *Jia Jin He* Collins J held (at para 69): **14.115**

> The authorities to which I have already referred make it plain that there is no question of any penalty involved in these proceedings. Furthermore, there has been no conviction of a criminal offence leading to a penalty. Of course, property cannot be recoverable unless, at the time it was acquired, it was obtained through unlawful conduct. That conduct must have been criminal at that time. To that extent, the prohibition against retrospectivity will apply, but only because the Act says that the property must be property which was obtained by criminal conduct. In those circumstances, it is quite clear that Article 7 has no application.

14.116 In *R (on the Application of the Director of the Assets Recovery Agency) v Paul Ashton* [2006] EWHC (Admin) 1064 Newman J also considered whether the civil recovery procedure offended Art 7 of the ECHR governing retrospectivity, and found that it did not. (Leave to appeal his judgment was subsequently refused.)

14.117 Similarly in *McGuffie* Lord Kinclaven stated (at para 127):

> In my opinion, on a fair valuation of all the circumstances, the orders sought by the Scottish Ministers in the present case do not amount to a retrospective criminal 'penalty' within the meaning of Article 7.

Article 8

14.118 In relation to Art 8, the right to family and personal life, Collins J in *Jia Jin He* held it added nothing to what he had said about proportionality in relation to Art 1.

Proportionality generally

14.119 In *Director of Assets Recovery Agency v John and Lord* [2007] EWHC 360 (QB) Tugendhat J found it doubtful that monies received from unlicensed street trading would amount to property obtained through unlawful conduct. He stated:

> 76. The provisions of s. 266 are to be contrasted with the way that the criminal law is framed. The penalty for unlicensed trading is set by Parliament. But it is not a mandatory penalty. Criminal statutes set a maximum penalty, and the courts impose a sentence within that maximum in accordance with the law on sentencing. Sentences must be proportionate to the offender's culpability and to the harm which the offence caused, was intended to cause or might foreseeably have caused, and fines must be proportionate to the offender's means: Criminal Justice Act 2003 ss. 143(1), 164(2) and (3). It cannot have been the intention of Parliament that a breach of a regulatory statute for which, on conviction, a fine of £50 pound is appropriate (that is the fine imposed on Mr John for each of his offences of unlicensed trading), should automatically also result in a civil recovery order in respect of all the money he received in making lawful sales while committing that offence.

14.120 For a broader discussion on proportionality in the civil recovery and confiscation context, see *Gilligan v The Criminal Assets Bureau* [1998] 3 IR 185 (in the context of the Irish Constitution); *Raimondo v Italy* [1994] 18 EHRR 371; and *McIntosh v Lord Advocate* [2001] 2 All ER 638.

E. Pension Schemes

Introduction

14.121 Pension policies can be of great value, but their actual value is often, pursuant to the terms of the pension policy, unrealisable until a certain age, or until the policy itself dictates or matures. Money paid into a policy tends to become locked in, with even the policy holder powerless to realise it, or in the alternative, an ability to realise it, but at a considerable undervalue due to the excessive penalties involved and incurred. Parliament appears to have acknowledged this practical problem and legislated for it accordingly within POCA. Not only is the realisation of pension schemes and policies important to the success of the Act and the recovery of the proceeds of crime, but it would also represent a considerable loophole in the legislation if those involved in criminal activity were aware that they could pay tens of thousands of pounds into pension schemes in the safe knowledge that it would place those funds beyond the reach of civil recovery and that in years to come those individuals could look forward to living off a nest egg representing the proceeds of ill-gotten gains.

Section 273(1) and (2) of POCA applies to recoverable property consisting of rights under **14.122** a pension scheme. A recovery order in respect of the property must, instead of vesting the property in the trustees for civil recovery, require the trustees or managers of the pension scheme to pay to the trustee within a prescribed period, the amount determined by the trustees or managers of the pension scheme to be equal to the value of the right, and to give effect to any other provision made within ss 273, 274, and 275. This is subject to what is said later in Pt 5 of the Act concerning consent orders (s 276), consent orders and pensions (s 277), and the limit on recovery (s 278).

The requirement of the trustee or managers of the pension scheme to pay to the trustee for **14.123** civil recovery an amount equal to the value of the rights of the pension scheme overrides the provisions of the pension scheme itself, to the extent that if they conflict with the provisions of the order, the order must take priority (see s 273(3)).

Subs (5) of s 273 provides that any statutory provisions, eg s 159 of the Pension Schemes **14.124** Act 1993, will not frustrate the enforcement authority's or the interim receiver's ability to pursue the recovery of the value of pension rights.

What does a pension scheme mean within this part of the Act?

A pension scheme means an occupational pension scheme or a personal pension scheme. **14.125** Under s 275(4), these expressions have the same meaning as in the Pension Schemes Act 1993.

References to a pension scheme also includes retirement annuity contracts; and annuity or **14.126** insurance policies purchased or transferred for the purposes of giving effect to rights under an occupational pension scheme or a personal pension scheme and/or an annuity purchase, for the purpose of discharging any liability in respect of a pension credit under s 29(1)(b) of the Welfare Reform and Pensions Act 1999.

'Trustees or managers'

In relation to an occupational pension scheme or a personal pension scheme, the 'trustees **14.127** or managers' mean either:

(a) in the case of the scheme established under a trust, the trustees
(b) in any other case, the managers (s 275(5)).

In relation to a retirement annuity contract or other annuity, references to the trustees **14.128** or managers are to the provider of the annuity, and in relation to an insurance policy references to the trustees or managers are to the insurer (see s 275(7)).

The Proceeds of Crime Act 2002 (Recovery from Pension Schemes) Regulations 2003

The Proceeds of Crime Act 2002 (Recovery from Pension Schemes) Regulations 2003 were **14.129** introduced by SI 2003/291 and came into force on 17 March 2003. These Regulations make provision as to the exercise by trustees or managers of pension schemes of their powers when a civil recovery order is made under s 273(2) of POCA and requires them to make a payment to the trustee for civil recovery in respect of the rights of a member of that scheme.

Calculation and verification of the value of rights under pension schemes

14.130 Regulation 2(1) applies where the High Court makes a pension recovery order (other than in respect of rights derived from a pension sharing transaction under a destination arrangement) in a pension scheme.

14.131 It provides for the calculation and verification of the cash equivalent of the value of pension rights which are recoverable property under the Act. This is by reference to the method applying for the purposes of the provision of information in respect of pensions on divorce, separation, and nullity under the Pensions on Divorce etc (Provision of Information) Regulations 2000, SI 2000/1048 and the equivalent regulations applying in Scotland and Northern Ireland.

14.132 A 'destination arrangement' means a pension arrangement under which some or all of the rights are derived, directly or indirectly, from a pension sharing transaction. A 'pension sharing transaction' means an order or provision falling within s 28(1) of the Welfare Reform and Pensions Act 1999 (activation of pension sharing)).

14.133 The trustees or managers of the pension scheme in respect of which the pension recovery order has been made must calculate and verify the cash equivalent of the value (at the valuation date of the rights which are the subject of the pension recovery order) and must pay to the trustee for civil recovery a sum equal to that cash equivalent (Regulation 3).

14.134 In relation to the calculation and verification by the trustees or managers of the cash equivalent referred to above:

(a) in the case of a pension scheme wholly or mainly administered in England and Wales, reg 3 of the Pensions on Divorce etc. (Provision of Information) Regulations 2000 (information about pensions and divorce: valuation of pension benefits), except para (2) thereof, shall have effect as it has effect for the valuation of benefits in connection with the supply of information and in connection with domestic and overseas divorce etc. in England and Wales, with the modification that, for 'the date on which the request for the valuation was received' in each case where it appears in that regulation, there shall be substituted 'the valuation date for the purposes of the Proceeds of Crime Act 2002 (Recovery from Pension Schemes) Regulations 2003';

(b) in the case of a pension scheme wholly or mainly administered in Scotland, reg 3 of the Divorce etc. (Pensions) (Scotland) Regulations 2000 (valuation), except para (11) thereof, shall have effect as it has effect for the valuation of benefits in connection with the supply of information in connection with divorce in Scotland, with the modification that, for 'the relevant date' in each case where it appears in that regulation, there shall be substituted 'the valuation date for the purposes of the Proceeds of Crime Act 2002 (Recovery from Pension Schemes) Regulations 2003'; and

(c) in the case of a pension scheme wholly or mainly administered in Northern Ireland, reg 3 of the Pensions on Divorce etc. (Provision of Information) Regulations (Northern Ireland) 2000 (information about pensions on divorce: valuation of pension benefits), except para (2) thereof, shall have effect as it has effect for the valuation of benefits in connection with the supply of information in connection with domestic and overseas divorce etc. in Northern Ireland, with the modification that, for 'the date on which the request for the valuation was received' in each case where it appears in that regulation, there shall be substituted 'the valuation date for the purposes of the Proceeds of Crime Act 2002 (Recovery from Pension Schemes) Regulations 2003.

Calculation and verification of the value of rights under destination arrangements

As stated above, 'destination arrangement' means a pension arrangement under which **14.135** some or all of the rights are derived, directly or indirectly, from a pension sharing transaction. Regulation 3(1) of the Proceeds of Crime Act 2002 (Recovery from Pension Schemes) Regulations 2003 applies where the High Court makes a pension recovery order in respect of rights derived from a pension sharing transaction under a destination arrangement in a pension scheme. The trustees or managers of the pension scheme in respect of which the pension recovery order has been made must calculate and verify the cash equivalent of the value at the valuation date of the rights which are the subject of the pension recovery order and must pay to the trustee for civil recovery a sum equal to that cash equivalent. Regulation 3 provides:

(3) In relation to the calculation and verification by the trustees or managers of the cash equivalent referred to in paragraph (2)—

    (a) in the case of a pension arrangement in a scheme that is wholly or mainly administered in either England and Wales or Scotland, regulation 24 of the Pension Sharing (Pension Credit Benefit) Regulations 2000 (manner of calculation and verification of cash equivalents) shall have effect as it has effect for the calculation and verification of pension credit for the purposes of those regulations; and

    (b) in the case of a pension arrangement in a scheme that is wholly or mainly administered in Northern Ireland, regulation 24 of the Pension Sharing (Pension Credit Benefit) Regulations (Northern Ireland) 2000 (manner of calculation and verification of cash equivalents) shall have effect as it has effect for the calculation and verification of pension credit for the purposes of those regulations.

Approval of manner of calculation and verification of the value of rights

Regulation 4 makes provision for circumstances where the person with the pension rights **14.136** which are recoverable property is a trustee or manager of the scheme in question. In such circumstances, an actuary must approve the method of calculation and verification of the cash equivalent value.

The manner in which the trustees or managers have calculated and verified the value of the **14.137** rights must be approved by:

(a) a Fellow of the Institute of Actuaries; or
(b) a Fellow of the Faculty of Actuaries.

Regulation 4 goes on to provide: **14.138**

(3) Where the person referred to in paragraph (2) is not able to approve the manner in which the trustees or managers have calculated and verified the value of the rights which are the subject of a pension recovery order, he must give notice in writing of that fact to the trustee for civil recovery and the trustees or managers of the scheme.

(4) Where the trustees or managers of the scheme have been given notice under paragraph (3), they must re-calculate and re-verify the value of the rights which are the subject of a pension recovery order for the purposes of regulation 2 or 3.

Time for compliance with a pension recovery order

14.139 Regulation 5 prescribes the period for paying the amount of those pension rights to the trustee for civil recovery:

> 5 (1) In this regulation, 'the prescribed period' means the period prescribed for the purposes of section 273(2)(a) of the Act.
>
> (2) Subject to paragraphs (3) and (4), the prescribed period is the period of 60 days beginning on the day on which the pension recovery order is made.

14.140 Under regulation 5(3), where an application for permission to appeal the pension recovery order is made within the period referred to in para (2), the prescribed period is the period of 60 days beginning on:

> (a) the day on which permission to appeal is finally refused;
> (b) the day on which the appeal is withdrawn; or
> (c) the day on which the appeal is dismissed, as the case may be.

14.141 Where the person referred to in regulation 4(2) gives notice, in accordance with regulation 4(3) and within the period referred to in para (2), to the trustee for civil recovery and trustees or managers of the scheme that he is unable to approve the manner in which the trustees or managers have calculated the value of the rights which are the subject of the pension recovery order, the prescribed period is the period of 60 days beginning on the day on which such notice is given (regulation 5(4)).

14.142 'Valuation date' means a date within the period prescribed by regulation 5 in respect of which the trustees or managers of the pension scheme decide to value the relevant person's pension rights in accordance with regulation 2 or 3.

Costs of the trustees or managers of the pension scheme

14.143 The trustees or managers of the pension scheme may recover costs incurred by them in:

> (a) complying with the recovery order, or
> (b) providing information, before the recovery order was made, to the enforcement authority or the interim receiver. (See s 273(4).)

Consequential adjustment of liabilities under pension schemes

14.144 A recovery order made by virtue of s 273(2) must require the trustees or managers of the pension scheme to make such reduction in the liabilities of the scheme as they think necessary in consequence of a payment made in pursuance of s 273(2).

14.145 Accordingly, by s 274(2), the order must require the trustees or managers to provide for the liabilities of the pension scheme to cease in respect of the respondent's recoverable property to which s 273 applies. For provision as to the exercise by trustees or managers of pension schemes of their powers see the Proceeds of Crime (Recovery from Pension Schemes) Regulations 2003, SI 2003/291.

14.146 Section 274(1) envisages that the recovery order itself will include a condition that stipulates that the trustees or managers of the pension scheme will reduce their liabilities to the extent they think necessary following the payment made under the order. Section 274(3) states that the trustees' or managers' powers include the power to reduce the amount of any benefit or future benefit to which the respondent is or may be entitled under the scheme, and any future benefit to which any other person may be entitled under the scheme in respect of that property.

Consent order: pensions

Section 277 of POCA envisages orders by consent being made where recoverable property **14.147** includes rights under a pension scheme. Section 277(2) states that:

A consent order made under section 276 [*which deals with consent orders generally in civil recovery, see para 14.17 above*]—
(a) may not stay the proceedings on terms that the rights are vested in any other person, but
(b) may include provision imposing the following requirement, if the trustees or managers of the scheme are parties to the agreement by virtue of which the order is made.

The requirement is that the trustees or managers of the pension scheme make a payment in **14.148** accordance with the agreement and give effect to any other provision made by virtue of s 277 in respect of the scheme (s 277(3)). Section 277(4) states:

The trustees or managers of the pension scheme have power to enter into an agreement in respect of the proceedings on any terms on which [a consent] order made under section 276 may stay the proceedings.

Section 277(6) makes it clear that a consent order made under s 276 overrides the provi- **14.149** sions of the pension scheme to the extent that they conflict with the requirements of the order.

The consent order may provide for the recovery by the trustees or managers of the scheme **14.150** (whether by deduction from any amount for which they are required to pay in pursuance of the agreement or otherwise) of costs incurred by them in complying with the order, or providing information before the order was made to the enforcement authority or interim receiver (s 277(7)).

F. Civil Recovery and Taxation

Summary of taxation provisions

Part 6 of POCA sets out the revenue functions and tax powers of the civil recovery scheme. **14.151** Pursuant to the Serious Crime Act 2007, these powers were extensively transferred to SOCA following the abolition of the ARA on 1 April 2008 (s 74(2) and Sch 8, para 93 SCA; and SI 2008/755). This includes ARA's power to issue tax assessments where the income can be linked to criminality.

Section 317(1) of POCA sets out the qualifying condition which must be satisfied before **14.152** the Director of SOCA can take over general Revenue functions (defined at s 323(1)). The condition is that the Director must have reasonable grounds to suspect that income, prof- its, or gains arising or accruing to a person (including a company) in respect of a chargeable period are chargeable to tax and arise or accrue as a result of that person's, or another's, criminal conduct. Criminal conduct is defined in s 326. If this condition is satisfied, then subs (2) allows the Director to serve a notice on HMRC that has the effect of vesting certain functions of the Revenue in the Director. The notice served will specify a number of things. These will include adequate details to identify the relevant person or company, the chargeable periods in question, and also the particular functions that the Director wishes to assume responsibility for. These may be some or all of the functions listed in s 323(1). The notice will also specify the particular tax periods during which the income, profits, or gains are suspected of arising as a result of criminal conduct.

14.153 By s 317(7), the tax function may be vested in both the Director and HMRC officers concurrently. This allows, among other things, routine work to be carried out by the HMRC notwithstanding that the functions are also vested in the Director.

14.154 Section 320 provides a right of appeal and all appeals against actions arising from the exercise by the Director of his Revenue functions will be to the Tax Tribunal. The right of appeal is equivalent to those available to taxpayers subjected to decisions made by HMRC.

14.155 Section 326 of POCA provides definitions and meanings for some of the terminology used in Pt 6 and in particular the terms 'criminal conduct' and 'criminal property.' For the purposes of Pt 6, 'criminal conduct' does not include an offence relating to a matter under the care and management of HMRC, for example, tax fraud.

15

THE SEIZURE AND RECOVERY
OF CASH

A. Introduction

15.01 The UK's first cash seizure provisions came into force on 1 July 1991 when Pt III of the Criminal Justice (International Co-operation) Act 1990 was enacted. That legislation proved to be necessary because the Drug Trafficking Offences Act 1986 (DTOA), together with similar provisions in other countries, had become a victim of their own success. Drug traffickers and money launderers could no longer risk transferring money from country to country by means of the electronic bank transfer system for fear of being detected, or the location of their money being discovered if they were arrested.

15.02 The money launderer became even more vulnerable following implementation of the First EC Money Laundering Directive, which required Member States to introduce legislation requiring financial institutions to keep proper records of transactions and report on money laundering. In consequence, Customs officers at ports and airports noticed that it was becoming increasingly common for large sums of money derived from drug trafficking to be imported into and exported from the UK in cash. They were powerless to intervene and detain such monies unless there was a prosecution for a drug trafficking offence ongoing, in which case the money could be the subject of restraint and confiscation orders. As a result, new legislation was required to combat the couriering of cash into and out of the UK.

The DTA

Part II of the Drug Trafficking Act 1994 (DTA) gave the police and Customs officers the **15.03** power to seize and detain for up to 48 hours drug trafficking money being imported or exported in cash. Magistrates' courts were given the power to order its further detention for periods of up to two years and, ultimately, to order its forfeiture.

The provisions of s 42 *et seq* of the DTA, although considered extensively in the first edition **15.04** of this work, are now consigned somewhat to history. The POCA regime has now been in operation for over seven years, and so the old legislation tends only to have application in terms of relevant case law that has transcended both schemes.

At the end of this chapter we consider the cash seizure provisions of the Anti–Terrorism, **15.05** Crime and Security Act 2001. Such seizures remain few and far between, with some anecdotal evidence that the police are in any event utilising POCA in such cases.

Finally, we outline the Control of Cash (Penalties) Regulations 2007 (SI 2007/1509), **15.06** which implements Art 3 of Community Regulation 1889/2005, and requires any person entering or leaving the EC and carrying cash amounting to €10,000 or more to declare that amount.

The POCA regime

While undoubtedly the DTA scheme for the seizure and forfeiture of cash met with some **15.07** success in terms of both the amounts seized and the message it sent out to would-be drug smugglers and their money couriers (not least because of its draconian nature), it was nevertheless restricted to money that represented or was intended for drug trafficking. In this regard the scheme was viewed by many as flawed, because it made no provision for the forfeiture of cash being imported or exported in relation to other forms of criminal conduct.

As a result, a new scheme under POCA was enacted which expanded the DTA regime to **15.08** include cash related to *all* unlawful conduct. It also went further, by expanding the meaning of 'cash', allowing cash found anywhere in the UK to be seized (not just that which was being imported or exported) and in addition, added new search provisions.

In this chapter we will consider the revised regime governing the law relating to the seizure, **15.09** detention, and forfeiture of cash under ss 289–303 of POCA (see Appendix 5 of this book). These sections came into force on 30 December 2002 (SI 2002/3015) and replace the earlier provisions found in ss 42–48 of the DTA 1994. They affect all cash seizures made on or after that date.

15.10 Sections 289–292 of POCA deal with the power to search premises and persons for cash (set out in the second part of this chapter), and ss 294–300 deal with the seizure and forfeiture of cash generally.

15.11 The relevant court forms in relation to cash seizures under POCA are found in the Magistrates' Court (Detention and Forfeiture of Cash) Rules 2002, SI 2002/2998, as amended by rr 91–96 of the Magistrates' Courts (Miscellaneous Amendments) Rules 2003, SI 2003/1236.

Civil proceedings

15.12 Although some debate ensued under the previous statutory provisions as to whether forfeiture provisions were civil or criminal, it is submitted that the new Act draws a line under such discussion. The Introduction to Pt 5 of POCA (Civil Recovery of the Proceeds Etc of Unlawful Conduct) states in terms that forfeiture proceedings will be civil proceedings before the magistrates' court:

Section 240(1) This Part has effect for the purposes of—

(a) . . . .

(b) enabling cash which is, or represents, property obtained through unlawful conduct, or which is intended to be used in unlawful conduct, to be forfeited in civil proceedings before a magistrates' court or (in Scotland) the sheriff.

15.13 This accords with the findings of courts under the DTA that the cash seizure provisions were civil in nature (see *R v Dover and East Kent Magistrates' Court ex p Steven Gore* (QBD, 23 May 1996); *R v Crawley Justices ex p Ohakwe* (1994) 158 JP Reports 78; and *Butler v UK (Application 41661/98)* (27 June 2002)).

UK Border Agency

15.14 The UK Border Agency (UKBA) took over the role of Customs at airports and ports throughout the UK from 5 August 2009. While the force and application of the cash forfeiture provisions will remain unchanged, the switch is likely to involve the handing over of responsibility from HMRC to the UKBA for cash seizures and investigations in relation to travellers found in possession of cash in excess of the minimum amount.

15.15 Section 26 of the Borders, Citizenship and Immigration Act 2009 makes various transfer provisions. The Scheme gives effect to the transfer of specified property, rights, and liabilities from the Commissioners for Revenue and Customs to the Secretary of State for the Home Department and the Director of Border Revenue in connection with the exercise of the Commissioners' functions which are extended concurrently to the Secretary of State and the Director with the Commissioners. The Secretary of State's functions will be exercised by delegation to the Chief Executive of UKBA.

Investigating the cash

15.16 The Serious Crime Act 2007 (SCA) introduces the concept of a formal detained cash investigation (ss 75–77). Schedule 10 of the SCA amends the relevant parts of POCA from 6 April 2008 to allow for the same.

15.17 Section 75 of the SCA alters s 341(3) of POCA to allow the production order provisions under Pt 8 of POCA to be used for investigating the provenance or intended destination of cash seized. Section 76 amends s 352(2) of POCA to allow for the search and seizure provisions under Pt 8 of POCA to be used for investigating the provenance or intended destination of cash seized. Section 77 gives effect to Sch 10 which makes further provision about the use of production orders and search and seizure warrants for detained cash investigations.

The detained cash investigation is intended to be an addition to the existing types of investigation, namely a confiscation investigation, civil recovery investigation, and money laundering investigation. **15.18**

Pursuant to s 79, Sch 11 gives accredited financial investigators powers to recover cash (as described by s 453). The term 'accredited financial investigator' is further defined by the Proceeds of Crime Act 2002 (References to Financial Investigators) (Amendment) Order 2009 (SI 2009/2707). **15.19**

B. The Seizure and Forfeiture of Cash

Preliminary matters

The provisions under ss 294–303 of POCA (set out in Appendix 5) establish a civil procedure by which money suspected of being either recoverable property or intended by any person to be used in unlawful conduct may be seized, detained, and forfeited (see s 294). The proceedings for forfeiture are civil (see s 240(1)(b)), the burden being on either the police, Revenue and Customs, or the relevant Agency to demonstrate that the property is recoverable or the conduct is unlawful, on the balance of probabilities (s 241(3)). As has already been mentioned, UKBA took over the role of Customs at airports and ports throughout the UK from 5 August 2009. While the force and application of the cash forfeiture provisions will remain unchanged, the switch is likely to involve the handing over of responsibility from HMRC to UKBA for cash seizures. **15.20**

The circumstances in which cash may be seized

Section 294(1) states: **15.21**

(1) A Customs Officer, a constable or an accredited financial investigator may seize any cash if he has reasonable grounds for suspecting it is—
   (a) recoverable property, or
   (b) intended by any person for use in unlawful conduct.

An officer may also seize an entire consignment of cash where he has reasonable grounds for suspecting part of it to be:

(a) recoverable property, or
(b) intended by any person for use in unlawful conduct, in circumstances where it is not reasonably practicable to seize only the 'suspicious' part (s 294(2)).

The minimum amount that may be seized: £1,000

Section 294 does not authorise the seizure of cash if it is for less than the 'minimum amount' (see s 294(3)). The minimum amount was originally set at £10,000, but was subsequently reduced on 16 March 2004 to £5,000 (SI 2004/420), and on 31 July 2006 to £1,000 following the introduction of the Proceeds of Crime Act 2002 (Recovery of Cash in Summary Proceedings: Minimum Amount) Order 2006, SI 2006/1699. **15.22**

Does the minimum amount need to be in the possession of a single person?

15.23 It is possible to foresee, particularly for inland seizures, the practical difficulties of linking cash seized from separate individuals and treating it as one amount. However, some judicial guidance may be derived from the decision of *Customs and Excise Commissioners v Duffy* The Times, 5 April 2002 (decided under the DTA) where the defendants, who had all been travelling to Malaga, were stopped by a Customs officer at Gatwick Airport. They were found with £20,000 collectively in cash. Of the three defendants stopped, it was found they were carrying £7,000, £7,000, and £6,000 respectively (the minimum amount under the DTA being £10,000). The Divisional Court held that a court should approach the Act having in mind that the cash might be with one individual, more than one individual, or in fact no individuals at all. Kennedy LJ said that the sums should not be aggregated if the individuals are otherwise apparently unconnected, but if it can be shown that the money comes from a common source or has a common destination, that may lead the court to conclude that in reality it is a single amount of cash.

15.24 It is submitted that the alternative would give rise to a situation developing where an individual involved in transferring large sums of cash could ask three individuals to carry, eg, £950 each (in total £2,850), in the knowledge that they would be able to avoid the bite of this legislation. Clearly it is important that the relevant Agency or the police should be able to show a nexus between the individuals or the cash concerned, eg that the contamination of the money in terms of residue of drugs matches, or that the travellers' tickets were booked at the same time, or that the individuals know each other, or have other ties. Any combination of these may suggest that the individuals were operating together and that the source of the money was therefore linked.

The meaning of 'cash'

15.25 The meaning of cash has been expanded under s 289(6) to include:

(a) notes and coins in any currency,
(b) postal orders,
(c) cheques of any kind, including traveller's cheques
(d) banker's drafts,
(e) bearer bonds and bearer shares.

Unlike the previous DTA regime, this entitles officers to seize cheques where the cheque is under suspicion. Where only part of the value of the cheque in question is under suspicion, s 296(2) allows an officer to pay that cheque into an interest bearing account, and release the part of the value of the cheque to which the suspicion does not relate (s 296(2)).

15.26 Cash also includes 'any kind of monetary instrument' (s 289(7)). Although 'monetary instrument' is yet to be defined by statutory instrument, it is submitted a 'monetary instrument' must be in such a form that it can be paid into an interest bearing account, so as to comply with the requirements of s 296(2). It follows that if it cannot be, then it is likely to fall outside of the seizure powers under POCA.

How is 'unlawful conduct' defined?

Under s 241 of POCA 'unlawful conduct' is defined as either: **15.27**

(1) Conduct occurring in any part of the United Kingdom which is unlawful under the criminal law of that part of the UK (s 241(1)); or
(2) Conduct which—
    (a) occurs in a country outside the United Kingdom and is unlawful under the criminal law of that country, and
    (b) if it occurred in a part of the United Kingdom, would be unlawful under the criminal law of that part [of the UK] (s 241(2)).

Does the 'unlawful conduct' have to be specified?

There is a requirement for the police or the relevant Agency to satisfy the court that the cash **15.28** relates to unlawful conduct, although that need not be limited to identifying one particular kind. Section 242(2)(b) reads:

(2) In deciding whether any property was obtained through unlawful conduct—
    (a) ...
    (b) it is not necessary to show that the conduct was of a particular kind if it is shown that the property was obtained through conduct of one of a number of kinds, each of which would have been unlawful conduct.

Provided the court is satisfied, on the balance of probabilities, that the cash relates, there- **15.29** fore, to unlawful conduct of one kind or another, it is not necessary to narrow the test to a single particular type. However, in practice most cases are likely to involve an allegation of a particular form of unlawful conduct, because the facts will dictate same, eg income from a shop where no tax has been declared, or cash with an unusually high contamination for drugs. It is also submitted that such a course is also preferable if the defendant is to know, notwithstanding these being civil proceedings, the case he has to answer.

This approach also appears to be in line with *R (Director of Assets Recovery Agency) v Green* **15.30** *2006* The Times, 27 February 2006, where Sullivan J held that in civil proceedings under Pt 5 of POCA, the applicant did not need to allege the commission of any specific criminal offence, but did have to set out the matters alleged to constitute the particular kind of unlawful conduct by which the property was obtained. He stated that if Parliament had wished the applicant to be able to recover property by simply alleging, and thereafter persuading the court, that, on the balance of probabilities, it had been obtained by some unspecified unlawful conduct, it could have said so, but did not. It follows to merely allege that the defendant has no identifiable lawful income, and therefore the cash 'must be' the proceeds of unlawful conduct is not enough; some evidence is required.

However, the decision of Sullivan J does not sit entirely comfortably with another first **15.31** instance decision. In *Muneka v Customs and Excise Commissioners* [2005] EWHC (Admin) 495 Moses J dismissed the suggestion that it was for the 'prosecution' (sic) to identify the criminal activity, the source of the money, or the criminal offence for which it is intended to use the money:

All that has to be shown is that the source of the money was a criminal offence in the United Kingdom and (*sic. or*) that it was intended for a criminal use either in the United Kingdom or elsewhere.

15.32   It is submitted that if there is a difference in emphasis, *Green* is to be preferred. *Green* was followed in *Szeptietowski* [2007] EWCA Civ 766 and *R v NW SW RC and CC* [2008] EWCA Crim 2, where Laws LJ held:

> 37. . . . it would be anomalous, not to say bizarre, if the Crown were not required to identify the class of crime in question in a criminal prosecution while the Director is so required in a civil enforcement suit. Sullivan J's description of the legislative purpose of POCA, adopted by Moore-Bick LJ, is surely no less apt as a guide for the application of Part 7 as it is for that of Part 5.
>
> 38. In short, we do not consider that Parliament can have intended a state of affairs in which, in any given instance, no particulars whatever need be given or proved of a cardinal element in the case, namely the criminal conduct relied on. It is a requirement, to use Sullivan J's expression, of elementary fairness.

15.33   Whilst it is correct to observe that the court in *NW* was considering civil recovery under Pt 5 of the Act in the context of s 340, it would be difficult to construe the cash forfeiture provisions, which also appear under Pt 5, in a different way.

How is 'recoverable property' defined?

15.34   'Recoverable property' is defined as property obtained though unlawful conduct (s 304) (ie property obtained through conduct which is unlawful under UK criminal law and/or the criminal law of a country outside the UK). To make full sense of this definition in the context of cash seizures, 'property' should be read as meaning 'cash' (and its various meanings under s 289(6)) (see s 232(1) and s 414: 'Property is all property wherever situated and includes—(a) money . . .').

15.35   Chapter 4 of Pt 5 of POCA sets out various definitions that apply to both the civil recovery scheme and the cash forfeiture provisions. It deals particularly with recoverable property, namely:

Property obtained through unlawful conduct	s 304
Tracing property	s 305
Mixing property	s 306
Recoverable property accruing profits	s 307
General and other exceptions and exemptions	ss 308 and 309
Granting interests	s 310
Obtaining and disposing of property	s 314

15.36   Under s 311, if the cash concerned is 'an asset of a company being wound up' or if there is a *prima facie*/arguable case that it is (or one of the other terms imposed by s 311), then an application for further detention may not be made unless the court that is dealing with the winding-up petition/bankruptcy gives leave.

The tracing of property

15.37   The Act envisages, under s 305, the tracing of property. Where the original property was obtained through unlawful conduct, any property subsequently obtained with it also potentially becomes 'recoverable property'. For example, a person steals a valuable painting (the original property), it is sold, and the cash received from the sale is later seized at an airport under POCA. Following an investigation the cash can be traced back to the stolen painting. The cash therefore becomes recoverable property, being the proceeds of a crime.

Mixed property

The Act also stipulates that where a person's 'recoverable property' is mixed with other property, **15.38** the portion of the mixed property that is said to relate to unlawful conduct becomes 'recoverable property' (see s 306). In terms of s 294, the recoverable property is likely to be mixed cash. For example, where there are two joint company directors, one uses the company account for legitimate monies, the other to launder the proceeds of crime. The 'honest' director withdraws a large sum and he is stopped going through the airport and the cash is seized. The portion of the cash which he has on him that relates to legitimate money from the business does not fall within the scheme; however, the portion which was paid in as part of the laundered proceeds of a crime does stand to be forfeited, whether that particular director knew about it or not.

Property that is not 'recoverable'

POCA also affords certain 'defences' under which property should not be considered **15.39** recoverable (see ss 304–310, SI 2003/336 and Chapter 13). General exceptions include a situation where a person disposes of recoverable property and the person who obtains it does so in good faith, for value, and without notice that it was recoverable property. In such circumstances the property may not be followed into that person's hands and, accordingly it ceases to be recoverable (s 308(1)).

Similarly, if in pursuance of a judgment in civil proceedings the defendant makes a pay- **15.40** ment to the claimant or the claimant otherwise obtains property from the defendant, that property ceases to be recoverable (see s 308(3)); or if a payment is made to a person in pursuance of a compensation order under s 130 of the PCC(S)A 2000, the property ceases to be recoverable (s 308(4)).

In cash seizure cases these are all matters that in practice will need to be raised by the **15.41** defendant/traveller. It may be that as part of their enquiries the police or the relevant Agency (or the court) will enquire of the defendant/traveller as to whether or not any of the exemptions or exceptions apply to the cash seized. Unless the court, police, or Customs are positively advised otherwise, they are likely to assume that they do not.

The re-seizure of cash

In *Chief Constable of Merseyside Police v Hickman* [2006] EWHC (Admin) 451; (The **15.42** Times, 7 April 2006) Mitting J held that money that had been seized pursuant to a criminal enquiry and s 19 of the Police and Criminal Evidence Act 1984, could be re-seized at any time under s 294 of POCA. There were no time limits on the exercise of the power to seize money under the cash forfeiture provisions of POCA, and there was no reason why the police should be prevented from 'seizing' cash already in their possession, the position being analogous to that of property found on an individual after arrest.

Ongoing criminal proceedings

In *R v Payton* (2006) 150 SJ 741, the Court of Appeal considered the difficulty of **15.43** where cash seizure proceedings may be ongoing and taking place either in advance of or contemporaneously with a defendant's criminal trial. The concern was that such proceedings would lead to a potential unfairness to the defendant if he was required to give or call evidence. To ensure that a defendant's entitlement to a fair trial was not compromised, the Court of Appeal stated that it was essential that there should be proper liaison between the police/cash seizing authority and the prosecuting authority, and in practice cash seizure cases are often adjourned pending the outcome of any criminal proceedings.

C. Practice and Procedure

The initial enquiry

15.44 The money may only be seized if the officer has reasonable grounds, upon enquiry, for suspecting the money is recoverable property or is intended by any person for use in unlawful conduct (s 294(1)). If the officer, or his senior officer, as the case may be, believes 'reasonable grounds' for such a suspicion do not exist, or conversely the explanation is credible, the cash should not be detained. It must be borne in mind that 'cash' also means traveller's cheques, cheques, and any other kind of monetary instrument.

15.45 In ascertaining whether the cash is recoverable or is intended by any person for use in unlawful conduct a short interview is often held. While the provisions of the Police and Criminal Evidence Act 1984 (PACE) do not apply in civil proceedings, officers should nevertheless consider what is best practice, particularly bearing in mind that at this stage it remains a possibility that, subject to further investigation, a criminal charge (eg money laundering) may arise. The signing/witnessing of an officer's notebook that 'the contents have been read back to me and I agree that they are true and accurate' therefore remains important for all parties, particularly if one considers that very often the person being questioned may subsequently change his story. The caution is not appropriate when acting solely under s 294.

15.46 At this preliminary stage there is no compulsion for an individual to stay and answer questions. If the individual elects to continue their journey or does not wish to answer any questions, that is their prerogative.

15.47 Once the decision to seize has been made, the individual should be informed that the matter will be listed before a magistrates' court within 48 hours.

Procedure prior to the first hearing and venue

15.48 The first application under s 295(4) for the extension of the period for which the cash (or any part of it) may be detained beyond the initial 48 hours may be made on Form A, and sent to the magistrates' court where the applicant wishes to make the application. Unlike the DTA, there is no restriction on which magistrates' court the applicant may use.

15.49 This is also reflected in SI 2003/638, which amends the magistrates' jurisdiction so that for the purposes of s 52 of the Magistrates' Courts Act 1980, any magistrates' court has jurisdiction to hear such an application, whether or not it relates to a matter arising within the commission area for which the court is appointed.

15.50 Where the reasonable grounds (under s 295(4)) for the suspicion leading to the seizure in question are connected to a previous order made under s 295(2) of the Act, then the application may be sent to the magistrates' court that made the previous order (r 4(2) of the Magistrates' Court (Detention and Forfeiture of Cash) Rules 2002, SI 2002/2998).

Under r 4(3) of the same rules, a copy of the written application and notification of the **15.51** hearing of the application should be given by the applicant to the person from whom the cash was seized (except where cash is seized as a result of an unattended despatch, eg an unattended letter or parcel, or where unattended cash is seized).

The first detention hearing for the seized cash

Under s 295(1) of POCA, while the police or a Customs/UKBA officer continue to have **15.52** reasonable grounds for suspicion that the cash seized falls under s 294, it may be detained, initially for a period of 48 hours (to allow further enquiries to be made).

At the first detention hearing the period for detention of the cash (or any part of it) may be **15.53** extended by the magistrates' court, but not for a period of beyond three months beginning with the date of the order (s 295(2)(a)). Thereafter, the period of detention may be extended on a three-monthly basis, but not beyond the end of a period of two years beginning from the date of the first order. In other words, the maximum order for continued detention, before having to return to the magistrates' court for a further order, is three months. The maximum period for the investigation is two years.

It should be noted that at this stage there is no obligation to notify any third party who may **15.54** be affected by the first application (see r 4(3) Magistrates' Court (Detention and Forfeiture of Cash) Rules 2002, SI 2002/2998). However, the rules envisage the magistrates' court giving notice of any order made by the court not only to the person from whom the cash was seized, but also to any other person known to be affected by the order (see r 4(9) as above).

Under the Act a single justice of the peace may exercise the powers of the magistrates' court **15.55** to make the first order extending the period (s 295(3)).

Unattended despatches

Where seized cash is found in a means of unattended despatch (eg an unattended letter or **15.56** parcel), copies of the written application and notification of the hearing of the application must be sent by either the police or Revenue and Customs/UKBA to the sender and intended recipient of the unattended item (r 4(4)).

Where the seized cash is contained in an unattended despatch, and the sender or intended **15.57** recipient is not known, the applicant (understandably) is not required to send out copies of the written application and notification (see r 4(5)).

Under the Magistrates' Courts Rules it is not in the court's power to decline to hear an **15.58** application solely on the ground that it has not been proved that the sender and intended recipient have been given a copy of the written application and notification of the hearing in unattended despatch cases (see r 4(6)).

Where unattended cash is seized (other than where the cash is found in an unattended **15.59** despatch), the applicant need not give a copy of the written application and notification of the hearing to any person (see r 4(7)).

The 48-hour rule

15.60   The 48-hour rule should be complied with in all cases. The Serious Organised Crime and Police Act 2005 (SOCPA), however, has amended the rule to allow for greater latitude in relation to the meaning of '48 hours'. Section 100 of SOCPA inserts into s 295 of POCA the following provision:

> (1B) In calculating a period of 48 hours in accordance with this subsection, no account shall be taken of—
>
> (a) any Saturday or Sunday,
> (b) Christmas Day,
> (c) Good Friday,
> (d) any day that is a bank holiday . . ., or
> (e) any day prescribed . . . as a court holiday . . . [in Scotland].

15.61   This section avoids the pitfall that formerly arose in terms of getting the matter before magistrates within 48 hours when the seizure took place at weekends (see *R v Uxbridge Magistrates' Court ex p Henry* [1994] Crim LR 581 and *Walsh v Customs and Excise Commissioners* The Times, 4 July 2001, both cases in which the Court found that the 48-hour time limit must be strictly complied with.)

15.62   It is perhaps worthwhile noting that the overriding purpose of POCA is to recover the proceeds of crime. To return, for example, £100,000 of cash that can be linked to unlawful conduct, on the basis that an officer was 10 minutes late in lodging an application, or on some other technicality, may, it is suggested, offend against the overall intention of Parliament. One remedy, presumably (and subject to abuse arguments), would be to return the money, and then re-seize it. (See also *Chief Constable of Merseyside Police v Reynolds* [2004] EWHC (Admin) 2862.)

The test the court will apply at further detention hearings

15.63   Under s 295(4), once an application has been made it is for the court to decide whether or not to make an order, if satisfied, in relation to any cash to be further detained, that either of the following conditions are met:

Condition 1:

> 295(5) . . . that there are reasonable grounds for suspecting that cash is *recoverable property* and that either—
>
> (a) its continued detention is justified while its *derivation* is further investigated, or consideration is given to bringing (in the UK or elsewhere) proceedings against any person for an offence with which the cash is connected, or
> (b) proceedings against any person for an offence with which the cash is connected have been started and have not been concluded. (Emphasis added)

If there are such reasonable grounds, that test/condition is met and the court may order a period of further detention.

Condition 2:

> 295(6) . . . that there are reasonable grounds for suspecting that the cash is intended to be used in *unlawful conduct* and that either—
>
> (a) its continued detention is justified while *its intended use is further investigated* or consideration is given to bringing (in the United Kingdom or elsewhere) proceedings against any person for an offence with which the cash is connected, or

(b) proceedings against any person for an offence with which the cash is connected have been started and have not been concluded. (Emphasis added)

Under s 295(4) either of the above conditions must be met. It is not necessary for both conditions to be met.

It is important to reiterate, therefore, that the officer must not only show that he has reason- **15.64** able grounds for suspecting that either the cash is recoverable property or the cash is intended to be used in unlawful conduct, but also that its continued detention is justified pending further investigation into its derivation or intended use; or consideration is being given to bringing proceedings against any person for an offence with which the cash is connected (or that proceedings against any person for an offence with which the cash is connected have been started and have not been concluded).

Interest

Under s 296, if cash is detained for more than 48 hours, it must at the first opportunity be **15.65** paid into an interest bearing account and held there; and the interest accruing on it must be added to it on its forfeiture or release.

It is suggested that this requirement could present some difficulty to law enforcement **15.66** officers. The banking of cash is not likely to be a problem; the banking of bearer bonds, banker's drafts, cheques and the like, is. In practical terms cheques can be 'stopped'. They are likely to be made payable to third parties. The above requirement therefore requires special arrangements to be put in place with the banks to ensure acceptance of any monetary instrument, without, presumably, adopting usual banking protocols.

Interest—what does 'at the first opportunity' mean?

Section 296(3) states that payment of money into an interest bearing account at the earliest **15.67** opportunity does not apply if the cash or, as the case may be, the part to which the suspicion relates, is required as evidence of an offence or evidence in proceedings under Chapter 3 of the Act.

One assumes that would cover a situation where the evidence was still being gath- **15.68** ered, eg forensic testing of the money. It follows that, if the police or the relevant Agency want to submit the money for forensic testing for traces of drugs, they would not be obliged to pay it into an interest bearing account until the results were back and the defence had been given the opportunity to test the money themselves (affording the defence the opportunity of testing the money themselves was always considered best practice in DTA cases, and avoids any argument that the defence were not given such an opportunity).

In cases where no forensic testing is required, and the cash is not required as a physical **15.69** exhibit, a strict interpretation of POCA appears to dictate that at the first opportunity after 48 hours have passed, in other words as soon as the banks open, the cash should be banked. It is submitted that an element of reasonableness should be implied, ie as soon as reasonably practicable. While that more lenient interpretation may afford the police or Revenue and Customs officers some further time, the failure to pay the money in at the first opportunity could later lead to criticism and potential compensation as s 302(2) provides:

> (2) If for any period beginning with the first opportunity to place the cash in an interest bearing account after the initial detention of the cash for 48 hours, the cash was not held in an interest bearing account while detained, the court may order an amount of compensation to be paid to the applicant.
>
> (3) The amount of compensation to be paid under subsection (2) is the amount the court thinks would have been earned in interest in the period in question if the cash had been held in an interest bearing account.

15.70 While in many cases the loss of interest will only be for a nominal amount, in cases where the cash seized is a more significant sum the potentially accruing interest is likely to be of more significance.

Release of money over which no suspicion attaches

15.71 Under s 296(2) the police or Customs officer must, on paying the seized cash into a bank account, release any part of that cash to which the suspicion does not relate.

D. Continued Detention Hearings: Practice

Form A

15.72 Applications for the continued detention of seized cash under s 295(4) may be made on Form A (see r 5(1) of the Magistrates' Court (Detention and Forfeiture of Cash) Rules 2002, SI 2002/2998, as amended by r 93 of the Magistrates' Courts (Miscellaneous Amendments) Rules 2003, SI 2003/1236).

15.73 On receipt of Form A the justices' clerk should fix a date for the hearing of the application and the court must then notify that date to the relevant Agency and every person to whom notice of the previous orders has been given (r 5(3)). It will be noted that because the justices' clerk is required to give seven days' notice for a continued detention hearing, Form A should not only reach the clerk prior to the existing order running out, but also at least eight or nine days earlier than that date, to allow him time to issue the hearing notice and comply with the seven-day requirement.

15.74 It is then the duty of the applicant to send a copy of the application to every person to whom notice of previous related orders made under s 295(2) of the Act has been given (see r 5(2)).

15.75 The Act, like the DTA before it, envisages a period of up to two years for the investigation to take place. The magistrates may allow a period up to a maximum of three months from the date of the order, but not beyond the end of a period of two years from the date of the first order (s 295(4)). It should be noted that, as in the initial detention application, the magistrates are entitled to conclude that only part of the cash seized should continue to be detained.

15.76 If the court refuses to grant a further detention, that will not necessarily lead to the release of the cash. The applicant is still at liberty to bring an application for forfeiture within 48 hours and/or an appeal, the effect of the magistrates' decision being to refuse a further extension, as opposed to ordering its release (see *Chief Constable of Lancashire Constabulary v Burnley Magistrates' Court* [2003] EWHC (Admin) 3308).

Form B

Form B requires the court to record the date of the seizure, the time of the seizure, the place **15.77**
of the seizure, the date of the latest order for continued detention of seized cash (if any), the
amount detained under the last order for continued detention, and amounts released since
the last order for continued detention (if any).

Under the Magistrates' Courts (Miscellaneous Amendments) Rules 2003, SI 2003/1236, **15.78**
the requirement to make an order for the continued detention of cash on Form B is omitted
and is no longer a requirement of the rules (r 92(2) and r 93(2)).

Form C

Form C relates to rr 4(9) and 5(6). It is a notice to persons affected by an order for contin- **15.79**
ued detention of seized cash. It reflects the Act, in that the person from whom the cash was
seized may apply for the release of the detained cash or any part of it under s 297 of the Act.
Under the Magistrates' Courts (Miscellaneous Amendments) Rules 2003, SI 2003/1236,
Form C is omitted from the Schedule and is no longer a mandatory requirement of the
rules (r 9(6)).

Service of documents

Under r 9 any notification or document required to be given or sent to any person under **15.80**
the new Magistrates' Court (Detention and Forfeiture of Cash) Rules 2002, SI 2002/2998
may be given by post or by fax to his last known address, or to any other address given to
that person for the purpose of service of documents under the rules (presumably including
solicitors).

Procedure at the continued detention hearing

Although the Magistrates' Courts Rules are themselves silent, Form A envisages the police **15.81**
or the Revenue and Customs officer applying for the order stating on oath that at least one
of the two grounds in s 295(4) is satisfied.

What if the correct forms have not been served or the proper procedure not followed?

Caution should be taken to ensure that the proper procedures set out in the Magistrates' **15.82**
Court (Detention and Forfeiture of Cash) Rules 2002 are followed. However, since the
introduction of the Magistrates' Courts (Miscellaneous Amendments) Rules 2003, SI
2003/1236 the requirement to use any of the forms is considerably diluted and, in
cases other than Form A and G, omitted This reflects the case law that had developed in
relation to cash seizure cases, which dictated that use of the forms was directory rather than
mandatory.

In *R v Luton Justices ex p Abecasis* The Times, 30 March 2000, the Court of Appeal held **15.83**
that Form C under the DTA was no more than a request to continue the existing order and
that it did not have to be served on the person whose cash has been seized. All that was

required, the Court held, is that the clerk to the justices should fix a date for the hearing and notify the person whose cash had been seized that the hearing was so listed. Where that was done, the substance of the rule was complied with. (See also *R (On the application of Gorvievski) v HM Customs & Excise* [2003] EWHC 2773 (Admin) where the court confirmed a technical failure to fully comply with the rules did not invalidate the order subsequently made). (See also *Halford v Colchester Magistrates' Court* (QBD, 25 October 2000)).

15.84   A similar problem arose in the POCA case of *Chief Constable of Merseyside Police v Reynolds* [2004] EWHC (Admin) 2862. In *Reynolds* an order for continued detention was made at 10am on 11 February 2004 for a further period of 90 days. It was argued, by way of case stated, that the order must have expired at midnight on 10 May 2004. The hearing for further detention had taken place on the morning of 11 May 2004. Furthermore, the request for an extension of time had not been served seven days prior to the hearing, as is required by r 5 of the Magistrates' Courts (Detention and Forfeiture of Cash) Rules 2002, SI 2002/2998.

15.85   In relation to the latter point the Court (Rose LJ and Leveson J) held that the requirement in r 5 was merely directory and not mandatory (following *Halford* and *Abecasis*) and as such had no merit.

15.86   In terms of the expiry period, the Court held 11 February should be excluded when calculating the 90-day period (by reference to *Marren v Dawson Bentley &Co* [1961] 3 All ER 270 and *Radcliffe and Bartholomew* [1892] 1 QB 161, which establish that the day a cause of action arises or an offence is committed is to be excluded in computing a limitation period and that the principle applied whether the statute in question was dealing with civil or criminal cases). For a similar decision on the application of the *Abecasis* principle, and the refusal of further detention on the merits, see *Chief Constable of Lancashire Constabulary v Burnley Magistrates' Court* [2003] EWHC (Admin) 3308 and *Gorgievski v Customs and Excise Commissioners* [2003] EWHC Admin 2773.

15.87   These cases should not of course be regarded as an invitation to the police or other officers to not comply with the Rules. Leveson J commented in *Reynolds* that such arguments 'are entirely avoidable if the application is not made at the last moment'.

Insolvency and further detention hearings

15.88   An application for an order for the further detention of any cash for which s 311(3) applies (assets subject to insolvency proceedings) may not be made under s 295 unless the appropriate court gives leave (s 311(2)).

Early release of the cash—to the person from whom the cash was seized

15.89   Section 297(2) of POCA authorises the court to release the cash prior to the expiration of a detention order. A magistrates' court may only direct the release of the cash under s 297 (either in whole or in part) if the following condition is met: the court must be satisfied, on an application from the person *from whom the cash was seized*, that the conditions in s 295(5) and (6) for the detention of the cash that is to be released are no longer met (s 297(2) and (3)). The burden at this interim stage is on the person from whom the sash was seized, to the civil standard (*R (on the application of the Chief Constable of Greater Manchester) v City of Salford Magistrates' Court and Sarwar and Sons (Knitwear Ltd)* [2008] EWHC 1651 (Admin)).

An application under s 297(3) of the Act for the release of detained cash must be made in **15.90** writing and sent to the magistrates' court (see r 6(1)). If the applicant (the person from whom the cash was seized) has been given notice of an order under s 295(2) (continued detention) in respect of the detained cash, then the application should be sent to the magistrates' court who sent him that notice. Once an application has been received, the court must send a copy of the application to the police or Customs (r 6(3)(a)), and every person to whom notice of the order made under s 295(2) of the Act has been given (r 6(3) (c)). The Justices' Clerk must then fix a hearing date (see r 6(4)).

Only a person from whom the cash was seized is entitled to make such an application under **15.91** s 297(3). A third party affected by the order therefore will have no right to do so (but does under s 301).

Form D

The requirement for the magistrates' court to make a direction for the release of the detained **15.92** cash on Form D if it is satisfied that the condition set out in s 297(3) has been met is omitted by the Magistrates' Courts (Miscellaneous Amendments) Rules 2003, SI 2003/1236 and is no longer a requirement, although in practice courts are still using the forms for administrative convenience.

Form D appears to envisage that the court will hear oral evidence and representations. **15.93**

The court may either order the immediate release of the money or the release of the money **15.94** on a date not more than seven days from the date of the direction, unless a later date is agreed by the applicant.

Cash cannot be released where s 298(4) of POCA applies (ie while forfeiture proceedings **15.95** are ongoing).

Applications for early release by victims or other owners

Section 301 is part of the supplementary provisions to the cash forfeiture regime, and **15.96** allows a person who claims that any cash detained under Chapter 3 of POCA belongs to him, to apply to a magistrates' court for the release of the cash (or a part of it) (s 301(1)).

The application may be made in the course of proceedings under s 295 (detention of seized **15.97** cash) or s 298 (forfeiture) or 'at any other time' (s 301(2)).

An application under s 301(1) of the Act for the release of detained cash must be made in **15.98** writing and sent to the magistrates' court concerned (see r 6(1)).

Section 301 is divided into two parts: **15.99**
(a) for victims of unlawful conduct (s 301(3)); and
(b) for other owners of the cash where s 295(5) and (6) is no longer met (s 301(4)).

Section 301(3): victims of unlawful conduct

15.100   Section 301(3) states:

(3) If it appears to the court . . . concerned that—
  (a) the applicant was deprived of the cash to which the application relates, or of property which it represents, by unlawful conduct,
  (b) the property he was deprived of was not, immediately before he was deprived of it, recoverable property, and
  (c) that cash belongs to him,
  the Court may order the cash to which the application relates to be released to the applicant.

All three requirements must be met. An example of where s 301(3) may apply would be if a third party was to come forward who claimed that the money had been stolen from him at an earlier time, ie he was the victim of an unlawful event.

Form E: Order for release under section 301(3)

15.101   The requirement for the magistrates' court to make a direction for the release of the detained cash on Form E, if it is satisfied that the condition set out in s 297(3) has been met, is omitted by the Magistrates' Courts (Miscellaneous Amendments) Rules 2003, SI 2003/1236 and the form itself is no longer a requirement, although is likely to be adopted for administrative convenience.

Section 301(4): third party applications/other owners

15.102   Section 301(4) states:

(4) If—
  (a) the applicant is not the person from whom the cash to which the application relates was seized,
  (b) it appears to the court . . . that that cash belongs to the applicant,
  (c) the court . . . is satisfied that the conditions in section 295 for the detention of the cash are no longer met or, if an application has been made under section 298 [forfeiture], the court decides not to make an order under that section in relation to that cash, and
  (d) no objection to the making of an order under this subsection has been made by the person from whom the cash was seized,
  the court . . . may order the cash to which the application relates to be released to the applicant or to the person from whom it was seized.

All four criteria must be met before release can be sanctioned. Section 301(4)(c) is implicit that there must no longer be any reasonable grounds for suspecting the cash is recoverable property and no longer any reasonable grounds for suspecting that the cash is intended for use in unlawful conduct.

Objection to release under section 301(4) from the person from whom the cash was seized

15.103   Section 301(4)(d) is important because if the person from whom the cash was seized objects to the third party's claim to being the true owner of the money, whatever the merits of the third party's claim, the court will not be able to release it. It is in effect a veto, held by the person from whom the cash was seized. Section 301(4)(d), according to the explanatory notes that accompany POCA, is intended to prevent the court from becoming embroiled in a complicated ownership dispute between the party from whom the cash was seized and the rightful owner of the cash prior to the forfeiture hearing.

Form F: Order for release under section 301(4)

Although the importance of Form F has diminished since its omission from the Magistrates' **15.104**
Courts (Miscellaneous Amendments) Rules 2003, SI 2003/1236, in practice courts are
still using the form for the purposes of administrative convenience where it appears to the
court that:

(a) the sum was not seized from the applicant;
(b) the sum (whether in full or in part) belongs to the applicant;
(c) the conditions in s 295 of POCA for detaining the sum are no longer met;
(d) the court has decided not to order forfeiture of the sum under s 298(2) of POCA; and
(e) no objection to the making of the order was made by the person from whom the sum
      was seized or alternatively the cash was unattended.

Form F anticipates that any release of the sum under s 301(4) will include any interest **15.105**
accruing thereon, as per s 296(1). Under Rule 6(7):

A Direction under section 297(2) of the Act and an Order under section 301(3) or (4) of the Act shall
provide for the release of the cash within seven days of the date of the making of the Order or Direction,
or such longer period as, with the agreement of the Applicant, may be specified, except that cash shall
not be released while section 298(4) [where a forfeiture application has been made and proceedings
have not been concluded] applies.

Joinder

Under r 6(5), at the hearing of an application under s 301(1) the court may, if it thinks fit, **15.106**
order that the applicant be joined as a party to all the proceedings in relation to the detained
cash.

Applications for the return of the cash: standard of proof

In *Customs and Excise Commissioners v Mukesh Shah* (1999) 163 JP 759 (a DTA case) the **15.107**
court accepted that it was for the applicant to satisfy the magistrates' on the balance of
probabilities to release the cash if they were satisfied that there are no, or no longer any,
grounds for its detention or, on an application made by any other person, the detention of
the cash is not for that or any other reason justified.

In many civil cases the degree of probability required to establish proof may vary according **15.108**
to the allegation to be proved (see *Hornal v Neuberger Products Ltd* [1957] 1 QB 247), and
the court is often reluctant, when considering claims by the Crown, to apply merely a 51/49
per cent test where an individual's property or other assets are in jeopardy (see *Bater v Bater*
[1950] 2 All ER 458 and *B v Chief Constable of Avon and Somerset* [2001] 1 All ER 562).

Can officers agree to the release of cash?

Yes. Under s 297(4) of POCA, a police or Revenue and Customs officer may (after notify- **15.109**
ing the magistrates' court under whose order the cash is being detained) release the cash
in whole or in part, if he is satisfied the detention of the cash is no longer justified. It is
always advisable therefore for a defendant to first write to either the police or the relevant
Agency and set out the defendant's case for the return of the cash prior to contemplating
court action.

Transfer of proceedings

15.110 Under r 10 of the Magistrates' Court (Detention and Forfeiture of Cash) Rules 2002, SI 2002/2998, any person who is a party to, or affected by, proceedings under Chapter 3 of Pt 5 of POCA may, at any time, make application to the court dealing with the matter for the proceedings to be transferred to a different petty sessions area (r 10(1)). Applications should be made in writing (r 10(2)) and should specify the grounds on which they are made. The magistrates' court must send a copy of the application to the parties to the proceedings and any other people affected by the proceedings and fix a date for the hearing of the application under rr 10(3) and (4).

Transfer: what test is to be applied?

15.111 Under r 10(5) the court may grant the application for transfer if it is satisfied that it would be more convenient or fairer for proceedings to be transferred to a different petty sessions area. Rule 10(6) sets out the steps that the magistrates' court should follow if the application is granted.

E. Applications for Forfeiture of Detained Cash

Forfeiture proceedings

15.112 When the police, Revenue and Customs, or relevant Agency have completed their enquiries into the provenance of the detained monies and consider they have sufficient evidence, on the balance of probabilities, to establish the cash or any part of it is:

(a) recoverable property or
(b) intended by any person for use in unlawful conduct,

an application for forfeiture on Form G should be made (see s 298 of POCA).

15.113 By s 298(2):

(2) The court may order the forfeiture of the cash or any part of it if it is satisfied that the cash or part—
　(a) is recoverable property, or
　(b) is intended by any person for use in unlawful conduct.

Form G

15.114 An application under s 298(1) for forfeiture of the detained cash may be made on Form G (r 7(1), as amended by the Magistrates' Courts (Miscellaneous Amendments) Rules 2003, SI 2003/1236 and sent to the Justices' Chief Executive to whom applications for the continued detention of the cash under s 295(4) of the Act have been sent (if no applications in respect of the cash have been made under s 295(4) then the application must be sent to the Justices' Chief Executive of the court before which the police or Customs wish to make the application).

15.115 Where the 'reasonable grounds for suspicion' that led to the initial seizure of the cash are connected to the 'reasonable grounds for suspicion' which led to the seizure of cash under another order (made under s 295(2)), the application should be sent to the Justices' Chief Executive for the magistrates' court that made the first order.

Form G should then be sent to every person to whom notice of any order made under **15.116** s 295(2) (continued detention) has been given, and to any other person identified by the court as being affected by the application.

Form G requires the police or Revenue and Customs officer to state the grounds for his **15.117** belief that the cash is recoverable property or is intended by any person for use in unlawful conduct.

It is the applicant's responsibility and not the court's to send a copy of the application to the **15.118** various parties. This may well therefore require an enquiry by the applicant to the court.

If the recipient of that notification is not the person from whom the cash was seized, but **15.119** someone who claims that the cash belongs to him, and the court decides not to make a forfeiture order, the recipient 'third party' of Form G may then apply to the court under s 301(4) for the release of the cash to them (as per Form G).

Effect of lodging an application

Once an application for forfeiture (Form G) has been made the cash may not be released **15.120** until any proceedings in pursuance of that application (including any proceedings on appeal) are concluded.

Power for prosecutors to appear in cash recovery proceedings

Section 84 of the Serious Crime Act 2007 permits both the Crown Prosecution Service **15.121** (CPS) and the soon to be abolished Revenue and Customs Prosecutions Office (RCPO) to take forward cash recovery proceedings on behalf of a constable or HMRC if asked to do so and it is considered appropriate. It inserts s 302A into POCA, which also allows designated staff who are not prosecutors, together with outside contractors to appear in cash seizure proceedings. The amendments made by this section are further amended by para 12 of Sch 11 to the Act to include accredited financial investigators. Previously these matters were exclusively dealt with by either the relevant police force's solicitors' office, or HMRC's solicitor's office.

F. The Hearing

Hearing for directions

Once Form G has been issued the justices' clerk must set a date for a directions hearing (see **15.122** r 7(4)). At the directions hearing, the court may give directions relating to the management of the proceedings, including the date of the hearing.

Importantly, under r 7(6) if neither the person from whom the cash was seized, nor any **15.123** other person who was affected by the detention of the cash, seeks to contest the application, the court may decide the application at the directions hearing. It is therefore imperative that parties attend directions hearings, or at least make it clear on the record that they intend to contest the hearing. Failure to do so may lead to the court making an order in the defendant's absence. This rule was tested in *Leigh v Uxbridge Magistrates' Court* [2005] EWHC (QBD) 1828 where Goldring J, while expressing no principle, quashed an order for forfeiture made by the magistrates' court and remitted the matter back to the justices in circumstances where it was apparent that the defendant had made it clear through his solicitors and counsel on previous occasions that he would be contesting the hearing, but nevertheless failed to attend the directions hearing.

15.124   For the non-appearance of the defendant, complainant, or both at the hearing of the complaint: see ss 55–57 of the Magistrates' Court Act 1980.

What type of directions may be ordered?

15.125   Rule 7(5) appears to give the court a wide discretion:

> The Court may give Directions relating to the management of the proceedings, including Directions as to the date of the hearing of the application.

The court will be concerned to ensure that any witnesses who may be required are available and therefore parties should be prepared to notify the court of what witnesses they are likely to be calling and the length of their evidence. Enquiries should be made about whether any evidence can be agreed or reduced to admissions, eg the date of the seizure and the amount of the cash. Enquiry should also be made about the service of witness statements by way of mutual disclosure.

15.126   Enquiries should be made as to whether or not any expert witnesses will be called (eg forensic scientists), and whether or not any interpreters are required.

The forfeiture hearing

15.127   The purpose of the hearing is to determine whether, in accordance with s 298(2), the detained cash is recoverable property; or is intended by any person for use in unlawful conduct. If the court is so satisfied, it may order its forfeiture under s 298.

Procedure at hearings made on complaint

15.128   Rule 11(1) states:

> At the hearing of an application under Chapter 3 of Part 5 of the Act (either searches for cash or seizure of cash), any person to whom notice of the application has been given may attend and be heard on the question of whether the application should be granted. The fact that any such person does not attend should not prevent the Court from hearing the application.

15.129   Rule 11(2) states:

> . . . proceedings on such an application shall be regulated in the same manner as proceedings on a Complaint, and accordingly for the purposes of these rules the application shall be deemed to be a Complaint, the Applicant a Complainant, the Respondents to be Defendants, and any notice given by the Justices' Chief Executive under Rules 5(3), 6(4), 7(4), 8(4) or 10(4) to be a Summons: but nothing in this rule should be construed as enabling a Warrant of Arrest to be issued for failure to appear to any such Notice.

15.130   The rules in relation to the hearing of a complaint, procedure, and the jurisdiction of the magistrates' court are set out at s 51 *et seq* of the Magistrates' Courts Act 1980.

15.131   Section 52 confirms jurisdiction; s 53 deals with procedure, and states that at the hearing of a complaint, the court shall, if the defendant appears, state to him the substance of the complaint. Section 54 sets out the adjournment provisions, which may take place 'at any time'; and s 55 confirms that if a defendant does not appear the court may proceed in his absence. Similarly, under s 56 where at the time and place appointed for the hearing or adjourned hearing of a complaint the defendant appears but the complainant does not, the court may dismiss the complaint or, if evidence has been received on a previous occasion, proceed in the absence of the complainant. By s 57, where neither party attends, the court may dismiss the complaint; and s 58 deals with the transfer of proceedings.

Order of evidence and speeches

Rule 14 of the Magistrates' Courts Rules 1981 sets out the order of evidence and speeches **15.132** in civil cases made on complaint:

(1) On the hearing of a complaint the complainant shall call the evidence and before doing so may address the court.
(2) At the conclusion of the evidence for the complainant, the defendant may address the court, whether or not he afterwards calls evidence.
(3) At the conclusion of the evidence, if any, for the defence, the complainant may call evidence to rebut that evidence.
(4) At the conclusion of the evidence for the defence and the evidence, if any, in rebuttal, the defendant may address the court if he has not already done so.
(5) Either party may, with the leave of the court, address the court for a second time, but where the court grants leave to one party it shall not refuse leave to the other.
(6) Where the defendant obtains leave to address the court for a second time, his second address shall be made before the second address, if any, of the complainant.

It is important to note that the applicant's only opportunity to fully address the court **15.133** without leave comes when he opens his case. From the applicant's point of view, therefore, it is important that he gives as full an opening as he can, although depending on the facts of the case, he may apply for leave to address the court again for a second time.

Similarly, if the defendant chooses to address the court in opening and before he calls **15.134** evidence he loses his opportunity to make a closing speech without further leave. The usual rules apply, in that either party may address the court on a point of law at any time.

Although the defendant is at liberty to make a submission of no case to answer after the **15.135** applicant's case, some caution should be exercised, because if it fails and the defendant has been asked to choose between calling evidence and making a submission, he will not be entitled to call evidence thereafter. See *Boyce v Wyatt Engineering* The Times, 14 June 2001.

Matters to be sworn under oath

By r 11(3): **15.136**

At the hearing of an application under Chapter 3 of Part 5 of the Act, the Court shall require the matters contained in the application to be sworn by the Applicant under oath, may require the Applicant to answer any questions under oath and may require any response from the Respondent to the application to be made under oath.

G. Rules of Evidence

Burden and standard of proof

The burden is on the applicant, to prove the criteria set out in s 298(2). The standard **15.137** of proof, however, is that applicable in civil proceedings (ie proof on the balance of probabilities (see s 240(1)(b)). Once the applicant has satisfied the court to the required standard, it is for the defendant to show, also on the balance of probabilities, that the suggestion advanced by the applicant is incorrect.

15.138 In *Butt v Customs and Excise Commissioners* (2002) 166 JP 173 money in the possession of the appellant's nephew was seized by Customs officers. The appellant's nephew had been travelling to Amsterdam on a single ticket with a large sum of cash in brown paper packages in a locked case. The defence argued that the justices had not borne in mind the remarks made by Lord Bingham in *B v Chief Constable of Avon and Somerset* [2001] 1 WLR 340 to the effect that in serious cases the difference between civil and criminal standards is 'in truth largely illusory'. In dismissing the appeal the Court held that Parliament had explicitly provided that the civil standard of proof should apply in proceedings under s 43 of the DTA, namely 'more probable than not'. A forfeiture order made under the 1994 Act, they stated, involved no aspersions on the character of the applicant. Indeed, in this case the justices made no finding that the monies actually belonged to the appellant. The proceeding was effectively an action *in rem*, the courts findings only applying to the cash.

15.139 While the case of *Butt* suggests that the standard of proof need only be on the balance of probability, in accordance with the civil standard under which POCA operates, some caution needs to be exercised. In *Butt* the Court was of the view that since it had not been established that the money belonged to the appellant, who was a third party applicant, the order for forfeiture could not involve aspersions on the character of the owner. If, on the facts, a case cast aspersions on the character of the owner, it is submitted, the consequences might demand the application of a slightly higher standard of proof than the mere balance of probabilities. Support for this view is drawn from *Hornell v Neuberger* [1957] 1 QB 247 where Morris LJ said:

> . . . it is, I think, clear from the authorities that a difference of approach in civil cases has been recognised (in terms of the burden of proof). Many judicial utterances show this. The phrase 'balance of probabilities' is often employed as a convenient phrase to express the basis upon which civil issues are decided . . . in some civil cases the issues may involve questions of reputation which can transcend in importance even questions of personal liberty . . . In English law the citizen is regarded as being a free man of good repute. Issues may be raised in a civil action which affect character and reputation, and these will not be forgotten by judges and juries when considering the probabilities in regard to whatever misconduct is alleged. There will be reluctance to rob any man of his good name: there will also be reluctance to make any man pay what is not due or to make any man liable who is not or not liable who is.

Are previous convictions admissible?

15.140 In contrast to the position in criminal proceedings, any previous conviction of a person claiming an interest in the money is admissible and adverse inferences may be made against him in relation to same.

15.141 The effect of previous convictions was illustrated in the DTA case of *Ali v Best* (1997) 161 JP 393. In March 1992 the appellant had been convicted of an offence of possessing one ounce of heroin with intent to supply. In August 1994 Customs officers at Dover stopped him as he was about to leave the country and a holdall in the boot of his car was found to contain £48,830 in cash. No drugs were found in the vehicle and no traces of drugs were found on the bank notes. The justices ordered the money to be forfeited, and the appellant appealed by way of case stated. The High Court dismissed the appeal, McCowan J commenting in delivering the judgment of the court:

> In my judgment, evidence of that previous conviction and the facts of it were clearly admissible. The question that remains is, how cogent was it? In my judgment, it did have some cogency. It certainly called for an answer. The answer that he gave, apparently in interview, was that the money had come from trading in Cypriot antiques and, as he told the Customs officer when stopped, he was intending to use it to buy a Mercedes or two. He did not, however, go into the witness box. In my judgment [counsel for the respondent] is entitled to rely on that fact that he did not choose to give any explanation on oath. This is not a criminal case, this is a civil case and in my judgment in those circumstances, this is a matter which can properly be relied upon by the respondent.

In *R v Isleworth Crown Court ex p Kevin Marland* (1998) 162 JPR 251 the Court held that in **15.142** civil cases the rules concerning the admission of previous convictions were less circumscribed because the underlying intention is not to protect one side but to be fair to both sides. If the facts of the previous conduct are sufficiently similar to the facts sought to be proved in the instant case as to be logically probative, then evidence of previous conduct is admissible and that would include spent convictions, subject only to the judge's discretion to exclude them on such grounds as oppression, unfairness, or surprise. Mrs Justice Smith held:

> . . . it matters not whether the evidence is of a conviction or whether it is of past conduct which has not resulted in the conviction . . . When exercising its discretion to admit spent convictions the Court must be satisfied that justice cannot otherwise be done. Justice means justice to both parties. These convictions were plainly of some relevance to the issues in the case . . . because of the lapse of time, they may be said to have less probative value than if they were more recent. Some tribunals might well have considered the prejudicial effect outweighed the probative value. However that is not to say that I think the decision to admit them was obviously wrong—I do not.

In *Customs and Excise Commissioners v T* (1998) 162 JP 193, Customs and Excise sought to **15.143** produce evidence that the defendant had previously been charged with the importation of drugs, albeit that when the matter came to trial the prosecution had offered no evidence against him. The Luton Magistrates had ruled that that evidence was not admissible. The magistrates were asked to state a case. In Lord Justice Staughton's judgment Customs and Excise were not precluded from relying on the evidence of the previous incident. There were no estoppels against them because of the acquittal, and the standard of proof required in the forfeiture proceedings was the civil and not the criminal standard. In so finding he ruled that the lower court had not been correct to rule that the evidence of the earlier incident was inadmissible, although what weight the court should have given that evidence would have clearly been dictated by the facts of the case.

Once, therefore, a previous conviction or previous alleged criminal conduct can be shown **15.144** to be relevant to the issues to be determined under the cash forfeiture provisions it may be admitted.

Is there a need for direct evidence of the unlawful conduct?

No. In *Butt v Customs and Excise* (2002) 166 JP Reports 173, the court held that in applica- **15.145** tions under s 43 of the DTA there was no need for direct evidence of connection to drugs for the purpose of discharging the burden of proof.

The drawing of inferences and illustrative cases

15.146   The drawing of inferences was a common thread through a number of cases under the DTA. In *Bassick and Osborne v Customs and Excise Commissioners* (1997) 161 JP 377, the magistrates came to the conclusion, having paid particular regard to the circumstances surrounding Bassick's possession of the cash seized, that it was more likely than not that the money directly or indirectly represented a person's proceeds of, or was intended by any person for use in, drug trafficking. Bassick was unemployed at the time he was stopped and on his way to Amsterdam with £21,520 in cash in various denominations, with a single flight ticket that had been bought shortly before the departure time of the aircraft. He possessed a note giving him instructions on how to reach an address in Amsterdam, and he had made no arrangements for his return journey or for his accommodation abroad. The magistrates had also noted his evasive demeanour and that of his witnesses when they testified. Accordingly the magistrates ordered forfeiture. There was nothing to suggest that either of the two defendants had been convicted of criminal offences involving drugs. There was nothing to suggest that they had been associated with people who were known to be connected with drug trafficking, nor was there anything to suggest that they were known to a person or persons in Amsterdam who were known to be so involved. On appeal Watkins LJ said:

> I can see no flaw in the way in which they (the Justices) approached it, and none in the decision which they reached upon it. It seems to me that there was ample material to allow them to come to the conclusion which they did . . . the overbearing fact is that these Justices simply did not believe Osborne and Bassick.

15.147   A similar decision was reached in *R v Dover and East Kent Magistrates' Court ex p Steven Gore* (QBD, 23 May 1996) where Auld LJ held:

> . . . the Magistrates were entitled and indeed bound, to take into account all the circumstances (of the case): the circumstances in which the money was seized; the amount of the money; the fact that it was contaminated albeit slightly with traces of cannabis or cannabis resin; the refusal of the applicant before caution to give an explanation as to who had given him the money, at a time when it might be expected that he would or could have given an explanation. The Magistrates were entitled to take into account the answers he gave in interview that I have summarised, an account which, putting aside any refusals to answer, raised more questions than it answered. I have no doubt that the Magistrates were entitled to apply the civil burden of proof to conclude as they did and to order the forfeiture of the money accordingly.

15.148   In *Muneka v Customs and Excise Commissioners* [2005] EWHC (Admin) 495, a case that was dealt with under s 298 of POCA and concerned an appellant who was stopped at Heathrow with £22,760 in cash in his possession while on his way to Albania via Hungary, Moses J held:

> In my judgement, in this context the fact that there was no explanation for the source of that money, no reasonable explanation as to why he was taking that cash to Albania, the fact that there were discrepancies in his explanations as to the source of the money and as to its final destination, taken together, did establish, both source and intention . . . on the balance of probabilities.

Hearsay in civil cases

15.149   The Magistrates' Courts (Hearsay Evidence in Civil Proceedings) Rules 1999, SI 1999/681, set out the rules applying to hearsay in magistrates' courts.

Those rules provide as follows: **15.150**

3(1) Subject to paragraphs (2) and (3), a party who desires to give hearsay evidence at the hearing must, not less than 21 days before the date fixed for the hearing, serve a hearsay notice on every other party and file a copy in the court by serving it on the justices' clerk.

3(2) Subject to paragraph (3), the court or the justices' clerk may make a direction substituting a different period of time for the service of the hearsay notice under paragraph (1) on the application of a party to the proceedings.

3(3) The court may make a direction under paragraph (2) of its own motion.

3(4) A hearsay notice must—
   (a) state that it is a hearsay notice;
   (b) identify the proceedings in which the hearsay evidence is to be given;
   (c) state that the party proposes to adduce hearsay evidence;
   (d) identify the hearsay evidence;
   (e) identify the person who made the statement which is to be given in evidence; and
   (f) state why that person will not be called to give oral evidence.

3(5) A single hearsay notice may deal with the hearsay evidence of more than one witness.

These Rules make provision for the requirements of the Civil Evidence Act 1995 in relation   **15.151**
to hearsay evidence in civil proceedings in magistrates' courts. They also make provision for:

- the procedure to call a witness for cross-examination on hearsay evidence (r 4);
- a notice requirement where a party tenders hearsay evidence (but does not call the person who made the statement to give oral evidence) and another party wishes to attack the credibility of the person who made the statement or allege that he has made another statement inconsistent with it (r 5);
- the service of documents required by the Rules (r 6).

However, a failure to comply with the duty to give notice should not affect the admissibility   **15.152**
of hearsay evidence (see s 1(1) of the Civil Evidence Act 1995 and s 1(2) which is specifically adopted by r 2(2)). It then becomes a question of weight for the justices to determine. In assessing the weight, all the relevant circumstances should be considered including the fact that the individual who makes the statement has not been tendered in cross-examination and therefore has not been tested. The desirability of serving a hearsay notice is obvious, as a party may find itself liable for costs if a witness statement tendered at the hearing reveals new evidence that the other side has not had the opportunity of exploring, or evidence that amounts to an ambush.

Section 4(2) of the Civil Evidence Act 1995 provides some guidance that may assist the   **15.153**
court when assessing what weight should be given to hearsay. That guidance includes:

   (i) Whether it would have been reasonable and practicable to have produced the person who made the statements rather than relying on a hearsay report of them;
   (ii) Whether the person who originally made the statements made them contemporaneously with the matters stated;
   (iii) Whether the evidence is multiple hearsay, in other words whether the hearsay witness is in fact repeating something which itself is hearsay;
   (iv) Whether anyone involved has a motive to conceal or misrepresent matters;
   (v) Whether the original statement was made for some purpose or produced in collaboration with others;
   (vi) Whether the attempt to rely on hearsay rather than calling the person who made the original statement is designed to prevent a proper evaluation of its weight by the court.

15.154 In the Crown Court the position in slightly different, although the same principle appears to apply. In *R v Wadmore and Foreman* [2006] EWCA Crim 686, a case that concerned an application for an anti-social behaviour order (ASBO), the Court of Appeal held that ASBOs amounted to civil proceedings in a criminal court. The Criminal Procedure Rules 2005 do not apply to civil cases. The Civil Procedure Rules 1998 do not apply in criminal courts. The Magistrates' Courts (Hearsay Evidence in Civil Proceedings) Rules 1999, SI 1999/681 do not apply to the Crown Court. The Court of Appeal therefore assumed, without deciding, that as the case was civil in nature, hearsay evidence was admissible under s 1 of the Civil Evidence Act 1995. There were no applicable procedural rules and the Court thought that the Magistrates' Court Rules should be applied by analogy.

Lies told by the defendant

15.155 In *Nevin v Customs and Excise Commissioners* (QBD, 3 November 1995), Smedley J stated:

> While the prescribed Civil Standard of proof would not, of course, allow the Justices to act without satisfactory evidence on the intended use of the money, they are not required to direct themselves, for example, in relation to lies told by a defendant, as the Judge would direct a jury in a criminal trial. That is not to say that they should overlook the possibility that lies may have the purpose of concealing something other than the misconduct presently alleged. But a suspect who gives an account of his reasons for carrying the money which the Justices reject as untruthful cannot complain if the Justices go on to infer from other relevant evidence, that by itself might not have been enough to satisfy them, that the true reason was for the use of [drug trafficking].

15.156 This passage was specifically referred to and approved by Moses J in *Muneka v Customs and Excise Commissioners* [2005] EWHC (Admin) 495, in which he stated:

> Those comments apply with added force in the context of this case where it is not necessary to identify any criminal activity such as drug trafficking; all that has to be identified is that the source was criminal activity or the intended destination was use for criminal activity. A lie in that context may well entitle the fact-finding body to infer what the source or intention for which the cash was to be used was in reality on the balance of probabilities.

15.157 In Moses J's judgment the fact that the appellant had lied was evidence upon which the district judge was entitled to conclude that the suggestions in relation to unlawful conduct being put to him were in fact true on the balance of probabilities:

> The District Judge was entitled to ask herself: why should this appellant have lied about the source and destination of that cash? He must have appreciated that such lies could have had no reasonable explanation, other than that the suggestions made to him as to their source and as to destination were in fact true.

15.158 Moses J went on to cite *Bassick and Osborne* [1993] 161 JP 377 as authority for the proposition that lies in a particular context may establish a positive case as to the source of the money.

Mass Spec expert reports

15.159 Previously, under the DTA regime, it would be commonplace in most s 43 applications for Customs to rely upon an expert's report from Mass Spec Analytical to demonstrate that the cash seized had traces, all be they microscopic, of drugs. That practice continues to operate in cases where the unlawful conduct may be related to drugs. The police have also used Mass Spec and their own Forensic Science Services to show traces of drugs on cash seized.

Mass Spec Analytical Ltd is a company that has for many years specialised in chemical **15.160** analysis using a method known as mass spectral analysis. The technique is extremely sensitive. It can detect one nanogram of a drug, that has been described in layman's terms as being approximately one million times less than a single grain of sugar. It cannot identify the precise quantity of the drug, although it can determine orders of magnitude.

It is now universally recognised by the forensic science services that all UK notes in general **15.161** circulation are likely to be contaminated with cocaine. This is not necessarily so with Ecstasy (MDMA) or cannabis (Tetrahydrachlorine). For further reading see: K A Ebejer, J Winn, J F Carter, R Sleeman, J Parker, and F Körber, *Forensic Science International*, 2007, 167, pp 94–101: The difference between drug money and a 'lifetime's savings'; S J Dixon, R G Brereton, J F Casale, and R Sleeman, *Analytica Chimica Acta*, 2006, 559, pp 54–63: Determination of cocaine contamination on banknotes using tandem mass spectrometry and pattern recognition; K A Ebejer, G R Lloyd, R G Brereton, J F Carter, and R Sleeman, *Forensic Science International*: Factors influencing the contamination of UK banknotes with drugs of abuse.

In *Thomas v Customs and Excise Commissioners* (1997) 161 JP 386, the defence argued that **15.162** when considering whether the cash was *intended* for use in drug trafficking the magistrates had been wrong to pay attention to evidence of traces of drugs on the notes. That could, it was submitted, only be relevant if the cash *represented* the proceeds of drugs trafficking. In *Thomas* the suggestion was that the cash was to be exchanged for drugs in the future. The Court rejected this argument on the basis that, although such evidence would normally relate to past dealing, it could also show that a source near to the carrier of the cash had contaminated the notes.

In *Compton v R* [2002] EWCA Crim 2835, a case which sought to criticise the methods **15.163** employed by Mass Spec, the Court of Appeal held that the range and weight of Mass Spec's database was 'sufficient for comparisons safely to be based on it'. A similar conclusion was reached in *Benn v R* [2004] EWCA Crim 2100 where doubts as to the validity of the methodology employed by Mass Spec and doubts as to the robustness of the findings because of the risks of innocent contamination were raised. (For further reading on drug contamination of bank notes see *Archbold News*, Issue 7, 16 August 2006.)

Mass Spec is currently developing the technology of identifying traces of explosives and **15.164** other prohibited substances on cash, as well as the linking of traces of drugs on money to drugs discovered in other police and Revenue and Customs operations.

For the value in criminal proceedings of Mass Spec reports see *R v Ali Hussain* [2005] **15.165** EWCA Crim 87.

Record of proceedings

Under r 11(4) there is a duty for the legal advisor and/or the court to keep a record of any **15.166** statements made under oath that are not already recorded in the written application.

In other words, the court must keep a record of proceedings, which may be later referred to in any appeal.

Form H: order for forfeiture

15.167 The requirement for the magistrates' court to use Form H is omitted by the Magistrates' Courts (Miscellaneous Amendments) Rules 2003, SI 2003/1236, and is no longer necessary for an order for the forfeiture of detained cash under s 298(2) and r 7(7).

Sensitive material

15.168 Although public interest immunity (PII) applications do not feature in magistrates' courts, exclusion of evidence on the grounds of public policy applies equally to civil proceedings as it does in criminal. The test is whether the production of a document or other piece of evidence would be 'injurious to the public interest'; ie whether the withholding of a document/information is necessary for the proper functioning of a government department. For example, the disclosure of the document may jeopardise an ongoing operation, or the methods deployed, or cooperation received from others in the investigation of an offence.

15.169 It is important to remember that the issue the court is having to decide is that set out in s 298(2), namely whether the seized cash is recoverable property; or is intended by any person for use in unlawful conduct. Considerations such as why the individual was stopped in the first place, or what information the police held on that individual, therefore fall away as being largely irrelevant to the test the court is having to apply, which focuses on the cash and its intended/previous purpose. (By analogy see *Hoverspeed v Customs and Excise Commissioners* [2002] EWCA Civ 1804 at paras 44–49.)

Joint owners

15.170 Under s 298(3), where the recoverable property belongs to joint owners, the order for forfeiture of the cash may not apply to any amount the court thinks is attributable to an innocent joint owner's share. Section 270(4) states:

> An excepted joint owner is a person who obtained the property in circumstances in which it would not be recoverable as against him; and references to the 'excepted joint owner's share' of the recoverable property are to so much of the recoverable property as would have been his if the joint tenancy had been severed.

In other words, the court must not forfeit the cash that is attributable to the innocent partner's share (eg if two business partners have a joint bank account, and one of those partners has been trading legitimately and paying legitimate money into it whereas the other one, unbeknown to the other, has been paying in drug trafficking proceeds, if the illegitimate partner were to withdraw all of the cash in the account and it was subsequently seized, the court would have to distinguish between the clean and the 'dirty' money. The court would be entitled to return to the innocent partner his share of the money.).

H. Costs and Compensation

15.171 The successful party may apply for his costs against the unsuccessful party. However, as in all costs matters, the court does have an element of discretion and would, for example, be entitled to refuse costs against a successful party whose behaviour had led the applicant to believe his case was stronger than it really was or where the case has been dismissed on a technicality rather than on the merits.

Costs payable at each application and not carried forward

In *R v Dover Magistrates' Court ex p Customs and Excise Commissioners* The Times, 12 **15.172** December 1995, a series of orders were made by the magistrates' court for continued detention of the money. During that period notice was given that an application for forfeiture had been lodged by Customs. Having put in that notice of application for forfeiture, Customs then gave notice that they did not intend to proceed with their application. Those representing the defendant applied for an order from the magistrates that Customs should pay the defendant's costs. The magistrates made the order, and said that if costs could not be agreed then they would assess the costs themselves. Subsequently, the magistrates made an order that the costs should be paid in accordance with the bill submitted by the defendant's solicitors. On appeal to the Divisional Court the issue was whether the defendant's bill included costs not only in relation to the proposed forfeiture hearing, but also in relation to the earlier continued detention hearings. Section 52(3) of the Courts Act 1971 provides that where:

> (b) a complaint is made to a Justice of the Peace acting for any area but the complaint is not proceeded with, a Magistrates' Court for that area may make such order as to costs to be paid by the Complainant to the Defendant as it thinks just and reasonable.

In the *Dover* case there was a complaint made to the justices asking for forfeiture. Under **15.173** s 64(1) of the Magistrates' Courts Act 1980:

> (1) On the hearing of a complaint a Magistrates' Court shall have power in its discretion to make such order as to costs that—
>
>   (a) on making the order for which the complaint is made, to be paid by the Defendant to the Complainant;
>
>   (b) on dismissing the complaint, to be paid by the Complainant to the Defendant, as it thinks just and reasonable . . .

The distinction between the two is that s 64 of the Magistrates' Courts Act deals with cases where the complaint has been heard and determined, whereas s 52 of the Courts Act deals with cases where the complaint is not proceeded with.

The Divisional Court had to determine whether or not there was one complaint initiated **15.174** by the first detention proceedings which continued up to and including the forfeiture proceedings; or whether there were separate complaints in respect of continued detention and forfeiture. Staughton LJ in the judgment of the court held that it was clear that there was more than one complaint: 'There was a complaint for forfeiture and at least one complaint if not more for detention'. He explained:

> First, in the circumstances of this case, the costs of detention proceedings fall to be dealt with under section 64. That says that where a complaint has succeeded the Court may award the costs to the Complainant, and where it has failed it may award the costs to the Defendant. That seems to me inconsistent with the court, in this case, awarding the costs of the detention proceedings, which have succeeded, to the Defendant. The second reason is this: it seems to me implicit in section 52 that what the Court may award is the cost of the proceedings in question. I cannot accept that section 52 gives the Magistrates carte blanche to award any other costs on any other matter whatsoever if they think it just and reasonable to do so. In my opinion the power relates to the cost of the proceedings in question.

15.175 It is therefore incumbent on the parties to ensure that costs are dealt with at the end of each individual application for continued detention. Costs may not be 'reserved' to later hearings, although it should be noted that once a forfeiture application has been lodged any hearing that takes place following the lodging of the application, eg a pre-trial review, forms part of the same application and therefore costs need not be dealt with until the hearing itself.

Costs under section 64 of the Magistrates' Courts Act 1980

15.176 The court has a discretion to make an award of costs in favour of the successful party. The successful party must specify the sum and such order must be such costs as the court thinks 'just and reasonable' (see *Orton v (1) Truro Crown Court and (2) West Cornwall Magistrates' Court* [2009] EWHC 168 (Admin)). The magistrates' court does not enforce these costs. There is no imprisonment in default. It is not treated as a fine. They merely create a civil debt between the applicant and the defendant. Enforcement is a matter for the county court, if the successful party thinks it is worth enforcing. When considering a costs order against a defendant, his means may be a relevant factor, because the court has to consider what sum is just and reasonable in the circumstances of the case. At this stage of the proceedings the court may be minded to infer that the defendant is of sufficient means if they have sat through a hearing where details of large sums of cash have been given. Conversely, if the applicant has just been awarded, by virtue of the court's finding, a large amount of money, then the court may not be minded to grant costs at all.

15.177 Pursuant to s 62(2) the amount ordered to be paid shall be specified in the order and s 62(3) confirms that the costs ordered shall be enforceable as a civil debt.

The issue when seeking to obtain defence costs

15.178 In *Perinpanathan v City of Westminster Magistrates' Court and 2 others* [2009] EWHC 762 (Admin) the test for the award of costs to a successful defendant was considered and set out. The Divisional Court adopted the words of Lord Bingham in *Bradford Metropolitan District Council v Booth* (CO/3219/99) The Times, 31 May 2000, a case where the local council had refused to renew Mr Booth's private hire operator's licence on the grounds Mr Booth had broken a condition, but in which Mr Booth had appealed to the magistrates' court and had been successful. He sought his costs on the basis that they should follow the event (CPR 44.3). Lord Bingham stated:

> 23. I would accordingly hold that the proper approach to questions of this kind can for convenience be summarised is three propositions:

> 24. (1) Section 64(1) confers a discretion upon a Magistrates' Court to make such order as to costs as it thinks just and reasonable. That provision applies both to the quantum of the costs (if any) to be paid, but also as to the party (if any) which should pay them.

> 25. (2) What the court will think just and reasonable will depend on all the relevant facts and circumstances of the case before the court. The court may think it just and reasonable that costs should follow the event, but need not think so in all cases covered by the subsection.

> 26. (3) Where a complainant has successfully challenged before justices an administrative decision made by a police or regulatory authority acting honestly, reasonably, properly

and on grounds that reasonably appeared to be sound, in exercise of its public duty, the court should consider, in addition to any other relevant fact or circumstances, both (i) the financial prejudice to the particular complainant in the particular circumstances if an order for costs is not made in his favour; and (ii) the need to encourage public authorities to make and stand by honest, reasonable and apparently sound administrative decisions made in the public interest without fear of exposure to undue financial prejudice if the decision is successfully challenged.

The Magistrates' Court in *Parinpanathan* had refused to award costs, on the basis that the cash seizure had been properly brought by the police. The Divisional Court concluded that they had acted properly, Goldring LJ commenting (at 29):   **15.179**

> . . . I accept that there is a difference between administrative decisions such as those referred to in *Bradford* and the present case. The distinction is limited, however. In one case a police officer (at possible risk to someone's livelihood) is saying that the person will not have an on-licence, for example. In the other, he is saying the person will not have his (or in this case her) money returned. In taking both decisions, it is crucial that the police act honestly, reasonably, properly, and on grounds that reasonably appear to be sound. In both cases there is a need to make and stand by honest, reasonable and apparently sound decisions in the public interest without fear of exposure to undue financial prejudice, in one case if the decision is successfully challenged, in the other if the application fails. There is a real public interest that the police seek an order for forfeiture if they consider that on the evidence it is more probable than not that the money was intended for an unlawful purpose. It would be quite contrary to the public interest if, due to fear of financial consequences, it was decided not to seek its forfeiture, but simply return the money. The public duty requires the police to make an application in such circumstances.

However, notwithstanding the court's refusal to pay costs to the successful party in this instance, the police or Revenue and Customs cannot assume that they may proceed with impunity. Goldring LJ made clear at para 33:   **15.180**

> . . . it should not be thought that those who bring these applications have carte blanche to make applications for forfeiture without any risk of costs being awarded against them. Such applications can result in grave injustice if not made honestly, reasonably, properly and on grounds that are sound. If applications are made inappropriately, the court should not hesitate to make an order for costs against the applicant.

Legal Services Commission funding

Pursuant to Sch 11 para 36 to POCA, the Access to Justice Act 1999 (AJA) was amended by POCA to insert at Sch 2 para 2(3) of the AJA a provision that allows for Legal Services Commission (LSC) funding to be obtained for an order or direction under ss 295, 297, 298, 301, or 302 of POCA (the cash forfeiture and supplementary matters provisions). In particular, this allows for advocacy to be met by LSC funding.   **15.181**

In practice, solicitors should complete a LSC Merits form and also the appropriate Means form. This may then be submitted to the relevant LSC office who will then decide whether or not it should be granted.   **15.182**

Practical difficulties might arise, including the fact that the claimant has just had a large amount of cash seized from him. This obviously gives rise to a question in relation to their means and will often lead to delay while the LSC investigate matters. Often as a result   **15.183** defendants in cash seizure cases are left either defending themselves or with their advisers sometimes acting on a conditional fee arrangement.

15.184 Quite why the cash seizure provisions are dealt with differently to those for civil recovery elsewhere under Pt 5 of the Act is not immediately clear. In civil recovery matters heard before the High Court, judges were fairly robust in resisting applications from the (former) Assets Recovery Agency (ARA) whilst LSC funding was being determined. It was in part as a result of the robust attitude of the judiciary that the amendments to the Serious Organised Crime and Police Act that now allow for restrained funds to be utilised to fund representation were introduced (based on arguments such as equality of arms etc). It could equally be argued that it is unfair for a defendant to have to respond to a complaint made by either the police or another Agency until his LSC funding has been determined.

May funds be released from the detained cash to fund continued detention and forfeiture applications?

15.185 The short answer appears to be No. In *Customs and Excise Commissioners v Harris* (1999) 163 JPR 408 Forbes J held:

> I am satisfied that there is no proper basis for extending to the Magistrates a power to make any order for the release of lawfully detained cash which has been seized pursuant to the provision of Section 42 of the 1994 Act, because of the absence of any specific Statutory power to make such an order and it is plain that the 1994 Act contains no provision empowering the Magistrates to make any such order.

And nor does POCA 2002.

Wasted costs

15.186 The power of the magistrates' court to make a wasted costs order is governed by s 145A of the Magistrates' Court Act 1980 and SI 1991/2096. Costs are further considered in Chapter 22.

Compensation

15.187 Under s 302(1) of POCA compensation may be paid to either the person from whom the cash was seized or the person to whom the cash belongs.

15.188 Section 302(1) states:

> If no forfeiture order is made in respect of any cash claimed under this Chapter, the person to whom the cash belongs or from whom it was seized might make an application to the Magistrates' Court for compensation.

15.189 Under s 302(4) if the court is satisfied, presumably on the balance of probabilities, that, taking account of any interest to be paid under s 296 the applicant has suffered a loss as a result of the detention of the cash, and that the circumstances are 'exceptional', the court may order compensation, or additional compensation, to be paid to him.

15.190 The amount of compensation to be paid under subs 4 is the amount the court thinks reasonable, having regard to the loss suffered and any other relevant circumstances (see s 302(5)).

This section applies to compensation for loss incurred as a result of the detention of the **15.191** cash. Therefore, if an individual has suffered loss for any other reason, there is no recourse under this section.

Section 302 does not define what 'exceptional circumstances' are, nor does it give any **15.192** indication as to the type of losses that would be considered appropriate. For example, ordinarily in a civil case the successful party would be entitled to claim their legal costs. That clearly does not come under the heading of compensation. Loss of earnings, however, in having to attend court in order to defend the forfeiture application, may be included. The question is whether or not loss of earnings would constitute 'exceptional circumstances'. 'Exceptional' has a dictionary meaning of 'not ordinary; uncommon; rare; hence, better than the average; superior; unusual; beyond the norm'.

The court will also need to satisfy itself, again on the balance of probabilities, that the loss **15.193** was 'as a result of the detention of the cash'.

Application for compensation

Under r 8(1) an application for compensation under s 302(1) must be made in writing **15.194** and sent to the Justices' Chief Executive before which the applicant wishes to make the application. However, under r 8(2), if the applicant has been given notice of an order under s 295(2) of the Act in respect of the cash which is the subject of the application, then the application must be sent to the Justices' Chief Executive who sent him that notice. The Justices' Chief Executive will send a copy of the application to either the police or the relevant Agency and then fix a date for the hearing of the application (see r 8(3)). Clearly therefore the Rules anticipate a separate and distinct hearing—the pre-requisite being an application in writing. (For further discussion on compensation applications, see Chapter 22.)

I. Appeals

Appeals against forfeiture

Section 299 of POCA was amended by s 101 of the Serious Organised Crime and Police **15.195** Act 2005 (SOCPA) because of an ambiguity as to its meaning. While the original s 299(1) appeared to allow 'any party to the proceedings' the ability to appeal against an order made under s 298, this was qualified by the words 'for the forfeiture of cash'. This meant that while any party may appeal an order for forfeiture there was no provision for the complainant (the police or HMRC) to appeal a refusal to grant forfeiture, although somewhat ironically a complainant could appeal an order for forfeiture.

The substituted s 299 now states: **15.196**

(1) Any person to proceedings for an order for the forfeiture of cash under section 298 who is aggrieved by an order under that section or by the decision of the court to make such an order may appeal.

In other words, both the complainant and the defendant now have a right of appeal from the magistrates' court hearing to the Crown Court. Such a hearing will normally be *de novo* (s 79(3) of the Supreme Court Act 1981), with the facts being re-examined in the court above, and with the opportunity for both parties to serve further evidence before the hearing takes place (while the original s 299(3) expressly stated that the appeal was by way of re-hearing, the substituted legislation does not).

15.197 The appeal is to the Crown Court and notice must be lodged before the expiration of 30 days from when the order or decision was made (substituted s 299(2)).

15.198 This section also has the effect of allowing the Crown Court to hear the appeal in the most appropriate way, for example, on a point of law only.

Can the 30-day period for the date of the appeal be extended?

15.199 It appears not. In *R v West London Magistrates' Court ex p Rowland Omo Lamai* (QBD, 6 July 2000), a DTA case, the High Court held that the 30-day period could not be extended by either a Crown Court or a magistrates' court; and that the 30-day deadline was a deadline without flexibility.

Funding the appeal

15.200 The provision under s 44(4) of the DTA for the release of cash in order to fund an appeal in DTA cases no longer exists under the corresponding provisions of s 299 (although it should be noted that substituted s 299(3) states that the court hearing the appeal may make 'any order it thinks appropriate'. It is anticipated that there is likely to be argument as to whether this can be extended to ordering release of part of the cash in order to fund the appeal, particularly where the appellant's arguments have merit, he can demonstrate that he has no other available funds, and that he requires representation, ie 'equality of arms' at the Crown Court. By implication ECHR arguments arise if such a request were refused without proper consideration).

Costs in appeal proceedings

15.201 For the Crown Court's powers to award costs in appeals brought from the magistrates' court, see rr 78.1 and 78.2 of the Criminal Procedure Rules.

Judicial review

15.202 While there remains obvious scope for judicial review proceedings in cash seizure cases, in *M v Bow Street Magistrates' Court* The Times, 27 July 2005 the court held that in proceedings under the Anti-Terrorism, Crime and Security Act 2001 it was premature to seek permission to challenge by way of judicial review a district judge's decision on a preliminary ruling when the judge had not yet determined any of the factual issues or received evidence in relation to the substantive matter. The Divisional Court held that it would be impossible to know precisely how the legal issues would arise until the evidence was heard and the facts were found. Appeals in cash seizure cases are further considered in Chapter 18.

J. Searches and Seizure of Cash

15.203 The second part of the regime under POCA deals with the power to search and seize cash found on either premises or on an individual. These provisions also came into force on

30 December 2002 (SI 2002/3015). Many of the procedural rules that apply to cash seizures under the seizure and detention provisions of s 294 apply equally to cash searches.

Cash on premises

Section 289 states: **15.204**

(1) If a Customs Officer, a constable or an accredited financial investigator who is lawfully on any premises has reasonable grounds for suspecting that there is on the premises cash—
    (a) which is recoverable property or is intended by any person for use in unlawful conduct, and
    (b) the amount of which is not less than the minimum amount, he may search for the cash there.

The minimum amount: £1,000

Under s 303, the 'minimum amount' is defined as the amount in sterling specified in an   **15.205**
order made by the Secretary of State (£1,000—SI 2006/1699) and for that purpose the amount of any cash held in a currency other than sterling must be taken to be the sterling equivalent.

These search powers can only be exercisable, therefore, if the suspected cash is thought to   **15.206**
exceed the threshold of £1,000.

The definition of 'cash'

Under s 289(6) cash means: **15.207**

(a) notes and coins in any currency,
(b) postal orders,
(c) cheques of any kind (including travellers cheques),
(d) bankers drafts,
(e) bearer bonds and bearer shares
found at any place in the UK.

Section 289(1) is only exercisable on private premises where the police or Revenue and   **15.208**
Customs have lawful authority to be present (see PACE 1984 and Customs & Excise Management Act 1979 (CEMA)). An officer could also be lawfully present on private premises if he is there at the invitation of the owner.

Cash on the suspect

Under s 289(2):   **15.209**

(2) If a Customs Officer, a constable or an accredited financial investigator has reasonable grounds for suspecting that a person (the suspect) is carrying cash—
    (a) which is recoverable property or is intended by any person to be used in unlawful conduct, and
    (b) the amount of which is not less than the minimum amount [£1,000], he may exercise the following powers.
(3) The officer, constable or accredited financial investigator may, so far as he thinks it necessary or expedient, require the suspect—
    (a) to permit a search of any article he has with him;
    (b) to make a search of his person.

This section does not require the person to submit to an intimate search or a strip search (within the meaning of s 164 CEMA 1979) (see s 289(8)). However, under s 289(4) an officer exercising his powers under s 289(3)(b) may detain the suspect for 'so long as is necessary for the exercise'.

15.210 Under s 289(5) the powers conferred by s 289(1) and (2) are exercisable only so far as is reasonably required for the purpose of finding cash and are exercisable by a Revenue and Customs officer only if he has reasonable grounds for suspecting the unlawful conduct in question relates to an assigned matter within the meaning of CEMA. Areas within the meaning of CEMA include drug trafficking, money laundering, and excise evasion.

Unlawful conduct

15.211 See s 241 at para 15.27 above.

Safeguards for the new search powers

15.212 The powers conferred by s 289 may only be exercised when the appropriate approval has been given unless it is not practicable to obtain that approval before exercising the power (s 290(1)).

15.213 The appropriate approval means the approval of a judicial officer or, if that is not practicable, the approval of a senior officer (s 290(2)). Under s 290(3)(a) a judicial officer means a justice of the peace.

15.214 A senior officer means, in relation to the exercise of the power by a Revenue and Customs officer, a Revenue and Customs officer of a rank designated by HMRC as equivalent to that of a senior police officer and in relation to the exercise of the power by a constable, a senior police officer (an inspector or above) (see s 290(4)). The grading and seniority of accredited financial investigators are framed by s 453.

15.215 If judicial approval is not obtained prior to a search, and cash is either not seized or is released before the matter comes before a court (ie within 48 hours) the officer concerned must prepare a written statement giving the particulars of the circumstances which led him to believe that the powers were exercisable and why it was not practicable to obtain the approval of a judicial officer (ie a magistrate). Once that is prepared they must submit it to 'the person appointed by the Secretary of State' (see s 290(6) to (8)).

15.216 There is therefore in effect a three stage process in exercising these searches in terms of prior approval:

(1) the officer concerned must seek the approval of a judicial officer (a magistrate) before exercising the power;
(2) if it is not practicable to obtain a magistrate's approval, the officer concerned should seek the approval of a senior officer; and
(3) the power to search may still be exercised if, in the circumstances, it is not practical to obtain the approval of either of the above before exercising the power (s 290(1)).

Report on exercise of powers

15.217 The report submitted to the 'appointed person', where judicial approval has not been sought, forms the basis of an annual report (s 291). The appointed person may draw general conclusions and make appropriate recommendations as to the circumstances and manner in which the powers conferred by s 289 are being exercised (see s 291(2)).

The Code of Practice

A Code of Practice exists for officers in connection with the exercise of the search powers **15.218** conferred by s 289 of POCA (The Proceeds of Crime Act 2002 (Cash Searches: Code of Practice) Order 2008, SI 2008/947).

Under s 292(6) a failure by an officer to comply with a provision of the Code does not of **15.219** itself make him liable to criminal or civil proceedings.

Under 292(7) the Code is admissible in evidence in criminal or civil proceedings and is to **15.220** be taken into account by a court or tribunal in any case in which it appears to the court or tribunal to be relevant.

The Code of Practice was introduced by The Proceeds of Crime Act 2002 (Cash Searches: **15.221** Code of Practice) Order 2002, SI 2002/3115 and came into force on 30 December 2002.

Procedure at hearings

Rule 11(1) states: **15.222**

At the hearing of an application under Chapter 3 of Part 5 of the Act (either searches for cash or seizure of cash), any person to whom notice of the application has been given may attend and be heard on the question of whether the application should be granted. The fact that any such person does not attend should not prevent the Court from hearing the application.

For further on procedure following the discovery and seizure of cash under the search powers, see para 15.44 *et seq* above.

K. Compatibility of the Forfeiture Provisions with the ECHR

In *Butler v UK* (Application 41661/98) (27 June 2002) the ECtHR took the view that **15.223** a forfeiture order was a preventative measure and could not be compared to a criminal sanction. The Court further held that the court proceedings:

... afforded the applicant ample opportunity to contest the evidence against him and to dispute the making of a forfeiture order and that the complaint before them was 'manifestly ill-founded'.

In short therefore, for the time being, this area of the law appears to be ECHR friendly.

L. Detention and Forfeiture of Terrorist Cash

Under Sch 1 of the Anti-Terrorism, Crime and Security Act 2001 an authorised officer may **15.224** seize any cash if he has reasonable grounds for suspecting that it is terrorist cash (see Pt 2 para 2(1)). The provisions that follow seizure reflect essentially the same provisions that are now set out under s 294 *et seq* of POCA. Whilst the authorised officer continues to have reasonable grounds for his suspicion, cash seized under Sch 1 may be detained initially for a period of 48 hours (para 3). That period may be extended by an order made by a magistrates' court, but the order may not authorise the detention of any of the cash beyond the end of the period of three months beginning with the date of the order and, in the case of any further order, beyond the date of the period of two years beginning with the date of the first order (see para 3(2)(a) and (b). Upon application for continued detention of the cash, a magistrates' court must be satisfied of the following two conditions:

(1) that there are reasonable grounds for suspecting that the cash is intended to be used for the purposes of terrorism and that either (a) its continued detention is justified while its intended use is further investigated or consideration is given to bringing (in the United Kingdom or elsewhere) proceedings against any person for an offence with which the cash is connected, or (b) proceedings against any person for an offence with which the cash is connected have been started and have not been concluded;

(2) that there are reasonable grounds for suspecting that the cash consists of resources of an organisation which is a prescribed organisation and that either (a) its continued detention is justified while investigation is made into whether or not it consists of such resources or consideration is given to bringing (in the United Kingdom or elsewhere) proceedings against any person for an offence with which the cash is connected, or (b) proceedings against any person for an offence with which the cash is connected have been started and have not been concluded;

(3) that there are reasonable grounds for suspecting that the cash is property earmarked as terrorist property and that either (a) its continued detention is justified while its derivation is further investigated or consideration is given to bringing (in the United Kingdom or elsewhere) proceedings against any person for an offence with which the cash is connected, or (b) proceedings against any person for an offence with which the cash is connected have been started and have not been concluded (see paras 5 through to 8 of Sch IV of the Anti-Terrorism Crime and Security Act 2001).

15.225 Like POCA, if cash is detained it must be held in an interest bearing account (para 4). The cash may be released in all or in part if the court is satisfied, on an application by the person from whom it was seized, that the conditions in para 3 for the detention of cash are no longer met (para 5(2)). However, the cash may not be released if an application for its forfeiture has been made under para 6 of Sch 1 or if proceedings have been started against any person for an offence with which the cash is connected (para 5(4)). Under para 6, forfeiture may be applied for and the court may order the forfeiture of the cash or any part of it if it is satisfied that the cash or any part of it is terrorist cash. An appeal against a decision of forfeiture may be made under para 7 of Sch 1 to the Crown Court. An appeal must be made within the period of 30 days beginning with the date on which the order is made and is by way of a rehearing (para 7(3)). Under para 9, a person who claims that any cash detained under the schedule belongs to him may apply to a magistrates' court for the cash or part of it to be released to him at any time during the course of the proceedings.

15.226 By para 10(1), if no forfeiture is made in respect of any cash detained under the schedule, the person to whom the cash belongs or from whom it was seized may make an application to the magistrates' court for compensation. If a forfeiture order is made in respect of only part of the detained cash under Sch 1, compensation may be sought in relation to the other part (para 10(9)). An 'authorised person' for the purposes of this part of the Act includes an officer of Revenue and Customs, a constable or police officer, or an immigration officer (para 19). The Magistrates' Courts (Detention and Forfeiture of Terrorist Cash) (No 2) Rules 2001 (SI 2001/4013) sets out the procedure to be followed for an application to a magistrates' court under Sch 1. The procedure very closely follows that provided for under the corresponding rules applicable to POCA, set out herein.

M. The Control of Cash (Penalties) Regulations

The Control of Cash (Penalties) Regulations 2007 (SI 2007/1509) came into force on 15 June 2007, and were made under s 2(2) of the European Communities Act 1972 (c68) to give effect to Community Regulation 1889/2005 which, under Art 3, requires any person entering or leaving the EC and carrying cash amounting to €10,000 or more to declare that amount. **15.227**

The intention is to introduce a harmonised control and information procedure for large-scale movements of cash in or out of the EC. **15.228**

The Regulations provide for penalties for failing to declare movements of cash and an appeal mechanism to the Tax Tribunal (reg 5). **15.229**

Cash is defined in SI 1889/2005 as including not only currency (banknotes and coins that are in circulation as a medium of exchange), but also 'bearer negotiable instruments including monetary instruments in bearer form such as travellers cheques, negotiable instruments (including cheques, promissory notes, and money orders) that are either in bearer form, endorsed without restriction, made out to a fictitious payee, or otherwise in such form that title thereto passes upon delivery, and incomplete instruments (including cheques, promissory notes, and money orders) signed, but with the payee's name omitted'. **15.230**

Regulation 3 gives effect to the obligation to create a system of penalties. Regulation 4 enables a person subject to a penalty to require a review of the decision to impose that penalty. Regulations 5, 6, and 7 create a right of appeal from the review decision to the Tax Tribunal, the powers of the tribunal in respect of the appeal, and a requirement that, save in the case of hardship, the penalty be paid as a condition of appealing. Article 4 of the Community Regulation creates a power to detain cash where there has been a breach of Art 3, and reg 8 enables the Commissioners to retain the amount of a proposed penalty from any money detained until determination of an appeal. **15.231**

In terms of the likely penalty and the discretion to impose same, the explanatory notes accompanying the Regulations state as follows: **15.232**

... the Commissioners for HMRC are being given the option of imposing a penalty not exceeding £5000 for non-compliance with the obligation to declare. This gives them the opportunity to exercise discretion to impose a lesser amount or to limit action to issuing a warning letter. Factors which would influence the action taken may include the amount of the undeclared cash in any particular case and the number of previous occasions that the person concerned has been identified as failing to comply with the obligation to declare.

16

THIRD PARTIES

A. Introduction

16.01 The draconian nature of confiscation law is such that restraint and confiscation orders will inevitably have an effect on parties, other than the defendant, who are in possession of, or hold an interest in, his realisable property. The purpose of this chapter is to consider the rights and obligations of third parties who find themselves holding realisable property subject to restraint and confiscation proceedings.

16.02 There is a body of case law within the Mareva/freezing injunction jurisdiction that suggests that the court's jurisdiction to make a freezing order against a third party is 'undoubted' (see *Dadourian Group International Inc v Azuri Ltd* [2005] All ER(D) 323 (April); (ChD 22 April 2005) and is exercised as, in effect, ancillary relief granted by the court in aid of, and as part of, the freezing order granted against the defendant to the substantive claim. Exercise of this jurisdiction could occur where there is good reason to suppose that the assets of the third party were, in truth, the assets of the injuncted defendant.

B. Restraint Orders

Jurisdiction to bind third parties

16.03 The power to restrain parties other than the defendant from dealing in his realisable property is found in s 41 of the Proceeds of Crime Act 2002 (POCA) (formerly s 26(1) of the Drug Trafficking Act 1994 (DTA), s 77(1) of the Criminal Justice Act 1988 (CJA 1988)).

16.04 Section 41(1) of POCA reads:

> If any condition set out in section 40 is satisfied the Crown Court will make an order (a Restraint Order) prohibiting any specified person from dealing with any realisable property held by him.

The intention of the legislation is that a restraint order may be made both against the defendant (or the person under investigation), and any other person holding realisable property.

16.05 These sections are intended to empower the court to prohibit third parties from dealing with realisable property. They are wide enough to restrain parties from dealing in assets in which the defendant holds an interest.

16.06 It is, of course, an essential prerequisite to restraining a third party that the defendant has some interest in the property: the prosecutor may not restrain assets in which the defendant has no interest whatever, except where the asset in question is a gift caught by the Acts.

Obligations of third parties

16.07 Once a third party is given notice or is served with a copy of a restraint order, he must not allow the defendant to deal with any realisable property caught by the order in a manner inconsistent with its terms. Any failure to do so will render the third party vulnerable to proceedings for contempt of court.

16.08 If the order contains any exceptions, the third party should only allow the defendant to avail himself of that exception once he has satisfied himself that the conditions precedent have been satisfied. For example, the release of monies to pay a defendant's general living expenses is frequently conditional upon him giving notice to the prosecutor of the source of any monies he intends to use for this purpose. A financial institution should always check with the prosecuting authority that conditions of this nature have been fulfilled before releasing money for such purposes.

The third party should also check whether he holds other assets belonging to the defendant **16.09** which, although not specifically named in the order, are caught by the general restraint provisions. These assets too should not be released to the defendant. A restraint order may specifically restrain the defendant from dealing with monies held in a current account at a particular bank. However, it may transpire that the defendant also holds a deposit account at the same bank, of which the prosecutor was unaware when he obtained the restraint order. In such circumstances the bank should also take steps to freeze that account.

A third party served with a restraint order would be well advised to seek legal advice on its **16.10** terms at an early stage. The third party has to steer a difficult course between preventing any dealing with assets properly caught by the order, and allowing defendants access to assets that are not strictly within its terms. Any failure to do the former may result in contempt proceedings being brought by the prosecutor, and any failure to do the latter may result in an action being brought against the third party by the defendant for breach of contract or other relief. In order to prevent being caught in this 'Catch 22' position, the third party should, when in doubt, make an application to the court under either r 59.3 of the Criminal Procedure Rules (Crown Court/POCA) or sc115.5(1) and Pt 23 of the Civil Procedure Rules (High Court, CJA/DTA).

In *Z Ltd v A-Z and Others,* sub nom *Mareva Injunction* [1982] QB 558; [1982] 2 WLR 288, **16.11** Lord Denning MR gave advice to third parties holding assets subject to Mareva (now freezing) injunctions, and similar principles, it is suggested, apply to restraint orders. At p 563 he said:

> As soon as the bank is given notice of the *Mareva* injunction, it must freeze the defendant's bank account. It not allow any drawings to be made on it, neither by cheques drawn before the injunction nor by those drawn after it. The reason is because, if it allowed any such drawings, it would be obstructing the course of justice as prescribed by the court granting the injunction, and it would be guilty of contempt of court. I have confined my observations to banks and bank accounts. But the same applies to any specific asset held by a bank for safe custody on behalf of the defendant, be it jewellery, stamps, or anything else and to any other person who holds any other assets of the defendants. If the asset is covered by the terms of the *Mareva* injunction, that other person must not hand it over to the defendant or do anything to enable him to dispose of it. He must hold it pending further order.

Specific guidance to the various kinds of third party most commonly affected by restraint **16.12** and confiscation orders is given later in this chapter.

Rights of third parties

Restraint and confiscation law has to strike a balance between ensuring that realisable prop- **16.13** erty in the hands of third parties are properly restrained on the one hand and ensuring that the third party does not suffer loss on the other. Inevitably this is a difficult balance to achieve, the two aims being to some extent in conflict. Third parties should, however, be aware of the rights they have in order to keep any potential loss suffered as a result of complying with any order to a minimum.

Reasonable costs and expenses

16.14 Most third parties will inevitably incur costs in complying with the terms of the order. In most cases, it will be necessary to take legal advice on the terms of the order, and in the case of orders affecting commercial organisations, the time of fee-earning staff will be occupied in setting up systems to ensure the order is complied with. Banks, for example, will have to put a 'freeze' on the defendant's bank accounts to prevent money being withdrawn from its branches by cheque or cash card. By r 59.2(5) of the Criminal Procedure Rules the court:

> . . . may require the applicant for a restraint order to give an undertaking to pay the reasonable expenses of any person, other than a person who is prohibited from dealing with realisable property by the restraint order, which are incurred in complying with the restraint order.

A similar provision was made under the CJA/DTA by sc115.4(1)).

16.15 It is usual for the prosecutor to give an undertaking to pay the reasonable costs and expenses of third parties (except the recipients of gifts caught by the Act), which are incurred:

(a) in ascertaining whether any assets caught by the order are within his possession or control; or

(b) in securing compliance with the terms of the order.

16.16 Typically such an undertaking is in the following terms:

> [The Prosecutor] will pay the reasonable costs of anyone other than the Defendant (and his wife) which have been incurred as a result of compliance with this Order including the costs of ascertaining whether that person holds any of the Defendant's assets SAVE THAT [the Prosecutor] will not pay any legal or accountancy costs so incurred without first giving their consent in writing.

This undertaking only extends to costs incurred for the purposes set out and for no other reason and only 'reasonable' costs and expenses are caught.

16.17 In the majority of cases, such issues can be resolved by agreement between the prosecutor and the third party concerned. Where the parties are unable to resolve any dispute as to liability or quantum, the third party should make an application to the court.

Restraint orders and the wife of the defendant

16.18 In *Re G (Restraint Order)* (QBD, 19 July 2001) Stanley Burnton J (as he then was) laid down guidelines for what should and should not be included in restraint orders. In respect of the wife of the defendant he found that s 77 of the CJA 1988 (which corresponds with s 26 of the DTA and s 41 of POCA) empowered the High Court (and now under POCA the Crown Court) to make a restraint order prohibiting any person from dealing with any realisable property. He stated such a person might be someone other than the defendant, provided he or she holds realisable property. He added:

> There are therefore two possible bases under the 1988 Act for making a restraint order prohibiting the wife of a defendant from dealing with a bank account in their joint names: (a) that the credit balance in the bank account constitutes realisable property; and (b) that the wife's interest in the joint bank account may be the result of a gift or gifts caught by Part VI of the 1988 Act.

On the same basis the real property in joint names may also be made the subject of a Restraint Order prohibiting both husband and wife from dealing with the property. Of course, in many cases basis (b) will be inapplicable, either because no gift has been made (as where the wife's interest results from her own earnings) or because of the requirement of section 74(10) that the gift must have been made after the earliest of the offences in question. In addition if a joint bank account is used for domestic expenses and has a modest credit balance, it is debatable whether the payments into the account made by the defendant are a 'gift' . . . if, as in the present case, a wife is to be prohibited from dealing with any property, the order should make clear on its face that she is the subject of the order. In the case of civil proceedings, this may be done by making her a Respondent to the application, and a defendant in the proceedings. RSC Order 115 Rule 2A would seem to prevent making the wife, against whom no criminal proceedings have been instituted and, as far as I am aware, is not to be charged, a defendant to proceedings such as the present. However, the 'Notice to the Defendant' at the beginning of the Restraint Order should be supplemented so as to become 'Notice to the Defendant and to (the wife)', giving the full name of the wife. It is not sufficient for the application of the Order for the wife to be found only in the operative paragraphs of the Order.

16.19 Stanley Burnton J went on to add that unless there is evidence that the wife has adequate separate means, it is essential that the order permits her to spend an adequate weekly sum on ordinary living expenses, and to pay for her separate legal advice and representation. It is not appropriate, he held, to rely on her right to apply to vary the order for this purpose. Lastly, he stated the order should include an undertaking by the prosecutor to serve the order and the witness statement in support on the wife as soon as practicable. Criminal Procedure Rule r 59.2(8) now makes such service mandatory (Sc115.4(3) applies to High Court DTA/CJA cases).

16.20 Stanley Burnton J added that the above considerations are equally applicable to anyone who is a cohabitee of the defendant.

Use of assets

16.21 The restraint order only prevents dealing in the property. Hence, a third party may continue to use an asset in such a way that does not constitute dealing in it. A wife may therefore continue to reside in a restrained property pending the making and enforcement of a confiscation order, and may continue to drive round in a restrained motor vehicle. What she may not do is attempt to sell the asset without first obtaining a variation order from the court.

What remedies are available to a person who denies the defendant has an interest in a restrained asset?

16.22 It may happen that a third party denies that the defendant has an interest in a restrained asset. If this is correct, and the asset does not constitute a gift caught by the Acts, then the asset will not constitute 'realisable property'. A third party who so contends would be entitled to apply to the High Court under the pre-POCA regime, and now the Crown Court under s 42(3) of POCA, for a variation releasing the asset in question from the terms of the order. It should be borne in mind that the function of the restraint order is to preserve the *status quo* pending the making and enforcement of a confiscation order. It does not take away title to property, but merely restrains any dealing in it. Accordingly, previously the High Court, and now for POCA cases the Crown Court, will not normally be willing to become embroiled in an argument as to ownership of property at the restraint stage, but will prefer issues as to the ownership of property to be resolved at the confiscation and enforcement stage.

16.23 Applications for the release of property should be confined at the restraint stage to those cases where the prosecution's evidence fails to establish any interest in the asset or where the applicant has clear and incontrovertible evidence that the defendant has no interest whatever in the asset. In *SCF Finance Co Ltd v Masri* [1985] 1 WLR 876 the Court of Appeal emphasised, in relation to freezing injunctions, that a mere assertion that a third party owns an asset need not be accepted without proper enquiry, and the court had jurisdiction in appropriate circumstances to order the trial of an issue in relation to any such dispute.

Living expenses

16.24 A wife is entitled to a sum from restrained funds in order to meet her weekly and monthly outgoings. If the defendant is in prison a figure will be fixed with her in mind. If the defendant is at liberty, a figure will be fixed for both him and his wife. 'Reasonable costs and expenses' will be met. School fees may be payable. But such items would cease to be allowable once the defendant was convicted, as per *Re Peters* [1998] 3 All ER 46 where the Court of Appeal held that payment for school fees for the defendant's son for a period after the result of his trial was known could not be allowed. As Mann LJ said at p 52:

> I fully understand that [the court below] may have been influenced by the disruption of the son's education should a confiscation order be made, but in my judgment there is, in the light of section 31(2) no room for the intrusion of sympathy.

16.25 In the majority of cases, such issues can be resolved by agreement between the prosecutor and the third party concerned. Where the parties are unable to resolve any dispute as to liability or quantum, the third party should make an application to the court.

Legal expenses

16.26 In *Re D* [2006] EWHC (Admin) 1519, the question of whether third parties who assert an interest in property that is the subject of a restraint order and which was due to be considered as part of a confiscation order have a right to receive legal funding from that property arose. There were a number of properties that were in the name of members of the defendant's family. It was part of the case against the defendant that that had been done deliberately in order to conceal the true situation, (namely that they were actually his benefit from his unlawful conduct). Counsel suggested that by virtue of s 82(4) of the CJA 1988 everyone who has an alleged interest in property should have the opportunity to establish the existence of that interest, and be provided with monies from the proceeds of the property, to pay for legal representation. Collins J described this as a 'quite hopeless submission'. He stated:

> The powers must be exercised to ensure that the third parties have a proper opportunity of pursuing their claim. That they will do in the way that any litigation is to be pursued. If they have the means, they will have to pay for it: if they do not have sufficient means, then they may apply for public funding. But what they cannot do is to obtain funding from the property which they are asserting they have an interest in when their interest is being disputed.

Restraint orders and limited companies

In *Re G (Restraint Order)* (2001) (above) Stanley Burnton J (as he then was) held, leaving **16.27** gifts aside, that there were two bases upon which a prosecutor may apply for a restraint order prohibiting dealings in the assets of a company controlled by a defendant, but against which no criminal charge is to be made. Namely:

(1) that the company holds realisable property within the meaning of (the applicable Act); and

(2) that the company has no genuine separate existence from the defendant, and is used by him as a device for fraud.

The corporate veil

In the case of (2) above, the court treats the assets of the company as if they were in the name **16.28** of the defendant. The court is said to pierce or 'lift the corporate veil'. The application to lift the corporate veil will often come in the witness statement that supports the application for the restraint order. The wording will be in similar terms to the following:

> I invite the Honourable Court to lift the corporate veil in respect of Tosca Limited as I believe the sole purpose of the company and its bank accounts was and continues to be to perpetrate a fraud and provide a conduit for its proceeds.

In *Re G* Stanley Burnton J held that while the phrase 'lifting the corporate veil' was helpful **16.29** shorthand, it had no place in an injunction (in the restraint order itself), because the object of that was to set out clear and specific prohibitions affecting the defendant and the other persons affected by the order and to impose equally clear obligations on the applicant. He stated as follows:

> If the evidence before the court raises a *prima facie* case justifying a lifting of the corporate veil, and to treat the property of the company as the property of the Defendant, the order should prohibit the company, in addition to the Defendant, from dealing with its property.

Notwithstanding Stanley Burnton J's above observation, it is commonplace to find within **16.30** a restraint order the following additional injunction:

> AND IT IS ORDERED THAT: The assets of Tosca Limited be treated as the personal assets of the Defendant

thus reflecting the fact that the court has in fact lifted the corporate veil over that company.

The principles relating to the lifting of the corporate veil in this context are no different **16.31** from those applicable in other areas of the law: see *Re H (Restraint Order: Realisable Property)* [1996] 2 All ER 391 and, more recently, *Trustor AB v Smallbone* [2001] 1 WLR 1177 (especially at para 23). In many cases, in addition, it will be appropriate to appoint a receiver under the power conferred by the relevant statute to take possession of the property of the company and to manage it (see *Re H* above).

It should also be noted that at the stage of the application for a restraint order without **16.32** notice, the courts will have no more than a *prima facie* case before it. The company in question may subsequently be able to establish that it has a legitimate existence as a legal person carrying on a lawful business. The order must therefore also be addressed to the company and the applicant's witness statement served on it, as required by Criminal Procedure Rules r 59.2(8) (or scl15.4(3) for CJA/DTA cases). The order should provide that the company should be entitled to spend up to a maximum sum (which is liable to be increased) on its separate legal advice and representation (as per Stanley Burnton J in *Re G*).

16.33 Stanley Burnton J also held that particular caution was required if it appeared that, in addition to engaging in fraudulent transactions, the company was carrying on a legitimate business that may be closed down by the order. In those circumstances it may not be appropriate to treat the assets of the company as those of the defendant. Freezing injunctions in civil proceedings normally contain an exception to the prohibition against dealing with property to enable the person restrained to deal with his assets in the ordinary course of business. A restraint order may be made subject to such a specified exception where appropriate.

16.34 Where the company is not a company limited by guarantee, but is merely a company which is a trading name for the defendant, eg Alfredo Germont trading as Alfredo Germont Fuels, it has no separate legal identity because it is not a registered company. It is therefore incorrect and unnecessary for it to be separately restrained. The restraint order itself would prevent the defendant from dealing with the assets of Alfredo Germont Fuels because he is prohibited from dealing with any assets that he holds.

Prosecutor does not have to give an undertaking in damages

16.35 In contrast to the position in relation to freezing injunctions, the prosecutor cannot be required to give an undertaking in damages. This provision is to be found in the Criminal Procedure Rules r 59.2(4) (POCA cases or scl15.4(1) CJA/DTA cases) and which states as follows:

> (4) The Crown Court must not require the applicant for a restraint order to give any undertaking relating to damages sustained as a result of the restraint order by a person who is prohibited from dealing with realisable property by the restraint order.

16.36 The sister provision under scl15.4(1) was considered by Otton J in *Re R (Restraint Order)* [1990] 2 All ER 569. The third party was the landlord of industrial premises let to the defendant who had installed plant machinery in them. When the defendant was charged with drug trafficking offences, a restraint order was made prohibiting him, *inter alia*, from disposing of or dealing in the plant machinery at the premises leased from the applicants. The landlord sought to distrain the plant machinery for arrears of rent, and arranged for it to be sold by auction. The landlord became aware of the restraint order two days before the auction, cancelled it, and sought an order against the prosecutor to be indemnified in respect of their loss. Otton J refused to make such an order, ruling that the court had no jurisdiction either by statute or in the exercise of its inherent jurisdiction to grant such relief.

Unsecured third party creditors

16.37 Defendants subject to restraint orders frequently owe money to unsecured third party creditors who are, understandably, anxious to get paid. Where the defendant is subject to a freezing order made in support of a civil claim, a third party creditor may intervene and apply for the order to be varied so as to enable, but not compel, the defendant to make payment of the amount owed. The reason for this is that a claimant who obtains a freezing order does not acquire an interest in the frozen assets, nor does he acquire precedence over other creditors of the defendant: see *Iraqi Ministry of Defence v Arcepey Shipping Co SA (The Angel Bell)* [1981] QB 65.

The position can be very different where a defendant's assets are frozen pursuant to a restraint order. Since its inception, confiscation legislation has made specific provision about the way in which the court must exercise its discretion to make, vary and discharge restraint and receivership orders. In *Re Peters* [1988] 3 WLR 182 the court described these provisions as 'a legislative steer' as to the manner in which the discretion should be exercised. Under the earlier legislation (which still applies to cases involving offences committed before 24 March 2003) the relevant provisions are to be found in s 82 of the CJA 1988 and s 31 of the DTA. Section 82(2) of the CJA 1988 and s 31(2) of the DTA provide: **16.38**

Subject to the following provisions of this section, the powers shall be exercised with a view to making available for satisfying the confiscation order or, as the case may be, any confiscation order that may be made in the defendant's case, the value for the time being of realisable property held by any person by means of the realisation of such property.

There are conflicting authorities as to the extent to which CJA and DTA restraint orders may be varied to enable third party creditors to be paid. In *Re W* The Times, 15 November 1990 Buckley J held at first instance that the legislative steer precludes the variation of a restraint order for such purposes. He ruled that the legislative steer gives priority to the satisfaction of a confiscation order over general creditors of the defendant. In *Re X* [2004] 3 WLR 906, however, Davis J came to the view that the interpretation Buckley J had given to the statutory provisions in *Re W* were incorrect, for the following three reasons: **16.39**

(1) section 77(1) was phrased in wide terms ('The High Court may by order (a Restraint Order) prohibit any person from dealing with any realisable property, subject to conditions and exceptions as may be specified in the order') and this discretion was preserved by s 77(2) (living expenses and legal expenses) and the unfettered discretion of s 77(6) (a Restraint Order may be varied in relation to any property);

(2) while Davis J accepted that the s 77 powers were subject to s 82 (the legislative steer), the phrase 'with a view to' in that section introduced a degree of elasticity;

(3) although s 82(6) of the CJA 1988 provides that no account shall be taken of any obligations of the defendant which conflict with the obligation to satisfy the confiscation order, s 82(6) only applies where a confiscation order has already been made; not at an earlier stage.

What further influenced Davis J in *Re X* was 'the clear distinction between after a confiscation order has been made and the position before one has been made'. A confiscation order is made after conviction. Before conviction Davis J was keen to stress that there was a presumption of innocence: **16.40**

The person who is the subject of the Restraint Order may be acquitted. It is difficult to think that Parliament could have intended to restrict the court's powers as a matter of jurisdiction in the way now contended for when the consequence might be the bankruptcy or ruin of the individual concerned before he has even been tried. That, indeed, to my mind is one explanation for the distinction between the wording of section 82(2) and section 82(6).

16.41 Furthermore he stated: 'Moreover, I would draw attention to section 82(4). The wording of that section is apt to extend to debts, given the wide definition of the word "property" in section 102' (para 22). He observed that s 82(4) stated that the powers of the court shall be exercised with a view to allowing any person other than the defendant to retain or recover the value of any property held by the defendant.

16.42 In relation to the 'legislative steer' Davis J concluded:

> That will always, indeed, be a highly material and important consideration. But it is not, in my view . . . a conclusive consideration in all cases (para 23).

16.43 In relation to 'discretion' he affirmed Simon Brown LJ's view in the case of *Re P* [2000] 1 WLR 473 that:

> a balance has to be struck between, on the one hand preserving the worth of the defendant's realisable property against the possibility that he may be convicted and a confiscation order made against him, and on the other hand, allowing him meantime to continue the ordinary course of his life.

16.44 As a result, Davis J refused to follow *Re W* holding that it had been wrongly decided. He found that these words conferred a wide discretion on the court, empowering it to sanction the payment of creditors over and above living expenses and legal fees. However, Davis J went on to refuse the release of funds on the particular facts of *Re X* applying the principles enunciated in the *Angel Bell* case (factually it was submitted that the claimed debt was not as a result of legitimate or *bona fide* trading, and therefore the payment requested should not be permitted)—in effect, therefore, the applicants were unsuccessful on their cause of claim (and this may be a clue as to why the decision was never appealed).

16.45 The position of unsecured third party creditors therefore remains somewhat uncertain under the old legislation. Arguably the *Re W* approach is to be preferred. In *Re X* Davis J failed to take into account two other similar cases, namely *Re M* [1992] QB 377 and *Re R* [2004] EWHC Admin 621. *Serious Fraud Office v Lexi Holdings PLC (In Administration)* [2008] EWCA Crim 1443 makes it clear that the effect of s 69(2)(c) is such that POCA restraint orders may not be varied to allow third party creditors of the defendant to be paid from restrained funds. In relation to restraint orders at least, it is clear that the decision of Buckley J in *Re W* remains good law. The court avoided making any observations as to whether the *Re W* or *Re X* approach was to be preferred in relation to restraint orders made under the old legislation, merely noting that the treatment of third party creditors had 'produced a number of judicial decisions, not all of which were reconcilable with each other'.

Unsecured creditors and POCA

16.46 The legislative steer under POCA is worded very differently from the old legislation. It is to be found in s 69(2) of the Act and provides:

> (2) The powers—
>   (a) must be exercised with a view to the value for the time being of realisable property being made available (by the property's realisation) for satisfying any confiscation order that has been or may be made against the defendant;
>   (b) must be exercised, in a case where a confiscation order has not been made, with a view to securing that there is no diminution in the value of realisable property;

(c) must be exercised without taking account of any obligation of the defendant or a recipient of a tainted gift if the obligation conflicts with the object of satisfying any confiscation order that has been or may be made against the defendant;

(d) may be exercised in respect of a debt owed by the Crown.

As will readily be appreciated, the legislative steer in s 69 is drafted much more tightly than under the previous legislation, and it was the construction of this section that fell to be determined in the case of *Lexi Holdings*.

In *Serious Fraud Office v Lexi Holdings PLC (In Administration)* [2008] EWCA Crim 1443   **16.47**
the Court held that restraint orders made under POCA may not be varied to permit defendants to pay off unsecured third party creditors. The Court also took the opportunity to give important guidance to practitioners on how applications to vary restraint orders, often involving complex points of law far removed from the usual work of the Crown Court, should be dealt with.

In *Lexi Holdings* a restraint order had been obtained by the Serious Fraud Office (SFO)   **16.48**
against an individual known as 'M' on the basis that he was subject to a criminal investigation into an offence of conspiracy to defraud the Cheshire Building Society and associated money laundering offences. The administrators of Lexi alleged it had been the victim of substantial frauds committed by M and others and judgment in default was eventually entered in its favour for some £625,250 plus interest. Lexi thereafter applied to the Central Criminal Court for the restraint order to be varied to permit M to satisfy the judgment. Lexi sought the variation both on the basis that it had a proprietary claim and as a *bona fide* judgment creditor. The application was opposed by the SFO, but the judge at first instance made the variation sought so as to allow payment to be made to Lexi from M's restrained assets. The judge held that the court had a 'reasonably wide discretion' under POCA 'to do justice'. He found that there was no significant change in statutory policy or underlying principle from the pre-2002 Act regime and agreed with the reasoning of Davis J in *Re X*. The SFO appealed, with permission, to the Criminal Division of the Court of Appeal.

The Court (Keene LJ, Davis J, and the Recorder of Swansea) allowed the SFO's appeal. The   **16.49**
court noted there were significant differences between the wording of the legislative steer in s 69 of POCA and under the previous legislation. Keene LJ said:

> It is true that some of the provisions in that section contain the phrase 'with a view to' which as has been said in several of the authorities indicates a degree of flexibility in the court's approach and simply gives a 'legislative steer.' Section 69(2)(c), however, is different. It does not contain that phrase and does appear to be in mandatory terms: the powers 'must be exercised without taking account of any obligation . . .' Moreover, the feature of its equivalent provision in the earlier legislation which so influenced Davis J. in Re X has changed: it is now clear that this provision does apply in the situation where there is a restraint order but no confiscation order in existence, because the words 'or may be made' have been added. This must be taken to represent a deliberate tightening up of the legislation by Parliament.

Keene LJ went on: **16.50**

> On the face of it, section 69(2)(c) does require the courts to ignore any debt owed by the restrained person to an unsecured third party creditor, so that the existence of such a debt would not empower the court to vary a restraint order unless there was no conflict 'with the object of satisfying any confiscation order.' On that last aspect, we are wholly unpersuaded

by [Counsel for Lexi's] argument about the meaning to be attached to those words. His contention that the 'object' is that of depriving the offender of the proceeds of crime is unsustainable. That is the object of the confiscation order itself, whereas this provision is referring to the object of 'satisfying' any confiscation order, i.e. providing a sufficient quantum of assets to meet the sum identified, already or in due course, in a confiscation order. Counsel's interpretation would render the presence of that word 'satisfying' unnecessary and would, in our judgment, distort the natural meaning of section 69(2)(c). If he were right, the provision would enable any third party creditor to obtain a variation of the restraint order and so to be paid and indeed Counsel submits that this is what should happen. The provision would in fact have virtually no effect in practice. In our view, the latter part of paragraph (c) is, as [Counsel for the SFO] argues, indicating merely that if the court can see that a confiscation order, existing or prospective, relates to an amount which the defendant has ample assets to meet, then it may be that a debt to a third party creditor can properly be allowed to be paid from the restrained assets.

16.51   The Court also noted that Lexi's argument appeared to be inconsistent with the procedures to be followed at the confiscation stage. Keene LJ said:

> . . . of the greatest significance, the payment of third party creditors at the restraint order stage seems to us to be inconsistent with the position which obtains at the confiscation order stage. Section 9 of the 2002 Act provides that the available amount of the defendant's assets when one comes to quantify the amount to be specified in the confiscation order is to be ascertained in the following way:
>
> (1) For the purpose of deciding the recoverable amount, the available amount is the aggregate of—
>
>   (a) the total of the values (at the time the confiscation order is made) of all the free property then held by the defendant minus the total amount payable in pursuance of obligations which have priority, and
>
>   (b) the total of the values (at that time) of all tainted gifts
>
> (2) An obligation has priority if it is an obligation of the defendant—
>
>   (a) to pay an amount due in respect of a fine or other order of a court which was imposed or made on conviction of an offence and at any time before the time the confiscation order is made, or
>
>   (b) to pay a sum which would be included among the preferential debts if the defendant's bankruptcy had commenced on the date of the confiscation order or his winding up had been ordered on that date.
>
> (3) 'Preferential debts' has the meaning given by section 386 of the Insolvency Act 1986 (c45).
>
> It will be seen that, when the court decides on the amount to be specified in the confiscation order, it has to use the total of the values of the property the defendant holds, less only 'priority' obligations such as fines and preferential debts. The existence of obligations owed to ordinary third party creditors is to be disregarded when a confiscation order is made. It seems to this court that it would have been wholly illogical for the legislature to have decided to allow third party debts to be paid during the period when assets are supposedly being preserved by a restraint order when such debts are to be left out of account at the stage when the confiscation order is made. We can see no reason why Parliament should have decided to allow unsecured creditors to reduce the assets during the restraint phase when such creditors could not reduce the assets at the confiscation stage. If that were the position, it would put a premium on well advised creditors getting in quickly during the restraint phase before their opportunity is lost, and we do not accept that that situation is one which was ever intended.

The Court emphasised that unsecured third parties were not necessarily left without a **16.52** remedy. It noted that a restraint order is essentially a temporary measure preserving assets pending the making and enforcement of a confiscation order. Keene LJ said:

> A restraint order is therefore performing a holding operation. Of course, it has to be acknowledged that that operation may, and has been known to, last a considerable time. Nonetheless, the limited duration of restraint orders is a relevant factor when considering its adverse effects on third party creditors and when seeking to ascertain the intention of Parliament. The restraint order will eventually be discharged and either replaced by some other order such as a confiscation order or not replaced at all.

The Court also noted that the potential harshness of s 69(2)(c) was mitigated to some **16.53** extent by other powers available to the Crown Court once an offender is convicted. As Keene LJ observed:

> . . . the court has the power under section 130 of the Sentencing Act to make a compensation order in favour of a person who has suffered loss resulting from the offence or any other offence which is taken into consideration. As (Counsel for the SFO) points out, such a compensation order takes priority over a confiscation order: see section 13(5) and (6) of the 2002 Act. Not every creditor will be helped by this provision, since he may not qualify under section 130, but some will be assisted. Indeed, if a victim of the defendant's criminal conduct has started or intends to start civil proceedings against him 'in respect of loss, injury or damage sustained in connection with the conduct', then the court, by virtue of section 6(6) need not make a confiscation order at all. The duty to make one where it is determined that the defendant has benefited from his criminal conduct becomes simply a power in those circumstances described in section 6(6). When one bears in mind that the criminal conduct leading to 'loss, injury or damage' may be *general* criminal conduct if the defendant has a criminal lifestyle and not merely the *particular* criminal conduct covered by the offences in question (plus those taken into consideration), it can be appreciated that a considerable number of persons may qualify as 'victims' for this purpose. This too must tend to reduce the number of third parties ultimately affected adversely by the 2002 Act.

Finally, the court noted that the victims themselves may benefit from the defendant's assets **16.54** being held under restraint pending the determination of the criminal proceedings. They too could lose out if the total value of the defendant's assets was reduced by claims by other third party creditors being entertained by the court at the restraint stage.

It is suggested that the Court's ruling in *Lexi* returns some much needed certainty into the **16.55** law relating to the release of restrained assets to pay unsecured third party creditors of a defendant. A similar decision from the Court of Appeal in relation to the old legislation would, it is submitted, be equally welcome. Advisers can now maintain a consistent approach to all applications to vary POCA restraint orders for such purposes, and defendants, victims, and creditors alike know where they stand in relation to such matters. This consistency of approach will ensure that no unsecured creditor can 'jump the gun' and gain an advantage over others, including a victim, by reducing the amount of assets available to meet compensation and confiscation orders.

This approach will also overcome the risk of abuse by associates of a defendant making **16.56** bogus third party claims at his behest with a view to reducing the fund available for confiscation. Although defendants are of course entitled to a presumption of innocence at the pre-conviction stage, one must remain mindful of the fact that, as Lord Donaldson MR observed in *Re O* [1991] 1 All ER 330:

> whatever may be the position in an individual case, the legislative contemplation is that restraint orders will be made in circumstances in which it is thought that some of those having interests in the property may well be of a dishonest disposition.

16.57   Of course, not all payments to third parties will fall foul of s 69(2)(c). There is, for example, no difficulty with a management receiver paying off trade debts with a view to retaining and preserving the value of the business of a company, since the payment of such a debt would preserve a greater asset in value. Similarly, there can be no objection to allowing rent or mortgage payments to be made either on the basis that it constitutes a living expense or because it preserves and maintains the defendant's interest in property. In both cases the value of the realisable property is not diminished or reduced in value overall because the payment allows a company to continue trading, making profits, and prevents the mortgagee foreclosing.

Third party claims and practice

16.58   In a postscript to the *Lexi Holdings* judgment, the Court gave some important guidance to practitioners as to how similar problems in relation to POCA restraint orders should be dealt with in the future. First, the court recognised that the issues arising in the *Lexi Holdings* case were not part of the daily work of most Crown Court judges. Where the points at issue are not unduly complicated, they could readily be dealt with in the Crown Court, but there would be other occasions in which the complexities of the case were such that it would be unwise for a Crown Court judge to attempt to determine the issues. In such circumstances Keene LJ suggested that:

> . . . where a relaxation of a restraint order is sought, consideration should be given to adjourning those variation proceedings to enable the issues to be determined in proceedings before a specialist Chancery Circuit Judge or High Court Judge of the Chancery Division. Alternatively, those arranging the listing of such cases in the Crown Court should seek to ensure that they are heard by a judge with the relevant experience and expertise.

16.59   Secondly, the Court reminded practitioners of their obligations under s 58(5) and (6) of POCA in cases where restraint orders had been made in relation to assets in respect of which they are litigating on behalf of third parties. These provisions require that the prosecutor and any receiver appointed under the Act are to be given the opportunity of making representations before it decides whether to stay third party litigation in relation to restrained assets or allow it to continue. The Court noted that this section had not been complied with in the instant case. In conclusion Keene LJ said:

> We entirely accept that the reason why section 58 was not drawn to the attention of those judges was because counsel appearing then for Lexi was himself unaware of it. It was an innocent oversight. Nonetheless, steps do need to be taken to ensure that the terms of section 58 are observed. Some thought might usefully be given to the possibility of creating a register or restraint orders and applications for such orders, though that would not have cured the problem in the present case, since all involved were aware of the existence of the restraint order. The SFO and other prosecuting authorities could usefully publicise more widely the general tenor of section 58, to increase the awareness of it in the legal profession, and no doubt the relevant Bar Associations could play a role. This is not just a matter for the criminal courts

and criminal lawyers: the duty under section 58 applies to all courts in which proceedings about such property take place and every so often those will be the civil courts. We shall direct that a copy of this judgment, together with a note drawing attention to this postscript, be sent to the Chairman of the Judicial Studies Board and to the Family and Civil Procedure Rules Committees.

C. Confiscation Orders

A confiscation order is an *in personam* order against the convicted defendant and not an **16.60** *in rem* order against specific items of property. The consequence of this is that third parties who hold an interest in realisable property do not have a right to be heard at the confiscation hearing in the Crown Court or to have counsel make representations to the court on their behalf. If, however, the defendant wishes the third party to be called as a witness on his behalf for the purpose of establishing the extent of his interest in realisable property, he may of course do so (see *Re Norris* below).

This may at first sight seem to be a denial of justice. However, this is not necessarily the case, **16.61** because the mere making of a confiscation order does not take away the owner's title to the property. It may be that the defendant will be able to satisfy the confiscation order by realising assets other than those in which a third party claims to have an interest. In this event the third party concerned will not be troubled further. It is only if the defendant fails to satisfy the order voluntarily and the Crown seeks the appointment of a receiver that a third party holding an interest in realisable property need become involved as a party to the proceedings.

No right to be heard at confiscation stage

So far as representation of a third party, such as a wife, in confiscation proceedings in the **16.62** Crown Court is concerned, there is no provision contained in POCA for representation or argument to be presented by the third party at the stage when the confiscation order is made.

In this respect the position is the same as that which existed under the CJA 1988 and DTA. **16.63** In *Re Norris* [2001] 1 WLR 1388 the House of Lords held that having convicted a person of a drug trafficking offence the Crown Court had to assess the value of his proceeds of drug trafficking and the amount of his realisable property for the purpose of making the necessary confiscation order. At that hearing the defendant's wife, who was not a party to the proceedings, had given detailed evidence on the defendant's behalf that the matrimonial home belonged either wholly or substantially to her. The judge disbelieved her evidence and made a confiscation order against the defendant on the basis that the house formed part of his realisable property. The House of Lords held that the assertion of an interest in the property by a third party (namely the wife) should be resolved at the enforcement stage. Their Lordships confirmed that a third party was not precluded from asserting his or her interest by reason of having previously made assertions as to the ownership of the property when called as a witness for the defence in the confiscation proceedings.

When making a confiscation order, therefore, the Crown Court must disregard what a **16.64** former wife may obtain in other proceedings over and above any interest which she holds at the time the confiscation order is made. The mere right of the wife to apply for relief under the Matrimonial Causes Act 1973 (MCA) does not amount to 'an interest' falling within the terms of s 69(3)(a) of POCA: see s 84(2)(f). At that stage, the Crown Court has no regard to, and makes no allowance for, any possible adverse consequences for a former spouse and her child when deciding the amount to be confiscated. The court's function is simply to conduct an arithmetical exercise to determine the assets available for confiscation: see *R v Ahmed and Qureshi* [2004] EWCA Crim 2599.

16.65   In that case Latham LJ stated:

> 11. . . . The court is merely concerned with the arithmetic exercise of computing what is, in effect, a statutory debt. That process does not involve any assessment, in our judgment, of the way in which that debt may ultimately be paid, any more than the assessment of any other debt. No questions therefore arise under Article 8 at this stage in the process.

> 12. Different considerations, will, however arise if the debt is not met and the prosecution determine to take enforcement action, for example by obtaining an order for a Receiver. As the House of Lords explained in *Re Norris* [2001] 1 WLR 1388, this is the stage of the procedure in which third party's rights can not only be taken into account but resolved . . . It would be at that stage that the court would have to consider whether or not it would be proportionate to make an order selling the home in the circumstances of the particular case . . . The court would undoubtedly be concerned to ensure that proper weight is given to the public policy objective behind the making of confiscation orders, which is to ensure that criminals do not profit from their crime. And the court will have a range of enforcement options available with which to take account of the rights of third parties such as other members of the Ahmed family.

16.66   By way of contrast with the position at the stage the confiscation order is made, POCA gives a right to an affected third party to make representations in relation to the making, variation etc of restraint orders and the enforcement of confiscation orders: see ss 42(3), 49(8), and 53(8). These provisions give effect to the requirement in s 69(3) to allow persons other than the defendant and the recipient of the tainted gift to retain or recover the value of his or her interests. Albeit POCA treats the function of the Crown Court at the confiscation stage as a limited one which does not involve the consideration of the practical effects of an order properly made on third party interests, if a property adjustment order is made in favour of a third party such as the wife, the Crown Court must have regard to it in determining the 'available amount'.

16.67   Similarly, if a property adjustment order is made after the confiscation order but before enforcement, the Crown Court must, on the application of the Crown Prosecution Service (CPS) or the defendant, have regard to it in adjusting 'the available amount' under s 23 of POCA.

Receivership proceedings

16.68   When this stage of the proceedings is reached, third parties claiming to hold an interest in realisable property have a right to be heard because a receivership order effectively extinguishes the property rights of those holding realisable property. However, the rights of third parties are protected in a number of ways.

16.69   Where the Crown applies for an enforcement receiver (under s 50 of POCA, s 29 DTA, s 80 CJA 1988), the court has the power to allow a third party claiming an interest in the property to reopen the question of ownership previously determined in the confiscation proceedings in the Crown Court, but should not permit the re-litigation of issues which had been decided in the Crown Court on the same, or substantially the same, evidence and submissions (see *Re Norris* [2001] 1 WLR 1388).

The right to be given notice of the proceedings

Section 50 of POCA, Criminal Procedure Rule 60.1(6)(b) (Sc115.7(2)(b) in CJA/DTA **16.70** cases) provides that the application seeking the appointment of a receiver must be served, *inter alia*, upon:

Any person holding any interest in the realisable property to which the application relates.

The application, together with the evidence in support, must be served not less than seven **16.71** days prior to the hearing date.

The right to make representations

Section 51(8) of POCA states: **16.72**

The court must not—
(a) confer the power mentioned in subsection (2)(b) or (c) in respect of property, or
(b) exercise the power conferred on it by subsection (6) in respect of property,
unless it gives persons holding interest in the property a reasonable opportunity to make representations to it.

A right merely to be given notice of the proceedings will, by itself, not be sufficient to protect the third party's interest in the property. Accordingly, s 51(8) of POCA provides that the court shall not exercise the powers given to it unless a reasonable opportunity has been given to persons holding an interest in the property to make representations to the court (s 29(8) of the DTA and s 80(8) of the CJA 1988).

It should be noted that the only persons who have a right to be given notice of and make **16.73** representations in receivership proceedings are those who have an interest in the defendant's realisable property. Thus, a bank holding a deposit account in the name of the defendant would have no right to make representations, whereas the defendant's spouse in whose name the matrimonial home was jointly held with the defendant clearly would.

What steps should be taken on behalf of the third party on receipt of an application to appoint an enforcement receiver?

The third party's solicitor should firstly go on the record by notifying the court, the prose- **16.74** cuting authority that issued the application, and the solicitors for the defendant, of his interest in the case. If the client is unable to fund the case privately and meets the eligibility criteria, an emergency application for Legal Service Commission (LSC) funding should be made. Once funding has been resolved, work should commence on preparing a witness statement setting out in detail the precise nature of the third party interest in the property. Where documentary evidence supporting the third party's claim exists (eg in relation to a spouse's interest in the matrimonial home) this should be produced and exhibited to the witness statement. If there are other persons who are in a position to confirm the extent of the third party's claim, witness statements should also be taken from them. Such independent corroboration is particularly important in cases where no documentary evidence exists confirming the third party's claim.

Seeking an adjournment

16.75 As third parties are only entitled to seven days notice of the hearing, there may be insufficient time to obtain LSC funding, conduct all the necessary enquiries, draft and serve witness statements, and brief counsel before the return date on the application. In such circumstances an adjournment should be sought. As the public interest requires that confiscation orders should be satisfied promptly, it may well be that the court would not be prepared to adjourn the entire receivership application. It is becoming increasingly common for the court to appoint a receiver to enable him to start realising assets that are free of third party claims. In order to protect the position of the third party, the court will then go on to order a stay on the receiver's powers of realisation in respect of those assets in which he claims an interest pending the determination of the claim. In order to ensure that the third party claim is determined expeditiously, the court may make directions as to how the case should proceed. The court may direct that the third party should serve his evidence in support within a specific time frame and that the prosecutor and defendant be at liberty to serve evidence in rebuttal within a specified period thereafter.

16.76 Before the hearing, it may be prudent for the third party to enter into negotiations with the prosecutor and defendant. In many cases, the fact of the third party having an interest in the asset will be beyond question, eg where the defendant and third party own a house in joint names. The real issue is more commonly the extent of the third party's interest. As all parties will be anxious to resolve the matter expeditiously and at minimum cost, it may well be that the prosecutor and defendant would be prepared to take a commercial view and not press for the highest amount for which they could argue.

Powers of the court and receiver in relation to third parties

16.77 Under s 69(3)(a) of POCA, the powers of a receiver must be exercised with a view to allowing a person, other than the defendant or a recipient of a tainted gift, to retain or recover the value of any interest held by him. It follows that the confiscation and enforcement powers conferred on the court and the receiver by the Act must be exercised with a view to allowing an innocent third party to retain or recover the value of any interest in realisable property held by him. Unlike the CJA 1988 and the DTA, it is now the duty of the Crown Court to ensure that the value of the third party's interests in realisable property is preserved, and that duty is in priority to the duty of the court to preserve assets for payment of a confiscation order.

16.78 It is important to remember that while there is no right to be heard at the confiscation hearing, a third party may be heard at the restraint stage of proceedings and then again at the enforcement stage.

16.79 It should also be noted that under s 84 of POCA, references to an interest in relation to land in England and Wales are to a legal estate, or equitable interest or power (see s 84(2)(f)). This means that mere rights such as a right of occupation are not protected under s 69(3)(a).

The role of the defendant

16.80 As already observed, the third party should serve his application and evidence on the defendant as well as the prosecutor and should also involve him in any negotiations. The reason for this is that the defendant has a clear interest in the outcome of the proceedings. The greater the interest the court rules the third party has in the asset, the less the defendant will have from the proceeds of sale to satisfy the confiscation order. Accordingly, he may well wish either to dispute the third party's claim in its entirety or at least argue that the extent of the third party's interest is not as great as that claimed. As there is such a potential conflict of interest between the defendant and third party, the practice of their being represented by the same solicitors should generally be discouraged, even when there remains a close relationship between the defendant and the third party.

The hearing

If the parties are unable to agree, the matter will usually be listed for hearing before a judge in chambers (unrobed) to determine: **16.81**

(a) whether the third party has any interest in the asset at all; and
(b) if so, the extent of that interest.

The third party, as applicant for relief, will normally open the proceedings and call his evidence, followed by the prosecution and defendant. Witness statement evidence will be admissible except to the extent that the court has required witnesses to attend for cross-examination under the Criminal Procedure Rules. Once all the evidence has been heard, the parties will have the right to make a closing address to the court in the usual way.

The court's order

The order the court makes will depend on its findings of law and fact. If the court finds that the third party is the sole owner of the property in dispute, then clearly it cannot be incorporated in the receivership order because it is not a realisable asset of the defendant. Equally, if the court rules that the defendant is the sole owner of the asset, the entire net proceeds of sale will be applied to the satisfaction of the confiscation order and the third party will get nothing. Such situations are deceptively simple, as the matter becomes increasingly more complex when the court rules that the third party does have some interest in the asset. **16.82**

In such circumstances, the court has a number of options under s 51 of POCA (or s 29 of the DTA and s 80 of the CJA 1988). Firstly, it could order the receiver to sell the asset and pay to the third party from the net proceeds of sale an amount proportionate to his interest in the property. If, for example, the net proceeds of sale of the property in question were £50,000 and the third party's interest in the property was found to be 50 per cent, £25,000 would go to the third party and £25,000 towards the satisfaction of the confiscation order. **16.83**

Alternatively, where the third party has the means to 'buyout' the defendant's interest in the property, the court may, under s 51(6)(a) of POCA (or s 29(6)(a) of the DTA and s 80(6) of the CJA 1988), order the third party to pay to the receiver an amount equivalent to the value of the beneficial interest of the defendant in that property or, as the case may be, of the recipient of a gift caught by the Act. The court may order under s 51(6)(b) of POCA (or s 29(6)(b) of the DTA and s 80(6) of the CJA 1988) that once such payment has been made, the defendant's interest in the property should be transferred to the third party and/or that the defendant's interest in the property be extinguished. **16.84**

16.85   Section 51(6) of POCA states:

> The court—
> (a) may order a person holding an interest in realisable property to make to the receiver such payment as the Court specifies in respect of a beneficial interest held by the Defendant or the recipient of a tainted gift;
> (b) may (on the payment being made) by order transfer, grant or extinguish any interest in the property.

Application of sums and third parties

16.86   Under s 54 of POCA, sums held by the receiver appointed by the Crown Court under s 50 of POCA which are the proceeds of the realisation of property under s 51, or sums in which the defendant holds an interest, must be applied as follows:

(1) they must be applied in payment for such expenses incurred by a person acting as an insolvency practitioner as are payable under this subsection by virtue of s 432;
(2) they must be applied in making any payments directed by the Crown Court; and
(3) they must be applied on the defendant's behalf towards satisfaction of the confiscation order. (See s 54(2).)

It follows therefore that where a third party had been successful in establishing their interest, that interest should be satisfied in terms of the repayment of any money owing in priority to satisfaction of the confiscation order.

16.87   Under s 54(3), if the amount payable under the confiscation order has been fully paid and any sums remain in the receiver's hands he must distribute them:

(3)
  (a) among such persons who held (or hold) interest in the property concerned as the Crown Court directs, and
  (b) in such proportions as it directs.
(4) Before making a direction under subsection (3), the Court must give persons who held, or hold, interests in the property concerned, a reasonable opportunity to make representations to it.

D. Specific Third Party Claims

Wives and cohabitees

16.88   Wives and cohabitees enjoy little more protection under the Acts than other third parties, and their rights to realisable property are proportionate to the interest they hold therein. Practitioners are perhaps more likely to find themselves advising wives on their position under confiscation legislation than any other third party. The first approach a solicitor is likely to get is immediately after a restraint order has been served. At this stage, the wife may well be in a state of some distress; not only may her husband be in custody facing serious criminal charges, but she may find herself served with a restraint order freezing all of her husband's realisable property, including items in which she may hold a joint interest. It is possible to give her some reassurance at this stage.

16.89   Firstly, although the matrimonial home may be subject to restraint or charging orders, she is entitled to remain in residence pending the conclusion of the proceedings. The restraint order merely prevents her from disposing of realisable property and does not prevent its use pending the determination of the proceedings against her husband. The same principle would apply to motor vehicles, namely that they may continue to be used by the wife, but not sold. The wife should be advised that if at any time she wishes to sell an asset, she must not do so, but should return to the solicitor forthwith. It may well be that if she wishes to move to a smaller house or buy a smaller motor vehicle, the prosecution and defendant would readily consent to a variation of the restraint order to enable her to do so, subject to the new asset being immediately made subject to restraint and any surplus funds being paid into an interest bearing account pending the conclusion of the proceedings. As well as being warned of the potential consequences of an unlawful sale, a wife should also be advised that, in so far as she is able, she should ensure that the asset is properly maintained in the interim. If she were to allow a property to deteriorate, or fail to keep up mortgage payments, this could provide a basis for the prosecution applying to appoint a pre-conviction management receiver.

Joint bank accounts can create particular problems when they are restrained. It may well be **16.90** that the wife's salary is paid into such an account, or that they contain other monies belonging solely to her. First, she should be advised to open a bank account in her sole name and arrange for all future salary payments, together with any other payments to which she alone is entitled, to be paid into that account. The prosecution should be notified that she intends to do this. Secondly, as to any monies belonging solely to her that are already in the account at the time the restraint order is served, she should be asked to provide documentary evidence (eg salary advice, letter from her employer, etc) to prove her entitlement. This should then be forwarded to the prosecution who will normally consent to the order being varied to release from the account monies belonging solely to her that do not constitute realisable property of the defendant. If the prosecution will not agree, an application to court should be considered.

The wife is also entitled, pending the conclusion of the criminal proceedings, to expect her **16.91** reasonable needs to be provided for. She would, therefore, be entitled to ask the court to vary the restraint order to allow reasonable sums to be released from the restraint order to pay the reasonable living expenses of herself and her family.

Restraint orders typically contain a proviso that spending limits for living expenses may be **16.92** increased on the following terms:

> The Defendant and Mrs Germont may agree with the (Prosecutor) that the above spending limits for living expenses should be increased, and the Defendant (and the Prosecutor) may agree this order may be varied in any respect but any such agreement must be in writing.

Where agreement cannot be reached in relation to living expenses the matter should be listed before the court for determination.

Once a confiscation order has been made, the position of the wife becomes less secure **16.93** because, as Henry J pointed out in *Re B* (QBD, 13 May 1991), the Acts make no special provision to protect the rights of the wife in the matrimonial home.

Property should form part of the confiscation order

In *R v Judge and Woodbridge* (1992) 13 Cr App R(S) 685, the court rejected the defen- **16.94** dant's contention that it was 'unfair and oppressive' to make a CJA confiscation order in an amount which would necessitate the sale of the matrimonial home. Similarly, in

R v Crutchley and Tonks (1994) 15 Cr App R(S) 627 the Court of Appeal ruled that the offender's home may be incorporated in a confiscation order to the extent that it forms part of his realisable property.

16.95 The court may give the wife the option of buying out her husband's interest in the property. She may be able to persuade the court to exercise its discretion under s 51(9) of POCA (or s 29(5) of the DTA or s 80(5) of the CJA 1988) to direct that the house should not be realised for a specific period to give her a reasonable opportunity either of finding alternative accommodation or raising the finance to buy out her husband's interest in the property. She may well also find the receiver, anxious to avoid a forced sale, will have some sympathy for her position and will be prepared to negotiate.

Matrimonial proceedings and the position under the CJA 1988 and DTA

16.96 The reader will now be familiar with the fact that, prior to the provisions of POCA coming into force, restraint and confiscation proceedings were governed by the CJA 1988 and the DTA. Under that earlier regime, whereas confiscation proceedings were conducted in the Crown Court, the jurisdiction over the making of restraint orders, the appointment of receivers, and the enforcement of confiscation orders rested with the High Court.

16.97 In that context, situations often arose where the claim of the divorced wife of a drug smuggler, money launderer, or other criminal, who sought ancillary relief under the MCA was in conflict with the claims of the Crown, represented either by the CPS or Customs and Excise, to the extent that the making of a property adjustment order in the ancillary relief proceedings would have the effect of reducing the amount available for confiscation.

16.98 In *Customs & Excise Commissioners v A* [2002] EWCA Civ 1039 [2003] Fam 55, the Court of Appeal clearly disposed of the suggestion that the jurisdiction of the family court under Part II of MCA was ousted by, or obliged to take second place to, proceedings to enforce orders under the DTA. It made clear that the broad scheme of the DTA, like that of its predecessor the Drug Trafficking Offences Act 1986 (DTOA), was governed by the intention that no one convicted of drug trafficking offences should be allowed to retain any part of the proceeds of his crime. This is recorded at para 14 of *Customs & Excise v A*, where Lord Donaldson in *Re Peters* [1988] QB 871 at 874D is quoted as saying:

> The broad scheme involves the making of confiscation orders at the time of sentencing and of prior protective orders. The latter are designed to pervent an accused rendering a confiscation order inappropriate or nugatory by disposing of his assets between the time when an information is about to be laid against him and the making of a confiscation order in the event of conviction.

16.99 However, at paras 12 and 13, Lord Justice Schiemann set out the position in relation to the jurisdiction of the court in civil proceedings to make an order under Part II of the MCA in any case involving assets acquired by or derived from criminal activities as follows:

> 12. . . . The court is not *obliged* to exercise its powers under section 23 or 24: section 25(1) gives it a discretion to do so;
>
> > (2) The fact that one or both of the parties to the marriage had been engaged in or convicted of trafficking in drugs is plainly a material circumstance of the case within section 25(1); and drug trafficking is almost certainly conduct which it would be inequitable to ignore.

(3) The court would plainly be bound to have regard to any drug trafficking confiscation order and the financial obligation which one or both of the parties had under any such order;

(4) The court equally and plainly must have regard to the extent to which the assets of the parties were the products of drug trafficking; and the extent to which their standard of living and respective financial contributions to the marriage derived from drug trafficking.

13. In short, in deciding whether to exercise its powers to make a property adjustment order under section 24 MCA 1973, the court would be bound fully to take into account any order made under DTA 1994 and to decide whether or not, in all the circumstances of the case it was appropriate to exercise the discretion under section 25 MCA to make a property adjustment order under section 24 MCA, or whether it was appropriate to decline to make such an order and to allow the DTA Order to be enforced. It is not difficult to envisage cases in which the latter would be the correct cause—an obvious example being where the matrimonial assets were the fruits of drug dealing in which both parties were engaged or complicit.

That, however, is a wholly different question from whether the terms of the DTA 1994 prevent the court exercising its MCA 1973 jurisdiction at all.

In *CPS v Richards and another* [2006] EWCA Civ 849, the Court of Appeal rejected a submission that the court was deprived of its jurisdiction under the MCA to make provision for a wife out of matrimonial assets, even though they were tainted. It held that where assets were tainted with the proceeds of crime and subject to confiscation they should not ordinarily, as a matter of public justice and public policy, be distributed. However, that was not to say that the court was deprived of the jurisdiction to make a distribution in favour of the wife, nor was it to say that no circumstances could exist in which such an order would be justified. **16.100**

As observed above, under the DTA and CJA 1988, the power to make a prior restraint order in relation to confiscation proceedings lay with the High Court. Section 26 of the DTA empowered the High Court to make a restraint order prohibiting any person from dealing with realisable property which might or would be subject to confiscation. It also empowered the High Court to appoint a receiver in respect of realisable property and manage it or otherwise deal with it as directed by the court. Sections 27 to 29 set out further powers of the High Court in dealing with restrained property. **16.101**

Section 31 of the DTA ('the legislative steer') provided that, in relation to decisions under ss 26 to 29: **16.102**

(2) Subject to the following provisions of this section, the powers should be exercised with a view to making available for satisfying a confiscation order or, as the case may be, any confiscation order that may be made in the defendant's case, the value for the time being in realisable property held by any person, by means of the realisation of such property . . .

(4) The powers shall be exercised with the view to allowing any person other than the defendant . . . to retain or recover the value of any property held by him.

(5) In exercising the powers, no account should be taken of any obligations of the defendant . . . which conflict with the obligation to satisfy the confiscation order.

In relation to this provision Schiemann LJ in *Customs & Excise v A* concluded: **16.103**

43. . . . there is nothing in the provisions of either MCA 1973 or DTA 1994 which requires the court to hold that either Statute takes priority over the other when the provisions of each are invoked in relation to the same property. Both statutes confer discretion on the

courts, which the court may or may not choose to exercise, to make orders. The terms of those orders will depend on the facts of the individual case . . .

44. Equally, it does not seem to me to be axiomatic that it is more in the public interest to enforce an order under section 31 DTA 1994 than to make a property adjustment order under section 24 MCA 1973. If the former has the effect of forcing a spouse to sell her home and become dependent on the state for housing and housing support in order to meet a confiscation order in relation to property which was not acquired by the profits of crimes; if the wife has made a substantial financial or other contribution to the acquisition of that property; if the crime involved is one of which she was ignorant and by which she is untainted, it seems to me that the public policy argument may well go the other way. Each case must depend on its own facts.

45. Accordingly, the fact that section 31(2)–(6) DTA 1994 require the court's powers for the realisation of property to be exercised in a particular way in enforcement proceedings under that Act does not, in my judgment, mean that by necessary implication that those subsections either exclude or take priority over powers of the court under MCA 1973 section 24. Unlike bankruptcy proceedings, the property which is subject to the confiscation order does not vest in the Receiver appointed under section 26 or 29 DTA 1994. It remains the property of the defendant drug trafficker, and is thus capable of being transferred to the defendant's former spouse under MCA section 24.

16.104 The question for the court in *Customs & Excise v A* was whether the judge was prohibited by the DTA from exercising his powers under the MCA on the basis that, once a confiscation order had been made, the DTA overrode and excluded the operation of the 1973 Act. In agreeing with the judgment of Schiemann LJ as quoted above, Judge LJ (as he then was) stated at para 92 that:

Looking at the matter generally, the outcome should not depend on whether an order made under the 1973 Act had been concluded in the wife's favour before the confiscation was made against her husband. Carried to its logical conclusion that would offer a material advantage to a spouse who rushed into divorce and ancillary relief proceedings as soon as she discovered the slightest grounds for suspicion that her husband was involved in drug dealing and a corresponding disadvantage if she delayed . . . A further consequence would be an unseemly competition between the prosecution and the Crown Court, where the wife would not be heard, and the solicitors acting for the wife in ancillary proceedings, from which the prosecution would be absent. First come, first served, would be unlikely to produce a just result. These are persuasive arguments for the view that, notwithstanding any perceived 'priority', the decision of the courts should not be confined to enforcement of a confiscation order first and exclusively, but even where a confiscation order has been made, provided the circumstances justify (for example, as here, where a wholly innocent spouse and property untarnished by drug dealing or its profits are involved), the enforcement process should at least acknowledge the existence of the 1973 Act and the power of the court to exercise its discretion by taking account of the interests of the innocent spouse as well as the criminal defendant.

16.105 The similar provisions of the CJA 1988 were explained *In Re X* [2004] EWHC 861 (Admin) at paras 10 to 12 per Davis J. He pointed out that s 82(2) and (4) of the CJA 1988 mirrored the terms of s 31(2) and (4) of the DTA. At paras 20 and 23 Davis J observed that the provision of s 82(2) requiring that the courts powers should be exercised 'with a view to' making available for satisfaction from any confiscation order the value of realisable property introduced 'a degree of elasticity' (para 20) so that:

the court certainly is required . . . to take into account what in *Re Peters* is called the 'legislative steer' to the effect that the value of realisable property should be maintained with a view to making it available to satisfy any confiscation order that may be made. But it is not, in my view . . . a conclusive consideration in all cases.' (para 23)

Given that, whereas confiscation proceedings were conducted in the Crown Court, it was **16.106** the High Court which had jurisdiction over the making of prior restraint orders and the subsequent enforcement of confiscation orders, and that the High Court had jurisdiction in respect of applications and orders under the MCA, it was recognised to be desirable that ancillary relief proceedings launched under the MCA and any resulting application to vary the restraint order be dealt with by a single High Court judge who was both a judge of the Family Division and a nominated judge of the Administrative Court.

Guidance for best practice in such situations was handed down by Munby J after consulta- **16.107** tion with the other judges of the Family Division who were also nominated judges of the Administrative Court in *W v H, and Her Majesty's Customs & Excise* [2004] EWHC 526.

In *W v H* it was stated that, as soon as it became apparent that an ancillary relief case **16.108** involved conflict with the Crown in relation to contemplated confiscation proceedings, the case should be transferred to the High Court to be listed for directions together with the Administrative Court proceedings before a judge of the Family Division who was also a nominated judge of the Administrative Court. At the same time directions were to be given for the participation of the CPS or Customs, and in particular for obtaining statements from them whether or not it was accepted that the wife had any, and if so what, beneficial interest in the assets claimed by her; whether or not it was accepted that she should be granted the ancillary relief sought; and whether or not it was asserted that any of the assets being claimed by her were acquired by criminal activity in which she was involved or were otherwise 'tainted' by her husband's criminal activities so far as she was concerned.

Factors to be taken into consideration

In *CPS v Grimes and Grimes* [2003] 2 FLR 510, Wilson J held that where the net proceeds **16.109** of sale of a former matrimonial home were held in an account in the name of two firms of solicitors; and the CPS, on the one hand, sought a direction that they be paid in partial satisfaction of a confiscation order made against the husband; and the wife, on the other hand, sought a direction either that she was the beneficial owner of one half of the fund or, alternatively, that half of the sum should be paid to her as a lump sum under s 23 of the MCA, the factors to be weighed against these competing arguments were (against the wife):

(1) that she already had a home;
(2) that some at least of the fund had effectively been contributed to by the husband's illicit income;
(3) the fact that the confiscation order had been made with reference to the whole fund;

and (for the wife)

(1) that she had no participation or knowledge of her husband's activities;
(2) that she had contributed to the ancillary costs of the property on the mortgage;
(3) her state of health;
(4) her poor financial position;

(5) the fact that a significant period of cohabitation preceded the marriage;

(6) she could expect no maintenance from her husband.

16.110 Wilson J found that the fact that the husband had not argued before the Crown Court that the wife had an interest in the property was of no significance. On the facts, the wife had established her equitable entitlement to a half-share, or in the alternative, an order for half a share would be made under s 23 of the 1973 Act.

16.111 In *Stodgell v Stodgell* [2009] EWCA Civ 243 the Court of Appeal considered two related applications for leave to appeal. They arose in the context of matrimonial claims for ancillary relief against a husband and father who had been convicted and made the subject of a confiscation order. The principal application was from the wife. She sought to challenge the decision of Holman J that her application for ancillary relief could not proceed until the confiscation order has been discharged, at which point it would be possible to see whether there are any other assets which she can attack.

16.112 A confiscation order under the CJA 1988 was made. That confiscation order was not appealed. The wife did not assert any proprietary interest in either the former matrimonial home or any other of the husband's assets. Her application was for ancillary relief pursuant to ss 21 to 25 of the MCA. Thus, it was an application for a discretionary order requiring the husband to make financial provision for her. The wife was not complicit in the husband's crime. The judge dealt with her on the basis that she was entirely innocent of it. The Court of Appeal confirmed that it was established by *Commissioners of Customs and Excise v A* [2003] 2 WLR 210 that neither an ancillary relief claim nor a confiscation order enjoys automatic priority, the one over the other. Hughes LJ, giving the judgement of the court, stated:

> 9. This case is a good illustration of the fact, that while non-complicity in the crime is a necessary condition for the wife to succeed in an ancillary relief claim as a matter of discretion where she is in competition with a confiscation order, such non-complicity is not a sufficient condition. She will also fail in a number of other circumstances, including where the husband's assets are reduced to nil by having to pay now what he ought to have paid years ago. This is not a case in which the confiscation order relates to surplus income derived from crime such as profits from drug trafficking. This is a case where the husband owed the Revenue the tax from years before his conviction . . . Penalties were incurred also because he failed to pay his debts. The spouses both lived well on a domestic economy which included the non-payment of tax and penalties . . .

> 10. For that reason, it is not critical that the Devon house and the London flat were not acquired from crime. What is critical, as it seems to me, is that they could not have been and cannot be preserved without non-payment of the tax and the penalties . . . That is not a question of treating a state creditor as in some way stronger than a private creditor. It is a question of ascertaining what are the assets available for distribution between husband and wife.

16.113 The Court also identified other factors of relevance:

(i) That the wife may be cast upon the state is a relevant factor—see *Customs and Excise v A*.

(ii) It was not a case of punishing the wife for the husband's crime. If one spouse turns out to be a spendthrift the result may be that the other suffers an absence of assets from which to seek ancillary relief. The same may happen if he turns out to be a criminal.

(iii) It would not be a legitimate exercise of the court's powers to use them in a manner which in effect requires the receiver to use up public funds on a search for assets in the hope that both the wife and the tax can be paid.

(iv) *White v White* [2000] UKHL 54 deals with the position as between husband and wife. To the extent that a wife has a proprietary interest in property, that property is not part of the husband's assets and his realisable assets are the smaller. In either case the wife is not in competition with the confiscation order, because her interest is vested and one never gets to the *Commissioners of Customs and Excise v A* question.

Matrimonial proceedings and the position under POCA

A number of significant changes to the confiscation regime were effected by POCA. In particular, jurisdiction over the making of restraint orders, the appointment of receivers, and the enforcement of confiscation orders is now exercised by the Crown Court, and the jurisdiction of the High Court has been removed. **16.114**

Section 41 of POCA confers on the Crown Court the power to make a restraint order **16.115** prohibiting any specified person from dealing with any realisable property held by him and the subsequent ss 41 to 60 deal with the Crown Court's powers in relation to restraint, receivers, and enforcement of confiscation orders.

Section 42(3) of POCA permits an application to discharge or vary a restraint order to be **16.116** made to the Crown Court by the person who applied for the restraint order or any person affected by that order (such as a wife).

Section 69 of POCA provides the following legislative steer to courts exercising powers **16.117** under ss 42 to 60:

(2) The powers—
    (a) must be exercised with the view for the value for the time being of realisable property being made available (by the property's realisation) for satisfying any confiscation order that has been made or may be made against the defendant;
    (b) must be exercised, in a case where a confiscation order has not yet been made with a view to securing that there is no diminution in the value of the realisable property . . .
(3) Sub-section (2) has effect subject to the following rule—
    (a) the powers must be exercised with a view to allowing a person other than the defendant or recipient of the tainted gift to retain or recover the value of any interest held by him . . .

By use of the phrase 'with a view to', the language of s 69 of POCA retains the same termi- **16.118** nology as that which appeared in s 31 of the DTA and there is nothing in the wording of POCA to suggest that the meaning of those words is different, or should be applied any differently, from the interpretation of the Administrative Court in *Customs & Excise v A*. The phrase retains such 'elasticity' as to permit a diminution in the available amount and it contemplates striking an appropriate balance between the same competing public policy considerations between confiscating the proceeds of crime and making proper financial provision for a wife, per para 42, *Webber v Webber and CPS* [2006] EWHC 2893 (Fam); (2007) 1 WLR 1052; (2007) 2 FLR 116, where the President of the Family Division held:

42. . . . For the reasons given in *Customs & Excise v A*, injustice may be caused by too rigid an application of the confiscation principle where the interests of an 'innocent' or former spouse are concerned. Removal of the discretion of the High Court to make financial provision in such circumstances would be a substantial change in the law and the juris-diction of the High Court and it is clear to me that the effect of MCA 1973 remains unaltered in that respect.

43. Thus, at the time that the matter came before me, it was clear that the High Court had the power to make a property adjustment order in favour of the wife to an extent which went beyond the half share conceded by the CPS not to be tainted as the proceeds of crime.

16.119   In *Webber v Webber* the President indicated:

52. . . . it was plainly preferable that the ancillary relief application should be disposed of first. By that means, on restoration of the adjourned hearing of the confiscation proceedings in the Crown Court [the judge] would be in a position to judge whether the amount available was 50% of the proceeds of sale, as conceded by the CPS, or required adjustment in the light of the findings of the High Court judge hearing the ancillary relief application.

16.120   It appears, therefore, that where an innocent wife has asked for her ancillary relief application to be dealt with at the same time as confiscation, the appropriate course is for the ancillary relief matter to be disposed of first by the High Court, thus enabling the Crown Court judge to make the appropriate determination in relation to what assets remained.

Property adjustment orders

16.121   In *Customs & Excise v A* [2002] EWCA Civ 1039, the Court of Appeal considered whether or not the court was precluded from making a property adjustment order under s 24 of the MCA when the property in question was also the subject of proceedings by HM Customs to enforce a criminal confiscation order made against the defendant in proceedings under the DTA, following his conviction and imprisonment for a drug trafficking offence.

16.122   In concluding that it was not so precluded, the Court found that Pt II of the MCA enables the court to make a wide range of orders, including financial provision orders (that is, orders for periodical payment and lump sums), as well as property adjustment orders, designed, on divorce, to regulate the financial position of the parties to the marriage. The basis upon which the court exercises its discretion to make financial provision and property adjustment orders is set out in s 25 of the MCA. In cases of divorce, Pt II of the MCA gives the parties to a marriage an unfettered right to apply to the court for financial provision and property adjustment orders. It follows, the Court held in *Customs & Excise v A*, that the court plainly has jurisdiction to entertain applications for ancillary relief by drug dealers or former spouses of drug dealers.

16.123   In *Customs & Excise v A*, the primary contention of the appellant was that the exercise of jurisdiction under the MCA is effectively ousted by and must take second place to proceedings to enforce orders made under the DTA. The court was able to extract the following propositions from s 25 of the MCA, namely:

(1)   the court is not obliged to exercise its powers under ss 23 or 24: s 25(1) gives it discretion to do so;

(2)   the fact that one or both of the parties to the marriage had been engaged in or convicted of trafficking in drugs is plainly a material circumstance of the case within s 25(1); and drug trafficking is almost certainly conduct which would be inequitable to ignore;

(3)   the court would plainly be bound to have regard to any drug trafficking confiscation order and financial obligation that one or both of the parties had under such an order;

(4) the court equally plainly must have regard to the extent to which the assets to the parties were the product of drug trafficking; and the extent to which their standard of living and respective financial contributions to the marriage derived from drug trafficking.

In short, the Court held that, in exercising its powers to make a property adjustment order under s 24 of the MCA, the court would be bound fully to take into account any order made under the DTA in deciding whether or not, in all the circumstances of the case, it was appropriate to exercise the discretion under s 25 of the MCA to make a property adjustment order under s 24, or whether it was appropriate to decline to make such an order and to allow the DTA order to be enforced.

The Court held it was not difficult to envisage cases in which the latter would be the correct course, an obvious example, it said, being where the matrimonial assets were the fruits of drug dealing in which both parties were engaged or complicit. The point the Court emphasised, however, was that that was a wholly different question on whether the terms of the DTA prevented the court exercising its MCA jurisdiction at all. **16.124**

The Court also held that it was not correct (as a general proposition) that an order under s 24 of the 1973 Act would be unassailable if the consequent transfer pre-dated an application under the 1994 Act. Such a conclusion would give open season to collusive agreements between dishonest former spouses. In such a situation, it would be open to the prosecution to apply for the order under the 1973 Act to be set aside on the grounds that the court had not been given full disclosure by the parties, or had not been told the assets transferred represented the proceeds of criminal conduct. **16.125**

Property adjustment orders: does POCA oust the MCA?

Under s 58(5) of POCA, if a court in which proceedings are pending in respect of any property is satisfied that a restraint order has been applied for or made in respect of the property, the court may either stay the proceedings or allow them to continue on any terms it thinks fit. Thus the legislative steer set out in s 69 may be applicable in family court proceedings where the court is considering a property adjustment order under s 24 or s 25 of the MCA. This has important significance following the case of *Customs & Excise v A*. In *Customs & Excise v A* the court concluded that the DTA and the MCA were on an equal footing. It is now arguable that the provisions of POCA oust the provisions of the MCA and therefore the effect of that part of the decision in *Customs & Excise v A* is questionable in relation to the new Act. **16.126**

Under s 69(3)(a) the powers of the court and receiver must be exercised with a view to allowing a person other than the defendant or recipient to retain or recover the value of any interest held by him. If s 69(3)(a) is not applicable, ie there is no need to protect any interest held by a third party, then the duty to preserve any realisable asset to pay the confiscation order would take priority over any other statutory power. **16.127**

Tainted funds in matrimonial cases

The starting point in relation to the issue of tainted funds in matrimonial cases are the two decisions of *Customs and Excise Commissioners v A* [2003] Fam 55; [2002] EWCA Civ 1039 **16.128** and *CPS v Richards* [2006] 2 FLR 1220; [2006] EWCA Civ 849. These were both cases in which a husband had been convicted of drug trafficking offences and there were confiscation proceedings against them. Each of the wives applied in ancillary relief proceedings under the MCA for a property adjustment order or a lump sum payment from assets of the husband. In *CPS v Richards*, it was successfully contended by the prosecution that public policy required that drug dealers were deprived of the fruits of their crimes and that those fruits should not be distributed to others, least of all those who had guilty knowledge of the origin of the assets. This court held that, where assets are tainted and subject to confiscation, they should ordinarily and as a matter of public policy not be distributed. In most cases, the fact that the assets were tainted was the decisive factor in any balance. In *Customs and Excise Commissioners v A*, the former wife obtained a property adjustment order, but this was on the basis of a specific finding by the judge that the house and the policies were not obtained with tainted funds, and that the wife herself had no knowledge of the husband's criminal activities.

16.129　The issue of matrimonial proceedings, tainted funds, and their interrelationship with the confiscation process was also considered in *Marion Gibson v RCPO* (2009) 2 WLR 471; (2008) 2 FLR 1672; (2009) QB 348. The case focused on the division of the matrimonial estate and home that Mr and Mrs Gibson had bought in 1990, which was registered in their joint names. At first instance, the deputy High Court judge referred at some length to the opinion of Baroness Hale of Richmond in *Stack v Dowden* [2007] UKHL 17, noting her observation that cases in which joint legal owners are to be taken to have intended that their beneficial interests should be different from their legal interests will be very unusual. He saw nothing to suggest that Mr and Mrs Gibson's intent at the time the property was purchased was that Mr Gibson should have a greater beneficial interest than 50 per cent. Nor had he seen anything to suggest that their initial intention subsequently changed. As between themselves, therefore, Mrs Gibson was the beneficial owner of 50 per cent of the equity in the property. The prosecution did not challenge this on appeal. It was also accepted that the burden was on the prosecution to displace Mrs Gibson's apparent beneficial interest; see *In Re Norris* [2001] 1 WLR 1388 at para 25.

16.130　The considerations in the Court of Appeal focused upon where a person had a mixed income, partly legitimate and partly the proceeds of crime. The issue was the effect of the taint on Mrs Gibson's half interest. At first instance the court considered whether she knew that the money was tainted, and if she did, whether that mattered. As to her knowledge, Mrs Gibson had given oral evidence at first instance and the deputy High Court judge had found her to be an evasive witness whose evidence was not credible. He found that she was well aware that a lot of cash, some of which she handled, was washing around the Gibson household well beyond that for which there may have been a legitimate explanation. He found that she had guilty knowledge, which in the context meant that she knew that money used to pay the mortgage was not legitimately earned.

16.131　The Court of Appeal held that the cases of *Customs and Excise Commissioners v A* [2003] Fam 55; [2002] EWCA Civ 1039 and *CPS v Richards* [2006] 2FLR 1220; [2006] EWCA Civ 849 did not apply in the instant case. Those cases concerned a husband's assets where the wife was seeking a discretionary order in her favour to transfer the assets to her. The court declined to exercise its discretion in the wives' favour because the assets were tainted and they were complicit. In the present case, Mrs Gibson was not applying for any transfer in her favour and for no exercise of the Court's discretion.

The Court found that the assets were hers without any court order in her favour. It was for **16.132** the prosecution to establish a public policy argument that would entitle the court to confiscate her assets, when she was not convicted; when no confiscation order had been made against her; and where there were no statutory confiscatory provisions in the DTA or otherwise on which the prosecution could rely. It had not done so.

As a result, the Court of Appeal rejected the Crown's arguments in relation to public policy. **16.133** It found there was powerful House of Lords *dicta* to the contrary in *In re Norris* [2001] 1 WLR 1388; [2001] UKHL 34 (at para 16). It also found support for its position in *R v Buckman* [1997] 1 Cr App R (S) 325, where Brooke LJ said (p 329) that the correct approach, where property is held in joint names, is for the court to start with the *prima facie* position as to where the beneficial interests lay and then go on to find whether there are gifts caught by the Act which ought then to increase the realisable value of the property within the meaning of s 6 of the DTA. On this basis, if Mrs Gibson's beneficial interests were not subject to gifts caught by the Act, and if they were not otherwise within the confiscatory ambit of the legislation, they did not fall to be confiscated. Furthermore, the Court held Mrs Gibson did not have to rely on illegality to establish her beneficial entitlement (see *Tinsley v Milligan* [1994] 1 AC 340).

Arden LJ observed: **16.134**

> when the court is considering what interests a husband and wife intended that they should have in a property in their joint names, the court is not exercising discretion as to what is fair. This point is made clear by Baroness Hale in *Stack v Dowden* at [61], where she emphasised that the search is for the result which the parties must, in the light of their conduct, be taken to have intended and not for the result which the court itself considers fair.

Equitable interests in the matrimonial home

In *Midland Bank plc v Cook* [1995] 4 All ER 562 the Court of Appeal held that where a **16.135** partner in a matrimonial home without legal title had established an equitable interest through direct contribution, the court would assess (in the absence of express evidence of intention) the proportion the parties were assumed to have intended for their beneficial ownership by undertaking a survey of the whole course of dealing between the parties relevant to that ownership and occupation of the property, and their sharing of its burdens and advantages. The court, the Court of Appeal held, should take into consideration all conduct that threw light on the question of what shares were intended. In particular, the Court held that a court was not bound to deal with the matter on the strict basis of a trust resulting from the cash contribution to the purchase price, and was free to attribute to the parties an intention to share the beneficial interest in some different proportions. The fact that the parties had neither discussed nor intended any agreement as to the proportions of their beneficial interest did not preclude the court from inferring one on general equitable principles (the Court of Appeal applying *Gissing v Gissing* [1970] 2 All ER 780 and *Grant v Edwards* [1986] 2 All ER 426). In *Cowcher v Cowcher* [1972] 1 WLR 425 the Court held that contributions to mortgage payments were to be treated as contributions to the purchase price of the property.

Trusts

16.136 For confiscation orders and family trusts see *R v Stannard* [2005] EWCA Crim 2717. In *R v Sharma* [2006] EWCA Crim 16, the Court of Appeal held that there was no room, where proceeds of crime were concerned, for the application of trust principles and the application of the normal legal consequences that might flow from the receipt of money for others. This was confirmed in *Revenue & Customs Prosecutors Office v May and Others* (2009) STC 2466, where the Court held that once it had been determined that particular property was a realisable asset, it could be recovered from any trust or company, irrespective of any legal obstacles or protections that might arise.

Banks

16.137 Banks and other financial institutions frequently find themselves affected by the terms of restraint orders, as they remain a popular repository for the proceeds of crime. The bank should, on receiving a restraint order, ensure that any accounts specified in the order which they hold are frozen forthwith. Further, if the restraint order is in purely general terms, any further accounts in which the defendant holds an interest of which they are aware should be similarly restrained. The bank is not, however, under an obligation to search through its records in an attempt to trace any other accounts the defendant may hold, unless the prosecuting authority is prepared to pay for the reasonable costs of such an exercise. If the order contains exceptions allowing, eg, the defendant to draw a specific weekly sum for general living expenses, the bank should ensure (by checking with the prosecution) that any preconditions to the release of such sums, such as the giving of notice to the prosecutor, have been complied with. Once such confirmation is forthcoming, the bank may release the sum allowed by the order and is not under any obligation to enquire into the purpose for which the defendant expends the money.

16.138 The bank is also entitled to look to the prosecutor for reimbursement of its reasonable costs and expenses in complying with the order. Inevitably, however, there will from time to time be cases that are of greater than average complexity and involve the bank in more work. In such cases the bank would be justified in seeking a higher payment.

16.139 The restraint order does not prevent the bank from exercising any existing rights it may have in relation to set off or to combine accounts. This principle is well illustrated by *Re K (Restraint Order)* [1990] 2 All ER 562. A restraint order was served on the Bank of India in respect of bank accounts that contained a total of £639,541.87. A separate account, however, had an overdraft of £337,585.59 and the bank applied to the court for a variation to the restraint order to enable it to combine the deposit and overdraft accounts so that the overdraft would be paid off leaving some £320,000 in the deposit accounts. Otton J allowed the application, ruling that a bank had an inherent right to combine the accounts and that by doing so it was merely carrying out an accounting exercise to determine the customer's indebtedness to the bank. The Court also ruled that, on the facts of the case, the bank had a right of set off and that the exercise of that right did not constitute disposing of or diminishing or in any way dealing with the money and that by so doing the bank was not in contravention of the restraint order.

16.140 A more difficult problem arises in relation to a bank that has an office within the jurisdiction of the court, but the account of the defendant is held at a branch overseas. If there is an agreement in force with the country in question, the account can be restrained by an order made in the courts of that jurisdiction, but considerable problems arise in relation to the defendant whose account is in a country where no such agreement exists. This problem arose in *Re M* (HC, 9 July 1993). M was charged with offences of VAT evasion and a restraint order was obtained under the CJA 1988 restraining him from dealing in any of his assets. M, who had been admitted to bail, subsequently absconded to Ireland and pre-conviction receivers were appointed to manage and preserve his assets. M had an account at a branch of the Bank of Ireland in Southampton and a copy of the order was subsequently served on that branch. He also had accounts at two branches of the Bank of Ireland in Ireland. Although a reciprocal enforcement agreement was in force between the UK and Ireland in relation to drug trafficking cases, no such agreement existed in relation to the CJA 1988. This placed the bank in an invidious position: if they refused to pay the money out to M, they would be vulnerable to an action for breach of contract by him; and if they did pay out they would have been vulnerable to proceedings for contempt of court by the prosecution. The bank therefore sought the court's directions, contending that they were not obliged to concern themselves with the order in so far as it concerned the accounts in Ireland.

16.141 Ognall J rejected the bank's argument that they need not concern themselves with the order at all, ruling that they must do everything lawfully within their power to restrain the monies held at their branches in Ireland. Ognall J said, at para 11E:

> We live in an age when funds may be transferred from jurisdiction to jurisdiction as rapidly as it takes me to speak this sentence and when banks are increasingly multi-national operations. In so far as a foreign bank sets up operations and registers within this jurisdiction, it not only submits itself *pro tanto* to the jurisdiction; in my judgment it should be treated as implicitly undertaking to do all that is necessary to cooperate to the fullest extent with the courts and law enforcement agencies of this country.

> I do not think it would be right to ease in any way the undoubtedly onerous burden resting upon the Bank to ensure that they do nothing that they are not strictly obliged to do under Irish law which would abet M's breach of that order and would allow him the benefit of his allegedly ill-gotten gains.

16.142 Ognall J refused the variation in the terms sought by the bank and only varied the order to the extent that it added the word 'lawfully' to that paragraph in the order dealing with its extraterritorial effect. It would have been inappropriate to expect the bank to do anything in relation to the accounts in Ireland which it could not do lawfully under Irish law, but it is now established that merely because an order relates to an account at an overseas branch of a bank does not mean that a financial institution served with a restraint order at its office within the jurisdiction can wholly disregard its terms.

Banks: no duty of care

16.143 In *Customs and Excise Commissioners v Barclays Bank plc* [2006] UKHL 28, Barclays Bank appealed against the decision that it owed a duty of care to Customs (a third party) to take reasonable care to ensure that no payments were made out of customer accounts that were subject to freezing injunctions. Customs had frozen two accounts while they sought payment of outstanding VAT, and the restraints specifically prohibited disposal of or dealing with any of the debtor companies' assets. The bank had been notified of the injunctions by fax. Only a matter of hours after receiving the freezing injunctions, Barclays had authorised transfers of substantial sums from the accounts. As a result Customs attempted to claim damages against Barclays for the sums paid out in breach of the freezing order.

16.144 The bank submitted that it did not owe a duty of care to avoid causing financial harm to another unless one had voluntarily undertaken responsibility towards that other person.

16.145 The House of Lords held that the presence or absence of a voluntary assumption of responsibility did not necessarily provide the answer in all cases. When the court granted Customs their application, the purpose was to protect Customs by preventing the companies from parting with their assets. The freezing injunctions were directed at the companies as opposed to the bank. Barclays, itself a third party, would be in contempt of court only if it knowingly failed to freeze customer accounts subject to the freezing injunctions and authorised transfers of sums from the accounts after being notified of the court orders (see *Z Ltd v A-Z and Others, sub nom Mareva Injunction* [1982] QB 558; [1982] 2 WLR 288, *A-G v Times Newspapers* [1991] 2 WLR 994 and *A-G v Punch Ltd* [2002] UKHL 50).

16.146 The Court held the failure to operate a system for freezing accounts did not mean that Barclays was liable to Customs who had obtained the orders. Notification of the order placed a duty on Barclays to respect the order of the court, but it did not of itself generate a duty of care to Customs. Having obtained a freezing order and notified the bank, Customs could expect that any responsible bank would respect the order, but it could not rely on the bank doing so.

16.147 Ultimately, Customs had to rely on the court to ensure that Barclays did not flout the orders and to punish Barclays if it did so. There was nothing that could be regarded as a voluntary assumption of responsibility by the bank for the way in which it would go about freezing the companies' accounts and there was nothing that involved Barclays in entering into any kind of relationship with Customs that required it to exercise such care as the circumstances required. The Court held that Barclays and Customs were about as far from being in a relationship 'equivalent to contract' as they could be, and therefore the court held that in the circumstances it would not be fair to hold that Barclays owed a duty of care to Customs.

The insolvent defendant: the position of the trustee in bankruptcy

16.148 It happens from time to time that defendants involved in offences to which POCA, the DTA, and the CJA 1988 apply are made bankrupt. There are a variety of reasons for this. If the defendant is in custody, he will not be earning any income and will be unable to run any business he might own. Further, he may well already be in financial difficulty at the time of committing the alleged offences and, indeed, his impecunious state may well provide an explanation for his offending in the first place.

16.149 In *R v Abdul Shahid* [2009] EWCA Crim 831 the Court of Appeal held that where a bankruptcy order had been made against an offender and all his assets were in the hands of his trustee in bankruptcy, it did not affect a judge's power to make a confiscation order. The Court found that whilst it might affect the enforcement of the confiscation order, it would not affect the making of it. For circumstances in which a court may interfere with a settlement following bankruptcy, see *Avis v (1) Turner (2) Avis* [2007] EWCA Civ 748.

POCA and the insolvent defendant

Under s 418 of POCA if a person is adjudged bankrupt in England and Wales the powers **16.150** conferred on a court by ss 41 to 67 of POCA, and the powers of a receiver appointed under ss 48 or 50 (enforcement receivers), must not be exercised in relation to:

(a) property which is for the time being comprised in the bankrupt's estate for the purposes of Part 9 of the Insolvency Act 1986;

(b) property in respect of which his trustee in bankruptcy may (without leave of the court) serve a notice under section 307, 308 or 308A of the 1986 Act (after acquired property, tools, tenancies etc);

(c) property which is to be applied for the benefit of creditors of the bankrupt by virtue of the condition imposed under section 280(2)(c) of the Insolvency Act 1986;

(d) in a case where a confiscation order has been made under section 6 or 156 of [POCA], any sums remaining in the hands of the receiver appointed under section 50 or 198 of [POCA] after the amount required to be paid under the confiscation order has been fully paid;

(e) in a case where a confiscation order has been made under section 92 of [POCA], any sums remaining in the hands of an administrator appointed under section 128 of [POCA] after the amount required to be paid under the confiscation order has been fully paid.

(See s 418(2) and (3).)

The basic rule is that if at the time a person is adjudged bankrupt under the Insolvency Act **16.151** 1986, a restraint order has previously been made, or a receiver or administrator has previously been appointed in respect of any of his property, that property is excluded from his estate for the purpose of the bankruptcy. That property first goes to satisfy the confiscation order, rather than being dispersed to creditors. In so doing the legislation prevents defendants from attempting to use the insolvency legislation to defeat the purpose of the confiscation regime. Under Sch 11 of POCA, if a restraint or receivership action is underway when the bankruptcy order is made, any unconfiscated property can be given to the creditors at a later date (see para 16 of Sch 11).

Section 32(1) of the DTA and s 84(1) of the CJA 1988 previously dealt with circumstances **16.152** where a person holding realisable property was adjudged bankrupt.

E. Conclusion

Anecdotally, prosecuting authorities are very conscious of the difficulties that restraint **16.153** orders can cause to innocent third parties and, in so far as the legislation allows, endeavour to deal with them fairly and in a way which takes account of their property rights. In the first instance, third parties and their solicitors who have any doubts as to their position, or who wish to deal with a particular asset, would be well advised to contact the prosecuting authority which obtained the restraint order to see if a mutually acceptable agreement can be reached.

17

INVESTIGATIONS

A. Introduction

If investigations by law enforcement agencies to trace the proceeds of criminal conduct are **17.01** to be truly effective, it is essential that they should have powers to compel third parties such as financial institutions, solicitors, accountants, etc to disclose information and produce documentation that may be relevant to their enquiries. Indeed, following the trail of the money often leads investigators to evidence of substantive offences such as frauds, drug trafficking, and the like.

17.02   In this chapter, we examine the powers of the court under the Proceeds of Crime Act 2002 (POCA) to make production orders, account monitoring orders, customer information orders, and search and seizure warrants compelling third parties to hand over material they hold to law enforcement authorities to assist their investigations into criminal conduct. We also examine the powers given to the Crown Court and a magistrates' court under the Serious Organised Crime and Police Act 2005 (SOCPA) to make financial reporting orders against persons convicted of certain criminal offences.

B. A Short History of the Legislative Provisions

17.03   Section 27 of the Drug Trafficking Offences Act 1986 (DTOA) gave circuit judges power to make production orders requiring persons to make material available to a constable to take away, or required them to give the constable access to it, if it was likely to be of substantial value to an investigation into drug trafficking. Section 28 made similar provision for a search warrant to be made authorising a constable to enter and search premises for material likely to be of substantial value to such an investigation. Section 30 empowered the High Court, on an application by a prosecutor, to make an order for the production of material in the possession of a government department. These provisions were re-enacted in ss 55, 56, and 59 of the Drug Trafficking Act 1994 (DTA).

17.04   Parliament chose not to make similar provision in relation to investigations into criminal conduct other than drug trafficking when it enacted the Criminal Justice Act 1988 (CJA 1988). In consequence, law enforcement agencies wishing to obtain material relevant to investigations into such offences had to rely on the more general provisions contained in the Police and Criminal Evidence Act 1995 which inserted new ss 93H and J into the 1988 Act making identical provision in relation to investigations into non drug trafficking offences.

17.05   The relevant provisions are now to be found in Pt 8 of POCA which came into force on 24 February 2003: see the Proceeds of Crime Act 2002 (Commencement No 4 Transitional Provisions and Savings) Order 2003, SI 2003/120. In addition to giving the Crown Court power to make production orders, Pt 8 also adds a number of additional powers to the investigator's armoury, in particular the power to apply for account monitoring orders and customer information orders.

C. Defining Investigations

17.06   Part 8 prescribes three types of investigation in relation to which these orders may be obtained: a confiscation investigation; a money laundering investigation; and a civil recovery investigation. These are defined in s 341 in the following terms:

(1) For the purposes of this Part a confiscation investigation is an investigation into—
   (a) whether a person has benefited from his criminal conduct, or
   (b) the extent or whereabouts of his benefit from criminal conduct.
(2) For the purposes of this Part a civil recovery investigation is an investigation into—
   (a) whether property is recoverable property or associated property,
   (b) who holds the property, or
   (c) its extent or whereabouts.

(3) But an investigation is not a civil recovery investigation if—
    (a) proceedings for a recovery order have been started in respect of the property in question,
    (b) an interim receiving order applies to the property in question,
    (c) an interim administration order applies to the property in question, or
    (d) the property in question is detained under section 295.
(4) For the purposes of this Part a money laundering investigation is an investigation into whether a person has committed a money laundering offence.

It would seem that the definition of 'confiscation investigation' in s 341(1) precludes **17.07** law enforcement agencies from seeking production orders to obtain information for the purpose of identifying legitimately acquired assets so as to make them available to satisfy a confiscation order. The information sought would neither relate to whether a person has benefited from criminal conduct nor the extent or whereabouts of his benefit from such conduct. In these circumstances, the appropriate remedy would be for the prosecutor to apply for a disclosure order in support of a restraint order under s 41(7) of POCA or, in a case to which the DTA or CJA 1988 applies, relying on the High Court's inherent jurisdiction. Disclosure orders are considered in more detail in Chapter 3. Further, a management or enforcement receiver can compel a defendant or third party to cooperate in the identification of realisable property. After conviction, an application for a financial reporting order can also be considered: see para 17.68 below.

D. Courts and Judges having Jurisdiction to Make Orders

Judges

In relation to a confiscation or money laundering investigation in England and Wales, **17.08** a judge entitled to exercise the jurisdiction of the Crown Court is empowered to make orders under Pt 8: see s 343(2)(a) of POCA.

In relation to a civil recovery investigation, only a judge of the High Court has jurisdiction **17.09** to make orders under Pt 8: see s 343(3) of POCA.

Courts

Similarly, s 343 of POCA provides that the court having jurisdiction in relation to confisca- **17.10** tion and money laundering investigations is the Crown Court and, in relation to civil recovery investigations, the High Court.

E. Production Orders

Jurisdiction to make the order

Section 345(1) of POCA gives a judge power to make a production order if he is satisfied **17.11** that all the requirements for making an order have been fulfilled. By s 345(2) applications for production orders must state that:

(a) a person specified in the application is subject to a confiscation investigation or a money laundering investigation, or
(b) property specified in the application is subject to a civil recovery investigation.

17.12 In accordance with s 345(3) the application must also state that:

   (a) the material is sought for the purpose of the investigation;

   (b) the order is sought in relation to material, or material of a description, specified in the application;

   (c) a person specified in the application appears to be in possession or control of the material.

Requirements for making the order

17.13 These are set out in s 346 of POCA which provides as follows:

   (1) These are the requirements for the making of a production order.

   (2) There must be reasonable grounds for suspecting that—

      (a) in the case of a confiscation investigation, the person the application for the order specifies as being subject to the investigation has benefited from his criminal conduct;

      (b) in the case of a civil recovery investigation, the property the application of the order specifies as being subject to the investigation is recoverable property or associated property;

      (c) in the case of a money laundering investigation, the person the application of the order specifies as being subject to the investigation has committed a money laundering offence.

   (3) There must be reasonable grounds for believing that the person the application specifies as appearing to be in possession or control of the material so specified is in possession or control of it.

   (4) There must be reasonable grounds for believing that the material is likely to be of substantial value (whether or not by itself) to the investigation for the purposes of which the order is sought.

   (5) There must be reasonable grounds for believing that it is in the public interest for the material to be produced or for access to it to be given having regard to—

      (a) the benefit likely to accrue to the investigation if the material is obtained;

      (b) the circumstances under which the person the application specifies as appearing to be in possession or control of the material holds it.

17.14 Most of these requirements are similar to those for obtaining production orders under the old legislation. In particular, there is no requirement that a person has been charged with a criminal offence—it is sufficient that there is a confiscation, money laundering, or civil recovery investigation taking place.

17.15 By s 345(4) the production order, once made, is an order either:

   (a) requiring the person the application for the order specifies as appearing to be in possession or control of material to produce it to an appropriate office for him to take away, or

   (b) requiring that person to give an appropriate officer access to the material,

within the period stated in the order.

17.16 The period specified for compliance is seven days unless the judges considers, on the facts of a particular case, that a longer or shorter period would be appropriate: see s 345(5). Section 349 requires information held on a computer to be produced in a visible and legible form.

17.17 Section 347 empowers the judge to make an order to grant entry to allow an appropriate officer to enter premises to obtain the material required to be produced under the order. By s 348(5) the appropriate officer may take copies of any material produced, or to which access is given, in compliance with a production order. Section 348(6) provides that material produced in compliance with a production order can be retained for as long as necessary in connection with the investigation for the purposes of which the order was made. If the appropriate officer has reasonable grounds for believing that the material may be required for the purpose of any legal proceedings and it might otherwise be unavailable for those purposes, he may retain it until the proceedings are concluded.

Legal professional privilege

Section 348(1) provides that a production order does not require a person to produce or give access to privileged material. By s 348(2) 'privileged material is defined as: **17.18**

any material which the person would be entitled to refuse to produce on grounds of legal professional privilege in proceedings in the High Court.

The mere fact that a lawyer is holding material on behalf of a client does not automatically mean that it is subject to legal professional privilege. In *R v Central Criminal Court ex p Francis and Francis* [1988] 3 All ER 775 the House of Lords held that documents were not subject to legal professional privilege if they were held with the intention of furthering a criminal purpose. This applies regardless of whether the intention was that of the person holding the documents or of any other person. Thus, a solicitor's file in relation to a conveyancing transaction on a property would not be subject to legal privilege in circumstances where the property was being purchased for a criminal purpose, for example, to launder the proceeds of drug trafficking. **17.19**

In *R (on the application of Miller Gardner Solicitors) v Minshull Street Crown Court* [2002] EWHC Admin 3077 the Divisional Court held that personal details held by a firm of solicitors, such as a client's name and address, telephone number, and date of birth, were not subject to legal professional privilege. **17.20**

Excluded material

Section 348(2) of POCA provides that a production order does not require a person to produce or give access to excluded material within the meaning of PACE. **17.21**

Government departments

A production order may be made in relation to material held by a government department as defined in the Crown Proceedings Act 1947 (see s 350(1) of POCA). The order may require any officer of the department (whether named in the order or not) who may for the time being be in possession or control of the material to which it relates to comply with it (see s 350(2)). **17.22**

Who may apply for a production order?

An application for a production order must be made by 'an appropriate officer'. This phrase is defined in s 378 of POCA (as amended by para 116 of Pt IV of Sch 8 to the Serious Crime Act 2007) and varies in accordance with the nature of the investigation in relation to which the application is made. By s 378(2), as so amended, in relation to confiscation investigations, the following are appropriate officers: **17.23**

(a) a member of SOCA's staff;
(b) an accredited financial investigator;
(c) a constable; and
(d) an officer of Revenue and Customs.

In relation to money laundering investigations, s 378(4) provides that accredited financial investigators, constables, and officers of Revenue and Customs are appropriate officers. As to civil recovery investigations, members of SOCA's staff along with the relevant directors are appropriate officers (see s 378(3) as so amended). The expression 'relevant director' **17.24** means the Director of Public Prosecutions, the Director of Revenue and Customs Prosecutions, and the Director of the Serious Fraud Office (see s 352(5A).

Procedure on applications: Crown Court

17.25 Applications for production orders may be made *ex parte* to a judge in chambers (see s 351(1)). Although there is no formal requirement either in the Act or in rules of court, a practice developed whereby applications to the Crown Court are made in the form of a written information prepared by the officer which is substantiated on oath by him in the presence of the judge. This procedure appears to have been given judicial approval in *R v Middlesex Guildhall Crown Court ex p Salinger* The Independent, 26 March 1992, a case involving similarly worded provisions in terrorism legislation. The Court gave the following guidelines:

(a) The application should be accompanied by a written statement upon which the office wishes to rely to persuade the judge that the statutory conditions have been fulfilled. The statement need not disclose the nature or source of sensitive information. The officer should appear before the judge and be prepared to supplement the statement by oral evidence. The judge should not normally enquire into the nature and identity of the source of information, but it may be necessary for the officer to amplify the nature of the information itself, particularly if it has not been fully disclosed in the written statement.

(b) If the judge decides to make the order, he should give directions as to what, if any information should be served with the order. This should normally be in writing and take the form of the written statement from the officer in support of the application. The information the judge requires the officer to give should be as full as possible without compromising security.

(c) If the judge decides it is inappropriate for any such information to accompany the order, he should consider whether it ought to be made available in the event of an application being made to vary or discharge the order.

The Court emphasised in its concluding words that the aim should be to provide as much information as possible, provided this is consistent with the security of the operation.

17.26 Any person affected by a production order may apply to have it varied or set aside under s 351(3). By r 56.4(2) of the Criminal Procedure Rules 2005 a person who proposes to apply for the variation or discharge of a production order must give a copy of the application, not later than 48 hours before making the application, to a constable at the police station specified in the order or, where the application was not made by a constable, to the office of the appropriate officer who made the application. Rule 56.4(3) provides that the judge may direct that these requirements need not be complied with if he is satisfied that the person making the application has good reason to seek a discharge or variation of the order as soon as possible and it is not practicable to comply with them.

17.27 In *R v Middlesex Guildhall Crown Court ex p Salinger* The Independent, 26 March 1992, the Divisional Court ruled that applications to vary or set aside production orders should, if possible, be made before the same judge who made the *ex parte* order, and it was desirable that the same officer that gave evidence at the *ex parte* hearing should attend. The court said that questions as to the nature or identity of the source of information should not be permitted and, if the nature of the information is sensitive in the sense that it may compromise the security of the investigation, the judge should not allow the questions. He should tell the respondent in such circumstances that he had been given information which satisfies him that the conditions are met, but that such information cannot be disclosed.

Procedure on applications: High Court

Applications for production orders or search warrants in support of civil recovery proceed- **17.28** ings are made to the High Court and are governed by the Civil Recovery Proceedings Practice Direction accompanying the Civil Procedure Rules.

The application must be made to a High Court judge by filing an application notice: see **17.29** para 8.1. By para 8.2, the application may be made without notice to the respondent. Paragraph 10 requires that the application must be supported with written evidence which must be filed with the application notice. Paragraph 10.2 provides that the evidence must set out all the matters on which the applicant relies in support of the application including the matters required to be stated in the Act and all material facts of which the court should be aware. By para 10.3 the applicant must also file with the application notice a draft of the order sought. If possible, this should be supplied to the court on disk in a form compatible with any word processing software used by the court.

The application will be heard and determined in private unless the judge directs otherwise **17.30** (see para 11.1).

An application for the variation or discharge of a production order or search warrant **17.31** made pursuant to a civil recovery investigation may be made by any person affected by it (see para 12.1). Any person making such an application must first notify the applicant under para 12.3. Paragraph 12.4 provides that any application for the variation of a production order or search warrant should be made to the judge who made the order or, if he is unavailable, to another High Court judge.

Complying with the order

One the order has been sealed by the court, the officer should serve it promptly on **17.32** the person or company to whom it is addressed. The recipient will normally have seven days in which to comply with the order unless the judge has exercised his discretion under s 345(5) to order a longer or shorter period. On no account should a person served with a production order divulge to a third party, particularly a client in relation to whom he is required to produce information, the fact that the order has been made. Any such disclosure could constitute an offence of prejudicing an investigation contrary to s 342.

It sometimes happens that information required to be disclosed under a production order **17.33** is held on a computer. This is dealt with in s 349 of POCA which provides:

(1) This section applies if any of the material specified in an application for a production order consists of information contained in a computer.
(2) If the order is an order requiring a person to produce the material to an appropriate officer for him to take away, it has effect as an order to produce the material in a form in which it can be taken away by him and in which it is visible and legible.
(3) If the order is an order requiring a person to give an appropriate officer access to the material, it has effect as an order to give him access to the material in a form in which it is visible and legible.

A person served with a production order may therefore have to print out the information covered by the order which he holds on computer or transfer it onto a disk or memory stick to allow the officer to take it away with him or have access to it.

17.34 In contrast to the position with restraint orders, there is no requirement for the prosecutor to give an undertaking to pay the costs of innocent third parties, such as financial institutions or professional advisers, incurred in complying with a production order. Any such costs will therefore have to be borne by those named in the order and may not be reclaimed from the applicant.

17.35 Once the appropriate officer has obtained material pursuant to a production order, it may be retained by him for so long as it is necessary to retain it (as opposed to copies of it) in connection with the investigation for the purposes of which the order was made (see s 348(6). However, by s 347(7):

(7) But if an appropriate officer has reasonable grounds for believing that—
    (a) the material may need to be produced for the purposes of any legal proceedings, and;
    (b) it might otherwise be unavailable for those purposes,
it may be retained until the proceedings are concluded.

Failure to comply with production orders

17.36 By s 351(7) of POCA:

Production orders and orders to grant entry have effect as if they were orders of the court.

The effect of this provision is that any breach of a production order may be dealt with by the Crown Court as a contempt of court and may lead to imprisonment, the imposition of a fine, or the sequestration of assets. The jurisdiction of the Crown Court to deal with breaches of its order as a contempt of court is considered in Chapter 6 above.

17.37 Where the production order is made by the High Court pursuant to a civil recovery investigation, any failure to comply with the order will, of course, fall to be dealt with by the High Court rather than the Crown Court.

F. Search and Seizure Warrants

17.38 Section 352 gives the court power to issue search and seizure warrants empowering appropriate officers to enter premises and seize material likely to be of substantial value to the investigation for the purpose of which the order is made. The requirements that must be fulfilled before a warrant may be issued are that a production order has already been made and has not been complied with and there are reasonable grounds for believing that the required material is on the premises, or that the requirements of s 353 have been met (see s 352(6)). Section 353 allows the court to issue search and seizure warrants in circumstances where it is not possible to make a production order. These instances include cases in which it is not practicable to communicate with a person in relation to whom a production order could be made, where consent would not be given without a warrant, or where the investigation might be seriously prejudiced if immediate entry to the premises could not be effected.

17.39 Appropriate officers should take great care to satisfy themselves that the statutory requirements have been satisfied before applying for a search warrant and give full and frank disclosure in the written statement in support. In *Power-Hynes v Norwich Magistrates Court* [2009] EWHC 1512 (Admin), a case concerning search warrants under PACE, Stanley Burnton LJ said:

> . . . They must make full and frank disclosure to the justice of the peace, or district or circuit judge of the facts justifying the application, which will include the justification for applying for a search warrant rather than another remedy, in the present case a production order under section 9 and Schedule 1 to PACE.

For additional requirements in relation to search warrants in support of civil recovery **17.40** investigations, see s 356 of POCA and Practice Direction: Civil Recovery (Proceeds of Crime Act 2002) Pts 5 and 8, s IV, reproduced at Appendix 14.

Further, appropriate officers should take great care to ensure that the written statement and **17.41** warrant set out clearly which conditions in ss 352 and 353 were relied on in obtaining the warrant and that it properly identifies the properties to be searched and the nature of the material for which the officer is entitled to search. If proforma statements and warrants are used, care should be taken both by the applicant and court officials to ensure that any provisions that are inapplicable are properly crossed out. In *Redknapp v Commissioner of City of London Police* [2008] EWHC 1177 (Admin) where the Divisional Court quashed a search warrant made under s 9 of PACE, Latham LJ said:

> . . . the first thing that has to be said is that the failures that I have already referred to are wholly unacceptable. This court has complained in the past about slipshod completion of application forms such as this, the last occasion being the judgment of Underhill J in *R (on the application of 'C') v The Chief Constable of 'A' Police and another* [2006] EWHC 2352 (Admin). The obtaining of a search warrant is never to be treated as a formality. It authorises the invasion of a person's home. All the material necessary to justify the grant of a warrant should be contained in the information provided on the form. If the magistrate or judge in the case of an application under section 9, does require any further information in order to satisfy himself that the warrant is justified, a note should be made of the additional information so that there is a proper record of the full basis upon which the warrant has been granted.

It is submitted that the same principles should apply to search warrants made under POCA **17.42** which can be equally intrusive.

G. Judicial Discretion

Even where the conditions set out in ss 345 or 352 have been met, the court retains a discre- **17.43** tion as to whether or not a production order or search warrant should be granted: note the use of the phrase 'a judge may' in ss 345(1) and 352(1). This was confirmed by the Divisional Court in *R v Crown Court at Southwark ex p Customs and Excise Commissioners* [1989] 3 All ER 673, where similar provisions in s 27 of the DTOA were considered. Watkins LJ said:

> . . . We see nothing in the words of section 27(2) of the 1986 Act to suggest that Parliament did not intend the circuit judge to have a discretion either to grant or to refuse an order although he be persuaded that the conditions contained in subsection (4) are satisfied. While we acknowledge that it is not easy to identify circumstances in which a judge might properly refuse to make an order when those conditions have been satisfied, we are not persuaded that this is a subsection in which 'may' can be construed as meaning 'must' or 'shall'.'

17.44   The judge had imposed a condition that the material obtained under the production order should not be removed from the jurisdiction without the leave of the court. The judge imposed the condition on the basis of evidence from an official of a bank affected by the order to the effect that there was a risk of reprisals against members of the bank's staff in Panama, their families, and properties. The court indicated that this evidence was 'unimpressive' and should not influence the court to exercise its discretion in favour of those who would use it to avoid compliance with an embarrassing order. Watkins LJ said:

> The courts of this country are not to be deflected from making orders in aid of the international battle against drug trafficking for fear of reprisals no matter from where the threat of them emanates.

17.45   In *R v Southwark Crown Court ex p Bowles* [1998] AC 641 the House of Lords in considering the powers under s 93H of the CJA 1988 to make production orders, emphasises the intrusive nature of such orders and the need for judges to scrutinise applications carefully before exercising the discretion to make an order. Lord Hutton cited the judgment of Bingham LJ (as he then was) in *R v Crown Court at Lewes ex p Hill* (1991) 93 Cr App R 60 where, in relation to similar powers under PACE, the court referred to the importance of achieving a balance between competing public interests. Bingham LJ said:

> The Police and Criminal Evidence Act governs a field in which there are two very obvious public interests. There is, first of all, a public interest in the effective investigation and prosecution of crime. Secondly, there is a public interest in protecting the personal and property rights of citizens against infringement and invasion. There is an obvious tension between these two public interests because crime could be most effectively investigated and prosecuted if the personal and property rights could be freely overridden and total protection of the personal and property rights of citizens would make investigation and prosecution of many crimes impossible or virtually so.

17.46   As Lord Hutton pointed out, Bingham LJ emphasised that circuit judges must exercise their powers with great care and caution to ensure the proper balance between these two competing public interests is maintained. The Divisional Court again referred to this balance in *Power-Hynes v Chief Constable of Norfolk* [2009] EWHC 1512 (Admin). Stanley Burnton LJ said:

> In a case such as the present, the Court is faced with two competing interests. The first is the public interest in prosecuting and preventing crime. That interest requires the Court to be sympathetic to the position of police officers applying for a search warrant, particularly in a case involving financial fraud, and to be realistic in its assessment of the compliance of the police with the obligations imposed by Parliament and set out in the provisions of PACE to which I have referred. The Court should not impose unrealistic or impracticable obligations on police officers seeking a search warrant or on the justice of the peace or district or circuit judge to whom application is made for the warrant.
>
> The second interest is that of the person or persons whose home or office or other business premises may be the subject of a search. A police search for materials is a very real and serious intrusion into the private life of those whose premises are searched and may be very distressing for them, and if it is to be justified the officers seeking the warrant must take diligent steps to ensure that the statutory requirements are satisfied.

17.47   The court must also take great care to ensure that the production order is not abused by its use in cases where an application under s 9 of PACE is more appropriate. The statutory requirements for obtaining a production order are less stringent than those for an order under PACE and there may be a temptation on the part of some investigators to rely on the POCA production order wherever possible. In particular:

(a) applications for production orders can be made without notice, whereas Sch 1 para 7 to PACE requires that applications under s 9 must be made on notice;

(b) section 9 applications must relate to a 'serious arrestable offence', whereas there is no such requirement in relation to applications for production orders;

(c) a s 9 order can only be made where there are reasonable grounds for believing that an offence has been committed; whereas a production order involves a lower threshold test, namely that there are reasonable grounds to suspect that a person has benefited from criminal conduct;

(d) applications under s 9 are further limited by a requirement that other methods of obtaining the material have failed or have not been tried because they were bound to fail; there is no similar requirement in relation to an application for a production order.

The House of Lords held in *R v Southwark Crown Court ex p Bowles* [1998] AC 641 that a **17.48** 'dominant purpose' test should be applied in determining whether a production order application or an application under s 9 is the most appropriate means of obtaining the required material. If the dominant purpose of the application is to obtain information in furtherance of a criminal investigation, s 9 should be used. If, however, the dominant purpose of the application is to obtain evidence in relation to an investigation into the proceeds of criminal conduct, a production order application may properly be made. Further, the House of Lords ruled that provided a production order had been obtained because the dominant purpose of the application was to progress an investigation into the proceeds of criminal conduct, it mattered not that evidence was found that assisted the criminal investigation: this could still be relied upon in a criminal trial. Lord Hutton said:

> I consider that if the true and dominant purpose of an application under section 93H is to enable an investigation to be made into the proceeds of criminal conduct, the application should be granted even if an incidental consequence may be that the police will obtain evidence relating to the commission of an offence. But if the true and dominant purpose of the application is to carry out an investigation whether a criminal offence has been committed and to obtain evidence to bring a prosecution, the application should be refused.

> I further consider that if the police discover evidence of the commission of an offence in the course of an investigation consequent upon an order properly made under section 93H, the fact that the evidence was discovered in this way would not be a reasons for the exclusion of the evidence under section 78 of PACE on the ground of unfairness at a trial where the prosecution sought to adduce such evidence.

H. Overseas Investigations

The Divisional Court held in *R v Crown Court at Southwark ex p Customs and Excise* **17.49** *Commissioners* [1998] 3 All ER 673 that a production order may be made for the purpose of obtaining material for use in an investigation into drug trafficking being undertaken overseas. On the application of a customs officer, production orders were made requiring the Bank of Credit and Commerce International to produce documents held by them in relation to General Manuel Noriega of Panama for use in proceedings in the USA. Although the judge made the orders, she imposed a condition requiring the Commissioners of Customs and Excise to undertake not to remove from the jurisdiction any documents obtained under the orders or to show or read them to a representative of any overseas law enforcement agency without the leave of the court. On an application for judicial review by the Commissioners, the Divisional Court ruled that the judge had no power to attach this condition to the order. Watkins LJ said:

> In our judgment there is nothing in section 27(1) of the 1986 Act which requires that the relevant investigation should necessarily be one being conducted by our customs officers. Suppose an investigation into drug trafficking be entirely into breaches of corresponding drug trafficking laws of other convention countries. In that situation it is surely not surprising that Parliament, in this day and age, should have legislated to permit a customs officer here to apply to a circuit judge for a production order in respect of the suspect passage of money laundered from drug trafficking abroad into a London bank account, no matter that such conduct only forms a comparatively small part of the trafficking being enquired into by a foreign law enforcement agency. It would, we think, be contrary to one of the purposes for which the 1986 Act was made which are, we believe, to advance the international cooperation to which this country is bound by the 1961 [Vienna Convention on Diplomatic Relations] to restrict the effect of section 27(1) in the manner for which the bank contended. There are no words either in section 27(1) or section 38(1) which suggest that the effect of section 27(1) should be so limited.

17.50 The Court emphasised that where the application is made solely or partly to assist an overseas investigation, this must be made clear in the information laid by the applicant in support of his application. Further, the court ruled that the applicant may not send any original documents taken up pursuant to the order to an overseas law enforcement agency without the leave of the court. Copies may, however, be provided.

I. Customer Information Orders

17.51 Customer information orders are a relatively new concept introduced by POCA and which put further powers at the disposal of investigators. Production orders on bank accounts can only be effective if the investigator has at least some information as to the identity of the account and the financial institution at which it is maintained. A customer information order requires a financial institution covered by the order to provide to an appropriate officer any customer information it has in relation to the person specified in the order (see s 363(5)). In relation to an individual, s 364(2) defines 'customer information' as information as to whether the person holds or has held an account with the institution named in the order and, if so, information as to:

(a) the account or account numbers;
(b) the person's full name;
(c) his date of birth;
(d) his most recent address and any previous addresses;
(e) the date or dates on which he began to hold the account or accounts and, if he has ceased to hold the account or any of the accounts, the date or dates on which he did so;

(f) such evidence of his identity as was obtained by the financial institution under or for the purposes of any legislation relating to money laundering;

(g) the full name, date of birth, and the most recent address and any previous addresses of any person who holds or has held an account at the financial institution jointly with him;

(h) the account number or numbers of any other account or accounts held at the financial institution to which he is a signatory and details of the person holding the other account or accounts.

Section 364(4) defines customer information in similar terms in relation to companies **17.52** or limited liability partnerships or similar bodies incorporated or otherwise established outside the UK.

Requirements for making orders

The requirements are set out in s 365. In all cases there must be reasonable grounds for **17.53** believing that the information will be of substantial value to the investigation (s 365(5) and that it is in the public interest for the information to be provided having regard to the benefit likely to accrue to the investigation if the information is obtained (s 365(6)). The other requirements vary according to the nature of the investigation in relation to which the information is being required:

(a) in a confiscation investigation, there must be reasonable grounds for suspecting that the person named in the application has benefited from criminal conduct (s 365(2));

(b) in a civil recovery investigation, there must be reasonable grounds for suspecting that the property specified in the application is recoverable or associated property and that the person holds some or all of the property (s 365(3));

(c) in a money laundering investigation, there must be reasonable grounds for suspecting that the person specified in the application has committed a money laundering offence.

Applications for customer information orders may be made *ex parte* to a Crown Court **17.54** judge and any person affected by an order once it is made may apply for it to be varied or set aside (see s 369(1) and (3) respectively). Section 369(7) (as amended by para 111 of Pt 4 of Sch 8 to the Serious Crime Act 2007) provides that an accredited financial investigator, member of SOCA's staff, a constable or Officer of Revenue and Customs may apply for a customer information order but only if he is a 'senior appropriate officer' or has been authorised to make the application by such an officer. Section 378(2) (as amended by para 116 of Pt 4 of Sch 8 to the Serious Crime Act 2007) defines a 'senior appropriate officer' as being a senior member of SOCA's staff, a police officer not below the rank of superintendent, an officer of Revenue and Customs designated by the Commissioners of Revenue and Customs as being of equivalent rank to superintendent, and an accredited financial investigator designated in an order made by the Secretary of State under s 453. Section 378(8) (as added by para 116 of Pt 4 of Sch 8 to the Serious Crime Act 2007) provides that a senior member of SOCA's staff is the Director General of SOCA or any member of SOCA's staff designated by the Director (whether generally or specifically) for this purpose.

Discharge and variation

17.55 By s 369(3) of POCA an application to vary or discharge a customer information order may be made by the person who applied for the order or by any person affected by it. The procedures to be followed on such applications are set out in r 62.2 of the Criminal Procedure Rules 2005. By r 62.2(1), where the application is made by a person other than the person who applied for the order he must, not later than 48 hours before the application is to be made, give a copy of the application to a police officer at the police station specified in the order or, where the application for the order was not made by a police officer, to the office of the appropriate officer who made the application. The notice must indicate the time and place at which the application is to be made.

Offences

17.56 It is an offence under s 366 for a financial institution to fail to comply with a customer information order without reasonable excuse (s 366(1)) or to knowingly or recklessly make a false statement when complying with such an order (s 366(3)). An offence contrary to s 366 is punishable by a fine not exceeding level 5 on the standard scale (see s 366(2)), and an offence contrary to s 366(3) is punishable on indictment with an unlimited fine (see s 366(4)).

J. Account Monitoring Orders

17.57 The court is empowered under ss 370 to 375 of POCA to make account monitoring orders on the application of an appropriate person. The particular value of these orders to investigators is that they impose an ongoing duty on the financial institution named in the order to provide information for a period of up to 90 days from the date on which the order is made. In contrast, production orders merely require the disclosure of information in the possession of the financial investigator when the order is served. If the officer requires further information after a production order has been complied with, he will have to apply to the court for another order.

17.58 An account monitoring order is defined in s 370(6) as:

> an order that the financial institution specified in the application for the order must, for the period stated in the order, provide account information of the description specified in the order to an appropriate officer in the manner, and at or by the time or times stated in the order.

The period stated in the order must not exceed 90 days (see s 370(7)).

17.59 The requirements that must be fulfilled before an account monitoring order can be made are set out in s 371 and are identical to those for making customer information orders. Again the application may be made *ex parte* to a judge in chambers, and affected parties have the right to apply to set aside or vary the order (see ss 373 and 375(2) respectively). Rule 62.1 of the Criminal Procedure Rules sets out the procedures that must be followed by affected parties who intend to apply for the order to be varied or discharged. As with customer information orders, the applicant must give at least 48 hours notice to the person who applied for the order (see r 62.1(2)).

K. Disclosure

By s 357(1) of POCA (as amended by para 108 of Sch 8 to the Serious Crime Act 2007) a judge may, on an application by a relevant authority make a disclosure order which is defined in s 357(4) as: **17.60**

> an order authorising the relevant authority to give any person the relevant authority considers has relevant information notice in writing requiring him to do, with respect to any matter relevant to the investigation for the purposes of which the order is sought, any or all of the following—
> (a) answer questions, either at a time specified in the notice or at once, at a place so specified;
> (b) provide information specified in the notice, by a time and in a manner so specified;
> (c) produce documents, or documents of a description specified in the notice, either at or by a time so specified or at once, and in a manner so specified.

A 'relevant authority' is defined in s 357(7) (as inserted by para 108 of Sch 8 to the Serious Crime Act 2007) as being, in relation to a confiscation investigation, a prosecutor and, in relation to a civil recovery investigation, a member of SOCA's staff or the relevant director. The term prosecutor includes the Director of Public Prosecutions, the Director of Revenue and Customs Prosecutions, and the Director of the Serious Fraud Office: see s 357(8).   **17.61**

Applications for disclosure orders may not be made in relation to money laundering investigations (see s 357(2)).   **17.62**

The requirements that must be fulfilled before an order can be made are set out in s 358 and are identical to those in relation to customer information orders and account monitoring orders, save that, as indicated above, they may not be made in relation to money laundering investigations. A person commits an offence under s 359 if he fails to comply with a disclosure order or knowingly or recklessly makes a false or misleading statement in response to such an order.   **17.63**

In *Serious Organised Crime Agency v Perry* [2009] EWHC 1960 (Admin) it was held that disclosure orders could be made where unlawful conduct was committed abroad provided the applicant for the order has reasonable grounds to believe that property obtained as a result of that unlawful conduct has been brought into the jurisdiction. In that case, the respondent had been convicted of offences of dishonesty in Israel and it was alleged that the proceeds of his unlawful conduct had been paid into bank accounts in England and Wales. Foskett J held that this was a sufficient basis for making an order under s 357. He said: **17.64**

> The case involves unlawful conduct committed abroad by someone who SOCA has reasonable grounds for believing has brought into the jurisdiction property obtained as the result of that unlawful conduct. In my judgment, that is sufficient to afford grounds for seeking and obtaining a disclosure order and the issue of 'information notices' pursuant to such an order. That conclusion would mean that the person in whose name the money or property in this jurisdiction is lodged may be open to a 'civil recovery investigation' even if he or she has no other connection with the jurisdiction. This seems to me to be the legislative purpose of the Act. If, contrary to that view, there needs to be some closer connection between the person in respect of whom the disclosure order is sought and the jurisdiction, it is in this case afforded by (a) the accounts in Mr Perry's name and those of his family members, (b) the past and present business interests here, (c) his postal address and (d) his past residence (together with that of his wife) in the jurisdiction and his liability, at least for a period, to UK tax.

It follows, therefore, that Mr. Perry and his family were, in my view, legitimate targets for a 'disclosure order' and, in consequence, for 'information notices'. Merely because they were (or may have been) outside England and Wales at the time the order was made (and not otherwise domiciled here) does not mean that an order could not be made. In other words, there was jurisdiction to make the order.

17.65 The judge expressed some concern about the practice of applications under s 357 being determined on the papers and, given the intrusive nature of disclosure orders, suggested that where complex points of law arise, the applicant should consider asking for an oral hearing (even on an *ex parte* basis).

L. Statements Made in Response to Orders

17.66 POCA restricts the use to which, pursuant to disclosure orders, customer information and orders and account monitoring orders may be put. By s 360, a statement made by a person in response to a requirement imposed on him under a disclosure order may not be used against him in criminal proceedings. Similar protection is afforded to financial institutions to comply with customer information orders (s 367) and account monitoring orders (s 372). These immunities do not, however, extend to confiscation proceedings, proceedings for contempt of court or perjury, or for an offence where, in giving evidence, a person makes a statement which is inconsistent with a statement made in complying with the order.

M. Code of Practice

17.67 Section 377 of POCA (as amended by para 114 of Sch 8 to the Serious Crime Act 2007) imposes an obligation on the Secretary of State to prepare a code of practice as to the use of the powers referred to in this chapter by the Director General of SOCA and his staff, accredited financial investigators, police officers, and officers of Revenue and Customs. This code was brought into force by virtue of SI 2003/334 on 24 March 2003. By s 377(6) a failure to comply with the Code does not of itself constitute a criminal offence, but by s 377(7) the code will be admissible in evidence and the court is entitled to take into account any failure to comply with its provisions in determining any question in the proceedings. Section 377A (as inserted by para 115 of Sch 8 to the Serious Crime Act 2007) imposes a similar obligation on the Attorney General to prepare a code of practice as to the exercise of these powers by the Director of Public Prosecutions, the Director of Revenue and Customs Prosecutions, and the Director of the Serious Fraud Office.

N. Financial Reporting Orders under the Serious Organised Crime and Police Act 2005

17.68 Section 76 of SOCPA gives the Crown Court and a magistrates' court jurisdiction to make a financial reporting order. Unlike production orders, account monitoring orders, and customer information orders, a financial reporting order may only be made after a defendant has been convicted of certain specified criminal offences. The explanatory note accompanying the Act describes the purpose of financial reporting orders in these terms:

Such orders may be imposed as ancillary orders for certain trigger offences and would enable the financial affairs of serious acquisitive criminals to be monitored from the point of sentence.

Jurisdiction to make the order

By s 76(1) a court sentencing or otherwise dealing with a person convicted of an offence **17.69** specified in s 76(3), may also make a financial reporting order. Section 76(2) restricts the court's jurisdiction to make the order to cases where it is:

satisfied that the risk of the person's committing another offence mentioned in subsection (3) is sufficiently high to justify the making of a financial reporting order.

In order to assess the risk of re-offending, it is submitted that the proper course is for the **17.70** court to look at the circumstances of the offence of which the defendant has been convicted, his role in its commission, and the nature of any previous convictions he may have.

Offences to which section 76 applies

By s 76(3) the offences are: **17.71**

(a) an offence under any of the following provisions of the Theft Act 1968—
    Section 15 (obtaining property by deception),
    Section 15A (obtaining a money transfer by deception),
    Section 16 (obtaining a pecuniary advantage by deception),
    Section 20 (2) (procuring execution of a valuable security, etc.),
(b) an offence under either of the following provisions of the Theft Act 1978—
    Section 1 (obtaining services by deception),
    Section 2 (evasion of liability by deception),
(c) any offence specified in Schedule 2 to the Proceeds of Crime Act 2002 ('lifestyle offences').

The 'lifestyle offences' referred to in s 76(3)(c) are set out in detail in para 8.55 above and **17.72** include most drug trafficking and money laundering offences. The Secretary of State may by order add to or delete offences from this list (see s 76(4).

A financial reporting order is not a penalty but a preventative measure intended to enable **17.73** the court to keep control over offenders who are likely to indulge in further criminal activity. It follows from this that Art 7 of the European Convention on Human Rights (ECHR) is not engaged and financial reporting orders can be made notwithstanding the fact that s 76 was not in force at the time of the commission of the relevant offences by the defendant: see *R v Adams* [2008] EWCA Crim 914 and *R v Wright* [2008] EWCA Crim 3207.

In the case of *Wright*, the appellant also contended that the judge adopted the wrong **17.74** approach in treating the order as an aid to enforcement of the confiscation order, that he was plainly wrong to conclude that there was a high risk of the defendant committing another specified offence, and that in reality such an order would have no utility. Before considering each of these points individually, the court noted the extent of the appellant's involvement in serious organised crime. Thomas LJ said:

This appellant is a career criminal on an enormous scale. He was convicted of offences of importing and supplying cocaine over a period of three years or thereabouts in the late 1990s.

The judge who made this order had presided over a trial which took something like three months and of which the appellant's evidence was a significant feature. He had heard the appellant give evidence that he had lived in effect throughout his adult life 'outside the system'—that is to say in such manner that there was no or virtually no recorded trace of his existence. He owned no property, he paid no tax, he had no social security or National Insurance or even perhaps national health identity, his passport was an Irish passport, he had no bank accounts, no car was registered in his name and so on. The judge also heard the appellant give evidence that whilst it was accepted he was a gambler on an enormous scale, he had lived almost entirely by cash and he was able, on the evidence, to put his hands on six figure sums of cash with the assistance of custodians, friends or associates, as and when he needed to.

The judge summed up the man he was dealing with in this way:

You lived anonymously, you were a master criminal, manipulative, influential and powerful.

And he added:

At various times you were the controlling mind and financial backbone behind an international drug smuggling ring which extended from South America in particular Colombia through the Caribbean and to these shores.

It was apparent that the appellant had lived for many years a lavish lifestyle in the United Kingdom and Spain and elsewhere, surrounded by a clique of loyal acolytes. In due course his benefit from drug trafficking was assessed in the confiscation proceedings at no less than £45 million. He was, in other words, one of the relatively rare major and criminal entrepreneurs to be caught and convicted. Catching him had not been straightforward. The investigation had been long and painstaking. When it got near to his associates this appellant decamped by private jet to North Cyprus where there is of course no extradition regime. He remained there for some years and it was only when he made the error (from his point of view) of returning not to this country but to Spain that he was traced and apprehended.

17.75 The Court also noted that at the confiscation hearing, the defendant adopted a policy of 'blanket non compliance'. He did not file a response to the prosecutor's statement and refused to give evidence.

17.76 Against this background, it is perhaps not surprising that the Court of Appeal dismissed the appeal against the financial reporting order. As to the first point taken by the appellant, the Court agreed that a financial reporting order should not be seen as ancillary to the enforcement of a confiscation order, although it noted that:

... an indirect effect of information given under the financial reporting order might turn out to be of some assistance to those who are seeking to enforce a confiscation order. The obvious case in which that might happen is if a prosecution for a money laundering offence followed and revealed into the public domain the existence of assets against which the order could be enforced. There may be other situations in which such indirect effect might occur.

17.77 The court expressed itself as being satisfied the judge had applied the statutory criteria correctly and rejected this ground of appeal. As to the suggestion that the appellant was incapable of committing further offences given that he was 61 years of age and serving a sentence of imprisonment of 30 years as a category A prisoner, the Court again found against the appellant. Thomas LJ said:

The judge gave proper consideration to the undoubted fact that at present at least the appellant is a category A prisoner and subject to the special restrictions which are imposed on such prisoners. He was satisfied that that would not necessarily prevent the appellant, no doubt with other people, from achieving what he wanted to achieve and we for our part entirely agree.

The Court was, however, at pains to emphasise that financial reporting orders should not **17.78** be made without careful consideration being given to what they are likely to achieve. Thomas LJ said:

> We should say that whilst this form of order is newly created it ought not to be thought that it is routinely to be made without proper thought. We do not seek to set out any general rules for when it will be appropriate or not. This is not the right place in which to do that. No doubt the paradigm case for such an order is the defendant with a history of unsatisfactory business or financial dealing who at some stage at least is likely to be at large and engaged in business, commercial or financial activity which would otherwise be unsupervised or unmonitored. But it is perfectly clear that the section embraces also the defendant who is going to be a prisoner and, at least in the case of the very exceptional facts of this prisoner, we have no doubt that an order can be appropriate.

Finally, the Court accepted that the order would have some utility in the case of the **17.79** appellant, Thomas LJ adding:

> We are quite sure that judges who are asked to make financial reporting orders should give careful consideration to whether it would actually achieve anything. They should certainly look at alternative powers which are available to financial investigators if they would have much the same effect. We have applied our minds to precisely that question in this case. It is the fact that if the appellant were to maintain a stance of total non co-operation with the financial reporting order and of disobedience to it, it no doubt would achieve nothing. We do not, however, think that there is any basis on which we should properly assume that that will be his stance, even if his stance in the confiscation proceedings was of that kind. This order is expressed to last ten years. It would be quite wrong to make the assumption that he will simply ignore it for all that time and court the risk of the penalties which would follow. Nor should we make any assumption as to the period which he will actually serve in prison. We simply do not know.

One of the alternative remedies the court considered was the ability of the prosecutor **17.80** to apply for variations to the restraint order requiring the defendant to make further disclosure statements. The court rejected this as an appropriate alternative saying:

> We certainly accept that to make repeated applications for variations of a restraint order with a view to obtaining a direction for disclosure by the defendant is not a realistic substitute for the financial reporting order. On the assumption that it is at least possible that the defendant will make some kind of compliance with the order, it seems to us that it may have, albeit limited, some utility. He will be on the spot and required to set out his financial position at regular intervals. There is a not fanciful possibility that something may emerge from what he says, if he says anything, which may be of value to those who are monitoring his finances and may enable either the commission of further offences to be avoided or deterred or, failing that, the commission of further offences to be detected.

Although the Court in *Wright* avoided giving guidance to judges as to the circumstances in **17.81** which it would be appropriate to make financial reporting orders, it is clear that such orders are not necessarily inappropriate in cases where the defendant is serving a long sentence of imprisonment. This said, the court must always take care to satisfy itself that a financial reporting order would serve a useful purpose and not make them as a matter or routine in every case where the statutory criteria are satisfied.

17.82   In *R v Adams* [2008] EWCA Crim 914 a financial reporting order was challenged on the additional ground that it was made not when the defendant was sentenced but at a subsequent hearing at which he was brought back before the court for a hearing in relation to the recovery of defence costs by the Legal Services Commission (LSC). The defendant contended that, when this hearing took place, the Court was *functus officio* so far as sentencing matters were concerned. The Court rejected this argument and dismissed the appeal Latham LJ saying:

> We take the view that the judge was entitled to make the order. When the matter came back before him, it matters not in what guise, he was dealing with the offender within the meaning of section 76. That gave him the jurisdiction and the power to make the order.

Duration of orders

17.83   By s 76(5) the order comes into force when it is made and has effect for the period specified in it, beginning on the date on which it is made. If the order is made by a magistrates' court, the duration of the order must not exceed five years (see s 76(6)). If the order is made by the Crown Court, its duration must not exceed 15 years, or 20 years if the defendant is sentenced to imprisonment for life (see s 76(7)). The duration of the order must be proportionate to the risk of re-offending and a lengthy order will rarely be justified against a defendant with few previous convictions who has not been convicted of a particularly serious offence.

Effect of a financial reporting order

17.84   By s 79(1) a person against whom a financial reporting order has been made must do the following:

> (2) He must make a report in respect of—
>   (a) the period of a specified length beginning with the date on which the order comes into force; and
>   (b) subsequent periods of specified lengths, each period beginning immediately after the end of the previous one.
> (3) He must set out in each report, in the specified manner, such particulars of his financial affairs relating to the period as may be specified.
> (4) He must include any specified documents with each report;
> (5) He must make each report within the specified number of days after the end of the period in question.
> (6) He must make each report to the specified person.

17.85   By s 81(1) 'the specified person' means the person to whom reports under the order are to be made. Section 82(2) empowers the specified person, for the purpose of doing either of the things mentioned in s 82(4), to disclose a report to any person who he reasonably believes may be able to contribute to doing either of those things. Similarly, by s 82(3), any other person may disclose information to the specified person or to a person to whom the specified person has disclosed a report, for the purpose of contributing to doing either of the things mentioned in s 82(4). Section 82(4) provides:

> The things mentioned in subsections (2) and (3) are—
> (a) checking the accuracy of the report or of any other report made pursuant to the same order,
> (b) discovering the true position.

By s 82(5) the specified person may also disclose a report for the purpose of the prevention, **17.86** detection, or investigation of criminal offences in the UK and elsewhere. Section 82(6) provides that any disclosure made under the section does not breach:

(a) any obligation of confidence owed by the person making the disclosure, or
(b) any other restriction on the disclosure of information (however imposed).

This is subject to an important provision in s 82(7) to the effect that the section does not authorise any disclosure in contravention of the Data Protection Act 1998 of personal data which is not exempt from its provisions.

Variation and revocation of financial reporting orders

By s 80(1), an application for the variation or revocation of a financial report order may be **17.87** made by the person in respect of whom it was made or by the person to whom reports are to be made under it. The application must be made to the court which made the order (s 80(2)) or, if the order was made on appeal, to the court which originally sentenced the person in respect of whom it was made.

Failure to comply with financial reporting orders

It is an offence under s 79(1) to include false or misleading information in a report or **17.88** otherwise to fail to comply with the order without reasonable excuse. The offence is punishable by imprisonment for a maximum of 51 weeks, a fine not exceeding level 5 on the standard scale, or both.

18

APPEALS

A. Introduction

18.01 The purpose of this chapter is to consider in more detail the practice and procedure of making an appeal against the various orders available to the court, including restraint and confiscation.

Transfer of powers from the High Court to the Crown Court

18.02 By s 91 of the Proceeds of Crime Act 2002 (POCA), the Criminal Procedure Rules now govern restraint, receivership, and confiscation applications made before the Crown Court. The procedure on appeal to the Court of Appeal from those orders and the procedure to be followed on appeal to the House of Lords came into force on 30 December 2002 (SI 2002/3015).

18.03 The Criminal Procedure Rules make provision for three types of appeals under POCA. The first is an appeal under s 31 of POCA to the Court of Appeal (and from there to the House of Lords under s 33 of POCA) by the prosecutor against a confiscation order or a failure of the Crown Court to make a confiscation order. The second is an appeal under s 43 of POCA to the Court of Appeal (and from there to the House of Lords under s 44 of POCA) in respect of decisions of the Crown Court about restraint orders. The third is an appeal under s 65 of POCA to the Court of Appeal (and from there to the House of Lords under s 66 of POCA) in respect of decisions of the Crown Court about receivers. The Rules relating to these appeals are considered at the relevant stages of the appeal process set out below, and a thumbnail guide is included at the conclusion of this chapter.

18.04 Restraint and receivership applications under the Drug Trafficking Act 1994 (DTA) and CJA 1988 are currently dealt with by the High Court and fall within its civil law jurisdiction. Therefore the appropriate rules of court relating to appeals are the Civil Procedure Rules (CPR). Due to the passage of time since the introduction of POCA, the number of DTA and CJA cases has declined considerably. As a result this chapter focuses exclusively on POCA, save for the essential practice and procedure under the earlier Acts, which is set out at the end.

Appeals distinguished

18.05 It is important that the difference between an appeal and an application to vary should be properly understood. An appeal is appropriate where there is a legal challenge to the order, either in whole or in part. An application to vary is appropriate where, eg in confiscation cases, assets are sold and those assets realise a lesser amount than that which was anticipated when the confiscation order was made, and therefore an application is made to the court to recognise this fact and reduce the original order.

The distinction is important because the Court of Appeal is not likely to view sympatheti- **18.06** cally an appeal made on the basis that assets to the value of the order are no longer available, when the same could be dealt with more expeditiously and economically by a judge on an application for a certificate of inadequacy (the application to vary in confiscation matters is usually referred to as either a certificate of inadequacy or a certificate of increase). Equally, a judge will not take kindly to being asked to act as a Court of Appeal by having to consider matters of law on the validity of the confiscation order that should more appropriately be determined by the Court of Appeal.

The Crown Court 'slip rule'

Under s 155(1) of the Powers of Criminal Courts (Sentencing) Act 2000 (PCC(S)A) both **18.07** the defendant and the Crown may apply to the Crown Court within 28 days to vary or remedy an order made on the basis that the factual conclusions determined by the Crown Court were incorrect.

B. Restraint Order Appeals: Practice and Procedure

Introduction

Now that the powers to make restraint orders have been transferred to the Crown **18.08** Court from the High Court, the general right of appeal that existed under the DTA and CJA 1988 no longer exists. Therefore specific rights of appeal have been incorporated into the Act.

Restraint orders: appeal by the prosecutor

If, on an application for a restraint order under POCA, the Crown Court decides not to **18.09** make an order, the person who applied for the order may appeal to the Court of Appeal against the decision (s 43(1)).

Section 43 applies where the Crown Court decides not to make a restraint order for what- **18.10** ever reason. On an appeal under s 43, the Court of Appeal may either confirm the decision or make such order as it believes is appropriate (see s 43(3)).

Restraint orders: general right of appeal

Section 43(1) is specifically directed at circumstances where a Crown Court decides not **18.11** to make a restraint order. There is no right of appeal therefore against the Crown Court's decision to make a restraint order. The aggrieved defendant may only appeal against the Crown Court's decision not to vary or discharge the restraint order on their application. In effect, therefore, this becomes a two tier process: firstly, a dissatisfied defendant must apply to the Crown Court for the variation or discharge of the restraint order; if that application fails then the second stage is to appeal to the Court of Appeal.

18.12 If an application is made under s 42(3) to discharge or vary a restraint order, or an order is made under s 41(7) (an order for the purpose of ensuring that the restraint order is effective), either the person who applied for the order or any person affected by it may appeal to the Court of Appeal in respect of the Crown Court's decision (s 43(2)).

18.13 It is important to realise that the application to vary or discharge is often the first time the Crown Court judge will have the opportunity of listening to and understanding the defendant's objections to the restraint order. This is because restraint orders are usually applied for on an *ex parte* (without notice) basis, so as to maintain the element of surprise and avoid any dissipation of assets prior to the matter being listed. Occasionally this is remedied by the setting of a 'return date' for the parties to attend *inter partes* (on notice).

Leave

18.14 By s 89(1) of POCA, an appeal to the Court of Appeal under Pt 2 of POCA lies only with the leave of that court.

18.15 Under r 73.1 of the Criminal Procedure Rules, leave to appeal to the Court of Appeal under s 43 of POCA will only be given where:

(a) the Court of Appeal considers that the appeal would have a real prospect of success; or
(b) there is some other compelling reason why the appeal should be heard.

18.16 Rule 73.2 of the Criminal Procedure Rules sets out the procedure for giving notice of appeal. The notice of appeal must be served on each respondent, any person who holds realisable property to which the appeal relates, and any other person affected by the appeal no later than seven days after the notice of appeal is served on the appropriate officer of the Crown Court. Rule 73.3 sets out the procedure for where a respondent is seeking leave to appeal, or wishes to ask the Court of Appeal to uphold the Crown Court's decision for different reasons from (or additional to) those given by the Crown Court.

18.17 Rules 73.4 to 73.6 of the Criminal Procedure Rules explain the procedure for amending, abandoning, staying, and striking out appeals.

Hearing the appeal

18.18 Subject to the rules made under s 53(1) of the Supreme Court Act 1981 (distribution of business between civil and criminal divisions), the criminal division of the Court of Appeal is the division to which appeals should be made (s 49(2)(a)).

18.19 Under r 73.7 of the Criminal Procedure Rules, every appeal will be limited to a review of the decision of the Crown Court, unless the Court of Appeal considers that in the circumstances of an individual appeal it would be in the interests of justice to hold a re-hearing. The Court of Appeal will allow an appeal where the decision of the Crown Court was:

(a) wrong; or
(b) unjust because of a serious procedural or other irregularity in the proceedings in the Crown Court.

18.20 The Court of Appeal may draw any inference of fact which it considers justified on the evidence (Criminal Procedure Rules r 73.7(4)). At the hearing of the appeal a party may not rely on a matter not contained in his notice of appeal unless the Court of Appeal gives permission (Criminal Procedure Rules r 73.7(5)).

The Proceeds of Crime Act 2002 (Appeals under Part 2) Order 2003

The Secretary of State has made certain corresponding provisions to the Criminal Appeal **18.21** Act 1968 to allow for the adoption of general procedures such as obtaining leave to appeal and transcripts (s 89(3)). The Proceeds of Crime Act 2002 (Appeals under Part 2) Order 2003, SI 2003/82 came into force on 24 March 2003. For a more detailed consideration analysis of this order, see para 18.86 below.

Restraint orders: appeal to the House of Lords

Following an appeal to the Court of Appeal under s 43, a further appeal lies to the House **18.22** of Lords under s 44 of POCA. The appeal may be made by any person who is a party to the proceedings before the Court of Appeal (and therefore includes the prosecution). The powers of the Court of Appeal are set out in s 44(3) and are either to:

(a) confirm the decision of the Court of Appeal, or
(b) make such order as it believes is appropriate.

An appeal to the House of Lords only follows from a decision of the Court of Appeal, and **18.23** only the parties to the Court of Appeal proceedings may appeal. Section 33(3) of the Criminal Appeal Act 1968 (limitation on appeal from the Criminal Division of the Court of Appeal) does not prevent an appeal to the House of Lords under Pt 2 of POCA (as per s 90(1)). For the procedure to be adopted when applying to appeal to the House of Lords, see r 71.10 of the Criminal Procedure Rules.

C. Receivership Order Appeals: Practice and Procedure

Appeals to the Court of Appeal in receivership proceedings

The general right of appeal under the DTA and the CJA 1988 no longer exists now that the **18.24** receivership provisions have been transferred to the Crown Court.

Appeal by the prosecutor

Under POCA if, on an application for a receivership order made under ss 48 to 51 of **18.25** POCA, the court decides *not* to make such an order, the person who applied for the order may appeal to the Court of Appeal against the decision (s 65(1)).

Applications under ss 48 to 51 are for: the appointment of a management receiver by the **18.26** Crown Court; the powers given to the management receiver by the Crown Court; the appointment of an enforcement receiver by the Crown Court; and the powers given to an enforcement receiver by the Crown Court.

Appeal by any party

If, on the other hand, the court *makes* an order under any of the above sections, the person **18.27** who applied for the order or any person affected by the order may appeal to the Court of Appeal in respect of the court's decision (s 65(2)).

Appeal: variation or discharge

18.28   On an application for an order under s 62 of POCA, namely, an application by either the receiver to the Crown Court for an order giving directions as to the exercise of the receiver's powers under s 62(2); or any person affected by action taken by the receiver, or any person who may be affected by the action the receiver proposes to take (s 62(3)), if the court decides *not* to make the order applied for, the person who applied for the order may appeal to the Court of Appeal against that decision under s 65(3).

18.29   Similarly, if on the other hand, the court makes an order under s 62, then the person who applied for the order or any person affected by the order, including the receiver, may appeal to the Court of Appeal in respect of the court's decision (s 65(4)).

18.30   Where an application is made to discharge or vary the powers of the receiver under s 63 of POCA, an appeal may be made to the Court of Appeal against the decision of the Crown Court by the person who applied for the order in respect of which the application was made; or any person affected by the court's decision; or the receiver.

18.31   In *R v Capewell* (2004) EWCA Civ 1628; (2005) 1 All ER 900, the Court of Appeal considered the question of discharging the receiver and noted that the following issues were likely to be relevant (para 50):

> On the question of discharge, cost is of course a factor, but it is not the primary issue. The overriding consideration is whether the receivership is still serving a valid purpose . . . The relevant questions for the court are likely to be:
>   i)   For what purposes, within the overall objective, was the receivership authorised?
>   ii) To what extent have those purposes been achieved or overtaken?
>   iii) To the extent that they have not yet been achieved or overtaken, is the continuation of the receivership (as opposed to a restraint order or some other order) necessary to achieve them?
>   iv) In any event, having regard both to the overall objective and to fairness to the defendant, is the additional cost of continuing the receivership proportionate to the likely financial gain?
>
> 52. We would add that fairness to the defendant cannot be measured purely in financial terms.

Leave

18.32   As in restraint cases, under s 89(1) of POCA an appeal to the Court of Appeal under Pt 2 of POCA lies only with the leave of that court.

18.33   Under r 73.1 of the Criminal Procedure Rules leave to appeal to the Court of Appeal under s 65 of POCA will only be given where:

(a) the Court of Appeal considers that the appeal would have a real prospect of success; or
(b) there is some other compelling reason why the appeal should be heard.

18.34   Rule 73.2 of the Criminal Procedure Rules sets out the procedure for giving notice of appeal. The notice of appeal must be served on each respondent, any person who holds realisable property to which the appeal relates, and any other person affected by the appeal, no later than seven days after the notice of appeal is served on the appropriate officer of the Crown Court. Rule 73.3 sets out the procedure for where a respondent is seeking leave to appeal or wishes to ask the Court of Appeal to uphold the Crown Court's decision for different reasons from (or additional to) those given by the Crown Court.

Rules 73.4 to 73.6 of the Criminal Procedure Rules explain the procedure for amending, **18.35** abandoning, staying, and striking out appeals.

Hearing the appeal

Subject to the rules made under s 53(1) of the Supreme Court Act 1981 (distribution of **18.36** business between civil and criminal divisions) the criminal division of the Court of Appeal is the division to which appeals should be made (see s 49(2)(a)).

Under r 73.7 of the Criminal Procedure Rules every appeal will be limited to a review of the **18.37** decision of the Crown Court unless the Court of Appeal considers that in the circumstances of an individual appeal it would be in the interests of justice to hold a re-hearing. The Court of Appeal will allow an appeal where the decision of the Crown Court was:

(a) wrong; or
(b) unjust because of a serious procedural or other irregularity in the proceedings in the Crown Court.

The Court of Appeal may draw any inference of fact that it considers justified on the **18.38** evidence. At the hearing of the appeal a party may not rely on a matter not contained in his notice of appeal unless the Court of Appeal gives permission (r 73.7(5) of the Criminal Procedure Rules).

The Proceeds of Crime Act 2002 (Appeals under Part 2) Order 2003

The Secretary of State has made certain corresponding provisions to the Criminal Appeal **18.39** Act 1968 to allow for the adoption of general procedures such as obtaining leave to appeal and transcripts (s 89(3)). The Proceeds of Crime Act 2002 (Appeals under Part 2) Order 2003, SI 2003/82 came into force on 24 March 2003. For a detailed analysis of this order, see para 18.86 below.

The powers of the Court of Appeal on receipt of an appeal against a receivership order

On an appeal under any of the heads of s 65, the Court of Appeal may either confirm the **18.40** decision or may make such order as it believes is appropriate (s 65(6)).

Appeal to House of Lords

An appeal also lies to the House of Lords from a decision of the Court of Appeal on an **18.41** appeal under s 65. It may be made by any person who was a party to the proceedings before the Court of Appeal and on appeal the House of Lords may confirm the decision of the Court of Appeal or make such order as it believes is appropriate. For the procedure to be adopted when applying to appeal to the House of Lords, see r 71.10 of the Criminal Procedure Rules.

It has already been noted that s 33(3) of the Criminal Appeal Act 1968 (limitation on **18.42** appeal from the Criminal Division of the Court of Appeal) does not prevent an appeal to the House of Lords under Pt 2 of POCA (s 90(1)).

Appeals by financial investigators under POCA

18.43 Section 68 of POCA extends appeals under restraint orders and management receivership orders to 'accredited financial investigators'. 'Accredited financial investigators' are defined as being:

(a) a police officer who is not below the rank of superintendent;

(b) a Revenue and Customs officer who is not below such grade as is designated by the Commissioners of Revenue and Customs as equivalent to that rank; or

(c) a person who falls within a description in SI 2003/172, eg certain employees of the Inland Revenue; the Financial Services Authority; the Department for Work and Pensions etc (specified by an order of the Secretary of State made under s 453 of POCA).

18.44 Section 68(1) gives the accredited financial investigator the power to make an application for a restraint order under ss 41 or 42 or the power to appeal a restraint order under ss 43 or 44. Similarly it gives the accredited financial investigator the power to apply for the appointment of a management receiver under ss 48 or 49 of POCA or appeal under ss 65 or 66 following an application for the appointment of a management receiver. It also extends to the accredited financial investigator the power to apply for variation or discharge of a management receiver under s 63 of POCA.

18.45 If such an application is made or appeal brought by an accredited financial investigator, any subsequent step in the application or appeal, or any further application or appeal relating to the same matter may be taken, made, or brought by a different accredited financial investigator providing they fall into or are authorised by the definitions set out in s 68(3) (as per s 68(4)). The purpose of this subsection is to ensure that no problems are created by, for example, the subsequent ill health of an investigator who makes an initial appeal concerning a restraint order.

D. Confiscation Order Appeals: Practice and Procedure

Appeals in confiscation order cases

18.46 Appeals against confiscation orders lie to the Court of Appeal (Criminal Division) (unless it is a rare High Court confiscation case, where the appeal will be to the Civil Division).

Confiscation appeals

18.47 Under s 87(2) of POCA, a confiscation order is subject to appeal until there is no further possibility of an appeal on which the order could be varied or quashed (for these purposes any power to grant leave to appeal out of time must be ignored).

Defendant's appeal

18.48 An appeal against a confiscation order lies as part of the sentencing process. In *R v Johnson* [1991] 2 QB 249 the Court of Appeal held that by virtue of s 9 of the Criminal Appeal Act 1968 (as amended), a person who has been convicted of an offence or indictment:

> . . . may appeal to the Court of Appeal against any sentence (not being a sentence fixed by law) passed on him for the offence, whether passed on his conviction or in subsequent proceedings.

'Sentence' in relation to an offence is defined in s 50(1) of the Criminal Appeal Act 1968 as including:

Any Order made by a court when dealing with an offender . . .

In *Johnson* the court therefore concluded that a confiscation order does form part of a sentence for the purpose of s 9 of the Criminal Appeal Act 1968.

The grounds must be drafted in terms of either mistake of law or mistake of fact. It should **18.49** be underlined that an appeal to the Court of Appeal must not be used merely to seek a rehearing where a confiscation ruling has been adverse to the client.

In *R v Hirani* [2008] EWCA Crim 1483, the Court of Appeal confirmed that it did have **18.50** jurisdiction in a confiscation appeal to substitute a new order in place of the original.

A right of appeal against the confiscation order in all cases

The right of appeal exists as a right against all matters determined by the Crown Court **18.51** at the confiscation hearing proceedings (*R v Emmett* [1998] AC 773) where Lord Steyn stated that there was a strong presumption that except by specific provision the legislature will not exclude a right of appeal as of right or with leave. He stated the starting point is that, unless the Act expressly or by necessary implication excludes a right of appeal, there is as a matter of jurisdiction a right of appeal against a confiscation order in all cases. In confiscation order matters there is no express ouster of the right of appeal contained in the various relevant Acts (as per Lord Scarman in *R v Cain* [1985] 1 AC 46, 55G–56D).

In *Emmett* the appellant asserted that his acceptance of an allegation in a prosecutor's state- **18.52** ment was the result of a mistake of law or fact, and therefore that acceptance should not be binding upon him on appeal. The Court of Appeal held that the burden rests upon an appellant who asserts that his acceptance of any allegation in a prosecutor's statement was the result of a mistake of law or fact to persuade the Court of Appeal that his assertion was correct. Lord Steyn added (at p 783):

> Lest it be thought, however, that my observations are some kind of open sesame to such appeals I would mention four matters. First, the question in such cases will not be what mistake Counsel made but what mistake the defendant made. Secondly, and particularly in regard to matters peculiarly within the knowledge of the defendant, the burden on the defendant of proving a mistake may not easily be discharged. Thirdly, the focus in such cases will be on a material and causatively relevant mistake viz. a material mistake which in fact induced the defendant to accept the correctness of a [prosecutor's] statement. Fourthly, even if the defendant can persuade the Court of Appeal on these three points, the Court of Appeal may still have to consider whether, absent a material mistake, the particular confiscation order would nevertheless have been inevitable. If that is the case, the appeal may have to be dismissed on the grounds that on a global view of the case no injustice can be shown.

Appeals involving the judge's discretion

The Court of Appeal has shown a marked reluctance to interfere in appeals that hinge on a **18.53** judge's power of discretion. Although the Court of Appeal does have the power to consider and interfere in matters involving the discretion of the trial judge, it will only do so in the following circumstances:

(1) where there has been a failure to exercise a discretion; or
(2) where the judge has failed to take into account a material consideration; or
(3) where the judge in the court below has taken into account an immaterial consideration (see *R v Quinn* [1996] Crim LR 516).

Confiscation orders: the Crown Court 'slip rule'

18.54 Under s 155(1) of the PCC(S)A both the defendant and the Crown may apply to the Crown Court on the basis that the factual conclusions determined by the Crown Court can be shown to be incorrect:

Subject to the provisions of this section, a sentence imposed, or other order made by the Crown Court when dealing with an offender may be varied or remedied by the Crown Court within the period of 28 days beginning with the day on which the sentence or other order was imposed or made.

18.55 The application of this section to confiscation cases was confirmed in the case of *R v Bukhari* [2008] EWCA Crim 2915, but only within the strict 28-day limit, thereafter the correct route was by way of appeal.

Appeal does not stop clock

18.56 Lodging an appeal in a confiscation order case does not stop the 'time to pay' period set by the Crown Court from running. The Court of Appeal took a robust approach to the period set for payment in the case of *R v May, Lawrence* [2005] EWCA Crim 97, where Keene LJ held at para 5 that the:

proposition that the time to pay a confiscation order runs from the date of the determination of an appeal was 'unsound in law'. In principle the fact that an appeal is pending does not operate so as to suspend the operation of any sentence or order.

He added at para 7 that:

There is no reason why steps preparatory to the raising of the money specified in the confiscation order should not have been taken while in (the defendant May's) appeal was pending. The appellant was not entitled to assume that his appeal would be successful and, as indicated above, as a matter of law time was running during that period. Moreover, it would be wrong as a matter of principle for appellants to be encouraged to believe that bringing an appeal would be likely to lengthen the time given for payment, even if the appeal was unsuccessful.

Confiscation orders and the Criminal Cases Review Commission

18.57 The Criminal Cases Review Commission is not a court of appeal and it is therefore unlikely that an application to it would slow or in any way inhibit the due processes of the confiscation scheme. This is reflected in the case law. In *Re P* (QBD, 6 November 1998) the defendant had been convicted in February 1995 of a conspiracy offence relating to drugs. On 17 July 1995 the court gave the receiver the right to sell properties owned by the defendant. Following that, on 6 October 1995, the Crown Court made a confiscation order against the defendant in the sum of £557,000 with an order that he serve four years' imprisonment in default of payment. In June 1997 the Court of Appeal dismissed the defendant's appeal against his conviction. On that occasion his counsel did not pursue any complaint against the confiscation order.

18.58 In 1998 the defendant sought to pursue his claim that he was innocent of the offence he had been convicted of with the Criminal Cases Review Commission (CCRC), and that, as a result, the confiscation order was wrongly made. He also lodged an application to the European Court of Human Rights. The defendant made an unsuccessful application to the court to have funds released from the bite of the restraint order to enable him to meet the expenses associated with those two applications. Laws J held:

> The fact is that, so far as the domestic criminal litigation is concerned in this case, Mr P is well past the end of the road. The Commission may, of course, investigate a matter after all other legal processes have been exhausted. Indeed that is their very role. However, it is quite clear to me that whilst they are doing so, and the fact that they are doing so, are no basis for altering, suspending or varying the affect of the restraint order and therefore, in effect, the execution of a confiscation order once that has been made. The same applies in relation to his application to the European Court of Human Rights.

18.59 In *Re C* (QBD, 14 May 2004), Owen J, relying on the dicta of Laws J in *Re P*, held that the fact the matter had been referred to the CCRC 'does not afford a reason why the law should not take its course'.

Fresh evidence

18.60 In *R v Stroud* [2004] EWCA Crim 1048, the Court of Appeal held that where a defendant sought to adduce fresh expert evidence on appeal against a confiscation order, the same considerations as to admissibility were to be considered as applied in appeals against conviction.

Prosecutor's appeal

18.61 If the Crown Court makes a confiscation order the prosecutor may appeal to the Court of Appeal in respect of that order (s 31(1)). Conversely, if the Crown Court decides not to make a confiscation order the prosecutor may appeal to the Court of Appeal against that decision (s 31(2)). The appeal may be on any ground (either a point of law or fact), for example, that the court has failed to take account of property that should be taken account of. The right of the prosecutor to appeal, including in cases which have been stayed as an abuse of process, was recently confirmed in *CPS v N, P and Paulet* (2009) EWCA Crim 1573 at 32.

18.62 Provisions for giving notice of appeal by the prosecutor are set out in r 72.1 of the Criminal Procedure Rules. Where a defendant is served with a notice of appeal under r 72.1, and wishes to oppose the granting of leave he must, not later than 14 days after the date on which he received the notice of appeal, serve on the registrar and on the appellant a notice (see r 72.2). Rule 72.3 of the Criminal Procedure Rules outlines the procedure to be followed when an appeal is to be either amended or abandoned.

18.63 Subject to the rules made under s 53(1) of the Supreme Court Act 1981 (distribution of business between Civil and Criminal Divisions) the Criminal Division of the Court of Appeal is the division to which appeals should be made (see s 49(2)(a)). The Secretary of

State has made certain corresponding provisions to the Criminal Appeal Act 1968 to allow for the adoption of general procedures such as obtaining leave to appeal and transcripts (s 89(3)).

18.64 There is, however, no prosecutor's right of appeal against an order or decision made by virtue of s 19 (no confiscation order made: reconsideration of case); s 20 (no confiscation order made: reconsideration of benefit); s 27 (where the defendant has absconded and he has been convicted or committed); or s 28 (where the defendant has absconded but he has neither been convicted nor committed) (see s 31(3)).

Leave

18.65 Like restraint and receivership appeals, under s 89(1) of POCA an appeal to the Court of Appeal under Pt 2 of POCA lies only with the leave of that court.

Appeal by the prosecutor: the Court of Appeal's powers

18.66 Under s 32 of POCA an appeal by the prosecutor to the Court of Appeal gives the Court of Appeal the power to confirm, quash, or vary the confiscation order (s 32(1)). For the exercise of these powers, see *R v Hockey* [2008] Crim LR 59; [2008] 1 Cr App R (S) 50.

18.67 If the appeal is on the grounds that the Court of Appeal has decided not to make a confiscation order, the Court of Appeal may confirm the decision or, if it believes the decision is wrong, it may itself proceed under s 6 of POCA to make a confiscation order (but in doing so ignoring s 6(1) to (3)), or it may direct the Crown Court to proceed afresh under s 6.

18.68 If the Crown Court is directed to proceed afresh, it must comply with any other directions the Court of Appeal may make in relation to the hearing (s 32(3)).

18.69 Under s 32(4), if the Court of Appeal makes or varies a confiscation order, or directs the Crown Court to go through the confiscation procedures afresh under s 6, and the Crown Court has, in the meantime, imposed a fine or an ancillary order set out within s 13(3) of POCA (eg a compensation order), then the court is required to have regard to the fine or order made.

The steps the court must take

18.70 If the Court of Appeal proceeds under s 6, or the Crown Court proceeds afresh pursuant to a direction by the Court of Appeal, then s 32(6) to (10) apply:

(6) If a court has already sentenced the defendant for the offence (or any of the offences) concerned, section 6 has effect as if his particular criminal conduct included conduct which constitutes offences which the court has taken into consideration in deciding his sentence for the offence or offences concerned.

(7) If an order has been made against the defendant in respect of the offence (or any of the offences) concerned under section 130 of the Sentencing Act (Compensation Orders)—
(a) the Court must have regard to it and,
(b) Section 13(5) and (6) . . . do not apply.

18.71 Section 13(6) states that the court must specify how much of the compensation is to be paid out of any sums recovered under the confiscation order; and the amount it specifies must be the amount it believes will not be recoverable because of the insufficiency of the person's means. This subsection only applies if the Crown Court makes both a confiscation order and an order for the payment of compensation under s 130 of the Sentencing Act against the same proceedings, and the court believes he will not have sufficient means to satisfy both the orders in full (s 13(5)).

By s 32(8):
18.72

Section 8(2) does not apply, and the rules applying instead are that the court must—
(a) take account of conduct occurring before the relevant date;
(b) take account of property obtained before that date;
(c) take account of property obtained on or after that date if it was obtained as a result of or in connection with conduct occurring before that date.

Section 8(2) limits the court to taking into account conduct occurring at the time that it makes its decision and taking account of property obtained at that time. Those restrictions do not apply where the Court of Appeal is proceeding under s 6, or the Crown Court is proceeding under s 6 as a result of a direction by the Court of Appeal, following a successful appeal by the prosecutor.

Section 32(9) provides:
18.73

(9) In Section 10—
   (a) the first and second assumptions do not apply with regard to property first held by the defendant on or after the relevant date; or
   (b) the third assumption does not apply with regard to expenditure incurred by him on or after the date;
   (c) the fourth assumption does not apply with regard to property obtained or assumed to have been obtained by him on or after that date.

Section 10 of POCA sets out the assumptions to be made in cases of criminal lifestyle.

Under s 32(10), s 26 of POCA applies in the circumstances mentioned in s 26(1), ie the **18.74** court is proceeding under s 6 in pursuance of either s 19 (where no confiscation order has been made and the court is reconsidering the case, or where no order has been made and the court is reconsidering what benefit there is) or the prosecutor applies under s 21, namely where an order has been made and the prosecutor is asking the court to reconsider the benefit.

The 'relevant date' for these purposes is the date on which the Crown Court decided not to **18.75** make a confiscation order (s 32(11)).

Corresponding provisions

The Secretary of State has made certain corresponding provisions to the Criminal Appeal **18.76** Act 1968 to allow for the adoption of general procedures such as obtaining leave to appeal and transcripts (s 89(3)). The Proceeds of Crime Act 2002 (Appeals under Part 2) Order 2003, SI 2003/82 came into force on 24 March 2003. For a detailed consideration of this order, see para 18.86 below.

Appeal to the House of Lords

Under s 33(1), an appeal lies to the House of Lords from a decision of the Court of Appeal **18.77** on an appeal under s 31 of POCA.

18.78 An appeal under this section lies at the instance of either the defendant or the prosecutor (if the prosecutor appealed under s 31); (see s 33(2)). On such an appeal, the House of Lords may itself confirm, quash, or vary the order (s 33(3)).

18.79 It will have been noted already that s 33(3) of the Criminal Appeal Act 1968 (limitation on appeal from the Criminal Division of the Court of Appeal) does not prevent an appeal to the House of Lords under Pt 2 of POCA (s 90(1)). For the procedure to be adopted when applying to appeal to the House of Lords, see r 71.10 of the Criminal Procedure Rules.

Powers of the House of Lords in such circumstances

18.80 On an appeal from the decision of the Court of Appeal to confirm the decision of the Crown Court not to make a confiscation order or from the decision of the Court of Appeal to quash a confiscation order the House of Lords may:

(a) confirm the decision, or
(b) direct the Crown Court to proceed afresh under s 6, if it believes the decision was wrong (s 33(4)).

18.81 It will be noted that the House of Lords has no power itself to proceed under s 6, unlike the Court of Appeal. Its powers under s 33 are limited to confirming, quashing, or varying the order of the Court of Appeal. If it elects to quash the order then it may remit the case to the Crown Court with directions to proceed afresh under s 6.

Where the Crown Court proceeds afresh

18.82 If proceeding afresh, the Crown Court must comply with any directions the House of Lords has made (s 33(5)). In similar terms to if the Court of Appeal orders the Crown Court to proceed afresh under s 6, if the Crown Court varies the confiscation order, or makes a confiscation order in pursuance of a direction by the House of Lords, it must have regard to any fine imposed on the defendant in respect of the offence concerned or in respect of any ancillary orders (which fall within s 13(3) of POCA). However, the Crown Court is not required to take account of an order if it has already taken account of the order in working out what the free property held by the defendant is (to avoid double counting) (ss 33(6)(b) and 32(4)(b)).

18.83 Section 33(8) to (12) is in identical terms to s 32(6) to (10) above and applies where the Crown Court is proceeding afresh under s 6 in pursuance of an election by the House of Lords.

18.84 For the purposes of s 33 the 'relevant date' is:

(a) in a case where the Crown Court made a confiscation order which was quashed by the Court of Appeal, the date on which the Crown Court made the order;
(b) in any other case, the date on which the Crown Court decided not to make a confiscation order (s 33(13)).

Attorney-General's appeal

18.85 In *A-G References Nos 114, 115, 116, 144 and 145 of 2002* the Court of Appeal held that it could properly hear applications by the Attorney-General to refer a sentence under s 36 of the CJA 1988, on the basis that a judge had wrongly refused to make a confiscation order and could consider evidence as required. Attorney-General's references may also be made under the same section where the confiscation is considered to be unduly lenient.

E. The Proceeds of Crime Act 2002 (Appeals under Part 2) Order 2003

Practice and procedure: appeals to the Court of Appeal

The Proceeds of Crime Act 2002 (Appeals under Part 2) Order 2003 (SI 2003/82) came **18.86** into force on 24 March 2003. It makes provisions that correspond with the provisions of the Criminal Appeal Act 1968 for the purposes of the three new appeal routes introduced by POCA, namely:

(1) an appeal under s 31 of POCA to the Court of Appeal (and from there to the House of Lords under s 33) by the prosecutor against a confiscation order or a failure of the Crown Court to make a confiscation order;

(2) an appeal under s 43 of POCA to the Court of Appeal (and from there to the House of Lords under s 44 of POCA) in respect of decisions of the Crown Court about restraint orders; and

(3) an appeal under s 65 of POCA to the Court of Appeal (and from there to the House of Lords under s 66 of POCA) in respect of decisions of the Crown Court about receivers.

Initiating procedure

Under Art 3(1) of the Proceeds of Crime Act 2002 (Appeals under Part 2) Order, a person **18.87** who wishes to obtain the leave of the Court of Appeal to appeal to the Court of Appeal under Pt 2 of POCA, ie confiscation, restraint, and appointment of receivers, shall give notice of their application for leave to appeal, in the manner directed by the Rules of Court. Such a notice of application for leave to appeal shall be given within:

(a) 28 days from the date of the decision appealed against, in the case of an appeal under section 31 of the Act [confiscation]; or

(b) 14 days from the date of the decision appealed against, in the case of an appeal under section 43 [restraint] or section 65 [receiverships] of the Act.

Under s 3(3) the time for giving notice may be extended by the Court of Appeal. Article 3 **18.88** reflects the provisions previously set out in s 18 of the Criminal Appeal Act 1968.

Disposal of groundless applications for leave to appeal

Under Art 4 of the Proceeds of Crime Act 2002 (Appeals under Part 2) Order, if it appears **18.89** to the Registrar that a notice of application for leave to appeal to the Court of Appeal does not show any substantial ground for appeal, he may refer the application for leave to the Court of Appeal for summary determination.

Where the case is so referred to the Court of Appeal, it may, if it considers that the appli- **18.90** cation for leave is frivolous or vexatious and can be determined without adjourning it for a full hearing, dismiss the application for leave summarily, without calling on anyone to attend the hearing. This provision corresponds with s 20 of the Criminal Appeal Act 1968.

Preparation of case for hearing

18.91   Once an application has been received, and subject to Art 4, Art 5 states as follows:

(1) The Registrar shall—

  (a) take all necessary steps for obtaining a hearing of any application for leave to appeal to the Court of Appeal under Part 2 of the Act of which Notice is given to him and which is not referred and dismissed summarily under Article 4;

  (b) where an application for leave to appeal to the Court of Appeal under Part 2 of the Act is granted, take all necessary steps for obtaining a hearing of an appeal; and

  (c) obtain and lay before the Court of Appeal in proper form all documents, exhibits and other things which appear necessary for the proper determination of the application for leave to appeal under Part 2 of the Act or the appeal under Part 2 of the Act.

18.92   This article corresponds with s 21 of the Criminal Appeal Act 1968 and provides that the Registrar must organise hearings for applications for leave to appeal and the appeals themselves. In the case of appeals in relation to confiscation orders, the Registrar must also organise documents and exhibits for the appeal and provide them, in accordance with the Rules of Court, to the parties. Under Art 5(2), a party to an appeal may obtain from the Registrar any document or thing, including copies or reproductions of documents, required for his appeal, in accordance with the Rules of Court. The Registrar may make charges in accordance with such rules for those documents (see Art 5(3)).

Right of defendant to be present

18.93   Under Art 6(1) of the Proceeds of Crime Act 2002 (Appeals under Part 2) Order 2003, the defendant will be entitled to be present, if he wishes, at the hearing of any appeal to the Court of Appeal to which he is a party, even though he may be in custody. However, if the defendant is in custody, he will not be entitled to be present:

(a) where the appeal is on some ground involving a question of law alone; or

(b) on an application for leave to appeal; or

(c) on any proceedings preliminary or incidental to an appeal, unless the Court of Appeal gives him leave to be present.

(See Art 6(2)). This article corresponds to s 22 of the Criminal Appeal Act 1968.

Rules of evidence in the Court of Appeal

18.94   For the purposes of an appeal under Pt 2 of POCA, the Court of Appeal may, if they think it necessary or expedient in the interests of justice:

(a) order the production of any document, exhibit or other thing connected with the proceedings, the production of which appears to them necessary for the determination of the appeal;

(b) order any witness to attend for examination and be examined before the Court of Appeal; and

(c) receive any evidence which was not adduced in the proceedings from which the appeal arises.

(See Art 7(1) of the Proceeds of Crime Act 2002 (Appeals under Part 2) Order.)

18.95   The Court of Appeal may, if they think it necessary or expedient in the interests of justice, order the examination of any witness whose attendance might be required under para (1)(b) to be conducted before any judge or officer of the court or other person appointed by the court for the purpose, and allow the admission of any depositions so taken as evidence before the court (See Art 7(3) of the Proceeds of Crime Act 2002 (Appeals under Part 2) Order).

Under Art 7(2) of the Order the Court of Appeal must, in considering whether to receive **18.96** any evidence, have regard in particular to:

(a) whether the evidence appears to the court to be capable of belief;
(b) whether it appears to the court that the evidence may afford any ground for allowing the appeal;
(c) whether the evidence would have been admissible in the proceedings from which the appeal lies on an issue which is the subject of the appeal; and
(d) whether there is a reasonable explanation for the failure to adduce the evidence in the proceedings giving rise to the appeal.

The above provisions reflect s 23 of the Criminal Appeal Act 1968.

General provisions

The Criminal Procedure Rules set out certain other general provisions to be adopted where **18.97** the circumstances dictate; the relevant rules are listed below:

Extension of time	r 71.1
Applications relating to bail, leave to be present, reception of evidence	r 71.2
Examination of witnesses in court	r 71.3
Supply of documentary and other exhibits	r 71.4
Registrar's power to require information from court of trial	r 71.5
Hearing by single judge	r 71.6
Determination by full court	r 71.7
Notice of determination	r 71.8
Record of proceedings and transcript	r 71.9
Appeal to House of Lords	r 71.10
Service of Documents	r 71.11

References to the European Court of Justice

The Court of Appeal has power to refer a case to the European Court of Justice at any time **18.98** before the determination of an appeal (see the Criminal Appeal (References to the European Court) Rules 1972, SI 1972/1786).

F. Appeals against Forfeiture Orders

Forfeiture appeals under POCA from the magistrates' court

Section 299 of POCA was amended by s 101 of the Serious Organised Crime and Police **18.99** Act 2005 (SOCPA) because of an ambiguity as to its meaning. While the original s 299(1) appeared to allow 'Any party to the proceedings' to appeal against an order made under s 298, this was qualified by the words 'for the forfeiture of cash'. This meant that while any party may appeal an order for forfeiture there was no provision for the complainant to appeal a *refusal* to grant forfeiture, although somewhat ironically a complainant could appeal an order *for* forfeiture.

18.100 The substituted s 299 now states:

> (1) Any person to proceedings for an order for the forfeiture of cash under section 298 who is aggrieved by an order under that section or by the decision of the court to make such an order may appeal . . .

In other words, both the complainant and the defendant now have a right of appeal from the magistrates' court hearing to the Crown Court. Such a hearing should be *de novo* (s 79(3) Supreme Court Act 1981), with the facts being re-examined in the court above, and with the opportunity for both parties to serve further evidence before the hearing takes place (whilst the original s 299(3) expressly stated that the appeal was by way of re-hearing, the substituted legislation does not).

18.101 The appeal is to the Crown Court and notice must be lodged before the expiration of 30 days from when the order or decision was made (substituted s 299(2)).

18.102 This section also has the effect of allowing the Appeal Court, and the Crown Court, to hear an appeal in an appropriate way, for example, on a point of law.

18.103 Appeals in relation to the cash seizure provisions, including whether the 30-day period can be extended; funding the appeal and judicial review, are further considered at para 15.195 *et seq* of Chapter 15.

18.104 It will have been seen from Chapter 15 (seizure of cash under POCA) that once an application for forfeiture has been made, the seized cash may not be released until any proceedings in pursuance of that application (including any proceedings on appeal) are concluded. Under the previous legislation (s 42(7)) the money was not to be released until the application or criminal proceedings were concluded.

Procedure on forfeiture appeals under POCA

18.105 The appeal is to the Crown Court; and notice must be lodged before the expiration of 30 days from when the order was made. It is a *de novo* hearing, the appeal being by way of rehearing (s 299(3)).

18.106 The judge sits usually with two lay magistrates. The judge must give reasons for the court's decision. The reasoning required will depend on the circumstances of the case but must be enough to show that the court has identified the main issues and how it has resolved them (see *R v Harrow Crown Court ex p Dave* [1994] 1 WLR 98). The Rules on hearing a complaint should be adopted as the procedure of the court for such a hearing.

Appeals in condemnation cases from the magistrates' court

18.107 Both HM Revenue and Customs and the defendant may appeal from the magistrates' court decision to the Crown Court, or in the alternative invite the court to state a case for the High Court on a matter of law (see Sch 3 para 11 to Customs & Excise Management Act 1979 (CEMA)). The Crown Court's jurisdiction and powers of disposal are set out in ss 45 to 48 of the Supreme Court Act 1981.

18.108 On appeal to the Crown Court the hearing is *de novo* (s 79(3) Supreme Court Act 1981) and involves a complete re-hearing of the original case, including oral evidence. Rule 63.2 of the Criminal Procedure Rules sets out the time limit (21 days) and the procedure (written notice to the magistrates' court), appears to have been adopted for use in complaint appeals, albeit the appeal is civil.

The procedure adopted at the hearing is the same as set out in the Magistrates' Courts Rules **18.109** above. Pending the re-hearing, there is no restriction on either Revenue and Customs or the defence obtaining more evidence and adducing new evidence at the appeal. Appeals in condemnation cases, including procedure, are further considered at para 23.130 *et seq* of Chapter 23.

Appeal from the magistrates' court to the High Court by way of case stated

Under the Magistrates' Court Act 1980, s 111(1):   **18.110**

Any person who was a party to any proceedings before a Magistrates' Court or is aggrieved by the conviction, order, determination or other proceeding of the Court may question the proceeding on the ground that it is wrong in law or in excess of jurisdiction by applying to the Justices to state a case for the opinion of the High Court on a question of law or jurisdiction involved . . .

The following points should be noted: **18.111**

(1) The application must be made in writing within 21 days of the sentence and must state the point of law upon which the opinion of the High Court is sought.
(2) There is no power to state a case until the magistrates have reached a final decision in the matter.
(3) The right to appeal to the Crown Court is lost once an application to state a case to the High Court is made (see Magistrates' Court Act 1980, s 111(4)).
(4) The magistrates are entitled to refuse to state a case once requested to do so, but that decision is itself reviewable by the High Court on an application for judicial review (see *R v Huntington Magistrates' Court ex p Percy* (1994) COD 323).

The relevant Criminal Procedure Rules are set out at Pt 64, and deal with, *inter alia*, the **18.112** making of the application; extension of the time limit; service of documents and content.

G. Appeals under Part 6 of POCA: Revenue Functions

An appeal in respect of the exercise by SOCA of general revenue functions shall be to the **18.113** 'Special Commissioners' (s 320(1)), now the First Tier Tax Tribunal. An assessor nominated to assist the Special Commissioners must have special knowledge and experience in the matter to which the appeal relates and must be selected from a panel of persons appointed for the purposes of s 320 by the Lord Chancellor.

This right of appeal is equivalent to those available to taxpayers subjected to decisions **18.114** made by the Revenue. All of the rules against actions arising from the exercise of his powers by SOCA of its revenue functions will be to the Special Commissioners and not to General Commissioners. The Taxes Management Act 1970 enables the Lord Chancellor to regulate by secondary legislation the administration of the Special Commissioner's hearing (s 320(4)).

From 1 April 2009 appeals will be heard by the First-tier Tribunal (Tax). This means **18.115** that the procedural rules of the new First-tier Tribunal (Tax) will apply. However, the

Tribunal has the discretion to disapply some or all of the new procedural rules and to apply some or all of the old procedural rules.

H. The Criminal Cases Review Commission

18.116 The Criminal Cases Review Commission (CCRC) may refer to the Court of Appeal any conviction or sentence. Such a reference is treated as an appeal by the person concerned under the Criminal Appeal Act 1995, s 9, provided that the conditions set out in s 13 of that Act are met. That provides that there is a real possibility that the conviction, finding, or sentence would not be upheld if the reference is made and, in the case of a sentence, on the basis of an argument on a point of law or information not raised in the proceedings. The appeal procedure must have been followed without success, or leave to appeal must have been refused, or there are exceptional circumstances that justify a reference, for a reference to be made.

18.117 If the CCRC forms a negative view about an application it will invite further representations or comments, usually within 20 working days. This period is non-statutory and may be extended upon application to the Commission. However, if further representations are not received within 20 working days (or any extension), or the representations raise no new issues, the case will be closed (see also *Re P* (QBD, 6 November 1998) above).

I. Appeals against Findings of Contempt of Court

Appeals in cases of findings of contempt of court by the High Court

18.118 Under para 21.4 of CPR Practice Direction 52, if an appeal under s 13 of the Administration of Justice Act 1960 is to be made (appeals in cases of contempt of court), the appellant must serve the appellant's notice on the court from whose order or decision the appeal is brought (r 52.4(3)). In the case of appeals from the Queen's Bench Division the notice must be served on the Senior Master of the Queen's Bench Division, and service may be affected by leaving a copy of the notice of appeal with the clerk of the lists. Permission is not required to appeal a committal for contempt of court; the defendant has the right of appeal to the Court of Appeal (Civil Division) either against the sentence imposed for contempt or the finding of contempt itself (see r 52.3 CPR).

18.119 The High Court has the power to grant bail pending the outcome of any appeal. See s 4 of the Administration of Justice Act 1960.

18.120 The powers of the Court of Appeal are found in s 13(3) of the Administration of Justice Act 1960, which reads:

> The court to which an appeal is brought under this section may reverse or vary the order or decision of the court below, and make such other order as may be just; and without prejudice to the inherent powers of any report referred to in subsection 2 of this section, provision may be made by rules of court authorising the release on bail of an appellant under this section.

18.121 There is a further provision for an appeal to the House of Lords under s 13(4) subject to leave.

Appeals in cases of findings of contempt of court by the Crown Court

Section 18A of the Criminal Appeal Act 1968 states that a person who wishes to appeal **18.122** under s 13 of the Administration of Justice Act 1960 from any order or decision of the Crown Court in the exercise of its jurisdiction to punish for contempt of court shall give notice of appeal in such manner as may be directed by the rules of court. Notice of appeal shall be given within 28 days from the date of the order or decision appealed against. The time for giving notice under this section may be extended either before or after expiry by the Court of Appeal (s 18A(3)).

The Court of Appeal may, if they think fit, grant an appellant bail pending the determi- **18.123** nation of his appeal (s 19 of the Criminal Appeal Act 1968). They may also revoke it (s 19(1)(b)).

J. Thumbnail Guide to the Appeal Provisions within the Criminal Procedure Rules

Part 63—Appeals from the Magistrates Court to the Crown Court against conviction or **18.124** sentence:

Notice of appeal	r 63.2
Documents to be sent to Crown Court	r 63.3
Entry of appeal and notice of hearing	r 63.4
Abandonment of appeal—notice	r 63.5
Abandonment of appeal—bail	r 63.6
Number and qualification of justices—appeal from youth court	r 63.7
Number and qualification of justices—dispensation	r 63.8
Disqualification of justices	r 63.9

Part 64—Appeal to the High Court by Way of Case Stated: **18.125**

Application to magistrates' court to state case	r 64.1
Consideration of a draft case by magistrates' court	r 64.2
Preparation and submission of final case for magistrates' court	r 64.3
Extension of time limit by magistrates' court	r 64.4
Service of documents on application to magistrates' court	r 64.5
Content of case stated by magistrates' court	r 64.6
Application to the Crown Court to state case	r 64.7

Part 65—Appeal to the Court of Appeal against ruling in Preparatory Hearing **18.126**
Part 66—Appeal to the Court of Appeal Against Ruling Adverse to the Prosecution
Part 67—Appeal to the Court of Appeal against order restricting reporting or public access
Part 68—Appeal to the Court of Appeal against Conviction or Sentence
Part 69—Reference to the Court of Appeal on a Point of Law
Part 70—Reference to the Court of Appeal of Unduly Lenient Sentence

18.127 Part 71—Appeal to the Court of Appeal under the POCA 2002: General rules:

18.128 Part 72—Appeal to the Court of Appeal under POCA 2002—Prosecutor's Appeal regarding Confiscation:

18.129 Part 73—Appeal to the Court of Appeal under POCA 2002: Restraint or Receivership Orders:

18.130 Part 74—Appeal to the House of Lords:

18.131 Part 75—Reference to the European Court:

K. CJA 1988 and DTA Appeals

Restraint and receivership: practice and procedure

18.132 Under both the DTA and CJA 1988, restraint orders are dealt with exclusively by the High Court and there is a general right of appeal against any such order made by the High Court to the Court of Appeal under s 16 of the Supreme Court Act 1981 (SCA).

18.133 Under s 16 of the SCA any person wishing to appeal a restraint or receivership order (in any of its forms) under the DTA or CJA 1988 has a general right of appeal to the Court of Appeal.

Part 52 of the Civil Procedure Rules and Practice Direction 52, which relates to appeals, **18.134** govern appeal procedure in the High Court. In the Queen's Bench Division an appeal from the High Court judge lies to the Court of Appeal. Permission is required to appeal from a decision of a High Court judge except where the appeal is in respect of a committal order (ie contempt and certain insolvency appeals and certain statutory appeals) (see r 52.3 CPR).

Permission should be sought at the hearing at which the decision to be appealed against **18.135** is made. If it is not, or if it is sought and refused, permission should be sought from the Court of Appeal. If permission is sought from the appeal court, it must be requested in the appellant's notice. Permission may be granted or refused, or granted in part and refused as to the rest (for obtaining permission to appeal, see Practice Direction 52 para 4.1 and r 52.3 CPR).

Rule 52.11(3)(a) and (b) sets out the circumstances in which the appeal court will allow an **18.136** appeal. The grounds of an appeal should set out clearly the reasons why r 52.11(3)(a) or (b) is said to apply (see Practice Direction 52 r 3.1). Rule 52.4 and para 5 of the Practice Directions deal with the appellant's notice (N161), which must be filed and served in all cases.

The appellant must file his notice at the appeal court either within the period specified by **18.137** the High Court or, if no such period is specified, within 14 days of the date of the decision appealed from. The notice must be served on each respondent as soon as practicable, and in any event not later than seven days after it is filed (Practice Direction 52 para 5.19 and r 52.4). Skeleton arguments must be filed with the appellant's notice unless it is impractical for the appellant's skeleton argument to accompany the appellant's notice, in which case it must be lodged and served on all respondents within 14 days of filing the notice (Practice Direction 52 r 5.9 and 5.19).

A respondent who wishes to ask the appeal court to vary the order of the lower court in any **18.138** way must appeal, and permission will be required on the same basis as for an appellant (Practice Direction 52 para 7.1). The respondent's notice must be filed either within a period specified by the lower court or, if no such period is specified, within 14 days (Practice Direction 52 para 7.7). The respondent's notice is form N162.

19

THE INTERNATIONAL ELEMENT

A. Introduction

Organised crime transcends national frontiers more than ever before. Improvements to **19.01** the public transport system make it easier to travel between countries, the advent of the internet and email allows for virtually instantaneous communication of criminal gangs across the world, and, as Ognall J observed in *Re M* (Unreported, 9 July 1993):

> We live in an age where funds may be transferred from jurisdiction to jurisdiction as rapidly as it takes me to speak this sentence.

It is increasingly common, therefore, to find a person prosecuted for criminal offences **19.02** in one country owning assets in another. The aims of the legislation would soon be defeated if criminals could invest their ill-gotten gains in an overseas country without the fear of the same being restrained and ultimately realised in satisfaction of a confiscation order. It is thus not surprising that the legislation bites on assets held all over the world: by s 62(2) of the Drug Trafficking Act 1994 (DTA) the Act 'applies to property whether it is situated in England and Wales or elsewhere'; s 102(3) of the CJA 1988 provides that Pt VI of the Act 'applies to property wherever situated'; and s 84(1) of the Proceeds of Crime Act 2002 (POCA) defines property as being 'all property wherever situated'.

B. International Assistance under the DTA and CJA 1988

19.03 The provisions of the DTA and CJA 1988 and the relevant subordinate legislation apply only to requests for international assistance made before 1 January 2006 and are not therefore considered in detail here. Section 39 of the DTA and s 96 of the CJA 1988 empowered Her Majesty The Queen to make Orders in Council enabling restraint orders to be made in the United Kingdom in support of overseas prosecutions and for confiscation orders made overseas to be enforced against UK held assets. Orders in Council were made under both Acts: the Drug Trafficking Act 1994 (Designated Countries and Territories) Order 1996, SI 1996/2880 under the DTA and the Criminal Justice Act 1988 (Designated Countries and Territories) Order 1991, SI 1991/2873 under the CJA 1988. These orders designated countries on whose behalf restraint orders could be obtained and enforcement action taken to enforce confiscation orders and modified the terms of the Acts for these purposes. For a detailed consideration of these Orders, the reader is referred to Chapter 25 of the second edition of this work.

C. Cooperation under POCA

Preliminary matters

19.04 Sections 443 and 444 of POCA permit Orders in Council to be made permitting the enforcement in the United Kingdom of orders made in other jurisdictions.

19.05 Section 443 relates to Scotland and Northern Ireland and s 444 to other jurisdictions. It is worthy of note that nothing in s 444 requires overseas countries to be designated before orders made in its courts may be enforced in the United Kingdom. The section (as amended by s 108 of the Serious Organised Crime and Police Act 2005 (SOCPA) and para 138 of Sch 8 to the Serious Crime Act 2007) provides:

(1) Her Majesty may by Order in Council—
    (a) make provision for a prohibition on dealing with property which is the subject of an external request;
    (b) make provision for the realisation of property for the purpose of giving effect to an external order.
(2) An order under this section may include provision which (subject to any specified modifications) corresponds to any provisions in Part 2, 3 or 4 or Part 5 except Chapter 3.
(3) An order under this section may include—
    (a) provision about the functions of any of the listed persons in relation to external requests and orders;
    (b) provision about the registration of external orders;
    (c) provision about the authentication of any judgment or order of an overseas court and of any document connected with such a judgment or order or any proceedings relating to it;
    (d) provision about evidence (including evidence required to establish whether proceedings have been started or are likely to be started in an overseas court);
    (e) provision to secure that any person affected by the implementation of an external request or the enforcement of an external order has an opportunity to make representations to a court in the part of the United Kingdom where the request is being implemented or the order is being enforced.
(4) For the purposes of subsection (3)(a) 'the listed persons' are—
    (a) the Secretary of State;
    (b) the Lord Advocate;

(c) the Scottish Ministers;
(d) SOCA;
(e) the Director of Public Prosecutions;
(f) the Director of Public Prosecutions for Northern Ireland;
(g) the Director of the Serious Fraud Office; and
(h) the Director of Revenue and Customs Prosecutions.

19.06 The removal of the requirement for designation is intended to expedite the process of obtaining restraint orders on behalf of overseas countries, enabling any country that identifies assets in the United Kingdom to forward a letter of request seeking a restraint order and, ultimately, confiscation of the property concerned.

19.07 Section 447 defines a number of the key expressions used in s 444. By s 447(1):

An external request is a request by an overseas authority to prohibit dealing with relevant property which is identified in the request.

19.08 By s 447(2):

An external order is an order which—
(a) is made by an overseas court where property is found or believed to have been obtained as a result of or in connection with criminal conduct, and
(b) is for the recovery of specified property or a specified sum of money.

19.09 By s 447(8) criminal conduct is defined as conduct which:

(a) constitutes an offence in any part of the United Kingdom, or
(b) would constitute an offence in any part of the United Kingdom if it occurred there.

19.10 On 1 January 2006 the Proceeds of Crime Act 2002 (External Requests and Orders) Order 2005, SI 2005/3181 ('the 2005 Order') came into force and all international requests made to the UK after that date are dealt with under its provisions. The 2005 Order has since been amended by the Proceeds of Crime Act 2002 (External Requests and Orders) (Amendment) Order 2008, SI 2008/302. The primary purpose of the 2008 Amendment Order is to delete references to the Assets Recovery Agency (ARA) and its Director following the abolition of the Agency by the Serious Crime Act 2007.

Action to be taken on receipt of an external request

19.11 When an external request is received by the Secretary of State in connection with criminal investigations or proceedings in the country from which the request was made and concerning relevant property in England and Wales he may, under Art 6(1) refer it to the Director of Public Prosecutions or the Director of Revenue and Customs Prosecutions to be processed. When the request appears to the Secretary of State to be made in connection with criminal investigations or proceedings which relate to an offence involving serious or complex fraud he may refer it to the Director of the Serious Fraud Office to be processed. The Director to whom the request is referred is described in the Order as 'the relevant Director': see Art 6(4).

Powers of the Crown Court to make restraint orders

19.12 The 2005 Order follows the scheme of POCA by transferring the jurisdiction to make restraint orders and enforce external confiscation orders from the High Court to the

Crown Court. By Art 7(1) the Crown Court may exercise the powers conferred by Art 8 to make restraint orders if either of the following conditions is satisfied:

(2) The first condition is that—
  (a) relevant property in England and Wales is identified in the external request,
  (b) a criminal investigation has been started in the country from which the external request was made with regards to an offence, and
  (c) there is reasonable cause to believe that the alleged offender named in the request has benefited from his criminal conduct.

(3) The second condition is that—
  (a) relevant property in England and Wales is identified in the external request,
  (b) proceedings for an offence have been started in the country from which the external request was made and not concluded, and
  (c) there is reasonable cause to believe that the defendant named in the request has benefited from his criminal conduct.

19.13 If either of these conditions is satisfied, the Crown Court may make a restraint order under Art 8(1) 'prohibiting any specified person from dealing with relevant property which is identified in the external request and specified in the order'. By Art 8(2) the order may be made subject to exceptions and such exceptions may in particular:

(a) make provision for reasonable living expenses and reasonable legal expenses in connection with the proceedings seeking a restraint order or the registration of an external order;
(b) make provision for the purpose of enabling any person to carry on any trade, business, profession or occupation;
(c) be made subject to conditions.

19.14 The terms of Art 8(2)(a) represent a significant departure from the position under the Act itself where, as we have seen, s 41(4) precludes the release of funds to meet legal expenses incurred in relation to the proceedings. It was held in *Customs and Excise Commissioners v S* [2005] 1 WLR 1338 that this prohibition included the restraint proceedings as well as the criminal prosecution. Article 8(2) represents a departure from this rule in relation to restraint orders sought pursuant to external requests, but only in relation to the restraint proceedings or the registration of an external order. The defendant would not, under Art 8(2), be able to apply for the release of restrained funds to defend the criminal proceedings in the overseas jurisdiction making the request.

19.15 Article 8(2)(c) empowers the court to impose conditions subject to which funds are released under Art 2(a) and (b). This would allow the court to release funds subject to the '65 per cent rule' whereby, if the prosecutor is not satisfied that the amount claimed has been actually, reasonably and properly incurred, the claim is referred for detailed assessment by a costs judge with 65 per cent of the sum claimed paid in the interim. Similarly, Art 8(2)(c) would empower the court to require a defendant to provide the prosecutor with banking records on a regular basis as a condition precedent to releasing funds for the purpose of allowing a business to continue trading legitimately pending the conclusion of proceedings.

19.16 The 2005 Order does not empower the Crown Court to make restraint orders prohibiting any dealing in assets located outside England and Wales. The House of Lords so held in dismissing an appeal by the Serious Fraud Office (SFO) in *King v Director of the Serious Fraud Office* [2009] UKHL 19. In that case a restraint order had been made against the defendant on the application of the SFO. It followed a request made by the National Prosecuting Authority of South Africa by whom he was being prosecuted for alleged fraud and exchange control offences. The restraint order related to all property held by the defendant, inside and outside England and Wales. In addition, it contained a disclosure provision requiring him to disclose all property he held, again both inside and outside England and Wales. The Crown Court judge found that because the Letter of Request from South Africa had requested an order that 'the defendants must not in any way dispose of, deal with or diminish the value of their assets whether they are in or outside England and Wales' it was their intention to seek a worldwide restraint order. The judge found he had power to make the order because the condition imposed by Art 7 of the 2005 Order, that relevant property in England and Wales should be identified in the request, was merely a 'gateway to the exercise of his jurisdiction'. He held that, once through the gateway, Art 8 gave the court power to make an order prohibiting the defendant from dealing with relevant property identified in the request regardless of whether it was located inside or outside England and Wales.

19.17 The defendant appealed against the judge's ruling to the Court of Appeal. The Court of Appeal allowed the appeal, holding that the 2005 Order did not give the Crown Court power to make restraint orders in relation to assets held outside England and Wales or to require the defendant to disclose assets held outside the jurisdiction. The Court held that Art 8(1) of the 2005 Order can only relate to relevant property held in England and Wales. The Court therefore quashed the restraint order made by the Crown Court and, in its place, substituted an order restraining the defendant from dealing with any of his assets in England and Wales.

19.18 The SFO appealed against this decision to the House of Lords, but the appeal was unanimously dismissed. Counsel for the SFO relied on the aims of the United Nations Convention against Illicit Traffic in Narcotic Drugs and Psychotropic Substances to which the UK became a signatory in 1988 and the European Convention on Mutual Assistance in Criminal Matters ratified in 1991. He drew attention to the fact that, a year later, the UK had ratified the Council of Europe Convention on Laundering, Search, Seizure and Confiscation of the Proceeds from Crime. Counsel submitted that these conventions committed the UK to give cooperation to the widest extent possible for the purposes of investigations and proceedings aimed at the confiscation of the instrumentalities and proceeds of crime. He contended that these obligations had been recognised by the Orders in Council made under the CJA 1988 and DTA which enabled external restraint orders to be made on a worldwide basis. It would, Counsel submitted, 'be extraordinary' to conclude that Parliament, when enacting POCA, intended to narrow the scope of the legislative powers to investigate and recover criminal assets.

19.19 Counsel for the defendant challenged the contention that restraint orders made pursuant to the 2005 Order had extra-territorial effect. He submitted that there was good reason why the scope of the 2005 Order should be restricted to assets held within the jurisdiction. He contended that if a country wishes to seek assistance from other countries in preserving or recovering property related to criminal activity, it made sense for its request to each of those countries to be restricted to the provision of assistance in relation to property located within its own jurisdiction. Counsel contended that if each country were requested to take steps to procure the preservation or recovery of property on a worldwide basis it would lead to a confusing and possibly conflicting overlap of international requests for assistance. He submitted that this would not only be confusing, but would involve significant and unnecessary multiplication of effort and expense.

19.20 The House of Lords found that there was 'obvious force' in the defendant's submissions. Their Lordships also noted the contents of the Explanatory Memorandum to the 2005 Order to the effect that it relates to property within the United Kingdom. Lord Phillips said:

> While this is not a legitimate aid to the interpretation of the language that Parliament has used it does counter [Counsel for the SFO's] submission that it would be extraordinary to conclude that Parliament had intended to restrict the scope of the Order in this way.

19.21 Lord Phillips reviewed all the powers the 2005 Order bestows on the Crown Court and said:

> These provisions amount to a clear and coherent scheme. From first to last the powers conferred by that part of the Order that relates to England and Wales can only be exercised in relation to property in England and Wales. Furthermore, no machinery is provided for exercise of those powers outside England Wales. In this respect there is a significant distinction between POCA, which deals with domestic orders, and the Order, which deals with external orders. Section 74 of POCA provides that if the prosecutor believes that there is realisable property situated in a country outside the United Kingdom he can ask the Secretary of State to forward a request for assistance in restraining dealing with the property or in realising the property. Had it been intended that external restraint orders or external orders should take effect outside the jurisdiction the order would surely have made provision similar to that in section 74 of the Act.

19.22 Lord Phillips said that he could 'see no logic' in the proposition that the requirement that the external request should relate to relevant property in England and Wales was a gateway that gave access to a worldwide jurisdiction. It followed from this that the Crown Court has no power to restrain assets held outside the jurisdiction when making a restraint order under the 2005 Order and no power to make a disclosure order requiring the defendant to disclose the existence of assets held outside England and Wales. The appeal by the SFO was therefore dismissed.

19.23 When seeking restraint, management receivership, and disclosure orders under the 2005 Order, prosecutors must therefore ensure that they are limited in extent to assets located in England and Wales. It is submitted that the House of Lords ruling in *King* must be a correct interpretation of the 2005 Order. To have held to the contrary could have resulted in overseas law enforcement agencies 'forum shopping' and choosing the Courts of England and Wales as a forum of convenience in which they can seek to restrain the defendant from dealing with all his assets located anywhere in the world simply because he has some tenuous connection with the country, for example, by holding one low value asset within the jurisdiction.

Ancillary orders

19.24 Article 8(1) empowers the court to make such order as it believes is appropriate for the purpose of ensuring the restraint order is effective. In the light of the decision of the House of Lords in *King v Director of the Serious Fraud Office* [2009] UKHL 17, it is submitted that this power is confined to making orders requiring the defendant to provide a disclosure statement disclosing all assets held by him within the jurisdiction.

Applications for and the discharge of restraint orders

By Art 9(1)(a) applications for restraint orders under the order can only be made by the **19.25** Director of Public Prosecutions, the Director of Revenue and Customs Prosecutions, or the Director of the Serious Fraud Office. The application may be made *ex parte* to a judge in chambers (see Art 9(1)(b).

The relevant Director and any person affected by the order may apply for the restraint order **19.26** to be varied or discharged. The order must be discharged if no external confiscation order is made (Art 9(5)), if no external confiscation order is registered within a reasonable time (Art 9(6)), or if proceedings for an offence are not started within a reasonable time when the order has been obtained on the basis that the defendant is subject to a criminal investigation (Art 9(7)).

Appeals

Article 10 makes provision for the relevant Director and parties affected by restraint orders **19.27** to appeal against decisions of the Crown Court to the Court of Appeal and Art 11 provides for a further appeal to the House of Lords.

Hearsay evidence

Article 13 makes provision for the admissibility of hearsay evidence in restraint proceed- **19.28** ings subject to the terms of ss 2 to 4 of the Civil Evidence Act 1995.

Management receivers

Articles 15 and 16 empower the court to appoint management receivers on the same basis **19.29** as under the 2002 Act. The provisions are not therefore considered in detail in this chapter. The application may be made at the same time as the application for a restraint order or any time thereafter (see Art 15(1)(b).

Procedural matters

Part 57.15 of the Criminal Procedure Rules 2005 provides that Pts 57, 59, 60, 61, and 71 **19.30** shall apply with the necessary modifications to applications under the 2005 Order in the same way as they apply to the corresponding provisions under Pt 2 of POCA.

It is important to note that the duty of full and frank disclosure applies equally to applica- **19.31** tions for restraints under the 2005 Order as it does to applications in domestic cases under POCA. The relevant Director should therefore be vigilant to ensure that the overseas authority on whose behalf he is making the application has provided all the information the court will require to discharge this duty. The court will not, however, discharge a restraint order on this basis unless the failure to give full and frank disclosure goes to a matter central to the proceedings. As Buxton LJ said in *Government of India v Ottavio Quattrocchi* [2004] EWCA Civ 40, a case decided under the old legislation:

> Complaint was made in the court below, and initially before us, that there had been non-disclosure of various matters, in particular before Moses J. First, there had been late

disclosure of the Indian statutory provisions, secondly, there had been a mistake about when Mr. Quattrocchi left India; and, thirdly, that Moses J had not been properly informed as to the status of these matters by the Crown Prosecution Service. All those matters did not affect the outcome of the case, as Counsel was fair enough to accept. If one needs to go further than that, one merely needs to refer to the authority of this court of *Brinks Mat Ltd v Elcombe* [1988] 1 WLR 1350 in which the principles to be followed by the court are set out: in particular that non-disclosure is not of itself a ground for refusing the application provided that it does not go to a central matter.

19.32 The Criminal Division of the Court of Appeal adopted a similar approach in *Director of the Serious Fraud Office v A* [2007] EWCA Crim 1927. The SFO obtained a restraint order against the defendant under the 2005 Order following receipt of a letter of request from Iran alleging that the defendant was guilty of a large scale fraud on an Iranian government agency, the State Purchasing Organisation, and offences of bribery or corruption of at least one of its officers. It was alleged that the defendant obtained $120 million dollars by means of the fraud and a corrupt relationship with the State Purchasing Organisation. Some of the money, it was alleged, could be traced to the purchase of a property in Mayfair, London. The Crown Court made a restraint order against the defendant on the application of the SFO. When making the order, the Judge had before him a copy of the letter of request which came from an Iranian judge who described himself as the 'judge appointed by the Head of the Judiciary in the Islamic Republic of Iran to investigate and take all necessary steps in the investigation of a serious and complex fraud committed against the State Purchasing Organisation'.

19.33 On an application by the defendant, the Crown Judge later discharged the restraint order on the basis that there had been a failure to give full and frank disclosure of all material facts. The failure which led the judge to discharge the order was that it had not been disclosed in the original letter of request that it came from the military branch of the Iranian judicial organisation. In discharging the order, the judge said:

> Having considered carefully the competing arguments in the authorities, I am firmly of the opinion that the fact that this external request emanated from the Military Branch of the Judicial Organisation is a matter which I would have taken into account in the exercise of my discretion. It is a factor which would have influenced the decision I would have come to. The jurisdiction I was being asked to exercise is exorbitant and its effects draconian. I view the lack of candour by the overseas authority very seriously indeed. It should have been made plain in the letter of request what the position was. The status of the requestor is not some minor matter which can be put into the category of mere oversight or lapse of memory, curable by subsequent disclosure. It goes to the heart of the matter and leads me without hesitation to discharge the restraint order.

19.34 The Court of Appeal allowed an appeal by the SFO against the judge's decision to discharge the order, holding that the non-disclosure complained of by the defendant was not material. Hughes LJ said:

> In the absence of any findings by the Judge on these issues of Iranian standards, the difficulty lies in ascertaining why he found that the fact that the investigating judge was in this instance operating within the framework of the military courts made a crucial difference to whether a restraint order should be made. If the investigating judge's explanation of his own position and of the nature of the investigation is correct, it is not easy to see why it should. *If* he is right,

it is not easy to see why it makes a significant difference that, as a career lawyer, he is in this instance investigating a case proceeding within the military court structure when he operates in a similar way in what he says is a parallel system of civil courts governed essentially by the same rules. *If* he is right, it is not easy to see why even if the investigator were a military officer that makes a significant difference where the trial will be before a properly constituted civil court. It might or might not be different if the defendant were being investigated by a biased or politically motivated officer with a view to a show trial with a pre-ordained end. But there is no finding that that is the case, or even that the contrary has not been sufficiently shown.

Hughes LJ concluded: **19.35**

> If the conclusion drawn in the Crown Court had been one of deliberate deception, then providing there was sufficient reason for reaching it that might well provide a basis for discharging the restraint order, but in the absence of such a conclusion and, if it be reached, consideration whether or no the order should stand on its merits, we are unable to say that the Judge directed himself correctly. The proper course is for the Judge's decision to discharge the restraint order to be quashed and the application for discharge to be remitted to the Crown Court for re-determination in the light of this judgment.

The decision in *Serious Fraud Office v A* notwithstanding, it is submitted that those charged **19.36** with the responsibility of applying for restraint orders on behalf of overseas law enforcement agencies should consider the letter of request with great care before proceeding to ensure that full and frank disclosure of all material facts has been given. The relevant Director is not merely a 'rubber stamp' for the requesting authority and, if the letter of request is defective or does not contain sufficient information, he should not hesitate to seek full and frank disclosure before proceeding.

The court will not, in deciding whether to make a restraint order, allow itself to become **19.37** embroiled in detailed argument as to the merits of the proceedings brought in the requesting country. In *Government of India v Ottavio Quattrocchi* [2004] EWCA Civ 40, a case concerning the old legislation, Buxton LJ said of the requirement that it must be shown that an external confiscation order may be made in the proceedings:

> Further, the statute says 'may'. That does not mean 'will be made'. All that is required is that in the future such an order may be made. Without trying to paraphrase the Act further, I would say in general terms that an external confiscation order can be made when the English court concludes, on evidence, that there is a reasonable possibility of an Indian confiscation order eventually occurring. That the matter should be put comparatively low is only to be expected when one is dealing with what is a preliminary act, that is to say a restraint or charging order. If it were necessary to obtain the level of proof for which Counsel argued, these valuable provisions would be rendered largely ineffective.

Applications to give effect to external orders

Articles 20 to 22 make provision for giving effect to external orders. By Art 2, 'external **19.38** order' has the meaning given to it in s 447(2) of POCA. Section 447(2) provides as follows:

(2) An external order is an order which—
  (a) is made by an overseas court where property is found or believed to have been obtained as a result of or in connection with criminal conduct, and
  (b) is for the recovery of specified property or a specified sum of money.

19.39   By Art 20(1), the relevant Director may make application to the Crown Court to give effect to an external order. The application shall include a request to appoint the relevant Director as the enforcement authority for the order and the application may be made *ex parte* to a judge in chambers (see Art 20(3)). By Art 20(2), no application to give effect to an external order may be made otherwise than in accordance with Art 20(1). This provision effectively precludes overseas law enforcement agencies from making their own direct applications to the Crown Court to give effect to their orders; such applications may only be made by the relevant Director.

19.40   Article 21 sets out the conditions that must be satisfied for the Crown Court to give effect to external orders. It provides:

(1) The Crown Court must decide to give effect to an external order by registering it where all of the following conditions are satisfied.

(2) The first condition is that the external order was made consequent upon the conviction of the person named in the order and no appeal is outstanding in respect of that conviction.

(3) The second condition is that the external order is in force and no appeal is outstanding in respect of it.

(4) The third condition is that giving effect to the external order would not be incompatible with any of the Convention rights (within the meaning of the Human Rights Act 1998) of any person affected by it.

(5) The fourth condition applies only in respect of an external order which authorises the confiscation of property other than money that is specified in the order.

(6) That condition is that the specified property must not be subject to a charge under any of the following provisions—

(a) section 9 of the Drug Trafficking Offences Act 1986;

(b) section 78 of the Criminal Justice Act 1988;

(c) Article 14 of the Criminal Justice (Confiscation) (Northern Ireland) Order 1990;

(d) section 27 of the Drug Trafficking Act 1994;

(e) Article 32 of the Proceeds of Crime (Northern Ireland) Order 1996.

(7) In determining whether the order is an external order within the meaning of the Act, the Court must have regard to the definitions in subsections (2), (4), (5), (6), (8) and (10) of section 447 of the Act.

(8) In paragraph (3) appeal includes—

(a) any proceedings by way of discharging or setting aside the order, and

(b) an application for a new trial or stay of execution.

19.41   The first condition, set out in Art 21(2), represents a major change from the position that applied under the old legislation to the extent that it requires that the external order was made on the conviction of the person named in it. This is in contrast to the position under the old Designated Countries and Territories Orders where external orders could be registered even if they were made in civil proceedings. Part V of the 2005 Order creates a separate regime for the enforcement of external orders made in civil recovery proceedings. Applications in relation to the enforcement of such orders may only be made to the High Court.

19.42   The third condition specifically requires the court to satisfy itself that giving effect to the order would not be incompatible with the convention rights of anyone affected by it. This was considered by the House of Lords in *Barnette v Government of the United States of America* [2004] UKHL 37, a case involving the old legislation. Under the old legislation, an external order could only be registered if the court was satisfied that enforcing the order in England and Wales would not be contrary to the interests of justice. In the case of *Barnette* it was contended that it would be contrary to the interests of justice to register the order because it would constitute a breach of the defendant's rights under Art 6 of the European Convention of Human Rights (ECHR). The breach complained of was that the US Court of Appeal had summarily dismissed an appeal by the appellant without considering it on the merits because the appellant's wife, Mrs Montgomery, with whom he was co-accused, had fled the jurisdiction and he had failed to comply with an order requiring him to give information and discovery. In consequence, the US Courts applied the 'fugitive disentitlement doctrine' to dismiss the appeal. The US Court of Appeal justified this doctrine in these terms:

> The rationales for this doctrine include the difficulty of enforcement against one not willing to subject himself to the court's authority, the inequity of allowing that 'fugitive' to use the resources of the courts only if the outcome is an aid to him, the need to avoid prejudice to the non fugitive part, and the discouragement of flights from justice.

It was submitted on behalf of the appellant that it was not in the interests of justice to register **19.43** the order because, if the ECHR had been applied in the USA, the order would have been in breach of Art 6 and Art 1 of Protocol 1. The House of Lords held that no such breach had occurred. Firstly, the Court noted that it was difficult to see how registration of the US order could constitute a direct breach of Art 6 since there could be no suggestion that the hearing afforded to the defendant in the registration proceedings failed to meet the requirements of the article. The Court also found that the application of the fugitive disentitlement doctrine did not amount to a breach of the appellant's human rights. Lord Carswell said:

> The fugitive entitlement doctrine is not an arbitrary deprivation of a party's rights to a hearing, but is intended to be a means of securing proper obedience to orders of the court. As Lord Woolf CJ said page 1928, para 35 of his judgment:
>
>> 'Where a party is guilty of contempt of court there may be no other sanction available if he is outside the jurisdiction of the court. The reason for the doctrine being applied by the United States Court of Appeal in Mrs. Montgomery's case was not to vindicate the dignity of the court, but because the court thought that it was the only available sanction which could achieve obedience to the orders of the court.'
>
> Although the application of the fugitive entitlement doctrine may be regarded as failing to secure all the protection required by Article 6 of the Convention, it is a rational approach which has commended itself to the Federal jurisdiction of the United States. As such it could not in my opinion be described by any stretch as a flagrant denial of the appellant's rights or a fundamental breach of that article. It follows that the appellant's argument based on the indirect engagement of the responsibility of the United Kingdom must fail.
>
> The same reasons are relevant in considering the issue of whether it was contrary to the interests of justice to enforce the confiscation order by registering the judgment of the US district court. As Stanley Burnton J and the Court of Appeal have pointed out in their judgments, the appellant was by no means shut out from taking part in the proceedings. The merits of her contentions had been fully considered at first instance and on appeal she filed a brief and was represented by counsel. When the issue of fugitive disentitlement was raised by the court she was able to file a brief relating to this issue. Moreover, it seems to me a material consideration that the US Court of Appeal found that she had been taking active steps to hide assets and transfer funds in an effort to evade the forfeiture judgment.

Registration of the order

19.44 Where the Crown Court decides to give effect to an external order, Art 22(1) provides that the court must:

(a) register the order in that court;
(b) provide for notice of the registration to be given to any person affected by it; and
(c) appoint the relevant Director as the enforcement authority.

19.45 If the order being registered is for a sum of money expressed in a currency other than sterling, the amount to be recovered is taken to be the sterling equivalent calculated in accordance with the rate of exchange prevailing at the end of the working day immediately preceding the day when the Crown Court registered the order: see Art 25(2). The sterling equivalent is to be calculated by the relevant director: see Art 25(3). The notice of registration required to be served under Art 22(1)(b) must specify the sterling amount that is required to be paid: see Art 25(4).

19.46 By Art 22(3), the Crown Court may cancel the registration of the order or vary the property to which it applies on the application of the relevant Director or any person affected by it and, under Art 22(4), must cancel the registration if it appears that the order has been satisfied.

Appeals

19.47 Article 23 makes provision for the relevant Director and any person affected by a registration to appeal to the Court of Appeal and Art 24 provides for a further appeal to the House of Lords.

Enforcement of the order

19.48 By Art 26(2), payment of the external order is due on the day notice of registration is served. If the registration of the order is subject to an appeal to the Court of Appeal or House of Lords, the duty to pay is delayed until the day on which the appeal is determined or withdrawn (Art 26(3)).

19.49 Further, by Art 26(4) a person affected by an external order can, once it has been registered, apply to the court for time to pay. If the person affected shows that he needs time to pay, the Crown Court may allow payment to be made in a specified period which must not exceed six months. If, within that period, the person can show 'exceptional circumstances' the court may approve a further extension provided the total period allowed for payment does not exceed 12 months: see Art 26(7).

19.50 Once an external order has been registered and any time to pay allowed by the Crown Court has expired, it may be enforced in similar ways to domestic confiscation orders: in particular Art 27 gives the court power to appoint enforcement receivers. As these provisions are in identical terms to those in relation to the appointment of enforcement receivers in domestic cases, considered in detail in Chapter 11 above, they are not considered separately in this chapter.

Outgoing requests: enforcement abroad

19.51 Thus far, we have considered only the position where an overseas jurisdiction seeks assistance in the restraint and realisation of assets located in England and Wales. POCA also makes provision for letters of request to be sent to overseas countries seeking similar assistance in cases where defendants being prosecuted in England and Wales hold assets overseas against which restraint and enforcement action is sought. This is dealt with in s 74 of POCA which makes provision both in respect of the position before and after a confiscation order is made. Section 74 (as amended by para 35 of Sch 8 to the Serious Crime Act 2007) provides:

(1) This section applies if—
    (a) any of the conditions in section 40 is satisfied,
    (b) the prosecutor believes that realisable property is situated in a country or territory outside the United Kingdom (the receiving country), and
    (c) the prosecutor sends a request for assistance to the Secretary of State with a view to it being forwarded under this section.
(2) In a case where no confiscation order has been made, a request for assistance is a request to the government of the receiving country to secure that any person is prohibited from dealing with realisable property.
(3) In a case where a confiscation order has been made and has not been satisfied, discharged or quashed, a request for assistance is a request to the government of the receiving country to secure that—
    (a) any person is prohibited from dealing with realisable property;
    (b) realisable property is realised and the proceeds are applied in accordance with the law of the receiving country.
(4) No request for assistance may be made for the purposes of this section in a case where a confiscation order has been made and has been satisfied, discharged or quashed.
(5) If the Secretary of State believes it is appropriate to do so he may forward the quest for assistance to the government of the receiving country.
(6) If property is realised in pursuance of a request under subsection (3) the amount ordered to be paid under the confiscation order must be taken to be reduced by an amount equal to the proceeds of realisation.
(7) A certificate purporting to be issued by or on behalf of the requested government is admissible as evidence of the facts it states if it states—
    (a) that property has been realised in pursuance of a request under subsection (3),
    (b) the date of realisation, and
    (c) the proceeds of realisation.
(8) If the proceeds of realisation made in pursuance of a request under subsection (3) are expressed in a currency other than sterling, they must be taken to be the sterling equivalent calculated in accordance with the rate of exchange prevailing at the end of the day of realisation.

19.52   Section 74 provides for a similar scheme to that applicable under the old legislation in relation to outgoing letters of request. Prior to the making of a confiscation order, a letter of request may only seek the restraint of assets held overseas by the defendant: see s 74(2). Once a confiscation order is made, however, the letter of request may seek both the restraint or assets and their realisation in satisfaction of the confiscation order. Once assets have been realised overseas in satisfaction of a confiscation order, the amount realised must be deducted from the amount due under the order: see s 74(6).

19.53   Section 74 is, of course, without prejudice to the right of the prosecutor to enforce the order by the employment of domestic remedies. He may, for example, require the defendant to bring back assets to the jurisdiction pursuant to a repatriation order, or an enforcement receiver may, pursuant to his order of appointment, require the defendant to sign such documents as are necessary to enable him to realise overseas assets and pay the proceeds into court in England and Wales. The remedy adopted by the receiver will inevitably depend on the facts of individual cases and the extent and speed of cooperation particular countries are able to offer. The letter of request route inevitably takes time and, if there is an immediate risk of dissipation, the prosecutor or receiver would be well advised to use the repatriation route in relation to a defendant who is within the jurisdiction and can be brought before the court swiftly for contempt of court should he refuse to comply. If, on the other hand, there is no risk of dissipation and an asset is located in a country that is able to respond effectively and expeditiously to a letter of request, the prosecutor should normally pursue the letter of request route specifically provided for under s 74.

D. Enforcement of POCA Confiscation Orders in Different Parts of the UK

19.54 Under the Proceeds of Crime Act 2002 (Enforcement in different parts of the United Kingdom) Order 2002, SI 2002/3133 orders made in England, Wales, Scotland, and Northern Ireland automatically have effect throughout the UK, but enforcement proceedings can only be brought if the orders are registered:

(a) in the Crown Court for England and Wales;
(b) the Court of Session for Scotland;
(c) the High Court for Northern Ireland.

19.55 Once registration is effective, the court has the same powers of enforcement it would have if the order had been made in that jurisdiction.

20

MONEY LAUNDERING

A. Introduction

No study of the law relating to the proceeds of crime would be complete without considering **20.01**
the provisions in the legislation that make the laundering of money a criminal offence.
The importance of this area of the law was underlined in *Bank of Scotland v A* [2001] 1
WLR 751 where the Court of Appeal stated:

> Money laundering is an increasingly common problem of large scale crime. It is of the
> greatest importance, in the public interest, that the police should be supported by financial
> institutions in their attempts to prevent money laundering and to detect it when it
> happens.

20.02   In this chapter we consider the money laundering provisions within the Proceeds of Crime Act 2002 (POCA) and the European directives relating to same. In the next chapter we look at the tipping-off provisions and the disclosure of suspicious transactions by the professions and the regulated sector.

20.03   The money laundering sections of Pt 7 of POCA came into force on 24 February 2003 (SI 2003/120). These principal money laundering offences do not have effect where the conduct constituting the offence began before 24 February 2003. In those cases the previous legislation, namely the Drug Trafficking Act 1994 (DTA), the Criminal Justice Act 1993 (CJA), and the Criminal Justice (International Co-operation) Act 1990, continue to have effect.

20.04   All of these Acts were introduced to meet the UK's obligation under Art 9 of the 1991 European Community Directive on the Prevention of the Use of the Financial System for the purpose of Money Laundering (Council Directive (EC) (1991/308)), which required contracting States to establish drug money laundering offences. This Directive, together with the Money Laundering Regulations 1993, was supplemented by the Council Directive (EC) 2001/97 (the second EC Directive) and the Money Laundering Regulations 2001, SI 2001/3641. (The international and domestic history of offences relating to laundering drugs money is considered in some detail by the House of Lords in *R v Montila* [2004] UKHL 50.)

20.05   The purpose of the 1991 Directive was the prevention of the use of the financial system for the purpose of money laundering. Article 2 provided that 'member states shall ensure that money laundering as defined in this Directive is prohibited'. Article 1 explained the phrase 'money laundering' embraced four different types of intentional conduct. These may be described as 'conversion or transfer', 'concealment or disguise', 'acquisition, possession or use', and 'participation'.

20.06   The second EC Directive, for its part, amended the 1991 Directive in a number of important ways. Paragraphs 1 to 15 of its recital explain the reasons why the steps required to combat money laundering needed to be enlarged. Paragraph 13 refers to evidence that the tightening of controls in the financial sector had prompted money launderers to seek alternative methods for concealing the origin of the proceeds of crime. Paragraph 14 speaks of trends towards the increased use by money launderers of non-financial businesses. And para 15 states that the obligations of the 1991 Directive concerning customer identification, record keeping, and the reporting of suspicious transactions should be extended to a limited number of activities and professions, which had been shown to be vulnerable to money laundering.

20.07   Article 1 of the 1991 Directive, as amended by the 2001 Directive, defines money laundering as meaning the following conduct when committed intentionally:

    (a) The conversion or transfer of property, knowing that such property is derived from criminal activity or from an act of participation in such activity, for the purpose of concealing or disguising the illicit origin of the property or of assisting any person who is involved in the commission of such activity to evade the legal consequences of his actions;

    (b) The concealment or disguise of the true nature, source, location, disposition, movement, rights with respect to, or ownership of property, knowing that such property is derived from criminal activity or from an act of participation in such activity;

(c) The acquisition, possession or use of property, knowing, at the time of receipt that such property was derived from criminal activity or from an act of participation in such activity;

(d) Participation in, association to commit, attempts to commit and aiding, abetting, facilitating and counselling the commission of any of the actions mentioned in the foregoing indents;

(e) Knowledge, intent or purpose required as an element of the above-mentioned activities may be inferred from objective factual circumstances.

Brooke LJ in *Bowman v Fels* [2005] EWCA Civ 226 emphasised that the 1991 and 2001 Council Directives were important to POCA's proper understanding. The Court interpreted 'so far as possible, the Act in the light of the wording and the purpose of the Directives in order to achieve the result pursued by the latter'. **20.08**

In his Lordship's judgment it was open to the UK Parliament to go further than the Directives and in some respects, in the Court's opinion, they did (see para 44). In particular, the UK legislation defined money laundering to include property known 'or suspected' to constitute or represent a benefit from criminal activity and apply it to the benefits of any type of criminal conduct (see s 330(3) of the 2002 Act). The extended definition of money laundering in the UK legislation (to embrace circumstances of suspicion) involved abandoning the distinction drawn in the Directives between money laundering and the requirement that the institutions and persons subject to the Directives should 'refrain from carrying out transactions which they know or suspect to be related to money laundering' (see also Case C-106/89 *Marleasing SA v LA Comercial Internacional de Alinentacion SA* [1990] ECR I-4135, para 8). **20.09**

The money laundering provisions of POCA were significantly amended by the Serious Organised Crime and Police Act 2005 (SOCPA). From 1 April 2006 the National Criminal Intelligence Service (NCIS) ceased to exist and its functions and staff were absorbed into the Serious Organised Crime Agency (SOCA). One of the difficulties with the reporting regime was that NCIS was inundated with insignificant and unnecessary suspicious activity reports (SARS) in relation to suspected money laundering or terrorist property offences. That burden remains for SOCA. **20.10**

Sections 364 and 415 of POCA are amended by s 107 of SOCPA so that the meaning of money laundering offences includes the principal money laundering offences that were in force before the 2002 Act. This will enable the investigation powers in Pt 8 of the Act to be used in investigating old money laundering offences. **20.11**

The Third EC Directive on Money Laundering (Directive 2005/60/EC) is considered at the end of this chapter. **20.12**

What is money laundering?

Money laundering is the process by which monies derived from criminal activities are converted into funds or assets which appear to have an apparently legitimate source. Money laundering was first made a criminal offence in relation to monies derived from drug trafficking by the Drug Trafficking Offences Act 1986 (DTOA). Subsequent legislation, notably the CJA 1988 and the DTA 1994 extended the number and ambit of these offences. POCA was intended to simplify and consolidate the existing statutory scheme. **20.13**

Why criminalise money laundering?

20.14   It has often been said that there would be fewer burglary offences committed if there were not those willing and able to receive and dispose of stolen property. Similarly, there would be less financially motivated crime committed if the criminal did not have at his disposal the means of concealing the origin of the proceeds of such offences by money laundering. The absence of legislation to prevent money laundering can result in a loss of confidence in a country's financial institutions as criminals invest and transfer the proceeds of crime through banks with impunity. Furthermore, legitimate banks do not wish to have accounts they maintain tainted with the proceeds of crime, and many have withdrawn from countries where money laundering has not been made illegal and where they are powerless to report suspicious transactions to law enforcement agencies without fear of an action for breach of confidence by the client. The absence of money laundering legislation can also serve to destabilise the political system of a country. The success of any terrorist organisation, for example, depends on its ability to raise and launder monies to fund their activities.

How is money laundered?

20.15   Money laundering techniques vary in their degree of sophistication from the most simplistic to the highly complex. In its simplest form, money laundering occurs where a relative of a criminal, motivated by a misplaced sense of loyalty, agrees to pass the proceeds of a criminal enterprise through a bank account. The most sophisticated laundering operations involve the creation of front companies, trusts, etc, and the creation of bogus transactions to give the impression that monies come from a legitimate source. Most money laundering schemes can, however, be divided into three stages regardless of the degree of complexity: placement, layering, and integration.

Placement

20.16   At the placement stage, the launderer disposes of the so-called 'dirty money'. Cash is the most common medium of exchange used for many types of criminal transactions, particularly those related to drugs. As cheques, credit cards, and other non-cash means are now used to finance the majority of legitimate transactions, the money launderer who carries out a large financial transaction in cash risks drawing undesired attention to his illegally acquired money. He thus attempts through placement to put his funds into the financial system unnoticed, for example by engaging a number of people to make a series of small deposits on his behalf (a process known as 'smurfing') or by physically transporting the cash out of the country. It is at the placement stage that illegally acquired funds are most vulnerable to detection.

Layering

20.17   After the funds have entered the financial system, the launderer further separates the illicit proceeds from their illegal source through layering. Layering occurs by conducting a series of financial transactions that, by reason of their frequency, volume, or complexities resemble legitimate financial transactions. The ultimate aim at this stage of the laundering process is to make tracing the funds back to their 'dirty' source as difficult as possible.

Integration

At the final integration stage, the launderer integrates the illicit funds into the economy. **20.18**
He does this in such a way that the funds at this juncture appear to have originated from an
entirely legal source, such as legitimate business earnings. At this stage the launderer has
provided a legitimate explanation for the criminally derived funds, and distinguishing
between legitimate and illicit funds proves extremely difficult, if not impossible to achieve.
The profits may then be invested in other criminal enterprises, or assets and property, or
used to support an extravagant lifestyle.

B. Money Laundering under the Proceeds of Crime Act 2002

Introduction

Part 7 of POCA introduces three principal money laundering offences: **20.19**

(a) s 327, concealing, disguising, converting, transferring, or removing from England and
     Wales criminal property;
(b) s 328, becoming concerned in an arrangement which a person knows or suspects
     facilitates the acquisition, retention, use, or control of criminal property by or on
     behalf of another person; and
(c) s 329, acquiring, using, or having possession of criminal property.

All of these money laundering offences apply to the laundering of an offender's own proceeds of crime, as well as those of someone else. The maximum sentence for these money
laundering offences is 14 years' imprisonment (see s 334).

Part 7 of POCA came into force on 24 February 2003 (SI 2003/120). The DTA and CJA **20.20**
money laundering offences continue to be the principal Acts for all offences committed
before that date (or which cross over that date), although these are becoming the exception
due to the passage of time since the introduction of POCA.

The ingredients of the offence

Sections 327 to 329 require proof that the conduct concerned involves 'criminal property'. **20.21**
Property is criminal property if it constitutes a person's benefit from criminal conduct, or
it represents such a benefit (whether directly or indirectly), and the alleged offender knows
or suspects that it constitutes such a benefit (s 340(3)).

In *R v Da Silva* [2006] EWCA Crim 1654, 2 Cr App R 35, the Court of Appeal held that **20.22**
for a defendant to be convicted of an offence under s 93A(1)(a) of the CJA, he or she must
think that there is a 'possibility, which is more than fanciful, that the relevant facts exist'.
This is subject, the Court held, to the further requirement that the suspicion so formed
should be of 'a settled nature'. The court added, in the absence of a statutory definition, the
dictionary definition would be likely to be an appropriate starting place.

The word 'suspect' is given various meanings in the Oxford English Dictionary. These include: **20.23**

(1) an impression of the existence or presence of;
(2) believe tentatively without clear ground;

(3) be inclined to think;

(4) be inclined to mentally accuse; doubt the innocence of;

(5) doubt the genuineness or truth of a suspected person.

20.24 In *K Ltd v National Westminster Bank* [2006] EWCA Civ 1039 the Court noted that there was no legal definition within the Act of what 'suspicion' or 'suspect' should be held to mean, but confirmed that if the definition in *Da Silva* was sufficient for criminal cases, it was also sufficient for civil cases (para 16).

Inchoate offences

20.25 Under s 340(11) of POCA, money laundering is an act which is not only defined by the three substantive offences, but is extended to all inchoate offences relating to them:

(11) Money laundering is an act which—

(a) constitutes an offence under sections 327, 328 or 329,

(b) constitutes an attempt, conspiracy or incitement to commit an offence specified in paragraph (a),

(c) constitutes aiding, abetting, counselling or procuring the commission of an offence specified in paragraph (a), or

(d) would constitute an offence specified in paragraph (a), (b) or (c) if done in the United Kingdom.

Proof

20.26 In *R v Saik* [2006] 2 WLR 993 it was confirmed that the *mens rea* required for an offence of conspiracy to launder money was knowledge of its illicit origins. The House of Lords held that a mere suspicion that property might be the proceeds of crime was insufficient to establish guilt of conspiracy to engage in money laundering. To establish guilt, the Court held the accused had to be aware that the property involved was in fact the proceeds of crime or, in the case of unidentifiable property, intend that it should be. Lord Nicholls held that Parliament could not have intended that a person would be liable for conspiracy where he lacked the knowledge required to commit the substantive offence. When knowledge of a material fact was an ingredient of a substantive offence, it was also an ingredient of the crime of conspiracy to commit that offence. He went on to state that the ingredient of the substantive offence in s 93C(2) of the CJA was that the property in question had to emanate from a crime (*R v Montila* [2004] 1 WLR 3141). The prosecution had to prove that the conspirator had intended or known that that fact would exist when the conspiracy was carried out. Hence, where the property had not been identified when the conspiracy agreement had been reached, the prosecution had to prove that the conspirator had intended that it would become the proceeds of criminal conduct.

20.27 In *R v Anwoir* [2008] 2 Cr App R 36 the Court of Appeal held (giving effect to *Director of the Assets Recovery Agency v Green* The Times, 27 February 2006 and *R v Craig* [2007] EWCA Crim 2913), that the Crown may prove the property was 'criminal property' by showing either that it derived from conduct of a specific kind (or kinds) and that conduct of that kind was unlawful, or by evidence that the circumstances in which the property was handled were such as to give rise to an irresistible inference that it could only be derived from crime (para 21). *Anwoir* was subsequently followed in *R v F* [2009] Crim LR 45.

Conspiracy

In *R v Ali Hussain* [2005] EWCA Crim 87, the Court of Appeal held that offences under **20.28** s 49(2) DTA and s 93C(2) CJA, required proof that a defendant was in fact dealing with the proceeds of drug trafficking or other criminal conduct. A jury could only convict of conspiracy if the defendant knew he was dealing with the proceeds of drug trafficking or other criminal conduct and mere grounds to suspect were not enough. The Court stated (at para 151) that the consequence of their decision was that the prosecution has a heavier burden to discharge than it would have in order to prove the substantive offence.

In *R v Montila* [2004] UKHL 50 the House of Lords decided that for offences under **20.29** s 49(2) of the DTA and s 93C(2) of the CJA, it must be proved that the property was in fact the proceeds of drug trafficking or of other criminal conduct (reversing the Court of Appeal's decision). It was not enough that the defendant has reasonable grounds to suspect that the property was the proceeds of drug trafficking or of other criminal conduct, when in fact it is not (or could not be proved to be so). Lord Hope, giving the considered opinion of the committee said at para 27:

> Sub-section (2) states that a person is guilty of an offence 'if knowing or having reasonable grounds to suspect that any property is . . . another person's proceeds of drug trafficking (s 49(2) of the 1994 Act) or of criminal conduct (s 93C(2) of the 1988 Act)' he does one or other of the things described to 'that property' for the purpose which the sub-section identifies. A person may have reasonable grounds to suspect the property is one thing (A) when in fact it is something different (B). But that is not so when the question is what a person knows. A person cannot know that something is A when in fact it is B. The proposition that a person knows that something is A is based on the premise that it is true that it is A. The fact that the property is A provides the starting point. Then there is the question whether the person knows that the property is A.

The Court said a further indication is to be found in the absence of any defence, if the **20.30** property which the defendant is alleged to have known or had reasonable grounds to suspect was another person's proceeds turns out to be something different. Subsequent events may show that the property that he was dealing with had nothing whatever to do with any criminal activity at all, but was the product of a windfall, such as a win on the National Lottery. See also *R v Harmer* [2005] EWCA Crim 1.

In *R v Hussain* the Court of Appeal concluded that *R v Singh* [2003] EWCA Crim 3712 **20.31** did not survive *Montila*. An intention to launder illicitly obtained money is not enough. The money must be proved to have been the proceeds of drug trafficking or other criminal conduct.

In *R v Saik* [2006] 2 WLR 993 the House of Lords found that a conspiracy to commit an **20.32** offence involved an agreement to convert another person's proceeds of criminal conduct. The agreement must be an agreement to do one or more of such acts for one or more of the stated purposes.

Another ingredient of the substantive offence is that the property in question must ema- **20.33** nate from a crime: *R v Montila* [2004] 1 WLR 3141. Lord Nicholls held that the criminal provenance of the property is in fact necessary for the commission of the offence. Hence, where the property has not been identified when the conspiracy agreement is reached, the prosecution must prove the conspirator intended that the property would be the proceeds of criminal conduct (para 23).

20.34 The phrase 'intend or know' in s 1(2) is a provision of general application to all conspiracies: in this context the word 'know' should be interpreted strictly and not watered down.

20.35 In *R v Suchedina* [2006] EWCA Crim 2543, the Court of Appeal held that where a conviction for conspiracy to commit money laundering offences had been obtained in circumstances where the jury had been directed that the offence was made, as to *mens rea*, by proof either of knowledge or of reasonable grounds for suspicion as to the illicit origins of the money, such a conviction could no longer be regarded as safe, in the light of the ruling in *R v Saik*. See also *R v R* [2006] EWCA Crim 1974.

The first money laundering offence: concealing etc

20.36 The intention of s 327 was to simplify and replace s 49 of the DTA and s 93C of the CJA. In so doing, POCA no longer distinguishes between the proceeds of drug trafficking in relation to money laundering and the proceeds of other crimes.

20.37 Under s 327(1) of POCA a person commits a money laundering offence if he:

(a) conceals criminal property;
(b) disguises criminal property;
(c) converts criminal property;
(d) transfers criminal property;
(e) removes criminal property from England or Wales or from Scotland or Northern Ireland.

In relation to s 327(1)(a) and (b) 'concealing' or 'disguising' criminal property includes concealing or disguising its nature, source, location, disposition, movement, or ownership of any rights with respect to it (s 327(3)).

20.38 In *R v Loizou* The Times, 23 June 2005 the Court of Appeal held, *obiter*, that the natural meaning of s 327(1) of POCA is that the property in question had to be criminal property at the time of the transaction. It was not sufficient that the property became criminal property within the meaning of the Act as a result of the transaction.

'Criminal property'

20.39 Criminal property is defined under s 340(3) as follows:

(3) Property is criminal property if—
(a) it constitutes a person's benefit from criminal conduct or it represents such a benefit (in whole or part and whether directly or indirectly), and
(b) if the alleged offender knows or suspects that it constitutes or represents such a benefit.

20.40 In *R v Gabriel* (2007) 1 WLR 2272 the Court of Appeal held that where a person in receipt of state benefits failed to declare income from a legitimate trade in goods to the Inland Revenue and the Department of Work and Pensions (DWP), his profits from the trade itself could not be said to constitute 'criminal property' within the meaning of s 340 of POCA. The failure to declare profits for the purposes of income tax may give rise to an offence, but that did not make the legitimate trading in goods an offence itself. The Court also held that where the prosecution allege that property is criminal property, it was sensible, by giving particulars either in advance or in opening, to set out the facts upon which they rely in the inferences that the jury will be invited to draw. *Gabriel* however was distinguished in *R v IK* (2007) EWCA Crim 491, where the Court found that a person who cheated the Revenue obtained a pecuniary advantage as a result of criminal conduct within the meaning of s 340(6) of POCA and the proceeds of cheating the Revenue could amount to 'criminal property' within the meaning of s 340(5). The difference between *Gabriel* and *IK*, the Court held, was that in *IK* the prosecution had established a *prima facie* case for cheating, and therefore the judge had been wrong to withdraw the count from the jury.

'Criminal conduct'

Criminal conduct is conduct which either constitutes an offence in any part of the UK, or would constitute an offence in any part of the UK if it occurred there (s 340(2)).   **20.41**

It is immaterial who carried out the conduct, who benefited from it, or whether the conduct occurred before or after the passing of POCA (see s 340(4)).   **20.42**

'Defences' to section 327(1)

Under s 327(2) a person does not commit such an offence if: **20.43**

(a) he makes an authorised disclosure under s 338 of POCA and (if the disclosure is made before he does the act mentioned in s 327(1)) he has the appropriate consent;
(b) he intended to make such a disclosure but has a reasonable excuse for not doing so;
(c) the act he does is done in carrying out a function he has relating to the enforcement of POCA or of any other enactment relating to criminal conduct or benefit from criminal conduct.

Occasionally either the police or other enforcement authorities will themselves take possession of criminal property in the course of their duties and either convert or transfer it pending or as part of a further investigation. Section 327(2)(c) gives such authorities an appropriate exemption from the s 327(1) offence.

Section 102 of the Serious Organised Crime and Police Act 2005 (SOCPA) amends Pt 7 of   **20.44**
POCA to introduce a new defence where overseas conduct is legal under local law. The amendment came into force on 1 July 2005. Section 327(2) has inserted into it the following defence:

(2A) Nor does a person commit an offence under sub-section (1) if (a) he knows, or believes on reasonable grounds, that the relevant criminal conduct occurred in a particular country or territory outside the United Kingdom, and (b) the relevant criminal conduct (i) was not, at the time it occurred, unlawful under the criminal law then applying in that country or territory, and (ii) is not of a description prescribed by an order made by the Secretary of State.
(2B) In sub-section (2A) 'the relevant criminal conduct' is the criminal conduct by reference to which the property concerned is criminal property.

Section 328 (Arrangements) and s 329 (Acquisition, Use and Possession) are amended in   **20.45**
identical terms.

The language used in POCA is different to that used in the CJA, in particular the draftsmen   **20.46**
of POCA do not use the word 'defence' in the relevant parts of the statute. Nevertheless, it is clear that an individual will not have committed the offence in question if one of the 'exemptions' set out in the Act apply. Arguably it will be for the Crown to show that they do not apply, and therefore the burden will be on the prosecution. Having said that, there

is something of an inevitability that in many cases the best evidence for applying the 'exemptions' will come from the defendant.

20.47   The use of a third party to lodge, receive, retain, or withdraw money from an account does not amount to a defence, where the defendant had given his full co-operation throughout the period of conversion: *R v Fazal* The Times, 26 June 2009.

Threshold amounts

20.48   Section 103 of SOCPA amends the threshold amounts in relation to money laundering. Section 327 (Concealing etc) inserts subsection (2C), which reads as follows:

(2C) A deposit-taking body that does an act mentioned in para (C) or (D) of sub-section (1) does not commit an offence under that sub-section if—
  (a) it does the act in operating an account maintained with it, and
  (b) the value of the criminal property concerned is less than the threshold amount determined under s 339A for the act.

20.49   Under section 327(1)(D) of POCA, a bank or other deposit-taking body would need to make a disclosure to obtain consent before proceeding with any transaction that was suspected of involving criminal property. The amendments will, in certain circumstances, allow deposit-taking bodies to continue to operate accounts without the need to seek consent in each case.

20.50   The amendments do not apply to the duty to make a disclosure in respect of the initial opening of an account or, as the case may be, the time when the deposit-taking body first suspects that the property is criminal property (see s 338(2A) of POCA, s 106(5) of SOCPA).

20.51   A bank or other deposit-taking body would not commit an offence in operating an account of a person suspected of money laundering when the amount of money concerned in the transaction is below £250 or such higher threshold amount as may be specified by a constable or Customs' officer (or by a person authorised by the Director General of SOCA).

20.52   Where a deposit-taking body requests a threshold amount higher than the £250 default threshold, one may be specified. This threshold amount of £250 may be varied by the Secretary of State.

20.53   Where a threshold amount (above the £250 default level) has been specified for an account, the specified amount may be varied by any of the officers who could have specified it. Different thresholds may be specified in relation to the operation of the same account (for example, a threshold could be specified for deposits that are higher than the threshold specified for withdrawals).

The second money laundering offence: arrangements

20.54   This section replaces s 50 of the DTA and s 93A of the CJA. Under s 328 of POCA a person commits an offence:

(1) . . . if he enters into or becomes concerned in an arrangement which he knows or suspects facilitates (by whatever means) the acquisition, retention, use or control of criminal property by or on behalf of another person.

It is for the prosecution to show not only that the person entered into an arrangement **20.55** which he knew or suspected would facilitate another person to acquire, retain, use, or control criminal property, but also that that person also knew or suspected that the property constituted or represented a benefit from criminal conduct.

'Defences' to section 328(1)

As noted elsewhere in this chapter, the language used in POCA is different from that used **20.56** in the CJA; in particular the draftsmen of POCA do not use the word 'defence' in the relevant parts of the statute. Nevertheless, it is clear that an individual will not have committed the offence in question if one of the 'exemptions' set out in the Act apply.

Under s 328(2) certain 'defences' therefore are afforded to a person who it is alleged com- **20.57** mitted such an offence as follows:

(a) he makes an authorised disclosure under s 338 and (if the disclosure is made before he does the act mentioned in subsection (1)) he has the appropriate consent;
(b) he intended to make such a disclosure but has a reasonable excuse for not doing so;
(c) the act he does is done in carrying out a function he had relating to the enforcement of any provision of POCA or of any other enactment relating to criminal conduct or benefit from criminal conduct.

The defences available and the requirement for authorised disclosure under s 338 mirror those found under s 327.

For a full consideration of the duties of disclosure in relation to s 328 and the Court of **20.58** Appeal decision in *Bowman and Fels* (2005) 2 Cr App R 19 (which held that s 328 was not intended to cover legal professionals conducting ordinary litigation), see Chapter 21.

Section 328 has after subsection (4) inserted a new defence, pursuant to SOCPA, which **20.59** reads as follows:

(5) A deposit-taking body that does an act mentioned in sub-section (1) does not commit an offence under that sub-section if (a) it does the act in operating an account maintained with it, and (b) the arrangement facilitates the acquisition, retention, use or control of criminal property of a value that is less than the threshold amount determined under s 339A for the act.

In *Squirrel Ltd v National Westminster Bank plc (Customs & Excise Commissioners interven-* **20.60** *ing)* [2005] 2 All ER 784, Laddie J held that once a bank suspected that a customer's account contained the proceeds of crime, it was obliged to report the matter to the relevant authority and not to carry out any transaction in relation to that account. Failing to do so would amount to an offence under s 328(1). That obligation remains the position unless and until consent for the transaction is given under s 335 of POCA, or if it were not, the relevant time limit had expired. Equally, if the bank told the customer why it was blocking the transaction or account, it would breach the tipping-off provisions set out at ss 333 and 338 of POCA. Laddie J noted that although the statutory provisions might cause hardship to companies, to force the bank to unblock the account would be tantamount to compelling it to commit a criminal offence and therefore sympathy for the company/customer's position could not override that consideration.

Questions of construction in relation to the money laundering provisions were further **20.61** considered in *K Ltd v National Westminster Bank plc* [2006] EWCA Civ 1039, in particular s 328. The bank found itself in a predicament when its customer asked it to make a payment which the bank suspected would facilitate the use of criminal property and leave it open to the allegation of becoming 'concerned in an arrangement'. The customer, following the bank's refusal, made a claim for an interim injunction requiring the bank to comply with its instructions. It was argued on behalf of the customer that the bank, by refusing to honour its customer's instructions, was acting in breach of the contract whereby the bank had agreed to follow its customer's instructions. The Court found that there could be no doubt that if a banker knows or suspects that money in a customer's account is criminal property and, without making disclosure or without authorised consent (if disclosure is made), he processes a customer's cheque in such a way as to transfer the money in question into the account of another person, then he was facilitating the use or control of that criminal property, and thus committing an offence under s 328 of the 2002 Act. The Court held it would be no defence to a charge under that section that the bank was contractually obliged to obey its customer's instructions (para 9):

> If the law of the land makes it a criminal offence to honour the customer's mandate in these cir-
> cumstances there can be no breach of contract for the bank to refuse to honour its mandate . . .

20.62 In *AP, U Limited v CPS, RCPO* [2007] EWCA Crim 3128, a case which essentially concerned the release of assets from restrained funds, the court confirmed that:

> Consent may relieve the bank of any criminal responsibility for a transaction in question; but
> that does not mean that in relation to others involved in the transaction, it may not amount
> to or form part of a dishonest money laundering scheme. (para 32)

The third money laundering offence: acquisition, use, and possession

20.63 Section 329(1) states that a person commits an offence if he:

(a) acquires criminal property;
(b) uses criminal property;
(c) has possession of criminal property.

20.64 Section 329 replaces s 51 of the DTA and s 93B of the CJA. In *Wilkinson, R (on the applica-tion of) v DPP* [2006] EWHC 3012 (Admin) an issue arose over the CPS's increasingly common practice of charging offences under s 329, as opposed to the offence of handling stolen goods. Arguably it is easier to prove a s 329 offence, because the *mens rea* is 'knowing or suspecting' as opposed to 'knowing or believing' (s 22 of Theft Act 1968). The Court held that if an offence was inappropriately charged the court should express a view and encourage (but no more) the CPS to charge a lesser offence. However, it was ultimately a matter for them and their own internal guidance.

20.65 In *CPS Nottinghamshire v Rose* [2008] EWCA Crim 239, the issue of whether s 329 charges were being brought in preference to handling stolen goods was returned to. The statistics did not bear out such an assertion, and the Court found nothing wrong in the Crown pro-ceeding with s 329 where it had the effect of simplifying the issues at the trial.

'Defences' to section 329(1)

20.66 The offence under s 329 is only committed if the person concerned knows or suspects the property which has been acquired or used or which he has in his possession, constitutes or represents his own or another's benefit from criminal conduct.

Under s 329(2) there are four specified exemptions available, as follows: **20.67**

(a) [the person] makes an authorised disclosure under s 338 and (if the disclosure is made before he does the act mentioned in s 338(1)) he has the appropriate consent;
(b) he intends to make such a disclosure but has a reasonable excuse for not doing so;
(c) he acquired or used or had possession of the property for adequate consideration;
(d) the act he does is done in carrying out a function he has relating to the enforcement of any provision of this Act or of any other enactment relating to criminal conduct or benefit from criminal conduct.

In relation to s 329(2)(c) a person 'acquires property for inadequate consideration' if the value   **20.68**
of the consideration is significantly less than the value of the property (see s 329(3)(a)).
A person also uses or has possession of property for inadequate consideration if the value of
the consideration is significantly less than the value of the use or possession (see s 329(3)(b)).

Further, it should be noted that the provision by a person of goods or services which he   **20.69**
knows or suspects may help another to carry out criminal conduct is not 'consideration'
under s 329(3)(c).

Section 329 is also amended by SOCPA from 1 July 2005 to include a new 'defence' (2C),   **20.70**
as follows:

(2C) A deposit-taking body that does an act mentioned in sub-section (1) does not commit an offence under that sub-section if (a) it does the act in operating an account maintained with it, and (b) the value of the criminal property concerned is less than the threshold amount determined under s 339A for the act.

Burden of proof

Under the CJA, the burden of proving the defence was with the defendant but, as in all   **20.71**
cases where a burden rests on the defence, the standard of proof was to the civil standard.
The burden was on the prosecution to prove the *mens rea* of the offence, but if the defendant wished to raise a defence to the effect that he did not know or suspect the nature of the
transaction, the burden of proof was upon him to do so on a balance of probabilities (see
R v Colle (1992) 95 Cr App R 67). The decision in *Colle* was approved by the Judicial
Committee of the Privy Council in *A-G of Hong Kong v Lee Kwong-Kut* [1993] AC 951. It
is unclear whether these decisions carry forward to POCA cases. The language used in
POCA is different to that used in the CJA; in particular the draftsmen of POCA do not use
the word 'defence' in the relevant parts of the statute. Nevertheless, it is clear that an individual will not have committed the offence in question if one of the 'exemptions' set out in,
eg, s 327(2) apply. Arguably it will be for the Crown to show that they do not apply, and
therefore the burden will be on the prosecution. Having said that, there is something of an
inevitability that in many cases the best evidence for applying the 'exemptions' will come
from the defendant.

Maximum penalty

Section 334 states: **20.72**

(1) A person guilty of an offence under section 327, 328 or 329 is liable—
(a) on summary conviction, to imprisonment for a term not exceeding six months or to a fine not exceeding the statutory maximum or to both, or

    (b) on conviction on indictment, to imprisonment for a term not exceeding 14 years or to a fine or to both.

(2) A person guilty of an offence under section 330, 331, 332 or 333 is liable—

    (a) on summary conviction, to imprisonment for a term not exceeding six months or to a fine not exceeding the statutory maximum or to both, or

    (b) on conviction on indictment, to imprisonment for a term not exceeding five years or to a fine or to both.

Authorised disclosures

20.73 All three of the new money laundering offences afford a 'defence' or exemption to an individual if disclosure is authorised under s 338 of POCA. Section 338(1) states that disclosure will be authorised if:

(1) ...

    (a) it is a disclosure to a constable, a customs officer or nominated officer by the alleged offender that property is criminal property,

    (b) ... [repealed SOCPA s 105, Sch 17]

    (c) the first [second or third] condition set out below is satisfied.

(2) The first condition is that the disclosure is made before the alleged offender does the prohibited act.

(2A) The second condition is that: [inserted by SOCPA s 106]

    (a) the disclosure is made while the alleged offender is doing the prohibited act,

    (b) he began to do the act at a time when, because he did not then know or suspect that the property constituted or represented a person's benefit from criminal conduct, the act was not a prohibited act, and

    (c) the disclosure is made on his own initiative and as soon as it is practicable after he first knows or suspects that the property constitutes or represents a person's benefit from criminal conduct.

(3) The third condition is that—

    (a) the disclosure is made after the alleged offender does the prohibited act,

    (b) he has a reasonable excuse for his failure to make the disclosure before he did the act, and

    (c) the disclosure is made on his own initiative and as soon as it is practicable for him to make it.

[As amended by the Terrorism Act 2000 and Proceeds of Crime 2002 (Amendment) Regulations 2007, SI 2007/3398, Reg 3, Sch 2, para 6 from 26 December 2007].

20.74 By s 338(6) references to 'the prohibited act', are to:

(a) an act mentioned in s 327(1) (ie the concealing, disguising, converting, transferring, or removing of criminal property), or

(b) an act mentioned in s 328(1) (where a person knows or suspects that an arrangement he has entered into will facilitate the acquisition, retention or use or control of criminal property), or

(c) an act mentioned in s 329(1) (where a person acquires criminal property, uses criminal property or has it in his possession).

20.75 For the 'defence' under s 338(1)(a)) to be successful, the disclosure must be made in the course of the defendant's employment (see s 338(5)).

20.76 It should be noted that an authorised disclosure is not to be taken to breach any restriction on the disclosure of information (however imposed) (see s 338(4)).

20.77 By s 339(1) the Secretary of State may prescribe the form and manner in which a disclosure under s 338 must be made. That order may include a request to the discloser to provide additional information specified in the form. This is considered more fully in Chapter 21.

Disclosure to a nominated officer

A nominated officer is a person nominated to receive disclosures under s 338 (see s 336(11)), **20.78** ie a person nominated to receive authorised disclosures relating to the money laundering offences under ss 327(1), 328(1), or 329(1), as the case may be.

The nominated officer will often be the person nominated by the alleged offender's **20.79** employer to receive authorised disclosures (see s 338(5)(a)).

Appropriate consent

The three new principal money laundering offences envisage that a person will have a **20.80** 'defence' if the disclosure is authorised under s 338 and the person involved has 'appropriate consent'.

Under s 335(1) the appropriate consent is defined as: **20.81**

(a) the consent of a nominated officer to do a prohibited act if an authorised disclosure is made to the nominated officer;
(b) the consent of a constable to do a prohibited act if an authorised disclosure is made to a constable;
(c) the consent of a customs officer to do a prohibited act if an authorised disclosure is made to a customs officer.

References to a 'prohibited act' are references to the offences mentioned in ss 327(1), 328(1), or 329(1), as the case may be (see s 335(8)).

Under s 335(1)(b), a constable includes a person authorised for the purposes of Pt 7 of **20.82** POCA by the Director General of SOCA (see s 340(13)).

By s 335(2), (3), and (4), a person must be treated as having the appropriate consent if he **20.83** makes an authorised disclosure to a constable or a customs officer and he does not receive, before the end of the 'notice period', a notice from a constable or customs officer that consent to the doing of the act is refused; or alternatively, before the end of 'the notice period', he does receive notice from a constable or customs that consent to the doing of the act is refused, but the 'moratorium period' has expired. POCA therefore envisages time limits under which customs or the police must respond to requests for consent.

For the right to ask for consent to be reviewed in the moratorium period and SOCA's **20.84** obligation to do so, see *R (UMBS Online) v Serious Organised Crime Agency* [2008] 1 All ER 465.

Notice period

Section 335(5) states: **20.85**

The notice period is the period of seven working days starting with the first working day after the person makes the disclosure.

Section 335 puts a proactive duty on the nominated officer or law enforcement agency concerned to respond within the time limit of seven days. Failure to do so will mean the person who has disclosed the information can go ahead with what may otherwise be a prohibited act and without an offence being committed.

Moratorium period

20.86 Under s 335(6) the moratorium period is the period of 31 days starting with the day on which the person receives notice that consent to the doing of the act is refused.

20.87 The effect of the moratorium period is that if a Customs officer or constable withholds consent within the seven working day period under s 335(5), then they are entitled to a further 31 calendar days in which to take further action in relation to the disclosures, for example seeking a court order to restrain the assets in question. However, if the discloser hears nothing more after the 31-day period has expired, then they can proceed with the transaction without the risk of committing any offence (a working day is defined as any day other than Saturday, Sunday, Christmas Day, Good Friday, or a Bank Holiday (see s 335(7)).

Consent from a nominated officer

20.88 Nominated officers must not give the appropriate consent to the doing of a prohibited act unless certain conditions set out in s 336(2)–(4) are satisfied (see s 336(1)). Those conditions are as follows:

(1) The discloser makes a disclosure that property is criminal property to a person authorised for the purposes of Part 7 by the Director General of SOCA, and such a person gives consent to the doing of the act (s 336(2)).

(2) The discloser makes a disclosure that property is criminal property to a person authorised for the purposes of Part 7 by the Director General of SOCA, and before the end of the notice period he does not receive notice from such person that consent to the doing of the act is refused (s 336(3)).

(3) The discloser makes a disclosure that property is criminal property to a person authorised for the purposes of Part 7 by the Director General of SOCA before the end of the notice period he receives notice from such a person that consent to the doing of the act is refused, and the moratorium period has expired (s 336(4)).

20.89 The nominated officer must very carefully adhere to the above conditions. Failure to do so may itself result in the committing of an offence by the nominated officer, for example, if he gives consent to a prohibited act in circumstances where none of the conditions are satisfied and the nominated officer knows or suspects that the act is prohibited under the money laundering regime (s 336(5)).

20.90 A nominated officer found to be guilty of such an offence stands liable, on summary conviction, to imprisonment for a term not exceeding six months, or to a fine not exceeding the statutory maximum, or to both; or on conviction on indictment, to imprisonment for a term not exceeding five years, or to a fine, or to both (see s 336(6)). The notice period and the moratorium period are identical to that set out under s 335(5) and (6), namely seven working days and 31 calendar days respectively (see s 336(7), (8), and (9)).

The prohibited act

20.91 The prohibited act referred to in s 336(1) is an act which falls under either s 327(1) (concealing etc), s 328(1) (arrangements for money laundering), or s 329(1) (acquisition, use, and possession of criminal property for money laundering) as the case may be (s 336(10)).

Protected disclosures

Disclosures under Pt 7 of POCA fall into two specified categories, either protected disclo- **20.92**
sures (under s 337) or authorised disclosures (under s 338). Authorised disclosures are
considered above.

Section 337 sets out three conditions under which disclosure will not be taken to breach **20.93**
any restriction on the disclosure of information (however imposed). The three conditions,
all of which must be satisfied, are as follows:

(1) That the information or other matter disclosed came to the person making the
    disclosure (the discloser) in the course of his trade, profession, business, or employ-
    ment (s 337(2));
(2) That the information or other matter:
    (a) causes the discloser to know or suspect, or
    (b) gives him reasonable grounds for knowing or suspecting,
that another person is engaged in money laundering (s 337(3));
(3) That the disclosure is made to a constable, a Customs officer, or a nominated officer
    as soon as is practicable after the information or other matter comes to the discloser
    (s 337(4)).

The first condition, s 337(2), exempts a person who receives information in the course of **20.94**
his trade or profession from any legal or other obligations that would otherwise prevent
him from making disclosure to the authorities. This protection extends beyond the regulated sector to include, eg, accountants or solicitors giving free advice.

In terms of the suggestion that disclosing information may breach confidentiality under- **20.95**
takings, s 104 of SOCPA adds the following:

4A. Where a disclosure consists of a disclosure protected under subsection (1) and a disclosure of either
    or both of—
    (a) the identity of the other person mentioned in subsection (3), and
    (b) the whereabouts of property forming the subject-matter of the money laundering that the
        discloser knows or suspects, or has reasonable grounds for knowing or suspecting, that other
        person to be engaged in,
the disclosure of the thing mentioned in paragraph (a) or (b) (as well as the disclosure protected under
subsection (1)) is not to be taken to breach any restriction on the disclosure of information (however
imposed).

Form and manner of disclosures

Under s 339 of the Act, the Secretary of State is permitted to prescribe the form and manner **20.96**
in which a disclosure under ss 330, 331, 332, or 338 must be made. An order under this
section may also provide that the form may include a request for the discloser to provide
additional information specified in the form. (See also Chapter 21.)

While s 339(3) anticipates that the Secretary of State may ask for the discloser to provide **20.97**
additional information, it does not create any criminal offence if the discloser refuses to
supply that additional information. Any additional information supplied appears, under
s 339(4), to have been given immunity from any restriction on the disclosure of information, such as confidentiality clauses in contracts.

Mode of trial

20.98   As these offences are triable either way, justices will be called upon to make decisions as to mode of trial. Case law suggests that rarely, if ever, will summary trial be appropriate. Further, the complexity of the case should also be taken into consideration. Money laundering cases frequently involve a detailed analysis of complex financial documentation which, together with the volume of evidence necessary to prove the case, means that any trial may be lengthy.

Money laundering offences under the DTA and CJA

20.99   The first money laundering offence to be created in the UK was in relation to the laundering of the proceeds of drug trafficking and was found in s 24 of the now repealed Drug Trafficking Offences Act 1986. It was re-enacted in s 50 of the DTA, which itself has now been revised by s 328 of POCA. Other offences were created by s 14 of the Criminal Justice (International Co-operation) Act 1990 and these, together with the former s 24 offence, were consolidated into Pt III of the DTA. These offences were introduced in compliance with the UK's obligations under Art 3(b) of the United Nations Convention Against Illicit Traffic in Narcotic Drugs and Psychotropic Substances ('the Vienna Convention'), which required contracting States to establish drug money laundering offences.

20.100   As a result of the transitional provisions governing POCA, all principal money laundering offences where the conduct commenced prior to 24 February 2003 (and ended before or after that date) will still be dealt with under the previous legislation of the DTA or CJA, as the case may be (SI 2003/120). However, due to the passage of time since the introduction of POCA, the number of DTA and CJA cases are now few and far between, and tend only to surface in the appellant courts, or in the context of confiscation. As a result we have not focused on the statutory procedures in this third edition, although the reader will find detailed analysis of the earlier statutory schemes in the two previous editions of this work.

C.   The EC Money Laundering Directives

20.101   On 10 June 1991 the Council of the European Communities issued a Directive (Council Directive (EC) (1991/308)) on the prevention of the use of the financial system for the purpose of money laundering. The Directive was issued because, in the words of the preamble:

> . . . lack of Community action against money laundering could lead Member States, for the purpose of protecting their financial systems, to adopt measures which could be inconsistent with completion of the single market; whereas in order to facilitate their criminal activities launderers could try to take advantage of the freedom of capital movement and freedom to supply financial services which the integrated financial area involves if certain co-ordinating measures are not adopted at Community level.

20.102   The Directive required Member States, by 1 January 1993, to introduce certain measures to prevent the financial system being used for money laundering. These included ensuring that money laundering is prohibited (Art 2); requiring credit and financial institutions to obtain evidence of identification of their customers (Art 3) and retain that evidence, together with records of transactions, for at least five years (Art 4); requiring such institutions to disclose to law enforcement authorities transactions which might be an indication of money laundering (Art 6) and that they refrain from carrying out transactions they know or suspect relate to money laundering (Art 7); and ensuring these institutions establish adequate procedures for internal control and communication in order to forestall and prevent money laundering transactions and for making their employees aware of the provisions of the Directive.

The definition of 'money laundering' in Art 1 covers only the proceeds of drug trafficking and **20.103** not those of any other crime. The reason for this is that Art 1 defined 'criminal activity' as being a crime specified in Art 3(1)(a) of the Vienna Convention. As this Convention is concerned with measures to combat drug trafficking, the definition of 'criminal activity' is confined to such offences. Article 15 of the Directive, however, allowed Member States to adopt stricter measures to prevent money laundering, and the preamble expressed the hope that they would extend it to cover other crimes. In consequence, certain countries, including the UK, have taken the opportunity to adopt 'all crime' money laundering legislation. Similarly, some countries, while not going so far as to extend the legislation to cover all crimes, have adopted legislation that covers other criminal activity, as well as that relating to drugs.

UK legislation to implement the Directive

The legislation introduced to compel disclosure of transactions relating to money launder- **20.104** ing and the establishment of systems within financial institutions to prevent money laundering comprise of the Money Laundering Regulations 1993, SI 1993/1933, the Money Laundering Regulations 2001, SI 2001/3641, Pt III of the DTA, and Pt 7 of POCA. The Money Laundering Regulations 2007 (SI 2007/2157) implement the EC Third Money Laundering Directive in the UK. This recent legislation reflects the recommendations of the international Financial Action Task Force which was set up to tackle money laundering on a worldwide basis.

The Money Laundering Regulations

The Money Laundering Regulations 1993, SI 1993/1933 gave effect to Arts 3, 4, 10, and **20.105** 11 of the Council Directive (EC) 1991/308 on prevention of the use of the financial system for the purpose of money laundering. These regulations came into force on 1 April 1994. The Regulations required that where business relationships are formed, or one-off transactions are carried out in the course of relevant financial business, the persons carrying out that business were required to maintain certain procedures for the purposes of forestalling or preventing money laundering (see regs 7, 9, 12, and 14). The Regulations also required relevant financial businesses to train their employees in procedures that would forestall or prevent money laundering.

The Money Laundering Regulations 2001, SI 2001/3641 supplemented the provisions of **20.106** the Money Laundering Regulations 1993 and give effect to Arts 12 and 13 of Council Directive (EC) 1991/308 on prevention of the use of the financial system for the purpose of money laundering.

The Money Laundering Regulations 2003 replaced the Money Laundering Regulations **20.107** 1993 and 2001 with updated provisions which reflected Council Directive (EC) 2001/97 (the second EC directive) and the amended Council Directive (EC) 91/308 on the prevention of the use of the financial system for the purpose of money laundering (the first directive). The 2003 Money Laundering Regulations came into force on 1 March 2004 (other than reg 10, which came into force on 1 April 2004). The regulated sector, including, but not limited to, accountants and auditors; tax advisers; dealers in high value goods (including auctioneers); casinos; estate agents; some management consultancy services; company formation agents; insolvency practitioners; legal advisers; and bureau de change; were all included within the regulated sector which required those businesses to establish procedures to confirm the identity of new clients and appoint a money laundering nominated officer to whom money laundering reports must be made. Firms within the sector also had to establish systems and procedures to forestall and prevent money laundering and provide relevant individuals for training or money laundering awareness courses.

20.108 The 2003 Regulations also revoked the Financial Services and Markets Act 2000 (Regulations relating to Money Laundering) Regulations 2001, SI 2001/1819).

20.109 The Proceeds of Crime Act 2002 and Money Laundering Regulations 2003 (Amendment) Order 2006 (SI 2006/308) extended important obligations upon professional advisers from a wide range of sectors, including tax advisers, accountants, auditors, insolvency practitioners, and legal advisers. Professionals who carry on relevant business were required to fulfil a range of obligations to prevent money laundering.

20.110 The Proceeds of Crime Act 2002 and Money Laundering Regulations 2003 (Amendment) Order 2006 came into force on 21 February 2006. It made various amendments to s 330 of POCA to encompass not only professional legal advisers but other relevant professional advisers as well (see reg 2(2)). Section 330 of POCA requires a person to make a disclosure in accordance with s 330(4) (as substituted by s 104(3) of SOCPA) where he knows or suspects, or has reasonable grounds for knowing or suspecting, that another person is engaged in money laundering and the information or other matter came to him in the course of a business in the regulated sector. Schedule 9 to that Act (as amended by the Proceeds of Crime Act 2002 (Business in the Regulated Sector and Supervisory Authorities) Order 2003, SI 2003/3074 has the effect of determining what is a business in the regulated sector. Failure to make such a disclosure is an offence under s 330(1).

The Third European Money Laundering Directive

20.111 The Third European Money Laundering Directive (Directive 2005/60/EC) came into effect on 15 December 2005 (see the EU Official Journal L 309 25 November 2005 at pp 15–36). The Directive required EU members to bring into force the laws, regulations, and administrative provisions necessary to comply with the new Directive by 15 December 2007.

The 2007 Regulations—summary

20.112 The Money Laundering Regulations 2007 (SI 2007/2157) came into force on 15 December 2007 as part of the UK's response to the third Money Laundering Directive. They replace the 2003 Regulations. The Regulations provide for various steps to be taken by the financial services sector and other persons to detect and prevent money laundering and terrorist financing.

The revised regulations include requirements that there be due diligence procedures in **20.113** place in relation to existing clients and customers and they require the financial, account-ancy, legal, and other sectors to take steps to prevent their services being used for money laundering or terrorist financing. The Regulations require firms to apply enhanced cus-tomer identification and monitoring measures, and require them to have appropriate anti-money laundering systems in place.

Most UK financial and credit businesses (banks, building societies, money transmitters, **20.114** bureaux de change, cheque cashers, pawn brokers, savings and investment firms) are cov-ered. In addition the Regulations cover independent legal professionals (when undertaking certain financial and property transactions) accountants, tax advisers, auditors, insolvency practitioners, estate agents, casinos, high value dealers (when taking cash of 15,000 or more) and trust or company service providers.

The 2007 Regulations require those businesses covered to put in place checks, controls, and **20.115** procedures in order to anticipate and prevent money laundering or terrorist financing, together with training staff in those procedures and in the law relating to money laundering and terrorist financing. They also require businesses to appoint a nominated officer or money laundering reporting officer to receive and consider internal disclosures and to make suspicious activity reports to SOCA. Where the business is a sole trader with no employees, the proprietor will be the person responsible for making the reports.

The Regulations also require businesses to put in place procedures to identify customers **20.116** and verify the customer's identity before entering into a business relationship or transac-tion, and to obtain information on the purpose or nature of the business relationship. These procedures are known in the regulations as 'customer due diligence' and also require businesses to conduct ongoing monitoring of the business relationship as appropriate.

The Regulations also specify the circumstances where businesses must undertake enhanced **20.117** measures, which include keeping records obtained in establishing customers' identities and of business relationships for five years.

Relevant persons

Obligations are imposed on 'relevant persons' (defined in reg 3 and subject to the exclu- **20.118** sions in reg 4), who are credit and financial institutions, auditors, accountants, tax advisers and insolvency practitioners, independent legal professionals, trust or company service providers, estate agents, high value dealers, and casinos.

Relevant persons are required, when undertaking certain activities in the course of busi- **20.119** ness, to apply customer due diligence measures where they establish a business relationship, carry out an occasional transaction, suspect money laundering or terrorist finance, or doubt the accuracy of customer identification information (reg 7). Relevant persons also have to undertake ongoing monitoring of their business relationships (reg 8).

Customer due diligence

Customer due diligence (CDD) measures (defined in reg 5) consist of identifying and **20.120** verifying the identity of the customer and any beneficial owner (as set out in reg 6), and obtaining information on the purpose and intended nature of the business relationship.

20.121   Regulation 9 sets out the general rule on the timing of the verification of the customer's identity and certain exceptions. Regulation 10 sets out when casinos must identify and verify their customers. Failure to apply such measures means that a person cannot establish or continue a business relationship with the customer concerned or undertake an occasional transaction (reg 11).

20.122   Regulation 12 provides an exception from the requirement to identify the beneficial owner for debt issues held in trust.

20.123   Relevant persons may apply simplified customer due diligence measures for the products, customers, or transactions listed in reg 13 and must apply enhanced measures in the four situations set out in regulation 14:

(1) A relevant person must apply on a risk-sensitive basis enhanced customer due diligence measures and enhanced ongoing monitoring—
   (a) in accordance with paragraphs (2) to (4);
   (b) in any other situation which by its nature can present a higher risk of money laundering or terrorist financing.
(2) Where the customer has not been physically present for identification purposes, a relevant person must take specific and adequate measures to compensate for the higher risk, for example, by applying one or more of the following measures—
   (a) ensuring that the customer's identity is established by additional documents, data or information;
   (b) supplementary measures to verify or certify the documents supplied, or requiring confirmatory certification by a credit or financial institution which is subject to the money laundering directive;
   (c) ensuring that the first payment is carried out through an account opened in the customer's name with a credit institution.
(3) A credit institution ('the correspondent') which has or proposes to have a correspondent banking relationship with a respondent institution ('the respondent') from a non-EEA state must—
   (a) gather sufficient information about the respondent to understand fully the nature of its business;
   (b) determine from publicly-available information the reputation of the respondent and the quality of its supervision;
   (c) assess the respondent's anti-money laundering and anti-terrorist financing controls;
   (d) obtain approval from senior management before establishing a new correspondent banking relationship;
   (e) document the respective responsibilities of the respondent and correspondent; and
   (f) be satisfied that, in respect of those of the respondent's customers who have direct access to accounts of the correspondent, the respondent—
      (i) has verified the identity of, and conducts ongoing monitoring in respect of, such customers; and
      (ii) is able to provide to the correspondent, upon request, the documents, data or information obtained when applying customer due diligence measures and ongoing monitoring.
(4) A relevant person who proposes to have a business relationship or carry out an occasional transaction with a politically exposed person must—
   (a) have approval from senior management for establishing the business relationship with that person;
   (b) take adequate measures to establish the source of wealth and source of funds which are involved in the proposed business relationship or occasional transaction; and
   (c) where the business relationship is entered into, conduct enhanced ongoing monitoring of the relationship.

(5) In paragraph (4), 'a politically exposed person' means a person who is—
    (a) an individual who is or has, at any time in the preceding year, been entrusted with a prominent public function by—
        (i) a state other than the United Kingdom;
        (ii) a Community institution; or
        (iii) an international body,
including a person who falls in any of the categories listed in paragraph 4(1)(a) of Schedule 2;
    (b) an immediate family member of a person referred to in sub-paragraph (a), including a person who falls in any of the categories listed in paragraph 4(1)(c) of Schedule 2; or
    (c) a known close associate of a person referred to in sub-paragraph (a), including a person who falls in either of the categories listed in paragraph 4(1)(d) of Schedule 2.
(6) For the purpose of deciding whether a person is a known close associate of a person referred to in paragraph (5)(a), a relevant person need only have regard to information which is in his possession or is publicly known.

Other obligations

Regulation 15 sets out the obligations on relevant persons in respect of their overseas **20.124** branches and subsidiaries. Regulation 16 imposes obligations in respect of shell banks and anonymous accounts. Regulation 17 lists the persons on whom relevant persons can rely to perform customer due diligence measures. Part 3 imposes obligations in respect of record-keeping (reg 19), policies and procedures (reg 20), and staff training (reg 21).

Supervision and registration

Part 4 deals with supervision and registration. Regulation 23 allocates supervisory author- **20.125** ities for different relevant persons. There are a number of supervisory authorities listed in the Regulations, including the Financial Services Authority (FSA), HM Revenue & Customs (HMRC), Office of Fair Trading (OFT), and a number of professional bodies. Businesses that are supervised by HMRC must apply to be registered, these include Money Service Businesses (MSBs) that are not supervised by the FSA; High Value Dealers (HVDs); Trust or Company Service Providers (TCSPs) and Accountancy Service Providers (ASPs) that are not supervised by the FSA or a designated professional body.

Regulation 24 sets out the duties of supervisors. MSBs, HVDs, and TCSPs that are not **20.126** otherwise registered are subject to a system of mandatory registration set out in regs 25 to 30. MSBs and TCSPs must not be registered unless the business, its owners, its nominated officer, and senior managers are 'fit and proper' persons: reg 28.

Regulation 35 enables supervisors to impose charges on persons they supervise. **20.127**

The Proceeds of Crime Act 2002 (Business in the Regulated Sector and Supervisory **20.128** Authorities) Order 2007, SI 2007/3287 makes amendments to the meaning of 'supervisory authority' provided by the new Pt 2 Sch 9 of POCA to reflect the requirement of the Directive that all sectors within its scope be effectively monitored for compliance, and the provision made by the Directive for accountants, auditors, legal professionals, and tax advisers to be monitored by a self-regulatory body.

Enforcement powers and penalties

Part 5 provides enforcement powers for certain supervisors, including powers to obtain **20.129** information and enter and inspect premises (regs 37 to 41). Civil penalties may be imposed by these supervisors under reg 42 on persons who fail to comply with the requirements of Pts 2, 3, and 4. Provision is made for reviews of and appeals against such penalties (regs 43 and 44).

20.130 Relevant persons who fail to comply with the requirements of Pts 2, 3, and 4 will also be guilty of a criminal offence: regs 45 to 47. Persons convicted of a criminal offence may not also be liable to a civil penalty.

21

DISCLOSURE OF SUSPICIOUS TRANSACTIONS

A. Introduction

Money laundering and confiscation law can only be truly effective if banks, financial **21.01** institutions, and professionals who handle money on behalf of clients, are compelled to disclose suspicious transactions to law enforcement authorities. The provisions of the Proceeds of Crime Act 2002 (POCA) and the related legislation encourage such disclosure by providing certain exemptions from criminal liability for money laundering and civil liability at the suit of the customer for any breach of confidentiality.

In this chapter we consider the thrust of the provisions of POCA in relation to disclosure **21.02** of suspicious transactions by the professions. The POCA provisions came into force on 24 February 2003.

POCA has been substantially amended in relation to money laundering and the disclosure **21.03** of suspicious transactions by virtue of the Serious Organised Crime and Police Act 2005 (SOCPA). According to the explanatory notes that accompany SOCPA, these amendments were designed to improve the effectiveness of the civil recovery scheme and ease the money laundering reporting requirements on the regulated sector.

21.04 As discussed in Chapter 20 of this book, many individuals launder money to conceal illegal activity, such as drug trafficking, tax evasion, and terrorism. It fuels criminal conduct, allowing drug dealers, smugglers, terrorists, arms dealers, and tax evaders to maintain control over their proceeds and ultimately to provide a legitimate cover for their sources of income. Law enforcement officials estimate that such individuals yearly launder $1 to $2 trillion worldwide through different types of financial institutions and businesses.

B. Disclosure of Suspicious Transactions under POCA

Businesses in the regulated sector

21.05 The legislation distinguishes between businesses within and those outside of the 'regulated sector'. The duty to report suspicious transactions under s 330 of POCA (below) is restricted to those businesses in the 'regulated sector'.

21.06 The original definition of the regulated sector found in Appendix 9 of the 2002 Act was replaced by the Proceeds of Crime Act 2002 (Business in the Regulated Sector and Supervisory Authorities) Order 2003, SI 2003/3074. This has subsequently been further substituted by the Proceeds of Crime Act 2002 (Business in the Regulated Sector and Supervisory Authorities) Order 2007, SI 2007/3287, which came into force on 15 December 2007. The activities defined as constituting business in the regulated sector include carrying out activities in the financial and property sectors; provision by way of business/or services by a body corporate or unincorporated; or, in the case of a sole practitioner, by an individual, trading which involves participation in a financial or real property transaction.

21.07 Businesses are included in the regulated sector if they engage in any of the following activities in the UK:

(a) the acceptance by a credit institution of deposits or other repayable funds from the public, or the granting by a credit institution of credits for its own account;

(b) the carrying on of one or more of the activities listed in points 2 to 12 and 14 of Annex 1 to the Banking Consolidation Directive by an undertaking other than—

    (i) a credit institution; or

    (ii) an undertaking whose only listed activity is trading for own account in one or more of the products listed in point 7 of Annex 1 to the Banking Consolidation Directive and which does not act on behalf of a customer (that is, a third party which is not a member of the same group as the undertaking);

(c) the carrying on of activities covered by the Life Assurance Consolidation Directive by an insurance company authorised in accordance with that Directive;

(d) the provision of investment services or the performance of investment activities by a person (other than a person falling within Article 2 of the Markets in Financial Instruments Directive) whose regular occupation or business is the provision to other persons of an investment service or the performance of an investment activity on a professional basis;

(e) the marketing or other offering of units or shares by a collective investment undertaking;

(f) the activities of an insurance intermediary as defined in Article 2(5) of the Insurance Mediation Directive, other than a tied insurance intermediary as mentioned in Article 2(7) of that Directive, in respect of contracts of long-term insurance within the meaning given by article 3(1) of, and Pt II of Schedule 1 to, the Financial Services and Markets Act 2000 (Regulated Activities) Order 2001;

(g) the carrying on of any of the activities mentioned in paragraphs (b) to (f) by a branch located in an EEA State of a person referred to in those paragraphs (or of an equivalent person in any other State), wherever its head office is located;

(h) the activities of the National Savings Bank;

(i) any activity carried on for the purpose of raising money authorised to be raised under the National Loans Act 1968 under the auspices of the Director of Savings;

(j) the carrying on of statutory audit work within the meaning of section 1210 of the Companies Act 2006 (meaning of 'statutory auditor' etc) by any firm or individual who is a statutory auditor within the meaning of Part 42 of that Act (statutory auditors);

(k) the activities of a person appointed to act as an insolvency practitioner within the meaning of section 388 of the Insolvency Act 1986 (meaning of 'act as insolvency practitioner') or article 3 of the Insolvency (Northern Ireland) Order 1989;

(l) the provision to other persons of accountancy services by a firm or sole practitioner who by way of business provides such services to other persons;

(m) the provision of advice about the tax affairs of other persons by a firm or sole practitioner who by way of business provides advice about the tax affairs of other persons;

(n) the participation in financial or real property transactions concerning—
    (i) the buying and selling of real property (or, in Scotland, heritable property) or business entities;
    (ii) the managing of client money, securities or other assets;
    (iii) the opening or management of bank, savings or securities accounts;
    (iv) the organisation of contributions necessary for the creation, operation or management of companies; or
    (v) the creation, operation or management of trusts, companies or similar structures,
by a firm or sole practitioner who by way of business provides legal or notarial services to other persons;

(o) the provision to other persons by way of business by a firm or sole practitioner of any of the services mentioned in sub-paragraph (4);

(p) the carrying on of estate agency work (within the meaning given by section 1 of the Estate Agents Act 1979 (estate agency work)) by a firm or a sole practitioner who carries on, or whose employees carry on, such work;

(q) the trading in goods (including dealing as an auctioneer) whenever a transaction involves the receipt of a payment or payments in cash of at least 15,000 euros in total, whether the transaction is executed in a single operation or in several operations which appear to be linked, by a firm or sole trader who by way of business trades in goods;

(r) operating a casino under a casino operating licence (within the meaning given by section 65(2) of the Gambling Act 2005 (nature of licence)).

The services referred to in subpara (1)(o) are: **21.08**

(a) forming companies or other legal persons;

(b) acting, or arranging for another person to act—
    (i) as a director or secretary of a company;
    (ii) as a partner of a partnership; or
    (iii) in a similar position in relation to other legal persons;

(c) providing a registered office, business address, correspondence or administrative address or other related services for a company, partnership or any other legal person or arrangement;

(d) acting, or arranging for another person to act, as—
    (i) a trustee of an express trust or similar legal arrangement; or
    (ii) a nominee shareholder for a person other than a company whose securities are listed on a regulated market.

The amendments to the meaning of a 'business in the regulated sector' provided by the new **21.09** Pt 1 of Sch 9 (as amended) reflect the changes to the scope of the regulated sector made by the EC's third money laundering Directive. The two major changes are the expanded definition of a trust or company service provider and the exemption for financial activity on an occasional or very limited basis.

21.10 POCA intends, therefore, that the businesses listed above will employ a higher level of diligence in handling transactions than other businesses.

Excluded businesses

21.11 A business is not in the regulated sector if it consists of:

(a) the issuing of withdrawable share capital within the limit set by section 6 of the Industrial and Provident Societies Act 1965 (maximum shareholding in society), or the acceptance of deposits from the public within the limit set by section 7(3) of that Act (carrying on of banking by societies), by a society registered under that Act;

(b) the issuing of withdrawable share capital within the limit set by section 6 of the Industrial and Provident Societies Act (Northern Ireland) 1969 (maximum shareholding in society), or the acceptance of deposits from the public within the limit set by section 7(3) of that Act (carrying on of banking by societies), by a society registered under that Act;

(c) the carrying on of any activity in respect of which a person who is (or falls within a class of persons) specified in any of paragraphs 2 to 23, 25 to 38 or 40 to 49 of the Schedule to the Financial Services and Markets Act 2000 (Exemption) Order 2001 is exempt;

(d) the exercise of the functions specified in section 45 of the Financial Services Act 1986 (miscellaneous exemptions) by a person who was an exempted person for the purposes of that section immediately before its repeal;

(e) the engaging in financial activity which fulfils all of the conditions set out in paragraphs (a) to (g) of sub-paragraph (3) of this paragraph by a person whose main activity is that of a high value dealer; or

(f) the preparation of a home information pack (within the meaning of Part 5 of the Housing Act 2004 (home information packs)) or a document or information for inclusion in a home information pack.

21.12 A business is also not in the regulated sector if it consists of financial activity where:

(a) the person's total annual turnover in respect of the financial activity does not exceed £64,000;

(b) the financial activity is limited in relation to any customer to no more than one transaction exceeding 1,000 euros, whether the transaction is carried out in a single operation, or a series of operations which appear to be linked;

(c) the financial activity does not exceed 5% of the person's total annual turnover;

(d) the financial activity is ancillary to the person's main activity and directly related to that activity;

(e) the financial activity is not the transmission or remittance of money (or any representation of monetary value) by any means;

(f) the main activity of the person carrying on the financial activity is not an activity mentioned in paragraph 1(1)(a) to (p) or (r); and

(g) the financial activity is provided only to customers of the person's main activity and is not offered to the public.

Failure to disclose: regulated sector

Under s 330 of POCA (as amended by s 104 of SOCPA) a person commits an offence if **21.13** each of the following conditions is satisfied:

> (2) The first condition is that he—
> > (a) knows or suspects, or
> > (b) has reasonable grounds for knowing or suspecting,
>
> that another person is engaged in money laundering.
>
> (3) The second condition is that the information or other matter—
> > (a) on which his knowledge or suspicion is based, or
> > (b) which gives reasonable grounds for such knowledge or suspicion,
>
> came to him in the course of a business in the regulated sector.
>
> (3A) The third condition is—
> > (a) that he can identify the other person mentioned in section 330(2) or the whereabouts of any of the laundered property, or
> > (b) that he believes, or it is reasonable to expect him to believe, that the information or other matter mentioned in section 330(3) will or may assist in identifying that that other person or the whereabouts of any of the laundered property.
>
> (4) The fourth condition is that he does not make the required disclosure to—
> > (a) a nominated officer, or
> > (b) a person authorised for the purposes of this Part by the Director General of the Serious Organised Crime Agency,
>
> as soon as is practicable after the information or other matter mentioned in sub-section (3) comes to him.
>
> (5) The required disclosure is a disclosure of (a) the identity of the other person mentioned in sub-section (2), if he knows it, (b) the whereabouts of the laundered property, so far as he knows it, and (c) the information or other matter mentioned in section 330(3).

The laundered property is the property forming the subject matter of the money laundering **21.14** that the individual knows or suspects (or has reasonable grounds for knowing or suspecting) that another person is engaged in (s 330(5A)). The 'reasonable grounds' element to the criteria introduces a negligence test to the legislation, which is also reflected in s 331.

Section 330 replaces s 52 of the DTA and is intended to create an obligation to report a **21.15** suspicion of money laundering to the authorities. In so doing, it widens the scope of the offences that it replaces under s 52 beyond reporting drug money laundering to reporting the laundering of the proceeds of *any* criminal conduct.

The obligation to disclose suspicions of money laundering will apply if the person required **21.16** to make a disclosure knows the identity of the person engaged in the money laundering offence, or the whereabouts of any of the laundered property, or information which may assist in uncovering the identity of the person engaged in the offence, or the whereabouts of any of the laundered property.

What test should the court apply?

Section 330(8) reads: **21.17**

> (8) In deciding whether a person committed an offence under this section the court must consider whether he followed any relevant guidance which was at the time concerned—
> > (a) issued by a supervisory authority or any other appropriate body,
> > (b) approved by the Treasury, and

(c) published in a manner it approved as appropriate in its opinion to bring the guidance to the attention of persons likely to be affected by it.

Under s 330(8) an appropriate body is any body which regulates or is representative of any trade, profession, business, or employment carried on by the alleged offender (see s 330(13)).

21.18 The British Bankers Association has set up a Joint Money Laundering Steering Group which has produced guidance notes on money laundering since 1990. It should be noted that guidance notes are just that, and cannot supplant the letter of the law, which the courts are bound to follow. Nevertheless s 330(8) provides that the court must at least take account of guidance notes issued by any supervisory authority providing that they have been approved by the Treasury.

'Defences' to failing to disclose in the regulated sector

21.19 A person does not commit an offence under s 330 if:

(6) ...
  (a) he has a reasonable excuse for not making the required disclosure;
  (b) he is a professional legal advisor or relevant professional adviser and—
    (i) if he knows either of the things mentioned in subsection (5)(a) and (b), he knows the thing because of information or other matter that came to him in privileged circumstances;
    (ii) the information or other matter mentioned in subs (3) came to him in privileged circumstances, or
  (c) subsection 7 or 7B applies to him.
(7) This subsection applies to a person if—
  (a) he does not know or suspect that another person is engaged in money laundering, and
  (b) he has not been provided by his employer with such training as is specified by the Secretary of State by order for the purposes of this Section.

21.20 Section 102 of SOCPA amends s 330 of POCA to insert a further defence:

(7A) Nor does a person commit an offence under this section if—
  (a) he knows, or believes on reasonable grounds, that the money laundering is occurring in a particular country or territory outside the United Kingdom, and
  (b) the money laundering—
    (i) is not unlawful under the criminal law applying in the country or territory, and
    (ii) is not of a description prescribed in an order made by the Secretary of State.

21.21 The Proceeds of Crime Act 2002 and Money Laundering Regulations 2003 (Amendment) Order 2006 (SI 2006/308) further inserts:

(7B) This subsection applies to a person if—
  (a) he is employed by, or is in partnership with, a professional legal adviser or a relevant professional adviser to provide the adviser with assistance or support,
  (b) the information or other matter mentioned in subsection (3) comes to the person in connection with the provision of such assistance or support, and
  (c) the information or other matter came to the adviser in privileged circumstances.

21.22 Subsection (7) confirms that an individual does not commit an offence if the individual does not know or suspect that the person is engaged in money laundering and he has not been provided by his employer with such training as is specified by the Act. It is therefore a reasonable excuse for an employee to raise that his employer has not given him adequate training, although the employers themselves may then find themselves in jeopardy of the money laundering regulations discussed in Chapter 20. Statutory Instrument 2003/171 specifies training for the purposes of POCA.

Subsection 7A provides that an offence is not committed where the money laundering has or **21.23**
is occurring outside the UK and money laundering is not unlawful in that particular country.

The language used in POCA is different to that used in the CJA 1988, in particular the **21.24**
draftsmen of POCA do not use the word 'defence' in the relevant parts of the statute.
Nevertheless, it is clear that an individual will not have committed the offence in question
if one of the 'exemptions' set out in the Act apply. Arguably it will be for the Crown to show
that they do not apply, and therefore the burden will be on the prosecution. Having said
that, there is something of an inevitability that in many cases the best evidence for applying
the 'exemptions' will come from the defendant.

Legal and professional privilege

Legal professional privilege therefore appears to survive POCA. An individual does not **21.25**
commit an offence under this section if he has a reasonable excuse for not making the
required disclosure; or he is a professional legal adviser and the information came to him in
privileged circumstances (s 330(6), or s 330(7) or (7B)).

Section 330(6)(b) (as substituted by s 104(3) of SOCPA) provides a defence where the **21.26**
person is a professional legal adviser or relevant professional adviser and the information or
other matter came to him in the circumstances set out in s 330(10).

'Relevant professional adviser' is defined by s 330(14), which is inserted by the Proceeds **21.27**
of Crime Act 2002 and Money Laundering Regulations 2003 (Amendment) Order 2006
(SI 2006/308) and includes accountants, auditors, and tax advisers who are members
of a professional body.

The effect of these amendments are to extend the defence available to professional legal **21.28**
advisers and to provide a defence for a person employed by, or in partnership with, a professional legal adviser or a relevant professional adviser. They came into force on 21 February
2006.

Section 330(10) states: **21.29**

Information or other matter comes to a professional legal advisor or relevant professional adviser in
privileged circumstances if it is communicated or given to him—
(a) by (or by a representative of) a client of his in connection with the giving by the advisor of legal
advice to the client,
(b) by (or by a representative of) a person seeking legal advice from the advisor, or
(c) by a person in connection with legal proceedings or contemplated legal proceedings.

However, s 330(10) does not apply to information or other matter that is communicated
or given to the legal adviser with the intention of furthering a criminal purpose (see
s 330(11) and *Francis and Francis v Central Criminal Court* [1988] 3 All ER 775 (HL)).

The important decision of *Bowman v Fels* [2005] EWCA Civ 226 in relation to profes- **21.30**
sional legal advisers is considered in detail below.

Failure to disclose: nominated officers in the regulated sector

Section 331 of POCA criminalises conduct where a nominated officer receives a report **21.31**
under s 330 which causes him to know or suspect, or gives reasonable grounds for knowledge

or suspicion, that money laundering is taking place, and where that nominated officer does not disclose that information 'as soon as practicable' after it comes to him.

21.32 A nominated officer is a person nominated to receive disclosures under s 338 (see s 336(11)), ie a person nominated to receive authorised disclosures relating to the money laundering offences under ss 327(1), 328(1), or 329(1), as the case may be.

21.33 The nominated officer will often be the person nominated by the alleged offender's employer to receive authorised disclosures (see s 338(5)(a)).

21.34 Section 331 states:

(1) A person nominated to receive disclosures under section 330 commits an offence if the conditions in subsections (2) to (4) are satisfied.

(2) The first condition is that he—

(a) knows or suspects, or

(b) has reasonable grounds for knowing or suspecting,

that another person is engaged in money laundering.

(3) The second condition is that the information or other matter—

(a) on which his knowledge or suspicion is based, or

(b) which gives reasonable grounds for such knowledge or suspicion,

came to him in consequence of a disclosure made under section 330.

(3A) The third condition is—

(a) that [the individual] knows the identity of the other person mentioned in subsection (2), or the whereabouts of any of the laundered property, in consequence of a disclosure made under s 330,

(b) that that other person, or the whereabouts of any of the laundered property, can be identified from the information or other matter mentioned in subsection (3), or

(c) that [the individual] believes, or it is reasonable to expect him to believe, that the information or other matter will or may assist in identifying that other person or the whereabouts of any of the laundered property.

(4) The fourth condition is that he does not make the required disclosure to a person authorised for the purposes of Part 7 [of POCA] . . . as soon as is practicable, after the information or other matter . . . comes to him. [as amended by s 104(4) of SOCPA].

21.35 The required disclosure must be made to either a person authorised by SOCA or in the form and manner prescribed under s 339 (see s 331(5)). The 'reasonable grounds' element of the criteria introduces a negligence test to the legislation.

21.36 The 'required disclosure' is a disclosure of: (a) the identity of the other person mentioned in s 3A(2), if disclosed to him under the applicable section, (b) the whereabouts of the laundered property, so far as disclosable to him under the applicable section, and (c) the information or other matter mentioned in s 3A(3).

21.37 By s 3A(5A), the 'laundered property' is the property forming the subject matter of the money laundering that the individual knows or suspects that other person to be engaged in.

'Defence' available

21.38 A person does not commit an offence under s 331 if he has a 'reasonable excuse' for not disclosing the information or other matter (see s 331(6)). Similarly, a new sub (6A) has been inserted after sub (6) which is in identical terms to the inserted defences available under s 330 (set out above).

As stated previously, the language used in POCA is different to that used in the CJA 1988; **21.39** in particular the draftsmen of POCA do not use the word 'defence' in the relevant parts of the statute. Nevertheless, it is clear that an individual will not have committed the offence in question if one of the 'exemptions' set out in the Act apply.

Considerations for the court

In deciding whether a nominated officer has committed an offence under s 331, the court **21.40** must consider whether he followed any relevant guidance which was at the time concerned issued by a supervisory authority or any other appropriate body and approved by the Treasury (see s 331(7)). An 'appropriate body' is a body which regulates or is representative of a trade, profession, business, or employment (see s 331(9)).

Failure to disclose: other nominated officers

Under s 332, it is an offence where a nominated officer receives a report under either s 337 **21.41** or s 338 (protected disclosures or authorised disclosures) which causes him to know or suspect that money laundering is taking place, and notwithstanding that, he does not disclose the report as soon as the information comes to him. The offence is committed if the following four conditions under s 332(1) to (4) are satisfied:

(1) that the person nominated knows or suspects that another person is engaged in money laundering;
(2) that the information or other matter on which his knowledge or suspicion is based came to him as a consequence of disclosure made under the applicable section;
(3) that—
  (a) he knows the identity of the other person mentioned in subs(2), or the whereabouts of any of the laundered property, in consequence of a disclosure made under the applicable section,
  (b) that other person, or the whereabouts of any of the laundered property, can be identified from the information or other matter mentioned in subsection (3) [(2) above], or
  (c) he believes, or it is reasonable for him to expect to believe, that the information or other matter will or may assist in identifying that other person or the whereabouts of any of the laundered property.
(4) that he does not make the required disclosures 'as soon as in practicable' after the information or other matter comes to him.

Under s 332(5) a nominated officer is required to disclose to SOCA in the form prescribed **21.42** by s 339.

By subs 5B the 'applicable section' is s 337 (protected disclosures), or s 338 (authorised **21.43** disclosures).

The laundered property is the property forming the subject matter of the money launder- **21.44** ing that the individual knows or suspects the other person to be engaged in (subs 5A).

No breach of confidentiality

Pursuant to s 104(7) of SOCPA, s 337 of the Proceeds of Crime Act (Protected Disclosures) **21.45** has inserted after subs (4) the following:

(4A) Where a disclosure consists of a disclosure protected under sub-section (1) and a disclosure of either or both of—
  (a) the identity of the other person mentioned in sub-section (3), and
  (b) the whereabouts of property forming the subject matter of the money laundering that the discloser knows or suspects, or has reasonable grounds for knowing or suspecting, that other

persons to be engaged in, the disclosure of the thing mentioned in paragraphs (a) or in (b) (as well as the disclosure protected under sub-section (1)) is not to be taken to breach any restriction on the disclosure of information (however imposed).

21.46   Authorised disclosures have a similar proviso under s 338(4).

'Defence' available

21.47   It will be noted that under s 332(6) an individual does not commit an offence if he has a reasonable excuse for not making the required disclosure. SOCPA inserts a new defence in the guise of s 332(7), which is in identical terms to that set out in s 330 above.

21.48   As stated above, the language used in POCA is different to that used in the CJA 1988; in particular the draftsmen of POCA do not use the word 'defence' in the relevant parts of the statute. Nevertheless, it is clear that an individual will not have committed the offence in question if one of the 'exemptions' set out in the Act apply. Arguably it will be for the Crown to show that they do not apply, and therefore the burden will be on the prosecution.

C. Professional Legal Advisers

Introduction

21.49   It will be noted that professional legal advisers continue to be exempt from the reporting obligations if the information or other matter comes to them in legally privileged circumstances. The defence of lack of training under s 330(7)(B) also remains, as does the defence of 'reasonable excuse'.

21.50   Section 330(9)(A) confirms that legal professional privilege is not lost when professional legal advisers, including solicitors and barristers, discuss matters with the nominated officers in their firms. Legal professional privilege remains intact whether or not the nominated officer is himself a professional legal adviser. The new provision allows professional legal advisers and relevant professional advisers to take advice from their nominated officers, without formal disclosure being made to the nominated officer. This amendment has the effect of giving some comfort to both the profession and also the client.

Bowman v Fels

21.51   The case of *Bowman v Fels* [2005] EWCA Civ 226, (2005) 2 Cr App R 19 raised important issues relating to the ambit of POCA and its application to the legal profession. Because of its importance the Bar Council, the Law Society, and the former National Criminal Intelligence Service (NCIS) were all granted permission to intervene in the appeal.

The facts

21.52   The underlying facts were relatively straightforward. The claimant lived with the defendant for 10 years in a house that was registered in the defendant's sole name. After their relationship ended she asserted a right to the beneficial interest in the property arising out of a constructive trust. Her case was that before the house was purchased the defendant had expressly agreed with her that they would buy the property jointly. The defendant resisted her claim and the matter was listed for trial at the Central London County Court.

The claimant's solicitors notified NCIS prior to the hearing of their suspicion that the defendant had included the cost of the work he had carried out at the property within his business accounts and his VAT returns, even though these were unconnected with his business. The claimant's solicitors believed that s 328 of POCA obliged them to make this disclosure and that it also prevented them from telling either their client or the defendant's solicitors what they had done.

The claimant's solicitors proceeded to make a 'without notice' application to the judge for **21.53** an order vacating the trial date, after they had been told by NCIS that it was unlikely that the requisite consent would be granted before the trial started. The judge granted their application. The defendant's solicitors were informed of the terms of the order, but not on what basis it had been made. They responded with an application that the judge's order should be set aside and the claimant's solicitors should be directed to disclose the basis of their application and the evidence they had tendered in support of it. They had guessed, correctly, why the application had been made (see para 4 of the judgment).

The issues

Bowman v Fels focused on the applicability or otherwise of s 328 of POCA in a case where **21.54** information came to the attention of the lawyer for one of the parties in the course of legal proceedings leading him to know or, more likely, suspect that the other party was engaged in money laundering. Potential issues arose from the decision and guidance given by the President of the Family Division in *P v P (Ancillary Relief Proceeds of Crime)* [2004] Fam 1.

In *Bowman v Fels* the Court was invited to determine whether s 328 of POCA (arrange- **21.55** ments in money laundering) meant that as soon as a lawyer acting for a client in legal proceedings discovered or suspected anything in the proceedings that may facilitate the acquisition, use, or control (usually by his client or his client's opponent) of 'criminal property', he must immediately notify NCIS (now SOCA) of his belief, if he was to avoid being guilty of the criminal offence of being concerned in an arrangement which he knew or suspected facilitated such an activity (see para 20).

The issue at the centre of the appeal was whether s 328 applied to the ordinary conduct of **21.56** legal proceedings. There was also a narrower issue, namely if it did, whether Parliament could be taken, without using clear words to that effect, to have intended to override the important principles underlying legal professional privilege and the strict terms on which lawyers are permitted to have access to documents disclosed in the litigation process (para 24 of the judgment delivered by Brooke LJ).

The judgment

The Court (Brooke LJ) found that s 330 was only relevant where information or other mat- **21.57** ters coming to the attention of a person in the course of a business in the regulated sector led him to know or suspect, or have reasonable grounds for knowing or suspecting, that another person is engaged in money laundering (see para 55).

The Court held that where legal professionals learn of information in privileged circum- **21.58** stances they are exempt from any obligation of disclosure. This suggests that they may continue to act as legal professionals, and continue the conduct of any legal proceedings or the giving of any legal advice, without making a disclosure, although clearly caution should be exercised.

21.59 *Per* the Court:

> . . . There seems to us to be considerable room for argument, although it is unnecessary to express any concluded view on this, that the protection intended in respect of the giving of legal advice must have been intended to cover advice given in the context of a transaction which the client was about to undertake; it cannot, in other words, have been envisaged that a legal professional would be 'carrying out a transaction' merely because he had advised in relation to it. (para 16.)

21.60 The Court went on to state:

> It cannot in our view have been conceived that the ordinary conduct of litigation to its ordinary conclusion, resolving the rights and duties of two parties according to law, could be said to involve the 'carrying out' of a 'transaction' related to money laundering. This would remain the case even if assets which happen to be the proceeds of money laundering might be the subject of claims in the proceedings, or be retained or used to satisfy any liability according to the outcome of the proceedings. The purpose of litigation—to resolve rights and duties according to law—and the public scrutiny to which it is subject, together with the presence and role of the judge, also distinguish legal proceedings from any 'transaction' that the European legislator can have had in mind, as well as offering safeguards against misconduct. (See para 62.)

21.61 The absence from s 328 of any equivalent protection to that contained in respect of the regulated sector in s 330(10) is a strong argument for a restricted understanding of the concept of 'being concerned in an arrangement' in s 328(1). The Court held that although s 328 applies to any person and is not limited like s 330 to the regulated sector, s 328 only applies if a person 'enters into or becomes concerned in an arrangement' which he knows or suspects facilitates the acquisition, retention, use, or control of criminal property. In the Court's view, it was improbable that Parliament had the ordinary conduct of legal proceedings in mind when drafting s 328 (or indeed ss 327 and 329).

21.62 The Court in *Bowman v Fels* commented that in *P v P* no distinction had been drawn between acting for a party in litigation (or, as it was put, seeking an arrangement from the court) and negotiating the settlement of a financial dispute (para 64). It was also assumed in *P v P* that a legal professional could become concerned in an arrangement prior to its execution, by, for example the act of negotiating it (see para 48 of *P v P*). However, in *Bowman v Fels* the Court held that a judgment or order is not an arrangement within the section and they found the word 'arrangement' to be a most unnatural use of language in this legal context (para 65). They stated that in s 328 the nature of the act is 'either entering into an arrangement or the vaguer concept of becoming concerned in an arrangement'. To enter into an arrangement involves a single act at a single point in time; so, too, on the face of it, does 'to become concerned' in an arrangement, even though the point at which someone may be said to have 'become' concerned may be open to argument.

21.63 As a result, the court rejected the notion that the ordinary pursuit or conduct of legal proceedings could give rise to an 'arrangement' which facilitated the acquisition, retention, use, or control of criminal property under s 328, (para 68), and thus distinguished and rejected *P v P*.

The court held that so far as UK domestic law was concerned, it was elementary that when   **21.64**
a lawyer is advising a client or acting for him in litigation, he may not disclose to a third
party any information about his client's affairs without his express or implied consent
(see para 78 and *R v Derby Magistrates' Court ex p B* [1996] 1 AC 487 at pp 503–508 and
Three Rivers DC v Bank of England (No 6) [2004] 3 WLR 1274, where the House of
Lords re-stated emphatically that legal advice privilege was just as important as litigation
privilege, and that for good policy reasons the law affords a special privilege to communications between lawyers and their clients which it denies to all other confidential
communications.

Conclusion

The Court concluded that the proper interpretation of s 328 is that it is not intended to   **21.65**
cover or affect the ordinary conduct of litigation by legal professionals. That included any
step taken by them in litigation, from the issue of proceedings and the securing of injunc-
tive relief or a freezing order up to its final disposal by judgment. Legal proceedings were
defined as a State-provided mechanism for the resolution of issues according to law.

The Court went on to consider the narrower issue of whether, on its true construction,   **21.66**
s 328 had the effect of overriding legal professional privilege and the terms upon which
lawyers are permitted to have access to documents disclosed in the litigation process. The
Court concluded that there was nothing in the language of s 328 to suggest that Parliament
expressly intended to override such privilege and formed the firm opinion that it would
require much clearer language than is contained in s 328 and its ancillary sections, before a
parliamentary intention could be gleaned to the effect that a party's solicitor is obliged, in
breach of his implied duty to the court, and in breach of the duty of confidence he owes to
his own client as the litigation solicitor, to disclose to SOCA a suspicion he may have that
documents disclosed under compulsion by the other party raised an issue under s 328.

As a result, the Court concluded that s 328 was to be interpreted as including legal proceed-   **21.67**
ings within its purview, and could not be interpreted as meaning that either legal professional privilege is to be overridden or that a lawyer is in breach of his duty to the court by
disclosing to a third party, external to the litigation, documents revealed to him through the
disclosure processes (see para 90).

Consensual resolution in a litigious context

In *Bowman v Fels*, the Court of Appeal considered the position where parties agreed to   **21.68**
dispose of the whole or any aspect of legal proceedings on a consensual basis. The consensual resolution of issues is an integral part of the conduct of ordinary civil litigation. There
is also within the Civil Procedure Rules a need to encourage cooperation and the value of
consensual settlement is underlined.

The Court commented that: **21.69**

> any consensual agreement can in abstract dictionary terms be called an arrangement. But we
> do not consider that it can have been contemplated that taking such a step in the context of
> civil litigation would amount to 'becoming concerned in an arrangement which . . . facilitates
> the acquisition, retention, use or control of criminal property' within the meaning of s 328.
> Rather it is another ordinary feature of the conduct of civil litigation, facilitating the resolution

of a legal dispute and of the parties' legal rights and duties according to law in a manner which is a valuable alternative to the court imposed solution of litigation and judgment.

The Court went on to state that the position could be different if one were concerned with a settlement which did not reflect the legal and practical merits of the parties' respective positions in the proceedings, and was known or suspected to be no more than a pretext for an agreement relating to the acquisition, retention, use, or control of criminal property.

POCA clauses

21.70   The Court in *Bowman v Fels* left open the permissibility or possibility of a POCA clause, whereby an arrangement might be entered into, but expressly made subject to it: 'not taking effect until authorised disclosure has been made pursuant to s 328 of POCA and appropriate consent is given or deemed to be given under s 335 of that Act'.

21.71   The Court commented that a question could arise whether the making of such an arrangement, even though its validity or implementation were to be made subject to the condition, could itself be a prohibited act within ss 328(1) and 338.

21.72   The Court stated (at para 103) that it remained uneasy about a clause which would disclose to all concerned (including the other party, who might well be the person suspected of money laundering activity) that money laundering was suspected.

21.73   It commented that, curiously, the prohibition on tipping off under s 333 only applied once a disclosure to the authorities has been made. In *Bowman v Fels*, the Court stated that both s 330(3)(c) and (4) and s 342(3)(c) and (4) preserve a broad freedom to make disclosure not merely to a client when giving legal advice, but to any person in connection with actual or contemplated legal proceedings, so it may be that a POCA clause would create no problem in the context of legal proceedings (see para 104), but clearly caution should be exercised.

21.74   It is also important to note that whilst the litigation in related processes may fall outside of the ambit of the offences, the property itself remains criminal property for the purposes of s 340(3) of POCA. Therefore any future dealings with the property after the terms of any judgment or settlement are carried out will require a re-examination of whether a report to SOCA is required. Solicitors will also need to advise their clients about their own position if ownership of criminal property by them falls outside a court order or other type of settlement covered by the exclusion. The s 329 offence of acquisition, use, and possession may be particularly relevant in these circumstances.

21.75   It should further be noted that neither common law legal professional privilege nor the s 330(6) exemption apply to communications made with the intention of furthering a criminal purpose.

Protection for judges

21.76   In relation to judges who suspect that the subject matter of the dispute may be criminal property, the Court of Appeal has made it clear that their judgments and orders will not constitute an 'arrangement' for the purposes of s 328 (see para 65 of their judgment). While the Court of Appeal does not expressly address the position of either arbitrators or mediators, it must be implied that the same considerations will be applied.

D. Suspicious Activity Reports: 'SARs'

Introduction

Suspicious Activity Reports (SARs) are one of the government's main weapons in the battle **21.77** against money laundering and other financial crimes. These reports generate leads that law enforcement agencies use to initiate money laundering investigations. A SAR should be made as soon as the knowledge or suspicion that criminal proceeds exist has arisen, especially if consent may be required, or at the earliest opportunity thereafter.

SOCA's preferred method for reporters to submit their suspicion is the SOCA Suspicious **21.78** Activity Report Form. SOCA prefers these forms to be submitted electronically, but hardcopy versions of the forms can be found on the SOCA website or can be obtained directly from SOCA. The Standard Form consists of six separate sheets ('modules').

SOCA do not usually acknowledge any SAR sent by fax, post, or by letter. Electronic **21.79** submissions through money.web, bulk submission, or through the SAR Online system will receive an acknowledgment which will include an automatically generated ELMER reference number.

Why is completing a SAR important?

One of the 'defences' to the money laundering offences in sections 327 to 329 is the making **21.80** of an authorised disclosure and the obtaining of appropriate consent.

An authorised disclosure (s 338) is a disclosure which is made: **21.81**

- before a person does the act prohibited by ss 327 to 329,
- while a person is doing the act prohibited by ss 327 to 329, the act having begun at a point when the discloser did not know or suspect that the property is the proceeds of crime and the disclosure being made on the discloser's own initiative as soon as practicable after he first knew or suspected that the property is the proceeds of crime, or
- after the act prohibited by ss 327 to 329 and is made on the discloser's own initiative as soon as practicable after the act

Appropriate consent is the consent of a constable, Customs officer, or SOCA officer to **21.82** proceed with a prohibited act (s 335).

A key element of consent is the specification of time limits within which the authorities **21.83** must respond to an authorised disclosure in circumstances where a consent decision is required. The law specifies that consent decisions must be made within seven working days. The seven-day notice period commences on the day after a disclosure is made and excludes bank holidays and weekends. The purpose of the seven-day notice period is to allow SOCA and its law enforcement partners time to risk assess, analyse, research, and undertake further enquiries relating to the disclosed information in order to determine the best response to the request for consent.

If nothing is heard within that time, then the discloser can go ahead with an otherwise **21.84** prohibited act without an offence being committed. If consent is withheld within the seven working days, then the authorities have a further 31 calendar days in which to take further action, such as seeking a court order to restrain the assets in question. The 31 days include Saturdays, Sundays, and public holidays.

21.85 It is an offence to undertake the act during this 'moratorium' period as the participant would not have the appropriate consent. The moratorium period enables SOCA to further their investigation into the reported matter using the powers within POCA in relation to the criminal property (eg imposing a restraint order). If nothing is heard after the end of the 31-day period, then the discloser can proceed with the transaction without committing an offence.

Notification of consent

21.86 In the first instance, a consent decision will usually be communicated to the reporter by telephone in order to provide the quickest possible response. SOCA will also send a letter by post recording the decision, but there is no requirement to wait for this letter in order to proceed with the prohibited act if consent has been granted verbally.

The legislative scheme

21.87 Section 339 of POCA (as amended by s 105 of SOCPA) states:

(1) The Secretary of State may by order prescribe the form and manner in which a disclosure under section 330, 331, 332 or 338 must be made.

(1A) A person commits an offence if he makes a disclosure under section 330, 331, 332 or 338 otherwise than in the form prescribed under subsection (1) or otherwise than in the manner so prescribed.

(1B) But a person does not commit an offence under subsection (1A) if he has a reasonable excuse for making the disclosure otherwise than in the form prescribed under subsection (1) or (as the case may be) otherwise than in the manner so prescribed.

(2) The power under subsection (1) to prescribe the form in which a disclosure must be made includes power to provide for the form to include a request to a person making a disclosure that the person provide information specified or described in the form if he has not provided it in making the disclosure.

(3) Where under subsection (2) a request is included in a form prescribed under subsection (1), the form must—

(a) state that there is no obligation to comply with the request, and

(b) explain the protection conferred by subsection (4) on a person who complies with the request.

Completing the form

21.88 A SAR should be made as soon as the knowledge or suspicion that criminal proceeds exist has arisen, especially if consent may be required, or at the earliest opportunity thereafter.

21.89 It is advisable to include as much Customer Due Diligence (CDD) detail as possible. The type of information likely to be of use to SOCA will be the person's full name, date of birth, passport number, National Insurance number, telephone numbers (home, business, and mobile), company name/registration number, email addresses, associated addresses, and postcodes, if you have this information. Current and previous addresses would also be of assistance.

You should also provide an initial summary that sets out the grounds for suspicion and, **21.90** where possible, any known links to criminality. If possible, detail chronologically the dates of individual transactions. Where you are suspicious because the activity deviates from the normal activity for that customer, business, or sector, you may need to explain what the normal activity is and how this differs. Include the value of the transactions involved, the origins/destination of the funds, and, if applicable, the associated crime number. Also, where applicable, give the reference numbers of any previous related SARs.

Limited Intelligence Value Reports

The Limited Intelligence Value Report (LIVR) is a briefer document to a full SAR and **21.91** allows financial institutions to adhere to their obligations under POCA when they have reasonable grounds to suspect money laundering, but in circumstances where they may only hold limited information or value in terms of law enforcement. They are of particular use for minor irregularities where there is nothing to suggest that the conduct is as a result of dishonest behaviour.

SOCA produces full guidance notes that relate to when LIVRs should be used, available **21.92** on their website. If you are not sure which form to use when making a report you should use the Standard Form.

E. Tipping Off

The offence of tipping off

If a person was to disclose to the subject of an investigation the fact that law enforcement **21.93** authorities had commenced an enquiry into his affairs, or that a production order had been obtained in relation to his bank accounts, or that a financial institution had disclosed a suspicious transaction, this could seriously prejudice the outcome of the enquiry. Accordingly, the legislation has been framed in such a way that such disclosures can in themselves give rise to criminal charges. POCA has been amended by the Terrorism Act 2000 and Proceeds of Crime Act 2002 (Amendment) Regulations 2007 (SI 2007/3398) to ensure investigations are not curtailed or prejudiced by way of 'tipping off'.

In the regulated sector a person commits an offence if: **21.94**

(1) ...
    (a) the person discloses any matter within subsection (2);
    (b) the disclosure is likely to prejudice any investigation that might be conducted following the disclosure referred to in that subsection; and
    (c) the information on which the disclosure is based came to the person in the course of a business in the regulated sector.
(2) The matters are that the person or another person has made a disclosure under this Part—
    (a) to a constable,
    (b) to an officer of Revenue and Customs,
    (c) to a nominated officer, or
    (d) to a member of staff of the Serious Organised Crime Agency authorised for the purposes of this Part by the Director General of that Agency,
of information that came to that person in the course of a business in the regulated sector.

(3) A person commits an offence if—
 (a) the person discloses that an investigation into allegations that an offence under this Part has been committed is being contemplated or is being carried out;
 (b) the disclosure is likely to prejudice that investigation; and
 (c) the information on which the disclosure is based came to the person in the course of a business in the regulated sector.

Sentence

21.95 The penalty for an offence under this section is, on summary conviction, a term not exceeding three months, or a fine not exceeding level 5 on the standard scale, or both; and on conviction on indictment, imprisonment for a term not exceeding two years, or to a fine, or to both.

'Defences' available

21.96 Sections 333B to 333D set out effectively the 'defences' available to a person who may be involved in a tipping-off offence. These sections provide:

333B Disclosures within an undertaking or group etc
(1) An employee, officer or partner of an undertaking does not commit an offence under section 333A if the disclosure is to an employee, officer or partner of the same undertaking.
(2) A person does not commit an offence under section 333A in respect of a disclosure by a credit institution or a financial institution if—
 (a) the disclosure is to a credit institution or a financial institution,
 (b) the institution to whom the disclosure is made is situated in an EEA State or in a country or territory imposing equivalent money laundering requirements, and
 (c) both the institution making the disclosure and the institution to whom it is made belong to the same group.
(3) In subsection (2) 'group' has the same meaning as in Directive 2002/87/EC of the European Parliament and of the Council of 16th December 2002 on the supplementary supervision of credit institutions, insurance undertakings and investment firms in a financial conglomerate.
(4) A professional legal adviser or a relevant professional adviser does not commit an offence under section 333A if—
 (a) the disclosure is to a professional legal adviser or a relevant professional adviser,
 (b) both the person making the disclosure and the person to whom it is made carry on business in an EEA State or in a country or territory imposing equivalent money laundering requirements, and
 (c) those persons perform their professional activities within different undertakings that share common ownership, management or control.

333C Other permitted disclosures between institutions etc
(1) This section applies to a disclosure—
 (a) by a credit institution to another credit institution,
 (b) by a financial institution to another financial institution,
 (c) by a professional legal adviser to another professional legal adviser, or
 (d) by a relevant professional adviser of a particular kind to another relevant professional adviser of the same kind.
(2) A person does not commit an offence under section 333A in respect of a disclosure to which this section applies if—
 (a) the disclosure relates to—
  (i) a client or former client of the institution or adviser making the disclosure and the institution or adviser to whom it is made,
  (ii) a transaction involving them both, or
  (iii) the provision of a service involving them both;

(b) the disclosure is for the purpose only of preventing an offence under this Part of this Act;

(c) the institution or adviser to whom the disclosure is made is situated in an EEA State or in a country or territory imposing equivalent money laundering requirements; and

(d) the institution or adviser making the disclosure and the institution or adviser to whom it is made are subject to equivalent duties of professional confidentiality and the protection of personal data (within the meaning of section 1 of the Data Protection Act 1998).

333D Other permitted disclosures etc

(1) A person does not commit an offence under section 333A if the disclosure is—

  (a) to the authority that is the supervisory authority for that person by virtue of the Money Laundering Regulations 2007 (SI 2007/2157); or

  (b) for the purpose of—

    (i) the detection, investigation or prosecution of a criminal offence (whether in the United Kingdom or elsewhere),

    (ii) an investigation under this Act, or

    (iii) the enforcement of any order of a court under this Act.

(2) A professional legal adviser or a relevant professional adviser does not commit an offence under section 333A if the disclosure—

  (a) is to the adviser's client, and

  (b) is made for the purpose of dissuading the client from engaging in conduct amounting to an offence.

(3) A person does not commit an offence under section 333A(1) if the person does not know or suspect that the disclosure is likely to have the effect mentioned in section 333A(1)(b).

(4) A person does not commit an offence under section 333A(3) if the person does not know or suspect that the disclosure is likely to have the effect mentioned in section 333A(3)(b).

In these sections 'relevant professional adviser' means an accountant, auditor, or tax adviser **21.97** who is a member of a professional body which is established for accountants, auditors, or tax advisers (as the case may be) and which makes provision for:

(a) testing the competence of those seeking admission to membership of such a body as a condition for such admission; and

(b) imposing and maintaining professional and ethical standards for its members, as well as imposing sanctions for non-compliance with those standards.

As stated elsewhere in this chapter, the language used in POCA is different from that used **21.98** in the CJA 1988; in particular the draftsmen of POCA do not use the word 'defence' in the relevant parts of the statute. Nevertheless, it is clear that an individual will not have committed the offence in question if one of the 'exemptions' set out in the Act apply. Arguably it will be for the Crown to show that they do not apply, and therefore the burden will be on the prosecution. Having said that, there is something of an inevitability that in many cases the best evidence for applying the 'exemptions' will come from the defendant.

Case law

The case law in this area is currently confined to the earlier legislation, the amendments **21.99** made by the Terrorism Act 2000 and Proceeds of Crime Act 2002 (Amendment) Regulations 2007 being relatively recent. The difficulties encountered by virtue of the tipping-off provisions were highlighted in *Bank of Scotland v A* [2001] 1 WLR 751, where the Court of Appeal stated:

> The tipping-off legislation which was the source of the problem with which this appeal deals, gave extensive powers to the police. Properly used they were beneficial. Misused they could

create unintended consequences. It is of the greatest importance that the use of those powers is confined to situations where it is appropriate. Institutions such as banks need to be able to ensure that they are not affected adversely or unnecessarily because of the existence of the police's powers.

21.100 In *A Bank v A Ltd (Serious Fraud Office, Interested Party)* The Times, 18 July 2000 (first instance), Laddie J held that a bank does not become a constructive trustee of money deposited with it merely because it entertains suspicions as to the provenance of the money. If a bank, being aware that a money laundering investigation was being conducted into the affairs of its customer, made an *ex parte* application for an order freezing the customer's funds on deposit with itself, such an order should not be made if the effect of the tipping-off legislation (s 93D of the CJA 1988) would be to prevent the order, skeleton arguments, witness statements, or transcripts from being disclosed to the respondent. The Court held that it was a fundamental principle that no one should be tried or deprived of his property without being told of the claims against him and having the opportunity to be heard; and the court should protect the rights and interests not only of those who were innocent, but also of those not proved to be guilty. The bank appealed Laddie J's decision.

21.101 The Court of Appeal (reported as *BS v A* [2001] 1 WLR 751) considered a situation where the police informed the bank that money laundering investigations were being conducted into activities closely associated with one of its customers, in consequence of which the bank was put in a dilemma: if it paid out, it might be liable to third parties as a constructive trustee, whereas if it did not, an action could be brought against the bank and it would be unable to defend itself because the police would object to the bank revealing what it had been told. The Court held that the question of what information could be revealed should have been capable of agreement between the bank, the police, and the Serious Fraud Office (SFO). Failing such agreement, the appropriate remedy was not to seek an *ex parte* order freezing the customer's account, but to seek an interim declaration under the Civil Procedure Rules 1998 r 25.1(1)(b).

21.102 In such an application the SFO would be the defendant and the court could set out what information it would be proper for the bank to rely on. The making of the application would protect the bank from criminal proceedings. In *BS v A* it was also held that the ability of the court to give directions would ensure that banks were not adversely affected by the 'tipping-off legislation' which gave extensive powers to the police, it being of the greatest importance that those powers were only used in situations where it was appropriate. The Court of Appeal added that the powers of the court were discretionary and an application should only be made where there was a real dilemma requiring the court's intervention: the making of an application should not be regarded as a substitute for a decision within the area of the bank's commercial responsibility.

22

COSTS, FUNDING ISSUES, AND COMPENSATION

A. Introduction

22.01 Restraint orders are made when the court is satisfied, amongst other things, that there is 'reasonable cause to believe' that the defendant has benefited from the criminal activity with which he is charged (s 40(2) of the Proceeds of Crime Act 2002 (POCA)). When the case comes to trial, however, the jury has to be satisfied of the defendant's guilt *beyond reasonable doubt* in order to record the conviction that is the essential prerequisite to a confiscation order being made. Sometimes a defendant who has been subject to a restraint order for a substantial period of time will be acquitted. Then the restraint order will promptly be discharged (s 42(6)), but he may have incurred costs in defending the proceedings and, together with other parties holding realisable property, have suffered a loss in complying with the terms of the restraint order.

22.02 The purpose of this chapter is to consider the rights of the defendant to seek costs and compensation against the prosecuting authority. We have divided it into various parts, including: issues relating to costs; legal fees and Legal Service Commission (LSC) funding (formerly legal aid); receivership costs; compensation for the acquitted defendant, and the power to award compensation under POCA. There is necessarily some overlap with other chapters to give the reader a complete overview of the costs and compensation regime within asset forfeiture law.

Costs and compensation distinguished

22.03 Orders for costs and orders for compensation are distinct. An order for costs is confined to ordering the payment of legal costs incurred by the defendant in restraint order proceedings, which may extend to related contempt or receivership hearings, but does not extend to any other costs or expenses he may incur as a result of the order. An order for compensation, on the other hand, seeks not to recompense the defendant for legal costs, but to compensate him for any loss he has suffered as a result of complying with the order. Persons other than the defendant who hold realisable property may seek a compensation order.

B. The Magistrates' Court and Costs

The power of the magistrates' court to order costs

22.04 The power of magistrates to award costs on the hearing of a complaint is contained in s 64 of the Magistrates' Courts Act 1980:

(1) On the hearing of a complaint, a magistrates' court shall have the power in its discretion to make such order as to costs—

    (a) on making the order for which the complaint is made, to be paid by the defendant to the complainant;

    (b) on dismissing the complaint, to be paid by the complainant to the defendant, as it thinks just and reasonable . . .

22.05 Under s 64(2), the amount of any sum ordered to be paid under s 64(1) shall be specified in the order, or order of dismissal, as the case may be. The costs ordered to be paid under this section shall be enforceable as a civil debt (s 64(3)).

The sum ordered should not be in excess of the proper costs incurred, nor should it be a **22.06** penalty in the guise of costs (see *R v Highgate Justices ex p Petrou* [1954] 1 All ER 406).

The amount of the costs must be fixed by the courts 'as part of the adjudication' (*R v* **22.07** *Pwllheli Justices ex p Soane* [1948] 2 All ER 815) and may include the expenses of the claimant's witnesses, as well as the fee of his solicitor. It follows that the same justices who reached the decision on hearing the complaint must make the award for costs.

An award for costs made by the magistrates' court under s 64 is not enforceable by the **22.08** magistrates' court, but in effect becomes a civil debt enforceable by the successful party on application to the county court.

Under s 52 of the Courts Act 1971, magistrates are entitled to award costs where an infor- **22.09** mation or complaint has not been proceeded with (s 52(3)(b)). Where a complaint is not proceeded with, a magistrates' court may make such order as to costs to be paid by the complainant to the defendant as it thinks is just and reasonable.

The power to award costs is limited to making an order as to the costs of proceedings on the **22.10** complaint in question and does not give the court authority to award costs which may have been incurred in other proceedings. For example, the power to award costs in a forfeiture application would only relate to the costs and hearings which occurred after the lodging of the application for forfeiture. It would not extend to the continued detention hearing that had taken place prior to the application for forfeiture. Each continued detention hearing is a separate application supported by an information in its own right, and costs should be applied for and dealt with at the time of the continued detention hearing (see *R v Magistrates' Court at Dover ex p Customs and Excise Commissioners* (1995) 160 JP 233).

There is no right to appeal to the Crown Court against a costs order by the magistrates (see **22.11** *R v Crown Court at Lewis ex p Rogers* [1974] 1 All ER 589).

The issue when seeking to obtain defence costs

In *Perinpanathan v City of Westminster Magistrates' Court and 2 others* [2009] EWHC 762 **22.12** (Admin) the test for the award of costs to a successful defendant was considered and set out. The Divisional Court adopted the words of Lord Bingham in *Bradford Metropolitan District Council v Booth* (CO/3219/99) The Times, 31 May 2000, a case where the local council had refused to renew Mr Booth's private hire operator's licence on the grounds Mr Booth had broken a condition, but in which Mr Booth had appealed to the magistrates' court and had been successful, He sought his costs on the basis that they should follow the event (CPR 44.3). Lord Bingham stated:

23. I would accordingly hold that the proper approach to questions of this kind can for convenience be summarised in three propositions:
24. (1) Section 64(1) confers a discretion upon a Magistrates' Court to make such order as to costs as it thinks just and reasonable. That provision applies both to the quantum of the costs (if any) to be paid, but also as to the party (if any) which should pay them.
25. (2) What the court will think just and reasonable will depend on all the relevant facts and circumstances of the case before the court. The court may think it just and reasonable that costs should follow the event, but need not think so in all cases covered by the subsection.

26. (3) Where a complainant has successfully challenged before justices an administrative decision made by a police or regulatory authority acting honestly, reasonably, properly and on grounds that reasonably appeared to be sound, in exercise of its public duty, the court should consider, in addition to any other relevant fact or circumstances, both (i) the financial prejudice to the particular complainant in the particular circumstances if an order for costs is not made in his favour; and (ii) the need to encourage public authorities to make and stand by honest, reasonable and apparently sound administrative decisions made in the public interest without fear of exposure to undue financial prejudice if the decision is successfully challenged.

22.13 The magistrates' court in *Perinpanathan* had refused to award costs, on the basis that the cash seizure had been properly brought by the police. The Divisional Court concluded that they had acted properly, Goldring LJ commenting (at 29):

> . . . I accept that there is a difference between administrative decisions such as those referred to in *Bradford* and the present case. The distinction is limited, however. In one case a police officer (at possible risk to someone's livelihood) is saying that the person will not have a licence, for example. In the other, he is saying the person will not have his (or in this case her) money returned. In taking both decisions, it is crucial that the police act honestly, reasonably, properly, and on grounds that reasonably appear to be sound. In both cases there is a need to make and stand by honest, reasonable and apparently sound decisions in the public interest without fear of exposure to undue financial prejudice, in one case if the decision is successfully challenged, in the other if the application fails. There is a real public interest that the police seek an order for forfeiture if they consider that on the evidence it is more probable than not that the money was intended for an unlawful purpose. It would be quite contrary to the public interest if, due to fear of financial consequences, it was decided not to seek its forfeiture, but simply return the money. The public duty requires the police to make an application in such circumstances.

22.14 However, notwithstanding the court's refusal to pay costs to the successful party in this instance, the police or Revenue and Customs cannot assume that they may proceed with impunity. Goldring LJ made clear at para 33:

> . . . it should not be thought that those who bring these applications have carte blanche to make applications for forfeiture without any risk of costs being awarded against them. Such applications can result in grave injustice if not made honestly, reasonably, properly and on grounds that are sound. If applications are made inappropriately, the court should not hesitate to make an order for costs against the applicant.

C. The Crown Court and Costs

Restraint and receivership proceedings

22.15 The power of the Crown Court to award costs in restraint and receivership proceedings is set out within r 61.19 of the Criminal Procedure Rules (CrimPR), which provides:

(2) The court has discretion as to—
   (a) whether costs are payable by one party to another;
   (b) the amount of those costs; and
   (c) when they are to be paid.
(3) If the court decides to make an order about costs—
   (a) the general rule is that the unsuccessful party will be ordered to pay the costs of the successful party; but
   (b) the court may make a different order.

Rule 61.20 states: **22.16**

(1) Where the Crown Court has made an order for costs in restraint proceedings or receivership proceedings it may either—
   (a) make an assessment of the costs itself; or
   (b) order assessment of the costs under rule 78.3.
(2) In either case, the Crown Court or the taxing authority, as the case may be, must—
   (a) only allow costs which are proportionate to the matters in issue; and
   (b) resolve any doubt which it may have as to whether the costs were reasonably incurred or reasonable and proportionate in favour of the paying party.

Rule 61.21 states, in relation to the time allowed for complying with an order for costs: **22.17**

(1) A party to restraint proceedings or receivership proceedings must comply with an order for the payment of costs within 14 days of—
   (a) the date of the order if it states the amount of those costs;
   (b) if the amount of those costs is decided later under rule 78.3, the date of the taxing authority's decision; or
   (c) in either case, such later date as the Crown Court may specify.

Rule 61.20(5) of the CrimPR states that the court must have particular regard to: **22.18**

(a) the conduct of all the parties, including in particular, conduct before, as well as during, the proceedings;
(b) the amount or value of the property involved;
(c) the importance of the matter to all the parties;
(d) the particular complexity of the matter or the difficulty or novelty of the questions raised;
(e) the skill, effort, specialised knowledge and responsibility involved;
(f) the time spent on the application; and
(g) the place where and the circumstances in which work or any part of it was done.

Costs in the Crown Court generally are dealt with at r 76 CrimPR (representation orders); **22.19** r 77 CrimPR (recovery of defence costs orders); and r 78 CrimPR (costs ordered against the parties).

The acquitted defendant and costs

In deciding whether the acquitted defendant has brought the proceedings and related **22.20** hearings upon himself, the Crown Court will no doubt be influenced by the manner in which the defendant has conducted his defence, in particular the circumstances that led to the defendant's acquittal that could have been raised by the defendant at an earlier stage of proceedings. If the Crown Court judge, having heard all the evidence during a lengthy trial, forms the view that it is appropriate to award the acquitted defendant his costs from central funds, it is unlikely that he would take the view that the defendant should bear the entire costs of the restraint order proceedings.

Costs against the defendant in confiscation order cases

Orders for the payment of costs should only be made where the defendant has the ability **22.21** to pay them following a confiscation hearing (*R v Ghadami* [1997] Crim LR 606). If a confiscation order is made in what the court finds to be the full value of the defendant's realisable property, no order for costs should be made. In *R v Szrajber* [1994] Crim LR 543, the defendant's benefit from the offences concerned was found to be £524,000, but his realisable property was valued at £407,188 and a confiscation order was accordingly made in this lesser sum. In addition, an order for the payment of costs was made in the sum of £65,428. The Court of Appeal quashed the order for costs on the basis that a confiscation order had been made in the full amount of the defendant's benefit from the offence, and accordingly he had no further assets at his disposal from which the order for costs could be made.

22.22 In *R v Smart* (2003) 2 Cr App R(S) 384, the Court determined that where a judge, having passed sentence, adjourned the proceedings in contemplation of a confiscation hearing and subsequently said he was reserving the question of costs until the issue of confiscation had been decided, he was exercising his lawful power to postpone part of the sentence, and the fact that he subsequently decided that there could be no confiscation proceedings because of a failure to meet the statutory pre-conditions for such, did not deprive him of his power to award costs.

Experts' reports and prosecution costs

22.23 In *Balshaw v the CPS* [2009] EWCA Crim 470, the defendant argued that the judge at first instance had been wrong to order the defendant to pay for the costs of a KPMG forensic report commissioned by the Thames Valley Police for use in confiscation proceedings, on the basis that s 18 of the Prosecutions of Offences Act 1985 only permitted the Crown Court to order costs to be paid by the accused to 'the prosecutor', and the Crown Prosecution Service (CPS) were 'the prosecutor', and not the police.

22.24 The Court of Appeal found that there was no principle that the CPS could only recover those fees that it had directly incurred. If the court was satisfied that the CPS would compensate the police for the costs of the report, it was proper for the court to make an order requiring the defendant to meet the costs of the report.

D. Receivership Costs

22.25 In most cases, costs will follow the event and the defendant will be required to pay a receiver's costs if he chooses to challenge an application and then loses that challenge. As with all costs decisions, it is a matter of discretion for the court. It is common for the court to order that the costs of the receiver (and, sometimes, the prosecutor) be 'Costs in the receivership'—that is to say, met out of the sums realised by the receiver. This empowers the receiver to realise sufficient assets to pay the costs awarded. In most cases, the receiver will assess his fees on a time-cost basis in accordance with the grade and experience of the fee earner employed.

22.26 There may be cases in which the defendant considers that the fees charged are excessive. The defendant's interests can be adversely affected by a large bill from a receiver; if he has assets available, they will usually be realised in addition to those required to satisfy the confiscation order. If no such assets are available, the receiver's costs will normally be met out of the assets that have been realised in satisfaction of the confiscation order.

22.27 One of the remedies for the aggrieved defendant is to seek an order from the court that the proper remuneration of the receiver be assessed by a costs or district judge. The defendant should not, however, embark upon this course unless satisfied that he has a reasonable prospect of reducing the receiver's charges substantially, because an unsuccessful application is likely to result in a further award of costs against him. The defendant would therefore be well advised to obtain expert evidence (preferably from a licensed insolvency practitioner) before seeking an order for taxation.

Receiver's costs in litigation

Often a court-appointed receiver will become embroiled in litigation as a third party and **22.28** sometimes by default. Costs are often said to be 'in the receivership' when either the prosecuting authority or the receiver is successful in litigation, although this expression is rarely, if ever, properly defined. The receiver will often have costs beyond merely instructing solicitors and counsel. They also have to incur costs in preparing witness statements and time in conference, giving instructions etc. Costs have often been awarded 'in the receivership' even when the receiver has been unsuccessful in litigation and this once again gives rise to the question as to who truly should bear those costs. In *Re Nossen's Letter Patent* [1969] 1 WLR 683, Lloyd-Jacob J stated that the established practice of the courts was to disallow any sums claimed in respect of the time spent by the litigant personally in the course of instructing his solicitors, but that, in the case of litigation by a corporation, that practice had not been strictly applied, it being recognised that, if expert assistance is properly required, it may well occur that the corporation's own specialist employees may be the most suitable or convenient experts to employ and that the direct costs incurred, but not a contribution to overheads, should, in principle, be recoverable. He expressed (at p 644) his conclusion this way:

> When it is appropriate that a corporate litigant should recover, on a party and party basis, the sum in respect of expert services of this character performed by its own staff, the amount must be restricted to a reasonable sum for the actual and direct costs of the work undertaken.

In *London Scottish Benefit Society v Chorley* (1884) 12 QBD 452; 13 QBD 872 (CA), Sir **22.29** Gordon Willmer went further and stated that the professional skill can be measured and recognised by law. In his judgment at pp 37–38, he said that costs are 'intended to cover remuneration for the exercise of professional legal skill'. In relation to other skills he said:

> Other professional people, who become involved in litigation and conduct their own case, may recover something in respect of their own professional skill in so far as they qualify as witnesses and are called as such. Nobody else, however, except a solicitor, has ever been held entitled to make any charge, as I understand it, in respect of the exercise of a professional legal skill . . .

In *Sisu Capital Fund Ltd v Tucker and Wallace* [2005] EWHC 2321 (Ch), Warren J accepted **22.30** that there may be cases where, in the fulfilment of his duties as an office holder, a receiver has to bring or defend litigation:

> The fact that he does so does not mean that it is part of his profession to conduct litigation in the way that it is part of the profession of a solicitor to do so. An office holder is not unique in this respect: trustees of family trusts or of pension funds have fiduciary duties, the fulfilment of which may require them to bring or defend proceedings. That sort of duty on the part of an office holder or other fiduciary does not, in my judgement, afford any basis for a

difference in treatment, vis-à-vis payment of costs by an opposing party, from any other litigant. (Paragraph 40 of the judgment.)

Nor in his Lordship's judgment did the fact that an office holder's remuneration was ultimately under the control of the insolvency court make any difference to the result. The real reason he was not able to recover his costs was because he was not a professional seeking to recover costs for time spent in respect of his area of expertise.

22.31 It therefore appears that if a receiver has costs that are incurred doing work as an expert as part of the litigation (for which, if he was not in office, an expert would have to be employed to carry them out) then those costs are recoverable out of the costs award and the receivership estate. Whether the receiver would be entitled to recover other costs would be determined by his original letter and order of appointment.

Payment of receiver's costs from receivership assets

22.32 In January 2007 the House of Lords gave its opinion in the appeal of *Capewell v HM Revenue and Customs* [2007] UKHL 2, (2007) 1 WLR 386, following the Court of Appeal's decision in a CJA (High Court) receivership case that r 69.7(2) of the Civil Procedure Rules (CPR) was designed to give the Court some discretion in relation to who would pay the court-appointed receiver's remuneration. The Court of Appeal had accordingly made an order requiring Customs be responsible for payment of the receiver's remuneration for part of the period of the receivership.

22.33 Customs appealed the Court of Appeal's ruling in relation to this. There was, prior to the introduction of the CPR, a considerable body of case law that supported the proposition that a receiver's costs should normally be met from the estate under management and the assets within the receiver's control: in *Hughes v Customs and Excise Commissioners* [2003] 1 WLR 177, it was held that, in the absence of any special statutory rules, the receiver appointed under the CJA was to be treated in the same way as his common law counterpart appointed under order of the court. It followed that a receiver was in principle entitled to recover his costs from the assets under his control, even where there had been no conviction and no confiscation order had yet been made. In *Hughes* the Court had followed the decision of the Court of Appeal in *Re Andrews* [1999] 1 WLR 1236. In that case, the defendant and his son had been charged with offences relating to their joint business, and restraint orders had been made. The son was convicted, but the defendant was acquitted and awarded his costs out of central funds. The taxing officer held that such costs did not include the costs of the receivership (amounting to some £10,000). The receiver sought to recover those costs out of the assets under her control. The defendant applied for an order that they be paid by the prosecutor. That application failed. The Court felt bound to apply the established common-law practice that the costs of a court-appointed receiver were paid out of realised assets, following *Boehm v Goodall* [1911] 1 Ch 155, at pp 161–162, where Warrington J stated:

> I think it is of the utmost importance that receivers and managers in this position should know that they must look for their indemnity to the assets which are under the control of the Court. The Court itself cannot indemnify receivers, but it can, and will, do so out of the assets so far as they extend, for expenses properly incurred; but it cannot go further.

The Court in *Andrews* held that its discretion in relation to 'the costs of and incidental to **22.34** proceedings in the High Court' (Supreme Court Act 1981, s 51) did not extend to the costs of a receivership. Ward LJ said that he reached this conclusion with 'unfeigned reluctance', because it was 'manifestly unfair' that the defendant, having been paid his trial costs out of public funds, should not be indemnified for the loss caused by the ancillary receivership proceedings (pp 1244B–1246H).

The central issue in *Capewell* therefore concerned whether the case of *Hughes* remained **22.35** good law as a result of the introduction of r 69.7 CPR.

In upholding Customs' appeal, and giving the judgment of the Court (with which all of **22.36** their Lordships concurred), Lord Walker stated:

> 27. In my opinion CPR 69.7 has not had that far-reaching and surprising result. The function of CPR 69 is to set out a procedural code applicable to the generality of receiverships of all types. Its text gives no indication that its draftsman had particularly in mind the new species of receiverships in support of restraint orders and confiscation orders. No doubt its provisions do in general apply to such receiverships but they cannot override the scheme inherent in the detailed provisions of CJA 1988. That scheme is for the receiver's remuneration and expenses to be paid out of the receivership assets, but in a way which counts towards satisfaction of any confiscation order, and subject to the statutory long-stop already mentioned. If an individual subject to a restraint order is not ultimately convicted and made subject to a confiscation order, section 89 of CJA 1988 gives a statutory right to compensation in some circumstances. But Parliament has deliberately framed the right to compensation in narrow terms. That is an aggrieved individual's only right to compensation as such. He would not normally have the benefit of an undertaking in damages since (as Simon Brown LJ observed in *Hughes* at para 50) a prosecutor cannot be required to give an undertaking in damages as a condition of obtaining the appointment of a receiver. An aggrieved individual's only other recourse would be to challenge the amount of the receiver's remuneration, as the respondent has done in this case. There is a similar scheme under POCA 2002 and the Crown Court (Confiscation, Restraint and Receivership) Rules 2003 (SI 2003/421) made under that Act, but in these new provisions it is made perfectly clear that receivership expenses and remuneration are to come out of the assets subject to the receivership.
>
> 28. The Court of Appeal was in my opinion wrong to suppose that CPR 69.7 has made (or could have made) a fundamental change either in the general law of receiverships, or in the position of receiverships under CJA 1988 and the other comparable statutory powers. I would allow this appeal on that ground. There is also a further, narrower ground for concluding that the order of the Court of Appeal cannot be upheld. In the original order appointing Mr Sinclair as receiver, Jackson J directed that 'the costs of the receivership' (which in this context must mean expenses and remuneration) were to be paid in accordance with the agreement letter of 21 November 2002. That order was not appealed at the time (although it was contemplated that an early application would be made for discharge of the receiver) nor has there been any subsequent application for permission to appeal from it out of time. A receiver takes on heavy responsibilities when he accepts appointment, and he is entitled to the security of knowing that the terms of his appointment will not be changed retrospectively—even if an appellate court later decides that the receivership should have been terminated at an earlier date.

As a result, the common law position in *Hughes* has now been re-affirmed, and all receiver- **22.37** ships under the DTA, CJA, and POCA legislation will proceed on the basis that the overall costs of the receivership will be drawn from assets within the receivership estate, even if the defendant is subsequently acquitted, not proceeded against, or the receivership is successfully discharged.

22.38 His Lordship defined 'remuneration' as the professional fees of the receiver and his own staff, and confined 'costs' to litigation costs and 'expenses' to all other expenditure necessarily or properly incurred by the receiver in the performance of his duties (para 7).

22.39 As a result of this judgment one of the basic principles of receivership survives, namely that the receiver is entitled to be indemnified in respect of his costs and expenses, and his remuneration, out of the assets in his hands as receiver. This principle is firmly reflected for POCA cases in the Criminal Procedure Rules, which provide:

> (5) A receiver appointed under section 48 of the 2002 Act is to receive his remuneration by realising property in respect of which he is appointed, in accordance with section 49(2)(d) of the 2002 Act.
> (6) A receiver appointed under section 50 of the 2002 Act is to receive his remuneration by applying to the magistrates' court officer for payment under section 55(4)(b) of the 2002 Act.

The receiver's lien

22.40 In *Sinclair v Glatt* [2009] EWCA Civ 176, the court held that a receiver appointed under s 77 of the CJA could recover costs from assets held by a third party with a beneficial interest, even where the defendant had only bare legal title.

E. Costs: High Court/Civil Cases

22.41 The general rule, as in all civil cases, is that costs follow the event, ie the acquitted defendant is entitled to have his costs of the restraint order proceedings paid by the prosecutor, there being no power to direct their payment from central funds (see *Re W (Drug Trafficking) (Restraint Order: Costs)* The Times, 13 October 1994). The question of costs remains a matter of discretion and where it can be shown that the defendant has behaved in such a way as to bring the proceedings upon himself, he can properly be left to pay his own costs.

22.42 If, of course, the defendant makes an unmeritorious application to either the High Court or the Crown Court in restraint proceedings (eg for a variation of the order) he can properly be ordered to bear not only his own costs, but also those of the prosecution, in respect of that one application.

Court's discretion and circumstances to be taken into account when exercising its discretion as to costs

22.43 Rule 44.3 of the CPR 1998 reads as follows:

> (1) The court has discretion as to—
>   (a) whether the costs are payable by one party to another;
>   (b) the amount of those costs; and
>   (c) when they are to be made.
> (2) If the court decides to make an order about costs—
>   (a) the general rule is that the unsuccessful party will be ordered to pay the costs of the successful party; but
>   (b) the court may make a different order.
> (3) . . .

(4) In deciding what order (if any) to make about costs, the court must have regard to all the circumstances, including—
   (a) the conduct of the party;
   (b) whether a party has succeeded on part of his case, even if he has not been wholly successful; and
   (c) any payment into court or admissible offers to settle made by a party which is drawn to the court's attention (whether or not made in accordance with Part 36).

(5) The conduct of the parties includes—
   (a) conduct before, as well as during, the proceedings, and in particular the extent to which the parties followed any relevant pre-action protocol;
   (b) whether it was reasonable for a party to raise, pursue or contest a particular allegation or issue;
   (c) the manner in which a party has pursued or defended his case or a particular allegation or issue;
   (d) whether a claimant who has succeeded in his claim, in whole or in part, exaggerated his claim.

(6) The orders which the court may make under this rule include an order that a party must pay—
   (a) the proportion of another party's costs;
   (b) a stated amount in respect of another party's costs;
   (c) costs from or until a certain date only;
   (d) costs incurred before proceedings have begun;
   (e) costs relating to particular steps taken in the proceedings;
   (f) costs relating only to a distinct part of the proceedings; and
   (g) interest on costs from or until a certain date including a date before judgment.

(7) . . .

(8) Where the court has ordered a party to pay the costs, it may order an amount to be paid on account before the costs are assessed.

Basis of assessment

Under r 44.4 of the CPR, where the court is to assess the amounts of costs (whether **22.44** by summary or detailed assessment) it will assess those costs either on the standard basis, or on an indemnity basis, but the court will not in either case allow costs which have been unreasonably incurred or are unreasonable in amount.

Where the amount of costs is to be assessed on the standard basis, the court will: **22.45**

(a) only allow costs which are proportionate to the matters in issue; and
(b) resolve any doubt that it may have as to whether costs were reasonably incurred or reasonable and proportionate in an amount in favour of the paying party.

Factors to be taken into account in deciding the amount of costs

Rule 44.5 of the CPR states: **22.46**

(1) The court is to have regard to all the circumstances in deciding whether costs were—
   (a) if it is assessing costs on the standard basis—
      (i) proportionately and reasonably incurred; or
      (ii) were proportionate and reasonable in amount, or
   (b) if it is assessing costs on the indemnity basis—
      (i) unreasonably incurred; or
      (ii) unreasonable in amount.

(2) . . .

(3) The court must also have regard to—
   (a) the conduct of all the parties including in particular:
      (i) conduct before as well as during the proceedings, and
      (ii) the efforts made, if any, before and during the proceedings in order to try and resolve the dispute;

(b) the amount or value of any money or property involved;

(c) the importance of the matter to all the parties;

(d) the particular complexity of the matter or the difficulty or novelty of the question raised;

(e) the skill, effort, specialised knowledge and responsibility involved;

(f) the time spent on the case; and

(g) the place where and the circumstances in which work or any part of it was done.

Interim costs orders

22.47 Most orders will include a provision for costs. Where the court makes an order that does not mention costs, the general rule is that no party is entitled to costs in relation to that order (see r 44.13(1)(a) CPR).

22.48 The Costs Practice Direction that supplements the Civil Procedure Rules sets out the meanings of common interim costs orders (see s 8):

(1) Costs in any event or simply 'costs': the party in whose favour the order is made is entitled to the costs in respect of the part of the proceedings to which the order relates, whatever other costs orders are made in the proceedings.

(2) Costs in the case, or costs in the application: the party in whose favour the court makes an order for costs at the end of the proceedings is entitled to his costs of the part of the proceedings to which the order relates.

(3) Costs deferred: the decision about costs is deferred to a later occasion, but if no later order is made the costs will be 'costs in the case'.

(4) Claimant's/defendant's costs in the case at application: if the party in whose favour the costs order is made is awarded costs at the end of the proceedings, that party is entitled to his costs of the part of the proceedings to which the order relates. If any other party is awarded costs at the end of the proceedings, the party in whose favour the final costs order is made is not liable to pay the costs of any other party in respect of the part of the proceedings to which the order relates.

(5) Costs thrown away: where, eg a judgment or order is set aside, the party in whose favour the costs order is made is entitled to the costs that have been incurred as a consequence. This includes the costs of:

(a) preparing for and attending any hearing at which the judgment order which has been set aside has been made;

(b) preparing for and attending any hearing to set aside the judgement or order in question;

(c) preparing for and attending any hearing at which the court orders the proceedings or the part in question to be adjourned;

(d) any steps taken to enforce a judgment or order which has subsequently been set aside.

(6) Costs of and caused by: where eg the court makes an order on an application to amend a statement of case, the party in whose favour the costs order is made is entitled to the costs of preparing for and attending the application and the costs of any consequential amendment to his own statement of case.

(7) Costs here and below: the party in whose favour the costs order is made is entitled not only to his costs in respect of the proceedings in which the court makes the order but also his costs in the proceedings in any lower court. In the case of an appeal from a divisional court the party is not entitled to any costs incurred in any court below the divisional court.

(8) No order as to costs or each party to pay his own costs: each party is to pay his own costs of the part of the proceedings to which the order relates whatever costs order the court makes at the end of the proceedings.

(9) Where, under r 44.3(8), the court orders an amount to be paid before the costs are assessed:

(a) the order will state that amount, and

(b) if no other date for payment is specified in the order r 44.8 (Time for Complying with an Order for Costs) will apply.

Two further costs order are: **22.49**

(10) Costs in the receivership: such a costs order implies that the costs of the application will be borne as part of the receivership, ie the receiver will be entitled to claim the costs of the hearing and related legal expenses out of the receivership funds which they manage or control. Where an issue remains over the amount to be paid these costs will be expressed as 'Costs in the receivership, subject to taxation'.

(11) Costs not to be enforced without further leave of the court or 'It is further ordered that the costs of this claim be paid by the claimant/defendant, but the determination of the claimant's/ defendant's liability to pay such costs shall be postponed pending further order'. Sometimes referred to as the 'pools coupon' order, it is primarily designed to deal with legally aided claimants who lose an application or matter. The order for costs anticipates that should, at some future point, the claimant/defendant come into funds, then the successful party would be at liberty to get the matter restored and seek their litigation costs.

F. Legal Expenses and Legal Funding

Community Legal Service funding

Much of POCA deals with criminal proceedings e.g. the money laundering offences in Pt **22.50** 7 of the Act. Representation for defendants in criminal proceedings under POCA is funded in the same way as any other criminal proceedings. Representation orders can be granted by the court or funding provided through the Criminal Defence Service. However, the Act also creates a number of types of civil proceedings for which Community Legal Service (CLS) funding is available. Section 36 of Sch 11 of POCA amends Sch 2 of the Access to Justice Act 1999 to bring a range of proceedings in the Crown Court and magistrates' court within the scope of CLS funding.

All High Court proceedings under Pt 5 of the 2002 Act and all proceedings under Pts 2, 5, **22.51** or 8 of the Act which have been brought within Sch 2 of the Access to Justice Act 1999 are civil proceedings for which CLS funding is available.

The availability of public funding for proceedings under the 2002 Act can be summarised **22.52** as follows:

(a) Proceedings which are 'criminal proceedings' within the meaning of section 12.2 of the Access to Justice Act 1999 are funded through the Criminal Defence Service. Application for a representation order must be made to the court.

(b) Proceedings under the Act which are in the High Court or are otherwise specified under Sch 2 of the Access to Justice Act 1999 are civil proceedings for which CLS funding is available. Applications for funding must be made to the Commission.

(c) Representation in any proceedings under the 2002 Act which do not fall under (a) or (b) above can only be funded in exceptional cases under s 6(8)(b) of the 1999 Act.

Funding criteria

Where CLS funding is available for proceedings under POCA, applications for legal **22.53** representation will be subject to the normal CLS criteria for scope, means and merits. CLS funding under POCA will only be available for clients who are financially eligible for such funding under the CLS (Financial) Regulations 2000 as amended. Where seized assets have not been taken into account on the basis that they are the subject matter of the dispute, success in the proceedings resulting in the release of assets to the client will be treated as a recovery or preservation. The statutory charge will then apply. Any assets so recovered must therefore be paid to the solicitor and on to the Commission—see Regs 18 and 20 of the CLS (Costs) Regulations 2000.

Funding and confiscation orders

22.54 When the court is deciding whether to make a confiscation order, the proceedings will be covered by CDS funding under the representation order for the substantive criminal proceedings which led to the court considering confiscation. If for any reason no representation order is in force, application may be made to the court for a representation order to cover the hearing concerning the confiscation order. Such matters come within the definition of 'criminal proceedings' under s 12(2)(b) of the Access to Justice Act 1999 since they concern 'proceedings before any court for dealing with an individual convicted of an offence (including proceedings in respect of a sentence order)'.

22.55 There are other specific types of proceedings under Pt 2 for which CLS funding in the Crown Court is available. These are:

(a) Section 41/restraint order proceedings. Section 41(7) allows the court to make such other order as is appropriate to make the restraint order effective. CLS funding is available for applications to discharge or vary under section 42(3). Such funding is available both to defendants and third parties affected by the restraint order.

(b) When a confiscation order is not satisfied, the Crown Court has power to appoint a receiver in respect of any realisable property. Under section 54(3) and 56(3) an enforcement receiver has power to distribute assets, but can only do so after giving persons who have an interest in the property concerned a reasonable opportunity to make representations. CLS funding is available to enable any such persons to be represented in hearings in the Crown Court as to the distribution of assets. Note that CLS funding is only available to third parties, not to the original defendant against whom the confiscation order was made (see paragraph 3(2)(a) of Schedule 2 of the Access to Justice Act 1999).

(c) Any person affected by an action that a receiver takes or proposes to take may apply to the Crown Court under section 62. CLS funding is available for such applications. Such funding is available to either a defendant or a third party.

(d) Under sections 48 to 53 the court may appoint and confer a range of powers on receivers. Under section 63 any person affected by an order under sections 48 to 53 may apply to the Crown Court to vary or discharge the order. CLS funding is available for such proceedings both to defendants and third parties.

(e) Sections 72 and 73 give the Crown Court power to award compensation to persons who have suffered loss as a result of orders made or actions done under Part 2 of the 2002 Act. Section 72 concerns compensation for serious default. CLS funding is available both to defendants and third parties in applications under this section. Section 73 concerns compensation where a confiscation order is varied under section 29 (defendant was an absconder) or where a confiscation order is discharged under section 30 (defendant acquitted or not proceeded against). CLS funding is not available to defendants who are claiming compensation under section 73 where the confiscation order was varied under section 29 (see paragraph 3(2)(b) of Schedule 2 of the Access to Justice Act 1999). Otherwise CLS funding is available to defendants and third parties for applications for compensation under sections 72 or 73.

Problems with confiscation funding and stays

In *Crown Prosecution Service v Susan Jane Campbell and Ors* [2009] EWCA Crim 997 the **22.56** facts were as follows. In February 2008 Susan Campbell had pleaded guilty to one count of money laundering. On 16 October 2008 the issue of Campbell's representation at the related confiscation proceedings was considered by the Crown Court judge dealing with the matter. After a detailed inquiry by Campbell's solicitors, the court accepted that a suitably qualified advocate could not, at that stage, be found to conduct the proceedings. The judge ordered that a transcript of the ruling be forwarded to the LSC and urged them to make an exception in this case to provide for adequate funding for an advocate, not least because substantial public funds, in the form of the potential confiscation order, were at risk. The LSC refused to make the requested exception.

On 20 February 2009 the confiscation proceedings came before the Crown Court. Campbell **22.57** was unrepresented at this hearing, despite there being a representation order in her favour. Her trial counsel had left the independent bar by the time of the confiscation proceedings and her solicitors were unable to find a suitably qualified replacement barrister willing to take the case due to the rate of remuneration under the applicable graduated fee structure: then a fixed daily rate of £178.25 or fixed half daily rate of £99.50 with no funding for preparation of the case unless it involved a very unusual or novel point of law or fact, which this case did not.

Campbell sought a stay of the confiscation proceedings on the basis that it would be **22.58** an abuse of process of the Court to proceed when she could not secure appropriate representation and therefore could not have a fair hearing. The judge at first instance found that any freshly instructed barrister would need to do approximately 80 hours of preparation before a final hearing and that the notion that Campbell could have a fair trial without representation was 'pie in the sky'. He then granted her application, stayed the proceedings, and made no confiscation order.

The Court of Appeal, refusing an adjournment, was unimpressed by the CPS's submission **22.59** that a review was going on into confiscation funding and an adequately funded advocate may be available for Campbell at some future point and the case remained stayed (see paras 8 and 44). The Court pointed out that the problem was not a new one, it having been identified by HHJ Mole QC a year previously (reported on BAILLI as *P* [2008] EW Misc 2 (EWCC).

The consultation paper in relation to counsel's fees was published in July 2009 and the **22.60** suggested rates therein were as follows:

The LSC are proposing to pay separate fees for confiscation proceedings where the POCA **22.61** pages run to more than 50 pages. The fees are banded according to the number of pages. For these purposes pages will include:

(a) the s 16 statement served and relied upon by the prosecution for the purpose of the confiscation hearing;

(b) documents served as part of the main trial bundle, where such documents are specifically relied upon and referred to in the s 16 statement but are not served again; and

(c) any defence expert report and the documents and exhibits attached, provided that the report had been obtained with the prior approval of the LSC, and any documents annexed to the report which have already been counted under either of the two sections above are excluded from the computation.

22.62 Where the page count exceeds 1,001, on completion of the hearing, the advocate will be entitled to immediate payment of the fees to which he would have been entitled if the page count had been between 750 and 1,000 pages.

Funding for enforcement

22.63 In *Taylor v City of Westminster Magistrates' Court* [2009] EWHC 1498, the court considered the extent to which a magistrates' court could make a representation order to provide public funding for a court advocate (as opposed to a solicitor alone). The facts were as follows: enforcement proceedings had been instituted against the claimant in 2008, and he had applied for and was granted a representation order by the magistrates' court. It covered a solicitor and was for the purposes of the confiscation enforcement proceedings. Subsequently, the claimant applied to have that order extended to include representation by an advocate. The basis of the application was that the issues for determination before the magistrates' court were such as to require an advocate as well as a solicitor. It was said, for example, that the proceedings before the magistrates' court involved a complex argument about delay by the prosecution in the application for his committal.

22.64 The claimant's application was refused, firstly by the Confiscation Order Unit of Her Majesty's Court Service and then subsequently on a renewed oral application before a District Judge. The judge, in refusing the request, relied upon reg 12 of the Criminal Defence Service (General) (Number 2) Regulations 2001, 2001 (SI 1473/2001).

22.65 In Pill LJ's judgement, the District Judge had been correct to refuse the extending of funding:

> 25.   . . . regulation 12 does not extend to confiscation enforcement proceedings in the Magistrates' Court, however serious the underlying events . . . The basic principle of interpretation is that a regulation such as this must be construed in context. That means that consideration must be given to this regulation in the context of the 2001 regulations themselves but also against the background legislative scheme, its scope and purpose. Confiscation enforcement proceedings are criminal proceedings for the purposes of the 1999 Act and the 2001 Regulations and fall within the scope of section 12(2)(b) of the 1999 Act. However, the confiscation legislation makes clear that enforcement of a confiscation order is deemed to be equivalent to the enforcement of a fine through the Magistrates' Court. That is far from being proceedings in the case of an indictable offence.

Funding in civil recovery cases

22.66 All proceedings under Chapter 2 of Pt 5 of POCA are civil proceedings for which CLS funding is available. This can apply to both a respondent against whom the agency is proceeding or a third party who claims to be an innocent owner of property (eg under s 281 a person who claims to be a victim of theft etc may apply to the court for a declaration that certain property is not recoverable property).

Being civil proceedings CDS funding is not available for any proceedings under Pt 5 of the **22.67**
2002 Act.

Funding in cash seizure cases

Chapter 3 of Pt 5 deals with the recovery of cash in summary proceedings. CLS funding is **22.68**
available for the following proceedings in magistrates' courts under Chapter 3 of Pt 5:

(a) Section 295. Application to extend the period during which seized cash may be
    detained.
(b) Section 297. Orders directing the release of the whole or any part of detained cash.
(c) Section 298. Applications for the forfeiture of detained cash.
(d) Section 301. Application by a person other than the person from whom the cash was
    seized, claiming ownership of detained cash and seeking its release.
(e) Section 302. Application for compensation for the detention of cash if no forfeiture
    order is made by the court.

Where the magistrates' court makes an order for forfeiture under s 29 any person aggrieved **22.69**
by the order may appeal to the Crown Court. CLS funding is also available for representation on such appeals.

Release of restrained funds to cover legal expenses under POCA

Under s 41(3) of POCA, a restraint order may be subject to an exception to allow for **22.70**
reasonable legal expenses; however, such an exception must *not* make provision for any
legal expenses that relate to an offence (which falls within s 41(5)) and are incurred by
either the defendant or a recipient of a tainted gift: see *S v The Commissioners of HM
Customs and Excise* [2004] EWCA Crim 2374, [2005] 1 WLR 1338, where the court said
(in para 47) that 'looking at the Act as a whole we are satisfied that Parliament intended to
make public funding available to question restraint orders' and that the order should make
clear that public funding is available.

Pursuant to s 41(5), the prohibition covers any offence mentioned in s 40(2) or (3), if the **22.71**
first or second condition (as the case may be) is satisfied (see below); or any offence (or any
of the offences) concerned, if the third, fourth or fifth condition is satisfied (below).

Section 40(2) states that the first condition is that a criminal investigation has been started **22.72**
in England and Wales with regard to an offence, and there is reasonable cause to believe the
alleged offender has benefited from his criminal conduct; and s 40(3) states that the second
condition is that proceedings for an offence have been started in England and Wales and
not concluded, and there is reasonable cause to believe the defendant has benefited from
his criminal conduct.

The third condition applies where an application by the prosecutor has been made **22.73**
under ss 19, 20, 27, or 28 of POCA and not concluded; or the court believes that such an
application is to be made, and there is reason to believe the defendant has benefited from
his criminal conduct (s 40(4)). (Section 19 applies when no order has been made and the
court is reconsidering the case; s 20 applies when no order has been made and the court
is reconsidering the benefit; s 27 applies where the defendant absconds and he has been

convicted or committed; s 28 applies where the defendant absconds and he has been neither convicted nor acquitted.)

22.74 The fourth condition is that an application by the prosecutor or the director has been made under s 21 and not concluded, or the court believes that such an application is to be made, and that there is reasonable cause to believe the court will decide under that section that the amount found under the new calculation of the defendant's benefit exceeds the relevant amount (see s 40(5)).

22.75 The fifth condition is that an application by the prosecutor has been made under s 22 and not concluded, or the court believes that such an application is to be made, and there is reasonable cause to believe the court will decide under that section the amount found under the new calculation of the available amount exceeds the relevant amount (see s 40(6)). (Section 21 applies where the confiscation order has been made and the court is reconsidering benefit, and s 22 applies where a confiscation order has been made and the court is reconsidering the available amount.)

22.76 In all of these circumstances, there is no opportunity for a defendant to avail himself of assets under restraint in order to fund his legal representation. He must therefore look to LSC funding, or assets elsewhere (the effect of the POCA provisions being confirmed in *Re S* (above) and *Ap and U Ltd v (1) Crown Prosecution Service (2) Revenue & Customs Prosecutions Office* [2007] EWCA Crim 3128, where the Court of Appeal held that Parliament was entitled to take the view that funds that might have criminal origins should not be used to pay lawyers for the benefit of a defendant who was either suspected of, or had been found to be, a criminal; and that Parliament had provided other means for defendants to have legal representation by the provision of state aid. It also held that the measure was not incompatible with any Convention rights).

22.77 However, there remain provisions for other legal costs to be met, eg legal charges in relation to conveyancing of property or litigation costs in ongoing proceedings, which are not connected to the criminal matters in question.

Drawing legal expenses from living expenses

22.78 In *Michael Joseph McInerney v Financial Services Authority* [2009] EWCA Crim 997 the judge made a restraint order against Mr McInerney under POCA in connection with alleged money laundering offences. The order restrained all known assets of McInerney, but allowed him £250 per week towards ordinary living expenses. In November 2008, McInerney applied to the LSC for public funding in order to review judicially the Financial Services Authority (FSA)'s decision to commence a prosecution of the money laundering offences.

22.79 On 12 February 2009, the LSC offered the requested public funding, subject to the condition that McInerney made a contribution of £117.66 per month from his 'income'. That assessment was made on the basis of his 'income' of £250 per week, that being the sum excluded as living expenses from the terms of the restraint order. McInerney's solicitors argued that the assessment of his income should have been 'nil' due to the restraint order. The LSC rejected this argument. Confirmation was then sought from the FSA that the monthly contribution could be paid to the LSC from the ordinary living allowance. The FSA responded that the payment of the contribution would be a breach of s 41(4) of POCA as it was not possible to make an exception to the order for any legal expenses. McInerney applied to Southwark Crown Court for a variation of the restraint order to make it clear that he was not prohibited from paying the £117.66 contribution. The court refused to make the variation requested. McInerney sought a variation (or a declaration) the effect of which would be to permit him to pay part of the money allowed to him for reasonable living expenses to the LSC as a contribution to the costs incurred in bringing the judicial review application.

22.80 The Court of Appeal rejected the defendant's request. It agreed with the judge at first instance: payments to the LSC are not ordinary living expenses and thus the defendant would be in contempt of court to pay money to the LSC and the LSC would be in breach of the restraint order to receive it. The court added that s 41(3)(a) makes a distinction between living expenses and legal expenses and if a contribution to the LSC is a legal expense, a payment to the LSC would not be a payment towards ordinary living expenses (para 33). As a result the court held (at para 38):

> In our view the judge was right. A contribution to the LSC to institute judicial review proceedings in connection with the offence in respect of which the restraint order was made is a 'legal expense'.

Release of restrained funds to cover legal expenses under the DTA and CJA

22.81 Most restraint orders contain provision for a defendant to spend money on legal expenses actually, reasonably, and properly incurred in the restraint proceedings and the related criminal proceedings provided that, before any monies are released for this purpose the defendant notifies the prosecuting authority in writing of the following matters:

(a) the source of the fund to be used to pay the said costs;
(b) the general nature of the costs incurred;
(c) the time spent and by whom in incurring the said costs;
(d) the hourly rate applicable to the costs incurred.

22.82 In the event the prosecuting authority considers the claim to be in respect of costs that have not actually, reasonably, or properly been incurred then the entitlement to draw such costs is usually restricted to 65 per cent of the amount claimed, and the whole claim for costs is then subject to detailed assessment on an indemnity basis in accordance with Pt 48 of the CPR (but without the provisions of s 48.8(2)(a) and (b) applying).

22.83 One of the difficulties that has arisen under the DTA and the CJA with the above provision is where a defendant wishes to draw upon restrained funds in preference to claiming LSC funding. In *RCPO v Briggs-Price and O'Reilly* [2007] EWCA Civ 568 where the Court of Appeal held that, where permitted, the court held a discretion to release restrained funds, notwithstanding the potential availability of LSC funding (para 51), the 'release of funds for the prospective appeal is properly within the terms of the order, and the statutory scheme', applying *Customs and Excise Commissioners v Norris* [1991] 2 QB 293.

22.84 The court added that the discretion should be exercised both in a judicial and proportionate way (para 50) and that the position might have been different had there not been excess funds available to meet both the confiscation order and the claim for private legal funding (para 46). The court also stated that if a line had to be drawn, in terms of the release of funds from restraint 'it was properly drawn when the defendant had exhausted all his remedies within the domestic proceedings' and it follows should not extend to European Convention or Criminal Cases Review Commission applications (para 53). It also added that in some cases funds would not be released 'if, for example, the application for which the release of funds was sought was manifestly unmeritorious; or if the sums sought to be expended were clearly disproportionate . . .' (para 54).

22.85 In two subsequent cases, *Re S* [2008] EWHC 1295 (Admin) and *Re L* [2008] EWHC 3321 (Admin) the High Court has ruled that payments of restrained funds for legal and living expenses should come to an end where confiscation orders remain unsatisfied long after all domestic avenues of appeal have been exhausted. For the unlawfulness of the release of funds, following the making of a restraint order, see *Re T* [2007] EWHC 3321 (Admin), and the related case of *RCPO v the Stoke Partnership* [2007] EWHC 1588.

Legal expenses and third parties

22.86 For commentary on the release of restrained assets to fund the legal expenses of third parties see *Re D* [2006] EWHC (Admin) 1519 and *RCPO v Stodgell* [2008] EWHC 2214.

G. Compensation

Compensation for the acquitted defendant under the DTA and CJA 1988

22.87 Section 18 of the DTA and s 89 of the CJA 1988, which are worded in identical terms, give the High Court jurisdiction, on an application by a person who held realisable property caught by an order, to order compensation to be paid to the applicant if, having regard to all the circumstances, it considers it appropriate to do so. The provisions thus enable not only the defendant, but also any person holding realisable property, to make an application for compensation. An application for compensation can only be made where criminal proceedings have been instituted against the defendant for a drug trafficking offence or an offence to which Pt VI of the CJA applies, as appropriate, and either:

(a) the proceedings do not result in his conviction for any such offence, or
(b) where he is convicted of one or more such offences—
    (i) the conviction or convictions concerned are quashed, or
    (ii) he is pardoned by Her Majesty in respect of the conviction or convictions concerned.

22.88 Section 18(1) of the DTA and s 89(1) of the CJA read as follows:

(1) The High Court may, on an application by a person who held property which was realisable property, order compensation to be paid to the applicant if, having regard to all the circumstances, it considers it appropriate to make such an order.
(2) The High Court shall not order compensation to be paid in any case unless the court is satisfied—
    (a) that there has been some serious default on the part of the person concerned in the investigation or prosecution of the offence or offences concerned, being a person mentioned in subsection (5) below; and

(b) that the applicant has suffered loss and consequence of anything done in relation to the property by or in pursuance of—
    (i) an order of the High Court or the County Court under this part of the Act [DTA ss 26–29]; or
    (ii) (applicable only in Scotland).

(3) The High Court shall not order compensation to be paid in any case where it appears to the Court the proceedings would have been instituted or continued even if the serious default had not occurred.

(4) The amount of compensation to be paid under this section shall be such as the High Court thinks just in all the circumstances of the case.

22.89 It is thus essential that the defendant should have been acquitted of all offences to which the restraint order proceedings relate. It is not sufficient that the court did not consider it an appropriate case for a confiscation order; there must be an acquittal before an application for compensation can be entertained.

Other conditions

22.90 An acquittal by itself will not be sufficient to found an application for compensation because, under s 18(2) of the DTA and s 89(2) of the CJA, two other conditions must also be satisfied. Firstly, it must be shown that there has been some 'serious default' on the part of a person mentioned in subs (5). Secondly, it must be shown that the applicant for compensation has suffered loss in consequence of anything done to the property as a result of an order made under the Acts. Subsection (3) imposes a further important restriction on the power of the court to award compensation, in that it provides that the court shall not order the payment of compensation where it appears that the proceedings would have been instituted or continued even if the serious default had not occurred. Rule 56.6 of the Criminal Procedure Rules deals with compensation on acquittal, and allows for notice of the acquittal to be served on the High Court.

How much compensation and by whom is it paid?

22.91 Subsection (4) gives the court a wide discretion as to the amount of compensation it may award, providing that the amount to be paid 'shall be such as the High Court thinks just in all the circumstances'. Subsection (5) deals with payment and provides:

(5) Compensation payable under this section shall be paid—
    (a) where the person in default was or was acting as a member of a police force, out of the police fund out of which the expenses of that police force are met;
    (b) where the person in default was a member of the Crown Prosecution Service or acting on behalf of the service, by the Director of Public Prosecutions;
    (c) where the person in default was a member of the Serious Fraud Office, by the Director of that Office;
    (d) where the person in default was an officer within the meaning of the Customs and Excise Management Act 1979, by the Commissioners of Revenue and Customs.

Procedure on applications

22.92 The procedure for making compensation applications is dealt with in RSC Ord 115 r 10, which provides that the application must be made in accordance with CPR Part 23, ie on an application notice served together with any supporting evidence on the person alleged to be in default and on the relevant authority not less than seven days prior to the date of the hearing. The witness statement in support (see CPR Part 22) should, of course, state all the facts relied on in support of the application including full details of the 'serious default' alleged. Any relevant documentation should be exhibited to the witness statement.

Compensation for the acquitted defendant under POCA

22.93   Section 72(1) of POCA sets out the three conditions that need to be satisfied before the Crown Court may make an order for payment of compensation. The amount the Crown Court may order to be paid is described as an amount 'it believes is just'.

22.94   The first condition is satisfied if a criminal investigation has been started with regard to an offence and proceedings are not started for the offence. Under POCA it is possible for a restraint order to be made as soon as the criminal investigation has been started, as distinct to under the DTA, where it was only possible to obtain a restraint order when proceedings had been started or were about to be. One of the main changes of POCA is that compensation will now be payable not only from when proceedings have been started, but from the beginning of the investigation itself. The first condition is also satisfied if proceedings for an offence are started against the person and they do not result in his conviction for the offence, or he is convicted of the offence but the conviction is quashed or he is pardoned in respect of it (see s 72(3)).

22.95   If a criminal investigation has been started with regard to an offence, and proceedings have not or are not started for that offence, the second condition is that in the criminal investigation there has been serious default by a person mentioned in s 72(9) of POCA and the investigation would not have continued if the default had not occurred (s 72(9) is in almost identical terms to subs (5) of the corresponding provisions of the DTA and CJA).

22.96   If proceedings for an offence are started against a person and they do not result in his conviction for the offence, or he is convicted of the offence but the conviction is quashed or he is pardoned in respect of it, the second condition is that in the criminal investigation with regard to the offence or in its prosecution there has been a serious default by a person who is mentioned in subs (9) and the proceedings would not have been started or continued if the default had not occurred.

22.97   The third condition is that an application is made under this section by a person who held realisable property and has suffered loss in consequence of anything done in relation to it by or in pursuance of an order under Pt 2 of the Proceeds of Crime Act (see s 72(6)).

22.98   Section 72 reflects largely the legislation under the DTA and the CJA, save that the provisions have been extended to cover the situation where the investigation is started, but proceedings have not been brought. It provides for compensation to be paid to a person whose property has been affected by the enforcement of the confiscation legislation. 'Serious default' is not defined in the Act and therefore each case will need to be determined on its own merits. It is not intended that compensation should be paid on acquittal as a matter of course.

Compensation for third parties

22.99   The Acts contemplate that both a compensation and confiscation order may be made against the same person in the same proceedings. In *Faithfull v Ipswich Crown Court* [2007]

EWHC 2763, a case which considered whether a Crown Court judge's decision in relation to compensation could be challenged by judicial review by a third party, and found that it could not (as there existed alternative civil court remedies), the Court held that decisions about confiscation and compensation were decisions about sentence, and as such were an integral part of the trial process, (*R v Maidstone Crown Court ex p Harrow LBC* [2000] QB 719 distinguished).

The Act does not contemplate that it shall operate as a means of compensating the **22.100** Crown where the Crown is the victim, eg by the evasion of duties and taxes, although a confiscation order may in practice have that effect. Compensating the Crown would only be necessary in cases where the Crown had suffered a loss and does not have a civil claim against the defendant. Such a purpose will be unnecessary in most cases, since the Crown remains entitled to the duties and taxes evaded, and perhaps to other civil remedies whether or not the defendant has been convicted (see *R v Smith (David)* [2001] UKHL 68).

Compensation in absconded defendant cases under POCA

Under s 73(1) where a court varies a confiscation order under s 29 of POCA (ie where a **22.101** defendant has absconded) or discharges a confiscation order under s 30 (where an absconded defendant is later tried for an offence and is acquitted on all counts) and application is made to the Crown Court by a person who held realisable property and has suffered a loss as a result of the making of the order, the court may order the payment of such compensation it believes is just.

In those circumstance compensation is payable to the applicant by the Lord Chancellor **22.102** (s 73(3)). It should be noted that this provision is not limited to serious default as in s 72.

Civil recovery compensation under POCA

Under s 283 of POCA, the scheme allows for compensation to be paid under Pt 5 of the **22.103** Act (Civil recovery of the proceeds etc of unlawful conduct).

Under s 283(1), where any property to which an interim receiving order (IRO) or prop- **22.104** erty freezing order (PFO) has at any time applied and where the court does not in the course of the proceedings decide that the property is recoverable property (or associated property), the person whose property it is may make an application to the court for compensation.

Section 283(1) does not apply if the court has made a declaration in respect of the property **22.105** under s 281 (Victims of Theft etc), or makes an order under s 276 (a consent order) (see s 283(2)).

If the court is satisfied that the applicant has suffered loss as a result of a PFO or IRO it may **22.106** require the enforcement authority to pay compensation to him. The amount of compensation to be paid under s 283 is the amount the court thinks reasonable having regard to the loss suffered and any other relevant circumstances (see s 283(9)).

22.107 Section 283 deals with cases where there has been a loss to owners of property in circumstances where that property has been made subject to a PFO or IRO, but has not in the end been deemed to be recoverable or associated property for two reasons:

(1) because the court has so determined, or
(2) because the claim or application has been withdrawn.

22.108 Under subs (1) the person whose property it is may apply to the court for compensation for any loss relating to that property. In those circumstances the court may order compensation to be paid by the enforcement authority under subs (5).

22.109 The measure of the compensation to be paid is at the court's discretion, having regard to all of the circumstances including any quantifiable losses suffered. If a claimant has himself contributed to the losses, for example through delays caused by himself, the court is entitled to take those facts into account.

Three-month time limit

22.110 If the court has decided not to make a recovery order in respect of the property, the application for compensation must be made within the period of three months beginning, in relation to a decision of the High Court, with the date of the decision or, if any application is not made for leave to appeal, within the date on which the application is withdrawn or refused or on which any proceedings on appeal are finally concluded (see s 283(3)).

22.111 If the proceedings in respect of the property have been discontinued, the application for compensation must be made within the period of three months beginning with the discontinuance (see s 283(4)).

Compensation for recovery of cash in summary proceedings

22.112 Under s 302 of POCA, when no forfeiture order is made in respect of any cash detained under Chapter 3, the person to whom the cash belongs or from whom it was seized may make an application to the magistrates' court for compensation. If the seized cash was not paid into an interest bearing account at the first opportunity following its initial detention, the court may make an order for compensation to be paid to the applicant (see s 302(2)).

22.113 The amount of compensation to be paid in those circumstances is an amount which the court thinks would have been earned in interest in the period in question if the cash had been held in an interest bearing account. It is therefore likely to be of relatively nominal value (see s 302(3)).

22.114 If the court is satisfied that the applicant has suffered any other loss as a result of the detention of the cash and that the circumstances are 'exceptional', the court may order compensation or additional compensation to be paid to him (see s 302(4)). In those circumstances the amount of compensation to be paid is the amount the court thinks reasonable, having regard to the loss suffered and any other relevant circumstances.

22.115 Where Revenue and Customs officials seize the cash, the compensation is to be paid by the Commissioners of Revenue and Customs (s 302(6)). If the cash was seized by a constable, the compensation is to be paid by the relevant police force.

It should be noted that if a forfeiture order is made in respect of any part of the cash **22.116** detained under ss 294 and 295 of POCA, the person to whom the cash belongs or from whom it was seized is entitled to claim compensation in relation to any part of the cash that is not ordered to be forfeited (see s 302(8)).

Compensation and the victims of crime

Section 130 of the Powers of Criminal Courts (Sentencing) Act 2000 provides: **22.117**

Compensation orders against convicted persons

(1) A court by or before which a person is convicted of an offence, instead of or in addition to dealing with him in any other way, may, on application or otherwise, make an order (in this Act referred to as a 'compensation order') requiring him—

(a) to pay compensation for any personal injury, loss or damage resulting from that offence or any other offence which is taken into consideration by the court in determining sentence; or

(b) to make payments for funeral expenses or bereavement in respect of a death resulting from any such offence, other than a death due to an accident arising out of the presence of a motor vehicle on a road;

but this is subject to the following provisions of this section and to section 131 below.

(2) ...

(3) A court shall give reasons, on passing sentence, if it does not make a compensation order in a case where this section empowers it to do so.

(4) Compensation under subsection (1) above shall be of such amount as the court considers appropriate, having regard to any evidence and to any representations that are made by or on behalf of the accused or the prosecutor.

Section 131(1) adds: **22.118**

The compensation to be paid under a compensation order made by a magistrates' court in respect of any offence of which the court has convicted the offender shall not exceed £5,000.

For the operation of s 130 in practice, see *RCPO v Duffy* [2008] EWHC 848 and the earlier **22.119** case of *R v Crutchley and Tonks* [1994] 15 Cr App R (S) 627.

In *R v Dorrian* (2001) 1 Cr App R(S) 135, the appellant submitted that the court had no **22.120** power to make a compensation order outside the period of 28 days following sentence in the absence of an expressly stated decision to postpone the compensation order as part of the sentence (s 47(2) of the Supreme Court Act 1981). It was conceded that there was a common-law power in the court to postpone any part of the sentence, but it was submitted that it must be expressly stated. In *Dorrian* there had been no express statement, but the making of the compensation order was postponed. The Court of Appeal was satisfied that s 72(5)(b) did not exclude compensation orders from the consideration of the court making the confiscation order, and that the sentencer had power to make a compensation order or to postpone the making of an order at the time of sentence. It also held that the appellant was correct in his submission that the section dealt with the manner in which funds were allocated if both of the orders were made. The exclusion of compensation orders from s 72A(9) provided protection for victims of crime. It meant they could benefit from a compensation order, where a confiscation order was made within the time limit provided. It was not however open to the Crown Court to make a compensation order 26 months after conviction where no common-law power had been exercised to postpone the making of such an order at the date of sentence. No reference was made at the time to the making of a compensation order, or postponing the making of such an order at the time, and accordingly the Crown Court had no power to do so more than two years after conviction. For those reasons the compensation order was not lawful and was quashed.

22.121 It follows that compensation orders may be made under s 130 of the Powers of the Criminal Courts (Sentencing) Act 2000 at the time of the confiscation hearing, provided that the court has postponed the making of such an order at the time of passing sentence using its common law jurisdiction. If at the time it postpones the confiscation order it is silent as to whether or not a compensation order will be made, it is not able to make one after the 28-day time limit has expired. It may be, in the light of the recent decisions concerning the purpose and intention of the legislation, that a failure to postpone is not as fatal as it may once have been (see *Sekhon* [2003] 3 All ER 508), although in relation to compensation orders this is untested territory. There should nevertheless be some acknowledgment as to the harsh consequences that *Dorrian* may have for a victim of crime on what may merely amount to a procedural irregularity.

23

CONDEMNATION AND RESTORATION

A. Introduction

23.01 In this chapter we give an overview of the law in relation to what some still describe as 'Bootlegging'. Whilst not strictly within the ambit of a book that has as its central focus the proceeds of crime, there is, nevertheless a nexus between the two. Cigarette and tobacco smuggling has been successfully deployed by criminal organisations to raise funds for many years, and the extremes to which individuals will go in order to evade the authorities are becoming increasingly sophisticated.

23.02 Nowadays the condemnation of goods covers a vast area in terms of legislation and, as a result, we have sought to concentrate on those areas that are typical of matters that regularly come before the courts. The notion of 'condemnation' has been explained in a number of authorities, including *Commissioners of Customs and Excise v Trustee of the property of Sokolow (a bankrupt)* [1954] 2 QB 336, 344 (Hilbery J) where, with reference to proceedings for the 'forfeiture and condemnation' of goods, it was said that their purpose is to determine the legality of the seizure.

23.03 The bifurcated jurisdiction adopted by the legislature in relation to the seizure, forfeiture, and condemnation of excise goods and vehicles under ss 49, 139, 141 and Sch 3 to the Customs and Excise Management Act 1979 (CEMA) on the one hand; and on the other, the discretionary power vested in the Commissioners of Revenue and Customs to restore, subject to such conditions (if any) that they think proper, anything forfeited or seized under s 152(b) of CEMA was recognised by Pill LJ in *Gora v Customs and Excise Commissioners* [2003] EWCA Civ 525, at para 57.

23.04 The present system in relation to forfeiture and restoration has not been without its critics. In *Customs and Excise Commissioners v Weller* [2006] EWHC 237 (Ch), Evans-Lombe J called for a 'statutory rationalisation of the procedure governing the forfeiture of goods by the Commissioners' (para 24). He stated that:

> It seems to me that the present system is confusing to the public and pregnant with the possibility of substantial injustice.

The problem of the two-track system of condemnation and forfeiture, followed by restoration, **23.05** was also subject to scrutiny by the Court of Appeal in *Gascoyne v Customs and Excise Commissioners* [2005] 2 WLR 222, para 5, where Buxton LJ said:

> The procedure has a number of elements which appear to have grown up over the years and which do not always easily fit with each other.

The courts merely seem to be highlighting the practical and very real problems that both **23.06** appellants, magistrates sitting in their civil jurisdiction, and Tax Tribunals have experienced. One proposal, which may or may not find favour in years to come, would be to introduce a unified condemnation and restoration procedure, which is less formal, less associated with the magistrates' and criminal courts (most first instance appeals are currently dealt with by the Crown Court), that perhaps operates under the auspices of the Tribunals Service.

Pursuant to s 50 of the Commissioners for Revenue and Customs Act 2005, references to **23.07** Commissioners of HM Customs and Excise, and HM Customs and Excise in the legislation, have been amended to Commissioners of HM Revenue and Customs, and HM Revenue and Customs respectively.

UK Border Agency

The UK Border Agency (UKBA) takes over the role of Customs at airports and ports **23.08** throughout the UK from 5 August 2009. While the force and application of the condemnation provisions will remain unchanged, the switch is likely to involve the handing over of responsibility from HMRC to the UKBA for seizures and investigations in relation to travellers found in possession of excise goods.

Section 26 of the Borders, Citizenship and Immigration Act 2009 makes various transfer **23.09** provisions. The scheme gives effect to the transfer of specified property, rights, and liabilities from the Commissioners for Revenue and Customs to the Secretary of State for the Home Department and the Director of Border Revenue in connection with the exercise of the Commissioners' functions which are extended concurrently to the Secretary of State and the Director with the Commissioners. The Secretary of State's functions will be exercised by delegation to the Chief Executive of UKBA.

The changes include: **23.10**

The liabilities and legal proceedings transferred in Parts II and III of this Scheme shall include statutory reviews and appeals pursuant to sections 14 and 16 of and Schedule 5 to the Finance Act 1994, condemnation proceedings pursuant to Schedule 3 to CEMA, requests, notices and appeals pursuant to the Freedom of Information Act 2000 and requests pursuant to the Data Protection Act 1998.

B. The Condemnation and Forfeiture of Goods

The statutory basis

The statutory basis for the forfeiture of goods improperly imported derives from s 49 **23.11** of CEMA. Section 49(1) sets out the circumstances under which goods shall be liable to forfeiture when they have been imported contrary to HM Revenue and Customs restrictions and where the goods in question are chargeable with duty:

(1) Where—

    (a) except as provided by or under the Customs and Excise Acts 1979, any imported goods, being goods chargeable on their importation with customs or excise duty, are, without payment of that duty—

        (i) unshipped in any port,

        (ii) unloaded from any aircraft in the United Kingdom,

        (iii) unloaded from any vehicle in, or otherwise brought across the boundary into, Northern Ireland, or

        (iv) removed from their place of importation or from any approved wharf, examination station or transit shed; or

    (b) any goods are imported, landed or unloaded contrary to any prohibition or restriction for the time being in force with respect thereto under or by virtue of any enactment; or

    (c) any goods, being goods chargeable with any duty or goods the importation of which is for the time being prohibited or restricted by or under any enactment, are found, whether before or after the unloading thereof, to have been concealed in any manner on board any ship or aircraft or, while in Northern Ireland, in any vehicle; or

    (d) any goods are imported concealed in a container holding goods of a different description; or

    (e) any imported goods are found, whether before or after delivery, not to correspond with the entry made thereof; or

    (f) any imported goods are concealed or packed in any manner appearing to be intended to deceive an officer,

those goods shall, subject to subsection (2) below, be liable to forfeiture.

(2) Where any goods, the importation of which is for the time being prohibited or restricted by or under any enactment, are on their importation either—

    (a) reported as intended for exportation in the same ship, aircraft or vehicle; or

    (b) entered for transit or transhipment; or

    (c) entered to be warehoused for exportation or for use as stores,

the Commissioners may, if they see fit, permit the goods to be dealt with accordingly.

23.12   These broad ranging provisions cover, subject to their own particular legislative provisions, the forfeiture of cigarettes and tobacco (see s 2 of the Tobacco Products Duty Act 1979), alcohol (the Alcoholic Liquor Duties Act 1979, particularly s 5 (spirits), s 36 (beer), s 54 (wine), and s 62 (cider)). They also cover a multitude of other excise goods, including bullion and coins (see *Allgemeine Gold-und Silberscheideanstalt v Customs and Excise Commissioners* [1980] 2 All ER 138 (CA)), pornography, vehicles, as well as goods prohibited from importation by virtue of matters as diverse as trade descriptions and UN sanctions orders.

Duty payable, unless for own use

23.13   UK excise duty is generally payable at the point of importation (see reg 12(1) of the Tobacco Products Regulations 2001, SI 1712/2001 for tobacco; reg 15(1) of the Beer Regulations 1993, SI 1228/1993 for beer; and reg 4(1) of the Excise Goods (Holding, Movement, Warehousing and REDS) Regulations 1992, SI 3135/1992 for wines and spirits).

23.14   As a result of the Divisional Court's decision in *R (Hoverspeed) v Customs and Excise Commissioners* [2002] 4 All ER 912, these Regulations were amended in 2002, pursuant to the Excise Goods, Beer and Tobacco Products (Amendment) Regulations 2002,

SI 2002/2692 and the Channel Tunnel (Alcoholic Liquor and Tobacco Products) (Amendment) Order 2002, SI 2002/2693 to insert a sub-regulation (1A) which makes provision for the cross-channel shopper who acquires and transports goods for his own use. This provides that no duty will be payable unless and until the goods are held or used for a commercial purpose by any person. Sub-regulation (1B) provides the definitions and criteria to be applied when considering whether (1A) applies (the regulations are set out below).

Importations for a commercial purpose

Excise duty only becomes payable if the goods are being imported for a commercial purpose (ie for forward sale or for money's worth or for profit). Article 8 of Council Directive (EC) 92/12 provides: **23.15**

> As regards products acquired by private individuals for their own use and transported by them, the principle governing the internal market lays down that excise duty shall be charged in the Member State in which they are acquired.

As a result, the amended Regulations confirm that duty and tax must be paid on the goods in the Member State in which they are acquired (see sub-reg (1B(d)).

In *The Netherlands v Joustra* C5-05 (ECJ, 23 November 2006), the Court held that for   **23.16** Art 8 of Directive 92/12 to have application, excise goods must have been acquired by private individuals for their own use and transported by them (para 332 of the judgment).

In *Joustra*, the Court rejected the argument that because the wine acquired by Mr Joustra   **23.17** was for his own use and that of members of a wine club, of which he was president, it fell within Art 8 of Directive 92/12 and therefore was not subject to Dutch excise duty on its importation (since French excise duty had already been paid on the goods). The ECJ found that the condition that goods should be for an individual's own use precludes acquisition of goods for the use of other private individuals. Where any goods have been acquired for the use of others, those goods cannot be considered to be held for strictly private purposes by the individual who has acquired them (see para 35 of the judgment). Nor is Art 8 applicable where the purchase and/or transportation of the excise goods is being carried out by an agent (para 41 of the judgment, reflecting *R v Customs and Excise Commissioners ex p Emu Tabac SARL* [1998] All ER (EC) 402, [1998] QB 971). The Court went on to conclude that Art 7(2) of the Directive applied to Mr Joustra. The Court stated that the Directive proceeded on the basis that goods not held for a private purpose must necessarily be regarded as held for a commercial purpose. As Mr Joustra was not holding the goods acquired for the wine circle for his own private purpose, he was to be regarded as holding them for a commercial purpose in the Netherlands. This was the case even though he was not acting with a view to making a profit (para 51). Accordingly excise duty was due in the Netherlands. Mr Joustra was, however, entitled to repayment of the French excise duty paid by him (see para 52 of the judgment).

Article 9 of the same Directive adds: **23.18**

> (1) Without prejudice to Article . . . 8, excise duty shall become chargeable where products released for consumption in a Member State are held for a commercial purpose in another Member State.

In *Hoverspeed* [2002] 3 WLR 1219, the Divisional Court held that the 1992 Order cor-   **23.19** rectly transposed the Directive in its definition of own use. Either goods were held for personal use within the meaning of Art 8 of the Directive or they were held for a commercial purpose under Art 9. The Court of Appeal's decision in *Hoverspeed* [2003] 2 WLR 950 confirmed the first instance decision. This was followed in the Divisional Court case of *Customs and Excise Commissioners v Newbury* [2003] 2 All ER 964; (2003) 1WLR 2131, where Hale LJ (approving the reasoning of Advocate General Ruis-Jarabo Colomer in *Emu Tabac*) held that:

> The object of the rules (in Directive 92/12) is to determine whether duty is payable in the country of origin or the country of destination. The general principle is the latter and Article 8 is an exception in which three conditions must be fulfilled: the products must be acquired by a private individual; the products must be acquired by private individuals for their own use; and the products must be transported by private individuals.

Civil proceedings

23.20 Actions for forfeiture and condemnation are actions *in rem* (against the property as opposed to the individual). Nobody stands in jeopardy and the action is by way of complaint heard, in the first instance, usually before a magistrates' court.

23.21 Paragraph 8 of Sch 3 to CEMA confirms that the proceedings are civil, and this was further confirmed in both *Goldsmith v Customs and Excise Commissioners* The Times, 12 June 2001 and *Mudie v Kent Magistrates' Court* [2003] EWHC (Civ) 237, 2 All ER 631, where the Courts held that condemnation matters do not involve the determination of a criminal charge and that none of the usual consequences of a criminal conviction apply. As a result Art 6 of the European Convention on Human Rights (ECHR) has no application (see para 23.139 below).

23.22 This is therefore one of the rare examples of the magistrates' court's civil jurisdiction, and because the proceedings are civil, the burden of proof is on the *balance of probabilities* and not the higher criminal test of 'beyond reasonable doubt'. Civil rules of evidence apply, including the admissibility of hearsay evidence, and there is no necessity for compliance with the Police and Criminal Evidence Act 1984 (PACE).

Legislative background

23.23 There have been various legislative changes in this area of the law over the years. For several years the Excise Duties (Personal Reliefs) Order 1992, SI 1992/3155 was followed, before it was amended by the Excise Duties (Personal Reliefs) (Amendment) Order 1999, SI 1999/1617. However, both of these Orders were revoked by the Excise Duties (Personal Reliefs) (Revocation) Order 2002, SI 2002/2691 on 1 December 2002 and replaced with a new set of Regulations following the Divisional Court's ruling in *R (Hoverspeed) v Customs and Excise Commissioners* [2002] 4 All ER 912 which held that the original Orders had failed to implement EC Directive (EC) 92/12 and had wrongly reversed the burden of proof by requiring the individual importing the goods to prove that they were for his own use.

23.24 It is as a result of these legislative changes, particularly the revocation of the 1992 Order (which included a presumption in favour of Customs), that requires case law before 1999 to be viewed with some caution. For example, *Customs and Excise Commissioners v Carrier* (1995) 4 All ER 38 and references to the presumption under Art 5(3) in the case of

R v Customs and Excise Commissioners ex p Kenneth Stephen Boxall (15 February 1996) (CO 1902/95) should be read in the light of the amended 1999 Order.

The revised legislative scheme

The Excise Goods, Beer and Tobacco Products (Amendment) Regulations 2002, SI 2002/ **23.25** 2692 came into force on 1 December 2002. It sought to correct any deficiency in the previous Regulations by amending the Excise Goods (Holding, Movement, Warehousing, and REDS) Regulations 1992, SI 2002/3135 to insert a specific provision in relation to 'own use':

> (1A) In the case of excise goods acquired by a person in another member State for his own use and transported by him to the United Kingdom, the excise duty point is the time when those goods are held or used for a commercial purpose by any person.

In other words, excise duty only becomes payable on the goods when they are held for a commercial purpose, or at the point in time when they become held or are used for a commercial purpose. This applies to both the traveller who imported them and/or by any other person who has possession or control of them.

SI 2002/2692 also amended the Beer Regulations 1993, SI 1993/1228 and the Tobacco **23.26** Products Regulations 2001, SI 2001/1712 in identical terms.

The effect of these amendments is to reassert that goods being brought into the UK for a **23.27** traveller's 'own use' are not subject to excise duty. This should ensure that goods purchased on cross-border shopping trips for an individual's own personal use are not subject to the payment of any excise duty (see the Divisional Court's judgment in *R (Hoverspeed) v Customs and Excise Commissioners* [2002] 4 All ER 912 at paras 107–109).

Gifts

The Excise Goods, Beer and Tobacco Products (Amendment) Regulations 2002 also altered **23.28** the pre-existing Regulations to define 'own use' to include personal gifts (para (1B)(b)). It is therefore permissible for a traveller to bring in larger than expected consignments of excise goods if he intends to give them away as personal gifts. Much will depend on the credibility of the traveller's story, the likelihood of the assertion, and the evidence the traveller is able to produce to support the claim.

Transfers for money's worth

Paragraph (1B)(c) of the Excise Goods, Beer and Tobacco Products (Amendment) **23.29** Regulations 2002 states that:

> If the goods in question are—
> (i) transferred to another person for money or money's worth (including any reimbursement of expenses incurred in connection with obtaining them), or
> (ii) the person holding them intends to make such a transfer,
> those goods are to be regarded as being held for a commercial purpose.

This comprehensive provision has the effect of catching any importation where the goods concerned are passed on in return for any payment, including any travel expenses. The transaction does not have to be for profit (indeed the legislation is broad enough to cover receiving payment at a loss), and it does not need to be for money, eg payment as a 'thank you' such as a dinner out would make the transfer commercial.

EU reaction

23.30   In previous years the EU Commission has expressed dissatisfaction with the UK in relation to its application of the forfeiture provisions, particularly against travellers who are bringing in items such as cigarettes and alcohol on behalf of friends and not for profit.

23.31   Such transactions only amount to minor fiscal offences and individually represent only a small loss to the Revenue. As a result the Commission sent to the UK a 'reasoned opinion' on the basis that in certain circumstances the penalties for smuggling tobacco and alcohol were disproportionate and represented an obstacle to the free movement of goods. This is part of the pre-litigation procedure set out in Article 226 of the EC treaty. Although the UK Government's initial reaction appeared to be one of defending their existing policies, anecdotally a slightly more relaxed approach has been adopted by officers at the ports, often resulting in first time offenders being given warnings, rather than having their goods seized in circumstances where the intended destination of the goods is to friends and family at cost price (see *Hoverspeed Ltd* [2003] 2 WLR 950).

What factors define 'commercial purpose'?

23.32   Paragraph (1B)(e) of the Excise Goods, Beer and Tobacco Products (Amendment) Regulations 2002 sets out a list of matters that may be taken into account by both Revenue and Customs/UKBA and, ultimately, the court, in making their determination as to whether the goods in question were being imported for a commercial purpose. These considerations are:

(a)   the person's reasons for having possession or control of the goods;

(b)   whether or not the person is a Revenue trader (as defined in s 1(1) of CEMA 1979);

(c)   the person's conduct, including his intended use of the goods or any refusal to disclose his intended use of the goods;

(d)   the location of the goods;

(e)   the mode of transport used to convey the goods;

(f)   any document or other information whatsoever relating to the goods;

(g)   the nature of the goods, including the nature and condition of any package or container;

(h)   the quantity of the goods; and in particular whether the quantity exceeds the guideline quantities (see para 23.39 below);

(i)   whether the person personally financed the purchase of the goods in question; and

(j)   any other circumstance which appears to be relevant.

23.33   Revenue traders, in the context of (b) above, are persons carrying on a trade or business involving the buying, selling, importation, exportation, or dealing in or handling of excise goods. If the person importing the goods had an obvious outlet through which he could sell the goods then that would be a matter that the court/Customs may wish to take account of.

23.34   Regard should be particularly given to (h), the quantity of the goods. If an individual is importing into the UK 100,000 cigarettes (eg in the boot of their car), there is a strong inference that they will not all be for personal use, although that inference may be rebutted if the individual is a heavy smoker, rarely travels abroad, or has sufficient means or another legitimate non-commercial reason for bringing the cigarettes in, eg gifts for family members at Christmas.

It should further be noted that under (j) this list is not intended to be exhaustive. **23.35**

In *R v Customs and Excise Commissioners ex p Mortimer* [1999] 1 WLR 17 the Court held **23.36** that Customs officers must take account of the above reasons when considering whether or not they should seize goods. As a result, in practice, a short interview will take place at the initial point of interception.

In *Mortimer* Lord Bingham stated at p 22: **23.37**

> . . . fairness demands that the importer has a fair opportunity to satisfy the Customs & Excise, despite the quantity of the goods involved, that he is not importing them for a commercial purpose. It is plain that the Customs & Excise have no discretion whether or not to give such a fair opportunity: it is something they must do.

Mortimer was decided under the now defunct Excise Duties (Personal Reliefs) Order 1992. As a result the mandatory presumption referred to therein no longer applies. Under the new regulations, the fact that the goods in question now exceed the Minimum Indicative Levels (the quantity guidelines) is something which HMRC and the court are merely entitled to have 'regard to'. The assertion, however, that the importer must have a 'fair opportunity' to satisfy Revenue and Customs/UKBA of his case remains, it is submitted, good law.

In the Divisional Court's judgment of *R (Hoverspeed) v Customs and Excise Commissioners* **23.38** [2002] 4 All ER 912, Brooke LJ stated that 'if no satisfactory explanation is forthcoming, then the national official may well conclude that the goods were indeed held for 'commercial purposes'. Refusal to provide an explanation, or a misleading explanation, may therefore both be factors that a court may take into account in deciding the issues it has to determine.

What are the minimum indicative levels?

The 'Minimum Indicative Level' is now a fairly dated term that relates to the guideline **23.39** quantities set by the EU. In effect, the expression refers to the guideline quantities set by the EU.

In May 2009 when travelling within the EU the quantities were: **23.40**

- 10 litres of spirits;
- 90 litres of wine;
- 20 litres of 'intermediate products';
- 110 litres of beer;
- 3,200 cigarettes;
- 400 cigarillos;
- 200 cigars;
- 3kg of any other tobacco products.

(See subreg (1B)(e) of the Excise Goods, Beer and Tobacco Products (Amendment) Regulations 2002.)

23.41   The levels set out mirror the minimum levels that may be adopted by Member States in EC Directive (EC) 92/12 (except those for cigarettes and hand-rolling tobacco, which are four and three times respectively above the levels set out in the original Directive).

23.42   Whilst difficult to quantify, the cigarette and tobacco levels represent around six months' usage for an average smoker (20 cigarettes a day x 182 days = 3,640 cigarettes).

23.43   Intermediate Products are defined in Art 17(1) of Council Directive (EC) 92/83. They include fortified wine, sherry, and port.

23.44   It should be emphasised that these levels are only a guide. There are no limits. Genuine shoppers are entitled to bring back greater quantities for their own use. Nor is it unheard of for bootleggers to bring back quantities below the guidelines or matching the guidelines, in an attempt to avoid having their goods being seized. In *Harrison v Revenue and Customs Commissioners* (2007) The Times, 8 January 2007, Lightman J held that where quantities less than the prescribed amount were brought into the UK, they could still lawfully be seized where there were ample other circumstances that justified Customs' decision.

23.45   It should further be noted:

- if a traveller has over these amounts he should declare the goods in the red channel;
- if the importer is under 17 the tobacco and alcohol allowances do not apply (ie there are no allowances);
- on transfer flights to other EU countries, it is only necessary to declare what is in hand luggage. Hold baggage contents need only be declared at the final destination;
- from certain EU countries (namely Estonia, Bulgaria, Lithuania, and Romania) other limits currently apply.

Travelling to the UK from outside the EU

23.46   Similar (albeit more restrictive) levels exist when travelling from a non-EU country (including the Canary Islands and the Channel Islands). Gibraltar is part of the EU, but is outside the EU customs territory, and therefore the 'outside the EU' levels apply. Similarly, although Cyprus is a member of the EU, any importation from an area not deemed under the control of the Government of the Republic of Cyprus is treated as a non-EU import. From 1 December 2008 the 'outside the EU' levels were (SI 2008/3058):

- 200 cigarettes or 100 cigarillos or 50 cigars or 250g of tobacco;
- 4 litres of still table wine;
- 16 litres of beer;
- 1 litre of spirits or strong liqueurs over 22% in volume or 2 litres of fortified wine, sparkling wine or other liqueurs;
- £340 worth of other goods, including perfumes, gifts, and souvenirs.

C. Detention, Seizure, and Condemnation

23.47   Section 139 of CEMA details the provisions as to detention, seizure, and condemnation of goods. Section 139(6) refers to Sch 3 of the Act as having effect for the purpose of forfeiture and condemnation proceedings.

The forfeiture provisions

Schedule 3 of CEMA sets out the relevant provisions relating to forfeiture, including **23.48** notice of seizure, notice of claim, and condemnation. A copy of Sch 3 may be found at Appendix 19.

Paragraph 7 of Sch 3 states that the forfeiture shall have effect as from the date when the **23.49** liability to forfeiture arose.

What does 'liable to forfeiture' mean?

The expression 'liable to forfeiture', which is littered throughout the relevant forfeiture **23.50** Acts and statutory provisions, denotes something different from 'shall be forfeited' or 'shall automatically be forfeited'. 'Liable' implies some form of discretion by those considering forfeiture, either at the time of seizure or later at court.

However, that initial elasticity may be somewhat illusory. Paragraph 6 of Sch 3 to CEMA **23.51** (see Appendix 19) states that if the court finds that the thing was at the time of seizure 'liable to forfeiture', the court shall (meaning must) condemn it as forfeit. The draconian nature of these provisions appears to be analogous to strict liability/absolute offences in the criminal sphere, where intention or state of mind becomes irrelevant. This was confirmed in the case of *De Keyser v British Railway Traffic and Electric Co Ltd* [1936] 1 KB 224, where it was held that the justices were bound to condemn prohibited goods and that they possessed no discretion to refuse to do so, eg on the grounds of hardship of an innocent owner.

While Sch 3(6) offers no discretion, it must now be read in the light of recent decisions, **23.52** particularly *Customs and Excise Commissioners v Newbury* [2003] 2 All ER 964; (2003) 1 WLR 2131, where arguments in terms of proportionality when condemning a vehicle, as well as the goods seized, were successfully raised.

Secondary forfeiture

Section 141(1) of CEMA states where anything has become liable to forfeiture under the **23.53** Customs & Excise Acts:

(a) any ship, aircraft, vehicle, animal, container (including any article of passengers' baggage) or other thing which has been used for the carriage, handling or concealment of the thing so liable to forfeiture, either at a time when it was so liable or for the purposes of the commission of the offence for which it later became so liable; and
(b) any other thing mixed, packed or found with the thing so liable,
shall also be liable to forfeiture.

This section once again highlights the draconian nature of the forfeiture provisions, by setting out the consequences for property found and used in connection with goods liable to forfeiture—hence the term 'secondary forfeiture'.

Any vehicle used in the transportation of excise goods where no duty has been paid will **23.54** itself be liable for forfeiture. Many travellers' motorcars have been forfeited as a result. Similarly, smaller quantities of goods that accompany larger importations of, eg tobacco or cigarettes, are themselves liable. So, where, eg, 60,000 cigarettes are being imported, together with 3 litres of gin and 1 litre of Bacardi, although the 3 litres of gin and the 1 litre of Bacardi may be understandably considered for personal use, because of s 141 and the provision as to any other thing mixed, packed, or found with the thing so liable, the spirits also become liable to forfeiture.

23.55 In *Travell v Customs and Excise Commissioners* (1997) 162 JP 181 the Divisional Court held that s 141(a) and (b) are to be read disjunctively.

23.56 The reference to 'any other thing' should be interpreted to include only things of a like kind. So, eg, where 90 kgs of hand-rolling tobacco are discovered in the suitcase of an individual, together with their travel alarm clock, the alarm clock is not an excise good, nor sufficiently similar to justify its forfeiture (see *R v Uxbridge Magistrates' ex p Webb* (1998) 162 JP 198 (DC)).

23.57 The application of the 'mixed, packed or found' rule must always be a question of fact and degree upon which the court must find. This is illustrated by *Travell*, where the Crown Court held that 365 obscene magazines found 'all over the Defendant's one bedroom flat' were also liable to forfeiture because they had been 'found with' 15 imported magazines containing indecent pictures of children. In *Webb* the defendant had imported six obscene videos in a suitcase. The magistrates fast forwarded through two of them and concluded that their content was obscene and that they were liable to forfeiture. They condemned all six videos on the basis that the other four were 'packed with' the two videos that had been viewed.

23.58 In *Customs and Excise Commissioners v Jack Bradley (Accrington) Ltd* [1959] 1 QB 219, the court held that where kerosene oil had been discovered in the fuel tanks of vehicles, the vehicles themselves would be liable to forfeiture since they had been 'used for the carriage' of the oil.

More than one person involved

23.59 Where excise goods belonging to two people are seized as being liable to forfeiture, the fact that one of them makes no claim under Sch 3 cannot trigger the operation of s 141(1)(b) of the Act so as to preclude the other person from arguing that none of the goods were liable to forfeiture. In *Fox v Customs and Excise Commissioners* The Times, 20 July 2002, Lightman J held:

> As a matter of common sense and as a matter of common justice it must be open to the owner of the seized goods (in this case Mr. Fox) to challenge the facts relied on to establish the liability to forfeiture of the other party's (in this case Mr. Everett) goods. It adds nothing to the point that the other party (in this case Mr. Everett) declined to make a claim or attend the hearing.

Transfers for money's worth and the gift provisions are considered at para 23.28 above.

Proof of certain other matters

23.60 Section 154 of CEMA deals with proof of certain other matters. Section 154(1) states:

An averment in any process in proceedings under the Revenue and Customs Acts—
(a) that these proceedings were instituted by the Order of the Commissioners shall, until the contrary is proved, be sufficient evidence of the matter in question;
(b) where in any proceedings relating to Revenue and Customs any question arises as to the place in which any goods have been brought or as to whether or not any duty has been paid or secured in respect of any goods, then the burden of proof shall lie upon the other party to the proceedings.

Stops at Coquelles

British Revenue and Customs/UKBA also operate in Coquelles, France as a result of **23.61**
agreements reached in relation to the Channel Tunnel. As a result, condemnation law also
applies to this 'satellite port', pursuant to the Channel Tunnel (Alcoholic Liquor and
Tobacco Products) (Amendment) Order 2002, SI 2002/2693.

D. Condemnation: Practice and Procedure

Initial seizure

In the case of *R v Customs and Excise Commissioners ex p Mortimer* [1999] 1 WLR 17, it was **23.62**
determined that:

• fairness required Customs officers to give the importer a full opportunity to satisfy them
  that the importation was not for a commercial purpose; and to alert the traveller to the
  consequences of his failure to take that opportunity;
• officers were obliged to make plain the purpose of any interview they conducted;
• where their purpose was both to investigate the possible commission of crime and to
  form a judgement for the purposes of forfeiture, they were required to inform the suspect
  accordingly (including cautioning him and informing him of his right to remain silent
  in respect of the criminal investigation);
• officers should explain that under the forfeiture regulations, in the absence of a
  satisfactory explanation of the traveller's intentions, the goods might be seized.

In *Mortimer*, the Court held that giving the traveller a fair opportunity meant two **23.63**
things:

(1) that the importer must have a full opportunity to say anything he wanted about his
    intentions in relation to the goods with a view to showing that his intentions were
    non-commercial, because he proposed to use them himself or give them to friends or
    relations as the case may be; and
(2) that he must be alerted to the possible consequences if he does not take advantage of
    the opportunity to satisfy Customs that the goods are not being imported for a com-
    mercial purpose.

This should mean, in practice, that he is told in general terms of the existence of the
Guideline quantities and of the consequence that the goods will be seized if Revenue and
Customs/UKBA are not satisfied with the explanation they are given.

These requirements are usually adhered to when the Revenue and Customs/UKBA **23.64**
officer reads to the traveller what is sometimes referred to as the 'Commerciality Statement',
which states:

> You have excise goods in your possession (control) which appear not to have borne UK
> duty.
>
> Goods may be held without payment of duty providing they have been acquired and are held
> for your own use. I suspect that you may be holding goods for a commercial purpose and
> not for your own use. I intend to ask you some questions to establish whether these goods are
> held for a commercial purpose.

> If no satisfactory explanation is forthcoming or if you do not stay for questioning it may lead me to conclude that the goods are not held for your own use but held for a commercial purpose and your goods (and vehicle) may be seized as liable to forfeiture.
>
> You are not under arrest and are free to leave at any time. Do you understand?

If yes, the officer should proceed with the short interview dealing with the issues set out at para 23.32 above, or explain the commerciality statement again. The person intercepted will also be issued with a Notice 1, which sets out the guidelines in terms of the guideline amounts.

23.65 It is submitted that best practice dictates that a note of any conversation should be made, preferably contemporaneously. The 'Commerciality Statement' should be used and referred to in any statement made by the stopping officer, along with Notice 1, which should be handed to the traveller, preferably before questioning, with the opportunity being given to read it.

23.66 The case of *R v Customs and Excise Commissioners ex p Kenneth Stephen Boxall* (15 February 1996), although decided before the 1999 amendment, is useful in confirming the procedure of how travellers found with excise goods in their possession should be treated. It repeats that the Revenue and Customs/UKBA must give the importer the opportunity to tell them why he has the goods in his possession, what he intends to do with them, and produce any document that relates to them. All of this must be done before they make any determination about whether to seize the goods in question as liable to forfeiture (see p 4F of the judgment). It should be emphasised, as it was in *Boxall*, that natural justice obliges the Revenue and Customs/UKBA to give the person concerned an opportunity to satisfy them that the goods were not imported for a commercial purpose. Not to do so would render the seizing of any excise goods unlawful.

Possible criminal proceedings

23.67 Section 139 of CEMA anticipates the possibility of criminal proceedings. There is the scope for charging individuals with an offence of evading duty contrary to s 170(1) and (2) of CEMA or the common law offence of cheating the Revenue. Within the statutory scheme each offence is punishable by up to seven years' imprisonment. If such proceedings are contemplated the codes and regulations set out in the Police and Criminal Evidence Act 1984 (PACE) should be followed.

23.68 However, it should be noted that for the purposes of a forfeiture hearing, a failure to follow PACE is not fatal, as the jurisdiction is civil and therefore falls outside of PACE's remit.

23.69 In *Mortimer*, Lord Bingham identified the practical difficulty Revenue and Customs officers may find themselves in if they were also investigating the possible commission of a crime. In such circumstances they would be obliged to caution the suspect and that would include the suspect being told that he does not have to say anything. The converse problem is that when dealing with the forfeiture aspect of the seizure, the importer is being actively encouraged to say anything that he wants to about the goods with a view to him showing that his intentions are non-commercial. Lord Bingham said there was no entirely simple answer to this practical problem. It would be incumbent on the interviewing officers to make plain the purposes of any interview and, if and when there are two purposes, to explain them both. There must be no watering down of the caution, nor must there be any watering down of the officers' duties in respect of warning the traveller about his failure to not take advantage of the opportunity to satisfy Customs that the goods are not being imported for a commercial purpose.

In *R v Payton* [2006] EWCA Crim 1226, the Court emphasised that nothing must be done **23.70** in civil proceedings that might prejudice the outcome of criminal proceedings. Thus if forfeiture proceedings are initiated it will generally be prudent to adjourn them pending the outcome of the criminal proceedings.

Notice of claim—the one-month time limit to appeal

Schedule 3 of CEMA states, at para 3, that: **23.71**

... any person claiming that anything seized as liable to forfeiture is not so liable shall within one month of the date of notice of seizure or, where no such notice has been served on him, within one month of the date of the seizure, give notice of his claim in writing to the Commissioners at any office of Revenue and Customs.

Paragraph 4 of the same Schedule states that any notice under para 3 should specify the **23.72** name and address of the claimant and, in the case of a claimant who is outside the UK, shall specify the name and address of a solicitor in the UK who is authorised to accept service of process and to act on behalf of the claimant.

Six-month time limit on HM Revenue and Customs/UKBA once notice lodged

Paragraph 6 of Sch 3 to CEMA (see Appendix 19) states that where a notice of claim in **23.73** respect of anything is duly given in accordance with paras 3 and 4 of the same Schedule, the Commissioners shall take proceedings for the condemnation of that thing, and if the court finds that the thing was at the time of seizure liable to forfeiture, the court shall condemn it as forfeited.

Accordingly, s 127 of the Magistrates' Court Act 1980 states: **23.74**

... a magistrates' court shall not try an information or hear a complaint unless the information was laid, or the complaint made, within 6 months from the time when the offence was committed.

In *Customs and Excise Commissioners v Venn* The Times, 24 January 2002, the Divisional **23.75** Court held that CEMA drew a distinction between the detention of goods and the provisions of Sch 3 in respect of forfeiture. Forfeiture depended on there being a seizure of the goods. Where a person gave notice under paras 3 and 4 of Sch 3, claiming that goods seized as liable to forfeiture were not so liable, it was incumbent on the Commissioners to take proceedings for the condemnation of that thing by a court; and where such proceedings were instituted by way of a complaint in a magistrates' court, time ran for the purposes of s 127 of the Magistrates' Court Act 1980 from the date of service of the notice, not from the date of seizure.

Preparation for the hearing—service of evidence

There are no rules for service of evidence in the magistrates' court in respect of civil com- **23.76** plaints. In the absence of such rules the court is able to regulate its own procedure (*Simms v Moore* [1970] 3 All ER 1). If relevant, all evidence is admissible, unless excluded by some other rule.

23.77 Prior to the hearing of any application for forfeiture at the magistrates' court, it is open to Revenue and Customs/UKBA to either make voluntary disclosure of the evidence upon which it seeks to rely, or, by correspondence with the defence, to ask for and arrange mutual disclosure.

23.78 Voluntary disclosure is useful in cases where, eg, the issues are straightforward, little is challenged, or where the witness in question, giving the statement, is unavailable to attend court. It enables his evidence to be agreed prior to the hearing.

23.79 Mutual disclosure can equally be of assistance where the issues are not straightforward and matters are challenged, so as to expedite matters at court and crystallise the arguments. This entails Revenue and Customs/UKBA and the other side coming to an agreement that Customs will reveal their case, ie statements, exhibits, interviews, etc, in return for the appellant revealing his case to Revenue and Customs/UKBA, including proofs of evidence. This has the advantage of both parties knowing what the other will say before the case comes to court, and avoids ambushes and costly adjournments.

Preparation for the hearing—dutiable goods

23.80 In *Boxall* (p 6E), the court held that para 6 of Sch 3 made it clear that it is for the court to consider whether the thing seized was at the time liable to forfeiture. Read with s 49(1), para 6 obliges the court to decide whether the goods are dutiable. On this question, the burden lies on Revenue and Customs/UKBA and, with the proceedings being civil, the court must be satisfied on the balance of probabilities (in the majority of cases there is little issue over the fact that the goods are dutiable, as they generally relate to excise products like cigarettes and tobacco).

The hearing—commercial purpose v own use

23.81 It will be incumbent upon the court to consider the evidence and determine the issue: namely whether the goods were imported for a commercial purpose, or for personal use.

23.82 In so doing they should consider the criteria set out in at para 23.32 above. The inclusion of 'any other circumstance that appears to be relevant' covers a multitude of matters, including frequency of travel. For example, an individual who travels abroad frequently does not need to 'stock up' on duty goods such as cigarettes, because they know they will have the opportunity to purchase more cigarettes on their next trip. Similarly, an individual who makes regular day trips with the sole purpose of bringing back excise goods may have difficulty persuading a court it is not for a commercial purpose, particularly if, for example, they do not smoke heavily, or are purchasing a variety of brands of cigarettes (smokers tend to stick to the same brand), or if they are using a hire car (in the knowledge that it will avoid their own vehicle being seized).

23.83 The court may also consider whether the defendant has been stopped before, or had knowledge of the guideline amounts, whether there had been any attempt to hide or conceal the items in question, and whether the traveller's story had changed since the initial stop.

23.84 Conversely, if the 'aggravating' matters outlined above do not feature in the defendant's case, or, for example, he has receipts for the purchases, it is a first time stop, and has verification that the goods are intended for a family party or similar, the court may consider that the importation lacks commerciality.

As has already been observed, the wording of the provisions are mandatory, akin to a **23.85** strict liability offence, and no discretion is afforded to the court in relation to the goods themselves if the court is satisfied on the balance of probabilities they were imported for a commercial purpose, as per *Fox v Customs and Excise Commissioners* (2002) 166 JP 578 at para 16, where Lightman J held:

> ... the statutory language is mandatory: where the goods are liable to forfeiture the Court is bound to condemn them.

However, in relation to secondary forfeiture under s 141, eg a traveller's vehicle, the court **23.86** is entitled to reach its independent judgment on proportionality, weighing up the evidence and the facts. In *Customs and Excise Commissioners v Newbury* [2003] 2 All ER 964; (2003) 1 WLR 2131, para 35, the court held:

> ... whether forfeiture would be so disproportionate as to be in breach of the particular claimant's rights under Article 1, Protocol 1 to the Convention ... can be resolved by the court. This is not strictly a question of discretion but a matter upon which the court is entitled to reach its own independent judgment.

In *Revenue and Customs Commissioners v Berriman and Teeside Combined Court* (2007) 4 All **23.87** ER 925; (2008) 1 WLR 2171 Customs sought, unsuccessfully, to challenge the finding in *Newbury* by arguing it had erroneously expanded the jurisdiction of the magistrates' court and was leading to unmanageable results (para 32). The court concluded that these arguments had 'much merit', but that *Berriman* was not the case in which to raise them. It found that it was bound by *Newbury*, and that the issues raised would be for a higher court to determine authoritively (para 36). It follows that there is still scope for argument in terms of the *Newbury* principle.

A useful summary of the statutory procedures to be followed is found in the judgement of **23.88** Lightman J in *Fox v Commissioners of Customs and Excise* [2003] 1 WLR 1331 at 9–11.

Court procedure: preliminary matters

Paragraphs 10(1) and (3) of Sch 3 to CEMA require that the claimant of the goods, ie the **23.89** defendant, swears on oath that the thing seized was, or was to the best of his knowledge and belief, his property at the time of the seizure (his solicitor may also take the oath on his behalf for the purposes of this section). Paragraph 10(3) states that if any part of that procedure is not complied with, the court shall (meaning must) give judgment for the Commissioners.

This means that if the defendant is not prepared to state on oath that the goods seized in **23.90** fact belonged to him and were his property, then the application for forfeiture on behalf of Revenue and Customs/UKBA will succeed. It is advisable that para 10(1) of Sch 3 to CEMA be dealt with at the outset of proceedings, because it may be considered pointless to sit through an entire case if the defendant was not prepared to swear on oath that the goods belonged to him or, alternatively, that he declared that the goods belonged to another for whom he was acting.

23.91 In giving judgment for Revenue and Customs/UKBA in such circumstances, the court will not have considered the facts of the matter. It in effect becomes condemnation by default. A question therefore arises whether or not s 141 would apply, it only having application where there is a finding that the goods are liable for forfeiture. In such circumstances it will be necessary to invite the court to consider the facts and decide whether any of the goods were so liable, in order for the secondary forfeiture provisions of s 141 to bite (see *Fox v Customs and Excise Commissioners* (2002) 166 JP 578).

Court procedure: condemnation by complaint

23.92 The procedural rules in relation to the hearing of a complaint and the jurisdiction of the magistrates' court are set out at s 51 *et seq* of the Magistrates' Courts Act 1980.

23.93 Section 52 confirms jurisdiction; s 53 deals with procedure, and states that at the hearing of a complaint, the court shall, if the defendant appears, state to him the substance of the complaint. Section 54 sets out the adjournment provisions, which may take place 'at any time'; and s 55 confirms that if a defendant does not appear the court may proceed in his absence. Similarly, under s 56 where at the time and place appointed for the hearing or adjourned hearing of a complaint the defendant appears but the complainant does not, the court may dismiss the complaint or, if evidence has been received on a previous occasion, proceed in the absence of the complainant. Section 57 states that where neither party attends, the court may dismiss the complaint; and s 58 deals with the transfer of proceedings.

Order of speeches

23.94 Once ownership of the goods has been established, the procedure to be followed is set out in the Magistrates' Court Rules 1981 at r 14, as follows:

(i) On the hearing of a complaint, the complainant shall call his evidence and before doing so may address the court.

(ii) At the conclusion of the evidence, for the complainant, the defendant may address the court, whether or not he afterwards calls evidence.

(iii) At the conclusion of the evidence, if any for the defence, the complainant may call evidence to rebut that evidence.

(iv) At the conclusion of the evidence for the defence and the evidence, if any, in rebuttal, the defendant may address the court if he has not already done so.

(v) Either party may, with the leave of the court, address the court a second time, but where the court grants leave to one party, it shall not refuse leave to the other.

(vi) Where the defendant obtains leave to address the court for a second time, his second address shall be made before the second address, if any, of the complainant.

23.95 It follows from the above that Revenue and Customs/UKBA only has one opportunity to address the court on the facts without further leave; and that is at the beginning of their case.

23.96 It should be noted that either party may, with the leave of the court, address the court a second time or, as in any proceedings, either party may address the court on a point of law at any stage.

23.97 Although the defendant is free to make a submission of no case to answer after the applicant's case, some caution should be exercised, because if it fails and the defendant has been asked to choose between calling evidence and making a submission, he will not be entitled to call evidence thereafter. See *Boyce v Wyatt Engineering* The Times, 14 June 2001.

It should also be noted that Revenue and Customs/UKBA has the opportunity to call **23.98** evidence in rebuttal should it wish to do so. This may occur in forfeiture cases where something has been suggested during the course of the defence case that is either new or was not put to the officer in the case at the first opportunity, and where the officer in the case believes that that aspect of the defence's case needs correcting.

The burden and standard of proof

It is for Revenue and Customs/UKBA to satisfy the court, on the balance of probabilities, **23.99** that the goods were imported for a commercial purpose (*R (Hoverspeed) v Customs and Excise Commissioners* [2002] 4 All ER 912 (DC) para 130/10).

This was illustrated in the VAT and Duties (now Tax) Tribunal case of *Bevins and Pyrah v* **23.100** *Customs and Excise Commissioners* [2005] (EO00903) where the Tribunal held that Customs had misapplied the law by incorrectly imposing the burden of proof on the travellers. Both the decision to seize the goods and the decision not to restore had been made on the basis that the travellers had not made out a satisfactory case that the goods were for their own use. It was held that following the decision in *Hoverspeed* such a positive burden could no longer apply; the burden in the first instance was on Customs to show that the goods were for a commercial use.

It is useful when addressing the court to remind them that they are sitting in their civil **23.101** jurisdiction and that the burden of proof is that of the 'balance of probabilities' and not that which they may be more familiar with, namely beyond reasonable doubt.

In other words, the defendant does not have to satisfy the court beyond reasonable doubt **23.102** that the goods were for his personal use, but only that it is more likely than not that they were. Equally however, HM Revenue and Customs/UKBA does not need to make them sure that the goods were being imported for a commercial purpose, but only satisfy them that it was more likely than not that that was the case.

In many civil cases the degree of probability required to establish proof may vary according **23.103** to the allegation to be proved (see *Hornal v Neuberger Products Ltd* [1957] 1 QB 247) and the court is often reluctant, when considering claims by the Crown, to apply merely a 51/49 per cent test where an individual's property or other assets are in jeopardy (see *Bater v Bater* [1950] 2 All ER 458 and *B v Chief Constable of Avon and Somerset* [2001] 1 All ER 562).

Hearsay in civil cases

The Magistrates' Courts (Hearsay Evidence in Civil Proceedings) Rules 1999, SI 1999/681 **23.104** set out the rules applying to hearsay in magistrates' courts. Those rules provide as follows:

3 (1) Subject to paragraphs (2) and (3), a party who desires to give hearsay evidence at the hearing must, not less than 21 days before the date fixed for the hearing, serve a hearsay notice on every other party and file a copy in the court by serving it on the justices' clerk.

(2) Subject to paragraph (3), the court or the justices' clerk may make a direction substituting a different period of time for the service of the hearsay notice under paragraph (1) on the application of a party to the proceedings.

(3) The court may make a direction under paragraph (2) of its own motion.

(4) A hearsay notice must—
    (a) state that it is a hearsay notice;
    (b) identify the proceedings in which the hearsay evidence is to be given;
    (c) state that the party proposes to adduce hearsay evidence;
    (d) identify the hearsay evidence;
    (e) identify the person who made the statement which is to be given in evidence; and
    (f) state why that person will not be called to give oral evidence.
(5) A single hearsay notice may deal with the hearsay evidence of more than one witness.

23.105 These Rules also make provision for:

- the procedure to call a witness for cross-examination on hearsay evidence (r 4);
- a notice requirement where a party tenders hearsay evidence but does not call the person who made the statement to give oral evidence, and another party wishes to attack the credibility of the person who made the statement or allege that he has made another statement inconsistent with it (r 5)
- the service of documents required by the Rules (r 6).

23.106 However, a failure to comply with the duty to give notice should not affect the admissibility of hearsay evidence (see s 1(1) of the Civil Evidence Act 1995 and s 1(2) which is specifically adopted by r 2(2)). It then becomes a question of weight for the justices to determine. In assessing the weight, all the relevant circumstances should be considered including that the individual who makes the statement has not been tendered in cross-examination and therefore has not been tested. The desirability of serving a hearsay notice is obvious as a party may find itself liable for costs if a witness statement tendered at the hearing reveals new evidence that the other side has not had the opportunity of exploring, or fresh evidence that amounts to an ambush.

23.107 Section 4(2) of the Civil Evidence Act 1995 gives some guidance that may assist the court when assessing what weight should be given to hearsay evidence. That guidance includes:

(a) whether it would have been reasonable and practicable to have produced the person who made the statements rather than relying on a hearsay report;
(b) whether the person who originally made the statements made them contemporaneously with the matters stated;
(c) whether the evidence is multiple hearsay, in other words whether the hearsay witness is in fact repeating something which itself is hearsay;
(d) whether anyone involved has a motive to conceal or misrepresent matters;
(e) whether the original statement was made for some purpose or produced in collaboration with others;
(f) whether the attempt to rely on hearsay rather than calling the person who made the original statement is designed to prevent a proper valuation of its weight by the Court.

23.108 In the Crown Court the position is slightly different, although the same principle appears to apply. In *R v Wadmore and Foreman* [2006] EWCA Crim 686, a case that concerned an application for an anti-social behaviour order, the Court of Appeal held that anti-social behaviour orders (ASBOs) amounted to civil proceedings in a criminal court. The Criminal

Procedure Rules 2005 did not apply to civil cases. The Civil Procedure Rules 1998 do not apply in criminal courts. The Magistrates' Courts (Hearsay Evidence in Civil Proceedings) Rules 1999 do not apply to the Crown Court. The Court of Appeal therefore assumed that as the case was civil in nature, hearsay evidence was admissible under s 1 of the Civil Evidence Act 1995. There were no applicable procedural rules and the Court thought that the Magistrates' Court Rules should be applied by analogy.

Previous convictions

In *Halford and Brooks [Senior]* The Times, 3 October 1991 the Court confirmed that in **23.109** civil proceedings a different approach to allegations of criminal behaviour may be taken, in that there is no right to silence and evidence of 'bad character' can be admitted (see also *Ali v Best* (1997) 161 JP 399H and *R v Isleworth Crown Court ex p Kevin Marland* (1998) 162 JPR 251).

Previous convictions can be proved by the production of a certificate of conviction, which **23.110** is admissible by virtue of ss 11 and 12 of the Civil Evidence Act 1968 (in force by virtue of the Civil Evidence Act 1968 (Commencement No 1) Order 1968, SI 1968/1734 and not repealed by the Civil Evidence Act 1995).

Where an individual is acquitted in criminal proceedings the evidence of those proceedings **23.111** is admissible (see *Customs and Excise Commissioners v T* (1998) 162 JP 193, citing *Hunter v Chief Constable of West Midlands* [1982] AC 529 (HL)).

Reasons for stopping the traveller

The only issue before the court is that concerning commercial or personal use. The action **23.112** is against the goods, *in rem*, and not against the individual. As a result the reason why an individual was stopped falls away as being irrelevant to the matter the court has to decide. Similarly, the seizure of the goods cannot be regarded as axiomatically invalid, merely because it occurred as a result of a check that was invalid or unlawful. See *Customs and Excise Commissioners v Atkinson, Dore and Binns* [2003] EWHC Admin 421; *Customs and Excise Commissioners v Newbury* [2003] 2 All ER 964; (2003) 1 WLR 2131 (at para 5); and *Hoverspeed v Customs and Excise Commissioners* [2002] EWCA Civ 1804 at paras 44–49, where the Court of Appeal ruled that no link between the legality of the stop and the legality of any subsequent seizure: '. . . can or should in our view be read into the provisions of CEMA' (para 48). In so finding the court held that it did not 'see any unfairness in the seizure of the goods liable to forfeiture, even though their presence happens only to be discovered in the course of an unlawful check. That may be bad luck, but it is not unfair'.

Power to stop the traveller

The power of Revenue and Customs to stop and search an individual and their vehicle **23.113** derives from ss 78, 163A, and 164 of CEMA.

Court should give reasons

The desirability for a court to give, at least, some brief reasons for its decision and the **23.114** necessity for the parties to prompt the court to do so if the court failed in this regard, was underlined in *R (on the application of Cleary) v Revenue and Customs Commissioners* [2008] EWHC 1987 (Admin).

Sensitive material

23.115 Although public interest immunity (PII) applications do not feature in magistrates' courts, exclusion of evidence on the grounds of public policy applies equally to civil proceedings as it does in criminal. The test is whether the production of a document or other piece of evidence would be 'injurious to the public interest'; ie, whether the withholding of a document/information is necessary for the proper functioning of a government department. For example, the disclosure of the document may jeopardise an ongoing operation, or the methods deployed, or cooperation received from others in the investigation of an offence.

E. Condemnation: Costs and Compensation

Costs

23.116 Under s 64(1) of the Magistrates' Courts Act 1980:

(1) On the hearing of a complaint, a Magistrates' Court shall have power in its discretion to make such order as to costs—
  (a) on making the order for which the complaint is made, to be paid by the Defendant to the Complainant;
  (b) on dismissing the complaint, to be paid by the Complainant to the Defendant,
as it thinks just and reasonable . . .

Pursuant to s 62(2) the amount ordered to be paid shall be specified in the Order and s 62(3) confirms that the costs ordered shall be enforceable as a civil debt, in other words, not administered by the magistrates' court.

23.117 It is always advisable to apply for costs on the same day and at the same time as the hearing of the forfeiture application. This is because such an order has to be made by the same Bench who made the order in relation to the forfeiture application.

23.118 Defence solicitors should advise their clients very cautiously about this aspect of the proceedings for three main reasons:

(1) Revenue and Customs are known to seek their full commercial costs in forfeiture proceedings, which can amount to several thousand pounds. It will sometimes be advisable to take a commercial view on whether to pursue litigation in cases where the value of the goods is not particularly high or where any prospective costs order is likely to make pursuing the claim prohibitive.
(2) Even if the defendant is successful, it will not necessarily follow that he will obtain a costs award if the court finds that Customs have acted honestly, reasonably, and properly, and in the public interest (following *Parinpanathan v City of Westminster Magistrates' Court and 2 others* [2009] EWHC 762 (Admin)).
(3) Revenue and Customs/UKBA would be entitled to object to such an order if, for example, the defendant had raised matters in the magistrates' court for the first time in dealing with the application for forfeiture which he had not mentioned, either at the time of seizure or subsequently in correspondence.

In exercising its discretion the court can take into account that Revenue and Customs/ **23.119**
UKBA are exercising their statutory function in condemnation matters. See *R v Uxbridge*
Justices ex p Metropolitan Police Commissioner [1981] 1 QB 829; *Bradford City Metropolitan*
District Council v Booth The Times, 31 May 2000; and *R (Chief Constable of*
Northamptonshire) v Daventry Magistrates' Court [2001] EWHC (Admin) 446.

Importantly, costs must not be used as a device to overcompensate the successful **23.120**
party, or punish the unsuccessful party (*R v Highgate Justices ex p Petrou* [1954] 1 All
ER 406).

The power of the magistrates' court to make a wasted costs order is governed by s 145A of **23.121**
the Magistrates' Court Act 1980 and SI 1991/2096.

LSC funding

Legal Service Commission (LSC) funding is not generally available for civil proceedings, **23.122**
although pursuant to the Access to Justice Act 1999 (AJA), a person may apply for public
funding as part of the Community Legal Service. Section 6(6) of the AJA, however, does
not permit the funding of services within Sch 2, and para 2(3) prohibits the funding of
advocacy in any proceedings in the magistrates' court. Condemnation proceedings in both
the magistrates' court and the Crown Court therefore appear to be excluded.

In *R (Mudie) v Kent Magistrates' Court* [2003] 2 All ER 631, the Court of Appeal confirmed **23.123**
that condemnation proceedings could not be extended to criminal proceedings, and therefore Criminal Defence Service funding was not available, although, as Laws LJ observed in
Mudie, there was nothing to prevent solicitors entering into conditional fee agreements in
condemnation proceedings (para 6).

Compensation

Under s 144: **23.124**

(1) Where, in any proceedings for the condemnation of any thing seized as liable to forfeiture under
the customs and excise Acts, judgment is given for the claimant, the court may, if it sees fit, certify
that there were reasonable grounds for the seizure.
(2) Where any proceedings, whether civil or criminal, are brought against the Commissioners, a law
officer of the Crown or any person authorised by or under the Customs and Excise Acts 1979 to
seize or detain any thing liable to forfeiture under the customs and excise Acts on account of the
seizure or detention of any thing, and judgment is given for the plaintiff or prosecutor, then if
either—
(a) a certificate relating to the seizure has been granted under subsection (1) above; or
(b) the court is satisfied that there were reasonable grounds for seizing or detaining that thing
under the customs and excise Acts,
the plaintiff or prosecutor shall not be entitled to recover any damages or costs and the defendant
shall not be liable to any punishment.
(3) Nothing in subsection (2) above shall effect any right of any person to the return of the thing seized
or detained or to compensation in respect of any damage to the thing or in respect of the destruction
thereof.

The plaintiff in such a scenario would be the aggrieved traveller or defendant, who had **23.125**
been successful in the magistrates' court, and now sought compensation. However, if the
bench has certified that, notwithstanding its finding against Customs, the original seizure

was nevertheless reasonable, then the aggrieved traveller or defendant will not be able to recover costs or damages in any subsequent compensation proceedings.

23.126   In the event of not succeeding with a forfeiture application therefore, Revenue and Customs/UKBA will always be anxious to ensure that the 's 144 certificate' as to the reasonableness of their original seizure is signed, to preclude any claim for compensation. This is equally so where the court has condemned (for example) tobacco, but refused to condemn the vehicle that was used to transport it (secondary forfeiture).

23.127   In *Revenue & Customs Commissioners v Dean Mark James (T/A M&D Enterprise)* (2008) EWHC 230 (QB), (2008) RTR 18, the court considered a matter where a vehicle has been seized at a time it was not in the possession or control of the claimant. Whilst the vehicle had been subsequently restored, the claimant sought to recover £25,000 by way of compensation for losses whilst he was deprived of its use. It was conceded that the original seizure was lawful. No notice of appeal in relation to the initial seizure had been served and, as a result, no condemnation proceedings had been instituted and no certificate under s 144 therefore made. The Court found that in such circumstances the condemnation of the goods were deemed to have occurred in favour of the Commissioners and the court had no power to re-open the question of legality of seizure where it had already been established by the operation of the law (applying *Gora v Customs and Excise Commissioners* (2003) EWCA Civ 525, (2004) QB 93 and *Gascoyne v Customs and Excise Commissioners* (2004) EWCA Civ 1162, (2005) Ch 215).

Refund for goods destroyed

23.128   Pursuant to paras 16 and 17 of Sch 3 of CEMA (Appendix 19), Revenue and Customs are entitled to destroy any perishable goods notwithstanding the fact that they may not have yet been condemned. It is common practice for Customs to destroy tobacco goods on the basis that they are perishable, prior to any hearing.

23.129   If this occurs, by para 17, Revenue and Customs are required to pay a successful appellant an amount equal to the market value of the thing at the time of its seizure. 'Market value' for these purposes was considered in *R (Revenue and Customs Commissioners) v Machell* [2005] EWHC 2593 (Admin) where Stanley Burnton J held that the market value was the retail price in the country of purchase, as opposed to the retail price in the UK. He also found that the travel costs of the importers were not a recoverable amount under para 17, as para 17 did not amount to compensation.

23.130   It will be noted that the court concluded (at para 26 of the judgement) that para 17 of Sch 3 was only directed towards reimbursement for destroyed *perishable* goods. Goods which were destroyed in error which were not perishable (such as alcohol) or by accident were therefore not covered.

F. Condemnation Appeals

23.131   Revenue and Customs/UKBA and the defendant may appeal from the magistrates' court decision to the Crown Court, or in the alternative invite the Court to state a case for the High Court on a matter of law (see Appendix 19 and para 11 of Sch 3 to CEMA).

The Crown Court's jurisdiction and powers of disposal are set out in ss 45 to 48 of the Supreme Court Act 1981.

Procedure

On appeal to the Crown Court the hearing is de novo (s 79(3) of the Supreme Court   **23.132**
Act 1981) and involves a complete rehearing of the original case, including oral evidence.
Rule 63.2 of the Criminal Procedure Rules gives a time limit of 21 days and the procedure
(written notice to the magistrates' court) appears to have been adopted for use in complaint
appeals, albeit the appeal is civil.

The procedure adopted at the hearing is generally the same as set out in the Magistrates'   **23.133**
Courts Rules above. Pending the rehearing, there is no restriction on either Revenue and
Customs/UKBA or the defence obtaining more evidence and adducing new evidence at
the appeal.

In *R (Customs and Excise Commissioners) v Maidstone Crown Court* [2004] EWHC (Admin)   **23.134**
1459, Customs sought judicial review of two decisions of the Crown Court in relation to
granting permission to appeal out of time. The original applications had been made without notice and were made after several months of delay. There was no proper explanation
as to why there had been a delay and the judge granted permission without giving
any reasons. Newman J held that it was incumbent on a judge in the proper exercise of his
discretion to consider the reasons given for any delay and to address the proposed merits of
the appeal in the light of said delay. Furthermore, a judge should in the interests of justice
give reasons for the grant or refusal of permission and communicate that decision to any
affected party.

Pre-hearing review

It is advisable to have some form of pre-hearing review at the appeal stage. There are a   **23.135**
number of reasons for this, which include:

* to assist the court with a time estimate; eg if there are four officers being called and two
  defendants that is likely to occupy a day, if not two days, of court time;
* to determine which witnesses are required, and ascertain their availability to give evidence;
* to notify any points of law that may prolong matters at the appeal hearing; and
* to deal with other matters that may or may not be relevant to the particular case, eg,
  whether or not an interpreter is required, etc.

Pending the hearing of an appeal

It should be noted that Art 12 of Sch 3 to CEMA states that pending the final determina-   **23.136**
tion by way of appeal of the matter, the goods in question should be left with Revenue and
Customs/UKBA (see Appendix 19).

G. Condemnation in the High Court

Although rare, as HMRC nearly always commences proceedings in the magistrates' court,   **23.137**
condemnation cases may be brought in the High Court. In such cases procedure is by
Claim Form and follows the Civil Procedure Rules. Costs are dealt with in CPR Part 44.

H. Condemnation and the ECHR

23.138 The legitimacy of forfeiture proceedings was considered in *Goldsmith v Customs and Excise Commissioners* The Times, 12 June 2001. In that case, the Divisional Court considered what application, if any, Art 6(2) of the ECHR had in relation to Sch 3 of CEMA. The Court found that because proceedings for the condemnation of goods as liable to forfeiture do not involve the determination of a criminal charge, none of the usual consequences of criminal conviction follow on from such proceedings. Therefore, even if the proceedings were proceedings to which the presumption of innocence in Art 6(2) of the ECHR applied, the burden of proof imposed on the importer of excise goods to rebut Customs' assertion that the importation was for a commercial purpose was proportionate, reasonable, and justified.

23.139 This issue had previously been considered in *Salabiaku v France* (1988) 13 EHRR 379, where the Court held that there was nothing particularly unfair in imposing a burden of proof on someone where the subject matter was something that he was particularly well placed to prove. See also *The Netherlands v Joustra* C5-05 (ECJ, 23 November 2006).

23.140 It will be noted that pursuant to Art 1 of Protocol 1 the right to property is not absolute and the State is permitted to secure property in order to control the use of it in accordance with the general interest or securing the payment of taxes and other contributions or penalties. Condemnation proceedings have also been found to be compliant with the ECHR and Art 6 in *Air Canada v UK* (1995) 20 EHRR 150, paras 61–63.

23.141 In relation to the condemnation of a vehicle and Art 1, see *Hopping v Customs and Excise Commissioners* (EOO 170) (2001), at para 29.246 below.

I. Useful Resources

23.142 Further information on condemnation may be found at <http://www.hmrc.gov.uk> under 'Individuals and Employees' and under 'Travel—Customs allowances'. In addition HMRC produce two helpful stand alone leaflets: Notice 1 'A Customs Guide for Travellers Entering the UK' and Notice 12A 'What you can do if things are seized by Customs'.

J. Red Diesel Cases

Introduction

23.143 Section 139 and Sch 3 to CEMA is intended to cover a myriad of circumstances where Revenue and Customs are entitled to bring proceedings for the condemnation of goods as forfeit.

23.144 Revenue and Customs are allowed, by law, to examine any vehicle, any oil in or on it, and to inspect, test, or sample any oil in the fuel supply. They are also entitled to require vehicle owners or anyone in charge of a vehicle to open a fuel tank or other sources of the fuel supply, so that the fuel may be located and inspected or tested or sampled. They are also entitled, by law, to require anyone in charge of the vehicle to produce any books or documents relating to the vehicle or about the oil carried in it. They are entitled to enter and inspect any premises (except private dwelling-houses) and inspect test and sample any oil on the premises whether in a vehicle or elsewhere. In short, their powers are wide reaching.

The legislative provisions

Red diesel is gas/heavy oil that carries a lower (rebated) rate of duty. It is commonly **23.145** referred to as 'red diesel' because of the red dye used in its production. The relevant law is found in the Hydrocarbon Oils Duties Act 1979 at ss 12(2) and 13(6). Section 12(2) reads:

No heavy oil on whose delivery for home use rebate has been allowed . . . shall:
(a) be used as fuel for a road vehicle; or
(b) be taken into a road vehicle as fuel . . .

Section 12(3) states:

(a) Heavy oil shall be deemed to be used as fuel for a road vehicle if, but only if, it is used as fuel for the engine provided for propelling the vehicle or for an engine which draws its fuel from the same supply as that engine; and
(b) heavy oil shall be deemed to be taken into a road vehicle as fuel if, but only if, it is taken into it as part of that supply.

Derv (fuel for a diesel engine road vehicle) is heavy oil that carries a higher rate of excise **23.146** duty than other heavy oils such as aviation kerosene, fuel oil, gas oil, and kerosene. It has now been replaced by the more environmentally friendly ultra low sulphur diesel (ULSD), which is also defined as a heavy oil.

By definition any oil which does not meet the criteria for classification as a light oil is a heavy **23.147** oil: see s 1(3) and (4) of the Hydrocarbon Oils Duties Act 1979. Section 13(6) states:

Any heavy oil—
(a) taken into a road vehicle as mentioned in s 12(2) above or supplied as mentioned in sub-section 12(2) or (3) above; or
(b) taken as fuel into a vehicle at a time when it is not a road vehicle and remaining in the vehicle as part of its fuel supply at a later time when it becomes a road vehicle,
shall be liable for forfeiture.

Because these matters, like the matters dealt with elsewhere in this chapter, are similar to **23.148** strict liability offences (although not criminal), the defendant's state of mind or mitigating circumstances tend to become irrelevant. The action is against the fuel, as opposed to the individual.

In *Customs and Excise Commissioners v Jack Bradley* [1959] 1 QB 219 (one of the few **23.149** reported cases on red diesel) Lord Parker held that where oil was being carried and was being consumed it became liable to forfeiture. Lord Parker held (at p 224):

The offence is the use of oil . . . one thing at least is clear, that oil is used when it is consumed . . .

It appears to follow, therefore, that even a vehicle that is shunted stands liable for forfeiture if the fuel is being used, for example, to create pressure, as opposed to propelling the vehicle.

Excepted vehicles

23.150 Excepted vehicles to the provisions of the Hydrocarbon Oils Duties Act are set out in Sch 1 to the Act. Schedule 1 reads:

(1) A vehicle is an excepted vehicle where—
    (a) it is not used on a public road, and
    (b) no licence under the Vehicle Excise and Registration Act 1994 is in force in respect of it.

Public roads are roads repairable at public expense.

23.151 Schedule 1(para 12) states as follows:

(1) A vehicle is an excepted vehicle if it is—
    (a) a road construction vehicle, and
    (b) used or kept solely for the conveyance of built-in road construction machinery (with or without articles or material used for the purposes of the machinery).
(2) In sub-paragraph 1 above 'road construction vehicle' means a vehicle:
    (a) which is constructed or adapted for use for the conveyance of built-in road construction machinery, and
    (b) which is not constructed or adapted for the conveyance of any other load except articles and material used for the purposes of such machinery.
(3) In sub-paragraphs (1) and (2) above 'built-in road construction machinery', in relation to a vehicle, means road construction machinery built-in as part of, or permanently attached to, the vehicle.
(4) In sub-paragraph (3) above 'road construction machinery' means a machine or device suitable for use for the construction or repair of roads and used for no purpose other than the construction or repair of roads.

23.152 Provided the vehicle a defendant operates satisfies all of the criteria at subss (1) to (4) above, it may be classed as a road construction vehicle and is able to use rebated heavy oil (red diesel) as fuel when travelling on a public road.

23.153 Depending on circumstances, vehicles excepted under the scheme include tractors, agricultural vehicles, gritters, mobile cranes, digging machines, work trucks, road construction vehicles, and road rollers (a question mark remains over street-lighting vehicles). In terms of penalties, the Misuse of Rebated Oil levy now has the maximum civil penalty of £500. The effect of the legislation is demonstrated by *Charles Michael Rush v Revenue & Customs Commissioners* (2007) (Vadt E01027), where the Tribunal held that even an honest mistake, such as erroneously using a fuel can containing red diesel to fuel a vehicle, was not in itself sufficient to establish a defence of reasonable excuse under the Finance Act 1994, s 10 to avoid liability for payment of civil penalties imposed by Customs.

23.154 In *Renfrewshire BC v Revenue and Customs Commissioners* (E00963) (2006) a VAT and Duties Tribunal held that a tractor was an 'excepted vehicle' when it was being used on a public road, within the meaning of Sch 1, when it was either travelling on its way to a site to perform an agricultural activity or its use on the road had some relationship or connection with such an activity (Lawtel, 24 August 2006). However, in *Jeff Potts v Revenue & Customs Commissioners* (2007) (Vadt E01065) the Tribunal determined that a farmer who, under a contract with a waste disposal company, used his tractor to transport effluent from a brewery and spread it on agricultural land was not using the tractor solely for agricultural purposes within the meaning of the Hydrocarbon Oil Duties Act 1979 Sch 1 para 2.

Compounding

Often in red diesel cases Revenue and Customs will offer to settle the matter upon the **23.155** payment of a settlement sum. This is known as compounding. The purpose of a compound settlement is to save time and money for Customs and the defendant, and avoid the need for legal proceedings. It is important to note that Revenue and Customs are only likely to offer a compound settlement where they have sufficient evidence to proceed to court. It is equally important to note that a compound settlement will not be offered in every case, and much will depend on what is being alleged.

Procedural requirements

Schedule 5 sets out the procedure that must be followed when a person takes a sample from **23.156** the motor vehicle for these purposes.

Section 32 of that Schedule states: **23.157**

Without prejudice to the admissibility of the evidence of the analyst [who analyses the sample and certifies it as red diesel] such a certificate shall not be admissible as evidence—

(a) unless a copy of it has, not less than 7 days before the hearing, been served by . . . the Commissioners on all other parties; or

(b) if any of those other parties, not less than 3 days before the hearing . . . serves notice on the Commissioners requiring the attendance at the hearing of the person by whom the analysis was made.

The main court procedural requirements for complaints, including appeals, are set out within the condemnation part of this chapter above, and apply equally to red diesel matters.

It is commonplace for somebody who is subject to a seizure to invite HMRC to conduct a **23.158** review of its decision, as a part of which the person whose property has been seized will have the opportunity to set out his reasons for disagreeing with the decision to seize the property as liable to forfeiture.

The vehicle and the fuel

Section 141 of CEMA applies, so if the fuel is liable for forfeiture, the vehicle being used to **23.159** carry it also becomes liable to forfeiture (secondary forfeiture). (See *Customs and Excise Commissioners v Jack Bradley (Accrington) Ltd* [1959] 1 QB 219, where the Court held that where kerosene oil had been discovered in the fuel tank of a vehicle, the vehicle itself would be liable to forfeiture since it had been 'used for the carriage' of the oil.)

Similar arguments in relation to 'bootlegging' matters arise here in terms of proportional- **23.160** ity, and whether it would be proportionate to condemn a vehicle with a value of, eg, £20,000, which was carrying a tank load of red diesel (value, eg, £35). See para 23.87 above and particularly *Customs and Excise Commissioners v Newbury* [2003] 2 All ER 964; (2003) 1 WLR 2131. Much will depend on the circumstances of the seizure: whether it is a first time 'offence'; whether warnings have been previously given; the quantities involved; whether HMRC officials/the court were deliberately misled; or whether there exist other 'aggravating' features. Conversely, if such circumstances do not exist, this may amount to a compelling reason not to order secondary forfeiture.

The civil burden

23.161 If the court finds on the balance of probabilities (these being civil proceedings) that the vehicles were carrying, handling, or concealing oil liable to forfeiture, then it has no discretion and must order forfeiture: see Sch 3(6) to CEMA (Appendix 19).

Criminal offences

23.162 While outside the auspices of this book, it is worth noting that the criminal law creates certain offences in relation to the use of oil (other than Derv) to fuel 'road vehicles'. This includes using any oil on which the Derv rate of duty has not been paid. It forbids the use of fully rebated kerosene to propel a vehicle, or fuel an engine (except one only providing heat).

23.163 The law goes further in that it makes it an offence to remove any designated chemical marker or dye from any oil (although how commonplace this is, is questionable). Similarly the law makes it an offence to obstruct any officer from Revenue and Customs from obtaining a sample of oil. For completeness, it is also an offence to mix any rebated or duty free oil with any oil on which no rebate has been allowed. In *R v Owens and Owens* (2006) 150 SJ 1188, it was held that any sample must be taken in the presence of the person concerned.

23.164 In the majority of cases the vehicle in question will be restored to the defendant on payment of an amount of money known as the 'restoration amount'. This amount will consist of a penalty for any additional offence committed (a penalty of £250 may be imposed for each offence, see s 13(1)(a) and (b) of the Hydrocarbon Oils Duties Act 1979) and an assessment for the duty rebate. If the offence is considered serious the vehicle may be seized and forfeited and may not be restored to the defendant.

K. Delivery Up

Introduction

23.165 The seizure of goods as liable to forfeiture does not mean that the individual from whom they were seized or the owner of the goods will be unable to regain control of the goods, even if that individual has accepted (or it has been found) that the goods were imported for a commercial purpose. Revenue and Customs are afforded a discretion to either restore the goods/thing seized or offer 'delivery up'.

The legislative provisions

23.166 The power to offer delivery up is found in para 16 of Sch 3 to CEMA (see Appendix 19).

23.167 This enables Revenue and Customs, prior to the condemnation of the goods/thing that has been seized, to return it upon payment of a sum not exceeding the value of the thing seized (including any duty or tax that was due).

23.168 The amount paid for delivery up is in effect a deposit. If the thing is later condemned by the court (or because a valid notice of claim/appeal is not received) the amount paid is forfeited. On the other hand, if the appeal is successful and the court finds in favour of the original owner, Revenue and Customs must return the sum. The benefit for the owner is that they have the use of the thing seized while the appeal against seizure is pending.

In terms of most goods/things, Revenue and Customs do not usually seek payment of more **23.169** than the retail value of the thing. The retail value can often be established from valuation guides, eg, for vehicles, Glass's Guide.

Practice

It should be noted that in practice Revenue and Customs do not normally offer 'delivery **23.170** up' if they would not subsequently be prepared to restore the goods (see below). Customs would argue that to do differently would negate the purpose of forfeiture. Nor should the offer of delivery up be construed as an admission by Revenue and Customs that they were wrong to seize the thing in the first place. The fact that the goods/thing is delivered up will not avoid the court proceedings or a final determination by the magistrates'. Revenue and Customs will undoubtedly pursue the court proceedings, not least because they would be liable for repayment of the sum paid (by way of refund) if they were not to.

L. Restoration

The statutory basis

Section 152(b) of CEMA allows for the restoration of goods that have been seized or **23.171** forfeited:

The Commissioners may, as they see fit—
(b) restore, subject to such conditions (if any) as they think proper, any thing forfeited or seized under [those] Acts.

Unlike 'delivery up', restoration will normally only take place once a seized thing has been **23.172** condemned, either following a hearing or because the thing has been deemed forfeit because no valid notice of claim/appeal has been lodged (see para 5 of Sch 3, Appendix 19). Revenue and Customs are entitled to impose such reasonable conditions 'as they think proper' as part of the agreement to restore. Common examples include the payment of a sum; production of an import licence (where one is required to import the thing); or re-labelling (where goods were seized under the Trades Description Act because they have false marks of origin). Unlike 'delivery up', a restoration amount is non-refundable.

Restoration is not automatic. Revenue and Customs may refuse to restore the goods/thing **23.173** concerned. That refusal is likely to lead in certain cases to complaint. The remedy is by way of an appeal to the First Tier Tax Tribunal ('the Tax Tribunal').

Appeals against non-restoration

Appeals against decisions not to restore the goods/thing are dealt with by the Tax Tribunal. **23.174** The Tax Tribunal derives its jurisdiction from s16(1) of the Finance Act 1994, which gives the Tribunal the power to review Commissioners'/Revenue and Customs' decisions in a number of areas.

Burden and standard of proof

In *Golobiewska v Customs and Excise Commissioners* The Times, 25 May 2005, the Court of **23.175** Appeal held that the effect of s 16(6) of the Finance Act 1994 was to impose the burden of proof on the appellant to establish, on the balance of probabilities, grounds showing that the vehicle should be restored. Such a burden was to the civil standard. See also *Szukala Trans Pthu Export-Import v Revenue and Customs Commissioners* (2006) 150 SJ 571 (below).

23.176   However, a distinction must be drawn where one of the factual issues is the question of own use/commercial purpose. In *Bevins and Pyrah v Customs and Excise Commissioners* [2005] (EO00903) the Tribunal held that Customs had misapplied the law by incorrectly imposing the burden of proof on the travellers. Both the decision to seize the goods and the decision not to restore had been made on the basis that the travellers had not made out a satisfactory case that the goods were for their own use. Following the decision in *Hoverspeed* (above, para 23.19) such a positive burden could no longer apply. The burden in the first instance was on Customs to show that the goods were for a commercial use.

Test of reasonableness

23.177   Section 16(4) of the Finance Act 1994 introduces a question of reasonableness for the Tribunal to consider and states:

> In relation to any decision as to an ancillary matter, or any decision on the review of such a decision, the powers of an Appeal Tribunal on an appeal under this section shall be confined to a power, where the Tribunal are satisfied that the Commissioners could not reasonably have arrived at it.

23.178   Appeals against non-restoration are ancillary (see Sch 5 para 2(r) of the Finance Act 1994; and s 14(1)(d) of the Finance Act 1994). It is the ancillary decision of HMRC not to restore the thing/goods that are subject to forfeiture, which is secondary in time (and thus ancillary) to the decision to condemn the goods as forfeit.

23.179   In short, the Tribunal is asking itself whether or not the Commissioners/HMRC acted reasonably in deciding to refuse to restore the goods/thing concerned. In *Szukala Trans Pthu Export-Import v Revenue and Customs Commissioners* (2006) 150 SJ 571, the Tribunal held that it was for the appellant to show that the decision was unreasonable. In order to be reasonable, a decision must be soundly based factually; and in this regard the Tribunal had a fact finding function. Since facts were not a matter of discretion but of evidence, if the decision of the reviewing officer was found to have been based on facts that were materially incorrect, his decision would be unreasonable and the Tribunal should direct a fresh review under s 16(4).

23.180   In *Ware v Customs and Excise Commissioners* (E00735) the Tribunal recognised a generally accepted test for what is reasonable: (para 18).

- Is this a decision that no reasonable panel of Commissioners could have come to?
- Has some irrelevant matter been taken into account?
- Has some matter which should have been taken into account been ignored?
- Has there been some error of law?

23.181   In *Gora* the Court of Appeal held that the issue of whether Customs reasonably arrived at their decision raised questions of *Wednesbury* reasonableness, as identified in *Customs and Excise Commissioners v J H Corbitt (Numismatists) Ltd* [1980] STC 231.

23.182   The case of *Associated Provincial Picture Houses Ltd v Wednesbury Corp* [1948] 1 KB 223 is reported extensively and it is not proposed to go into it in any detail within this chapter, the main principles being espoused by Lord Greene MR at p 229 of the judgment, which are also commented upon by Lord Lane at p 663 of his judgment in the case of *Corbitt*. (See also the Court of Appeal decision of *John Dee Ltd v Customs and Excise Commissioners* [1995] STC 941.)

Proportionality

In *Lindsay v Customs and Excise Commissioners* [2002] EWCA Civ 267, the Court of **23.183** Appeal considered the circumstances in which a failure to offer restoration to a person of his vehicle, which was found to have carried forfeited excise goods, would be unreasonable and disproportionate. Lord Phillips MR held that the aim of the Commissioners' policy was the prevention of the evasion of excise duty that was imposed in accordance with European Community law. He stated that was a legitimate aim under Art 1 of the First Protocol of the Convention (para 55). He went on to note that the trade in smuggled cigarettes was massive and the free movement of persons under Community law greatly facilitated the elicit importation of excise goods, making the smuggler's detection less likely. He also stated that the public were warned that if vehicles were used for smuggling, those vehicles might be forfeited and therefore anybody using their vehicle for smuggling was taking a calculated risk.

He added that as a general policy those who used their vehicles for commercial smuggling **23.184** could not be heard to complain if they then lost their vehicles. In those circumstances, the value of the vehicles did not need to be taken into account (see paras 60–63 of the judgment). However, he also stated that where the importation was not for profit each case had to be considered on its own facts, and introduced a proportionality test. In setting out the factors that should be taken into account, Lord Phillips MR stated at para 64:

> The Commissioners' policy does not, however, draw a distinction between the commercial smuggler and the driver importing goods for social distribution to family or friends in circumstances where there is no attempt to make a profit. Of course, even in such a case the scale of importation, or other circumstances, may be such as to justify forfeiture of the car. But where the importation is not for the purpose of making a profit, I consider that the principle of proportionality requires that each case should be considered on its particular facts, which would include the scale of the importation, whether it is a 'first offence', whether there was an attempt at concealment or dissimulation, the value of the vehicle and the degree of hardship that will be caused by forfeiture.

In *Aykut Ates v Customs and Excise Commissioners* (2002) (EOO 188) the Tribunal held that **23.185** the Commissioners had not acted proportionately when refusing to restore a vehicle used for smuggling to its owner, in circumstances where it was accepted that the owner had lent the car to a friend, and was himself innocent of any smuggling and did not know the use to which the vehicle was being put. The facts suggested that the appellant had been duped into lending his vehicle. Customs had taken the view that in lending his vehicle the appellant had taken a risk that the third party concerned would take the vehicle abroad, and as such there were no exceptional circumstances that justified departing from the policy that vehicles used in smuggling would not be restored to the owner.

The appellant appealed on the basis that that was an unreasonable decision because it did **23.186** not enable his exceptional circumstances to be taken into account, circumstances which he maintained had been unreasonably rejected because of Customs' stated policy. Secondly, he maintained that the seizure of his car was disproportionate in relation to the amount of duty evaded.

23.187 The Tribunal held that it was right for the Commissioners to have a policy, provided that they did not fetter their discretion when applying it. In exercising that discretion, the Commissioners must strike a fair balance between the demands of the general interest of the community and the requirements for the protection of the individual's fundamental rights. In the Tribunal's judgment, it was unreasonable to refuse to restore a vehicle in circumstances where the owner was unaware that it was being used for smuggling. Once it had been accepted that the appellant was innocent, the amount of the alcohol imported and the other circumstances relating to the driver became irrelevant.

Jurisdiction

23.188 It should be noted that the above is the limit of the Tribunal's jurisdiction. It is not entitled to, and will not, act as a court of appeal from the magistrates' decision on the question of forfeiture itself. It may, however, hear evidence about the seizure if it is relevant in assisting with the question of whether the ancillary non-restoration decision was correct (see the guidance provided by the Court of Appeal in *Gascoyne* below).

23.189 In *Lindsay*, the Tribunal purported to direct that if a vehicle could not be restored, the Commissioners should pay compensation. On appeal, Lord Phillips MR stated (para 607):

> The Tribunal directed that Mr. Lindsay's vehicle should be restored to him and that, if this were not possible, the Commissioners should pay him compensation. In so doing they purported to be exercising jurisdiction conferred by s 16(4) of the 1994 Act. That sub-section expressly spells out the powers of the Tribunal in the circumstances of this case. They include the power to direct that the decision appealed against ceased to have effect and to require the Commissioners to conduct a further review of the original decision in accordance with the Directions of the Tribunal. [Counsel] sought to persuade us that was all that the Tribunal had done. The decision appealed against was that the vehicle should not be restored. If that decision ceased to have effect, it followed, inevitably, that the vehicle would have to be restored and the Tribunal had done no more that give this Direction. I do not agree. The Tribunal have done more than direct that [the Customs officer's] decision ceased to have effect. They have purported to reverse it. That is something that they have no jurisdiction to do.

23.190 However, the Tribunal's power to direct that a payment should be made when restoration of the goods was not possible was re-visited in *Powell v Revenue and Customs* (2005) (EOO 900) in the context of compensation (see para 29.240 below).

Personal/commercial use

23.191 The Tribunal is not directly concerned with the question of personal use or commercial importation. That is an issue principally within the confines of the condemnation proceedings/the magistrates' court. (See *Gora v Customs and Excise Commissioners* [2003] EWCA Civ 525 (CA) where Pill LJ recognised that the Tribunal procedure was not intended to enable the appellant to challenge the deemed condemnation of forfeit goods if no claim had been made under Sch 3 to CEMA (see para 58)).

In *Gascoyne v Customs and Excise Commissioners* [2005] 2 WLR 222 (CA), Buxton LJ held **23.192**
(at para 46 *et seq*):

> I do not think it can have been intended that the exporter before the Tribunal would have a
> second bite at the cherry of lawfulness, having failed in condemnation proceedings or let them
> go by default . . . the reason why the importer cannot have that liberty is not because of the terms
> of the statute, but because of normal English law rules of *res judicata* or abuse of process.

The reasoning in *Gascoyne* was confirmed by Lindsay J in *Customs and Excise Commissioners* **23.193**
v Demack and Eatock [2005] EWHC 330 (Ch), in which the Court found that Tax Tribunals
should not undo findings of fact made by the magistrates in earlier forfeiture proceedings.
In *Johnstone v Customs and Excise Commissioners* [2005] EWCA Admin 115, the High
Court established that if an appellant advances grounds of appeal against non-restoration
based on personal use then he has neither advanced a valid ground for restoration nor a
valid ground of appeal before the Tax Tribunal. Moses J stated (at para 12 *et seq*):

> Unfortunately, as I have said, they went on to consider that which has been advanced by
> Mr. Johnstone, namely that these cigarettes were not for commercial use; they were for per-
> sonal use. That was not a matter for the Tribunal at all. It is no ground for restoration to say
> to the Commissioners: these cigarettes were for personal use. This is not a ground upon
> which restoration can be made.
>
> In the instant case no ground whatever for restoration was advanced. All that was said was
> that the cigarettes were for personal use. But that issue was solely a matter for the Magistrates'
> or an appeal to the Crown Court. It was not a matter for the reviewing officer; it was not a
> matter for the Tribunal; and it is not a matter for the court. If all someone importing ciga-
> rettes such as this does is to persist in saying they are for personal use, the correct response is
> to say: 'You have advanced no ground whatever for restoration in the exercise of powers
> under section 152(b)'. That, in my judgment, is the view which the Tribunal ought to have
> taken. But unfortunately, in an excess of kindness, they did look yet again at the issue of
> whether the grounds were for personal use and decided yet again that they were not. That, as
> I have said, was not a matter for them.

The judgment of Buxton LJ in *Gascoyne* raises the question of how a Tribunal should pro- **23.194**
ceed where the appellant has not been afforded a hearing at the condemnation proceedings
stage. While most appellants have their 'day in court' at the condemnation hearing, and
thus have had the opportunity to make and to argue points on own use/commercial
purpose etc (ie a fair hearing pursuant to the ECHR), in cases when no condemnation
proceedings have taken place the position will be different. In *Gascoyne* Buxton LJ held (at
para 49 *et seq*):

> The ECHR jurisprudence itself creates a great deal more difficulty in relation to the deeming
> provisions under paragraph 5 of Schedule 3. One's instincts, if no more, suggest that the
> extent to which it was held in *Gora v Customs and Excise Commissioners* [2004] QB 93 CA
> that those provisions necessarily prevent any further consideration of the legality of the sei-
> zure was an excessive limitation . . . Lord Phillips in *Lindsay* at paragraph 64 of his judgment
> (states) that the principle of proportionality requires that each case should be considered on
> its particular facts . . . As it seems to me, for an importer to be completely shut out in the
> only Tribunal before which he has in fact appeared from ventilating the matters that are
> deemed to have been decided against him because of paragraph 5 of Schedule 3 does
> not adequately enable him to assert his Convention rights. In my view, therefore, in a case
> where the deeming provisions under paragraph 5 are applied the Tribunal can re-open those

issues: so that a Tribunal will always have very well in mind considerations of, or similar to, abuse of process in considering whether such issues should in fact be ventilated before it. The mere fact that the Applicant has not applied to the Commissioners, and therefore there have been no condemnation proceedings, would not in my view be enough. But in my judgment it goes too far to say that the deeming provisions have always, in every case, got to be paramount.

23.195   Lindsay J in *Customs and Excise Commissioners v Demack and Eatock* [2005] EWHC 330 (Ch) suggests, following *Gascoyne*, that in deemed seizure cases the Tribunal could re-open the evidence and make findings of fact on the matter. See also *William McGuiness v Customs and Excise Commissioners* [E00793], and *Customs and Excise Commissioners v Dickinson* The Times, 3 December 2003, where the Court held it remained open to an importer to raise the issue of personal use for the purposes of seeking to invoke the discretionary procedure of restoration.

23.196   Anecdotally, Tribunals have appeared reluctant to see their jurisdiction curtailed in the way that the decision in *Gascoyne* anticipates. Part of the problem is the conflicting messages being sent out in terms of case law. The position was re-examined once again in detail by Evans-Lombe J in the case of *Customs and Excise Commissioners v David Weller* [2006] EWHC 237. In *Weller* the Tribunal proceeded on the basis that it had jurisdiction to consider whether the seized goods were for the appellant's personal use, in a case where there had been no condemnation proceedings and condemnation had not been challenged (para 1).

23.197   His Lordship described the present system as being two track. The first track was to challenge the lawfulness of the forfeiture to the magistrates' court with an appeal to the Crown Court and then to a Divisional Court of the High Court. The second track was to seek the return of the goods forfeited with an appeal to the (Tax) Tribunal and thereafter to the High Court if unsuccessful (para 10).

23.198   His Lordship proceeded to review both the cases of *Gascoyne* and *Gora*. He noted that Buxton LJ took the view that where there had been deemed forfeiture it was a potential breach of the importer's rights under Art 6 of the ECHR to prevent him from seeking to re-open the issue of whether the original forfeiture was lawful as a reason, or one of the reasons, why his forfeited goods should be returned to him. Buxton LJ had not sought to limit what sort of facts would be relevant to the decision, beyond a recommendation that a Tribunal 'will always have very well in mind considerations of, or similar to, abuse of process'.

23.199   In *Weller* Evans-Lombe J referred specifically to the case of *Revenue and Customs Commissioners v Smith* (QBD, 17 November 2005). In *Smith*, Lewison J was dealing with a case where an importer was stopped at Dover by Customs officers with 2,000 litres of beer, 250 litres of wine, and four litres of spirits in a Toyota Land Cruiser, without having paid duty. He did not give a notice of appeal to the Commissioners under para 3 of Sch 3 to CEMA, but sought to raise the validity of the seizure on appeal with the Tax Tribunal following the Commissioners' refusal to review its decision not to return the forfeited goods to him.

The Tribunal permitted him to raise such an argument. Lewison J, however, set aside the **23.200** Tribunal's ruling. Having referred to Buxton LJ's judgment in *Gascoyne* at para 76, Lewison J stated:

> It is, in my judgment, clear from that passage that in the run-of-the-mill case where there has been a failure to give a paragraph 3 notice invoking the condemnation proceedings, the [provisions] will operate against the applicant in any subsequent appeal to a Tribunal. The Tribunal's function, therefore, is analogous to a sentencing court once a defendant has been convicted. No matter that the defendant still protests his innocence of the charge against him, the function of a sentencing court is to accept mitigation but not to question the original conviction.
>
> Lord Justice Buxton's reference to abuse of power or to considerations analogous to abuse of process are, in my view, references to the well-known principle that it may be an abuse of process to raise in one Tribunal matters that could and should have been raised in another. So the relevant questions will always be, first, could the applicant have raised the question of lawfulness of forfeiture in other proceedings and, if the answer to that question is yes, why did he not do so? In the light of his reasons for not raising the matter in condemnation proceedings, the Tribunal can then answer the question, should he have done so and if the answer to the question is 'yes', then it will be, in most cases, an abuse of process for him to raise the question before the Tribunal.

Evans-Lombe J agreed with this approach. Whether an importer is able to raise the validity **23.201** of the forfeiture on a review to a Tribunal will depend on two questions:

(1) Did the importer have a realistic opportunity to invoke the condemnation procedure?
(2) If he did, are there nonetheless reasons, disclosed by the facts of the case which should persuade the Commissioners or the Tribunal to permit him to re-open the question of the validity of the original seizure on an application for return of the goods?

Evans-Lombe J stated in *Weller* that the first question would almost always be answered in **23.202** the affirmative, since facts would have to be very unusual to base a conclusion that the importer was prevented, in the 30 days succeeding forfeiture, from giving notice to Customs to initiate condemnation procedure in the magistrates' court (see para 16).

It would appear, therefore, that the issue in relation to the Tribunal's jurisdiction has been **23.203** both clarified and curtailed as a result of the judgments in *Weller* and *Smith*.

Recent cases in which the first tier Tribunal have found it appropriate to review Customs' **23.204** decisions notwithstanding a failure to pursue condemnation proceedings include *Peet v Revenue and Customs Commissioners* [2007] LTL 12.7.07 (permitted to re-open on the grounds of human rights) and *Foster v Revenue and Customs Commissioners* [2008] (VADT E 01124), where Customs' reasons had been deemed 'obscure'.

The High Court has subsequently found that failing to pursue condemnation due to **23.205** cost and inconvenience is not necessarily a legitimate ground for raising 'own use' arguments on restoration (see *Customs and Excise Commissioners v Dawkin* [2008] EWHC 1972 (Ch)).

Case law

23.206 In *Robert Brookes v Customs and Excise Commissioners* (2005) (E00847) the Tribunal found a materially different set of facts on the evidence to those previously established by Customs. The Tribunal took the view that because the facts that they found were so different to those found by Customs, and because the new facts might have impacted upon Customs' decision not to offer restoration, it could only be concluded that the earlier review had been unreasonably arrived at within the meaning of s 16(4) of the 1994 Act.

23.207 In *Crocker v Revenue and Customs Commissioners* (18 October 2005) (EO0926) the appellant had her motor vehicle intercepted at Dover Docks on 5 May 2001. Travelling in the vehicle were the appellant's husband and two others. The three men concerned were found to be carrying over 20kg of hand-rolling tobacco as well as some other excise goods. Both the vehicle and the goods were seized. The appellant maintained that while she had been aware that her husband and the others had been making a trip abroad, she was unaware that her vehicle was to be used for the trip.

23.208 Customs refused to offer unconditional restoration of the vehicle because it believed that the appellant knew her vehicle was to be used; and furthermore that she was not a genuine third party owner because the car had shared insured drivers and the appellant did not have sole and absolute control over the vehicle (although it was registered in her name).

23.209 The Tribunal accepted the appellant's evidence that she did not know her vehicle was to be used and that she would not have consented had she known. They also accepted that the appellant needed use of the vehicle for herself and her children (including on the day it was seized) and therefore would not have let her husband use it had she known.

23.210 The Tribunal found that Customs had formed its view on 'remarkably scanty information' (para 23 of the judgment). It dismissed the suggestion that the appellant had not made it clear that the vehicle had been taken without her permission and the mere fact that her husband was bringing something back for her did not mean and could not be taken to imply that she knew her vehicle was being used.

23.211 In relation to the ownership of the vehicle, the Tribunal acknowledged that Customs do not want vehicles being returned to 'wrong doers' (para 24 of the judgment). This, they said, was a perfectly reasonable aim for the Commissioners to have. However, it went on to state that all policies must bend to the facts and be capable of being enforced with sufficient flexibility to take account of the facts of each case. Lady Mitting found:

> ... the situation which we have, because the Respondents have disposed of the vehicle, is that Mrs. Crocker has lost an asset worth £2,775 and received just £306 in lieu. Surely it cannot be right that she should be penalised merely because to give her vehicle back unconditionally would have a side effect of allowing her husband to regain access to it? If this is the view which (Customs) took, then we consider this to have been unreasonable.

On the above basis the Tribunal found that the decision to offer only conditional restoration of the vehicle to Mrs Crocker was unreasonable and directed that a further review be carried out.

23.212 In *Frost and Mason v Customs and Excise Commissioners* (2005) (72) (E00872) the Tribunal found that the reviewing officer's decision was unreasonably arrived at because of the hardship suffered by the loss of the vehicle. The vehicle in question was required by the traveller's wife to care for her grandchild and her father-in-law. The Tribunal ordered further reviews to consider the question of exceptional hardship. (For financial hardship see *Tilburn v Revenue and Customs Commissioners* (2006) (E00989).)

The case of *Custom and Excise Commissioners v Mark Mills* [2007] EWHC 2241 (Ch) **23.213** provides an example of the unusual circumstances in which a Tribunal may consider the question of own use *despite* the lack of condemnation proceedings.

In 2006, Mr Mills' £12,000 Volvo was seized when he and his business partner, Mr Kerry, **23.214** failed to declare 43.5kgs of hand-rolling tobacco upon their return from Belgium. Despite Mr Mills maintaining that his share (21.75kgs) was for his and his wife's personal use, neither man challenged the seizure through condemnation proceedings at the magistrates' court.

The Tax Tribunal at first instance found that Mr Mills' share was for his 'own use' and that **23.215** any challenge to the seizure in the magistrates' court would have been bound to fail due to the mixing of Mr Mills' goods with Mr Kerry's: Mr Mills' intended use of his portion of the tobacco becoming irrelevant, and thus he could not have prevented his car being condemned. (Mr Mills' goods were mixed with Mr Kerry's and that may have resulted in them being automatically forfeited under s 141(1)(a) and (b) of CEMA.)

The High Court reached the same conclusion, via a different route. Mr Mills was not **23.216** bound by Mr Kerry's failure to appeal the seizure. Rather, he could have prevented his goods/car from being condemned by proving that Mr Kerry's goods were not for a commercial purpose (see *Fox v HMCE* [2002] EWHC 1244 (Admin)). It would therefore not be an abuse to consider 'own use' at the Tribunal stage (para 36). As a result, where goods are condemned as a result of being mixed, packed, or found with other goods liable to forfeiture, the question of 'own use' may remain a live issue.

It follows that solicitors must be cautious to ensure that the 'commercial purpose' point is **23.217** not unwittingly conceded in correspondence. If an appellant unequivocally acquiesces to 'commercial purpose' (arising from deemed forfeiture), he cannot then rely on *contra* arguments at the restoration stage (para 38). (See also *HMRC v James* [2008] EWHC 230, where the High Court again approved a robust approach to reopening the question of lawfulness during restoration proceedings (paras 31 and 36), although this was somewhat diluted by two recent Tribunal decisions which, albeit on specific facts, suggest a softening in approach where condemnation proceedings are initially commenced but then withdrawn (*Foster* (2008) (E01124) and *(1) David Owens (2) Mandy Owens* (2008) (E01096)).)

It should also be noted that the Tribunal's finding that Mr Mills imported 21.75kg for his **23.218** personal use remains open to criticism. On one view, it placed insufficient weight on the fact that the seized amount was seven times the guideline quantities. Indeed, the High Court believed that the 'own use' finding was both 'wrong' and 'surprising' (paras 43 and 45).

Therefore, *Mills* should not be viewed as a green light for individuals to import tobacco **23.219** vastly in excess of the guideline quantities—3,200 cigarettes, 3kg of hand-rolling tobacco—on the assumption that they will be able to establish own use at the restoration stage.

23.220   Other recent first tier cases, which demonstrate the way the restoration provisions work in practice, include: *Sanczyk v Revenue and Customs Commissioners* (2006) (E00972) where the Tribunal determined that a decision not to restore a vehicle to its Polish owner, in circumstances where he spoke little English and therefore did not understand his vehicle was being seized was unreasonable, and should be referred for a further review; *Cleary v Revenue and Customs Commissioners* (2008) (VADT E 01136), where HMRC's decision to refuse to restore a vehicle was found to be proportionate in circumstances where other vehicles were available to the appellant, and thus arguments in relation to exceptional hardship had little application; and *Pierhead Purchasing Ltd v Revenue and Customs Commissioners* [2008] (E01138), where trivial errors on administrative documentation were considered not to be grounds to refuse restoration.

M. Restoration: Practice and Procedure

Formal departmental reviews

23.221   Appeals to the Tribunal are against a formal review decision by the Revenue and Customs. Appeals can only be brought by a person who has first requested a formal department review (see the Finance Act 1994, s 16(2)). Persons able to request a review include those affected by the decision, or persons who are liable to pay any duty or penalty in relation to it; together with persons on behalf of whom an application is made (see s 14(2) of the Finance Act 1994).

Tribunal procedure

23.222   The procedure before the Tax Tribunal is governed by the Tribunal Procedure (First-tier Tribunal) (Tax Chamber) Rules 2009 ('the Tax Chamber Rules') (SI 2009/273).

Time limits

23.223   Section 14(1) of the Finance Act 1994 requires a request for a review to be made in writing within 45 days from the date of the original decision (s 14(3)). While the Commissioners are not obliged to carry out a review if the request is received outside the 45-day limitation period, s 16(1)(b) does afford some scope for out-of-time requests where the Commissioners have agreed to undertake a review after the end of the 45-day period.

23.224   Within 45 days of receiving the request for a review, HMRC must complete their formal review (Finance Act 1994, s 15(2)). Once the 45-day period expires, the original decision shall be assumed to be upheld and the individual looking to appeal will have an immediate right to pursue that appeal. The 45-day period afforded to Customs cannot be extended. The appeal itself must be served within 30 days of the date of the document containing the disputed decision (see para 203 of The Transfer of Tribunal Functions and Revenue and Customs Appeals Order 2009 (SI 2009/56), which amends s 16(1) of the Finance Act 1994). It may also be extended by r 5(3)(a)), subject to r 20(4), per the Tax Tribunal website:

> You will normally have 30 days to appeal a disputed HMRC decision. If you make use of HMRC's review process you will have 30 days to appeal from the date they tell you the outcome. The time limit runs from both the original decision and any decision following review. The letter you receive from

HMRC, both the original decision and any decision following review, will confirm the time you have for appealing.

If you are making your appeal outside the time limit, you must give reasons to the tribunal in writing.

Lodging the appeal and the statement of case

Rule 20 of the Tax Chamber Rules 2009 states an appeal to the Tribunal should be brought **23.225** by a notice of appeal and the notice of appeal must include:

(a) the name and address of the appellant;
(b) the name and address of the appellant's representative (if any);
(c) an address where documents for the appellant may be sent or delivered;
(d) details of the decision appealed against;
(e) the result the appellant is seeking; and
(f) the grounds for making the appeal.

Rule 20(3) provides: **23.226**

The appellant must provide with the notice of appeal a copy of any written record of any decision appealed against, and any statement of reasons for that decision, that the appellant has or can reasonably obtain.

In terms of Customs lodging their case in reply, r 25 provides as follows: **23.227**

Respondent's statement of case
25.—(1) A respondent must send or deliver a statement of case to the Tribunal, the appellant and any other respondent so that it is received—
    (a) in a Default Paper case, within 42 days after the tribunal sent the notice of the appeal or a copy of the application notice or notice of reference; or
    (b) in a Standard or Complex case, within 60 days after the tribunal sent the notice of the appeal or a copy of the application notice or notice of reference.
(2) A statement of case must—
    (a) in an appeal, state the legislative provision under which the decision under appeal was made; and
    (b) set out the respondent's position in relation to the case.
(3) A statement of case may also contain a request that the case be dealt with at a hearing or without a hearing.
(4) If a respondent provides a statement of case to the Tribunal later than the time required by paragraph (1) or by any extension allowed under rule 5(3)(a) (power to extend time), the statement of case must include a request for an extension of time and the reason why the statement of case was not provided in time.

Rules 26 and 27 set out the procedure to be followed depending upon whether the appeal **23.228** has been designated as a basic, standard, or complex case, including considerations in terms of disclosure. It is anticipated that the more complex cases will be referred to the Upper Tribunal for determination.

While Tribunal procedures tend to be less formal than court procedures, failure to disclose **23.229** a certain document may lead to it being excluded from the hearing (see *David Kirk v Customs and Excise Commissioners* (14042)). The risk in non-disclosure is that if the Tribunal is minded to admit any late document, the Revenue and Customs are likely to ask for more time to consider it and that may lead to an adjournment and a possible costs award (see *Customs and Excise Commissioners v Gus Merchandise Corp* [1992] STC 776 at 781–782). The first tier decision of *Jason Smith v Revenue and Customs Commissioners*

(2007) (LTL 25.4.07) suggests that Tax Tribunals are entitled to consider matters that were not known to the Commissioners at the time the decision was made.

23.230   In terms of disclosure generally, legal privilege applies (see *Three Rivers DC (Respondents) v Governor of the Bank of England* [2004] UKHL 48 at 114–117 and *Alfred Crompton Amusement Machines Ltd v Customs and Excise Commissioners* [1974] AC 405 in relation to internal correspondence between officers and the legal section of Customs).

Failure to comply with directions

23.231   Extensions of time may be sought under r 5(3); however the importance of complying with the directions of the Tribunal and the requisite time limits was emphasised by *Customs and Excise Commissioners v Young* [1993] STC 394 where the Commissioners lost the appeal because they had served documents 12 days late.

Pre-hearing directions

23.232   Pre-hearing directions are not uncommon in non-restoration appeals and these may be ordered by the Tribunal of its own volition, or following a request of one of the parties (r 6). Often, however, directions are agreed by consent and this can avoid the necessity of a hearing.

23.233   Where directions cannot be agreed or where there is a matter of substance which needs to be dealt with, a hearing can be arranged that will usually be heard before a Tribunal judge.

Preparation for the hearing

23.234   In practice, usually each party is responsible for preparing its own bundle for the hearing, although in practice Revenue and Customs usually take a lead in relation to this. Rule 15 deals with the procedure in terms of evidence and submissions.

The hearing

23.235   Consideration in terms of whether the hearing should be in private or in public is set out in r 32. Usually the hearing will be in public. The correct terms of address for the Tribunal judge and any lay members are Sir or Madam, as appropriate. It is not usual for counsel to stand when addressing the Tribunal.

23.236   During the hearing the judge and any other member of the Tribunal may put questions to any witness called to give evidence. While officers are entitled to refer to their notebooks when giving evidence, they should make it clear whether the notes were made contemporaneously or not (*Mori Mohal Indian Restaurant v Customs and Excise Commissioners* (1992) VAT TR 188).

23.237   Under r 33, if neither party or if only one party attends, then the Tribunal is entitled to go on and hear the matter in any event. Shorthand writers may only be present if permitted by the Tribunal (see *Empire Stores Ltd v Customs and Excise Commissioners* (1992) VAT TR 271).

Judgment

23.238   A decision will not necessarily be given immediately and it is usual for there to be a delay while the Tribunal judge prepares his decision (the rules suggest 28 days or as soon as practicable thereafter, r 35). While there has been complaint in the past about the length of the delay, Moses J held in *R v Customs and Excise Commissioners ex p Dangol* [2000] STC 107 (QBD) that a party could only seek judicial review of a delay in issuing a decision if they could demonstrate that the delay caused an injustice.

Parties are entitled to have a decision set aside if, eg, there is a procedural irregularity. **23.239** However, that must be done within 28 days of the release of the decision (r 38). There is no power to set a decision aside outside of that period, the only recourse then being to appeal (see *Mohammed Razaq v Customs and Excise Commissioners* (14949)).

N. Restoration Appeals

Rule 39 outlines the procedure to be followed for permission to appeal the Tax Tribunals **23.240** decision. Appeals must be filed within 56 days (see r 39(2)).

O. Restoration: Costs and Compensation

Compensation

Traditional thinking has always maintained that the Tax Tribunal does not have any juris- **23.241** diction to entertain claims for compensation and such matters are entirely within the remit of the county court (see *Lindsay*, considered above at para 23.184). However, this was called into question by *Powell v Revenue and Customs Commissioners* (2005) (EOO 900), where the Tribunal held that a power to pay compensation when restoration was no longer possible was a necessary part of the structure of the legislation, pursuant to s 152(b) of CEMA. The Tribunal found (at paras 102, 109, 112, and 113) that there is a right of appeal to the Tribunal on the question of quantum of compensation and the reasonableness of the payment offered in restoration proceedings where goods have been destroyed. The Tribunal's power would be to return the decision to Customs for review if it found the offer to be unreasonable. It has no power to make its own order in substitution of Customs' decision. It only has the power to keep reviewing the decisions of Customs and if they are unreasonable then returning them for further re-review.

Costs

Costs are dealt with by r 29 CPR. As with all civil proceedings costs usually follow the **23.242** event, provided that they are reasonable and have been properly incurred. The Tribunal may decide that costs are not reasonable where the conduct of a party has been improper or where issues have been raised late in the day and without proper notice. Litigants in person are unable to recover their costs in respect of time spent on the case, per *Melina Serpes v Revenue and Customs Commissioners* (VADT20906)(2008).

The withdrawal of a party from an appeal will not usually save them from having to pay **23.243** costs unless, eg, they do so as a result of new evidence of which they were previously unaware (see *JJ McGinty v Customs and Excise Commissioners* (1995) V&DR 193).

Pursuant to *Burgess v Stafford Hotel Ltd* [1993] 3 All ER 222 costs may be awarded on an **23.244** indemnity basis where the conduct of a party has been unconscionable.

P. The ECHR and Restoration

23.245 It is well established that pursuant to s 2(1) of the Human Rights Act 1998, a court or tribunal 'must take account' of decisions of the European Commission and Court. Guidance on how matters should be approached is provided by *Hoverspeed Ltd* [2002] EWHC Admin 1630 at paras 186–189, and for the court's approach in relation to proportionality see *Lindsay v Customs and Excise Commissioners* [2002] EWCA Civ 267.

23.246 In *Gora* the Court of Appeal upheld the conclusions of the Tribunal that a decision not to restore seized goods did not involve a criminal charge for the purposes of Art 6 of the Convention (para 48).

23.247 In *Hopping v Customs and Excise Commissioners* (2001)(EOO 170), the Tribunal held that the policy of 'use it and lose it', namely seizing and refusing to restore to the owner a vehicle used for bootlegging, was proportionate in that a fair balance existed between the legitimate aim pursued and the means employed. The Tribunal commented that seizure and the refusal to restore the vehicle are, on first impression, direct violations of the owner's fundamental right of peaceful enjoyment of his vehicle (Art 1 of Protocol 1 of the ECHR); and that the Commissioners' policy was capable of being arbitrary to the point of being extravagant (para 28), particularly where the financial loss resulting from the refusal to restore an expensive car could many times exceed the loss of revenue sought from the operation.

23.248 Whilst this decision should be treated with some caution, due to the passage of time, it nevertheless provides a helpful list of criteria which demonstrate that the means employed tend to balance up the aim pursued. The Tribunal found:

(1) The policy was a suitable way of preventing smuggling. Take away the vehicle and it can be no longer used for bootlegging.
(2) To refuse to restore is even-handed. It is the course of action that is blind to the value of the vehicle and to the financial means of the owner. It treats all bootleggers alike.
(3) The owner who makes a bootlegging trip to France and whose vehicle is taken will know the score before he embarks on his smuggling operations. In a real sense he ventures his vehicle as one of the stakes of his dishonest enterprise. He foregoes his claim to any unqualified fundamental right of peaceful enjoyment of the vehicle before he sets off on his trip.
(4) So long as the seizure and refusal to restore the vehicle does not cause physical suffering or result in excessive inconvenience to defenceless third parties, its impact will be directed at the owner (see para 28).

23.249 Sir Steven Oliver QC added at para 29:

Every case will have to be dealt with on its own facts. But in principle we do not see a lack of balance when the factors set out above are brought into the reckoning. Where the owner is the driver he risks losing the vehicle when he sets out to bootleg. He takes the risk and loses when he is caught.

Q. Useful Resources

A copy of the Tribunal Procedure (First-tier Tribunal) (Tax Chamber) Rules 2009 (SI **23.250**
2009/273), together with the Finance Act 1994, may be found at <http://www.opsi.gov.
uk> and further information on the first tier Tax Tribunal may be found at <http://www.
tribunals.gov.uk/Tax>.

APPENDICES

APPENDIX 1

THE PROCEEDS OF CRIME ACT 2002
Sections 6–18 (as amended)

PART 2

Confiscation Orders

6 Making of order

(1) The Crown Court must proceed under this section if the following two conditions are satisfied.

(2) The first condition is that a defendant falls within any of the following paragraphs—

  (a) he is convicted of an offence or offences in proceedings before the Crown Court;

  (b) he is committed to the Crown Court for sentence in respect of an offence or offences under section 3, 4 or 6 of the Sentencing Act;

  (c) he is committed to the Crown Court in respect of an offence or offences under section 70 below (committal with a view to a confiscation order being considered).

(3) The second condition is that—

  (a) the prosecutor asks the court to proceed under this section, or

  (b) the court believes it is appropriate for it to do so.

(4) The court must proceed as follows—

  (a) it must decide whether the defendant has a criminal lifestyle;

  (b) if it decides that he has a criminal lifestyle it must decide whether he has benefited from his general criminal conduct;

  (c) if it decides that he does not have a criminal lifestyle it must decide whether he has benefited from his particular criminal conduct.

(5) If the court decides under subsection (4)(b) or (c) that the defendant has benefited from the conduct referred to it must—

  (a) decide the recoverable amount, and

  (b) make an order (a confiscation order) requiring him to pay that amount.

(6) But the court must treat the duty in subsection (5) as a power if it believes that any victim of the conduct has at any time started or intends to start proceedings against the defendant in respect of loss, injury or damage sustained in connection with the conduct.

(7) The court must decide any question arising under subsection (4) or (5) on a balance of probabilities.

(8) The first condition is not satisfied if the defendant absconds (but section 27 may apply).

(9) References in this Part to the offence (or offences) concerned are to the offence (or offences) mentioned in subsection (2).

7 Recoverable amount

(1) The recoverable amount for the purposes of section 6 is an amount equal to the defendant's benefit from the conduct concerned.

(2) But if the defendant shows that the available amount is less than that benefit the recoverable amount is—

  (a) the available amount, or

  (b) a nominal amount, if the available amount is nil.

(3) But if section 6(6) applies the recoverable amount is such amount as—

  (a) the court believes is just, but

  (b) does not exceed the amount found under subsection (1) or (2) (as the case may be).

(4) In calculating the defendant's benefit from the conduct concerned for the purposes of subsection (1), any property in respect of which—
    (a) a recovery order is in force under section 266, or
    (b) a forfeiture order is in force under section 298(2),
must be ignored.

(5) If the court decides the available amount, it must include in the confiscation order a statement of its findings as to the matters relevant for deciding that amount.

8 Defendant's benefit

(1) If the court is proceeding under section 6 this section applies for the purpose of—
    (a) deciding whether the defendant has benefited from conduct, and
    (b) deciding his benefit from the conduct.

(2) The court must—
    (a) take account of conduct occurring up to the time it makes its decision;
    (b) take account of property obtained up to that time.

(3) Subsection (4) applies if—
    (a) the conduct concerned is general criminal conduct,
    (b) a confiscation order mentioned in subsection (5) has at an earlier time been made against the defendant, and
    (c) his benefit for the purposes of that order was benefit from his general criminal conduct.

(4) His benefit found at the time the last confiscation order mentioned in subsection (3)(c) was made against him must be taken for the purposes of this section to be his benefit from his general criminal conduct at that time.

(5) If the conduct concerned is general criminal conduct the court must deduct the aggregate of the following amounts—
    (a) the amount ordered to be paid under each confiscation order previously made against the defendant;
    (b) the amount ordered to be paid under each confiscation order previously made against him under any of the provisions listed in subsection (7).

(6) But subsection (5) does not apply to an amount which has been taken into account for the purposes of a deduction under that subsection on any earlier occasion.

(7) These are the provisions—
    (a) the Drug Trafficking Offences Act 1986 (c. 32);
    (b) Part 1 of the Criminal Justice (Scotland) Act 1987 (c. 41);
    (c) Part 6 of the Criminal Justice Act 1988;
    (d) the Criminal Justice (Confiscation) (Northern Ireland) Order 1990 (S.I. 1990/2588 (N.I. 17));
    (e) Part 1 of the Drug Trafficking Act 1994 (c. 37);
    (f) Part 1 of the Proceeds of Crime (Scotland) Act 1995 (c. 43);
    (g) the Proceeds of Crime (Northern Ireland) Order 1996 (S.I. 1996/1299 (N.I. 9));
    (h) Part 3 or 4 of this Act.

(8) The reference to general criminal conduct in the case of a confiscation order made under any of the provisions listed in subsection (7) is a reference to conduct in respect of which a court is required or entitled to make one or more assumptions for the purpose of assessing a person's benefit from the conduct.

9 Available amount

(1) For the purposes of deciding the recoverable amount, the available amount is the aggregate of—
    (a) the total of the values (at the time the confiscation order is made) of all the free property then held by the defendant minus the total amount payable in pursuance of obligations which then have priority, and
    (b) the total of the values (at that time) of all tainted gifts.

(2) An obligation has priority if it is an obligation of the defendant—
   (a) to pay an amount due in respect of a fine or other order of a court which was imposed or made on conviction of an offence and at any time before the time the confiscation order is made, or
   (b) to pay a sum which would be included among the preferential debts if the defendant's bankruptcy had commenced on the date of the confiscation order or his winding up had been ordered on that date.

(3) "Preferential debts" has the meaning given by section 386 of the Insolvency Act 1986 (c. 45).

10 Assumptions to be made in case of criminal lifestyle

(1) If the court decides under section 6 that the defendant has a criminal lifestyle it must make the following four assumptions for the purpose of—
   (a) deciding whether he has benefited from his general criminal conduct, and
   (b) deciding his benefit from the conduct.

(2) The first assumption is that any property transferred to the defendant at any time after the relevant day was obtained by him—
   (a) as a result of his general criminal conduct, and
   (b) at the earliest time he appears to have held it.

(3) The second assumption is that any property held by the defendant at any time after the date of conviction was obtained by him—
   (a) as a result of his general criminal conduct, and
   (b) at the earliest time he appears to have held it.

(4) The third assumption is that any expenditure incurred by the defendant at any time after the relevant day was met from property obtained by him as a result of his general criminal conduct.

(5) The fourth assumption is that, for the purpose of valuing any property obtained (or assumed to have been obtained) by the defendant, he obtained it free of any other interests in it.

(6) But the court must not make a required assumption in relation to particular property or expenditure if—
   (a) the assumption is shown to be incorrect, or
   (b) there would be a serious risk of injustice if the assumption were made.

(7) If the court does not make one or more of the required assumptions it must state its reasons.

(8) The relevant day is the first day of the period of six years ending with—
   (a) the day when proceedings for the offence concerned were started against the defendant, or
   (b) if there are two or more offences and proceedings for them were started on different days, the earliest of those days.

(9) But if a confiscation order mentioned in section 8(3)(c) has been made against the defendant at any time during the period mentioned in subsection (8)—
   (a) the relevant day is the day when the defendant's benefit was calculated for the purposes of the last such confiscation order;
   (b) the second assumption does not apply to any property which was held by him on or before the relevant day.

(10) The date of conviction is—
   (a) the date on which the defendant was convicted of the offence concerned, or
   (b) if there are two or more offences and the convictions were on different dates, the date of the latest.

11 Time for payment

(1) The amount ordered to be paid under a confiscation order must be paid on the making of the order; but this is subject to the following provisions of this section.

(2) If the defendant shows that he needs time to pay the amount ordered to be paid, the court making the confiscation order may make an order allowing payment to be made in a specified period.

(3) The specified period—
  (a) must start with the day on which the confiscation order is made, and
  (b) must not exceed six months.
(4) If within the specified period the defendant applies to the Crown Court for the period to be extended and the court believes there are exceptional circumstances, it may make an order extending the period.
(5) The extended period—
  (a) must start with the day on which the confiscation order is made, and
  (b) must not exceed 12 months.
(6) An order under subsection (4)—
  (a) may be made after the end of the specified period, but
  (b) must not be made after the end of the period of 12 months starting with the day on which the confiscation order is made.
(7) The court must not make an order under subsection (2) or (4) unless it gives—
  (a) the prosecutor
an opportunity to make representations.

12 Interest on unpaid sums

(1) If the amount required to be paid by a person under a confiscation order is not paid when it is required to be paid, he must pay interest on the amount for the period for which it remains unpaid.
(2) The rate of interest is the same rate as that for the time being specified in section 17 of the Judgments Act 1838 (c. 110) (interest on civil judgment debts).
(3) For the purposes of this section no amount is required to be paid under a confiscation order if—
  (a) an application has been made under section 11(4),
  (b) the application has not been determined by the court, and
  (c) the period of 12 months starting with the day on which the confiscation order was made has not ended.
(4) In applying this Part the amount of the interest must be treated as part of the amount to be paid under the confiscation order.

13 Effect of order on court's other powers

(1) If the court makes a confiscation order it must proceed as mentioned in subsections (2) and (4) in respect of the offence or offences concerned.
(2) The court must take account of the confiscation order before—
  (a) it imposes a fine on the defendant, or
  (b) it makes an order falling within subsection (3).
(3) These orders fall within this subsection—
  (a) an order involving payment by the defendant, other than an order under section 130 of the Sentencing Act (compensation orders);
  (b) an order under section 27 of the Misuse of Drugs Act 1971 (c. 38) (forfeiture orders);
  (c) an order under section 143 of the Sentencing Act (deprivation orders);
  (d) an order under section 23 of the Terrorism Act 2000 (c. 11) (forfeiture orders).
(4) Subject to subsection (2), the court must leave the confiscation order out of account in deciding the appropriate sentence for the defendant.
(5) Subsection (6) applies if—
  (a) the Crown Court makes both a confiscation order and an order for the payment of compensation under section 130 of the Sentencing Act against the same person in the same proceedings, and
  (b) the court believes he will not have sufficient means to satisfy both the orders in full.

(6) In such a case the court must direct that so much of the compensation as it specifies is to be paid out of any sums recovered under the confiscation order; and the amount it specifies must be the amount it believes will not be recoverable because of the insufficiency of the person's means.

Procedural matters

14 Postponement

(1) The court may—
 (a) proceed under section 6 before it sentences the defendant for the offence (or any of the offences) concerned, or
 (b) postpone proceedings under section 6 for a specified period.
(2) A period of postponement may be extended.
(3) A period of postponement (including one as extended) must not end after the permitted period ends.
(4) But subsection (3) does not apply if there are exceptional circumstances.
(5) The permitted period is the period of two years starting with the date of conviction.
(6) But if—
 (a) the defendant appeals against his conviction for the offence (or any of the offences) concerned, and
 (b) the period of three months (starting with the day when the appeal is determined or otherwise disposed of) ends after the period found under subsection (5),
the permitted period is that period of three months.
(7) A postponement or extension may be made—
 (a) on application by the defendant;
 (b) on application by the prosecutor;
 (c) by the court of its own motion.
(8) If—
 (a) proceedings are postponed for a period, and
 (b) an application to extend the period is made before it ends,
the application may be granted even after the period ends.
(9) The date of conviction is—
 (a) the date on which the defendant was convicted of the offence concerned, or
 (b) if there are two or more offences and the convictions were on different dates, the date of the latest.
(10) References to appealing include references to applying under section 111 of the Magistrates' Courts Act 1980 (c. 43) (statement of case).
(11) A confiscation order must not be quashed only on the ground that there was a defect or omission in the procedure connected with the application for or the granting of a postponement.
(12) But subsection (11) does not apply if before it made the confiscation order the court—
 (a) imposed a fine on the defendant;
 (b) made an order falling within section 13(3);
 (c) made an order under section 130 of the Sentencing Act (compensation orders).

15 Effect of postponement

(1) If the court postpones proceedings under section 6 it may proceed to sentence the defendant for the offence (or any of the offences) concerned.
(2) In sentencing the defendant for the offence (or any of the offences) concerned in the postponement period the court must not—
 (a) impose a fine on him,
 (b) make an order falling within section 13(3), or
 (c) make an order for the payment of compensation under section 130 of the Sentencing Act.

(3) If the court sentences the defendant for the offence (or any of the offences) concerned in the postponement period, after that period ends it may vary the sentence by—
   (a) imposing a fine on him,
   (b) making an order falling within section 13(3), or
   (c) making an order for the payment of compensation under section 130 of the Sentencing Act.

(4) But the court may proceed under subsection (3) only within the period of 28 days which starts with the last day of the postponement period.

(5) For the purposes of—
   (a) section 18(2) of the Criminal Appeal Act 1968 (c. 19) (time limit for notice of appeal or of application for leave to appeal), and
   (b) paragraph 1 of Schedule 3 to the Criminal Justice Act 1988 (c. 33) (time limit for notice of application for leave to refer a case under section 36 of that Act),
   the sentence must be regarded as imposed or made on the day on which it is varied under subsection (3).

(6) If the court proceeds to sentence the defendant under subsection (1), section 6 has effect as if the defendant's particular criminal conduct included conduct which constitutes offences which the court has taken into consideration in deciding his sentence for the offence or offences concerned.

(7) The postponement period is the period for which proceedings under section 6 are postponed.

16 Statement of information

(1) If the court is proceeding under section 6 in a case where section 6(3)(a) applies, the prosecutor must give the court a statement of information within the period the court orders.

(2) If the court is proceeding under section 6 in a case where section 6(3)(b) applies and it orders the prosecutor to give it a statement of information, the prosecutor must give it such a statement within the period the court orders.

(3) If the prosecutor believes the defendant has a criminal lifestyle the statement of information is a statement of matters the prosecutor believes are relevant in connection with deciding these issues—
   (a) whether the defendant has a criminal lifestyle;
   (b) whether he has benefited from his general criminal conduct;
   (c) his benefit from the conduct.

(4) A statement under subsection (3) must include information the prosecutor believes is relevant—
   (a) in connection with the making by the court of a required assumption under section 10;
   (b) for the purpose of enabling the court to decide if the circumstances are such that it must not make such an assumption.

(5) If the prosecutor does not believe the defendant has a criminal lifestyle the statement of information is a statement of matters the prosecutor or the Director believes are relevant in connection with deciding these issues—
   (a) whether the defendant has benefited from his particular criminal conduct;
   (b) his benefit from the conduct.

(6) If the prosecutor gives the court a statement of information—
   (a) he may at any time give the court a further statement of information;
   (b) he must give the court a further statement of information if it orders him to do so, and he must give it within the period the court orders.

(7) If the court makes an order under this section it may at any time vary it by making another one.

17 Defendant's response to statement of information

(1) If the prosecutor gives the court a statement of information and a copy is served on the defendant, the court may order the defendant—
   (a) to indicate (within the period it orders) the extent to which he accepts each allegation in the statement, and

   (b) so far as he does not accept such an allegation, to give particulars of any matters he proposes to rely on.

(2) If the defendant accepts to any extent an allegation in a statement of information the court may treat his acceptance as conclusive of the matters to which it relates for the purpose of deciding the issues referred to in section 16(3) or (5) (as the case may be).

(3) If the defendant fails in any respect to comply with an order under subsection (1) he may be treated for the purposes of subsection (2) as accepting every allegation in the statement of information apart from—

   (a) any allegation in respect of which he has complied with the requirement;

   (b) any allegation that he has benefited from his general or particular criminal conduct.

(4) For the purposes of this section an allegation may be accepted or particulars may be given in a manner ordered by the court.

(5) If the court makes an order under this section it may at any time vary it by making another one.

(6) No acceptance under this section that the defendant has benefited from conduct is admissible in evidence in proceedings for an offence.

18 Provision of information by defendant

(1) This section applies if—

   (a) the court is proceeding under section 6 in a case where section 6(3)(a) applies, or

   (b) it is proceeding under section 6 in a case where section 6(3)(b) applies or it is considering whether to proceed.

(2) For the purpose of obtaining information to help it in carrying out its functions the court may at any time order the defendant to give it information specified in the order.

(3) An order under this section may require all or a specified part of the information to be given in a specified manner and before a specified date.

(4) If the defendant fails without reasonable excuse to comply with an order under this section the court may draw such inference as it believes is appropriate.

(5) Subsection (4) does not affect any power of the court to deal with the defendant in respect of a failure to comply with an order under this section.

(6) If the prosecutor accepts to any extent an allegation made by the defendant—

   (a) in giving information required by an order under this section, or

   (b) in any other statement given to the court in relation to any matter relevant to deciding the available amount under section 9,

the court may treat the acceptance as conclusive of the matters to which it relates.

(7) For the purposes of this section an allegation may be accepted in a manner ordered by the court.

(8) If the court makes an order under this section it may at any time vary it by making another one.

(9) No information given under this section which amounts to an admission by the defendant that he has benefited from criminal conduct is admissible in evidence in proceedings for an offence.

THE PROCEEDS OF CRIME ACT 2002
Sections 40–42 (as amended)

Restraint Orders

40 Conditions for exercise of powers

(1) The Crown Court may exercise the powers conferred by section 41 if any of the following conditions is satisfied.

(2) The first condition is that—
    (a) a criminal investigation has been started in England and Wales with regard to an offence, and
    (b) there is reasonable cause to believe that the alleged offender has benefited from his criminal conduct.

(3) The second condition is that—
    (a) proceedings for an offence have been started in England and Wales and not concluded, and
    (b) there is reasonable cause to believe that the defendant has benefited from his criminal conduct.

(4) The third condition is that—
    (a) an application by the prosecutor has been made under section 19, 20, 27 or 28 and not concluded, or the court believes that such an application is to be made, and
    (b) there is reasonable cause to believe that the defendant has benefited from his criminal conduct.

(5) The fourth condition is that—
    (a) an application by the prosecutor has been made under section 21 and not concluded, or the court believes that such an application is to be made, and
    (b) there is reasonable cause to believe that the court will decide under that section that the amount found under the new calculation of the defendant's benefit exceeds the relevant amount (as defined in that section).

(6) The fifth condition is that—
    (a) an application by the prosecutor has been made under section 22 and not concluded, or the court believes that such an application is to be made, and
    (b) there is reasonable cause to believe that the court will decide under that section that the amount found under the new calculation of the available amount exceeds the relevant amount (as defined in that section).

(7) The second condition is not satisfied if the court believes that—
    (a) there has been undue delay in continuing the proceedings, or
    (b) the prosecutor does not intend to proceed.

(8) If an application mentioned in the third, fourth or fifth condition has been made the condition is not satisfied if the court believes that—
    (a) there has been undue delay in continuing the application, or
    (b) the prosecutor does not intend to proceed.

(9) If the first condition is satisfied—
    (a) references in this Part to the defendant are to the alleged offender;
    (b) references in this Part to the prosecutor are to the person the court believes is to have conduct of any proceedings for the offence;
    (c) section 77(9) has effect as if proceedings for the offence had been started against the defendant when the investigation was started.

41 Restraint orders

(1) If any condition set out in section 40 is satisfied the Crown Court may make an order (a restraint order) prohibiting any specified person from dealing with any realisable property held by him.

(2) A restraint order may provide that it applies—
  (a) to all realisable property held by the specified person whether or not the property is described in the order;
  (b) to realisable property transferred to the specified person after the order is made.

(3) A restraint order may be made subject to exceptions, and an exception may in particular—
  (a) make provision for reasonable living expenses and reasonable legal expenses;
  (b) make provision for the purpose of enabling any person to carry on any trade, business, profession or occupation;
  (c) be made subject to conditions.

(4) But an exception to a restraint order must not make provision for any legal expenses which—
  (a) relate to an offence which falls within subsection (5), and
  (b) are incurred by the defendant or by a recipient of a tainted gift.

(5) These offences fall within this subsection—
  (a) the offence mentioned in section 40(2) or (3), if the first or second condition (as the case may be) is satisfied;
  (b) the offence (or any of the offences) concerned, if the third, fourth or fifth condition is satisfied.

(6) Subsection (7) applies if—
  (a) a court makes a restraint order, and
  (b) the applicant for the order applies to the court to proceed under subsection (7) (whether as part of the application for the restraint order or at any time afterwards).

(7) The court may make such order as it believes is appropriate for the purpose of ensuring that the restraint order is effective.

(8) A restraint order does not affect property for the time being subject to a charge under any of these provisions—
  (a) section 9 of the Drug Trafficking Offences Act 1986 (c. 32);
  (b) section 78 of the Criminal Justice Act 1988 (c. 33);
  (c) Article 14 of the Criminal Justice (Confiscation) (Northern Ireland) Order 1990 (S.I. 1990/2588 (N.I. 17));
  (d) section 27 of the Drug Trafficking Act 1994 (c. 37);
  (e) Article 32 of the Proceeds of Crime (Northern Ireland) Order 1996 (S.I. 1996/1299 (N.I. 9)).

(9) Dealing with property includes removing it from England and Wales.

42 Application, discharge and variation

(1) A restraint order—
  (a) may be made only on an application by an applicant falling within subsection (2);
  (b) may be made on an ex parte application to a judge in chambers.

(2) These applicants fall within this subsection—
  (a) the prosecutor;
  (b) ....
  (c) an accredited financial investigator.

(3) An application to discharge or vary a restraint order or an order under section 41(7) may be made to the Crown Court by—
  (a) the person who applied for the order;
  (b) any person affected by the order.

(4) Subsections (5) to (7) apply to an application under subsection (3).

(5) The court—
  (a) may discharge the order;
  (b) may vary the order.

(6) If the condition in section 40 which was satisfied was that proceedings were started or an application was made, the court must discharge the order on the conclusion of the proceedings or of the application (as the case may be).
(7) If the condition in section 40 which was satisfied was that an investigation was started or an application was to be made, the court must discharge the order if within a reasonable time proceedings for the offence are not started or the application is not made (as the case may be).

THE PROCEEDS OF CRIME ACT 2002
Sections 48–51 (as amended)

Management receivers

48 Appointment

(1) Subsection (2) applies if—
   (a) the Crown Court makes a restraint order, and
   (b) the applicant for the restraint order applies to the court to proceed under subsection (2) (whether as part of the application for the restraint order or at any time afterwards).
(2) The Crown Court may by order appoint a receiver in respect of any realisable property to which the restraint order applies.

49 Powers

(1) If the court appoints a receiver under section 48 it may act under this section on the application of the person who applied for the restraint order.
(2) The court may by order confer on the receiver the following powers in relation to any realisable property to which the restraint order applies—
   (a) power to take possession of the property;
   (b) power to manage or otherwise deal with the property;
   (c) power to start, carry on or defend any legal proceedings in respect of the property;
   (d) power to realise so much of the property as is necessary to meet the receiver's remuneration and expenses.
(3) The court may by order confer on the receiver power to enter any premises in England and Wales and to do any of the following—
   (a) search for or inspect anything authorised by the court;
   (b) make or obtain a copy, photograph or other record of anything so authorised;
   (c) remove anything which the receiver is required or authorised to take possession of in pursuance of an order of the court.
(4) The court may by order authorise the receiver to do any of the following for the purpose of the exercise of his functions—
   (a) hold property;
   (b) enter into contracts;
   (c) sue and be sued;
   (d) employ agents;
   (e) execute powers of attorney, deeds or other instruments;
   (f) take any other steps the court thinks appropriate.
(5) The court may order any person who has possession of realisable property to which the restraint order applies to give possession of it to the receiver.
(6) The court—
   (a) may order a person holding an interest in realisable property to which the restraint order applies to make to the receiver such payment as the court specifies in respect of a beneficial interest held by the defendant or the recipient of a tainted gift;
   (b) may (on the payment being made) by order transfer, grant or extinguish any interest in the property.

(7) Subsections (2), (5) and (6) do not apply to property for the time being subject to a charge under any of these provisions—

    (a) section 9 of the Drug Trafficking Offences Act 1986 (c. 32);

    (b) section 78 of the Criminal Justice Act 1988 (c. 33);

    (c) Article 14 of the Criminal Justice (Confiscation) (Northern Ireland) Order 1990 (S.I.1990/2588 (N.I. 17));

    (d) section 27 of the Drug Trafficking Act 1994 (c. 37);

    (e) Article 32 of the Proceeds of Crime (Northern Ireland) Order 1996 (S.I. 1996/1299 (N.I. 9)).

(8) The court must not—

    (a) confer the power mentioned in subsection (2)(b) or (d) in respect of property, or

    (b) exercise the power conferred on it by subsection (6) in respect of property,

    unless it gives persons holding interests in the property a reasonable opportunity to make representations to it.

(8A) Subsection (8), so far as relating to the power mentioned in subsection (2)(b), does not apply to property which—

    (a) is perishable; or

    (b) ought to be disposed of before its value diminishes

(9) The court may order that a power conferred by an order under this section is subject to such conditions and exceptions as it specifies.

(10) Managing or otherwise dealing with property includes—

    (a) selling the property or any part of it or interest in it;

    (b) carrying on or arranging for another person to carry on any trade or business the assets of which are or are part of the property;

    (c) incurring capital expenditure in respect of the property.

Enforcement receivers

50 Appointment

(1) This section applies if—

    (a) a confiscation order is made,

    (b) it is not satisfied, and

    (c) it is not subject to appeal.

(2) On the application of the prosecutor the Crown Court may by order appoint a receiver in respect of realisable property.

51 Powers

(1) If the court appoints a receiver under section 50 it may act under this section on the application of the prosecutor.

(2) The court may by order confer on the receiver the following powers in relation to the realisable property—

    (a) power to take possession of the property;

    (b) power to manage or otherwise deal with the property;

    (c) power to realise the property, in such manner as the court may specify;

    (d) power to start, carry on or defend any legal proceedings in respect of the property.

(3) The court may by order confer on the receiver power to enter any premises in England and Wales and to do any of the following—

    (a) search for or inspect anything authorised by the court;

    (b) make or obtain a copy, photograph or other record of anything so authorised;

    (c) remove anything which the receiver is required or authorised to take possession of in pursuance of an order of the court.

(4) The court may by order authorise the receiver to do any of the following for the purpose of the exercise of his functions—

    (a) hold property;

     (b) enter into contracts;

     (c) sue and be sued;

     (d) employ agents;

     (e) execute powers of attorney, deeds or other instruments;

     (f) take any other steps the court thinks appropriate.

(5) The court may order any person who has possession of realisable property to give possession of it to the receiver.

(6) The court—

     (a) may order a person holding an interest in realisable property to make to the receiver such payment as the court specifies in respect of a beneficial interest held by the defendant or the recipient of a tainted gift;

     (b) may (on the payment being made) by order transfer, grant or extinguish any interest in the property.

(7) Subsections (2), (5) and (6) do not apply to property for the time being subject to a charge under any of these provisions—

     (a) section 9 of the Drug Trafficking Offences Act 1986 (c. 32);

     (b) section 78 of the Criminal Justice Act 1988 (c. 33);

     (c) Article 14 of the Criminal Justice (Confiscation) (Northern Ireland) Order 1990 (S.I.1990/2588 (N.I. 17));

     (d) section 27 of the Drug Trafficking Act 1994 (c. 37);

     (e) Article 32 of the Proceeds of Crime (Northern Ireland) Order 1996 (S.I. 1996/1299 (N.I. 9)).

(8) The court must not—

     (a) confer the power mentioned in subsection (2)(b) or (c) in respect of property, or

     (b) exercise the power conferred on it by subsection (6) in respect of property,

unless it gives persons holding interests in the property a reasonable opportunity to make representations to it.

(8A) Subsection (8), so far as relating to the power mentioned in subsection (2)(b), does not apply to property which—

     (a) is perishable; or

     (b) ought to be disposed of before its value diminishes.

(9) The court may order that a power conferred by an order under this section is subject to such conditions and exceptions as it specifies.

(10) Managing or otherwise dealing with property includes—

     (a) selling the property or any part of it or interest in it;

     (b) carrying on or arranging for another person to carry on any trade or business the assets of which are or are part of the property;

     (c) incurring capital expenditure in respect of the property.

THE PROCEEDS OF CRIME ACT 2002
Section 69 (as amended)

Exercise of powers

69 Powers of court and receiver

(1) This section applies to—
    (a) the powers conferred on a court by sections 41 to 59 and sections 62 to 67;
    (b) the powers of a receiver appointed under section 48 or 50.

(2) The powers—
    (a) must be exercised with a view to the value for the time being of realisable property being made available (by the property's realisation) for satisfying any confiscation order that has been or may be made against the defendant;
    (b) must be exercised, in a case where a confiscation order has not been made, with a view to securing that there is no diminution in the value of realisable property;
    (c) must be exercised without taking account of any obligation of the defendant or a recipient of a tainted gift if the obligation conflicts with the object of satisfying any confiscation order that has been or may be made against the defendant;
    (d) may be exercised in respect of a debt owed by the Crown.

(3) Subsection (2) has effect subject to the following rules—
    (a) the powers must be exercised with a view to allowing a person other than the defendant or a recipient of a tainted gift to retain or recover the value of any interest held by him;
    (b) in the case of realisable property held by a recipient of a tainted gift, the powers must be exercised with a view to realising no more than the value for the time being of the gift;
    (c) in a case where a confiscation order has not been made against the defendant, property must not be sold if the court so orders under subsection (4).

(4) If on an application by the defendant, or by the recipient of a tainted gift, the court decides that property cannot be replaced it may order that it must not be sold.

(5) An order under subsection (4) may be revoked or varied.

THE PROCEEDS OF CRIME ACT 2002
Sections 294–303A (as amended)

CHAPTER 3

Seizure and detention

294 Seizure of cash

(1) A customs officer, a constable or an accredited financial investigator, may seize any cash if he has reasonable grounds for suspecting that it is—

    (a) recoverable property, or

    (b) intended by any person for use in unlawful conduct.

(2) A customs officer, a constable or an accredited financial investigator, may also seize cash part of which he has reasonable grounds for suspecting to be—

    (a) recoverable property, or

    (b) intended by any person for use in unlawful conduct,

    if it is not reasonably practicable to seize only that part.

(3) This section does not authorise the seizure of an amount of cash if it or, as the case may be, the part to which his suspicion relates, is less than the minimum amount.

(4) This section does not authorise the seizure by an accredited financial investigator of cash found in Scotland.

295 Detention of seized cash

(1) While the customs officer, a constable or an accredited financial investigator, continues to have reasonable grounds for his suspicion, cash seized under section 294 may be detained initially for a period of 48 hours.

(1A) The period of 48 hours mentioned in subsection (1) is to be calculated in accordance with subsection (1B).

(1B) In calculating a period of 48 hours in accordance with this subsection, no account shall be taken of—

    (a) any Saturday or Sunday,

    (b) Christmas Day,

    (c) Good Friday,

    (d) any day that is a bank holiday under the Banking and Financial Dealings Act 1971 in the part of the United Kingdom within which the cash is seized, or

    (e) any day prescribed under section 8(2) of the Criminal Procedure (Scotland) Act 1995 as a court holiday in a sheriff court in the sheriff court district within which the cash is seized.

(2) The period for which the cash or any part of it may be detained may be extended by an order made by a magistrates' court or (in Scotland) the sheriff; but the order may not authorise the detention of any of the cash—

    (a) beyond the end of the period of three months beginning with the date of the order,

    (b) in the case of any further order under this section, beyond the end of the period of two years beginning with the date of the first order.

(3) A justice of the peace may also exercise the power of a magistrates' court to make the first order under subsection (2) extending the period.

(4) An application for an order under subsection (2)—

    (a) in relation to England and Wales and Northern Ireland, may be made by the Commissioners of Customs and Excise, a constable or an accredited financial investigator,

(b) in relation to Scotland, may be made by the Scottish Ministers in connection with their functions under section 298 or by a procurator fiscal,

and the court, sheriff or justice may make the order if satisfied, in relation to any cash to be further detained, that either of the following conditions is met.

(5) The first condition is that there are reasonable grounds for suspecting that the cash is recoverable property and that either—

(a) its continued detention is justified while its derivation is further investigated or consideration is given to bringing (in the United Kingdom or elsewhere) proceedings against any person for an offence with which the cash is connected, or

(b) proceedings against any person for an offence with which the cash is connected have been started and have not been concluded.

(6) The second condition is that there are reasonable grounds for suspecting that the cash is intended to be used in unlawful conduct and that either—

(a) its continued detention is justified while its intended use is further investigated or consideration is given to bringing (in the United Kingdom or elsewhere) proceedings against any person for an offence with which the cash is connected, or

(b) proceedings against any person for an offence with which the cash is connected have been started and have not been concluded.

(7) An application for an order under subsection (2) may also be made in respect of any cash seized under section 294(2), and the court, sheriff or justice may make the order if satisfied that—

(a) the condition in subsection (5) or (6) is met in respect of part of the cash, and

(b) it is not reasonably practicable to detain only that part.

(8) An order under subsection (2) must provide for notice to be given to persons affected by it.

296 Interest

(1) If cash is detained under section 295 for more than 48 hours (calculated in accordance with s 295(1B)), it is at the first opportunity to be paid into an interest-bearing account and held there; and the interest accruing on it is to be added to it on its forfeiture or release.

(2) In the case of cash detained under section 295 which was seized under section 294(2), the customs officer, a constable or an accredited financial investigator, must, on paying it into the account, release the part of the cash to which the suspicion does not relate.

(3) Subsection (1) does not apply if the cash or, as the case may be, the part to which the suspicion relates is required as evidence of an offence or evidence in proceedings under this Chapter.

297 Release of detained cash

(1) This section applies while any cash is detained under section 295.

(2) A magistrates' court or (in Scotland) the sheriff may direct the release of the whole or any part of the cash if the following condition is met.

(3) The condition is that the court or sheriff is satisfied, on an application by the person from whom the cash was seized, that the conditions in section 295 for the detention of the cash are no longer met in relation to the cash to be released.

(4) A customs officer, a constable or an accredited financial investigator, or (in Scotland) procurator fiscal may, after notifying the magistrates' court, sheriff or justice under whose order cash is being detained, release the whole or any part of it if satisfied that the detention of the cash to be released is no longer justified.

Forfeiture

298 Forfeiture

(1) While cash is detained under section 295, an application for the forfeiture of the whole or any part of it may be made—

(a) to a magistrates' court by the Commissioners of Customs and Excise, a constable or an accredited financial investigator,

(b) (in Scotland) to the sheriff by the Scottish Ministers.

(2) The court or sheriff may order the forfeiture of the cash or any part of it if satisfied that the cash or part—

(a) is recoverable property, or

(b) is intended by any person for use in unlawful conduct.

(3) But in the case of recoverable property which belongs to joint tenants, one of whom is an excepted joint owner, the order may not apply to so much of it as the court thinks is attributable to the excepted joint owner's share.

(4) Where an application for the forfeiture of any cash is made under this section, the cash is to be detained (and may not be released under any power conferred by this Chapter) until any proceedings in pursuance of the application (including any proceedings on appeal) are concluded.

299 Appeal against decision under section 298

(1) Any party to proceedings for an order for the forfeiture of cash under section 298 who is aggrieved by an order under that section or by the decision of the court not to make such an order may appeal—

(a) in relation to England and Wales, to the Crown Court;

(b) in relation to Scotland, to the Sheriff Principal;

(c) in relation to Northern Ireland, to a county court.

(2) An appeal under subsection (1) must be made before the end of the period of 30 days starting with the day on which the court makes the order or decision.

(3) The court hearing the appeal may make any order it thinks appropriate.

(4) If the court upholds an appeal against an order forfeiting the cash, it may order the release of the cash.

300 Application of forfeited cash

(1) Cash forfeited under this Chapter, and any accrued interest on it—

(a) if forfeited by a magistrates' court in England and Wales or Northern Ireland, is to be paid into the Consolidated Fund,

(b) if forfeited by the sheriff, is to be paid into the Scottish Consolidated Fund.

(2) But it is not to be paid in—

(a) before the end of the period within which an appeal under section 299 may be made, or

(b) if a person appeals under that section, before the appeal is determined or otherwise disposed of.

Supplementary

301 Victims and other owners

(1) A person who claims that any cash detained under this Chapter, or any part of it, belongs to him may apply to a magistrates' court or (in Scotland) the sheriff for the cash or part to be released to him.

(2) The application may be made in the course of proceedings under section 295 or 298 or at any other time.

(3) If it appears to the court or sheriff concerned that—

(a) the applicant was deprived of the cash to which the application relates, or of property which it represents, by unlawful conduct,

(b) the property he was deprived of was not, immediately before he was deprived of it, recoverable property, and

(c) that cash belongs to him,

the court or sheriff may order the cash to which the application relates to be released to the applicant.

(4) If—

(a) the applicant is not the person from whom the cash to which the application relates was seized,

(b) it appears to the court or sheriff that that cash belongs to the applicant,

(c) the court or sheriff is satisfied that the conditions in section 295 for the detention of that cash are no longer met or, if an application has been made under section 298, the court or sheriff decides not to make an order under that section in relation to that cash, and

(d) no objection to the making of an order under this subsection has been made by the person from whom that cash was seized,

the court or sheriff may order the cash to which the application relates to be released to the applicant or to the person from whom it was seized.

302 Compensation

(1) If no forfeiture order is made in respect of any cash detained under this Chapter, the person to whom the cash belongs or from whom it was seized may make an application to the magistrates' court or (in Scotland) the sheriff for compensation.

(2) If, for any period beginning with the first opportunity to place the cash in an interest-bearing account after the initial detention of the cash for 48 hours (calculated in accordance with s 295(1B)), the cash was not held in an interest-bearing account while detained, the court or sheriff may order an amount of compensation to be paid to the applicant.

(3) The amount of compensation to be paid under subsection (2) is the amount the court or sheriff thinks would have been earned in interest in the period in question if the cash had been held in an interest-bearing account.

(4) If the court or sheriff is satisfied that, taking account of any interest to be paid under section 296 or any amount to be paid under subsection (2), the applicant has suffered loss as a result of the detention of the cash and that the circumstances are exceptional, the court or sheriff may order compensation (or additional compensation) to be paid to him.

(5) The amount of compensation to be paid under subsection (4) is the amount the court or sheriff thinks reasonable, having regard to the loss suffered and any other relevant circumstances.

(6) If the cash was seized by a customs officer, the compensation is to be paid by the Commissioners of Customs and Excise.

(7) If the cash was seized by a constable, the compensation is to be paid as follows—

   (a) in the case of a constable of a police force in England and Wales, it is to be paid out of the police fund from which the expenses of the police force are met,

   (b) in the case of a constable of a police force in Scotland, it is to be paid by the police authority or joint police board for the police area for which that force is maintained,

   (c) in the case of a police officer within the meaning of the Police (Northern Ireland) Act 2000 (c. 32), it is to be paid out of money provided by the Chief Constable.

(7A) If the cash was seized by an accredited financial investigator who was not an officer of Revenue and Customs or a constable, the compensation is to be paid as follows—

   (a) in the case of an investigator—

       (i) who was employed by a police authority in England and Wales under section 15 of the Police Act 1996 (c. 16) and was under the direction and control of the chief officer of police of the police force maintained by the authority, or

       (ii) who was a member of staff of the City of London police force,

           it is to be paid out of the police fund from which the expenses of the police force are met,

   (b) in the case of an investigator who was a member of staff of the Police Service of Northern Ireland, it is to be paid out of money provided by the Chief Constable,

   (c) in the case of an investigator who was a member of staff of a department of the Government of the United Kingdom, it is to be paid by the Minister of the Crown in charge of the department or by the department,

   (d) in the case of an investigator who was a member of staff of a Northern Ireland department, it is to be paid by the department,

   (e) in any other case, it is to be paid by the employer of the investigator.

(7B) The Secretary of State may by order amend subsection (7A).

(8) If a forfeiture order is made in respect only of a part of any cash detained under this Chapter, this section has effect in relation to the other part.

302A Powers for prosecutors to appear in proceedings

(1) The Director of Public Prosecutions or the Director of Public Prosecutions for Northern Ireland may appear for a constable or an accredited financial investigator in proceedings under this Chapter if the Director—

    (a) is asked by, or on behalf of, a constable or (as the case may be) an accredited financial investigator, to do so, and

    (b) considers it appropriate to do so.

(2) The Director of Revenue and Customs Prosecutions may appear for the Commissioners for Her Majesty's Revenue and Customs or an officer of Revenue and Customs in proceedings under this Chapter if the Director—

    (a) is asked by, or on behalf of, the Commissioners for Her Majesty's Revenue and Customs or (as the case may be) an officer of Revenue and Customs to do so, and

    (b) considers it appropriate to do so.

(3) The Directors may charge fees for the provision of services under this section.

(4) The references in subsection (1) to an accredited financial investigator do not include an accredited financial investigator who is an officer of Revenue and Customs but the references in subsection (2) to an officer of Revenue and Customs do include an accredited financial investigator who is an officer of Revenue and Customs.

303 "The minimum amount"

(1) In this Chapter, the minimum amount is the amount in sterling specified in an order made by the Secretary of State after consultation with the Scottish Ministers.

(2) For that purpose the amount of any cash held in a currency other than sterling must be taken to be its sterling equivalent, calculated in accordance with the prevailing rate of exchange.

303A Financial investigators

(1) In this Chapter (apart from this section) any reference in a provision to an accredited financial investigator is a reference to an accredited financial investigator who falls within a description specified in an order made for the purposes of that provision by the Secretary of State under section 453.

(2) Subsection (1) does not apply to the second reference to an accredited financial investigator in section 290(4)(c).

(3) Where an accredited financial investigator of a particular description—

    (a) applies for an order under section 295,

    (b) applies for forfeiture under section 298, or

    (c) brings an appeal under, or relating to, this Chapter,

any subsequent step in the application or appeal, or any further application or appeal relating to the same matter, may be taken, made or brought by a different accredited financial investigator of the same description.

THE PROCEEDS OF CRIME ACT 2002
Schedule 6

POWERS OF INTERIM RECEIVER AND ADMINISTRATOR

Seizure

1   Power to seize property to which the order applies.

Information

2(1)   Power to obtain information or to require a person to answer any question.

(2)   A requirement imposed in the exercise of the power has effect in spite of any restriction on the disclosure of information (however imposed).

(3)   An answer given by a person in pursuance of such a requirement may not be used in evidence against him in criminal proceedings.

(4)   Sub-paragraph (3) does not apply—

(a)   on a prosecution for an offence under section 5 of the Perjury Act 1911, section 44(2) of the Criminal Law (Consolidation) (Scotland) Act 1995 or Article 10 of the Perjury (Northern Ireland) Order 1979 (false statements), or

(b)   on a prosecution for some other offence where, in giving evidence, he makes a statement inconsistent with it.

(5)   But an answer may not be used by virtue of sub-paragraph (4)(b) against a person unless—

(a)   evidence relating to it is adduced, or

(b)   a question relating to it is asked,

by him or on his behalf in the proceedings arising out of the prosecution.

Entry, search, etc.

3(1)   Power to—

(a)   enter any premises in the United Kingdom to which the interim order applies, and

(b)   take any of the following steps.

(2)   Those steps are—

(a)   to carry out a search for or inspection of anything described in the order,

(b)   to make or obtain a copy, photograph or other record of anything so described,

(c)   to remove anything which he is required to take possession of in pursuance of the order or which may be required as evidence in the proceedings under Chapter 2 of Part 5.

(3)   The order may describe anything generally, whether by reference to a class or otherwise.

Supplementary

4(1)   An order making any provision under paragraph 2 or 3 must make provision in respect of legal professional privilege (in Scotland, legal privilege within the meaning of Chapter 3 of Part 8).

(2)   An order making any provision under paragraph 3 may require any person—

(a)   to give the interim receiver or administrator access to any premises which he may enter in pursuance of paragraph 3,

(b)   to give the interim receiver or administrator any assistance he may require for taking the steps mentioned in that paragraph.

Management

5(1) Power to manage any property to which the order applies.

(2) Managing property includes—

   (a) selling or otherwise disposing of assets comprised in the property which are perishable or which ought to be disposed of before their value diminishes,

   (b) where the property comprises assets of a trade or business, carrying on, or arranging for another to carry on, the trade or business,

   (c) incurring capital expenditure in respect of the property.

PROCEEDS OF CRIME ACT RESTRAINT ORDER

DISOBEDIENCE TO THIS ORDER IS A CONTEMPT OF COURT WHICH IF YOU ARE AN INDIVIDUAL IS PUNISHABLE BY IMPRISONMENT OR IF YOU ARE A BODY CORPORATE IS PUNISHABLE BY SEQUESTRATION OF YOUR ASSETS AND BY IMPRISONMENT OF ANY INDIVIDUAL RESPONSIBLE

IN THE CROWN COURT
SITTING AT SOUTHWARK

Before His Honour Judge Bullingham sitting in Private

No. ....

Dated ....

IN THE MATTER OF ALFREDO GERMONT (Defendant)

AND

IN THE MATTER OF THE PROCEEDS OF CRIME ACT 2002

RESTRAINT ORDER PROHIBITING DISPOSAL OF ASSETS

TO: (1) **Mr Alfredo Germont (the Defendant)**

    (2) **Mrs Voiletta Valery (wife of the Defendant)**

    (3) **Traviata Trading Enterprises Limited (a company controlled by the Defendant)**

    (4) **Mr Giorgio Germont (father of the Defendant)**

PENAL NOTICE

If you the Defendant, Mrs Violetta Valery, Traviata Trading Enterprises Limited or Mr Giorgio Germont disobey this Order you may be held to be in contempt of court and may be imprisoned, fined or have your assets seized.

Any other person who knows of this order and does anything which helps or permits the Defendant, Mrs Violetta Valery, Traviata Trading Enterprises Limited or Mr Giorgio Germont to breach the terms of this Order may also be held to be in contempt of court and may be imprisoned, fined or have their assets seized.

IMPORTANT: NOTICE TO THE DEFENDANT, MRS VIOLETTA VALERY, TRAVIATA TRADING ENTERPRISES LIMITED AND MR GIORGIO GERMONT

This order prohibits you, the Defendant, from dealing with your assets. It prohibits Mrs Violetta Valery from dealing with the assets identified in paragraph 7 of this Order. It prohibits Traviata Trading

Enterprises Limited from dealing with the assets identified in paragraph 8 of this Order. It prohibits Mr Giorgio Germont from dealing with the assets identified in paragraph 9 of this Order.

The order is subject to the exceptions contained in the order. You should read it all carefully.

You are advised to consult a solicitor as soon as possible. Under paragraph 2 of schedule 2 of the Access to Justice Act 1999, as amended by paragraph 36 of schedule 11 of Proceeds of Crime Act 2002, you may be entitled to Community Legal Service Funding in respect of this Order. Your solicitor will be able to provide you with the appropriate forms. You should contact the Head Office of the Legal Services Commission (LSC), 4 Abbey Orchard Street, London SW1P 2BS, who will be able to advise you as to any public funding available. In relation to LSC funding (formerly Legal Aid) general enquiries may be directed to the LSC telephone helpline: 0800 085 6643.

If you are a defendant in criminal proceedings to which this Order is ancillary and you have the benefit of a Representation Order then your solicitor may be able to give you advice and assistance within the scope of that Representation Order.

You have a right to ask this court to vary or discharge this order (see paragraph 20 below). If you wish to do this you must serve the application and the witness statement in support of the application on the Revenue and Customs Prosecutions Office and the Defendant, Mrs Violetta Valery, Traviata Trading Enterprises Limited and Mr Giorgio Germont at least two clear working days before the date fixed by the Crown Court for the hearing of the application.

There is an interpretation section at paragraphs 33 and 34 of this order.

THE ORDER

1. This is a Restraint Order made against Mr Alfredo Germont ("the Defendant"), Mrs Violetta Valery, Traviata Trading Enterprises Limited and Mr Giorgio Germont on 1st September 2009 by His Honour Judge Bullingham on the application of the Revenue and Customs Prosecutions Office ("the Prosecutor"). The Judge read the witness statements listed in Schedule A and accepted the undertakings set out in Schedule B at the end of this order.

2. This order was made without notice to the Defendant, Mrs Violetta Valery, Traviata Trading Enterprises Limited and Mr Giorgio Germont. The Defendant, Mrs Violetta Valery, Traviata Trading Enterprises Limited and Mr Giorgio Germont have a right to apply to the court to vary or discharge the order—see paragraph 20 below.

OPTIONAL—RETURN DATE PROVISION

3. There will be a further hearing of this matter on 14th September 2009 ("the return date") when the Prosecutor will apply for the continuation of this order. The Defendant, Mrs Violetta Valery, Traviata Trading Enterprises Limited, Mr Giorgio Germont and any other person affected by this order are entitled to appear and to object to the continuation of this order or to ask for it to be varied.

DISPOSAL OF OR DEALING WITH ASSETS

3. The Defendant must not:—
   (1) remove from England and Wales any of his assets which are in England and Wales whether in his own name or not and whether solely or jointly owned; or
   (2) in any way dispose of, deal with or diminish the value of any of his assets whether they are in or outside England and Wales whether in his own name or not and whether solely or jointly owned.

4. Paragraph 3 applies to all the Defendant's assets whether or not the assets are described in this order or are transferred to the Defendant after the order is made, are in his own name and whether they are solely or jointly owned. For the purpose of this order the Defendant's assets include any asset which he has the power, directly or indirectly, to dispose of or deal with as if it were his own. The Defendant is to be regarded as having such power if a third party holds or controls the asset in accordance with his direct or indirect instructions.

5. This prohibition includes the following assets in particular:—
   (a) the property known as "Traviata", 123 The Esplanade, Torquay, Devon registered at HM Land Registry under title number DN12345 or the net sale money after payment of any mortgages if it has been sold;
   (b) the property and assets of the Defendant's business known as Traviata Trading Enterprises Limited carried on at 123 The Esplanade, Torquay, Devon or the sale money if any of them have been sold;
   (c) the assets of a company called Traviata Trading Enterprises Limited (company number 12345), registered address 123 The Esplanade, Torquay, Devon;
   (d) the shares held by the Defendant in the company called Traviata Trading Enterprises Limited (company number 12345), registered address 123 The Esplanade, Torquay, Devon;
   (e) any money in the account numbered 12345678 at Anytown Bank PLC, 1 Main Street Torquay, held in the name of the defendant;
   (f) any money in the account numbered 98765432 at Anytown Bank PLC, 1 Main Street, Torquay, held in the name of Mrs Violetta Valery;
   (g) any money in the account numbered 22334455 at Anytown Bank PLC, 1 Main Street, Torquay, held in the name of Mr Giorgo Germont;
   (h) A Rolls Royce motor vehicle registered number AG 123 registered in the name of the defendant;
   (i) A motor vessel named "Hispaniola", registered in the joint names of the Defendant and Mrs Violetta Valery;
   (j) A racehorse named "Nabucco", registered in the joint names of the Defendant and Mr Giorgio Germont;
   (k) cash totalling £175,000 currently in the possession of the Metropolitan Police Service;
   (l) the property known as "The Heights", Marbella, Spain.

AND IT IS ORDERED THAT:—

6. The assets of Traviata Trading Enterprises Limited be treated as the personal assets of the Defendant.]

7. Mrs Violetta Valery must not:—
   (1) remove from England and Wales or
   (2) in any way dispose of or deal with or diminish the value of the following assets —
       (i) any monies in the account numbered 98765432 at Anytown Bank PLC, 1 Main Street Torquay, held in the name of Mrs Violetta Valery;
       (ii) a motor vessel named "Hispaniola", registered in the names of the Defendant and Mrs Violetta Valery.

8. Traviata Trading Enterprises Limited (a company in the Control of the Defendant) must not:—
   (1) remove from England and Wales or
   (2) in any way dispose of or deal with or diminish the value of the following assets —
       (a) The assets of the company called Traviata Trading Enterprises Limited (Company number 12345) registered address 123 The Esplanade, Torquay, Devon;
       (b) Any monies in the account numbered 66778899 at Anytown Bank PLC, 1 Main Street, Torquay, held in the name of Traviata Trading Enterprises Limited.

9. Mr Giorgio Germont must not:—
   (1) remove from England and Wales; or
   (2) in any way dispose of or deal with or diminish the value of the following assets —
       (a) Any monies in the account numbered 22334455 at Anytown Bank PLC, 1 Main Street, Torquay Devon;
       (b) A racehorse called "Nabucco" registered in the names of the defendant and Mr Giorgio Germont.

RENTAL INCOME

10. Any rent received by the Defendant in respect of the properties set out in paragraph 5 (a) and (l) above shall be dealt with in the following manner:—
    (a) the tenant shall pay rent to the Defendant in the form of a cheque, standing order or other inter bank transfer;
    (b) the Defendant shall pay the cheque or other payment into bank account number 12345678 at Anytown Bank PLC, 1 Main Street, Torquay in the name of the Defendant ("the account");
    (c) the sums received shall be used by the Defendant each and every month to pay mortgage instalments upon the properties set out in paragraph 5 (a) and (l) above in such amounts as the mortgagees shall require; and
    (d) any surplus held in the account or accounts shall be held restrained in the account subject to this order.

11. The Defendant shall keep records of rent received and sums paid to the mortgagees, such records to include:—
    (a) the name and address of the tenant from whom each sum is received and the date of receipt;
    (b) the amount paid to the mortgagee and the date of the payment;
    (c) bank statements of the account or accounts into which rents are received and from which mortgage instalments are made;

AND the Defendant shall supply to the Prosecutor each and every calendar month within 14 days after the end of the month a copy of the said records relating to that month.

DISCLOSURE ORDERS

PROVISION OF INFORMATION

12. The Defendant must serve a witness statement certified by a statement of truth on the Prosecutor within 21 days after this order has been served on him setting out all his assets and all assets under his control whether in or outside England and Wales and whether in his own name or not and whether solely or jointly owned, giving the value, location and details of all such assets. The witness statement must include:
    (1) the name and address of all persons including financial institutions holding any such assets;
    (2) if the Defendant alleges that any third party or financial institution holds an interest in any such asset then he must identify the nature and extent of that interest, and the name and address of the person who is alleged to hold it;
    (3) details of the Defendant's current salary or other form of income, identifying the amounts paid, by whom they are paid and the account or accounts into which such sums are paid;
    (4) the names and numbers of all accounts held by or under the control of the Defendant, together with the name and address of the place where the account is held and the sums in the account;
    (5) details (including addresses) of any real property in which the Defendant has any interest, including an interest in any of the net sale money if the property were to be sold. These details must include details of any mortgage or charge on the property;
    (6) details of all National Savings Certificates, unit trusts, shares or debentures in any company or corporation, wherever incorporated in the world, owned or controlled by the Defendant or in which he has an interest;
    (7) details of all trusts of which the Defendant is a beneficiary, including the name and address of every trustee;
    (8) particulars of any income or debt due to the Defendant including the name and address of the debtor;
    (9) details of all assets over £1,000 in value received by the Defendant, or anyone on his behalf, since 1st September 2003 identifying the name and address of all persons from whom such property was received;

(10) details of all assets over £1,000 in value transferred by the Defendant, or anyone on his behalf, to others since 1st September 2003, identifying the name and address of all persons to whom such property was transferred; and

(11) In the event that any Claim Form, Petition, Statutory Demand, Application Notice, Enforcement Notice, Seizure Notice or other civil court process is pending or is at any time during the currency of this order served upon him or brought to his attention, the Defendant shall forthwith provide a copy of the process to the Prosecutor.

13. (1) Subject to any further order of the court any information given in compliance with this order shall only be used:—

    (a) for the purpose of these proceedings;

    (b) if the Defendant is convicted, for the purposes of any confiscation hearing that may take place; and

    (c) if a confiscation order is made, for the purposes of enforcing that order, including any receivership proceedings.

(2) Paragraph 13 (1) does not prevent the Prosecutor or counsel instructed by the Prosecutor from considering any information disclosed in compliance with this order for the purposes of discharging the Prosecutor's disclosure obligations in the criminal proceedings (to which these proceedings are ancillary) whether under the Criminal Procedure and Investigations Act 1996 or the common law.

(3) There shall be no disclosure of any material disclosed in compliance with this order to any co-defendant in the criminal proceedings.

(4) However, nothing in this paragraph shall make inadmissible any disclosure made by the Defendant in any proceedings for perjury relating to that disclosure.

14. The Defendant must serve a witness statement certified by a statement of truth upon the Prosecutor within 21 days after this order has been served on him setting out the following matters:—

(1) the name and address of every tenant in the properties referred to in paragraph 5 (a) and (l) above; and

(2) the amount of rent paid by each tenant, details of any arrears of such rent and the manner in which the rent is usually paid.

15. (1) Subject to any further order of the court any information given in compliance with this order shall only be used:—

    (a) for the purpose of these proceedings;

    (b) if the Defendant is convicted, for the purposes of any confiscation hearing that may take place; and

    (c) if a confiscation order is made, for the purposes of enforcing that order, including any receivership proceedings.

(2) Paragraph 15 (1) does not prevent the Prosecutor or counsel instructed by the Prosecutor from considering any information disclosed in compliance with this order for the purposes of discharging the Prosecutor's disclosure obligations in the criminal proceedings (to which these proceedings are ancillary) whether under the Criminal Procedure and Investigations Act 1996 or the common law.

(3) There shall be no disclosure of any material disclosed in compliance with this order to any co-defendant in the criminal proceedings.

(4) However, nothing in this paragraph shall make inadmissible any disclosure made by the Defendant in any proceedings for perjury relating to that disclosure.

REPATRIATION

16. (1) The Defendant must within 21 days after being asked to do so in writing by the Prosecutor bring any moveable asset in respect of which he has an interest, which is outside England and Wales, to a location within England and Wales.

(2) The Defendant must inform the Prosecutor of the location within England and Wales within 7 days of the arrival of the assets.

(3) If the asset is cash or credit in a financial institution it must be paid into an interest bearing account and the account holder, location and account number be notified to the Prosecutor within 7 days.

SERVICE BY AN ALTERNATIVE METHOD

17. The Prosecutor shall have permission to serve this order and the witness statement of listed in Schedule A and any further orders or applications or other paperwork relating to this claim by serving the same on Mr Giorgio Germont c/o Messrs Dodson and Fogg, Solicitors, 2 Main Street, Torquay, Devon by pre-paid first class post.

18. The service referred to in paragraph 17 above shall be considered to be good and sufficient service upon the said Mr Giorgio Germont on the second day after posting.

EXCEPTIONS TO THIS ORDER

19. (1) This order does not prohibit the Defendant, on the proviso that he is not in prison, from spending up to £250 a week towards his ordinary living expenses, up to the date of the making of any confiscation order. Before starting to withdraw money in respect of his living expenses, the Defendant must contact the Prosecutor to nominate a bank account or source of income from which such monies will be drawn and must obtain the consent of the Prosecutor in writing to the use of that account or income for that purpose.

(2) This order does not prohibit Mrs Violetta Valery, on the proviso that she is not in prison, from spending up to £250 a week towards her ordinary living expenses, up to the date of the making of any confiscation order. But before spending any money Mrs Violetta Valery must contact the Prosecutor to nominate a bank account or source of income from which such monies will be drawn and must obtain the consent of the Prosecutor in writing to the use of that account or income for that purpose.

(3) This order does not prohibit the Defendant from spending any money he may receive by way of state benefit from the Department for Work and Pensions and/or Her Majesty's Revenue and Customs.

(4) This order does not prohibit the Defendant from spending towards his ordinary living expenses any sum earned by him whilst he is in prison.

(5) The Defendant and Mrs Violetta Valery may agree with the Prosecutor that the above spending limit be varied or that this Order be varied in any other respect, but any such agreement must be in writing.

(6) This order does not prohibit the Defendant from dealing with or disposing of any of his assets in the ordinary and proper course of business, including operating bank account number 667788999 at Anytown Bank PLC, 1 Main Street, Torquay, held in the name of Traviata Trading Enterprises Limited for this purpose. However, to do this, the Defendant must supply to the Prosecutor within 7 days after being asked:—

(a) the following accounting records of the business:—

(i) entries from day to day of all sums of money received and expended by the business and the matters in respect of which the receipt and expenditure takes place;

(ii) a record of the assets and liabilities of the business, including debts owed to and by the business; and

(iii) if the business involves dealing in goods, statements of stock held by the business.

(b) bank statements, cheque stubs, paying in books, bank transfer documentation and any correspondence with the bank in relation to the business bank account.

(7) This order does not prevent:—

(a) any person from paying any money in satisfaction of the whole or part of any confiscation order which may be made against the Defendant; or

(b) the levy of distress upon any goods subject to this order for the purpose of enforcement of any confiscation order which may be made against the Defendant.

VARIATION OR DISCHARGE OF THIS ORDER

20. Anyone affected by this order may apply to the court at any time to vary or discharge this order (or so much of it as affects that person), but they must serve the application and the witness statement in support of the application on the Prosecutor and the Defendant, Mrs Violetta Valery, Traviata Trading Enterprises Limited and Mr Giorgio Germont at least two clear working days before the date fixed by the Crown Court for the hearing of the application.

EFFECT OF THIS ORDER

21. A person who is an individual who is ordered not to do something must not do it himself or in any other way. He must not do it through others acting on his behalf or on his instructions or with his encouragement.

22. A person who is not an individual which is ordered not to do something must not do it itself or by its directors, officers, partners, employees or agents or in any other way.

PARTIES OTHER THAN THE DEFENDANT

Effect of this order

23. It is a contempt of court for any person notified of this order knowingly to assist in or permit a breach of this order. Any person doing so may be imprisoned or fined. He is also at risk of prosecution for a money laundering offence.

Set off by banks

24. This order does not prevent any bank from exercising any right of set off it may have in respect of any facility which it gave to the Defendant before it was notified of this order.

Withdrawals by the Defendant

25. No bank need enquire as to the application or proposed application of any money withdrawn by the Defendant if the withdrawal appears to be permitted by this order.

Cash in the custody of Her Majesty's Revenue & Customs or the Serious Organised Crime Agency

26. This Order does not apply to any cash while it is seized or detained by Her Majesty's Revenue & Customs or the Serious Organised Crime Agency under Part 5 of the Proceeds of Crime Act 2002, or while it is detained or forfeited by order of a court under that Part. "Cash" is to have the meaning given to it by section 289(6) of that Act.

Existing Charges

27. This order does not prevent any financial institution or other charge holder from enforcing or taking any other steps to enforce an existing charge it has in respect of a property or properties so secured, providing that the said financial institution gives written notice to the defendant, the Prosecutor and any other affected third party no later than 21 days before any such application is made. If any evidence is to be relied upon in support of any such application, the substance of it must be communicated to the Prosecutor in advance.

Persons outside England, Wales, Scotland and Northern Ireland

28. (1) Except as provided in paragraph (2) below, the terms of this order do not affect or concern anyone outside the jurisdiction of this court, Scotland or Northern Ireland.

    (2) The terms of this order will affect the following persons in a country or state outside the jurisdiction of this court, Scotland or Northern Ireland:—

(a) a person to whom this order is addressed or the officer or agent appointed by power of attorney of such a person;

(b) any person who:—

    (i) is subject to the jurisdiction of this court, Scotland or Northern Ireland;

    (ii) has been given written notice of this order at his residence or place of business within the jurisdiction of this court, Scotland or Northern Ireland; and

    (iii) is able to prevent acts or omissions outside the jurisdiction of this court, Scotland or Northern Ireland which constitute or assist in a breach of the terms of this order; and

(c) any other person, only to the extent that this order is declared enforceable by or is enforced by a court in that country or state.

Enforcement in Scotland and Northern Ireland

29. This order shall have effect in the law of Scotland and Northern Ireland, and may be enforced there, if it is registered under the Proceeds of Crime Act 2002 (Enforcement in Different Parts of the United Kingdom) Order 2002.

Assets located outside England and Wales

30. Nothing in this order shall, in respect of assets located outside England and Wales, prevent any third party from complying with:—

    (1) what it reasonably believes to be its obligations, contractual or otherwise, under the laws and obligations of the country or state in which those assets are situated or under the proper law of any contract to which it is a party; and

    (2) any orders of the courts of that country or state, provided that reasonable notice of any application for such an order is given to the Prosecutor;

    unless those assets are situated in Scotland or Northern Ireland, in which case this order must be obeyed there.

UNDERTAKINGS

31. The Prosecutor gives to the court the undertakings set out in Schedule B to this order.

DURATION OF THE ORDER

32. This order will remain in force until it is varied or discharged by a further order of this court.

INTERPRETATION

33. Reference to the "Defendant" means Mr Alfredo Germont. Reference to an asset belonging to the Defendant includes any property in which the Defendant has an interest and any property to which the Defendant has a right.

34. A period of time expressed as a number of days shall be computed as clear days as defined in rule 57.2 of the Criminal Procedure Rules 2005.

COSTS

35. The costs of this order are reserved.

COMMUNICATIONS WITH THE COURT

All communications to the court about this order should be sent to the Southwark Crown Court quoting the case number. The office is open between 9am and 5pm Monday to Friday. The telephone number is.

ADDRESS OF THE PROSECUTOR FOR SERVICE AND ANY COMMUNICATION IN RESPECT OF THESE PROCEEDINGS

All communications to the Prosecutor about this order should be sent to (insert name, address, telephone and fax numbers of prosecutor).

COURT STAMP

SCHEDULE A

WITNESS STATEMENTS

(1) Witness Statement of [NAME] dated [DATE].

SCHEDULE B

UNDERTAKINGS GIVEN TO THE COURT BY THE PROSECUTOR

(1) The Prosecutor will serve upon the Defendant, Mr Giorgio Germont, Mrs Violetta Valery and Traviata Trading Enterprises Ltd:—
   (a) a copy of this order; and
   (b) a copy of the witness statement containing the evidence relied upon by the Prosecutor, and any other documents provided to the court on the making of the application.

(2) Anyone notified of this order will be given a copy of it by the Prosecutor.

(3) The Prosecutor will pay the reasonable costs of anyone other than the Defendant, Mrs Violetta Valery, Traviata Trading Enterprises Limited and Mr Giorgio Germont which are incurred as a result of this order including the costs of finding out whether that person holds any of the Defendant's assets, save that the Prosecutor will not without an order of the court be obliged to pay any legal or accountancy costs so incurred unless the Prosecutor first gives its consent in writing.

MANAGEMENT RECEIVERSHIP ORDER

DISOBEDIENCE OF THIS ORDER IS A CONTEMPT OF COURT WHICH IF YOU ARE AN INDIVIDUAL IS PUNISHABLE BY IMPRISONMENT OR IF YOU ARE A BODY CORPORATE IS PUNISHABLE BY SEQUESTRATION OF YOUR ASSETS AND BY IMPRISONMENT OF ANY INDIVIDUAL RESPONSIBLE

IN THE CROWN COURT

SITTING AT SOUTHWARK

Before His Honour Judge Bullingham sitting in Private

No. ....

Dated ....

IN THE MATTER OF ALFREDO GERMONT (Defendant)

AND

IN THE MATTER OF THE PROCEEDS OF CRIME ACT 2002

ORDER APPOINTING A MANAGEMENT RECEIVER

IMPORTANT: NOTICE TO THE DEFENDANT, ALFREDO GERMONT, MR. GIORGIO GERMONT, MISS VIOLETTA VALERY AND TRAVIATA TRADING ENTERPRISES LIMITED AND ANYONE IN POSSESSION OR CONTROL OF THE DEFENDANT'S ASSETS

1. This Order appoints a Receiver to manage the assets of the Defendant subject to the Restraint Order made by His Honour Judge Bullingham on 1st September 2009.

2. This order varies the Restraint Order made against the Defendant, Mr Giorgio Germont, Miss Violetta Valery and Traviata Trading Enterprises Limited by His Honour Judge Bullingham on 1st September 2009.

3. If the Defendant or any person in possession or control of his assets disobeys this order or obstructs the Receiver he or she may be guilty of contempt of court and may be sent to prison or fined or have his assets seized.

4. There is an interpretation section at page 4 of this Order.

THE ORDER OF APPOINTMENT

An application was made today by the Revenue and Customs Prosecutions Office to the Crown Court sitting at Southwark for the appointment of a Management Receiver over the assets of the Defendant to enforce the Restraint Order made against him by His Honour Judge Bullingham on 1st September 2009.

The Judge read the witness statement of [insert name] made on the 5th day of November, 2009.

As a result of the application THE COURT APPOINTS [insert name and address of receiver] as Management Receiver ["the Receiver"] of the realisable property of the Defendant including those listed in the Schedule to this Order and including the assets and the business and undertakings of Traviata Trading Enterprises Limited.

And it is Ordered that:—

1. The assets of Traviata Trading Enterprises Limited be treated as the personal assets of the Defendant.
2. The Receiver shall have the following powers without prejudice to any existing powers vested in her whether by statute or otherwise:—
    a. Power to take possession of, preserve, manage, collect, let charge and sell the assets of the Defendant and Traviata Trading Enterprises Limited.
    b. Power to appoint solicitors, counsel, attorneys, accountants or other agents to advise and/or act on behalf of the Receiver in any part of the world.
    c. Power to discharge all and any costs, charges and expenses of the receivership out of the assets and/or the proceeds of realisation thereof.
    d. Power to bring proceedings in the name of or on behalf of the Defendant and/or Traviata Trading Enterprises Limited, within or without the jurisdiction, against any person having possession of the realisable property of the Defendant and/or Traviata Trading Enterprises Limited for possession thereof or for the payment or delivery up thereof.
    e. Power to execute all such documents in the name of and on behalf of the Defendant and/or Traviata Trading Enterprises Limited as may be necessary to take possession of, preserve, manage, collect, let, charge and/or sell realisable property.
    f. The Defendant, Traviata Trading Enterprises Limited and all other persons in possession of the assets of the Defendant shall take all such reasonable and necessary steps as may be required by the Receiver to enable the receivership to be conducted and the sale of the Defendant's assets to proceed, including but without prejudice to the generality of the foregoing:—
        (i) Providing the Receiver forthwith upon request by the Receiver with such information and documents relating to the management of the said assets as the Receiver so requires.
        (ii) Signing and delivering to the Receiver in accordance with the instructions of the Receiver letters of authority to financial institutions or any other person or body holding any asset of the Defendant authorising the Receiver to receive information or effect the transfer of any asset to the Receiver's control.
        (iii) Executing and delivering within 4 days of being instructed to do so by the Receiver powers of attorney to the Receiver in such form and in such manner as the Receiver directs.
3. No information provided to the Receiver under the powers conferred on the Receiver by this Order shall be used in evidence in the prosecution of an offence alleged to have been committed by the person required to make that disclosure or by any spouse of that person.
4. The costs of the Receivership shall be paid in the Receivership in accordance with the letter of agreement as exhibited to the witness statement of (insert name) made on the 1st day of November 2009.
5. The Receiver shall act in accordance with the letter of agreement as exhibited to the witness statement of (insert name) made on the 1st day of November 2009 and the Receiver shall supply to the Defendant copies of the accounts and reports supplied to the Revenue and Customs Prosecutions Office in accordance with the said letter of agreement.
6. In this Order the realisable property of the Defendant or the Defendant's assets include but is not limited to the assets specified in the Schedule to this Order.

Effect of this Order on Persons outside England, Wales, Scotland and Northern Ireland

7. The terms of this Order do not affect or concern anyone outside England and Wales, Scotland and Northern Ireland until it is declared enforceable or is enforced by a court in the relevant country and then they are to affect him only to the extent they have been declared enforceable or have been enforced, UNLESS such a person is:

   a. a person to whom this Order is addressed or an officer or an agent appointed by power of attorney of such a person; or

   b. a person who is subject to the jurisdiction of this court or Scotland or Northern Ireland and (i) has written notice of this order at his residence or place of business within the jurisdiction of this court or Scotland and (ii) is able lawfully to prevent acts or omissions outside the jurisdiction of this court or Scotland which constitute or assist in a breach of the terms of this Order.

THE COSTS OF THIS ORDER

8. Costs reserved.

DURATION OF THIS ORDER

9. This Order shall remain in force until is is varied or discharged by further Order of this Court.

INTERPRETATION OF THIS ORDER

10. In this Order "the Defendant's assets" or "assets of the Defendant" means any property in which the Defendant has any interest or to which the Defendant has any right and any property held by any other person to whom the Defendant has made a tainted gift caught by the Proceeds of Crime Act 2002, including but not limited to all property set out in the Schedule hereto.

13. Reference to selling a property includes charging, disposing, transferring, or conveying the legal and/or beneficial interest in the property to the purchaser of it.

14. Reference to the Receiver means [insert name and address of the receiver]

15. Reference to the Defendant means ALFREDO GERMONT.

VARIATION OR DISCHARGE OF THIS ORDER

16. The Defendant (or anyone notified of this Order) may apply to the court at any time to vary or discharge this Order (or so much of it as affects that person), but anyone wishing to do so must first inform the Receiver and the Revenue and Customs Prosecutions Office giving 2 clear days notice in writing.

DATED this the 5th day of November, 2009.

All communications to the Receiver about this Order should be sent to [insert name, address and telephone number of the receiver].

All communications to the Court about this Order should be sent to the Chief Clerk at Southwark Crown Court [insert address]. The offices are open between 10am and 4.30pm Monday to Friday. The telephone number is [insert number].

The address for service and telephone number of [insert name of prosecutor] for any communication in respect of these proceedings is:

[insert address and telephone number of the prosecutor].

SCHEDULE TO THE RECEIVERSHIP ORDER MADE ON 5TH NOVEMBER 2009

(a) The Defendant's interest in a company known as Traviata Trading Enterprises Limited;

(b) Anytown Bank PLC account number 12345678 in the name of the Defendant;

(c) Anytown Bank PLC account number 98765432 in the name of the Defendant and Violetta Valery;

(d) Anytown Bank PLC account number 22334455 in the name of Giorgio Germont;

(e) Anytown Bank PLC account number 66778899 in the name of Traviata Trading Enterprises Limited;

(f) The Defendant's interest in all that property and land known as "The Heights" Marbella, Spain;

(g) The Defendant's interest in a Rolls Royce motor vehicle registered number AG 123 registered in the name of the Defendant;

(h) The Defendant's interest in a motor vessel named "Hispaniola" registered in the names of the Defendant and Violetta Valery;

(i) A racehorse named "Nabucco" registered in the names of the Defendant and Giorgio Germont;

(j) A quantity of cash found on the defendant when arrested totalling £175,000 in Sterling bank notes.

APPENDIX 9

ENFORCEMENT RECEIVERSHIP ORDER

DISOBEDIENCE TO THIS ORDER IS A CONTEMPT OF COURT WHICH IF YOU ARE AN INDIVIDUAL IS PUNISHABLE BY IMPRISONMENT OR IF YOU ARE A BODY CORPORATE IS PUNISHABLE BY SEQUESTRATION OF YOUR ASSETS AND BY IMPRISONMENT OF ANY INDIVIDUAL RESPONSIBLE

IN THE CROWN COURT

SITTING AT SOUTHWARK

Before His Honour Judge Bullingham sitting in Private

No. ....

Dated ....

IN THE MATTER OF ALFREDO GERMONT (Defendant)

AND IN THE MATTER OF THE PROCEEDS OF CRIME ACT 2002

ORDER APPOINTING A RECEIVER OVER THE ASSETS OF THE DEFENDANT

IMPORTANT: NOTICE TO THE DEFENDANT AND ANYONE IN POSSESSION OR CONTROL OF HIS ASSETS OR NAMED IN THIS ORDER

1. This order appoints a Receiver over the assets of the Defendant to enforce the confiscation order made against the Defendant at the Crown Court sitting at Southwark on 7th January, 2010. This means that the Receiver must, subject to the terms of this order, collect the Defendant's assets and sell enough of them to pay the confiscation order.
2. If the Defendant or any person in possession or control of his assets disobeys this order or obstructs the Receiver he or she may be guilty of contempt of court and may be sent to prison or fined or have his assets seized.
3. There is an interpretation section at page 5 of this order.

THE ORDER OF APPOINTMENT

An application was made today by the Revenue and Customs Prosecutions Office to the High Court for the appointment of an Enforcement Receiver over the assets of the Defendant to enforce the Confiscation Order made by the Crown Court at Southwark on 7th January, 2010 in the sum of £1,000,000.

The Revenue and Customs Prosecutions Office and the Defendant were represented by Counsel. Violetta Valery was represented by Counsel.

The Judge read the witness statements of [insert name of prosecutor] made 1st April, 2010, Alfredo Germont made on 10th April, 2006 and Violetta Valery made on 12th April 2010.

As a result of the application THE COURT APPOINTS [insert name of Receiver] to act as an Enforcement Receiver to take possession of, or otherwise deal with, all the assets of the Defendant including, but not limited to, those listed in the Schedule to this Order.

It is Ordered that:

1. The Defendant, Violetta Valery and all other persons having possession of the Defendant's realisable property do forthwith deliver up to the Receiver possession of all such realisable property, together with all deeds, books, documents and papers relating thereto, but without prejudice to the rights of any encumbrancer.

2. The Receiver shall have the following powers without prejudice to any existing powers vested in him whether by statute or otherwise:—

    (a) Power to take possession of, preserve, manage, collect, let, charge and sell the assets of the Defendant;

    (b) Power to apply the net proceeds of the realisation of the Defendant's realisable property towards satisfaction of the Confiscation Order made against the Defendant by the Crown Court sitting at Southwark on 7th January, 2010;

    (c) Power to appoint Solicitors, Counsel, Attorneys, Accountants or other Agents to advise and/or act on behalf of the Receiver in any part of the world;

    (d) Power to discharge all and any costs, charges and expenses of the Receivership out of the assets and/or the proceeds of realisation thereof;

    (e) Power to institute, defend or compromise proceedings in connection with the realisation of the Defendant's assets;

    (f) Power to bring proceedings in the name of or on behalf of the Defendant, within or without the jurisdiction, against any person having possession of the realisable property of the Defendant for possession thereof or the payment or delivery up thereof;

    (g) Power to execute all such documents in the name of and on behalf of the Defendant and Violetta Valery as may be necessary to take possession of, preserve, manage, collect, let, charge and/or sell realisable property;

    (h) After satisfaction of the Confiscation Order power to apply out of the realisable property such sum as is required in satisfaction of the legal costs of then Revenue and Customs Prosecutions Office ordered by Paragraph 9 of this Order;

    (i) Power to settle debts and liabilities of the Defendant from the assets of the Defendant; and

    (j) Power to manage the realisable property of the Defendant including the leasing, letting and/or granting of a licence in any real property forming part of the realisable property.

3. The powers of the Receiver shall not be exercisable in relation to any tainted gifts made by the defendant to Violetta Valery until agreement between the parties or further order and that part of the application by the Revenue and Customs Prosecutions Office for the appointment of a receiver in respect of such gifts do stand adjourned generally with the following directions:—

    (a) Any evidence from Violetta Valery to be served by 3rd May, 2010;

    (b) Any evidence from the Revenue and Customs Prosecutions Office in reply to be served within 14 days thereafter;

    (c) The application be listed on the first open date thereafter on a date fixed through the list office at the convenience of the parties.

4. The Defendant, Violetta Valery and all other persons in possession of the assets of the Defendant shall take all such reasonable and necessary steps as may be required by the Receiver to enable the receivership to be conducted and the sale of the Defendant's assets to proceed, including but without prejudice to the generality of the foregoing-

    (a) Providing the Receiver forthwith upon request by the Receiver with such information and documentation relating to the said assets as the Receiver requires;

    (b) Signing and delivering to the Receiver in accordance with the instructions of the Receiver, Letters of Authority to financial institutions or any other person or body holding any assets of the Defendant authorising the Receiver to receive information or effect the transfer of any asset to the Receiver's control; and

    (c) Executing and delivering within four days of being instructed to do so by the Receiver power of Attorney to the Receiver in such form and in such manner as the Receiver directs.

5. The costs of the receivership shall be paid in the receivership in accordance with the letter of agreement as exhibited to the witness statement of [insert name of prosecutor].

6. The receiver shall act in accordance with the letter of agreement as exhibited to the witness statement of [insert name of prosecutor] and the Receiver shall supply to the Defendant copies of any accounts and reports supplied to the Revenue and Customs Prosecutions Office in accordance with the said letter of agreement.

7. The Receiver shall be allowed remuneration in accordance with the aforesaid letter of agreement.

8. In this order the realisable property of the Defendant or the Defendant's assets includes but is not limited to the assets specified in the Schedule to this Order.

THE COSTS OF THIS ORDER

9. The costs of and occasioned by the orders made on 1st September 2009, 5th November, 2009 and by this application shall be paid by the Defendant to be subject to detailed assessment by a costs judge if not agreed.

EFFECT OF THIS ORDER ON PERSONS OUTSIDE ENGLAND, WALES, SCOTLAND AND NORTHERN IRELAND

10. The terms of this order do not affect or concern anyone outside England, Wales, Scotland and Northern Ireland until it is declared enforceable or is enforced by a court in the relevant country and then they are to affect him only to the extent they have been declared enforceable or have been enforced, UNLESS such person is:

    (a) A person to whom this order is addressed or an officer or an agent appointed by power of attorney of such a person; or

    (b) A person who is subject to the jurisdiction of this court and—

        (i) Has been given written notice of this order at his residence or place of business within the jurisdiction of this court; and

        (ii) Is able lawfully to prevent acts or omissions outside the jurisdiction of this court which constitute or assist in a breach of the terms of this order.

DURATION OF THIS ORDER

11. This order will remain in force until it is varied or discharged by further order of this Court.

INTERPRETATION OF THIS ORDER

12. In this order "the Defendant's assets" or "assets of the Defendant" means any property in which the Defendant has any interest or to which the Defendant has any right and any property held by any person to whom the Defendant has made a tainted gift caught by the Proceeds of Crime Act 2002 including but not limited to all property set out in the Schedule hereto.

13. Reference to selling a property includes charging, disposing transferring or conveying the legal and/or beneficial interest in the property to the purchaser of it.

14. Reference to the receiver means [insert name and address of the receiver].

15. Reference to the defendant mean Alfredo Germont.

DATED this the 15th day of April, 2010.

SCHEDULE

[List all known realisable assets of the Defendant subject to the order]

APPENDIX 10

LETTER OF AGREEMENT BETWEEN PROSECUTOR AND RECEIVER

Dear

RE: REGINA -v- ALFREDO GERMONT

APPOINTMENT OF RECEIVER—PROCEEDS OF CRIME ACT 2002

I am writing to enquire as to whether you would be prepared to act as receiver in the above case of which the Revenue and Customs Prosecutions Office has the conduct under the provisions of the Proceeds of Crime Act 2002.

Mr Germont has been arrested and charged with alleged drug trafficking offences contrary to the Customs and Excise Management Act 1979. He is currently awaiting trial at the Crown Court sitting at Southwark. The Revenue and Customs Prosecutions Office wishes to apply for your appointment as a management receiver under section 48 of the Proceeds of Crime Act 2002 for the purpose of managing and preserving his realisable property pending the determination of these proceedings.

A restraint order was granted over the defendant's assets on 1st September 2009 by His Honour Judge Bullingham. A copy is attached at Annex A to this letter.

Mr Germont owns a company known as Traviata Trading Enterprises Limited which apparently operates as an import and export business. He is now in prison on remand. Traviata Trading Enterprises is in essence a cash and carry business. It is now felt appropriate that this business should be run by an independent person appointed by the court so as to ensure the business is properly managed.

You will appreciate that your appointment is dependent on an order being made by the Crown Court pursuant to section 48 of the Proceeds of Crime Act 2002. On appointment you become an officer of the Court and accordingly draw your authority and powers from the Court. In this connection I would refer you to Part 60 of the Criminal Procedure Rules 2005 which you may find helpful.

As a condition of being nominated by the Revenue and Customs Prosecutions Office your consent to adhere to a standard practice is requested, the provisions of which appear below. We request that you agree to:

INTERPRETATION

For the purposes of this letter, the term "defendant" means the subject of the criminal investigation or the criminal proceedings, the alleged offender or suspect, the restrained party or the offender as the context requires in accordance with the proceeds of crime legislation and other relevant legislation.

CAPEWELL GUIDELINES

You must at appointment and thereafter at every stage of the Receivership consider the list of matters set out as an appendix to the judgment of the Court of Appeal in *Capewell* [2005] EWCA Civ 964; [2005] 1 All ER 900. If you are not able to comply with any of the requirements for the conduct of the receivership there set out, you must notify this office so that the matter can if necessary be referred to the Court.

CONDITIONS OF APPOINTMENT

1. Records

(a) keep separate financial records for each matter or estate in respect of which you are appointed;

(b) keep such other financial records as are required to explain the receipts and payments entered in the records described in paragraph (a) above, including an explanation of the source of any receipts and the destination of any payments, and from day to day enter in those records all the receipts and payments you make;

(c) obtain and keep bank statements relating to any bank account held relevant to your appointment.

2. Produce Accounts

You must produce on demand, without prior notice and at any time, to any officer of the Revenue and Customs Prosecutions Office, HM Revenue and Customs or the Serious Organised Crime Agency if appropriate, any accounts, books or other records kept by yourself in relation to the receivership and this duty to produce and inspect shall extend to:-

(a) production and inspection at your premises; and

(b) production and inspection of any financial records of the kind described in paragraph 1 above; and any such demand may require you to allow an officer of the Revenue and Customs Prosecutions Office or HM Revenue and Customs or of the Serious Organised Crime Agency if appropriate, to remove or take copies of any accounts or financial or administrative documents kept in relation to the administration of the matter or the estate regardless of where they may be situated.

3. Initial and Bi-monthly/Quarterly Reports

You must serve on the Court, RCPO and the defendant 28 days after your appointment as Receiver and [bi-monthly/quarterly thereafter] a report containing the following information:

(a) the work done in the receivership (including a receipts and payments account);

(b) the overall cost of the receivership to date;

(c) a summary and detailed breakdown of the matters to which the overall costs to date relate;

(d) the projected remuneration, costs and expenses until the next report; and

(e) if possible, an estimate of the likely final receivership bill.

Each report shall contain a statement that you believe that your costs are reasonable and proportionate in all the circumstances. If for any reason it is not possible to fulfill any of the above reporting requirements, you should as soon as reasonably practicable give a written explanation of why that is the case, to be served on the Court, RCPO and the defendant.

4. Monthly bills

In addition you must serve on RCPO and the defendant 28 days after your appointment and monthly thereafter, bills/statements of account containing the following information:

(a) all remuneration, costs and expenses incurred in the relevant period;

(b) a summary and detailed breakdown for the matters to which the remuneration and those costs and expenses relate;

(c) projected remuneration, costs and expenses until the next bill; and

(d) if possible an estimate of the final Receivership bill.

Each bill/statement shall include a written request from you to RCPO and the defendant that the amount owing in respect of the relevant period be drawn down by you from restrained funds within your management, in accordance with the provisions contained in paragraph 7 below.

5. Report findings and revised cost estimates

(a) You must report directly to RCPO on all findings and steps taken in the administration of the receivership. Your initial and subsequent reports should always provide to the best of your ability an estimate of the value of the assets which have been taken or can be taken into your possession and you must report at once if there is any substantial diminution of the value of such assets as estimated in any earlier report. You must inform the Court and RCPO and all parties if the final receivership costs are likely to be disproportionate to the proceeds of realisation. This necessarily involves close attention throughout the receivership to the estimated value of the assets comprised in the estate;

(b) You must inform the court, RCPO and the defendant if at any stage it appears to you that it is no longer necessary in order to preserve any part of the assets comprised within the receivership to maintain any particular powers of management. You must also inform the court, RCPO and the defendant if at any time you become of the opinion that it is no longer necessary for you to remain in office, for example, if the assets in the estate can adequately be preserved by way of a restraint order alone; and

(c) In addition:

    (i) if it appears that any initial costs estimate given by you will be exceeded by (insert amount); or

    (ii) that any subsequent costs estimate will be exceeded by (insert amount): or

    (iii) that costs amounting to in excess of (insert amount) not already projected for are likely to be incurred, then

a statement to this effect should be served on the court, RCPO and the defendant immediately.

6. Your Powers

RCPO will be making application for you to be given, inter alia, the following powers:

(a) Power to take possession of, preserve, get in, collect and sell the realisable property;

(b) Power to appoint solicitors, counsel, attorneys, accountants or other agents to advise and/or act on your behalf in any part of the world. However, any instruction of solicitors, counsel or other agent is also subject to obtaining specific prior consent in writing from RCPO unless the Court otherwise so orders;

(c) Power to realise so much of the realisable property as is necessary to meet your remuneration and expenses;

(d) Power to bring proceedings in your own name against any person having possession of realisable property of the defendant for possession thereof of for payment or delivery up thereof;

(e) Power to institute defend or compromise proceedings in connection with the sale of the defendant's assets;

(f) Power to manage the realisable property of the defendant including the leasing, letting and/or granting of a licence in any real property forming part of the said realisable property;

(g) Power to carry on the business currently carried on by the defendant known as Traviata Trading Enterprises Limited;

(h) Power to continue any contract entered into by the said business;

(i) Power to take all steps reasonably necessary to ascertain the beneficial ownership of the property situated at 123 The Esplanade, Torquay, Devon;

(j) Power to enter premises to search for or inspect anything as authorised by the court and to make or obtain a copy, photograph or other record of anything so authorised and to remove anything which you are required or authorised to take possession of in pursuance of the order of the Court; and

(k) Power to receive and read all correspondence (including email) addressed to the defendant or Traviata Trading Enterprises Limited.

7. REMUNERATION AND EXPENSES

(a) It is proposed to seek an order from the Court that your remuneration in this matter should be paid out of the assets (including money at the bank) which come within your control during the course of this receivership;

(b) It is also proposed to seek an order from the Court that your costs and expenses in this matter (to include any legal costs, charges or other disbursements) shall be met from the assets (including money at the bank) which come within your control during the course of this receivership;

(c) Following submission of your monthly bill(s) and before drawing down any remuneration, costs or expenses in respect of that period, you must first obtain the written approval of RCPO (such approval not to be unreasonably withheld) and the defendant to such payment being made and, in default of agreement, your entitlement to draw down such remuneration, costs and expenses shall be determined by the Court;

(d) In all cases RCPO reserves the right to insist upon a detailed assessment of all your remuneration, costs and expenses and the cost to you of any lawyers or agents you may instruct;

(e) If lawyers or other agents are instructed by you, you should ask for monthly bills or fee notes. You should endeavour to keep a close control on such fees and satisfy yourself that the legal or other agency costs being incurred are reasonable and proportionate in the circumstances;

(f) Agreement by RCPO to any monthly payments shall not operate as a waiver of its right to require a detailed assessment of your remuneration, costs and expenses (including disbursements to solicitors, agents or other persons instructed by you in connection with the receivership) at a later stage and shall not prejudice any right RCPO may have to claim repayment of such sums to the estate in the event the same would have been payable under the insurance referred to in paragraph 8 below;

(g) It is proposed to seek a provision in the order of appointment that you should be allowed to draw remuneration and pay any expenses from any realisations every calendar month provided that monthly bills/statements of account for the relevant period have been submitted to and approved by RCPO in advance, such payments being drawn down within 28 days of the approval of RCPO being given;

(h) RCPO requires, as provided in paragraph 4 above, to the extent that the same is permitted under the order of appointment or any further order of the Court, that you submit bills/interim statements of account every calendar month and should draw down payment in the amount approved by RCPO and the defendant from the funds then held by you in the receivership within two weeks of such approval. In the event that there are insufficient funds available for payment, you should consult with RCPO and with the defendant as to the realisation of property comprised in the receivership for the payment of interim costs;

(i) Subject to the provisos set out below, should your reasonable remuneration, costs and expenses exceed the sum realised, RCPO is prepared to indemnify you to the extent of a sum inclusive of your remuneration, costs and expenses up to a sum of (insert amount) although exclusive of VAT, and less any sums available to you from the property under your management. The indemnity is conditional on the following provisions:

  (a) It is your responsibility to inform RCPO immediately if the value of the assets comprised in the estate may become insufficient to cover your remuneration, costs and expenses and your right to indemnity is conditional on performance by you of this obligation;

  (b) It is also a condition of recovery under this indemnity that any work done or expenses incurred which fall within the scope of the indemnity must have been notified to RCPO within two calendar months of the date on which the work was done or the expenditure incurred;

  (c) It is also a condition of such recovery that your render a bill of your final remuneration, costs and expenses within 28 days of the discharge of the receivership in respect of work done to the date of discharge;

  (d) RCPO will only indemnify you as above if you have complied with any requirement it may make that you should first seek to obtain payment by the use of funds or realisation of property comprised within the receivership (including steps to enforce your lien over such funds or property);

(e) RCPO will only indemnify you as above in respect of additional remuneration, costs and expenses incurred after you become aware that you might need to call on this indemnity if such additional remuneration, costs and expenditure has been expressly authorised in writing by RCPO before being incurred; and

(f) RCPO may require you to permit it (subject to approval of the court where necessary) to conduct or defend in your name any litigation which may give rise to such additional remuneration, costs and expenditure (including the settlement of the litigation).

These provisions apply to remuneration, costs and expenditure arising both before and after the discharge of the receivership (including costs and expenditure incurred in enforcing any lien or claim by you for remuneration against assets comprised in the estate).

NOTE: In the case where the defendant has absconded or absented himself from proceedings the Court will be asked to make provision that you be entitled to apply for an order permitting you to draw periodic sums in respect of your remuneration, costs and expenses until further order without having on each such occasion to make a specific application to the court provided that on each such occasion you have taken reasonable steps to contact the defendant through his solicitors and at his last known address.

8. SECURITY

You should confirm in writing prior to accepting this appointment that you have sufficient security in place to cover your liability for your acts and omissions as a receiver. You should confirm in writing that you have insurance in place which covers the legal expenses incurred by you in respect of litigation brought by you (including litigation to enforce any lien or secure your remuneration) or brought against you by the defendant or any other person and also covers any costs awarded against you in any proceedings whether by yourself, the defendant or any other person.

In addition, the court may direct that you give such security as it determines or file and serve evidence of your security.

9. CONFIDENTIALITY

(a) You will undertake to abide and procure that any of your employees, servants and agents abide by the provisions of:—
   (i) the Official Secrets Acts 1911 to 1989; and
   (ii) section 182 of the Finance Act, 1989.

(b) You will keep secret and not disclose and shall procure that your employees, servants and/or agents keep secret and do not disclose any information of a confidential nature obtained by you by reason of the receivership except information which is in the public domain otherwise than by failure by yourself to comply with the requirement to retain confidentiality aforesaid.

(c) the duty described in paragraph 9(b) to keep secret and prohibiting the disclosure of confidential information shall not apply to disclosure of such information to an employees, servant and/or agent who needs to be in possession of that information to enable yourself as Receiver to discharge and fulfil your duties under the receivership and provided always that such disclosure is made in confidence and is subject to a duty of confidence which is enforceable in law by the Receiver in the event of a threatened or actual breach.

(d) You will ensure that all your employees, servants and/or agents so far as appropriate, are aware of, and comply with the requirements in paragraphs 9 (a) & (b) and in any instance of a threatened or actual breach of confidence mentioned in paragraphs 9 (b) & (c) you will at your own cost apply for appropriate civil process, relief and remedy, to protect the confidentiality of the information or restrict its further dissemination and disclosure and, shall inform and keep fully informed the

Revenue and Customs Prosecutions Office of any such instance and of the proceedings and their progress.

(e) The duty of confidentiality shall not determine with the conclusion of the receivership.

(f) Further, in paragraph 9(b) "information of a confidential nature obtained by you by reason of the receivership" includes information coming to the knowledge of yourself or your employees, servants, agents and/or sub-contractors prior to your formal appointment as Receiver, by virtue of any dealings with the Revenue and Customs Prosecutions Office including visits and/or meetings with members of the Revenue and Customs Prosecutions Office and/or investigating officers in the employ of HM Revenue and Customs or the Serious Organised Crime Agency.

10. Variation of Standard Provisions

Any variation of these provisions must be consented to in writing by the Revenue and Customs Prosecutions Office.

11. Discharge

Upon concluding the receivership you will inform the Revenue and Customs Prosecutions Office and, in conjunction with that Office, apply to the Crown Court for your discharge. Your powers to receiver property cease upon discharge of the receivership but your obligations to account and your rights to enforce payment of your remuneration, costs and expenses against property comprised within the estate and to exercise any lien will continue.

12. Witness statement and draft order

Your attention is drawn to the witness statement which RCPO intend to submit to the Court in support of its application for your appointment and to the terms of the draft order.

13. Contents of letter of acceptance

Finally, we would require a letter from you confirming acceptance of the terms of this proposed appointment together with the following information:

(a) a table setting out the hourly rates of each grade of fee earner you propose to employ in the conduct of the receivership; and

(b) if it is possible to do so, an estimate of how much the Receivership is likely to cost; alternatively a statement by you that it is not possible to estimate the likely cost of the Receivership together with an explanation of why this is not possible.

I am most grateful for your assistance in this matter and look forward to hearing from you at your earliest convenience.

Yours sincerely

[Prosecutor]

VARIATION OF RESTRAINT ORDER

DISOBEDIENCE OF THIS ORDER IS A CONTEMPT OF COURT WHICH IF YOU ARE AN INDIVIDUAL IS PUNISHABLE BY IMPRISONMENT OR IF YOU ARE A BODY CORPORATE IS PUNISHABLE BY SEQUESTRATION OF YOUR ASSETS AND BY IMPRISONMENT OF ANY INDIVIDUAL RESPONSIBLE

IN THE CROWN COURT

SITTING AT SOUTHWARK

Before His Honour Judge Bullingham sitting in Private

No. ....

Dated ....

IN THE MATTER OF ALFREDO GERMONT (Defendant)

AND

IN THE MATTER OF THE PROCEEDS OF CRIME ACT 2002

ORDER

UPON HEARING Counsel for the Defendant and Counsel for the Revenue and Customs Prosecutions Office.

AND UPON READING the witness statement of Alfredo Germont made on the 30th day of November, 2009.

IT IS ORDERED THAT

1. The restraint order made by His Honour Judge Bullingham on the 1st day of September, 2009 ("the Restraint Order") be varied to the following extent—
   (a) The amount payable to the Defendant by way of general living expenses pursuant to paragraph 19 of the order be increased from £250 per week to £350 per week, to be paid from account number 12345678 held in the name of the Defendant at Anytown Bank PLC; and
   (b) The period for compliance with paragraph 12 of the Order be extended to 1600 hours on 20th December 2009.
2. The Defendant has permission to sell all that property and land known as "Traviata" 123 The Esplanade, Torquay, Devon ("the property")

PROVIDED THAT

(i) The Defendant must provide the Revenue and Customs Prosecutions Office with two independent valuations in respect of the property. The Revenue and Customs Prosecutions Office reserves the right to obtain further independent professional property valuations if it wishes to verify those provided by the the Defendant;

(ii) The Defendant must not sell the property for an amount less than its market value as confirmed by the highest valuation obtained under sub-paragraph (i) above;

(iii) The Defendant shall not pay any fees and charges from the gross sum obtained from the sale of the property (including but not limited to legal fees, agents fees, search fees and charges) without obtaining the prior written consent of the Revenue and Customs Prosecutions Office. The Revenue and Customs Prosecutions Office may withhold its consent for the payment of fees and charges that are unreasonable or are improperly incurred;

(iv) The Defendant will instruct Messrs. Thorn and Partners, Solicitors, 1a High Street, Torquay, Devon to act for him on the sale of the property and undertakes not to terminate their retainer in respect thereof save with the written consent of the Revenue and Customs Prosecutions Office or the permission of the court;

(v) The gross proceeds of the sale of the property less:
   a. The total amount required to discharge any mortgages and charges that were registered in relation to the property prior to 1st September 2009; and
   b. The amount required to pay any fees and/or charges for which the prior consent of the Revenue and Customs Prosecutions Office has been obtained in accordance with sub-paragraph (iii) above

must be paid into an interest bearing account in the name of Messrs. Thorn and Co. The net proceeds will be subject to the terms of the restraint order.

(vi) Within two working days of receiving the net proceeds of sale into their interest bearing account, Messrs. Thorn and Co will inform the Revenue and Customs Prosecutions Office in writing of the date on which the net proceeds of sale were received and the amount of those proceeds. Messrs. Thorn and Co will also provide the Revenue and Customs Prosecutions Office with a completion statement in relation to the said sale.

(vii) Within three working days of the Revenue and Customs Prosecutions Office receiving written confirmation that the net proceeds of sale have been paid into an interest bearing account subject to the terms of the restraint order, the Revenue and Customs Prosecutions Office will apply to HM Land Registry for the removal of the restriction registered against the property.

3. The restraint order will remain in force in relation to the net proceeds of sale pending the conclusion of these proceedings.

4. Paragraph 2 of this Order will cease to have effect if the sale of the property does not take place by 4pm on 31st January, 2009.

5. Costs reserved.

DATED this the second day of December, 2009.

APPENDIX 12

CERTIFICATE OF INADEQUACY

Claim DTA No. 1234 of 2005

IN THE HIGH COURT OF JUSTICE
QUEEN'S BENCH DIVISION
Administrative Court

Before the Honourable Mr Justice Vosper sitting in Private

IN THE MATTER OF ALFREDO GERMONT (Defendant)

AND

IN THE MATTER OF THE DRUG TRAFFICKING ACT 1994

ORDER

UPON HEARING Counsel for the Defendant and Counsel for the Revenue and Customs Prosecutions Office

AND UPON READING the witness statement of Alfredo Germont made on 1st October, 2007.

IT IS CERTIFIED THAT the value of the Defendant's realisable property is inadequate for the payment of the amount remaining to be recovered pursuant to the confiscation order ("the order") made against him in the sum of £1,000,000 by the Crown Court sitting at Southwark on 15th January, 2010 for the following reasons:—

(a) By order of this Honourable Court made on 30th January, 2010 it was determined that Violetta Valery had a 50% interest in all that property and land known as "Traviata", 123 Esplanade, Torquay and in consequence thereof only 50% of the proceeds of sale were available to meet the order; and

(b) The Crown Court in making the order determined that the Defendant's Rolls Royce motor vehicle registration number AG 123 was valued at £75,000 whereas upon sale by the Receiver realised only £35,750.

There be no order for costs.

DATED this the 14th day of June, 2010.

APPENDIX 13

EXTRACT FROM PRACTICE DIRECTION ON POCA PARTS 5 AND 8

SECTION III—APPLICATIONS UNDER PART 8 OF THE ACT IN RESPECT OF CIVIL RECOVERY INVESTIGATIONS AND DETAINED CASH INVESTIGATIONS

How to apply for an order or warrant

8.1

An application for an order or warrant under Part 8 of the Act in connection with a civil recovery investigation or (where applicable) a detained cash investigation must be made—

(1) to a High Court judge;
(2) by filing an application notice.

8.2

The application may be made without notice.

Confidentiality of court documents

9.1

CPR rules 5.4, 5.4B and 5.4C do not apply to an application under Part 8 of the Act, and paragraphs 9.2 and 9.3 below have effect in its place.

9.2

When an application is issued, the court file will be marked 'Not for disclosure' and, unless a High Court judge grants permission, the court records relating to the application (including the application notice, documents filed in support, and any order or warrant that is made) will not be made available by the court for any person to inspect or copy, either before or after the hearing of the application.

9.3

An application for permission under paragraph 9.2 must be made on notice to the appropriate officer in accordance with CPR Part 23.

(CPR rule 23.7(1) requires a copy of the application notice to be served as soon as practicable after it is filed, and in any event at least 3 days before the court is to deal with the application.)

Application notice and evidence

10.1

The application must be supported by written evidence, which must be filed with the application notice.

10.2

The evidence must set out all the matters on which the appropriate officer relies in support of the application, including any matters required to be stated by the relevant sections of the Act, and all material facts of which the court should be made aware.

10.3

There must also be filed with the application notice a draft of the order sought. This should if possible also be supplied to the court on disk in a form compatible with the word processing software used by the court.

Hearing of the application

11.1

The application will be heard and determined in private, unless the judge hearing it directs otherwise.

Variation or discharge of order or warrant

12.1

An application to vary or discharge an order or warrant may be made by—

(1) the appropriate officer; or
(2) any person affected by the order or warrant.

12.2

An application under paragraph 12.1 to stop an order or warrant from being executed must be made immediately upon it being served.

12.3

A person applying to vary or discharge a warrant must first inform the appropriate officer that he is making the application.

12.4

The application should be made to the judge who made the order or issued the warrant or, if he is not available, to another High Court judge.

EXTRACT FROM PRACTICE DIRECTION ON POCA PARTS 5 AND 8

SECTION IV—FURTHER PROVISIONS ABOUT SPECIFIC APPLICATIONS UNDER PART 8 OF THE ACT

Production order

13.1

The application notice must name as a respondent the person believed to be in possession or control of the material in relation to which a production order is sought.

13.2

The application notice must specify—

(1) whether the application is for an order under paragraph (a) or (b) of section 345(4) of the Act;
(2) the material, or description of material, in relation to which the order is sought; and
(3) the person who is believed to be in possession or control of the material.

13.3

An application under section 347 of the Act for an order to grant entry may be made either—

(1) together with an application for a production order; or
(2) by separate application, after a production order has been made.

13.4

An application notice for an order to grant entry must—

(1) specify the premises in relation to which the order is sought; and
(2) be supported by written evidence explaining why the order is needed.

13.5

A production order, or an order to grant entry, must contain a statement of the right of any person affected by the order to apply to vary or discharge the order.

Search and seizure warrant

14.1

The application notice should name as the respondent the occupier of the premises to be subject to the warrant, if known.

14.2

The evidence in support of the application must state—

(1) the matters relied on by the appropriate officer to show that one of the requirements in section 352(6) of the Act for the issue of a warrant is satisfied;
(2) details of the premises to be subject to the warrant, and of the possible occupier or occupiers of those premises; and

(3) the name and position of the member of the staff of the appropriate officer who it is intended will execute the warrant.

14.3

There must be filed with the application notice drafts of—

(1) the warrant; and
(2) a written undertaking by the person who is to execute the warrant to comply with paragraph 13.8 of this practice direction.

14.4

A search and seizure warrant must—

(1) specify the statutory power under which it is issued and, unless the court orders otherwise, give an indication of the nature of the investigation in respect of which it is issued;
(2) state the address or other identification of the premises to be subject to the warrant;
(3) state the name of the member of the staff of the appropriate officer who is authorised to execute the warrant;
(4) set out the action which the warrant authorises the person executing it to take under the relevant sections of the Act;
(5) give the date on which the warrant is issued;
(6) include a statement that the warrant continues in force until the end of the period of one month beginning with the day on which it is issued; and
(7) contain a statement of the right of any person affected by the order to apply to discharge or vary the order.

14.5

An example of a search and seizure warrant is annexed to this practice direction. This example may be modified as appropriate in any particular case.

14.6

Rule 40.2 applies to a search and seizure warrant.

(CPR rule 40.2 requires every judgment or order to state the name and judicial title of the person making it, to bear the date on which it is given or made, and to be sealed by the court.)

14.7

Upon the issue of a warrant the court will provide to the appropriate officer—

(1) the sealed warrant; and
(2) a copy of it for service on the occupier or person in charge of the premises subject to the warrant.

14.8

A person attending premises to execute a warrant must, if the premises are occupied produce the warrant on arrival at the premises, and as soon as possible thereafter personally serve a copy of the warrant and an explanatory notice on the occupier or the person appearing to him to be in charge of the premises.

14.9

The person executing the warrant must also comply with any order which the court may make for service of any other documents relating to the application.

Disclosure order

15.1

The application notice should normally name as respondents the persons on whom the appropriate officer intends to serve notices under the disclosure order sought.

15.2

A disclosure order must—

(1) give an indication of the nature of the investigation for the purposes of which the order is made;
(2) set out the action which the order authorises the appropriate officer to take in accordance with section 357(4) of the Act;
(3) contain a statement of—

    (a) the offences relating to disclosure orders under section 359 of the Act; and
    (b) the right of any person affected by the order to apply to discharge or vary the order.

15.3

Where, pursuant to a disclosure order, the appropriate officer gives to any person a notice under section 357(4) of the Act, he must also at the same time serve on that person a copy of the disclosure order.

Customer information order

16.1

The application notice should normally (unless it is impracticable to do so because they are too numerous) name as respondents the financial institution or institutions to which it is proposed that an order should apply.

16.2

A customer information order must—

(1) specify the financial institution, or description of financial institutions, to which it applies;
(2) state the name of the person in relation to whom customer information is to be given, and any other details to identify that person;
(3) contain a statement of—

    (a) the offences relating to disclosure orders under section 366 of the Act; and
    (b) the right of any person affected by the order to apply to discharge or vary the order.

16.3

Where, pursuant to a customer information order, the appropriate officer gives to a financial institution a notice to provide customer information, he must also at the same time serve a copy of the order on that institution.

Account monitoring order

17.1

The application notice must name as a respondent the financial institution against which an account monitoring order is sought.

17.2

The application notice must—

(1) state the matters required by section 370(2) and (3) of the Act; and
(2) give details of—

(a) the person whose account or accounts the application relates to;

(b) each account or description of accounts in relation to which the order is sought, including if known the number of each account and the branch at which it is held;

(c) the information sought about the account or accounts;

(d) the period for which the order is sought; and

(e) the manner in which, and the frequency with which, it is proposed that the financial institution should provide account information during that period.

17.3

An account monitoring order must contain a statement of the right of any person affected by the order to apply to vary or discharge the order.

INTERIM RECEIVING ORDER UNDER SECTION 246 OF POCA 2002

CO No. 123 of 2010

IN THE HIGH COURT OF JUSTICE
QUEEN'S BENCH DIVISION

Before the Honourable Mr Justice Bellini sitting in Private

IN THE MATTER OF MR ALFREDO GERMONT (Respondent)

AND

IN THE MATTER OF THE PROCEEDS OF CRIME ACT 2002

INTERIM RECEIVING ORDER

Penal Notice

IF ALFREDO GERMONT FAILS TO COMPLY WITH THE TERMS OF THIS ORDER HE MAY BE HELD IN CONTEMPT OF COURT FOR WHICH HE MAY BE FINED AND BE IMPRISONED OR HAVE HIS ASSETS SEIZED

ANY OTHER PERSON WHO KNOWS OF THIS ORDER AND DOES ANYTHING WHICH HELPS OR PERMITS ALFREDO GERMONT TO BREACH THE TERMS OF THIS ORDER MAY ALSO BE HELD TO BE IN CONTEMPT OF COURT AND MAY BE IMPRISONED, FINED OR HAVE THEIR ASSETS SEIZED.

To: ALFREDO GERMONT

An application having been made to the High Court pursuant to section 246 of the Proceeds of Crime Act 2002 by the Director of the Serious Organised Crime Agency ("the Director").

And upon reading the witness statement of **Tony Foot** dated 22 July 2010,

And Upon Hearing Counsel for the Director,

THE COURT IS SATISFIED that the relevant requirements for making an interim receiving order are fulfilled.

Important Notice

TO THE RESPONDENT ALFREDO GERMONT AND TO ANYONE IN POSSESSION OR CONTROL OF THE RESPONDENTS PROPERTY

A. This Order appoints an Interim Receiver over certain property of the Respondents, limited to the property specified in Schedule 2 to this Order. This Order prohibits the Respondents from dealing with that property.
B. The Order is subject to the exclusions at the end of this Order.
C. You should read all of this Order carefully. You are advised to consult a solicitor as soon as possible.

D. You may be entitled to Community Legal Service Funding in respect of this Order. You are referred to section 6 of the Access to Justice Act 1999 and the Guidance to solicitors and applicants seeking Community Legal Service funding for proceedings under the Proceeds of Crime Act 2002 involving the Serious Organised Crime Agency.

E. Subject to the provisions of section 245C of the Proceeds of Crime Act 2002 and the Proceeds of Crime Act 2002 (Legal Expenses in Civil Recovery Proceedings) Regulations 2005, you may be entitled to the release of restrained funds to pay for legal representation in connection with this Order. A request for the release of a sum in respect of reasonable legal expenses must be made in writing to the Director of the Serious Organised Crime Agency and before any release can be made certain conditions must be fulfilled. You and your legal adviser are referred to Part 3 of the Proceeds of Crime Act 2002 (Legal Expenses in Civil Recovery Proceedings) Regulations 2005 (SI 3382 of 2005).

F. Further to the provisions of section 245C of the Proceeds of Crime Act 2002, you may be entitled to the release of restrained funds to meet your reasonable living expenses or to carry on any trade, business, profession or occupation. A request for the release of property or an asset to meet reasonable living expenses or to carry on any trade, business, profession or occupation can either be made to the Director of the Serious Organised Crime Agency, in the first instance or to the Court pursuant to section 245B of the Proceeds of Crime Act 2002.

G. You have a right to ask this Court to vary or discharge this Order.

H. If the Respondent or any person in possession or control of the property specified in Schedule 2 to this Order disobeys this Order or obstructs the Receiver he or she may be guilty of contempt of court and may be sent to prison or fined or have their assets seized.

I. There is an interpretation section at page x of this Order.

AS A RESULT OF THE APPLICATION THE COURT MAKES THE FOLLOWING ORDERS: —

The Order of Appointment:

1. THE COURT APPOINTS Ivan I. Dere as Interim Receiver ("the Receiver") of the property listed in Schedule 2 to this Order.

Order for the detention, custody, preservation and possession of property:

2. The Respondent must not:
   (i) remove from England and Wales any Schedule 2 property which is in England and Wales whether in their own name or not and whether solely or jointly owned; or
   (ii) in any way dispose of or deal with or diminish the value of any of the Schedule 2 property whether it is in or outside England and Wales whether in the Respondents own name or not and whether solely or jointly owned.

3. Pursuant to section 250 of the Proceeds of Crime Act 2002, the Respondent shall as soon as reasonably practicable:

   (i) on the demand in writing of the Receiver co-operate in procuring the transfer of the monies specified as item iv of Schedule 2 to this Order to such account as is specified by the Receiver;
   (ii) bring such property as is specified by the Receiver to the offices of the Receiver at Blueberry House, Strawberry Lane, London N1 1AA or to such other place as the Receiver specifies or place it in the custody of the Receiver; and
   (iii) do anything he/she is reasonably required to do by the Receiver for the preservation of the property.

4. Unless otherwise agreed in writing by the Receiver, the Respondent and all other persons having possession of the Schedule 2 property shall forthwith deliver up to the Receiver possession of all such assets, together with all deeds, books, documents and papers relating thereto, but without prejudice to the rights of any encumbrancer and SAVE THAT any person in lawful occupation of any real property is not required, until further order, to give physical possession of the real property to the Receiver.

Disclosure:

5. Within 72 hours of personal service of this order, to the best of his ability, the Respondent must inform the Receiver in writing of all of his assets worldwide exceeding £1000 in value whether in his own name or not and whether solely or jointly owned, giving the value, location and details of all of his assets. The Respondent must then provide this information in a witness statement certified by a statement of truth within 14 days after being personally served with this Order.

6. Nothing in this Order shall make inadmissible any disclosure made by the Respondent in any proceedings for perjury relating to that disclosure.

7. If the provision of the information required by paragraph 5 is likely to incriminate the Respondent, he may be entitled to refuse to provide it, but he is recommended to take legal advice before refusing to provide the information. Wrongful refusal to provide the information is a contempt of court and may render the Respondent liable to be imprisoned, fined or have his assets seized.

Powers of the Receiver:

8. In accordance with Schedule 6 to the Proceeds of Crime Act 2002, the Receiver shall have the following powers without prejudice to any existing powers vested in him whether by statute or otherwise:-

  (i) Power to seize property to which this Order applies;

  (ii) Power to take possession of and manage any property to which this Order applies;

  (iii) Power to enter and search any premises in the United Kingdom in which the Receiver believes or has reasonable grounds to believe that material relevant to his duties under the Act may be located and take the following steps:

    (a) carry out a search for or inspection of anything described in this Order, which shall include, but not be limited to, Suite 1, 2 Commercial Road, Torquay TQ1 1RR;

    (b) to have Police assistance, if required, when carrying out service of this Order and a search for or inspection of anything described in this Order;

    (c) make or obtain a copy, photograph or other record of anything so described in this Order;

    (d) remove anything which he is entitled to take possession of in pursuance of this Order or which may be required as evidence in proceedings for civil recovery;

    (e) effect and maintain insurance.

  (iv) Power to appoint solicitors, counsel, attorneys, accountants or other agents to advise and/or act on behalf of the Receiver in any part of the world;

  (v) Power to bring proceedings in the name of or on behalf of the Respondent and any other person within or without the jurisdiction, against any person having possession of the property of the Respondent for possession thereof or for the payment or delivery up thereof;

  (vi) Power to execute all such documents in the name of and on behalf of the Respondent and any other person as may be necessary to manage Schedule 2 property;

  (vii) Power to require the Respondent, and all other persons in possession of the property of the Respondent to take all such reasonable and necessary steps as may be required by the Receiver to enable the receivership to be conducted, including but without prejudice to the generality of the foregoing:

    (a) providing the Receiver forthwith upon request by the Receiver with such information and documents including any questions put to them by the Receiver relating to the management of the said property as the Receiver so requires;

    (b) to sign and deliver to the Receiver in accordance with the instructions of the Receiver letters of authority to financial institutions or any other person or body holding any asset of the Respondent authorising the Receiver to receive information or effect the transfer of any such property to the Receiver's control;

    (c) to execute and deliver within 4 days of being instructed to do so by the Receiver power of attorney to the Receiver in such form and in such manner as the Receiver directs.

9. Nothing in this Order shall prevent any person claiming legal professional privilege in relation to the matters set out therein, particularly in relation to communications between the legal adviser and his or her client, or communications made in connection with or in contemplation of legal proceedings and for the purposes of those proceedings. However in such circumstances any person claiming legal professional privilege must still give to the Receiver access to any premises he may enter in pursuance of paragraph 8 and give to the Receiver any assistance he may require pursuant to this order.

Duties of the Receiver:

10. Pursuant to section 247(2)(a) of the Proceeds of Crime Act 2002, the Receiver shall consider such information and documents as are obtained by him in pursuance of this Order to establish whether or not the Schedule 2 property is recoverable property or associated property, and if the latter, to what extent the property comprises associated property.

11. Pursuant to section 247(2)(b) of the Proceeds of Crime Act 2002, the Receiver shall take all reasonable and necessary steps to establish whether or not any other property is recoverable property (in relation to the same unlawful conduct), and if it is, who holds it.

12. In accordance with section 255(1) of the Proceeds of Crime Act 2002, the Receiver must inform the Director and this Honourable Court as soon as reasonably practicable if he thinks that:
    (i) any property to which the Order applies by virtue of a claim that it is recoverable property is not recoverable property;
    (ii) any property to which this Order applies by virtue of a claim that it is associated property is not associated property;
    (iii) any property to which the Order does not apply is recoverable property (in relation to the same unlawful conduct) or associated property; or
    (iv) any property to which the Order applies is held by a person who is different from the person it is claimed holds it, or if he thinks that there has been a material change in circumstances.

13. In accordance with section 255(2) of the Proceeds of Crime Act 2002, the Receiver shall provide to this Honourable Court a report of his findings and shall serve copies of that report on the Director of the Serious Organised Crime Agency and on any other person who holds any property to which the Order applies or who may otherwise be affected by the report.

Orders relating to service:

14. Permission is given to the Serious Organised Crime Agency to comply with their undertaking relating to service on the Respondent by serving a copy of the Application Notice, the witness statement of Tony Foot dated 1 July 2010, and this Order on the last known solicitors for the Respondent, namely Messrs Tryitt and Sea, Green House, Blue Road, Torquay TQ1 1LN.

The Receiver's liability:

15. If the Receiver deals with any property which is not property to which this Order applies, and at the time he deals with the property he believes on reasonable grounds that he is entitled to do so in pursuance of the Order, the Receiver will not be liable to any person in respect of any loss or damage resulting from his dealing with the property except so far as the loss or damage is caused by his negligence.

16. The Receiver is required to have sufficient security or insurance to cover any liability for their acts or omissions as a Receiver. If the Receiver has appropriate insolvency practitioners' bond or guarantee, then no specific order concerning the security will be necessary from the Court. If, however, the insurance comes in some other form, then provided this form is acceptable, the Court will need to make some direction that the security can be given in this other form.

The effect of this Order:

17. A person who is an individual who is ordered not to do something must not do it himself or herself or in any other way. He or she must not do it through others acting on his or her behalf or on his or her instructions or with his or her encouragement.

18. A person which is a corporation and which is ordered not to do something must not do it by its directors, officers, employees or agents or in any other way.

19. Pursuant to Schedule 6(2) to the Proceeds of Crime Act 2002, no answer given by a person to the Receiver in pursuance of paragraph 6 above shall be used in evidence in criminal proceedings against the person, SAVE:

    (i) on a prosecution for an offence under section 5 of the Perjury Act 1911, section 44(2) of the Criminal Law (Consolidation) (Scotland) Act 1995 or Article 10 of the Perjury (Northern Ireland) Order 1979 (false statements); or

    (ii) on a prosecution for some other offence where, in giving evidence, he or she makes a statement inconsistent with it. (But an answer may not be used against a person unless evidence relating to it is adduced, or a question relating to it is asked, by him or her or on his or her behalf in the proceedings arising out of the prosecution).

Third parties:

20. It is a contempt of court for any person notified of this Order knowingly to assist in or permit a breach of this Order. Any person doing so may be sent to prison, fined or have his or her assets seized. He or she is also at risk of being prosecuted for a money-laundering offence.

The effect of this Order on persons outside England, Wales and Scotland

21. The terms of this Order do not affect or concern anyone outside England, Wales and Scotland until it is declared enforceable or is enforced by a court in the relevant country and then they are to affect him or her only to the extent they have been declared enforceable or have been enforced, UNLESS such person is:

    (i) a person to whom this Order is addressed or an officer or an agent appointed by power of attorney of such a person; or

    (ii) a person who is subject to the jurisdiction of this court and (i) has been given written notice of this Order at his or her residence or place of business within the jurisdiction of this court and (ii) is able lawfully to prevent acts or omissions outside the jurisdiction of this court which constitute or assist in a breach of the terms of this Order.

Undertakings:

22. The Director gives to the Court the undertakings set out in Schedule 1 to this Order.

Duration of this Order:

23. This Order will remain in force until it is varied or discharged by further Order of this court.

Variation or discharge of this Order:

24. The Respondent (or anyone notified of or affected by this Order) may apply to the court at any time to vary or discharge this Order (or so much of it as affects that person), but anyone wishing to do so must first inform the Serious Organised Crime Agency giving at least 2 clear days' notice in writing.

The costs of the Receivership:

25. The Receiver may charge for his services and shall prepare and serve accounts in accordance with the letter of nomination as exhibited to the witness statement of Tony Foot dated 1 July 2010.

The costs of this Order:

26. The costs of this Order are reserved.

Communications with the Receiver:

27. All communications to the Receiver about this Order should be sent to Ivan I. Dere of Blueberry House, Strawberry Lane, London N1 1AA, telephone number 0207 000 1111 quoting the Respondent's name.

Communications with the Serious Organised Crime Agency:

28. All communication to the Director of the Serious Organised Crime Agency about this Order should be sent to the Serious Organised Crime Agency, PO Box 8000, London, SE11 5EN, telephone number 0370 496 7622, quoting reference: **GERMONT**.

Communications with the Court:

29. All communication to the Court about this Order should be sent to Administrative Crown Office, Royal Courts of Justice, Strand, London, WC2A 2LL quoting the case number. The office is open between 10am and 4:30pm Monday to Friday. The telephone number is 020 7947 6000.

Interpretation of this Order:

30. "Property" is all property wherever situated and includes:
    (i) money;
    (ii) all forms of property, real or personal, heritable or moveable; and
    (iii) things in action and other intangible or incorporeal property.

31. Any reference to a person's property (whether expressed as a reference to the property he or she holds or otherwise) is to be read as follows:
    (i) In relation to land, it is a reference to any interest which he or she holds in the land.
    (ii) In relation to property other than land, it is a reference –
        (a) to the property (if it belongs to him or her), or
        (b) to any other interest which he or she holds in the property.

32. "The Respondents recoverable property" or "recoverable property of the Respondent" means property that has been obtained through unlawful conduct, or property that represents such property.

33. "Associated property" means property of any of the following descriptions (including property held by the Respondent) which is not itself recoverable property –
    (i) any interest in the recoverable property,
    (ii) any other interest in the property in which the recoverable property subsists,
    (iii) if the recoverable property is a tenancy in common, the tenancy of the other tenant,
    (iv) if (in Scotland) the recoverable property is owned in common, the interest of the other owner,
    (v) if the recoverable property is part of a larger, but not a separate part, the remainder of that property.

34. "Unlawful conduct" includes conduct occurring in any part of the United Kingdom which is unlawful under the criminal law of that part.

35. The power to 'manage any property' includes:
    (i) selling or otherwise disposing of assets comprised in the property which are perishable or which ought to be disposed of before their value diminishes;
    (ii) where the property comprises assets of a trade or business, carrying on, or arranging for another to carry on, the trade or business;
    (iii) incurring capital expenditure in respect of the property;
    (iv) in respect of any illegitimate business, ceasing the operation of that business.

36. "Dealing" with property includes (1) disposing of it, (2) removing it from the United Kingdom, (3) relinquishing or cancelling or varying any signing authority over any bank accounts over which he has signing authority or in respect of which he is a signatory on the mandate irrespective of whether there is any money in such accounts, (4) relinquishing or cancelling or varying any power of attorney, directorship, office as trustee or other arrangement pursuant to which he has control of any asset which is not held in his name, or (5) relinquishing, cancelling or varying any arrangements whereby he is empowered to deal with assets which are not in his own name.

37. "Document" means anything in which information of any description is recorded.

38. Reference to selling or otherwise disposing of assets comprised in the property which are perishable, or which ought to be disposed of before their value diminishes, includes charging, disposing, transferring or conveying the legal and/or beneficial interest in the property to the purchaser of it.

39. "Act" refers to the Proceeds of Crime Act 2002.

Reference to the Receiver means:

Ivan I. Dere of Blueberry House, Strawberry Lane, London N1 1AA.

Reference to the Respondent means:

MR ALFREDO GERMONT

DATED this 20th day of July 2010.

SCHEDULE 1

Undertakings given to the Court by the Director of the Serious Organised Crime Agency

1. The Director will arrange to serve on the Respondent, ALFREDO GERMONT, a copy of this Order together with a copy of the witness statement containing the evidence relied on by the Applicant when obtaining this Order. Service will take place as soon as practicable after the Order is sealed.

SCHEDULE 2

(i) The proceeds derived from the sale of the land and property situated at 1 Royal Road, Brixham BX2 1PP registered at HM Land Registry in the name of A Germont with title number TQ11111, and any property acquired from said proceeds.

(ii) The following motor vehicles:
   (a) Mercedes SL500 with number plate ALFREDO 1 registered in the name of Mr Alfredo Germont;
   (b) BMW X5 with number plate ALFY 2 registered in the name of Mr Alfredo Germont;

(iii) The boat currently being constructed by Boatworks Ltd and located at its premises at Haven Quay, New Road, Brixham BX2 1TT.

(iv) Monies which have been credited to or have passed through the following accounts:

Account holder	Institution	Sort Code	Account
Mr Alfredo Germont	Lloyds TSB	00-00-00	12131415
Mr Alfredo Germont	Halifax	00-10-00	654321
Mr A & Mrs T Germont	Lloyds TSB	00-99-02	000011111
Mr A & Mrs T Germont	Co-Op Bank	00-11-11	22223333

AND

(v) Any other such property that the Interim Receiver may believe to be either Recoverable or Associated Property within the meaning of the Act, so long as the Interim Receiver gives notice of this Order to the appropriate person holding or in control of said property.

PROPERTY FREEZING ORDER

If you, AlfredoGermont, or you, Violetta Valery (otherwise Valery Violetta), disobey this order you may be held to be in contempt of court and may be imprisoned, fined or have your assets seized.

Any other person who knows of this order and does anything which helps or permits the respondents to breach the terms of this order may also be held to be in contempt of court and may be imprisoned, fined or have their assets seized.

PROPERTY FREEZING ORDER

(Section 245A of the Proceeds of Crime Act 2002)

POCA no. 107 of 2010

IN THE HIGH COURT OF JUSTICE

QUEEN'S BENCH DIVISION

ADMINISTRATIVE COURT

Before the Honourable Mr Justice Bullingham Sitting in Private

Between

THE DIRECTOR OF THE SERIOUS ORGANISED CRIME AGENCY (Applicant)

and

ALFREDO GERMONT (First Respondent)

and

VIOLETTA VALERY

(OTHERWISE VALERY VIOLETTA) (Second Respondent)

TO THE FIRST REPONDENT

AND TO THE SECOND RESPONDENT

Upon reading the witness statement of Tony Foot dated the 10th day of January 2010,

And Upon Hearing Counsel for the Director of the Serious Organised Crime Agency ("the Director"),

THE COURT IS SATISFIED that the relevant requirements for making a Property Freezing Order are fulfilled.

THIS ORDER

1. This is a Property Freezing Order made against Alfredo Germont 'the First Respondent' and Violetta Valery (otherwise Valery Violetta) 'the Second Respondent' on 11th January 2010 by Mr Justice Bullingham following an application on behalf of the Serious Organised Crime Agency ("the Agency").

2. This Order prohibits the First Respondent and Second Respondent from dealing with the property and assets set out herein.

3. The Order is subject to the exclusions at the end of this Order.

4. You should read all of this Order carefully. You are advised to consult a solicitor as soon as possible.

5. Subject to the provisions of section 245C of the Proceeds of Crime Act 2002 and the Proceeds of Crime Act 2002 (Legal Expenses in Civil Recovery Proceedings) Regulations 2005, you may be entitled to the release of restrained funds to pay for legal representation in connection with this Order. A request for the release of a sum in respect of reasonable legal expenses must be made in writing to the Director of the Serious Organised Crime Agency and before any release can be made certain conditions must be fulfilled. You and your legal adviser are referred to Part 3 of the Proceeds of Crime Act 2002 (Legal Expenses in Civil Recovery Proceedings) Regulations 2005 (SI 3382 of 2005).

6. Further to the provisions of section 245C of the Proceeds of Crime Act 2002, you may be entitled to the release of restrained funds to meet your reasonable living expenses or to carry on any trade, business, profession or occupation. A request for the release of property or an asset to meet reasonable living expenses or to carry on any trade, business, profession or occupation can either be made to the Director of the Serious Organised Crime Agency, in the first instance, pursuant to paragraph 12 of this Order, or to the Court pursuant to section 245B of the Proceeds of Crime Act 2002.

7. The First Respondent and Second Respondent and any other person affected by this Order have a right to apply to the Court to vary or discharge it.

Disposal of or dealing with assets

8. The First Respondent must not until further order of this Court:-
   (a) remove from England and Wales any of the property or assets set out in paragraph 9 below, whether in his own name or not and whether solely or jointly owned; or
   (b) in any way dispose of or deal with or diminish the value of any of the property or assets set out in paragraph 9 below, whether in his own name or not and whether solely or jointly owned.

9. Paragraph 8 applies to the following property and assets:
   i. The proceeds of the sale of the property situated at 6 Simpson Avenue, Springfield, Torquay TQ1 1AB, previously registered at HM Land Registry in the name of the First Respondent, with title number TQ123456;
   ii. The property situated at 12 Marge Way, Springfield, Torquay TQ2 2AB, and registered at HM Land Registry in the name of the First Respondent, with title number TQ98765;
   iii. Vehicle Registration No. TS02 ACB, a BMW X5 Sport Automatic registered to the First Respondent at Flat 1, 22 Seaview Rise, Paignton TQ6 1PT;
   iv. The following bank accounts
      a. National Westminster Bank account number 12345678 sort code 00-10-00 in the name of the First Respondent;
      b. HSBC account number 98765432 sort code 10-00-10 in the name of the Second Respondent.

10. The Second Respondent must not
    (i) remove from England and Wales; or
    (ii) in any way dispose of or deal with or diminish the value of any of
       i. The proceeds of the sale of the property situated at 6 Simpson Avenue, Springfield, Torquay TQ1 1AB, previously registered at HM Land Registry in the name of the First Respondent, with title number TQ23445;
       ii. The property comprising the land at the back of 12 Marge Way, Springfield, Torquay TQ2 2AB, and registered at HM Land Registry in the name of the First Respondent, with title number TQ98765;
       iii. Vehicle Registration No. TS02 ACB, a BMW X5 Sport Automatic registered to the First Respondent at Flat 1, 22 Seaview Rise, Paignton TQ6 1PT;
       iv. The following bank accounts
          a. National Westminster Bank account number 12345678 sort code 00-10-00 in the name of the First Respondent;

    b. HSBC account number 98765432 sort code 10-00-10 in the name of the Second Respondent.

Disclosure of information

11. The First Respondent must:
    (i) inform the Agency in writing within 72 hours of service of this Order on the First Respondent of all his assets whether in or outside England and Wales and whether in his own name or not and whether solely or jointly owned, giving the value, location and details of all such assets;
    (ii) confirm the information in a witness statement which must be verified by a statement of truth and served on the Agency within 21 days after this Order has been served on the First Respondent.

The information in the witness statement must include:

a. the name and address of all persons including financial institutions holding any such assets;
b. details of the First Respondent's current salary or other form of income, identifying the amount paid, by whom it is paid and the account or accounts into which it is paid;
c. the names and numbers of all accounts held by or under the control of the First Respondent, together with the name and address of the place where the account is held and the sums in the account;
d. details (including addresses) of any real property in which the First Respondent has any interest, including an interest in any of the proceeds of sale if the property were to be sold. These details must include details of any mortgage or charge on the property;
e. details of all National Savings Certificates, unit trusts, shares or debentures held by the First Respondent in any company or corporation wherever incorporated in the world, owned or controlled by the First Respondent or in which he has an interest;
f. details of all trusts of which the First Respondent is a beneficiary, including the name and address of every trustee;
g. particulars of any income or debt due to the First Respondent including the name and address of the debtor;
h. details of all assets over £2,000.00 in value received by the First Respondent or anyone on his behalf since the 11th January 2004 identifying the name and address of the person from whom such assets were received;
i. details of all assets over £2,000.00 in value transferred by the First Respondent or anyone on his behalf to others since 11th January 2004 identifying the name and address of all persons to whom such property was transferred.

12. The Second Respondent must:
    (i) inform the Agency in writing within 72 hours of service of this Order on the Second Respondent of all her assets whether in or outside England and Wales and whether in her own name or not and whether solely or jointly owned, giving the value, location and details of all such assets;
    (ii) confirm the information in a witness statement which must be verified by a statement of truth and served on the Agency within 21 days after this Order has been served on the Second Respondent.

The information in the witness statement must include:

a. the name and address of all persons including financial institutions holding any such assets;
b. details of the Second Respondent's current salary or other form of income, identifying the amount paid, by whom it is paid and the account or accounts into which it is paid;
c. the names and numbers of all accounts held by or under the control of the Second Respondent, together with the name and address of the place where the account is held and the sums in the account;
d. details (including addresses) of any real property in which the Second Respondent has any interest, including an interest in any of the proceeds of sale if the property were to be sold. These details must include details of any mortgage or charge on the property;

e. details of all National Savings Certificates, unit trusts, shares or debentures held by the Second Respondent in any company or corporation wherever incorporated in the world, owned or controlled by the Second Respondent or in which she has an interest;

f. details of all trusts of which the Second Respondent is a beneficiary, including the name and address of every trustee;

g. particulars of any income or debt due to the Second Respondent including the name and address of the debtor;

h. details of all assets over £2,000.00 in value received by the Second Respondent or anyone on his behalf since the 11th January 2004 identifying the name and address of the person from whom such assets were received;

i. details of all assets over £2,000.00 in value transferred by the Second Respondent or anyone on his behalf to others since 11th January 2004 identifying the name and address of all persons to whom such property was transferred.

13. Subject to any further Order of the court any information given in compliance with this Order shall only be used for the purpose of these proceedings and any subsequent civil recovery proceedings.

14. However, nothing in this paragraph shall make inadmissible any disclosure made by the Respondents in any proceedings for perjury relating to that disclosure.

Costs

15. The costs of this Order are reserved.

Variation or Discharge of this Order

16. The First Respondent or the Second Respondent may agree with the Agency that this Order be varied in any respect but any such agreement must be in writing.

17. Anyone affected by this Order may apply to the Court at any time to vary or discharge this Order (or so much of it as affects that person), pursuant to section 245B of the Proceeds of Crime Act 2002, but they must first inform the Agency and anyone named on the first page of this Order giving 2 clear days notice. If any evidence is to be relied upon in support of the application it must also be served giving 2 clear days notice.

Interpretation of this Order

18. A person who is an individual who is ordered not to do something must not do it himself or herself or in any other way. He or she must not do it through others acting on his or her behalf or on his or her instructions or with his or her encouragement.

19. A person that is a corporation and which is ordered not to do something must not do it by its directors, officers, employees or agents or in any other way.

Parties other than the Respondents

20. *Effect of this order.* It is a contempt of court for any person notified of this Order knowingly to assist in or permit a breach of the Order. Any person doing so may be sent to prison, fined, or have his assets seized. He is also at risk of prosecution for a money laundering offence.

21. *Set off by banks.* This Order does not prevent any bank from exercising any right of set off it may have in respect of any facility which it gave to the Respondents before it was notified of the Order.

22. *Withdrawals by the respondent.* No bank need enquire as to the application or proposed application of any money withdrawn by the Respondents if the withdrawal appears to be permitted by this Order.

23. *Persons outside England Wales and Scotland.*

    (1) Except as provided by in paragraph (2), the terms of this Order do not affect or concern anyone outside the jurisdiction of this court or Scotland.

    (2) The terms of this Order will affect the following persons in a country or state outside the jurisdiction of this court or Scotland:-

        a. a person to whom this Order is addressed or an officer or an agent appointed by power of attorney of such a person; or

        b. any person who:-

            i. is subject to the jurisdiction of this court,

            ii. has been given written notice of this Order at his residence or place of business within the jurisdiction of this court, and

            iii. is able lawfully to prevent acts or omissions outside the jurisdiction of this court which constitute or assist in a breach of the terms of this Order.

        c. any other person only to the extent that this Order is declared enforceable or is enforced by a court in that country.

24. *Assets located outside England and Wales.* Nothing in this Order shall, in respect of assets located outside England and Wales, prevent any third party from complying with:-

    a. what it reasonably believes to be its obligations, contractual or otherwise, under the laws and obligations of the country or state in which those assets are located or under the proper law of any contract between itself and the Respondents or any of them, or

    b. any Orders of the courts of that country or state, provided that reasonable notice of any application for such an Order is given to the Agency.

COMMUNICATIONS WITH THE COURT

All communications to the court about this order should be sent to The Administrative Court Office, Royal Courts of Justice, Strand, London WC2A 2LL quoting the case number. The office is open between 10am and 4pm Monday to Friday. The telephone number is 020 7947 6653.

Undertaking given by the Agency to the Court

The Agency will as soon as practicable serve upon the First and Second Respondents:-

a. A copy of this Order,

b. The witness statement containing the evidence relied on by the Agency and any other documents provided to the Court on the making of the application.

ADDRESS AND TELEPHONE NUMBER OF THE AGENCY FOR SERVICE AND ANY COMMUNICATION IN RESPECT OF THESE PROCEEDINGS

The Director

Serious Organised Crime Agency

PO Box 8000

London

SE11 5EN

Tel: 0370 496 7622

APPENDIX 17

CIVIL RECOVERY ORDER BY CONSENT

CLAIM NUMBER: CO/0000/2010

IN THE HIGH COURT OF JUSTICE

QUEEN'S BENCH DIVISION

ADMINISTRATIVE COURT

IN THE MATTER OF A RECOVERY ORDER

PURSUANT TO SECTION 266 OF THE PROCEEDS OF CRIME ACT 2002

Between

THE DIRECTOR OF THE SERIOUS ORGANISED CRIME AGENCY (Claimant)

and

ALFREDO GERMONT (First Respondent)

VIOLETTA VALERY (Second Respondent)

TRAVIATA TRADING ENTERPRISES LTD (Third Respondent)

GIORGIO GERMONT (Fourth Respondent)

ORDER FOR DISPOSAL BY CONSENT

UPON THE APPLICATION of the Director of the Serious Organised Crime Agency issued on [insert date]

AND BY THE CONSENT of the Claimant and the First, Second and Third Respondents,

AND UPON READING THE FIRST WITNESS STATEMENT of Ivor Edake dated / /2010

AND THE SETTLEMENT AGREEMENT DATED / /2010, attached hereto marked Schedule Two

IT IS ORDERED THAT

1. A Recovery Order is made in respect of the property listed in the first schedule to this Order, marked Schedule One (the "**Scheduled Property**").

2. The Scheduled Property shall vest in the Trustee for Civil Recovery (the "**Trustee**"), namely Tony Foot of the Serious Organised Crime Agency, PO Box 8000, London SE11 5EN, forthwith upon the making of this Order.

3. The Trustee shall have the following powers without prejudice to any other powers he may have by virtue of statute or by implication of law:
   a. power to transfer, convey and/or sell the Scheduled Property or any part of it or interest in it;
   b. power to incur expenditure for the purpose of:
      i. acquiring any part of the Scheduled Property, or any interest in it, which is not vested in him; and
      ii. discharging any liabilities, or extinguishing any rights, to which the Scheduled Property is subject;

    c. power to manage the Scheduled Property including:
        i. selling or otherwise disposing of assets comprised in the Scheduled Property which are perishable or which ought to be disposed of before their value diminishes;
        ii. where the Scheduled Property comprises assets of a trade or business, carrying on, or arranging for another to carry on, the trade or business;
        iii. incurring capital expenditure in respect of the Scheduled Property;
    d. power to start, carry on or defend any legal proceedings in respect of the Scheduled Property;
    e. power to make any compromise or other arrangement in connection with any claim relating to the Scheduled Property;
    f. for the purposes of, or in connection with, the exercise of any of his powers, power by his official name to do any of things mentioned in sub-clause (g) below and power to do any other act which is necessary or expedient;
    g. the things mentioned in sub-clause (f) above are:
        i. holding, entering or seizing the Scheduled Property;
        ii. entering into contracts;
        iii. suing and being sued;
        iv. employing agents; and
        v. executing a power of attorney, deed or other instrument.

4. Upon the Trustee taking possession of the Scheduled Property, the Interim Receiving Order made by this Court on 1 April 2009 shall be discharged and the proceedings brought under case number CO/0000/2009 shall be stayed as against all the Respondents.

5. There be no order for the costs of these proceedings or for the costs of the proceedings relating to the Interim Receiving Order obtained on 1 April 2009 (case number CO/0000/2009).

Dated this   day of October 2010

....

For the Claimant   For the Second Respondent

....

For the First Respondent   For the Third Respondent

SCHEDULE ONE

Property subject to a Recovery Order pursuant to Section 266 of the Proceeds of Crime Act 2002

1. The sum of £15,000 held in an account numbered [*insert number*] in the name of the [*insert respondent*] at [*insert location*] branch of [*insert bank*].

2. Zurich Investment Bond 00000 held in the name of the First Respondent.

3. Scottish Provident Investment Bonus Growth policy number 000000 held in the joint names of the First Respondent and the Second Respondent.

4. Funds held by Traviata Trading Enterprises Ltd to the order of the First Respondent with a value at April 2010 of £100,000 plus any interest accrued since that time.

5. AMP Pearl policy held in the name of the First Respondent.

6. Northern Rock policy number 000000 held in the name of the Second Respondent as trustee with a value as at 1st September 2010 of £5000.

7. 5.99% of the current value of the Mercedes 220CE with licence plate numbered TY10 MSW.

8. The real property situate at 11 Simpsons Lane, Springfield, Torquay under Land Registry Number TQ12345678.

FINANCIAL REPORTING ORDER

In the Crown Court

At Torquay   Case No: T2010 0000

                                              Court Code:

FINANCIAL REPORTING ORDER

(Section 76 of the Serious Organised Crime and Police Act 2005)

The offender: ALFREDO GERMONT   Date of birth: 10th August 1955

was convicted on the 1st April 2010 of Conspiracy to Import and Supply Cocaine.

The Court was satisfied that the risk of the offender's committing another offence listed in section 76(3) of the Serious Organised Crime and Police Act 2005 was sufficiently high to justify the making of a Financial Reporting Order.

On 29th July 2011, the Court ordered that the offender be subjected to a Financial Reporting Order, the details of which are specified in the attached Schedule, for a period of **10** years from the date of the making of the order.

Breach of this Order is punishable with imprisonment and/or a fine.

AN OFFICER OF THE CROWN COURT

Date:

SCHEDULE

Details of the Financial Reporting Order

(Any requirement(s) imposed by the court under section 79 of the Serious Organised Crime and Police Act 2005 must be listed here)

The Court orders that a defendant subjected to a Financial Reporting Order must do the following:

1. Within one month of 29th July 2011 make a report to the specified person namely, The Serious Organised Crime Agency Financial Reporting Officer.

2. Thereafter, within 28 days of the end of each succeeding period of 6 months, make further reports to the specified person.

3. This order shall have effect until 31st July 2021.

4. The report shall be in writing and may be delivered by hand or posted to The Financial Reporting Officer, c/o Deputy Director Proceeds of Crime, PO Box 8000, London SE11 5EN.

5. Each report shall include (if applicable):
   a. Schedule of any current salary or other form of income (save for that which passes through his account held with the Prison Service or any sum earned from prison employment, providing said sum does not exceed £1000 in any six month period), identifying the amount paid, by whom it is paid and the account or accounts into which such sums are paid. The report shall include copies of all payslips for the relevant period.
   b. Schedule of all accounts held by the defendant, or to which the defendant is a signatory, including the name in which the account is held, the balance in the account and the name and address of the place where the account is held, together with copies all statements from such accounts for the period in question.
   c. Schedule (including addresses) of any real property in which the defendant has any interest, including an interest in any of the net sale money if the property were to be sold. These details must include details of any mortgage or charge on the property.
   d. Schedule of any rental income from property, the property to which it relates, the details of who pays the rental income and into which account paid.
   e. Schedule of all beneficial interests the defendant may hold in all business concerns and companies, whether trading or dormant including shares or debentures held in any company or corporation wherever incorporated in the world. If the business is trading to provide annual accounts.
   f. Details of all National Savings Certificates and unit trusts.
   g. Schedule of all assets or property of any value, currently held or received by the defendant or anyone on his behalf since 01/04/2010, identifying the name and address of the person from whom such asset was received.
   h. Particulars of all trusts of which the defendant is a trustee, giving the names and addresses of the beneficiaries thereof and particulars of those of which they are beneficiary, giving the names and addresses of the trustees thereof.

APPENDIX 19

CONDEMNATION AND FORFEITURE OF GOODS

SCHEDULE 3 OF THE CUSTOMS AND EXCISE MANAGEMENT ACT 1979
PROVISIONS RELATING TO FORFEITURE

Sections 139, 143, 145

Notice of seizure

1 (1) The Commissioners shall, except as provided in sub-paragraph (2) below, give notice of the seizure of any thing as liable to forfeiture and of the grounds therefore to any person who to their knowledge was at the time of the seizure the owner or one of the owners thereof.

 (2) Notice need not be given under this paragraph if the seizure was made in the presence of —
 (a) the person whose offence or suspected offence occasioned the seizure; or
 (b) the owner or any of the owners of the thing seized or any servant or agent of his; or
 (c) in the case of anything seized in any ship or aircraft, the master or commander.

2 Notice under paragraph 1 above shall be given in writing and shall be deemed to have been duly served on the person concerned—
 (a) if delivered to him personally; or
 (b) if addressed to him and left or forwarded by post to him at his usual or last known place of abode or business or, in the case of a body corporate, at their registered or principal office; or
 (c) where he has no address within the United Kingdom [or the Isle of Man], or his address is unknown, by publication of notice of the seizure in the London, Edinburgh or Belfast Gazette.

Notice of claim

3 Any person claiming that any thing seized as liable to forfeiture is not so liable shall, within one month of the date of the notice of seizure or, where no such notice has been served on him, within one month of the date of the seizure, give notice of his claim in writing to the Commissioners at any office of [Revenue and Customs].

4 (1) Any notice under paragraph 3 above shall specify the name and address of the claimant and, in the case of a claimant who is outside the United Kingdom [and the Isle of Man], shall specify the name and address of a solicitor in the United Kingdom who is authorised to accept service of process and to act on behalf of the claimant.

 (2) Service of process upon a solicitor so specified shall be deemed to be proper service upon the claimant.

Condemnation

5 If on the expiration of the relevant period under paragraph 3 above for the giving of notice of claim in respect of any thing no such notice has been given to the Commissioners, or if, in the case of any such notice given, any requirement of paragraph 4 above is not complied with, the thing in question shall be deemed to have been duly condemned as forfeited.

6 Where notice of claim in respect of any thing is duly given in accordance with paragraphs 3 and 4 above, the Commissioners shall take proceedings for the condemnation of that thing by the court,

and if the court finds that the thing was at the time of seizure liable to forfeiture the court shall condemn it as forfeited.

7   Where any thing is in accordance with either of paragraphs 5 or 6 above condemned or deemed to have been condemned as forfeited, then, without prejudice to any delivery up or sale of the thing by the Commissioners under paragraph 16 below, the forfeiture shall have effect as from the date when the liability to forfeiture arose.

Proceedings for condemnation by court

8   Proceedings for condemnation shall be civil proceedings and may be instituted—

(a) in England or Wales either in the High Court or in a magistrates' court;
(b) in Scotland either in the Court of Session or in the sheriff court;
(c) in Northern Ireland either in the High Court or in a court of summary jurisdiction.

9   Proceedings for the condemnation of any thing instituted in a magistrates' court in England or Wales, in the sheriff court in Scotland or in a court of summary jurisdiction in Northern Ireland may be so instituted—

(a) in any such court having jurisdiction in the place where any offence in connection with that thing was committed or where any proceedings for such an offence are instituted; or
(b) in any such court having jurisdiction in the place where the claimant resides or, if the claimant has specified a solicitor under paragraph 4 above, in the place where that solicitor has his office; or
(c) in any such court having jurisdiction in the place where that thing was found, detained or seized or to which it is first brought after being found, detained or seized.

10 (1) In any proceedings for condemnation instituted in England, Wales or Northern Ireland, the claimant or his solicitor shall make oath that the thing seized was, or was to the best of his knowledge and belief, the property of the claimant at the time of the seizure.

(2) In any such proceedings instituted in the High Court, the claimant shall give such security for the costs of the proceedings as may be determined by the Court.

(3) If any requirement of this paragraph is not complied with, the court shall give judgment for the Commissioners.

11 (1) In the case of any proceedings for condemnation instituted in a magistrates' court in England or Wales, without prejudice to any right to require the statement of a case for the opinion of the High Court, either party may appeal against the decision of that court to the Crown Court.

(2) In the case of any proceedings for condemnation instituted in a court of summary jurisdiction in Northern Ireland, without prejudice to any right to require the statement of a case for the opinion of the High Court, either party may appeal against the decision of that court to the county court.

12 Where an appeal, including an appeal by way of case stated, has been made against the decision of the court in any proceedings for the condemnation of any thing, that thing shall, pending the final determination of the matter, be left with the Commissioners or at any convenient office of customs and excise.

Provisions as to proof

13 In any proceedings arising out of the seizure of any thing, the fact, form and manner of the seizure shall be taken to have been as set forth in the process without any further evidence thereof, unless the contrary is proved.

14 In any proceedings, the condemnation by a court of any thing as forfeited may be proved by the production either of the order or certificate of condemnation or of a certified copy thereof purporting to be signed by an officer of the court by which the order or certificate was made or granted.

Special provisions as to certain claimants

15 For the purposes of any claim to, or proceedings for the condemnation of, any thing, where that thing is at the time of seizure the property of a body corporate, of two or more partners or of any number of persons exceeding five, the oath required by paragraph 10 above to be taken and any other thing required by this Schedule or by any rules of the court to be done by, or by any person authorised by, the claimant or owner may be taken or done by, or by any other person authorised by, the following persons respectively, that is to say—

(a) where the owner is a body corporate, the secretary or some duly authorised officer of that body;

(b) where the owners are in partnership, any one of those owners;

(c) where the owners are any number of persons exceeding five not being in partnership, any two of those persons on behalf of themselves and their co-owners.

Power to deal with seizures before condemnation, etc

16 Where any thing has been seized as liable to forfeiture the Commissioners may at any time if they see fit and notwithstanding that the thing has not yet been condemned, or is not yet deemed to have been condemned, as forfeited—

(a) deliver it up to any claimant upon his paying to the Commissioners such sum as they think proper, being a sum not exceeding that which in their opinion represents the value of the thing, including any duty or tax chargeable thereon which has not been paid;

(b) if the thing seized is a living creature or is in the opinion of the Commissioners of a perishable nature, sell or destroy it.

17 (1) If, where any thing is delivered up, sold or destroyed under paragraph 16 above, it is held in proceedings taken under this Schedule that the thing was not liable to forfeiture at the time of its seizure, the Commissioners shall, subject to any deduction allowed under sub-paragraph (2) below, on demand by the claimant tender to him—

(a) an amount equal to any sum paid by him under sub-paragraph (a) of that paragraph; or

(b) where they have sold the thing, an amount equal to the proceeds of sale; or

(c) where they have destroyed the thing, an amount equal to the market value of the thing at the time of its seizure.

(2) Where the amount to be tendered under sub-paragraph (1)(a), (b) or (c) above includes any sum on account of any duty or tax chargeable on the thing which had not been paid before its seizure the Commissioners may deduct so much of that amount as represents that duty or tax.

(3) If the claimant accepts any amount tendered to him under sub-paragraph (1) above, he shall not be entitled to maintain any action on account of the seizure, detention, sale or destruction of the thing.

(4) For the purposes of sub-paragraph (1)(c) above, the market value of any thing at the time of its seizure shall be taken to be such amount as the Commissioners and the claimant may agree or, in default of agreement, as may be determined by a referee appointed by the Lord Chancellor (not being an official of any government department [or an office-holder in, or a member of the staff of, the Scottish Administration]), whose decision shall be final and conclusive; and the procedure on any reference to a referee shall be such as may be determined by the referee.

(5) The Lord Chancellor may make an appointment under sub-paragraph (4) only with the concurrence—

(a) where the proceedings referred to in sub-paragraph (1) were taken in England and Wales, of the Lord Chief Justice of England and Wales;

(b) where those proceedings were taken in Scotland, of the Lord President of the Court of Session;

(c) where those proceedings were taken in Northern Ireland, of the Lord Chief Justice of Northern Ireland.

(6) The Lord Chief Justice of England and Wales may nominate a judicial office holder (as defined in the Constitutional Reform Act 2005) to exercise his functions under this paragraph.

(7) The Lord President of the Court of Session may nominate a judge of the Court of Session who is a member of the First or Second Division of the Inner House of that Court to exercise his functions under this paragraph.

(8) The Lord Chief Justice of Northern Ireland may nominate any of the following to exercise his functions under this paragraph—

(a) the holder of one of the offices listed in the Justice (Northern Ireland) Act 2002;

(b) a Lord Justice of Appeal (as defined in section 88 of that Act).]

ATTORNEY-GENERAL GUIDANCE TO PROSECUTING BODIES ON THEIR ASSET RECOVERY POWERS UNDER THE PROCEEDS OF CRIME ACT 2002

Issued 5 November 2009

PROCEEDS OF CRIME ACT 2002
SECTION 2A (CONTRIBUTION TO THE REDUCTION OF CRIME)
JOINT GUIDANCE GIVEN BY THE SECRETARY OF STATE
AND HER MAJESTY'S ATTORNEY GENERAL

This guidance is given by the Secretary of State to the Serious Organised Crime Agency (SOCA), and by the Attorney General to the Director of Public Prosecutions, the Director of Revenue and Customs Prosecutions, the Director of the Serious Fraud Office and the Director of Public Prosecutions for Northern Ireland, in accordance with section 2A of the Proceeds of Crime Act 2002. In the case of the Director of Public Prosecutions for Northern Ireland, the guidance is given by the Attorney General in her capacity as Attorney General for Northern Ireland. In this guidance, as in section 2A, SOCA and the Directors are referred to as "relevant authorities".

1. The reduction of crime is in general best secured by means of criminal investigations and criminal proceedings. However, the non-conviction based asset recovery powers available under the Act can also make an important contribution to the reduction of crime where (i) it is not feasible to secure a conviction, (ii) a conviction is obtained but a confiscation order is not made, or (iii) a relevant authority is of the view that the public interest will be better served by using those powers rather than by seeking a criminal disposal.

2. In any case where proceeds of crime have been identified but it is not feasible to secure a conviction, or a conviction has been secured but no confiscation order made, relevant authorities should consider using the non conviction-based powers available under the Act.

3. In any case where it appears that a conviction might be secured, relevant authorities will consider whether or not it is in the public interest to conduct a criminal investigation and (at a later stage, if sufficient evidence is obtained) a prosecution. In these circumstances relevant authorities may also consider whether or not the public interest might be better served by using the non conviction-based powers available under the Act, applying the principle that a criminal disposal will generally make the best contribution to the reduction of crime.

4. Any assessment of where the public interest lies should include consideration of all relevant factors. The Code for Crown Prosecutors (in Northern Ireland, the Code for Prosecutors) lists some of the factors that might be relevant in deciding whether or not a prosecution is in the public interest. The same factors might also be relevant in considering, at any stage, whether or not the non conviction-based powers should be used. A vital underlying consideration is the need to retain public confidence in the criminal justice system as a whole, and in the fair and proper use of the non conviction-based powers. In particular, care must be taken not to allow an individual or body corporate to avoid a criminal investigation and prosecution by consenting to the making of a civil recovery order, in circumstances where a criminal disposal would be justified under the overriding principle that the reduction of crime is generally best served by that route, and in accordance with the public interest factors in the relevant prosecutors' Code.

5. For illustrative purposes only, the following is a non-exhaustive list of circumstances in which use of the non-conviction based powers might be appropriate because it is not feasible to secure a conviction:

    a. The only known criminality is overseas, and there is no extra-territorial jurisdiction to pursue a criminal case in the courts of England & Wales or Northern Ireland.

    b. There is no identifiable living suspect who is within the jurisdiction or realistically capable of being brought within the jurisdiction.

    c. Proceeds of crime can be identified but cannot be linked to any individual suspect or offence.

    d. A law enforcement authority considers that an investigation could not generate sufficient evidence to create a realistic prospect of conviction.

    e. A criminal investigation has been conducted but the prosecuting authority considers that there is insufficient evidence to create a realistic prospect of conviction.

    f. A prosecution has been conducted but has not resulted in a conviction.

6. Again for illustrative purposes only, the following is a non-exhaustive list of circumstances in which a conviction is feasible, but use of the non conviction-based powers might better serve the overall public interest:

    a. Using non-conviction based powers better meets an urgent need to take action to prevent or stop offending which is causing immediate harm to the public, even though this might limit the availability of evidence for a future prosecution.

    b. It is not practicable to investigate all of those with a peripheral involvement in the criminality, and a strategic approach must be taken in order to achieve a manageable and successful prosecution.

    c. Civil recovery represents a better deployment of resources to target someone with significant property which cannot be explained by legitimate income.

    d. The offender is being prosecuted in another jurisdiction and is expected to receive a sentence that reflects the totality of the offending, so the public interest does not require a prosecution in this country.

7. These are examples, and are not intended to include all of the circumstances in which the non conviction-based powers may be used. Every case is different, and must be decided by the relevant authority on its own facts. SOCA is able to seek advice from the relevant prosecuting authority before making a decision, where necessary.

8. In using the non conviction-based powers, relevant authorities must have regard to, and seek to minimise, any potential prejudice to a related or potential criminal investigation or criminal proceedings. So far as it is practicable to do so, the relevant authority should:

    a. Liaise with any relevant law enforcement and/or prosecuting authorities before exercising any of its operational functions (other than the seizure of cash), in order to enquire whether doing so would prejudice a criminal investigation or criminal proceedings, and give due weight to any advice so received;

    b. Keep under review the extent to which taking, continuing or refraining from any course of action has a potential to prejudice a criminal investigation or criminal proceedings and avoid such prejudice where possible; and

    c. Ensure where possible that information relevant to a criminal investigation or criminal proceedings is disclosed to the relevant law enforcement or prosecution authority at the earliest practical opportunity.

9. This guidance does not prohibit a criminal investigation by a law enforcement authority being carried out at the same time as a civil recovery and/or tax investigation. Nor does it prevent civil recovery and/or tax proceedings being instituted where a criminal investigation by a law enforcement authority is being carried out at the same time into unrelated criminality, subject to the duty on relevant authorities to seek to minimise prejudice to criminal investigations and proceedings. Similarly this guidance does not prohibit criminal proceedings being instituted or carried on by a prosecuting authority at the same time as a civil recovery and/or tax investigation is carried out.

10. In no circumstances may criminal and civil/tax proceedings be carried on at the same time in relation to the same criminality. Where criminal proceedings have been stayed by a court, or cannot progress for example because the defendant has absconded, they are not being carried on for the purposes of this prohibition.

11. A relevant authority may agree to accept a reduced sum in satisfaction of a civil recovery claim if satisfied that:

    a. The sum is reasonable, having regard to all relevant circumstances including the chances of recovering the full amount claimed and the time and public funds likely to be expended in attempting to do so; and

    b. Accepting the reduced sum would not damage public confidence.

INDEX